THE OFFICIAL GUIDE TO MBA PROGRAMS

Edited by Charlotte Kurst

Inquiries concerning this publication should be directed to:
GMAT Program Direction Office, Educational Testing Service, CN 6106,
Princeton, New Jersey 08541-6106.

USA: 0-446-38437-2
CAN: 0-446-38438-0

In association with Warner Books, Inc., a Warner Communications Company

Contents

The Graduate Management Admission Council

The Graduate Management Admission Council (GMAC) is an organization of graduate business and management schools sharing a common interest in professional management education. The Council provides information to schools and prospective students to help both make reasoned choices in the admission process. It also provides a forum for the exchange of information through research, educational programs, and other services among the broad constituency of individuals and institutions concerned with management education.

The Council has three basic service objectives:

1. To enhance the management admission process by:

   ■ developing and administering appropriate assessment instruments;

   ■ developing other services and materials related to the selection process;

   ■ informing schools and students about the appropriate use of such instruments and materials;

   ■ providing opportunities for the exchange of information between students and schools.

2. To broaden knowledge about management education by:

   ■ conducting educational research;

   ■ disseminating information about relevant research;

   ■ encouraging the development and exchange of information by professionals in the field.

3. To promote the highest standards of professional practice in the administration of management education programs and related activities by:

   ■ developing appropriate standards of practice;

   ■ offering educational programs and publications to provide essential knowledge, skills, and values;

   ■ providing other opportunities for professional development.

Member Schools

Atlanta University
Graduate School of Business Administration

Babson College
M.B.A. Program

Boston College
Graduate School of Management

Boston University
School of Management

Bowling Green State University
College of Business Administration

Brigham Young University
Graduate School of Management

Carnegie-Mellon University
Graduate School of Industrial Administration

College of William and Mary
School of Business Administration

Columbia University
Graduate School of Business

Cornell University
The Samuel Curtis Johnson
Graduate School of Management

Dartmouth University
Amos Tuck School of Business Administration

Duke University
Fuqua School of Business

East Carolina University
School of Business

Emory University
Graduate School of Business Administration

Florida State University
College of Business

Georgia Institute of Technology
College of Management

Georgia State University
College of Business

Hofstra University
Graduate School of Business

Indiana University (Bloomington)
M.B.A. Program

Kent State University
Graduate School of Management

Marquette University
College of Business Administration

Massachusetts Institute of Technology
Sloan School of Management

Michigan State University
Graduate School of Business Administration

New York University (New York City)
Graduate School of Business Administration

Northeastern University
Graduate School of Business Administration

Northwestern University
J.L. Kellogg Graduate School of Management

Ohio State University
College of Administrative Science

The Pennsylvania State University (University Park)
Graduate Programs in Business Administration

Purdue University (West Lafayette)
Krannert Graduate School of Management

Rutgers, The State University of New Jersey
Graduate School of Management

San Francisco State University
Graduate School of Business

Seton Hall University
W. Paul Stillman School of Business

Southern Methodist University
Edwin L. Cox School of Business

Stanford University
Graduate School of Business

State University of New York at Buffalo
School of Management

Syracuse University
School of Management

Texas A&M University
College of Business Administration

Texas Christian University
M.J. Neeley School of Business

Tulane University
A.B. Freeman School of Business

The University of Alabama
Graduate School of Business

University of Arizona
College of Business and Public Administration

University of California, Berkeley
Graduate School of Business Administration

University of California, Los Angeles
Graduate School of Management

The University of Chicago
Graduate School of Business

University of Cincinnati
College of Business Administration

University of Connecticut (Storrs)
School of Business Administration

University of Denver
Graduate School of Business and Public Management

University of Georgia
College of Business Administration

University of Hawaii at Manoa
College of Business Administration

University of Illinois at Chicago
College of Business Administration

The University of Kansas
School of Business

University of Maryland
College of Business and Management

The University of Michigan (Ann Arbor)
The School of Business Administration

University of Minnesota (Minneapolis)
Graduate School of Management

University of Missouri—Columbia
College of Business and Public Administration

University of Missouri—St. Louis
School of Business Administration

The University of North Carolina at Chapel Hill
Graduate School of Business Administration

University of Notre Dame
College of Business Administration

University of Oklahoma
College of Business Administration

University of Pittsburgh
Graduate School of Business

University of Rhode Island
College of Business Administration

University of Rochester
Graduate School of Management

University of South Carolina
College of Business Administration

University of South Florida
College of Business Administration

University of Southern California
Graduate School of Business Administration

The University of Tennessee, Knoxville
College of Business Administration

The University of Texas at Austin
Graduate School of Business

The University of Tulsa
College of Business Administration

University of Utah
Graduate School of Business

University of Virginia
The Colgate Darden Graduate School
  of Business Administration

University of Washington
Graduate School of Business Administration

University of Wisconsin—Milwaukee
School of Business Administration

Vanderbilt University
Owen Graduate School of Management

Virginia Polytechnic Institute and State University
College of Business

Washington State University
College of Business and Economics

Washington University (St. Louis)
Graduate School of Business Administration

The Wharton School (University of Pennsylvania)
Graduate Division

Whether your interest stems from professional commitment or curiosity, the fact that you have opened this book means you already have some idea of the importance of a graduate degree in management* to today's society, the business community, and potentially to your own future success. Now you need hard facts.

This edition of *The Official Guide to MBA Programs* has been developed to provide the realistic information and pragmatic decision-making assistance you need—organized in a need-to-know sequence. In the following pages, you will find:

■ a detailed overview of the management degree's background, nature, benefits, and selection factors;

■ "Key Facts," pertinent information about programs and schools prepared in chart form for at-a-glance comparison;

■ in-depth descriptions of more than 520 graduate management programs throughout the world, including addresses you can use to obtain more information and application forms.

In this edition an attempt has been made to answer the wide range of questions that may arise as you evaluate your options for satisfying your personal criteria and career goals.

Graduate Management Degrees: How Important and Why

Over the past two decades, the M.B.A. degree has grown in both popularity and impact. From 5,000 M.B.A. graduates in 1965, the number has increased to 21,000 in 1970, 45,000 in 1977, and in 1983, to 65,000. While the yearly increase in M.B.A. graduates continues, however, the growth rate has begun leveling off as increasing competition and the changing economy affect the M.B.A. supply/demand ratio. As managerial positions continue to be filled by an estimated 70,000 1986 M.B.A. graduates, still greater employer selectivity awaits graduating classes of the future. As a result, prospective M.B.A. candidates must become equally selective in their choice of both school and program to meet the newly defined needs that exist in the public sector and non-profit organizations, as well as in private firms.

To keep pace with this evolving demand, colleges and universities are developing a fast-rising number of programs. In fact, a potential candidate for the M.B.A. degree can now choose a graduate program in management from about 850 different institutions, and the variety of programs has broadened each year.

For many who seek an M.B.A. degree the goal is not just getting ahead in the business arena, but getting in at all. Specialized skills, knowledge, and mind-set are associated with the graduate management degree. As a result, it may be a corporate hiring prerequisite, particularly in top companies with potential "fast track" or management development/training programs. Although future success depends on the individual, the M.B.A. graduate's initial competitive edge is reflected in starting salaries that can be considerably higher than the current rate for some bachelor's degrees.

With today's changing pattern of supply and demand, salary expectations will fluctuate. According to the College Placement Council's 1985 *Salary Survey**, yearly salary offers for M.B.A. graduates with nontechnical undergraduate degrees and no experience averaged $28,584; those having technical undergraduate degrees had beginning salary offers averaging $30,444. Although the career paths of M.B.A. graduates frequently call for mobility, the highest-paid jobs are usually found in those areas with the highest cost of living—primarily the Northeast, mid-Atlantic, and Pacific regions, as well as in the noncontinental United States and abroad.

Whatever the location, however, there are some new M.B.A. graduates who will start below or above the salaries in the average range. The fact is that differences in individual salaries are the result of many factors, including:

■ the type of industry, its geographic location, whether it is in the public or private sector, its size, and its profitability;

■ the applicant's M.B.A. functional concentration, academic standing, work experience, age, and individual characteristics;

■ the recruiting pattern of the school attended and the employer's perception of that school.

To qualify for the opportunities afforded by the M.B.A. degree, applicants must be willing to invest both time and money. Candidates come directly from undergraduate studies in both business and non-business majors and, increasingly, from the business world itself.

There has been a dramatic increase in the number of women enrolling in M.B.A. programs. A rarity little more than a decade ago, female M.B.A. students are today the most rapidly growing group on the graduate business campus. They represented more than 30 percent of all 1985 M.B.A. graduates, compared with only 7 percent in 1974. Students enrolled in part-time programs are also a significant force in graduate business schools. Figures from a survey of students taking the Graduate Management Admission Test (GMAT) in 1983-84 show that more than 45 percent of U.S. students intended to study part time.

---

* Graduate management degrees have several different names and focuses, as indicated in the school description section. Abbreviations for some of the different degree names are listed on page 14. However, we will use M.B.A. in this *Guide* to refer to all generalized, professional graduate degrees in management.

---

*The *Salary Survey* is a study of beginning salary offers made to graduating students during the recruiting period September through June. The Survey reports offers, not acceptances, with no limit on the number of offers per student. The data are submitted by 187 placement offices throughout the United States.

What Factors Are Fueling the Fire?

Behind the demand for graduate management degrees are factors reflecting changes through all of society. For one thing, the nature of business itself has changed. Corporations are responding to shifts in overseas competition and the world economy by expanding in both complexity and international scope. Advances in electronic technology have moved the computer out of the back room and into the executive suite. The electronic office, electronic mail, teleconferencing, information network terminals in briefcase-size as well as on desktops — these and still more technological developments are quickening the pace of business by providing new managerial tools for decision making, communication, and centralized control. At the same time, social pressures are accelerating change by opening new managerial career opportunities for such traditionally underrepresented groups as women. There are also other outside pressures: an inflationary/recessionary economy, soaring energy costs, environmentalists' demands, and the vagaries of bureaucracy all require more managerial problem-solving and planning responses. Government as well as public and nonprofit sectors needs management skills to develop more efficient ways of allocating limited resources.

As corporations, organizations, and government learn to live with the new way of doing business in today's world, new hiring expectations and needs have developed. Not only business in general, but the managerial decision-making response itself, has been affected, thereby creating increased demand in all sectors of society for the combination of analytical/strategic skills with which the M.B.A. curriculum is associated. A candidate who has been graduated from an M.B.A. program will have to demonstrate on-the-job worth. Many employers, however, feel that the degree at least testifies to proven drive, conceptualization capabilities, and exposure to an overview of the managerial state-of-the-art.

"From the prospective employer's point of view, the degree means pre-screened quality. We get the best of both worlds — top undergraduates, who have matured while acquiring still more superior skills. Good input, good output — good for us!"

In addition, many companies in fast-developing fields believe that M.B.A. managerial candidates are better equipped than those with a bachelor's degree to assimilate new business subjects and job responsibilities more quickly, particularly when the M.B.A. graduate in question has prior job experience. When these personal qualities and knowledgeability are combined in an individual who meets additional hiring criteria, recruiters and personnel directors may even feel that they're satisfying two objectives with one stroke.

The broad spectrum of different programs at different schools makes career and placement generalizations impractical. Nevertheless, for business students attuned to recent developments in the competitive business world and economy, the graduate management degree can serve as an effective bridge to the middle and upper reaches of authority. Many M.B.A. programs can be tailored to maximize personal marketability — opening the right doors to executive opportunities in the industries and locations most wanted.

Prospective M.B.A. candidates would be wise, however, to carefully scrutinize their objectives. Whether involving the allocation of limited resources, problem solving, or the direct motivation of people, managerial jobs differ greatly. Before investing the time and money in pursuing a particular avenue of graduate management training, candidates should make sure it leads to those jobs that interest them most.

Deciding to Study for an M.B.A.: Some Personal Considerations

Combining marriage and an M.B.A. education poses a special challenge that prospective applicants may wish to consider. All married M.B.A. students must deal with the problem of dividing their time and responsibilities. In dual-career marriages, however, there may be an additional issue of priority. Are simultaneous studies affordable? If not, which (if either) partner's education should be financed first? What would happen if one were asked to relocate away from the other's school or existing career? If possible, these and similar questions should be considered before entering an M.B.A. program.

Caution is also advised for the person in mid-life who is considering graduate management education. M.B.A. programs are rigorous, particularly for someone with little recent academic experience. A more pertinent consideration, however, is whether the program will be worth the investment in time, money, and energy. In the case of a person who has already achieved a measure of success in a given field, it may be more profitable in the long run to continue on an existing career path — with perhaps some additional nondegree training or courses.

Men and women returning to the work force after years of absence should investigate the long-run career and salary potentials available to them before making the commitment to an M.B.A. program; many employers are looking primarily for people with recent work experience or a particular set of individual characteristics.

Persons struggling with the impact of career decisions on family life may find the services of a career counseling center particularly helpful. For additional information on career counseling, students may wish to contact Catalyst at 250 Park Avenue South, New York, NY 10003. Catalyst is a national not-for-profit organization that works with corporations and individuals to develop career and family options.

2 The Graduate Management Program: Contents, Requirements, Options

Commonly used as media and personnel shorthand for all graduate management degrees, the term M.B.A. is actually just one of several names referring to different master's programs with different approaches to preparing students for professional careers in management. Degrees granted by schools described in this book are listed by name on page 14; you will have to study the individual school descriptions to determine the particular emphasis offered in their graduate management program. For discussion purposes here, the Master of Business Administration will be used to refer to all generalized graduate management programs. It is important, however, to remember that your selection of both school and program will, in fact, define what the degree will mean for you.

Professional Management: What the Program Prepares You For

A practical starting point for understanding the nature of all M.B.A. programs is defining their common career goal: professional management. Preparation may be for short-term goals, as in entry-level managerial positions, as well as for long-term career objectives in professional management. From a broad point of view, professional management is the effective organization and direction of resources including people, money, materials, and technology to achieve business and organizational goals.

As a manager, for example, you might manage

People: By setting goals for a sales force and directing efforts to achieve the goals, you would be managing people.

Money: As an investment counselor, you would manage a client's stock portfolio to increase its value and yield high dividends.

Natural Resources: If employed by a timber company, you would manage forests to provide enough wood for present and future customers, while keeping the forest environmentally sound.

Businesses: As a business operations manager, you might manage personnel, accounting systems, production and development functions, or marketing operations, to provide goods and services at prices customers want, and at a profit to the business.

Institutions: As a hospital administrator, you would manage people, equipment, money, and other resources to deliver health care to people at an affordable price.

Government: As a manager in government, you might manage people, money, or resources in government-funded programs or areas calling for formulation or implementation of policy impacting on the public domain.

In practice, the professional manager is concerned with planning, profitability, and efficiency. This could involve day-to-day supervisory and problem-solving skills, long-range business strategy and planning, or a combination of both (as in smaller organizations with less functional segmentation, or at higher levels of senior management). Typically, the managerial career path places more emphasis on detailed technical expertise at entry levels, more on human resource management at middle management levels, and more on organizational overview and planning at higher levels where economic, political, competitive, regulatory, and cultural factors become more complex.

Professional management as a career can be looked at two ways— by industry, or in terms of functional specializations that cross over industry lines. Management school areas of concentration generally follow functions, such as accounting, finance, marketing, general management, operations, and other fields of specialization discussed in Chapter 7, under careers. Although some schools offer specialized programs and combinations intended for a very specific career path, you may choose a management program with a flexible concentration or major that can lead to a variety of industries and jobs. One caution, however: don't enter an M.B.A. program thinking of professional management as a blank check to be filled in at some future date. To make sure you're headed toward the career path that will be best for you later, you need to base your educational strategy on some personal career planning—a process that includes realistically assessing your own qualities and goals as well as evaluating the environment in which you wish to practice management. You may fine-tune your direction as you acquire more information, but you will at least avoid miscalculation by default.

In addition to the different management functions, you will also find that while schools teach all theories, different programs are geared to preparing you for different management techniques. Management by objectives, for example, is a multi-level technique by which managers motivate employees to pursue personal goals in the process of working toward company goals and subgoals. In some cases, traditional philosophies of employment management are being challenged in some areas by the new goals and techniques of human resources management. This represents a move from carefully monitored work performance in a structured organizational hierarchy, to open-ended job responsibilities designed to increase productivity by allowing rank-and-file workers more room for creativity in areas now restricted to managers.

"The chief job of managers in the next decade will be to manage change. Unlike orchestra leaders, managers not only conduct the score; they must write it, too."

As you consider a career in management, however, remember that there is no one right way. A variety of leadership talent is needed in both the private and public sectors, and differences in technique are really options permitting flexibility to meet specific organizational needs. In most cases, the managerial structure still reflects a progression from competence in some specialty, to competence in managing that specialty, and then to the ability and authority to make decisions based on the total picture—integrating planning, organization, direction, and control for the good of the organization as a whole.

The M.B.A. Program: Adaptability to Different Needs

Just as there is no single definition of management, no single program can be right for everyone. Even within the area of generalized business management, graduate schools vary in terms of curriculum, program, and the teaching methods used. The factors to consider in evaluating alternative graduate degree programs and different schools are discussed in the following section. Remember: your ability to perform effectively in business will hinge on your learning experience. So as you read the following pages and study the school descriptions in this book, concentrate first on identifying the type of instruction most suited to your career plan; work or educational background; and personal interests, capabilities, and needs.

Graduate management programs vary not only in name, but in direction. When comparing an M.B.A. with an M.S.B.A. or other graduate program, it is important to bear in mind that the difference refers to the degree of specificity. It reflects the administration's general philosophy. As a result, a program may be oriented more to general management, or geared more to a specific function, industry, or career path through emphasis on "tools courses" such as quantitative methods and computer programming. Most full-time M.B.A. programs are designed to cover a broad spectrum of management subjects over a period of two years. Bear in mind, of course, that a two-year program can take three or four years of part-time study.

Basic course curricula and requirements reflect the faculty's judgment of the courses every student should have to meet the program's overall goals. Curricula vary in the number of credit hours and courses required. Between 36 and 60 hours are typically needed to complete the total program, although a heavy undergraduate background or degree in business may significantly reduce credit hour requirements—depending on the policy of the individual school.

Curricula also differ in their emphasis on "core" vs. "elective" courses. "Core" courses are generally required during the early part of the program to give students a thorough grounding in fundamental business concepts and functions, such as accounting, finance, marketing, operations, and employee relations. "Tools courses" may be included in the core curriculum to supplement the theoretical foundation with a practical methodological base. "Electives," which may generally be chosen later in the program, differ from core courses in that they focus on areas of advanced or more highly specialized areas of functional concentration.

Some schools subscribe to the theory that managers should be generalists and offer a fixed curriculum with no provision for electives or a field of concentration. Other schools combine general courses, electives, and a field of concentration. Still others may favor specialization to the extent of encouraging students to virtually custom-design their own course mix to suit individual career objectives and interests. In some cases, the curriculum also requires an internship or field work in the student's area of concentration—often a useful source of future contacts as well as hands-on experience and training. The value of the different approaches depends on your own priorities. Do you want a cross-discipline foundation to keep more career options open? Do you want the head start of exposure to a particular field? Do you want to test the waters in a number of fields to better assess your own aptitude and preferences?

Some curricula are highly quantitative—dealing with numbers. In programs with this strong mathematical orientation, courses typically use mathematical modeling as a primary decision-making tool. Curriculum differences are also reflected in research and examination requirements, a factor to consider if you want to capitalize on your particular strengths and learning style. For example, some schools provide both a thesis and nonthesis option within their graduate management program. Others require oral or written comprehensive examinations, a minimum grade-point average, or demonstrated proficiency in one or more subjects they consider especially vital.

One educator's view of generalists: *"They are not trained to do computer programming. They are trained to do the unexpected."*

Teaching methods differ from one graduate institution to another. Although day-to-day course work will vary according to the nature of the subject matter and classroom dynamics, a particular school's teaching emphasis will generally lean toward either a pragmatic application orientation or toward the theoretical approach.

Application-oriented techniques typically use case studies, which are analyzed extensively through the interaction of informal debates and student role playing, usually in smaller seminars. Courses may emphasize interaction with the business community—through guest speakers, through internships that use governmental agencies or local businesses as an extended laboratory, or through teleconferencing with business leaders across the country. In some programs, the concept of reality testing takes the form of hands-on experience for academic credit in the actual management of ongoing projects such as the school's own educational fund.

In contrast, the theoretical approach emphasizes underlying general concepts or theories derived from models based on research. The focus here is on an understanding of basic business constructs that cut across many industries and fields. Because of the broad nature of the subject matter, courses frequently utilize lectures presented to hundreds of students at a time. Management decision games may also be used, sometimes with heavy emphasis on computer simulations based on the heavily developed theoretical and statistical framework. However, while you need to know what the terminology implies, the two approaches are not mutually exclusive. Most schools use both methods; the difference is in the proportion of the mix. You will need to determine the right mix for your own learning style and objectives, and then take that into consideration as you make your selection of schools. Remember, there is no one right way for everyone. Your primary concern should be personal challenge.

Full-Time vs. Part-Time

In many cases, your selection of school will be determined in part by whether you plan to attend full time or part time. In its early days, graduate management education was geared primarily toward full-time students. Today, however, there are many schools which offer, and sometimes concentrate on, programs designed for students who attend on a part-time basis—because of economic necessity, time constraints, or to advance their careers. You may wish to evaluate a school's full-time or part-time offerings in terms of the availability of its support systems, how well its scheduling compares with your needs, and its potential for interaction with both faculty and other students. As a general rule, however, the decision to attend a particular school part time will be based on its program, not on differences in curriculum. If your options are open, however, it would be wise to consider the benefits and disadvantages of both full- and part-time studies in the context of your personal situation and goals.

If you have the time and money, a full-time program offers the following:

■ a shortened time period before graduation;

■ total immersion in studies, with more time for study and peer discussions;

■ a more well-rounded school life, with increased opportunities to make friendships and build faculty relationships.

In some instances, however, personal circumstances prohibit attending full time. Perhaps you are already employed and don't choose to give up two years of experience,

salary, and promotion possibilities. In that case, a part-time program offers distinctive advantages:

■ an opportunity to broaden your career options without interrupting your present earning capabilities;

■ stretching of costs for tuition, books, and materials over a longer period of time;

■ benefits to your current job performance from a day-to-day application of your studies;

■ a learning experience many feel is more realistic and meaningful, since both faculty and students are frequently part of the job world;

■ a signal to your employer that you are motivated and ambitious;

■ a chance to have your tuition fully or partially paid as part of a management development program by your present employer.

Realistically, however, you should be prepared for the fact that the pressures created by adding part-time studies to your present schedule can be difficult to handle. Not only you, but your marriage, your family, and your job can be strained by the constant extra demand on your energy and attention. You will probably be able to give less time to your studies and research than you would on a full-time basis, and even then you may find your efforts limited by fatigue and lack of access to people and facilities.

Many schools, due to increased awareness of these factors, have developed programs designed to minimize part-time student difficulties. Among these are programs that offer courses via interactive closed-circuit or public television channels, in special commuter railroad cars, on the premises of employers' plants and offices, and in a variety of scheduling plans that utilize campus facilities through summer and holiday periods and on weekends year-round. Some schools also allow you to enter at any term, so you needn't wait for the traditional September admission. Utilizing one or more of these special programs can enable you to cut down the time required to earn a graduate management degree on a part-time basis.

You may also qualify for advanced standing on the basis of undergraduate work. As a general rule, however, you can expect a part-time program to take at least four years, based on a course load of two courses per semester, two semesters per year.

"Night school students who are also working are more likely than M.B.A. candidates with no business experience, to challenge the professor as to the relevance or practicality of an example. And the professors know it."

Other Graduate Program Alternatives

Before committing yourself to the M.B.A. track, you may also wish to look into other types of graduate management degrees available for both full-time and part-time students. Some degrees concentrate on generalized business courses without the M.B.A. degree's additional program breadth; others focus on more specific areas or specialized career paths. You can investigate which programs will lead you to different goals by reading the school descriptions and "Key Facts" section of this *Guide* and through discussions with various school representatives.

Although their names reflect a general difference in direction, degrees most similar to the M.B.A. are the Master of Science in Management (M.S.M.), the Master of Science in Business Administration (M.S.B.A.), and the Master of Public and Private Management (M.P.P.M.).

If you have more closely defined your intended field of concentration, you may also be interested in some of the more specialized programs, such as the Master of International Management (M.I.M.), the Master of Public Administration (M.P.A.), the Master of Health Administration (M.H.A.), the Master of Science in Accounting (M.S.A.), and the Master of Science in Taxation (M.S.T.). Listed on the next page are the names and abbreviations of other degree programs offered by schools included in this *Guide*.

B.A.—Bachelor of Arts
B.A./M.B.A.—Bachelor of Arts/Master of Business Administration
B.B.A.—Bachelor of Business Administration
B.S.—Bachelor of Science
D.B.A.—Doctor of Business Administration
D.P.A.—Doctorate of Public Administration
Ed.D—Doctor of Education
Ed.S.—Educational Specialist in Business Administration
E.M.B.A.—Executive Master of Business Administration
J.D.—Juris Doctor
J.D./M.Acc.—Juris Doctor/Master of Accountancy
J.D./M.B.A.—Juris Doctor/Master of Business Administration
J.D./M.P.A—Juris Doctor/Master of Public Administration
M.A.—Master of Arts
M.A.A.E.—Master of Arts in Applied Economics
M.Ac.—Master of Accountancy
M.Acc.—Master of Accountancy or Master of Accounting
M.Acco.—Master of Accounting
M.A.C.T.—Master of Arts in College Teaching
M.Ad.—Master of Administration
M.A.E.—Master of Arts in Applied Economics
M.Arch./M.B.A.—Master of Architecture/Master of Business Administration
M.A.S.—Master of Accounting Science, Master of Applied Science, or Master of Actuarial Science
M.B.A.—Master of Business Administration
M.B.A./C.P.A.—Master of Business Administration/Certified Public Accountant
M.B.A./J.D.—Master of Business Administration/Juris Doctor
M.B.A./M.A.—Master of Business Administration/Master of Arts
M.B.A./M.A.I.S.—Master of Business Administration/Master of Arts in International Studies
M.B.A./M.C.R.P.—Master of Business Administration/Master in City and Regional Planning
M.B.A./M.E.—Master of Business Administration/Master of Engineering
M.B.A./M.H.A.—Master of Business Administration/Master of Health Administration
M.B.A./M.P.H.—Master of Business Administration/Master of Public Health
M.B.A./M.S.W.—Master of Business Administration/Master of Social Work
M.B.A./Ph.D.—Master of Business Administration/Doctor of Philosophy
M.B.E.—Master of Business Economics or Master of Business Education
M.B.I.S.—Master of Business Information Systems
M.B.S.—Master of Business Studies
M.C.S.M.—Master of Computer Systems Management
M.D./M.B.A.—Medical Doctor/Master of Business Administration
M.E.—Master of Engineering
M.E./M.B.A.—Master of Engineering/Master of Business Administration
M.H.A.—Master of Health Administration
M.I.B.—Master of International Business
M.I.B.S.—Master of International Business Studies
M.I.M.—Master of International Management
M.I.N.—Master of Insurance

M.L.S.—Master of Library Science
M.L.S./M.B.A.—Master of Library Science/Master of Business Administration
M.M.A.—Master of Management and Administration
M.M.R.—Master of Marketing Research
M.M.S.—Master of Management Studies
M.O.B.—Master of Organizational Behavior
M.O.D.—Master of Science in Management and Organization Development
M.P.A.—Master of Professional Accountancy, or Master of Professional Accounting, or Master of Public Administration
M.P.Acc.—Master of Professional Accounting
M.P.E.R.—Master of Personnel and Employee Relations
M.P.H.—Master of Public Health
M.P.M.—Master of Public Management or Master of Project Management
M.P.P.M.—Master in Public and Private Management
M.Pr.A.—Master of Professional Accountancy
M.P.S.H.Ad.—Master of Professional Studies in Hotel Administration
M.S.—Master of Science
M.S.A.—Master of Science in Accountancy or Accounting or Master of Science in Administration
M.S.Ac.—Master of Science in Accounting
M.S./Accy.—Master of Science in Accountancy
M.S.B.—Master of Science in Business
M.S.B.A.—Master of Science in Business Administration
M.S.:B.M.—Master of Science in Business Management
M.S.:B.O.M.—Master of Science in Business Organizational Management
M.Sc.—Master of Management Science or Master of Science
M.S.C.I.S.—Master of Science in Computer Information Systems
M.S.F.—Master of Science in Finance
M.S.I.—Master of Science in Insurance
M.S.I.A.—Master of Science in Industrial Administration
M.S.I.M.—Master of Science in Industrial Management
M.S.I.S.—Master of Science in Computer-Based Information Systems or Master of Science in Information Systems
M.S.M.—Master of Science in Management
M.S./M.I.S.—Master of Science/Management Information Systems
M.S.O.B.—Master of Science in Organizational Behavior
M.S.O.D.—Master of Science in Organizational Behavior and Development
M.S.P.A.—Master of Science in Professional Accounting
M.S./Ph.D.—Master of Science/Doctor of Philosophy
M.S.R.E.—Master of Science in Real Estate and Urban Affairs
M.S.T.—Master of Science in Taxation
M.S.Tax—Master of Science in Taxation
M.T.—Master of Taxation
M.T.X.—Master of Taxation
M.U.P.—Master of Urban Planning
Ph.D.—Doctor of Philosophy

Joint programs: Both time and money can sometimes be saved by combining your M.B.A. with a master's degree in another academic discipline, rather than taking both degree programs separately. Joint programs normally require 3 to 4 years to complete on a full-time basis, and as much as 10 years part-time. Examples include the M.B.A. and law (M.B.A./Juris Doctor), engineering (M.B.A./Master of Engineering), social work (M.B.A./Master of Social Work), and management in the arts (M.B.A./Master of Arts). The mix of M.B.A. and companion-program courses varies according to the field and the particular school. The value of joint programs to individuals also varies. In some cases, integrating the two disciplines may be appropriate, depending on future career objectives. Another student, however, might profit more by the opportunity to sample the full range of potential specializations in his or her field, and only then make the commitment to a particular graduate-level concentration. If you are considering a joint program, seek the advice of people who have pursued this educational path.

Another factor to weigh when considering joint programs is that you may have to go through the application/admission process separately for each of the two schools of study. Schools listing these programs will be found in the "Key Facts" section. The program requirements for each school will be detailed in its individual description in this *Guide.* Study them carefully; admissions criteria may be very different for different graduate schools within the same institution.

Executive M.B.A. programs: If you have already acquired experience and demonstrated promise in your current middle-management position, you may consider entering an executive M.B.A. program. More than 100 schools now offer executive M.B.A. programs. Participants in executive programs are generally sponsored by their employers, who pay the entire cost. Although they are composed of the same basic curricula, these programs may require fewer credit hours than regular M.B.A. programs, due to the advanced business backgrounds of

most participants. You should, however, be aware that the change in the number of hours may change the program format and degree title. Program structure varies, usually based on the premise that the employer must give up some of your working time to compensate for your after-hours and free-time commitment.

Overseas studies: If you plan to work for an American company that does business abroad, or for a foreign employer, you might seek out an M.B.A. program that combines studies here and in an overseas school. One caveat: these programs are not the equivalent of a Master in International Management. You would be exposed to a regular M.B.A. curriculum, but you would spend a term or more in each location.

Doctoral programs: Many business schools also offer Ph.D. or D.B.A. degrees, which lead to teaching careers at colleges and universities. While some doctoral programs feature elements common to the M.B.A. program, in others they are conducted on a totally separate and different basis. In contrast to many academic fields, there is a critical shortage of business school faculty members holding doctoral degrees. The American Assembly of Collegiate Schools of Business (AACSB) estimates that three faculty openings were available for each new doctoral graduate in 1984. Fields such as accounting and management information systems show even higher vacancy rates. This employment demand is reflected in starting faculty salaries, which compare favorably to those available in private industry and surpass those paid to faculty in most other academic disciplines.

Business Faculty Careers: A Logical Choice, a booklet published by AACSB, provides additional information on faculty careers in business. A copy may be obtained by completing the postcard in the back of this *Guide.*

The Guide to Doctoral Programs in Business & Management, published by AACSB, is the only guide to Ph.D. and D.B.A. programs at more than 80 business schools in the United States and Canada. Included

is specific information on admissions, fields of study, degree requirements, expenses, financial assistance, and placement of graduates, by school. A copy may be obtained by completing the postcard in the back of this publication and including a check for $10 ($15 outside the U.S.).

The National Doctoral Fellowship Program in Business and Management, sponsored jointly by the AACSB and the Graduate Management Admission Council, offers significant financial assistance to qualified first-year doctoral students. For more information, contact AACSB, 605 Old Ballas Road, Suite 220, St. Louis, MO 63141 (314-872-8481) or complete the postcard in the back of this publication.

3 Choosing a School

Identifying the specific type of program you want is just the first step in determining your selection of a business school. Your eventual range of choices will actually be shaped by a number of factors—some a matter of necessity, some of compatability with personal interests and expectations, and some primarily concerned with optimizing your admission chances in an increasingly competitive and selective field. Obviously, the number of applications to a particular school or program will affect its ability to winnow out anyone but the brightest students with the best potential for success. In some cases, your choice will be restricted by finances, by a geographic preference, or by the number of schools offering the program you want within part-time or commuting range. Whatever your choice parameters, the task of making the best selection of a graduate management school is one that can have significant impact on subsequent job placement, starting salary, and potential career.

Placement office records are one effective way of comparing the career paths of graduates of different schools. You would do well, however, to bear in mind that these statistics also reflect the individual students' class rank and pre-M.B.A. experience, the school's geographic location, and the many other factors outlined in the Preface to this book.

Accreditation

Ranking schools on the basis of which is best is a highly subjective process dependent on relatively unscientific survey data, word of mouth about a school's reputation, and—the most relevant factor—your individual needs. Another factor to consider is accreditation, which means simply that the school's program meets certain basic standards in curriculum, faculty qualifications, and admissions selectivity.

There are six major regional accrediting organizations: the New England Association of Schools and Colleges (NEASC), the Middle States Association of Schools and Colleges (MSASC), the North Central Association of Schools and Colleges (NCACS), the Northwest Association of Schools and Colleges (NASC), the Western Association of Schools and Colleges (WASC), and the Southern Association of Schools and Colleges (SASC).

While most of the approximately 800 United States colleges and universities offering M.B.A. degrees hold institution-wide accreditation, 216 have also met the standards of the American Assembly of Collegiate Schools of Business (AACSB). AACSB is recognized by the U.S. Department of Education and the Council on Postsecondary Accreditation as the sole accrediting agency for baccalaureate and master's degree programs in business. The AACSB accreditation process is implemented by business school administrators and corporate officials who have detailed knowledge of management education. By applying measurements that have wide acceptance in the educational community, the AACSB accreditation process assures that a school has met certain minimum standards in areas such as faculty resources and qualifications, curriculum, intellectual climate, admission policy, degree requirements, library and computer facilities, and physical plant. Schools holding AACSB accreditation are periodically revisited by AACSB to ensure that these quality standards are upheld. See the "Key Facts" section of this *Guide* for information on those schools that have achieved AACSB accreditation.

Program/Resources Evaluation

Certain facilities and services offered by schools relate directly to how much benefit you will receive from your educational experience, and should be considered when comparing programs. Among these, some of the most important are the school's support system, faculty makeup and student/faculty ratio, and the placement office. To evaluate the support system, you will want to find out how extensive and accessible the business school and/or university library and computer facilities are. Relevant information about the faculty includes the number of both full-time and part-time professors, the difference (if any) in the qualifications of the two groups, the number of professors with doctoral degrees and/or extensive business experience, the student/faculty ratio, and average class size.

Job placement services can be a particularly important adjunct to a program for your future career. You should know whether the department provides individual counseling (on career possibilities, pay scales, resume preparation, and interview techniques, for example) and how active it is in generating and arranging job interviews with recruiters. The placement office should also be prepared to supply fairly extensive information on local and national companies and on the starting salaries and types of jobs attained by recent graduates.

Personal Criteria

The final element to be considered in selecting a school is how compatible it is with your personal qualities, interests, and needs. This involves questions only you can answer. For example, will your personality fit (or flourish) in this type of campus life? With these social and cultural opportunities? In these living accommodations? Will you be comfortable with the size of the classes? In this geographic location? With the type of students the program attracts? Will the work pace stretch you enough without bending you out of shape?

And perhaps most critical, do the tuition and associated expenses fit your budget? If assistantships, scholarships, loans, and work/study programs are available, will you qualify? (See "Financing Graduate Management Education," page 25.)

Researching Your Options

The more information you can gather—about a school's program, character, resources, and compatibility with your personal criteria—the more accurate your selection will be and the better your admission chances. For a start, you may use this book as a basic reference to identify the programs that interest you, and then write for bulletins, financial aid information, and applications. There are also a number of other fact-finding avenues you can use to find out what you need to know as rapidly, efficiently, and painlessly as possible.

MBA FORUMS

There are always some questions that can only be asked in person and answered individually. Multiply your ability to do this by over 75 schools at a time, and you can readily see why over 7,000 prospective applicants each year attend MBA Forums. Held in several major cities each fall, MBA Forums are sponsored by the Graduate Management Admission Council (GMAC) to enable you to speak directly with representatives from graduate management schools across the country. Special workshops are conducted at each MBA Forum to help attendees understand more clearly the M.B.A. and Ph.D. admission process, programs of study, potential career paths, and job search strategies. Each workshop is followed by a discussion session where attendees can ask questions and request additional information. Current workshops are entitled, "The MBA and You, " "MBA Careers, " and "Doctoral Programs." Each workshop lasts about 60 minutes. A representative of the Graduate Management Admission Council will also be available to answer questions about the Graduate Management Admission Test and to provide copies of the test information bulletin and registration form.

MBA Forums are an efficient, money-saving way to acquire a balanced perspective about your options, as well as specific information about an evenly balanced cross-section of national, regional, and local schools. While a similar mix of backgrounds and interests characterizes the potential M.B.A. candidates who attend the forums, it is interesting to note that 42 percent of the 1985 MBA Forum attendees were women and 22 percent were minority group members. Sixty-one percent planned on enrolling in a full-time program, 29 percent in a part-time program, 2 percent in an executive M.B.A. program, and 3 percent in doctoral programs.

See the inside back cover for the dates of the 1986 MBA Forums and the cities in which they will be held. For more information about these and future forums, write: National Coordinator of Forums, CN 6106, Princeton, New Jersey 08541-6106.

CAREER DAYS AND ON-CAMPUS VISITATIONS

There may be other opportunities for you to participate in an exchange of questions and information without investing time and money in visits to different schools. Both schools and professional organizations sponsor career days to bring together school representatives and would-be M.B.A. students. These events serve the same purpose as the MBA Forums, although more selectively and on a smaller scale. Representatives of business school programs also visit undergraduate campuses to talk with students about their programs. Campus placement offices can usually provide information about scheduled visitations.

VISITS TO SCHOOLS

Personal visits to schools that interest you are often the best way to gather firsthand information. Plan ahead, since you will probably have to give the admissions office time to make arrangements—including, if possible, a guided tour. You will want to see the classroom and lecture facilities, living and dining accommodations, the business or university library, and support service facilities such as the placement and guidance offices. In addition to getting an accurate picture of the environment and the type of students who attend, you may also be able to arrange interviews with school officials and combine information gathering with an opportunity to improve your chances for admission. You should ask whether the purpose of the interview is to evaluate you or to give you program information. Although other important factors will be used to evaluate your admission potential, make the most of interviews by observing a few common-sense rules:

■ *Do your homework first.* Read the catalog carefully so that you can focus on the important questions that demonstrate knowledgeability and prior thought. Never ask questions that reading the catalog could answer; you would be wasting your interviewer's time and making yourself appear unprepared. Questions you will want to ask include your specific admission chances, recommended first-year programs, potential areas of concentration, the amount and nature of corporate recruiting on campus, placement results, financial aid availability, and the extent of campus social and cultural life.

■ *Sell yourself*. Make sure you provide your interviewer with the type of information that can influence his or her decision—including well-articulated answers to questions about why you want a graduate management degree, why that particular school interests you, and your long-range career goals. Your undergraduate record and personal interests will also be of interest, as will the unspoken message conveyed by the conservative, business-like way you dress.

TALKING WITH SCHOOL ALUMNI AND NEARBY MANAGEMENT FACULTY

For a more personal view of a school than is available elsewhere, talk to its students or graduates. School admissions, placement, or alumni offices can usually give you names of people to contact. Faculty members of nearby undergraduate or graduate business programs may also be able to provide a meaningful and helpful perspective on questions relating to your educational and career strategy.

BUSINESS ASSOCIATES AND FRIENDS

You may find excellent sources of information among associates who have attended M.B.A. programs or are earning their degrees part time. If you are working, check with your supervisor and/or personnel officer about your employer's promotion policy for M.B.A. graduates or people enrolled in part-time M.B.A. programs. In addition, if you or your family have friends who are managers, you might ask their advice about M.B.A. education in relation to what they know about you.

4 What It Takes to Get In

The Admissions Process

A broad range of objective and subjective criteria are evaluated in the admissions process of graduate business schools. The process of selection is not an exact science. Different schools have varying standards and goals on which they base their evaluation process, which means that your chances for selection will differ from school to school. What's more, a particular school's reputation, location, and costs may increase its overall desirability—with the result that it will draw applications from a disproportionately large number of would-be students across the country. Obviously, the more students who apply for a limited number of openings, the more selective the admissions process will become. Accordingly, you will need to utilize every means at your disposal to optimize your admission chances at the schools that best fit your needs.

Major selection criteria: Among the many criteria that are considered by business schools in the selection process, are the following:

■ your undergraduate record and related indications of past academic performance,

■ your scores on the Graduate Management Admission Test (GMAT),

■ your accomplishments or experience at work, in the military, or in campus and community activities,

■ the overall quality of your application and recommendations,

■ intangibles such as your motivation, maturity, and leadership abilities, as suggested by a variety of information.

None of these criteria, in itself, is likely to be the sole determinant of your candidacy. Admissions boards will look at them in combination with one another—strengths balanced against weaknesses—from the perspective of that particular school's admission policy, institutional goals, and past experience. All facets of your application will be considered.

Your Undergraduate Record

Your academic standing will be viewed within the framework of your undergraduate program's quality and competitiveness, and the particular courses you took. Some schools set an acceptance standard for minimum grade-point average (GPA). Some also set standards for your rank in your class—accepting only candidates from the top 10 percent down to the upper 50 percent. Extracurricular activities and special projects you have performed also enter into the evaluation of your undergraduate record. So will your course load, the relative ease or difficulty of the courses you took, and whether your grade level rose, dropped, or remained static. Your undergraduate grades, grade trends, and ranking are likely to carry especially heavy weight if you plan to enter graduate school immediately after obtaining your bachelor's degree, since you will have little or no work record. Generally, one or more transcripts of your undergraduate courses and grades will be required with your application, and grades for courses in progress must be reported. If you think your undergraduate record may exclude you from a program you would like to attend, it might be wise to check with the school's admission officers to see if they can suggest alternate courses of action.

Programs accept students from all undergraduate majors. In fact, prospective applicants taking the GMAT in 1983-84 represented a wide variety of undergraduate fields: 4.7 percent were majoring in the humanities, 16.1 percent in the social sciences, 19.1 percent in science and engineering, 36.5 percent in business and commerce, 4.4 percent in other major fields (approximately 19 percent did not respond to the survey item).

At some schools, undergraduate courses in algebra, calculus, economics, or basic business subjects may be required as foundation for particularly specialized or quantitative programs. You may be admitted without these courses, but you may be required to take them before you are classified as a regular student in the graduate school. (Of course, if you already meet these criteria, you will have a good head start in the graduate program, with perhaps some advanced academic standing that will enable you to complete your studies in less time.) Some schools also like to see students with backgrounds in psychology and experimental science, and nearly all are concerned with whether an applicant has a good written and oral command of English. The important fact to remember is that an undergraduate degree in business is not required. A technical undergraduate degree coupled with an M.B.A. is a frequent combination, but undergraduate majors in the sciences, social sciences, or humanities account for a large percentage of M.B.A. candidates today.

The Graduate Management Admission Test (GMAT)

More than 180,000 potential M.B.A. candidates each year take the Graduate Management Admission Test, which is required for admission to most graduate business schools. The GMAT is not a test of knowledge in specific subjects—for example, it does not test knowledge of economics or accounting. Instead, it provides a standardized measurement for general verbal and mathematical abilities that are developed over a long period of time and are associated with success in the first year of study at graduate schools of management. There are no passing or failing scores, and undergraduate preparation in business is not required to take the GMAT. International students should bear in mind that the test is given only in English.

The current GMAT consists of eight separately timed sections, each containing 20 to 35 multiple-choice questions. The total testing time is four hours.

The *quantitative* sections of the test measure basic mathematical skills and understanding of elementary concepts, and the ability to reason quantitatively, solve quantitative problems, and interpret graphic data.

The *verbal* sections of the test measure the ability to understand and evaluate what is read and to recognize basic conventions of standard written English.

The GMAT yields three scores—verbal, quantitative, and total—each of which is reported on a fixed scale. Verbal and quantitative scores range from 0 to 60, although scores below 10 and above 46 are rare. Total scores are reported on a scale ranging from 200 to 800, but extreme scores (below 250 and above 700) are uncommon. You will receive a report of your GMAT scores, along with a percentile rank for each score, showing the percentage of examinees tested in the past three years who scored below your scores.

In the "Key Facts" section of this book, you will note that many schools have reported the middle 80 percent range of GMAT scores for their entering students. While it may be tempting to interpret this range as an approximation of the quality of the school, resist the temptation. GMAT scores are only one criterion suggesting quality, and there are many other aspects of quality that may be more relevant to you. By the same token, don't assume that you have no chance of being admitted if your GMAT score was below the range for the school of your choice. If everything else in your application looks good, you may still be a successful candidate for admission.

Although you can repeat the GMAT, you should note that your three most recent GMAT scores will be included on your score report and probably averaged by the school. Unless your scores seem unusually low compared with other indicators of your ability, or unless there are other reasons to believe that you did not do your best on a test for which scores have been reported, taking the GMAT again is unlikely to result in a substantial increase in your scores. In fact, there is a chance that your scores may decline.

The GMAT is offered on four Saturdays each year—usually in January, March, June, and October—at centers throughout the world. See the chart below for the test dates for 1986-87, 1987-88, and 1988-89. Because some examination centers fill rapidly, early registration is advised. For details on the test and registration requirements, contact an undergraduate counseling office or graduate admissions office. You may also request a *GMAT Bulletin of Information* by writing to: Graduate Management Admission Test, CN 6101, Princeton, New Jersey 08541-6101. The Graduate Management Admission Council publishes *The Official Guide for GMAT Review* which includes test-taking strategies and sample tests as an aid to preparation. Instructions for ordering this publication are found on page 605.

GMAT Test Dates

1986-87	1987-88	1988-89
October 18	October 17	October 15
January 24	January 23	January 28
March 21	March 19	March 18
June 20	June 18	June 17

Graduate Management Admission Search Service (GMASS)

One time-saving way to consolidate and extend your search-and-selection efforts is to receive information from local, regional, and national business schools that are already interested in you—including some you may not have otherwise discovered. Offered free of charge by the Graduate Management Admission Council, the Graduate Management Admission Search Service is designed to accomplish just that.

In order to participate, you must take the Graduate Management Admission Test (GMAT). Using information obtained from your GMAT registration form, the GMASS makes your name and address available to graduate management institutions that have expressed an interest in persons with characteristics similar to yours. For example, a school might be interested in men or women who have particular undergraduate majors, have work experience, reside in certain states, have undergraduate averages or GMAT scores within certain ranges, or have combinations of these or other characteristics. If you meet their specified criteria, they may mail you information about their programs, admission procedures, and financial aid opportunities. Turn-around time between the test date and initial mailings is approximately 10 weeks. Complete information on the service and how you may register for it is contained in the *GMAT Bulletin of Information*.

Work or Military Experience

Although few schools specifically require work experience, many agree that it is of great value to students in their studies and career planning, and thus can be an important factor in the admission process. Whether the work or military experience is during undergraduate school or after, full-time or part-time, it can be an important indicator of the applicant's motivation and leadership qualities. Some schools, however, prefer applicants directly from college, when their basic academic skills and study habits are still fresh.

In a survey of GMAT test takers conducted in 1983-84, some 40 percent of the prospective applicants reported having between one and seven years of work experience; 14 percent had between one and seven years of work experience; 14 percent had between eight and ten years of experience. Students who had less than one year of experience made up almost 22 percent of the group and another 23 percent did not respond to the survey item.

Your Application

The admissions criteria discussed up to this point have one thing in common: they're past history. In contrast, the preparation, contents, and timing of your application reveal a great deal about the person you are now and can be in the future. Many admissions boards are very conscious of this fact. To them, your application is an important part of the total package you present. And remember, it is the total package that will determine whether or not you are admitted. If they're not quite convinced, your application may clinch it.

Think of your application in terms of answering questions that admissions officials will be asking themselves about you—questions that reflect your potential for success in graduate management education and in your future career. These questions might include the following:

■ *Have you identified your career goals?* Show admissions officers that you've given serious thought to your reasons for pursuing an M.B.A. education, and they're likely to consider your application in a more favorable light. Clearly articulating your career goals can gain you a definite advantage, especially if you can show how an M.B.A. would be useful in achieving them. If you haven't yet made a career decision, try to identify areas of particular interest or skills you want to acquire for career advancement. Then use these points to demonstrate why you feel an M.B.A. program would meet your individual needs.

■ *Are you serious about your application?* Don't just tell them—show them that you're serious—by making your application as complete, accurate, and meticulously prepared as possible. Technically, you'll meet most requirements if your application is neatly written or typed. In reality, that's not good enough. Typing is essential. If you're willing to invest in your graduate education, start by investing in a professional-looking typing job if you can't do it yourself. (Hint: if you make an extra copy to use as a rough pencil draft, it's easier.) Good written English, organized thoughts and paragraphs also demonstrate your organizational skills.

■ *Are you careful about details?* If you don't answer all the questions, or if your answers are incomplete or inaccurate, the response will be predictable: no. And while it may seem obvious, remember that the people who will be reviewing your application are highly educated; poor grammar, incorrect punctuation, and misspellings will flag their attention. To be on the safe side, get a pre-typing quality check from a friend, relative, coworker, or anyone whose written communications skills you respect.

■ *Are you willing to do more than is required?* Most schools will be pleased to accept additional information from you such as a resume; a statement about something that wasn't asked but might give a better idea of your motivation, interests, or abilities; or a clarification of something in your credentials that might be confusing. It is unwise, however, to include extraneous material. If you need a reply to an inquiry, ask the question in a separate letter rather than including it with your application.

■ *Do you plan ahead?* Time will tell—literally. The deadline for admission applications is usually indicated in the school catalog. For full-time programs that begin in the fall, you should apply at least 6 to 10 months in advance (some say as much as a year ahead)—particularly if you're a student applying from outside the U.S., or if you will also be applying for an assistantship or financial aid. Lead times are usually shorter for programs that begin at other times of the year and for most part-time programs. However, many schools observe a common reply date. In any event, be sure to see whether the schools that interest you have rolling admissions—admissions throughout the year. If they do, an early application will most likely assure you of an early response, so you will have a better idea of your options and can avoid the necessity for delay tactics while waiting to hear about admission elsewhere. As a general rule, remember: evaluations can't be completed until all your credentials, GMAT results, and other materials arrive, so you'll be doing yourself a disservice if you don't plan ahead. This includes finding out well in advance when and where you can take the GMAT and making all necessary arrangements to have your test scores sent to all schools to which you're applying.

Recommendations

Recommendations can be extremely important in confirming or augmenting your other credentials, or in interpreting your grades or background. Although some schools may require only one recommendation, you may wish to provide several—but make sure you check with the school first.

Some schools may tell you the type of person to use as a reference and may provide rather detailed evaluation forms. In general, the most meaningful recommendations are written by professors, employers, student advisers, and alumni you have known in a business or academic context—providing they know you well, respect you, and can contribute specific comments rather than vague generalizations. The stature or fame of the person recommending you is usually less important than what he or she has to say. Of course, even the best recommendation will be valueless if your reference procrastinates past the deadline. For these reasons, you should be very careful in choosing the people you ask to recommend you. And *do ask*—before you list their names.

Providing your references with a brief outline of your background and material about the admissions procedure used by the school is one way to increase the effectiveness of their recommendations. It will require additional effort on your part, but they may welcome the assistance in making their recommendations more meaningful. If they do wish this help, avoid adjectives and concentrate on specific experiences that demonstrate why you would make a good business school candidate and a good manager.

Assessing Your Chances for Admission

All the steps and guidelines discussed in this chapter are designed to help you elicit a favorable response to the number one question posed by candidates: will I be admitted to the school of my choice? Remember, though, that you can help increase your chances by fine-tuning your own decision-making process first to ensure maximum compatibility between your goals and those of the school. Knowing the number of spaces available at a school—and the number of applicants—may also help you set realistic expectations for your admission to a specific program. At this point, a brief review is in order to make sure you have taken all possible steps.

1. Do you have a clear picture of your career goals? If not, have you explored all the possibilities, or would additional work experience help clarify your objectives?

2. Have you researched schools that offer M.B.A. programs in areas most compatible with your career goals?

3. Do you have a strong academic record? If not, have you explored the possibility of other academic endeavors that might help offset it?

4. Did you take the Graduate Management Admission Test?

5. Have you identified the most meaningful references from your academic and work experiences?

6. Have you identified the type of M.B.A. program most consistent with your objectives?

7. Have you contacted the admissions personnel and discussed your particular qualifications?

A great deal of your personal resources, time, and effort must be invested in ensuring the success of your application to graduate school. Considering the amount of money you may be investing after acceptance, giving it anything less than your best try would be cheating yourself.

5 Financing Graduate Management Education

For many people in today's economy, the financial aspects of earning an M.B.A. are a major decision factor. The impact of changing financial aid expectations and rising costs must be kept in mind as you weigh the substantial investment required against the promise of a more interesting career and greater financial rewards than you would otherwise be likely to obtain. Later chapters discuss aid programs for special interest groups; this chapter, however, is concerned with what you can expect to pay and what avenues are open to finance it.

- *The cost factor:* The costs of individual school programs are included in many of the school descriptions in this *Guide*. In general, however, graduate management school costs can range from less than $2,000 for tuition alone to more than $18,000 with tuition, room, board, books, and travel to and from school included.

    Perhaps the greatest single cost determinant is whether you enter a full- or part-time program. Part-time candidates are able to distribute tuition costs over a longer period of time, with the result that budgeting is easier and on-going costs can usually be covered out of current income. If you are working, you may even get your company to pay for your studies through a tuition reimbursement plan. Some organizations even provide leaves of absence, with pay and tuition, for full-time M.B.A. study. Attending a state school can also help keep costs down. Other than that, money-saving techniques are generally the same ones undergraduates rely on—using college meal tickets or eating in the college cafeteria and living in the dorm. If you are married and need family quarters, costs will, of course, be higher.

- *Estimating financial need:* On page 28 is a chart for calculating your costs at three different graduate management schools and the income you will be able to apply toward those costs.

Most of the schools described in this book have supplied estimated costs for attending their graduate management programs. You can use these figures as a guide for computing your costs. Unspecified expenses can usually be obtained by consulting the school's literature. You will want to keep in mind that the cost of goods and services varies greatly in different regions and that the costs published in this *Guide* were supplied by the schools in the fall of 1985 and may be estimated for the following academic year. It is also wise to allow for some tuition increase each year to account for inflation.

Next, calculate your cash resources. Some students are surprised to learn that loan and financial aid officers may expect M.B.A. candidates to convert any assets—cars, stocks, bonds, trust funds—as well as personal savings toward the cost of their education. If you are married, your spouse's income should be included as well. In addition, parents or a "supporter" (someone who claims a student as a dependent) may be expected to contribute money. According to current federal standards, a student is classified as "dependent" if he or she meets any one of the following criteria for the current and/or previous year: (a) was or will be claimed by a parent or supporter as a U.S. income tax exemption, (b) received or will receive $750 or more for support from a parent or supporter, (c) lived or will live with a parent or supporter for more than six weeks. If a student is declared a dependent and is applying for certain government funds, schools weigh the parents' or supporter's ability to give financial help—not their willingness. This is also true in some cases for students applying for nongovernment monies. Check with financial aid officers of individual schools about their policies concerning this matter.

Finally, to determine your financial need, subtract your cash resources from your total expenses.

Sources of Financial Aid

Graduate business students generally turn to four different types of financial aid resources:

- scholarships and fellowships,
- teaching and research assistantships,
- loans, and
- self-help employment and work/study programs.

Whether or not you can find the money to attend graduate school depends a great deal on how much searching you are willing to do. Start by reading school catalogs and talking to financial aid officers. One of the following publications on financial aid may also be a good initial step in your search.

- *Financial Aid for Higher Education Catalog.* William C. Brown Co., 2460 Kerper Blvd., Dubuque, IA 52001.

- *Need a Lift?* ($1), National Emblem Sales Division, American Legion, Box 1055, Indianapolis, IN 46206.

SCHOLARSHIPS AND FELLOWSHIPS

Scholarships and fellowships are highly coveted and fiercely sought, since they amount to "free money"—funds which do not require repayment and which are not considered income for tax purposes. Sometimes linked to particular fields of study, they are awarded on the basis of merit, on the basis of merit and need, and on the basis of need alone. Some grants apply only to tuition and fees; others provide money for living expenses as well. Applications for grants are only considered after you have been accepted for admission. As a general rule, they are terminated if a specified level of scholarship is not maintained.

Funding through scholarships and fellowships is available from a broad range of sources, including colleges, foundations, businesses, professional and civic organizations, and state and federal governments. The financial aid office at the schools of your choice can supply you with information on available grants and how to apply. In addition, scholarships may even be available from your local chamber of commerce, veteran's organization, or your parent's employer.

In some cases, special scholarship opportunities and programs are available to minorities. Sources include the following:

- ASPIRA, 114 E. 28th St., New York, NY 10016

- Consortium for Graduate Study in Management, 101 North Skinker Blvd., Box 1132, St. Louis, MO 63130

- *Financial Aid for Minorities in Business,* Garrett Park Press, P.O. Box 190, Garrett Park, MD 20896 ($3 per copy; make check payable to Garrett Park Press)

- *Financing Your Graduate Management Education,* Graduate Management Admission Council, 11601 Wilshire Blvd., 10th Floor, Los Angeles, CA 90025

- League of United Latin American Citizens (LULAC), National Educational Services Centers, Inc., Suite 716, 400 First St., N.W., Washington, DC 20001

- McKnight Programs in Higher Education in Florida, 201 E. Kennedy Blvd., Suite 1510, Tampa, FL 33602

- Minority Admissions Recruitment Network (MARN), Atlanta University Graduate School of Business, Central Office, P.O. Box 244, Atlanta, GA 30314

- National Black MBA Association, Inc., 111 East Wacker Drive, Suite 600, Chicago, IL 60601

School counselors who advise minority groups and aid officers may be able to inform you of other sources. Many schools have specific scholarships for minority group applicants; be sure to ask the representatives about these possibilities.

Financial aid programs aimed at encouraging women's enrollment in graduate management schools and aiding their subsequent management careers are available from businesses, foundations, professional organizations and local chapters of such organizations as the American Association of University Women (AAUW). Graduate schools may also administer scholarships and other aid earmarked for women; you can find out by checking with their financial aid offices.

TEACHING AND RESEARCH ASSISTANTSHIPS

Many schools offer assistantships to qualified students. Students are generally asked to work a given number of hours per week in return for a flat fee salary, and sometimes remission of tuition. Depending on how the school structures the position, the pay may or may not be taxable.

Duties will vary according to the school and department need. As a teaching assistant, you might evaluate and grade papers, tutor undergraduate students, and even teach undergraduate seminars and courses—all providing valuable insight into the classroom process. As a research assistant, you would probably help faculty members on research projects, which can be extremely interesting in terms of both the project and the close collaboration involved.

Although they may add to your income, assistantships have one drawback: time. Some require so much time that accepting an assistantship can detract from your academic work and cause you to take longer finishing your degree. For this reason, some schools do not offer assistantships to M.B.A. candidates.

LOANS

Borrowing money has traditionally been the major source of financial aid at some institutions. Loans vary in amount, rate of interest, and schedule of repayment, and are granted by schools, banks, and other lending institutions, and state and federal governments.

The U.S. Department of Education has two major loan programs applicable to graduate management students: the National Direct Student Loan (NDSL), which is administered by the schools; and the Guaranteed Student Loan (GSL/PLUS Loans), which are low-interest loans made by a lender such as a bank or other financial institution and insured by the federal government or a state guaranteeing agency.

Because policies are subject to change, the current status of programs should be checked at the time of application. The most recent regulatory decisions, however, allow qualified students who are U.S. citizens enrolled at least half-time in graduate school to borrow up to a total of $12,000 from the NDSL program, less any amount previously borrowed for undergraduate or graduate studies, through their schools. Interest is five percent, and repayment begins six months after you leave school or drop below half-time status. The amount of the payment depends on the size of your debt, but usually you must pay at least $30 per month (less if the school agrees to a lesser amount due to extraordinary circumstances). You are allowed up to 10 years for repayment.

Qualified students enrolled at least half-time in graduate school may borrow up to $25,000 from the GSL program, less any amount previously borrowed. The maximum loan in a given year is $5,000. However, you may have to show financial need, which may limit the size of your GSL. Interest is eight percent of the balance for new borrowers. For students who currently have a seven or nine percent GSL, the rate on additional loans will continue to be seven or nine percent. Loan repayment begins 6 months after you leave school if your interest rate is eight or nine percent, and 9 to 12 months after you leave school if your interest rate is seven percent. Some state and local lenders may restrict borrowing on this plan, but the lender generally must allow you at least 5 years to repay the loan and may allow you up to 10 years.

Meant to provide additional funds for educational expense, PLUS loans are available from lenders such as banks, credit unions, or savings and loan associations. The interest rate for these loans is 12 percent. Graduate students or their parents may borrow up to $3,000 per year to a total of $15,000, although PLUS borrowers do not have to show need. An insurance premium of up to one percent per year of the outstanding balance of the loan is usually collected in advance by the lender. Repayment begins within 60 days, although borrowers who are full-time students, on active military duty, or a volunteer with certain qualified service organizations such as the Peace Corps or VISTA are entitled to a deferment of principal payments. All borrowers must begin paying the interest within 60 days. Graduate students are also eligible to borrow up to $3,000 a year from the Auxiliary Loan Program to Assist Students, commonly referred to as ALAS. The interest rate on ALAS loans is 12 percent.

Check with school financial aid officers for any applicable budgetary restrictions or for information about school "aid package" requirements. For full details about federal loan programs, write for *The Student Guide: Five Federal Financial Aid Programs,* from the Public Documents Distribution Center, Dept. DEA-87, Pueblo, Colorado 81009 or simply complete and return the reply card found in the back of this *Guide.*

SELF-HELP AND WORK/ STUDY PROGRAMS

A wide variety of part-time job opportunities is available at some schools to supplement assistantships or otherwise take up your financial slack. Graduate students at some schools can work part time in the computer room, mail room, or library; as waiters; or as dorm or residence hall advisers or counselors—sometimes in return for free room. The federal government also offers the College Work Study (CWS) program, through which you can work with a public or private nonprofit agency on a part-time basis, or during summers and school vacation periods. Since traditional part-time jobs are usually scarce in college communities, you may also create your own part-time job by filling some basic or innovative service need. Like assistantships, however, part-time jobs of all types have the same potential drawback: they can cut into your academic and personal time. For this reason, some M.B.A. programs limit the number of hours you can work. Summer jobs can help offset expenses, but don't count on them for major financial help, as well-paying summer jobs are at a premium.

Applying for Financial Aid

Applications for financial aid often have deadlines that precede school application deadlines, so plan ahead! Most M.B.A. schools require financial aid applicants to submit a written statement to support their claims. This is a prerequisite if you are applying for federal or state monies. Applications generally must be made each year you are in school and wish to receive funds.

In an effort to standardize these applications, many schools use the Graduate and Professional School Financial Aid Service (GAPSFAS) as their need analysis service, while others use the Financial Aid Form (FAF) published by the College Scholarship Service (CSS) of the College Board. Students using either system answer questions about personal and family finances on a standardized form. Both GAPSFAS and CSS send their reports on the applicant's estimated resources to the schools requested by the applicant. The schools in turn decide how much (if any) and what kind of aid will be given. Information about GAPSFAS or CSS and the necessary forms can be obtained from the schools you are considering or by filling out and returning the appropriate business reply card found in the back of this book. Caution: Check with aid officers to determine which form is used.

How to Determine Financial Need

Your decision to pursue a professional management degree may depend on finding sufficient funds. The guide below suggests how to analyze your own specific financial situation. The individual school descriptions in this book will help you complete this guide; additional information can be found in school brochures.

EXPENSES	SCHOOL 1	SCHOOL 2	SCHOOL 3
1. Student's tuition and fees	$_____	$_____	$_____
2. Student's books	$_____	$_____	$_____
3. Student's equipment and supplies	$_____	$_____	$_____
4. Spouse's (or prospective spouse's) direct educational expenses—tuition, fees, books equipment, supplies	$_____	$_____	$_____
5. Rent or mortgage, including heat, utilities	$_____	$_____	$_____
6. Food and household supplies	$_____	$_____	$_____
7. Clothing, laundry, and cleaning	$_____	$_____	$_____
8. Auto insurance premiums	$_____	$_____	$_____
9. Other transportation expenses	$_____	$_____	$_____
10. Medical and dental expenses	$_____	$_____	$_____
11. Child care	$_____	$_____	$_____
12. Debt repayment (amount to be repaid in next academic year)	$_____	$_____	$_____
13. Other expenses	$_____	$_____	$_____
14. Total expenses (add lines 1-13)	$_____	$_____	$_____
RESOURCES			
15. Personal savings or assets	$_____	$_____	$_____
16. Student's academic year employment	$_____	$_____	$_____
17. Spouse's academic year employment	$_____	$_____	$_____
18. Summer savings	$_____	$_____	$_____
19. Financial assistance from parents (and other relatives)	$_____	$_____	$_____
20. Scholarships, fellowships, grants	$_____	$_____	$_____
21. Loans	$_____	$_____	$_____
22. Other income	$_____	$_____	$_____
23. Total resources (add lines 15-22)	$_____	$_____	$_____
24. Minus total expenses (line 14)	−$_____	−$_____	−$_____
25. Excess/Shortfall (subtract line 24 from line 23)	$_____	$_____	$_____

6 Considerations for Minority Group and Foreign Students

With the change in consciousness levels throughout today's society, both the public and private sectors of the business community have changed accordingly. Increased pressure from federal government agencies and organizations representing minority group and foreign students has not only pushed many companies into relaxing the barriers that formerly kept minority group members out of corporate managerial structures—in many cases, there is now active corporate recruiting to create a more equitable balance. With the opening of these new horizons, the practical career goals of people in these previously underrepresented groups have soared accordingly. There is now far more incentive to invest the time, money, and effort necessary to prepare for career opportunities that were previously unavailable. The M.B.A. degree can also provide foreign students with a means for obtaining a solid management background. In this chapter, we will discuss how a graduate management degree relates to realistic admissions and career expectations for minority group members and foreign students.

> *"We are over the hump of having sex or race be a ticket to employment. Companies are in a more realistic mode of hiring people for their skills and background."*
> An Assistant Dean of Placement

Minority Group Students

Most graduate management schools today encourage applications from Black, American Indian, and Asian-American students. In their attempt to achieve better enrollment balances, many schools are targeting special funds, recruitment efforts, and placement services to attract members of these minority groups—often competing directly with corporations seeking to hire qualified students in these categories as soon as they complete their undergraduate studies. Faced with today's financial

aid squeeze, many students already burdened with an undergraduate debt load may be tempted by the lure of a good early job. However, for minority students whose sights are firmly set on significantly better jobs, higher salaries, and faster career advancement over the long run, the recruitment tug of war can be extremely beneficial when seeking admission.

Most schools are firmly committed to boosting their enrollment of students from minority groups. The primary factor limiting these applicants appears to be money. To help offset the financial hurdle, a number of recruitment/aid programs have been developed that are funded by major nonprofit foundations. Major programs designed to encourage enrollment of students from minority groups in business and management programs are listed on page 26 of this book and described in the GMAC brochure, *Financing Your Graduate Management Education—Information for Minority Candidates,* which is available by writing to the Graduate Management Admission Council, 11601 Wilshire Blvd., Suite 1060, Los Angeles, CA 90025-1748. General information for applicants from minority groups who are contemplating an M.B.A. program is provided in the booklet, *The MBA, Access to Opportunity.* Currently, two editions are available: one for Black students and one for Hispanic students. When requesting a copy from the GMAC address given above, students should specify which edition they would like to receive.

Once in the job market, M.B.A. graduates from minority groups have been attaining starting salaries at least as high as other graduates for comparable work. In fact, they sometimes earn more—partially due to the demand for qualified M.B.A. graduates from minority groups and also because these graduates tend to have more work experience than other graduates. Many M.B.A. executives from minority groups who are seeking career advancement are also buttressing their job expertise in a

number of ways—for example, by networking to gain greater insight into different companies' social norms, and, with increasing frequency, by answering the call of the executive recruiter.

Additional information about companies or fields that employ M.B.A.s may be available from the following:

■ *Black Collegian* (Journal). Black Collegian Services, Inc., 1240 S. Broad, New Orleans, LA 70125.

■ *Black Enterprise* (Journal). Earl G. Graves Inc., 130 Fifth Ave., New York, NY 10011.

■ *The NSBE Journal,* The National Society of Black Engineers, 1240 S. Broad, New Orleans, LA 70125.

■ National Black MBA Association, 111 East Wacker Drive, Suite 600, Chicago, IL 60601.

Foreign Students

Foreign students applying to M.B.A. programs in the United States have special concerns about the admission process, financial assistance, and housing. To address these concerns, the Graduate Management Admission Council has prepared a pamphlet titled *International Guide to Graduate Management Programs.* Any student registering for the GMAT from outside the United States will automatically receive a copy of the pamphlet together with his or her score report.

Foreign students represent between 10 and 20 percent of the student body in most graduate management schools. They face the same fast-paced challenge as their peers and are usually expected to meet most schools' regular admission requirements. In addition, they must provide admissions committees with evidence that they can understand rapidly spoken idiomatic English, participate actively in discussion, read widely and quickly, and write reports and other required materials. Completion of all undergraduate work is sometimes required before a foreign student can even apply for admission.

Because command of the language is so vital, most graduate business and management schools require foreign students whose undergraduate training was not conducted in English to demonstrate their proficiency by submitting scores achieved on the Test of English as a Foreign Language (TOEFL), which is administered by Educational Testing Service several times a year throughout the world. Schools that require the TOEFL of foreign applicants may have widely differing minimum score limits. This will depend to some extent upon the facilities for English language study at the school, the number of foreign students enrolled, and the rigor of the program. It is also important to remember that the GMAT, required by all the schools described in this book, is given only in English. Copies of the TOEFL *Bulletin* are usually available at United States educational commissions and foundations, United States Information Services (USIS) offices, binational centers, and private organizations, such as the Institute of International Education (IIE). Students who are unable to obtain a *Bulletin* locally should request one *well in advance* from TOEFL, CN 6151, Princeton, NJ, 08541-6151, USA. A business reply card for requesting a TOEFL *Bulletin* is found at the back of this book.

An additional test, the Test of Spoken English (TSE), has been developed to measure students' ability to speak English. An increasing number of educational institutions are now requiring the TSE. Information on this test may be obtained by writing to the TOEFL address given above.

Foreign students applying to business and management schools should submit their applications a year before the program begins. The extra time is necessary because of the longer processing time required, particularly since foreign students' undergraduate transcripts are usually not written in English. Many schools require that a translation of transcripts be submitted with the application. Even after translation, admissions officers spend additional time evaluating courses and credit systems that differ greatly from undergraduate programs in the United States. Students should check application deadlines carefully and mail all materials via air mail.

Admissions policies differ between schools, and within schools, for domestic and foreign applicants. In addition, all M.B.A. programs in the United States do not use the same standard criteria in making admission decisions, and many programs have more qualified candidates than they can accommodate. Students should review the literature from each institution about its admission policies and practices to determine its particular focus. Schools also differ in how much and what kind of special assistance and financial aid they will provide. Some let foreign students forge their own way; others may have special advisers and programs to help foreign students deal with housing, finances, personal adjustment, and questions relating to immigration. As a general rule, however, most graduate management schools will not provide financial aid for the first year of a foreign student's studies. Some schools may require evidence of sufficient funds before reviewing a student's application. This type of information, along with the number of foreign students enrolled in the school, can be obtained by writing to the schools at the addresses indicated in the school descriptions in this *Guide*.

Although most federal financial aid programs require that recipients be U.S. citizens or have permanent resident status, other loans, grants, and fellowships may be available. Students should check first with their home government, a local U.S. consulate, and other advisers. The following publication may be useful in providing information on graduate management programs and aid opportunities: *A Selected List of Major Fellowship Opportunities and Aid to Advanced Education for Foreign Nationals,* available without charge from the National Science Foundation, 18th & G Sts. N.W., Washington, DC 20550, Att'n: Publications Office.

All students who are not United States citizens or permanent residents must maintain a visa status that allows registration as a student. To secure a visa for study in the United States, students must obtain a Certificate of Eligibility from the college or university that has offered admission. This certificate cannot be issued to a student accepted for admission until evidence of satisfactory proficiency in the English language and documentation of adequate financial support is on file.

Two types of visas are available for foreign students studying in the U.S.:

■ A Student Visa (F-1) is obtained with an I-20 Certificate of Eligibility issued by the school the student plans to attend. With an F-1 visa the student must enroll in a full-time program at the school that issued the Certificate of Eligibility used to secure the visa. If the student is accompanied by a spouse or child, he or she enters on an F-2 visa. F-2 visa holders, however, may not be employed while in the United States.

■ An Exchange-Visitor Visa (J-1) is obtained with an IAP-66 Certificate of Eligibility issued by the school or a sponsoring agency. This visa is required for students sponsored by certain agencies, foundations, and governments. Students who have other sources of funding may obtain the IAP-66 on request. In most cases, Exchange Visitors must leave the United States at the conclusion of their program of study, may not change their visa status, and may not apply for permanent residency in the United States until they have returned to their home countries for at least two years. The spouse of an Exchange Visitor enters on a J-2 visa and may, in some cases, obtain permission to work.

It is extremely difficult—often impossible—to change visa status after arrival in the United States. If a student obtains a Tourist Visa (B-2) from the U.S. Consul, it will be impossible to change to F-1 student status after arrival in the U.S., unless the words "Prospective Student" appear on the B-2 visa stamp in the student's passport.

Foreign students should be aware of the great diversity that exists in housing accommodations available to graduate students in the United States. Many universities provide at least some housing on campus and may give international students preference for it. Students should keep in mind, however, that it is their responsibility to make housing arrangements after they have been admitted.

On-campus housing can range from a dormitory room, which is shared with another student, to a small apartment, to a reasonably sized three-bedroom apartment for a family. The monthly rent for on-campus accommodations may be substantially less than the rate for off-campus housing, and this can make it an attractive alternative.

Many graduate students live off campus, either by themselves or with a small group of students in a house or apartment. Most universities have offices that list available rooms, apartments, and houses; provide maps of the local area; and give students advice on reasonable rents and lease arrangements. Rents throughout the United States vary greatly depending on location and demand. For an estimate of housing costs and specific information about on- and off-campus housing at particular institutions, review the schools' publications or write to the admissions office.

Since the United States does not have a national health plan, the potential cost of health care for foreign students who are not insured may be extraordinarily high. Some sponsoring organizations provide health insurance, and universities may also offer insurance plans. It is very important to review these plans. Some provide hospital coverage (major medical) while others provide only simple coverage for use of the student health center on campus.

Married students should find out if the plan being considered will cover spouse and family or if supplemental insurance will be needed. Health insurance costs may well exceed $800-$1,000 for each year of the M.B.A. program. It is recommended that all individuals planning to study in the U.S. have adequate health insurance.

Due to immigration laws, international students are severely limited in their ability to work while in the U.S. as students. Some schools may offer the option of working on campus as a teaching assistant, resident assistant, or office worker to students who have the necessary skills, but off-campus employment is very difficult to find and may not be permitted by a student's visa status. Job opportunities for spouses may also be restricted by visa status.

Employment opportunities in the United States for international students who have completed their program of study are definitely limited, unless the students have strong prior technical training. In addition, very few firms visit campuses to recruit students for international positions outside the United States. Necessarily then, a foreign student's job search will be largely independent of the formal recruiting/interviewing process. Many international students enter an M.B.A. program knowing that they will return to their former employer or family business when they have completed their program of study. No international student should enter a M.B.A. program with the assumption that he or she will find employment in the United States.

FINAL CHECKLIST FOR FOREIGN APPLICANTS

To be sure that you have completed all the necessary steps in the admission process, review the steps in the list below.

✓ Institution's application form. All questions answered. Form signed.

✓ Academic credentials from all postsecondary institutions attended (official documents, with notarized translation if necessary).

✓ Employment history summary.

✓ Essay/statement of purpose in attending school.

✓ Letters of recommendation.

✓ Application fee, in United States dollars.

✓ GMAT registration submitted. Institutions to receive scores correctly designated.

✓ TOEFL registration submitted. Institutions to receive scores correctly designated.

✓ Financing arranged for total period of study.

✓ Financial aid applications filed with those institutions that have requested one (some colleges do not accept applications for aid from foreign applicants).

7 The Goal: Careers in Management

There is no one best career for all M.B.A. students. There are, however, substantial data available from school job counseling and placement offices, organizations such as the Association of MBA Executives, and through private studies, about the nature and potential of different management careers.

In terms of specific career outlook, it is wise always to remember that the ostensibly hard numbers of hiring and salary trends actually reflect differences in job function, geography, and a candidate's academic standing, major, age, and work experience. They may also indicate peaks of demand vs. supply that will change as vacuums are filled and new areas of opportunity arise. And—one final caution—they may be overrated due to the unrealistically high expectations sometimes fueled by recruiters, and the simple fact that problems may unexpectedly surface in a particular career slot or industry. You will be wise to assess your own qualities and goals, and then investigate the realities of the job market at the time of your graduation to see how your personal characteristics relate to the opportunities that exist. In terms of specific jobs, you will want to know where they lead after entry level, and how healthy and growing the particular organization is.

A few elements of what employers look for in M.B.A. graduates seem clear. It appears that employers prefer applicants who have had work experience and who offer a firm foundation in the fundamental areas of management, accounting/finance, and marketing. In addition, it is apparent that most employers are seeking candidates who can provide general administrative abilities rather than narrow technical expertise and who appear to have long-range management potential.

As a starting point for evaluating your options, study the following discussion of management careers in different businesses and industries, in the public sector and not-for-profit organizations, and in entrepreneurial endeavors. Bear in mind, though, that the progressions illustrated are not fixed. As a neophyte, you can offer only potential. Your individual advancement depends on your ability to produce results, work successfully with your colleagues, and learn from experience, as well as on the economic climate and the size and growth of your organization.

Managerial Functions

While there is no "typical" management career, there are certain similarities in the way responsibilities are handled and delegated as an M.B.A. moves up the management ladder. Sometimes as an entering M.B.A. you will participate in a training program; in other cases you will be required to learn on the job. As you advance, different skills are required. At entry level, you would most likely be using a particular technical skill. As you move up, you would then have increased decision-making authority for that area—possibly supervising those in your former functional capacity, guiding their work, and developing subordinates. This can be an extremely important point, since you'll be demonstrating your worth not as a technician, but as executive material with the broad administrative skills employers want—particularly if your background is strong in the functional areas of finance/accounting, marketing, and general management.

As your scope of responsibility increases, you might supervise people who perform a number of different functions, or assume greater responsibility for relationships with other companies and organizations. At this level, and those that follow, you would be increasingly responsible for policy making, long-term planning, major financial decisions, and the overall allocation of personnel, materials, and investments.

Management Careers in Business and Industry

Accounting

Although accounting represented only eight percent of all M.B.A. placements in 1983, economic factors point to a rise in accounting's importance, due to increased control consciousness, fiscal awareness, and a need for greater security. Accounting's broad hiring pattern is due to the fact that it is fundamental to virtually all organizations—first in classifying, analyzing, measuring, and planning an organization's costs and revenues, and then in designing systems to make the organization's financial procedures more efficient and accurate.

M.B.A. graduates who go into accounting may work as public accountants (C.P.A.s) after certification or as accountants on the staffs of businesses and other organizations. Corporate staff accountants might serve as financial analysts or internal auditors involved in such areas as resource allocation, management information systems, and on some aspects of financial planning and control. Their jobs can be oriented toward budgeting and analysis or toward planning and forecasting. The audits of publicly held companies are primarily handled by large public accounting firms; however, both large and small accounting firms have consulting divisions that enable them to meet a wide range of financial and nonfinancial consulting needs.

Additional information about careers in accounting may be obtained from the following sources:

American Institute of Certified Public Accountants, 1211 Avenue of the Americas, New York, NY 10036

American Society of Women Accountants, 35 East Wacker Drive, Chicago, IL 60601

Institute of Certified Management Accountants, 10 Paragon Drive, Montvale, NJ 07645

National Association of Accountants, 10 Paragon Drive, Montvale, NJ 07645

National Society of Public Accountants, 1010 N. Fairfax St., Alexandria, VA 22314

Finance

The broad area of finance provides more jobs than any other field for M.B.A. graduates. In 1983, 25 percent of all new M.B.A.s went into finance. Finance encompasses all areas of money management, from analyzing how a business uses its monetary and other resources, to raising new capital investments. The diversity of opportunities within the field points M.B.A. graduates down several promising career paths. Among these are commercial banking; financial management in a variety of businesses and other organizations; and investment banking, which includes the high prestige areas of corporate finance, trading, and the more entrepreneurial environment of sales.

M.B.A.s working in commercial banks, savings and loan associations, or other related institutions are typically involved in making credit and loan decisions, servicing loans, managing the bank's cash resources, and directing or advising companies or individuals on investments, trusts, and estates. According to data compiled by the Association of MBA Executives, 9 percent of 1983 M.B.A. graduates found jobs in consumer banking.

Within corporations, the finance function is concerned with measuring in dollars how effectively the company is using its resources; whether it is obtaining optimal value for its money; the amount of cash necessary to pursue certain enterprises; and how those enterprises should be financed.

Competition for positions is particularly keen in investment banking, which is frequently identified with Wall Street and the securities markets. The limited number of positions are primarily filled by new M.B.A.s recruited from full-time programs and further trained in internal development programs. As a whole, investment banks advise corporations, municipalities, individual investors, and other major clients on how to invest their funds profitably. The banks are also directly involved in underwriting, that is, helping their clients obtain financing for major

projects and enterprises. In addition, investment banks are involved in arranging and financing corporate mergers and acquisitions.

Within the investment banking industry, corporate-finance division spots are sometimes thought to offer more chances to work more closely with senior partners while putting together major corporate debt and equity offerings; trader's jobs and sales division spots, on the other hand, are frequently associated with significantly higher earning potential.

Additional information about careers in the fields of finance and banking may be available from the following organizations:

American Bankers Association, Banking Education Network, 1120 Connecticut Ave., N.W., Washington, DC 20036

Board of Governors, Federal Reserve System, Personnel Department, Washington, DC 20551

National Association of Bank Women, Inc., National Office, 500 N. Michigan Ave., Suite 1400, Chicago, IL 60611

Human Resources Management

In 1982, three percent of all M.B.A. graduates entered jobs in the functional area of personnel. Future graduates, however, may well find even broader opportunities in this field of concentration. Due to changes in the strategic as well as the operational concerns of today's employers, the traditional managerial function of personnel administration is in many cases being transformed by a new concept that links productivity with work enrichment or enlargement.

This new broader concept has come to be known by several different names, including human resources management, manpower administration, manpower planning, and other titles. Whatever its name, human resources management reflects a new policy-making orientation that extends far beyond the traditional personnel areas of recruitment, selection, compensation, training, and labor relations. Added to these are new requirements for developing and implementing policies in such areas as human resource planning and forecasting, equal employment opportunity and affirmative action, personnel development and career planning, and organization development. The human resources manager must also relate broader policies to the specific management problems and personnel needs of different organizational areas, such as accounting, sales and marketing, finance, general administration, production, and long-range planning. Growing in both the public and private sectors, the trend toward human resources management has been caused by a variety of internal and external pressures. Demands for greater efficiency and cost savings have put new emphasis on reducing excessive employee turnover and improving productivity. At the same time, the increasing size, complexity, and technological orientation of many organizations have created a need for more long-range planning and formulation of human resource policies designed to interact with and reinforce overall organizational objectives. Affirmative action programs have required modifications in personnel recruiting, selection, and management development. These, in turn, are echoed by changing expectations on the part of established as well as new employees for more career planning, better work climate, and personal work environment.

Because many organizations are finding that their traditional personnel practices aren't geared to meeting these new needs, new managerial talent is being sought for positions such as manager of human resource planning and career development, human resources manager, management resources and development consultant, director of affirmative action planning, manager of managerial inventory and placement, manager of organizational development, human resource forecaster, and so forth. As a result, the skills and techniques of personnel/human resources management may well open the door for M.B.A. graduates to a broader variety of entry-level jobs.

Additional information concerning the area of human resource management may be obtained from the following organization:
American Society for Personnel
  Administration
606 N. Washington St.
Alexandria, VA 22314.

International Business

With the increasing globalization of business, a specialized variation on general business administration has emerged as a distinctive and high-growth-potential managerial career field. Basically, multinational M.B.A.s are involved in managing imports and exports for consumer firms (who generally offer more jobs and higher salaries), industrials, and banks. In the public sector, international business also extends to a growing number of local, national, and internationally based government agencies.

International business can be viewed as a management function as well as a specialized career field, depending on company size. Most jobs offering direct and immediate international involvement are found at larger banks and corporations, which seek M.B.A. graduates of specialized international business programs. It is also possible to move into international management through staff line advancement within a firm. Smaller banks and corporations tend to view international work as a junior middle-management function, to be entrusted to graduates of conventional M.B.A. programs only after several years of project work and orientation tours of duty in the company's different domestic components. The job title for such an entry-level spot might be financial analyst.

In conducting its international business, a company will typically have to deal with at least two sets of national laws, cultural practices, and transportation/import-export regulations. As a result, international business programs frequently stress diversified interdisciplinary mixtures that extend beyond basic business and economics into areas of foreign policy and international politics. Undergraduate degrees in such technical fields as engineering can also be helpful for certain specialized international business career paths.

Not surprisingly, multinational M.B.A.s typically travel abroad for a significant portion of the year. As a rule, consumer firms require more overseas travel than their industrial counterparts. Either way, command of at least one foreign language is usually a must. Prior experience in living outside the U.S., while considered potentially helpful, is generally not required.

Management Consulting

Although management consulting has been one of the most highly valued M.B.A. career paths for several years, consulting jobs are harder to find. For example, only 8 percent of 1983 M.B.A. graduates landed consulting spots.

Consulting is also extremely demanding work, generally requiring long hours and travel. To a large extent, consultants draw on a variety of independent outside sources to study a particular problem and recommend an appropriate course of action. (Consultants at one major firm are expected to be out on assignment one to four workdays each week). Initial assignments are usually to a consulting team and designed to provide close support and guidance from an experienced team member. These sometimes involve an introductory training program, seminars, and discussion groups. Soon the new consultant can work without direction, with regular work reviews and salary increases based on performance. Consulting is also somewhat of a "make or break" field; few firms hold on to those whose performance is less than superior.

The greatest number of job opportunities for consultants is in management consulting firms, where an M.B.A. graduate generally provides special expertise sought by corporations. This may utilize specialization in a limited field, such as marketing or computer operations, or a broad overview approach to a wide variety of organizational problems.

As mentioned above, some consulting operations are part of accounting firms. Wherever they are based, however, all require challenge-oriented people who are able to solve complex business problems. In addition, M.B.A.s who join consulting firms have had substantial work experience.

A source of information on careers in the field of management consulting is the Institute of Management Consultants, Inc., 19 W. 44th St., Suite 810-811, New York, NY 10036.

Management Information Systems

With the rapid evolution of computer technology, organizations in all areas of both the private and public sectors have turned to new data processing techniques to support their operations, management, and decision-making functions with needed information. The result, broadly termed management information systems, combines information analysis, system design and implementation (typically based on the use of computer hardware and software), manual procedures, a database, and management/decision models. For M.B.A. graduates, it represents an increasingly important field of concentration that incorporates technological expertise with management, organizational, and behavioral concepts. According to the Association of MBA Executives, some six percent of all 1983 M.B.A. graduates found jobs in the field of information systems.

As the embodiment of what is known as the "systems approach" —viewing an organization as many interacting subparts of a complex whole—information systems management combines the analytical framework and computer-based methodology for the analysis, design, implementation, and management of complex information systems. For management information specialists, a number of career paths exist in firms in general business, nonprofit and government organizations, and companies that produce and/or market data processing goods and services. Positions are found in areas including accounting, EDP auditing, data administration, consulting, communications system management, marketing, production, and systems analysis/design.

Whether in a management information systems (MIS) group or a user group within a business/governmental organization, entry-level jobs typically involve use of the computer-based information system (frequently as systems analysts and designers). On the other hand, senior managers focus more on coordinating various technical functions, serving as the MIS department/corporate management interface, and on using information derived from computer technology as a decision-making and planning tool. There is, in addition, a relatively recent managerial function found usually in large organizations, where a database administrator is needed to determine what data will be collected and stored, who can access the system, and what standards will be developed for the system's maintenance and use. Because of the sensitive corporate priority issues involved, this is typically a senior-level position.

The following organizations may provide information about the various career opportunities in the field of management information systems:

American Federation of Information Processing Societies, 1899 Preston White Drive, Reston, VA 22091

Association for Educational Data Systems, 1201 16th St., N.W., Washington, DC 20036

Association for Systems Management, 24587 Bagley Rd., Cleveland, OH 44138.

Marketing

There is a steady flow of M.B.A. graduates into marketing, which accounted for 22 percent of all 1983 placements. The field of marketing encompasses private enterprise, nonprofit institutions, and public institutions. Involving both technical and nontechnical products as well as services, it is primarily concerned with determining consumers' desires, creating products and services to fill these desires, and the functions of sales and distribution. Often based on market research, it is also closely tied to advertising, as well as to such promotionally oriented aspects as packaging.

Product management (also known as brand management) for a large company is a major career path within marketing. A product manager has total responsibility for a single product—generally one of many products made by a company that produces a large number of different products. The job generally encompasses the promotion and distribution of the product, as well as internal coordination of design, manufacturing, and packaging. M.B.A. graduates typically enter this field as product (brand) assistants assigned to a three-to-five-person group that functions as a business within a business. Each group would take complete responsibility for sales, advertising, finance, market research, and other aspects of manufacturing and selling its product. Other excellent employment opportunities exist in the marketing field; these include positions such as account executive, market research analyst, planning analyst, market analyst, sales representative, and media planner.

Students may wish to write the associations listed below for additional information on marketing careers:

American Marketing Association, 250 S. Wacker Dr., Suite 200, Chicago, IL 60606

Marketing Research Association, Suite 600, 111 E. Wacker Dr., Chicago, IL 60601

Operations Management

Only four percent of all M.B.A. graduates in 1983 went into the field of general operations management. Broadly speaking, these M.B.A. graduates were concerned with all the activities occurring between the production and the consumption of goods and services. This wide-ranging responsibility deals specifically with developing and managing an efficient combination of people, machines, and raw materials to produce the firm's product. It involves all systems through which work is planned, performed, and assessed in all areas of an organization—and can include accounting procedures, computer systems, human resource planning, marketing services, and indeed the whole range of the firm's functional activities.

M.B.A. graduates particularly suited to the operations management field combine a good sense of general management with an ability to apply systems to specific operational tasks. This function can involve building a work flow model through the use of a simple chart, or designing a sophisticated computer model. For example, the operations manager of a small company might concentrate on the working and coordination of all internal systems, with involvement in designing systems to plan and measure company growth, organize reporting and information flow, or track expenses and revenues. In a larger company, the operations manager might be responsible for similar work on a divisional or departmental basis and would probably concentrate on one particular area of operations.

Entrepreneurial Ventures

Entrepreneurial business is a viable career alternative for many M.B.A.s who prefer the challenge and self-defined rewards of independence. There are currently over 10 million entrepreneurial businesses—businesses founded and run by owner-managers. They can range from franchises or service firms to companies built around the invention, manufacture, or marketing of a new or competitive product. As a group, entrepreneurial enterprises can often be categorized by their degree of risk and return. Some may involve a large initial investment and substantial risk of failure, but offer very high rewards if they succeed. Other ventures might require a lesser investment and lesser risk, without the really high rewards.

Although it is possible to start your own business immediately upon graduation from an M.B.A. program, the broad range of skills and knowledgeability required to succeed influences most people to wait until they have gained business experience in other companies. They can then take their knowledge and experience (along with their increased range of contacts and established credit rating), and apply them to a business of their own.

Management Careers Outside Business

An increasingly large number of M.B.A.s today are choosing to apply their managerial skills to government, educational institutions, health care institutions, philanthropic organizations, and the arts. The growing demand for improved management talent in many of these organizations is linked closely to the economy, since more effective operations may often be a matter of survival and accountability to public sources of funds. Below, we look at a few of these fields. For information about specific school programs that may offer electives or special programs geared to any of these fields, please consult the "Key Facts" section and school literature.

Arts Management

In addition to finding increasing acceptance in creative industries, such as publishing, television and film, many M.B.A. graduates are choosing careers associated with the fine and performing arts. Symphonies, dance and theater companies, and museums alike are faced with diminishing subsidies along with many of the same operational and financial decisions of large businesses. These organizations are now looking for men and women who, in addition to being capable administrators, are knowledgeable and sensitive to the needs of artists and the arts.

The overall responsibilities of an arts manager are to coordinate the business factors and the artistic goals of the organization, and to build and maintain a sound financial foundation for its continuing development. For example, the responsibilities of an associate director of a community arts council, museum, or symphony might include budget analysis or marketing. In the arts, marketing encompasses researching the artistic interests of a particular local community, audience development, publicity, promotion, and distribution. This may mean planning a tour or arranging a cross country radio broadcast. Other duties might be organizing subscription campaigns, negotiating contracts with artists, helping to accommodate set designs to the budget, and maintaining a staff and the facility itself.

For M.B.A.s interested in diversifying within the arts field, there is opportunity for movement among the art forms. In fact, advancement from a staff or associate position to top management has been traditionally accomplished through a series of jobs with increasing responsibility in different types of art institutions.

Educational Administration

As the budgetary problems of educational institutions increase, due to tightening funds, diminishing enrollments, and growing regulatory complexity, many school systems and private educational systems are filling middle- and senior-level management positions with M.B.A.s. Among the many M.B.A. management skills that have found enhanced opportunities to contribute in this environment, specialization in finance is particularly prized for the management of large departments and frequently in the direct line of academic administration itself. While many M.B.A. positions appear to be in large educational institutions, even small schools have found management skills to be of great use in delivering educational programs with increased efficiency and effectiveness.

Government

The government and nonprofit areas of the public sector represent a vast managerial opportunity. The need for M.B.A.s and people with similar graduate management degrees extends to both the political and administrative sectors of government at all levels. Students in this field most commonly have— besides an appreciation for finance, accounting, organizational structure, and management techniques— an instinctive feel for policy issues and a desire to participate in an efficiently run government.

Recent graduates working in government—federal, state, or local— have degrees in public policy, public administration, or public and private management. In the wide variety of governmental positions now available to professional managers, there are opportunities to suit virtually any field of interest or specialization. For example, an M.B.A. in the Environmental Protection Agency of one city uses financial analysis techniques to project the effect of proposed regulatory legislation on business. Such a financial specialist might also analyze departmental agencies to identify and solve costly operational problems, or could function as a revenue forecaster.

In view of new federal policies aimed at restricting excessive bureaucratic expansion, many other areas of government are in particular need of trained managers to achieve maximum impact with the fewest possible resources. There are also several M.B.A.s now serving as members of Congress, and a number of recent graduates with M.B.A.s or similar master's degrees in public policy, public administration, or public and private management work at the federal, state, and local levels. Recent M.B.A. jobs in government include special assistant to a city mayor and policy analyst on energy and transportation issues for a large city. Individuals might also analyze department agencies to identify and solve operational problems with major financial implications, improve agency efficiency and cost-effectiveness, or forecast potential revenues.

Health Care Administration

Few industries are growing as rapidly as health care. For the management graduate this means new opportunities in hospitals, medical education centers, health maintenance organizations, and government agencies.

Health administrators play a key role in containing costs, continually improving the quality of care, and increasing access to services. If you choose to specialize in health care administration, you might further concentrate your training in financial management, information processing, quality control, system engineering, personnel management, or labor relations. An initial assignment might, for example, be responsibility for the efficient functioning of all out-patient services. Alternatively, studies could be focused on health care policy making, leading to a job in a state or federal health department. This could involve planning health services by analyzing how the health needs of a community could best be met with available resources.

Graduates in health administration tend to stay in their first job about two years before moving to another institution. Entry level positions are frequently as a staff member at a large hospital or assistant administrator at a medium-sized hospital. The next step may be to a position as an assistant or associate administrator in a larger institution. With significant additional experience, this could lead to a chief executive or vice president title.

For many women and men a major attraction of this field is the fact that graduates often are given broader job responsibility earlier than in the private sector. Despite these advantages, career counselors advise students considering this specialty to examine whether they truly have a strong desire to improve the health of individuals and the effectiveness and efficiency of health care delivery services. This is considered one of the essential prerequisites of any health-related job.

Nonprofit Agencies

In recent years, a wide variety of nonprofit organizations have realized that good business management is critical to their survival. Even though they don't operate to earn a profit for their stockholders, they must achieve their goals within a defined budget. As a result, they generally have the same type of managerial problems as for profit organizations. While these positions may not pay salaries as high as those in large corporations, they can provide opportunities for more creativity, earlier overall responsibility, and personal satisfaction.

Challenging jobs can be found in such nonprofit organizations as philanthropies, foundations, professional associations and councils, libraries, and youth centers. Some enterprising graduates have created their own opportunities after recognizing the increasing need for management expertise in advocacy groups concerned with such areas as urban development, environmental problems, and community affairs. Others have entered alternative businesses, such as food cooperatives— many marketing themselves to institutions that had never before considered using M.B.A. talent.

Graduate Schools of Management

In addition to the capsule comparisons of schools and programs provided in "Key Facts" to help you begin your search, you will need in-depth data on the different full- and part-time programs offered in order to make your decisions. You will find these detailed descriptions following the "Key Facts" pages, listed in alphabetical order by school name.

All schools that require the Graduate Management Admission Test of substantially all applicants were invited to provide information for this book. The GMAC defines "substantially all" as "all applicants for the master's program except those who by virtue of visual or physical handicaps are unable to write the test (even with the special arrangements available for candidates with disabilities), or who because of late application are accepted provisionally, contingent upon their presenting a satisfactory score at the next administration of the test."

More than 520 schools chose to submit descriptions of their management programs. Because the information was provided by the schools themselves, the GMAC is not able to guarantee its accuracy.

The descriptions include general information about the schools and details about the programs of study, admission policies, expenses, financial assistance, and placement. Addresses for future correspondence are also given.

As an added feature for your convenience, the *Guide* also includes six reply cards that you can send to schools to request a catalog, admissions materials, or financial aid information. Additional reply cards allow you to request GAPSFAS and CSS forms as well as several useful publications. The reply cards are found inside the back cover of this book.

Key Facts about Graduate Schools of Management

Key Facts provides capsule information about the more than 520 schools included in this book. A more detailed description of each school is found on the page listed before the school's name. In order to use this section accurately to make some preliminary choices of graduate schools, it will be helpful to read the descriptions below. These paragraphs explain the individual segments of the tables beginning on page 44 and the method by which the information was gathered.

Schools were asked to provide separate data for the full- and/or part-time programs offered. Full-time programs are indicated in the "Key Facts" section by the designation (F) following the school's name; part-time programs by a (P). Because many schools do not separate their information into full- and part-time categories, some did not designate a category. The data about these schools may pertain to a full- or part-time program or may include both. The description of each of these schools, which appears on the page given after the school's name, should include information on the types of programs offered by the school. A blank space in any category indicates that the school did not supply the data—either because it is not available or it is regarded as confidential.

Programs of Study. There will be an entry under "General Management Program" if the school's curriculum emphasizes management in general, rather than concentration in any one functional area. The categories under "Concentrations" do not refer to single courses within the core curriculum, but rather to advanced material that forms a major or concentration. Under "Joint Degrees" the schools have indicated any programs that they offer in conjunction with other graduate schools of their universities.

Doctoral Program. The enrollment of the school's doctoral program, either full-time or part-time, is given in this column.

Other Options. Schools indicated here whether students may take courses for credit in other schools of the university.

Entrance Dates. Schools were asked to indicate all those months in which students may begin a master's program.

Deferred Admit Policy. A deferred admit policy guarantees to a potential student the right to enroll in a future class at a date mutually agreed to by the student and the school. The number of variations on this policy precludes their being listed here. Schools that offer such programs to prospective students are indicated in this column. Students should request specific information from the school of their choice.

Length of Study. The figure in this column refers to the minimum number of months in which a student with a normal course load could expect to complete a master's program. A two-year, full-time program with two semesters of 15 weeks and the usual academic holidays may require 18 months for the master's degree. Part-time program length reflects normal part-time course loads.

Applicants/Enrollment for 1984-85. Schools were asked to give the actual (or approximate) number of students who applied for admission for the 1984-85 academic year and the number of those who enrolled for the first time during that year.

Characteristics of the 1984-85 Entering Class. Schools were asked to provide the following data:

- The percentage of students from minority groups (including American Indian/Alaskan Native, Black, Hispanic, Asian-American, and Puerto Rican) in the class that entered the program during 1984-85.

- The percentage of women students in that class.

- The percentage of foreign students in that class.

- The average age of the students when they entered the program.

- The percentage of students who had undergraduate degrees in the Humanities (includes English, other languages, philosophy, and fine arts); Social Science (includes economics, sociology, psychology, political science, history, education, and government); Business and Commerce (includes accounting, management, business education, industrial relations, marketing, and finance); Science and Engineering (includes mathematics, architecture, biological and physical sciences, statistics, and all engineering disciplines); and other fields.

- The percentage of students who had already attained a graduate degree.

- The range of GMAT scores of the middle 80 percent of their entering students—to obtain this range, the schools eliminated the 10 percent of students who scored on the top end of the distribution and the 10 percent who scored on the low end.

- The range of TOEFL scores for the middle 80 percent of entering students using the same procedure detailed above.

- The range of grade-point average for the middle 80 percent of entering students—schools could elect to use either two-year or four-year grade-point averages.

- The percentage of entering students who had full-time *continuous* work experience of one or more years.

- The percentage of students who entered the program directly from undergraduate school.

April 15. An entry in this column indicates a school that adheres to a common annual date of April 15 prior to which no applicant for fall term admission to a graduate management program would be required to accept or reject offers of admission or financial assistance. The purposes of this standard date are to reduce confusion among applicants for admission to graduate management programs, to eliminate certain competitive aspects among schools (which are not in the applicant's best interests), and to make the application-admission process more orderly.

Financial Assistance. Schools were asked to indicate all those forms of financial assistance offered to master's students. It cannot be assumed, however, that a school will offer a particular form of aid in all its programs.

GAPSFAS. Schools were asked to indicate if they require applicants for financial aid to file through the Graduate and Professional School Financial Aid Service (GAPSFAS), a central need analysis agency (see page 27 for further information on GAPSFAS).

Placement Service. Schools indicate whether they maintain their own placement service as opposed to using a university-wide placement service.

Placement Data Available. Many schools publish placement data which contains information about starting salaries, placement in various career fields, number of employers interviewing on campus, and geographical areas in which graduates are placed. Schools that make such data available to applicants upon request are indicated here.

AACSB. While most M.B.A. programs are offered by schools that have institutional accreditation, some programs have also met the standards of the American Assembly of Collegiate Schools of Business (AACSB), the national accrediting agency for baccalaureate and master's degree programs in business administration. AACSB accreditation standards address such considerations as faculty resources, the curriculum, admissions, and library, computer, classroom and other support facilities. M.B.A. programs accredited by AACSB are designated by a dot in this column.

Programs of Study Offered

Page	School Name and Page Number (F) = Full-time program (P) = Part-time program	General Management Program	Accounting	Arts Administration	Behavioral Sciences	Economics	Finance	Health Services	International Business	Management Information Systems	Management	Marketing	Production/Operations Management	Public Policy or Administration	Quantitative Analysis	Real Estate and Insurance	Transportation	M.B.A./J.D.	M.B.A./Engineering	Other Joint Degrees	Total Doctoral Enrollment	Students Can Take Courses for Credit in Other Schools of University	January	February	March	April	May	June	July	August	September	October	November	December
ALABAMA																																		
80	Alabama A&M University (F)	●	●			●	●		●	●	●											●	●					●			●			
92	Auburn University (F)	●																			10	●	●		●			●			●			
367	Samford University (P)	●																		●														
413	Troy State University Dothan/Fort Rucker (F)	●																					●		●			●			●			
422	University of Alabama (Tuscaloosa) (F)	●				●	●	●	●	●	●	●				●	●					●								●				
423	University of Alabama at Birmingham (P)	●	●					●													12	●	●		●						●			
424	University of Alabama in Huntsville (F)	●			●				●		●												●		●			●			●			●
500	University of North Alabama (P)	●																				●	●					●			●			
522	University of South Alabama																																	
ALASKA																																		
425	University of Alaska, Anchorage																																	
ARIZONA																																		
81	American Graduate Sch. of Inter'l Mgt. (F)								●													●						●		●				
87	Arizona State University	●	●			●	●		●	●	●	●	●			●	●	●			110	●	●								●			
305	Northern Arizona University	●							●													●							●	●	●			
427	University of Arizona (F)		●		●	●	●	●			●	●	●	●	●	●	●				108										●			
ARKANSAS																																		
88	Arkansas State University (F)	●																				●							●	●	●			
428	University of Arkansas (F)	●	●			●	●				●	●	●	●	●						80	●	●					●			●			
429	University of Arkansas at Little Rock (F)	●				●	●				●	●										●									●			
429	University of Arkansas at Little Rock (P)	●				●	●				●	●				●						●									●			
441	University of Central Arkansas (F)	●																			0	●	●						●	●	●			
CALIFORNIA																																		
95	Azusa Pacific University (F)	●				●		●			●	●										●	●								●			
115	California Lutheran University (P)	●																				●				●					●			
116	California Polytechnic State University (F)	●																				●	●								●			
117	California State College, Bakersfield (P)	●																				●			●			●			●			
118	California State Polytechnic U., Pomona (P)	●	●		●	●	●		●		●	●		●	●							●	●		●						●			
119	California State University, Chico (F)	●	●																			●	●								●			
120	California State University, Dominguez Hills (F)	●									●											●	●								●			
121	California State University, Fullerton (P)	●	●			●	●						●									●				●					●			
122	California State University, Hayward																																	
123	California State University, Long Beach (P)	●							●							●						●									●			
124	California State University, Los Angeles (P)	●	●		●	●	●	●	●	●	●	●			●							●			●			●						
125	California State University, San Bernardino																																	
126	California State University, Stanislaus (P)	●																				●	●	●							●			
139	Chapman College (F)		●			●	●				●	●										●						●		●				
139	Chapman College (P)		●		●	●	●															●						●						
143	Claremont Graduate School (F)	●			●	●	●		●	●	●	●		●						●	25	●	●					●			●			
143	Claremont Graduate School (P)	●			●	●	●		●	●	●	●		●						●	25	●	●					●			●			
200	Golden Gate University (F)	●	●	●			●	●	●	●	●	●		●	●	●						●	●								●			
200	Golden Gate University (P)	●	●	●										●	●	●				●	60	●	●								●			
207	Holy Names College (P)								●													●		●							●			

– 44 –

Deferred Admit Policy: School Offers This Option to Students	Length of Study: Minimum Number of Months to Obtain Degree	Applicants/Enrollment for 1984-85: Number of Students Who Applied for Admission	Number of Students Who Enrolled for the First Time	Percentage of Minority Students	Percentage of Women Students	Percentage of Foreign Students	Average Age of Students at Matriculation	Humanities	Social Sciences	Business and Commerce	Science and Engineering	Other Fields	Percentage Having Graduate Degree	Range of Middle 80% of Students' GMAT Scores	Range of Middle 80% of Students' TOEFL Scores	Range of Middle 80% of Students' Undergraduate GPA	Percentage of Students Having One or More Years of Full-Time Work Experience	Percentage of Students Entering Directly from Undergraduate School	April 15: Common Date for Applicant Reply	Financial Assistance: Scholarships/Fellowships	Teaching/Research Assistantships	Loans	GAPSFAS: Required for Financial Aid	Separate Placement Service for Management Students	Placement Data Available: Starting Salaries	Career Placement	Campus Interviews	Geographic Placement	AACSB: Master's Program Accredited by	Page Number
	18			90	28	59													•	•	•									80
	12	105	27	0	44	9	27	0	4	33	30	33		480-590		2.51-3.54	22	78			•								•	92
																														367
	18	26	17	8	20	5	32	10	15	65	5	5	10				95	10				•			•	•		•		413
•	21	150	50	5	35	15	25	15	20	25	35	5	10	510-670	540-620	3.0-3.8	40	60	•	•	•	•			•	•	•	•	•	422
•	18	125	100	8	38	4								450-590		2.5-3.6					•								•	423
	12	76	73	12	37	4		1	5	52	32	10	1	400-580		2.4-3.7	76	20			•									424
	12	85	70	6	49	3	30	4	5	75	16			480-530		2.6-3.6	95	5												500
																													•	522
																														425
•	12	1,800	1,800	2	33	26	25	17	42	33	8		4	430-620	513-637	2.71-3.72	68	34	•	•		•		•	•	•	•	•		81
	12	1,688	322	5	34	3	26							560-640		3.3-3.6				•	•	•			•	•	•	•	•	87
•	12			8	28	14	29	4	16	48	20	12	4	420-600	527-607	2.5-3.7	88	20	•	•	•	•			•	•		•	•	305
	21	400	82	17	33	6	25	10	40	25	20	5	5	550-600	540-560	3.1-3.45	40	50	•	•	•			•					•	427
	9	40	30	5	25	10	28							380-520	560-580	2.6-3.7	55	43	•	•	•	•							•	88
•	36	34	10	0	20	20	25							500-700	550-600	2.8-3.9	50	50	•	•	•								•	428
•	12	3	3	0	0	0	23			100			0	530-540		2.69-3.50	0	100							•	•	•	•	•	429
•	24	58	36	0	33	0	29	3	3	43	30	21	0	480-600		2.65-3.44	57	30	•						•	•	•	•	•	429
	12	30	20	3	20	10			5	85	10		0	400-500	560-620	2.75-3.25	50	20	•				•			•	•			441
•	12			85	25	77	25										25			•	•	•			•	•	•	•		95
	30																							•						115
	9	250	51	2	42	2	28	20	20	30	25	5	3	430-570		2.74-3.61	60	40	•	•	•	•			•	•	•	•		116
	12	150	120	20	40	25	30	2	10	30	50	8	5	460-530	560-580	2.8-3.2	90	5		•		•			•	•	•			117
	12	151	123		27	9	28		9	41	18	32	3	450-550	580-600	2.5-3.5	80	10				•			•	•				118
•	84	100	50	10	40	10	26	10	10	50	20	10	5	500-540	550-600		20	50	•	•	•	•		•					•	119
	12	300	150	10	20	10	28			70	10	20					85	15	•		•	•	•							120
	12	643	103		38																								•	121
																													•	122
	12	872	292	27	40	15	27	7	24	40	21	8	2	440-610		2.76-3.64	85	10	•	•	•	•			•	•	•		•	123
	12	302	68		37	15	28	17	17	58	7	1	8	420-580	557-595	2.7-3.6	91	11	•	•	•	•			•	•	•		•	124
																														125
	18	94	78	6	51	15	30	44	12	39	25	19	6	433-530	513-560		73	27									•	•		126
•	16	50	25	5	35	5	30	3	5	85	5	2	5	500-650	500-600	2.9-3.3	85	70	•	•	•				•	•	•			139
•	30	100	50	10	20	0	35	3	5	85	2	5	1	500-650	500-600	2.9-3.3	90	30		•	•				•	•	•			139
•	16		61	3	25	34	26	8	31	43	7	11		500-650	560-650	3.0-3.5	72	28	•	•	•				•	•	•	•		143
	24		37	3	32		26	8	19	43	27	3		500-650	560-650	3.0-3.5	92	8	•	•	•				•	•	•	•		143
•	12	96	37	18	11	15	25	10	10	65	10	5	5	440-495	550-600	2.25-3.5	25	75												200
•	20	2,073	1,617	48	49	15	29	15	10	50	15	10	25	435-495	545-595	2.25-3.5	80	20			•	•								200
•	24	17	8	25	75	13	36	12	37	37	12		0				100	0		•		•								207

*See page 43 for explanation

School Name and Page Number (F) = Full-time program (P) = Part-time program	General Management Program	Accounting	Arts Administration	Behavioral Sciences	Economics	Finance	Health Services	International Business	Management Information Systems	Management	Marketing	Production/Operations Management	Public Policy or Administration	Quantitative Analysis	Real Estate and Insurance	Transportation	M.B.A./J.D.	M.B.A./Engineering	Other Joint Degrees	Total Doctoral Enrollment	Students Can Take Courses for Credit in Other Schools of University	January	February	March	April	May	June	July	August	September	October	November	December
209 Humboldt State University (F)	•																				•								•				
243 Loma Linda University	•			•		•					•										•				•		•			•			
250 Loyola Marymount University (P)	•	•			•	•		•	•	•	•										•									•			
283 Monterey Institute of International Studies		•				•		•			•									0	•									•			
323 Pacific States University (F)		•						•		•											•						•			•			
360 Saint Mary's College of California (P)	•			•	•	•															•				•			•			•		
368 San Diego State University (F)	•	•		•		•		•	•	•	•	•		•							•									•			
369 San Francisco State University	•	•				•			•	•	•					•					•								•				
370 San Jose State University (P)	•	•		•							•										•					•			•				
370 San Jose State University (P)	•	•		•							•										•	•	•	•	•	•	•	•	•	•	•	•	•
372 Santa Clara University	•														•						•		•			•							
381 Sonoma State University (F)	•				•			•		•	•								•		•								•				
392 Stanford University (F)	•									•							•			87	•									•			
416 United States International University (P)	•			•					•	•										75	•	•			•		•						
435 University of California, Berkeley (F)	•	•			•	•	•	•		•	•	•			•				•	75	•									•			
435 University of California, Berkeley (P)				•	•	•				•	•									0	•									•			
436 University of California, Davis (F)	•	•				•				•	•						•	•		0	•									•			
437 University of California, Irvine (F)	•	•		•		•				•	•	•	•			•				30	•									•			
438 University of California, Los Angeles (F)	•	•	•	•	•	•	•	•	•	•	•	•	•		•		•	•	•	116	•									•			
438 University of California, Los Angeles (P)	•	•	•	•	•	•	•	•	•	•	•	•	•		•						•									•			
439 University of California, Riverside (F)	•				•					•											•									•			
468 University of Judaism (P)	•																				•					•				•			
471 University of La Verne	•									•											•	•	•	•	•				•	•		•	•
517 University of San Diego	•	•								•									•		•						•	•	•				
518 University of San Francisco (F)	•					•				•	•								•		•									•			
518 University of San Francisco (P)	•					•				•									•		•						•		•	•			
526 University of Southern California (F)		•				•		•	•	•	•	•		•	•		•		•		•									•			
586 Whittier College (P)	•			•						•									•		•	•		•	•					•			
COLORADO																																	
153 Colorado State University (F)		•		•				•	•	•											•									•			
338 Regis College (P)		•		•				•	•												•				•								
445 U. of Colorado (Boulder & Colorado Springs) (F)		•	•		•			•	•	•	•			•	•					67	•								•				
445 U. of Colorado (Boulder & Colorado Springs) (P)		•						•	•	•	•										•								•		•		
446 University of Colorado at Denver	•	•		•	•	•				•				•	•						•									•			
451 University of Denver	•	•						•	•						•		•				•					•				•			
CONNECTICUT																																	
184 Fairfield University (P)						•															•									•			
350 Sacred Heart University (P)	•	•		•	•	•		•		•											•				•		•		•				
432 University of Bridgeport		•		•	•	•		•	•	•	•								•	112	•			•						•			
447 University of Connecticut (F)	•	•		•		•	•	•	•	•	•				•		•	•	•		•									•			
447 University of Connecticut (P)	•			•						•	•				•						•						•	•	•				
458 University of Hartford (P)		•		•	•	•	•	•	•	•	•	•		•							•									•			
577 Western Connecticut State University (P)		•				•		•		•			•								•	•	•	•	•	•	•	•	•	•	•	•	•

Characteristics of 1984-85 Entering Class

Deferred Admit Policy (School Offers This Option)	Min. Months to Degree	Applied for Admission	Enrolled First Time	% Minority	% Women	% Foreign	Avg Age at Matric.	% Humanities	% Social Sciences	% Business & Commerce	% Science & Eng.	% Other Fields	% Having Graduate Degree	GMAT Range (mid 80%)	TOEFL Range (mid 80%)	GPA Range (mid 80%)	% w/ 1+ Yrs Work Exp.	% Directly from Undergrad	April 15 Common Reply	Scholarships/Fellowships	Teaching/Research Assistantships	Loans	GAPSFAS Required	Separate Placement Service	Starting Salaries	Career Placement	Campus Interviews	Geographic Placement	AACSB Accredited	Page
	18	30	26	8	38	8		12	12	23	31	22	12	450-548	554-566	2.71-3.30	77	15	●	●	●	●			●	●	●			209
	12	22	10	50	80	50	25		10	80	10		20	320-550			90	50	●	●		●		●	●	●	●	●		243
	12	500	200	5	40	5	27	5	10	40	30	5	5	500-600	600-650	3.3-3.5	95	5											250
●	15	213	79	7	51	22	25	50	40	10	0	0	2			3.2-3.4	60	40	●		●				●	●	●			283
●	16	718	151		26	97	23		13	45	39	3	2	375-505		2.2-3.3	10	88	●											323
●	21	255	152	8	32	7	33	20	26	31	22	1	5	470-660	550-580	2.7-3.5	95	10	●	●		●							360
	12	1,263	450	3	39	12	25	5	20	50	20	5	11	520-620	560-600	3.0-3.5			●	●	●	●						●	368
	12	800	250		41	14	28	10	20	40	25	5	4	450-620		2.7-3.7	80	17	●	●	●	●		●				●	369
	12	520	407		40		29	10	14	38	24	13		449-574		2.98-3.52	80	23	●	●					●	●	●	●	●	370
	12	238	205		27		33	7	11	40	28	14	13	473-577		2.95-3.56	95	5	●	●					●	●	●	●	●	370
●	12	830	481		40		26	2	8	40	46	4	14	450-680		2.6-3.8	85	15					●		●	●	●	●	●	372
●	12	110	66	17	36	15	36	15	33	40	10	2	5	400-580		2.9-3.9	90	15								●	●		381
●	21	4,160	319	14	26	14	27	27	30	13	30	0	13				93	5	●	●		●	●	●	●	●	●	●	392
●	20	500		15	25	35	29						10	300-600		3.0-3.5	60	20				●		●	●	●	●	●	416
●	21	2,361	245	22	32	17	26	10	15	26	25	24	20	580-680	600-680	3.3-3.9	95	5	●										435
	27	322	110	22	25	5	27	15	20	11	44	10	42	590-690		3.3-3.9	100												435
	24	175	49	11	40	6	28	15	15	25	35	10	8	605-615		2.9-3.5	90	10		●	●	●			●	●	●	●	436
●	18	600	124	4	42	13	25	5	33	20	18	24	12	510-620	580-630	3.0-3.8	88	12		●	●	●		●	●	●	●	●	437
	21	3,303	373	12	40	19	26	14	34	18	33	1	11	550-710	600-650		95	5	●	●	●	●			●	●	●	●	438
	33	350	51	10	45	8	31	14	28	12	47		31	550-720			100	0	●	●	●	●			●	●	●	●	438
	18	140	50	6	40	25	28	10	19	40	31	0	3	420-600	540-630	2.95-3.75				●	●	●			●	●	●	●	439
●	21	25	10	0	65	20	30	40	40	10		10	20							●	●				●	●	●	●	468
●	18														280-630	2.5-3.9				●									471
		350	93		35	10	26	15	6	32	23	20	4	450-630		2.46-3.50	90	10		●	●	●			●		●	●	517
●	12	670	180	33	33	25	27	10	10	50	20	10	10	470-570	590-620	2.5-3.5	85	15		●	●	●			●		●		518
●	24	330	90	25	33	0	28	10	10	50	20	10	10	470-570	590-620	2.5-3.5	95	5		●					●		●		518
●	24	1,462	330	18	36	11	26	4	9	32	21	10					80	20		●	●	●	●		●	●	●	●	526
●	24	39	21	4	51	9	27	26	14	41	13	6	0	500-640	550-675	2.75-3.5	85	15	●		●	●							586
●	12	250	100	5	40	10	27	5	10	44	26	15	4	490-575	570-610	3.1-3.5	70	30					●	●	●	●	●	●	153
●	19		150				34							475-525			99	1	●			●	●			●	●		338
●	12	490	177	4	30	<1	27							480-660						●	●	●						●	445
	15	167	88	2	50	0	32	15	15	25	25	20	5	480-580		2.75-3.5	98	10				●						●	445
	24	611	334		45		30			50				480-660			99	5		●	●	●							446
●		497	349	5	37	12			15	16	37	22	9				75	25	●	●	●	●	●	●	●	●	●	●	451
●	18	90	60		49		29	16	14	60	10		5	460-560		2.8-3.4	90	10	●	●									184
	24	1,124	1,100	6	50	1	32										99	1			●					●	●		350
●	9	563	240	2	35	15	28	13	21	40	23	3	5	440-580		2.7-3.3	15	90	●	●	●					●	●		432
	16	480	110	7	45	10	26	15	15	35	30	5	10	530-600	530-580	2.9-3.1	60	40	●				●	●	●	●	●	●	447
		500	350	10	50		28	20	10	25	35	10	15	520-610		2.9-3.1	100	0										●	447
●	28	481	413		40	24	25	2	13	58	10	17	3	360-580	503-585	2.47-3.55	95	5	●	●		●			●		●		458
	18	161	102		50		35										80				●	●			●	●	●		577

*See page 43 for explanation

School Name and Page Number (F) = Full-time program (P) = Part-time program	General Management Program	Accounting	Arts Administration	Behavioral Sciences	Economics	Finance	Health Services	International Business	Management Information Systems	Management	Marketing	Production/Operations Management	Public Policy or Administration	Quantitative Analysis	Real Estate and Insurance	Transportation	M.B.A./J.D.	M.B.A./Engineering	Other Joint Degrees	Total Doctoral Enrollment	Students Can Take Courses for Credit in Other Schools of University	January	February	March	April	May	June	July	August	September	October	November	December
599 Yale University (F)	●																●		●	60	●									●			
DELAWARE																																	
450 University of Delaware (F)	●																	●					●							●			
450 University of Delaware (P)	●																		●				●							●			
592 Wilmington College	●																						●		●					●		●	●
DISTRICT OF COLUMBIA																																	
83 American University (F)		●		●	●		●			●					●		●							●		●				●		●	
193 George Washington University (F)		●		●	●	●		●		●			●				●			160	●	●				●	●	●	●				
195 Georgetown University (F)	●																●													●			
208 Howard University (F)	●					●				●											●					●				●			
385 Southeastern University (F)	●	●			●	●		●		●	●	●	●								●					●					●		
453 University of the District of Columbia (F)	●	●			●	●		●	●	●	●			●	●						●					●				●			
453 University of the District of Columbia (P)	●	●			●	●		●	●	●	●			●	●						●					●				●			
FLORIDA																																	
186 Florida Atlantic University (F)	●	●			●																●					●				●			
187 Florida International University (P)	●	●				●		●	●												●					●				●			
188 Florida State University (F)	●	●			●					●	●			●		●				48										●			
229 Jacksonville University						●				●	●										●					●				●			
312 Nova University (P)	●	●		●		●	●	●	●	●		●								350	●	●			●			●		●			
345 Rollins College (F)	●																				●									●			
345 Rollins College (P)	●																				●									●			
363 St. Thomas University (F)		●				●	●	●	●		●										●					●				●			
397 Stetson University (F)	●	●																					●				●			●			
442 University of Central Florida																																	
456 University of Florida	●	●		●	●	●	●	●	●	●	●	●			●		●		●	80	●									●			
481 University of Miami		●		●	●	●	●	●	●	●	●	●	●	●			●	●		11	●						●	●		●			
525 University of South Florida (F)		●			●	●		●	●	●	●										●									●			
525 University of South Florida (P)		●			●	●		●	●	●	●										●									●			
572 Webber College (F)	●									●											●					●				●			
572 Webber College (P)	●									●											●		●			●						●	●
GEORGIA																																	
91 Atlanta University (F)	●	●				●				●	●	●									●									●			
93 Augusta College																																	
102 Berry College (P)	●																				●		●		●			●		●			
180 Emory University (F)	●																●	●		0	●								●				
196 Georgia College (F)	●									●											●	●		●		●				●			
197 Georgia Institute of Technology (F)	●	●		●	●	●				●	●	●		●			●	●		10	●									●			
198 Georgia Southern College (F)	●																				●						●			●			
199 Georgia State University		●		●	●	●	●	●	●	●	●		●	●		●				155	●	●		●		●				●			
270 Mercer University Atlanta (P)		●			●				●	●	●										●	●		●		●				●			
271 Mercer University Macon (P)	●				●					●	●				●						●	●		●		●				●			
373 Savannah State College (F)	●																				●						●			●			
457 University of Georgia (F)		●	●	●	●	●		●	●	●	●	●	●	●	●		●			120	●								●				

School Offers This Option to Students	Min. Months to Obtain Degree	No. Applied for Admission	No. Enrolled First Time	% Minority	% Women	% Foreign	Avg Age at Matriculation	Humanities	Social Sciences	Business and Commerce	Science and Engineering	Other Fields	% Having Graduate Degree	GMAT Range	TOEFL Range	Undergrad GPA Range	% With 1+ Yrs Full-Time Work Exp	% Entering Directly from Undergrad	Common Date April 15	Scholarships/Fellowships	Teaching/Research Assistantships	Loans	Required for Financial Aid	GAPSFAS	Separate Placement Service	Starting Salaries	Career Placement	Campus Interviews	Geographic Placement	Master's Program Accredited (AACSB)	Page Number
•	21	1,522	185	13	45	16	27	30	42	8	20		25	500-640	560-620		98	1		•	•	•	•		•		•	•		•	599
	24	80	24	1	35	3	28	2	5	36	30	27	5	460-610	520-633	2.7-3.7	87	13	•	•	•	•			•		•	•	•	•	450
	60	127	54	2	28	0	28	7	2	43	43	5	8	460-650		2.7-3.7	90	10	•						•		•	•	•	•	450
•																	98	2		•	•	•									592
																															83
	12	1,038	318	7	37	5	26	37	20	36	7		11	520-550	550-580	2.8-3.2	70	30	•	•	•						•			•	193
	21	480	66	8	30	22	26	19	59	4	18	0	6	510-660	557-653	2.75-3.80	72	28	•	•	•	•		•	•	•	•	•		•	195
	17	515	78	98	51	27	27	16	7	53	2	22	3	330-490		2.40-3.48	67			•	•	•	•	•		•		•		•	208
•	12		129			59																									385
•	18	100	80	80	30	30	27	10	20	60	10		5				90	60	•						•						453
•	18	60	50	80	30	30	30	10	20	60	10						90	20	•						•						453
	12	184	112	9	38	7	27	1	5	60	30	4	5	480-550	500-600	3.0-3.6	80	20	•	•	•					•	•	•	•	•	186
	18	922	229	6	37	7	32													•					•	•	•	•	•	•	187
	12	171	31	<1	26	0	23	<1	10	77	<1	<1	<1	480-610		2.86-3.73	48	32	•	•										•	188
	18	36	22	55	40	2	27	10	20	61	8	1	2	350-580	540-590	2.5-3.5	92	8		•		•			•	•	•	•	•	229
•	18	600	450	12	40	4	32		20	50	20	10	15	425-500	520-580	2.8-3.4	98	2			•	•									312
	24	165	50	5	35	16	24	15	15	45	15	10	1	500-600	550-600	2.9-3.3	58	42	•						•		•	•	•	345
	24	126	78	5	45	0	26	15	15	40	20	10	2	500-600	550-600	2.9-3.3	90	10	•						•		•	•	•	345
	9																									•					363
•	12	85	29																							•					397
																														•	442
	16	800	112	6	30	10	24	5	25	43	20	7	3	530-660	597-617		50	50		•	•				•		•	•	•	•	456
•	10	620	187	20	39	27	25	4	20	63	6	12	2					30	•	•	•	•		•		•	•	•	•	481
	16	400	150	5	45	5	27	10	10	50	20	10	10	500-550		3.0-3.4	40	60									•		•	525
	16	500	250	5	45	5	28	5		60	30	5		500-550		3.0-3.4	80	20									•		•	525
	12	10	5	20	0	40	24		100					500-550	575-625	3.2-3.6	100	0	•			•				•				572
•	24	25	20	10	15	15	25	2	3	90	3	2	0	450-550	550-600	3.0-3.5	95	5	•			•				•				572
•	18	256	52	100	56	3	25	25	18	34	20	3	<1	620-320		3.64-2.31	53	23	•	•	•	•		•	•	•	•	•	•	91
																															93
•	12	40	30	10	50	10	30	15	15	40	20	10	5				90	10	•											102
	18	500	110	2	33	14	25	22	25	26	22	5	5	500-630	550-650	2.5-3.6	65	35	•	•			•			•	•	•	•	180
	12	267	151	12	47	3		5	15	45	30	5	20	400-600	500-550	2.4-3.6	85	15	•	•	•					•	•	•	•	196
•	18	250	80	7	30	19	26		16	21	48	15	6	440-650	580-630	2.5-3.6	51	49	•	•			•			•	•	•	•	197
•	12			4	29	11	24	7	5	67	19	2	0	450-550	550-670	2.50-3.58	75	25	•	•	•					•	•	•	•	198
	12	2,880	1,135	9	36	4	32											90	10	•	•	•			•					•	199
•	21	380	230				30						<1	410-510	530-550	2.3-3.0	95	1												270
	15	40	30	10	25	7	29	15	20	35	30		5	410-540	480-580	2.55-3.25	70	15	•											271
	12	120	100	41	42	28	28	9	9	63	18	1	2	300-425	500-578	2.7-3.5	90	48		•	•			•		•	•	•		373
	12	385	73	2	28	20	24	10	8	45	21	16		490-690		2.90-3.85	34	66		•	•			•		•	•	•	•	457

*See page 43 for explanation

Programs of Study Offered

School Name and Page Number
(F) = Full-time program
(P) = Part-time program

Page	School Name	Gen Mgmt Program	Accounting	Arts Administration	Behavioral Sciences	Economics	Finance	Health Services	International Business	Mgmt Info Systems	Management	Marketing	Production/Operations Mgmt	Public Policy or Admin	Quantitative Analysis	Real Estate and Insurance	Transportation	M.B.A./J.D.	M.B.A./Engineering	Other Joint Degrees	Total Doctoral Enrollment	Students Can Take Courses for Credit in Other Schools	Jan	Feb	Mar	Apr	May	Jun	Jul	Aug	Sep	Oct	Nov	Dec
562	Valdosta State College (F)	●																					●		●			●			●			
562	Valdosta State College (P)	●																					●		●			●			●			
573	West Georgia College	●																			0	●	●		●			●			●			
	HAWAII																																	
138	Chaminade University of Honolulu (F)	●																					●			●			●			●		
459	University of Hawaii at Manoa	●	●			●	●		●	●	●	●	●		●			●		●			●							●				
	IDAHO																																	
105	Boise State University	●	●			●	●				●	●											●		●						●			
211	Idaho State University	●																					●		●					●	●			
464	University of Idaho (F)	●																					●		●					●	●			
464	University of Idaho (P)	●																					●		●					●	●			
	ILLINOIS																																	
111	Bradley University (F)	●																					●								●			
111	Bradley University (P)	●																					●								●			
163	De Paul University		●			●	●		●	●	●	●	●		●			●		●			●		●			●			●		●	
174	Eastern Illinois University	●																					●					●		●				
194	George Williams College (P)	●			●						●									●			●			●		●		●	●			
202	Governors State University (P)	●																					●					●	●	●				
213	Illinois Benedictine College	●	●			●	●		●	●	●	●											●		●			●		●	●			
214	Illinois Institute of Technology (F)									●	●												●											
214	Illinois Institute of Technology (P)	●	●				●			●	●	●	●				●				8		●											
215	Illinois State University (F)	●																					●					●		●	●			
233	Keller Graduate School of Management (P)	●	●				●			●		●												●		●		●			●		●	
237	Lake Forest Grad. School of Management																																	
242	Lewis University (P)	●			●						●	●											●							●	●			
252	Loyola University of Chicago (F)	●	●				●		●	●	●	●	●											●				●			●			●
252	Loyola University of Chicago (P)	●	●				●			●	●	●	●										●					●			●			●
306	Northern Illinois University (F)	●	●				●			●	●	●	●		●								●					●		●			●	
306	Northern Illinois University (P)	●	●				●			●	●	●	●		●													●		●			●	
311	Northwestern University (F)	●	●	●	●	●	●	●	●	●	●	●	●	●	●	●	●			●	90	●	●								●			
311	Northwestern University (P)	●	●	●	●	●	●	●	●	●	●	●	●	●	●	●	●	●	●	●		●	●		●		●				●			
346	Rosary College (P)	●	●		●	●	●		●	●	●	●	●					●	●				●						●	●	●			
364	Saint Xavier College (P)								●		●	●											●	●						●	●			
371	Sangamon State University (P)	●																					●		●				●					
386	Southern Illinois U. at Carbondale (F)	●	●		●		●			●	●	●	●					●			19		●					●						
387	Southern Illinois U. — Edwardsville (F)	●	●			●	●			●	●	●	●										●		●	●				●				
387	Southern Illinois U. — Edwardsville (P)	●	●			●	●			●	●	●											●		●	●				●				
443	University of Chicago (F)		●		●	●	●		●	●	●	●	●		●	●			●		144		●								●			
465	University of Illinois at Chicago (F)		●			●	●		●	●	●	●	●						●				●		●						●			
465	University of Illinois at Chicago (P)		●			●	●		●	●	●	●	●						●				●		●		●				●			
466	U. of Illinois at Urbana-Champaign (F)	●	●		●	●	●		●	●	●	●						●	●	●	50		●							●				
578	Western Illinois University (F)	●	●		●	●	●				●	●					●						●								●			

Table: Characteristics of 1984-85 Entering Class

School Offers This Option to Students	Min. Months to Obtain Degree	No. Who Applied	No. Enrolled First Time	% Minority	% Women	% Foreign	Avg Age at Matriculation	Humanities	Social Sciences	Business and Commerce	Science and Engineering	Other Fields	% Having Graduate Degree	GMAT (Middle 80%)	TOEFL (Middle 80%)	Undergrad GPA (Middle 80%)	% With 1+ Yrs Full-Time Work Exp.	% Entering Directly from Undergrad	April 15 Common Reply Date	Scholarships/Fellowships	Teaching/Research Assistantships	Loans	GAPSFAS Req'd for Financial Aid	Separate Placement Service	Starting Salaries	Career Placement	Campus Interviews	Geographic Placement	AACSB Accredited	Page
	12	64	39	30	20	2	30	10	10	60	20		2	420-600	500-600	2.7-3.4	90	20	●		●	●				●	●			562
	18	31	12	30	20	0	30	10	10	60	20		0	420-600	500-600	2.7-3.4	90	20	●		●	●				●	●			562
●	12	35	20	5	40	10	30		10	80	10		5	470-520	540-570	2.8-3.5	95	5	●	●	●	●	●				●			573
	15																99	1			●					●	●			138
	21	235	113	50	33	9	30	13	13	31	19	24	15	480-630		2.51-3.73	100		●	●	●	●				●	●	●	●	459
	12	210	199		40		32							450-550		2.8-3.5	90	10	●	●									●	105
●	12	63	48		19	8	25	4	8	52	29	7	6	450-590	513-570	2.76-3.70	25	48	●		●				●	●	●	●	●	211
	9	47	11	0	36	9	31	18	0	45	18	18	0	470-620		2.6-3.6	73	27	●	●	●				●	●	●			464
	28	29	19	0	26	0	35	5		89	5		0	440-580		2.5-3.5	100	0			●									464
	18	15	12		25	13			12	62	26			420-580		2.60-3.52	65	35	●	●	●				●	●	●		●	111
	18	56	46		25	13			12	62	26			420-580		2.60-3.52	65	35	●	●	●				●	●	●		●	111
●	12	2,091	1,051	5	35	1	25	15	10	50	10	15	1	480-590		3.0-3.4	90	10	●		●	●	●						●	163
	12																				●									174
	20	113	61	7	59	3	32										95	5	●		●					●	●	●		194
	12	125	80	27	35	23	33																							202
●	18	224	177		37	1	30	9	14	46	29	2	5	375-575		2.4-3.65	99	1			●									213
	24																													214
	12	250	150	10	20	10	30	5	5	20	60	10	15	475-525	550-600	2.9-3.2	90	10			●	●								214
	12	270	100	0	10	5	26	10	23	46	13	11							●		●								●	215
	15	365	236	10	33	2	31	10	26	41	15	8	15	450-600	560-600	2.5-3.3	90	10	●		●			●		●		●	233
	15																													237
	24	178	150					12	14	46	24	4	2				99	1			●	●		●						242
	15	100	40	<1	48	10	25	20	20	30	10	20	5	500-570	550-600	3.2-3.6	50	90			●	●		●	●	●		●	252
	15	1,100	450	<1	45	2	26	10	10	38	10	32	10	470-550	550-600	2.8-3.3	90	10	●		●			●		●	●		252
●	8							4	5	54	11	26							●	●	●					●	●		●	306
●	12							4	5	54	11	26							●	●	●					●	●		●	306
●	12	3,000	470	11	35	12	26	12	45	16	22	5	5	510-750	580-620	3.1-3.6	95	5	●						●	●	●	●	●	311
	30	1,350	450	7	46	2	27	20	25	30	20	5	15	540-740		3.0-3.8	98	2			●								●	311
	18	245	187	5	54		30	27	18	37	13	21	14			2.6-3.6	95	5		●	●					●	●			346
	24	113	44	8	40	1		5	25	60		10	4	450-500			100	0			●									364
	16	146	80	6	32	5	31	10	14	43	27	6	5	410-610		2.4-3.6	98	2		●	●	●								371
	14.5		28		32	39				57		43		451-580		2.73-3.75			●	●	●							●	386
	9	48	23	10	28	50	26	5	10	40	15	30	5	450-600	550-600	3.75-4.50	25	33	●	●	●				●	●	●	●	387
	18	125	77	5	30	7	32	10	10	25	30	25	15	410-600	550-600	3.75-4.50	99	0	●	●	●				●	●	●	●	387
●	18	2,647	502	10	20	16	25	7	8	25	23	37	8	580-740		3.1-3.8	80	27	●				●	●		●	●	●	●	443
●	18	450	100	10	35	7	25	35	10	30	18	7	10	500-620	580-630	3.1-3.7	75	24	●	●	●				●	●	●	●	465
●	24	600	150	8	35	5	28	24	14	20	32	10	20	500-620		3.1-3.7	98	2							●	●	●	●	465
	16	580	108	11	34	23	25			53		47	4	550-660	577-623	3.0-3.6	69	31	●	●	●			●		●	●	●	466
●	12	75	50	5	31	35	24	5	5	8	5	3		390-580	550-600					●	●	●							●	578

*See page 43 for explanation

Programs of Study Offered

School Name and Page Number	General Management Program	Accounting	Arts Administration	Behavioral Sciences	Economics	Finance	Health Services	International Business	Management Information Systems	Management	Marketing	Production/Operations Management	Public Policy or Administration	Quantitative Analysis	Real Estate and Insurance	Transportation	M.B.A./J.D.	M.B.A./Engineering	Other Joint Degrees	Total Doctoral Enrollment	Students Can Take Courses for Credit in Other Schools of University	January	February	March	April	May	June	July	August	September	October	November	December
INDIANA																																	
97 Ball State University (P)	•									•											•												
218 Indiana Central University	•																				•				•		•			•			
219 Indiana State University	•																				•						•			•			
220 Ind. U. (Bloomington & Indianapolis) (F)	•	•	•	•	•	•		•	•	•	•	•	•	•	•	•	•	•		157	•									•			
220 Ind. U. (Bloomington & Indianapolis) (P)	•					•			•	•	•			•							•									•			
221 Indiana University at South Bend (P)	•																				•					•				•			
222 Indiana University Northwest (P)	•																				•								•				
224 Indiana U. — Purdue U. at Fort Wayne (P)	•			•						•	•										•				•				•	•			
334 Purdue University (West Lafayette) (F)	•	•		•					•	•	•	•		•						116	•									•			
335 Purdue University Calumet (P)	•	•			•	•					•	•									•						•			•			
455 University of Evansville (P)	•																				•					•			•				
506 University of Notre Dame (F)	•	•		•				•	•		•			•							•								•	•			
IOWA																																	
164 Drake University (F)										•				•							•	•							•				
164 Drake University (P)										•				•							•	•							•				
255 Maharishi International University (F)	•	•																			•									•			
352 St. Ambrose College (P)	•	•				•				•	•	•									•	•				•			•				
467 University of Iowa (F)		•		•	•	•	•		•	•	•	•		•			•	•	•	148	•	•							•	•			
467 University of Iowa (P)		•		•	•	•	•		•	•	•	•		•			•	•	•		•								•	•			
KANSAS																																	
181 Emporia State University (F)	•																	•			•						•		•				
191 Fort Hays State University (F)		•			•	•			•	•	•										•						•		•				
232 Kansas State University (F)	•	•																			•						•		•				
329 Pittsburg State University (F)	•	•		•						•											•						•		•				
329 Pittsburg State University (P)	•	•		•						•											•						•		•				
469 University of Kansas (F)	•			•	•				•	•			•	•						34	•						•		•				
469 University of Kansas (P)	•																												•				
568 Washburn University	•																				•						•			•			
587 Wichita State University (F)	•	•		•	•	•		•	•	•	•			•	•						•	•								•			
587 Wichita State University (P)	•	•		•	•	•		•	•	•	•			•	•						•	•								•			
KENTUCKY																																	
100 Bellarmine College (P)	•			•	•	•		•	•		•										•	•			•				•				
175 Eastern Kentucky University (F)	•																				•						•		•				
175 Eastern Kentucky University (P)	•																				•						•		•				
284 Morehead State University (F)	•																				•							•	•				
284 Morehead State University (P)	•																				•							•	•				
286 Murray State University (F)	•																				•							•	•				
286 Murray State University (P)	•																				•						•	•	•				
307 Northern Kentucky University (P)	•															•					•								•	•			
470 University of Kentucky	•	•				•		•	•	•	•	•								90	•						•		•				
472 University of Louisville	•																				•							•	•				
579 Western Kentucky University (F)	•																				•					•			•				
579 Western Kentucky University (P)	•																				•					•			•				

- 52 -

School Offers This Option to Students	Minimum Number of Months to Obtain Degree	Number of Students Who Applied for Admission	Number of Students Who Enrolled for the First Time	Percentage of Minority Students	Percentage of Women Students	Percentage of Foreign Students	Average Age of Students at Matriculation	Humanities	Social Sciences	Business and Commerce	Science and Engineering	Other Fields	Percentage Having Graduate Degree	Range of Middle 80% of Students' GMAT Scores	Range of Middle 80% of Students' TOEFL Scores	Range of Middle 80% of Students' Undergraduate GPA	Percentage of Students Having One or More Years of Full-Time Work Experience	Percentage of Students Entering Directly from Undergraduate School	Common Date for Applicant Reply	Scholarships/Fellowships	Teaching/Research Assistantships	Loans	Required for Financial Aid	Separate Placement Service for Management Students	Starting Salaries	Career Placement	Campus Interviews	Geographic Placement	Master's Program Accredited by	Page Number
●	12	169	107	4	27	10	28	12	8	54	22	4	3				95	5			●			●					●	97
		80	72	3	26	1	30	12	4	41	27	13	1	360-570			95	5			●				●	●	●	●		218
																													●	219
●	18	1,046	250	8	30	14	26	10	28	40	22			501-650	570-630	2.75-3.65	57		●	●	●	●		●	●	●	●	●	●	220
●	36	392	75	6	38	0	28	19	12	36	33			501-650		2.88-3.78	70	30	●		●	●		●	●	●	●	●	●	220
	36	150	90	10	20	10	32		5	4	5	5	10			3.2-4.0	98	2												221
●	36	128	77	6	35	2	26	8	8	38	33	13	3	410-600		2.39-3.43	88	12	●		●			●						222
	36	123	85	6	24	2	28	8	5	46	33	8	15	425-590		2.4-3.5	92	8									●			224
●	11	700	164	8	32	17	24	10	5	38	42	5	10	530-660	560-627	2.90-3.86	57	43	●	●	●	●		●	●	●	●	●	●	334
●	18	120	45	10	30	5	28		10	20	60	10	5	460-630		2.9-3.8	80	10			●			●			●	●		335
	12		50	5	50	5	27			60	30	10	2	425-525	560-600	2.8-3.5	95	5						●		●	●	●		455
	11		141	3	18	9	23	20	28	22	28	3	2	510-610	310-333		49	51		●				●		●	●	●		506
	12	113	53	33	30	32	26	8	9	74	8	2		400-590		2.69-3.62	10	80	●		●		●		●	●	●	●	●	164
	30	137	110	30	29	0	30	3	8	62	14	13		410-590		2.55-3.74	95	2					●		●	●	●	●	●	164
	22		25	4	12	40	34	18	9	55	18		0	450-570	570-600	2.8-3.5	91	9	●	●	●	●				●	●		●	255
	32	133	120	20	27	1	30	5	5	60	25	5		450-475		3.2-3.7	95	5	●		●	●								352
●	12	326	122	5	33	25	1	20	25	40	15		2	470-630		2.8-3.8	45	50	●	●	●		●		●	●	●	●	●	467
																													●	467
	12	130	30		35	25				5	80	5	10					35		●	●				●		●	●		181
	12	15	10		40	5	25	2	3	90	3	2		350-450		2.8-3.8	40	60			●				●	●	●	●		191
●	12	128	75	3	37	40	25	10	10	50	20	10	4	420-610	550-623	2.8-3.5	30	70	●		●			●	●	●	●	●	●	232
	12	36	22	5	41	10	29	5	12	69	12	2	7	380-550	575-640	2.65-3.60	65	35	●		●			●						329
	36	70	27	0	42	0	30	11	8	45	24	12	9	400-600		2.50-3.60	75	25	●		●			●						329
●	12	418	223	4	38	6	28	12	16	48	14	10	14	450-640	596-625	3.0-3.8	60	33	●		●	●		●	●	●	●	●	●	469
●	48	198	129		40		30	9	17	27	41	6	19	460-600		2.7-3.9	81	2						●					●	469
	12	27	23		37		37							480-520		3.0-3.4	97	1												568
	18	247	157	4	38	4	36	17	3	52	20	8					95	5		●	●	●	●		●	●	●	●	●	587
	24	247	157	4	38	4	36	17	3	52	20	8					95	5		●	●	●	●		●	●	●	●	●	587
	24	138	73	8	32	1	29	10	16	52	18	4	8	500-520		2.9-3.4	90	10			●						●			100
	10		8	39	30	1	25			86		14					59	41			●									175
	50		15	39	30	1	25			86		14					59	41			●									175
	9	204	68	5	30	55	25	5	5	70	10	10	5	350-500	530-570	2.5-3.3	35	75	●		●				●	●	●		284
	24	86	62	2	35	4	30	5	10	50	25	10	10	425-575		2.6-3.3	95	15	●						●	●	●		284
●	12	177	21	0	52	14	27	5	0	62	19	14	5	380-550		2.73-3.48	29	14	●		●	●			●	●	●	●	●	286
●	12	177	25	0	36	0	28	0	4	60	32	4	4	390-610		2.85-3.35	96	4	●		●	●			●	●	●	●	●	286
	33	85	50	5	33	10	31										95	5						●			●			307
	12	353	75	2	2	10	25	4	20	50	16	10	12				50	50	●	●	●	●	●	●	●	●	●	●	●	470
	24	340	139																	●						●				472
	14	40	25		50		28												●	●	●									579
		12	10		50		35																							579

School Name and Page Number

(F) = Full-time program
(P) = Part-time program

Page	School Name	General Management Program	Accounting	Arts Administration	Behavioral Sciences	Economics	Finance	Health Services	International Business	Management Information Systems	Management	Marketing	Production/Operations Management	Public Policy or Administration	Quantitative Analysis	Real Estate and Insurance	Transportation	M.B.A./J.D.	M.B.A./Engineering	Other Joint Degrees	Total Doctoral Enrollment	Students Can Take Courses for Credit in Other Schools of University	January	February	March	April	May	June	July	August	September	October	November	December
	LOUISIANA																																	
230	Grambling State University (F)	•								•												•	•					•			•			
246	Louisiana State U. in Baton Rouge	•																		•	95	•	•							•				
247	Louisiana State U. in Shreveport (P)	•																				•	•					•		•				
248	Louisiana Tech University (F)		•			•	•				•	•		•							66				•			•			•			•
251	Loyola University, New Orleans (P)	•												•								•	•					•		•				
267	McNeese State University (P)	•																				•	•					•		•				
296	Nicholls State University (F)	•																				•	•					•		•				
302	Northeast Louisiana University (F)	•																				•	•					•		•				
310	Northwestern State U. of Louisiana	•								•	•											•	•					•		•				
383	Southeastern Louisiana University	•																				•	•					•		•				
414	Tulane University (F)	•	•		•	•	•	•	•	•	•	•			•			•		•		•	•								•			
414	Tulane University (P)	•	•		•	•	•	•	•	•	•	•			•					•		•	•								•			
498	University of New Orleans (F)	•	•	•		•	•								•						12	•	•					•		•				
498	University of New Orleans (P)	•	•	•		•	•								•							•	•					•		•				
529	University of Southwestern Louisiana (P)	•	•			•	•				•	•										•	•					•			•			
	MAINE																																	
210	Husson College (P)	•																				•	•								•			
410	Thomas College (P)	•	•							•	•	•	•									•				•					•			
474	University of Maine at Orono (F)		•			•					•	•										•	•					•	•		•			
474	University of Maine at Orono (P)		•			•					•	•										•	•					•	•		•			
	MARYLAND																																	
249	Loyola College (P)	•	•			•	•				•	•	•									•	•					•			•			
285	Mount Saint Mary's College (P)	•	•		•						•											•	•				•	•			•			
366	Salisbury State College (P)	•																				•				•		•			•			
430	University of Baltimore (F)		•			•	•		•	•	•	•	•					•				•	•					•			•			
430	University of Baltimore (P)		•			•	•		•	•	•	•	•					•				•	•					•			•			
477	University of Maryland (F)	•	•		•		•		•	•	•	•	•	•	•			•	•	•	75	•	•								•			
477	University of Maryland (P)	•	•		•		•		•	•	•	•	•	•	•			•	•	•	0	•	•								•			
	MASSACHUSETTS																																	
82	American International College (F)	•																																
90	Assumption College (F)	•																				•	•					•	•		•			
90	Assumption College (P)	•																				•	•					•	•		•			
96	Babson College (F)	•	•		•	•	•		•	•	•	•			•							•	•								•			
96	Babson College (P)	•	•		•	•	•		•	•	•	•			•							•	•					•			•			
101	Bentley College (F)		•		•	•	•			•	•		•									•	•								•			
101	Bentley College (P)		•		•	•	•			•	•		•									•	•								•			
106	Boston College (F)	•	•	•		•	•		•	•	•	•						•		•	•		•								•			
106	Boston College (P)	•	•		•		•		•	•	•	•						•		•	0	•	•								•			
107	Boston University (School of Management)	•	•			•	•	•	•	•	•	•	•	•				•	•	•		•	•					•			•			
145	Clark University (F)	•	•		•		•		•		•	•										•	•					•			•			
145	Clark University (P)	•	•		•	•	•		•		•	•										•	•					•			•			
264	Massachusetts Institute of Technology (F)		•		•	•	•	•	•	•	•	•		•							78	•	•								•			

School Offers This Option to Students	Minimum Number of Months to Obtain Degree	Number of Students Who Applied for Admission	Number of Students Who Enrolled for the First Time	Percentage of Minority Students	Percentage of Women Students	Percentage of Foreign Students	Average Age of Students at Matriculation	Humanities	Social Sciences	Business and Commerce	Science and Engineering	Other Fields	Percentage Having Graduate Degree	Range of Middle 80% of Students' GMAT Scores	Range of Middle 80% of Students' TOEFL Scores	Range of Middle 80% of Students' Undergraduate GPA	Percentage of Students Having One or More Years of Full-Time Work Experience	Percentage of Students Entering Directly from Undergraduate School	Common Date for Applicant Reply (April 15)	Scholarships/Fellowships	Teaching/Research Assistantships	Loans	Required for Financial Aid (GAPSFAS)	Separate Placement Service for Management Students	Starting Salaries	Career Placement	Campus Interviews	Geographic Placement	Master's Program Accredited by (AACSB)	Page Number
	14																			●	●						●			203
●	24	600	120	7	32	7	27	6	5	37	40	12	5	450-600		2.70-3.30		40	●	●	●	●		●	●	●	●	●	●	246
	12	150	100	10	45	5	30	10	7	32	26	25	10	450-575	550-700	2.3-3.2	80	20	●	●	●				●	●				247
	12		94																										●	248
●	12	185	120	12	30	5	26	10	15	50	20	5	10	430-520	560-640	2.9-3.3	75	25	●						●	●	●	●	●	251
	12	43	38	8	12	7		10	10	35	30	15	1				72	15		●	●				●	●				267
	12	60	38	4	32	17	24	5	0	63	30	2	4	380-516	567-690	2.4-3.6	20	80	●	●	●				●		●			296
	18	65	42	0	40	20	26	10	20	50	20		3	475-525	575-600			15	70		●								●	302
	12	20	15	20	50	20	28	25		50	25						90	25	●	●	●					●	●		310
	12	60	45	20	50	25	26		10	60	20	10	20	400-500	500-530	2.7-3.5	33	70	●	●	●			●	●	●	●	●	●	383
	21	425	97	4	26	20	24	10	23	24	40	3		470-660		2.4-3.6	50	50	●	●	●	●		●		●			●	414
	48	80	40	8	47	2	27	18	4	20	58			480-660		2.5-3.5	95	5			●								●	414
	12			8	35	6	29	12	9	40	32	7	8	440-560	570-610	2.7-3.5	80	20	●	●	●								●	498
	28			8	35		29	12	9	40	32	7	8	440-560		2.7-3.5	80	20											●	498
	16		60	10	35	5	27	10	10	30	45		5	450-550		2.5-3.5	90	20	●	●	●									529
●	24		80	1	30	5	33							425-550		2.6-3.2	90	10								●	●	●		210
	24	135	93																	●	●					●	●	●	●	410
●	12	75	25																		●								●	474
●	28	75	25																		●								●	474
	12	460	230	10	35	1	27	10	15	40	15	20	10				95	20		●	●				●	●	●	●		249
	12	120	85	5	35	2	32	5	11	58	16	10	16	440-560		2.9-3.4	95	5		●	●									285
	16	20	14	0	36	7	30							480-590		2.6-3.2	100	0	●								●			366
	10	750	500	10	25	5	29	18	19	45	17	1	1	460-500	550-600	2.75-3.25	90	40	●						●	●	●	●	●	430
	24	750	500	10	25	5	29	18	19	45	17	1	1	460-500	550-600	2.75-3.25	90	40	●						●	●	●	●	●	430
●	16	600	120	14	32	13	26	12	34	31	23		7	500-640	580-650	2.8-3.6	65	35	●	●	●	●		●	●	●	●	●	●	477
●	36	400	120	12	41	2	30	15	22	30	33		12	500-640	620-680	2.7-3.6	92	8	●	●	●			●	●	●	●	●	●	477
●		80	40	10	40	15	28	5	5	90								30			●	●		●						82
		7	5	1			20			40	40		20									●		●						90
		54	32	14				13	19	59	9													●						90
●	9	507	192		35	31	25	6	33	46	13	2	12				65	35	●	●	●	●		●	●	●	●	●	●	96
●	21	724	428		38		28	7	21	46	19	7					95	5	●						●	●	●	●	●	96
●	9		49	3	46	15	25	6	16	53	15	10	3	475-565	510-600	2.8-3.6	75	25		●	●	●					●		●	101
●	21		360	3	43	3	29	9	6	56	26	3	9	485-585	510-600	2.9-3.6	99	1		●	●	●					●		●	101
	72	500	86	20	38	20	25	13	39	22	26	0	5	490-650	610-660	2.7-3.6	78	22	●	●	●	●		●	●	●	●	●	●	106
	72	350	115	2	43	0	29	32	29	17	22	0	10	510-670		2.8-3.7	93	7	●						●	●	●	●	●	106
●	16			5	50	15	27	20	34	17	17	0	13	540-590	580-620	3.0-3.4	75	25		●	●	●			●	●	●	●	●	107
●	12	40	20	20	35	20	25	10	65	12	12	0	10	450-600		2.5-3.5	25	65		●	●			●				●	●	145
●	12	120	83		43	8	32	20	25	10	40	5	15	480-620		2.8-3.4	95	0		●	●			●			●	●	●	145
●	18	1,331	200	10	22	26	26	7	22	22	47	2	14				84	16	●		●	●		●	●	●	●	●	●	264

*See page 43 for explanation

School Name and Page Number
(F) = Full-time program
(P) = Part-time program

Page	School Name	General Management Program	Accounting	Arts Administration	Behavioral Sciences	Economics	Finance	Health Services	International Business	Management Information Systems	Management	Marketing	Production/Operations Management	Public Policy or Administration	Quantitative Analysis	Real Estate and Insurance	Transportation	M.B.A./J.D.	M.B.A./Engineering	Other Joint Degrees	Total Doctoral Enrollment	Students Can Take Courses for Credit in Other Schools of University	Jan	Feb	Mar	Apr	May	Jun	Jul	Aug	Sep	Oct	Nov	Dec
297	Nichols College (P)	●	●			●	●			●	●	●			●							●	●				●				●			
304	Northeastern University (F)	●	●		●	●	●	●	●	●	●	●	●		●	●						●	●						●		●			
304	Northeastern University (P)	●	●		●	●	●	●	●	●	●	●	●		●	●						●		●								●		●	
365	Salem State College (P)	●																				●	●								●			
379	Simmons College (F)	●																				●									●			
379	Simmons College (P)	●																				●									●			
384	Southeastern Massachusetts University (P)	●	●		●	●	●				●	●									0	●	●								●			
399	Suffolk University																																	
473	University of Lowell (F)	●	●		●	●					●	●	●									●	●				●				●			
473	University of Lowell (P)	●	●		●	●					●	●	●									●	●				●	●						
478	University of Massachusetts (Amherst) (F)	●	●				●		●				●																		●			
478	University of Massachusetts (Amherst) (P)	●																				●									●			
479	University of Massachusetts at Boston (P)	●	●			●	●	●	●	●	●	●										●									●			
581	Western New England College (P)	●	●			●	●				●	●										●							●	●	●			
595	Worcester Polytechnic Institute									●	●		●		●							●	●								●			
	MICHIGAN																																	
84	Andrews University (F)	●	●					●														●	●		●		●				●			
86	Aquinas College (P)	●			●				●													●					●		●		●			
135	Central Michigan University (F)																				0	●					●	●		●	●			
135	Central Michigan University (P)																				0	●					●	●		●	●			
176	Eastern Michigan University (P)	●	●	●	●	●	●		●	●	●	●			●							●									●			
204	Grand Valley State College (F)	●	●				●				●	●										●					●				●			
204	Grand Valley State College (P)	●	●				●				●	●										●					●				●			
254	Madonna College (P)										●									●		●					●				●			
275	Michigan State University		●		●	●	●				●	●	●				●			●	158	●	●		●						●			
276	Michigan Technological University (F)				●								●									●									●			
308	Northern Michigan University (F)	●																				●					●		●		●			
313	Oakland University (P)	●																				●					●	●			●			
351	Saginaw Valley State College (P)		●			●	●				●	●										●					●				●			
452	University of Detroit	●	●			●	●		●	●	●	●				●						●					●	●			●			
482	University of Michigan (Ann Arbor) (F)	●	●		●	●	●		●	●	●	●	●					●		●	90	●									●			
482	University of Michigan (Ann Arbor) (P)	●	●		●	●	●		●	●	●	●			●							●									●			
483	University of Michigan — Dearborn (F)	●					●			●	●		●								0	●	●								●			
483	University of Michigan — Dearborn (P)	●					●			●	●		●								0	●									●			
484	University of Michigan — Flint (P)	●									●											●									●			
571	Wayne State University (P)		●		●	●	●			●	●	●										●					●				●			
580	Western Michigan University (F)	●				●	●				●	●										●					●			●	●			
580	Western Michigan University (P)	●				●	●				●	●										●					●			●	●			
	MINNESOTA																																	
151	College of St. Thomas (P)	●						●	●		●			●								●		●			●				●			
257	Mankato State University (F)	●	●			●	●		●		●	●				●						●		●				●			●			
273	Metropolitan State University (P)	●																				●				●				●			●	
354	St. Cloud State University	●																				●			●						●			●

Characteristics of 1984-85 Entering Class

Deferred Admit (School Offers Option)	Min. Months to Degree	No. Applied	No. Enrolled First Time	% Minority	% Women	% Foreign	Avg. Age	Humanities	Social Sciences	Business & Commerce	Science & Engineering	Other Fields	% Having Grad. Degree	GMAT (mid 80%)	TOEFL (mid 80%)	GPA (mid 80%)	% w/ Work Exp.	% Direct from Undergrad	April 15 Reply	Scholarships/Fellowships	Teaching/Research Assistantships	Loans	GAPSFAS Required	Separate Placement Service	Starting Salaries	Career Placement	Campus Interviews	Geographic Placement	AACSB Accredited	Page
	12		70	1	30	1	29	10	15	40	25	10	1	400-600		2.5-3.5	99	1				•		•						297
•	15	800	180	9	50	15	24	25	25	30	15	5	10	480-620	580-610	2.8-3.5	70	30		•	•	•	•	•	•	•	•	•	•	304
•	18	1,200	450	10	35		28	15	15	30	30	10	15	480-620		2.7-3.4	100	0				•	•	•	•	•	•	•	•	304
	30	170	40	3	50		30	15	50	8	19	8	12	470-580			95	2	•		•	•								365
	12	155	63	4	100	1	33	39	36	19	4	2	18	460-620		2.2-3.9	100	0	•			•		•	•	•	•	•		379
	24	130	59	4	100	1	33	39	36	19	4	2	18	460-620		2.2-3.9	100	0	•			•		•	•	•	•	•		379
	36	50	35	3	10	0																								384
																														399
•	12	20	10		40	50	24	10	20	30	30	10		425-550	525-575	2.7-3.3	20	80	•		•									473
•	22	177	87	1	35	15	26	8	16	26	44	6	10	425-600		2.5-3.5	85	15	•											473
	21	450	85	1	43	25	27	19	20	34	24	3		530-540	560-580	3.1-3.3	56	35			•	•	•							478
	36	30	20	0	35	0	27	22	28	25	14	7	11	530-540			82	10											•	478
•	24	199	75	17	29	15	30	3	7	44	14	28	4	460-530	513-583	2.6-3.5	84	13			•	•	•		•	•	•	•		479
		260	216																							•	•			•	•	581
•	18	75	34		17	6	30	11		9	76	4	29				95	5			•				•	•	•	•		595
	12	124	22	60	30	53	27			80	5	15	2				51	49	•	•	•				•	•	•	•		84
		158	123	8	43		30	10	20	30	35	5	2	350-500		2.6-3.5	100	3		•	•	•			•	•	•			86
									15	70	15																			135
									20	20	60																			135
•	16					10	32			25		10		450-600	500-600	2.6-3.4	90	15			•	•							•	176
	12	14	9	3	34	6	25	10	10	40	20	20	10	450-610		2.9-3.7	40	40	•	•	•	•	•		•	•	•	•		204
	24	74	41	3	27	4	32	2	10	45	30	13	10	450-610		2.86-3.65	99	10	•	•	•	•	•		•	•	•	•		204
•	11	134	84	7	65	1	34	5	4	26	17	48		370-540		2.4-3.6	100	0	•			•				•				254
•	15	900	250	5	30	17	26			47	9	44				2.9-3.8				•	•				•	•			•	275
•	15	45	20	25	20	15	26			100			15	490-600	540-640	2.9-3.4	90	10		•	•	•								276
	12	30	30	10	25	5	28		5	75	20		0	450-550		2.6-3.6	80	20	•	•	•									308
•	16	280	157	1	41	1	27	6	12	34	40	8	5	480-620	570-630	2.7-3.5	77	10			•	•				•	•	•		313
	24	72	54	4	43	6	30	5	4	48	30	13	3	420-550		2.35-3.58	83	11				•				•	•			351
	36	381	150		40	10	30										75	25											•	452
•	20	1,910	374	10	26	15	25	25	25	22	28			549-693	568-662	2.8-3.9	72	28	•	•		•	•	•	•	•	•	•	•	482
•		446	246	4	32		28	25	25	22	28			551-675	597-597	2.7-3.7	100							•	•	•	•	•	•	482
•	18	236	82	1	37	3	25	10	10	0	64	15	1	500-575		3.0-3.8	90	10	•	•	•	•								483
•	32	236	82	1	37	3	25	10	10	0	64	15	1	500-575		3.0-3.8	90	10	•	•	•	•								483
•	30	116	78	5	30		27	2	5	41	52		6	470-620		2.5-3.8	100		•			•								484
	12	1,400	600	10	30	2	28	5	5	40	25	25	13	407-591		2.56-3.59	90	10		•	•	•			•	•	•	•		571
	15			20	45	5	24	10	10	40	30	10	10				40	10		•	•								•	580
	30	400	200	20	45	0	30	9	9	50	30	2	20				90												•	580
•	33			5	33	1	31	24		41	35		5	480-620			99	1				•		•						151
	9	135	104	4	27	22	31						10	374-554		2.4-3.4	60	40		•	•				•	•	•	•		257
•	27	61	45	7	34	1	35	10	30	35	15	10	8			2.6-3.4	99	1				•		•						273
	12	90	50							40	40	20					90													354

*See page 43 for explanation

| | | Programs of Study Offered | | | | | | | | | | | | | | | | Joint Degrees | | | Doctoral Program | Other Options | Entrance Dates | | | | | | | | | | | |
| | | Concentrations | | | | | | | | | | | | | | | | | | | | | | | | | | | | | | | | |
Page	School Name and Page Number (F) = Full-time program (P) = Part-time program	General Management Program	Accounting	Arts Administration	Behavioral Sciences	Economics	Finance	Health Services	International Business	Management Information Systems	Management	Marketing	Production/Operations Management	Public Policy or Administration	Quantitative Analysis	Real Estate and Insurance	Transportation	M.B.A./J.D.	M.B.A./Engineering	Other Joint Degrees	Total Doctoral Enrollment	Students Can Take Courses for Credit in Other Schools of University	January	February	March	April	May	June	July	August	September	October	November	December
485	University of Minnesota (Minneapolis) (F)	●	●				●			●	●	●		●		●	●	●				●						●			●			
485	University of Minnesota (Minneapolis) (P)	●	●				●			●	●	●										●	●		●						●			
486	University of Minnesota Duluth (P)	●																				●		●				●			●	●		
593	Winona State University (P)																					●			●						●			●
	MISSISSIPPI																																		
162	Delta State University (F)	●																				●	●					●	●	●				
162	Delta State University (P)	●																				●	●					●	●	●				
228	Jackson State University	●	●																							●		●					●	
278	Millsaps College (P)	●																				●						●			●			
279	Mississippi College (P)	●																				●						●			●			
280	Mississippi State University (F)				●	●				●	●	●			●						101	●						●			●			
487	University of Mississippi (F)	●																●			30	●						●	●	●				
527	U. of Southern Mississippi (Hattiesburg) (F)				●	●				●	●			●								●						●			●			
528	U. of Southern Mississippi — Gulf Coast (P)	●				●				●												●		●		●		●			●		●	
591	William Carey College (P)	●								●	●											●						●		●			●	
	MISSOURI																																		
94	Avila College (P)	●	●		●		●		●	●	●	●	●									●						●			●			
136	Central Missouri State University (F)	●																				●						●		●				
136	Central Missouri State University (P)	●																				●						●		●				
166	Drury College (F)	●																				●					●				●			
166	Drury College (P)	●																				●					●				●			
189	Fontbonne College (F)	●																				●									●			
262	Maryville College — St. Louis (P)	●					●				●	●										●			●	●		●			●	●		
303	Northeast Missouri State U. (F)		●																			●						●			●			
309	Northwest Missouri State U. (F)	●			●	●	●													●		●						●			●			
344	Rockhurst College (P)		●				●				●	●	●								0	●						●			●			
358	Saint Louis University	●	●		●	●	●		●	●	●				●					●	52	●						●			●			
382	Southeast Missouri State University	●																				●						●			●			
390	Southwest Missouri State University (F)	●	●			●	●			●	●	●								●		●						●			●			
488	University of Missouri — Columbia	●	●	●		●	●			●	●	●						●	●	●	17	●						●		●				
489	University of Missouri — Kansas City (P)	●	●				●				●	●	●									●									●			
490	University of Missouri — St. Louis	●	●		●	●	●				●											●						●		●				
570	Washington University (F)	●	●		●	●	●	●	●	●	●	●						●		●	12	●									●			
570	Washington University (P)	●	●		●		●	●	●	●	●	●	●									●					●				●			
	MONTANA																																		
491	University of Montana																																		
	NEBRASKA																																		
158	Creighton University (F)	●																●				●						●						
492	University of Nebraska at Omaha (F)	●	●			●	●				●	●			●	●						●						●		●				
493	University of Nebraska — Lincoln (F)		●		●	●	●	●		●	●	●	●	●	●					●	150	●	●					●	●	●	●			
	NEVADA																																		
494	University of Nevada, Las Vegas (P)	●	●		●										●							●									●			
495	University of Nevada, Reno (F)	●	●			●	●		●	●	●	●																			●			
495	University of Nevada, Reno (P)	●	●			●	●		●	●	●	●																			●			

Characteristics of 1984-85 Entering Class

Column groups: **Deferred Admit Policy** (School Offers This Option to Students) · **Length of Study** (Minimum Number of Months to Obtain Degree) · **Applicants/Enrollment for 1984-85** (Number Who Applied / Number Who Enrolled First Time) · **Characteristics of 1984-85 Entering Class** (%Minority, %Women, %Foreign, Avg Age at Matriculation, Percentage with Degree in: Humanities / Social Sciences / Business and Commerce / Science and Engineering / Other Fields, %Having Graduate Degree, Range of Middle 80% GMAT, Range of Middle 80% TOEFL, Range of Middle 80% Undergraduate GPA, %Having 1+ Years Full-Time Work Experience, %Entering Directly from Undergraduate School) · **April 15*** (Common Date for Applicant Reply) · **Financial Assistance** (Scholarships/Fellowships, Teaching/Research Assistantships, Loans) · **GAPSFAS** (Required for Financial Aid) · **Placement Service** (Separate Placement Service for Management Students) · **Placement Data Available** (Starting Salaries, Career Placement, Campus Interviews, Geographic Placement) · **AACSB** (Master's Program Accredited by) · **Page Number**

Def	Mos	Appl	Enr	%Min	%Wom	%For	Age	Hum	SocSci	Bus/Com	Sci/Eng	Other	%Grad	GMAT	TOEFL	GPA	%Work	%Direct	Apr15	Schol	T/R Asst	Loans	GAPSFAS	Sep Plc	Start Sal	Career	Campus	Geog	AACSB	Page
●	12	511	158	2	32	18	26	49		8	31	12	8	450-760	550-620	2.6-4.0	70	15		●	●	●		●	●	●	●	●	●	485
●	18	494	411	3	35	15	28		24	52	24		12	450-710	550-600	2.6-4.0	90	10											●	485
●	18	51	27	0	43	3	29	15	6	34	22	23	0	460-670		3.00-3.89	100	0		●	●	●			●	●	●	●		486
	15	43	27	21	22	1	28													●	●	●	●							593
	12	26	21	15	31	12	25			69	12	19		360-510		2.7-3.7	46	54	●		●	●								162
	21	50	30	23	40					7	10			390-570		3.0-3.5	67	33	●		●	●								162
				90	50	30	25		10	80	10		5	250-350		2.5-3.1	50	30							●	●				228
	12		65	4	43	2	29	2	7	68	10	13	9	450-520		2.8-3.4	82	18		●	●	●					●		●	278
	24	72	38	8	40		30			40	45	15		385-470			95	5												279
●	12	210	70	5	40	20	25	20	10	40	20	10	10	440-530	570-625	2.75-3.40	40	60	●		●	●				●	●	●	●	280
	12	150	50	8	30	10	25	15	5	50	25	5	5	440-580	550-600	2.75-3.65	30	35	●	●	●	●				●	●	●	●	487
	12	120	70	10	35	20	24	5	5	55	30	5	5	430-570	580-610		50	55			●	●				●	●	●		527
●	12	200	150	20	20	5	37	5	15	40	30	10	15	450-550	560-620	2.9-3.7	90	10	●	●	●	●		●						528
	18	35	26	19	12	12	33			19			4				96		●	●		●								591
●	9	58	51	4	50	0	33	13	16	43	12	16	2	360-476	560-590	2.6-3.5	96	4	●			●								94
	12	200	100	7	40	50	24	2	3	90	2	3	2				40	60		●	●	●		●	●	●	●	●		136
	36	40	20	8	30	10	26	2	3	90	2	3	2				80	20		●	●	●		●	●	●	●	●		136
●	12						33							480-590	550-650	3.2-3.8	92	7	●			●			●	●	●	●		166
●	24						33							480-590	550-650	3.2-3.8	92	7	●			●			●	●	●	●		166
	12	35	30	3	17	6	28	10	3	80	7	0	7				90	10				●				●				189
	16	195	174	6	37	2	35	11	8	40	36	5	4				99	3				●				●				262
	12	20	10		60	20	25	10	20	70			10			3.3-3.7	20	70	●			●				●	●			303
●	12													400-420					●	●	●	●								309
●	16	300	280	5	40	1	28	10	5	50	30	5	2	440-580	540-560	2.8-3.4	99	5				●				●	●			344
●	12	608	204	9	36	12	25	10	10	50	25	5	15	450-550	500-550	2.5-3.5	80	15	●	●	●	●							●	358
	12																				●	●								382
	12	139	75		24	7								420-590		2.70-3.75			●	●	●	●				●	●	●		390
	12	374	136		23	16		14	14	45	22	5		560-620		2.80-3.50				●	●	●		●	●			●	488
	12	300	220	20	50	15	29	15	30	35	10	10	10	400-480		2.5-3.0	90	15											●	489
●	16	490	190		40			8	10	52	25	5	11	470-610		2.7-3.7	85		●			●				●		●		490
●	18	552	126	13	32	11	25	28	19	25	13	15	3	510-650	580-630	3.0-3.6	60	40	●			●			●	●	●	●	●	570
●	32	210	94	6	38	3	28	24	21	25	15	15	3	510-660	580-630	2.8-3.7	95	5	●			●							●	570
																													●	491
	12	229	122	5	25	5	28	5	10	40	25	20	5				85	15	●		●	●				●	●		●	158
	18	125	50	10	38	5	29	8	9	46	24	13		500-580	577-617	2.8-3.5	99	5				●					●		●	492
●	12	108	25																●	●	●	●					●		●	493
	12																		●	●	●	●			●	●	●	●		494
	14	41	32	2	19	16	26	0	4	58	28	10	0	400-540		3.23-3.70	18	23	●	●	●	●							●	495
	27	56	45	1	43	0	32	9	10	45	18	18	4	470-700		2.78-3.33	69	0	●	●	●	●							●	495

*See page 43 for explanation

Page	School Name and Page Number	General Management Program	Accounting	Arts Administration	Behavioral Sciences	Economics	Finance	Health Services	International Business	Management Information Systems	Management	Marketing	Production/Operations Management	Public Policy or Administration	Quantitative Analysis	Real Estate and Insurance	Transportation	M.B.A./J.D.	M.B.A./Engineering	Other Joint Degrees	Total Doctoral Enrollment	Students Can Take Courses for Credit in Other Schools of University	January	February	March	April	May	June	July	August	September	October	November	December
NEW HAMPSHIRE																																		
160	Dartmouth College (F)	•																	•		0	•									•			
288	New Hampshire College (F)	•	•			•			•	•		•										•			•		•		•		•			•
288	New Hampshire College (P)	•	•			•			•	•		•										•			•		•		•		•			•
330	Plymouth State College (F)	•	•			•				•		•										•	•	•	•	•	•	•	•	•	•	•	•	•
330	Plymouth State College (P)	•	•			•				•		•										•	•	•	•	•	•	•	•	•	•	•	•	•
341	Rivier College (P)	•																			0	•						•		•				
496	University of New Hampshire	•	•		•	•	•			•	•	•		•				•		•		•									•			
NEW JERSEY																																		
185	Fairleigh Dickinson University	•	•		•	•	•		•		•	•	•							•		•								•	•			
281	Monmouth College	•	•			•	•				•	•	•									•	•							•	•			
282	Montclair State College (P)		•			•	•				•	•		•								•	•								•			
340	Rider College (P)	•	•			•	•				•	•										•		•							•			
348	Rutgers, The State U. of N.J. (Newark) (F)	•	•			•	•		•	•	•	•	•		•			•	•	•	77	•						•			•			
348	Rutgers, The State U. of N.J. (Newark) (P)	•	•			•	•		•	•	•	•	•		•			•	•	•	77	•			•						•			
349	Rutgers University — Camden (P)	•																				•	•								•			
376	Seton Hall University (F)	•	•			•	•		•	•	•	•			•			•				•						•			•			
376	Seton Hall University (P)	•	•			•	•		•	•	•	•			•			•				•							•		•			
398	Stevens Institute of Technology (F)	•			•	•				•	•										14	•									•			
398	Stevens Institute of Technology (P)	•			•	•				•	•											•									•			
411	Trenton State College (P)	•								•												•	•								•			
NEW MEXICO																																		
177	Eastern New Mexico University (F)	•	•			•	•				•	•										•												
289	New Mexico Highlands University (P)	•																				•	•		•	•		•			•		•	
290	New Mexico State University (F)	•	•			•	•				•	•										•	•					•		•	•			
497	University of New Mexico	•	•		•	•	•		•	•		•						•		Joint		•								•	•			
582	Western New Mexico University (F)	•																				•							•		•			
NEW YORK																																		
79	Adelphi University (P)		•		•	•	•	•	•	•		•	•									•								•	•	•		
98	Baruch College	•	•			•	•		•	•	•	•	•	•	•			•		•	137			•				•		•			
129	Canisius College (P)	•	•			•					•	•									0					•		•			•			
146	Clarkson University (F)	•	•			•				•	•											•									•			
149	College of Insurance (P)	•														•						•				•					•			
150	College of Saint Rose (P)	•	•						•													•							•		•			
154	Columbia University (F)	•	•	•		•	•		•	•	•	•	•	•				•	•	•	100	•									•			
156	Cornell U. (Johnson Grad. Sch. of Bus.) (F)	•	•		•	•	•		•	•	•	•	•		•			•	•	•	26	•								•				
157	Cornell U. (School of Hotel Admin.) (F)				•		•				•	•									7	•									•			
190	Fordham University at Lincoln Center (F)	•	•	•			•				•	•			•							•						•			•			
190	Fordham University at Lincoln Center (P)	•	•	•			•				•	•			•							•						•			•			
206	Hofstra University (F)	•	•				•			•	•	•	•		•							•								•	•			
206	Hofstra University (P)	•	•				•			•	•	•	•		•							•								•	•			
245	Long Island University (Dobbs Ferry)	•																																
256	Manhattan College (P)		•				•		•	•	•	•									0	•	•							•		•		

Table: Characteristics of 1984-85 Entering Class

Deferred Admit Policy (School Offers This Option to Students)	Length of Study (Min. Months to Obtain Degree)	No. Applied for Admission	No. Enrolled First Time	% Minority	% Women	% Foreign	Avg Age at Matric.	Humanities	Social Sciences	Business and Commerce	Science and Engineering	Other Fields	% Having Graduate Degree	Mid 80% GMAT	Mid 80% TOEFL	Mid 80% Undergrad GPA	% w/ 1+ Yrs Full-Time Work Exp	% Entering Directly from Undergrad	Common Date for Applicant Reply (April 15*)	Scholarships/Fellowships	Teaching/Research Assistantships	Loans	Required for Fin. Aid (GAPSFAS)	Separate Placement Service	Starting Salaries	Career Placement	Campus Interviews	Geographic Placement	AACSB Accredited	Page Number
	18	1,650	171	5	28	12	25	20	47	11	20	2	4	560-730	560-630	2.7-3.7	95	7	•	•		•	•	•	•	•	•	•	•	160
•	9	420	168	2	33	45	25	5	5	45	25	10	5	440-590	525-580	2.5-3.4	70	15		•	•	•	•	•	•	•	•	•		288
•	18	550	300	5	25	0	28	5	5	40	30	10	5	460-630		2.5-3.6	98	0		•		•	•	•	•	•	•	•		288
•	9	35	27		15	41	28	10	10	65	5	10	4	350-500		2.30-3.08	59	41	•	•	•	•				•	•			330
•	18	82	64		33	0	34	18	22	31	18	11	3	390-590		2.30-3.78	89	11	•	•	•	•				•	•			330
•	30	161	158	9	35	6	34	5	7	54	29	5	4	420-518	500-530	2.4-3.1	94	6		•		•				•	•	•		341
•	21	94	23	0	26	13	26	26	30	0	35	9	8				83	17	•	•		•				•	•	•		496
	18		1,075	7	40	1	30														•	•									185
	15	393	264											425-500	525-550	2.8-3.2	75	25		•		•		•	•	•	•	•		281
	21	365	64	5	34	3	29	14	14	31	30	11	9	490-620	550-575	2.67-3.63	92	0	•	•	•	•	•							282
	12	254	179	5	40	5	25	3	9	58	19	11	10				90	10						•	•	•	•			340
•	15	617	201	13	37	3	26	37	9	24	22	8	11	430-640	550-700	2.71-3.51	85	15		•	•	•	•	•	•	•	•	•	•	348
•	40	1,050	492	13	37	3	28	37	9	24	22	8	11	490-650		2.70-3.65	95	5			•		•	•	•	•	•	•	•	348
•	36	90	55	7	21		29							380-550			90		•			•			•	•	•	•		349
•	24	35	20	2	40	3	24	20	20	40	20		0	475-510	500-520	2.80-3.25	10	90	•	•	•				•	•	•	•	•	376
•	40	700	275	7	40	7	28	20	20	40	20		5	490-530	500-540	3.0-3.2	80	20		•					•	•	•	•	•	376
•	18	150	20	8	17	25	24		30	20	50		5			3.0-3.8	50	50	•	•	•	•		•		•	•	•		398
•	36	250	30	7	20	10	28		30	20	50		5			3.0-3.8	80	10	•	•	•	•		•		•	•	•		398
•	12	45	20	10	55	5	30	10	15	50	20	5	3	490-580	520-600	2.6-3.7	95	5	•						•	•	•	•		411
	12																														177
	15																80	20												289
	12	158	68	5	45	5	28	7	13	55	12	13	5	395-580		2.81-3.78	52	48	•	•	•	•			•		•	•	•	290
•	12	430	376	7	41	5	31							520-580			70	30	•	•	•	•		•	•				•	497
	12		20	30	30	25	28		10	80		10	10				70	30	•	•	•					•	•		•	582
•		508	324		36	1	28	9	15	26	17	35	7				95	5	•	•										79
•		2,000	600		47		27			27	73			435-620		2.56-3.56				•	•	•		•	•	•	•	•	•	98
•	32	200	120	5	30	1	26	12	13	50	25			420-600		2.7-3.3	85	10		•	•	•							•	129
•	10	180	45	0	29	5	24		31	38	18	13	0						•	•	•				•	•	•	•		146
•	24	40	32	4	3	0	27	20	20	50	5	4	1	400-500		2.5-3.5	75	10			•									149
•	18	65	30	1	30	1	30	10	10	50	10	20	1	480-580	500-600	2.9-3.5	80	15			•					•				150
•	16	3,100	640	14	35	16	26	20	35	18	26	1	7	550-690	600-630	2.9-3.8	81	19	•	•	•	•	•	•		•	•	•	•	154
•	21	1,500	225	8	29	22	25	9	38	8	35	9	5	680-590	620-580	3.5-3.1	81	19	•	•		•	•	•		•	•	•	•	156
•	18	160	40	1	33	10	27	28	25	33	10	5	2	425-590	550-640	2.5-3.5	98	<1	•	•	•	•		•		•	•	•	•	157
	12	240	80	5	45	3	25	10	43	33	14		5	480-650	590-610	2.8-3.2	90	10		•	•				•	•	•	•	•	190
	24	1,190	402	5	48	3	25	10	43	33	14		5	480-650	590-610	2.8-3.2	90	10		•	•				•	•	•	•	•	190
	12	230	80	2	45	3	23	8	28	45	14	5	1	450-650	550-650	3.0-3.7	50	50	•	•	•			•					•	206
	16	1,245	375	2	45	2	26	8	15	50	20	7	2	450-600		2.8-3.4	70	30	•					•					•	206
																														245
	24	59	34																											256

*See page 43 for explanation

- 61 -

Programs of Study Offered

Concentrations | **Joint Degrees** | **Doctoral Program** | **Other Options** | **Entrance Dates**

Page	School Name and Page Number	General Management Program	Accounting	Arts Administration	Behavioral Sciences	Economics	Finance	Health Services	International Business	Management Information Systems	Management	Marketing	Production/Operations Management	Public Policy or Administration	Quantitative Analysis	Real Estate and Insurance	Transportation	M.B.A./J.D.	M.B.A./Engineering	Other Joint Degrees	Total Doctoral Enrollment	Students Can Take Courses for Credit in Other Schools of University	January	February	March	April	May	June	July	August	September	October	November	December
258	Marist College (P)	●	●		●		●		●	●				●								●	●					●			●			
292	New York Institute of Technology (P)	●	●				●		●	●	●											●	●					●			●			
293	New York University (New York City) (F)		●		●	●	●		●	●	●	●			●					●	121	●	●					●			●			
293	New York University (New York City) (P)		●		●	●	●		●	●	●	●			●					●	80	●	●					●			●			
294	New York University (Purchase) (P)	●				●																●									●			
295	Niagara University (P)	●																				●	●					●			●			
331	Polytechnic Institute of New York (P)		●						●	●			●	●								●	●					●			●			
343	Rochester Institute of Technology (F)		●		●		●				●	●										●			●			●			●			●
343	Rochester Institute of Technology (P)		●		●		●				●	●										●			●			●			●			●
347	Russell Sage College (P)		●				●															●				●		●		●	●			
353	St. Bonaventure University (P)	●	●				●				●	●										●	●					●		●	●			
355	St. John Fisher College	●	●		●		●		●	●	●											●						●			●			
356	St. John's University																																	
393	State University of New York at Albany (F)																																	
394	State University of New York at Buffalo (F)	●	●		●	●	●		●	●	●	●	●					●		●	80	●	●					●			●			
394	State University of New York at Buffalo (P)	●																				●						●			●			
395	State U. of New York Maritime College																●					●	●	●	●	●	●	●	●	●	●	●	●	●
401	Syracuse University (F)	●	●		●	●	●		●	●	●	●	●		●			●	●	●	40	●	●				●		●		●			
401	Syracuse University (P)	●	●		●		●		●	●	●	●	●		●			●				●	●				●		●		●			
415	Union College (F)	●	●					●	●	●									●		1	●				●		●			●			
415	Union College (P)	●	●						●	●									●			●	●								●			
515	University of Rochester (F)		●			●	●				●	●	●							●	55	●	●								●			
515	University of Rochester (P)		●			●	●				●	●	●							●		●	●								●			
	NORTH CAROLINA																																	
85	Appalachian State University (F)		●		●	●			●	●	●	●			●	●						●						●		●				
128	Campbell University (P)	●																				●						●		●				
167	Duke University	●	●															●	●	●		●									●			
169	East Carolina University	●	●			●			●	●			●									●						●		●	●			
179	Elon College	●																						●							●			
272	Meredith College (P)	●																				●						●			●			
300	North Carolina Central University (F)		●			●			●	●	●											●									●			
327	Pfeiffer College (P)	●																				●						●	●		●			
336	Queens College (P)	●																				●						●			●			
501	U. of North Carolina at Chapel Hill (F)	●	●	●	●		●	●	●	●	●				●	●		●			60	●									●			
502	U. of North Carolina at Charlotte (P)	●																				●								●				
503	U. of North Carolina at Greensboro (F)					●					●	●		●								●						●		●				
504	U. of North Carolina at Wilmington (P)	●																				●						●		●				
567	Wake Forest University (F)	●														●						●									●			
576	Western Carolina University (F)	●																				●						●		●				
576	Western Carolina University (P)	●																				●						●		●				
	NORTH DAKOTA																																	
505	University of North Dakota (F)																					●	●					●		●				

School Offers This Option to Students	Minimum Number of Months to Obtain Degree	Number of Students Who Applied for Admission	Number of Students Who Enrolled for the First Time	% Minority	% Women	% Foreign	Avg Age at Matriculation	Humanities	Social Sciences	Business and Commerce	Science and Engineering	Other Fields	% Having Graduate Degree	Range Middle 80% GMAT	Range Middle 80% TOEFL	Range Middle 80% Undergrad GPA	% Having 1+ Yrs Full-Time Work	% Entering Directly from Undergrad	Common Date for Applicant Reply (April 15)	Scholarships/Fellowships	Teaching/Research Assistantships	Loans	Required for Financial Aid (GAPSFAS)	Separate Placement Service	Starting Salaries	Career Placement	Campus Interviews	Geographic Placement	Master's Program Accredited by (AACSB)	Page Number
●	16	84	59	2	39	5	27	18	16	36	27	3	19	420-610		2.4-3.7	90	10	●		●	●				●	●	●	●	258
●	2	323	256	15	32	10	32	10	20	40	25	5	10	400-530		2.6-3.7	85	10		●		●					●	●		292
	15	2,648	448	8	48	25	25	14	38	24	21	3	15	560-670		2.90-3.68	82	13	●	●	●	●	●	●		●	●	●	●	293
	15	2,121	862	7	35	7	26	14	38	24	21	3	15	550-670		2.95-3.75	87	9	●			●		●		●	●	●	●	293
●	36	132	58	2	43	7	27						9	520-680		2.8-3.7	100	0	●					●		●	●	●		294
●	36			5	25	2	32			50							95	5		●	●	●								295
●																	98	2				●					●	●		331
●	18	106	26	5	26	3	29	11	19	50	19	1		470-650	525-580	2.5-3.8	90	10	●	●	●			●		●	●	●	●	343
●		176	92	5	41	2	29	9	9	40	32	10		450-650	525-580	2.5-3.8	90	10	●	●				●		●	●	●		343
							30	15	25	60				475-575			98				●	●					●	●		347
	12	63	50		30	2			16	9	55	20		420-600		2.66-3.72	80	20			●	●								353
	21		70	8	38	1	30	11	14	48	16	11	9	400-560		2.4-3.5	94	4				●								355
																													●	356
																													●	393
	12	725	213	3	29	29	24	7	19	46	17	11		450-610	540-583	2.6-3.6					●	●			●		●	●	●	●	394
	40	200	128	1	41	0	29	5	8	38	23	26		440-640		2.29-3.71	100	0						●		●	●	●	●	394
	60	40	30																										●	395
●	12	740	123	3	33	15	24	15	25	34	23	3		475-635	570-630	2.7-3.6	60	40	●	●	●	●		●		●	●	●	●	401
●		200	120		33		27	10	20	30	35	5	10	450-630		2.5-3.5	97	3						●		●	●	●	●	401
	24	76	13	23	23	23													●	●										415
	24	64	53																●											415
●	18	493	114	13	22	29	25	8	37	22	28	5	10	470-650	550-640	2.5-3.6	58	42		●	●	●		●		●	●	●	●	515
●	30	113	87	10	34	5	27	3	10	20	60	7	20	470-660		2.6-3.4	95	5			●			●		●	●	●		515
	12	350	100		45	5	25		5	80	5	10	1	450-780	500-600	2.9-3.9	45	60	●	●	●					●	●		●	●	85
●	24	95	45	20	18	15	35	3	3	82	12		5	400-550		2.8-3.4	90	10	●							●	●	●	●		128
●	21	1,100	249	8	30	13	24	22	27	30	17	4	1	540-650	577-647	2.8-3.7	58	38	●	●			●	●		●	●	●	●	●	167
	12	145	94	5	37	1	24	5	10	40	25	20	15	420-550		2.5-3.5	75	25	●		●	●							●	169
	15	83	42		35		30	12	9	43	29	7	5	440-580		2.36-3.72	90	10			●	●							●	179
●	24	61	47	14	100		28	15	13	32	9	32	4	590-376		2.28-3.58	96	4		●		●						●		272
	18	25	15							100				480-640		2.53-2.99		100	●	●	●					●	●	●	●	300
●	24	50	40	15	20	10	26	10	20	50	10	10	5	400-500		2.6-3.0	100	5	●								●			327
	16	107	77	12	45	<1	30		10	25	60	5		460-560	480-520	2.8-3.7	99	1		●		●								336
●	24	1,100	168	5	33	8	26	7	31	25	28	9	1	530-615	587-615	2.8-3.8	92	7	●	●		●				●	●	●	●	●	501
	24	250	105	3	30	2	26	15	13	45	22	5	15	500-580		2.8-3.2	85	15			●								●	502
●	21	317	190	6	41	4	29	7	28	33	32	0	4	420-600	550-600	2.34-3.49	85	5	●	●	●	●							●	503
	24	58	34	3	34	1	27	12	8	30	33	17	3	440-600		2.46-4.00	100	0												504
●	21		100	3	30	11	25	17	17	39	20	3	4	500-600	550-650	2.8-3.3	67	33	●	●	●	●	●	●		●	●	●	●	567
●	12	52	15	3	28	10			10	15	65	10	5	430-550			30	70			●	●				●	●	●	●	576
●	30	80	20	3	37	1		10	15	30	35	10	5	430-550			90	10											●	576
	12	29	15	0	40	13	27	0	21	71	8	0	0	420-560		2.65-3.43		36	●	●	●	●				●	●	●	●		505

*See page 43 for explanation

Programs of Study Offered

School Name and Page Number
(F) = Full-time program
(P) = Part-time program

Pg	School Name	Gen. Mgmt Prog.	Accounting	Arts Admin.	Behav. Sci.	Economics	Finance	Health Svcs.	Int'l Business	Mgmt Info Sys.	Management	Marketing	Prod./Oper. Mgmt	Public Policy/Admin	Quant. Analysis	Real Est./Ins.	Transportation	M.B.A./J.D.	M.B.A./Eng.	Other Joint Deg.	Total Doctoral Enroll.	Courses in Other Schools	Jan	Feb	Mar	Apr	May	Jun	Jul	Aug	Sep	Oct	Nov	Dec
OHIO																																		
89	Ashland College (P)	•																				•					•			•	•			
110	Bowling Green State University (F)	•					•		•	•	•	•	•									•						•	•	•				
110	Bowling Green State University (P)	•					•		•	•	•	•										•						•	•	•				
130	Capital University (P)																			•		•			•						•			
133	Case Western Reserve University (F)	•	•		•		•	•		•	•	•	•							•	172	•	•					•		•				
133	Case Western Reserve University (P)	•	•		•		•	•		•	•	•	•							•		•	•					•		•				
148	Cleveland State University (F)		•			•	•		•	•	•	•	•		•							•	•		•			•		•				
148	Cleveland State University (P)		•		•	•	•	•	•	•	•	•	•	•	•							•	•		•			•		•				
231	John Carroll University (P)	•								•												•												
234	Kent State University (F)	•	•		•	•		•	•	•	•	•			•		•				98	•						•		•				
234	Kent State University (P)	•	•		•	•		•	•	•	•	•	•	•	•		•				98	•	•					•		•				
274	Miami University (F)		•		•	•			•	•		•			•						0									•				
315	Ohio State University (F)	•	•			•		•	•		•	•			•	•	•	•			108	•						•		•				
315	Ohio State University (P)	•	•			•		•	•		•	•			•	•	•	•			•	•						•		•				
316	Ohio University (F)	•					•		•	•	•											•	•		•			•		•				
421	University of Akron (P)		•				•		•	•		•	•									•	•					•		•				
444	University of Cincinnati (F)		•				•		•	•	•	•	•		•						60	•	•					•		•				
444	University of Cincinnati (P)		•				•		•	•	•	•			•						0	•	•					•		•				
449	University of Dayton (P)	•																		•		•					•	•		•				
530	University of Steubenville (P)	•																				•			•					•				
541	University of Toledo (F)	•	•		•		•	•	•	•	•	•	•		•			•				•	•					•		•				
541	University of Toledo (P)	•	•		•	•	•	•	•	•	•	•	•	•	•		•	•				•	•					•		•				
596	Wright State University		•			•	•			•	•	•										•	•					•	•		•			
597	Xavier U. (Grad. Prog. in Hosp. & Hlth Ad.) (F)	•	•		•	•	•	•		•	•	•	•	•	•	•						•						•		•				
598	Xavier U. (Grad. Sch. of Business) (F)		•		•	•		•	•	•	•	•		•							0	•						•		•				
598	Xavier U. (Grad. Sch. of Business) (P)		•		•	•		•	•	•	•	•		•							0	•						•		•				
602	Youngstown State University (F)	•	•			•					•	•										•	•		•			•		•				
602	Youngstown State University (P)	•	•			•					•	•										•	•		•			•		•				
OKLAHOMA																																		
103	Bethany Nazarene College (F)	•																				•						•		•				
137	Central State University (F)	•	•			•	•			•	•										0							•		•				
317	Oklahoma City University (F)		•	•			•			•	•	•								•	0							•		•				
318	Oklahoma State University (F)	•				•				•	•											•						•	•				
318	Oklahoma State University (P)	•				•				•	•											•						•	•				
320	Oral Roberts University (F)	•	•			•	•		•	•							•					•						•	•		•			
320	Oral Roberts University (P)	•	•			•	•		•	•							•					•						•	•		•			
507	University of Oklahoma (F)	•	•		•	•		•	•	•	•	•	•	•	•		•			•	27	•						•		•				
543	University of Tulsa	•	•		•	•	•		•	•	•		•		•						0	•	•					•		•				
OREGON																																		
321	Oregon State University (F)	•																				•	•		•			•		•			
332	Portland State University (F)	•	•			•				•	•							•			8	•	•			•			•		•		•	
332	Portland State University (P)	•	•			•				•	•							•			8	•	•			•			•		•		•	

Deferred Admit Policy: School Offers This Option to Students	Length of Study: Minimum Number of Months to Obtain Degree	Applicants/Enrollment for 1984-85: Number of Students Who Applied for Admission	Number of Students Who Enrolled for the First Time	Percentage of Minority Students	Percentage of Women Students	Percentage of Foreign Students	Average Age of Students at Matriculation	Humanities	Social Sciences	Business and Commerce	Science and Engineering	Other Fields	Percentage Having Graduate Degree	Range of Middle 80% of Students' GMAT Scores	Range of Middle 80% of Students' TOEFL Scores	Range of Middle 80% of Students' Undergraduate GPA	Percentage of Students Having One or More Years of Full-Time Work Experience	Percentage of Students Entering Directly from Undergraduate School	April 15: Common Date for Applicant Reply	Scholarships/Fellowships	Teaching/Research Assistantships	Loans	GAPSFAS: Required for Financial Aid	Placement Service: Separate Placement Service for Management Students	Starting Salaries	Career Placement	Campus Interviews	Geographic Placement	AACSB: Master's Program Accredited by	Page Number
	24	108	87	11	22	10	27		4	72	17	7	2				89	5	•		•			•		•	•			89
•	12	90	47	2	30	19	23	4	4	77	11	4	0	450-580	543-610	2.6-3.5	17	83	•	•	•	•	•			•	•	•	•	110
•	24	94	51	2	29	4	27	6	0	53	31	4	6	450-610		2.7-3.7	86	14	•							•	•	•	•	110
	30	282	167	1	10	0	35			40		60	1				100	0												130
•	11	470	150	4	32	16	25	17	25	44	12	2	11	500-630	560-640	2.6-3.7	70	30	•	•	•	•				•	•	•	•	133
•	29	510	205	3	34	1	28	25	20	26	27	2	15	480-630		2.5-3.7	95	5				•				•	•	•	•	133
•	9	35	29	5	30	10	26	10	25	35	20	10	10	400-540	530-590	2.4-3.5	75	25			•	•				•	•	•	•	148
•	18	285	240	8	30	7	30	8	27	39	21	5	18	390-550	540-590	2.3-3.5	98	1								•	•	•	•	148
	24	106	84	5	44		29	7	24	51	17	1	12	440-580		2.4-3.5	95	5	•											231
•	20	117	48	0	46	31	25	10	12	44	27	7	0	450-650	560-620	2.8-3.8	45	55	•	•						•	•	•	•	234
	36	90	64	2	44	2	24	15	9	52	19	7		450-650		2.8-3.8	87	13								•	•	•	•	234
•	12	300	60	2	35	20	26	12		63	27	8	<1				50	50		•	•	•				•	•	•	•	274
	21	744	105	10	32	21	25	8	8	51	25	8	5	520-650	575-640	3.0-3.7	60	40	•	•				•		•	•	•	•	315
	21	107	64	0	29	2	28	2	2	64	29	3	5	520-650		3.0-3.7	100	0								•	•	•	•	315
•	10	236	90	3	26	48	25	5	15	60	20	0	5	450-600	520-580	2.6-3.4	20	70	•	•	•			•			•		•	316
•	9	470	315	1	31	10		8	8	57	27		20	480-580	550-600	2.5-3.2	90	10			•								•	421
	15	257	139	8	32	9	28	1	7	47	41	4	1	500-600	580-620	3.1-3.3	30	70	•					•		•	•	•	•	444
	30	257	65	4	32	0	28	1	7	47	41	4	1	500-600		3.1-3.3	80	20	•					•		•	•	•	•	444
•	12	450	345	3	37	2	28	10	10	55	20	5	2	450-550	560-570	2.75-3.50	85	10		•	•	•				•	•	•	•	449
	24	25	20	10	20	4		10	10	75	5	0	5				95	5	•											530
	9	100	50	5	30	10	29		15	50	25	10	5	460-540		2.9-3.3	20	50		•	•	•					•	•		541
	9	500	250	5	30	10	29		15	50	25	10	5	460-540		2.9-3.3	80	25		•	•	•					•	•		541
•	12	470	280	9	31	5								460-580		2.8-3.6				•	•	•							•	596
•	24	119	41	4	46	0	28	14	9	44	34	4	22	380-550		2.52-3.68	63	41						•		•	•	•	•	597
	12							18	12	27	30	13	3	450-570	500-550	2.75-3.30	60	40		•	•					•	•	•		598
	24			7	32	7	25	18	12	27	30	13	10	440-550	500-550	2.75-3.30	90	10				•				•	•	•		598
	12	51	45	3	38	8	27	14	19	37	10	20	1	350-610	520-545	2.45-3.55	90	10	•	•	•	•				•	•	•	•	602
	12	145	130	2	33		28	5	13	41	20	21	2	340-600		2.45-3.60	95	5	•	•				•		•	•	•	•	602
	18	34	28	18	24	44	29	9	9	50	15	17	9	420-300	507-553	2.33-3.72	70	30	•							•	•	•	•	103
	12	308	205																											137
	12							5	5	65	15	10					60	40		•		•				•	•			317
	48		76		25	24	4	4	46	14	8	4		480-590		3.0-3.6					•	•				•	•	•	•	318
	48		50		36	4	2	9	21	16	2	4		480-590		3.0-3.6													•	318
	12	85	35	10	33	12	26	12	0	70	18	0	8	400-570	540-620	2.7-3.6	33	67	•	•	•			•		•	•	•	•	320
	24	75	34	10	38	0	30	4	22	63	4	7	6	400-570		2.7-3.5	100	0	•							•	•	•	•	320
•		117	56	2	32	11	27										73			•	•	•	•	•		•	•	•	•	507
•	12	278	189	11	37		27	10	10	45	30	5	3	450-650		3.0-3.5	85	15		•	•					•	•	•	•	543
	12	161	37	3	22	24	26	9	21	42	22	6	3	460-610	543-610	2.83-3.68	84	27	•		•					•	•	•	•	321
	15	55	30	5	50	15	30	20	35	25	15	5	20	510-610	560-580	3.00-3.45	70	30		•	•	•							•	332
	15	480	150	10	45	10	33	20	30	25	20	5	15	500-630	560-580	2.95-3.50	90	10		•	•	•							•	332

*See page 43 for explanation

	School Name and Page Number (F) = Full-time program (P) = Part-time program	General Management Program	Accounting	Arts Administration	Behavioral Sciences	Economics	Finance	Health Services	International Business	Management Information Systems	Management	Marketing	Production/Operations Management	Public Policy or Administration	Quantitative Analysis	Real Estate and Insurance	Transportation	M.B.A./J.D.	M.B.A./Engineering	Other Joint Degrees	Total Doctoral Enrollment	Students Can Take Courses for Credit in Other Schools of University	January	February	March	April	May	June	July	August	September	October	November	December
		Programs of Study Offered — Concentrations																**Joint Degrees**			**Doctoral Program**	**Other Options**	**Entrance Dates**											
389	Southern Oregon State College	•	•								•	•											•		•			•			•			
508	University of Oregon (F)	•	•				•		•		•	•	•		•			•				•	•					•			•			
512	University of Portland																																	
590	Willamette University (F)	•				•	•				•	•	•		•	•		•				•								•				
	PENNSYLVANIA																																	
104	Bloomsburg University (F)	•																				•						•			•			
104	Bloomsburg University (P)	•																				•						•			•			
114	Bucknell University	•	•				•		•	•	•		•	•								•		•				•			•			
127	California University of Pennsylvania	•																				•						•			•			
132	Carnegie-Mellon University (F)	•	•		•	•	•		•	•	•	•	•	•	•			•		•	56	•									•			
144	Clarion University of Pennsylvania (F)	•	•																			•								•	•			
165	Drexel University	•	•		•	•	•		•	•	•	•	•		•							•	•		•			•			•			
168	Duquesne University (F)	•															•		•		0	•									•			
168	Duquesne University (P)	•															•		•		0	•									•			
173	Eastern College (F)	•				•		•														•									•			
173	Eastern College (P)	•			•		•	•			•											•									•			
192	Gannon University								•	•		•	•	•								•							•		•			
223	Indiana University of Pennsylvania																																	
236	Kutztown University (P)	•																			0													
239	La Roche College (F)				•						•											•					•				•			
239	La Roche College (P)				•						•											•					•				•			
240	La Salle University (P)		•				•	•			•	•			•			•				•						•			•			
241	Lehigh University (F)	•	•	•	•	•	•			•	•	•	•	•							15	•						•			•			
263	Marywood College								•	•	•	•										•									•			
325	Penn. State U. (University Park) (F)	•	•		•	•	•	•	•	•	•	•	•	•	•	•	•		•	•	102	•								•				
326	Penn. State U. (Capitol Campus) (F)	•																				•					•				•			
326	Penn. State U. (Capitol Campus) (P)	•																				•									•			
328	Philadelphia Coll. of Textiles and Science (P)	•	•			•	•	•			•	•										•									•			
342	Robert Morris College (P)	•	•						•		•	•		•								•						•		•			•	
357	Saint Joseph's University (P)		•				•	•			•	•	•									•					•				•			
378	Shippensburg University	•	•				•		•		•	•				•						•							•	•	•			
403	Temple University (F)	•	•			•	•		•		•	•		•	•			•	•	•	78	•						•			•			
403	Temple University (P)	•	•			•	•		•		•	•		•	•			•	•	•	25	•						•			•			
511	University of Pittsburgh (F)	•	•				•		•	•	•	•	•	•				•		•	40	•	•								•			
511	University of Pittsburgh (P)	•	•				•			•	•	•	•								40					•					•			
520	University of Scranton	•	•				•				•											•		•					•	•	•			
564	Villanova University (P)	•																				•					•				•			
584	Wharton School (U. of Pennsylvania) (F)		•	•			•	•	•	•	•	•		•	•	•		•	•	•	400	•									•			
588	Widener University (P)	•	•			•	•	•	•		•	•						•	•			•									•			•
600	York College of Pennsylvania (P)	•																			0	•												
	RHODE ISLAND																																	
113	Bryant College (P)	•	•				•	•			•	•										•	•								•			
333	Providence College (P)	•																				•						•			•			

Characteristics of 1984-85 Entering Class

Deferred Admit Policy: School Offers This Option to Students	Length of Study: Min. No. of Months to Obtain Degree	Applicants: No. Who Applied for Admission	Enrollment: No. Who Enrolled for the First Time	% Minority Students	% Women Students	% Foreign Students	Avg. Age at Matriculation	Humanities	Social Sciences	Business and Commerce	Science and Engineering	Other Fields	% Having Graduate Degree	Range Middle 80% GMAT	Range Middle 80% TOEFL	Range Middle 80% Undergrad GPA	% Having 1+ Yrs Full-Time Work Exp.	% Entering Directly from Undergraduate School	April 15* Common Date for Applicant Reply	Scholarships/Fellowships	Teaching/Research Assistantships	Loans	GAPSFAS Required for Financial Aid	Separate Placement Service for Mgmt Students	Starting Salaries	Career Placement	Campus Interviews	Geographic Placement	AACSB Accredited	Page No.
	9	26	20	4	30	10	32			50		50	10	450-540	500-540	2.6-3.5	60	40	●	●	●	●								389
	24	263	59		20	33	27	20	5	45	25	5		563-633	500-650	2.8-3.8	50	50											●	508
																													●	512
●	21	150	75	8	32	7	27	13	23	21	19	24		480-520			75	25	●	●		●	●	●		●	●	●	●	590
	12	15	12	8	50	16	28	16	16	50	8	8					50	50			●	●					●	●		104
	12	48	31	2	20	20	29	8	21	55	7	9	3				52	44	●			●					●	●		104
																					●	●								114
	16	40	25	8	20	20	26		20	60		20	4	400-500	500-550	2.8-3.8	50	40				●								127
●		800	131	10	25	8	25	7	8	30	55	0		600-640	590-640	3.0-3.5	70	30	●	●	●	●	●	●	●	●	●	●		132
	24	200	70	5	52	15	22	10		75	10	5	2	400-450	500-540	2.75-3.00	90	20				●								144
●	24	1,194	350	6	33	8	26	11	9	58	16	4	6	440-680		2.75-3.75	79	20	●			●		●	●	●	●	●	●	165
●	24	65	49	<1	36	<1	27	10	10	40	25	15	<1	450-620	500-550	2.5-3.5	54	25				●							●	168
●	48	235	104	<1	38	<1	27	10	10	40	25	15	<1	450-620	500-550	2.5-3.5	54	25				●							●	168
●	18	23	19	0	20	10	26	0	30	20	0	50	10	460-570		2.91-3.79	75	25		●	●	●	●							173
●	18	22	19	20	30	10	32	0	10	60	0	30	0	340-600		2.60-3.70	80	20				●	●							173
●	18	150	88	5	30			10	20	40	20	10	5	400-550			80					●					●			192
																														223
	18	45	30				29	20	20	35	10	15		410-610			98	2												236
		4	4	0	50	0	27	75	0	25	0	0	0				50	50	●			●								239
●	25	64	40	0	63	0	30	5	68	18	0	9	9				100	0	●	●		●								239
●	18	600	326	7	40	2	29	18	20	50	10	2	8	450-580			99	1			●		●		●		●			240
●	12	210	48	5	30	10	26	5	5	40	40	10	10	520-600	530-590	3.1-3.6	40	35		●	●	●			●	●	●	●	●	241
	24	100	75	11	22	11	32			100			10				95	30	●	●	●	●			●	●	●	●	●	263
●	21	550	136	11	36	21	25	36	21	38	28		2		560-610	2.6-3.6	66	34	●	●	●	●		●	●	●	●	●	●	325
	18	181	130														90	10		●	●	●	●			●	●			326
	30																90	10		●	●	●	●			●	●			326
																														328
●	24	287	95	4	33	2	27	5	6	42	30	17	8	450-545		2.4-3.4	98	2	●	●	●			●		●	●			342
●	17	596		2	45	10	30							400-600			90				●	●				●	●			357
	12	170	88	2	39	2	29	8	12	63	14	3	2	420-600		2.70-3.56	81	19		●	●	●			●	●	●			378
	12	243	93	18	42	2	23	15	25	40	10	10	2	525-580	550-600		35	65		●	●	●	●		●	●	●		●	403
	12	1,104	478	12	38	2	26	30	6	33	25	6	8	510-590	550-600		80	20							●	●	●		●	403
●	11	840	231	6	43	18	25	9	10	33	31	17	10	500-710	447-653	2.7-3.9	56			●	●			●		●	●			511
●	26		200				29			34	43	23		490-710		2.7-3.9	90					●				●			●	511
	15		100																●		●									520
●	24	489	238		52		26	6	10	43	34	7	5	450-590		2.6-3.6	95	5		●	●	●							●	564
●	16	3,900	700	12	27	20	26	11	14	20	20	35	10	530-690	550-690	3.0-3.8	96	4	●	●	●	●	●	●	●	●	●	●	●	584
	24	425	289		32	1	32	5	4	53	27	4	7				95	5			●	●				●	●			588
●	18	40	32	1	10	1	25	2	5	60	30	3	0	400-540		2.7-3.3	85	2	●	●		●				●	●	●		600
●	36	190	33		3	<1	30																				●	●		113
	14																													333

*See page 43 for explanation

- 67 -

Column legend for the table below:
- GMP = General Management Program
- Concentrations: Acc = Accounting, AA = Arts Administration, BS = Behavioral Sciences, Econ = Economics, Fin = Finance, HS = Health Services, IB = International Business, MIS = Management Information Systems, Mgmt = Management, Mktg = Marketing, POM = Production/Operations Management, PPA = Public Policy or Administration, QA = Quantitative Analysis, REI = Real Estate and Insurance, Trans = Transportation
- Joint Degrees: JD = M.B.A./J.D., Eng = M.B.A./Engineering, OJD = Other Joint Degrees
- TDE = Total Doctoral Enrollment
- SCT = Students Can Take Courses for Credit in Other Schools of University
- Entrance Dates: Jan–Dec

(F) = Full-time program (P) = Part-time program

Page	School Name	GMP	Acc	AA	BS	Econ	Fin	HS	IB	MIS	Mgmt	Mktg	POM	PPA	QA	REI	Trans	JD	Eng	OJD	TDE	SCT	Jan	Feb	Mar	Apr	May	Jun	Jul	Aug	Sep	Oct	Nov	Dec
513	University of Rhode Island (F)		•				•		•	•	•	•	•	•	•				•			•	•					•	•		•			
513	University of Rhode Island (P)		•				•		•	•	•	•							•									•	•		•			
	SOUTH CAROLINA																																	
142	Citadel (P)	•																				•						•		•				
147	Clemson-at-Furman M.B.A. Program (P)	•																			0	•						•		•				
523	University of South Carolina (F)	•	•			•	•	•		•	•		•			•			•		120	•	•					•		•				
523	University of South Carolina (P)	•	•			•	•	•		•	•	•			•	•			•		120	•	•					•		•				
594	Winthrop College (P)	•																				•						•		•				
	SOUTH DAKOTA																																	
524	University of South Dakota (F)	•	•				•									•			•	•		•	•					•			•			
524	University of South Dakota (P)	•																				•	•					•			•			
	TENNESSEE																																	
170	East Tennessee State University (F)	•	•																			•						•		•				
269	Memphis State University		•			•	•			•	•	•			•		•				53	•						•			•			
277	Middle Tennessee State University	•	•			•	•	•		•	•	•			•						0	•						•	•	•	•			
404	Tennessee State University (P)	•	•			•	•				•	•			•							•	•					•			•			
405	Tennessee Technological University (F)	•																				•	•	•				•			•			
534	U. of Tennessee at Chattanooga (P)	•	•			•	•			•	•	•	•									•					•			•	•	•		
535	U. of Tennessee, Knoxville (F)		•			•	•			•	•	•				•	•				75							•			•			
535	U. of Tennessee, Knoxville (P)		•			•	•			•	•	•				•	•				75							•			•			
563	Vanderbilt University (F)	•	•		•		•		•		•	•				•	•	•		9	•						•			•			
	TEXAS																																	
99	Baylor University		•				•		•	•	•	•										•						•		•				
171	East Texas State University (Commerce) (P)	•			•																	•	•					•	•	•				
172	East Texas State U. at Texarkana (F)	•																				•	•					•		•				
238	Lamar University (F)	•																				•	•					•		•				
238	Lamar University (P)	•																				•	•					•		•				
301	North Texas State University	•	•			•			•	•	•	•		•	•						158	•						•		•				
324	Pan American University	•	•							•	•	•										•						•		•				
339	Rice University (F)	•	•		•	•	•	•	•	•	•	•	•					•		3	•							•					
362	St. Mary's University (Texas) (F)	•			•	•	•	•	•	•	•											•						•		•				
362	St. Mary's University (Texas) (P)	•			•	•	•	•	•	•	•											•						•		•				
388	Southern Methodist University (F)	•	•	•	•	•			•	•	•			•			•	•	•			•						•					
388	Southern Methodist University (P)	•	•	•	•	•			•	•	•			•								•						•					
391	Southwest Texas State University (F)	•																				•	•					•	•		•			
396	Stephen F. Austin State University	•					•		•		•	•										•	•					•	•		•			
400	Sul Ross State University (F)	•	•						•		•											•	•					•	•		•			
406	Texas A&M University (F)	•	•		•		•		•	•	•	•	•	•	•		•	•			104	•						•		•				
407	Texas Christian University (F)	•	•			•	•			•	•											•	•					•	•		•			
407	Texas Christian University (P)	•	•				•			•	•											•	•					•	•		•			
408	Texas Southern University (F)	•	•													•	•					•	•					•	•	•				
409	Texas Tech University (F)	•	•			•	•		•	•	•					•	•	•		69		•	•					•	•	•	•			
412	Trinity University (P)	•				•	•			•	•											•	•							•				

School Offers This Option to Students (Deferred Admit Policy)	Minimum Number of Months to Obtain Degree (Length of Study)	Number of Students Who Applied for Admission	Number of Students Who Enrolled for the First Time	% Minority	% Women	% Foreign	Avg Age at Matriculation	Humanities	Social Sciences	Business and Commerce	Science and Engineering	Other Fields	% Having Graduate Degree	Range of Middle 80% GMAT	Range of Middle 80% TOEFL	Range of Middle 80% Undergrad GPA	% Having One or More Years Full-Time Work Experience	% Entering Directly from Undergraduate School	Common Date for Applicant Reply (April 15)	Scholarships/Fellowships	Teaching/Research Assistantships	Loans	Required for Financial Aid (GAPSFAS)	Separate Placement Service for Management Students	Starting Salaries	Career Placement	Campus Interviews	Geographic Placement	Master's Program Accredited by (AACSB)	Page Number
●	12	132	52	10	40	20	26	15	18	32	32	3	10	400-600		2.5-3.7	65	35	●	●	●	●			●	●	●	●	●	513
●	24	224	44	10	40	5	30	15	18	32	32	3	10	400-600		2.5-3.5	90	10	●			●			●	●	●	●	●	513
	24	43	29	16	53	1								400-600		2.6-3.5	95	1			●								142
	12	144	59	<1	<1	<1	34	6	5	49	37	3	7	430-610		2.3-3.6	95	5				●			●	●	●	●	●	147
●	24	1,419	498	2	26	27	25	15	30	45	8	2	5	470-620	550-600	2.7-3.8	41	59	●	●	●	●		●					●	523
●	48	241	104	1	32	5	28	11	15	14	44	16		470-630	550-620	2.8-3.8	100		●					●	●	●	●	●	●	523
	24	105	72	7	31	2	32	6	9	61	22	2	1	420-530		2.5-3.7	82	18			●					●	●	●	594
●	12	70	40		12	20	26	5	15	65	10	5	5	420-590		2.75-3.50	50	40	●	●	●				●		●	●	●	524
●	27	100	55		25	2	29	5	10	60	20	5	10	420-590		2.75-3.50	80	10							●		●	●	●	524
	12	165	90	1	35	8	28	6	8	48	25	13	3	370-610	520-570	2.5-3.6	74	26	●	●	●				●		●	●	●	170
	12	325	216																										●	269
	12	120	107	7	41	5	28	10	11	63	12	4	3	380-586		2.41-3.67	75	17			●	●			●	●	●	●	●	277
	12	150	75	33	30	10	30	15	20	40	15	10	10	375-550	510-550	2.5-3.5	80	25		●	●					●	●		404
	12	115	45	4	42	9	26	0	13	53	27	7	2	403-562	561-632	2.53-3.57	53	31	●	●	●	●	●	●	●	●	●	●	●	405
	12	225																												534
●	18	420	60	12	30	12	27	12	13	44	21	10	10	540-580	530-590	3.2-3.6	74	26	●	●	●	●			●	●	●	●	●	535
●	48	50	25	5	33	0	33	10	10	20	50	10	25	540-580		3.0-3.5	100	0	●	●	●	●			●	●	●	●	●	535
	18	596	164	2	29	4	24	13	29	31	25	2	2	510-680		2.63-3.77	39	61	●	●	●	●	●	●	●	●	●	●	●	563
	12	300	195		27	10	24	11	11	59	8	10		490-630		2.8-3.0				●	●	●			●	●	●	●	●	99
	18	250		30	34	18	30	1	5	71	13	10		390-540		2.5-3.65	80	15		●	●	●			●	●	●		●	171
	12	90	75	11	51	5	34	5	5	50	30	10	5				99	5	●	●	●				●	●	●	●		172
	12	30	15	20	50	10	30	10	10	30	40	10	10	470-570	520-570	2.7-3.3	90	15	●	●	●				●	●	●	●		238
	24	75	40	20	50	10	33	10	10	30	40	10	10	470-570	520-570	2.7-3.3	90	15	●	●	●				●	●	●	●		238
	12	635	254	20	40	10	25	5	10	73	5	7	10				60	40	●	●	●				●	●	●	●		301
	24	40	19	30	30	30	34	20		60	10	10	20	460-560	560-630	2.8-3.4	70	20	●	●			●		●	●	●	●		324
●	21	390	57	3	37	19	25	10	39	14	33	4	11	560-690	600-640	2.60-3.67	65	35	●	●		●		●	●		●	●		339
●	12			20	30	8	28													●	●	●			●	●	●	●	●	362
●	24			20	30	0	30													●	●	●			●	●	●	●	●	362
	12	600	147	5	38	7	25	14	8	37	33	8	4	510-670		2.75-3.75	68	28	●	●	●				●	●	●	●	●	388
	36	400	125	5	35	3	27	15	10	30	39	6	10	510-670		2.75-3.75	100	0			●	●			●	●	●	●		388
	12	185	63	23	45	7	32	10	15	50	20	5	10	410-550	555-570	2.8-3.5	60	35		●	●	●			●	●	●			391
	12	100	55	15	30	15	33	10	25	50	25		5	410-580	500-610	2.9-3.5	60	40	●	●	●								●	396
●	12	200	55	45	12	35	24	1	3	85	10	1	2	420-500	510-520	3.0-3.5	20	70		●	●	●				●	●			400
	15	420	132		30		25	9	9	30	42	10									●	●	●			●	●	●	●	●	406
●	12	210	75	5	38	15	25	15	15	40	20	10	5	440-540	590-630	2.6-3.4	50	30			●	●			●	●	●	●	●	407
	36	195	55	5	40	1	27	15	15	40	20	10	5	440-540		2.6-3.4	90	10											●	407
●	12	257	82	95	35	60	28	3	7	77	10	3	5			3.25-2.75	95	30	●		●	●							●	408
	12	287	260	15	10	20	26	5		70	10		15				80	60		●	●	●		●					●	409
●	15	70	30	5	50	10	27	20	20	20	20	20	10	470-570	580-600	3.0-3.5	50	50	●						●	●				412

*See page 43 for explanation

Page	School Name and Page Number (F) = Full-time program (P) = Part-time program	General Management Program	Accounting	Arts Administration	Behavioral Sciences	Economics	Finance	Health Services	International Business	Management Information Systems	Management	Marketing	Production/Operations Management	Public Policy or Administration	Quantitative Analysis	Real Estate and Insurance	Transportation	M.B.A./J.D.	M.B.A./Engineering	Other Joint Degrees	Total Doctoral Enrollment	Students Can Take Courses for Credit in Other Schools of University	Jan	Feb	Mar	Apr	May	Jun	Jul	Aug	Sep	Oct	Nov	Dec
448	University of Dallas																																	
461	U. of Houston - Clear Lake (F)	●	●				●															●	●					●			●			
461	U. of Houston - Clear Lake (P)	●	●				●															●	●					●			●			
462	U. of Houston - University Park																																	
516	University of St. Thomas (F)	●					●		●		●	●										●	●					●			●			
516	University of St. Thomas (P)	●				●			●		●	●										●	●					●			●			
536	University of Texas at Arlington	●	●			●	●		●	●	●	●			●	●					60	●						●			●			
537	University of Texas at Austin (F)	●	●		●		●	●	●	●	●	●	●		●	●				●	250	●								●				
538	University of Texas at Dallas (P)		●		●	●	●		●	●	●	●									73	●					●				●			
539	University of Texas at San Antonio	●	●						●													●					●		●		●			●
540	University of Texas at Tyler (P)	●																			0	●								●	●			
574	West Texas State University	●	●		●	●	●			●	●	●		●								●									●	●		
	UTAH																																	
112	Brigham Young University (F)		●		●		●					●						●	●	●											●			
544	University of Utah (F)	●	●		●	●	●				●							●	●	●											●			
544	University of Utah (P)	●			●		●											●	●	●	0	●									●			
561	Utah State University (F)	●	●						●													●	●		●			●			●			
561	Utah State University (P)	●																				●	●		●			●			●			
	VERMONT																																	
545	University of Vermont (F)	●																													●			
	VIRGINIA																																	
134	CBN University (F)																			●		●	●			●					●			
152	College of William and Mary (F)	●	●			●	●				●	●	●							●		●	●								●			
230	James Madison University	●																			0	●	●					●	●		●			
253	Lynchburg College in Virginia	●																				●						●			●			
261	Marymount College of Virginia		●		●	●			●	●	●			●														●			●			
299	Norfolk State University	●			●					●												●						●			●	●		
319	Old Dominion University (P)	●				●	●	●		●	●	●	●		●	●						●						●			●			
377	Shenandoah College and Conservatory	●																				●						●			●			
514	University of Richmond (P)	●																●			0	●						●			●			
546	University of Virginia (F)	●																●		●	15										●			
565	Virginia Commonwealth University (F)		●		●	●		●		●					●	●					24	●					●	●	●		●			
565	Virginia Commonwealth University (P)		●		●	●		●		●					●	●					24	●					●	●	●		●			
566	Virginia Polytechnic Inst. and State U. (F)	●	●		●	●	●			●	●	●	●		●						93	●									●			
566	Virginia Polytechnic Inst. and State U. (P)	●	●		●		●			●	●	●			●						0	●									●			
	WASHINGTON																																	
178	Eastern Washington University (F)	●	●			●	●	●	●	●	●	●	●		●					●		●	●			●				●				
201	Gonzaga University	●																●	●								●	●	●		●			
322	Pacific Lutheran University	●						●														●			●						●			
359	Saint Martin's College (F)	●																		●		●	●			●				●	●			
359	Saint Martin's College (P)	●																		●		●	●			●				●	●			
374	Seattle Pacific University (P)	●																				●									●			
375	Seattle University (P)				●	●	●		●	●	●	●			●							●			●			●			●			

Characteristics of 1984-85 Entering Class

School Offers This Option to Students	Min. Months to Degree	Applied	Enrolled First Time	% Minority	% Women	% Foreign	Avg Age	Humanities	Social Sciences	Business & Commerce	Science & Engineering	Other Fields	% Grad Degree	GMAT Range (mid 80%)	TOEFL Range (mid 80%)	GPA Range (mid 80%)	% Full-Time Work Exp	% Direct from UG	Common Date for Applicant Reply	Scholarships/Fellowships	Teaching/Research Assistantships	Loans	Required for Financial Aid	Separate Placement Service	Starting Salaries	Career Placement	Campus Interviews	Geographic Placement	AACSB Accredited	Page
																														448
	12	100	70	5	30	5	30	5	5	35	40	15	2	500-600	550-600	2.8-3.3	50	50	●	●		●			●	●	●	●	●	461
	24	390	281	4	35	5	32	6	6	37	43	8	2	500-600	550-600	2.8-3.3	50	50	●	●		●			●	●	●	●	●	461
																													●	462
●	15	12	11	0	45	64	28	0	0	82	18	0	0	390-460	513-610	2.42-3.1	50	50	●	●	●	●			●	●	●	●	●	516
●	19	123	69	7	22	4	28	0	0	46	27	27	4	380-600	573-617	2.47-3.50	80	20	●	●	●	●			●	●	●	●	●	516
●	12	1,336	433	5	42	21	32	8	14	43	32	3	8	460-610	550-600	2.8-3.7	95	5	●	●	●	●			●	●	●	●	●	536
	12	2,080	430	10	30	12	25	22	10	45	23		5						●	●	●			●					●	537
	20	442	209	5	60	11	31												●	●	●	●	●		●	●	●	●	●	538
	18	541		15	39		30										95	5				●			●	●	●	●	●	539
	24	50	25	10	40	5	35	5	5	60	30		2	450-550		2.9-3.5	90	10												540
	18	100	40	10	40	15	30	20	20	10	40	10	2				90	15						●		●	●			574
	24	541	300	1	10	7	27	5	16	41	15	18	3	520-650		3.2-3.7	60		●	●	●	●		●	●	●	●	●	●	112
	9	213	64	1	27	3	26	16	16	37	15	13	3	490-640	600-650	2.90-3.85	66	40	●	●	●	●			●	●	●	●	●	544
	18	151	42	2	20	0	28	10	0	54	24	12	10	480-610		3.20-3.81	83	17	●				●		●	●	●	●	●	544
●	9	165	50	10	15	12	26	25	7	46	15	7	1	470-580	510-530	3.1-3.6	35	80	●	●	●				●	●	●	●	●	561
●	24	110	25	10	15		31	5	3	62	19	11		470-580		3.1-3.6	98	0	●										●	561
	24	53	18	5	39	11	28	11	11	22	50	5	0	490-630		2.64-3.50			●		●						●			545
●	21	45	23				30						5				80	10	●		●				●	●	●			134
●	17	325	84	5	38	3	26	23	23	25	4	25	3	500-680	580-640	2.7-3.6	64	36	●	●	●	●	●		●	●	●	●	●	152
	24	142	71	5	32	6	27			33	33	33					80	20	●	●	●				●	●	●	●	●	230
	24	117	95	14	26	8	31							580-350			96	4		●	●									253
	12						32										95			●	●									261
	14	49	10	85	30	30	24	0	10	85	5	0	0	260-370	500-620	2.5-3.5	50	50	●	●	●	●								299
	12	326	210	5	20	5	28	10	10	50	20	10	5	450-540	550-610	2.8-3.4	75	25	●	●	●	●		●	●	●	●	●	●	319
●	24	18	10	23	30	19	40													●	●	●							●	377
	12	207	103	2	25	1	26	11	11	33	29	16	1	480-620		2.6-3.6	95	2	●	●	●				●	●		●		514
	21	1,214	241	9	26	8	26	12	38	20	28	2	18	540-690	603-637	2.5-3.6	98	2	●	●	●			●	●	●	●	●	●	546
	12	68	40	5	37	3														●	●	●							●	565
	24	378	221	5	37	3														●	●	●							●	565
●	15	285	104	4	33	13	26	1	8	49	35	7	9	490-640	613-653	2.76-3.75	62	38	●	●	●				●	●	●	●	●	566
●	24	134	72	3	40	6	29	13	15	50	17	5	11	470-630		2.47-3.77	88	2	●	●									●	566
	12	131	94	9	28	9		12	11	40	18	19	1							●	●	●			●	●		●	●	178
●	12	92	33	3	31	6	28		3	77	20		3	410-560		2.61-3.70	76	24	●		●	●			●	●	●	●		201
●	15	133	98	8	31	12	30	1	8	46	26	19	10	450-620	577-587	2.66-3.68	88	8	●		●	●							●	322
●	12	8	2	10	30	20	33	10	10	60	10	10	5	480-540		2.9-3.4	100	5		●		●								359
●	12	35	12	10	30	20	33	10	10	60	10	10	5	480-550		2.9-3.4	100	5		●		●								359
	24	32	37	2	30	1	33	10	30	30	20	10	1	430-620		2.9-3.75	95	1	●			●	●							374
		400	195				32																●						●	375

*See page 43 for explanation

Concentrations • Joint Degrees • Doctoral Program • Other Options • Entrance Dates

School Name and Page Number
(F) = Full-time program
(P) = Part-time program

Page	School Name	General Management Program	Accounting	Arts Administration	Behavioral Sciences	Economics	Finance	Health Services	International Business	Management Information Systems	Management	Marketing	Production/Operations Management	Public Policy or Administration	Quantitative Analysis	Real Estate and Insurance	Transportation	M.B.A./J.D.	M.B.A./Engineering	Other Joint Degrees	Total Doctoral Enrollment	Students Can Take Courses for Credit in Other Schools of University	Jan	Feb	Mar	Apr	May	Jun	Jul	Aug	Sep	Oct	Nov	Dec
548	University of Washington (F)	•	•		•	•	•		•	•	•	•	•	•	•			•		•	100	•									•			
569	Washington State University (F)	•	•		•		•				•	•	•		•						30	•						•		•				
583	Western Washington University (F)	•																				•						•			•			
583	Western Washington University (P)	•																				•						•			•			
WEST VIRGINIA																																		
260	Marshall University (F)	•																				•	•						•	•	•			
575	West Virginia University (F)	•	•			•												•				•								•				
585	Wheeling College (F)	•																		•		•					•		•	•	•			
585	Wheeling College (P)	•																		•		•					•		•	•	•			
WISCONSIN																																		
259	Marquette University (P)	•	•		•	•	•			•	•	•	•					•				•	•					•						
552	University of Wisconsin — Eau Claire	•																				•						•			•			
553	University of Wisconsin — La Crosse (F)	•																				•						•			•			
554	University of Wisconsin — Madison (F)		•	•	•	•		•	•	•	•	•	•	•		•	•	•			117	•	•					•			•			
555	University of Wisconsin — Milwaukee (F)	•	•		•		•	•		•		•	•								35	•	•				•				•			
556	University of Wisconsin — Oshkosh (P)	•	•																			•						•			•			
557	University of Wisconsin — Parkside (P)	•	•			•	•			•	•	•		•								•						•			•			
558	University of Wisconsin — Whitewater (F)		•			•	•	•			•	•	•									•						•			•			
558	University of Wisconsin — Whitewater (P)		•			•					•	•	•									•						•			•			
WYOMING																																		
560	University of Wyoming (F)	•	•			•												•				•	•						•		•			
AUSTRALIA																																		
161	Deakin University (P)	•									•													•										
291	New South Wales Inst. of Tech. (P)		•				•		•		•	•		•																				
420	University of Adelaide (P)	•			•	•					•	•	•											•										
480	University of Melbourne	•	•		•	•	•			•	•	•	•	•							15			•										
499	University of New South Wales (F)	•	•		•	•	•		•	•	•	•	•	•							28	•			•									
533	University of Sydney (P)		•			•	•																	•	•									
549	University of Western Australia	•	•		•						•										10	•	•		•									
BELGIUM																																		
109	Boston University Brussels (F)	•								•	•											•							•		•			
109	Boston University Brussels (P)	•								•	•											•							•		•			
183	European University									•	•									•		•	•			•							•	
CANADA																																		
131	Carleton University (F)						•		•	•												•									•			
155	Concordia University (F)	•																•				•	•			•					•			
155	Concordia University (P)	•																•				•	•			•					•			
159	Dalhousie University (F)	•	•		•		•		•		•	•			•	•	•					•									•			
159	Dalhousie University (P)	•	•		•		•		•		•	•			•	•	•					•									•			
265	McGill University (F)	•	•		•	•	•		•	•	•	•			•	•				•	18	•									•			
265	McGill University (P)	•	•		•	•	•		•	•	•	•			•	•				•		•	•				•				•			
266	McMaster University (F)	•	•		•	•	•		•	•	•		•								10	•									•			
266	McMaster University (P)	•	•		•	•	•		•		•	•	•								3	•									•			

Table: Characteristics of 1984-85 Entering Class

School Offers This Option to Students	Min. Months to Obtain Degree	# Applied for Admission	# Enrolled First Time	% Minority	% Women	% Foreign	Avg Age	Humanities	Social Sciences	Business and Commerce	Science and Engineering	Other Fields	% Having Graduate Degree	GMAT Range (Mid 80%)	TOEFL Range (Mid 80%)	Undergrad GPA Range (Mid 80%)	% With 1+ Yrs Full-Time Work Exp.	% Entering Directly from Undergrad	Common Date for Applicant Reply (April 15)	Scholarships/Fellowships	Teaching/Research Assistantships	Loans	Required for Financial Aid	GAPSFAS	Separate Placement Service	Starting Salaries	Career Placement	Campus Interviews	Geographic Placement	Master's Program Accredited (AACSB)	Page Number
	18	900	250	11	33	11	28	10	29	25	27	9	10	530-640	580-620	2.90-3.58	90	10	●	●	●	●					●	●	●	●	●	548
	12	525	85	10	30	20	28	10	20	40	15	15	5	500-580	580-620	3.0-3.6	35	65	●	●		●								●	569
	12																				●	●									583
	24	60	39	15	35	15	33	10	13	46	20	11	15	430-630		2.6-3.55	95	5			●	●									583
	12	158	76	49	38	11	33	5		53	28	15		450-575				80		●	●	●	●			●	●	●	●		260
●	14	356	132	2	37	9	26	4	6	54	29	7	6	490-650	593-657	2.7-3.8	51	49	●	●	●	●					●	●		●	575
	20		2		0																	●					●	●			585
	24		32		28																	●					●	●			585
●	24	373	148		35	6	26	6	10	44	34	6	8	510-600	590-630	3.10-3.55	92	5	●	●	●	●					●	●	●	●	259
●	12	73	38	0	53	10	30													●	●						●	●			552
	15	75	28		43	12		5	10	50	20	15	5	430-600	550-580	2.75-3.50	70	25	●	●	●					●	●	●	●	●	553
	12	1,073	259	9	36	14	25			47		53		532-604	591-628	3.18-3.63	63	37	●	●	●			●		●	●	●	●	●	554
●	18	800	356	1	34	18		6	16	54	23	1	9	470-630	520-640	2.74-3.68				●	●	●						●		●	555
●	12	230	180	1	33	4	30	5	15	50	20	10	5	440-580	540-600	2.7-3.5	90	5	●	●	●	●								●	556
	15						32							450-570		2.6-3.6	90	10	●	●	●	●									557
	12	100	80	5	4	10		12	10	40	20	8		450-650	560-620	2.5-3.5	20	80		●	●	●								●	558
	30	160	100		30			5	10	25	50	10	4	450-600		2.6-3.4	100	0												●	558
●	9																				●					●	●	●	●	●	560
	24	425	64		8	2	36	5	5	20	50	20	8	520-660			100	0	●												161
	36	150	58		8		18	5	5	42	45	3	8				100														291
	21	120	35		20	12	29		20	28	42	10	20				100														420
	20	313	71		34			21	8	28	42	1	23				100			●								●	●		480
●	21	330	87		21	23	29	20		18	45	17	14	460-680			89	11	●	●	●			●		●	●	●			499
●	36	220	33		20	10	31	5	20	10	40	5	20	595-680			100	0	●												533
	21	125	60	12	11	13	30	5	5	25	55	10	100				90	10													549
●	11	75	34		35	70	26							450-650			70	30		●	●	●		●		●	●	●			109
●	22	106	83		25	85	33						5	450-650			98	2		●	●	●		●		●	●	●			109
	12				25	65	28	5	10	30	50	5	20	450-480	520-580	2.6-3.8	40	45						●				●			183
	12	62	10		60	40	26			90		10	30	570-590	550-570		60	40		●	●	●									131
●	18	386	69		36	3	25		50	35	10	5	15				40	60	●	●	●	●		●			●	●			155
●	60	257	72		22	3	25		50	35	10	5	15				75	25	●												155
	16	450	95		30			15	20	25	30	10	5	480-640	590-650	3.1-3.8	40	40	●	●						●	●	●	●		159
	96	62	10		35			15	20	25	30	10	5	480-640	590-650	3.1-3.8	40	40								●	●	●	●		159
●	24	750	120		28	26	25		33	25	37	2	3				40	60		●	●			●			●				265
●	36																							●							265
	16	512	123		30	1	25	9	30	30	26	4		520-640						●	●	●	●								266
	40	169	70		26		28		16	24	58	2		520-630																	266

Programs of Study Offered

School Name and Page Number	General Management Program	Accounting	Arts Administration	Behavioral Sciences	Economics	Finance	Health Services	International Business	Management Information Systems	Management	Marketing	Production/Operations Management	Public Policy or Administration	Quantitative Analysis	Real Estate and Insurance	Transportation	M.B.A./J.D.	M.B.A./Engineering	Other Joint Degrees	Total Doctoral Enrollment	Students Can Take Courses for Credit in Other Schools of University	January	February	March	April	May	June	July	August	September	October	November	December
268 Memorial University of Newfoundland (F)	●																				●									●			
268 Memorial University of Newfoundland (P)	●																				●	●				●				●			
337 Queen's University at Kingston																																	
361 Saint Mary's University (Nova Scotia) (F)	●	●			●	●		●		●	●			●							●	●				●				●			
361 Saint Mary's University (Nova Scotia) (P)	●	●			●	●		●		●	●			●							●	●				●				●			
380 Simon Fraser University (F)																	●													●			
380 Simon Fraser University (P)																	●													●			
418 Université de Sherbrooke (F)	●																													●			
426 University of Alberta (F)	●																	●	●		●									●			
426 University of Alberta (P)	●																					●				●				●			
433 University of British Columbia (F)	●	●		●		●		●	●	●	●		●	●		●					●									●			
434 University of Calgary (F)	●	●		●	●			●		●	●	●								0	●									●			
476 University of Manitoba (F)	●	●		●	●					●	●			●	●															●			
476 University of Manitoba (P)	●	●		●	●					●	●			●	●															●			
510 University of Ottawa																																	
519 University of Saskatchewan (F)	●																				●	●								●			
542 University of Toronto (F)	●	●		●		●		●		●	●						●			40										●			
542 University of Toronto (P)	●	●		●		●				●	●	●					●				●	●								●			
550 University of Western Ontario																																	
551 University of Windsor		●		●		●		●	●	●				●			●				●								●	●			
589 Wilfrid Laurier University (P)	●																												●	●			
601 York University	●	●	●	●	●	●		●	●	●	●	●	●		●					30	●	●			●					●			
ENGLAND																																	
217 Imperial Coll. of Sci. & Tech. (U. of London) (F)	●	●		●	●	●		●	●	●	●	●	●	●	●																●		
235 Kingston Polytechnic (P)	●																							●									
244 London Business School (F)	●																			36											●		
244 London Business School (P)	●												●									●											
417 United States Int. Univ. — Europe (F)	●			●																	●	●			●		●			●			
431 University of Bath (F)	●																			120											●		
463 University of Hull (F)	●			●					●	●				●						8										●			
475 U. of Manchester Inst. of Sci. & Tech.		●		●	●	●		●		●	●									40											●		
521 University of Sheffield (F)	●																			10											●		
547 University of Warwick (F)	●	●		●	●	●			●		●		●							60											●		
FRANCE																																	
225 INSEAD	●							●														●								●			
HONG KONG																																	
140 Chinese University of Hong Kong (F)	●					●		●	●	●																				●			
140 Chinese University of Hong Kong (P)	●					●			●	●																				●			
460 University of Hong Kong	●																													●			
INDONESIA																																	
226 Institut Pengembangan Manajemen (F)	●																					●								●			
IRELAND																																	
419 University College Galway (P)	●																													●			

Characteristics of 1984-85 Entering Class

Deferred Admit Policy	Min. Months to Degree	Applied	Enrolled	% Minority	% Women	% Foreign	Avg Age	Human.	Soc. Sci.	Bus./Comm.	Sci./Eng.	Other	% Grad Degree	GMAT Range	TOEFL Range	GPA Range	% Work Exp.	% Direct	April 15	Schol./Fellow.	TA/RA	Loans	Req. for Aid	GAPSFAS	Sep. Placement	Starting Salaries	Career Placement	Campus Interviews	Geographic Placement	AACSB	Page
●	9	35	10	12	20		24		20		50		10	450-640			50	50	●	●											268
	30	60	23	40			26	35	35	20	10		10	470-640			92	8	●												268
																															337
●	18	210	38	20	20		25	8	11	36	41	4	7	500-580	586-650	3.0-3.8	80	20		●	●	●									361
●	40		10	30	0		30	25	50		25		13	520-600		2.9-3.5	100	0													361
	24	36	10			75	22			100			100				2	90		●	●										380
	32	96	24	3			34		8	75	15	2	95				100														380
	24	160	30	10	20	10	29	50	10	15	20	5	95				100	0			●	●					●	●	●	●	418
	16	231	41		20	10	27	0	15	7	56	5	17	561-650					●		●									●	426
		62	24	25	0		28	0	12	21	50	17	4	560-660					●											●	426
	16	660	100					26	19	34	21						88			●	●	●			●						433
	18	220	75	32					21	15	51	13	16	520-660		3.00-3.78	100	0		●	●	●			●	●	●	●	●	●	434
	18	185	40	28	5		26	44		23	33		12	500-610		2.82-3.68	55	45	●												476
	40	124	39	25			28	15		26	46	13	15	520-640		2.84-3.83	82	18	●												476
																															510
●	9	202	30	0	20	20	18	13		27	53	7	17	400-600			65	33	●	●								●			519
●	9	764	148	32	10		25	9	7	28	36	20	6	570-650		3.2-3.7	40	60		●	●				●	●	●	●	●		542
●	27	231	84	47			29	9	7	17	57	10	19		580-660	3.2-3.7	100								●	●	●	●			542
																															550
●	12	250	45																												551
	24	113	36	33				18	7	21	39	11	11				100			●								●			589
●	18	1,710	525	30			27	14	9	35	26	17		600-620	600-620		45	50		●	●	●			●		●	●	●		601
●	12	630	86	19	50		24						98				41	48	●			●				●	●	●	●		217
	30	29	22	14			31	4	4	23	31	38	4	480-655			100	0	●								●				235
	21	500	110	20	30		27	9	6	30	51	4	5	560-710			98	2					●		●						244
	30	200	60	28			31	11	13	30	43	3	5	550-680			100						●								244
	16	61	26	15	75		25	5	5	50	30	10	5	400-580	550-650	2.7-3.5	50	30					●	●							417
●	12	1,000	30	10	33	60	26	10	15	30	20	25	10				70	30													431
●	12	300	35	20			25	10	15	40	30	5	5	520-620			70	25													463
●	12	700	75			30	34	15	40	30	15		5	500-590	600-635		60	40				●								475
●	12	250	30	35	70		25	15	20	15	50		20	530-560	580-600		35	55													521
	12	750	68	9	31		27	20	19	16	40	5	16	540-620			72	32				●					●	●	●		547
	10	1,600	300	15	75		27			30	40	30					85	15	●						●		●	●	●		225
	22	306	47	19			23	3	13	8	22	1		540-620			45	55	●	●	●	●	●		●			●			140
	34	338	52	17			27		6	14	30	2		530-610			100	0	●	●	●		●								140
	36	358	358						30	40	30		100						●												460
●	12	128	48	19	0		34	8	15	17	52	8	65				100	0			●		●				●				226
	24	65	26	4	0		30	0	4	31	65	0	15				100	0	●												419

*See page 43 for explanation

- 75 -

Programs of Study Offered

School Name and Page Number
(F) = Full-time program
(P) = Part-time program

Page	School Name	General Management Program	Accounting	Arts Administration	Behavioral Sciences	Economics	Finance	Health Services	International Business	Management Information Systems	Management	Marketing	Production/Operations Management	Public Policy or Administration	Quantitative Analysis	Real Estate and Insurance	Transportation	M.B.A./J.D.	M.B.A./Engineering	Other Joint Degrees	Total Doctoral Enrollment	Students Can Take Courses for Credit in Other Schools of University	January	February	March	April	May	June	July	August	September	October	November	December
ISRAEL																																		
108	Boston U. — Ben Gurion Univ. of the Negev	●																						●		●					●			
402	Tel Aviv University		●		●		●	●	●	●	●	●			●	●					30	●		●					●		●			
NETHERLANDS																																		
182	Erasmus University Rotterdam (F)	●																				●										●		
298	Nijenrode, The Netherlands Sch. of Bus. (F)	●																														●		
NEW ZEALAND																																		
509	University of Otago (F)	●																			10				●									
SCOTLAND																																		
205	Heriott-Watt University (F)	●	●		●	●	●		●	●	●	●			●							●										●		
205	Heriott-Watt University (P)	●	●		●	●	●		●	●	●	●			●							●										●		
454	University of Edinburgh (F)				●		●		●	●	●										10											●		
531	University of Stirling (F)	●	●		●	●	●		●		●	●			●					●	25										●			
532	University of Strathclyde (F)	●																														●		
532	University of Strathclyde (P)	●																														●		
SINGAPORE																																		
287	National University of Singapore (P)	●					●		●		●	●			●														●					
SOUTH AFRICA																																		
440	University of Cape Town (F)	●	●		●	●	●			●	●	●	●		●						4													
559	University of the Witwatersrand																																	
SPAIN																																		
212	IESE (F)	●	●		●	●	●		●		●	●	●		●						15											●		
SWITZERLAND																																		
183	European University								●	●										●		●	●	●			●					●		
216	IMEDE (F)	●	●		●	●	●		●	●	●	●			●						0		●											
227	International Management Institute (IMI) (F)	●	●		●	●	●		●	●	●	●			●															●				
314	Oekreal Foundation (P)	●	●		●	●	●		●	●	●	●			●	●							●	●	●	●	●	●	●	●		●	●	●	●
THAILAND																																		
141	Chulalongkorn University (F)	●					●		●		●											●							●					

Deferred Admit Policy	Length of Study (Min. Months)	No. Applied for Admission	No. Enrolled First Time	% Minority	% Women	% Foreign	Avg. Age at Matriculation	Humanities	Social Sciences	Business and Commerce	Science and Engineering	Other Fields	% Having Graduate Degree	Range GMAT (Middle 80%)	Range TOEFL (Middle 80%)	Range Undergrad GPA (Middle 80%)	% w/ 1+ Yr Full-Time Work Exp.	% Entering Directly from Undergrad	April 15 (Common Reply Date)	Scholarships/Fellowships	Teaching/Research Assistantships	Loans	Required for Financial Aid (GAPSFAS)	Separate Placement Service	Starting Salaries	Career Placement	Campus Interviews	Geographic Placement	AACSB Accredited	Page Number
●	11						29													●										108
	16						30	7	44		48	1		425-650			90			●	●			●				●		402
	20	302	60	21	37	43	27	20	10	25	15	30	74				49	15	●					●		●	●	●		182
●	12	45	17	8	40	8	25			100			0				50	50												298
	15	60	22	10	15	20	35		25				80	550-600			100													509
	12	108	7	14	14	57	30						71				100		●	●										205
	24	52	10		20		36						80				100		●	●										205
●	12	450	45		30	40	27	21	29	16	27	7	10				65	60	●	●		●				●	●	●		454
●	12	575	59		30	68	31	10	10	45	25	10	93				75	25												531
●	12	800	67	40	15	50	29						90				100			●		●								532
●	36	120	76		10		30						80				95													532
		204	78				31		4	23	68	5	21	560-620			100	0	●	●										287
●	12	445	61		5	10	30	6	9	21	39	25	96	579-592			99	15		●		●		●		●	●	●		440
																														559
●	21	209	52		20	80	26	2	19	28	45	16					53	47						●		●	●	●	●	212
	12	75	40	25	65		28	5	10	30	50	5	20	450-480	520-580	2.6-3.8	40	45						●			●			183
●	11	400	68	20	88		30	13	14	42	31	1	100				100	0						●		●	●	●	●	216
	9	400	49	15	95		33	10	14	21	39	16	88	450-600			100				●		●	●						227
●	24	1,200	100			15	35			50	40	10	80	520-600	580-630		100				●			●			●	●		314
	20	142	58	55	9		26	12	26	31	31		7				59	41						●		●	●	●		141

*See page 43 for explanation

The Schools of Business of Adelphi University consist of the School of Business Administration and the School of Banking and Money Management. The former offers curricula that lead to the Master of Business Administration (M.B.A) and the Master of Science (M.S.) in accounting, and the latter offers curricula that lead to the Master of Science in banking and money management.

PROGRAMS OF STUDY

The Master of Business Administration degree program consists of a maximum of 51 credits and a minimum of 39 credits. This flexibility is intended to accommodate students with varied academic backgrounds, including those who have earned an advanced degree and are considering a graduate business degree. Concentrations may be pursued in 12 areas of study: accounting, banking and financial markets, business economics, corporate finance and investments, hospital and health care management, human resource management and personnel administration, international business, logistics, management, marketing, organizational behavior, and public management. The M.B.A. program is being offered on two commuter railroad lines on selected morning and evening trains and at five locations in Nassau, Queens, and Suffolk counties.

A 30-credit Master of Science degree program in accounting is designed to prepare students for careers in public and private accounting. Successful completion of the program reduces New York State's C.P.A. work experience requirement to one year.

The M.B.A./C.P.A. program is designed for students without prior accounting knowledge who desire to obtain C.P.A. certification within the context of a graduate M.B.A. program. Completion of this program also reduces the state's C.P.A. work experience requirement to one year.

The Master of Science degree program in banking and money management consists of a maximum of 48 credits and a minimum of 36 credits. The number of credits required depends upon the academic background of the student. The program is designed to provide a thorough understanding of significant banking and monetary problems, issues, and challenges, including technical aspects of the operation of financial institutions and markets. Courses cover financial aspects of commercial and Federal Reserve banking, savings banks, savings and loan associations, mutual funds, and others.

Courses for all programs offered on campus are scheduled in the late afternoon and evening. Off-campus courses are given during the evening hours.

ADMISSION

Admission to all degree programs is open to those students who have completed an undergraduate degree at an accredited college or university and who demonstrate the maturity and intellectual ability to participate in a rigorous academic program. No specific courses are required for admission. Students applying for the M.S. program in accounting should have undergraduate accounting preparation.

Among the factors considered are the individual's accomplishments in his or her previous academic work, the quality of the institutions attended, the academic discipline studied, and the score on the Graduate Management Admission Test (GMAT).

To apply for admission, students are required to submit an application, official transcripts from institutions previously attended, and Graduate Management Admission Test scores. Foreign students whose native language is not English are required to take the Test of English as a Foreign Language (TOEFL) and file a financial affidavit. Prospective foreign students are encouraged to submit their credentials by the following dates: fall term, April 1; spring term, November 1; summer term, March 1. All other applicants should forward their credentials early enough for an admission decision and to ensure appropriate guidance in course selection. August 15 is the deadline for the fall term; December 15 for the spring term; and May 15 for the summer term.

EXPENSES

The cost of tuition is $209 per credit; the application fee is $20; and the university fee for full-time students is $150. Tuition and fees are subject to change.

FINANCIAL ASSISTANCE

Graduate assistantships are awarded to exceptional students on the basis of their undergraduate grade-point average, GMAT scores, and professional experience. Assistants, who are expected to work 20 hours per week in academically related areas, receive full tuition remission.

PLACEMENT

The Schools of Business, in conjunction with the University Career Service Center, offer a career planning and referral service to all students and alumni interested in obtaining employment. Assistance is given in securing career information, writing resumes, preparing cover letters, interviewing techniques, and planning job campaigns.

CORRESPONDENCE

For additional information or to request an application for admission, please write or call

Office of the Dean
Schools of Business
Adelphi University
Box 701
Garden City, New York 11530
Telephone: 516-663-1177

The Master of Business Administration degree (M.B.A.) program at Alabama A&M University was started in 1970 with the support of Pennsylvania State University, College of Business Administration. Since then it has grown to an average enrollment exceeding 160, which includes a large number of international students. The program is now part of the Department of Graduate Studies and Research, which also administers a closely coordinated Master of Science (M.S.) program in economics. The School of Business has over 30 full-time faculty members. Undergraduate majors are available in finance, accounting, business administration, economics, marketing, management, business education, and office administration. Alabama A&M is a land-grant, state institution, accredited by the Southern Association of Colleges and Schools. It is located on a scenic site in northeast Huntsville, a city of 150,000.

PROGRAM OF STUDY

The M.B.A. program has recently been thoroughly revised to meet the needs of tomorrow's executive. It is structured to train an aware and competent individual to handle both the technical and human aspects of management in modern public or private organizations. Its basic organizational structure is grounded on finance, marketing, accounting, economic theory, and quantitative skills.

The program is suitable for students whose specialization is in business as well as those whose primary occupation is in another field but who wish to gain sufficient business knowledge to qualify for management positions.

Forty-two credit hours are required, of which 12 hours are from the student's selected area of concentration (marketing, management, finance, accounting, logistics, computer science, or database management). The maintenance of a minimum B average is necessary for graduation. Although the recommended course load is 9 hours per semester for a full-time student, a maximum of 12 hours is permitted. Therefore, it is possible to complete the program in three regular semesters and one summer session.

ADMISSION

Applicants must hold a bachelor's degree, or equivalent, from an accredited college or university. It is not necessary, however, that the degree be in a business area. In addition to completed application forms, the following must be forwarded directly to the Dean, School of Graduate Studies: an official transcript from each university or college attended, scores on the Graduate Management Admission Test (GMAT), three letters of recommendation, and in the case of foreign students, scores from the Test of English as a Foreign Language (TOEFL).

Admission to graduate study is based on an evaluation of all the credentials submitted to determine if the student has sufficient background and potential for successful graduate study. The School of Graduate Studies requires a minimum grade-point average of 2.5 out of a maximum of 4.0 for admission. A high score on the GMAT may partially compensate for not achieving this minimum. Meeting the minimum requirements, however, does not guarantee admission.

EXPENSES

Out-of-state tuition for 1985 (subject to change) was $70 per semester hour.

FINANCIAL ASSISTANCE

A limited number of graduate assistantships and other types of financial aid are available. To apply for these, students must write to the Dean, School of Graduate Studies.

PLACEMENT

An active on-campus placement service provides informative exhibits and on-campus recruitment programs by national, regional, and local companies, as well as by government agencies.

CORRESPONDENCE

An informative booklet entitled *MBA Program*, which includes application forms, is available upon request. Please write or call

Chairperson
Department of Graduate Studies
  and Research
School of Business
Alabama A&M University
Normal, Alabama 35762
Telephone: 205-859-7221
or
Dean
School of Graduate Studies
Alabama A&M University
Normal, Alabama 35762
Telephone: 205-859-7302

AMERICAN GRADUATE SCHOOL OF INTERNATIONAL MANAGEMENT

GLENDALE, ARIZONA

Commonly known as Thunderbird, American Graduate School of International Management is located in Glendale, Arizona, adjacent to Phoenix. It was founded in 1946 under the name of American Institute for Foreign Trade, and later was known as Thunderbird Graduate School of International Management. A private, nonprofit institution, the school is accredited by the North Central Association. Enrollment is limited to approximately 1,000 students per semester. Foreign students from over 50 countries account for a fourth of the enrollment. The faculty-student ratio is approximately 1 to 13.

Thunderbird continues its role as the premier graduate management school in the United States devoted exclusively to educating men and women for international careers. Its principal objectives are to provide an academically sound and pragmatically relevant master's degree program in international management to a new generation of global executives, and to foster international understanding by developing constructive, sympathetic, and mutually satisfactory business and cultural relations among peoples of the world.

PROGRAMS OF STUDY
The Master of International Management degree (M.I.M.) is awarded after the successful completion of 42 semester hours of work, usually requiring three terms in residence. Within this framework, there are minimum requirements for three academic departments.

• *Department of Modern Languages*— All students are expected to achieve conversational proficiency, as well as functional reading ability, in one of the languages taught at the school, in addition to their native language. English as a second language, Spanish, French, German, Brazilian Portuguese, Mandarin Chinese, Japanese, and Arabic are currently offered. This requirement can be waived in part or in whole upon examination by the department to determine the level of the student's proficiency at the time of admission. The audio-lingual system of instruction is employed.

• *Department of International Studies*— Students are required to take at least nine semester hours of work, concentrating in a major world area (Latin America, Western Europe, Far East, Africa, Middle East) or on global issues. Students who have developed backgrounds in one or more areas may petition for a partial waiver of the requirements.

• *Department of World Business*—Students are required to take the basic principles of the following subjects: accounting, marketing, management, statistics, micro-macroeconomics, and computer systems. They are also required to take 15 hours of 400-500-level instruction. Waivers of 300-level courses may be granted based on prior education.

Students meeting the minimum requirements of each department may then choose from a wide range of advanced courses in international and area studies, international banking, finance, commerce, and so forth. A total of 42 hours of study is required of all students, regardless of the number of elective hours resulting from waivers. Three hours of graduate study may be accepted in transfer.

In addition, through Thunderbird Management Center, American Graduate School offers nondegree executive development programs for persons involved in or entering international management. These programs include intensive training in languages, cross-cultural communications, socioeconomic issues, and international business transactions. Courses are scheduled to suit the convenience of the students or their sponsoring company or agency.

ADMISSION
Students may enter in January, June, or August and are encouraged to apply at least nine months before the term for which consideration is requested. Matriculants must hold at least the equivalent of an American bachelor's degree from a recognized institution of higher education. The basic criteria for admission consideration are undergraduate grades (preferably 3.0 or higher in last two years), scores on the Graduate Management Admission Test (GMAT), letters of recommendation, and extracurricular and job experience. Foreign students must earn scores above 450 on the Test of English as a Foreign Language (TOEFL) and provide proof of financial ability to cover a year of study.

EXPENSES
An application fee of $40 is required of all applicants. Tuition and student fees for a regular semester are $3,235 and $2,380 for a summer session. Books and supplies cost about $200 per term. Students who room on campus (approximately half) must also board on campus. Total cost for room and board averages $1,500 per single person per regular semester and $1,100 for a summer session.

FINANCIAL ASSISTANCE
Approximately 20 assistantships and scholarships are available each term for applicants having an undergraduate grade-point average higher than 3.5 and a GMAT score of at least 500. With rare exception, these grants cover one-half tuition, for two successive terms only, without continuance. Smaller grants are available for a limited number of continuing students who have high scholastic averages and who are active in campus activities.

PLACEMENT
Thunderbird operates a Career Services Center for students and alumni that is visited yearly by recruiters representing nearly 300 national and international organizations. The center enjoys an enviable record of nearly 40 years of successful placement in the international field.

CORRESPONDENCE
For further information, write or phone
  Dean of Admissions
  American Graduate School
    of International Management
  Glendale, Arizona 85306
  Telephone: 602-978-7210

American International College (AIC) is located in Springfield, Massachusetts, a city of 165,000 persons. The college, founded in 1885, is a medium-sized, accredited, coeducational institution, which has more than 15,000 alumni. Enrollment currently approximates 2,700, including 1,500 full-time undergraduates and another 1,200 graduate and part-time students. AIC offers programs leading to undergraduate and graduate degrees in the Schools of Arts and Sciences, Psychology and Education, and the Division of Nursing, as well as in the School of Business Administration. Since 1954, the School of Business Administration has offered a graduate program designed to meet the needs of students seeking academic preparation for middle- and upper-level management positions in profit and nonprofit organizations.

PROGRAM OF STUDY

At American International College students can earn a Master of Business Administration (M.B.A.) degree on either a full- or part-time basis. Both day and evening programs are offered and have the same academic standards and requirements. M.B.A. courses are taught year round, during day and evening, allowing students to accelerate their progress. The M.B.A. program consists of 18 courses or 54 semester hours; 15 courses are required and 3 are elected. A full-time student taking a minimum of 4 courses (12 credit hours) per semester can complete degree requirements in 4 semesters or 18 months. Students with undergraduate degrees in business may receive advanced-standing credit for up to 6 courses (18 hours) and complete their studies in 3 semesters or one calendar year. Students with undergraduate degrees in majors other than business usually take all 18 courses, although waivers may be granted on an individual basis.

The M.B.A. program will help students learn how to assess and take charge of situations, ask the right questions, and understand the economic, functional, behavioral, legal, ethical, and quantitative aspects of business. Since quantitative analysis is restricted to a minimum in the required core courses, students can select a greater concentration in the more behavioral aspects of business. For those who excel in mathematics, however, there are ample elective courses from which to choose. Undergraduate work in liberal arts, science, education, engineering, or business, for example, can be strengthened through M.B.A. core courses and individually selected electives.

ADMISSION

Qualified men and women who hold bachelor's degrees from accredited colleges and universities will be considered for admission. Admission criteria consist of an evaluation of undergraduate transcripts, personal references, Graduate Management Admission Test (GMAT) scores, and work experience. If the applicant's native language is not English, proof of scores on the Test of English as a Foreign Language (TOEFL) must also be supplied.

EXPENSES

Tuition is $165 per credit hour, or $495 per course. Tuition rates are the same for all students, regardless of residency. Books and supplies are estimated at $30 per course. Room and board on campus is $2,651 per year.

FINANCIAL ASSISTANCE

Graduate students with demonstrated financial need may apply for aid from the National Direct Student Loan Program or the College Work-Study Program. Veterans Administration benefits are also available. Many corporations will help employees continue their education; prospective students should check with their company personnel office for details.

PLACEMENT

Personnel recruiters from private industry and government conduct job interviews in the college's Placement and Career Development Office throughout the academic year.

CORRESPONDENCE

For further information, write or call
    Charles F. Maher
    Academic Dean
    Dean, School of Business
        Administration
    American International College
    1000 State Street
    Springfield, Massachusetts 01109
    Telephone: 413-737-7000

The Kogod College of Business Administration offers programs of graduate study leading to the Master of Business Administration (M.B.A.) and Master of Science (M.S.) degrees in various specialized fields of interest. All programs are available on a full- or part-time basis. M.B.A. and M.S. degree candidates totaled 673 in the fall 1985 session. Executives from business and government organizations form a substantial portion of the student body. The college is a member of the Middle Atlantic Association of Colleges of Business Administration and the American Assembly of Collegiate Schools of Business.

The campus is located in a quiet suburban environment just off Washington's "Embassy Row" and 15 minutes from the White House. Washington offers unique opportunities for research because of its many highly specialized libraries and data sources. Most large businesses, unions, trade associations, and professional associations maintain large offices in the city. These offices are particularly interested in supplying information as part of their business-government liaison activities.

PROGRAMS OF STUDY

The M.B.A. program is in the tradition of the nation's top schools, has exacting entrance standards, and presents a demanding challenge for students. The program is designed for individuals motivated toward high-level positions in large organizations, both public and private. Graduates are expected to have acquired a broad understanding of the wide responsibilities of a high-level manager. All graduates are required to demonstrate knowledge of a core area that includes accounting, finance, marketing, statistics, quantitative methods, international business, management information systems, economics, organizational behavior, and management. The program consists of 13 core courses, 4 courses in the area of concentration, and 3 elective courses. Areas of concentration include accounting, finance, international business, marketing, operations analysis, personnel and industrial relations, procurement management, and real estate and urban development. Special areas of concentration may also be arranged.

Up to 12 semester hours of graduate-level courses may be transferred into the M.B.A. program if earned with a grade of B or higher at an accredited institution within five years prior to admission. Up to 24 semester hours may be waived for students who have completed the appropriate undergraduate or graduate courses with a grade of B or higher at an accredited institution within five years prior to admission. The combination of transferred and waived courses cannot exceed a total of 24 semester hours. A minimum of 36 semester hours must be taken in residence for the 60-credit M.B.A. program and a minimum of 30 hours in residence for the M.S. degrees.

The Kogod College of Business Administration recognizes the growing demand for programs that provide advanced study in specialized areas of professional business management. The Master of Science program was created for students who have this specific need. The M.S. is awarded in accounting, finance, health/fitness management, international business, marketing, operations analysis, personnel and industrial relations, procurement management, public relations management, real estate and urban development, and taxation. Depending on a student's educational and professional background, the M.S. programs require between 30 and 51 semester hours.

ADMISSION

Students may enter in the spring, summer, or fall. Basic criteria for admission to all degree programs are a bachelor's degree from a regionally accredited institution with a grade-point average of 3.0 in the final two years, an acceptable Graduate Management Admission Test (GMAT) score, and letters of recommendation. Extracurricular activities and job experience are also considered. Applicants for the M.S. in accounting and taxation may substitute successful completion of the entire C.P.A. examination for the GMAT.

EXPENSES

Tuition for the 1985-86 academic year was $288 per credit hour.

FINANCIAL ASSISTANCE

Graduate scholarships, assistantships, and loan funds are available. Applications must be received no later than February 1 for scholarships and assistantships and April 1 for loans.

PLACEMENT

The university's Career Center provides assistance to students in all phases of career planning, that is, resume preparation, interview techniques, and job strategy. Assistance in obtaining interviews with employers is provided both on and off campus. The Kogod College of Business Administration provides assistance for part-time jobs, internships, and summer employment.

CORRESPONDENCE

For further information, write or call
Kogod College of Business
Administration
Office of Student Affairs
The American University
4400 Massachusetts Avenue, N.W.
Washington, D.C. 20016
Telephone: 202-885-1908

Established in 1874, Andrews University is a private institution of higher learning offering undergraduate, graduate, master's, and doctoral programs in liberal arts, religion, and technology. All of these programs are accredited by the North Central Association of Colleges and Schools. The university's student body numbers close to 3,000; approximately one-sixth of these students are involved in graduate-level study. The Andrews educational community is dedicated to the concept of excellence and high standards in all of its academic programs. The School of Business operates with a strong commitment to standards established by the American Assembly of Collegiate Schools of Business.

PROGRAM OF STUDY
The Master of Business Administration (M.B.A.) program is a professional program of study designed to provide advanced study for students interested in a career in professional management. It aims to provide an opportunity for men and women to develop knowledge, understanding, abilities, and attitudes that will constitute a foundation for their growth into competent and responsible business administrators. The program leading to the M.B.A. degree is designed both for those students whose undergraduate preparation is in nonbusiness areas as well as for students with undergraduate training in business. Special programs of study are offered for those desiring to follow a career in health-care administration, those with an undergraduate accounting major preparing to take the C.P.A. examination, and those with a background in computers desiring graduate course work in computer and information science.

ADMISSION
To qualify for admission, the student must meet all three of the following criteria:

• A baccalaureate degree or equivalent from an accredited university or senior college.
• A formula score of at least 1,000, computed by multiplying the undergraduate overall grade-point average by 200 and adding the product to the Graduate Management Admission Test (GMAT) score.
• Scores on the Test of English as a Foreign Language (TOEFL) are required for foreign students.

Applications for admission are accepted on a continuous basis, and qualified students may enroll for any quarter, beginning in mid-September, early January, or mid-March. For those students who enter the program without prior course work in business, the M.B.A. degree is a two-year (seven-quarter) program. The graduate curriculum is divided into two parts: preparatory courses and advanced courses. The preparatory courses approximate three quarters of work, while the advanced courses require a minimum of four quarters. Those students who have satisfactory undergraduate backgrounds in business administration may enter directly into the advanced section of the program.

EXPENSES
Tuition for 1985-86 was $130 per credit hour. Housing is available on campus; a dormitory room with 21 meals per week costs $1,004 per quarter. Married housing is also available.

FINANCIAL ASSISTANCE
Information regarding loans and grants can be obtained by contacting the Financial Aid Office at Andrews University. Several grants-in-aid are available to students in the M.B.A. program who have demonstrated high scholastic achievement and potential. The university offers a work program for students desiring part-time employment.

CORRESPONDENCE
For further information or to make formal application, write or call
Graduate Admissions Director
Andrews University
Berrien Springs, Michigan 49104
Telephone: 616-471-3497 or
Toll free: Nationwide, 800-253-2874
          In Michigan, 800-632-2248

Appalachian State University, one of the 16 constituent members of the University of North Carolina system, has the largest College of Business in the state. Appalachian enrolls some 10,000 students. The John A. Walker College of Business has 2,500 undergraduates and about 250 graduate students. Appalachian State University is located in Boone, North Carolina, among the most popular year-round living-vacation areas in the East. Boone, at 3,333 feet, is situated in the heart of the Blue Ridge of the Appalachian Mountains. The Blue Ridge Parkway is six miles from campus. The average summer temperature is 69 degrees; daytime highs average in the low-to-middle 70s. Mount Mitchell, the highest point in the eastern United States, is some 40 miles away.

PROGRAMS OF STUDY
The Master of Business Administration (M.B.A.) program at Appalachian State University provides a curriculum offering professional training for executive positions in business, industry, and government. The degree also prepares students for doctoral study leading to careers in teaching and research. The program is designed both for those who hold baccalaureate degrees in business administration and for those who have earned degrees in other disciplines.

For students with satisfactory undergraduate preparation in business, the M.B.A. program consists of a minimum of 36 semester hours of advanced course work. A minimum of 12 months is needed to complete the program. For students without adequate undergraduate preparation in business, undergraduate prerequisite courses must be completed. The student should be able to complete these prerequisites in 12 months or less.

The 36-semester-hour program includes 24 semester hours of required courses in quantitative methods, economics, finance, accounting, marketing, and management, with the remaining 12 semester hours to be chosen as approved electives.

Three additional programs of study are also offered: the Master of Science in accounting, the Master of Arts in economics and business with a major in business teacher education and options in either secondary teaching or two-year college teaching, and a Master of Arts in economics. All programs require a minimum of 36 semester hours, except the M.S. in accounting which requires a minimum of 30 semester hours. All programs require a background in the proposed field of study. No foreign language is required for any program.

ADMISSION
Admission is open to all qualified men and women who hold a bachelor's degree from an accredited undergraduate institution. Previous academic work, employment experience, and motivation for professional graduate work are given very careful consideration. An interview is not required, but applicants with particular questions are encouraged to visit the school. All applications are processed on a continuous basis in order of receipt; therefore, they should be submitted as early as possible.

Applications are accepted at any time; however, entry in the fall semester minimizes scheduling problems. Applications for fall entry and all supporting documents should be received by August 1. The application must include an official score report on the Graduate Management Admission Test (GMAT). For regular admission, the applicant should have 450 or better on the GMAT and a 2.8 (4.0 scale) or better undergraduate grade-point average. An admissions formula is used so that a higher score on one index may compensate for a lower score on another. Students whose first language is not English must report a score of 500 or above on the Test of English as a Foreign Language (TOEFL).

EXPENSES
Tuition for full-time graduate students is $481.25 per semester for in-state students and $1,278.25 per semester for out-of-state students. Part-time fees (one to seven hours) are $154.00 for in-state students and $1,113.00 for out-of-state students. Fees are subject to change.

Appalachian State University maintains 14 residence halls providing housing for some 4,000 students. In addition, the university provides apartment living in the Mountaineer Apartment complex, consisting of 90 apartment units available to both married and single upperclass students on a first-come, first-served basis. A descriptive brochure and application can be obtained from the Appalachian State University Office of Housing Operations.

FINANCIAL ASSISTANCE
A number of assistantships are available upon recommendation of one of the four departments in the College of Business. These appointments require service to the departments in research assistance or other assigned duties. Stipends for assistantships range from $1,500 to $2,500 for nine months, with a typical stipend of $2,500. Scholarship funds are also available. Application for financial aid should be made by letter. Preference is given to those applicants with high academic standing. Assistantship appointments are generally made by July 15, and scholarships are usually awarded in April.

CORRESPONDENCE
For further information, please write or call

Assistant Dean and Director of
  Graduate Studies
John A. Walker College of Business
Appalachian State University
Boone, North Carolina 28608
Telephone: 704-262-2057

Founded in 1922, Aquinas College is a career-oriented liberal arts college with a Catholic/Christian tradition. About 3,000 full- and part-time students, ranging in age from 18 to 80, take classes on its wooded 70-acre campus in Grand Rapids, and at extension sites in Lansing and Muskegon. Aquinas is accredited by the North Central Association of Colleges and Schools.

Aquinas College's graduate program in management is a logical outgrowth of the college's successful undergraduate evening program in business administration. Begun in 1969, continuing education degree programs—designed for working adults—have provided hundreds of business men and women with the opportunity to complete a degree entirely in the evening. In the process, the college has developed a special understanding of the needs and expectations of adult students.

Market research in the mid-1970s indicated that area organizations (profit and nonprofit) saw a need for graduate studies that would help employees improve their ability to communicate within an organization, understand individual personalities and group dynamics, be able to structure goals and objectives, motivate and evaluate individual and group performance, and develop the skills to effect alternative modes of planning, problem solving and decision making.

In short, a humanistic (or, in business administration terms, a behavioral) management program was called for—a program that would combine technical efficiency with an understanding of human behavior within an organizational framework. That is the kind of graduate program Aquinas has designed.

PROGRAM OF STUDY

The Aquinas Graduate Management Program, which leads to the Master of Management degree, focuses on human behavior within organizations—the people side of management. The Aquinas program is based on the concept that it is people working together who accomplish organizational objectives. This approach is based on the understanding that the study of management should be generic, that is, common to all organizations, and as a consequence the Aquinas program serves a broad range of professional managers and administrators in business and industry, government, social and health agencies, and educational institutions.

Instructors in the Graduate Management Program are selected for their academic preparation and their extensive practical experience gained from their activities in business, industry, and a variety of nonprofit organizations. The faculty have management experience and academic background in such fields as business administration, public administration, educational administration, economics, sociology, psychology, communication, and ethics. The faculty include both Aquinas full-time instructors and adjunct instructors who are practicing professionals in the Grand Rapids and Lansing areas. The multidisciplinary nature of the faculty guarantees an exciting and stimulating view of management processes—a view grounded in theory and tempered with practical experiences.

Because most of the students are employed full time, the Graduate Management Program is designed as an evening program with all courses needed for the degree offered in the evening or occasionally on Saturday mornings. It is possible to complete the degree in as few as seven semesters if the student enrolls for two courses in each of the three terms (fall, winter, summer) scheduled each year. However, students may set their own pace and have seven years from the date of their first registration to complete degree requirements.

ADMISSION

Admission requirements follow.

(1) A bachelor's degree from a college or university accredited by a regional association such as North Central. No prerequisites are required, regardless of undergraduate major.

(2) Evidence of interest, aptitude, and ability to undertake graduate studies in management, which includes:

• previous work experience,
• a minimum acceptable score at the 40th percentile on the Graduate Management Admission Test (GMAT),
• a minimum undergraduate grade-point average of 2.75 on a 4.00 marking system,
• a personal interview with program admissions officers, and
• three references (to be contacted only if necessary).

Final acceptance is determined by the Admissions Committee of the Graduate Management Program.

EXPENSES

Tuition per semester hour was $149 for the 1985-86 school year. Certain classes have materials fees which are listed in the current semester schedule.

FINANCIAL ASSISTANCE

All degree candidates who wish to apply for financial assistance must be enrolled on at least a half-time basis (six credits per semester). Students may be eligible to receive assistance from the Michigan Tuition Grant Program, the National Direct Student Loan Program, and the Guaranteed Student Loan Program. A Graduate Management Program Scholarship Fund also awards scholarships to selected students who have successfully completed at least one course in the program. Students wishing to apply for financial aid may contact the Financial Aid Office directly.

PLACEMENT

Placement services are provided to all Aquinas students through the Career Development Office.

CORRESPONDENCE

For further information, or to request a catalog and application for admission, please write or call

Director
Graduate Management Program
Aquinas College
Grand Rapids, Michigan 49506
Telephone: 616-459-8281 (in Metro Grand Rapids); 800-541-5410 (in Michigan); 800-545-0055 (outside Michigan)

Arizona State University has a resident enrollment of more than 40,558. The College of Business Administration enrolls approximately 9,800 undergraduate and 2,000 graduate students per semester. Instruction in the College of Business Administration is provided by 230 full-time faculty members. Both the undergraduate and graduate programs in business administration are accredited by the American Assembly of Collegiate Schools of Business.

PROGRAMS OF STUDY

The Master of Business Administration (M.B.A.) degree curriculum has both breadth and flexibility. Students with undergraduate backgrounds in general education or engineering, as well as business administration, are admitted.

The M.B.A. curriculum is divided into two sections. The basic program, consisting of 24 hours of course work, is required of all students who have not previously earned academic credit in specified business study areas (accounting, economics, finance, business law, management, marketing, and statistics). A minimum of 36 semester hours is required for the advanced program. A student who has met the requirements of the basic program may be admitted directly into the advanced program and may complete requirements for the degree in one calendar year.

The Master of Quantitative Systems program provides study that concerns the application of decision and information systems in business, government, and social agencies. The areas of specialization include business statistics, business planning, and computer information systems. Prerequisite courses in business administration and in the area of specialization are required. The professional program of study consists of 30 semester hours.

The Master of Accountancy program is available for those students who wish to obtain professional competency in accounting theory and practice or taxation. It is designed to prepare men and women for positions in public accounting, managerial accounting, governmental agencies, and college and university teaching. A student must meet all regular requirements for admission plus a minimum number of hours of prerequisite courses in accounting. The professional program of study requires 30 hours of accounting and related courses. An option is available that allows students to specialize in taxation courses.

The Master of Health Services Administration program prepares individuals seeking careers as administrators of hospitals and health care organizations. The program consists of a minimum of 45 semester hours: 15 hours of business administration, 24 hours of health services administration, and 6 hours of electives.

The Master of Science in economics degree is offered for those who desire careers as professional economists or who wish to take additional preparation for doctoral study. A minimum of 30 semester hours in economics is required, including a research requirement of 3 to 6 hours. A maximum of six semester hours of graduate courses in related fields may be applied toward the degree.

The M.B.A. for Executives program is designed to prepare working executives for higher levels of responsibility and accomplishment. It offers mature managers a broad perspective of the profession—its fundamentals, tools, concepts, and styles—in a learning setting with a select group of students who have demonstrated significant managerial achievement. One unique feature of the program is that courses are offered on Friday afternoons and Saturday mornings.

A minimum of 30 semester hours of credit beyond the master's degree is required of all doctoral students, exclusive of the dissertation and the prerequisite business courses generally required for admission to graduate study in business.

The Ph.D. in business administration prepares candidates for scholarly careers in leading educational institutions and for positions in business and government organizations where advanced research and analytical capabilities are required. Areas of concentration include accounting, finance, logistics, management, marketing, and decision information systems. The Ph.D. in economics is also available.

ADMISSION

Applicants may be admitted to regular classification if they hold a baccalaureate or graduate degree and have attained an average of B+ or better in the last two years of study. Letters of recommendation are encouraged but not required.

All students applying for business administration programs are required to take the Graduate Management Admission Test (GMAT) before admittance. Applicants for economics degree programs are to submit Graduate Record Examinations (GRE) scores. All applicants for doctoral degree programs must have three letters of recommendation.

EXPENSES

Students classified as residents of Arizona who enroll for more than six semester hours of course work are subject to fees in the amount of $495 per semester. Students classified as nonresidents who register for 12 or more semester hours pay nonresident tuition and fees amounting to $1,922 per semester; students who register for 7 to 11 hours pay a prorated tuition. The rate for students taking six hours or less is $53 per semester hour.

FINANCIAL ASSISTANCE

Approximately 80 graduate assistantships and fellowships are available. These programs provide stipends of from $2,250 to $9,000 per academic year plus the waiver of nonresident tuition; 10 to 20 hours per week of service are required.

PLACEMENT

Career Services has a well-qualified, full-time staff who assist alumni and graduates in obtaining positions. Representatives of well-known firms schedule interviews regularly.

CORRESPONDENCE

For further information, write
Director of Graduate Studies
College of Business Administration
Arizona State University
Tempe, Arizona 85287

The Master of Business Administration (M.B.A.) degree program at Arkansas State University provides a curriculum offering professional training for careers in business management. Emphasis in the course of study is on problem solving and decision making. The M.B.A., a professional degree program consisting of 30 semester hours, is designed to be completed in one calendar year by most students with an undergraduate major in business. For nonbusiness majors, the program can generally be completed in two years. The program is accredited by the American Assembly of Collegiate Schools of Business.

PROGRAM OF STUDY

All applicants must have completed the following foundation courses, or their equivalent, as a minimum: College Algebra, Principles of Macroeconomics, Principles of Microeconomics, Statistics, Business Communications, Operations Management, Principles of Marketing, Legal Environment of Business, Principles of Accounting I and II, Introduction to Computer Information Systems, Principles of Management, and Business Finance. The student must be within six hours of completing the foundation courses before taking graduate courses.

The following graduate courses are required in the M.B.A. program: Acct. 50023, Current Accounting Problems; Econ. 50333, Advanced Business Cycles and Forecasting or Econ. 50313, Economics of Industry; Fin. 50723, Advanced Management of Finance; Mgmt. 51423, Managerial Policies; Mktg. 52023, Marketing Policies; and Mgmt. 51433, Management Science. The M.B.A. core provides the student with the behavioral skills, analytical tools, and environmental considerations that condition and impact decision making.

The remaining 12 hours may be elected from graduate-level courses in business as approved by the student's adviser. A maximum of three semester hours may be elected from selected senior-level courses. A thesis is optional. A comprehensive written examination must be taken in the final enrollment period. An acceptable score on this examination is a requirement for the awarding of the degree.

ADMISSION

Admission requires a bachelor's degree from an accredited university. Admission status is determined by undergraduate grade-point average and score on the Graduate Management Admission Test (GMAT). The M.B.A. adviser will evaluate a student's transcripts, prescribe the needed foundations, and compute the required GMAT score. Admission may be either with full qualifications or on a provisional basis. To establish admission with full qualifications to the M.B.A. program, applicants must submit a score on the Graduate Management Admission Test. Entering M.B.A. students will be admitted with full qualifications if they have a total of at least 950 points based on the formula: 200 times the overall grade-point average plus the GMAT score; or at least 1000 points on the formula: 200 times the grade-point average on the last 60 hours plus the GMAT score. Foreign applicants whose native language is not English must submit a score of 550 or higher on the Test of English as a Foreign Language (TOEFL).

EXPENSES

The registration fee for the fall or spring semester is $395 for Arkansas residents taking a full academic load (12 hours or more). Non-Arkansas residents pay $895. The registration fee for a five-week summer term is $190 for residents and $430 for nonresidents.

Students enrolled in fewer than 12 hours during a regular semester (or fewer than 6 hours during a five-week summer term) are classified as part-time students for fee payment. Part-time state residents pay $33 per credit hour, and part-time nonstate residents pay $75 per credit hour. (Fees are subject to change.)

FINANCIAL ASSISTANCE

A limited number of assistantships are available to well-qualified candidates. These require a 2.5 overall grade-point average plus a 2.75 in the last 60 hours, or a 3.0 in the major field. Assistants must work 15 hours per week with professors in the College of Business Administration. The stipend is $4,250 for nine months. Summer assistantships are also available. Applicants with undergraduate degrees from other institutions are encouraged to apply.

Information concerning other financial aids, including loans, is available from the Financial Aid Office, Arkansas State University, State University, Arkansas 72467.

CORRESPONDENCE

For additional information, please write or call

Director of Graduate Studies
College of Business
Arkansas State University
P.O. Drawer 2220
State University, Arkansas 72467
Telephone: 501-972-3416

ASHLAND COLLEGE

ASHLAND, OHIO

Ashland College, founded in 1878, is independent, coeducational, and affiliated with the Brethren Church. Beautifully landscaped, the college has over 35 buildings most of which are new, contemporary, and functional. Ashland College has, from its beginning, blended professional education (particularly business administration, economics, and teacher education) with the liberal arts. Therefore, it was appropriate that it respond to the rapid changes in the method and environment of business by establishing a Master of Business Administration (M.B.A.) program in 1978. Over 450 students are enrolled.

PROGRAM OF STUDY

The Ashland College M.B.A. program, established as a two-year course of evening and Saturday study, is designed to provide a solid theoretical understanding while developing usable skills within the broad spectrum of management problems. As such, the emphasis in the program is not on the development of functional expertise areas, such as accounting, production, marketing, and other specialized areas of business or economics. Rather, emphasis comes from the perspective of management, the executive's view of the organization—how functions interact and react to external pressures so that the organization can survive and meet its goals and objectives. The program is designed for middle and top management individuals, generally company-sponsored persons from Ohio firms. Further, the program provides opportunities for supervised in-company research on a specific problem and encourages the exchange of ideas, insights, and information among participants. Graduate studies include evening seminars with guest speakers from government, business, and academia. A total of 36 semester hours completed with a 3.0 cumulative grade-point average is required for the awarding of the Master of Business Administration degree. A program of study may be started in January, May, or September.

The program of graduate studies in business administration has been approved by the Ohio Board of Regents and accredited by the North Central Association of Colleges and Schools. The M.B.A. program also holds membership in the American Assembly of Collegiate Schools of Business.

ADMISSION

Selection is determined by the M.B.A. faculty and directors based upon academic achievement, business experience, future potential, score on the Graduate Management Admission Test (GMAT), and an interview with the M.B.A. Director or committee. All areas will be weighed carefully and evaluated in the context of the candidate's desire, personality, enthusiasm, and availability to meet the demanding class schedule.

Candidates can be any age but must demonstrate ability to do intensive graduate-level work. Those candidates with inadequate backgrounds in business administration will be required to correct their deficiencies either by undergraduate "bridging" courses or by successfully completing the new Post-Baccalaureate Pre-M.B.A. program. The Post-Baccalaureate Pre-M.B.A. consists of eight different modules relating to specific subjects in business.

Specific requirements for M.B.A. admission are as follows:
- proof of graduation from an accredited undergraduate college or university,
- a cumulative grade-point average of 2.6 or above (4.0 system) in undergraduate work,
- an overall score of 450 or better on the GMAT,
- two letters of recommendation from former professors or other persons qualified to estimate the applicant's ability to pursue successfully a program of graduate study in business,
- compliance with minimum course requirements as outlined, and
- work experience (submit resume or vita).

All of the above factors will be considered in determining the eligibility of a candidate for admission. The M.B.A. program committee will treat these factors in a flexible manner; for example, a small deficiency in grade-point average may be overcome by a higher GMAT score or by professional attainment.

EXPENSES
For 1985-86

Tuition, per semester credit hour	$142
Audit fee, per semester credit hour	71
Graduation fee (paid last semester prior to graduation)	25
Schedule change fee	5
Transcript fee	2
Late registration fee	25

All tuition, fees, and other charges are set by the college and subject to change.

FINANCIAL ASSISTANCE

Information concerning financial aid may be obtained through agencies such as the Veterans Administration, from banks, or by consulting the Ashland College financial aid director.

Some private companies will help subsidize the advanced continuing education of their employees through tuition-reimbursement programs. For information on such programs students should see the personnel officer at their place of employment. M.B.A. students should also be aware that certain educational expenses are tax-deductible.

PLACEMENT

A centralized placement service, which provides contact with representatives of large numbers of national and regional companies, is available to all students and alumni of the college. The M.B.A. Director, the faculty, and the Placement Office work together in assisting students as requested.

CORRESPONDENCE

For additional information, please write or call
Director
Graduate Studies in Business
  Administration
Ashland College
Ashland, Ohio 44805
Telephone: 419-289-4142,
  extension 5236
In Ohio: 800-882-1548

Assumption College is a small (approximately 2,000 full-time equivalent students) private liberal arts college with professional programs on the graduate level. It is located in Worcester, Massachusetts, the second largest city in the New England States and an important corporate center.

PROGRAM OF STUDY

The Master of Business Administration (M.B.A.) program at Assumption has been designed to provide professional preparation for men and women already employed who wish to study part time. The primary goal of the M.B.A. program is to provide opportunity for qualified persons to develop the knowledge, skills, abilities, and competencies that will constitute a foundation for career growth and development in business, government, or other organizations.

The M.B.A. program at Assumption consists of 36 semester hours (12 courses of work at the graduate level). Program courses are arranged according to the following levels:

Level II Core (24 credits)
MBA300 Managerial Economics
MBA301 Human and Organizational
          Behavior
MBA302 Marketing Strategy
          Development
MBA303 Financial Strategy
          Development
MBA304 Financial and Operations Strategy Development
MBA305 Production and Operations
          Strategy Development
MBA306 The Management of
          Information
MBA307 Business Ethics

Level III Electives (9 credits)
MBA401 Human Resources
          Management
MBA405 Accounting for Governmental
          and Nonprofit Organizations
MBA406 Financial and Tax Aspects of
          Business Combinations
MBA407 Tax Aspects of Management
          Decisions
MBA420 Marketing Research Seminar
MBA425 International Marketing
MBA440 Inventory and Materials
          Management
MBA489 Management Practicum
MBA490 Legal Frameworks of Business
Other electives are in the process of development.

Level IV Integrative Experience (3 credits)
MBA501 Organizational Strategy
          Development

For those students who enter the M.B.A. program at Assumption with no prior background in the area of business administration, additional work at the prerequisite and "common body of knowledge" levels is required.

Prerequisites
CS13 Introduction to Computer Science
EC107 Statistics
MA17 Calculus I

Level I Common Body of Knowledge (waivable)
MBA202 Quantitative Methods
MBA203 Microeconomics
MBA204 Macroeconomics
MBA205 Financial Accounting
MBA206 Managerial Accounting
MBA207 Administration and
          Management
MBA208 The Marketing System
MBA209 The Financial System

ADMISSION

Men and women graduates of accredited colleges or universities who have earned bachelor's degrees in arts and sciences are eligible for admission. The student's cumulative grade-point average should be at least 2.75.

The Assumption M.B.A. program is open to students from any field of undergraduate study. For those persons without an appropriate undergraduate background certain prerequisites and common body of knowledge courses (Level I) are required (see above). Candidates are also asked to submit official Graduate Management Admission Test (GMAT) scores.

EXPENSES

Tuition, per credit hour $143
Computer use 25
Parking   5
Assumption College does not maintain housing for graduate students. The office of the Dean of Student Affairs assists students whose homes are not within commuting distance to find housing in the vicinity.

CORRESPONDENCE

For further information or to request an application for admission, please write or call

Associate Dean of Academic Affairs
Graduate Office
Assumption College
500 Salisbury Street
Worcester, Massachusetts 01609
Telephone: 617-752-5615, extension 387

ATLANTA UNIVERSITY

ATLANTA, GEORGIA

Atlanta University is composed of a group of graduate schools in arts and sciences, business administration, education, library studies, and social work with over 1,000 full-time students. It is located in attractive surroundings less than five minutes from downtown Atlanta, Georgia, a city of 450,000 that is rapidly expanding.

The Graduate School of Business, established in 1946, offers a two-year high-quality program of study designed to prepare qualified candidates for management careers in the public and private sectors both nationally and internationally. Accredited by the American Assembly of Collegiate Schools of Business (AACSB), it has a full-time student enrollment of approximately 200 from 20 states and 6 foreign countries. Approximately 40 percent of the students enter with significant work experience. The school is housed in a three-story, air-conditioned building which is convenient to student parking and contains modern classrooms and a computer facility to facilitate a comprehensive learning environment for students. Dormitory facilities are available for single graduate students. Approved housing is available within the city in privately owned apartments. Bus and rapid rail service to the campus are convenient.

PROGRAM OF STUDY

The M.B.A. curriculum embodies a formal integrated sequence of courses that provides concentrations in accounting, quantitative methods, finance, management, and marketing. Data processing applications are emphasized in each area of concentration. A concentration in management information systems was implemented in fall 1984. The program is open to students with bachelor's degrees in engineering, liberal arts, and sciences as well as business.

Completion of the M.B.A. program requires a minimum of 60 semester hours. A maximum of six credit hours may be transferred from an accredited graduate business program. Full-time students generally complete the program in four semesters.

During the first year, students participate in a comprehensive set of core courses intended to provide a broad foundation in basic managerial disciplines and functions. Emphasis is upon fundamental concepts and theories and the mastering of analytical techniques. The second year is devoted to advanced quantitative courses and electives. A minimum of 15 semester hours of elective courses in no more than two disciplines is required to acquire a concentration.

The background of the school's faculty reflects a healthy and diverse mixture of outstanding academic accomplishments and solid practical experience. The methods of instruction include case analysis, lectures, seminars, computer games, direct interface with firms, and other innovative teaching techniques designed to equip students with strong abilities in decision making. Clarity of both written and oral communications is emphasized. Each student has available a program of counseling and professional seminars to help build a career plan tailored to his or her career objectives.

ADMISSION

Students are admitted to either a fall semester beginning in early September or a spring semester beginning in early January. A summer term is available in June. Applicants must have obtained a bachelor's degree from a recognized institution of higher learning. Admission is based on scholastic achievement; Graduate Management Admission Test (GMAT) scores; school, civic, and professional activities; letters of recommendation; and work experience. All foreign applicants whose native language is not English are required to perform acceptably on the Test of English as a Foreign Language (TOEFL).

Application forms and official transcripts from each undergraduate school attended and other supporting materials should be forwarded to the Office of the Registrar, Atlanta University. Applications are due June 1 for the fall semester, October 1 for the spring semester, and May 1 for the summer semester.

EXPENSES

Per year	All students
Nonrefundable application fee	$ 30
Tuition (30 semester hours at $160 per semester hour)	4,800
Room and board	3,856
Fees (matriculation, health services)	125
Laundry and incidentals	2,530
Books and supplies	625

FINANCIAL ASSISTANCE

Financial assistance is available to students from the university through graduate assistantships and direct student loans. The Business School provides a number of full scholarships through its Executive Management Scholarship Program (EMSP) and Minority Engineers in Management Program (MEMP). Under these programs full tuition benefits are given. Brochures may be obtained by writing to the Coordinator of EMSP, School of Business. University financial assistance information may be obtained directly from the Office of Financial Aid. Deadline for applications is March 1.

PLACEMENT

The university maintains a placement office with a professional staff who interact with over 800 businesses, financial institutions, governmental agencies, and educational institutions for placement of graduates. The business school operates its own program which places students in internship positions during the summer. The placement service of the school is rated as one of the most outstanding in the country.

CORRESPONDENCE

For further information, write or call
Graduate School of Business
Administration
Atlanta University
Atlanta, Georgia 30314
Telephone: 404-681-0251,
extension 391 or 393

Auburn, chartered in 1856, is the state's land-grant institution. The university now serves the objectives of teaching, research, and service through 13 schools and colleges including a graduate school. Approximately 3,100 of the university's 19,000 students are enrolled in the College of Business, which was established in 1967. The college's undergraduate and graduate programs are accredited by the American Assembly of Collegiate Schools of Business. The 110 faculty members emphasize both teaching and research. The campus of 1,900 acres, located in the city of Auburn, is approximately a two-hour drive from the metropolitan areas of Atlanta and Birmingham. Library facilities include access to over 1.1 million bound volumes, and academic computing facilities include an IBM 3033 as well as mini-computer laboratories. Terminal and mini-computer facilities are available in the College of Business.

PROGRAMS OF STUDY

Six graduate programs of study are offered: the Master of Business Administration (M.B.A.), Master of Science in business administration and in economics (M.S.), Master of Accountancy (M.Ac.), Master of Arts in College Teaching (M.A.C.T., economics), and Doctor of Philosophy in applied economics.

The M.B.A. program is intended to prepare talented and strongly motivated students for middle- and upper-level staff positions in private and public enterprises. Courses are taught by the method appropriate to the subject matter in small clases of 10 to 20 students. The program is designed both for students who have an undergraduate degree in business and those who do not. Applicants are encouraged to complete courses in introductory statistics and differential calculus prior to admission. However, deficiencies in these areas, which are not included in the foundation set, may be met by course work after entering the program. Foundation or prerequisite courses in business, if needed, are built into the program itself. The program consists of 32 quarter hours of accelerated foundation courses and 50 hours of advanced work. Segments of the foundation course hours may be waived by strong academic achievement in selected undergraduate business courses. The advanced work includes 40 hours of required courses and 10 hours of business electives selected according to student interests.

The Master of Science in business is a thesis program designed for persons wishing to specialize in such areas as human resources, industrial/operations management, and management information systems. This program requires a minimum of 50 quarter hours of graduate work, including a thesis. Information concerning degrees in economics should be obtained by direct correspondence with the department.

The Master of Accountancy is a professional nonthesis degree program. At least 45 hours of advanced courses, 35 of which are in accounting, are selected with the approval of the student's advisory committee.

ADMISSION

Graduation with a bachelor's degree from an accredited college or university is required for admission. Selection for the M.B.A. and M.S. in business programs depends on Graduate Management Admission Test (GMAT) scores and undergraduate college grades. International students must provide scores on the Test of English as a Foreign Language (TOEFL). All test scores must be submitted before the admission application can be evaluated. Admission and entrance to the program is available at any one of the four quarters of the academic year. Approximate due dates for completing applications for the various quarters are late May for summer, early September for fall, mid-December for winter, and early March for spring.

EXPENSES

Full-time tuition per quarter (fall 1985) was $365 for an Alabama resident and $835 for a nonresident. Out-of-state fees are waived for students with graduate assistantships of one-fourth or more. Student housing arrangements are available both on and off campus. The minimum rate, as of fall 1985, for a one-bedroom unfurnished apartment on campus (excluding the cost of electricity) was $2,460 per calendar year.

FINANCIAL ASSISTANCE

A number of graduate assistantships are awarded on the basis of merit and according to department needs. Awards are generally for nine months. Stipends are about $450 per month for a one-third work load, and the student is permitted to carry a full load of graduate courses consisting of 10 quarter hours and not exceeding 15 quar-

ter hours. Applications for graduate teaching and research assistantships may be secured from the Director of the M.B.A. Program, College of Business.

PLACEMENT

Campus-wide Placement Services offers the major source of placement assistance. In 1984-85, Placement Services was visited by 400 recruiters from business, government, and other agencies seeking to hire graduates. In addition, faculty of the College of Business maintain contact with outside agencies.

CORRESPONDENCE

For information, please write or call
  Director, M.B.A. Program
  College of Business
  Auburn University
  Auburn University, Alabama 36849-3501
  Telephone: 205-826-4030

AUGUSTA COLLEGE

AUGUSTA, GEORGIA

Augusta College is a nonresidential, coeducational, state-supported college offering both baccalaureate and master's degrees. The campus is situated within close proximity of the Medical College of Georgia where a variety of professional and graduate programs are offered in the health fields. A close working relationship exists between the two institutions.

Augusta College is an urban institution of 4,000 students. The college is located in Augusta, Georgia, a growing metropolitan area of over 350,000 people, which is 150 miles east of Atlanta.

PROGRAM OF STUDY

The principal objectives of the Master of Business Administration (M.B.A.) degree are to provide a modern management science oriented program, which will enable the graduate to apply the more advanced techniques of decision making now essential in the operation of business and other organizations. It is also a requirement that each candidate for the M.B.A. degree become well prepared in all of the functional areas of business and institutional administration. Careful control of admission and instructional standards attempts to ensure that persons awarded the degree by Augusta College have achieved a high level of excellence.

Students entering the program with the Bachelor of Business Administration degree normally will be able to complete the Master of Business Administration degree with as few as 56 quarter hours. The program, however, is designed to accommodate students from other backgrounds, and a series of prerequisite courses is offered to provide these students with the necessary background.

The particular courses needed by an individual student are determined in consultation with an adviser in the School of Business Administration and are influenced by the student's previous experience. A specific set of 36 quarter hours of core courses is required of all students. These courses build a common base of understanding and analytical competence necessary for effective managerial performance. The core courses stress the learning of concepts and analytical thought appropriate in a rapidly changing environment. In addition to the core, a student develops an individualized elective program of 20 quarter hours in the fields of accounting, health services administration, or management.

The M.B.A. at Augusta College is offered as an evening program, enabling students to pursue graduate study while obtaining work experience in the wide variety of industries and health care institutions located in the area.

ADMISSION

Admission to the program is based on meeting the general requirements for all graduate students including (1) completion of a bachelor's degree in an accredited college; (2) a minimum grade-point average of 2.5 on a 4.0 scale; (3) satisfactory scores on the Graduate Management Admission Test (GMAT); and (4) submission of three letters of recommendation, two official college transcripts, and an application for admission to the graduate program. In order to register, students must be sure that all application materials are on file one month prior to the beginning of the quarter.

EXPENSES

Expenses will vary for each student. The quarterly matriculation fee is determined as follows:

Quarter hours scheduled	Resident	Nonresident
12 or more	$320	$960
Less than 12, per hour	27	81

In addition, the following nonrefundable fees must be paid: an application fee of $10 with each initial application, a student service fee of $20 per quarter, and an athletic fee of $25 per quarter. Fees and charges are subject to change at the end of any quarter.

FINANCIAL ASSISTANCE

Augusta College is interested in students with ability and ambition. The college makes every effort within its means to give financial aid to capable and promising students who would otherwise be unable to attend. Information on scholarships, loan funds, student assistantships, and work-study programs may be obtained by writing to the Director of Student Financial Aid, Augusta College, Augusta, Georgia 30910.

PLACEMENT

The college operates the Office of Career Planning and Placement to assist students and alumni in obtaining suitable employment.

CORRESPONDENCE

For further information, write or call
Graduate Office
School of Business Administration
Augusta College
2500 Walton Way
Augusta, Georgia 30910
Telephone: 404-737-1565

Avila College, founded in 1916, is a Catholic college that seeks to provide for the intellectual, spiritual, and social growth of all its members. The college includes men and women of many faiths and welcomes a diversity of religious convictions. Programs at the graduate and undergraduate levels are accredited by the North Central Association. The school's present enrollment is approximately 2,000.

Total offerings of the school include programs in the traditional fields of liberal arts plus programs in selected professional areas, including relatively large programs in business and nursing. Graduate studies at this time are restricted to the areas of business, education, and psychology.

The physical plant consists of 11 modern buildings, all attractively placed around a central quadrangle and conveniently located in close proximity to ample parking facilities. A spacious continuing education center, a modern theater, and a small art gallery enhance the physical facilities of the campus, and theater and musical performances and special lectures enrich the regular educational programs of the school. The greater Kansas City metropolitan area provides a multitude of opportunities for further expansion of the student's total educational experience.

Although full-time graduate students in business can be accommodated, the majority of the graduate business courses are scheduled during the evening hours to serve the needs of the relatively large percentage of part-time students. The faculty consists of a combination of academic and career business, economic, and legal professionals.

PROGRAM OF STUDY

The Master of Business Administration (M.B.A.) program is designed to provide men and women with management and leadership skills that they can utilize in relation to a broad range of institutions. Students holding undergraduate degrees in business and nonbusiness fields may enroll in the program, which varies in length from 24 to 48 hours depending upon the background of the individual student.

Eight concentrations are provided in the program—accounting, administration, finance, human resource management, international business, management information systems, marketing, and operations management. The administration concentration is designed to provide opportunities for the individual student to pursue a total program of a general management nature. Concentrations in most of the other areas require nine graduate hours in the area of concentration beyond the basic course.

The accounting concentration is designed to serve the needs of individuals with diverse career objectives ranging from those who desire a general management program with a special emphasis in the field of accounting to those who want to prepare for the C.P.A. or C.M.A. examinations and have either substantial or no formal education in accounting. Accounting courses are also offered as the alternate means of satisfying the experience requirement for the C.P.A. certificate in states where this provision exists.

Students who do not have an adequate undergraduate background in areas generally considered to comprise a common body of knowledge basic to the study of business must secure this background via graduate courses offered particularly for this purpose. Courses designed to serve these needs include Economic Concepts, Business Legislation, Financial Accounting, Statistics, Quantitative Analysis, Management Processes, Marketing Management, and Financial Management I.

All M.B.A. students conclude their study programs with a policy course entitled Corporate Strategy and Planning, and all students must complete a minimum of 24 hours of graduate courses in addition to satisfying the common body of knowledge requirement. Although the specific courses included in the study programs of the students vary in relation to the background and career objectives of the students, the following are typical of the other courses used in completing the degree: Business, Government, and Society; Organizational Behavior; Managerial Accounting; Managerial Economics or Aggregate Income Analysis; Management Seminar; Marketing Strategy; and Financial Management II.

Students pursuing the accounting concentration typically include Accounting Theory, Advanced Tax Accounting, Advanced Cost Accounting, and Advanced Auditing in their study programs.

ADMISSION

Admission requirements to Avila's M.B.A. program are a baccalaureate degree from an accredited institution and at least 1,000 points based on a formula: 200 times the grade-point average on the last 60/90 semester/quarter hours (4.0 system) plus Graduate Management Admission Test (GMAT) score. Foreign students should have a minimum score of 550 on the Test of English as a Foreign Language (TOEFL) and 450 on the GMAT. Students not meeting these requirements may petition for admission.

EXPENSES

Selected relevant expenses for 1985-86 are outlined below:

Tuition, per credit hour . . . . $ 140
Room and board in
  residence hall, per semester . . . 1,100

FINANCIAL ASSISTANCE

Only limited financial assistance is available at this stage of development of the Avila College; however, the college does have a full-time Office of Financial Aid.

CORRESPONDENCE

For information, please write or call
  M.B.A. Office
  Avila College
  11901 Wornall Road
  Kansas City, Missouri 64145
  Telephone: 816-942-8400

Azusa Pacific, founded in 1899, is an inter-denominational Christian university offering 30 undergraduate degrees, 9 graduate programs, and a wide variety of cultural, athletic, and ministry opportunities. The campus is located in a suburban hillside setting 30 miles east of Los Angeles. Stationed in the midst of a diverse complex of corporate, Christian nonprofit, and independent businesses, the university provides an ideal setting for students pursuing professional careers in business management.

Azusa Pacific University (APU) has a graduate enrollment of 616 full-time and 274 part-time students, 109 of whom are pursuing a Master of Business Administration (M.B.A.) in the School of Business and Management. The School of Business and Management, academically and physically an integral part of APU, provides advanced professional education for the business, government, and private non-profit sectors in a personable atmosphere offering opportunities for close relationships with teaching faculty.

The Academic Computer Center is equipped with a Hewlett-Packard Model 300 permitting COBOL, RPG Data Base, Pascal, and FORTRAN applications. SPSS is available for application of statistics to quantitative course work and project research. The center also utilizes IBM compatible (COMPAQ) microcomputers.

The university library system maintains a collection of 88,954 books, 317,263 microforms, 3,433 media aids, 500 periodicals and "Dialogue," an electronic information retrieval system.

APU is accredited by the Western Association of Schools and Colleges and is an institutional member of the American Assembly of Collegiate Schools of Business.

PROGRAMS OF STUDY

The primary aim of the M.B.A. program is to develop professional managers dedicated to service and integrity in business, education, government, religious organizations, and service agencies. The M.B.A. program consists of 12 courses totaling 36 units for students with a bachelor's degree in business and 57 units for students without a bachelor's degree in business. The program entails 12 to 21 months of academic work which must be completed within 5 years. M.B.A. students must select an emphasis in entrepreneurial, international, or nonprofit business.

The entrepreneurial emphasis is designed primarily for American students already involved in a business setting. Partly in response to the rise of the free enterprise spirit and the proliferation of privately owned small businesses, this emphasis recognizes the beneficial effects of entrepreneurial attitudes in the world of management.

The international emphasis features a curriculum design that emphasizes the functional specialities of business (accounting, finance, marketing). This emphasis encourages the student to explore the applications and ramifications of traditional business topics.

The nonprofit emphasis is uniquely designed for personnel of organizations whose goals are service-oriented, particularly those in Christian ministries. This emphasis features a curriculum with courses in management, fund raising, promotional strategies, planned giving, administrative practices, and leadership styles.

The School of Business and Management is seeking new ways to meet the needs of management careers. Currently under study is the formulation of a new Master of Ministry Management degree.

ADMISSION

The basic policy for admission to the M.B.A. program is to select men and women whose capabilities fit them to be trained for a career in business. Applicants must hold a bachelor's or higher degree from an accredited college or university with minimum grade-point average of 3.0. Provisional admission may be granted to applicants whose average is at least 2.5.

All applicants must file a university application, pay a $30 application fee, and submit official transcripts from every college or university previously attended. In addition, a letter of recommendation and a personal interview are required.

Foreign applicants must submit a minimum score of 500 on the Test of English as a Foreign Language (TOEFL) or the completion of Level 9 in English Language School or a Michigan Test score of 82, proof of health, translation of their transcripts, and proof of adequate funds for two years of study.

EXPENSES

Tuition is $150 per unit. No on-campus graduate housing is available. The cost for an academic year, including room and board, books and supplies, personal expenses, and nine units of tuition, is estimated at $11,270.

FINANCIAL ASSISTANCE

Financial aid is available in the form of employment, Guaranteed Student Loans, National Direct Student Loans, grants, and scholarships. For more information, contact the Office of Student Financial Services.

PLACEMENT

The university provides career counseling and information on national and local companies.

CORRESPONDENCE

For further information, write or call
Graduate Admissions Office
Azusa Pacific University
Citrus and Alosta
Azusa, California 91702
Telephone: 818-969-3434, ext. 3414

BABSON COLLEGE
WELLESLEY, MASSACHUSETTS

Babson College, founded in 1919 by financier Roger W. Babson, is located in Wellesley, Massachusetts, just 12 miles from Boston. An independent, coeducational institution, Babson is accredited by the New England Association of Schools and Colleges. Its undergraduate and graduate programs in business are accredited by the American Assembly of Collegiate Schools of Business (AACSB). Babson College is recognized for its leadership in management education and its emphasis on entrepreneurial studies. Through integration of lectures, seminars, case problems, the conference method, and individual projects, the student learns to appreciate management problems and approach problem solving critically within a practical frame of reference.

PROGRAM OF STUDY
The Babson M.B.A. can be completed through a program of full- or part-time study. Two semesters and two accelerated summer sessions allow students to study throughout the calendar year.

The program consists of 20 courses—13 required and 7 elected. Individuals who have successfully completed business-related courses may be awarded advanced standing credit for up to 10 of the 13 required M.B.A. courses. Advanced standing may be granted if the following criteria are met:
• the grade earned must be B− or better in a course taken at a regionally or nationally accredited college or university;
• the course must carry at least three semester hours of credit; and
• the course content must be substantially similar to Babson's equivalent course.

Normally the full-time program requires two years for completion. However, the advanced standing policy makes it possible for some students to complete the program in a minimum of one year.

Specialized electives provide students with the opportunity to apply their classroom knowledge to professional business situations. The Management Consulting Field Experience allows consulting teams of four to six graduate students to work with faculty advisers to solve actual problems for business firms and for government and nonprofit organizations. Participation is competitive and limited to students who have completed at least one half of the M.B.A. program.

In the International Management Internship Program students work individually on projects in international business organizations for two summer months. Participation requires completion of at least one half of the M.B.A. program, one or more courses in the international curriculum, and acceptance by the selection committee. The Domestic Management Field Experience for International Students allows selected students to be assigned to summer internships with U.S. industrial or service organizations. Independent research may be undertaken for academic credit with the approval of a faculty adviser, the graduate dean, and the appropriate division chairman. In addition, electives in entrepreneurial studies are offered for students who seek either to become entrepreneurs or to work with entrepreneurs in some special capacity such as consultant, financial analyst, or venture capitalist.

ADMISSION
Applicants must have earned an undergraduate degree (or in the case of a foreign student, its equivalent) from a nationally or regionally accredited college or university. In addition, all applicants must submit results of the Graduate Management Admission Test (GMAT), official transcripts of undergraduate and graduate work, and resumes that document work experience. Foreign students from non-English-speaking countries must submit scores from the Test of English as a Foreign Language (TOEFL) and official English translations of all pertinent documents.

EXPENSES
Annual tuition for a standard load of five courses is $8,220 plus $177 for student fees for full-time graduate students. Part-time evening graduate students pay $822 per course. Expenses are subject to change. A limited number of on-campus apartments and rooms for unmarried students, as well as on-campus apartments for married students, are currently available.

FINANCIAL ASSISTANCE
Financial aid deadlines are March 1 for September registration and November 1 for January. Full-time students may apply for financial aid. All awards are based on demonstrated need. Applicants for financial aid are required to submit a Babson Financial Aid Application and a Graduate and Professional School Financial Aid Service (GAPSFAS) form.

Graduate assistantships and part-time employment as well as residential staff positions are available. The program is approved for veterans' benefits, and many part-time students receive financial assistance through company-sponsored educational plans.

In addition, several alternative options are available through loan programs. For forms and additional information, contact the Office of Financial Aid.

PLACEMENT
The Office of Career Services actively assists students in planning and managing their careers as well as in searching for permanent employment on receipt of the master's degree. Representatives from many organizations visit the campus each year. Assistance is also available to alumni who seek a change in employment.

CORRESPONDENCE
For further information or to request an application for admission, please write or call

Director of Graduate Admission
Babson College
Babson Park (Wellesley),
 Massachusetts 02157
Telephone: 617-235-1200, extension 4317

Ball State University enrolls over 17,000 students and is located in Muncie, Indiana, a city of 84,000. The College of Business has about 4,500 undergraduate and over 400 graduate students in 6 departments with a total faculty of more than 100. The Bureau of Business Research is an area center for business, labor, and government research.

PROGRAMS OF STUDY

The primary objective of the Master of Business Administration (M.B.A.) program is that of educating men and women for management positions in business, industry, and government. The program is designed to provide breadth of preparation in the various functional areas of business. Classes are scheduled at night so that students can pursue any program on a part-time or full-time basis. Students may begin at any quarter.

The M.B.A. program is available to those students holding baccalaureate degrees in areas other than business administration as well as to those who hold degrees in business. The time required for completion of the program will vary according to the background of study presented by the candidate and will range from a minimum of one year to a maximum of two years.

The foundational areas required for the program include the following: principles of economics, business statistics, management, data processing, accounting, finance, business law, marketing, and basic calculus. Students holding undergraduate degrees in business normally will have completed all of these foundational requirements. The student who has not completed course work in any of these areas will remove the deficiencies as soon as scheduling permits by taking appropriate undergraduate courses or by taking graduate survey courses especially designed for this purpose.

Requirements for the degree beyond the foundational areas include the following:
- completion of a minimum of 45 quarter hours of graduate credit as approved by the graduate adviser or as many additional hours as necessary to complete the degree requirements (This minimum of 45 hours must be completed within a 6-year period);
- completion of the following core of courses—managerial finance, marketing management, national income analysis,

managerial economics, managerial accounting, production management, management information systems, statistics for business decisions, organizational behavior, and business policy for a total of 33 quarter hours (Substitutions for core courses may be approved by the graduate adviser should the candidate present evidence of having completed equivalent courses);
- an additional 12 quarter hours of elective course work to meet the minimum requirements for the degree and a four-quarter-hour course in international business (The elective courses will permit the student to develop a limited degree of depth in an area and provide flexibility for meeting individual needs. The elective hours include a three-quarter-hour course on methods of research in business);
- a minimum grade-point average of 3.0 (A = 4.0).

ADMISSION

To be admitted to the program, a student must demonstrate high promise of success in a graduate business degree program. The scores on the Graduate Management Admission Test (GMAT) are required. The minimum standards for consideration for admission to all graduate programs in business at the master's level are (1) a baccalaureate degree from an accredited college or university and (2) a minimum composite score of 1,000 points computed by multiplying the undergraduate grade-point average overall (based on a 4.0 grading system) by 200 and adding the GMAT score or demonstration of high promise as evidenced by trends and patterns in college and employment. International students also must score at least 550 on the Test of English as a Foreign Language (TOEFL).

The student's application will not be considered until the following materials are at Ball State: (1) transcripts from all undergraduate or graduate institutions sent by those institutions (one to the Office of Admission and another to the Office of the Associate Dean, College of Business), (2) a completed Graduate Application, (3) a statement of work experience, and (4) a GMAT score. All materials must be on file, and the student must have received a letter of acceptance before beginning graduate work.

A specialized master's degree also may be pursued in management. All master's degree admission requirements are the same. The Master of Science program

requires about 30 quarter hours in a specialty and 15 quarter hours of electives approved by the appropriate departmental adviser beyond the foundational areas. A liberal arts master's degree in economics also is available.

EXPENSES

Unmarried, in-state, full-time students without assistantships have minimal total expenses of at least $5,160 per academic year. New university housing is available for both married and single students.

	Indiana Resident	Out-of-State
Tuition and fees	$2,072	$4,760
Room and board	2,088	2,088
Books and personal expenses	1,000	1,000
Total	$5,160	$7,848

FINANCIAL ASSISTANCE

Thirty-two graduate assistantships paying $3,310 each for the academic year are available. Fees are reduced for graduate assistants, and out-of-state tuition is eliminated. The Office of Student Financial Aids should be contacted about loans.

PLACEMENT

The university Placement Office is in communication with a large number of employers, many of whom visit the campus one or more times each year. Counseling is available to aid each student in the development of individualized objectives and job search strategies.

CORRESPONDENCE

For further information, write or call
Graduate Coordinator,
    College of Business
Ball State University
Muncie, IN 47306
Telephone: 317-285-1931

Baruch College is a senior college of the City University of New York (CUNY) located in the Gramercy Park area of New York City. The forerunner of Baruch College was the School of Business and Civic Administration established in 1919. In 1953, the school was named in honor of Bernard M. Baruch, the statesman and financier. In 1968, the school was designated an independent senior college of CUNY. Baruch currently enrolls 15,000 students and has a teaching staff of over 600. Baruch's School of Business and Public Administration, the largest in the world, is the only City University unit that awards both the Bachelor and Master of Business Administration degrees. It also conducts the City University's Ph.D. program in business.

Baruch's undergraduate and graduate programs are accredited by the American Assembly of Collegiate Schools of Business (AACSB). Baruch is the only New York City college, public or private, having both the B.B.A. and M.B.A. programs in accountancy so accredited. The *Gourman Report* ranks Baruch's School of Business and Public Administration as one of the top 20 in the country. Baruch's graduate programs enroll approximately 2,500 men and women who represent over 200 colleges and universities, from this country and abroad. The instructional staff includes members of the permanent faculty and specialists drawn from New York City's vast resources in business and public service.

PROGRAMS OF STUDY
Baruch College offers graduate programs leading to the following degrees: the M.B.A.; the M.B.A. in health care administration (jointly with Mt. Sinai School of Medicine), accredited by the Commission on Education for Health Services Administration; the Master of Public Administration (M.P.A.), accredited by the National Association of Schools of Public Administration and Affairs; the Master of Science (M.S.) in education; the Master of Science in industrial and labor relations (jointly with Cornell University); the Master of Science in statistics, computer methodology, operations research, industrial and organizational psychology, quantitative economics, taxation, and marketing; and the Juris Doctor/Master of Business Administration (J.D./M.B.A.) and the Juris Doctor/Master of Public Administration (J.D./ M.P.A.) (jointly with New

York Law School and Brooklyn Law School). The M.P.A. program offers four specializations: budgeting and financial management, human services management, policy analysis, and public management generalist. The M.B.A. program offers specializations in accountancy, business administration and policy, computer systems, economics, finance and investments, health care administration, industrial psychology, international business, management, marketing, operations research, statistics, and taxation.

The program requires the completion of courses covering a common body of knowledge (30 credits). This requirement may be satisfied by courses taken at the undergraduate level. In addition, the program includes at least 15 credits in the major, 15 credits outside the major, and 6 credits in a thesis or thesis alternative.

Candidates for the Ph.D. in business select a major and minor from among the following: accountancy, consumer behavior, finance, industrial psychology, operations management, and organizational behavior. Candidates must complete at least 60 credits of graduate work, take an examination consisting of a position paper and an oral examination on the paper, pass an oral and written examination in the major field, and submit and defend a dissertation.

ADMISSION
A bachelor's degree from an accredited college or university is required. For the M.B.A. or an M.S. in marketing or taxation programs, the Graduate Management Admission Test (GMAT) is also required. For the M.S. program in computer methodology, industrial and labor relations, industrial and organizational psychology, operations research, quantitative economics, or statistics, or for the M.B.A. program in industrial psychology, either the GMAT or the Graduate Record Examinations (GRE) is acceptable. The M.P.A. program requires the GRE. Admission to the Ph.D. program requires a bachelor's degree with a 3.20 average or better in the undergraduate major or a master's degree with superior performance from an accredited college or university. Applicants must take the GMAT or GRE. International students must also take the Test of English as a Foreign Language (TOEFL).

EXPENSES
For New York State residents, full-time tuition (12 credits or more) is $950.00 per semester; part-time, $82.00 per credit. For nonresidents, full-time tuition is $1,600.00 per semester; part-time tuition is $136.00 per credit. All students pay an $11.35 activity fee per semester. These charges are subject to change.

Baruch College does not have dormitories or housing facilities. Cost-of-living figures vary widely, depending on the student's place of residence.

FINANCIAL ASSISTANCE
Financial aid is available through a wide variety of sources. A number of fellowship and research assistantships are awarded each year; selection is competitive. In addition, students may be eligible for financial aid through various state and federal programs, including the New York State Tuition Assistance Program (TAP), New York State loans, College Work-Study Program, National Direct Student Loans (NDSL), and the CUNY Graduate Tuition Waiver Program. For information and applications, contact the Financial Aid Office.

PLACEMENT
The Career Planning and Placement Office offers the benefits of an active association with more than 150 major corporations in the New York City area. Students are assisted with resume writing and interview preparation. Faculty members help in placing graduates with leading firms.

CORRESPONDENCE
For further information, please write or call

Office of Graduate Admissions
Baruch College, Box 276
17 Lexington Avenue
New York, New York 10010
Telephone: 212-725-3078

Baylor University, chartered by the Republic of Texas, is the oldest Texas university in continuous existence since its founding. Today, Baylor is one of the nation's major church-related universities and provides both liberal arts and professional education in the context of a Christian environment. Baylor is located in central Texas in the thriving city of Waco, which has a population of approximately 110,000 and is only a few hours' drive from such centers as Dallas, Houston, and San Antonio. By today's standards, Baylor is a medium-sized university, with approximately 10,000 students on the main campus. About 195 students are enrolled in the graduate business programs with seminars averaging between 15 and 25 students.

PROGRAMS OF STUDY

The Hankamer School of Business offers the following degree programs: Master of Business Administration (M.B.A.), Master of Taxation, Master of Science in economics, M.B.A./M.I.S., and Master of International Management. Graduate programs are accredited by the American Assembly of Collegiate Schools of Business (AACSB).

The Master of Business Administration program has nationally recognized faculty members who seek to develop in the student an understanding of business and the management process. The concentration in entrepreneurship at the graduate level is one of the few such programs in the country. The small class size also allows optimum interaction between students and professors, and the placement office has been very successful in placing graduates in firms throughout the world. The M.B.A. degree may be earned under either a one- or two-year program. For admission to the one-year program, the applicant must have an undergraduate business degree consisting of 30 hours of business courses. The development of expertise in a specific area of business may be achieved through field concentrations, which include three elective courses in the area of interest.

The Master of Taxation program is designed to equip graduates with the technical knowledge and human skills necessary to enter and lead in the rapidly expanding and changing field of taxation. A distinctive feature of this program is an optimal four-and-one-half-month internship with the tax department of either a major public accounting firm or industrial enterprise.

The Master of International Management degree has become a valuable credential in the fields of international business and government service. The interdisciplinary Master of International Management degree provides management opportunities for men and women who are interested in international economic and political affairs.

ADMISSION

Applicants must have a bachelor's degree from an accredited college or university. They must complete the Graduate Management Admission Test (GMAT) with a minimum score of 450 to qualify for the M.B.A., Master of Taxation, or Master of International Management programs, and a minimum score of 450 to qualify for the Master of Science in economics. To be accepted, the applicant must have a 2.7 (4.0 system) overall grade-point average plus the GMAT score, or a 3.0 (4.0 system) grade-point average in the last 60 hours, plus the GMAT score. A combined score of 900 on the verbal and quantitative portions of the Graduate Record Examinations General Test may be substituted for the GMAT for admission to the Master of Science in economics program or a 1050 for admission to the Master of International Management program.

EXPENSES

Semester hour................. $ 116
On-campus housing,
    per semester 1,285
Off-campus housing,
    per month............... 400-900*
*Depending on the accommodations chosen.

FINANCIAL ASSISTANCE

The Hankamer School of Business offers three types of financial assistance: graduate assistantships, work-study assistantships, and graduate fellowships. The graduate assistantships are valued at $6,176 including 36 hours of tuition and a cash stipend of $1,000. They entail work assignments of 10 to 20 hours per week as a laboratory assistant, research assistant, or instructor. Work-study assistantships pay at least $3,500 per year. The work-study assistant pays his or her own tuition but receives a 25 percent discount from the regular tuition rate. Each work-study assistant is assigned to a progressive business firm for approximately 20 hours per week for 12 months. Nonservice graduate fellowships valued at $5,325 are also offered. Applications should be filed by March 1 for the following academic year. Part-time employment is available on and off the campus for both students and their spouses.

PLACEMENT

The Baylor University Placement Office is available to assist students in the master's programs in obtaining the best job opportunities available. Each year over 230 firms, governmental agencies, and schools conduct interviews in the Baylor Placement Office. The Placement Office is also willing to assist graduates who decide to change jobs after graduation.

CORRESPONDENCE

For further information on the graduate programs offered at Baylor, write
    Associate Dean for Graduate Programs
    Hankamer School of Business
    Baylor University
    Waco, Texas 76706

Bellarmine College, a private, liberal arts college under Catholic auspices, is located in the suburban, eastern section of Louisville, Kentucky. The college has an enrollment of about 2,800 students.

Bellarmine is known for its distinctive educational programs conducted in an atmosphere of small classes and maximum instructor-student interaction. The faculty in the graduate and undergraduate business programs is composed of men and women who combine academic qualifications with practical management experience.

PROGRAM OF STUDY

The Master of Business Administration (M.B.A.) program offered by Bellarmine College is essentially a broad-based course of study in business management with emphasis on the nature of managerial responsibility in a changing world. The program is directed to the professional training of qualified individuals either to fill managerial positions in corporate business enterprises or to head their own business organization. It is also designed to be of benefit to those pursuing careers in government, health, and educational administration. Additionally, the program provides a valuable opportunity for those already in responsible management positions to update their skills and advance further within the organization.

To obtain an M.B.A. degree students must complete 36 hours of graduate credits in business administration and/or related fields. Of these 36 hours, 21 are in the core curriculum. The remaining 15 hours include 6 hours in integrative courses and the remainder in electives. Students with strong undergraduate backgrounds in accounting, quantitative techniques, and the social sciences are encouraged to seek waivers of the appropriate core courses.

ADMISSION

The criteria for admission are as follows:
- an undergraduate degree from an accredited institution;
- satisfactory scores on the Graduate Management Admission Test (GMAT);
- letter of application (career objectives, etc.);
- letter of recommendation;
- a 2.75 undergraduate grade-point average;
- satisfactory completion of the preparatory phase consisting of the common body of knowledge (courses in accounting, business administration, economics, and mathematics). Applicants who have completed equivalent undergraduate or graduate courses may obtain waivers on a course-by-course basis. Waivers may be obtained also on the basis of an examination.

Application deadlines for the fall, spring, and summer sessions are August 1, December 1, and May 1.

EXPENSES

Tuition is currently $155 per semester hour. In many cases, tuition is paid by the organization sponsoring the participant.

FINANCIAL ASSISTANCE

A graduate assistantship valued at over $5,200 is available. This appointment requires service to the M.B.A. program in administrative assistance or other assigned duties. Applications for financial aid should be made by letter to the M.B.A. Director, W. Fielding Rubel School of Business. Preference is given to those applicants with high academic standing. Appointments are generally made by August 1.

CORRESPONDENCE

To register or to obtain additional information, contact
Office of Admissions and Records
Bellarmine College
Newburg Road
Louisville, Kentucky 40205
Telephone: 502-452-8131

BENTLEY COLLEGE

WALTHAM, MASSACHUSETTS

Founded in 1917, Bentley College is an independent, coeducational institution recognized internationally for its excellence in professional business education. The 107-acre campus is ideally located only nine miles from Boston and its historical, cultural, and academic resources. In 1985, the college enrolled 1,700 graduate students and 5,975 undergraduate students. The Bentley College faculty is a rich blend of 188 full-time and 140 adjunct members.

PROGRAMS OF STUDY
Bentley College Graduate School offers five programs leading to the Master of Science degree in Accountancy, Computer Information Systems, Finance, and Taxation and a Master of Business Administration (M.B.A.) program. Each program is an intensive learning experience intended to help persons achieve professional performance requiring technical and professional competence, and professional ethics.

The Master of Science in Accountancy (M.S.A.) program is designed for persons seeking to become professional accountants. The program is structured to enable every student to develop competence in each of the basic areas within accounting.

The Master of Science in Computer Information Systems (M.S.C.I.S.) program is designed to enable persons to be capable of developing complex information systems. It best serves postexperience students whose current job and career direction require professional competence in this field.

The Master of Science in Finance (M.S.F.) program is intended for individuals who seek to expand their knowledge of corporate finance. The M.S.F. student usually holds a significant position in the finance function of a large enterprise, has a strong accounting background, and is interested in those aspects of finance that influence managerial decision making.

The Master of Science in Taxation (M.S.T.) program is designed to help individuals become competent professional tax advisers and consultants, tax executives in private and public enterprises, and leaders in the tax field.

The Master of Business Administration (M.B.A.) program is intended for individuals who already have a specialization in business or who want to acquire a broad educational base for renewing, changing, or launching a career in management.

The programs vary in length from a 12-course to a 20-course sequence. Advanced standing can reduce the total to a minimum of 10 courses for those whose previous education covers the foundation areas.

Over 90 percent of all students have had full-time work experience. Over one third of the students have graduate degrees or professional certifications prior to entering Bentley.

Two courses constitute a full load for part-time students. Four courses constitute a full load for full-time students. Each three-credit course meets once a week.

Since the school's offerings are programs leading to degrees:
• a student must be accepted into a program; there is no special student status;
• application for admission must be made in advance.
Matriculation may begin in September or January.

ADMISSION
To apply for admission to a program, an applicant is expected to submit a completed application form (factual information should be complete, and evidence of a match between Bentley and the applicant should be carefully presented); have transcripts submitted for all academic work beyond high school; take the Graduate Management Admission Test (GMAT) early enough for the results to be considered by the Admissions Committee. (Bentley College Graduate School Code No. is R3096.) For M.S.F. and M.S.T. applicants, GMAT score or evidence of successful completion of the C.P.A., bar examination, or receipt of an appropriate master's or doctor's degree may be submitted.

Applicants whose native language is not English, and who have not earned a degree in a college where instruction is in English, are also required to take the Test of English as a Foreign Language (TOEFL) and request that the score be sent to Bentley College.

The number of students the school can accept in one semester is limited. The deadline for submission of a completed application file is June 15 (fall semester) and November 1 (spring semester). Written notification is July 15 (fall) and November 30 (spring).

EXPENSES
Tuition for 1985-86 is $720 per course. Expenses are subject to change. Applications must be accompanied by a $25 non-refundable fee.

FINANCIAL ASSISTANCE
Financial assistance is available in the form of scholarships, loans, the College Work-Study Program, and graduate assistantships. Many students receive financial aid from their employers. The programs are approved for veterans' benefits. Graduate students may also apply for positions as resident assistants in the undergraduate housing facilities.

PLACEMENT
Career planning is available for all students. On-campus recruiting is available for students in the last year of their program. A job locator service is available to assist students in finding part-time employment.

CORRESPONDENCE
For additional information, write
Graduate School
Bentley College
Waltham, Massachusetts 02254
Telephone: 617-891-2108

Berry College facilities stand unmatched in vastness and beauty by other private institutions in the United States. Gracing some 500 acres of attractively landscaped terrain on which much of the natural beauty—dogwood, redbud, and many other species of trees—has been retained, the Berry College campus adjoins the school's 30,000-acre domain of forests, fields, mountains, lakes, and streams, providing a peaceful atmosphere conducive to intellectual and spiritual growth. From the log cabin area of earlier days to the Gothic Ford quadrangle and the later Georgian structures, beauty, charm, and peace abound. These features and others combine to form a truly unique environment for learning.

Although campus housing is available, graduate students are not required to reside on campus. Room assignments are made by the director of residence life.

PROGRAM OF STUDY

The Master of Business Administration (M.B.A.) degree at Berry College, which requires a minimum of 60 quarter hours, is a generalist degree designed to provide each student with a broad general background in significant managerial areas. The graduate program in business administration is accredited by the Southern Association of Colleges and Schools.

Upon satisfactory completion of prerequisite work, if any, and upon completion of the general requirements for admission to graduate school, an applicant will be given regular admission status.

The M.B.A. program consists of 45 quarter hours of required courses that provide a fundamental understanding of business problems and practices, and 15 quarter hours of electives that permit specialization in an area of interest. Each required course may be waived, depending upon the undergraduate and/or graduate courses that the individual student has previously completed. Any student receiving a waiver must substitute an elective course for each of the required courses waived.

No final oral examination is required for the M.B.A. degree; nor is a thesis required. A general policy course, BUS 685 (Business Policy) is required of all students.

The time limit on earned credit that can be accepted toward fulfilling the requirements for the master's degree is six years.

The number of students in each class is kept to a minimum. The classes usually include from 9 to 25 students; the average is about 15. The small classes allow students self-expression and individual attention.

ADMISSION

Application for admission to graduate studies must be filed with the dean of admissions no later than 30 days before the beginning of each quarter. All transcripts, references, and test scores must be in the admissions office at least 10 days prior to the beginning of the quarter for which admission is sought.

To be admitted as a student in good standing, the applicant must present (1) a completed application with a $30 nonrefundable application fee, (2) a baccalaureate degree from a regionally accredited college or university, (3) three references from persons in a position to attest to his or her ability to perform successfully in a quality graduate program, (4) two official transcripts from each undergraduate and graduate institution attended, and (5) satisfactory scores on the Graduate Management Admission Test (GMAT).

An applicant seeking a graduate degree in a specialization different from his or her undergraduate major may be granted conditional status while satisfying undergraduate deficiencies. An applicant meeting the first two regular admission requirements, but showing a deficiency in one or more of the additional requirements, may seek enrollment with conditional status. An applicant from a nonaccredited institution may be considered for conditional admission. Applicants not desiring to work toward the master's degree may apply for special status.

A maximum of 15 quarter hours of graduate credit earned at another institution may be accepted toward the master's degree at Berry College provided: (1) the credit has been earned at a regionally accredited graduate institution within five years of the date on which the master's degree requirements are completed; (2) the work is acceptable as credit toward a comparable program at Berry College; (3) the courses to be transferred are approved by the Director of Graduate Studies and the head of the department in which the specialization is being taken; and (4) the courses to be transferred carry a grade of B or better.

EXPENSES

Tuition and textbook expenses for the 60 quarter hours are approximately $7,000.

CORRESPONDENCE

For additional information on the program of study offered by Berry College, write or call
   Director
   Graduate Studies in Business
   Berry College
   Mount Berry, Georgia 30149
   Telephone: 404-232-5374, extension 2233

BETHANY NAZARENE COLLEGE

BETHANY, OKLAHOMA

The Division of Business at Bethany Nazarene College initiated the graduate program leading to the Master of Science in Management (M.S.M.) degree during the academic year 1979-80. The program is housed in a new million-dollar facility equipped with the latest learning devices.

PROGRAM OF STUDY

The M.S.M. degree program is designed for the student who is working on a full-time basis. The class schedule rotation permits the student to complete the program in two years. Classes are offered two nights per week, and one class is offered each in June and July. A student may accelerate graduation by enrollment in cognate areas or by transfer of credit.

The curriculum of studies is designed to meet career objectives of individuals who occupy or aspire to the following:
- mid-management level positions—managers of functional areas of business or segments of a corporation;
- individuals who are in the nonprofit, service related organization who assume managerial responsibility; and
- individual owners, operators, or managers of traditional small-business entities.

The unique feature of the program is the area of professional specialization. A student may enroll in this area of field studies more than one time. The field studies concept permits a student to identify a problem related to his or her work experience and develop an appropriate solution to the problem at hand. This course may be on an arranged basis simulating a laboratory experience model.

ADMISSION

An applicant must fulfill the following requirements in order to be admitted to a graduate program:
- hold a baccalaureate degree from a regionally accredited college or university,
- have completed the necessary undergraduate hours in the area of concentration,
- submit a completed application for admission to graduate studies 30 days prior to enrollment,
- have an official transcript of all post-secondary work sent to the Office of Graduate Studies,
- take the English Usage Test or request that the score be sent to the Office of Graduate Studies (This test is waived if the applicant scored 20 or better on the ACT, made a B or better in Freshman English II (or its equivalent), or was admitted to a teacher education program at the undergraduate level),
- have earned a grade-point average of 3.00 in the major field and 2.50 in the last 60 hours of undergraduate work (based on 4.00 scale),
- submit a score of 425 or better on the Graduate Management Admission Test (GMAT) before enrollment.

EXPENSES

Tuition is currently $104 per semester credit hour. Normal general fees are assessed. Limited college housing is available; however, students usually make personal housing arrangements.

FINANCIAL ASSISTANCE

A limited number of scholarships are available to the graduate student with stipends from $200 to $500. Information may be obtained from the Director of Financial Aid.

PLACEMENT

Graduates work with the career center on campus for placement opportunities.

CORRESPONDENCE

For further information, write or call
Director of Graduate Studies
Bethany Nazarene College
Bethany, Oklahoma 73008
Telephone: 405-789-6400

Established in 1976, the graduate degree curriculum in business administration was developed to prepare the student to accept leadership responsibility within the business organization. The School of Business (Business Administration) is located in Sutliff Hall. Students are required to live off campus. Enrollment in this program is limited; therefore, admission to the courses is selective. The faculty consists of 16 members, with a student population of approximately 110.

PROGRAM OF STUDY

A Master of Business Administration (M.B.A.) degree is comprised of two levels of courses. Level I consists of background courses or experiences that are prerequisite to Level II. Students whose undergraduate major was in business administration are likely to have had most, or perhaps all, of the courses of Level I; they may be exempted from courses that duplicate their undergraduate work. Level I must be completed before entering the Level II program.

Level II consists of 36 semester hours of graduate credit, of which 30 are prescribed and 6 are elected. No thesis is required.

The school operates on the semester system, and instruction begins in late August. Courses are available in the evenings; the program serves both full-time and part-time students.

ADMISSION

Applicants for the M.B.A. degree must complete the application form (including the $10 application fee), hold a baccalaureate degree from an accredited college or university with an overall quality-point average of 2.50 or higher (A = 4), complete the Graduate Management Admission Test (GMAT) with a total of 450 or higher, and provide two letters of recommendation and a statement of experience in business.

EXPENSES

Full-time basic fees (9 to 15 credits), per semester

Pennsylvania resident	$800.00
Nonresident	891.00

Part-time basic fees (fewer than 9 credits or over 15 credits), per credit

Pennsylvania resident	89.00
Nonresident	99.00
Student activity fee (optional)	45.00

Student union fee, per semester

(9 + credits)	10.00
Degree fee	10.00

Health Service fee

(4 to 8 credits)	8.50
(9 + credits)	17.00

FINANCIAL ASSISTANCE

Assistance is available in the form of Federal Fellowships (in selected areas), the National Direct Student Loan Program, and the Pennsylvania Higher Education Assistance Agency Loan Program. Inquiries should be addressed to the Director of Financial Aid.

A limited number of graduate assistantships are available through the School of Graduate Studies. Inquiries should be directed to the Dean of Graduate Studies.

PLACEMENT

Graduate students are eligible to utilize the services of the Placement Office after having been accepted as candidates for the master's degree. Inquiries should be addressed to the Director of Placement.

For foreign students an I-20 form is required together with a minimum score of 550 on the Test of English as a Foreign Language (TOEFL). There are no special application deadlines or deposit. A Foreign Student Advisor and an International Education Committee are available on campus.

CORRESPONDENCE

For further information, write or call
Dr. Daniel C. Pantaleo
Dean
College of Graduate Studies
Bloomsburg University
Bloomsburg, Pennsylvania 17815
Telephone: 717-389-4004

PROGRAMS OF STUDY

The College of Business offers programs of study leading to the Master of Business Administration (M.B.A.) degree (30 hours) or the Master of Science in Accounting (33 hours). The objectives of these programs, predominantly offered at night, are to further prepare candidates for careers in their chosen fields. The M.B.A. program emphasizes the traditional approach of the development of managerial generalists, with a common body of functional knowledge given to all students. While there is no area of emphasis or major available in the M.B.A. program, once a student satisfies the functional core of courses, electives to achieve a minor degree of concentration are possible.

ADMISSION

Admission will be granted to applicants who hold a bachelor's degree from an accredited college or university and who meet the standards set by the College of Business of Boise State University. A foundation of prerequisite knowledge in basic fields of business administration is common to all graduate programs. Students presenting a bachelor's degree in business or accounting normally will have completed most of these requirements in their undergraduate programs. Students who have completed a bachelor's degree in nonbusiness fields such as the sciences, engineering, and the liberal arts must demonstrate proficiency in business prerequisites. These prerequisites may be fulfilled by satisfactory completion of course work in these areas, or by successfully passing the acceptable College-Level Examinations Program (CLEP) examination and any other local departmental requirements.

All applicants must meet the following requirements before being accepted with regular status in the graduate program:
- possession of a bachelor's degree from an accredited institution;
- achievement of an acceptable formula based on cumulative undergraduate grade-point average (GPA) and score on the Graduate Management Admission Test (GMAT) — 200 × GPA + GMAT must equal 1,000;
- completion of prerequisite courses or their equivalent in accounting, communication, economics, production management, statistics, business law, marketing, management, finance, data processing, and college mathematics.

By application, students who are deficient in prerequisites may enroll in the graduate program and begin their course of prerequisite study immediately, with unclassified or provisional status.

Students may be admitted for the fall term (August), spring term (January), or summer term (June). A student may commence the program without scheduling difficulties at the beginning of any term. Admission correspondence should be addressed to the Dean of Admissions, Boise State University, Boise, Idaho 83725.

EXPENSES

Per semester,

estimated	Resident	Nonresident
Tuition	none	$ 950
Institutional fees	$ 664	664
Board and room	1,800	1,800
Books and supplies	200	200
	$2,664	$3,614

FINANCIAL ASSISTANCE

Limited numbers of scholarships, fellowships, and assistantships are available. Contact the Dean of the College of Business for details.

National Direct Student Loans at 5 percent interest are available from Boise State University by filing the CSS Financial Aid Form before March 1 preceding fall registration. Students must demonstrate financial need. The maximum loan is $1,500 per year with a $12,000 aggregate maximum, including amounts borrowed as undergraduates.

Guaranteed Student Loans at 7, 8, and 9 percent are available from lenders in the community (banks, credit unions, etc.). The maximum loan is $5,000 per year if the student attends full time. A $25,000 aggregate limit, including undergraduate loans, is in effect.

Short-term emergency loans are available by applying to the Financial Aid Office. These loans must be repaid within 90 days.

The College Work-Study Program provides opportunities for on-campus employment while students are enrolled. Students must demonstrate financial need by filing the CSS Financial Aid Form.

The Job Location and Development Office assists students in securing part-time employment opportunities off campus.

CORRESPONDENCE

For further information, write or call
Graduate Program Coordinator
Boise State University
Boise, Idaho 83725
Telephone: 208-385-1125

Boston College, a university comprised of 13 colleges, schools, and institutes, is located in Chestnut Hill, Massachusetts, within sight of downtown Boston. The Master of Business Administration (M.B.A.) program may be completed either on a full-time or a part-time basis. There are openings for 90 full-time and 45 part-time students each September and for 90 part-time students each January.

PROGRAMS OF STUDY

The Boston College M.B.A. program is designed to provide students with the analytical and decision-making skills required by a successful manager. It also uniquely emphasizes the next critical step in the managerial process: implementation skills. Through open critical self-evaluation and group interaction, the M.B.A. program strives to create settings that challenge a participant's skills and support the further development and refinement of these skills.

The M.B.A. program includes a full-time and part-time option and requires 54 course credits for graduation. The first 30 credits make up the core curriculum. The core begins with a broad introduction to the history of economic thought and business history, along with an initial forecast of future political and economic development and a description of the organizational principles upon which this core curriculum itself was built.

The core curriculum includes 8 three-credit courses in accounting, computer information systems, economics, finance, international management, marketing, production, and statistics, as well as 3 two-credit courses in human resources management, organization studies, and perspectives on management.

Throughout the core program, in classes and in special integrative activities, students will repeatedly be required to perform professionally, whether in terms of oral or written presentation or in terms of managing a group to accomplish certain tasks. Students will receive feedback about their managerial style and will be asked to experiment toward increasingly responsible and effective modes of management. The core prepares students, not only to think effectively, but to act effectively under conditions of complexity, uncertainty, and interruptions.

After completing the core courses, students take two capstone courses in policy and environmental analysis during the second half of their program, along with six elective courses. Of the six electives, a maximum of four can be taken in a concentration area. Concentrations are offered in the following areas: strategic management, environment and policy, accounting, computer science, marketing management, financial management, and organizational studies. The concentrations may include approved courses from other areas of the M.B.A. program as well as approved courses offered by other colleges and schools of the university.

A full-time option is a two-year program. Core courses meet during the day; electives are offered in the late afternoon and evening. The part-time program is generally completed in three and one half to four years. Part-time students typically take courses two evenings a week and often take a course during the summer session. Full-time applicants are accepted in the spring for September classes. Part-time applicants are accepted both during the spring for September and the fall for January classes.

The program is designed for people with broad liberal arts backgrounds; engineering, mathematical and scientific training; education, nursing, and business undergraduate degrees. It is also designed to be of interest to students who already hold relevant master's degrees in fields other than management or business administration.

Other degrees offered include a Master of Science in finance, joint J.D.-M.B.A. and M.S.W., M.B.A.-Ph.D. in sociology, and an Advanced Certificate in Management.

ADMISSION

Admission to the graduate programs is open to all qualified men and women who hold bachelor's degrees from accredited colleges and universities. No specific undergraduate major or series of courses is required for entrance, but it is strongly recommended that students complete some mathematics, computer science, and economics courses in undergraduate school. The admission decision is based on a combination of factors rather than on any one factor. Consideration is given to academic record; recommendations; scores on the Graduate Management Admission Test (GMAT); potential for leadership in business as evidenced by part-time or full-time work experience, military service, or community or extracurricular activities; and statements on the application form concerning the reason for pursuing a course of study in business.

EXPENSES

Application fee	$ 30
Tuition, per credit hour	288
Books and supplies, per course	50

FINANCIAL ASSISTANCE

Boston College administers the full range of federal and state financial aid programs (Guaranteed Student Loans, National Direct Student Loans, Work-Study, Massachusetts Graduate Grants, etc.). Students should make application by April 22 to the University Financial Aid Office. A limited number of graduate and research assistantships, which carry tuition remission, are also available.

PLACEMENT

The Career Services Office of the Graduate School provides individual career counseling, alumni contacts, job search skills workshops, research capabilities on potential employers, and liaison to other career services throughout the university. It also attempts to be the main source of information about placement activities on campus. The majority of on-campus interviews are handled through the university's main Career Center, but job openings are received in the GSOM Career Services Office. Students are encouraged to keep a current copy of their resume on file for potential matching with such job postings. The Career Services Office also attempts to increase employer awareness of the M.B.A. program and its unique approach to graduate management training.

CORRESPONDENCE

For further information, please write or call

Director of Admissions
Graduate School of Management
Boston College
Chestnut Hill, Massachusetts 02167
Telephone: 617-552-3920

The School of Management at Boston University, located in metropolitan Boston along the Charles River, is one of the country's oldest management educators. Founded in 1915, the school offers Master of Business Administration (M.B.A.) programs in general management, health care management, and public management; a Master of Science in Management Information Systems (M.S./M.I.S.) program, and a Doctor of Business Administration (D.B.A.) program. The school emphasizes a strong general management foundation as the key to long-term growth. The 106 faculty members integrate a blend of proven teaching techniques to help students develop their highest potential.

PROGRAMS OF STUDY
The first half of the M.B.A. program requires rigorous core courses in accounting, organizational behavior, marketing, finance, operations management, quantitative methods, economics, and information systems. The second half includes a management policy course and electives.

The public management option stresses the skills required for managing government agencies and nonprofit institutions. The health care management option focuses on health service delivery and is accredited by the Accrediting Commission on Education for Health Services Administration. A specialization in health financial management is also available. Both the public and health care management options are based on the core M.B.A. curriculum. The School of Management offers September and January 14-week semesters and 2 seven-week summer sessions. The full 16-course M.B.A. degree program can be completed in two years of full-time (four courses), or four years of part-time (one or two courses) study. Summer study can speed this process. A thesis is not required.

The program features flexible transfer between full- and part-time study. Candidates with appropriate course work may qualify for advanced standing by waiver examination. Candidates who have completed relevant graduate course work may apply for transfer of credit.

Formal dual degree programs are offered with the College of Engineering in manufacturing engineering, the Graduate School of Arts and Sciences in economics, the School of Public Communication in broadcast administration, and the School of Law. The M.B.A. with concentration in health care management combined with the J.D. is offered with the Center for Law and Health Sciences.

The M.S./M.I.S. program teaches both organizational and technical information systems skills in a one-year, three-semester format. Designed for students with a degree in management (or its equivalent), the M.S./M.I.S. program includes eight technical and four applications courses, plus a two-semester required field experience. Purchase of a professional-grade personal computer is required for this program. Courses ensure a common understanding of management problems, an ability to integrate computerized information systems with managerial needs, as well as a sound practical and theoretical understanding of management information systems.

ADMISSION
Admission to the M.B.A. program is granted on a rolling basis in September and January; to the M.S./M.I.S. and doctoral programs, only in September. An applicant must have earned a bachelor's degree from a fully accredited college or university and must evidence strong academic ability and the potential to succeed in a managerial role as demonstrated by management-related work or extracurricular experience. No specific undergraduate majors are required except for the M.S./M.I.S. program, which requires an undergraduate background in management. The Graduate Management Admission Test (GMAT) is required.

Current M.B.A. students average 27 years of age, and the class is evenly divided between males and females. Three quarters of the student body have undergraduate degrees in liberal arts, and the rest in business/management, engineering, or other fields. Mean undergraduate grade-point average and GMAT score are 3.2 and 85th percentile, respectively. About one quarter of the student body hold previously earned graduate degrees. Admission deadline for September is May 1 for full-time students, July 15 for part-time. Deadline for January is December 1. International applicants should contact the School of Management for admissions and deadline information.

EXPENSES
During 1984-85, tuition and fees were $1,264 per course. Books and supplies for a full-time student cost about $600. Limited on-campus housing facilities are available through the Boston University Housing Office; numerous apartments are available off campus.

FINANCIAL ASSISTANCE
Financial aid deadline is March 15 for September admission. Students who are U.S. citizens or permanent residents may apply for financial aid. Awards based on need and merit are in the form of scholarship and/or work-study. Applicants requesting financial aid must file a form with the Graduate and Professional School Financial Aid Service (GAPSFAS). Students are urged to investigate outside loan opportunities. The faculty select a limited number of entering full-time students to serve as research assistants.

PLACEMENT
The school's Career Planning and Placement Office provides a full range of services for M.B.A. candidates and alumni. The office is visited by more than 200 companies and nonprofit organizations annually.

CORRESPONDENCE
For further information or to request an application for admission, please write or call
Graduate Management
   Admissions Office
Boston University School of
   Management
685 Commonwealth Avenue, Room 133
Boston, Massachusetts 02215
Telephone: 617-353-2670
Health Care Management,
   Telephone: 617-353-2730
Public Management,
   Telephone: 617-353-2312
Doctoral Program,
   Telephone: 617-353-2670
Master of Science in Management
   Information Systems,
   Telephone: 617-353-3522

Metropolitan College
BOSTON UNIVERSITY –
BEN GURION UNIVERSITY OF THE NEGEV
BEER SHEVA AND TEL AVIV, ISRAEL

Boston University and Ben Gurion University of the Negev began their joint graduate management program for the Master of Science in Management (M.S.M.) degree in September 1985. The program brings students and faculty from Israel, the United States, and around the world to the Ben Gurion University campus in Beer Sheva and Tel Aviv for an intensive 12-month program of graduate studies in management.

Boston University has offered its graduate management program abroad since 1972. The program at Ben Gurion University brings the same experience and international orientation to graduate management studies. Students may live on campus, participate in all university activities and facilities, and receive a joint diploma upon successful completion of the program.

The M.S.M. program operates on a trimester basis, with three equal terms of 14 weeks each. Students living outside Israel who participate in the program normally pursue a full-time program of studies requiring three trimesters (one year) of course work. Admission for full-time students is normally for September. Part-time students may begin in September or January. Classes meet in the late afternoon. The language of instruction is English. The faculty include Boston University professors in residence and Ben Gurion University professors.

PROGRAM OF STUDY
The Master of Science in Management (M.S.M.) degree program emphasizes management in general rather than concentration in any one functional area. The program consists of 12 courses, plus a mathematics requirement. The required courses emphasize the basic managerial tools and disciplines of computers, quantitative methods, economics, behavioral science, and accounting. The program stresses the application of these tools and disciplines within the major management functions of finance, marketing, and operations management and provides exposure to the development of management policy and strategy and to the management of international business.

Candidates for the M.S.M. degree must complete the following 12 courses: financial and managerial accounting, financial management, the economic environment, economic decision analysis, quantitative methods, operations management, marketing management, human behavior in organizations, management policy, computers for management, international business, and one elective course. Students must also satisfy a mathematics requirement.

ADMISSION
The university grants admission for full-time study only in September. Part-time students may normally begin study in September or January. Applicants for degree candidacy must hold a bachelor's degree or equivalent. Occasional exception to this requirement is made for persons with substantive academic preparation and exceptional work experience. No particular field of undergraduate study is required. Applicants must submit official scores of the Graduate Management Admission Test (GMAT) and two letters of reference. Applicants whose native language is not English and who have not completed a major portion of their education at English-speaking institutions must also submit the results of the Test of English as a Foreign Language (TOEFL).

Students who have not been admitted to degree candidacy may apply as special students to enroll in a maximum of four courses. Special students may be in the process of preparing an application for admission to degree candidacy or may be taking courses for professional enhancement.

EXPENSES
Tuition for full-time students was $2,200 per semester in 1985-86. Living expenses are generally low in Israel. An application fee of $50 must accompany the application for admission. Students may live either in university dormitories where the semester charge is about $500, or in neighboring Beer Sheva or Tel Aviv.

Tuition and fees are payable at time of registration in Beer Sheva.

FINANCIAL ASSISTANCE
Partial scholarship assistance may be available to degree candidates based on financial need and academic promise.

CORRESPONDENCE
Further information and application forms are available from
  Director
  Overseas Graduate Management
    Program
  Boston University Metropolitan College
  755 Commonwealth Avenue
  Boston, Massachusetts 02215
  Telephone: 617-353-2987
    or
  Director
  Boston University Joint Programs
  Ben Gurion University of the Negev
  P.O. Box 653
  Beer Sheva, Israel

Since 1972 Boston University has offered its graduate management degree program in Brussels. In 1980, the Vrije Universiteit Brussel (VUB) and Boston University inaugurated a joint program for the Master of Science in Management (M.S.M.) degree. In 1985, the two universities began a second program for the Master of Science in Computer Information Systems (M.S. in C.I.S.). This cooperative effort marks the first such joint graduate programs in Europe. Students utilize VUB campus facilities and benefit from the academic and administrative resources of Boston University.

The programs emphasize the international dimensions of management. Student internships with multinational corporations lend a pragmatic, work-study approach. The city of Brussels with its international organizations and multinational firms provides a unique setting for the program. More than 1,000 students have studied in the Brussels programs, and nearly 400 have earned their master's degree.

The university operates on a semester plan with an added summer session. Students may enter in September, January, and May and pursue the program either part time or full time. The entire program may be completed in one year of full-time study or two years of part-time study. Classes meet during the evening. The language of instruction is English.

The Brussels programs stress an international perspective, a practical work-study approach, and rigorous and pragmatic courses. A faculty with international management experience, students from many nations, and a location in Brussels enhances the international experience. The practical work-study approach includes evening classes and internships in a multinational corporation or international organization. The rigorous, pragmatic courses stress seminars, a case-study approach, and knowledge and skills applicable on the job.

PROGRAMS OF STUDY

The Master of Science in Management (M.S.M.) degree program emphasizes management in general rather than concentration in any one functional area. The program consists of 12 courses and a requirement in mathematics. The required courses emphasize the basic managerial tools and disciplines of quantitative methods, economics, behavioral science, and accounting. The program stresses the application of these tools and disciplines

within the major management functions of finance, marketing, and operations management and provides exposure to the development of management policy and strategy and to international business.

The Master of Science in Computer Information Systems (M.S. in C.I.S.) degree program trains managers to work with computer-based management and decision support systems. The program requires completion of 10 four-credit courses and satisfaction of four prerequisites.

Master of Science in Management (M.S.M.) degree candidates may earn the Certificate in Computer Information Systems concurrently by taking four designated C.I.S. courses beyond the M.S.M. degree requirements.

ADMISSION

Admission to the M.S.M. and M.S. in C.I.S. programs is granted in September, January, and May. Applicants for degree candidacy must hold a university diploma or its equivalent. Occasional exception to this requirement is made for persons with substantive academic preparation and exceptional work experience. No particular undergraduate study is required for admission. Scores obtained on the Graduate Management Admission Test (GMAT) and three letters of reference are required of all applicants. The results of the Test of English as a Foreign Language (TOEFL) are required of applicants whose native language is not English and who have not received a major portion of their education at institutions where English is the language of instruction.

Following a personal interview, an individual may enroll as a special student for a maximum of four courses. A special student is generally one who is either taking courses solely for professional enhancement or is in the process of preparing an application for admission to degree candidacy.

EXPENSES

Tuition is assessed on a per course basis and is payable in Belgian Francs (BF); thus it is based on current exchange rates at the time or registration. In 1985 the tuition rate for each course was 26,500 Belgian Francs or approximately $470. The application fee is 2,000 Belgian Francs, and the registration fee each semester is 1,000 Belgian Francs. Students

taking 12 credits or more in a semester are assessed a full-time student fee of 15,000 Belgian Francs per semester.

Tuition and fees are to be paid in full at time of registration for courses. The Trustees of Boston University reserve the right to change tuition charges and fees.

The university does not provide housing for students but is able to advise students seeking accommodations. There is generally an ample supply of apartments in Brussels.

FINANCIAL ASSISTANCE

Tuition scholarships will be awarded within funding limitations on the basis of academic merit and financial need. Application information is available from the administrative office listed below. The internship program provides an additional source of assistance.

CORRESPONDENCE

For further information, write or call
  Boston University Brussels
  17A Avenue de la Toison d'Or, Bte 69
  1060 Brussels, Belgium
  Telephone: 02-511-18-06
      or
  Director, Graduate Management
    Program
  Boston University, Metropolitan
    College
  755 Commonwealth Avenue—
    Room 202
  Boston, Massachusetts 02215
  Telephone: 617-353-2987

Bowling Green State University is located in Bowling Green, Ohio, 20 miles south of Toledo, and situated on a 1,250-acre campus with over 100 buildings. Facilities available to the graduate student include a contemporary nine-story library and a well-equipped university computer center with three mainframe computers (IBM 4381, Decsystem 2060, VAX-11/780, and VAX 11/785) and terminals in the business administration building to offer the most current methods in information processing to the student. Additionally, four personal computer labs are available on campus. The College of Business Administration building also features the latest equipment for management education, including closed-circuit television, behavioral laboratories, and special lecture rooms with student response systems.

The university operates on the semester plan along with 2 five-week summer sessions. Students may enter at the beginning of any academic term. The graduate programs may be completed on a full-time or part-time basis; courses are offered in both day and evening schedules. Each student's program is individually designed.

PROGRAMS OF STUDY

The Master of Accountancy is a professional degree program designed to provide candidates with technical and theoretical education in accounting at the graduate level. The program fulfills both immediate and long-run objectives: preparation for the Certified Public Accountant examination, if desired, and studies in depth in specialized areas of accounting and related disciplines, which may be elected to prepare the student for any of the facets of the accounting profession. Graduates of an accredited school of business administration, with concentration in accounting, may complete the degree in one academic year. For graduates in other fields, the program may require up to two years, depending upon undergraduate background.

The Master of Business Administration (M.B.A.) program's broad, integrated curriculum provides the student with an understanding of the major facets of business operations. Tool courses (managerial accounting, statistics, organization behavior, and operations research) prepare candidates for management courses in the functional areas: marketing, finance, and operations. Synthesizing courses in economic policy and business policy and a business research project complete the core. Beyond the core, the student may design his or her program to abet educational and career objectives by pursuing studies in accounting, economics, finance, information systems, international business, management, marketing, operations research, statistics, and other options. For the student who is able to devote full time to the M.B.A. degree program, the amount of time required will vary from one to two calendar years, depending upon experience and training.

The executive M.B.A. seminars are a unique seminar series leading to the M.B.A. degree. They comprise a rigorous, concentrated, and centralized program resulting in the M.B.A. degree after completion of 6 two-week seminars over a three-year period. Candidates must be nominated by their employers and should hold substantial responsibility in their own organizations. Diverse educational backgrounds and career patterns are sought for this program, and a class might include corporate vice presidents and other senior executives, controllers, mid-level managers, engineers, and technical directors.

The Master of Science in applied statistics is a program to develop statistical proficiencies at both the theoretical and applied levels to prepare the candidate for service in education, government, or business, or to pursue additional graduate work in statistics at the doctoral level.

The Master of Organizational Development program provides an effective framework for research and study and is aimed directly at the skill and knowledge requirements of the professional manager to organize and maintain human resources for highest performance. The program is designed to be completed on the manager's own time and can be undertaken as a full-time or part-time course of study with weekend class offerings to aid working managers.

ADMISSION

The basic requirements for admission are a bachelor's degree from an accredited college or university, an undergraduate record that indicates an ability to complete the graduate program successfully, and satisfactory scores on the Graduate Management Admission Test (GMAT).

Foreign students must establish English proficiency and take the Test of English as a Foreign Language (TOEFL).

FINANCIAL ASSISTANCE

Both teaching and nonteaching graduate assistantships are available from the university in amounts ranging from $2,716 to $5,572 for an academic year. Most positions permit registration for approximately 12 hours of graduate work per semester and provide a waiver of instructional and nonresident fees. Formal application for an assistantship should be submitted before March 1 preceding the desired academic year of appointment.

PLACEMENT

The university maintains a large, well-staffed placement office. Businesses throughout the United States and Canada as well as governments and other institutions send interviewing representatives to the university.

CORRESPONDENCE

For further information, write or call
    Director
    Graduate Studies in Business
    Bowling Green State University
    Bowling Green, Ohio 43403
    Telephone: 419-372-2488

Bradley University was founded in 1897 by Mrs. Lydia Moss Bradley. Privately endowed, it has an enrollment of approximately 5,000 students. The College of Business Administration enrolls approximately 1,000 students. The Master of Business Administration (M.B.A.) program is approaching an enrollment of 130 students and is fully accredited.

The Bradley University campus is located in Peoria, Illinois, a city of 130,000 midway between Chicago and St. Louis. The Peoria metropolitan area is the second largest in the state with a population of more than 340,000.

Murray M. Baker Hall houses the facilities for the College of Business Administration. Computer terminals and a micro-computer laboratory are available to all students in the college. Dormitory housing is available for single students, and university apartments or university-approved apartments and rooms are available in nearby residences. The M.B.A. program is open to both full- and part-time students. Twenty-five M.B.A. degrees are conferred each year. Class sizes range from 20 to 50.

PROGRAM OF STUDY
The M.B.A. program has a strong management orientation emphasizing the role of the manager as a decision maker as well as one who deals with and accomplishes goals through people. The 36-credit-hour core program focuses on management in functional areas; integration is achieved through two policy courses.

The curriculum normally involves a minimum of two years for students who have an undergraduate degree outside business. Prerequisites may be satisfied through special pre-M.B.A. courses and undergraduate courses. Students who majored in business as undergraduates may complete the program in three semesters.

The management core consists of work in operations research, accounting, economics, management theory, finance, marketing, operations, and social and business policy. Students may elect two courses either for the purpose of some specialization or to add breadth to their background. Courses outside business may be elected with permission of the student's adviser.

Various instructional modes are used; the case method, problem analysis, group discussions, and computer simulations supplement the traditional lecture method. Most courses are offered in the evenings, although some courses are offered during the day and on weekends. Excellent computer facilities are available.

ADMISSION
Applicants must have a baccalaureate degree from an accredited institution. The admission process includes the application form, fee card, transcripts, references, Graduate Management Admission Test (GMAT) score, and Test of English as a Foreign Language (TOEFL) score (for foreign students only). The GMAT is required of all applicants. Students seeking admission should complete the application process not less than two months before the beginning of a semester.

EXPENSES
Estimated expenses are as follows:

Application fee	$ 20
Tuition, full-time, per semester	3,150
Tuition, part-time, per credit hour	172
Room, per semester	850
Meals, per semester (estimated)	850

FINANCIAL ASSISTANCE
Graduate assistantships are available. Applications must be received by March 1 or November 1 for full consideration. Assistantships range in value from tuition remission only up to tuition remission and a stipend of $3,000.

Research assistants work directly with faculty members on creative projects. Work requirements range from 10 to 20 hours per week.

Scholarships are also available for highly qualified students. Loan funds are sometimes available after a student has been at Bradley for one semester.

Applicants for assistantships are encouraged (not required) to schedule an interview with the Director of the M.B.A. program.

PLACEMENT
Graduates of the M.B.A. program receive individual attention in their career planning activity. The Placement Center has an extensive library of employer information.

Students of the program may qualify for summer co-op positions. These employment opportunities often lead to permanent positions.

CORRESPONDENCE
For additional information on the M.B.A. program offered at Bradley, please write to
 Graduate School Office
 Bradley Hall
 Room 118
 Bradley University
 Peoria, Illinois 61625

Brigham Young University, established in 1875 and sponsored by The Church of Jesus Christ of Latter-day Saints (Mormon), is a coeducational institution established for the purpose of promoting high standards of scholarship and the development of religious faith, high moral character, and responsible citizenship. Brigham Young University has a student body of 26,000 from all 50 states and 70 foreign countries. Instruction is offered in over 150 different subject areas by 15 colleges and graduate schools.

The Master of Business Administration (M.B.A.), the Master of Accountancy (M.Acc.) and the Master of Organizational Behavior (M.O.B.) programs are accredited by the American Assembly of Collegiate Schools of Business. The Institute of Public Management's Master of Public Administration (M.P.A.) program is listed by the National Association of Schools of Public Affairs and Administration (NASPAA) as meeting graduate study guidelines for the M.P.A degree. The Master of Health Administration (M.H.A.) is a new program, having begun in fall 1984.

PROGRAMS OF STUDY

The M.B.A. degree requires four semesters of full-time study. The curriculum has been designed to give the student a general management education and depth in area(s) bearing specifically on professional interests. Students who complete the program will have (1) acquired an understanding of business and management tools and principles that have significance in a changing environment, (2) developed advanced knowledge in a field of concentration, (3) achieved an understanding of the utilization of quantitative methods and behavioral sciences in the solution of business problems, (4) obtained skills in critical analysis and careful reasoning, and (5) strengthened ability to communicate effectively.

The M.P.A. degree is awarded upon completion of 64 semester hours of approved graduate credit. The M.P.A. degree is a two-year professional degree supported by studies in administrative and organization analysis, political environment of public administration, interpersonal behavior, public policy and decision making, public finance and personnel administration, and quantitative methods for decision making.

The M.Acc. degree is awarded upon completion of a three-year professional program which normally begins in the junior year of the undergraduate program and culminates at the end of the fifth year in the Graduate School of Management. Students entering the M.Acc. program with a bachelor's degree in accounting will ordinarily complete the program in less than three years. Students receive training in the areas of financial/audit, management accounting, management advisory services, and taxation.

The Master of Organizational Behavior is a two-year professional degree program designed to prepare those people who plan to pursue careers in organizational development, management training, or personnel administration—in business, education, public administration, or hospital administration. The program develops professional skills in areas such as decision making, leadership, motivation, organization design, and management of conflict and change.

The M.H.A. program is designed to prepare graduates for professional management careers in the health services industry. It is a four-semester program followed by an eight-month administrative residency.

ADMISSION

Applicants to the programs are carefully evaluated in four areas: (1) previous academic performance (minimum of 3.0 on a 4.0 scale); (2) completion of the bachelor's degree (except for students applying to the Master of Accountancy program); (3) test scores on the Graduate Management Admission Test (minimum 500); and (4) work experience, extracurricular activities, leadership potential, motivation, and maturity. Programs actively recruit good students from a large number of different undergraduate majors. Program directors should be contacted for specific requirements. International students must receive a minimum score of 550 on the Test of English as a Foreign Language (TOEFL).

Application deadlines are February 15 for financial aid applications and April 15 for international student applications (International students should contact the International Students Office for special requirements). June 15 is the university's final date for application.

In accordance with the beliefs of The Church of Jesus Christ of Latter-day Saints, all students are expected to maintain high standards of integrity and morality during their period of residence. Students are also expected to abstain from the use of alcohol, tobacco, and drugs.

EXPENSES

Estimated expenses for single students:

Nonrefundable application fee ..	$ 25
Tuition (1985-86)	2,700
Room/board (on campus).	2,300
Books and supplies	450
Personal expenses.	650

A nonmember of The Church of Jesus Christ of Latter-day Saints pays $4,050 tuition. This disparity is similar to the higher tuition that the graduate schools of state universities charge to nonresidents.

Expenses for married students will vary with family size.

FINANCIAL ASSISTANCE

The Graduate School of Management provides financial aid to qualified students through the following: GSM Scholarship Fund, private scholarship donations (to the GSM), assistantship awards, and loan assistance.

PLACEMENT

The Graduate School of Management utilizes the University Placement Center, as well as a GSM placement coordinator, to assist both students and alumni in finding suitable positions. Each year more than 400 firms and agencies interview on campus.

CORRESPONDENCE

For further information, write or call
Brigham Young University
Graduate School of Management
730 Tanner Building
Provo, Utah 84602
Telephone: 801-378-4121

Bryant College, founded in 1863, prepares men and women to take an active part in society and to progress by their own competence toward leadership positions in the world of business and public service. The Graduate School is located on Bryant's campus in suburban Smithfield in an ultramodern unistructure. The campus is only 15 minutes from Providence.

PROGRAMS OF STUDY

The graduate Master of Business Administration (M.B.A.) evening programs, which are available both full-time and part-time, on- and off-campus, provide undergraduates and mature employed persons with the advanced academic background necessary for increased responsibilities and leadership in the business world. There are 1,450 graduate students enrolled.

Candidates who fulfill the graduate foundation requirements can attain the M.B.A. degree in an extended year of full-time study or in two years of part-time study. The academic year comprises fall and spring semesters and a summer session. Students must maintain a cumulative average of B (3.0 on the 4.0 system) to maintain their status as degree candidates.

The M.B.A. with a concentration in management comprises 10 graduate advanced management courses including 4 electives, and, if needed, up to 10 graduate foundation courses.

The M.B.A. with the accounting concentration is primarily intended for accounting majors who want to prepare themselves for careers in public accounting as well as for the C.P.A. exam. The professional managerial courses will be of great value to accounting majors as preparation for private accounting. This concentration, open to nonbusiness majors, includes 12 graduate advanced courses (2 accounting courses, 6 management courses, 2 accounting electives and 2 management electives). Candidates may need undergraduate courses in accounting and taxes, as well as graduate foundation courses.

The M.B.A. with a concentration in finance consists of 42 semester hours of advanced study and, if necessary, up to 24 semester hours of graduate foundation courses. The advanced core program consists of 36 semester hours of required advanced courses and 6 semester hours of finance electives.

M.B.A. programs are offered with concentrations in computer information systems, entrepreneurship, and public management. These programs are designed to educate and train professional practitioners for executive roles in the public and private sector. These concentrations include a minimum of 36 semester hours of graduate advanced courses and, if necessary, up to 30 hours of foundation courses.

The M.B.A. health care management concentration provides students with the latest techniques and management development in this field. The Bryant approach is a professional managerial approach to health care, in distinct contrast to the social science, public health on-the-job training approach of many advanced programs in health administration. It is intended only for students who are presently employed in the broad field of health care and desire to upgrade their professional skills. The program includes 36 semester hours of advanced graduate course credit and, if necessary, up to 30 hours of graduate foundation courses.

The Graduate School of Bryant College has developed a program for a Certificate of Advanced Graduate Studies (CAGS) at the graduate level of education that is designed to meet the special needs of experienced managers in business, government, and nonprofit organizations. The CAGS program consists of a group of five related courses selected by the experienced manager to fill his or her advanced educational needs.

CAGS courses are advanced graduate courses; therefore, it is necessary for the student to satisfy any prerequisites for these courses. Candidates must be fully qualified professionally, holding a master's degree or a certification of its equivalent in business, law, or other professional field. The requirements must be completed in three years. The CAGS program is offered with concentrations in accounting, finance, health care management, management, and taxation.

The Master of Science in Taxation (M.S.T.) provides a framework of technical and professional knowledge that will assist students in developing the expertise needed to understand the difficult and complex tax structure. The program also prepares graduate students to become professional tax consultants or to staff tax

positions in private enterprise and public service. The diversified program of five required and five elective courses will give students a solid foundation on which to build their tax expertise.

Tax candidates, except holders of a J.D. degree or a C.P.A., must attain acceptable scores on the Graduate Management Admission Test (GMAT). They should also have a minimum of two years of tax experience.

ADMISSION

Admission requirements comprise a bachelor's or a graduate degree from an accredited institution, acceptable scores on the GMAT (for public management candidates, the Graduate Record Examinations (GRE) may be substituted), and an interview. The following should be sent to the Graduate Office: completed application, official transcripts of all undergraduate and graduate study, GMAT or GRE scores, and letters of recommendation (optional).

EXPENSES

Application fee, nonrefundable . . . . . $ 30
Tuition, M.B.A., per credit hour . . . 112
Tuition, M.S.T., per credit hour 125
In-residence fee 20

PLACEMENT

Active career planning and job placement services are available to all graduate students and alumni. Many corporations and government agencies visit the campus to interview students. There is no charge for these services.

CORRESPONDENCE

For further information, write or call
Dean of the Graduate School
Bryant College
Smithfield, Rhode Island 02917
Telephone: 401-232-6231

PROGRAM OF STUDY

Bucknell serves the graduate and professional education needs of business administration students through a Master of Science in Business Administration (M.S.B.A.) program. The M.S.B.A. program stresses the development and integration of knowledge, skills, and perspectives that together provide a solid foundation for managerial effectiveness.

Candidates for Bucknell's M.S.B.A. degree complete seven graduate-level courses and a master's essay, for an equivalent of eight course units. College graduates whose undergraduate work has included core courses in economics and business (see prerequisite courses, under admissions requirements, below) can complete the M.S.B.A. program in one year. The program also serves the needs of part-time students.

Each student in the program works closely with the M.S.B.A. Program Coordinator and faculty members to develop a specific course program within the following guidelines:

Areas of Concentration—Students complete at least two courses, within an approved area of concentration. Students select among areas such as finance, marketing, management information systems, and accounting.

Research Methods and Analysis—Students complete a required course in Research Methods, covering topics in research design, information and data systems design, analytical models, and statistical techniques. This course leads directly to application in the design and execution of the master's essay.

Elective Courses—Students may use two elective courses, either to increase depth in their chosen area of concentration or to explore related topics in other disciplines. The faculty may recommend certain electives in the light of prior core business education (see admissions requirements, below).

M.S.B.A. Integrative Core—All M.S.B.A. students complete a two-semester course sequence, devoted to general management analysis and problem solving. The first course in the sequence, Managerial Economics, examines the competitive structure of markets; determination of prices and output; and the eco-

nomic, social, legal, and cultural environments in which organizations operate. The second course, Strategic Management, stresses diagnosis and resolution of general management problems. This "capstone perspective" course requires integration of knowledge from concentration areas with research and analytical skills.

Model Program (Full-time students)*

Fall Semester	Spring Semester
Managerial Economics (Core)	Strategic Management (Core)
Course in Concentration	Course in Concentration
Elective Course	Elective Course
Research and Analysis (Methods)	Master's Essay

*Part-time students must complete Managerial Economics and Research Methods and Analysis within their first two semesters in the Bucknell M.S.B.A. program.

ADMISSION

Bucknell's M.S.B.A. program is a small, highly selective one, depending for its effectiveness on close working relationships between students and faculty. M.S.B.A. admission decisions will be based on evidence of academic capacity and accomplishment in general, and on specific evidence of motivation and accomplishment in prerequisite core business and economics courses.

Applicants must have a bachelor's degree from an accredited U.S. college or university, or certification of equivalent achievement from a foreign institution. Official transcript(s), verifying grade-point averages and conferral of the baccalaureate degree, and official notification of scores on the Graduate Management Admission Test (GMAT) must be filed with the Office of Graduate Studies before admission to the M.S.B.A. program can be confirmed. Applicants whose undergraduate work was not done in English must also submit scores on the Test of English as a Foreign Language (TOEFL).

Applicants with undergraduate majors in business administration, accounting, or management will normally have met prerequisite core course guidelines in economics and business. Applicants with other undergraduate majors will be accepted provided that they have completed prerequisite courses in mathematics/statistics, economics, financial/managerial accounting, and in the functional area that will be the candidate's area of concentration

before admission to the M.S.B.A. program. Students who have not also met guidelines in other functional areas or in organization and management may meet those guidelines after being admitted to the program. All candidates for admission to the M.S.B.A. program should consult with the M.S.B.A. Program Coordinator concerning prerequisites. (Bucknell offers the possibility of special graduate student status to those who are completing certain prerequisite courses.)

FINANCIAL ASSISTANCE

Full-time students admitted to the M.S.B.A. program may be eligible for stipends and partial-tuition scholarships based on obligations to assist faculty members in their teaching and research activities. Applicants interested in such assistantships should consult with the M.S.B.A. Program Coordinator.

PLACEMENT

The Bucknell University Office of Career Planning and Placement serves undergraduate and graduate students and alumni in arranging contacts and interviews with potential employers and maintaining a file of appointments and occupational literature.

CORRESPONDENCE

For further information and application materials, contact

Coordinator of Graduate Studies
Bucknell University
Lewisburg, Pennsylvania 17837

CALIFORNIA LUTHERAN UNIVERSITY

THOUSAND OAKS, CALIFORNIA

California Lutheran University is a liberal arts university located in Thousand Oaks, California. Situated in suburban Ventura County only 40 miles northwest of Los Angeles, the university draws upon the vast cultural, professional, recreational, and social opportunities of one of the nation's largest cities. Near the campus are significant industrial and research centers concentrating on technology.

PROGRAM OF STUDY

The basic purpose of the graduate program in business administration is to provide students with the education and training for careers as professional managers in the environments of business, education, government, religious organizations, and service agencies. The program is designed to provide a liberalizing influence on the art and science of management that will develop innovative and responsible leadership. It is hoped that this imaginative leadership will not only bring about the most efficient use of the resources available but also the fulfillment of its members and the society it serves.

To accomplish these objectives, all students will be involved with the common body of knowledge characteristic of all the environments of leadership, including

- an understanding of the economic, legal, political, and social strategic factors;
- an understanding of the concepts, processes, and institutions in finance, production, and distribution;
- a basic understanding of the concepts and methods of accounting, quantitative methods, and information systems;
- an understanding of organization theory, interpersonal relationships control and motivational systems, and communications;
- a study of administrative processes under conditions of uncertainty, including integrating analysis and policy determination at the management level;
- an understanding of ethical values and systems with emphasis on their use in the decision-making process.

The program is not essentially sequential or hierarchical in structure but may be entered at many points. Thus, the program will not require the cumulative addition of new courses and repetition of earlier courses each year.

Courses are offered during fall, spring, and summer semesters. Since most students are full-time professional employees, classes are scheduled for late afternoon and evening hours.

A program of 42 semester units of course work is required for the M.B.A. degree. Additional course work may be required in individual cases. Normally, required courses include quantitative methods, managerial economics, managerial accounting, organizational theory and development, behavioral sciences for management, social ethics, law for business executives, marketing theory, financial principles and policies, and computer use in management decision making.

ADMISSION

Admission to the degree program is contingent upon sound scholarship in the applicant's undergraduate program and normally successful professional experience. Application for admission to graduate studies should be submitted at least 30 days prior to the term in which the applicant wishes to begin graduate work. Official transcripts of all prior college work should be submitted. Candidates should also submit scores from the Graduate Management Admission Test (GMAT) and arrange for an interview with the director of the program. A foundation program for those who do not have academic or work experience in economics, business administration, or management should be completed before the student enters the M.B.A. program. If all the requirements for admission to the M.B.A. graduate program are met, the applicant will be granted regular graduate standing. If all the criteria are not met, applicants may under certain circumstances enroll in graduate courses.

International students whose native language is not English are required to submit scores of the Test of English as a Foreign Language (TOEFL). The minimum score accepted is 550.

EXPENSES

Tuition for 1985-86 was $155 per semester credit for all students. Room and board on campus for graduate students is not available. The university will assist students in locating housing in the community.

PLACEMENT

The Career Planning and Placement Center is available to assist students in realizing their career objectives and finding employment.

CORRESPONDENCE

For further information on graduate studies at California Lutheran University, please write

Director
Graduate Program in Business
  Administration
California Lutheran University
Thousand Oaks, California 91360

Cal Poly's methods of education and dedication to occupationally centered curricula have created for the university a distinctive role in higher education. Its statewide and national reputation has made it one of the most popular campuses in California. Cal Poly is particularly noted for its special emphasis on and excellence in such applied fields as agriculture, architecture, business, engineering, and science and mathematics.

The Cal Poly campus consists of over 5,000 acres adjacent to San Luis Obispo, a community of 35,000 located on U.S. Highway 101, midway between San Francisco and Los Angeles, and 12 miles from the beaches and marine facilities of California's central coast.

PROGRAM OF STUDY

The Cal Poly Master of Business Administration (M.B.A.) program prepares students for careers in all phases of management. The program is broad in nature, requiring advanced study and research in most business disciplines. The program is intended for full-time students from a variety of undergraduate backgrounds. It features close faculty-student relationships and limited class sizes. The primary goals of the program can be described as follows:

* to provide an integrated understanding of the principles of the various business disciplines (Cal Poly's approach to M.B.A. education is purposely aimed at fostering this integrated understanding);
* to develop an expertise in assembling and analyzing relevant facts as a basis for significant business decisions (The student should obtain analytical, planning, and forecasting skills to provide a basis for effective managerial decisions); and
* to promote the ability to work with other people through an understanding of human values, motivations, and organizational structures (The student should understand the essential elements of interpersonal relations, individual and group behavior, and the design of effective organizations).

The purpose of the first year of the two-year program is to build a broad understanding of the concepts and principles of business administration. The first-year courses comprise the material that is commonly referred to as the business core or common body of knowledge. Exceptionally well-qualified students with undergraduate business administration degrees may be exempt from the first year of the M.B.A. program. For other students, the first-year courses provide the framework for the second-year curriculum.

During the program's second year, there are three areas of emphasis to the course work: (1) the development of analytical, planning, and forecasting skills; (2) the development of skills to enhance interpersonal and organizational effectiveness; and (3) electives.

Following completion of the program, the Cal Poly M.B.A. will have acquired abilities in two somewhat diverse areas: planning skills and interpersonal and organizational skills. Very few managers excel in both areas. There is probably a natural tendency for different types of people to be proficient in only one of these areas. Those who are able to master two such diverse skills have a high probability of becoming top managers. The training of the Cal Poly M.B.A. will provide an exceptional foundation for managerial growth.

ADMISSION

The Admissions Committee selects men and women whose intellectual abilities and personal characteristics are suited for careers in management. The primary factors considered in the admission process are the applicant's (1) undergraduate academic record, (2) achievement on the Graduate Management Admission Test (GMAT), and (3) management potential as evidenced by previous work experience, community or college extracurricular activities, and evaluations of professors and/or supervisors. No specific undergraduate majors are preferred for admission to the program; however, some mathematical background is desirable. A policy of rolling admissions is followed, with the earliest decisions being made in January. Applications should be submitted by April 15. Applications after this date may be accommodated on a space-available basis.

EXPENSES

Fees of about $700 per year must be paid by students who are residents of the state of California. For nonresident students, tuition is also charged, raising the total to about $4,700 per year. (Fees are subject to change.) Books and supplies are additional expenses. Most students live off campus. There are, however, residence halls on campus offering room and board for $3,000 per academic year.

FINANCIAL ASSISTANCE

The principal sources of financial assistance are federally funded loan programs. A large percent of students in the M.B.A. program finance part of their education in this manner. Funds are available so that a limited number of well-qualified students may supplement their financial resources by assisting faculty members with their research work. In addition, graduate assistantships are available to a few second-year M.B.A. students.

PLACEMENT

A centralized placement service is available to all students and alumni of the university providing contact with representatives of large numbers of national and regional companies. The Placement Office assists students in obtaining the most suitable employment consistent with preparation and experience.

CORRESPONDENCE

For further information or to request an application, please write or call
M.B.A. Director
School of Business
California Polytechnic State University
San Luis Obispo, California 93407
Telephone: 805-546-2637

California State College, Bakersfield, was opened in 1970 as the nineteenth campus of the California State Universities and Colleges. The college offers a broad program of studies at the undergraduate level in the humanities, behavioral and natural sciences, and selected professional areas, and at the graduate level in business, public administration, English, history, behavioral science, and education. Enrollment in the fall of 1985 was approximately 4,000 students; about 300 students were seeking graduate degrees in the School of Business and Public Administration.

The college is located at the southern end of the San Joaquin Valley in an area that benefits from a temperate climate. The college campus is situated in the southwest sector of Bakersfield, a community of about 200,000 population. The college's location is approximately 110 miles from Los Angeles adjacent to the California coastal region and Yosemite and Sequoia National Parks.

The college operates on a three-course, three-term plan and permits a normal student load of three courses of five quarter units each. Most of the graduate courses in the School of Business and Public Administration are scheduled during the evening hours.

PROGRAMS OF STUDY
The School of Business and Public Administration offers three types of master's degrees: a Master of Business Administration (M.B.A.), Master of Public Administration (M.P.A.), and Master of Science (M.S.) in administration and health care management. Each of these three degrees is designed to provide a broad foundation of knowledge for individuals who wish to obtain professional assignments in business, government, or the health care field.

Each of these three master's degrees requires one or two years (45 to 100 quarter units) of college study beyond the baccalaureate degree depending upon a student's prior formal education. For the M.B.A., M.P.A., and M.S. degrees, the student must complete (or have completed) an integrated foundation set of core courses. For the M.B.A. program only, recent completion of a baccalaureate program in business administration at a school that is a member of the American Assembly of Collegiate Schools of Business (AACSB) will often suffice. The foundation core includes courses in statistics, economics, management, budgeting, and administrative processes in government or health care management. In the second year of the graduate component of the program, M.B.A. students must complete six required courses and three elective courses covering advanced facets of the management of modern business entities. M.P.A. and M.S. health care management students take six required courses and three electives to complete their degree programs, as well as advanced courses oriented toward public sector management and its problems. A total of 45 quarter units of graduate course work beyond the foundation requirements is prescribed for each of the M.B.A., M.P.A., and M.S. degree options. A formal thesis is not required; all graduate courses require the student to develop specific research and communication competencies.

The graduate option in business administration conforms to the standards established by the AACSB, and the program is accredited by that organization. The option in public administration permits specialization in the areas of political science and the behavioral sciences and seeks to reinforce the knowledge of social forces essential to the public administrator.

ADMISSION
The minimum requirement for admission is a baccalaureate degree from an accredited four-year institution of higher learning with (1) a satisfactory grade-point average (based upon a four-point scale) that conforms to at least one of the following: (a) a grade-point average of 2.50 in all undergraduate course work or (b) a grade-point average of 2.75 in all upper-division course work; and (2) a satisfactory score on the Graduate Management Admission Test (GMAT) for those selecting the business administration option or the Graduate Record Examinations (GRE) for those selecting the public administration or health care management option. An overall grade-point average of 3.0 in all graduate courses applied toward the degree is required. Applications for admission to the college for the fall quarter may be submitted to the Admissions Office through the month of September, for the winter quarter through the month of December, and for the spring quarter through the month of March.

EXPENSES
Currently, California residents are charged $111 for 0-6.0 units or $191 for 6.1 or more units per quarter in fees for materials, services, and student activities. In addition, students who do not qualify as California residents pay an additional $84 per unit, per quarter. Fees are subject to change without prior notice.

PLACEMENT
Limited funds are available for loans to needy and deserving students. Some graduate assistantships are also available each quarter. Further information about financial assistance can be obtained from the Financial Aids Office of the college.

CORRESPONDENCE
For further information, write to
Graduate Program Coordinator
School of Business and Public
Administration
California State College, Bakersfield
9001 Stockdale Highway
Bakersfield, California 93311-1099

California State Polytechnic University, Pomona, is located in a rural setting on 1,300 acres of land, surrounded by rolling hills. One of the largest educational facilities in the state college system, the campus represents a blending of tile-roofed Spanish ranch buildings and modern classroom buildings. The campus is less than an hour's drive from metropolitan Los Angeles.

Cal Poly is a coeducational state institution with an enrollment of over 17,000 students. Seven departments comprise the School of Business Administration: accounting; operations management; management and human resources; computer information systems; finance, real estate, and law; marketing management; and hotel and restaurant management. Cal Poly is accredited by the Western Association of Schools and Colleges.

PROGRAMS OF STUDY
The Master of Business Administration (M.B.A.) program provides professional education for managerial positions in business, industry, and government. The degree program also enables those students already in responsible positions to update their skills for advancement in the organization. The M.B.A. curriculum is comprehensive, and each course is planned to interrelate all functional areas of business. The specific objectives are as follows:
- to develop a better understanding of the manager's responsibilities within the firm and society,
- to assist the student in developing an analytical approach to decision making and planning,
- to improve skills in interpersonal relations and in speaking and writing effectively and professionally, and
- to develop a sound theoretical understanding of organizational behavior and a management perspective for problem solving.

A minimum of 48 units is required for the M.B.A. degree. A student whose undergraduate degree is not in business will be expected to complete additional prerequisites in the first year of the program. The degree program will vary in length depending upon the academic background of the student. The average candidate who is employed and attending Cal Poly part time can complete the program in six quarters, enrolling in two classes each quarter. The full-time student may complete the M.B.A. in one year. All core courses are offered in the evening with the majority of classes meeting one night a week. A thesis or project is required.

A career M.B.A. program is available that permits specializations in accounting, finance, marketing, human resources, operations management, and other areas.

Graduate students are also offered the Master of Science in Business Administration (M.S.B.A.) degree program in EDP auditing, which requires a minimum of 45 quarter units.

The M.S.B.A. with the EDP auditing option is designed for students who wish to pursue a career in this area. The program is for business decision makers, information systems technical specialists and managers, and professionals in accounting and EDP auditing. The objectives of the program are to develop an understanding of the role and scope of EDP auditing and its relationship to an organization, to develop the ability to plan and conduct audits and to report the findings, and to prepare for careers in the EDP auditing profession. A strong academic background in accounting and information systems is necessary. A thesis or project is required.

ADMISSION
The M.B.A. and the M.S.B.A. programs are open to students who hold a bachelor's degree from an accredited college or university.

Students are admitted each quarter. Selection will be on the basis of evidence of ability to perform at a high academic level. The following criteria are considered: the undergraduate grade-point average, scores on the Graduate Management Admission Test (GMAT), work experience, letters of recomendation, and the applicant's personal statement or interview. A minimum GMAT score of 450 is required. A Test of English as a Foreign Language (TOEFL) score of 580 is required for foreign students.

An applicant who wishes to register for graduate study must file application forms and be accepted by the office of Admissions and Records. In addition, two sets of official transcripts must be received by the college no later than four weeks preceding the first day of scheduled classes.

EXPENSES
Fees vary with the number of units carried and are subject to change by the Board of Trustees. Resident students normally pay approximately $150-$250 per quarter. Nonresident students will pay an additional $84 per quarter unit for up to 15 units. Housing is not available on campus for graduate students.

FINANCIAL ASSISTANCE
Students are eligible for various grants and loans administered by the college. For further information, contact the Financial Aids Office.

PLACEMENT
Many representatives from business, industry, and government recruit annually through the Career Planning and Placement Office.

CORRESPONDENCE
For further information, write
Dr. Madeline Currie
Director of Graduate Programs
School of Business Administration
California State Polytechnic University, Pomona
Pomona, California 91768

California State University, Chico, founded in 1887, is the second oldest state university in California. Located in the middle of the North Sacramento Valley, the town of Chico is noted for its beauty. Chico Creek, a cool mountain stream, passes through the 2,400-acre municipal park occupying the center of town. The university campus is built around this park and presents one of the most beautiful campus settings on the Pacific Coast. In addition, the capital of California, Sacramento, and the financial center of the West Coast, San Francisco, are both readily available to students.

Approximately 14,000 students are enrolled in the various programs of the university, including a total of 1,900 graduate students. The School of Business has approximately 2,600 majors, of whom 200 are Master of Business Administration (M.B.A.) or Master of Science (M.S.) students.

PROGRAMS OF STUDY
The School of Business offers the M.B.A. degree, an M.B.A. with an emphasis in accounting, and an M.S. degree in accountancy at the graduate level. These degree programs have the following objectives:
• to provide an opportunity for well-qualified students from any discipline to develop a greater understanding of the process of administration in the role of the business manager in society,
• to provide a program based on a solid foundation of knowledge in both quantitative methods and the behavioral sciences and a broad program aimed at competence for general administration and management,
• to provide an underlying structure that will enable the professional business manager to develop his or her own personal frame of reference by which to interpret management in a changing environment.

The M.B.A. program requires from one to two years of graduate study beyond the baccalaureate degree. The exact amount of work, 30 to 60 semester units, will depend upon the student's background. The first-year courses are designed to provide the nonbusiness graduate with an understanding of the basic functions of management. The second year of study is designed to provide an in-depth investigation of business while providing sufficient flexibility so that students may better meet their own professional objectives.

The objective of the M.S. degree in accountancy is to prepare students for careers as professional accountants. The M.S. degree offers the opportunity for greater depth in the field of accounting than the M.B.A. through its specialized course offerings.

It is the policy of the School of Business to maintain small classes at the graduate level. By maintaining small class size, the learning relationship between the professor and the student is amplified to the benefit of both parties.

A final research project is required of all M.B.A. students. This project is not of the magnitude of a thesis; however, it does require an original investigation in a particular business specialization.

ADMISSION
The M.B.A. program is open to qualified students who hold a bachelor's degree in any field from an accredited four-year college or university. Admission to the M.B.A. program is based upon the student's ability to perform at a satisfactory level. For most students this ability will be demonstrated by grade-point average and scores on the Graduate Management Admission Test (GMAT). The minimal requirements for admission to the program are as follows:
• grade-point average for the last 30 hours of work.................... 3.00
• grade-point average for the last 60 hours of work.................... 2.75
• Graduate Management Admission Test total score.................... 500

A student who presents ample justification in relation to a deficiency in either the grade-point average or GMAT scores may satisfy admission requirements by achieving a satisfactory value on an admission index. This admission index incorporates the verbal and quantitative scores on the GMAT, the undergraduate grade-point average for the last 60 units, and an index of the undergraduate institution's relative performance on the GMAT. Additionally, foreign applicants must achieve a score of 550 on the Test of English as a Foreign Language (TOEFL).

Application for admission to both the M.B.A. and M.S. programs should be submitted to the Graduate School office on the Chico campus. Fall semester applications should be submitted no later than March 1 of the previous year, and spring semester applications should be submitted no later than October 15 of the previous year.

EXPENSES
California residents have a charge of $344.50 for 15 or more units and $224.50 for 6 or fewer units per semester for materials and services, student activities, and university union. In addition, students who do not qualify as California residents pay $126 per unit plus the same flat rate as California residents. Foreign students pay the same amount as nonresidents, that is, $344.50 or $224.50 plus $126 per unit.

FINANCIAL ASSISTANCE
Limited funds are available for loans to needy or deserving students through the Student Aids Office. In addition, a substantial number of graduate assistantships are available each semester. Application forms are available from the School of Business.

PLACEMENT
Some 125 national and regional firms send recruiters to California State University, Chico, to interview graduate students who are completing their work. The University Placement Office is available to aid both the student and the interviewing firm.

CORRESPONDENCE
For additional information, please write
    Graduate Coordinator
    School of Business
    California State University, Chico
    Chico, California 95929

California State University, Dominguez Hills, is one of the 19 campuses in the California State Universities and Colleges system. The university is divided into five schools and has a current enrollment of approximately 7,700 full-time equivalent students.

The Master of Business Administration (M.B.A.) program started in the spring quarter of 1972. Enrollment in the fall term 1985 was approximately 300 students. The M.B.A. program is housed in the School of Management. Classes are scheduled in the evening and on Saturday. While most students attend part time, the program is designed to accommodate the full-time student as well.

PROGRAMS OF STUDY
The Master of Business Administration program is designed to meet the professional needs of two groups: recent college graduates who plan careers in business and college graduates already employed who desire to extend their business understanding and potential. The focus of the program is on the management function; all parts of the program relate to decision making within the corporate enterprise. The program is divided into two phases, and the course of study leading to the M.B.A. involves the successful completion of between 30 and 54 semester units of course work with a grade-point average of 3.0 (B) or better. Students with a baccalaureate in business administration will be admitted automatically to phase II. All other students will have their records evaluated, and credit will be granted for equivalent phase I course work satisfactorily completed at other colleges and universities. The program consists of the following courses:

General M.B.A.
Phase One (24 semester units)
ACC 530 Principles of Accounting . . . . . . (3)
BUS 505 Social and Legal
    Environment of Business. . . . (3)
CIS 571 Introduction to Information
    Systems . . . . (3)
ECO 501 General Economic Theory . . . . (3)
FIN 561 Financial Management . . . . (3)
MGT 510 Management Theory . . . . (3)
MKT 551 Marketing Systems. . . . . (3)
QMS 521 Quantitative Methods I . . . . (3)

Phase II (30 semester units)
ACC 531 Managerial Accounting. . . . . . . (3)
BUS 590 Seminar in Business Policy . . . . (3)
FIN 563 Financial Decision Analysis . . . (3)
FIN 583 Managerial Economics . . . . (3)
FIN 585 Seminar in Multinational
    Business. . . . . (3)

MGT 513 Foundations of Human
    Behavior in Organizations . . (3)
MKT 552 Marketing Management . . . . . . (3)
QMS 523 Quantitative Methods II . . . . . . (3)
QMS 522 Production Operations . . . . (3)
BUS 595 Graduate Seminar:
    Special Topics . . . . (3)
BUS 594 Independent Study
    in Business. . . . . (3)

M.B.A. with Management Information Systems concentration *(30 semester units)*
Phase I (same as above)

Phase II (Required: 21 semester units)
ACC 531 Managerial Accounting. . . . . . . (3)
BUS 590 Seminar in Business Policy . . . . (3)
FIN 563 Financial Decision Analysis . . . (3)
FIN 585 Seminar in Multinational
    Business. . . . . (3)
MGT 513 Foundations of Human
    Behavior in Organizations . . (3)
MKT 552 Marketing Management . . . . . . (3)
QMS 522 Production Operations . . . . (3)

plus three Computer Information Systems (CIS) courses (9 semester units) to be selected from the following:
CIS 572 Legal Aspects of Computer
    Systems . . . . (3)
CIS 573 Business Microcomputer
    Software . . . . (3)
CIS 575 Management Information
    Systems and Data Base
    Concepts . . . . (3)
CIS 576 Decision Support Systems
    and Modeling . . . . (3)
CIS 577 Office Automation . . . . (3)
CIS 578 EDP Audit, Control and
    Security . . . . (3)
CIS 579 Information Systems Policy and
    Resource Management . . . . . (3)
CIS 595 Advanced Topics for
    Management Systems . . . . . . (3)

ADMISSION
Eligibility is determined by the American Assembly of Collegiate Schools of Business (AACSB) formula based on a combination of the undergraduate grade-point average (last two-year minimum of 2.75) used in conjunction with the Graduate Management Admission Test (GMAT) score (minimum 450) for a total of 1,000 (two-year grade-point average) points.

EXPENSES
As of the fall semester 1986, fees for full-time students will be $350 per term for residents of California and $126 per unit for nonresidents. Fees are subject to change without prior notice by the Board of Trustees.

The university provides housing on campus. The Office of Student Housing provides information and applications for on-campus living facilities for students.

FINANCIAL ASSISTANCE
Limited financial assistance is available. Students may apply to the Office of Financial Aid for work-study jobs, loans, and scholarships.

PLACEMENT
The university offers a placement service to assist students seeking jobs in the fields of business, industry, government, and teaching. In addition, the Placement Office offers vocational counseling and a career planning service.

CORRESPONDENCE
Information concerning the Master of Business Administration program may be obtained from
    M.B.A. Coordinator
    School of Management
    California State University,
      Dominguez Hills
    Carson, California 90747

California State University, Fullerton, is one of 19 institutions in the publicly supported California State Universities and Colleges system. The Fullerton campus was established in 1957, and the School of Business Administration and Economics offered its first formal classes in 1959. The campus is strategically located on the periphery of Los Angeles, one of the largest metropolitan areas in the nation. The suburban location of California State University, Fullerton, is within easy driving distance of beaches, mountains, deserts, and the cultural centers of the Los Angeles metropolitan area.

The university has an enrollment of about 23,000 students. Graduate students as a group comprise about 20 percent of the student body. The School of Business Administration and Economics enrolls about 500 graduate students, the majority of whom are part-time students pursuing the Master of Business Administration (M.B.A.) degree. The school also offers master's degrees in economics, management science, and taxation.

The university's computer center, the school's minicomputers and many on-line terminals provide ample computing power to satisfy most student and faculty research needs. The university system's distributed computing network and the school's arrangements with private industry offer computing capability for more demanding projects. The university library, the libraries of the surrounding universities, and the statewide, interlibrary loan system are all available for graduate research.

PROGRAMS OF STUDY
The School of Business Administration and Economics offers two plans for the M.B.A. degree. The M.B.A./generalist plan is designed for students with little or no course work in business administration. The curriculum surveys the entire field of business administration, preparing students for general management responsibilities. The plan is structured, keeping students together for most of their classes, and must be completed within three years. Courses may not be waived, although limited substitution of more advanced courses is allowed. This format requires a substantial and sustained commitment from students over the three-year period.

The M.B.A./specialist plan is designed for students with recent course work (or an undergraduate degree) in business administration, for those who wish to include a specialized area of concentration in their curriculum, and/or for those unable to follow the structure of the M.B.A./generalist plan. Some courses may be waived on the basis of equivalent undergraduate course work. The program is not structured, and five years are allowed for completion. The areas of concentration are accounting, business economics, finance, international business, management, management science, and marketing.

The M.B.A. program is scheduled especially for students who are employed full time. Courses are offered during the late afternoon and evening. Most students enroll on a part-time basis, taking two courses (six or seven units) per semester.

ADMISSION
Admission to the M.B.A. program requires the following:
- a bachelor's degree from an accredited institution,
- satisfactory combination of grade-point average (GPA) and score on the Graduate Management Admission Test (GMAT). The combination of GPA and GMAT must yield a score of at least 950 according to one of the following formulas: (A) if overall undergraduate GPA is at least 2.5 and GMAT score is at least 450, then score = (GPA × 200) + GMAT; (B) if overall undergraduate GPA is below 2.5 or GMAT is below 450, then score = (GPA × 200) + GMAT − 50; (C) if GPA is based on the last 60 semester units, then score = (GPA × 200) + GMAT − 100. (Due to limited facilities and resources, a score higher than 950 may be required of all applicants.)
- Foreign students must have a Test of English as a Foreign Language (TOEFL) score of at least 550 and must submit a financial statement to the Admissions Office. Foreign students may apply only during November for fall admission or during August for spring admission.

EXPENSES
Resident graduate students pay a fee of about $365 per semester. Foreign and non-resident graduate students are charged an additional $126 per unit. These figures are approximate and subject to change. Books and supplies are additional expenses.

There are two private dormitories adjacent to campus and numerous apartments with a wide range of rents.

FINANCIAL ASSISTANCE
A few graduate assistantships are available paying about $6,000 per academic year. The student is expected to work approximately 20 hours per week. Applications for these assistantships are accepted prior to May 15 for positions starting in September. Full-time graduate students may borrow under federal programs. Because the university is located in a large metropolitan area, there are opportunities for either part-time or full-time employment.

PLACEMENT
The University Placement Office actively supports students seeking part-time and career employment.

CORRESPONDENCE
Requests for catalogs and applications should be addressed to the Admissions Office. Specific questions about curriculum should be addressed to
Associate Dean, M.B.A. Program
School of Business Administration
and Economics
California State University, Fullerton
Fullerton, California 92634
Telephone: 714-773-2211

The location of California State University, Hayward, in the rolling foothills overlooking San Francisco Bay offers its students many educational and recreational advantages. The climate of the region is moderate and provides a pleasant environment for study as well as an opportunity to utilize the recreational potential of the ocean to the west and mountains to the east. The proximity of Cal State to San Francisco and other Bay Area cities makes available the museums, libraries, art galleries, aquariums, and other cultural and educational resources of the metropolitan area. There are also plays, musicals, concerts, and the entire range of cosmopolitan entertainment for which San Francisco is famous. These aspects of student life are an important complement to academic efforts and contribute to a broadening college experience.

California State University, Hayward, operates on the quarter system with each quarter approximately 10 weeks in length. Enrollment in extension courses or in the summer session does not constitute enrollment in a quarter. One semester unit is equivalent to one and one-half quarter units of credit.

Cal State is accredited by the Western Association of Schools and Colleges and is a member of the Council of Graduate Schools in the United States. The Bachelor of Science in business administration, the Master of Business Administration, and the Master of Science programs are accredited by the American Assembly of Collegiate Schools of Business (AACSB).

PROGRAMS OF STUDY
The School of Business and Economics initiated the Master of Business Administration (M.B.A.) program in 1968 and added the Master of Science in Business Administration (M.S.B.A.) in 1972. Classes, scheduled from 8 a.m. through 10 p.m., accommodate both day and evening students.

The objective of the Master of Business Administration program at California State University, Hayward, is twofold. Upon completion of the program the student will understand the theory and concepts of modern business and have a knowledge of the techniques and processes of enterprise management. Completion of the program will also serve as an intermediate step toward the doctorate. Ten concentrations are available in the Master of Business Administration program: accounting, finance, information systems,

international business, management sciences, marketing, new ventures/small business, operations research, personnel/industrial relations, and taxation.

The Master of Science programs enable students to concentrate more time in courses that represent their area of specialization. This degree may be viewed as a terminal degree program that prepares individuals for work as analysts in business, government, or other organizations, or serves as the initial step in a program of more advanced study. Concentrations currently offered are quantitative business methods and taxation.

The master's degree may be based on a bachelor's degree in the arts, science, engineering, or business. Those students who have received their bachelor's degree in a field other than business can be classified after completing or otherwise satisfying certain prerequisites in business, economics, and quantitative methods. Forty-five quarter units are required for the M.B.A. or M.S.B.A., of which 32 units must be in residence. No more than 5 units may be accepted for thesis work, and a maximum of 13 units may be in transfer course credit.

ADMISSION
The university operates on the quarter system. Application for the fall, winter, spring, and summer quarters will be accepted beginning in January, September, November, and March, respectively.

Admission is based on a baccalaureate degree from an accredited university, a 2.75 grade-point average in the last 90 quarter units of undergraduate work and a score of 500 on the Graduate Management Admission Test (GMAT). Applications of students who do not meet these admission standards will be given to the Graduate Admission Committee for further evaluation. Foreign applicants are also required to submit official Test of English as a Foreign Language (TOEFL) scores.

EXPENSES
Approximate expenses, per quarter, are as follows:

	State residents	Out-of-state residents
Fees	$250	$84/unit

Most students live off campus; however, there is a residence hall next to the cam-

pus, offering room and board for approximately $3,000 per academic year (three quarters). A housing service on campus maintains a listing of off-campus housing.

FINANCIAL ASSISTANCE
Eligible students can obtain a maximum loan of $750-$1,500 per quarter from the National Direct Student Loan Program.

PLACEMENT
The university operates an effective placement service. Because of its location in one of the country's best labor markets and the strong local reputation of the School of Business and Economics, most graduates have little trouble finding suitable employment.

CORRESPONDENCE
Information may be obtained from
  School of Business and Economics
  Student Service Center
  California State University, Hayward
  Hayward, California 94542
  Telephone: 415-881-3323

California State University, Long Beach, observed its thirtieth anniversary in 1979. With an enrollment of 33,000 students from every state and 90 countries, the university offers graduate study in 50 separate master's degree programs. Varied professional and liberal arts programs permit a wide range of career and cultural opportunities. Located on the hilltop portion of the 322-acre campus overlooking the Pacific Ocean, the School of Business Administration is housed in a three-story, two-building complex. Physical facilities feature lecture and seminar classrooms, an accounting laboratory, a production management laboratory, extensive data processing and information retrieval facilities, and an advanced and sophisticated marketing laboratory. The moderate Mediterranean climate of southern California provides a climate conducive to academic work.

PROGRAMS OF STUDY
The School of Business Administration provides degree-oriented graduate study leading to completion of the Master of Business Administration (M.B.A.) or the Master of Science (M.S.) degree. Geared to the needs of the employed, courses are scheduled during the evening hours. A program of breadth, the M.B.A. provides individualized study in accounting, finance, management and human resources management, marketing, and quantitative systems. Each student completes required courses in Management Information Systems, Business Research Methodology, and Integrated Analysis, the capstone course. Specialized preparation is provided by the M.S. programs in accounting, finance, human resources management, management, marketing, or operations management. A certificate in international business is also offered and may be pursued concurrently with the graduate degree. The M.B.A. and M.S. programs require a minimum of 33 units following prerequisites. Neither thesis nor comprehensive examination is required within the M.B.A. program, with the capstone course, Integrated Analysis, serving the essential process of integration of the program. A thesis may be included to further develop research competencies. The M.S. program permits election of comprehensive examination, thesis, or the integration course. Prerequisites for the M.B.A. or the M.S. degrees include completion of the common body of knowledge, characteristic of programs accredited by the American Assembly of Collegiate Schools of Business (AACSB). Graduates of

AACSB-accredited programs normally will have met such prerequisites. Graduates with degrees in fields other than in business otherwise eligible for admission may complete prerequisite courses through accelerated graduate courses or through more extensive upper-division work.

ADMISSION
Dual application to the Office of Admissions and Records and to the Graduate Office, School of Business Administration, is necessary. Transcripts of all previous study are required by each office. Applications may be requested from the Office of Admissions and Records. Graduate Management Admission Test (GMAT) results must be forwarded to the School of Business Administration by Educational Testing Service. Two indicators of high promise for graduate study in business are combined according to the following formula: cumulative grade-point average × 200 + GMAT score. The minimum qualifying score yielded by such computation is 1,050 points. If greater promise for success appears to be indicated, the last 50 percent of all course work may be utilized in the computation. The resultant score must be at least 1,125 points. This combination of indicators of high promise is employed with consistency. The Test of English as a Foreign Language (TOEFL) with a minimum score of 550 is required for all foreign applicants whose native language is not English. The Examination in English as a Second Language is required for all visa students for whom English is the second language.

The university operates on an early semester plan. The fall semester begins in late August and the spring semester in late January. Graduate students in business administration may enter in either semester. All application materials must have been received by the School of Business Administration Graduate Office by April 30 for fall admission or October 15 for spring admission.

EXPENSES
Tuition is not charged to legal residents of California. Resident graduate students pay fees and expenses of approximately $330 for the normal 12 units per semester for a full-time student pursuing a master's degree. Students enrolled for 6 or fewer units, half time, would pay approximately $210. Nonresidents of California, foreign or domestic, must pay the basic fees, which are approximately $330 for full-time

and $210 for part-time, plus $126 per unit. All fees are subject to change. Students must be prepared to meet expenses for fees at registration. Other expenses are variable and must be estimated individually and included in the total cost of graduate study.

Residence hall accommodations are limited. Students living in a residence hall pay approximately $3,700 for room and board for an academic year. A single student living off campus with shared housing will find expenses higher. Married students living off campus will require careful financial planning for housing and transportation.

FINANCIAL ASSISTANCE
Nonteaching graduate assistant positions are available within the School of Business Administration. Information concerning financial aid may be obtained from the Financial Aid Office.

PLACEMENT
The Career Planning and Placement Center facilitates employment processes for students, alumni, and job recruiters.

CORRESPONDENCE
For additional information on graduate programs in business or for the *Graduate Handbook,* write to
> School of Business Administration
> Director of Graduate-Undergraduate Studies
> California State University, Long Beach
> Long Beach, California 90840
> Telephone: 213-498-4514

California State University, Los Angeles, one of the 19 institutions in the publicly supported system of California State Universities and Colleges, operates on a year-round quarter system. The university is a multipurpose institution of more than 30,000 students; postbaccalaureate study accounts for approximately 30 percent of the enrollment. The campus is located adjacent to the financial, commercial, and manufacturing centers of the metropolitan complex. Beach and mountain resorts, other recreational facilities, and a wide variety of cultural opportunities are within a short drive.

The School of Business and Economics is located in a recently constructed complex of air-conditioned classrooms, faculty offices, and a computer center. Approximately 20 percent of the 5,000 students enrolled in the school are at the graduate level. Both the graduate and undergraduate programs are accredited by the American Assembly of Collegiate Schools of Business (AACSB).

PROGRAMS OF STUDY
The Master of Business Administration (M.B.A.) program (52 quarter units) emphasizes breadth of education. Graduate courses in the fields of accounting, economics, finance, management, marketing, and the application of quantitative techniques in business decision making are required. The candidate also chooses as an area of concentration one of the following: accounting, business economics, business information systems, finance, international business, management, marketing, or office administration. Competency must be demonstrated by the successful completion of an eight-hour comprehensive examination in the last quarter of the program. The examination covers four of the six fields in the common core, including the area of concentration.

The Master of Science in Accounting (M.S.Ac.) program (45 quarter units) is designed with options to meet specific professional objectives in financial (public) accounting, management accounting, business taxation, and information systems.

The Master of Science in Business Administration (M.S.B.A.) program (45 quarter units) is a specialized in-depth degree with options in business information systems, finance, international business, management, marketing, and business economics. Major emphasis is on leadership development as well as

research, including the completion of a thesis.

The Master of Arts in Business Education program (45 quarter units) is designed to meet the needs of business education teachers in secondary schools and community colleges.

The Master of Arts in Economics program (45 quarter units) provides for advanced study of economic theory and research for students who wish to pursue a career in business, the public sector, or teaching.

The Master of Science in Health Care Management is an interdisciplinary program designed to prepare students for mid-level or department head positions in health care facilities.

The programs vary from one to two years of full-time study, depending upon undergraduate preparation. A student with an undergraduate degree in business normally completes the master's degree in one year of full-time study or one and a half years of half-time study. Classes are scheduled from 8 a.m. to 10 p.m. The major portion of the strictly graduate offerings, however, are scheduled during the 4 to 10 p.m. period. Students may enter the programs at the beginning of any academic quarter—January, March, June, or September.

ADMISSION
For admission to California State University, Los Angeles, applicants must have a baccalaureate degree from an accredited institution or equivalent academic preparation as determined by an appropriate campus authority. Applicants must have a grade-point average of at least 2.5 (4.0 = A) in their last 90 units attempted and must be in good standing at the last college attended.

An applicant from a non-English-speaking country also must have a minimum score of 550 on the Test of English as a Foreign Language (TOEFL).

In addition to university admission requirements, applicants to the M.B.A., M.S.Ac., and M.S.B.A. programs in the School of Business and Economics must satisfy criteria outlined below. The School of Business and Economics examines the academic ability and managerial potential of each candidate, taking into consider-

ation all academic work, Graduate Management Admission test (GMAT) scores, letters of recommendation, work experience, level of responsibility, and other factors that may have a bearing upon the individual's potential for success. Applicants are evaluated on the merits of their application in comparison with all other applicants for the quarter.

Admission requirements to the other graduate programs may be obtained from the Graduate Programs Office of the School of Business and Economics.

EXPENSES
The quarterly fees (tuition) for the academic year for California residents are $224 for 6.1 or more units, $144 for 0-6.0 units. Nonresidents (including residents and citizens of foreign countries) are charged additional fees of $84 per unit. Additional expenses are for books, supplies, and nominal student activities fees. Although the university maintains no student housing, accommodations are available near the campus.

FINANCIAL ASSISTANCE
The university offers a limited number of graduate assistantships. Information concerning financial aids may be requested from the Office of Financial Aids.

PLACEMENT
The university operates a Career Development and Placement Center to assist students and graduates seeking full-time and part-time positions in the business, industry, government, and teaching fields.

CORRESPONDENCE
For additional information, please write or call
  Graduate Programs Office
  School of Business and Economics
  California State University, Los Angeles
  Los Angeles, California 90032
  Telephone: 213-224-2727

California State University, San Bernardino, is one of the 19 campuses in the California State Universities and Colleges system. Students on the San Bernardino campus enjoy the intimacy of a small university, yet have available the resources of one of the largest and most progressive systems of higher education in the country.

Distinctive features of the educational program at San Bernardino include its 3/3 academic plan and the preponderance of small classes. All of the graduate classes are taught by regular faculty, and each class has a maximum of 20 students. A graduate student is considered a full-time student by taking two courses each quarter. Each course offers five quarter units of credit and meets four hours per week which gives further opportunity for student research and in-depth study of specific topics.

PROGRAMS OF STUDY
The School of Business and Public Administration offers two separate graduate degree programs: the Master of Business Administration (M.B.A.) and the Master of Public Administration (M.P.A.). Both programs provide course flexibility to prepare for a career in administration in the private or public sector. The major objective is to provide the student with the tools of decision making, an understanding of the total administrative system, and a capacity for understanding interrelationships.

The Master of Business Administration program consists of nine courses including six required core courses covering the broad spectrum of management and three elective courses in a selected concentration. All of the courses are offered in the evening to allow the student to complete the program on a part-time basis. Prerequisite courses in the areas of economics, mathematics, and management are required prior to taking M.B.A. courses. Each applicant is advised on an individual basis regarding deficiencies and given an opportunity to meet prerequisite requirements through course work, credit by examination, or waiver based upon work experience.

The minimum requirements for the M.B.A. degree are a B average in graduate courses and a passing grade on a comprehensive examination covering the concentration.

ADMISSION
Applicants must hold a baccalaureate degree from an accredited institution. In addition, admission to classified graduate standing requires the following combination of grade-point average (GPA) and test score on the Graduate Management Admission Test (GMAT): GMAT score plus 200 × GPA on the last 90 sequential quarter units (60 semester units) of course work (including postbaccalaureate course work) equals or exceeds 1,020. Entering students can begin course work in the fall, winter, or spring quarter. Summer classes are available on a limited basis.

EXPENSES
California residents pay fees of approximately $162 (one course) to $247 (three courses) per quarter. Foreign and nonresident graduate students pay approximately $583 (one course) to $1,507 (three courses) per quarter. There is also a $35 application fee.

FINANCIAL ASSISTANCE
The Office of Financial Aid advises students on the availability of scholarships, loans, tuition refund plans, and part-time employment as well as procedures and qualifications to apply for such assistance. Paid graduate assistant positions are available for new students. For information contact Jennifer McMullen, Administrative Aide, at the address below.

PLACEMENT
All facilities of the Placement Office are available to M.B.A. candidates and alumni. Many national, regional, and local business firms make regular recruiting trips to the campus in search of business administration graduates.

CORRESPONDENCE
For additional information, write to
Director of Graduate Studies
School of Business and Public Administration
California State University, San Bernardino
5500 State College Parkway
San Bernardino, California 92407

CALIFORNIA STATE UNIVERSITY, STANISLAUS

TURLOCK, CALIFORNIA

California State University, Stanislaus, one of the 19 California State Universities and Colleges, was founded by an act of the California Legislature in 1957 and commenced operation in temporary quarters in 1960. Following the occupancy of its permanent campus in 1965, the university entered a period of growth that has brought the enrollment to about 4,300 students. Located in the San Joaquin Valley, 13 miles south of Modesto and 102 miles southeast of San Francisco, Turlock is a stable residential community (population 40,000) offering many advantages for family living, recreation, and cultural activity.

The School of Business Administration has primary responsibility within the university for the preparation and continuing education of business administrators. The school offers two degree programs: one leading to the Bachelor of Science in business administration; the other leading to the Master of Business Administration (M.B.A.) degree. Courses in the M.B.A. program are offered during the evening only. Courses are offered both on the Turlock Campus and the Stockton Campus (45 miles to the north). There are approximately 200 students enrolled in the M.B.A. program.

PROGRAM OF STUDY

The M.B.A. program is a professional graduate-level program in business and administration. The program has been established to assist professionally oriented men and women in preparing for responsible managerial and staff positions in business, governmental agencies, and other organizations, and for the recognized business professions, and to assist persons already holding responsible positions to prepare for advancement in management.

The M.B.A. is awarded upon satisfactory completion of core and elective courses. Before beginning the core courses, students are required to have taken the courses listed in the foundation or their equivalents. Generally, students with a bachelor's degree in business administration will not need to take the foundation courses. The M.B.A. program includes the following elements:

• M.B.A. foundation program—Principles of Accounting; Computers in Business; Law, Environment, and Ethics; Business and Economic Environment; Management of Financial Resources; Seminar in the Administrative Process; Marketing Fundamentals; Seminar in Management Science for Business; Quantitative Business Methods I;

• M.B.A. core program—Managerial Accounting Seminar; Computer Information Systems; Seminar in the Management of International Business; Business Policy; Managerial Finance; Business Organization, Theory, and Behavior; Marketing Management; Production and Operations Management;

• area of specialization—an approved sequence of courses, tailored to meet each student's unique needs and interests, totaling a minimum of six semester units (students may draw upon the resources of other schools in the university, as appropriate, in developing this part of their program).

The M.B.A. program does not require a thesis; however, a research project (three units) is required. There is no foreign language requirement, but there is a requirement for proficiency in English. Applicants whose native language is not English must take the Test of English as a Foreign Language (TOEFL) and have a minimum score of 550, with part scores of at least 54, reported directly from the testing service.

The members of the faculty complement their academic achievements with up-to-date perspectives on management acquired through their involvement in business and government, through their service as consultants, and in previous positions as business executives. Their research and teaching extends into the international aspects of business from which have evolved courses dealing with the international dimensions of management education.

Instruction is offered in small classes with heavy emphasis placed on student participation. Case problem analysis, simulation exercises, group projects, lecture-discussions, and independent research are all employed as effective aids to learning.

ADMISSION

Qualified individuals holding a bachelor's degree from an accredited college or university can be admitted to the programs. Each applicant must submit the following to the Admissions Office: (1) a fully completed application form (Parts A and B of the Standard California State University Application) and (2) two copies of official transcripts from each college attended.

The following is to be submitted to the Director of Graduate Programs, School of Business Administration: (1) three letters of recommendation from faculty and other sources and (2) the score on the Graduate Management Admission Test (GMAT), which should be sent directly from the testing service.

EXPENSES

Fees depend upon the number of units for which each student is enrolled. California residents will normally pay approximately $650-$679 per year. Out-of-state students will pay a higher fee.

PLACEMENT

The university operates an active placement program for the assistance of its students.

CORRESPONDENCE

Inquiries should be addressed to
Director, Graduate Studies
School of Business Administration
California State University, Stanislaus
Turlock, California 95380
Telephone: 209-667-3287

CALIFORNIA UNIVERSITY OF PENNSYLVANIA

CALIFORNIA, PENNSYLVANIA

Beginning as a one-building private academy in 1852, California University of Pennsylvania has grown into a 147-acre campus surrounding the community of California, located about 35 miles south of Pittsburgh in the foothills of the Allegheny Mountains. As a normal school, it became a member of the Commonwealth System in 1914. It has continued to grow and diversify over the years, becoming a state teacher's college in 1928 and a multipurpose state college in 1959. The university has an enrollment of 4,500 students, most of whom are enrolled full time.

PROGRAM OF STUDY

The Master of Science degree program in business administration is professionally oriented and designed to prepare individuals to assume management positions in industry, business, and government. The program is particularly appropriate for working individuals who are interested in developing managerial skills as part of a planned program for professional growth. The courses are offered primarily in the evenings. Students may enroll on a full-time or part-time basis. The program emphasizes the practical approach to management problems as well as providing a rigorous examination of management theory.

The degree requires the completion of an undergraduate core and a graduate core. The undergraduate core courses provide a foundation in the basic concepts needed for the program. These courses must be completed with a B or better grade. Undergraduate core courses may be waived, or equivalent courses taken recently at an accredited four-year college or university may be accepted as substitutes. The graduate core, consisting of a minimum of nine required and four elective courses, contains offerings in the fields of management, finance, marketing, organization, industrial relations, accounting, economics, and production.

The program is designed primarily for persons holding business administration, economics, industrial management, engineering, industrial technology, or other similar undergraduate degrees. These individuals will normally have taken appropriate undergraduate course work and can be excused from some or all of the courses in the undergraduate core. Students who have deficiencies in undergraduate preparation will be required to complete both the undergraduate and graduate cores. By pursuing the studies on a part-time basis, a student would normally take about two years to complete the graduate core courses.

ADMISSION

Admission to the program is open to qualified students with baccalaureate degrees in almost any field. Admission is possible in the fall, spring, and summer terms and is based on the undergraduate record, Graduate Management Admission Test (GMAT) scores, and any work experience related to the program. Because of the rolling admissions policy, no rigid deadline has been established for submitting applications for admission. However, as early as possible, each applicant should file with the Graduate Office, an application for admission accompanied by official transcripts from all institutions at which he or she has taken undergraduate and graduate courses.

EXPENSES

The estimate of expenses (subject to change by the Board of Trustees) as of March 15, 1985 was as follows:

Application fee	$ 20
Tuition, full-time student for 9 to 15 semester credit hours	
In-state	785
Out-of-state	830
Tuition, part-time student, per semester credit hour	
In-state	87
Out-of-state	92
Room and board, per semester	1,000
Books and supplies, per semester	150

FINANCIAL ASSISTANCE

A limited number of graduate assistantships are available to full-time graduate students. A graduate assistant is expected to devote full time to his or her studies and work related to the assistantship. Graduate assistants are assigned to various departments or service areas to assist in research and other professional duties. Course fees are waived for graduate assistants.

PLACEMENT

The services of the Placement Office are available to California University of Pennsylvania graduate students and alumni.

CORRESPONDENCE

For further information, write or call
Coordinator, Graduate Program
Business and Economics Department
California University of Pennsylvania
California, Pennsylvania 15419
Telephone: 412-938-4371/4372

Campbell University is a liberal arts university located in Buies Creek, a rural community of 500 people approximately 30 miles south of Raleigh, North Carolina. It is one of seven colleges owned by the North Carolina Baptist State Convention.

Founded in 1887 as Buies Creek Academy by Dr. James Archibald Campbell, it achieved a wide reputation as a good, private secondary school. In 1925 title to the school was acquired by the Baptist State Convention at which time the name of the school was changed to Campbell College in honor of its founder. In the spring of 1958, the Baptist State Convention authorized a change of status from junior to senior college and in 1975 approved the launching of three graduate programs in law, education, and business administration. On June 6, 1979, Campbell College changed its name to Campbell University.

Business has been and continues to be one of the major programs at Campbell University. Evidence of this is the fact that Campbell University ranks high among the private colleges in North Carolina in the number of graduates who have fulfilled business major requirements. The graduate program in business has been prepared with a commitment toward continuing to meet the needs of students in the business field.

PROGRAM OF STUDY
The major objective of the graduate program in business is to develop the student's analytical, critical, problem-solving, and decision-making capabilities and to provide the basic knowledge needed for the solution of business problems. The Master of Business Administration (M.B.A.) program is designed to accommodate the needs of students having a bachelor's degree in business and students with degrees in other fields.

Candidates with undergraduate degrees in business administration should allow two full years for completion of the requirements; candidates who did not major in business administration should allow three years. Persons enrolling in graduate courses are expected to have completed the following undergraduate courses:

Course	Semester Hours Credit
Principles of Accounting	6
Principles of Economics	6
Principles of Management	3
Principles of Marketing	3
Corporate Finance	3
Computer Science	3
Statistics	3

In order to earn the Master of Business Administration degree, candidates must satisfy the following course requirements:

Course	Semester Hours Credit
BA 600—The Management Process	3
BA 610—Quantitative Methods	3
BA 620—Financial Analysis	3
BA 630—Economic Analysis and Policy	3
BA 631—Economic Analysis and Policy	3
BA 640—Marketing Management	3
BA 650—Advanced Management Accounting	3
BA 660—Legal Environment	3
Electives	6
Total	30

ADMISSION
Students are admitted to the school's 30-semester-hour, evening M.B.A. program only on a part-time basis and may normally enter the program during either the fall or spring semester.

Evening classes are scheduled on the campus of Campbell University, at Fort Bragg, Rocky Mount, Raleigh, and Goldsboro, North Carolina.

Applicants to graduate study in business may be admitted to full standing by meeting the following requirements:
- a bachelor's degree from an accredited institution of higher education,
- a minimal grade-point average of 2.70 on a 4.00-point scale on all undergraduate work,
- sufficient courses or work in the chosen area to qualify for graduate study in that area, and
- satisfactory scores on the Graduate Management Admission Test.

EXPENSES
The cost of instruction has been set at $85 per semester hour. The college reserves the right to change the cost of instruction when this change is deemed necessary.

CORRESPONDENCE
For additional information on the M.B.A. program at Campbell, please write or call
Admissions Office
Campbell University
Box 546
Buies Creek, North Carolina 27506
Telephone: 919-893-4111

Canisius College is located in Buffalo, New York, at the center of a large industrial complex called the Niagara Frontier. The college, now over 100 years old, is an urban, coeducational institution with a full complement of undergraduate major concentrations.

The School of Business Administration became a separate administrative entity within the college in 1958, and it offers rigorous preparation in the areas of accounting, finance, economics, management, and marketing. A large portion of business school graduates seek to further their formal education after receiving their baccalaureate degrees.

The members of the School of Business Administration faculty hold graduate degrees from more than 45 different universities, and the diversity of their fields of specialization gives considerable breadth and depth to the curriculum of the school. Excellence in teaching is emphasized at Canisius College; a quality library, an on-campus computer center equipped with a VMS VAX 11/780 "super" minicomputer, and a computational laboratory equipped with IBM and Apple personal computers provide the necessary research outlets for both faculty and students in the School of Business Administration.

PROGRAM OF STUDY

The Master of Business Administration (M.B.A.) curriculum is professional in nature. The courses offered are application oriented as well as theoretical. The objective of the program is to educate efficient, forward-looking managers for business, industry, and government. The program is open to any qualified holder of a bachelor's degree from a recognized college or university regardless of undergraduate major field of study. It is an evening M.B.A. program and can be completed in eight semesters (three semesters per year). The M.B.A. program is made up of 16 courses of three credit hours each and allows for an area of concentration. Course waivers and substitutions are granted according to established criteria.

The M.B.A. program is comprised of the following:

	Credit hours
Part 1: Basic Courses	
Management Information Systems/Computer Programming Applications	3
Statistical Methods for Business Decision Making	3
Financial Accounting	3
Analysis of Microeconomic Decision Making	3
Analysis of Macroeconomic Theory and Policy	3 15
Part II: Core Courses	
Managerial Accounting	3
Organizational Behavior	3
Management Science	3
Managerial Finance	3
Marketing Management	3
Operations Management	3
Human Resources Management	3
Managerial Environment	3 24
Part III: Advanced-Level Courses	
Accounting: 3 electives offered regularly	
Finance: 4 electives offered regularly	
Management: 3 electives offered regularly	
Marketing: 4 electives offered regularly	
Choose any two courses	6
Part IV: Business Policy	3 3
	48

ADMISSION

The Admissions Committee takes into consideration, among other things, the undergraduate quality-point average and scores on the Graduate Management Admission Test (GMAT). Each applicant must submit these items: (1) a completed application form and appropriate fee, (2) official GMAT scores, (3) two official transcripts of all previous college work, and (4) other information requested by the Admissions Committee. A background knowledge of calculus is a prerequisite for the program. A candidate lacking such background is required to obtain it during his or her first semester in the program.

Eligible students may enter in the fall, spring, or summer semester. Preferred consideration is given to applications received by June 1 for fall, October 1 for spring, and March 1 for summer.

EXPENSES

Application fee, nonrefundable	$ 20
Tuition, per credit hour (1984-85)	200
Fees, per credit hour	5

Additional expenses for books, supplies, and so on may average $40 per three-hour course.

CORRESPONDENCE

For further information, write or call
Director, M.B.A. Program
Canisius College
Buffalo, New York 14208
Telephone: 716-883-7000,
   extensions 470, 471

Capital University, founded in 1830, now has approximately 2,500 students. The university is composed of Arts and Sciences, Conservatory of Music, School of Nursing, Law School, and the Graduate School of Administration. The campus is located about midway between the center and the city limits of the capital city of Ohio, a metropolitan area of approximately one million people.

The Graduate School of Administration, which offers the Master of Business Administration (M.B.A.) degree program, was authorized in 1971. The first course offerings at the graduate level came during the 1972-73 academic year.

PROGRAM OF STUDY

The M.B.A. program emphasizes the professional management development of individuals already engaged in managerial careers. Toward this end the degree program includes a common core of studies focusing on analytical and behavioral techniques and on institutional and environmental considerations confronting business and the business man or woman. Individual specialization is afforded through a series of elective specialties. The student is expected to acquire a broad understanding of business concepts and operations and to develop his own philosophy of leadership, characterized by analysis and originality.

The M.B.A. program requires successful completion of 40 semester hours in an approved curriculum. To encourage program flexibility for the student, no comprehensive examination, thesis, or foreign language is required. Courses in fall, winter, and summer semesters are scheduled for the evenings (6:00 p.m. and after) and on some Saturdays. Maximum graduate load is two courses per semester, making program completion possible in 24 months.

The degree candidate must complete a total of 32 semester hours (eight courses) over four major areas: managerial philosophy, analytical methods, management of functional business areas, and policy, plus 8 semester hours in elective courses. A special research paper is a degree requirement of all M.B.A. candidates.

Appropriate graduate credit may be granted for transfer to the M.B.A. program by presentation of official transcripts. No more than three courses, maximum of nine semester hours, may be transferred to M.B.A. requirements.

ADMISSION

Admission will be granted to those students satisfying basic qualifications and showing high promise of success in the graduate program and in the business community. Basic qualifications include (1) a baccalaureate degree with an above average grade-point ratio from an accredited institution; (2) a knowledge of basic concepts and terminology in the fields of the social sciences, business, and quantitative methods; (3) significant work experience and full-time employment concurrent with the program enrollment; and (4) satisfactory scores on the Graduate Management Admission Test (GMAT). The second requirement may be satisfied by taking one or more specialized, graduate-level prerequisite courses offered by the Graduate School of Administration. Applicants with a thorough knowledge in only portions of an area may be asked to complete specific reading assignments or to attend the relevant portion of the prerequisite course. Prerequisite courses are designed in modular form to facilitate student preparation for entrance into the program. Required prerequisite knowledge may be gained by enrolling in an entire classroom course, needed modules of a particular classroom course, or all or any portion of a course on a tutorial basis. Applicants must also complete the M.B.A. application form and supply official transcripts of all college work.

EXPENSES

Basic expenses for the academic year are as follows:

M.B.A. tuition, per semester
hour of credit $150
Application fee. 25
Graduation fee (due the final
semester) 20

Housing is the student's own responsibility.

PLACEMENT

The university placement office will serve students in the M.B.A. program and alumni. However, since the students average 31 years old and all are employed while in the program, they are urged to first seek advancement with their present employers, rather than seeking new positions.

CORRESPONDENCE

For further information or to request an application, please write to

Dr. Richard L. Pinkerton, Dean
Graduate School of Administration
Capital University
Columbus, Ohio 43209

Carleton University's School of Business offers a Master of Management Studies (M.M.S.) degree program. The school, one of 11 academic units in the Faculty of Social Sciences, has an excellent academic staff representing a broad cross-section of disciplines and backgrounds. Because of its location in Ottawa, the school provides students with unique opportunities to interact with government and industry.

PROGRAM OF STUDY

The focus of the M.M.S. program is applied research directed toward developing productivity and innovation in Canadian business. The program of studies will develop in students the conceptual and methodological skills required to undertake, manage, and evaluate business research. It is designed to prepare students for managerial and policy roles in Canadian business. The applied research skills developed in the M.M.S. program are deemed to be essential if Canadian business is to be more productive and innovative in the increasingly competitive and complex world economy.

The M.M.S. program requires successful completion of the equivalent of 10 half-courses. Students must complete seven half-courses of which at least five must be at the 500 level or above and a thesis equivalent to three half-courses.

The areas of specialization within the program are business information systems, finance, management, and marketing. The business information systems area is designed for students interested in systems analysis, decision support systems, computer auditing, and management information systems. The finance area will prepare graduate students for research in business finance, investment management, and the management of financial institutions. The management area is designed for students interested in personnel management, operations management, human resource development, and management of organizations. The marketing area is designed to provide students with specialized skills in domestic and international marketing analysis and planning, marketing policy, market opportunity assessment, and new product development.

ADMISSION

Admission to the program will be judged primarily on the applicant's ability to undertake successfully advanced studies and research in business, prospects for completion of the program, experience, and achievement.

Applicants are required to have the equivalent of an honor's bachelor's degree in commerce, business, management, administration, or the equivalent, with a minimum of high second-class standing. Applicants are expected to have had credits in mathematics and the core courses in functional areas of business.

In addition, applicants are expected to have had an upper-level course sequence in their proposed area of business specialization, and to have an adequate grounding in at least one supporting fundamental discipline such as economics, psychology, sociology, mathematics, anthropology, or computer science.

The school requires that all applicants submit scores obtained in the Graduate Management Admission Test (GMAT) offered by Educational Testing Service of Princeton, New Jersey. A superior GMAT score will be required for admission. All applicants whose native tongue is not English must be tested for proficiency in the English language and obtain an adequate score on the Test of English as a Foreign Language (TOEFL).

The school's admission policy is governed by the availability of graduate student space. Possession of the minimum admission requirements does not, in itself, guarantee acceptance. Advanced standing may be granted for required courses only if previous work is judged to be equivalent to courses required in the program. Advanced standing and transfer of credit must be determined on an individual basis in consultation with the supervisor of graduate studies and must also be approved at the time of admission by the Dean of the Faculty of Graduate Studies and Research. In general, a grade of B− or better is required in equivalent courses to obtain advanced standing.

EXPENSES

The fee schedule for a full-time student in a master's program, published below, was in effect for the academic year 1984-85 and is subject to change.

Canadian Citizens and Landed Immigrants

	First Term	Second or Subsequent Terms
Tuition	$672.60	$201.40
Student Sickness/ Accident Insurance	5.40	5.40
Students' Association	20.15	6.05
Athletics	25.50	7.60
Health	7.40	2.20
University Centre	6.65	2.00
Total composite fee (per term)	$737.70	$224.65

Foreign Students	*September through August*
Tuition Fees	$ 8,587.80*
Books	500.00
Lodging	4,200.00
Food	1,800.00
Bus Fare	360.00
Medical/Hospital Insurance	357.00
Miscellaneous	1,500.00
Estimated cost (12 months)	$17,304.80

*The current tuition fees are $8,587.80 or $2,862.60 per term. A bursary of $300 for full-time students is possible for the third consecutive term of full-time study, but this will be confirmed prior to each registration.

FINANCIAL ASSISTANCE

Students accepted for full-time study are automatically considered for teaching or research assistantships. In addition, Carleton University provides a large number of fellowships, grants, and scholarships. A booklet providing details of awards, application procedures, and eligibility is available from the Graduate Studies and Research office. March 1 is the last date for receipt of completed applications for financial assistance.

PLACEMENT

The school has undertaken to make specific provisions for career counseling and placement of its graduate students.

CORRESPONDENCE

For an application for admission to the M.M.S. program or for further information, please write or call

Professor George H. Haines, Jr.
Supervisor of Graduate Studies
Carleton University
Ottawa, Ontario
Canada, K1S 5B6
Telephone: 613-564-4373

The purpose of the Graduate School of Industrial Administration (GSIA) is to provide a unique graduate education in management to men and women of outstanding promise and to support pioneering research in management, economics, and industrial administration. GSIA programs emphasize fundamental concepts in order to provide a basis for dealing with contemporary problems and for continuing growth into the next century. GSIA is committed to a strong practical orientation and an underlying belief in the importance of a broad intellectual base that draws on many disciplines. The school's small size (104 faculty members, 360 students) makes possible close informal contact with student colleagues and with faculty members working on a wide variety of problems. Joint degree programs are offered with the Carnegie-Mellon University (CMU) School of Urban and Public Affairs and the University of Pittsburgh's School of Law. CMU's departments of computer science, psychology, and statistics all have outstanding faculties and extensive programs of courses and research. GSIA students may choose electives from any of the university's graduate departments.

PROGRAMS OF STUDY

The two-year Master of Science (M.S.) program is designed to prepare men and women for rapid advancement and outstanding performance in general management. Master's students gain experience in the application of analytical concepts and methods to the solution of management problems. The curriculum is designed to complement these analytical capabilities with an understanding of economic, technological, political, behavioral, and international environments. The first-year curriculum's emphasis on behavioral science is based on extensive formal and informal small group work. These groups grow into the successful management teams of GSIA's management game. In this unique game, student managers make decisions under conditions close to those in the real world, deal with each other and a variety of outside agencies, and live with the results. Opportunities for project work with local corporations and small businesses offer further emphasis on practical applications.

Doctoral programs in economics, business administration, operations research, organizations and social behavior, politics and political economy, and systems sciences prepare students for careers in research and education. Candidates for the Doctor of Philosophy (Ph.D.) degree can enter the program directly after completing their undergraduate work and earn the degree in three years. The doctoral programs stress early involvement in research. Each student has a faculty advisory committee to aid in the design of a program. Students combine courses, independent study, and research in preparation for the qualifying examinations. To earn the Ph.D. the student must perform satisfactorily on qualifying examinations, prepare a research paper during the first two years, as well as submit a dissertation to the faculty and defend it in an oral examination.

Several programs for experienced managers, including the intensive six-week program for executives, provide students and faculty with an opportunity for beneficial interaction with outstanding management practitioners.

The School of Urban and Public Affairs (SUPA) M.S. program, which prepares students for public sector management, specializes in applications of quantitative analytic techniques to solving urban and national problems. The SUPA faculty and courses are interdisciplinary, ranging from engineering to behavioral and management science. Interested students should contact SUPA Admissions.

ADMISSION

The Admissions Committee accepts students for full-time study beginning each September. The application deadline is March 15. Applicants for the M.S. program should submit scores on the Graduate Management Admission Test (GMAT); Ph.D. applicants may submit either GMAT scores or scores from the Graduate Record Examinations (GRE). GSIA's students come from all undergraduate backgrounds. Applicants must have a good background in mathematics, including differential and integral calculus. Counsel about mathematics preparation is available from the GSIA Director of Admissions.

EXPENSES

Tuition is $10,608 per academic year. Costs of housing, meals, books, and personal expenses are about $7,000 more. About $1,800 is added for each dependent.

FINANCIAL ASSISTANCE

GSIA makes every attempt within its resources to assist qualified applicants. The principal sources of aid for U.S. master's program students are the federally funded loan programs. Approximately 80 percent of the students finance part of their education through these programs. Many master's program students supplement their financial reserves by part-time research work with faculty members. Also, a limited number of scholarships are awarded each year. Since Ph.D. candidates are expected to devote full time to study and research, GSIA offers them substantial fellowships and stipends.

PLACEMENT

GSIA master's program graduates have achieved key management positions in manufacturing, financial institutions, commerce, and major consulting organizations, while GSIA doctorates appear on the faculty rosters of leading universities. The median annual starting salary for master's graduates without significant work experience was over $37,000 in 1985. GSIA's Placement Office assists students with full-time employment after graduation and summer employment between the first and second year.

CORRESPONDENCE

For further information on the programs offered by the Graduate School of Industrial Administration, write or call

GSIA Director of Admissions
Carnegie-Mellon University
Pittsburgh, Pennsylvania 15213
Telephone: 412-578-2272

Case Western Reserve University was established on July 1, 1967, by the federation of Western Reserve University and Case Institute of Technology. The university is located in Cleveland's University Circle area. Situated within this 500-acre region is probably the most extensive concentration of educational, scientific, medical, artistic, musical, and cultural institutions in the United States.

The university's Weatherhead School of Management offers programs leading to the Master of Business Administration (M.B.A.) and Master of Accountancy (M.Acc.) degrees. The M.B.A. degree offers a general management core curriculum, permits students to concentrate in one of ten possible elective sequences, and integrates hands-on management training in Cleveland's industrial, service, and health organizations as part of the student's degree requirements.

The Weatherhead School of Management has an unusually strong faculty. Two of its departments were recently rated among the top ten percent of such departments in the country. The school is relatively small, having 60 faculty members and 980 graduate students in business administration and management. In addition to close faculty relationships, the school has educational relationships with close to 50 companies having sales or assets of over $100 million in the Cleveland area, as well as a large number of health systems and entrepreneurial enterprises. These relationships provide opportunities for students to relate to real management problems and to obtain future employment.

PROGRAMS OF STUDY
The program of study leading to the M.B.A. degree has been designed to accommodate differing undergraduate backgrounds. For individuals with no previous work in business or management, the full program requires 60 semester hours of credit generally accomplished in two academic years of work. For those with undergraduate degrees in business or a management-related field, the master's degree can be obtained in 36 semester credit hours of work generally completed in 11 calendar months. Part-time evening study can ordinarily be followed at a pace of 12 to 15 credit hours each year. Each student has available a program of counseling and professional seminars to help build a career plan tailored to the individual.

Elective sequences are available in accounting, entrepreneurship and innovations management, finance, industrial relations, management information systems, management policy, marketing management, operations management, and organization development. Students electing the health management option will devote approximately 12 credit hours to specialized work in this area.

The M.Acc. program requires 36 hours of course work for students with undergraduate degrees in accounting and 60 hours for students with undergraduate majors in business subjects other than accounting. Students with majors in fields other than business will be required to take additional courses beyond the 60-semester-hour amount as indicated by the circumstances of their degree background, experience, and related accreditation requirements.

In addition, the Weatherhead School of Management offers the Master of Science (M.S.) and Doctor of Philosophy (Ph.D.) in operations research, the Ph.D. in management, and the M.S. and Ph.D. in organizational behavior. Information on these programs is available through the Dean of Graduate Studies.

ADMISSION
Candidates with qualified records from accredited schools and acceptable scores on the Graduate Management Admission Test (GMAT) will be considered for admission to the fall semester beginning late in August, the spring semester beginning the middle of January, or the summer session beginning the middle of June. Credentials for admission to the part-time program should be on file at least 30 days prior to registration. Applicants to the full-time program should refer to the Weatherhead School catalog for deadline dates.

International applicants must submit official copies, in English, of all transcripts showing course work and degrees completed, GMAT score, Test of English as a Foreign Language (TOEFL) score, and an affidavit of financial support for the entire course of study. International students may enter the full-time M.B.A. or M.Acc. program in August only.

EXPENSES
Per semester, approximately
Tuition (part-time rate:
  $357 per credit hour) . . . . $ 4,275
Room and board 1,700
Books and supplies 200
  Total $6,175

FINANCIAL ASSISTANCE
Scholarships, assistantships, and loans are available. Cleveland-area companies have funded a large number of full- and half-tuition scholarships to applicants of unusual promise. Assistantships range from $4,500 to $9,500 including tuition. Government loans may be made up to a maximum of $7,200 a year. Assistance for first-year students is available based on merit and/or need.

PLACEMENT
The Office of Career Planning and Placement at the Weatherhead School works closely with the faculty and administration to provide a total placement program for each student. As part of their programs, entering students meet with the placement director to discuss work experience, interests, and career goals. The school's size gives students a chance to establish ongoing relationships with both the director and faculty advisers. The office sponsors a variety of career development and placement services, including the off-campus interview program, recruiter receptions, the Alumni Network, career seminars and workshops, resume books, the internship program, and the placement library.

CORRESPONDENCE
For information about the M.B.A. or M.Acc. programs, write or call
  Director of Admissions
  Weatherhead School of Management
  Case Western Reserve University
  Cleveland, Ohio 44106
  Telephone: 216-368-2030

CBN University, founded in 1977, is a Christian graduate university allied with the Christian Broadcasting Network. The Graduate School of Business Administration is dedicated to the Glory of God and His Son, Jesus Christ. It is founded upon the principle that God, the fountainhead of all wisdom, reveals Himself through Jesus Christ, the incarnate Word of God, and the Bible, His written word. The objective of the business school is to discover and teach Biblical truth as the foundation for effective, modern management practice.

Fully accredited by the Southern Association of Colleges and Schools in 1984, CBNU Graduate School of Business is dedicated to the training of men and women who understand people and can lead them, who have a broad vision of business and its environment, and who will hold to high moral standards in the business world. It is one of seven graduate schools and institutes that together comprise CBN University.

The university is located in Virginia Beach, Virginia, an area rich in history and culture. Its campus is adjacent to the international headquarters of the Christian Broadcasting Network, and the entire facility comprises some 685 acres of woods, gardens, and buildings of stunning Georgian architecture, the centerpiece of which is the two-year-old library, one of the finest in the Southeast. Activities and fellowship, both planned and spontaneous, are a large part of student and faculty life. A low (10:1) student-faculty ratio and the intense personal interest in the students shared by all faculty members assures a close, caring student-teacher relationship in an exciting Christian atmosphere.

PROGRAM OF STUDY
The Master of Business Administration (M.B.A.) program is oriented toward the management-of-people skills so desperately needed nationally and internationally in business today. The curriculum has as its heart the study of Christian principles of management. Leadership styles as described in current secular literature are compared to Biblical principles, with emphasis placed on areas of congruence and careful evaluation exerted on areas of incongruence. Business ethics, people management, and communication skills are broad areas given great stress in all courses.

In addition, specific business functions (marketing, finance, computers, personnel) are given individual attention in separate courses. These courses select from what is excellent in secular or traditional material, but test such material against the yardstick of God's Truth. Each functional area course is composed of current professional material and is structured within a framework of Christian principles of leadership, management ethics, people management, and communication.

The five foundation courses of the curriculum are perhaps unique among graduate business schools. Two such courses are Christian Witnessing in a Business Environment and Christian Foundations of Business. The former seeks to train students in how to witness in the business field—where behavior quite different from street evangelism is called for. The course covers both personal testimony and living a witness, since business associates are often more attuned to how we live than to what we say. The second course, Foundations, examines the place of business in God's world and how we should live in the face of the pressures and conditions peculiar to the business scene, and takes the student into a personal confrontation with the daily challenges of business ethics.

The school operates on a four-quarter system, with new students accepted for entrance in either the fall or spring quarters. Seventy-two credit hours are required for the M.B.A. degree, including 18 required courses (57 credit hours), 9 credit hours of electives, plus a culminating experience (practicum, internship, or thesis) of 6 credit hours, or an additional 6 credit hours of electives followed by written and oral comprehensive examinations.

ADMISSION
The M.B.A. program is open to graduates of any undergraduate discipline. Business school applicants for regular status should have a minimum grade-point average of 3.00. Selection is comprehensive and gives weight to many factors. Special attention is given to the applicants' readiness for the program.

EXPENSES
Tuition for the 1985-86 academic year was $90 per credit hour. The estimated total cost for tuition, fees, books, and living expenses ranges from $2,800 per quarter for single students to $5,200 per quarter for a family of four, based on a normal course load of 12 credits per quarter.

FINANCIAL ASSISTANCE
A variety of types of financial aid are available. Most, but not all, are need-based. Applications for financial aid are to be submitted after the student is accepted into the program.

PLACEMENT
The university maintains its own placement office and offers many services including placement file maintenance, resume assistance, interview training, and job leads. Future services being developed are on-site interview coordination, placement database, and internship development and assistance.

CORRESPONDENCE
For further information, write or call
Office of Admissions
CBN University
Virginia Beach, Virginia 23463
Telephone: 804-424-7000

Central Michigan University, founded in 1892, is located in Mt. Pleasant, approximately 65 miles north of Lansing. The community consists of 22,000 people. The university is located in the center of Michigan near the industrial centers of Midland, Saginaw, and Bay City. Approximately 17,000 students were on the campus during the 1984-85 academic year. The graduate school enrollment, on campus, is about 2,500.

PROGRAM OF STUDY
The graduate program for the M.B.A. has as its purposes: (1) to develop characteristics for leadership in the administration of business and industry; (2) to attain both breadth and depth in the study of business; (3) to apply the requisite tools and skills in analysis, interpretation, and expression; (4) to develop an understanding of the background and evolution of American business and the interrelationships of the various areas; and (5) to acquire an awareness of the responsibilities of business to society.

A student is required to have prerequisites equivalent to the common body of knowledge in business, as defined by the American Assembly of Collegiate Schools of Business. This requirement includes satisfactory work in the following fields: accounting, administration, business environment and public policy, economics, finance, marketing, statistics, and techniques of decision making.

The degree requirements consist of a core of 27 hours and general electives of 9 hours.

ADMISSION
To be considered for admission to the M.B.A. program, students must first be admitted to the School of Graduate Studies. The application for admission should be sent to the School of Graduate Studies at least six weeks prior to the beginning of the first semester of anticipated enrollment.

Following admission to the School of Graduate Studies, the undergraduate grade-point average and the Graduate Management Admission Test (GMAT) score are the primary criteria used in the admission decision. The GMAT measures aptitude for graduate study in business and not achievement or knowledge in any specific subject-matter area. Students with nonbusiness undergraduate degrees can score well without having taken any prior business courses. As the GMAT must be taken before admission to the M.B.A. program, students should arrange to take the test prior to or concurrent with their application. The test is given four times a year at Central Michigan University as well as at other colleges and universities throughout the nation. A decision on admission to the M.B.A. program is not made until the GMAT score has been received. Foreign students must also submit a satisfactory score on the Test of English as a Foreign Language (TOEFL) before admission status can be determined.

EXPENSES
The tuition and local fees for full-time graduate students who are residents of the state of Michigan are $63.50 per semester hour. Nonresidents pay $138.00 per hour. There is a registration fee of $25.00 per semester.

The university offers housing for single graduate students in the residence halls. Graduate students may arrange for off-campus accommodations in apartment houses near the campus. Married students may apply for campus apartments, but the number available is limited in relation to the demand. Room and board in the university residence halls for single students is $2,350 for the two semesters. The cost for married students will vary with the size of the apartment needed. The university reserves the right to revise rates when necessary. Housing applications and additional information may be obtained from the Director of Housing.

FINANCIAL ASSISTANCE
Graduate fellowships of $4,000 are available to students who have an outstanding academic record.

Graduate assistantships that pay $5,000 to $6,000 for two semesters with remission of tuition (depending on the applicant's training) are available. Graduate assistants must teach an average of 6 hours per semester or perform equivalent services and may be enrolled in 6 to 10 hours of graduate study. To be chosen, they must have an overall average of 2.5 and have 3.00 in their field of specialization. Applications should be submitted by February of the year preceding the student's expected starting date. There is some opportunity for part-time work in the area because some graduate courses are scheduled in the evenings.

PLACEMENT
The placement office of the university provides help in attempting to place potential graduates and alumni. A great number of nationally known organizations, as well as smaller companies, governmental agencies, and schools, visit the campus to interview students. No charge is made for this service.

CORRESPONDENCE
For additional information, write to
Dr. Robert D. Hanson
Associate Dean
School of Business Administration
Central Michigan University
Mt. Pleasant, Michigan 48859

Central Missouri State University (CMSU) is located approximately 50 miles southeast of the Kansas City metropolitan area in Warrensburg, Missouri, a county seat. The university, founded May 10, 1871, is now in its second 100 years of operation. The growth in the university's physical plant reflects the institution's growth in enrollment. The university has some of the finest educational facilities in the country. The faculty numbers approximately 500. The main campus of 935 acres includes Pertle Springs, a 340-acre recreational and instructional park; Skyhaven Airport, also used for instruction; and the central campus, comprising residential and instructional buildings, play and drill fields, the University Stadium, the Museum, and the University Union.

The Master of Business Administration (M.B.A.) program may be completed either on a full-time or a part-time basis on the central Warrensburg campus or as a part of continuing education courses conducted in the Kansas City metropolitan/suburban area. The program is open to students from all parts of the world.

Applicants are considered equally without regard to race, sex, religion, creed, or national origin, and may have a liberal, scientific/engineering, or other professional degree. Currently, about 150 students are enrolled in the program.

Numerous openings are available for new students. The university operates on the semester plan with students being able to enter the program at the beginning of any academic semester—August, January, or June.

PROGRAM OF STUDY

The Master of Business Administration (M.B.A.) program is designed to meet the professional needs of recent college graduates who plan careers in business and college graduates already employed who desire to extend their business understanding and potential. The focus of the program is on decision making within the corporate enterprise; it is designed to prepare students professionally for responsible careers in business and other organizations, including public corporations, educational systems, nonprofit institutions, and government. The degree is conferred upon satisfactory completion of 33 to 57 semester hours depending upon student background.

The background courses presuppose no prior knowledge of business. This enables the school to select students with diverse backgrounds of experience and education. Realizing that some entering students will have acquired extensive knowledge in some subject areas of the background courses, the faculty has established a course waiver policy. To receive a waiver of a course, the student is asked to present evidence that he or she has successfully completed the course or an equivalent.

The core course requirements of the program are designed to enable the student to integrate concepts, skills, and principles. Perspective and depth of insight are increased as the student deals with complex organizational problems. Every attempt is also made to strengthen the student's analytical and communicative skills. Elective courses enable the student to develop depth in one or more areas of special interest. Because of this, each student is encouraged to play an important role in the early designing of his or her graduate program, seeking the guidance and counsel of an adviser and other College of Business and Economics faculty members.

The curriculum for the M.B.A. program emphasizes self-development. Although the program is comprehensive, it is not overly specialized, providing for student flexibility in elective selections. At the completion of the program, the student should be well informed in the functional areas of business. He or she should also have a knowledge of quantitative methods and data processing currently in use, an understanding of business applications of the behavioral sciences, and proficiency in oral and written English.

ADMISSION

Applicants for admission to the M.B.A. program must submit the following:
- a completed application form and
- transcripts of all college-level work indicating completion of a bachelor's degree.

Applicants are required to hold a baccalaureate from an accredited institution recognized by CMSU. In addition, students must have a Graduate Management Admission Test (GMAT) score and undergraduate grade-point average that totals a minimum of 950 based on the following formula: 200 × undergraduate overall grade-point average + GMAT = 950 or 200 × the grade-point average on last 60 hours + GMAT = 1,000.

EXPENSES

Fees at CMSU are exceptionally low, making a graduate degree from the university within the financial means of almost everyone.

FINANCIAL ASSISTANCE

A number of graduate assistantships are available for qualified graduate students in the College of Business and Economics and throughout the university. Assistantships provide students with the opportunity to teach, do research, or assist in an administrative capacity. In addition, each year CMSU administers almost $11 million in scholarships, federal and state insured loans, outright grants, and student employment programs.

CORRESPONDENCE

For further information on the M.B.A. program offered at Central Missouri, please write to

Coordinator, M.B.A. Program
College of Business and Economics
Central Missouri State University
Warrensburg, Missouri 64093
Telephone: 816-429-4289

Central State University, established in 1890, is the oldest state educational institution in Oklahoma. An urban renewal project in the 1960s expanded the campus to approximately 200 acres and provided an opportunity to add many new buildings. Most buildings have been built in the last 20 years. Although there are eight institutions of higher education in the metropolitan Oklahoma City area, more students from Oklahoma City attend Central State than any other school. Approximately 80 percent of the students commute. The university has placed major emphasis on superior instruction, with most professors teaching at the undergraduate as well as the graduate level. Very few graduate teaching assistants are employed. In the fall of 1985 total enrollment exceeded 13,000 students; over 3,700 of these were graduate students. Thirty-two percent of the total enrollment is in the College of Business.

PROGRAM OF STUDY

The College of Business Administration offers the Master of Business Administration (M.B.A.) degree as well as providing graduate courses for students pursuing graduate degrees in other colleges of the university. The M.B.A. degree at Central State University is designed for students who desire a broad preparation for executive and administrative positions in business, industry, government, and education. Areas of emphasis offered are accounting, economics, finance, management, and marketing. Courses in the M.B.A. program deal with problems faced by modern business institutions and assist the student in developing the ability to cope effectively with these problems. The College of Business Administration also provides an opportunity for persons who are employed full time to obtain a M.B.A. degree by offering the program at night as well as during the day.

ADMISSION

Admission standards for the M.B.A. degree are the same for all students whether they attend full time or part time. Admission is based on the overall undergraduate grade-point average and the student's score on the Graduate Management Admission Test (GMAT). Admission standards for international students, in addition, include a score of 550 on the Test of English as a Foreign Language (TOEFL). Applications for international students must be received by July 1, November 1, or April 1 for admission to the succeeding semester.

EXPENSES

Tuition and fees per semester hour are
    Residents of Oklahoma $20.55
    Nonresidents of Oklahoma 56.95
University-owned housing consists of 158 apartments for married students, their spouses and/or children, and four residence halls for single students. For further information, write to the Housing Office.

FINANCIAL ASSISTANCE

Central State University has very few graduate assistantships; however, the same forms of financial aid are available to graduate students that are provided for undergraduate students. For information write to the Office of Student Financial Aids.

PLACEMENT

The university has several means of assisting the student with placement. The College of Business offers a career day each year during which representatives from about 70 companies visit the campus to interview students. The College of Business also publishes vita for all graduating students. The unversity provides full placement services through the Placement Office.

CORRESPONDENCE

For further information or to request an application for admission, please write or call
    Dean of the Graduate College
    Central State University
    100 North University Drive
    Edmond, Oklahoma 73034
    Telephone: 405-341-2980, extension 2678

CHAMINADE UNIVERSITY OF HONOLULU

HONOLULU, HAWAII

Chaminade University is located on an 60-acre tract of land in the St. Louis Heights area, about two miles from Waikiki Beach, three miles from downtown Honolulu, and one mile east of the main campus of the University of Hawaii. The school was established in 1955 and offers both undergraduate and graduate programs in business administration, on a part-time and full-time basis. Approximately 2,000 day and evening students are enrolled in the various programs. The university is accredited by the Accrediting Commission for Senior Colleges and Universities of the Western Association of Schools and Colleges.

PROGRAM OF STUDY

The degree of Master of Business Administration (M.B.A.) is a professional degree designed to meet the needs of individuals in business, institutions, and the government to prepare them for increasing executive responsibilities. The degree program is practice oriented, designed to develop scholarship including interpretation, organization, evaluation, and application of knowledge to business. The graduates of this program are expected to demonstrate
- a broad knowledge of policies and techniques of business administration;
- the ability to evaluate operations, diagnose problems, and specify action by intelligent analysis of business systems;
- the ability to apply appropriate quantitative and other research methodology in specifying action for decision making in business.

The Master of Business Administration curriculum of Chaminade University requires the completion of 30 semester hours of course work. The M.B.A. program is presented in 10-week accelerated semesters (45 clock hours) with each student being permitted to take up to 6 semester hours each session. The student is required to complete five core courses to assure comprehensive coverage of the broad field of business.

M.B.A. Core Requirements	Credits
BU 600 Management of Business Systems	3
BU 610 Managerial Accounting	3
BU 620 Statistical Analysis for Business Decisions	3
BU 630 Marketing Systems	3
BU 640 Managerial Economics	3

Besides the core requirements, 15 additional hours of course work must be fulfilled. This includes BU 705 and any four other courses on the following list (additional electives will be developed in accordance with student demands):

	Credits
BU 701 Entrepreneurship	3
BU 702 Business Law	3
BU 704 Personnel Management	3
BU 705 Business Policy Seminar	3
BU 712 Financial Management	3
BU 722 Data Processing Systems	3
BU 730 Advanced Marketing Problems	3
BU 740 National Economic Policy	3
BU 770 Contemporary Tax Issues	3
BU 771 Estate Planning and Taxes	3
BU 772 Federal Taxation of Real Estate	3
BU 773 Taxation of Small Businesses	3
BU 780 Special Topics	3

Two courses (six semester hours) per 10-week accelerated semester are considered a full-time load and will be the maximum each student will be allowed to carry. Courses are offered in the evening.

ADMISSION

Applications will be accepted from individuals who have earned a bachelor's degree with an overall grade-point ratio of 3.0 or better on a 4.0 scale. Prerequisite courses in accounting, statistics, economics, marketing, finance, and management are also required.

All M.B.A. applicants must take the Graduate Management Admission Test (GMAT) prior to admission. An applicant from a foreign country or one who speaks English as a second language must also take the Test of English as a Foreign Language (TOEFL) and achieve a score of 550. A personal interview may be requested as part of the admission process. Candidates for this degree are selected from a list of qualified applicants. Semesters start in October, January, April, and July.

EXPENSES

Application fee, submitted with application, nonrefundable ... $ 30
Tuition, per credit hour 130
Total cost (30 credits) $3,900

CORRESPONDENCE

For further information, write or call
Chairman
M.B.A. Program
Chaminade University of Honolulu
3140 Waialae Avenue
Honolulu, Hawaii 96816
Telephone: 808-735-4744

The goal of Chapman College is to provide liberal and professional learning of distinction within a caring and value-centered community. In 1861, the college was founded by the Christian Church (Disciples of Christ) as a private, non-profit, coeducational institution. The campus is in Orange, a pleasant community of 90,000, within easy access to the abundant recreational, cultural, and employment opportunities of Southern California. Orange is 30 miles southeast of Los Angeles and 90 miles north of San Diego. The college is accredited by the Western Association of Schools and Colleges, and the School of Business and Management is a member of the American Assembly of Collegiate Schools of Business. The School of Business and Management offers the Bachelor of Arts in economics; the Bachelor of Science in accounting, business economics, finance, international business, management, management science, and marketing; the Master of Business Administration (M.B.A.); Economic Forecast Conferences; and public issues programs.

PROGRAM OF STUDY

Through the School of Business and Management, Chapman College offers a program of day and evening classes leading to the Master of Business Administration degree. The program is specifically designed for those now holding, or ultimately seeking, administrative positions in business. The purpose of the program is to develop professional competence and capability in the functional areas of business administration. The goal is to provide the student with the knowledge and perspective needed for success in the dynamic, changing world of business administration.

The M.B.A. program consists of three segments. The first segment comprises the 24-credit M.B.A. core courses. The following classes in business administration theory and practice are required of all candidates: MGSC 511, Statistical Decision Theory; FIN 517, Managerial Finance; ACTG 520, Managerial Accounting; MRKT 604, Marketing Management; MGSC 612, Operations Research; MGMT 613, Organization Theory; BUS 616, Research Methods in Business Administration; and BUS 675, Administrative Policy and Strategy. The second segment comprises the 12-credit elective courses. The candidate may choose 4 courses from a selection of 31 elective courses. Twenty-four of the 36 credits must

be taken in residence, and students must maintain an overall grade-point average (GPA) of 3.0 in all course work. The third segment of the program comprises the comprehensive examination, which is designed to test the extent to which the student has achieved the objectives of the program. The test should be taken in the final semester before graduation, and the candidate must achieve an acceptable grade.

ADMISSION

Prior study in business or economics is not a requirement for admission to the program. To be admitted to the program, students must (1) hold a baccalaureate degree from an accredited college or university; (2) take the Graduate Management Admission Test (GMAT) and have the results sent to the Graduate Division by Educational Testing Service; (3) have a grade-point average in the last 60 graded semester credits earned prior to the baccalaureate degree that multipled by 200 and added to the score achieved on the GMAT must equal 1,000 or higher (GPA × 200 + GMAT = 1,000) *or* have a score of 500 or higher on the GMAT. Students with an advanced degree from an institution that was accredited at the time the degree was awarded will be admitted to full standing providing they also achieve a score of at least 450 on the GMAT.

As a prerequisite, the applicant must present evidence of knowledge of concepts of accounting, economics, management and marketing, business statistics, and computer science. Acceptable evidence may consist of (1) completed undergraduate courses, (2) experience, or (3) satisfactory scores on an examination. Deficiencies must be removed prior to advancement to candidacy.

International students must submit the following before admission: (1) application for graduate studies; (2) application fee; (3) transcripts from all colleges attended; (4) completed financial form; (5) verification of English competency: Test of English as a Foreign Language (TOEFL) with a minimum score of 550, ESL level 9, or Michigan Test with a minimum score of 90. Deadlines for receipt of all application materials for international students are December 15 for spring and April 15 for fall and summer.

EXPENSES

The tuition is $250 per credit (1985-86), with an application fee of $25. Tuition discounts are available to students who pre-register. Students whose employers pay a portion of, or all their tuition, may be eligible for the deferred tuition plan. On-campus housing and a meal plan are available.

FINANCIAL ASSISTANCE

Graduate assistantships are awarded each semester and are renewable on request by the student with the recommendation of the supervising department or division. The grant covers full tuition costs up to a maximum of 18 credits, all of which must be fully acceptable toward the student's degree program.

California Guaranteed Student Loans and California Graduate Fellowships are available to students. Applications may be obtained from the Student Financial Aid Office. Part-time employment is available through the Student Financial Planning and Career Planning and Placement Offices.

PLACEMENT

The services of the Career Planning and Placement Office are available to students and alumni. Many large business firms recruit on campus in search of business administration graduates.

CORRESPONDENCE

Address inquiries to
    Director of Graduate Admissions
    Graduate Admissions Office
    333 N. Glassell
    Orange, California 92666
    Telephone: 714-997-6786

The Chinese University of Hong Kong was founded in 1963. The campus of the university is located on a beautiful hillside in Shatin, New Territories. Graduate studies in business administration began in 1966 with the establishment of The Lingnan Institute of Business Administration.

Because of the increasing demand in Hong Kong for people with formal business education, The Chinese University of Hong Kong, with the support of several local businessmen, initiated an evening three-year program of studies leading to the Master of Business Administration (M.B.A.) degree. This program began in September 1977.

The use of the name "The Lingnan Institute of Business Administration" has been discontinued, and both of the university's M.B.A. programs are now offered by the Division of Business Administration, Graduate School. The two M.B.A. programs have a unified faculty.

PROGRAMS OF STUDY

The major objective of the M.B.A. programs is to prepare men and women for responsible administrative and executive positions in business, government, and other organizations. In addition, the evening studies program aims to supplement the experience of practicing managers with the knowledge and theory of management.

The two-year M.B.A. program requires two years of full-time study, and classes are held on the university's campus at Shatin. Under the two-year M.B.A. program, there are three options: a general program, a specialization program in marketing and international business, and a specialization program in organization and policy studies.

Students enrolled under the general program are required to take core courses and a series of four integrative courses, and also to write a master's thesis or a business research report. Other than the above requirements, students are given opportunities to take certain elective courses according to their own interests.

The curricula of specialization programs permit each student to waive certain basic courses (depending upon his or her undergraduate studies) and require him or her to take some functional seminars, integrative courses, and specialized courses in the programs' specialized field. Each student in the specialization programs must write

a master's thesis or a business research report on a topic relating to his or her specialized field. The minimum number of credits required to complete the two-year M.B.A. program is 54.

The class sessions of the three-year M.B.A. program are held in the evenings and are designed to provide business management education to practicing managers and other professional people. Classes are held in the Town Centre at Tsim Sha Tsui East, Kowloon. The three-year program consists of 18 courses, each carrying 3 credits toward a minimum credit requirement of 54, equivalent to that required for the full-time program. Each calendar year is divided into three trimesters of 13 working weeks. Two or three courses are offered in each trimester, but individuals can elect to take one course per trimester and proceed at a slower pace. Completion of the 18 courses, however, must be within five consecutive years in order to qualify for the Master of Business Administration degree. Each student in the three-year program is also required to write a master's thesis or a business research report. This program offers core and elective courses similar to those of the two-year program.

ADMISSION

A first degree from a recognized university or a professional qualification judged to be the equivalent of a first degree is required of all applicants. Applicants who wish to be admitted to the specialization programs must be holders of bachelor's degrees in business administration. Although students without work experience are accepted in the two-year program, those with a year or more of full-time work experience in business or government are preferred. The three-year program entrance requirements are basically similar to those for the two-year program. However, applicants to this program are expected to have at least three years of significant full-time work experience after obtaining their undergraduate degrees. Applicants who have professional or similar qualifications equivalent to a degree and have a minimum of three years of postqualification work experience may also apply for admission.

Application for admission begins on January 2 and ends on February 28 each year. A complete application should include the following: two application forms, two official transcripts of undergraduate work, two confidential recom-

mendations, and Graduate Management Admission Test (GMAT) score.

After the selection committee has reviewed all applications, those with suitable credentials will be invited to take the language test, which is administered by the Graduate School of The Chinese University. Fluency in written and spoken Chinese and English is required for admission to either program. After review of their scores from the GMAT and the language test, selected applicants will be interviewed by a panel of faculty members.

EXPENSES

Tuition for the two-year program will be HK$4,800 in 1986-87, payable in two installments. Tuition for the three-year program will be HK$10,500 in 1986-87, payable in three installments. In addition, a caution money of HK$200 is charged to students of both programs.

Full-time single students of the two-year program can apply for rooms in the graduate hostel. Charges ranged from HK$900 to HK$1,350 per semester in 1985-86. A limited number of rooms are available to married students (without children) at different rates, and ranged from HK$770 to HK$1,035 per month in 1985-86. Charges for 1986-87 are under review.

FINANCIAL ASSISTANCE

A number of scholarships are awarded to students of the two-year program each year on the basis of academic achievement. Other forms of financial assistance available to students of the two-year program include the Hong Kong Government bursaries and loans administered by the Joint Universities Committee on Student Finance (available only to citizens of Hong Kong) and Graduate School scholarships and bursaries. In addition, students may apply for loans from funds established by the Board of Trustees and the program's alumni.

Second- and third-year students of the three-year program may apply for loans from the program's Financial Assistance Scheme. The amount of each applicant's loan is not to exceed 50 percent of the yearly tuition fee.

CORRESPONDENCE

For further details, write to
Admissions Office
M.B.A. Programs
The Chinese University of Hong Kong
Shatin, N. T., Hong Kong

The Graduate Institute of Business Administration of Chulalongkorn University (GIBA) is a joint academic endeavor among the J.L. Kellogg Graduate School of Management of Northwestern University, the Wharton School of the University of Pennsylvania, and Chulalongkorn University. Its primary objective is the development of efficient management personnel who will foster a climate of growth as well as strengthen the business administration infrastructure on which the future of Asian countries must depend. The teaching staff are selected mainly from leading members of both Kellogg and Wharton, complemented by supporting staff from Chulalongkorn University. The school occupies the fourth, fifth, and sixth floors of Vidyabhathna Building of Chulalongkorn University and is located on Soi Chulalongkorn 12 in Bangkok, Thailand.

GIBA offers a Master of Business Administration (M.B.A.) program designed to produce graduates in business administration who are comparable in knowledge and ability with those from leading business schools in the United States.

PROGRAM OF STUDY

The two-year M.B.A. program offers the students an opportunity to become totally involved in developing management skills applicable to both the public and private sectors of today's society. Teaching is by case study, balanced with lectures, seminars, and group work. The case study method involves active discussion of authentic business situations and is intended to develop managerial skills and knowledge so that students can readily apply their classroom experience to real-world managerial problems.

The M.B.A. curriculum is a tightly integrated program resembling those taught at both Kellogg and Wharton. Some adaptations have been made to suit the Asian environment. The overall program consists of 10 core and 14 supportive courses in the following areas: accounting, finance, industrial relations, management information systems, management policy, managerial economics and decision science, marketing, operations management, organization behavior, quantitative methods, and law. The program offers double majors; thus allowing the students to follow courses in two specialized fields of study throughout the program. In any one program, one of the two specialized fields will be international business. The second specialized field (finance, marketing, operations, personnel, or one other field) will change from year to year. The courses offered in this program are taught by faculty members from both Kellogg and Wharton as well as by qualified Thai counterparts. The program is operated on a quarter system. The academic year consists of 3 ten-week quarters; each quarter is further divided into 2 five-week periods, and in each period at least two courses of study are presented concurrently.

ADMISSION

By design, M.B.A. classes are limited in number, thus offering students the rare educational experience of close personal relationships with faculty and other students. Approximately 50 students are admitted to the program each year. Only those candidates whose academic ability, intellectual capacity for graduate study in management, managerial talent, motivation, and personal characteristics indicate that they are suited for management courses are admitted. A candidate must hold a bachelor's degree or its equivalent from an accredited institution. The Graduate Management Admission Test (GMAT) is required of all applicants. Applicants whose native language is not English must submit a score on the Test of English as a Foreign Language (TOEFL).

Admission is granted upon a successful interview with the representative of Kellogg and with the GIBA Admissions Committee, which is comprised of alumni of Northwestern University and the University of Pennsylvania, as well as GIBA senior administrative staff. All candidates are required to sit for interviews.

EXPENSES

Tuition, per credit hour, is $85.50.

FINANCIAL ASSISTANCE

Financial assistance is available through scholarships and long-term, low-interest loans. Although GIBA has no resources of its own to provide scholarships, it makes every attempt to assist qualified students who would otherwise be unable to attend. Through GIBA's assistance, a number of full scholarships have been made available by major business corporations, both to students who are in their employ and to those who are not.

PLACEMENT

GIBA offers career planning and placement services with active on-campus recruitment from major corporations. The aim of the placement program is to bring students and employers together in mutually beneficial relationships. GIBA's placement services supplement rather than substitute for the student's own efforts in identifying and obtaining the job best suited to his or her qualifications and career plans.

CORRESPONDENCE

For further information, please contact
Admission Office
Graduate Institute of Business
Administration
Chulalongkorn University
Vidyabhathna Building, 5th Floor
Soi Chulalongkorn 12
Phyathai Road, Bangkok 10500
Thailand
Telephone: 2142581-2

THE CITADEL

CHARLESTON, SOUTH CAROLINA

PROGRAM OF STUDY

The Master of Business Administration (M.B.A.) program is designed to provide broad professional training in business administration so that students will be better equipped with knowledge and skills for future executive careers. It aims to give the student a knowledge of theories, techniques of analysis, and methods of control that are common to all business, as well as an awareness of the social and human considerations in today's economic society.

The M.B.A. program is designed for students having a bachelor's degree in liberal arts, engineering, or sciences, as well as those with degrees in business administration. Students with degrees in business administration are eligible to enroll in graduate courses provided the specific course prerequisites have been met. Students with degrees in other fields must first complete the foundation course program outlined below. If some of the courses in the foundation course program have been completed, the student may proceed with the master's program while completing the remainder of the foundation course program. The courses generally will be offered in the evenings for people employed in the Charleston area. For this reason a student will usually take no more than two courses per semester.

In order to meet the standards of the American Assembly of Collegiate Schools of Business (AACSB), students must be instructed in the core areas of economics, accounting, statistics, business law, business finance, marketing, management, and business policy. In order to meet these standards the following undergraduate courses are required for the foundation course program: principles of economics, principles of accounting, statistics, principles of marketing, business finance, management, business law, and business policy.

The requirements for the graduate course program are 30 semester hours of graduate study, including seven required courses and three elective courses. No thesis is required. The required courses are as follows: managerial economics, management theory, managerial accounting, financial management, marketing administration, quantitative methods for business decision making, and business policy.

In addition to the above, three of the following must be elected: economic policy, computer information systems, financial institutions, investment policies, organization behavior and administration, legal aspects of business, consumer behavior and marketing research, production planning and control, contemporary accounting theory and advanced problems, and administrative communication theory.

Transfer credit may be approved for any of the foundation courses, and up to six hours credit for graduate courses may be approved for transfer, provided the graduate credits were earned within five years prior to admission at AACSB-accredited institutions. Courses completed in the University of South Carolina MBA-ETV program may be approved for credit. Correspondence courses will not be approved for credit.

A grade of A, B, or C will be considered passing for a graduate course. If a grade of F or WF (withdrawal failing) is received on a graduate course, the student—except in unusual circumstances—must withdraw from the program. An incomplete grade must be completed within the next academic semester. A grade of WP (withdrawal passing) earns no credit.

The Master of Business Administration degree will be conferred upon the successful completion of 30 hours of graduate credit with a grade-point ratio of 3.0 or better.

ADMISSION

Applicants will be admitted to the Master of Business Administration program on the basis of scholastic ability for graduate study, qualities of character, motivation, and other attributes appropriate to administrative responsibility. Anyone holding a bachelor's degree from an accredited college or university is eligible for consideration. Prior study in business or economics is not a requirement for admission. In the selection process the Admissions Committee will carefully appraise the following:

● academic record—the official transcripts of all colleges and universities previously attended will be examined not only for the overall grade average but also for trend of grades and areas of particular scholastic strengths,

● scores on the Graduate Management Admission Test,

● references—at least two letters of reference, preferably from faculty members of the undergraduate school attended (if these are not easily available, references from associates in business or the military services may be substituted),

● a personal interview with a designated representative of the college.

EXPENSES

Costs will include a $15 application fee, $70 for each graduate credit hour, and a registration fee of $5 for each semester or summer-school term.

CORRESPONDENCE

For further information, contact
M.B.A. Coordinator
Department of Business Administration
The Citadel
Charleston, South Carolina 29409

Established in 1925, The Claremont Graduate School (CGS) is affiliated with a group of five undergraduate colleges which together form the Claremont Colleges. The other colleges are Pomona, Scripps, Claremont McKenna, Harvey Mudd, and Pitzer. The Claremont Colleges base their association on the cluster concept, combining the strengths of the small college with those of a large university.

CGS emphasizes flexibility in its programs and permits students to take relevant graduate courses in the school's other graduate programs. The academic resources are many and varied. The Honnold Library System contains approximately 1,250,000 volumes. A major new Academic Computing Center offers state-of-the-art DEC, IBM, and Hewlett Packard equipment. Los Angeles, with its major cultural opportunities, lies only 30 minutes to the west.

PROGRAMS OF STUDY

The Claremont Graduate School's Graduate Management Center has three programs, differentiated on the basis of managerial experience: Business Administration, Executive Management, and Advanced Management.

The Business Administration Program is intended for those who are planning to begin or are in the early stages of their management careers. It offers two professional master's degrees: Master of Business Administration (M.B.A.) and Master of Business Economics (M.B.E.), both of which can be pursued on a full- or part-time basis. The curricula expose students to strategic management, international management, management theory, accounting, economics, finance, information science, marketing, and organizational behavior. Each degree requires 60 credits of course work: 11 core courses and 4 electives. The M.B.E. requires that all electives be taken in economics. The M.B.A. allows students to design a concentration of electives tailored to their individual career objectives. No thesis is required. The program also offers Doctor of Philosophy (Ph.D.) degrees designed to meet the needs of students who contemplate careers in teaching and research. (Information in the "Key Facts" section refers to the M.B.A./M.B.E. degrees only.)

The Executive Management Program is designed to provide managerial education to the seasoned, working executive. It

offers a 12-unit certificate, a 32-unit Master of Arts in management, a 48-unit Executive M.B.A., a 32-unit Advanced Executive M.B.A., and a Ph.D. in executive management. Prospective applicants may request a special brochure from the Associate Director, Executive Management Program.

The Advanced Management Program is designed to provide residential noncredit education for management at the policy level.

The unique design of the Graduate Management Center, which allows for extensive interaction of senior faculty with experienced managers enrolled in the Executive and Advanced Management programs, improves faculty awareness of current needs and practices in the business sector and enriches the curricula of all three management programs. The center also draws upon resources of other CGS programs in the humanities, economics, information science, public policy studies, mathematics, psychology, education, government, and international relations. These disciplines have developed and strengthened such subject areas as communication, ethics, and organizational history, and have allowed for a more sophisticated emphasis on analytical and verbal skills than professional schools typically provide. Methods of instruction vary with subject areas and preferences of faculty.

ADMISSION

All applicants for admission to the Business Administration Program must submit (1) completed application form, (2) transcripts of all college-level work showing the satisfactory completion of a bachelor's degree, (3) scores on the Graduate Management Admission Test (GMAT), (4) three recommendations, (5) current resume, and (6) statement of purpose. International applicants are also required to submit official Test of English as a Foreign Language (TOEFL) scores. No previous business-related courses are required. Admission is based on test scores, transcript quality, and leadership potential. Experience, business or military, is a significant factor. Students are admitted on a rolling admission basis for the fall, spring, or summer semesters.

EXPENSES

Tuition for full-time students was $7,950 in 1985-86 and $350 per unit for part-time study. The Claremont Graduate School reserves the right to change tuition and other fees at any time.

FINANCIAL ASSISTANCE

Merit scholarships and fellowships are available to the most outstanding master's and Ph.D. students. Loans and work-study opportunities are also available to qualified students.

PLACEMENT

Complete placement services are available, including individualized career counseling, career development, and job placement utilizing state-of-the-art computerization. Large sophisticated databases, computerized job matching, and laser-prepared cover letters facilitate the job search. Career fairs, alumni networking, and career-exploration seminars help identify skills. Mock interviews and practice sessions help prepare applicants for interviews.

CORRESPONDENCE

Inquiries should be addressed to
    Associate Director
    Business Administration Program
    The Claremont Graduate School
    Claremont, California 91711
    Telephone: 714-621-8073

CLARION UNIVERSITY OF PENNSYLVANIA

CLARION, PENNSYLVANIA

Clarion University of Pennsylvania was established in 1867. A coeducational university, it is one of the 14 institutions in the state university system of Pennsylvania. Located in northwestern Pennsylvania, the university has an enrollment of 5,600 students. Most of the students attend full time. The campus has grown significantly during the past 10 years; as a result, the majority of the physical plant consists of new buildings constructed within this period.

PROGRAM OF STUDY

The major objective of graduate study in the College of Business Administration is to provide those enrolled with the opportunity to develop a basic core of knowledge concerning the theory, techniques, and practices of administering business activities. In addition to studying the basic core of knowledge, candidates for the degree will have the opportunity for some in-depth study in a particular area of interest.

The program is designed to accommodate candidates with undergraduate degrees in fields other than business administration, as well as graduates from business degree programs. Candidates with undergraduate degrees other than business administration must take at least 30 credits of foundation courses that make up the undergraduate common body of knowledge in business administration. Persons in this category are encouraged to apply for the program and discuss their specific requirements with the Director of the M.B.A. program. Foundation requirements may be removed by course work at Clarion or other approved institutions.

The program leading to the degree is based on a total requirement of 33 credits beyond the foundation courses, which are determined at the time of admission. Twenty-four credits of this 33 are specifically required courses. All students must take courses in organizational structure and behavior, quantitative analysis for business decisions, management accounting, managerial economics, financial management, production management, marketing decision making, and a capstone course in business policy. The remaining nine credits in the program are elected, permitting the student to design the program to particular objectives with the approval of the M.B.A. Director.

A maximum of 9 hours credit toward the 33 credits required for the M.B.A. degree may be transferred from other accredited graduate programs with the approval of the M.B.A. committee. No graduate credit is granted for correspondence courses. Subject to the regulations governing the transfer of credits, the entire program must be taken in residence. The maximum time for completion of the degree program is six calendar years from the date of first enrollment.

Students can enroll in the program on either a full-time or part-time basis. Graduate classes are scheduled in late afternoon and evening and on weekends to accommodate the part-time enrollment.

ADMISSION

Admission to the M.B.A. program is open to qualified graduates of recognized colleges or universities accredited by a regional or general accrediting agency. There are three major requirements for consideration of admission to the program. They are (1) a generally satisfactory undergraduate record, (2) acceptable scores on the Graduate Management Admission Test, and (3) three letters of recommendation from the applicant's professors and/or employer.

EXPENSES

Expenses are listed as of August 26, 1985 and are subject to change.

	In-state Students	Out-of-state Students
Application fee	$ 10	$ 10
Tuition, per semester hour	89	99
Nine semester hours or more	800	891
Room and board, per semester, as available	1,005	1,005
Books and supplies	200	200

FINANCIAL ASSISTANCE

The School of Business Administration awards a number of graduate assistantships annually. These carry stipends of $1,550 or $3,100, depending on services rendered. Basic fees (tuition) are waived.

PLACEMENT

The college maintains an Office of Career Planning and Placement. This office is visited annually by representatives of leading companies. Alumni are kept informed of placement opportunities.

CORRESPONDENCE

For further information, please write or call

Dean of Graduate Studies
Telephone: 814-226-2337
        or
Director of the M.B.A. Program
Clarion University of Pennsylvania
Clarion, Pennsylvania 16214
Telephone: 814-226-2626

Clark University is an urban, independent university of liberal arts, founded in 1887 as a graduate institution. By design, the university has remained small, offering students the rare educational experience of close personal relationships between and among the faculty and students. The university has approximately 2,000 undergraduate and 750 graduate students. The Graduate School of Management enrolls approximately 50 full-time and 350 part-time students in its Master of Business Administration (M.B.A.) program.

The campus is located in Worcester, a city of 185,000 people in central Massachusetts, within an hour's drive of Boston. The city has a diversified industry and is distinguished as an educational center. The 10 schools of higher education in the Worcester area, which enroll more than 10,000 students, have formed the Worcester Consortium for Higher Education. Clark students are permitted to register at the other institutions for special courses and topics, and shuttle buses operate between the schools.

PROGRAMS OF STUDY

Clark offers graduate programs leading to the M.B.A. or the Master of Health Administration (M.H.A.) degree and a five-year B.A./M.B.A. program.

The M.B.A. program is not solely committed to the study of business organizations. The faculty believes the study of management applies to all organizations, not-for-profit as well as profit. M.B.A. students are interested in careers in business, government, health care, education, and other settings.

The M.B.A. program requires 18 graduate credits for the degree, equivalent to four semesters of full-time graduate study. The 16 credits are organized into four categories of course work and independent study (courses meet for 14 weeks, 3 hours a week, unless otherwise indicated):

1) Required background courses are designed to introduce students to the fundamental language, concepts, and skills underlying the core functional fields of management. Students with previous course work or experience in these areas may elect to waive these courses. Background courses are MGMT 301, Managerial Accounting and Finance; MGMT 302, Quantitative Methods; MGMT 303, Managerial Economics; MGMT 304, Introduction to Management Information Systems; and MGMT 310, Organization Behavior.

2) Required core management courses, intended to provide students with basic background knowledge and skills in several important functional areas, are MGMT 330, Marketing Management; MGMT 340, Financial Management; MGMT 350, Operations Management; MGMT 360, Business Policy; MGMT 362, Corporate Social Responsibility; and MGMT 390, Management Analysis and Communication.

3) Seminars and electives are designed to meet three objectives: they focus students more intensively on advanced topics in a particular functional area (e.g., seminar in marketing research); they provide students an opportunity to integrate previous course work by applying their knowledge/skills to a particular problem area (e.g., small business management); or they provide students an opportunity to explore important related topics in management (e.g., international business).

The M.B.A. program exposes all students to a broad general management orientation. Students wishing to focus on a particular area of management can do so by concentrating their elective courses in that area. Fields in which the M.B.A. program offers a wide selection of electives include human resource management, marketing, finance, accounting, organization development, and operations management.

ADMISSION

Admission to the M.B.A. program is open to all students who have a bachelor's degree or its equivalent and who show potential for success. Official transcripts of previous college and/or university work are required as well as three letters of recommendation. Additional criteria used in evaluating an applicant's potential include degree of achievement in previous undergraduate/graduate work and performance on the Graduate Management Admission Test (GMAT).

EXPENSES

For the year 1985-86, tuition for all courses was $750 per course. The other charges are a $25 nonreturnable application fee and a $25 diploma-publication fee. The cost of room, board, books, and sundries totals about $4,000 for one year.

CORRESPONDENCE

Inquiries should be sent to
Dean
Graduate School of Management
Clark University
950 Main Street
Worcester, Massachusetts 01610

Clarkson University was founded in 1896. About 60 percent of the students are enrolled in the School of Engineering; the remainder are about equally divided between the School of Science and the School of Management. The university's 200 faculty members promote technical and professional competence, but recognize the need for an adequate liberal arts background as a preparation for citizenship and life enjoyment.

The School of Management, which is 56 years old, has risen to prominence in the last 15 years. Its 45-member faculty represents all areas of the United States, and its members are dedicated to excellence in teaching and quality in research. A close personal relationship between students and faculty is encouraged. Students also benefit from the small, friendly community, the excellent climate, outdoor recreation, and the variety of placement opportunities.

Current enrollment at Clarkson is about 3,700 undergraduate and 350 graduate students. Graduate enrollment in the School of Management ranges from 100 to 120 students, approximately 60 of whom attend full time.

Located in the center of the St. Lawrence Valley, Potsdam is bounded on the northwest by the St. Lawrence River and on the southeast by the Adirondack State Park. It is primarily a recreational and dairy-farming area. Skiing (downhill and cross-country), ice-skating, ice hockey, snowshoeing, hiking, canoeing, hunting, and fishing are some of the popular outdoor activities. The climate is dry and cool with adequate, but not excessive, snowfall.

In addition to the students at Clarkson University, about 5,000 students are enrolled at the State University of New York College at Potsdam, so the community of scholars is approximately 9,000 in a town of about 10,000 permanent residents. This provides an excellent student-oriented atmosphere and valuable social and cultural facilities. The nearest large cities are Syracuse, New York (140 miles), Ottawa, Ontario (90 miles), and Montreal, Quebec (100 miles).

PROGRAMS OF STUDY

Clarkson University offers programs leading to the Master of Business Administration (M.B.A.) degree and the Master of Science (M.S.) degrees in Accounting and Industrial Management. These programs are accredited by the American Assembly of Collegiate Schools of Business (AACSB).

Requirements for the M.B.A. or M.S. degrees include 27 semester hours of credit in foundation courses covering the following: accounting, computer science and information systems, corporate finance, economics, law and society, management principles, marketing principles, operations or production management, and quantitative methods (statistics and calculus). Foundation courses can be waived in subjects in which a student has completed equivalent courses as an undergraduate.

Beyond the foundation, the M.B.A. program consists of 32 credits. Of the total, 20 credits comprise a core of modules covering the essential skills and knowledge base required to be an effective manager. The core consists of a series of interrelated modules that build upon one another and provide students with an integrated view of management. The core modules stress practice of analytical and creative thinking, communication, interpersonal and administrative skills. In addition, current trends in management are discussed and analyzed.

Beyond the core, students in the M.B.A. program select 4 three-credit electives. Building on the existing strengths in the School of Management, elective courses are offered in accounting, economics, finance, management information systems, marketing, and production management.

The M.S. degree in Accounting provides concentrated study for those interested in accounting. Beyond the 27-credit foundation, the program consists of 30 credits.

The M.S. in Industrial Management (M.S.I.M.) offers specialized, in-depth study in a specific area of the student's choice. Beyond the foundation, students may concentrate in manufacturing management by taking course work in such areas as computer-integrated manufacturing, quality control and industrial statistics, manufacturing planning and control, management of technology, and production management.

Students may also concentrate in management information systems within the M.S.I.M. by taking courses in information systems management, database organization, development of computer-based decision support systems, human factors, and systems analysis and design.

ADMISSION

Admission to M.B.A. and M.S. programs is open to qualified students with a baccalaureate degree. The Graduate Management Admission Test (GMAT) is required and should be taken at an early date. Completed applications, transcripts, test scores, and references will be reviewed after October 1 for January admission or after February 15 for summer or September admission. No deadlines are set, but early applicants are given preference. Applicants from non-English-speaking countries must submit scores on the Test of English as a Foreign Language (TOEFL).

EXPENSES

Tuition for full-time attendance is $7,900. Living costs for one year of study are estimated at $5,000 exclusive of tuition, but may vary by 20 percent, depending on the choice of housing and miscellaneous expenses.

FINANCIAL ASSISTANCE

A number of teaching and research assistantships are available on a competitive basis, ranging from tuition remission (for 30 credit hours) to additional stipends for students with outstanding academic credentials. The University Financial Aid Office will help candidates to secure loans, but few funds are available on a need basis. Foreign students must secure a guarantee of adequate financial support before arrival.

CORRESPONDENCE

For information or to request an application for admission, please write or call
Dean of the Graduate School
Clarkson University
Potsdam, New York 13676
Telephone: 315-268-6613

CLEMSON-AT-FURMAN M.B.A. PROGRAM

FURMAN CAMPUS, GREENVILLE, SOUTH CAROLINA

In 1969, Clemson University, a state-supported, land-grant university, and Furman University, a private liberal arts school, combined their resources to create a graduate educational program in business administration geared toward management and professional personnel in the Piedmont area of South Carolina. Subsequently, Clemson University assumed administrative responsibility for the Master of Business Administration (M.B.A.) program and the name was changed to the Clemson-at-Furman M.B.A. Program. As the name implies, the program is still offered on the Furman campus in Greenville where expansion of the business-industrial complex has provided the opportunity for beneficial interaction between the business and academic communities.

Although Clemson University is the policy-making body for the Clemson-at-Furman M.B.A. Program, the program still makes use of Furman University's faculty and facilities so that, in effect, the resources of both institutions are still available to the graduate student.

PROGRAM OF STUDY
The Master of Business Administration program has as its principal goal the preparation of candidates for positions of responsibility in business, government, and industry. It is designed to provide the student with a broad professional training that will enable him or her to deal more effectively with a rapidly changing business and social environment. To this end, it stresses a general viewpoint instead of limiting the student to one area of specialization. The Clemson-at-Furman M.B.A. Program operates an active adjunct professorship program, with selected corporation presidents meeting once each semester with individual classes. By this means business and industrial leaders become directly involved in the process of educating men and women for positions of leadership.

The program is open to both full-time and part-time students. Since all classes are offered during evening hours, individuals may undertake graduate-level education as part-time students without the necessity of terminating employment.

Graduates of engineering and liberal arts schools, as well as business administration graduates, are encouraged to enroll. Applicants for the M.B.A. program who have an undergraduate background in business or economics are normally permitted direct entry into graduate-level courses. Graduates of engineering or liberal arts schools who have no substantial background in business must present academic credits in each of the following areas before enrollment in graduate course work: principles of accounting and control systems, introduction to statistics, principles of economics, business management and organization, business finance, legal environment of business, quantitative methods, and management data systems.

Students whose undergraduate work includes the above courses in business and economics may complete the requirements for the M.B.A. degree in one calendar year of full-time study. Part-time students having the necessary prerequisites may be able to complete the program in two or three years depending on the number of courses taken each semester. M.B.A. students must complete a minimum of 30 credit hours of graduate-level work. The following courses are required: managerial economics, statistical analysis of business operations, managerial accounting and information systems, operations management, financial management, managerial problems in marketing, organization theory and behavior, and managerial policy. In addition, six semester hours must be selected from the following courses: research and communications, legal and social environment of business, international business management, financial markets and institutions, and industrial relations.

A student may transfer up to six hours toward the master's degree provided the work was taken at an approved graduate school. The transfer of credits must be approved by the Admissions Committee.

ADMISSION
All applicants for admission to the program must hold a bachelor's degree from an accredited college or university; the degree may be in any academic discipline. Applicants may enter the program for the fall semester, the spring semester, or the summer session.

Students are admitted to the program as candidates for the M.B.A. degree on the basis of interest, aptitude, and capacity for business study as indicated by previous academic records, scores on the Graduate Management Admission Test (GMAT), letters from employers and faculty members, and pertinent information from the student's application. A thorough effort is made to determine the applicant's potential for graduate study in business. The program seeks those who possess the capacity for creative and analytical thinking as well as a high level of motivation for graduate study and a career in business administration.

The Clemson-at-Furman M.B.A. Program is accredited by the American Assembly of Collegiate Schools of Business (AACSB) as well as the Southern Association of Colleges and Schools.

EXPENSES
Tuition is $125 per credit hour. A nonrefundable, nonrecurring fee of $15 must accompany each application. A diploma fee of $6.50 is payable upon completion of the program.

FINANCIAL ASSISTANCE
Low-interest, federally sponsored loans are available for students attending on at least a half-time basis.

PLACEMENT
The placement offices of both Furman University and Clemson University are available to assist graduate students in obtaining either full- or part-time employment.

CORRESPONDENCE
For further information, write or call
Director
Clemson-at-Furman M.B.A. Program
Furman University Campus
Greenville, South Carolina 29613
Telephone: 803-294-2090 or 2091

Cleveland State University is a distinctly urban university, created in 1964 to fill a need for higher education facilities in the Cleveland area. The university is coeducational and has an enrollment of over 18,000 students. More than 1,200 full- and part-time students are enrolled in the five graduate business programs.

PROGRAMS OF STUDY

The program leading to the degree of Master of Business Administration (M.B.A.) began in 1970. It is designed for students whose undergraduate preparation is in nonbusiness areas, as well as for students with undergraduate training in business. The program is designed to meet the needs of both full-time and part-time students. The M.B.A. program is accredited by the American Assembly of Collegiate Schools of Business (AACSB). All courses taken for graduate credit will be offered both in the daytime and evening. The curriculum consists of three sections: (1) 11 basic courses (44 hours) that can be waived if the student has had a background of courses in business, (2) 6 core courses (24 hours), and (3) 5 electives and one research project (24 hours). The total curriculum is 23 courses (92 quarter hours).

The Master of Accountancy and Financial Information Systems degree develops competent accountants who are knowledgeable in financial information systems, making them able to provide and interpret sophisticated financial information for the business community. The program will accommodate evening students on a full- or part-time basis. The curriculum consists of 9 foundation courses (36 hours), which can be waived with appropriate business background, 4 foundation courses (16 hours), and 12 core courses (48 hours).

The Master of Computer and Information Science program is a professional degree program specifically designed to combine a thorough education in computer and information science with an application area in business, engineering, science, or mathematics. The program is open to full- and part-time evening students. Students lacking prior computer science background must take a 56-hour preparatory program. The basic master's program consists of 45 hours beyond the prerequisites.

The College of Business Administration and the Department of Political Science offer a jointly sponsored and administered program leading to the degree of Master of Public Administration (M.P.A.). The principal objective of this program is to prepare graduates for administrative positions in government, nonprofit, public service organizations, and in health care administration. The program is designed primarily for part-time evening students wishing to enter into or to enhance a career in government. The curriculum for the M.P.A. program consists of 56 hours of study.

The Master of Labor Relations and Human Resources program consists of 64 credit hours beyond the baccalaureate degree. The program is designed to enroll students who are currently working. It is expected that the majority of enrollees will be part-time students taking courses in the evening. All students are required to have training in micro- and macroeconomics. The program is divided into four sections: (1) statistics and methodology (8 credit hours), (2) required core (28 credit hours), (3) elective courses (20 credit hours), and (4) Research Seminar in Labor Relations and Human Resources (MLR 690, 8 credit hours).

ADMISSION

Students are admitted to graduate programs in the fall (September), winter (January), spring (March), and summer (June) quarters. Applications and credentials should be submitted not later than six weeks before the beginning of the term. A nonrefundable application fee of $25 must accompany all applications for graduate study at the university.

In addition to submitting transcripts from each college or university attended, students must have a total of at least 950 points based on the formula: 200 × the overall grade-point average plus the Graduate Management Admission Test (GMAT) score; or at least 1,000 points based on the formula: 200 × the upper-division grade-point average plus the GMAT score.

EXPENSES

For 13-16 credit hours (full time)	*Resident of Ohio*	*Nonresident of Ohio*
Instructional fee	$ 649	$ 649
General fee	89	89
Tuition surcharge		738
Total	$ 738	$1,476
1-12 credit hours, each	$ 57	$ 114

FINANCIAL ASSISTANCE

Assistantships are available carrying a stipend of up to $1,500 per quarter in addition to waiver of fees. Recipients will be expected to assist faculty, and only full-time graduate students will be considered. The university participates in the National Direct Student Loan Program.

PLACEMENT

The full services of the Career Planning and Placement Center are available to graduate business students. Individual counseling assistance in placement is provided.

CORRESPONDENCE

For further information, write or call
  Dean, College of Graduate Studies
  Cleveland State University
  Rhodes Tower 1209
  Cleveland, Ohio 44115
  Telephone: 216-687-3592

THE COLLEGE OF INSURANCE

NEW YORK, NEW YORK

The College of Insurance, established in 1962, can trace its genesis to 1901 and the establishment of the Insurance Society of New York. Accredited by the Middle States Association, the New York City private college now offers degrees on the master's, bachelor's, and associate's levels.

The college is located in the heart of New York City's downtown financial and insurance district, within walking distance of the New York Stock Exchange, historic Trinity Church (where the college commencement ceremonies are held), South Street Seaport, and the World Trade Center. Conveniently located near public transportation, the college is just a short ride away from the Broadway and Lincoln Center theaters, Greenwich Village, Chinatown, and the uptown department stores, boutiques, and restaurants.

PROGRAM OF STUDY

The college's Master of Business Administration (M.B.A.) program encompasses 39 graduate credits (33 credits if a thesis is elected). Twenty-seven of these credits are required core courses in the areas of economics, management theory, financial management, and quantitative techniques. Twelve are selected from electives in the areas of insurance management and risk management.

While the M.B.A. program is designed for the typical graduate of a Bachelor of Business Administration program, an accelerated series of preparatory courses has been formulated for those persons holding bachelor's degrees in fields other than business administration. All applicants must also have or acquire a fundamental knowledge of insurance at the survey level.

The M.B.A. program is expressly tailored for insurance personnel or those dealing with the insurance industry. The program aims to enable the student to identify the central issues in insurance and to understand the economic, social, and political environment in which it functions; to develop skills in problem solving; to acquire analytical abilities; to improve communication skills; to evaluate and appreciate the role of behavioral science in the managerial function; to explore the financial, sociological, managerial, and other functions of the business entity; and to increase managerial competence and professional prestige.

ADMISSION

The minimum requirement for admission to the M.B.A. program is a bachelor's degree. Candidates must also meet the following conditions:

• in general, the college encourages applicants with undergraduate records at the B level or better, particularly in economics and business subjects;

• each applicant must have achieved a score satisfactory to the Graduate Admissions Committee on the Graduate Management Admission Test (GMAT) as an indication of ability to pursue graduate study successfully;

• foreign applicants are also required to submit official Test of English As a Foreign Language (TOEFL) scores;

• a personal interview may be required for admission.

Application deadlines are July 15 for the fall semester and December 15 for the spring semester. An application fee of $25 is required when the application is submitted, and a $25 registration fee is required each term when one or more courses are taken. A $25 student activity fee is also charged each semester.

EXPENSES

Graduate-level tuition is $180 per credit hour for employees of organizations sponsoring The College of Insurance and $195 per credit hour for all others. Tuition for courses taken at the undergraduate level is $150 per credit hour for employees of organizations sponsoring the college and $162 per credit hour for all others. These tuition fees were in effect for the 1985-86 academic year.

FINANCIAL ASSISTANCE

Students in the M.B.A. program are generally employed in the insurance industry and attend classes after work. Because the M.B.A. degree is awarded in the field of insurance, a high proportion of students have their tuition paid by their employers. Other forms of financial aid available include the New York State Tuition Assistance Program, the federally sponsored Guaranteed Student Loans, and Veterans Administration education benefits for those who qualify.

CORRESPONDENCE

Applications for admission to the program should be directed to

Graduate Admissions Committee
The College of Insurance
101 Murray Street
New York, New York 10007

THE COLLEGE OF SAINT ROSE

ALBANY, NEW YORK

The College of Saint Rose (CSR), an independent, coeducational liberal arts college, has an enrollment of over 3,000 students. Of this number, 850 are graduate students, the majority of them attending part time. The college offers the Master of Arts, Master of Science, Master of Science in Education, and Master in Business Administration (M.B.A.) in 21 fields of education, special education, the liberal arts, and business administration. Founded in 1920, CSR is fully accredited and has been offering graduate-degree programs since 1949.

CSR is characterized by academic strength and openness to innovation as well as by traditions of service, respect for the individual, and commitment to values. Located in a residential neighborhood of Albany, the college has all the advantages of an urban campus. A mixture of large, new modern buildings and traditional homes surrounds the campus green, creating an environment that is conducive to personal as well as professional growth and enrichment. Student involvement is full and varied; graduate students serve on college committees and are active in all areas of college life. Although CSR gives highest priority to excellence in teaching, members of the faculty are engaged in a number of research projects, often in cooperation with students.

PROGRAM OF STUDY

Designed to serve the professionally engaged person who wishes to pursue a degree through part-time study, the M.B.A. program is characterized by a strong general approach to the field of management. Foundation requirements may be satisfied by approved undergraduate work or by appropriate graduate-level work. Selected courses, which are part of the regular CSR curriculum, are offered in the evening each semester. Graduate applicants are eligible to register for these courses in order to fulfill foundation requirements. Students complete a minimum of 36 graduate credits in advance work in the following areas: accounting, business environments, business policy, data systems, economics, finance, marketing, operations management, organizational theory and behavior. There are also several elective options in accounting, business ethics, entrepreneurship, and human resource management. A capstone course, taken at the end of the program, provides an overall synthesis of material covered in earlier courses. Students also participate in a workshop/seminar each semester, exploring further dimensions of the managerial sciences.

The college operates on the semester system and provides fall, spring, and selected summer offerings. The M.B.A. program is designed for the part-time evening student. Degrees are awarded in May of each year.

ADMISSION

CSR welcomes applications from men and women in or preparing for managerial positions, or from any fields in which the insights, understandings, attitudes, and managerial skills appropriate for business administration are of value. Applicants should submit the following materials:
- the application form together with the application fee,
- official transcripts from all colleges attended (sent directly to the Graduate School from the other institutions),
- scores from the Graduate Management Admission Test (GMAT),
- two letters of recommendation for graduate study from college professors or from professional supervisors.

A personal interview is encouraged but not required.

Foreign students or students whose native language is not English must submit scores on the Test of English as a Foreign Language (TOEFL).

When all credentials are complete, the application will be reviewed by the program committee on admissions. In order to be considered for the M.B.A. program, an applicant should have earned a minimum index of 3.0 on a scale of 4.0 in his or her undergraduate major.

EXPENSES

Tuition is $146 per credit hour. Other academic fees include the one-time application fee of $15 and a registration fee of $7 per semester.

FINANCIAL ASSISTANCE

Because the M.B.A. program is designed to serve the needs of the part-time student, financial aid opportunities are limited. Students who are enrolled for six hours are eligible to apply for National Direct Student Loans as well as loans through the New York Higher Education Assistance Corporation Program. All inquiries should be addressed to the Office of Financial Aid.

PLACEMENT

All graduate students are encouraged to take advantage of the services of the CSR Career Center. These services include placement advice and information; interviews with representatives from business, industry, and government; and yearly placement seminars.

CORRESPONDENCE

For further information on the M.B.A. program at the College of St. Rose, please write or call
Graduate Dean
The College of Saint Rose
432 Western Avenue
Albany, New York 12203
Telephone: 518-454-5136

The College of St. Thomas is a private, four-year liberal arts college located in St. Paul, Minnesota. It lies at almost the center of the Minnesota Twin Cities metropolitan area, within easy commuting distance of both St. Paul and Minneapolis downtown districts.

A self-proclaimed "teaching" college—one primarily concerned with the instruction of its 3,800 plus undergraduates—St. Thomas also operates two postgraduate programs. These are the Graduate Programs in Management and the Graduate Programs in Education.

The Graduate Programs in Management faculty is composed of full-time members of the business administration, economics, and quantitative methods departments and full-time professionals in business, health care, energy, or government sectors who teach on a part-time basis. Though all classes are held evenings and Saturdays, the Graduate Programs in Management make full use of the college's facilities. The college's extensive O'Shaughnessy Library, one of the leading small college facilities of its kind in the northern Midwest, is available for use by graduate students. Academic departments and students also use the college's Computing Center (part of an intercollegiate computer system) and the professionally staffed Audio-Visual Center, which provides a full range of audio and graphic-visual services.

PROGRAMS OF STUDY

The College of St. Thomas' Graduate Programs in Management offer a Master of Business Administration (M.B.A.) program as well as a Master in International Management (M.I.M.). There are four formal M.B.A. program adaptations designed to meet the managerial needs of students from both the profit and nonprofit sectors. M.B.A. specializations in health care management, government contracts, and public management differ from the M.B.A. specialization in business management in the application of topics to profit and nonprofit organizations. The M.B.A. program integrates the fundamental managerial concepts, processes, disciplines, techniques, and tools that are common in differing organizational applications.

The M.B.A. program is professional rather than research oriented. The program requirements offer a good blend of theoretical and professionally applied courses to exercise the students in tools, methods, and techniques for decision making. The program's objective is to educate efficient, professional, and contemporary managers for business, industry, government, and health care organizations.

The M.I.M. program, like the M.B.A., is designed to prepare working professionals for successful managerial careers. The M.I.M. program is focused specifically toward careers in international business and emphasizes extensive study in international management disciplines, intercultural communications, and foreign languages.

These programs are open to any student holding a bachelor's degree from an accredited institution, regardless of undergraduate major. The Graduate Management Admission Test (GMAT) is required of all students. The M.B.A. program can be completed in three years. The program is made up of 14 courses of three semester credit hours each and allows for six elective hours within three areas of concentration.

The M.B.A. program outline and content is as follows:

I.	Foundation	4 courses
II.	Management Core	3 courses
III.	Functional Management	4 courses
IV.	Concentration	2 courses
V.	Policy	1 course

The M.I.M. program consists of a four-part curriculum:

I.	Foundation	6 courses
II.	Area and Language Studies	3 courses
III.	International Management Disciplines	4 courses
IV.	Capstone	1 course

ADMISSION

Admission into the program is based upon four criteria:

- undergraduate degree and grade-point average,
- GMAT scores,
- responsibility and accountability in professional work,
- motivation to complete a graduate program in management.

Eligible students may enter any one of three semesters—fall, spring, or summer. Preferred consideration is given to applications received by July 1 (fall), December 1 (spring), and April 1 (summer).

EXPENSES

Application fee, nonrefundable .. $ 15
Tuition, per semester credit hour . 185
It is expected that additional expenses for books and classroom materials would amount to approximately $40 per three-hour course.

CORRESPONDENCE

For information on the Graduate Programs in Management and applications, write or call

Director of M.B.A. Admissions
Graduate Programs in Management
College of St. Thomas
St. Paul, Minnesota 55105
Telephone: 612-647-5327

The College of William and Mary is a coeducational, state-supported institution with an enrollment of about 6,300 students. About 20 percent are engaged in graduate-degree programs. Located in Williamsburg, Virginia, the college is adjacent to the restored area of Colonial Williamsburg. Chartered in 1693, the College of William and Mary in Virginia is a small, modern university, oriented toward breadth of curricula and high academic standards.

PROGRAMS OF STUDY
The Master of Business Administration (M.B.A.) program objective is development of the broadly educated professional manager. Knowledge is acquired and skills are developed in managerial areas of problem analysis, evaluation and decision, and implementation of these decisions within the social and economic environment of contemporary American life. The case method is emphasized but not used exclusively.

The M.B.A. program requires 62 semester credit hours. Of the total, 41 hours are required courses including the common body of knowledge basic to modern business and managerial practice. The remaining 21 hours are in elective areas of marketing and distribution, management and organization, applied economics, finance, operations management, and accounting and control. No student may accumulate more than 12 credit hours in any one elective area; this policy encourages the development of the broadly educated manager rather than the specialist.

The M.B.A. program is open to any qualified holder of a bachelor's degree, regardless of the undergraduate field of study. Applicants with undergraduate business administration, computer science, engineering, or science majors may be granted waivers from selected common body of knowledge courses. Such waived courses must be replaced with an elective from the same discipline. Students with exceptional academic backgrounds may be granted advanced standing, which can reduce program requirements by up to 15 credit hours.

The normal program of study requires four academic semesters, although this may be reduced through summer session attendance and advanced standing. The M.B.A. program has about 225 full-time students. M.B.A. classes average about 25 students, providing a superior learning environment and excellent rapport between students and professors.

A combined M.B.A.-J.D. program, offered in conjunction with the Marshall-Wythe School of Law, permits students to complete both degree requirements in four academic years. Candidates must meet the admission requirements for each program and make a separate application to each school.

In late 1981 the business school moved into a renovated building solely for the business program. This facility provides specialized computer, classroom, and study areas for the M.B.A. program. M.B.A. students use an IBM model 370/158 and PRIME 750 computers with over 40 terminals in the business school.

The Professional Resource Center, located in Chancellors Hall, includes computer facilities, microfiche readers and printers, current business periodicals, and reference materials as well as space for individual study and research. The college's Swem Library contains over 500,000 classified volumes and since 1936 has been a selective depository receiving publications of agencies of the U.S. government. More than 3,000 periodicals are received regularly.

ADMISSION
Applications are accepted for August and January admission. An applicant must hold a bachelor's degree from an accredited institution. In addition, an official score report on the Graduate Management Admission Test (GMAT) taken within the past five years is required.

EXPENSES
The tuition and general fee for full-time graduate study is $1,285 per semester for Virginia residents and $3,224 per semester for others. Summer session students from Virginia are charged $92 per semester hour. Nonresident tuition is $221 per semester hour. A nonrefundable application fee of $15 is required.

There are limited living facilities on campus for graduate business students. Nearby housing is relatively plentiful, however, and M.B.A. students often share apartment expenses. Approximately $250 per month is needed for shared housing plus minimum personal expenses.

FINANCIAL ASSISTANCE
Most financial assistance is oriented toward certifiable financial need. Graduate scholarship and fellowship funds are available from state and private sources. In addition, the business school currently awards a limited number of research assistantships. These awards provide up to $4,600 and remission of tuition. Through the college's Office of Student Aid, assistance is available under the National Direct Student Loan Program, the Guaranteed Student Loan Program, and various programs for federal beneficiaries.

Part-time employment opportunities within the community are comparatively good; however, first semester students are encouraged not to work part time.

PLACEMENT
The college placement office assists students and alumni in obtaining suitable employment. National and middle-Atlantic region corporations and governmental agencies actively recruit at the college.

CORRESPONDENCE
For further information, write or call
Director of Admissions and
Financial Aid
School of Business Administration
College of William and Mary
Williamsburg, Virginia 23185
Telephone: 804-253-4102

COLORADO STATE UNIVERSITY

FORT COLLINS, COLORADO

The origin of Colorado State University (CSU) can be traced to an act of the Territorial Legislature in 1870, six years before Colorado became a state. The first students registered in 1879. In the same year the Colorado General Assembly accepted the provisions of the Morrill Act of 1862. This laid the foundation for the development of CSU as a land-grant institution. Graduate study in some areas has been available for many years; the first master's degree was granted in 1893.

The College of Business was formed on January 1, 1966. A Department of Business had operated under the College of Science and Arts for 10 years prior to the granting of college status. The first master's degrees with a major in business were given in 1964. Graduate work in business had been available for some time, but the degrees had been granted under the auspices of the Economics Department. Current enrollment is approximately 230 students per semester. Each student is assigned an adviser to assist in developing a program of study.

PROGRAMS OF STUDY

The programs at the graduate level in business lead to the degree of Master of Science (M.S.) in business and Master of Business Administration (M.B.A.). Students may enroll in any semester including the summer.

Students with a bachelor's degree in business may expect a program of 30 semester credits with a thesis or 32 semester credits without the optional thesis. Thesis credit is limited to six hours. Such a program could lead to completion of the M.S. degree with a business specialization in one calendar year.

Students with a bachelor's degree in a subject other than business may expect a program of 30-32 semester credits plus missing pregraduate business courses. Such a program ordinarily requires four semesters to complete and leads to the M.B.A. degree.

The M.B.A. program includes a sequence of pregraduate core courses in business law, microeconomics, computer language, business statistics, accounting, finance, management, marketing, and production. Accelerated courses have been designed for nonbusiness degree holders so they can complete accounting, finance, and management pregraduate requirements in one-semester courses. All of the other pregraduate courses are also one-semester courses. One or more of these pregraduate courses can be waived on the basis of previous course work or proficiency.

The graduate courses in the M.B.A. program are as follows:
- *tool areas*—statistical decision making, methods in general business research, computer applications in decision making, and managerial economics;
- *general courses*—managerial accounting, business financial policy, management, and marketing strategy;
- *integrating course*—business policy, plus electives.

The M.S. degree program provides an opportunity for in-depth study in the specialized fields of accounting and taxation, finance, management, management information systems, and marketing. It is designed to prepare students for positions of executive leadership in these specialized business areas.

ADMISSION

In evaluating requests for admission, emphasis is placed on undergraduate grade performance and performance on the Graduate Management Admission Test (GMAT). Recommendations from faculty, work experience, and similar factors will be examined before making an admission decision. Students are admitted in September, January, and June. A minimum score of 550 on the Test of English as a Foreign Language (TOEFL) is required of international applicants.

EXPENSES

Minimum estimates of costs for one academic year:

	In-state	Out-of-state
Tuition and fees (nine months)	$1,756	$4,889
Room and board (minimum)	2,742	2,742
Books and supplies	320	320
Personal expenses	710	710
Total for academic year	$5,528	$8,661

FINANCIAL ASSISTANCE

A limited number of graduate teaching assistantships are available. These include tuition remission and a cash stipend. Duties range from nominal to substantial service and are usually related directly to stipend size. Tuition scholarships are also available.

PLACEMENT

The university maintains its own Placement Office, visited annually by representatives of many companies from all sections of the country. The Placement Office also keeps interested alumni informed of opportunities as they arise and maintains a credentials service for alumni use throughout their careers.

CORRESPONDENCE

Applicants should submit transcripts, GMAT scores, and three letters of recommendation to
    Associate Dean
    College of Business

Catalogs and admissions forms are available from
    Graduate School
    Colorado State University
    Fort Collins, Colorado 80523

Located on the main campus at Morningside Heights, Columbia University's Graduate School of Business enjoys a close association with the business and financial community of the nation's largest city. Students are encouraged to utilize the many opportunities to hear and meet outstanding business leaders and to visit industrial and financial organizations. Columbia's location permits the school to staff some classes with adjunct faculty who are key managers of Fortune 500 firms, entrepreneurial businesses, and major not-for-profit organizations. Their daily contact with the business community forms an integral part of classroom exchange.

PROGRAMS OF STUDY

Programs leading to the Master of Business Administration (M.B.A.) and Doctor of Philosophy (Ph.D.) degrees in business are available on a full-time basis to qualified men and women. There is no evening program. Combined degree programs at the master's level are offered with the Schools of Journalism, Law, Architecture, International Affairs and Public Administration, Public Health, Engineering, and Social Work, and at both the master's and doctoral levels with Teachers College.

A unique feature of the Business School is its operation on a trimester basis. A student may begin studying at any one of three times—in summer, fall, or spring. He or she may complete degree requirements in 4 consecutive terms, or a period of 16 months, or may elect not to attend the school for any one 4-month period, thereby completing the degree in a period of 20 months.

The M.B.A. program is designed to provide professional education in the liberal tradition of academic instruction. The M.B.A. curriculum provides the student with a breadth of preparation through the general management approach of the core courses. At the same time, study in depth in one of the fields of business permits the student to make an immediate contribution to an employer. To complete the degree, the student takes 20 courses. Eight are required courses concerned with the environment in which business operates, the internal organization and administration of business firms, the quantitative tools used in measurement and control, and the characteristics of business policy formation. The Master of Business Administration candidate also completes approximately five courses in an area of concentration selected from the following: accounting, banking, business economics and public policy, finance, operations management, marketing, international business, management science, management of organizations, corporate relations and public affairs, and public and not-for-profit management. It is possible to choose a concentration other than one of those listed above, including one that may be composed partially of courses offered in other graduate faculties of the university. The remaining courses are completed in elective work either within the Graduate School of Business or in related graduate courses in other faculties of the university.

The doctoral degree program is designed primarily for those students who wish to pursue a career in teaching and research. Complete information may be obtained from the Office of Doctoral Studies, Room 213, Uris Hall.

A special master's degree program is available for executives at the middle management level who are sponsored by their companies. Details may be obtained from the Office of the Master's Degree Program for Executives, 218 Uris Hall.

ADMISSION

A bachelor's degree or the equivalent is the minimum entrance requirement. All candidates for admission are required to take the Graduate Management Admission Test (GMAT). A personal interview is not mandatory, although candidates may be requested by the Committee on Admissions to appear for such an interview. Applicants in the New York area are encouraged to request an interview.

The Committee on Admissions selects those students who show the greatest promise of achieving successful careers in business. The academic record, the GMAT score, evidence of leadership ability, managerial potential, and letters of recommendation are the main criteria used in making selections.

Students who have completed undergraduate or graduate courses equivalent to required course work in the Graduate School of Business may receive exemptions through a proficiency examination or transcript analysis. Exemption permits the substitution of an elective for the required course but does not reduce the degree requirements.

EXPENSES

Figures per term for 1985-86

Tuition	$5,640
Fees	180
Books	275
Room and board	2,768
Approximate total	$8,863

FINANCIAL ASSISTANCE

M.B.A. candidates who are U.S. citizens or permanent residents may apply for the Tuition Loan Plan, a program that provides assistance to help meet tuition costs. Applications are available after a student has been admitted. A number of fellowships and scholarships are available to M.B.A. candidates. Fellowship awards are made on the basis of academic excellence, but the stipend accompanying each award is adjusted according to the financial need of the students. Scholarships are granted on the basis of need alone.

PLACEMENT

The school provides a comprehensive placement service for graduating students and alumni. Over 300 corporations, financial institutions, and nonprofit organizations visit the school in the fall and spring to conduct over 10,000 employment interviews. Placement staff are available at all times for guidance and counseling. Students also have access to the Alumni Counseling Board, a network of M.B.A. graduates.

CORRESPONDENCE

For further information, please write or call

Business School Admissions Office
105 Uris Hall
Columbia University
New York, New York 10027
Telephone: 212-280-5568

Montreal is the second largest city in Canada, with a population of nearly three million, of whom roughly two thirds are French speaking. It boasts all the attractions of a large cosmopolitan area: many theaters and museums, a rich musical life, numerous places of historic interest, and beautiful parks. Concordia University is one of four universities in the Montreal area. It was formed in 1974 when Sir George Williams University and Loyola College of Montreal merged.

PROGRAMS OF STUDY

Concordia's Faculty of Commerce and Administration is one of Canada's leading business schools and enjoys an international reputation. The school offers programs of study and research leading to the Ph.D. in Administration and a Master of Business Administration (M.B.A.) in two configurations: the Professional M.B.A. and the M.B.A. Executive Option.

The Ph.D. in Administration program is offered in collaboration with the three other universities in Montreal. The joint nature of the program gives the student access to a large number of highly qualified scholars with a wide range of expertise. Since this is a bilingual program with some courses being given in English and others in French, applicants must demonstrate a level of competence that would allow them to read technical material and to follow lectures and discussions in both languages. Students in the program may write reports, examinations, and their thesis in English or in French.

The M.B.A. Executive Option is designed for executives with wide experience at the senior management level. This intensive program takes two years to complete while maintaining full-time employment. Admission standards are selective. Preference will be given to candidates who have completed undergraduate studies and who have a number of years of business experience.

The objective of Concordia's Professional M.B.A. Program is to develop knowledgeable, trained professionals, highly skilled in the art and science of business management and ready to accept its challenges.

The program is given in two parts. Part I courses provide the basic foundations in the technical skills of management (11 courses). Part II consists of three compulsory courses, five or more elective seminars which allow each student to pursue his or her particular interest, and a major research paper. While lectures, seminars, and independent study make up most of the program, use is also made of the case method of instruction in which actual business problems in need of professional solutions are brought into the classroom.

Students who have a Bachelor of Commerce or related degree may be exempted from certain Part I courses. The minimum degree requirement is 45 credits, including at least one 3-credit course or seminar in each discipline. The timetable options are flexible: day, evening, part-time, and full-time.

ADMISSION

Admission is possible in the fall (September), winter (January), and summer (May). Applications to the program will be accepted up to June 30 for fall admission, October 30 for winter admission, and February 28 for summer admission.

An applicant for admission to the Concordia M.B.A. program must have a bachelor's degree with high standing, or qualifications accepted as equivalent by the Board of Graduate Studies; a satisfactory performance on the Graduate Management Admission Test (GMAT); and three letters of reference. Preference is given to applicants with at least two years of business experience. Upon admission to the program, competence in business mathematics must be demonstrated by either passing the Business Mathematics Examination or by taking an appropriate level mathematics course.

Applicants whose native tongue is not English or French and who are not Canadian citizens or landed immigrants are required to achieve a satisfactory performance in the Test of English as a Foreign Language (TOEFL) before being considered for admission. This requirement will be waived for foreign students completing their undergraduate degree at a university where English or French is the language of instruction.

EXPENSES

Term fee	$ 10
Tuition fee, per credit	
Canadians and students with permanent resident status	10
International students	195

FINANCIAL ASSISTANCE

Most full-time students are eligible to apply for financial assistance from the university in the form of teaching fellowships, assistantships, and scholarships. Additional information will be supplied upon request.

PLACEMENT

The M.B.A. program office seeks to provide placement opportunities for M.B.A. graduates. Each year an M.B.A. profile book is published and distributed to several hundred companies. The Guidance Services provide job hunting workshops specifically designed for M.B.A. students. Recruitment activities take place both on campus and off campus.

CORRESPONDENCE

For further information or to request an application for admission, please contact
M.B.A. Program
Faculty of Commerce and
 Administration
Concordia University
1455 de Maisonneuve Blvd. West
Room GM 201-9
Montreal, Quebec H3G 1M8 Canada
Telephone: 514-848-2717

Established in 1946, the Johnson Graduate School of Management offers graduate programs designed to provide an educational foundation for men and women who plan to pursue management careers in the private sector. In 1964, the school moved into the newly built Malott Hall, a building designed to meet the special requirements of graduate study in management. A new wing, completed in January 1977, provides additional lecture halls and office and library space. In 1984, the school received a $20 million endowment gift from the Johnson family of Racine, Wisconsin. This endowment, the largest single gift ever given to an American graduate school of management, has given the school its new name.

The school's faculty of 42 and full-time student enrollment of 480 enjoy the opportunities of a diversified university. The school emphasizes flexibility in its programs and permits students to take relevant graduate courses in the university's 50 other graduate schools and departments. Students may live in graduate dormitories, university apartments, or private dwellings and apartments off campus.

PROGRAMS OF STUDY

The school offers a two-year Master of Business Administration (M.B.A.) program requiring completion of 60 credits of course work and four semesters in residence. No thesis is required, but the assignment of papers is frequent. The first year consists of core courses in the basic areas of management and a few electives; in the second year each student designs a concentration of elective courses tailored to his or her individual career objectives. Methods of instruction in the school vary with subject areas and the preferences of instructors. Frequent guest lectures by practicing managers are an integral part of the curriculum.

The school operates on the semester system, and instruction begins in late August. No part-time or evening programs are available.

In cooperation with the Cornell Law School, the school conducts a combined program in management and law, a four-year program leading to the M.B.A. and the Juris Doctor (J.D.). Candidates for admission to the combined programs must satisfy the admission requirements of both schools.

The school's Doctor of Philosophy degree program in business is designed to meet the needs of students who contemplate careers in teaching or research.

ADMISSION

The school welcomes applications from men and women who will have received the baccalaureate degree or its equivalent by the time of enrollment. Candidates are urged to pursue a broad education at the undergraduate level. Applicants for the M.B.A. degree must take the Graduate Management Admission Test (GMAT); the October administration of this test is recommended, but the January and March tests will also meet the April 1 application deadline. Applicants for the combined program in administration and law must also take the Law School Admission Test (LSAT). Two letters of evaluation and transcripts for any academic work taken for credit beyond the secondary level are required. Prior full-time work experience is an important criterion in the admission process. Personal evaluative interviews are a part of the application process. These are conducted on campus, with 1,000 alumni interviewers worldwide, or on toll-free phone lines. Applications for admission should be completed by April 1. Chances for admission after that date are somewhat reduced. Each entering class has approximately 225 students.

EXPENSES

Tuition and fees for the 1985-86 academic year were $11,100. Total costs, including living expenses, but excluding transportation, came to about $18,250 for the single student. For the married student without children, the cost averaged from $3,000 to $3,500 more. The approximate expense for each child was $1,650 for the academic year.

FINANCIAL ASSISTANCE

Financial assistance in the form of scholarships and loans is available to students in the school. Applicants for financial assistance are required to submit their requests for aid through the Graduate and Professional School Financial Aid Service (GAPSFAS) no later than February 1. Awards are based on a combination of merit and need.

PLACEMENT

The school's Office of Career Services coordinates several hundred recruiting visits each year by national and multinational corporate employers. An active career forum brings more than 200 executives to the school, enabling students to discuss career opportunities in various industries and fields of work. In addition, career counseling, summer job search assistance, and alumni placement are ongoing services of this office.

CORRESPONDENCE

For further information or to request an application for admission, write or call
Office of Admissions
Johnson Graduate School of
    Management
Malott Hall
Cornell University
Ithaca, New York 14853
Telephone: 607-256-2327
Toll-free during academic year:
800-252-6326 (New York State)
800-847-2082 (all other states)

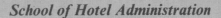

Cornell University's School of Hotel Administration offers a program leading to the degree of Master of Professional Studies in Hotel Administration (M.P.S. H. Ad.) The program is designed for students who have hospitality-industry experience and hold bachelor's degrees in other academic areas. The M.P.S. program was developed in 1972 to meet the continuing need in the hospitality industry at both the corporate and operational levels for men and women equipped with a variety of professional and academic skills. On average, 80 students are enrolled in the two years of the program at any given time.

The first of its kind, Cornell University's School of Hotel Administration was established in 1922 and has remained foremost among the numerous hospitality-education programs established in more recent years. The 5,000 alumni of the undergraduate and graduate programs are recognized as leaders in all segments of the hospitality field and other business fields. Their close and continuing association with the school provides invaluable resources for current information and placement opportunities.

The School of Hotel Administration is located on Cornell University's scenic Ithaca, New York, campus. Students in the M.P.S. program are encouraged to make use of the vast academic and cultural resources offered by the university.

PROGRAM OF STUDY

The two-year M.P.S. program provides extensive professional training in disciplines pertinent to the hospitality industry. The core curriculum includes courses in the areas of financial management, properties management, food and beverage management, human resources management, marketing, and computer applications.

In their second year of study, students write a monograph on a topic of their selection under the direction of a faculty adviser. In addition to the core curriculum, students are required to concentrate in one of the following nine areas: financial management, foodservice-systems management, hospitality management, human resources management, management information systems, management sciences, project development and design, marketing management, or small-business development.

ADMISSION

Applicants are required to have had experience in the hotel, restaurant, or tourism fields. They are not required to have baccalaureate degrees in hotel administration. In addition to the Graduate Management Admission Test (GMAT), applicants are required to complete the graduate school application form, submit two letters of recommendation, and arrange for a personal interview with a representative of the School of Hotel Administration.

Candidates are admitted for the fall term only. Applications for admission must be filed by February 15. The deadline for submitting supporting documents and fulfilling the personal-interview requirement is February 15.

EXPENSES

Tuition and fees for the 1985-86 academic year were $10,500. Living expenses are estimated at an additional $7,150 for the nine-month academic year, plus approximately $3,000 more for a married student and $1,700 for each child. (These figures do not include transportation to and from the university.) Both tuition and expenses are expected to increase for the 1986-87 academic year.

FINANCIAL ASSISTANCE

A portion of the school's scholarship funds are available for students enrolled in the Master of Professional Studies program. However, there are many applicants for financial assistance, and the funds are limited. Every graduate student who wants to be considered for financial assistance must complete a form from the Graduate and Professional School Financial Aid Service (GAPSFAS) by March 1.

Awards are based on financial need and scholastic ability. In addition, teaching assistantships are available to qualified students in their second year. The assistantships are based on academic qualifications and are independent of need.

PLACEMENT

Job opportunities for graduates of the School of Hotel Administration have been plentiful throughout the school's history. Numerous corporations send their representatives to the school each year to interview students for positions.

The program provided by the Hotel School, the numerous contacts made during the two years of the M.P.S. program, and the admirable record of Cornell graduates in the industry have combined with the efforts of the school's placement office to produce an enviable record—95 percent employment of graduates of the undergraduate and graduate programs throughout the history of the school.

CORRESPONDENCE

Requests for application forms and inquiries about interview arrangements, the school's program, requirements for graduation, and financial aid should be directed to

Director
Master of Professional Studies Program
School of Hotel Administration
Statler Hall
Cornell University
Ithaca, New York 14853
Telephone: 607-256-7245

Creighton University is a privately endowed, coeducational institution operated by the Jesuit Order. Founded in 1878, it is located in Omaha, Nebraska. Its courses and curricula are open to qualified students without regard to race, color, national or ethnic origin, handicap, sex, religion, or age. Over 6,000 students are presently enrolled in the university, and approximately 250 students are enrolled in graduate programs in the College of Business Administration. The college is an accredited member of the American Assembly of Collegiate Schools of Business (AACSB).

PROGRAMS OF STUDY

Creighton's graduate programs are designed to assist individuals to become proficient in technical topics as well as to develop creative and professional leadership qualities. The Creighton graduate will have had the opportunity to specialize in an area of particular interest while being exposed to a broad-based approach to business topics and issues. The College of Business Administration offers three distinct master's programs in order to meet the specific requirements of students with varying interests and professional needs: the Master of Business Administration (M.B.A.), the Master of Professional Accountancy (M.P.A.), and the Master of Computer Systems Management (M.C.S.M.).

Since M.B.A. students have differing management responsibilities and hence differing practical course needs, Creighton University's modular Master of Business Administration program has a distinct advantage over conventional programs: it has flexibility in selection of courses. Each student selects courses that meet his or her interests and needs in order to provide a broad background in the fundamental areas of business. Creighton's program is divided into six modules: policy, accounting, decision sciences, economics, finance, and marketing. Students must complete the four courses in the policy module and take one course from each of the remaining five modules. The courses are not sequential, and the student may select any course in a module that best fits his or her academic needs. Two 700-level electives from any of the courses available (including an independent study and research option) round out the program.

The Master of Professional Accountancy curriculum is designed to provide a significant educational experience for students seeking advanced study in the field of accountancy. Candidates are exposed to each major segment of the accounting discipline. As an alternative to the M.B.A. for those who have chosen accounting as a career path, the M.P.A. emphasizes that management and accounting are not separate disciplines when applied to actual situations. M.P.A. students must take six required courses, three from the policy module and three from the accounting module. The M.P.A. students must select four additional courses in the systems audit area or the taxation area or a combination of both areas. One 700-level elective from the M.B.A. or M.C.S.M. course offerings is also required.

The Master of Computer Systems Management degree is designed to prepare qualified individuals for administrative careers in information systems management. The curriculum is structured to combine rigorous study of computer hardware and software with course work in organizational issues facing the computer professional. Students must take seven courses in computer systems work as well as three courses in supporting areas such as policy and one 700-level elective from any of the courses available.

All programs are comprised of 33 semester credit hours of graduate-level courses. Most course offerings are held one evening per week in the fall and spring semesters and two evenings per week during summer sessions.

ADMISSION

Enrollment in the graduate programs is open to any student who meets the following requirements: (1) a baccalaureate degree from an accredited institution; (2) high scholastic achievement at the undergraduate level; (3) evidence of character, aptitude, and capacity for graduate study; and (4) an acceptable score on the Graduate Management Admission Test (GMAT). Applicants who were graduated from universities in non-English-speaking countries must submit scores from the Test of English as a Foreign Language (TOEFL). A minimum score of 500 is required.

Applicants from nonbusiness undergraduate areas may be required to take up to 24 semester hours of foundation courses in the areas of accounting, economics, business law, statistics, finance, marketing, organizational theory, and operations management. These courses are waived in each subject area for students who have satisfactorily completed equivalent courses prior to admission to the program. M.P.A. students must add two semesters of intermediate and one semester of advanced accounting to the above foundation courses in order to be prepared to take the graduate-level accounting work. M.C.S.M. students are required to have most of the above foundation courses and six hours of college mathematics (algebra and calculus) and two three-hour courses in programming.

EXPENSES
Tuition in the graduate program was $162 per semester credit hour at the foundation level and $175 at the graduate level for the 1985-86 academic year.

FINANCIAL ASSISTANCE
Students accepted for admission to Creighton University may apply for financial assistance under the student loan program. Graduate research assistantships are available through the College of Business Administration. Many employers pay tuition in whole or in large part for their personnel.

CORRESPONDENCE
For additional information, write or call
College of Business Administration
Creighton University
Omaha, Nebraska 68178
Telephone: 402-280-2853

Dalhousie University's School of Business established a Master of Business Administration (M.B.A.) program in 1967 and has since added a joint program in cooperation with the Faculty of Law, leading to a combined L.L.B.-M.B.A. degree. Students enrolled in the university's M.P.A. program also take a number of courses in the School of Business. There are about 340 students in these programs, of whom approximately 250 are full-time M.B.A. candidates.

Dalhousie started the first English M.B.A. program in eastern Canada. The school was established primarily to serve the Atlantic provinces; however, since students come from all parts of Canada, the United States, Europe, Africa, and the Near and Far East, the program has avoided a purely parochial, regional focus.

PROGRAMS OF STUDY

The objectives of the program are to develop in students sound knowledge of the concepts, theories, and basic tools required by managers; skill in analyzing business problems; facility in making sound decisions; and flexibility in the changing business environment. The program is designed to emphasize the practical applications of course material, and students are encouraged to become involved in consulting and research activities while at the university. Various student, faculty, and business organizations facilitate this kind of activity both during the regular academic year and in the summer months.

Instructional methods include case study, lectures, seminars, and field projects. Practical experience in computer applications is also included in the program. The Master of Business Administration degree may be obtained by attending full time for two academic years or by taking a part-time program which must be completed within six calendar years. The core program in the first year includes exposure to accounting, behavioral sciences, economics, finance, marketing, operations research, and statistics. The second year provides students with electives in such subjects as marketing, finance, control, law, taxation, personnel administration, management science, international business, and transportation. All core classes are available in late afternoon or evening sessions for the benefit of students in the part-time program.

The combined L.L.B.-M.B.A. degree may be obtained after four years of study in the business and law schools. The first year of the program is normally spent in the School of Business; the second year in the Law School; the third and the fourth years are divided between the two schools. Further information on this program will be supplied on request.

ADMISSION

Students entering the program need not hold an undergraduate degree in commerce or business. The normal requirement is an average of B or better in the final two years of undergraduate study, but the admissions committee tries to assess applicants on the basis of potential rather than purely on past academic performance. Submission of scores on the Graduate Management Admission Test (GMAT) is required as an aid in selection. A knowledge of English and sound background in mathematics are of prime importance. A student whose mother tongue is not English must take the Test of English as a Foreign Language (TOEFL). Students are admitted only in the fall term, and applications should be submitted no later than May 31 (April 30 for non-Canadian students).

EXPENSES

Estimated expenses, per year (1985-86), are as follows:

Tuition	$1,704
Foreign students (differential)	1,700
Room and board	3,200
Books and supplies	450

FINANCIAL ASSISTANCE

The School of Business Administration and the university award a limited number of scholarships to first- and second-year students on the basis of academic excellence. No application is required, but candidates hoping to be considered should be sure all documentation is complete no later than April 30. Outstanding candidates wishing to be nominated for one of two very prestigious awards, the Killam and Bank of Nova Scotia scholarships, should be sure all documentation is complete by mid-February. Students may apply for several external fellowships and scholarships including awards made by Xerox, General Mills, Lever Brothers, and Canada Mortgage and Housing. Canadian students may, in their second year, be employed by the school as research assistants or markers. Under Canada Immigra-

tion Regulations, students must have proof of full support before entering Canada to pursue their studies.

PLACEMENT

The federal government's Employment Centre maintains an on-campus placement service, and the School of Business actively cooperates with this service through its Business Placement Centre.

CORRESPONDENCE

For further information or to request an application for admission, please write to
Coordinator, M.B.A. Programme
School of Business Administration
Dalhousie University
Halifax, Nova Scotia, Canada B3H 1Z5

The Amos Tuck School of Business Administration at Dartmouth College, founded in 1900, is the oldest graduate school of business in America. It is located in Hanover, New Hampshire, a picturesque New England town and a major educational, cultural, and medical center. Tuck School's Master of Business Administration (M.B.A.) program is a full-time, two-year course of study designed to provide high-quality professional preparation for men and women seeking careers in management. Each September a class of 165 students enters the school.

The Murdough Center has classrooms of advanced design, the business and engineering library, computer facilities, small group study rooms, and an outstanding career resource library. The school has acquired 50 IBM personal computers, 16 MacIntosh computers, and peripheral equipment for the exclusive use of Tuck students. The close proximity of dormitories to classrooms and faculty offices provides an opportunity to study management in a uniquely supportive environment. Attractive single- and double-story, duplex housing facilities located close to Hanover are available for married students.

The school's curriculum takes advantage of the most accessible time-shared computing system in the world. A wide range of regional manufacturing and commercial establishments offers students perspective on the business community. An executive-in-residence program and an active calendar of visiting speakers provide many opportunities for students to interact with managers from all sectors.

PROGRAMS OF STUDY
The curriculum exposes students to key issues in the various functional fields of business. It also offers a core of courses with a general management perspective to demonstrate the interrelationships of specialized fields and the contributions of mathematics and the behavioral sciences to the analysis of decision problems. The school's primary objective is to develop the capacity of its students to make sound managerial decisions. Courses particularly stress the learning of concepts and habits of analytical thought that are appropriate in a rapidly changing environment.

The first-year program consists of a specific set of courses required of all students. These courses build a common base of understanding and analytical competence necessary for performance in any managerial role.

In the second year the student develops an individualized program of elective courses, seminars, and opportunities for independent study. The required course in business policy challenges the student with complex, cross-functional cases from the point of view of top management, in both a national and an international setting.

Professors use many teaching methods at Tuck, in various combinations, to suit the purposes of their courses. The case study method is popular because it is so well suited to the teaching of analytical decision making. With all teaching forms there is extensive student participation.

Persons holding undergraduate engineering degrees may wish to consider the M.B.A./M.E. program offered jointly with Dartmouth's Thayer School of Engineering.

ADMISSION
Tuck welcomes applications from men and women who hold or are about to receive their baccalaureate degrees from any accredited college or university in this country or abroad. A solid foundation in the social, physical, or natural sciences, the humanities, or engineering is appropriate background for the program. The quality of an applicant's past academic experience, maturity and sense of commitment to professional education, and personal qualities of leadership and administrative ability form an important part of the evidence considered for admission. In preparation for Tuck's M.B.A. program, a student is urged (but not required) to take college courses in economics, finite mathematics, calculus, and English.

To apply, a student must submit an application, recommendations, transcripts of all academic work, and results from the Graduate Management Admission Test (GMAT). The Test of English as a Foreign Language (TOEFL) is required of all applicants whose native language is not English. Decisions are rendered on a rolling basis; applications should be completed by April 15.

In a typical year Tuck students hold bachelor's degrees from 110 different colleges and universities and come from 40 states and several foreign nations; 96 percent have a year or more of full-time work experience. Women made up 28.5 percent of the enrollment in 1985-86.

Tuck does not accept transfer students, and it does not grant advanced standing to students on the basis of work done elsewhere.

EXPENSES
Expenses for the 1985-86 academic year:

	Single	Married
Tuition	$11,000	$11,000
Books	750	750
Living expenses	7,700	11,750
Total	$19,450	$23,500

FINANCIAL ASSISTANCE
Tuck has a program that includes scholarships and a variety of deferred-payment loans to assist students whose resources fall short of costs. All applicants for financial aid must file the form of the Graduate and Professional School Financial Aid Service (GAPSFAS). Tuck actively encourages applications from minority group members.

PLACEMENT
All students may participate in the school's active placement program, which each year provides many opportunities for challenging and rewarding employment. In 1985 more than 150 companies from all sections of the country scheduled recruiting dates at Tuck to interview graduating students for permanent employment, and many of these firms also recruited first-year students for summer jobs.

CORRESPONDENCE
For further information, write or call
Director of Admissions
Amos Tuck School of Business
    Administration
Dartmouth College
Hanover, New Hampshire 03755
Telephone: 603-646-3162

At the official opening of the university in 1978, the Premier of the State of Victoria had this to say about Deakin: "It is Geelong's University, it is Australia's University, but in a very real sense it is Victoria's newest and in many senses most exciting university. . . . Today Deakin stands for an education philosophy unique in Australia and rare in the world. . . ."

By 1985 the university had some 6,000 students studying in five schools. The School of Management was fortunate to acquire a nucleus of experienced staff and a well-established degree program.

Deakin University is located on 82-hectare site at Waurn Ponds on the outskirts of the city of Geelong, 60 kilometers from the state capital (Melbourne) and adjacent to the picturesque Bellarine Peninsula. Geelong still caters to much of Victoria's wheat and wool trade, and port facilities line the bay. The region provides facilities for almost every type of sport.

PROGRAM OF STUDY

The Deakin Master of Business Administration (M.B.A.) program is designed specifically for persons employed full time and is available only in the off-campus mode. On-campus attendance is required only for the residential schools. These occupy one weekend in each of the first two years and one week in each of the final two years. Students normally undertake two units in each semester, a pace that enables a capable student to graduate in four years of part-time study.

The M.B.A. teaching materials have been prepared by course teams whose membership includes academic staff employed by Deakin and consultants from other universities, professional bodies, and the world of business and government. The subject specialists are supported by editors, designers, media specialists, and educational advisers.

The difficulties of working students are fully taken into account in the preparation of course materials, in the tutorial arrangements, and in the rules governing the M.B.A. program. For example, a participant who is given a promotion, faces increased responsibility, or changes jobs, is able to postpone M.B.A. studies and return when that particular career challenge has passed. Candidates offered a place in the M.B.A. program are provided with an orientation package that introduces them to the "off-campus" studies program and the resources available, and also provides some initial information on study techniques.

The first two years of the four-year, part-time M.B.A. program provide a set of analytical tools sufficiently fundamental to be relevant to a broad range of management problems. Economics, organizational behavior, legal studies, accountancy, and a variety of quantitative methods (including statistics, decision sciences, and computer methods) are among the very basic skills necessary for competent decision making in both public and private organizations. This part of the program seeks to develop a familiarity with fundamental concepts and an ability to adapt them to diverse and changing decision contexts.

The final two years of the program stress the functional fields of management (marketing, finance, production, personnel management and labor relations) and also emphasize management policy and the individual project. These are the major integrating courses in the program, pulling together skills gained in both the basic disciplines and in the functional fields.

The M.B.A. program is not committed to any single method of instruction, although in the "off-campus" mode, major emphasis is placed upon carefully structured study guides provided for each course.

Wherever possible students are organized into local study groups that provide support and the mechanism for completing those assignments that may be submitted either by groups or individuals.

Study-guide reading, individual problem solving, taped lectures, the Delphi approach, project work, research reports, and case discussion activities are all part of the learning experience of the M.B.A. program. In addition, some courses emphasize group projects as a means of exposing students both to real-world management problems and to the experience of decision making within a group context.

ADMISSION

Students are enrolled from a wide variety of backgrounds and disciplines. The Admissions Committee wishes to attract and train those individuals with the greatest potential as managers and will therefore look beyond purely academic credentials. Leadership skills, motivation, maturity, strength of commitment, and quality of experience to date are among the criteria considered in addition to academic records.

The educational requirement for entrance to the M.B.A. program is a recognized degree and diploma or professional qualification deemed equivalent. Selection of candidates for admission to the M.B.A. program will also be based upon a detailed application form completed by the candidate, personal reference from present or former employers and teachers, and the results of the Graduate Management Admission Test (GMAT).

The off-campus M.B.A. program begins in late February to early March each year. Completed application forms should be filed by October 31.

EXPENSES

No tuition fees are payable by Australian residents. All students are required to pay a general service fee and can expect to pay for text books, a microcomputer, and any travel and accommodation expenses incurred during workshops.

CORRESPONDENCE

For further information on the programs of study offered by the School of Management, write or call

Off-Campus Operations
Deakin University
Victoria 3217, Australia
Telephone: 052-471155

Cleveland, the home of Delta State University, is located in the heart of the Mississippi Delta approximately 110 miles south of Memphis, Tennessee. Delta State University was founded in 1924 as Delta State Teachers College. The growth and expanding function of the school is evidenced by changes in name to Delta State College in 1954 and to Delta State University in 1974. The School of Business is one of five schools authorized within the academic program. The university enrolls approximately 3,500 students and is accredited by the Southern Association of Colleges and Schools. The School of Business has 35 full-time faculty members and enrolls approximately 1,000 undergraduate and 75 graduate students.

PROGRAM OF STUDY

The objective of the Master of Business Administration program is to provide a broad professional education to prepare graduates for responsible positions in education, business, and government. The program was designed originally for working people in the area who wish to pursue graduate study on a part-time basis. Required courses for the degree continue to be available in the evening with classes meeting one night a week from six to nine o'clock. The program requires completion of 33 semester hours of graduate credit consisting of 21 hours in business and economic core courses, 6 hours of approved electives in business and/or economics, and 6 hours of electives that may be chosen from areas other than business and economics. The core requirements are managerial accounting, managerial economics, financial management, management problems, marketing seminar, business research, and statistics.

ADMISSION

Admission to the program is open to graduates of accredited colleges and universities who indicate promise of success in postgraduate study. Students must have completed or complete with grades of C or higher a minimum of 36 semester hours in undergraduate foundation courses consisting of accounting principles, principles of economics, business policies, finance, management, marketing, introduction to data processing, statistics, business law, and production management.

Students must submit scores from the Graduate Management Admission Test (GMAT). To be fully admitted requires a minimum of 950 points based on the formula: 200 times the undergraduate quality-point average (4.00 system) plus the GMAT score.

EXPENSES

University fees are $500 per semester. Students desiring to live in university dormitories pay $720 per semester for room, board, and laundry. Part-time students scheduling fewer than nine semester hours pay $53 per semester hour. Out-of-state fees per semester for non-Mississippi residents are $591 added to the above fees. These fees were in effect for the 1985-86 academic year.

FINANCIAL ASSISTANCE

Assistantships are available to qualified full-time graduate students. Graduate students do not teach but assist faculty members approximately 10 hours per week. Applications are available from the Dean, School of Graduate Studies.

PLACEMENT

The university maintains a Placement Office to assist students and alumni. A number of well-known companies regularly visit the campus seeking qualified candidates.

CORRESPONDENCE

Address inquiries to
  Dean
  School of Business
  Delta State University
  Cleveland, Mississippi 38733
  Telephone: 601-846-4200

DePaul University is a private coeducational institution founded in 1898. Since then it has matured and widened its scope to embrace eight major academic divisions. The College of Commerce was established as a separate school within the university in 1912. The university enrolls approximately 13,000 students who are about evenly divided between its Lincoln Park Campus on the north side of Chicago and the Loop Campus at Jackson Boulevard and Wabash Avenue in the downtown area.

The master's programs in business are conducted in the air-conditioned Frank J. Lewis Center in the heart of downtown Chicago. The best laboratory available—the dynamic commercial and financial center of Chicago—is just outside its doorstep. The Graduate School of Business has an enrollment of approximately 2,500 students, most of whom are studying on a part-time evening basis.

Students currently enrolled in the programs completed their undergraduate studies in institutions throughout the United States and in many foreign countries. Approximately 50 percent have undergraduate degrees in business or economics, while the remaining 50 percent have undergraduate degrees in various other nonbusiness subjects.

The Graduate School of Business offers evening programs of study leading to the degrees of Master of Business Administration (M.B.A.), Master of Science in Accountancy (M.S.A.), and Master of Science in Taxation (M.S.T.), and a day program leading to the degree of Master of Accountancy (M.Acc.). The programs are accredited by the American Assembly of Collegiate Schools of Business (AACSB). Degrees may be pursued on a full-time or part-time basis except the M.Acc. degree, which is available only to full-time students.

In addition, the Graduate School of Business, in conjunction with the Computer Science Department of the Graduate Division of Liberal Arts and Sciences, offers a joint Master of Science in Management Information Systems (M.S./M.I.S.) degree program.

PROGRAMS OF STUDY

The emphasis of the M.B.A. program is on decision making as the characteristic function of business administration. The program's purpose is to integrate the several functional areas of business and the contributions they make to the development of administrative competence.

Students who possess an undergraduate degree in business are required to take 52 quarter hours of course work. If the student has earned an undergraduate degree in an area other than business, a maximum of 92 quarter hours of course work may be necessary depending on the student's academic background. The student has the opportunity to enroll for approximately one third of his or her course work in one of the following areas of specialization: management accounting, association management, business economics, entrepreneurship, finance, international business, operations management, human resources management, systems, marketing, or quantitative methods.

The objective of the Master of Science in Accountancy degree is to provide a formal integrated sequence of courses at the graduate level that emphasizes intensive study of topics relevant to the work of a professional accountant, as well as allows the student ample opportunity to explore advanced topics of interest. It is expected that after completing the program the student would be well prepared to take the C.P.A. exam. The program is intended to serve the needs of holders of undergraduate degrees with nonaccounting backgrounds.

This program consists of 52 quarter hours of course work for the business undergraduate, of which 48 quarter hours are in accountancy. The nonbusiness undergraduate may be required to take a maximum of 92 quarter hours of course work depending on academic background.

The M.S.T. program emphasizes planning and decision making for the professional in the field of taxation. It is the purpose of the program to integrate a sound technical competence, an appreciation of the social and governmental aspects of taxation, and an awareness of the other relevant functional areas of business.

The program consists of 52 quarter hours of course work, of which 44 quarter hours are in the field of taxation and the rest in other related business subjects. If the student has earned an undergraduate degree in a nonbusiness area, a maximum of 92 quarter hours of course work may be necessary, depending on academic background.

The M.Acc. is a professional degree in accounting and auditing. It prepares students for positions in public accounting, business, and the public sector. Applicants are expected to have an undergraduate degree in accountancy.

The program consists of a minimum of 52 quarter hours, of which 40 quarter hours are in graduate accountancy courses and the rest in related business subjects.

The joint M.S./M.I.S. program provides a balanced curriculum to develop technological competency and managerial capability. It requires 120 quarter hours, a portion of which may be waived by examination or prior course work.

ADMISSION

Applicants for admission must possess a baccalaureate degree from a regionally accredited institution and give evidence of aptitude for successful study in business as indicated by the Graduate Management Admission Test.

DePaul University operates on a quarter plan. Accepted candidates may begin their program in the autumn, winter, spring, or summer quarter (except for the M.Acc. program, which has entrance only in the autumn).

EXPENSES

Each graduate course carries four quarter hours of credit; tuition per course is $656 (for the academic year 1985-86).

FINANCIAL ASSISTANCE

Graduate assistantships, which provide stipends of $3,200 to $3,500 plus a complete tuition grant, are available. Appointees generally assist with research.

PLACEMENT

The facilities and services of the Placement Bureau of DePaul University are available to all master's candidates. About 100 nationally known firms send representatives to the university for interviews with interested students.

CORRESPONDENCE

For information, write or call
Director, Graduate School of Business
DePaul University
25 East Jackson Boulevard
Chicago, Illinois 60604-2287
Telephone: 312-341-8810

DRAKE UNIVERSITY

DES MOINES, IOWA

Drake University is a private, nonsectarian institution whose College of Business Administration, founded in 1888, enjoys a rich heritage in intensely personal high-quality education for business. Although master's degrees have been granted by Drake University since 1883, the Master of Business Administration (M.B.A.) program was initiated in 1968 and currently has approximately 320 candidates pursuing graduate work in business. Located in Des Moines, the capital of Iowa, the university offers an abundance of educational and cultural opportunities in the metropolitan community.

PROGRAMS OF STUDY

The primary objective of the Drake M.B.A. program is to prepare qualified individuals for responsible administrative and executive positions in business organizations. This aim recognizes the need to integrate the various functional areas of business, to understand the wide variety of relationships, and to be able to analyze evolving administrative situations. The basic philosophy of Drake's M.B.A. program, therefore, reflects the general management point of view and is oriented toward preparing students for responsible positions in management. The Drake M.B.A. program is not intended to provide training of a specialized nature.

The Drake M.B.A. program consists of three elements:
  • the prerequisites consist of basic academic instruction in those areas considered the common body of knowledge in business and administration and should include courses in economics, finance, marketing, management, mathematics, accounting, and computers;
  • 12 M.B.A. courses of 3 credits each have been developed and integrated into a unified program;

Along with the above described general management M.B.A. program, a student may elect to take sufficient accounting credits to qualify for the C.P.A. examination. If this option is selected, a minimum of 18 credits beyond the basic course in accounting is required.

The faculties of the Law School and the College of Business Administration offer a joint program leading to the J.D. and M.B.A. degrees. It should be pointed out that the M.B.A. section of the joint program is ancillary to the law segment. The major product of the joint program is individuals trained to practice law with an in-depth knowledge of business. Students in the joint program should complete the requirements in three years and three summers, that is, six regular semesters and three summer terms.

ADMISSION

Applicants for the M.B.A. program must meet the following admission requirements:
  • hold a baccalaureate degree from an accredited institution (No particular undergraduate field of study is required; however, a good background in English and mathematics is desired and expected);
  • present a satisfactory record of undergraduate scholastic achievement;
  • show evidence of good character, aptitude, and capacity for graduate study;
  • present acceptable scores on the Graduate Management Admission Test (GMAT); and
  • satisfy the general requirements for admission to the School of Graduate Studies of Drake University. (A score on the Graduate Record Examinations (GRE) or Miller Analogies Test (M.A.T.) is not required.)

Applicants for the Drake University combined J.D.-M.B.A. program must meet the requirements of and be admitted to both the Law School and the M.B.A. program in the School of Graduate Studies. Admission requirements to the Law School include an acceptable score on the Law School Admission Test. For the complete admission requirements, please write to Dean, The Law School.

EXPENSES

The appropriate expenses for a full-time student for the fall or spring semester are as follows:

Tuition	$3,315
Room and board	1,485
Books and supplies	475
Total	$5,275

Tuition for summer term is $150 per credit hour.

FINANCIAL ASSISTANCE

Financial assistance is available for qualified students who otherwise would find it economically impossible to pursue their graduate study at Drake.

M.B.A. graduate research assistantships are awarded to a limited number of M.B.A. students with excellent undergraduate records and high GMAT scores. Guaranteed student loans and National Direct Student Loans are also available.

Full-time graduate students may combine a part-time position in business or at the university with their studies. Administrative or management trainee positions are generally available in banking, insurance, communications, manufacturing, and other industries in the Des Moines area as well as teaching and laboratory assistantships on campus. These opportunities are intended to be a meaningful work experience and not just income creating.

PLACEMENT

Drake University has a central placement service. Its services are available to all Drake graduate students, as well as alumni. Over 250 business firms actively recruit on the Drake campus each year.

CORRESPONDENCE

For further information or to request an application for admission, write or call
  Director, Graduate Programs
    in Business
  Drake University
  Des Moines, Iowa 50311
  Telephone: 800-362-2416 toll free from Iowa
  800-247-2135 toll free from Illinois, Nebraska, South Dakota, Wisconsin, Minnesota, Missouri
  515-271-2187 from all other locations

Since 1891, Drexel has enjoyed a very favorable reputation as a quality institution. Realizing the need for a full-time Master of Business Administration (M.B.A.) program in such a concentrated industrial area, Drexel inaugurated its full-time day M.B.A. program in the fall of 1965 to complement its existing evening program. In 1974, the M.B.A. offerings were extended into a weekend M.B.A. program. The College of Business and Administration also offers the Master of Science (M.S.) degree in all the major fields of business concentration: accounting, taxation, finance, management, marketing, and economics. Effective October 1980, the President and Board of Trustees approved the inauguration of a Doctor of Philosophy (Ph.D.) curriculum in business administration. The college is housed in a modern, air-conditioned, five-story building offering the utmost in convenience.

PROGRAMS OF STUDY
In order to qualify for the degree of Master of Business Administration, each candidate must complete a first-year program consisting of fundamental concepts and quantitative tools in the areas of accounting, economics, law, finance, human resource management, organizational theory, management information systems, marketing, calculus, and statistics. First-year requirements may be satisfied by taking the designated course or equivalent at an accredited college, as a regularly enrolled student in the M.B.A. program, on a self-study basis, or by special examination. Although the program stresses the study of broad, executive management responsibilities, a limited specialization is offered to equip graduates to make an early contribution to management.

After satisfaction of the first-year requirements, each M.B.A. candidate must complete 48 quarter credits distributed as follows: core program (12 quarter credits) and postcore program (36 quarter credits) consisting of an area of concentration (12 quarter credits), professional electives (15 quarter credits), and business electives (9 quarter credits).

The weekend M.B.A. was developed particularly for graduate students who have at least two years of managerial experience. Under this program, students who do not require first-year courses may complete their entire degree by attending on weekends. The student should be able to complete the degree in approximately two years, although the period of study may be lengthened or shortened at the student's option.

The Master of Science program is designed to respond to the growing demand for trained management personnel at all levels of government and business. These programs allow for a greater degree of specialization than that permitted by the nature of the M.B.A.

In order to qualify for the M.S. degree each candidate must complete the following elements:
- the same first-year program required in the M.B.A. program and
- 48 quarter credits of second-year courses consisting of 6 to 12 credits of core courses, 18 to 27 credits of specialization courses, and 12 to 18 credits of electives depending on the area of specialization chosen.

The Master of Science programs in taxation and accounting are designed to meet the needs of those men and women who plan careers in tax consulting, public accounting, private industry, or government.

All full-time M.B.A. and M.S. students have the option of participating in cooperative education, enabling them to get three months of practical experience working off campus with career professionals. All programs require a minimum of 48 quarter credits of advanced studies.

The Ph.D. program requires a minimum of 45 quarter credits above the M.B.A. degree. Each candidate must select a primary and secondary field of concentration, pass a series of qualifying examinations, and prepare a publishable dissertation. All candidates will be required to teach and to work in an appropriate level position as part of the program.

ADMISSION
In order to qualify for admission to any of the graduate programs in the College of Business and Administration, candidates must submit application, transcripts, recommendations, and Graduate Management Admission Test (GMAT) scores to the Graduate Admissions Office. The candidate's qualifications must meet the admissions standards set by the Accreditation Council of the American Assembly of Collegiate Schools of Business. In general, however, students entering the graduate programs of the College of Business and Administration exceed these standards. For example, a typical student entering the graduate programs of the College of Business and Administration will score in the vicinity of the 60th percentile on the GMAT and have a grade-point average in his or her junior-senior years placing him or her in the top 30 percent of his or her class. The applicant should ask the authorities of all colleges and universities attended to forward to Drexel's Office of Graduate Admissions official transcripts of all prior collegiate work. This material must be on file six weeks before the contemplated enrollment date.

EXPENSES
Tuition is $191 per credit hour (subject to change). Each application is to be accompanied by a nonrefundable application fee of $10. A general university fee of $215 per academic year for full-time study and $108 for part-time study covers library and medical services for full-time students and library services for part-time students.

FINANCIAL ASSISTANCE
There are a limited number of graduate assistantships and fellowships available in the full-time (day) M.B.A. and Ph.D. programs.

PLACEMENT
Facilities of the Graduate Placement Office are available without charge to all graduate students. This office maintains contacts with industrial firms, educational institutions, and professional organizations and recommends qualified persons for positions.

CORRESPONDENCE
For further information or to request an application for admission, write or call
Drexel University
Office of Graduate Admissions 1-212
Philadelphia, Pennsylvania 19104
Telephone: 215-895-2400

Drury College was founded in 1873 as a liberal arts college dedicated to the individual development of each student. The Breech School of Business Administration, dedicated in 1960, was the result of a gift by Ernest R. Breech, a former Drury student. Ernie Breech served as President of Bendix Corporation, Chairman of the Board of the Ford Motor Company, Board Chairman of TWA, and is a member of the American Automobile Hall of Fame. The Breech School offers a program leading to the degree of Master of Business Administration (M.B.A.) and functions at the undergraduate level to provide training in business administration, accounting, and economics.

PROGRAM OF STUDY
The objective of the Master of Business Administration (M.B.A.) program is to offer professional training for the person who is already employed in a management capacity or who plans to embark on a career in management.

The M.B.A. program consists of 31 semester hours of graduate courses preceded by a total of 24 hours of prerequisite study in economics, accounting, statistics, personnel, marketing, and finance for the student who has had no prior background in economics and business administration at the undergraduate level. When the applicant has had an undergraduate program in either economics or business administration, up to 24 hours of credit may be accepted toward fulfillment of the prerequisite courses. However, a minimum of one full calendar year's graduate study at the Breech School is required of all M.B.A. candidates. In addition to full-time students, the M.B.A. program is designed so that individuals who are employed may successfully pursue graduate study on a part-time basis in the evening.

The M.B.A. program has a broad managerial orientation rather than that of the business specialist. The objective of the training is to prepare each student for the ultimate responsibility of managing an entire business enterprise as well as to make the student a more effective manager at lower levels in the organization. The courses in the M.B.A. curriculum are organized to emphasize four areas of management competency: internal enterprise management, relating the enterprise to its market environment, relating the enterprise to its nonmarket environment, and business research and quantitative analysis.

Decision making and effective communications are given particular emphasis in the M.B.A. program. Although experience is indispensable in effective managerial decision making, a good grasp of the process through professional training will enable a person to learn the lessons of experience rapidly in a business career. Instruction in all areas of the graduate curriculum focuses on the following aspects of the decision-making process: defining problems and issues in complex situations; determining what problems need managerial decisions; making decisions about plans, policies, and operations; and developing programs to implement the decisions.

The case method of instruction is used extensively with an emphasis upon orderly problem solving and an integration of the student's knowledge. Clarity of both written and oral communication is emphasized. Students participate in such experiences as game competition using computer applications, sensitivity training in human relations, and preparation of extensive business reports to broaden their understanding of the managerial function.

ADMISSION
Only individuals who hold a baccalaureate degree from an accredited four-year college or university are accepted into the program. Admission to the M.B.A. program is based upon these factors:
- the applicant's undergraduate record,
- performance on the Graduate Management Admission Test (GMAT), and
- progress in work experience if the applicant has been out of school for some time.
  The Test of English as a Foreign Language (TOEFL) is required of all foreign students.

Students normally enter the M.B.A. program in the fall semester beginning in September. Early application is advised, since classes are kept small to facilitate personal development of each student.

EXPENSES
Graduate tuition is $105 per credit hour, or a total of $3,255 for the program of 31 graduate class hours. A discussion of other fees and expenses is contained in the M.B.A. bulletin.

FINANCIAL ASSISTANCE
Some limited financial assistance is available for full-time graduate students in the form of loans. Applicants with superior undergraduate records who are interested in financial assistance should contact the Director of the Breech School for details of the financial aid program.

PLACEMENT
The Breech School cooperates with the Drury College Placement Office, which coordinates an active recruiting program by leading national and regional firms. Placement personnel have developed an excellent rapport with industry in recent years in the placement of Drury graduates.

CORRESPONDENCE
For further information, write to
  Director, Breech School of Business
    Administration
  Drury College
  Springfield, Missouri 65802
  Telephone: 417-865-8731

Duke University is located in Durham, North Carolina, a city with a population of approximately 110,000. Durham, along with nearby Raleigh and Chapel Hill, form the "Research Triangle," a major center of education, technology, and the arts. The Fuqua School of Business (FSB), established in 1969, is located on Duke's main campus. With an entering class of approximately 225 students, the school is able to devote personal attention to the students while maintaining its excellent national reputation. The Fuqua School is exclusively a graduate school; there are no undergraduate business or management majors at Duke.

The philosophy and programs of the school are future oriented. The study of past and current business practices is de-emphasized, and stress is placed instead on developing the student's capacity for general problem solving. The Master of Business Administration (M.B.A.) program is designed to help the student develop a base from which learning will continue.

PROGRAMS OF STUDY

The purpose of formal course work in the M.B.A. program is to develop the student's intellectual capacity to solve real business and economic problems. Because of the rapid social and technological changes taking place within society, programs that focus exclusively on current business practice, even the best current business practice, will surely produce students likely to become professionally obsolete in a relatively few years. The educational experience has been structured to provide career education for professional managers. Varied teaching methodologies challenge the student to study the problems of economic enterprise and decision making from the perspective of the entire organization. There are several major idea streams that run through the program:
- managerial economics and a systems view of decision making in a firm,
- strategic problems in the management of complex organizations,
- human behavior within organizations,
- design of organization structures and information systems for the coordination and control of the firm's activities, and
- quantitative analysis and its application in the solution of management problems.

The Fuqua School makes extensive use of computer technology in the delivery of management education. All first-year courses incorporate the use of the personal computer as a decision-making tool. The school offers unsurpassed computing facilities.

In cooperation with the Duke University School of Law, the School of Forestry and Environmental Studies, and the Institute of Policy Sciences and Public Affairs, programs leading to combined degrees are offered by the Fuqua School of Business. Applicants for combined programs must submit a separate application to each school involved.

The Doctor of Philosophy program builds on an education equivalent to that of the Duke M.B.A. program. It requires one additional year of course work, including two courses in advanced mathematics. The remainder of this year is made up of courses outside the school and of tutorials that are tailored to the student's individual interests and needs. A comprehensive examination and an original dissertation are also required.

ADMISSION

An applicant for admission to the M.B.A. program should have a baccalaureate degree from a recognized institution. No specific majors or areas of concentration are required or preferred for admission to the program. The applicant is encouraged to submit evidence of work experience, military service, and community or extracurricular activities. The admission process includes an evaluation of academic record (emphasis on the last two years), score from the Graduate Management Admission Test (GMAT), personal recommendations, work experience where applicable, and leadership in extracurricular activities.

A policy of rolling admissions is followed, with the earliest decisions being made in January. Candidates may begin the M.B.A. program only in September. Applications should be submitted before April 1.

EXPENSES
Approximate expenses for a single student for 1985-86 are as follows:

Tuition	$10,100
Books and supplies	530
Living expenses	6,244
Health fee	190

FINANCIAL ASSISTANCE
The school offers a program that includes scholarships, fellowships, and various types of loans. Scholarships and fellowships are awarded primarily on merit. Loans are available to those students whose resources are insufficient to cover the cost of their education. Applications for financial aid should accompany the application for admission and should be submitted by March 1 to guarantee full consideration. All financial aid applicants must file the form of the Graduate and Professional School Financial Aid Service (GAPSFAS).

PLACEMENT
The FSB Placement Office offers specific counseling and placement activities designed to enhance the student's career search. Each year representatives from national and multinational financial institutions, accounting firms, and industrial and commercial organizations visit Duke, providing full-time and summer employment opportunities for FSB students and alumni.

CORRESPONDENCE
For further information, write or call
Director of Admissions
Fuqua School of Business
Duke University
Durham, North Carolina 27706
Telephone: 919-684-5874
    or 919-684-4266

DUQUESNE UNIVERSITY

PITTSBURGH, PENNSYLVANIA

Duquesne University, founded in 1878, established its School of Business and Administration in 1913. An integral part of Pittsburgh's renaissance, the new facilities of the school are within walking distance of industry—large and small—retail stores, major professional associations, union headquarters, research centers, and governmental units. These advantages, combined with easy access to the cultural facilities of the city, provide an educational opportunity and a laboratory for the development of business leaders.

PROGRAM OF STUDY

The Master of Business Administration (M.B.A.) program is structured to provide course work for students who can devote full time to graduate study for a period of two years (four semesters) or for students who are employed full time and who can complete the program over a period of eight semesters.

Courses leading to the M.B.A. are viewed as part of a professional program leading to a professional terminal degree. The program is entirely management oriented for decision-making objectives; it is directed to the preparation of competent men and women for general management careers in business and public administration. The curriculum emphasizes a broad managerial approach rather than concentration in major fields.

The program consists of three phases as follows:

CORE IA: 6 credits (may be waived)
501 Mathematical Foundations for Management
502 Computer Fundamentals for Quantitative Management Techniques
503 Statistics as a Basis for Managerial Decision Making

CORE IB: 14 credits
511 Quantitative Analysis for Management Decisions
512 Foundations of Accounting and Control
513 Economics for Managers
514 Financial Control of Organizations
515 Management Information Systems
518 Law for the Executive
519 Managerial Marketing Strategies

CORE II: 15 credits required course work
521 Environment of Business
522 Financial Management
523 Operation Research
524 Organizational Behavior in Management
529 Managerial Decision Making

CORE III: 21 credits elective course work

Students accepted from undergraduate schools accredited by the American Assembly of Collegiate Schools of Business (AACSB) are eligible for waivers of Core I courses for a total of 20 credits. Other accepted students may obtain the waiver through examination. All students must petition for a waiver and take the examination prior to entering the program.

ADMISSION

Applicants are admitted in August and January; admission in August is preferred. Candidates who have completed undergraduate work at an accredited institution with a superior academic record and who have achieved appropriate scores on the Graduate Management Admission Test (GMAT) are eligible for admission. No specific undergraduate field of concentration is required. A high level of skill in written and oral English is important.

EXPENSES

Tuition is $194 per credit hour. A university fee is $11 per credit hour. Estimated cost of books and supplies for full-time students is $500. Dormitory accommodations (room and board) range from $1,421.00 (double) to $1,701.50 (single) per semester.

FINANCIAL ASSISTANCE

Graduate assistantships are available in amounts up to $3,500 or tuition each year. Graduate assistants are assigned to tasks for which they are qualified.

PLACEMENT

The full services of the Career Planning and Placement Center are available to graduate business students. Individual counseling and assistance in placement are provided.

CORRESPONDENCE

For additional information, write or call
Assistant Dean
Graduate School of Business and Administration
Duquesne University
Pittsburgh, Pennsylvania 15282
Telephone: 412-434-6276

EAST CAROLINA UNIVERSITY

GREENVILLE, NORTH CAROLINA

East Carolina University, founded in 1907, is a state-supported, coeducational university with an enrollment of about 14,000 students. The university has grown rapidly in recent years and has expanded its offerings in undergraduate, graduate, and professional programs including a medical school. East Carolina University is one of 16 constituent institutions that comprise The University of North Carolina.

East Carolina University is located in Greenville, North Carolina, a growing town of about 44,000. It is the dominant university in the coastal plain region of North Carolina. The Greenville area offers a wide range of outdoor recreational activities, including hunting, boating, fishing, camping, sightseeing, and swimming on nearby beaches. The university provides a wide range of cultural opportunities, including artistic events, popular entertainment, lecture and theater series, and the East Carolina University Summer Theater.

The School of Business has an enrollment of about 1,000, including approximately 70 full-time and 110 part-time graduate students.

PROGRAM OF STUDY
The purpose of the Master of Business Administration (M.B.A.) program is to offer professional training to qualified applicants who aspire to careers as efficient and responsible administrators. The program is structured for qualified applicants with baccalaureate degrees from regionally accredited institutions in non-business as well as business fields. The M.B.A. program emphasizes the development of analytical skills, problem solving, and decision making so that graduates can function effectively within changing environments.

The M.B.A. degree requires between 36 and 54 semester hours depending on the applicant's academic background. Most full-time students require between 12 and 24 months to complete the program, while part-time students require 2 to 4 years.

Course requirements for the M.B.A. degree include two groups: common body of knowledge and breadth requirements. The common body of knowledge requirement includes nine required courses covering the functional areas of business; the social, political, and economic environment of business; the basic concepts of accounting, quantitative methods, and

information systems; and organization theory and behavioral analysis. For those students who may have completed comparable work in other degree programs, some of the common body of knowledge courses may be waived.

To complete the breadth requirement, each student must complete nine courses beyond the common body of knowledge with no more than six semester hours in a field of specialization. Courses required as part of the breadth requirement include business policies, business research, economic analysis, international business, statistical analysis, management science, and financial management. Areas of specialization include accounting, finance, management, marketing, management science, and information systems.

ADMISSION
Students are admitted who demonstrate a high promise of successfully completing the M.B.A. degree program. The decision is based on a combination of factors including the following: (1) grade-point average (4.0 system) × 200 + Graduate Management Admission Test (GMAT) score ≥ 950 or (2) grade-point average of upper-division work (4.0 system) × 200 + GMAT score ≥ 1,000.

Application for admission to the M.B.A. degree program requires the following information to be sent to the Dean of the Graduate School, East Carolina University, Greenville, North Carolina 27834: (1) completed application forms, (2) two official transcripts of all work beyond high school, and (3) a satisfactory GMAT score.

EXPENSES
It is estimated that the average North Carolina resident student incurs necessary expenses of approximately $2,700 to $2,900 for room, meals, tuition, fees, and books during an academic year (two semesters). The cost of lodging, meals, and books may vary considerably according to individual requirements. Nonresidents of North Carolina should add $2,846 to this estimate.

FINANCIAL ASSISTANCE
The School of Business currently has available numerous graduate assistantships with stipends of either $2,100 or $4,200 for 9 or 18 hours of work per week, respectively. Loans are available to students through two plans: the National Direct Student Loan Program and the East Carolina University Loan Program.

PLACEMENT
The university provides a placement center to assist students in finding employment. The center maintains contact with a large number of business and industrial firms and other potential employers.

CORRESPONDENCE
For further information or to request an application for admission, please write or call

Director of Graduate Studies
School of Business
East Carolina University
Greenville, North Carolina 27834
Telephone: 919-757-6970

EAST TENNESSEE STATE UNIVERSITY

JOHNSON CITY, TENNESSEE

Located in the foothills of the Great Smoky Mountains, East Tennessee State University is close to the Appalachian Hiking Trail, near water sports in the TVA recreational areas, and within 40 minutes of the Beech Mountain ski slopes. Johnson City is the major urban center of upper East Tennessee. In contrast with the contemporary growth are the locations where the first settlers in the state chose to live and carve out their place in American history. As part of the Tri-Cities, Johnson City is a city on the move, growing and progressing.

PROGRAMS OF STUDY

The program for the Master of Business Administration (M.B.A.) includes managerial accounting, economics of business decisions, applied macroeconomics, financial management, operations management, statistical analysis, organizational theory and behavior management, organizational communications, marketing management, policy formulation, and two College of Business electives.

For those students with no previous formal academic preparation in business administration, the following courses, or their equivalent, must be completed before undertaking the advanced graduate courses for either the M.B.A. or Master of Accountancy (M.Acc.): essentials of accounting/finance, essentials of economics, essentials of management/marketing, essentials of computers and statistics, and essentials of law for graduates. Upon completion of course work, successful completion of a written comprehensive case analysis is required to demonstrate the student's mastery and understanding of business administration.

For the Master of Accountancy program, those students with no previous formal academic preparation in accountancy must complete the following foundation courses, or their equivalent, before undertaking the advanced graduate courses: policy and strategy formulation, intermediate accounting, cost accounting, income taxes, auditing, advanced accounting, and accounting information systems. All candidates for the Master of Accountancy degree must complete a minimum of 33 hours of graduate work, including 27 semester hours of work open only to graduate students. Course requirements for the degree are as follows:

Accounting Courses—accounting theory, advanced managerial accounting, auditing theory, tax research and planning, accounting policy, and accounting electives.

Accounting Environment Courses—financial management, statistical analysis, economics of business decisions, and College of Business elective.

The successful completion of a designated capstone accounting course toward the end of the program is required. This course focuses on the integration of accounting subject matter with that of other areas of the curriculum. No comprehensive final examination or thesis is required.

ADMISSION

Students admitted to these programs must hold a bachelor's degree from an accredited college or university. In addition to submitting an application and transcripts, all students applying for these programs will take the Graduate Management Admission Test (GMAT) before being enrolled in classes. The criteria for admission shall be the candidate's performance on the GMAT, undergraduate grade-point average, and practical experience. Prior to first registration a candidate must have a conference with the Associate Dean for Graduate Business Studies to discuss his or her program and to determine program prerequisites.

EXPENSES
Average semester expenses:

Tennessee students (registration fee)	$ 612
Out-of-state students (registration fee and tuition)	1,074
Part-time graduate students (11 or fewer quarter hours)	
Tennessee students, per credit hour	61
Out-of-state students, per credit hour	94
Housing (single students)	
Residence halls (double occupancy)	385-437
Apartments (double occupancy)	490

Several meal plans are available in the university dining facilities. The cost of the meal plans is based on 15 meals per week or 21 meals per week. Meals may be purchased on an individual basis. Prices are subject to change.

FINANCIAL ASSISTANCE

The financial aid program of the school includes cooperative education, scholarship, assistantships, and loans.

CORRESPONDENCE

For additional information, please write or call
Dr. James H. Potts
Associate Dean for Graduate
  Business Studies
ETSU Box 21250A
Johnson City, Tennessee 37614
Telephone: 615-929-5314

East Texas State University (ETSU), founded in 1889, has become a multipurpose state university. Current enrollment is approximately 7,000 students.

The university is located in Commerce, a community of approximately 8,800 population 60 miles east of Dallas via an interstate highway. This location offers the advantages of a relaxed, informal atmosphere in which to live and study, plus easy access to major cultural, commercial, and recreational centers, including several large lakes.

East Texas State University has a modern campus that consists of more than 80 academic and residential buildings, which provide the facilities for the 32 academic departments that compose three colleges and the Graduate School. The university library contains an extensive selection of important research materials from a wide variety of fields including a special business services section. In addition, the university maintains modern and efficient computer facilities. Excellent, moderately priced housing accommodations are available for both single and married students.

The College of Business and Technology consists of seven departments: Accounting, Aerospace Studies, Economics/ Finance, General Business, Industry and Technology, Marketing/Management, and Office Administration/ Business Education. Graduate business degrees include the Master of Business Administration, the Master of Science in business education, and the Master of Science and Master of Arts degrees in economics. In 1970, the College of Business and Technology moved into a new $2.2-million complex. The building houses the university computer center as well as student-centered classrooms that are equipped with the latest equipment. Two additional buildings are used to house individual components of Aerospace Studies and Industry and Technology.

PROGRAM OF STUDY

ETSU's Master of Business Administration (M.B.A.) program focuses upon the problem-solving and decision-making responsibilities of modern management and is aimed at providing broad-based preparation for careers in administration in either the public or the private sector. More specifically, the M.B.A. program is designed to ensure a basic knowledge of essential business functions; to develop individual's analytical decision-making skills; to increase an individual's ability to adjust to rapidly changing social, eco-

nomic, technological, and political conditions; and to provide the foundation and encouragement essential for continuing professional self-development.

For most persons who hold baccalaureate degrees in business, the requirements for the M.B.A. degree include the completion of 12 graduate courses in business and economics. Persons who have degrees in disciplines other than business are required to complete additional background courses to insure a common body of knowledge. It is possible to begin graduate business programs during the fall, spring, or summer semesters and to complete these programs in one calendar year.

More than 200 individuals are presently enrolled in graduate degree programs in business. To meet the needs and schedules of these students, the College of Business Administration offers a variety of program alternatives designed to allow flexibility in pursuit of the degree, including evening classes in Dallas and day and evening classes in Commerce. Students may attend graduate programs in business full time or part time according to their professional objectives and personal lifestyles.

ADMISSION

To be admitted to the M.B.A. and M.S. in business education programs, applicants must possess a baccalaureate degree and achieve either: (a) 950 points based on the formula 200 × the undergraduate grade-point average + the Graduate Management Admission Test (GMAT) score, or (b) 1,000 points based on the formula 200 × the junior-senior (last 20 courses) grade-point average + the GMAT score. Official transcripts and GMAT scores must be received prior to admission.

Applicants for admission to the M.A. or M.S. program in economics may contact the Dean's Office of the College of Business and Technology concerning the use of Graduate Record Examinations (GRE) scores in lieu of GMAT scores. Official transcripts and GMAT/GRE scores must be received prior to admission.

International applicants must submit a Test of English as a Foreign Language (TOEFL) score of at least 500, official transcripts from all schools attended, and a sponsor's statement (ETSU special form).

EXPENSES

The following is an estimate of the expenses for a single student per semester for 12 credit hours:

Tuition and fees
Texas resident...............$ 321
Nonresident 1,617
Room and board.............. 1,181
Books and supplies   175

FINANCIAL ASSISTANCE

A number of graduate assistantships that require part-time teaching, laboratory instruction, research, and/or other institutional services are available on a competitive basis. The stipend for graduate assistantships is $5,000 for nine months, and the out-of-state portion of the tuition charge is waived for recipients of graduate teaching assistantships. Department heads administer the graduate assistantship program, and applications should be submitted directly to the department head of the appropriate department. Scholarships and student loans are administered through the Financial Aid Office.

PLACEMENT

An effective University Placement Service assists graduate students in career planning and in obtaining responsible positions in business, industry, government, education, and other professional areas.

CORRESPONDENCE

Inquiries should be addressed to
Assistant Dean
College of Business and Technology
East Texas State University
Commerce, Texas 75428
Telephone: 214-886-5190

East Texas State University at Texarkana was established in 1971 as a component of East Texas State University, which has its main campus in Commerce, Texas. Texarkana is located on the Texas-Arkansas boarder. State Line Avenue divides the city, which is operated by two city governments, each with its own mayor, police department, and fire department. Texarkana is 152 miles from Little Rock; 112 miles from Hot Springs, Arkansas; 175 miles from Dallas, Texas; and 75 miles from Shreveport, Louisiana.

East Texas State University at Texarkana was established on the campus of Texarkana Community College as a method of expanding and complementing the offerings of that 50-year-old college, and bringing increased educational opportunity to citizens of an approximate 12-county area containing a population of almost 300,000.

Three hundred and twenty-three students constituted the initial enrollment of fall 1972. This number has steadily increased to approximately 1,200 students.

East Texas State University at Texarkana, like the community colleges of the region, is primarily a commuter institution with a majority of its students coming from a nine-county area in extreme Northeast Texas and three counties in Southwest Arkansas. The typical student is approximately 31 years of age, is married, has children, usually holds a full-time job, and is primarily interested in those courses or programs that will provide the skills and knowledge associated with career advancement. Understandably, time is a precious commodity to these students. They frequently find that it is very difficult to attend courses that are highly structured in terms of time and place.

In view of these factors, ETSU-Texarkana is making a significant commitment to the development of instructional delivery systems and curricula that make portions of courses and programs somewhat "time free," stress competencies generally expected in various professional fields, and call for student participation in internships, field experiences, and action research projects focused on industry, business, school, or community problems.

PROGRAMS OF STUDY

ETSU-Texarkana offers both the Master of Business Administration (M.B.A.) and the Master of Science (M.S.) in business administration. Both programs focus upon the problem-solving and decision-making responsibilities of modern management

and are aimed at providing broad-based preparation for careers in administration in either the public or the private sector.

The M.B.A. program is designed to ensure a basic knowledge of essential business functions; to develop analytical decision-making skills; to increase the ability to adjust to rapidly changing social, economic, technological, and political conditions; and to provide the foundation essential for continuing professional self-development.

For persons with baccalaureate degrees in business, the requirements for the M.B.A. degree include the completion of 12 graduate courses in business and economics. Persons with degrees in disciplines other than business are required to complete additional background courses (or submit acceptable College-Level Examination Program (CLEP) scores in lieu of such course work) to ensure a common body of knowledge.

The M.S. in business administration is more flexible and permits taking a narrower base of courses to specialize in specific disciplines such as management or marketing. This program requires the completion of eight graduate courses in business administration plus four graduate courses in an area other than business administration.

It is possible to begin graduate business programs during the fall, spring, or summer semesters and to complete these programs in one calendar year.

ADMISSION

To be admitted to either the M.B.A. or M.S. in business administration program, applicants must possess a baccalaureate degree and one of the following:
- an undergraduate grade-point average (GPA) of 2.5 on a 4.0 scale, plus a Graduate Management Admission Test (GMAT) score of 450,
- at least 950 points based on the formula: $200 \times$ undergraduate GPA + GMAT score,
- at least 1,000 points based on the formula: $200 \times$ GPA on last 60 undergraduate hours + GMAT score.

International students on F-1 Visa must submit a $25 application fee, score 550 or above on the Test of English as a Foreign Language (TOEFL), be approved for admission to the program by the Program

Director, and submit all forms and transcripts required for admission at least 60 days prior to registration.

EXPENSES
The following is an estimate of the expenses for a single student per semester:
Tuition and fees
  Texas residents . . . .$ 275
  Nonresident 1,575
Books and supplies 150

FINANCIAL ASSISTANCE
The financial assistance program of the school includes scholarships and loans.

PLACEMENT
The university maintains a placement office to serve students and graduates.

CORRESPONDENCE
Inquiries concerning the programs in management offered at ETSU-Texarkana should be addressed to
Dr. Ernest L. Carlton
Program Director for Administration
  Disciplines
East Texas State University at
  Texarkana
P.O. Box 5518
Texarkana, Texas 75501
Telephone: 214-838-6514

Eastern is a coeducational, Christian, liberal arts college founded in 1952 as Eastern Baptist College. Early in 1972, the name of the college was changed to Eastern College. The college is located in St. Davids, in the western suburbs of Philadelphia, Pennsylvania, on a 92-acre campus.

A recognition that the business sector has pervasive influence in society prompted the college to begin an undergraduate program in economics and business administration in 1966. Since 1972, the business curriculum has almost tripled and now includes four majors. The Master of Business Administration (M.B.A.) degree was first offered in January 1982, and now there are approximately 200 students in the undergraduate business program and over 100 in the graduate programs.

Eastern College seeks to provide education that is rooted in a unifying Christian world view in order to prepare graduates for lives of leadership and service in all segments of society. The goal of the M.B.A. program is to educate business leaders who will possess a sense of Christian values and moral and ethical responsibility in addition to well-developed professional and interpersonal skills.

Faculty members at Eastern College are dedicated to combining scholarship and experience with a genuine interest in their students as individuals. Attention to students' particular needs and counseling in academic, career, and personal areas have been and will continue to be priorities for the faculty. Small class size and availability of faculty outside of class provide many opportunities for students to question, to discuss, and to develop their own understanding.

PROGRAMS OF STUDY

Eastern College offers a standard Master of Business Administration (M.B.A.) degree, an M.B.A. in economic development, an M.B.A. with a concentration in business ethics, and joint M.B.A./M.Div. and M.B.A./M.A.R. degrees with Eastern Baptist Theological Seminary. Courses are scheduled in the late afternoon and evening in order to maximize opportunity for employed students.

The core curriculum for students in the part-time program includes accounting, economics, finance, organizational behavior, marketing management, quantitative decision making, and Christian business ethics. Four concentrations are available for specialization: health administration, human resources management, marketing, and finance.

The M.B.A. in economic development prepares dedicated Christians to serve as administrators and entrepreneurs in the inner city and throughout the less developed world. Graduates of the college have the technical expertise and spiritual vision to serve the socially disinherited and oppressed. This curriculum includes a core of business courses plus courses in economic development, cultural anthropology, appropriate technology, entrepreneurship, and international marketing.

The business ethics concentration adds courses in ethics, Christian social responsibility, and theology and the corporation to the core and allows students to choose a corporate or entrepreneurship emphasis. The joint M.B.A./M.Div., M.B.A./M.A.R. degree programs include both college and seminary course requirements.

The graduate programs are approved by the Pennsylvania Department of Education. Eastern College is accredited by the Middle States Association of Colleges and Secondary Schools and is a member of the American Assembly of Collegiate Schools of Business.

ADMISSION

To be admitted to the M.B.A. program the student must meet the following criteria:

- a bachelor's degree in any field from an accredited college or university,
- a 2.5 overall undergraduate grade-point average,
- a score of at least 425 on the Graduate Management Admission Test (GMAT),
- a Test of English as a Foreign Language (TOEFL) score of 500 or above,
- and a total of at least 950 points based on the formula: 200 times the overall grade-point average plus the GMAT score.

A limited number of individuals who do not meet the above criteria may be granted provisional admission by the M.B.A. Committee for up to two semesters. Continuance in the program will be determined by the student's performance in the graduate courses.

EXPENSES

Tuition and fees (subject to change)
   Application fee (nonrefundable). . $ 15
   Tuition, per semester hour
    (includes fees). 175

FINANCIAL ASSISTANCE

Financial assistance is available for students in need. The financial aid program offers assistance in the form of scholarships, assistantships, and Guaranteed Student Loans.

PLACEMENT

Formal placement facilities are not available; however, assistance is provided by the faculty in arranging employment opportunities.

CORRESPONDENCE

For further information, please write or call
   Director
   M.B.A. Program
   Eastern College
   St. Davids, Pennsylvania 19087
   Telephone: 215-341-5847

EASTERN ILLINOIS UNIVERSITY

CHARLESTON, ILLINOIS

Eastern Illinois University, established in 1895 to serve the educational needs of the citizenry, is organized as a public institution. The primary aim of the university's programs is to provide excellent instruction and an educational environment that will produce broadly educated, responsible citizens who are prepared to serve and to lead in a free society.

PROGRAM OF STUDY

The Master of Business Administration (M.B.A.) program is designed to serve the student who has completed a bachelor's degree in nonbusiness fields, as well as the graduate with a concentration of undergraduate courses in business. The time needed to complete the program depends upon the student's course background and course load. All requirements for graduation, as stated in the Graduate School Catalog, must be met.

The basic philosophy of the M.B.A. program reflects the general management point of view. The program is meant to ensure a sound knowledge of the basic business functions: accounting, production, finance, and marketing.

The program is designed to develop ability in methods and processes of analysis, particularly in identifying problems, obtaining relevant facts, and rendering judgment and action based on careful, systematic, and scientific analysis of data. The student is expected to communicate ideas, proposals, findings, conclusions, and judgments by oral and written means—clearly, concisely, reliably, concretely, and coherently. The program provides the means for an understanding of the social conscience. The general background enables the student to continue his or her learning and development in a continuously changing world.

Students with business undergraduate degrees normally have a satisfactory command of elements of understanding fundamental to entry into graduate study for the degree. They may be prepared to launch immediately into phase II (graduate-level courses). Students who do not have undergraduate degrees in business are expected to make up deficiencies by completing phase I (undergraduate-level courses). The phase I courses must be completed or substantially completed before the student enrolls in phase II courses.

The program is flexible enough to take into account the diversity of undergraduate backgrounds of the students. A student who has an undergraduate degree in business administration with a major in one of the functional areas will not take the functional course in that area at the graduate level but will substitute an approved elective. For this reason each student accepted for the M.B.A. program must meet initially with the Coordinator of Graduate Business Studies to prepare an approved program and schedule courses to allow for individual circumstances.

Phase II includes the following three-credit courses: operations management, managerial accounting control, marketing management, operations research, financial management, administrative policy, information systems, and organizational behavior. A course in business research methods and six hours of electives are also required. The student may elect courses in business or related subjects with the approval of the Coordinator of Graduate Business Studies.

The student may elect to complete a thesis for three to six semester hours or independent study for three to six semester hours. The combined total of thesis and independent study may not exceed nine semester hours.

ADMISSION

An applicant for admission to the Graduate School must (1) satisfy all general admission requirements of the university, (2) hold a bachelor's degree from an accredited college or university, (3) submit to the Graduate School a complete and official transcript of work completed at each college or university attended, and (4) submit the results of the Graduate Management Admission Test (GMAT). Foreign students must submit a Test of English as a Foreign Language (TOEFL) score of at least 550. All applications for admission should be made to the Graduate School.

Requirements for admission to the Master of Business Administration program are based on a combination of undergraduate grade-point average and score on the Graduate Management Admission Test. Those requirements are (1) a score of 450 or more on the GMAT and a grade-point average of 2.75 (4.0 scale) for the last 60 semester hours of undergraduate credit; or (2) a total of 1,000 points based on the

formula: 200 × junior-senior grade-point average plus GMAT score, with the proviso that a minimum GMAT score of 400 must be attained.

An applicant should meet the following deadlines for completed applications, transcripts, GMAT and TOEFL scores:

Fall semester . . . . July 1
Spring semester . . . . December 1
Summer term . . . . April 15

EXPENSES

Tuition and fees, per semester (subject to change)
Full-time (12 or more semester hours)
  resident student . . . . $ 628.00
Part-time resident student,
  per hour 48.95
Full-time nonresident
  student 1,534.00
Part-time nonresident student,
  per hour 104.45

FINANCIAL ASSISTANCE

A limited number of graduate assistantships are available. Applications may be obtained from the Graduate School. Applications for assistantships for the following year must be submitted to the Coordinator of Graduate Studies by March 1.

PLACEMENT

The facilities of the Director of Placement at Eastern Illinois University are available for use by students and alumni.

CORRESPONDENCE

Initial correspondence concerning the M.B.A. program at Eastern Illinois should be directed to
  Coordinator of Graduate Business Studies
  School of Business
  Eastern Illinois University
  Charleston, Illinois 61920
  Telephone: 217-581-3028

EASTERN KENTUCKY UNIVERSITY

RICHMOND, KENTUCKY

Eastern Kentucky University is a coeducational public institution of higher education. Richmond, the county seat of Madison County, is an expanding community of approximately 20,000 population. A rural atmosphere in close proximity to Lexington, Cumberland Lake, and the Daniel Boone National Forest makes Richmond an ideal location for both study and recreation.

PROGRAMS OF STUDY

The College of Business offers programs leading to the Bachelor of Business Administration and the Master of Business Administration (M.B.A.) degrees. The M.B.A. degree program is broad in nature and aimed at development of general competence in the functions of management. It provides for study in breadth in selected functional areas and for concentrated study in a specialized field of the student's choice.

All M.B.A. students must satisfy requirements for the common body of knowledge (CBK) and complete 27 graduate hours beyond the CBK. Of these 27 graduate hours, 24 must be reserved exclusively for graduate students (6xx level of instruction). Except for business policy, courses in the CBK normally will be taken prior to graduate-level instruction.

Students who have an undergraduate background in business must have completed the equivalent of the business core as described in the current *General Catalog* and a mathematics course. Business policy is part of the CBK and will be taken as a capstone course at or near the final semester of the M.B.A. program. For students without an academic background in business, an accelerated curriculum covers the common body of knowledge. The CBK may be satisfied in part by participation in the College-Level Examination Program (CLEP).

In addition to the common body of knowledge, at least 27 semester hours must be taken in the fields of accounting, economics, business, and office administration. Managerial economics and business research and report writing are required of all students and count as 6 of the 27 hours.

ADMISSION

Applicants to the Master of Business Administration programs must (1) hold a bachelor's degree from an accredited institution, (2) have at least a minimum grade-point average of 2.4 on a 4.0 (A) basis, (3) achieve a minimum score of 350 on the Graduate Management Admission Test (GMAT), and (4) provide indicators of success in graduate study by the combination of their grade-point average and GMAT score as follows: at least 950 points based upon the formula: 200 × the overall grade-point average + the GMAT score or at least 1,000 points based on the formula: 200 × the upper-division grade-point average + the GMAT score.

EXPENSES

Tuition, per semester
Full-time (minimum of nine semester hours), resident student . . . .$ 522
Full-time, nonresident student 1,494

FINANCIAL ASSISTANCE

A limited number of graduate assistantships are available. Stipends for assistantships currently amount to $3,100 per year (10 months). Out-of-state tuition is waived for those holding assistantships.

PLACEMENT

The facilities of the Director of Placement at Eastern Kentucky University are available for use by students and alumni.

CORRESPONDENCE

For information on the program of study offered by Eastern Kentucky University, please write or call

Dean of Graduate School
Eastern Kentucky University
Richmond, Kentucky 40475
Telephone: 606-622-1742

EASTERN MICHIGAN UNIVERSITY

YPSILANTI, MICHIGAN

Eastern Michigan University (EMU), founded in 1849, is a coeducational institution located near the Detroit metropolitan area. University growth and function are related directly to the large industrial, educational, research complex in southeastern Michigan. The graduate program in business, established in 1953, enrolls approximately 800 men and women in evening only classes.

PROGRAMS OF STUDY

Eastern Michigan University offers four graduate business programs: the Master of Business Administration (M.B.A.), the Master of Science in Accountancy (M.S.A.), the Master of Science in Computer-Based Information Systems (M.S.I.S.), and the Master of Science in Organizational Behavior and Development (M.S.O.D.). These programs require 60-72 semester hours of graduate-level courses; however, students with undergraduate business degrees will usually be able to complete a program within one year of full-time study. Applicants with nonbusiness undergraduate degrees may need several graduate foundation courses prior to enrolling in the core-level courses. Calculus and linear algebra are deficiencies that must be completed first or prior to entering the program. Students may elect to take tests to excuse them from some foundation courses or submit College-Level Examination Program (CLEP) scores.

The M.B.A. program is designed to establish a broad understanding of business functions, the relationship of business to society as a whole, and the impact of legal forces on business. The program is also designed to provide sufficient specialization for the student to perform in a specific job area, such as accounting, accounting information systems, finance, computer-based information systems, operations research, decision sciences, management, organization development, marketing, international or general business.

The M.S.A. program is designed to develop an individualized advanced specialization in accounting. Upon admission to the program the student will prepare a proposed program of course work and present it to the M.S.A. Advisory Committee for review. Once approved, this program becomes the student's degree requirements.

The M.S.I.S. is a program of study for students seeking a solid background in computer systems analysis, management of computer-related activities, modeling and computer simulation, and database management.

The M.S.O.D. program is designed to train organizational development practitioners to evaluate and develop organizational cultures, to be more resourceful in solving personnel development problems, and to assist the organization in adapting to ongoing change, both internal and external.

ADMISSION

Admission is granted to those graduates of regionally accredited institutions whose undergraduate grade-point average and Graduate Management Admission Test (GMAT) scores indicate a high promise of success in graduate business studies. Precise grade-point average and GMAT requirements vary from program to program; specific program information is available from the address below. Applications, transcripts, and GMAT scores should be submitted no later than 30 days before the beginning of a term (60 days for foreign students).

Foreign student requirements are in addition to the above: (1) proof of degree from an accredited college overseas and submission of official transcripts or mark sheets, (2) Test of English as a Foreign Language (TOEFL) minimum score of 550 or Michigan Test ELI minimum of 85, (3) statement of financial responsibility, and (4) two letters of recommendation. Please take note that the I-20 form for the F-1 Visa cannot be issued until the student has been admitted to a degree program. EMU never issues provisional I-20s.

EXPENSES

Per semester	Michigan	Nonresident
Registration fee	$ 20	$ 20
Tuition (12 hours)	760	1,765
Room and board	1,310	1,310
Books and supplies	350	350

Residence hall space is available as are off-campus student apartments. The supply of married student campus housing is very limited. Rent for on-campus apartments varies from $230-$300 per month; off-campus rents range from $250-$500 per month. Inquiries should be directed to the Director of Housing.

FINANCIAL ASSISTANCE

A limited number of graduate assistantships are available for full-time graduate students. Assistantships require 20 hours of work per week and carry a stipend of $3,800 to $4,000 for two semesters, in addition to a maximum of 16 hours of paid tuition. Inquiries regarding these programs should be addressed to the head of the department in which the student intends to specialize. Students who need part-time employment should apply to the Placement Office. Foreign students are expected to devote full time to study.

CORRESPONDENCE

For further information concerning the graduate business programs, write to
    Coordinator
    Graduate Business Programs
    517 Pray-Harrold Building
    Eastern Michigan University
    Ypsilanti, Michigan 48197

Eastern New Mexico University offers a balanced program combining both general and specialized learning. This task is accomplished through effective organization of human and physical resources in various services, colleges, and schools.

The College of Graduate Studies is university wide in its scope and serves to coordinate all graduate programs offered by the university. The dean assumes general responsibilities relating to admissions, record keeping, appointments of advisers and graduate committees, approval of degree programs, and final approval of theses.

PROGRAM OF STUDY

The College of Business offer a curriculum leading to a Master of Business Administration (M.B.A.) degree. This program is designed for either the thesis or nonthesis plan. Students are prepared for responsible managerial positions in an increasingly complex business environment. Emphasis is placed on the development of managerial generalists rather than specialists and requires study in all major areas of business. The course of study for the M.B.A. degree must follow a structured degree plan guided by the catalog requirements, developed by the student's advisory committee, approved by the Dean of the College of Business, and finally approved by the Dean of Graduate Studies. The program consists of three groupings: (A) leveling courses, (B) business core courses—21 credit hours, (C) area of emphasis/elective courses—12 credit hours.

Entry into the M.B.A. program in the College of Business requires that all applicants have a common background of basic concepts and skills used in subsequent courses and in business. Each applicant's undergraduate transcript will be evaluated to determine which foundation courses are required, if any. The following Eastern New Mexico University undergraduate courses, or their equivalent, are minimum leveling requirements for the M.B.A. degree:

Acct 201-203	Elementary Accounting
BAd 315	Business Law I
Econ 221-222	Principles of Economics I and II
Fin 311	Corporation Finance
Mgt 301	Principles of Management
Mkt 301	Principles of Marketing
Stat 213	Statistics I
CIS 151	Intro to CIS

All of the following seven core courses must be completed for graduate credit by each candidate:

Acct	551	Managerial Accounting
BAd	501	Business and Society
CIS	500	Applications in Business Information Systems
Fin	541	Advanced Managerial Finance
Mgt	501	Survey of Management Science
Mgt	513	Advanced Studies in Organizational Behavior Theory
Mkt	517	Marketing Administration

The student who has an undergraduate concentration in one of the fields listed in the M.B.A. core or has taken an equivalent course in a bachelor's degree program may not take the course pertaining to that field as a core requirement. Course substitutions, with the recommendation of the student's advisory committee, will be made as necessary in the core requirement.

ADMISSION

Applicants holding a baccalaureate degree from any accredited college or university may apply for admission to the Graduate School. Admission requirements of the Graduate School must be met before the applicant may be admitted to the M.B.A. program. To be granted regular admission in the Graduate School, the applicant must have a 2.7 grade-point average (out of a possible 4.0). For students who do not meet this requirement, provisional or unclassified admission is available. In addition to the Graduate School admission requirements, admission to the M.B.A. program must be obtained. All applicants must submit acceptable scores from the Graduate Management Admission Test (GMAT) at least one month prior to the student's first enrollment. The College of Business considers both the undergraduate grade-point average (GPA) and the score on the GMAT in deciding upon a student's admission. As a general guideline the applicant should score a total of 950 or more based on the formula: 200 × undergraduate GPA + the GMAT score, to be eligible for admission.

EXPENSES

Per semester*	New Mexico Resident	Nonresident
Full time (12 or more credits)	$393.00	$1,245.00
Part time (11 or fewer credits), per credit	32.75	103.75

*Subject to change

FINANCIAL ASSISTANCE

Graduate assistantships are available to applicants eligible for regular admission who have a Bachelor of Business Administration or similar degree. Other financial assistance is available through the Office of Financial Aids.

PLACEMENT

The University Placement Office services the College of Business Administration. Numerous firms and agencies interview on campus.

CORRESPONDENCE

Inquiries should be addressed to
    Graduate Coordinator
    College of Business Administration
    Eastern New Mexico University
    Portales, New Mexico 88130
    Telephone: 505-562-2252

In 1982, Eastern Washington University celebrated its 100th year as an educational institution. The university is located in Cheney, Washington, 16 miles southwest of the city of Spokane, the central city in the region of northwestern U.S.A. known as the Inland Empire. Although Eastern is a regional university, students come from all of the United States and many foreign countries. Enrollment in the university is approximately 8,000 students; about 1,100 are engaged in graduate studies. Eastern's School of Business has an enrollment of 1,200. The graduate and undergraduate business administration programs are accredited by the American Assembly of Collegiate Schools of Business (AACSB). The School of Business has its headquarters in the modern three-story Ceylon S. Kingston Hall; however, the M.B.A. program courses are offered entirely at night in the Eastern Washington University Spokane Center primarily for the convenience of working men and women. Metropolitan bus service, direct no-toll phone lines between Spokane and the Cheney campus, and a growing number of resident courses in various disciplines offered in Spokane emphasize the close relationship of Eastern to the city.

PROGRAM OF STUDY

The Master of Business Administration (M.B.A.) program is designed to provide advanced study for persons interested in a career in professional management. The aims of the program are (1) to develop an understanding of the nature and complexities of the business decision-making process in a world of change and uncertainty, (2) to promote an understanding of the place of business organizations in the larger society in which they operate, (3) to provide meaningful learning experiences for students and practicing administrators of profit and not-for-profit organizations, and (4) to give students with undergraduate degrees in all fields an opportunity to learn and understand useful managerial theories and concepts, as well as analytical tools and methods.

The M.B.A. program is divided into three areas of study. A basic program consisting of 46 hours of course work (11 courses) is required of all students having baccalaureate degrees in areas other than business administration. The basic program is designed to ensure that entering nonbusiness students have knowledge of micro- and macroeconomic theory, accounting principles, quantitative analy-

sis, finance, marketing, business law, management, business social responsibility, and the use of computers in business. Undergraduate transcripts are reviewed by the School of Business faculty to determine which of the basic program courses the student needs. Students who have a baccalaureate in business administration will usually not undertake the basic program unless their transcripts indicate a deficiency in the business common body of knowledge. The advanced program is begun only after all basic program requirements have been met. The advanced program consists of 36 hours (nine courses) covering the methods of business research, financial management, business decision analysis, marketing management, organization and management theory, administrative controls, management information systems, managerial economics, and administrative policies. In the third area, the student elects one of three options to complete the master's studies in keeping with his or her career objectives: (1) a thesis and 4 hours of electives, (2) a comprehensive research report and 4 hours of electives, or (3) 12 hours of electives. An oral examination on the student's total program must be completed during the final quarter.

ADMISSION

To be admitted to the M.B.A. program, a candidate must hold a four-year baccalaureate degree in any field of specialization from an accredited college or university. Admission is based on a combination of the student's undergraduate grade-point average and score on the Graduate Management Admission Test (GMAT). In accordance with present program requirements and national accreditation standards (AACSB), master's level business courses are reserved exclusively for students who have been formally admitted to the M.B.A. program or other master's degree programs. International students must demonstrate English language competency by taking the Test of English as a Foreign Language (TOEFL).

EXPENSES

Graduate quarterly tuition for residents of the state of Washington is $570 for full-time study (10 or more credit hours) and $57 per credit hour for part-time (fewer than 10 hours). Nonresident full-time graduate tuition is $1,698 per quarter. Reduced fees are available to approved Vietnam veterans. All fees are subject to change.

FINANCIAL ASSISTANCE

Financial assistance for graduate students is available through programs such as National Direct Student Loans, Guaranteed Student Loans, student work-study employment, and a limited number of scholarships where there is exceptional financial need. A limited number of graduate assistantships are also available.

PLACEMENT

The university provides career planning and placement services for formally admitted master's students who have advanced to candidacy. The Career Planning and Placement Office offers workshops, seminars, discussion groups, and presentations to provide awareness of the present employment picture, career planning, applying for a job, and interviewing techniques. A library of occupational information is available. The Placement Office arranges and schedules interviews with personnel recruiters from business and industry. The M.B.A. Association (students) publishes a newsletter each quarter in which information about the M.B.A. program and careers is disseminated.

CORRESPONDENCE

For further information or to request an application for admission, please write
M.B.A. Program Director
School of Business
Eastern Washington University
Cheney, Washington 99004
Telephone 509-458-6413

ELON COLLEGE

ELON COLLEGE, NORTH CAROLINA

Elon College, founded by the Christian Church in 1889, is one of North Carolina's foremost private schools. Located in the heart of the state's heavily industrialized Piedmont region, the college lies adjacent to the city of Burlington, approximately halfway between Greensboro and Durham. With a total enrollment of 2,900 undergraduate and graduate students, the college emphasizes close interaction between students and faculty in an environment conducive to participatory learning. Limited enrollment and an advantageous location offer students a unique opportunity to enjoy a college-town ambience and benefit from small classes, while having access to a sophisticated business sector and outstanding cultural facilities.

PROGRAM OF STUDY

The Master of Business Administration (M.B.A.) program at Elon College is designed to enhance the technical skills and theoretical dimensions useful for career development. Theory and practice are stressed throughout the program, with particular emphasis being placed upon problem solving and the analysis of cases. The program is arranged so that students may enroll on either a full-time or part-time status; all courses are offered during evening hours, and approximately 50 percent of the students elect to attend part time while pursuing their careers.

The program consists of a minimum of 12 courses and a maximum of 17 courses, and it is divided into three parts: basic studies, core curriculum, and electives. The basic studies segment is composed of fundamental courses in accounting, economics, inferential statistics, and computer science. It is designed to prepare students for advanced work in the core curriculum and electives. There are five basic studies courses, and one or more of these may be waived on the basis of an applicant's educational background and/or career experience. Waiver of all basic studies courses leaves a student with a minimum program of study made up of 12 courses taken from the core curriculum and electives. A full-time student needing no basic studies courses may complete the program in three semesters. Part-time status and/or the need for basic studies courses lengthens the time commensurately.

The core curriculum is required of all students, and it consists of the following seven advanced courses: quantitative decision methods, statistical analysis, manage-rial economics, managerial accounting, financial management, marketing management, and business policy. Five additional courses are chosen from the following electives: organizational behavior, organizational development and theory, business communications, operations management, management information systems, business and society, legal environment of business, international business, special topics, and independent study. The latter two elective courses allow particular interests to be developed.

ADMISSION

Both part-time and full-time applicants are evaluated according to the same admission standards. The key elements are undergraduate record, scores on the Graduate Management Admission Test (GMAT), recommendations, and professional experience. The undergraduate grade-point average is multiplied by 200, and the product is added to the GMAT score. A minimum of 950 total points is required for consideration.

International applicants are subject to the same criteria as domestic applicants, with the additional condition that they perform adequately on the Test of English as a Foreign Language (TOEFL).

EXPENSES
Per academic year

Tuition (Residents and Nonresidents of N.C.), per semester hour	$ 110
Room	920
Board	1,350
Books	500
Deposit	50

Many students in the M.B.A. program live off campus. Single, full-time M.B.A. students may choose to reside in a college dormitory and/or take meals in a college facility.

FINANCIAL ASSISTANCE

Students enrolled full time in the M.B.A. program are eligible for financial assistance from the following sources: institutional work-study program, college work-study program, and student loan program.

Information concerning these programs may be obtained from the Office of Admission and Financial Planning.

PLACEMENT

The College Placement Office assists graduate students in obtaining employment. Many major organizations conduct interviews on campus each year, and frequent placements are made as a result of steady liaison between the business department and the private sector.

CORRESPONDENCE

For additional information concerning the M.B.A. program at Elon College, please write or call

Director, M.B.A. Program
Department of Business and Accounting
Campus Box 2176, Elon College
Elon College, North Carolina 27244
Telephone: 919-584-2238

Emory University is located in a residential suburb six miles from downtown Atlanta, the financial and business center of the growing Southeast. In 1954, the Master of Business Administration (M.B.A.) degree program was initiated at Emory University, building upon an already solidly established Bachelor of Business Administration program dating from 1919. When the American Assembly of Collegiate Schools of Business (AACSB) began accrediting master's programs in 1961, Emory's was one of the first 16 graduate business schools approved.

The School of Business Administration enrolls approximately 220 M.B.A. students, all of whom study full time. Students come from a wide variety of academic disciplines and represent all regions of the United States and several foreign countries. In addition, the school enrolls approximately 300 undergraduate students in the Bachelor of Business Administration program and 80 business executives in a program that permits them to earn an M.B.A. without career interruption (executive M.B.A. program).

The Emory School of Business Administration plays an important role in regional and national business activities. The school is proud of the recognition it receives from the business community. Through generous endowments, the John H. Harland Chair of Business Administration, the Georgia Power Professorship, and the Charles H. Kellstadt Chair of Marketing were established recently. Also, a group of Atlanta-based and regional business firms has made available some of their senior executives for the Management Conference Board, which provides consultation, seminars, on-site visits, distinguished lecturers, and other kinds of support for the school.

PROGRAMS OF STUDY

The M.B.A. program at Emory provides its students with a broad professional education and acquaints them with the theory, principles, and techniques of analysis; organization; planning; and control common to all institutions. Over and above this base, students are able to develop their talents in areas of special interest, whether these be accounting, finance, marketing, or management.

The course work consists of 31 semester-credit hours of core requirements and 27 semester-credit hours of electives. The first year of the program consists largely of required core courses in the areas of accounting, marketing, finance, management, quantitative skills, economics, business environment, and computer skills. Most first-year courses are taught in sections of 30 to 35 students, thus permitting frequent exchange between teacher and student and among the students themselves. In the second year, course work dealing with managerial strategy completes the core sequence. Students may pursue areas of interest through a variety of electives that are sufficient in number to permit strong specialization for those who so desire it. Concentration in accounting is available for students desiring preparation for a professional accounting career within the framework of an M.B.A. program. The teaching methods used include lecture, discussion, the case method, and team learning. Applicants who have completed the equivalent of the core courses may receive waivers that will permit them to choose more electives.

Recent graduates of undergraduate business schools accredited by the AACSB may enter the Emory M.B.A. program at the start of the summer semester and complete 14 courses required for the M.B.A. degree in one calendar year (three semesters). Several joint degree programs are offered through the School of Business Administration, including programs with the Schools of Law, Public Health, and Theology.

ADMISSION

New students are admitted to the School of Business Administration in the fall semester of each year. The results of the Graduate Management Admission Test (GMAT); official transcripts of all previous undergraduate, graduate, and professional work; and two letters of recommendation are required. Applicants from non-English-speaking countries must submit scores on the Test of English as a Foreign Language (TOEFL) and a statement of financial resources. Because admission is competitive, it is advisable that candidates submit applications and all supporting documents by April 15. Candidates who wish to be considered for fellowships and research assistantships must be accepted for admission by March 1.

There are no prerequisite courses for admission, although M.B.A. students find that it is helpful to have taken introductory courses in economics, accounting, calculus, and statistics prior to enrollment.

EXPENSES

Application feea.............. $ 25
Tuition and fees, each semester.. 4,200

FINANCIAL ASSISTANCE

Fellowships, loans, and assistantships are granted on the basis of academic and professional achievement. Graduate business students are also eligible to apply for awards from the National Direct Student Loan and the College Work-Study programs through the University Financial Aid Office.

PLACEMENT

The resources of an active Graduate Business School Placement Office are available to M.B.A. candidates. Over 120 companies send representatives to the campus to interview M.B.A. candidates. Job opportunities for the M.B.A. candidates have exceeded the number of graduates available. Graduates have had ample opportunity to start careers with advancement potential, both in the Southeast and throughout the nation.

The school also works closely with local, regional, and national firms and professional societies in placing graduate students in summer employment between their first and second year in the program.

CORRESPONDENCE

For further information, write or call
M.B.A. Program
School of Business Administration
Emory University
Atlanta, Georgia 30322
Telephone: 404-727-6311

The Kansas Board of Regents authorized the first business program at Emporia State University in 1905, and in 1941 a Master of Science degree in business administration was first offered by the college. The Master of Business Administration (M.B.A.) degree program is now a part of the graduate program of this university of 6,000 students. The School of Business is by invitation an associate member of the American Assembly of Collegiate Schools of Business (AACSB). The university is accredited by the North Central Association of Secondary Schools and Colleges. The M.B.A. program has an enrollment of approximately 100, including a number of night school graduate students.

The School of Business is housed in air-conditioned Cremer Hall, which is convenient to student parking, the Memorial Student Union, and William Allen White Library. The library, completed in 1971, is a beautiful air-conditioned structure with well-lighted study rooms, individual carrels, and open stacks for most materials.

PROGRAM OF STUDY
The Master of Business Administration program is designed to meet the needs of students preparing for middle management or technical jobs or to teach business administration on the college level. The M.B.A. program can be completed in one year by the student with an undergraduate business degree. For others, the program will require two years.

The M.B.A. degree provides the mature student with a broad education in business administration as well as the opportunity for considerable depth of study in one area through elective courses. The required courses include MG 853, Behavioral Aspects of Management; AC 834, Seminar in Managerial Accounting; FI 850, Seminar in Financial Management; MG 801, Business Policy and Strategic Management; MK 864, Marketing Management; BA 770, Operations Research; and MG 845, Management and Organization Theory. In addition to the 20 semester hours of required courses listed above, the candidate must complete 15 hours of electives that permit him or her to obtain graduate credit in such areas as accounting, data processing, marketing, management, or finance, according to his or her needs and interests. On the other hand,

the student may choose to broaden his or her understanding of business administration through other electives available in the School of Business.

ADMISSION
The one-year M.B.A. course of study is designed for students who have completed an undergraduate degree in business. For those who do not have a business undergraduate major, it would be necessary to undertake a required core of business subjects in the following areas: accounting, nine hours; economics, six hours; business law, three hours; marketing, three hours; management, three hours; business finance, three hours; statistics, three hours; and data processing, three hours. Students who have an undergraduate business major but have deficiencies in the above areas would have the opportunity to take the necessary courses before starting on the M.B.A. program. Before full admission is made to the program, the student is required to take the Graduate Management Admission Test (GMAT). Admission follows the criteria established by the AACSB, using the GMAT scores and the undergraduate grade-point average. Application for admission to the graduate M.B.A. program should be sent to the School of Graduate and Professional Studies.

EXPENSES

Per semester	Residents	Nonresidents
Total fees	$ 595	$1,183
Books and supplies	125	125
Room and board	910	910
	$1,630	$2.218

Students enrolled for six semester hours or less pay $41.00 per hour if they are Kansas residents, and $80.25 per credit hour if they are nonresidents.

FINANCIAL ASSISTANCE
A number of teaching and research assistantships are offered in the School of Business each year to qualified graduate students. Emporia industries and business firms are especially cooperative in offering employment to mature students. Inquiries should be addressed to the Director of Financial Aids.

PLACEMENT
The School of Business and the Placement Office work closely with business and governmental organizations in securing employment for graduate students. Each fall and spring many personnel representatives visit the campus to interview students.

CORRESPONDENCE
For further information or to obtain an application for admission, please write to
 Director
 M.B.A. Program
 School of Business
 Emporia State University
 Emporia, Kansas 66801
 Telephone: 316-343-1200, station 456

The Rotterdam School of Management is located in Rotterdam itself. The school was initiated in 1969 in Delft by a joint effort of a number of large Dutch-based multinationals like Shell and Unilever. In 1984 the school merged with Erasmus University in Rotterdam and moved into a new building on the campus of the university. The Rotterdam School of Management offers an international program in general management that leads to a Master's Degree of Business Administration. The 80 faculty members integrate a blend of teaching techniques to help students develop their highest potential.

PROGRAM OF STUDY

The program is oriented toward a general management point of view and incorporates three basic characteristics:

• A practical orientation—the School maintains regular contacts with managers in business, industry and government. It emphasizes the importance of decision making, analysis of complex organizational problems in relation to their environment and problem solving. Special attention is devoted to technology, innovation and their relation to organizational change.
• Teamwork—Students are encouraged to form groups in dealing with business problems as a regular requirement for the courses.
• Attention to development of social skills, communication, and technical skills, for example, working in small groups on cases.

Educational objectives are to train graduates for work in management in national or international jobs in profit and non-profit organizations. The balance between theory and practice is reflected in the teaching style; staff and students deal with important management questions together, which leads to joint research and discussion. Staff members fulfill more the role of tutor than that of authorative expert. Case studies, simulations, and projects demand a high degree of independent work from the student.

The M.B.A. program is a full-time day program; it offers an integrated study that develops an understanding of the fundamental areas of business. Courses are arranged according to the following main fields:

Trimester 1: Information, Communication, and Organization—Course 1: Management Information Systems and Computers; Course 2: Business Methods; Course 3: Communication in and by Organizations; Course 4: Managerial Economics. Projects: Simulation and Field Projects

Trimester 2: Functional Areas of Management—Course 1: Finance and Accounting; Course 2: Marketing Management; Course 3: Operations Management; Course 4: Social Aspects of Management; Course 5: Legal Aspects of Management (Students are required to take four of these five courses.)

Trimester 3: Organization and Strategy—Course 1: Organizational Development and Change; Course 2: Management Support Systems; Course 3: Strategic Management; Course 4: Management of Technology

Trimester 4: International Business Environment—Course 1: A. Economics of International Competition; B. Political and Cultural Environment of the Firm; Course 2: A. Business in its European Competitive Legal Environment; B. Industrial Economics; Courses 3, 4, 5: Elective or project

Trimester 5: Electives—Four electives are to be selected

Trimester 6: Final Project—Seminar: Ethics; Seminar: Methodology; Project: Field Project

ADMISSION

Admission requirements include a university degree from an accredited institution (Dutch students need the degree of Doctorandus, Meester, or Ingenieur) and acceptable scores on the Graduate Management Admission Test (GMAT). The Admission Committee evaluates each student's ability for management studies and his or her motivation. Since multidisciplinary workgroups form an important part of the learning process, the total student population should reflect a sufficient range of previous studies and interests relevant to the study of management. An application will not be evaluated until GMAT scores have been received.

EXPENSES

Basic expenses for one academic year (in Dutch guilders) are as follows:

Tuition and admission fee	ƒ 6000.–
Additional expenses (books, excursions, for example)	ƒ 1500.–
Housing, living, and traveling expenses	ƒ 12500.–
Total expenses, approx.	ƒ 20000.–

Most Dutch students live in student houses; universities do not usually have a campus. There is an office at the Erasmus University of Rotterdam which organizes housing in various parts of Rotterdam. Foreign students need to report to the Alien Registration Office and those who want to travel to countries for which they need a visa are advised to get the visa in their home country.

PLACEMENT

The Rotterdam School of Management organizes placement activities several times a year. Students are interviewed by recruitment officers from a wide variety of organizations. For many students this often turns out to be the starting point of their career. A period of practical training with a company may be the beginning of a successful career. Approximately 33 percent of graduates find jobs in industry, 25 percent with banks and insurance companies; about 15 percent work in some branch of public administration and 15 percent set up their own business. An active organization at the school keeps in touch with former students and follows their careers.

CORRESPONDENCE

For further information, write or call
Ms. Anita Noordzij, Public Relations M.B.A.
Rotterdam School of Management
Erasmus University Rotterdam
P.O. Box 1738
3000 DR Rotterdam, The Netherlands
Telephone: 31-10525511, extension 4011

EUROPEAN UNIVERSITY

ANTWERP and BRUSSELS, BELGIUM – MONTREUX, SWITZERLAND

Europe's largest business school, the European University, offers career-oriented graduate programs that provide the needed theoretical background with practical examples and experiences to solidify managerial skills. In coordination with local industry, the university offers the students numerous opportunities to exercise analytic abilities.

Belgium is the economic, political, and geographical heart of Europe, with both the Economic Community and NATO headquarters located there. Brussels is a multilingual, multinational city, and is a frequent choice for international firms to situate their European headquarters.

Antwerp and Brussels are also within easy reach of such major European cities as Paris and London, making them a convenient location from which to travel for either tourist or business purposes.

Montreux is a beautiful city in Switzerland located nearby Geneva on the Lac Leman. It is the site of a large number of conventions for the economic, political, and cultural world. The university is located on the waterfront in the center of town.

European University was founded in 1973 and has grown into Europe's largest privately sponsored business school. Its faculty of 136 specialists in business functions serve a student body of approximately 1,800.

PROGRAMS OF STUDY

Today more than 25 percent of the world's nonagricultural output is accounted for by multinationals. These firms not only take a lion's share of global manufacturing, they also dominate many modern sectors, that is, those industries with the highest growth in terms of both sales and technological development. In short, the international aspects of business provide a highly exciting if complex subject for study. In order to prepare the future manager adequately for the demands of an international business career, the European University organizes an intensive program covering several aspects of international operations. The emphasis falls on international finance and marketing, both highly interesting specialist functions. Of course, before the student embarks on the more complex analysis of international operations, a solid foundation in the traditional management disciplines is established. Students who do not wish to take the full Master of Business Administration

(M.B.A.) program can also combine the international business subjects into a separate package leading to a postgraduate certificate rather than the M.B.A. degree.

European University has a Master of Business Administration program in international management which effectively taps the resources of the international communities in Belgium and Switzerland. The program consists of 15 required courses which a full-time student can complete in one academic year. Some internship opportunities are available for students maintaining a grade-point average of 3.6 or more.

The master's degree program in Management Information Systems (M.I.S.) combines essential managerial skills with data and computer communication abilities. A full-time student can complete the program, which consists of 15 courses, in one academic year.

The Master of Business Communication and Public Relations program, offered in Brussels and Montreux, is a 15-course, 10-month graduate program of study designed to increase management communication efficiency and improve public relations skills. Interviewing, negotiations, sales techniques, and media are covered. European University's graduate program in hotel administration in Montreux enjoys the support of the Swiss hotel industry and the city of Montreux. Internships in hotels are available. The program consists of 15 courses combining the specifics of the hotel trade with general management, and can be completed in one academic year.

ADMISSION

An applicant must hold a bachelor's degree from a recognized or accredited institution. Candidates must submit Graduate Management Admission Test (GMAT) scores, as well as Test of English as a Foreign Language (TOEFL) scores if their mother tongue is not English. Individuals of all undergraduate disciplines are encouraged to apply. Admission is open for all three terms in the academic year. The first term starts in the first week of October, the second term in the first week of January, and the third term after Easter.

EXPENSES

Costs are estimated for the 1986-87 academic year and are influenced by dollar exchange rate fluctuations. Tuitions and fees are subject to change without notice.

In Belgium

Tuition and fees (full program)...	$ 3,300
Room and board, per academic year	5,000
Books and supplies	550
Total	$ 8,850

In Switzerland

Tuition and fees (full program)...	$12,500
Room and board, per academic year	11,000
Books and supplies	800
Total	$24,300

FINANCIAL ASSISTANCE

Based on potential and financial need, the university grants partial and full scholarships to a limited number of applicants.

CORRESPONDENCE

For further information, write to the Dean of Admissions at the campus of your choice.

Amerikalei 131
2000 Antwerp, Belgium

Rue de Livourne 116-120,
1050 Brussels, Belgium

Grand-Rue 42, 1820
Montreux, Switzerland

Fairfield University was founded in 1942 by the Jesuit Order in the United States. It is the inheritor of a tradition of learning and scholarship that dates back to 1540 when St. Ignatius Loyola founded the Society of Jesus (the Jesuits) on the principle of active service in the world.

The School of Business at Fairfield was established in 1978. For 30 years, the university offered an undergraduate program in various areas of business administration through a department within the College of Arts and Sciences. As the reputation of the program grew, the increasing offerings became so extensive that the Board of Trustees authorized a separate School of Business.

Two other factors contributed to the founding of the School of Business: the status of Fairfield County as the fastest-growing corporate headquarters area in the United States and the selection of Fairfield University by the National Council of Savings Institutions as the site for the Center for Financial Studies. This center is the national site for the continuing education programs for association members.

PROGRAMS OF STUDY

The Master of Science (M.S.) in financial management program consists of a core and an area of specialization. The group of courses in the core requires no prior training in business and consists essentially of the common body of knowledge as defined by the American Assembly of Collegiate Schools of Business (AACSB). Completing the core will make it possible for the student with a nonbusiness oriented background of education and experience to complete the M.S. program successfully.

The core courses are essentially intensive introductions to the subject areas which would have been covered if a student had earned a Bachelor of Business Administration (B.B.A.) or a Bachelor of Science (B.S.) in a business major at the undergraduate level. Therefore, selected core courses may be waived for many students admitted into the program. Such waivers may be granted when the quality of preparation of the student justifies the waiver on the basis of previous course work or on the successful completion of a written qualifying examination.

The specialization courses are designed to provide qualified, mature individuals with the opportunity to strengthen their managerial competency in the area of corporate financial management. The program is intended to meet the needs of the corporate community for middle-management personnel by providing a broad understanding of the role of finance in corporate management and specific training in the techniques appropriate to this particular management function.

The program, therefore, takes as its focus the corporation, its objectives, and its strategies. Although not designed to prepare individuals for careers in the financial markets and institutions per se, the program will be of value to persons engaged in those activities as well as those either entering or currently employed in the specific field of financial management.

The program seeks to blend broadly focused courses such as those dealing with ethical dynamics, environmental, and legal issues with specialized offerings such as those in capital budgeting, monetary policy, and portfolio analysis.

The program is designed to accommodate those individuals who are now employed in the corporate area. Classes are conducted on Tuesday, Wednesday, and Thursday evenings and on Saturdays to enable each student to select up to four courses from among several options each semester while continuing full-time employment.

The university has a DEC 2060 computer system with a large number of interactive terminals for student use.

A certificate program for advanced study in finance is also offered. This program is available to those with a Master of Business Administration degree or a Master of Science in a business speciality.

ADMISSION

Students who hold a bachelor's degree in any field from an accredited college or university and who have demonstrated their ability or potential to do high-quality academic work are encouraged to apply.

Consistent with normal requirements of the AACSB, the criteria for admission to the program will be an appropriate undergraduate grade-point average and an appropriate score on the Graduate Management Admission Test (GMAT). In addition, the admissions process requires complete official transcripts of all college work, two letters of recommendation, and a self-evaluation of work experience.

EXPENSES

The schedule of fees for the Master of Science in financial management program is as follows:

Application fee (due with the
application for admission) . . . $ 25
Registration fee, payable each
semester 15
Tuition, per course hour 185

FINANCIAL ASSISTANCE

A number of full scholarships have been made available by major business corporations. A student may apply for a scholarship after having been accepted into the program.

CORRESPONDENCE

For applications and additional information, write or call

Committee on Graduate Admissions
School of Business
Fairfield University
Fairfield, Connecticut 06430
Telephone: 203-254-4070

Fairleigh Dickinson University is an independent, nonsectarian, coeducational institution offering undergraduate, graduate, and professional degree programs in business administration, dentistry, education, engineering, liberal arts, and sciences. Founded in 1942, the university has grown to three major campuses in northern New Jersey, a campus in England, and another on St. Croix in the U.S. Virgin Islands. The university's enrollment of more than 15,000 students is divided among full-time undergraduates, part-time undergraduates, and graduate students.

The Samuel J. Silberman College of Business Administration is located on all three main campuses and currently enrolls approximately 3,700 graduate students. Courses are scheduled during late afternoons and evenings and on Saturdays. Classes are offered year round during two semesters and three summer sessions. Flexible scheduling, full- and part-time studies, and three campus locations offer convenience to working and nonworking students.

PROGRAMS OF STUDY
Offered on three campuses in the New York metropolitan area, minutes from many of the nation's corporate headquarters, the university's Master of Business Administration (M.B.A.) programs are geared to advancing the administrative skills of men and women in varied business and industrial settings. The M.B.A. programs are designed for three types of individuals: managers who wish to broaden their educational base, employees who wish to enter the field of management, and students seeking a career in business administration. Theory and practice are melded in a series of courses addressing management techniques. Case studies, guest lectures by professionals in industry, and adjunct faculty with extensive expertise enhance the practicability of the course offerings. A broad selection of majors, based on a common core of knowledge, emphasizes the general and special areas of business practice and management applications.

The M.B.A. program requires between 36 and 60 credits depending on the student's undergraduate major and concentration in the M.B.A. program. Up to 15 credits of prerequisites may be waived if appropriate courses have been completed with a grade of B or better on the undergraduate level. The remaining credits consist of core courses, required courses for the major field, and the necessary number of electives to complete the total credit requirements.

The M.B.A. degree is offered in the following areas: accounting, accounting and taxation, economics, finance, human resource administration, industrial management, international business, management, marketing, pharmaceutical-chemical studies, and quantitative analysis.

In addition to these evening M.B.A. programs, four special weekend M.B.A. programs are offered on the Rutherford campus. The M.B.A. in management programs (for executives, bank managers, data processing professionals, scientists, engineers, and technical managers) are designed for professionals in these fields with five to seven years' experience, depending on the specialization. Courses are given in five-week modules of one Friday afternoon and four Saturdays or five Saturdays, depending on the program. Students go through the program as an integrated group, beginning in September or February, completing three module courses each semester. An M.B.A. in management for hospitality managers is also available on the Rutherford Campus.

The College of Business Administration offers a Master of Arts in economics; the Public Administration Institute offers a Master of Public Administration (M.P.A.).

ADMISSION
Students may apply for full- or part-time studies; applications are accepted for the fall, spring, and summer sessions. Applications should be sent to the campus of choice and will be reviewed on a rolling basis.

Applicants for matriculation must file a graduate studies application and nonrefundable application fee; credentials for all postsecondary-school academic work, including an official transcript from an accredited institution of higher learning through the baccalaureate degree; and official score reports from the Graduate Management Admission Test (GMAT). Letters of recommendation may be required.

EXPENSES
Tuition is charged on a per-credit basis; the tuition rate for graduate courses during the 1985-86 academic year was $202 per credit hour. For the weekend M.B.A. in management programs, there is a flat fee.

CORRESPONDENCE
For further information, please write or call

Graduate Admissions Office
Fairleigh Dickinson University
Florham-Madison Campus
Madison, New Jersey 07940
Telephone: 201-377-4700

Graduate Admissions Office
Fairleigh Dickinson University
Rutherford Campus
Rutherford, New Jersey 07070
Telephone: 201-460-5000

Graduate Admissions Office
Fairleigh Dickinson University
Teaneck-Hackensack Campus
1000 River Road
Teaneck, New Jersey 07666
Telephone: 201-692-2000

Florida Atlantic University is located in the heart of the most rapidly growing area in Florida and the nation. Once a resort city for millionaires, Boca Raton is becoming a thriving city with well-planned industrial development, mostly in the high technology or research-oriented areas. Within an hour's drive are West Palm Beach, Fort Lauderdale, and Miami with their varied commercial, recreational, and cultural activities.

The university was established in the fall of 1964 as the first upper-division and graduate university to be established in the nation. The undergraduate division enrolled the first freshman class in 1984, and the university now offers full four-year undergraduate and expanded graduate programs.

The undergraduate and graduate business programs are accredited by the American Assembly of Collegiate Schools of Business (AACSB). The college currently enrolls 3,397 undergraduate and 814 graduate students. The faculty is distinguished for its research endeavors, participation in professional organizations, and community service.

PROGRAMS OF STUDY
Graduate programs offered include the Master of Accounting (M.Acc.), the Master of Business Administration (M.B.A.), the Master of Public Administration (M.P.A.), the Master of Applied Science in computer systems (M.A.S.), and the Doctor of Philosophy in public administration (Ph.D.).

All graduate programs are open to applicants who hold baccalaureate degrees in any field from an accredited institution. Students who do not have undergraduate degrees in business will be required to complete a core of undergraduate courses prior to full admission.

The M.Acc. is designed to meet the Florida C.P.A. fifth-year educational requirement and consists of 30 semester credits of graduate work. Undergraduate preparation may be required before admission.

The M.B.A. program is designed to provide general competence for students preparing for managerial careers in business. Tracks are available in accounting and finance for the student who wishes to specialize. The program consists of 40 semester credits of graduate work, with substitutions made for those following a specific track. An examination is required prior to admission to candidacy.

A student who has completed all the required preparatory courses can complete the M.B.A. in three semesters of full-time attendance. Classes are available during the day and evening on the Boca Raton campus and during evening hours at the Broward Campus and West Palm Beach center.

The college also offers a Master of Applied Science degree program in computer and information systems and a Master of Public Administration program. Each program requires one year of full-time course work for students entering with all prerequisite requirements met.

Additionally, a Ph.D. in public administration is offered in conjunction with Florida International University.

ADMISSION
Applications for admission may be made at any time; the program may be started in August, January, or May. Completed applications should be received one month prior to the desired entrance date. Applicants to all graduate programs must submit official transcripts of previous undergraduate and graduate work. Applicants to the M.B.A. and M.Acc. programs must submit scores from the Graduate Management Admission Test (GMAT). M.P.A. and M.A.S. applicants must submit scores from the Graduate Record Examinations (GRE). Foreign applicants are required to submit scores on the Test of English as a Foreign Language (TOEFL).

Minimum admission requirements include a B average in the last two years of work on the undergraduate degree and a score of 450 on the GMAT or 1,000 on the GRE. However, mature work experience, trend of undergraduate grades, and other measures of high promise of success will be considered.

EXPENSES
The tuition fee for Florida residents is approximately $50 per semester hour; for nonresidents, it is approximately $150 per semester hour. Out-of-state tuition fees may be waived for fellowship and assistantship holders. Residence hall rent is approximately $500 per semester, subject to change. There is no on-campus housing for married students, but there are many apartment buildings in Boca Raton and nearby communities. Several meal plans are available in the main cafeteria at varying prices.

FINANCIAL ASSISTANCE
A limited number of fellowships and assistantships are available. Tuition waivers and waivers for the out-of-state portion of fees are also available. The university participates in a wide variety of loan programs. Applications can be obtained from the Office of Student Financial Aid, Florida Atlantic University, Boca Raton, Florida 33431.

PLACEMENT
The university maintains a placement office which is visited by several hundred business and government employers each year. The college also acts as a referral center for requests from prospective employers.

CORRESPONDENCE
For further information concerning the master's programs, please write or call
Director of Student Services
College of Business and Public
  Administration
Florida Atlantic University
Boca Raton, Florida 33431
Telephone: 305-393-3650

Established in 1972, Florida International University's College of Business Administration offers graduate programs designed to provide the student with advanced professional education for managerial careers in business and government. Currently, the university has two campus locations. The main campus, Tamiami, is located 10 miles west of downtown Miami on the Tamiami Trail. The Bay Vista campus is located on a 106-acre site in North Dade County on Biscayne Bay. Florida International, a member institution of the State University System of Florida, is an accredited member of the Southern Association of Colleges and Schools.

Approximately 500 admitted students are enrolled in the graduate programs of the school. Florida International attracts students from all parts of the nation and many foreign countries.

PROGRAMS OF STUDY

The College of Business Administration offers five master's degree programs: Master of Business Administration (M.B.A.), Master of Science in Management (M.S.M.), Master of International Business (M.I.B.), Master of Accounting (M.Acc.), and Master of Science in Taxation (M.S.T.). The objective of the M.B.A. program (42 semester hours plus prerequisites) is to provide the student with a general background in the concepts and processes of administration. The program is oriented toward the private sector. The M.I.B. program (39 semester hours plus prerequisites) is designed to prepare individuals for successful careers in the international field, either working abroad or at home for multinational corporations. The Master of Science in Management program provides an in-depth educational experience for the student desiring greater specialization in a particular area. Concentrations are available in the following areas: finance and management information systems. The length of the M.S.M. program depends upon the selected concentration and the applicability of the student's undergraduate courses. There is no thesis requirement in the programs.

The M.Acc. program is designed to prepare students for entry and accelerated advancement in the accounting profession and to provide the additional formal education needed by persons already in accounting and other fields seeking a career change, advancement, or both. The M.S.T. program is designed to prepare students for either entry or advancement in the highly specialized area of taxation. The curriculum is flexible in order to provide students with a background in the various aspects of the tax area. Both programs require a minimum of 30 semester hours.

The school operates on the semester system, and students may begin in August, January, or May. Students must meet the admission standards prior to registration. All of the graduate programs are designed for part-time evening students.

ADMISSION

Undergraduate preparation in business or economics is not required for admission to the M.B.A., M.I.B., or M.S.M. programs. To be eligible for admission, the applicant must hold a baccalaureate degree from a regionally accredited college or university. Additionally, admission to the programs will be based upon a combination of the score on the Graduate Management Admission Test (GMAT) and the upper-division grade-point average. Decisions on admission to the program will not be made until the applicant's GMAT scores, official transcripts, and application for graduate admission have been received and evaluated. (All students must take the GMAT.)

Foreign students whose native language is not English will be required to establish proficiency in English. Proficiency may be verified by a minimum score of 500 on the Test of English as a Foreign Language. Foreign students should direct their admission inquiries to the Office of International Admission.

EXPENSES

The application fee (one-time nonrefundable charge) is $15. Tuition fees for graduate work are $48.18 per semester hour for Florida residents and $142.68 per semester hour for non-Florida residents. On-campus housing is available. For additional information, contact the Director of Housing.

FINANCIAL ASSISTANCE

In order to qualify for aid, a student must be fully admitted to the graduate program. Further information may be obtained from the Office of Financial Aid.

PLACEMENT

The Career Resources Center is the focal point of career planning and related programs for students and alumni. These programs are intended to help students develop their career objectives, to assist individuals in locating the most advanced positions for which they are qualified, and to provide alumni with the opportunity to audit their career effectiveness and make critical career decisions. Career planning and placement services include one-to-one counseling, group guidance in the form of workshops, on-campus recruiting of students by employers, a career information library, and assistance to students in developing personal and professional data to be presented to employers.

CORRESPONDENCE

For further information, please write to
Graduate Coordinator
College of Business Administration
Florida International University
Tamiami Trail
Miami, Florida 33199
Applications for admission, catalogs, and test application packets may be requested from
The Office of Admissions and Records
Primera Casa Rm. 130
Florida International University
Tamiami Trail
Miami, Florida 33199
Telephone: 305-554-2363

FLORIDA STATE UNIVERSITY

TALLAHASSEE, FLORIDA

Florida State University is one of nine state-supported universities in the Florida system and one of only two authorized for full programs of graduate study. The student body exceeds 22,000; approximately one in six is a graduate student. The campus is situated on 343 acres of rolling land less than one mile from the state capitol complex. The campus buildings represent a harmonious blending of the traditional and the modern.

The College of Business, which occupies new modern facilities, is accredited by the American Assembly of Collegiate Schools of Business (AACSB) at the undergraduate and graduate levels. Graduate student enrollment is approximately 250, including approximately 50 Ph.D. students.

PROGRAMS OF STUDY

The Master of Business Administration (M.B.A.) program emphasizes the knowledge and skills required for scientific management. There are two program options available to students depending on their background. Both options are full-time, lock-step programs. For the nonbusiness bachelor's degree holder, the program of studies is 60 semester hours (four semesters of 15 hours each). A limited number of summer internships are available for the two-year students. For those students with an undergraduate degree in business, the program consists of 39 semester hours to be completed in the fall, spring, and summer semesters.

The Master of Accounting (M.Acc.) program provides advanced study for those seeking careers in professional accounting as Certified Public Accountants or as controllers and accounting executives in industry and government. The usual prerequisite for admission is an undergraduate degree in business with a major in accounting. Applicants who present other undergraduate degrees will be required to complete preparatory work in accounting and business administration. The program consists of 11 courses and normally can be completed in one year of full-time study.

The College of Law and the College of Business offer a joint program leading to the J.D. and M.B.A. degrees. Applicants must fulfill entrance requirements of both colleges.

The Doctor of Philosophy program is intended to prepare candidates for university teaching and research and for administrative and research positions in the pub-

lic and private sectors. The program includes mastery of a major area of concentration; proficiency in a supporting area; competency in the use of analytical, communicative, and logical reasoning processes; and competency in mathematics and economics. Each candidate will complete a dissertation.

ADMISSION

Requirements for admission consideration include an acceptable bachelor's degree, scores on the Graduate Management Admission Test (GMAT), letters of recommendation, and the candidate's personal statement. Business experience is a positive factor but is not required. International students must also submit scores from the Test of English as a Foreign Language (TOEFL).

Admission to the M.B.A. program is in the fall semester only. The application deadline is May 1. Admission to the M.Acc. is in the fall, spring, or summer. Application deadlines are June 1 for fall, October 1 for spring, and March 1 for summer. Normally, notification will be received within one month of receipt of a completed application.

Admission to the Ph.D. program is normally in the fall. Application deadline is May 1.

EXPENSES

Application fee . . . . $ 15
Tuition, per semester hour
    Florida resident 47
    Nonresident 141
    Health services fee 39
Housing costs vary based on the type of housing sought. The university maintains dormitories and apartments for graduate students. Further information is provided with the application materials.

FINANCIAL ASSISTANCE

At the master's level there are a number of College of Business fellowships available. These fellowships are awarded on a competitive basis with awards normally made by April 1.

A limited number of university fellowships of $6,000 are awarded in a university-wide competition. The university fellowship holders receive a waiver of out-of-state tuition. The university fellowship application deadline is January 15.

Doctoral students receive an annual stipend of approximately $9,000. Duties include both research and teaching in the second and third year.

PLACEMENT

The College of Business Placement Office will assist all graduate students in identifying and communicating with national and regional firms and agencies for employment opportunities. A broad range of firms recruit at the university. Resumes of graduating students are published by the M.B.A. Association and distributed to over 200 firms.

CORRESPONDENCE

For further information or to request an application for admission, please write or call
    Ms. Dale Williamson
    Director of Master's Program
    College of Business
    Florida State University
    Tallahassee, Florida 32306-1042
    Telephone: 904-644-3090 (or 6458)

FONTBONNE COLLEGE

ST. LOUIS, MISSOURI

Fontbonne College is a private, coeducational, liberal arts/career-oriented institution located in Clayton, Missouri. Clayton is a beautiful, residential suburb of St. Louis. Fontbonne was founded in 1923 and is sponsored by the Sisters of St. Joseph of Corndelet. The college welcomes men and women of different religious backgrounds. Programs at the graduate and undergraduate levels are accredited by the North Central Association. The college has graduate studies leading to the Master of Science in communication disorders, Master of Arts, Master of Fine Arts in art, and Master of Business Administration.

PROGRAM OF STUDY

The Master of Business Administration (M.B.A.) program is designed to provide men and women with practical managerial and leadership skills. Emphasis is also placed on internship experience and the development of writing and research skills through thesis research. Students holding undergraduate degrees in business and nonbusiness fields may enroll in the program, which varies in length from 30 to 60 credit hours depending upon the background of the student. Graduate courses are taught on Saturdays. The minimum length of time for completion of the degree is one calendar year. Students may also enroll on a part-time basis.

Students must complete the Preparatory Core requirement which consists of 30 undergraduate credit hours taken within the content areas specified: management, marketing, accounting, finance, economics, and statistics/computer science. A minimum of one course is required from each of the content areas; there is no restriction on the distribution of the remaining credit hours within the content areas. Based upon an evaluation of the student's application, undergraduate transcripts, and relevant work experience, students may place out of some or all of the Preparatory Core requirements.

Having completed the Preparatory Core, the M.B.A. program is arranged so that students can complete it in 52 calendar weeks by attending Saturday-only classes. Students are allowed to enroll for up to nine hours of graduate credit during the fall and spring semesters. During the summer semester the students can enroll for up to 12 hours of graduate credit.

The fall schedule contains the Tactical Core. The student is required to choose from the following courses: (1) Managerial Accounting or Financial Management, (2) Seminar in Marketing Management or Seminar in Human Resources Management, (3) Operations Management or Special Topics in Business Law. The spring schedule contains the Strategic Core. The following courses are required: (1) International Management, (2) Seminar in Social Responsibility and Business Ethics, (3) Administrative Policy and Strategic Planning. The summer schedule contains the Capstone Core. It includes the following courses: (1) Graduate Internship, (2) Comprehensive Examinations, (3) Directed Readings in Business Administration, and (4) Thesis Research.

ADMISSION

Admission requirements to Fontbonne's M.B.A. program are a bachelor's degree from an accredited institution of higher education. Students must submit the following to the Office of Admissions before being formally admitted: (1) official transcript from the institution granting the bachelor's degree, (2) scores from the Graduate Management Admission Test (GMAT), (3) a completed application form with a nonrefundable $20 fee, (4) three letters of recommendation. International students must also submit an official letter of financial assurance by their government or a letter of financial guarantee and a letter of credit from their bank. International applicants who have completed their undergraduate degree at a college or university in the United States must complete an interview with the M.B.A. Admissions Committee prior to acceptance. International applicants who have completed their undergraduate degree outside the United States must submit the official score reports of the Test of English as a Foreign Language (TOEFL) and GMAT prior to acceptance.

EXPENSES

Selected relevant expenses for 1985-86 are outlined below:

Tuition, per credit hour $170
Room and board in resident hall,
per semester . . . . $1,335-$1,495

FINANCIAL ASSISTANCE

Only limited financial assistance is available at this stage of development. However, the college does have a full-time Office of Financial Aid.

CORRESPONDENCE

For information, please write or call
M.B.A. Office
Dr. William Friedman
Fontbonne College
6800 Wydown Boulevard
St. Louis, Missouri 63105
Telephone: 314-862-3456 or 314-889-1400

FORDHAM UNIVERSITY AT LINCOLN CENTER
NEW YORK, NEW YORK

The Graduate School of Business Administration was established by Fordham in 1969 after a half-century of providing undergraduate business education for young men and women. The school is located in the Lowenstein Center on the Lincoln Center campus in mid-Manhattan. The academic year consists of three terms and extends from September through July. Most of the classes are given in the evening. Full-time students can complete the program in four terms, while students with full-time positions can do so in three years by taking two courses each term.

The Graduate School of Business Administration also offers its Master of Business Administration (M.B.A.) degree in Westchester at its graduate center, located at Marymount College in Tarrytown, New York. The Tarrytown center is a branch of Fordham University, complementing the Rose Hill and Lincoln Center campuses.

Classes at Tarrytown are taught by the faculty of the Graduate School of Business Administration and are scheduled for the easy commuting convenience of residents of and professionals working in Westchester, Putnam, Rockland, and Dutchess counties in New York, northern New Jersey, and southern Connecticut.

PROGRAMS OF STUDY
Two programs are offered that lead to the M.B.A. degree: a program in business management and a program in professional accounting. In each case the program consists of three parts:
- a common body of knowledge (core courses) essential for managers of business firms and other organizations,
- a series of courses in various functional areas of business (concentrations) that enable the development of expertise in an area of interest to the student,
- a series of courses from which students select according to their interests (electives). These courses provide breadth to the program and enable students to supplement the core and concentration with courses consistent with career objectives.

The program consists of 54 graduate credits (60 graduate credits for the M.B.A. in professional accounting). Exemptions may be granted against core requirements for a limited number of courses taken elsewhere.

Concentrations are offered in accounting, finance, management, marketing, and quantitative methods. In addition, several courses in international business are offered to supplement functional concentrations.

ADMISSION
Requirements for admission are as follows:
- possession of a baccalaureate degree from an accredited institution;
- scores on the Graduate Management Admission Test (GMAT).

Credentials that must be submitted for admission are a bachelor's degree from an accredited institution and GMAT scores. No specific undergraduate major is preferred. Applicants are evaluated on their capacity to pursue demanding and sustained graduate-level studies as evidenced by previous academic records and GMAT scores and by professional and other business experience.

The final date for submitting credentials is July 1 for the fall term, November 1 for the winter term, and March 1 for the spring term.

In addition to the requirements listed above, international students must also submit the results of the Test of English as a Foreign Language (TOEFL) if the applicant's native language is not English. If a student visa is required, the final date for submitting credentials is July 1 for the fall term, November 1 for the winter term, and February 1 for the spring term.

EXPENSES
Tuition for the year 1985-86 is $235 per credit or $705 for a three-credit course. Living expenses are expected to be at least $8,500 a year. No university housing is provided for graduate students.

FINANCIAL ASSISTANCE
A limited number of assistantships are available to full-time students who are not engaged in outside work. These involve tuition awards and require 16 hours of work per week. Applications should be made to the Dean two months prior to the beginning of the term.

Further information concerning New York State and federal financial aid programs may be obtained from the Financial Aid Office, Room 220.

PLACEMENT
The Career Planning and Placement Center works closely with students in the Graduate School of Business by providing individual counseling, workshops, on-campus recruiting, and job listings. The center also offers placement assistance to alumni.

CORRESPONDENCE
For further information regarding the M.B.A. program, please write or call
Director of Admissions
Graduate School of Business
Fordham University at Lincoln Center
New York, New York 10023
Telephone: 212-841-5432

FORT HAYS STATE UNIVERSITY

HAYS, KANSAS

Fort Hays State University, founded in 1902, is a state, tax-assisted liberal and applied arts university established and maintained by the state to serve the people of Kansas. Fort Hays State is situated at the hub of a vast, unique geographical region—the Great Plains. It is the only college or university in western Kansas offering both undergraduate and graduate degree programs. More than 5,500 students attend the university.

PROGRAM OF STUDY

The Master of Business Administration (M.B.A.) is a professional degree program for those aspiring to responsible positions in business and industry. The program is offered by Fort Hays State University under the direction of the Graduate School and the Department of Business Administration. The purpose of the M.B.A. program is to develop professional capability in functional areas of business administration. The goal is to provide the student with the knowledge and perspective needed for success in the rapidly changing world of business management. The 36 hours of course work consist of 24 hours of core courses, 9 hours of specialization courses, and 3 hours of research. Normally, the program is completed in three semesters of full-time study or three years of part-time study.

ADMISSION

Admission criteria for the M.B.A. degree program include undergraduate academic performance, completion of undergraduate prerequisite requirements with a minimum overall B (3.00) average, scores from the Graduate Management Admission Test (GMAT), and letters of recommendation. Admission criteria for international students are identical to those of domestic students with the addition of adequate performance on the Test of English as a Foreign Language (TOEFL) and a minimum score of 450 on the Graduate Management Admission Test.

EXPENSES

Fees per academic semester for all students:
Residents of Kansas,
per credit hour $41.75
Nonresidents of Kansas,
per credit hour 81.00
The university maintains on-campus dormitories; information about housing may be obtained from the University Housing Office.

FINANCIAL ASSISTANCE

A limited number of graduate assistantships are available. Graduate assistantship duties include teaching and nonteaching responsibilities.

PLACEMENT

The University Career Planning and Placement Office assists graduates in obtaining full-time employment. Regional and national companies come to the campus each fall and spring to conduct interviews.

CORRESPONDENCE

For further information or to request an application for admission, please write or call
Dean
Graduate School
Fort Hays State University
Hays, Kansas 67601
Telephone: 913-628-4236

GANNON UNIVERSITY

ERIE, PENNSYLVANIA

Gannon University is a privately endowed, coeducational institution located in Erie, Pennsylvania. It has an enrollment of 4,200 students, 500 of whom are enrolled in graduate study. The graduate program leading to the Master of Business Administration (M.B.A.) degree has an enrollment of 325 students. During the M.B.A. program's 15-year history, over 600 graduates have filled management positions in business and industry throughout the country. In addition to full-time students, the M.B.A. program enrollment includes management personnel from a large number of business and industrial establishments in the Erie metropolitan area.

PROGRAM OF STUDY
The graduate program in business administration is designed to provide advanced studies for the prospective or practicing manager who wishes to continue his or her preparation for responsible and effective participation in the management profession.

More specifically, the objectives of the program are
• to provide advanced studies in, and an understanding of, the quantitative and behavioral foundations of modern approaches to the management of both small- and large-scale organizations;
• to provide educational experiences that will lead to the development of an understanding of the functional areas of management;
• to provide educational experience in the process of analysis, research, and decision making that will lead to the development of the capabilities required in the effective performance of the primary functions of the manager in formulating and implementing solutions to management problems;
• to develop the graduate student's capacity for independent study and continued professional growth;
• to develop the graduate student's professional attitudes as a responsible member of the management community;
• to provide the student with opportunities to evaluate the responsibilities of the management profession in the light of personal and social values.

The program requires 48 semester hour credits of course work. These 48 credits include 18 credits from Level I, the Foundation Sequence (these courses can be waived either by undergraduate course work or by challenge examinations); 15 credits from Level II, the MBA Core; and 12 credits from Level III, the Electives. Within Level III the student will complete a research project. Level IV includes a three-credit capstone course, Cases in Business Policy, and the comprehensive exam. The elective credits can be structured to include an area of concentration compatible with the student's background and interests. These concentrations include finance/brokerage, human resources/personnel, marketing/advertising, management science/systems, entrepreneurial management, public administration, and health services administration.

ADMISSION
To be accepted as a degree status student the applicant must have obtained a bachelor's degree or equivalent from any accredited college or university. The degree may be in any field. No previous college study in business is required. The M.B.A. program is designed to serve the needs of graduates of liberal arts, science, and engineering programs as well as business and economics graduates. An applicant must have earned an overall grade-point average of 2.5 (on a 4.0 scale) or a 3.0 in the major field of study. Applicants are required to take the Graduate Management Admission Test (GMAT). A score of 450 or higher is required. Applicants who fail to meet all of these requirements will be considered for provisional status. Students may enter the program at the start of the fall, spring, or summer sessions.

EXPENSES
The tuition fee is $165 per credit hour. College-approved accommodations are available near the campus.

FINANCIAL ASSISTANCE
Assistantship positions in various offices are available for students enrolled in the M.B.A. program. There are positions available in the M.B.A. Office and the School of Graduate Studies. The Small Business Development Center (SBDC) also has graduate assistantships available to qualified students. Full-time students may be eligible for National Direct Student Loans and Work-Study Program grants. Opportunities for full-time and part-time employment in the Erie area are available to graduate students.

PLACEMENT
The graduate program in business administration cooperates with the Placement Office of Gannon University to assist graduates in obtaining suitable positions with the regional and national business and industrial organizations that visit the university to conduct interviews.

CORRESPONDENCE
Prospective applicants may write
   Director, M.B.A. Program
   Gannon University
   University Square
   Erie, Pennsylvania 16541
   Telephone: 814-871-7567
   Toll Free in Pennsylvania: 800-352-0988
   Out of State: 1-800-458-0871

The location of The George Washington University provides an ideal setting for study and research in administration. A recent publication of the Library of Congress shows over 300 library and reference facilities in the Washington metropolitan area. Students attending the university also have unique opportunities for interchange of ideas with experts from business, government, and various national and international organizations.

The student body is truly heterogeneous, composed of members from a variety of academic and professional preparations. The wide range of age and experience represented in the classroom provides a setting for interaction directed toward meshing theory and practice. Students may attend classes on either a full- or part-time basis, and graduate classes are scheduled for both day and evening. There are 2,200 men and women enrolled in the master's programs and 160 in the doctoral programs.

PROGRAMS OF STUDY

The School of Government and Business Administration is dedicated to academic excellence through the study, teaching, and research of management and policy in the public and private sectors, both within the United States and internationally. The school practices a multidisciplinary approach with flexibility in educational programming in the belief that such is essential to dealing with the complexities of today's organizational society. The school offers preparation of both the generalist and the specialist for professional careers, and seeks to improve the quality and character of the individual as citizen, professional, and scholar as well.

The Master of Business Administration (M.B.A.) program provides a depth of understanding in one field of instruction and a broad exposure to subjects and issues at the general management level. Fields of instruction are offered in the areas of business economics and public policy; finance and investments; general management systems; information systems management; international business; management planning and control; management of science, technology, and innovation; marketing; organizational behavior and development; personnel management; procurement and contracting; and quantitative analysis for decision making. In addition to individual course examinations, a thesis embodying the results of independent study of an important problem in the major area of interest is often recommended in certain fields of instruction.

A complete M.B.A. program consists of 60 semester hours for students with no previous background in business administration or related fields. Students who have undergraduate backgrounds in either business or accounting may complete the M.B.A. program by taking the minimum requirement of 33 semester hours.

The traditional doctoral program prepares the candidate for teaching and research. Although the fulfillment of these requirements is essential, an exclusive orientation to these objectives no longer satisfies other pressing needs. Thus, the Doctor of Business Administration/Doctor of Public Administration program has been designed to prepare graduates to conduct independent research, teach at the college level, and hold positions of major responsibility in industry and government.

An applicant for doctoral study should have a master's degree in a relevant field. Before reaching candidacy, a student must demonstrate his or her capacity for creative scholarship by passing qualifying examinations. Each program is individually arranged within the context of the student's background and career objectives. A dissertation is required as evidence of ability to perform scholarly research and to interpret and present its results.

ADMISSION

Candidates for graduate degrees offered through the School of Government and Business Administration must hold baccalaureate degrees from regionally accredited undergraduate institutions. Admission is granted on a highly competitive basis. Previous academic history, performance on the entrance examination, letters of reference, motivation and aptitude to do graduate-level work, and professional experience are all taken into consideration. Doctoral applicants are also required to have three letters of recommendation sent on their behalf by university faculty members under whom they have studied. Scores on the Graduate Management Admission Test (GMAT) must be submitted by all applicants.

Deadlines for receiving applications and supporting credentials are May 1 for the fall semester, November 1 for the spring semester, and April 1 for the summer sessions. However, because of limited class size, applicants are advised to complete their applications before the deadlines given above.

EXPENSES

The tuition, although subject to change, was $275 per semester hour for the 1985-86 academic year. Each graduate course is three semester hours. A deferred payment plan is available.

FINANCIAL ASSISTANCE

The university makes every effort to provide financial assistance to highly qualified full-time candidates who would otherwise be unable to pursue their educational goals. A limited number of graduate teaching assistantships and fellowships are available. Some loans are also provided to help meet tuition and living expenses. A booklet containing information about financial aid programs may be obtained by writing to the Office of Student Financial Aid.

PLACEMENT

A Career Services Center is maintained for all students and alumni of the university. Recruiters from both private and public sector concerns visit the campus each year. Many faculty members maintain a close relationship with the business community, and the placement program benefits from this relationship.

CORRESPONDENCE

For further information, write or call
  Office of Enrollment Development
    and Admissions
  School of Government and Business
  Administration
  The George Washington University
  Washington, D.C. 20052
  Telephone: 202-676-6584

George Williams College is a privately endowed, coeducational institution in Downers Grove, Illinois. Set on a 200-acre wooded campus near the cultural opportunities of Chicago, the college has an enrollment of 1,150 students, 512 of whom are enrolled in graduate study. The graduate program leading to the Master of Business Administration (M.B.A.) or Master of Science in Administration and Organizational Behavior has an enrollment of 120. Students attending the evening and weekend program include management personnel from a large number of business, industrial, and hospital organizations in the Chicago metropolitan area, as well as full-time students.

PROGRAMS OF STUDY

The M.B.A. and Master of Science degrees in Administration and Organizational Behavior are competency-based curricula, designed to develop professional managers, administrators, and consultants who can use the tools of research and knowledge in managing organizations capable of effective action in today's society. The degrees provide a foundation in basic areas of management knowledge and skills, but the major focus of the department is on the management of human resources in administration and organizational improvement.

The Master of Business Administration degree requires the completion of a 32-credit management core, plus advanced work in one of four concentrations: management and organizational behavior, institutional management (community service or health care), human resources development, or organizational development. The M.B.A. core consists of principles of administration, management process, marketing, economic policy, management decision making, finance, management policy, and accounting.

Students in the M.B.A. program can choose a concentration in one of four tracks.

● The management/organizational behavior track emphasizes developing basic line management skills and knowledge with advanced work in organizational behavior. This track is most appropriate for students preparing for management positions.

● The institutional management track emphasizes developing basic management skills and knowledge within community or social service agencies. This track combines courses in management skills and knowledge with courses in social work, counseling psychology, health education, and so forth, and is most appropriate for students preparing for administration in social services and community organizations.

● The human resources development track emphasizes developing skills and knowledge in the personnel function. This track concentrates on areas such as manpower planning and development, training and development, and human resources management; it is most appropriate for students preparing for work in personnel management.

● The organizational development track emphasizes developing group facilitation, consultation and organizational systems, intervention skills, and knowledge. This track concentrates on such areas as group dynamics, conflict management, and organizational assessments and is most appropriate for students preparing for work as internal or external consultants.

The Master of Science degree offers a more specialized behavioral curriculum in each of the four above tracks. The program also offers experiences in action-oriented management and organizational research characterized by extensive student-faculty collaboration on applied research and professional publishing.

Management internships are also available, geared to the individual student's level of experience.

ADMISSION

The basic requirements for admission include a bachelor's degree from an accredited college or university. Additional requirements include a completed application, four letters of recommendation, official transcripts from each college or university attended, an interview with departmental faculty, and scores from the Graduate Management Admission Test (GMAT).

EXPENSES

The tuition fee is $163 per credit hour or $6,336 per year for full-time students. Dormitory and married student apartments are available on campus.

FINANCIAL ASSISTANCE

Full-time students may be eligible for several scholarships, grants, and work-study programs.

CORRESPONDENCE

For information and application forms, prospective applicants may contact

Dr. Peter F. Sorensen, Jr.
Director, Graduate Studies
Graduate School of Management and Organizational Behavior
George Williams College
555 - 31st Street
Downers Grove, Illinois 60515-9960
Telephone: 312-964-3100, extension 386

Georgetown University is the oldest Jesuit institution of higher learning in the United States. Established in 1789 by Bishop John Carroll, the university is now known throughout the world for the superior quality of its graduate and undergraduate programs.

PROGRAMS OF STUDY

Georgetown University offers programs leading to the degrees of Master of Business Administration (M.B.A.) and Master of Science in Taxation (M.S.-Tax); in conjunction with the Georgetown Law Center, a four-year program leading to a J.D.-M.B.A. is offered.

The M.B.A. program is a two-year, full-time, nonthesis program designed for the liberal arts, science, or technical graduate. The school seeks to enable its students to assume policy-making positions in business or government and to become leaders in society. Emphases are on acquiring a thorough knowledge of the skills traditional to business management and on the integration of those skills with the social sciences and ethical and philosophical systems. The primary curricular focus is course work in the traditional functional areas of management and business policy, finance and economics, marketing, accounting and quantitative methods, and strategic planning. The curriculum builds on the traditional strengths of Georgetown; a major objective of the program is the integration of the theory and practice of management with the program themes of international business, business-government relations, business ethics, and communication skills.

The M.S.-Tax program is a 30-credit, nonthesis, part-time, evening program designed for individuals holding an undergraduate or graduate business degree with an accounting major (or the equivalent). The school provides these students with additional professional training for tax-related careers in public accounting, business, and government. The program includes course work in taxation, including corporate partnership, estate, gift, trust, and international taxation. Research skills and written and oral communication of the results are emphasized in all courses. Students may take two courses per semester on a year-round basis, and the program can be completed in 21 months.

Library holdings include 1,300,000 volumes, 850,000 microforms and government documents, and 12,000 periodicals. Georgetown's Washington location is excellent for the study of business due to the research resources of the federal agencies and departments; trade associations; and regional, national, and international businesses. Computer facilities include the Business Information Systems Laboratory, which has IBM personal computers and many business and statistical software packages. The university maintains an IBM mainframe, a minicomputer, CMS remote terminals, and an extensive library of statistical packages and data files. Graduate business students have use of an entire floor with study carrels and a lounge in Old North.

ADMISSION

New students are admitted to graduate business programs in the fall semester of each year. Applications are encouraged from interested students with a bachelor's degree from an accredited college.

Admission to the programs is by competitive review. Applications must be supported by three recommendations, official transcripts of all postsecondary course work, and results from the Graduate Management Admission Test (GMAT). Applicants whose native language is not English must submit a Test of English as a Foreign Language (TOEFL) score, and foreign nationals must submit a statement of financial resources. The application fee for fall 1986 is $30. Applicants to the M.B.A. program need no previous business education. Knowledge of calculus is required prior to enrollment. The deadline for receipt of all M.B.A. application materials for consideration for regular admission is February 15. Applications received between February 15 and May 1 are evaluated on a space-available basis. The application deadline for the M.S.-Tax program is June 1.

EXPENSES

Tuition for the M.B.A. program was $7,460 for the 1985-86 academic year. Tuition for the M.S.-Tax program was $933 per course for the 1985-86 academic year. Health insurance, housing, books, supplies, transportation fees, and other personal expenses are additional. On-campus housing for graduate students is very limited; most students live off campus. The Off-Campus Housing Office provides assistance in location of suitable housing.

FINANCIAL ASSISTANCE

About 50 percent of M.B.A. students receive full- or partial-tuition scholarships and/or federally sponsored loans. Research assistantships are available through the M.B.A. fellows program; fellows receive full-tuition scholarships. Scholarship awards are based on merit. For M.S.-Tax students, financial assistance is available through long-term, low-interest loans awarded on the basis of need. Financial aid applicants are required to file the Graduate and Professional School Financial Aid Service (GAPSFAS) form with Educational Testing Service.

PLACEMENT

The university maintains an active center for career counseling and placement, and a large number of national and regional firms recruit on campus. The School of Business Administration also directly assists its graduate students in obtaining employment.

CORRESPONDENCE

For further information, please write or call
Graduate Business Admissions
School of Business Administration
105 Old North Building
Georgetown University
Washington, D.C. 20057
Telephone: 202-625-4201

The home of Georgia College is on the fall line of the Oconee River, less than a dozen miles from the geographic center of Georgia. It is approximately 100 miles from Augusta, Atlanta, Albany, and Columbus, and 30 miles from Macon. The community, which has a population of over 25,000, is located in a setting of natural beauty, and is long known as a center of history and culture.

Milledgeville was laid out in 1803 and in the following years was designated as the capital of Georgia, remaining the seat of government until 1868. Its physical layout and the arrangement of public buildings coincided in time with the organization of Washington, D.C., and the town is somewhat reminiscent of the nation's capital during the early part of the 19th century.

In January 1967 the Board of Regents of the University System of Georgia authorized The Women's College of Georgia to admit male students in the 1967-68 fiscal year, to expand its curriculum and physical facilities, and to provide residence halls for men. Nondormitory male students were admitted, however, to regular undergraduate classes for the first time in the spring quarter, 1967. The new name, Georgia College at Milledgeville, was adopted by the Board later in March 1967. In October 1971 the Board of Regents changed the name to Georgia College.

A graduate program was initiated in the summer of 1958, and the first Master of Education was granted in 1959. The first courses in the Master of Business Administration (M.B.A.) degree program were offered in the winter quarter of 1969. In the 1984-85 academic year, 88 graduate business degrees were awarded.

Since January 1932, the college has operated as a unit of the University System of Georgia under one Chancellor and a Board of Regents. The School of Business was established as a separate entity September 15, 1977.

PROGRAMS OF STUDY
The School of Business offers graduate studies leading to the Master of Business Administration (M.B.A.) degree and the Master of Science in Administration (M.S.A.) degree. The two degree programs are designed to prepare graduates to compete successfully in the domain of private and public enterprise. The programs encourage the intellectual leadership and general development of the graduate student in the selected area of study.

The basic M.B.A. program consists of 60 quarter hours of graduate work for the student with a background in management. Other students have individually prepared programs requiring up to 90 quarter hours to complete.

The M.S.A. program consists of 35 quarter hours in administration and 35 quarter hours of electives. All M.S.A. students complete a total of 60 quarter hours for the degree.

The programs are offered entirely in the evening, and the typical student will require six quarters for completion of either degree. Part-time students are enrolled in the program for longer periods of time.

The M.S.A. degree is offered off campus at Robins Air Force Base, Warner Robins, Georgia.

The M.B.A. degree is offered on the main campus in Milledgeville, at the External Degree Program Center in Macon, and at the Graduate Center at the Warner Robins Air Force Base.

ADMISSION
Entrance into either the M.B.A. or M.S.A. program is open to all qualified students who show promise of success in graduate business study. Admission is based on the applicant's previous academic record, work experience, and related information.

The applicant is required to furnish an acceptable score on the Graduate Management Admission Test (GMAT). In certain specialized areas of the M.S.A. program other recognized graduate admission test scores are acceptable.

All admission materials should be submitted not less than three weeks prior to admission to courses. A student may begin in any quarter.

EXPENSES
Full-time students who are Georgia residents pay a matriculation fee of $27 per quarter hour plus health and activity fees. Out-of-state residents, as well as those taking off-campus courses and contract courses, are charged an additional fee based on the rate applicable in the specific domain. The college comptroller will furnish the rate in the applicable area. Room and board vary from $500 to $645, depending on options selected. All

expenses are based on a quarterly rate. Active-duty military personnel and their dependents pay in-state rates. All fees are subject to change without notice.

FINANCIAL ASSISTANCE
A limited number of graduate assistantships of $3,000 are awarded to qualified applicants. These assistantships include out-of-state fee waiver and stipend.

Minority students who are residents of Georgia may apply for a Regent's Opportunity Scholarship, an award of $2,500.

Graduate students may request information about grants, scholarships, loans, and work-study programs from the Director of Financial Aid, Parks Hall, Georgia College.

PLACEMENT
Georgia College maintains a full-time Director of Placement. Students may use the placement services without charge.

CORRESPONDENCE
For further information about the programs of study offered by Georgia College, please write or call
Dr. Tom Pritchett, Coordinator
Graduate Programs in Business
Georgia College
Milledgeville, Georgia 31061
Telephone: 912-453-5115 or 912-453-5497
or
Dr. Bruce C. Brumfield, Director
Centers and Off-Campus Programs
Georgia College
Milledgeville, Georgia 31061
Telephone: 912-932-5599

The Georgia Institute of Technology was founded in 1885 to bring technological education and training to Georgia and the Southeast. Located on nearly 300 wooded acres, Georgia Tech houses the Colleges of Management, Architecture, Engineering, and Science and Liberal Studies. The student body of 11,000 represents every state and 60 foreign countries in a metropolitan, coeducational academic community. Georgia Tech regularly enrolls the nation's highest per capita number of National Merit and National Achievement scholars for a public institution.

The Graduate Management Program of the College of Management awards the Master of Science in Management (M.S.M.) and the Doctor of Philosophy (Ph.D.) in management degrees.

PROGRAM OF STUDY
The Master of Science in Management program is designed to develop technical skills and analytical abilities for management. This emphasis is calculated to meet the demands of business' most difficult contemporary problems, the management of technical/economic projects and solution of highly complex problems in every administrative area. The applicability of quantitative/analytical skills is virtually limitless, as the excellent placement record of the alumni demonstrates.

The curriculum of the M.S.M. includes a very broad core and a generous body of electives. These two features allow students with good analytical ability from any undergraduate major to enter the program and, within two years, to acquire a thorough knowledge of business entities and functions, plus a concentration in one of eight areas: economics, accounting, finance, general management, human resource management, management science, marketing, or production and operations management. Courses from industrial and systems engineering, information and computer science, mathematics, and engineering may be incorporated in the concentration area as complements to management electives.

The course work is challenging and requires good mathematics aptitude. Entering students need a working knowledge of one-variable calculus and linear algebra; otherwise, there are no prerequisites. Use of computers is stressed; knowledge of a computer language is recommended.

ADMISSION
Applicants must possess a bachelor's degree from an accredited institution and must submit transcripts of all previous college work, Graduate Management Admission Test (GMAT) scores, three letters of evaluation, and an autobiographical sketch. No cutoff scores are used in evaluating applications. Facility in basic calculus and linear algebra must be in evidence. For applicants with substantial work experience, the employment record becomes a major consideration.

Admission requirements and deadline differ for international applicants. An international applicant must submit a Test of English as a Foreign Language (TOEFL) score of 600, Michigan score of 90, or equivalent score on another examination. In addition, the international applicant must submit a financial affadavit of support. The deadline for an international applicant (including proof of English proficiency) is March 1.

EXPENSES
Tuition and fees for 1985 were $529 and $1,564 per quarter for state residents and nonresidents, respectively. Dormitories and meal plans are available.

FINANCIAL ASSISTANCE
Scholarships, assistantships, work-study, and out-of-state tuition waivers are available. Ph.D. stipends are $7,800 plus an out-of-state fee waiver. The President's Fellowship is the most prestigious award, which carries a stipend of $10,000 for the first calendar year and a waiver of all tuition and fees. One or two are usually granted each year. Assistantships are granted to approximately 20 percent of each entering class. Each offers a stipend of $4,500 for nine months plus a waiver of out-of-state fees and requires a one-third time work commitment.

A minority fellowship program is available to Georgia residents. An extensive and liberal loan program and college work-study funds are available to U.S. citizens who demonstrate need. Most financial aid programs have a February 15 deadline.

PLACEMENT
The M.S.M. graduate can explore his or her career interests with many of the 600 employers who deal directly with the Placement Center. These employers represent a substantial number of the Fortune 500 as well as regional organizations. The college, through its Management Career Services Office, assists the placement of its graduates by publishing the Graduate Management Resume Booklet, hosting a number of firms for career seminars, and cohosting a Georgia M.B.A. career fair annually. The college also boasts a strong alumni network to assist in placement of the students. In past years, Georgia Tech graduates have been placed in major metropolitan areas. The average starting salary in 1985 was $32,600.

CORRESPONDENCE
For further information or to request an application for admission, please write or call
Director of Graduate Admissions
Mail Code: MBA
College of Management
Georgia Institute of Technology
Atlanta, Georgia 30332
Telephone: 404-894-2604

Georgia Southern College (GSC), the premier senior college in the University System of Georgia, serves approximately 7,000 students, including approximately 1,000 graduate students. The 457-acre campus is located in Statesboro, 50 miles west of Savannah and 210 miles southeast of Atlanta.

The Georgia Southern College School of Business has offered graduate study leading to the Master of Business Administration (M.B.A.) degree since 1968. The School of Business is accredited at the graduate and undergraduate level by the American Assembly of Collegiate Schools of Business (AACSB).

PROGRAM OF STUDY

Georgia Southern College's School of Business offers a comprehensive M.B.A. program that emphasizes the fundamental knowledge and skills underlying modern administration and management, and applies these with emphasis upon the area of managerial and executive decision making.

The GSC M.B.A. program requires a year and a half of full-time study, yet is flexible enough to accommodate part-time students. Classes are moderate in size to create an optimum environment for learning. The program of study includes 40 quarter hours of core requirements designed to introduce students to the functional areas and the analytical tools of modern decision making. In addition to the required courses, students choose elective courses in fields of special interest. Normally a student will have an opportunity to take three electives, however, individually designed programs may vary. Students whose undergraduate preparation did not include the necessary foundation course work will be expected to enroll in these courses or remove the deficiencies by examination prior to beginning graduate course work. An oral examination is also required of all candidates for the degree.

ADMISSION

For unqualified admission to the Graduate School to pursue graduate work leading to the Master of Business Administration, the applicant must have completed requirements for the bachelor's degree from a college or university accredited by the proper regional accrediting association. The undergraduate academic record combined with satisfactory scores on the Graduate Management Admission Test (GMAT) must demonstrate that the applicant has the potential for successful performance in the M.B.A. program.

International students are required to submit scores on the Test of English as a Foreign Language (TOEFL) for admission. The college also requires an additional English language proficiency examination upon enrollment.

EXPENSES

Schedule of quarterly fees for 1985-86 (subject to change):

Matriculation fee	$ 320
College fee	94
Room (maximum residence hall)	280
Meals (maximum plan)	350
Nonresident fee	640
Total	$1,684

FINANCIAL ASSISTANCE

The college provides a variety of financial assistance opportunities for eligible graduate students. A limited number of graduate assistantships are awarded on a competitive basis. (The current stipend is $4,000 for nine months, plus a waiver of nonresident fees.) Specific programs are available for minority and veteran applicants.

Information on scholarships and need-based grants and loans may be obtained by contacting the Financial Aid Office. Information on graduate assistantships may be obtained from the Graduate School or M.B.A. Program Coordinator.

PLACEMENT

The college maintains an active placement office that provides placement services for graduate and undergraduate students.

CORRESPONDENCE

For further information on the program of study offered at Georgia Southern College, write or call

M.B.A. Program Coordinator
School of Business
Georgia Southern College
Landrum Box 8002
Statesboro, Georgia 30460
Telephone: 912-681-5106
   or
Graduate School
Landrum Box 8113
Telephone: 912-681-5384

Georgia State University is located in Atlanta, Georgia, only two blocks from the center of the principal downtown financial district of the metropolitan area. The College of Business Administration was the original constituent of the institution. There are more than 190 full-time members of the faculty of the school. Some 2,320 students are enrolled in the master's programs and 155 in the doctoral programs of the school. Approximately 6,000 men and women are enrolled in the undergraduate programs.

Since the university does not provide housing facilities, graduate students must make their own arrangements for suitable accommodations, which are available throughout the metropolitan area.

PROGRAMS OF STUDY

The College of Business Administration offers the following graduate business degree programs: Master of Business Administration (M.B.A.), Master of Actuarial Science (M.A.S.), Master of Business Administration/Master of Health Administration (M.B.A./M.H.A.), Master of Business Information Systems (M.B.I.S.), Master of Insurance (M.I.N.), Master of Professional Accountancy (M.P.A.), Master of Science (M.S.), Master of Science in Real Estate and Urban Affairs (M.S.R.E.), Master of Taxation (M.T.X.), Doctor of Philosophy (Ph.D.) in economics, and Ph.D. in business administration.

The M.B.A. program requires the completion of 95 quarter credits of graduate-level work. Of the 95 hours, 20 quarter hours may be exempted through examinations. All M.B.A. students must complete a 55-quarter-hour core curriculum. The remaining 20 quarter hours can be completed through a major in one area or through electives.

The M.B.A./M.H.A. program requires the completion of 115 quarter hours of graduate-level work. All other master's degree programs require 60 quarter hours of course work in addition to preparatory work. Preparatory course requirements vary according to degree program.

All master's degrees require that 45 quarter hours be completed in residence. A 3.0 grade-point average must be maintained throughout the program. The master's programs may be pursued on a full- or part-time basis. The courses in these programs are generally scheduled during both the day and the evening.

The Doctor of Philosophy in business administration regulations require the completion of three fields of study. Two of these, economic theory and analysis and quantitative methods, are required. The major area of concentration may be selected from those listed below. Certain course work, but no examination, is required in a related area.

The major field for the Ph.D. may be chosen from the following: accountancy, actuarial science, decision sciences, finance, health administration, industrial relations, information systems, insurance and risk management, international business, land economics and urban affairs, management, management information systems, and marketing. Other requirements are the dissertation seminar examination, the dissertation, and the final oral examination. The Ph.D. in business administration also has the computer competency-foreign language requirement.

The Doctor of Philosophy in economics program requires written preliminary examinations in economic theory and two elective fields. Students must complete graduate work in economic history, mathematics for economists, advanced economic statistics, and applied economics. They must also demonstrate competency in mathematics or computers as research tools or a foreign language. The preliminary oral examination, dissertation seminar examination, dissertation, and its oral defense are the final requirements.

ADMISSION

An applicant to any master's degree program offered by the college must have a bachelor's degree from an accredited college or university and an acceptable combination of undergraduate grade-point average (GPA) and Graduate Management Admission Test (GMAT) scores. For example, a 2.78 or a 3.00 GPA for the last two years and a 480 total GMAT score would meet the fundamental master's admission requirements. Higher grades can offset lower test scores and vice versa. Some specialized (non-M.B.A.) programs have higher requirements. Doctoral criteria are substantially higher. Applications should be submitted as far as possible in advance of the desired time of admission.

All applicants must submit transcripts of all prior collegiate credit and satisfactory scores on the GMAT. In some cases, other tests and an interview may be required. All these elements together must indicate to the Graduate Admissions Committees that the applicant has a favorable prospect for successful completion of his or her program.

In addition to meeting the regular admission requirements, an international applicant whose native language is other than English must submit official scores on the Test of English as a Foreign Language (TOEFL). Applicants needing a student visa are required to show financial capability for their full degree program.

FINANCIAL ASSISTANCE

Scholarships and loan sources are available in relatively modest quantity. Many part-time and other employment opportunities are available for master's level students both in the university and in nearby business firms. Graduate teaching and research assistantships are available for doctoral students.

CORRESPONDENCE

For further information, write or call
  Doctoral Programs
  College of Business Administration
  University Plaza
  Atlanta, Georgia 30303-3087
  Telephone: 404-658-3379

  Master's Programs
  College of Business Administration
  University Plaza
  Atlanta, Georgia 30303-3087
  Telephone: 404-658-2606

GOLDEN GATE UNIVERSITY

SAN FRANCISCO, CALIFORNIA

Founded in 1901, and having its main campus in San Francisco's financial district, Golden Gate University offers day and evening programs leading to the bachelor's, master's, and doctoral degrees in management, public administration, and law. With an enrollment of 10,500, it is the third largest independent university in California. The university is accredited by the Western Association of Schools and Colleges, and its School of Law is approved by the American Bar Association and accredited by the Association of American Law Schools and the State Bar of California. The university operates on a year-round, trimester schedule.

Golden Gate University's central educational objective is the preparation of skilled professionals capable of effective managerial decision making in the context of present-day society. To help achieve this objective, the university emphasizes in its curricula the synthesis of managerial theory and practice and extensively utilizes the case method of study. For the same purpose, it includes on its faculty both full-time academics and part-time teacher-practitioners drawn from among high-level professionals in the subject areas covered. Further ties to the business and public communities are maintained through professional curricular advisory committees and through the university's Career Planning and Placement Center.

To allow for maximum interaction between students and instructors, enrollment in graduate classes is generally limited to 24 students. Discussion in graduate seminars is enriched by students who already hold responsible managerial positions and who are studying part time for advanced degrees.

Curricular programs are supported by the university's two main library facilities: the general business library and the law library. The general library is one of the country's most complete and current collections of materials in business management, accounting, taxation, public administration, transportation, international business, and related areas. The law library, in addition to a comprehensive collection of general law books, maintains special sections on taxation law and administrative decisions and regulations.

PROGRAMS OF STUDY
The graduate programs of Golden Gate University lead to M.B.A., M.P.A., M.A., M.S., M.S.P.A., and Ph.D. degrees in the following areas: accounting (M.B.A. and M.S.P.A.), acquisition, procurement, and contract management (M.S.), arts administration (M.A. and M.B.A.), banking (M.S. and M.B.A.), finance (M.B.A.), financial planning (M.B.A.), financial planning—tax concentration (M.S.), financial services (M.S. and M.B.A.), health services management (M.B.A. and M.P.A.), high technology management (M.B.A.), human resources management (M.S., M.B.A. and M.P.A.), information systems (M.S. and M.B.A.), international management (M.B.A.), investments (M.S. and M.B.A.), management (M.B.A. and Ph.D.), marketing (M.B.A.), project and construction management (M.B.A.), public administration (M.P.A. and Ph.D.), public relations and public affairs (M.S.), real estate (M.S. and M.B.A.), risk management and insurance (M.S. and M.B.A.), taxation (M.S.), telecommunications management (M.S. and M.B.A.), and transportation and physical distribution management (M.B.A.).

The School of Law offers the J.D. and LL.M. (tax) degrees, as well as joint M.B.A./J.D. degrees offered in conjunction with other graduate schools of Golden Gate University.

ADMISSION
Golden Gate University has a rolling admissions policy for most programs: new students may enroll at the beginning of any one of the three annual trimesters (September, January, or May). Applicants for admission to the full-time general M.B.A. program (Nagel T. Miner Program) and full-time M.S.-tax program (John Cordell Williams Program) must submit their applications and supporting documents, including transcripts, recommendations and Graduate Management Admission Test (GMAT) scores, no later than July 1 for admission in the fall term beginning in September.

Admission to the graduate programs is based on an evaluation of both quantitative and qualitative criteria, including undergraduate grade-point average, test scores, recommendations, and personal statement. The Admissions Office bases its decision on the aggregate of all factors giving evidence of each applicant's readiness to undertake graduate-level study at the university. The admission decision is made without regard to age, sex, race, creed, color, physical handicap, or national or ethnic origin.

EXPENSES
Tuition (1985-86) for master's-level courses, excepting tax courses, was $168 per semester unit, and for tax courses $200 per unit. Tuition rates are subject to change for the 1986-87 and subsequent academic years.

FINANCIAL ASSISTANCE
The National Direct Student Loan Program, State or Federal Guaranteed Student Loan Program, emergency loans, and veterans' benefits are the major sources of financial assistance available to qualifying graduate students at Golden Gate University. The Federal College Work-Study Program and deferred payment plan for tuition are also available.

PLACEMENT
The university maintains a Career Planning and Placement Center which provides career information and job placement services to current students and alumni. Students in the university's full-time M.B.A. program may also participate in the Mentor Program, through which each M.B.A. candidate is introduced to a senior executive from the business community who has volunteered to act as a career adviser for students in the program.

CORRESPONDENCE
For further information, write or call
  Director of Admissions
  Golden Gate University
  536 Mission Street
  San Francisco, California 94105
  Telephone: 415-442-7272

Gonzaga, a Jesuit institution of higher learning, was founded in 1887. In 1921 the university opened the School of Business Administration, and in 1931 the Graduate School was established. Gonzaga is one of the 28 Jesuit colleges and universities in the United States and is noted for its tradition of academic excellence. The Jesuit tradition of academic excellence is over four centuries old and emphasizes one's rational involvement in the intellectual and social issues of the contemporary world. Gonzaga University provides the opportunity for men and women to participate in the cultural and technological aspects of education.

Gonzaga's campus, spread over 60 landscaped acres, includes 31 major buildings. Its student body represents 47 states and 47 foreign countries; total enrollment is 3,400.

PROGRAMS OF STUDY

The Master of Business Administration (M.B.A.) is a broad-based course of study concerned with the nature of managerial decision responsibility in a rapidly changing world. The program permits emphases on the behavioral sciences for the purpose of better understanding the human element in organization. It also emphasizes the nature of social responsibilities and the need for involvement in the total society in which business operates.

Three elements are woven throughout the program; first, an understanding of the economic and analytical nature of decision processes; second, an appreciation of the broad range of managerial functions within an organization; and third, recognition of the policy and social responsibilities that accompany decisions affecting social and economic systems.

The program is designed to be of maximum convenience and benefit to employed men or women who wish to expand their knowledge, develop their ability, increase their understanding of the business world, and prepare for advancement. All courses required for graduation are offered in the evening or late afternoon; the degree can be taken on either a full-time or part-time basis.

Thirty-three hours of graduate business administration courses are required. The following seven courses totaling 21 credits comprise the core curriculum: Marketing Problems; Problems in Financial Management; Operations Planning and Control;

Administration Theory and Organization Behavior; Managerial Accounting; Business, Government, and Society; and Policy and Administration. The 12 credits of electives may be chosen from any of the graduate-level course offerings. No more than two of the elective courses may be taken from the same subject area.

In cooperation with the School of Law, the School of Business Administration offers the M.B.A./Juris Doctor. The total combined credits for this program must be 114. This represents a reduction of 9 credits from the 123 that would be required if both degrees were to be earned separately.

ADMISSION

All applicants must have a bachelor's degree, with an acceptable grade-point average, from an accredited college or university; a satisfactory score from the Graduate Management Admission Test (GMAT); and two letters of recommendation. Prerequisite deficiencies in accounting, economics, finance, marketing, organization theory, quantitative methods, and operations analysis may be satisfied by taking the foundation courses.

Foreign students must submit a score report from the Test of English as a Foreign Language (TOEFL).

EXPENSES

For 1985-86

Tuition, per semester hour	$180
Application fee, nonrefundable	20
Tuition deposit, credited toward first semester tuition, nonrefundable	100
Matriculation fee, payable on first registration only	25
Books and supplies (two semesters)	900

A limited number of graduate assistantships are available to full-time students. The university has a program of scholarships, loans, and jobs to help meet demonstrated financial needs of qualified students.

PLACEMENT

A complete placement service is provided to assist graduates in securing employment and to aid students seeking jobs while attending the university. Interviews for full-time employment with national corporations, local business firms and government agencies are arranged by the center. The center also assembles and maintains individual portfolios for Gonzaga graduates.

CORRESPONDENCE

For applications for admission and graduate assistantships and additional information on the graduate programs offered at Gonzaga, write or call

Graduate Director
School of Business Administration
Gonzaga University
Spokane, Washington 99258
Telephone: 509-328-4220

Governors State University, located 35 miles south of Chicago, was established in 1969 to provide upper division and graduate studies to the rapidly developing region. The College of Business and Public Administration was established when the university opened, and offers graduate degrees in business administration and public administration. These programs are accredited through the North Central Association of Colleges and Secondary Schools.

There are currently 250 graduate students pursuing master's degrees in the College of Business and Public Administration. The college curriculum is designed with the understanding that students enrolled are seeking management careers in the public or private sector. Accordingly, the college offers rigorous programs that will challenge students and provide them with the preparation to assume positions of leadership and responsibility.

The campus is situated on 753 acres in Will County, Illinois, in a picturesque environment.

PROGRAMS OF STUDY

The primary objective of the Master of Business Administration (M.B.A.) is to provide a quality professional degree that meets the needs of students and the standards of the business community. The program includes a preparatory core that is intended to provide students with a common background. Twenty-one hours of core courses are required, as well as 12 hours of business electives. M.B.A. students may select their electives from a specific functional area or pursue electives that broaden their management skills. Classes are offered in the evening hours.

A Master of Public Administration (M.P.A.) is offered to those interested in a managerial career in the public sector. The curriculum is designed to teach the techniques and methods of personnel management, budgeting, and organization. The program consists of 12 hours of preparatory course work, 24 hours of required core courses, 6 hours of elective credit, and a master's research paper.

Students in the College of Business and Public Administration are required to maintain a grade-point average of 3.0 (on a 4.0 scale) to remain in good standing.

ADMISSION

Admission to the M.B.A. program is open to those holding a baccalaureate degree from an accredited institution. Acceptance to the program will be based on academic history, results of the Graduate Management Admission Test (GMAT), career experience, and petition letters from the applicant.

M.P.A. applicants are admitted on the basis of their undergraduate academic performance, past experience, and applicant petition letters.

Applicants whose native language is not English are required to take the Test of English as a Foreign Language (TOEFL) and have the score forwarded to the university before admission evaluation. A minimum score of 550 is required for admission to the college.

Applications may be submitted up to one year before planned entry into the program. Application deadlines are established three weeks prior to on-campus registration. Students not meeting minimum requirements may contact the university for further information.

EXPENSES

Tuition for graduate courses during academic year 1985-86 was $44 per credit hour for state residents and $144 for out-of-state students. There is a $20 student fee per trimester. Parking fees and books average $350 per year.

On-campus housing is not available; therefore, cost of living will vary considerably according to location and travel expenses. Living expenses for one year for single independent students average $7,500; for married students, the average is $9,000.

FINANCIAL ASSISTANCE

Graduate research and staff assistantships are awarded to qualified students by the college on an annual basis. Tuition (including out-of-state) is waived for those students holding full-time assistantships.

PLACEMENT

The Placement Office assists university students and alumni in preparing for a job search and securing career employment. A yearly forum is conducted to assist students in preparing their job search.

CORRESPONDENCE

Address inquiries to
College of Business and Public Administration
Governors State University
University Park, Illinois 60466
Telephone: 312-534-5000
or
Office of Admissions
Governors State University
University Park, Illinois 60466
Telephone: 312-534-5000

Founded in 1901, Grambling State University seeks to provide opportunities for its students to develop intellectually and to acquire appropriate job skills and self-actualization. Grambling State University is fully accredited by the Louisiana State Board of Trustees and the Southern Association of Colleges and Schools.

PROGRAM OF STUDY
The Master of Business Administration (M.B.A.) at Grambling State University is designed to prepare students to apply relevant computer technology, quantitative techniques, and administrative skills to the information processing and other business problems of an organization. With the two options of computer information systems and general administration, the educational elements of the M.B.A. program focus on the functional areas of business and administration, as well as technical topics in the computer field and their applications. The M.B.A. program consists of 33 semester hours for students with appropriate undergraduate courses in the common body of business knowledge. Students are admitted after graduating from any undergraduate major, and work experience is not required. Generally, full-time resident students with no previous business background will complete the requirements within two years. For those who have undergraduate business courses, this can be reduced.

ADMISSION
The M.B.A. program at Grambling State University is open to students with any undergraduate degree: physical science, engineering, social sciences, education, liberal arts or business.

Applicants are to submit transcripts of all previous academic work as well as scores from the Graduate Management Admission Test (GMAT). Those applicants whose native language is not English will need to submit scores from the Test of English as a Foreign Language (TOEFL). Applications for admission to Grambling State University are due 90 days prior to registration for course work.

EXPENSES
Tuition and fees estimated for the 1986-87 academic year (subject to change without notice):

	In-State	Out-of-State
3 semester hours	$1,084	$1,084
6 semester hours	1,189	1,393
9 semester hours	1,294	1,616
12 semester hours	1,399	1,839

FINANCIAL ASSISTANCE
Assistantships, as well as three federally supported financial aid programs, are available for M.B.A. students at Grambling State University. Assistantships are awarded to students based on the combination of an applicant's GMAT scores and previous academic record. Transcripts and GMAT scores must be submitted to the Division of Graduate Studies no later than May 15 to be considered for an assistantship. The federally supported financial aid programs that are available at Grambling State University are College Work-Study, National Direct Student Loans, and Guaranteed Student Loans. Because approximately four to six weeks are required for the university to receive loan checks, it is advisable that students apply early.

PLACEMENT
The university maintains a Career Planning and Placement Center which assists graduating seniors and students in securing full-time employment commensurate with their education, skills, interests, and abilities.

CORRESPONDENCE
For further information, write or call
Dr. Hubert Tolman, Assistant Director
College of Business, M.B.A. Program
Grambling State University
P.O. Box 1176
Grambling, Louisiana 71245
Telephone: 318-274-2434

Grand Valley, a public coeducational state institution of higher education, was initiated by action of the Michigan legislature in 1960. Classes began in 1963 with an enrollment of 226. Since then Grand Valley has experienced steady but marked growth. The 1985 fall enrollment was 7,600. Grand Valley offers over 75 undergraduate and 20 graduate areas of concentration.

Grand Valley's 876-acre campus is nestled amidst rolling hills, deep ravines, and farmland in the Grand River Basin of rural Ottawa County. The campus is near Allendale, 12 miles west of Grand Rapids (the second largest population center in Michigan), and within easy driving distance of Holland, Grand Haven, and Muskegon. On-campus housing is available to single students in three residence halls and an apartment complex. Additional housing is available adjacent to the campus in privately owned apartments.

PROGRAMS OF STUDY

The F.E. Seidman School of Business was established in June 1973. Current enrollment is 1,000 undergraduate and 350 graduate students. The mission of the F.E. Seidman School of Business is to prepare students to deal with business and administration problems of today and tomorrow. The college expects its graduates to be farsighted, forward-looking leaders and managers having good judgment and effective decision-making and problem-solving skills; to be able to cope effectively with the rapid rate of personal, social, and technological change that will characterize the future; and to be cognizant of the ways in which their roles in management and society increasingly are affected by social control through public policy. To fulfill its mission the Seidman Graduate Division

• offers courses that help develop the ability and willingness to perceive, identify, and analyze problems, communicate appropriate alternate solutions, make decisions, and implement and monitor the results;

• provides a flexible program that requires students to specify career objectives, plan their programs, select courses and other resources judged to be most appropriate for their program goals, and complete their studies either on or off campus;

• ensures that opportunities exist for students to elect graduate courses involving public policy analysis that are relevant to their professional and career interests;

• offers a self-assessment program that will assist students in the development of the capacity, educational base, and desire for a lifetime of continuing personal growth and professional development;

• makes it possible for individuals who are employed full time to complete their programs at times other than the normal daytime college hours.

Students can emphasize management, accounting, finance, marketing, personnel and labor relations, or taxation in their studies.

The Master of Business Administration (M.B.A.) and Master of Science in Taxation (M.S.T.) programs consist of 33 semester hours of appropriate graduate course credit and can be completed in one calendar year if a person has completed all the background area requirements and studies full time in the Seidman School. If the student has not completed background studies, the master's programs can be completed in approximately two calendar years. Those who intend to study part time and who have completed the background studies requirements can expect to complete the graduate program within two years by electing two graduate courses each semester.

ADMISSION

The school's programs are open to individuals who have a bachelor's degree from an accredited college or university. No particular undergraduate major is necessary. Students are admitted as candidates for the master's degree in business administration or taxation on the basis of interest, aptitude, and capacity for study as indicated by previous academic record, work experience, Graduate Management Admission Test (GMAT) scores, pertinent information from the student applications, and, if judged necessary, letters of reference and a personal interview. Prospective students should hear from the college concerning admission within two weeks after their application is complete.

EXPENSES

The tuition rate for the 1985-86 academic year for graduate students who were Michigan residents was $73 per credit hour. For non-Michigan residents the 1985-86 tuition rate was $166 per credit hour. New students must pay a one-time application fee of $15.

FINANCIAL ASSISTANCE

Financial aid for students is available in the form of graduate assistantships, scholarships, and loans. In some instances a student may be given a research assistantship. Application forms for financial aid will be sent upon request to applicants for admission. Information on veterans' benefits can be obtained from the Records Office.

PLACEMENT

The Placement Office works with employers and with graduates in finding the right person for the right job. Employers frequently fill their personnel needs by arranging interviews on campus as well as contacting the Placement Office to describe available job openings. Students seeking part-time employment may also use the Placement Office to locate jobs.

CORRESPONDENCE

Inquiries concerning the programs of study offered at Grand Valley State College should be addressed to
F.E. Seidman School of Business
Grand Valley State College
Allendale, Michigan 49401

Heriot-Watt University, granted its University Charter in 1966, celebrated in 1985 the centenary of Heriot-Watt College, recalling 100 years of achievement in teaching and research in technology, management, trade, and commerce. The university is committed to maintaining and enhancing its pioneering drive towards new applications of its expertise, and to combining the highest academic standards with the commercial impetus of a business.

The university is situated in the heart of Edinburgh, administrative capital of Scotland, international financial center, and hub of "silicon glen," and also on the new Riccarton campus of mature woodland, park, and loch on the city's outskirts. Until the relocation of the entire university to the new campus is completed in the early 1990s, the Faculty of Economic and Social Studies, including the specially equipped M.B.A. Management Suite, remains in the city center. The university has some 3,600 students of whom approximately 550 are on first degree, diploma, and master's courses or research in the Faculty of Economic and Social Studies.

PROGRAM OF STUDY

The Master of Business Administration (M.B.A.) degree course, introduced in October 1985, is a broadly based, intensive program, covering the full range of management subjects and calling on the expertise of the whole faculty of Economic and Social Studies. It is geared to the requirements of young executives in industry and commerce who have at least two years' responsible experience and are ready for an additional injection of management skills in preparation for more senior positions. It is particularly suitable for specialists such as engineers and accountants who wish to move into management. The M.B.A. degree is postgraduate in its academic standards, but it is not required or assumed that students will have previously studied business or management at a university. Each subject is taught from basic foundations, progressing rapidly to up-to-date material. All classes use participative methods for roughly half the class time to make the most of students' experience. The M.B.A. may be taken full time or part time.

The full-time M.B.A. course covers a period of 12 months, beginning in October. The first nine months are spent on six core classes (business policy, business economics, marketing, organizational behavior, operations management and quantitative methods, accountancy and finance) and two elective classes taught over the university's normal academic year in 3 ten-week terms and formally assessed by examination. In the final three months, each candidate undertakes a project, submitting a dissertation by the end of September.

The part-time M.B.A. program has a timetable tailored to the practical needs of managers and their firms. It is a two-year, day-release course, with teaching concentrated into Mondays and Fridays, and fully integrated with the full-time course. The project and dissertation are completed at the end of the second year.

ADMISSION

The full- and part-time M.B.A. courses are open to honors graduates in any subject, or those with equivalent professional qualifications. Candidates must also have at least two years of responsible work experience. All candidates will be required to take the Graduate Management Admission Test (GMAT). Applicants whose first language is not English must also provide evidence of proficiency in the English language. Selection will also depend upon the provision of satisfactory references and in some cases on the result of an interview.

EXPENSES

Fees for the M.B.A. course are currently (1985-86) £1632 for UK and other EEC residents, and £3410 for overseas residents. For the part-time course, the tuition fees per year are half the full-time fees. The fees are subject to annual review. Other expenses for accommodations, books, and general living expenses are estimated to be about £4400 a year.

FINANCIAL ASSISTANCE

E.S.R.C. postgraduate studentships for good honors graduates resident in Britain are available through a national pool competition.

PLACEMENT

The university has a Careers Advisory Service, which offers M.B.A. students information and advice.

CORRESPONDENCE

For further information, please contact
The MBA Course Director
Department of Business Organization
Heriot-Watt University
35 Grassmarket
Edinburgh EH1 2HT, Scotland
United Kingdom

Founded in 1935, Hofstra is a private, nonsectarian university located in a suburban community 25 miles east of Manhattan. Students find that Hofstra's proximity to New York City offers them excellent job opportunities and a business and cultural environment second to none.

Graduate courses at the Hofstra School of Business are predominantly taught by full-time faculty members whose backgrounds are rich in both scholarly and business activities. In addition to more than 80 full-time faculty members, the school employs approximately 30 part-time professors who have been selected on the basis of academic and professional achievements. The programs offered by the School of Business are accredited by the American Assembly of Collegiate Schools of Business (AACSB).

Current enrollment is approximately 200 full-time and 800 part-time M.B.A. students. Hofstra offers 2 four-month semesters, a one-month January session, and 2 five-week summer sessions.

PROGRAMS OF STUDY

Master of Business Administration (M.B.A.) students may attend classes in the day or evening program on a part-time or a full-time basis. Specializations are offered in certified public accounting, certified managerial accounting, taxation, finance, management, management science, marketing, and international business. A program leading to both the Juris Doctor and M.B.A. is also offered.

Two plans of study are provided within the M.B.A. program. Students can satisfy degree requirements by selecting Option A and completing a 36-credit program (plus prerequisites) that includes a master's thesis, or by selecting Option B and completing a 39-credit program (plus prerequisites) that includes a seminar on research design in lieu of the thesis. Each student completes a core, a specialization, and either a master's thesis or a business research seminar. The total number of semester hours necessary depends upon the student's previous education. Students who have satisfactorily completed equivalent course work at the undergraduate level will have prerequisite courses waived. Students who have not completed equivalent course work may be required to take up to 24 semester hours of intensive survey courses.

The core of the M.B.A. program is designed to give students a broad-based background in business at the graduate level. Courses in organization theory, macroeconomic theory, statistics, marketing management, managerial finance, and general business allow students to see problems in a broader perspective, integrate the various elements of business, and communicate more readily with staff and line managers in other functional areas.

Specialized courses comprise between 25 and 40 percent of the degree requirements and are designed to give graduate students proficiency in one field of business.

For students who select Option A, the capstone of the M.B.A. degree program is the thesis in which students may elect to work as a group (under faculty supervision) or independently to solve complex administrative problems, examine applications of theories, or comment on the effectiveness of new business techniques. Research findings are published in a volume of the *Hofstra University Yearbook in Business* series or by a commercial publisher. M.B.A. candidates who select Option B register for a graduate research seminar during their final semester.

ADMISSION

Hofstra University seeks to enroll in its M.B.A. program those candidates who demonstrate both strong potential for success in a rigorous academic program and qualities that portend the ability to make a significant contribution to the management profession.

Admission to the M.B.A. program is competitive, and the admission decision is based on an evaluation of all materials submitted by the individual student. All applicants are required to submit an official report of scores obtained on the Graduate Management Admission Test (GMAT) and official transcripts of previous undergraduate and graduate course work. In addition, applicants are encouraged to submit supporting credentials such as letters of recommendation, statements on professional objectives, and resumes describing work experiences. Foreign students must also submit official scores from the Test of English as a Foreign Language (TOEFL). The average GMAT score of students recently entering the program was 530; the average grade-point average, 3.2. Students may commence study in the fall, spring, or summer. It is suggested that applicants seeking admission for the fall semester apply by April 1. Those students seeking admission for the spring or summer semesters should make application at least 60 days in advance of the semester in which they wish to begin study. Foreign students are advised to file their applications well in advance of these deadlines due to the additional time required to process them.

EXPENSES

Tuition for 1985-86 was $205 per credit hour, plus registration fees ranging from $31 for part-time students to $151 for full-time students. On-campus housing is available in the forms of dormitory rooms and campus-owned apartments, with prices ranging from approximately $750 to $1,050 per semester. Books and supplies are estimated at $300 per year.

FINANCIAL ASSISTANCE

There are a number of M.B.A. fellowships, scholarships, and other financial aid awards available for full-time and part-time students. In addition, the university sponsors a Minority Fellowship Program for M.B.A. candidates. The Financial Aid Form (FAF) of the College Scholarship Service and Hofstra's own financial aid form should be submitted no later than April 1 for the fall semester and no later than December 1 for the spring semester in order to ensure a student's full consideration for available funds.

PLACEMENT

Major businesses and other institutions regularly visit the School of Business to recruit M.B.A. graduates. In addition, the university's reputation and its proximity to New York City facilitate direct contact between students and prospective employers. The M.B.A. Placement Coordinator also serves alumni of the school. An annual resume book published by the M.B.A. Student Association is distributed to *Fortune 500* and other companies.

CORRESPONDENCE

For further information, write or call
    Office of Graduate Admissions
    Holland House
    Hofstra University
    Hempstead, New York 11550
    Telephone: 516-560-6707
    or
    Susan McTiernan
    Director of M.B.A. Programs
    105 Heger Hall
    Hofstra University
    Hempstead, New York 11550

HOLY NAMES COLLEGE

OAKLAND, CALIFORNIA

Holy Names College (HNC), founded more than 100 years ago in Oakland, California, is an independent, Catholic institution, which offers men and women of all faiths and ages an opportunity to obtain an excellent education in liberal arts, preparation for certain professions, and an enriched life. As a small, cosmopolitan institution of higher learning drawing upon the richness of the San Francisco Bay Area, HNC fosters a sense of world community through its faculty and students representing diverse cultures.

In 1981 the faculty and administration of the college undertook to formulate the Weekend College (known as WECO) in recognition of the needs of working men and women who want to complete a college degree, but who find weekday or evening classes inconvenient or incompatible with career and family responsibilities. Within a nontraditional time-frame the Weekend College programs reflect to the men and women enrolled in them the aims and values of Holy Names College: to provide an environment and process that foster an individual, personal development that embraces the intellectual, spiritual, cultural, and social spheres of life; the acquisition of career skills for professional work as an integral part of a total life; a liberal arts orientation that recognizes the benefit of human experience and the values that give meaning and order to life.

PROGRAM OF STUDY
The degree is designed to combine academic quality, flexibility, and the opportunity for advanced and specialized training. The degree may be completed in two years or less based upon the fundamental undergraduate curriculum in business administration or upon undergraduate study in other fields. A concentration is offered in management science.

Weekend College at HNC offers an opportunity to earn a degree from Holy Names College by enrolling in the specially designed classes that meet every other weekend, three trimesters per year. This design provides many adult students an alternative means of completing their education. Classes offer opportunities for personal and cultural enrichment, as well as highly specialized skills for improving capabilities. Students who do not plan to work toward a degree are also welcome to enroll in Weekend College credit courses.

The degree candidate must complete a total of 11 courses (33 units) in the M.B.A. program, exclusive of the foundation courses that include Elementary Accounting I and II, Statistics, Macro- and Microeconomics, Calculus, and Computer Programming. HNC has a large, modern IBM computer lab and a separate accounting lab. Counseling and advising are readily available to each WECO student, and all instructors may be reached at the college or at home by phone in case of need for information or clarification. Personal attention, excellence of education, and convenience are the hallmarks of the Weekend College M.B.A. program.

ADMISSION
Application is made through the Graduate Division. Qualifications for admission to the Graduate Division are as follows: a bachelor's degree, or its equivalent, conferred by an institution of recognized academic standing; an undergraduate record of satisfactory scholarship (an overall grade-point average of 2.6 and 3.0 in the major); a completed application; and the payment of a $25 application fee. Applicants must submit Graduate Management Admission Test (GMAT) scores. Information about the GMAT may be obtained from Educational Testing Service.

The Graduate Council admits students on an ongoing basis, as files are completed, but it is prudent for students to complete the application well in advance of the semester or summer in which study is to begin. Two official copies of the transcripts indicating the completion of the bachelor's degree and two letters of recommendation complete the requirements for application.

EXPENSES
Tuition and basic fees for 1985-86
Graduate and postgraduate students
   Tuition, per unit $207
   Registration and library fee 15
The college maintains dormitories for on-campus residents. Information about housing may be obtained from the Director of Residents.

FINANCIAL ASSISTANCE
Limited numbers of scholarships, fellowships, loans, grants, assistantships, and work-study opportunities are available for HNC graduate students. For more information, contact the Office of Financial Aid at 415-436-1327.

CORRESPONDENCE
For further information, please write or call
   The Weekend College Office
   Holy Names College
   3500 Mountain Boulevard
   Oakland, California 94619
   Telephone: 415-436-1120

Howard's first Commercial School was opened on January 18, 1870 and operated for four years in conjunction with the old Freedmen's Savings Bank and Trust Company. After the bank closed, the school was discontinued until 1903, when it was reopened to offer college-level courses leading to the Bachelor of Science degree. This arrangement continued until the School of Commerce and Finance was established in 1919.

The school's beginning in the Reconstruction era eventually led to the birth in January 1970 of the current School of Business and Public Administration. The Board of Trustees authorized the admission of the first class in September 1970. Today, although the school is much larger and expanding rapidly, its philosophy does not differ from the ideals and goals set in 1870.

As a unit of Howard University, the school is accredited by the Middle States Association of Schools and Colleges. The undergraduate and Master of Business Administration (M.B.A.) programs are accredited by the American Assembly of Collegiate Schools of Business (AACSB).

PROGRAMS OF STUDY

Students with or without undergraduate degrees in business administration can be accommodated in the M.B.A. program. The M.B.A. degree is offered in three areas: general business administration, health services administration, and labor/management relations. Applicants holding an undergraduate degree in business administration may complete the M.B.A. program in 39 credit hours, while those without the business degree can complete the program in a maximum of 60 credit hours. The Master of Public Administration (M.P.A.) program offers the degree in five areas. These programs may be completed in 48 credit hours.

The objective of the general business administration M.B.A. program is to prepare the student for a managerial career in a profit-oriented business in a changing society. The M.B.A. degree in health services administration is designed to prepare the student for managerial careers in voluntary agencies, hospitals, health planning, health maintenance organizations, or other health-related areas.

The M.P.A. curriculum attempts to provide the student with an awareness of the political processes involved in a democratic government. The general M.P.A.

program emphasizes policy formulation, policy analysis and program development, and implementation within a public agency. The urban M.P.A. emphasizes urban complexities and problems. Attention may be given to human services, land use, transportation, solid waste disposal, or other problems.

ADMISSION

Admission to graduate study in business and public administration is open to all persons holding a baccalaureate degree or its equivalent from a nationally or regionally accredited college or university situated either in the United States or abroad. The applicant is responsible for complying with all rules and regulations of the school. Applications are accepted for both the fall and spring semesters; fall semester applicants should apply by April 1, while spring applicants must apply by November 1. Applicants seeking admission to the M.B.A. and M.P.A. programs are required to present Graduate Management Admission Test (GMAT) scores prior to admission. An applicant with a foreign transcript which has no grade-point average must score a minimum of 450 on the GMAT. In addition to test scores, applicants must also present an official transcript, a resume, two letters of recommendation, and an autobiographical sketch.

EXPENSES

A nonrefundable application fee of $25 is required. The budgets for the 1985-86 school year were

Budget for two semesters	Single Student Living Off Campus
Graduate Tuition	$ 3,400
Fees	365
Books and supplies	358
Room rent	4,683
Board (Food)	1,743
Personal	975
Local transportation	1,140
Total for year	$12,664

Most of the graduate students live in off-campus housing.

FINANCIAL ASSISTANCE

Limited financial aid is available in all programs to qualified graduate students. Research assistantships and scholarships are awarded to students on the basis of need and/or merit. These students must enroll full time (at least nine credit hours) to receive any form of assistance. Applicants must submit a Graduate and Professional School Financial Aid Service

(GAPSFAS) form. Financial aid is also available through the Howard University Financial Aid and Student Employment Office.

PLACEMENT

The School of Business and Public Administration has housed within its division a Placement Office. The Director of this office schedules recruiters throughout the academic year who, in turn, provide employment information and opportunities to business and public administration students. The university maintains a Career Planning and Placement Office that serves the entire university.

CORRESPONDENCE

All requests for further information or applications for admission should be forwarded to

Graduate Programs Office, Suite 575
School of Business and Public Administration
Howard University
Washington, D.C. 20059
Telephone: 202-636-5109

Founded in 1913, Humboldt State University is accredited by the Western Association of Schools and Colleges. As one of the 19 campuses of the California State University System, the university is located 275 miles north of San Francisco in a spectacular setting of redwood forests, rivers, mountains, rangelands, and ocean beaches—the heart of an outdoor paradise nationally famous for its beautiful scenery and recreation. The College of Business and Economics was founded in 1969 when the university was reorganized. While relatively small in numbers of students and staff, the school emphasizes a quality program, which is delivered in an informal atmosphere of close faculty and student contact.

PROGRAM OF STUDY

The curriculum is designed to assure the opportunity to grasp basic and advanced understanding of business operations. For those who have majored in other fields there are the introductory requirements (Group A). Group A consists of 33 semester units of course work that cover the common body of knowledge recommended by the American Assembly of Collegiate Schools of Business (AACSB).

Evidence of satisfactory preparation in the areas of accounting, business law, economics, finance, management, marketing, data processing, mathematics, and statistics is necessary. (Any deficiencies in this course work (Group A) may be met at the university by taking the appropriate courses.)

The M.B.A. core (Group B) is built around the analytical tools and the basic disciplines that are available to modern management for solving problems. The Group B course work includes 27 semester units in marketing, organizational theory, managerial accounting, organizational policy, finance, information systems, and microeconomic analysis.

The student may choose four semester units from specialized graduate seminars to satisfy the Group C requirements. In addition, a thesis or graduate research project is required.

The program accommodates both full- and part-time students. Group A courses are offered day and night. Group B courses are offered at night only.

Time required to complete the program varies upward from a minimum of one year, depending upon course work to be completed and the full- or part-time status of the student.

ADMISSION

The formula for admission is as follows: the upper-division grade-point average (GPA) multiplied by 200, added to the Graduate Management Admission Test (GMAT) score, must total 1,050 or more [(GPA × 200) + GMAT = 1,050].

Where exceptional abilities or qualifications are demonstrated, the applicant may request special consideration in the event the minimum score requirement is not met.

Additional requirements for admission are as follows:
- a minimum grade-point average of 2.50, based on the last 90 quarter units or 60 semester units of undergraduate studies completed prior to application for admission;
- an acceptable baccalaureate degree from an accredited institution or equivalent academic preparation as determined by the appropriate college authorities;
- a minimum score of 550 on the Test of English as a Foreign Language (TOEFL) for foreign students.
Applications for admission are accepted on a continuous basis, and qualified students may enroll any semester, beginning in late August or early January.

EXPENSES

There is a one-time, nonrefundable $35 application fee. Registration and tuition fees for out-of-state students are approximately $4,200 per academic year. For the California resident, there are only registration fees, approximately $700 per academic year for 1985-86. Other expenses vary according to the individual student.

FINANCIAL ASSISTANCE

Graduate assistantships are available. Certain funds may be available to the student through government loans and through a limited number of scholarships. Part-time employment may be available in the community or at the university. The university placement office assists in locating part-time jobs in the area.

PLACEMENT

Local and national firms recruit on the campus, although the majority of M.B.A. graduates find employment through their own efforts, with the assistance of experienced faculty, or with the assistance of the university placement office (open to graduate students and to alumni).

CORRESPONDENCE

Students desiring application packets should address
  Mr. Donald G. Clancy
  Director of Admissions
  Humboldt State University
  Arcata, California 95521
Students who want information about the M.B.A. program should consult the university catalog or address
  Director, M.B.A. Program
  College of Business and Economics
  Humboldt State University
  Arcata, California 95521
  Telephone: 707-826-3546

Husson College is a private, nonprofit institution of higher education located in Bangor, a commercial and financial center in eastern Maine with a metropolitan population of 100,000. Founded in 1898, Husson has a long-standing historical commitment to education for leadership in business, and that heritage provides a strong and supportive environment for the graduate business program, which was established in 1978.

The college grants the Bachelor of Science degree in accounting, business administration, business education, office administration, and nursing. The Graduate Studies Division offers programs of study leading to the degree of Master of Science in Business (M.S.B.). The M.S.B. program is designed primarily for the education of management generalists. More specialized concentrations are available in health care administration and business education, however, and the curriculum contains sufficient flexibility to allow students to develop informal concentrations in a variety of areas through judicious selection of electives.

Most students in the M.S.B. program are fully employed individuals who enroll in classes on a part-time basis. A small percentage elect a full-time course of study and complete the degree requirements in 12 months. Students come into the program from a wide variety of academic backgrounds and career experiences. Most are mature, highly motivated individuals with 8 to 10 years of work experience. This diversity enriches classroom interaction and provides a dynamism often missing in more traditional graduate programs. Average class size is 15 to 20 students. Classes with more than 25 students are rare, and many have only 10 to 12 students. Small class size facilitates close and informal interaction between students and faculty who work together in common inquiry.

Graduate courses meet in the evenings or on Saturdays to accommodate the needs of those whose employment or family responsibilities preclude enrollment in a daytime program. The M.S.B. program is delivered on Husson's main campus in Bangor and at the college's educational center in Portland, Maine. Students can fulfill the degree requirements at either site.

Husson College is accredited by the New England Association of Schools and Colleges, Inc.

PROGRAM OF STUDY

The principal objective of the M.S.B. program is to develop in students a broad capacity to exercise managerial decision-making skills in rapidly changing contexts. This objective implies the ability to use effectively available tools of research, analysis, problem solving, and communications. To this end, the program requires the successful completion of 12 graduate courses (36 credits) with a cumulative average of 3.0 or better. The required core curriculum consists of the following courses: Management Communications, Research Methods, Managerial Accounting, Managerial Economics, and Policy and Strategy. Students are also required to take either Business Law or Corporate Strategy and Public Policy and one of the following: Financial Management, Marketing Management, or Production Management. Students select four electives from a wide range of specialized courses and may, with permission, substitute electives for core courses in which they have advanced undergraduate preparation.

The 36-hour degree requirement applies to all students regardless of undergraduate background. No undergraduate prerequisites in business, accounting, or related fields are stipulated (international students excepted), and individuals with baccalaureate degrees in any discipline are welcome to apply for admission.

ADMISSION

To be admitted to the M.S.B. program at Husson College, the applicant must have earned a baccalaureate degree from an accredited college or university and show promise of ability and motivation to pursue graduate studies. The Graduate Executive Committee makes admissions decisions based on the following factors:
- a personal interview with the Dean,
- a review of undergraduate transcripts,
- scores on the Graduate Management Admission Test (GMAT), and
- letters of recommendation.

International students are required to obtain a minimum score of 550 on the Test of English as a Foreign Language (TOEFL) and to take undergraduate prerequisite courses in English and business.

EXPENSES

Registration fee (per semester).....	$ 5
Application fee	25
Tuition, per credit hour	110

PLACEMENT

Husson College operates an Office of Career Counseling, the services of which are available to graduate students.

CORRESPONDENCE

For further information, please write or call
Dean
Graduate Studies Division
Husson College
Bangor, Maine 04401
Telephone: 207-947-1121, extension 224

Idaho State University (ISU) is an institution of about 7,000 students. In addition to the College of Business, the university has colleges in arts and sciences, education, health-related professions, and pharmacy; a school of engineering; a vocational-technical school; and a Graduate School.

The university is located in Pocatello, a community of 56,000. Pocatello is a pleasant community serving as the transportation, industrial, and trade center of southeastern Idaho. It is also quite convenient to the Idaho National Engineering Laboratory, which is a major energy research center in this country. The surrounding area provides ideal opportunities for all forms of outdoor recreation including access to some of the finest skiing in the country.

The Master of Business Administration (M.B.A.) program at Idaho State, offered since 1968, provides the student with the advantages of a small, quality program. The typical M.B.A. class is a diverse, cosmopolitan group that represents all regions of the U.S. and numerous foreign countries. The informal, friendly atmosphere maximizes the amount of interaction between students and faculty, providing an ideal educational environment. Close interaction among members of the student body, many of whom work in the business community, strengthens and expands the knowledge derived from the classroom, presenting a broad spectrum of practical business experience in addition to a strong academic program.

Graduate classes normally have fewer than 30 students and are taught by a relatively young graduate faculty, all of whom hold the Doctor of Philosophy (Ph.D.) degree and have considerable professional experience in their respective fields. ISU's M.B.A. program is accredited by the American Assembly of Collegiate Schools of Business (AACSB).

PROGRAM OF STUDY

The M.B.A. program consists of undergraduate core equivalent courses, a set of M.B.A. core classes, and electives. All M.B.A. students are required to have the equivalent of the undergraduate core in business. Students from an undergraduate business program will normally have completed this requirement. Students with deficiencies in this area make them up during the program.

The M.B.A. program has a broad-based administrative emphasis, permitting a limited degree of specialization in one of the functional areas of business administration. The M.B.A. core is composed of eight courses that provide for the development of key conceptual, analytical, and behavioral skills as well as study in the basic functional areas of business. The student has an additional six credit hours of elective course work that may be chosen from courses throughout the university to meet particular interests or goals.

ADMISSION

Admission to the M.B.A. program is open to any student holding a bachelor's degree, in any field of study, from an accredited institution. All applicants are required to submit two official copies of the undergraduate transcript(s) and to take the Graduate Management Admission Test (GMAT).

Admission to the graduate program is granted only to students showing high promise of success in postgraduate study. No admission is granted until the College of Business has received the applicant's transcripts, GMAT scores, and a completed application for admission.

The College of Business uses various measures of high promise, including the candidate's performance on the GMAT, upper-division grade-point average, and work experience. Ordinarily such measures, along with other reasonable indications of promise, will be used in combination rather than trying to arrive at a final judgment on the basis of a single criterion.

The minimum requirement that must be met in order to be considered for admission is defined by the following formula: 200 × the last two years grade-point average (4.0 system) + the GMAT score = at least 1,000 points. In addition, a minimum raw score of 22 on each part of the GMAT is required. Meeting this requirement does not assure admission; many factors are weighed in such a decision.

EXPENSES

Although tuition costs are subject to change, the fees for the 1985-86 school year can be used as a guide: $687 per semester for resident graduate students or $1,637 per semester for nonresidents. Part-time students, taking seven credits or less, pay $67.25 per credit. Room and board for single students is about $1,146 per semester. On-campus apartments for married students start at $208 per month. Off-campus housing is abundant.

FINANCIAL ASSISTANCE

The College of Business has a limited number of teaching/research assistantships available. Information may be obtained by writing to the College of Business. Student loans and some university scholarships are also available to graduate students in business. Information on these may be obtained from the Financial Aid Office.

PLACEMENT

Idaho State University maintains a placement service which assists students in placement activities. Many national and regional area firms visit the campus for interviews during the year, and graduates generally are readily placed.

CORRESPONDENCE

For further information, write or call
M.B.A. Director
College of Business
Box 8020
Idaho State University
Pocatello, Idaho 83209
Telephone: 208-236-2504

Instituto de Estudios Superiores de la Empresa (University of Navarra)

IESE

BARCELONA, SPAIN

Instituto de Estudios Superiores de la Empresa (IESE), founded in 1958 and located in Barcelona, is the Graduate School of Business Administration of the University of Navarra, which has its main campus in Pamplona. In addition to the bilingual (English-Spanish) Master of Business Administration (M.B.A.) described here, IESE offers a Spanish M.B.A. section (called M.E.D.), a doctoral program, management development programs throughout Spain and in various other countries, and a continuing education program for its alumni. Both IESE's Spanish M.B.A. and doctoral programs are the oldest in Europe. The bilingual M.B.A. was first offered in 1980. Since IESE's foundation, members of the Harvard Business School faculty have collaborated, forming part of IESE's M.B.A. Supervisory Council. M.B.A. students number about 300, or about 150 per academic year. In the first year there are three sections, one taught in English and two in Spanish. In the second year, English-speaking students—after formal language training for nine months and three months work on a project in a Spanish company between the two academic years—are expected to be able to follow course work in Spanish or English, as offered at the choice of the instructors.

PROGRAM OF STUDY

The bilingual M.B.A. program is a full-time course of 21 months starting in September of each year. Its aim is to prepare tomorrow's managers to lead businesses and other organizations successfully within an increasingly complex environment. The program is based on the premise that a successful manager needs more than sheer knowledge and a great willingness to act. To obtain the desired results a manager has to be good at the analytical level, have the interpersonal skills needed to work through colleagues and subordinates, and possess the emotional competence to accept full responsibility and to take tough decisions. He or she must be able to make sound judgments about specific situations and the people involved.

To develop such essential management skills, the M.B.A. program relies on three basic elements:
• a structured first academic year (nine months divided into three quarters) that strongly focuses on the functional areas of a business organization;

• a practical project to be carried out in a company, closely associated with IESE, during the three-month summer term, under the double supervision of a faculty member and a manager of the company sponsoring the project;
• a diversified second academic year (nine months divided into two semesters) composed mainly of elective courses, where the student can concentrate on his or her principal areas of interest. Many of the courses strongly accent policy aspects of business problems.

During the second year about 20 percent of the students will spend one term studying at foreign centers. Exchange arrangements exist with outstanding business schools in North America and Europe.

Three further elements contribute to the program's distinctive character.
• Its unique international orientation, facilitated by the program's bilingual format, results in graduates who speak with a working level of fluency the two most important western business languages and who are thoroughly at home in the cultures that these languages represent. As a consequence, graduates from IESE are in demand from multinational corporations.
• IESE is heavily committed to active pedagogic methods, especially the case method.
• The learning process works at different levels (individual, group, and full class) but is always closely supervised by a member of the faculty (tutorial system). The participants form study groups, heterogeneous by design, to facilitate the exchange of points of view, experience, and knowledge. The groups meet daily, after individual study, to discuss the cases that will be analyzed subsequently in the general sessions.

ADMISSION

Prerequisite is a completed university degree course or its equivalent. Further requirements are a completed application form; transcripts of university grades; a copy of the degree, title, or diploma; Graduate Management Admission Test (GMAT) scores; Test of English as a Foreign Language (TOEFL) scores unless the candidate's mother tongue is English or a sufficient command of English is evident from other sources or facts; and three recommendations. An interview is desirable but not obligatory; the same is true for

meaningful previous work experience. IESE is looking for students who are highly motivated to become successful leaders in internationally oriented organizations.

EXPENSES
Tuition, including registration fee and all educational materials (books, cases, etc.) cost Ptas. 775,000 per academic year in 1986-87. Cost of living for a single student is estimated at $450 per month; for a married student $700. The three-month summer project is remunerated and should take care of the cost of living during that period.

FINANCIAL ASSISTANCE
IESE itself can offer only a reduction in tuition. There are some scholarships and grants available (usually tied by their sources to students of certain nationalities). The arrangement of personal loans, often on concessionary terms (not available for students from all countries) is the most common source of financing. This emphasis on loans reflects IESE's belief that students should consider a loan as a business-like investment in their own future. Experience shows that it is a highly profitable one.

PLACEMENT
A large number of companies and organizations, multinational and national, recruit on the campus. The number of firm job offers has always far exceeded the number of graduates looking for placement.

CORRESPONDENCE
For further information, write
M.B.A. Admissions Office
IESE, University of Navarra
Avenida Pearson, 21
08034 Barcelona, Spain

ILLINOIS BENEDICTINE COLLEGE

LISLE, ILLINOIS

The Master of Business Administration (M.B.A.) program at Illinois Benedictine College was instituted to meet the needs of the rapidly growing residential and industrial population in the western suburbs of Chicago.

The primary objectives of the Master of Business Administration program at Illinois Benedictine College are the following:

• to enable men and women in business and management to combine the study of management principles, analytical concepts, and problem solving with worthwhile experience;

• to provide individuals with the practically oriented conceptual knowledge needed to solve current problems and the ability to foresee and solve problems in a changing environment;

• to provide managers with an awareness of the ethical considerations in decision making and to encourage a commitment to improving the social and environmental conditions in our society.

In order to accomplish these objectives, the college has made a commitment of its resources to provide the following:

• a program of graduate study that is academically sound and practically oriented,

• a program of graduate study that is broad in scope and has a major emphasis on planning and decision making as the characteristic functions of professional management,

• a faculty with strong academic credentials as well as relevant business experience,

• library and computer facilities necessary for advanced study in business,

• an administration committed to quality education and a concern for each student associated with the program, and

• convenient evening and weekend course offerings for business professionals.

PROGRAM OF STUDY

The M.B.A. curriculum assumes no prior course work in business. Candidates with previous academic course work in business or related areas will be evaluated on an individual basis, and appropriate adjustments in program requirements may be made through transfer credit (based on previous graduate course work), course waivers (based on previous undergraduate course work), and course substitution (based on nonacademic experience).

The curriculum consists of 16 courses: 12 required and 4 electives. Electives may be selected in one area to develop a specialization or in several areas to develop further knowledge in a variety of fields. Formal concentrations are available in financial management, marketing, human resource and operations management, management information systems, and health care management.

Required courses include the following: Financial Accounting, Economics, Business Law, Organizational Behavior, Data Processing and Management, Quantitative Methods I, Quantitative Methods II, Managerial Accounting, Economics for Business Decisions, Financial Management, Marketing Management, and Ethics and Business Policy.

ADMISSION

In general, applicants must have a bachelor's degree from an accredited college or university and show high promise of success. Admission to the program will be based on undergraduate grades, trend of undergraduate grades, recommendations, scores earned on the Graduate Management Admission Test (GMAT), and other pertinent data supplied by the applicant. A personal interview with the director of the program may be required. Foreign applicants are also required to submit official Test of English as a Foreign Language (TOEFL) scores.

Admission to the program is open to individuals with any undergraduate major and without regard to race, color, age, sex, or creed.

EXPENSES

Tuition for 1985-86 was $540 per course.

CORRESPONDENCE

For further information, call or write
Director of the M.B.A. Program
Illinois Benedictine College
5700 College Road
Lisle, Illinois 60532
Telephone: 312-960-1500

ILLINOIS INSTITUTE OF TECHNOLOGY

CHICAGO, ILLINOIS

Illinois Institute of Technology (IIT), a private coeducational university of about 6,500 students, is dedicated to excellence in education for professional practice and research—in engineering, computer science, applied science and mathematics, law, business and public administration, design and architecture—through programs that distinctively emphasize advanced technology.

The School of Business Administration, established in 1970, focuses on educating managers for complex and technology-intensive organizations in a rapidly changing society. Courses in the M.B.A. program are taught at IIT's 120-acre main campus located three miles south of Chicago's Loop, or at the Downtown Center, 77 South Wacker, which also houses IIT Chicago-Kent College of Law.

PROGRAMS OF STUDY

IIT's M.B.A. programs are designed for individuals from a wide variety of academic and professional backgrounds. The program's emphasis on traditional business education combined with the university's technological orientation prepares graduates for career advancement in business and finance within the context of rapidly changing technology and increasingly competitive world markets. The focus is on helping students gain an understanding of the complex strategic and organizational issues created by change in technology, advances in information management, and the globalization of the economy.

IIT's M.B.A. Program with the Management Internship Option is a course of study designed to help students gain practical, on-the-job experience while working toward the degree. The program is a two-year, full-time day offering. Students entering the program in the summer of 1986 will intern full time during the fall 1986 and summer 1987 semesters and will complete the program in the spring of 1988. In addition to internship income, qualified applicants may be eligible for half-tuition Dean's scholarships for three semesters of full-time study.

IIT's M.B.A. offerings at the Downtown Center include specializations in accounting, finance, human resources management, information resources management, management sciences, marketing, and operations management. All classes are held in the evening.

The M.B.A. for Technology Managers is designed to provide engineers, scientists, and allied professionals with the skills necessary to assume managerial roles in technology-based business and industry. Specializations include research and engineering management, information resources management, industrial management, and business marketing. This curriculum is offered at IIT's extension sites in Naperville and Rolling Meadows.

The Weekend M.B.A. for Technology Executives is designed to strengthen the business skills of individuals assuming leadership roles in the management of complex technology in competitive world markets. This two-year program meets on Friday and Saturday of alternate weekends. Admission to this program generally requires five years experience in industry, preferably with at least two years of supervisory responsibility.

IIT also offers the Master of Science in operations research and a Doctor of Philosophy in management sciences. (Additional information may be obtained from the address below.)

ADMISSION

IIT's M.B.A. programs are open to all qualified men and women having a bachelor's degree from an accredited institution. No specific undergraduate major or series of courses is required for entrance. All applicants must meet IIT requirements for admission to graduate study; M.B.A. candidates must also take the Graduate Management Admission Test (GMAT) before entering the program or at the next possible date. Admission is based on a combination of past academic records, GMAT score, work experience, and references.

EXPENSES

1985-86

Tuition: $246 per credit hour ($3,695 for full-time students)

Room and board: $3,310-$4,203 (varies by room, meal plan)

FINANCIAL ASSISTANCE

A limited number of graduate assistantships are awarded each year; recipients receive a full-tuition scholarship and a stipend and are required to work up to 20 hours per week. The M.B.A. with a Management Internship provides a form of aid by guaranteeing a paid position for two semesters.

PLACEMENT

IIT maintains a Placement Office which is visited annually by representatives of over 500 companies, and which arranges for interviews between graduating students and industry representatives and assists alumni who are looking for better positions.

CORRESPONDENCE

For information, write or call
Director, M.B.A. Programs
IIT School of Business Administration
IIT Center
Chicago, Illinois 60616
Telephone: 312-567-5878

Illinois State University (ISU) is a state-supported institution serving over 19,000 students. The College of Business was established as a separate college in 1967 and now has about 4,700 majors and enrolls over 6,500 persons in its courses each year.

PROGRAM OF STUDY

The Master of Business Administration (M.B.A.) degree program in the College of Business at Illinois State University provides its graduates with professional preparation for a wide variety of challenging and rewarding positions with managerial and administrative responsibility. Lectures, seminars, cases, computer games and simulations, role playing, and report writing provide the student with practical approaches to the solution of business problems. These approaches are solidly based on a theoretical structure that provides the student with an understanding of organizational systems, managerial processes, interpersonal relations, and individual and group behavior within the firm, as well as the behavior of consumers and the effects of the economic, political, and social environment external to the firm. The program allows each student to develop a specialization in a particular area such as finance, management, human resources management, decision systems, not-for-profit management, and accounting.

All M.B.A. candidates must complete 24 hours of professional core courses and 12 hours of electives. The electives should be selected considering the student's career objectives. Completion of the degree within 36 hours assumes an appropriate background "knowledge base" in business, economics, and mathematics. Additional course work will be necessary for students who lack undergraduate prerequisites in these areas.

M.B.A. Summary

Course Title	Credit Hours
Quantitative Methods for Managerial Decisions	3
Research Methodology	3
Legal Aspects of Business Decisions	3
Advanced Marketing Management	3
Financial Management	3
Organizational Structure and Systems	3
Business Problems and Policy	3
Managerial Accounting	3
Graduate electives	12
Total program hours	36

ADMISSION

The M.B.A. degree program serves students having a bachelor's degree in business administration and students having degrees in other disciplines. Each applicant must

• comply with admission requirements and procedures of the Graduate School of Illinois State University (information on these requirements can be found in the Graduate Catalog);

• possess a baccalaureate degree from a regionally accredited university or college;

• offer satisfactory evidence of completion of or plans to complete the undergraduate "knowledge base" prerequisite to the M.B.A. program (this deficiency can be removed by additional course work at ISU); and

• complete with acceptable results the Graduate Management Admission Test (GMAT).

Admission generally follows the criteria established by the American Assembly of Collegiate Schools of Business (AACSB) using the undergraduate grade-point average and the GMAT score.

EXPENSES

Tuition and fees for each semester for students who register for 12 or more semester hours are approximately $730 for Illinois residents and $1,530 for nonresidents. Resident students who register for fewer than 12 semester hours must pay $42.50 per credit hour plus a total of from $79.50 to $93.50 in general fees. Nonresidents registering for fewer than 12 hours must pay $127.50 per credit hour plus from $42.50 to $93.50 in general fees.

FINANCIAL ASSISTANCE

The Departments of Management and Marketing, Finance and Law, Business Education and Office Administration, and Accounting offer some graduate assistantships to suitably qualified candidates. Those applicants not qualifying for an assistantship may be employed as student workers. Other financial aids are also available. For further information regarding assistantships, please write to the Director of Graduate Programs in the College of Business, Illinois State University.

PLACEMENT

The department cooperates with the university placement office and takes an active interest in the placement of its graduates. Each year, over 125 companies interview at Illinois State University, reflecting the entire spectrum of locational opportunity, company size and type, and position availability.

CORRESPONDENCE

For further information on graduate study in business at Illinois State University, please write to

Director of Graduate Programs
College of Business
Illinois State University
Normal, Illinois 61761

International Management Development Institute (IMEDE), located in Lausanne, Switzerland, was established in 1957 under the guidance of members of faculty of the Harvard Business School as an independent foundation under the patronage of the University of Lausanne. IMEDE was founded specifically to serve multinational companies that wish to develop managerial knowledge and skills in their executives. Having gained an enviable reputation for the quality of its educational programs for experienced executives, IMEDE introduced in 1972 a yearlong M.B.A. program, concentrating two academic years into 12 months. The program starts in January and runs through December of each year.

The recognition IMEDE enjoys is due in large part to the quality of its faculty. In 1971 the faculty was enlarged to its present size of 20 and modified in its national background. The nationalities represented since 1971 have been American, British, Canadian, Dutch, French, German, Iranian, Israeli, Italian, Nicaraguan, Norwegian, South African, and Swiss.

PROGRAM OF STUDY
As a result of its constant interaction with the international business community, IMEDE believes that, in order to respond to the increasing complexity and changing nature of business problems, the IMEDE Master of Business Administration (M.B.A.) participants must develop the following managerial capabilities:

• An international know-how—IMEDE M.B.A. participants work interactively in a truly international environment. The class of 65 to 70 participants includes 20 to 25 different nationalities and works with a faculty of 10 from at least five different countries. This provides a unique training ground to understand managers from a large range of cultures and to interact, resolve business problems, and negotiate solutions in a context similar to that of international business.

• Interpersonal skills—IMEDE M.B.A. participants develop the interpersonal skills needed to provoke action and results in the business organizations of the 1980s by placing considerable emphasis on communication and negotiation. Throughout the program, IMEDE M.B.A. participants must present and defend their solutions to business problems in front of their fellow participants, the faculty, or corporate executives.

• Integrative capabilities—IMEDE M.B.A. participants develop the ability to adopt a multidisciplinary point of view in responding to the increased complexity and changing nature of the management problems of the eighties. Over the year, IMEDE M.B.A. participants progress through a sequence of nine issue-oriented modules of increasing complexity and breadth. Each module combines various functional disciplines such as management accounting, decision analysis, human resource management, marketing, finance, operations management, strategic analysis and planning, environment analysis, as well as the newer fields of knowledge needed in today's management problems. In addition, IMEDE M.B.A. participants work in small study groups that combine a wide range of experiences and background disciplines, thus forcing them to break out of their individual specialty and to explore more fully the alternative dimensions of business problems.

• Thorough analytical capabilities—In all the activities of the IMEDE M.B.A. program, through discussions, communication and feedback, participants are continuously forced to discipline their approach to problem solving, thus developing thorough analytical skills.

• A practical orientation—The IMEDE M.B.A. program relies heavily on active learning through case analysis and consulting projects. The latter represents substantial consulting assignments performed in companies by teams of M.B.A. participants under the guidance of the faculty. These consulting projects allow the participants to apply their interactive and interpersonal skills in an actual business context.

• An ability to operate under pressure—The IMEDE M.B.A. program concentrates within 12 months (one calendar year) what would take two academic years in most other M.B.A. programs. Participants thus develop an ability to operate under intense work pressure. They also learn to establish their priorities in order to deal simultaneously with several tasks which place conflicting demands on their time.

ADMISSION
Admission is based upon an assessment of an individual's overall potential to pursue an ambitious career in business administration successfully. In making these judgments, the admissions committee will evaluate the applicant's academic achievements, score on the Graduate Management Admission Test (GMAT), work experience, and motivation. Applicants are expected to have a bachelor's degree from an American university or its equivalent in other countries. Two years of full-time work experience are also considered an essential minimum requirement. The average age of the participants is 29. The program is conducted in English, and a high level of proficiency in this language is necessary. Applicants may be private or company sponsored.

EXPENSES
The fee amounts to Sw.Fr. 28'000. This fee includes tuition, as well as lunch at IMEDE five days a week. The approximate total cost of the year of study for a single student is estimated at Sw.Fr. 50'000.

FINANCIAL ASSISTANCE
Participants are expected to secure their own sources of financing.

PLACEMENT
The school provides placement service to assist nonsponsored participants in their search for employment.

CORRESPONDENCE
For further information, write or call
Information Service
IMEDE
P.O. Box 1059
CH-1001 Lausanne, Switzerland
Telephone: 4121-26-71-12
Telex 25871

IMPERIAL COLLEGE OF SCIENCE AND TECHNOLOGY (UNIVERSITY OF LONDON)

LONDON, ENGLAND

The Department of Management Science at Imperial College was first established in 1955. The term management science, first used in the early fifties, highlights the department's concern with an analytical approach to all problems of concern to management. From being confined to production and inventory in the early days, management scientists have moved into marketing and distribution, finance, manpower planning, investment analysis, cash and foreign exchange management, purchasing, facilities design, corporate planning, planning for new technology, profitability and productivity analysis, as well as other functions of management.

The department has excellent computing and library facilities; it is housed on a modern campus that includes halls of residence and good recreational facilities.

PROGRAMS OF STUDY

The department offers a master's program in management science leading to the award of the Master of Science (M.Sc.) degree of the University of London, and a research program in management science leading to the award of the M.Phil. or Ph.D. degree. The Diploma of the Imperial College (D.I.C.) is normally awarded on the completion of the M.Sc., M.Phil., or Ph.D. degree.

The M.Sc. course is a 12-month, intensive, full-time program that begins in October each year. Time spent on the course is divided into three sections: core subjects, elective subjects, and project. The compulsory core subjects provide the essential background to the course and are assessed by examinations. More than 40 elective subjects are offered from which students may choose those most appropriate to their individual career aspirations. All electives are assessed on course work. The project presents students with an opportunity to study a field of particular interest in depth and may be theoretical or practical.

Courses are taught mainly by series of lectures, tutorials, seminars, and group discussions; students will be involved in syndicate work and oral presentation.

Students who would like to carry out research in management science are invited to apply for admission to the Research Program. On joining this program each student will have the opportunity of either contributing to an ongoing research project or exploring a new problem, perhaps in collaboration with a sponsoring organization. The duration of the M.Phil. program is usually two years and that of the Ph.D. three years or more. Degrees are awarded after the candidate has successfully presented a thesis and passed an oral examination.

ADMISSION

For the M.Sc. in management science applicants should possess a first or second class honors degree from a British university or equivalent qualification, preferably with some business experience. Applicants should also have a sufficient competence in mathematics.

For direct entry into the M.Phil. program an M.Sc. in management science is desirable. Alternatively a candidate must have a first or upper-second class honors degree in engineering, science, or economics from a British university, in which case part of the M.Sc. course may need to be followed during the first two terms of study.

For the Ph.D. program candidates must first register for the M.Phil. program, and then, after some 18 months of study, a transfer to the Ph.D., backdated to the registration date, can be considered after an evaluation of the candidate's work.

For all courses applicants must complete an application form, provide two references, and take the Graduate Management Admission Test (GMAT).

EXPENSES

Tuition fees for 1985-86 were £5,400 p.a. for overseas students and £1,632 for British students. (These fees are subject to increases.) Living expenses, including accommodations, board, and books, are at present around £4,500 p.a.

FINANCIAL ASSISTANCE

The department is recognized by the SERC for the tenure of its awards, although these are restricted to candidates normally resident in the United Kingdom. The department is a participant in the Business Graduates' Association bank loan schemes that allow students to benefit from lower interest rates.

PLACEMENT

The department works in close liaison with Imperial College Appointments Board to help students find jobs appropriate to their qualifications and interests. The college has many contacts in most leading British companies and a wide range of overseas companies.

CORRESPONDENCE

For further information and an application form, write to
   The Registrar
   Imperial College of Science and
      Technology
   London SW7 2AZ, United Kingdom
   Telephone (International)
      +44 1 589 5111
   Telex 261503

Indiana Central University, founded as a coeducational, private, liberal arts institution in 1902, is affiliated with the United Methodist Church. The university is located in a residential area about 15 minutes from the heart of Indianapolis. This location has many advantages for the student both academically and professionally as Indianapolis is the government, financial, and business hub of the state. Indiana Central University is fully accredited by the North Central Association of Colleges and Secondary Schools.

The Master of Business Administration (M.B.A.) programs are designed to focus upon the decision making and communication responsibilities of modern business executives. Two part-time programs, an evening and an executive, are offered. The M.B.A. programs are administered by an M.B.A. council through the graduate school of the university.

PROGRAMS OF STUDY
The executive M.B.A. program is a two-year program designed for the manager who has been vocationally active for at least 10 years. Classes meet on selected Fridays and Saturdays from 8 a.m. to 5 p.m. This program does not use the regular academic calendar. The curriculum is highly structured; all students are enrolled in identical core course sequences. The program consists of 40 semester hours with core courses that are the same as the evening program.

The evening program consists of 33 semester hours of core courses and 9 hours of elective courses. This program utilizes class time from 5:30 to 8:30 p.m. Monday through Thursday. The school year consists of two 14-week semesters and two 7-week summer sessions. The normal course load is two classes in each regular semester and one class in either of the two summer sessions.

The evening program is open to anyone who meets the entrance requirements. Students are provisionally admitted to the program until they have successfully completed six courses with a grade-point average of at least B. At this point, students are admitted to candidacy or are placed on probation. The probational student must follow the path designated by the M.B.A. Council as to how degree candidacy can be achieved.

To ensure academic proficiency, the M.B.A. candidate must attain the grade of B in all core courses. Those attaining a B– may be required to take a comprehensive exam. Those attaining a C + or below are required to repeat the course and attain the grade of B.

There are no general survey courses in the core program. Thirty-three core hours of integrated, computer-augmented courses are required for graduation. Students are required to use various computer software for decision-making purposes due to the comprehensiveness and depth of the programs and cases assigned. One course is entirely devoted to decision making using a simulated computerized economic model.

ADMISSION
The university admits students of any race, color, national, and ethnic origin to all the rights, privileges, programs, and activities generally accorded or made available to students at the university. It does not discriminate on the basis of race, color, national, and ethnic origin in administration of its educational policies, admissions policies, scholarship, and loan programs. The university welcomes applications from men and women who have graduated with a minimum of a baccalaureate degree from an accredited institution.

A minimum undergraduate grade-point average of 7.000 (C +) is required. The student's major and the last two years of undergraduate work will be emphasized in the evaluation of undergraduate credits. The Graduate Management Admission Test (GMAT) is required for admission to the evening program.

Students without academic proficiency in accounting/finance, economics, or mathematics/statistics will be required to take basic courses in these areas before being fully admitted to the program. Some of these courses may be counted toward the M.B.A. degree.

Students with an undergraduate average between C + and B may be required to take preliminary courses in order to build up academic deficiencies.

EXPENSES
The current tuition is $98 per credit hour. At this rate the M.B.A. degree tuition fee is $4,116. A $5 registration fee is charged each time the student registers. Currently, most students are commuters who have full-time occupations. Residency is possible for those students who wish to pursue full-time study during the evening.

FINANCIAL ASSISTANCE
Financial assistance is available through the guaranteed student loan package for those who qualify.

PLACEMENT
A full-time director coordinates both job placement upon graduation and part-time employment for students currently enrolled in the university. Career counseling and placement are available to any student enrolled at Indiana Central. The placement director coordinates the interview between students and firms visiting the campus as well as directing students to part-time employment.

CORRESPONDENCE
For further information, write or call
   Director, M.B.A.
   Graduate School
   Indiana Central University
   1400 East Hanna Avenue
   Indianapolis, Indiana 46227
   Telephone: 317-788-3368 (S-T-U-D-E-N-T)
      or 317-788-3340

Indiana State University, established in 1865, first opened its doors to students in 1870. During more than a century of distinguished service, the university has become widely recognized for the outstanding quality of its programs, facilities, staff, and graduates. As a multipurpose university, Indiana State provides a great variety of higher education opportunities.

Today, the 91-acre main campus is conveniently located in midtown Terre Haute, Indiana. The 11,600 students enrolled at the university enjoy modern, pleasant facilities dedicated to education, housing, study, sports, culture, and recreation. Fields of instruction include undergraduate, graduate, and adult education programs. Degree programs are offered in a broad range of disciplines at the associate, baccalaureate, master's, educational specialist, and doctoral levels.

The Center for Research and Management Services engages in the basic research activities for the School of Business. Through the center, the students are acquainted with research purposes and practices and are provided with the opportunity to work closely with the faculty and outside business groups in research activities. The advanced facilities of the computer center are also available to students.

PROGRAM OF STUDY

The School of Business offers a program leading to the degree of Master of Business Administration. The program is accredited by the American Assembly of Collegiate Schools of Business (AACSB).

The objective of the Master of Business Administration program is to provide breadth of knowledge and understanding of the process and problems of the professional manager working within the framework of the free enterprise system. The program recognizes four primary areas of student development: (1) instruction in the major functions of the business enterprise, (2) instruction in the uses and application of decision-making tools, (3) instruction in the significant areas of the business environment, and (4) instruction in the formulation and administration of business policy. The curriculum is designed to meet the needs of students who seek academic preparation and achievement in business,

regardless of their undergraduate academic training. Students who have the prerequisite background can expect to complete the program of study in a minimum of 36 graduate credit hours. Students who lack the necessary background are required to take the appropriate management foundation courses in addition to the core program.

ADMISSION

Requests concerning admission to graduate study should be addressed to the Dean of the School of Graduate Studies. Application must be made 30 days prior to first registration. Unconditional admission requires a minimum undergraduate index of 2.5 (4.0 = A) and satisfactory scores on the Graduate Management Admission Test (GMAT).

EXPENSES

Residents of Indiana pay a combined contingent, student service, and building facilities fee of $61 per semester hour during the regular 1985-86 academic year. Nonresident students pay $134 per hour for on-campus study during the regular academic year.

Room and board costs are $2,176 for the 1985-86 academic year. One- and two-bedroom apartments for married students range in cost from $176 to $242 monthly.

FINANCIAL ASSISTANCE

The university offers a number of graduate assistantships. The stipend for the academic year ranges from $2,800 to $3,300 with remission of all except nominal service fees. Generally, qualification for an assistantship requires an overall undergraduate index of at least 2.75 (4.0 = A). A number of university fellowships are available for qualified graduate students (those who have had teaching, research, or comparable experience). The university fellowship stipend for the academic year ranges

from $3,200 to $4,500 with remission of all except nominal service fees. A minimum overall undergraduate grade-point index of 2.75 is required for fellowships.

Graduate students interested in securing a loan should contact the director of the Office of Student Financial Aids. Admission to the School of Graduate Studies is prerequisite to the processing of an application for a loan.

CORRESPONDENCE

For further information, write or call
Director, M.B.A. Program
School of Business—East Tower
Indiana State University
Terre Haute, Indiana 47809
Telephone: 812-237-2000

The Graduate School of Business at Indiana University prepares its graduates for the responsibility of leadership positions in business by providing a dynamic, professional environment for its Master of Business Administration (M.B.A.) candidates. The program emphasizes a balance between developing the student's skills needed for technical specialization and developing the conceptual skills necessary in general management.

The full-time program (enrollment, 600) is located in Bloomington, 50 miles south of Indianapolis in the rolling hills of southern Indiana. With a total enrollment of over 30,000 students, Indiana University–Bloomington is a major center for higher education.

PROGRAMS OF STUDY
The Master of Business Administration program at Indiana University requires approximately 50 semester credit hours. The program is designed recognizing that it is essential for today's executive to be fully versed in all functional areas of business. The first semester of the program concentrates on the quantitative, economic, accounting, and computer skills needed to understand the functional areas of marketing, finance, and operations management presented in the second semester. In the second year of the program, the student is given the opportunity to specialize in one of 15 career paths. Either through examination or adequate prior course work, a student may be exempted from one or more of the core courses which are replaced with electives enhancing the flexibility and direction of the student's program. Part-time students desiring evening courses normally enroll at the Indianapolis campus (enrollment, 500).

Emphasized in the program is the need for executives to be well-trained in the utilization of computers. The Computer Literacy Program provides the knowledge, experience, and conceptual framework necessary for the use of the computer as a management tool. The M.B.A. student is encouraged to make use of the extensive system implemented in the program, which includes the VAX system; an electronic mail system; a microcomputer lab for database, spreadsheets, statistics, and linear programming; and the Dow Jones News/Retrieval, an excellent source of up-to-the-minute information on business issues.

Unique program options include a five-week summer session in Washington, D.C., the Undergraduate Honors Program, and the M.B.A./J.D. program. Indiana University also offers an executive M.B.A. program and doctoral programs of study.

ADMISSION
Admission to the M.B.A. program is highly selective and is designed to identify those applicants who have the maturity, ability, and interest to successfully meet the rigors of the program. Individuals with academic backgrounds in science, engineering, and liberal arts, as well as business, are encouraged to apply. Although the curriculum is structured to accommodate nonbusiness undergraduates, it is expected that each student is familiar with both differential and integral calculus before entering the program.

Undergraduate grade-point average, scores from the Graduate Management Admission Test (GMAT), work experience, extracurricular activities, community involvement, career objectives, and letters of recommendation are all carefully considered in the admission decision. The average grade-point average and GMAT scores for the last entering class are 3.35 and 75-80th percentile respectively. Work experience prior to entering the program is strongly encouraged.

EXPENSES
The minimum budget for one academic year for a single graduate student residing in university housing is approximated to be:

Tuition and fees, resident	$1,905
Tuition and fees, nonresident	5,044
Room and board	2,763
Books and supplies	425
Personal expenses	1,200
Total (Indiana resident)	$6,293
Total (nonresident)	$9,432

FINANCIAL ASSISTANCE
Nearly 40 percent of the M.B.A. students are awarded graduate assistantships or associate instructorships. These awards are based on merit and skill without regard for financial need. Awards range from $1,300 to $4,305 per academic year plus partial or full fee remission. The typical assistantship requires 10 hours per week of administrative or departmental service in return for a half-tuition fee remission and $1,300 stipend per academic year.

Additional sources of aid, such as loans and work-study employment, are available from the Office of Scholarships and Financial Aid through the university.

PLACEMENT
The Indiana University School of Business has developed one of the most effective and comprehensive facilities in the nation for the placement of its graduates who are employed in prominent positions throughout the world. Over 300 firms from every region of the country interview at the Business Placement Office (BPO).

CORRESPONDENCE
Prospective students interested in receiving more information or requesting an application packet are encouraged to write to
Director of Admissions and
Financial Aid
Graduate School of Business
Room 254
Indiana University
Bloomington, Indiana 47405

The purpose of the program leading to the Master of Science (M.S.) degree in business administration at Indiana University at South Bend is to prepare the qualified candidate for a professional career in business management. The program thus provides high-level graduate education for persons who have demonstrated a potential for assuming responsible business leadership in a dynamic environment.

The M.S. program in business administration is designed to accommodate adults who are employed in positions of responsibility and who are pursuing graduate education concurrently with their employment. Most of these candidates will enter the M.S. program because either their present or future positions will require increased managerial competence.

PROGRAM OF STUDY

The M.S. program is keyed to the needs of the candidate who has just assumed or is preparing to assume additional broad managerial responsibilities. The candidate's work experience is considered an integral part of the total educational experience and is pursued simultaneously with the course work on which the program is built. Consequently, candidates who are employed normally should plan to restrict their formal classroom load to no more than six credit hours per semester.

The program, building on this experience base, provides a broad foundation of theory and tools required for modern managerial decision making. This study is followed by work in the functional areas that emphasizes their interrelationships in administrative policy decision. There is only limited opportunity for specialization; instead the program seeks to further develop the initiative and creativity of the candidates to bring their potentialities to the highest level.

The sequence of courses is paced over a three-year period, although students may accelerate the pace. The degree must be completed within five years from the date of admission to the M.S. program. Individual circumstances will be weighed for any extensions requested.

The basic M.S. program consists of 45 credit hours covering five areas of competence. Minimum requirements in each area are shown below:

Area of Competence	Minimum Units* Required
Theory of the firm and information systems: systems analysis, statistics, legal environment, micro-economics.	4
Functional areas: finance, marketing, production	3
Business environment: organization behavior, macro-economics, management accounting	3
Managerial coordination: administrative policy.	1
In-depth study and specialization: electives (which may be selected from the categories above)	4
Total units required	15

*A unit normally consists of three hours of graduate credit.

ADMISSION

Admission to the M.S. in business administration program is limited to students of demonstrated aptitude, ability, and scholarship. Applicants must hold a baccalaureate degree and must take the Graduate Management Admission Test (GMAT). Some applicants—generally those with little or no academic background in business areas—will be required to supplement the basic M.S. program with additional graduate or undergraduate work. Additional course work could total a maximum of 12 credit hours. A placement exam is used to determine each candidate's entry level.

A committee on admissions acts individually on each application to the program and selects for admission only those who show strong promise for success in graduate study. The committee takes into account the applicant's: (a) performance on the GMAT, (b) undergraduate scholastic record, (c) three letters of recommendation, (d) professional activities and performance, including management work experience, and (e) other evidence that may indicate the applicant's aptitude for graduate study. Foreign students must submit a $35 application fee and the International Application for Admission as well as the materials mentioned above.

Candidates may begin the program in January, May, or August. Deadlines for submission of applications have been established as follows:

Fall Semester .... July 1
Spring Semester .... November 1
Summer Sessions .... April 1

Foreign student deadline is May 16 for fall, September 15 for spring, and February 15 for summer sessions.

EXPENSES

Per credit hour	In-state	Out-of-state
Tuition	$59.50	$131.50

PLACEMENT

Information about employment in specific career fields is available from any of these locations: placement offices, deans' offices, and/or department chairmen.

CORRESPONDENCE

For application forms, write to
Dr. John R. Swanda, Jr.
Indiana University at South Bend
1700 Mishawaka Avenue
P.O. Box 7111
South Bend, Indiana 46634

The Indiana University Northwest (IUN) Division of Business and Economics has an aggressive, dynamic, multidisciplinary Master of Science in Business Administration (M.S.B.A.) degree program. This program has been designed to serve contemporary needs and conceptualized to address futuristic perspectives. Students will acquire the knowledge and skills they may expect to utilize as effective administrative and managerial scientists in their daily endeavors. The program appeals specifically to persons already employed who wish to acquire increased competence and breadth in decision making. The various disciplinary areas of the M.S.B.A. degree emphasize instruction in using the tools, concepts, and languages of a number of diverse fields. Thus the recipient of the degree will gain a comprehensive background in contemporary administrative and managerial techniques.

PROGRAM OF STUDY

Each M.S.B.A. candidate is required to complete a minimum of 42 graduate-level credit hours. Each student's program will be tailored to meet his or her individual needs and desires. To be graduated, a student must maintain a 3.0 (A = 4.0) average at all times. Students usually enroll in two graduate courses during any one semester.

All students will complete a common body of knowledge (CBK) in the field of business administration. In certain cases, several courses in the CBK may be waived as individual case histories are reviewed.

The M.S.B.A. degree has been designed so that graduates of the program are generalists with a broad, integrated education in business theories and applications. Thus the only area of concentration offered is general administration.

ADMISSION

Admission to the M.S.B.A. program is limited to students who demonstrate an exemplary level of aptitude, ability, and scholarship. The M.S.B.A. program is designed to be a significant challenge for all those admitted; therefore, a strong foundation in the courses that constitute the CBK and associated areas will enhance the student's prospects of success. Applicants must hold baccalaureate degrees, take the Graduate Management Admission Test (GMAT), provide one letter of reference, and pass a stringent review by the Graduate Committee. Each applicant must arrange to have one official transcript from each school he or she has attended forwarded to the Office of Graduate Studies in Business.

Candidates may enter the program during the fall, spring, or summer. It is recommended that the GMAT be taken in January, March, or June for admission in the following fall semester and in October for the following spring semester.

The admissions committee acts individually on each applicant and selects for admission only those who show promise for success in a dynamic graduate studies program. The committee takes into account the applicant's performance on the GMAT, undergraduate scholarship record, any graduate scholarship record, professional activities and performance, and such other evidence the candidates may submit to indicate aptitude for study at the graduate level.

EXPENSES

Fees are paid at the time of registration each semester and are subject to action by the Board of Trustees. Currently, Indiana residents pay $59.50 per graduate credit hour and nonresidents pay $131.50 per graduate credit hour. It is the practice of many firms in Indiana, Illinois, and Michigan to reimburse their employees for the cost of acquiring the M.S.B.A. degree.

PLACEMENT

IUN has a comprehensive Placement Bureau that is available to all M.S.B.A. students and alumni.

CORRESPONDENCE

For further information about the M.S.B.A. program offered at Indiana University Northwest, write or call

Peter F. Kesheimer
Director of Graduate Studies
Division of Business and Economics
Indiana University Northwest
3400 Broadway
Gary, Indiana 46408
Telephone: 219-980-6635

INDIANA UNIVERSITY OF PENNSYLVANIA

INDIANA, PENNSYLVANIA

Indiana University of Pennsylvania (IUP) is the fifth largest university in Pennsylvania and has been cited in a prominent national publication as one of the 50 universities in the entire country where a student can still obtain a superior education at a moderate cost. The university has a distinguished history of over 110 years of service to the state and the nation. The university's location combines the advantages of a lovely rural setting within easy commuting distance into a major metropolitan center. Indiana, Pennsylvania is a community of 26,000 about 55 miles northwest of Pittsburgh and 30 miles north of Johnstown. Situated in the Allegheny foothills, the school enjoys a moderate climate conducive to study year round and offers a wide variety of historical, cultural, and recreational facilities.

PROGRAM OF STUDY

The Master of Business Administration (M.B.A.) program is intended to serve the needs of junior and intermediate level business executives seeking additional knowledge and skills to do a more efficient job of problem solving and managerial decision making. The M.B.A. program also prepares students seeking advanced training in business management prior to entry into a business career.

Applicants holding degrees in business administration may usually enter directly into a 33-semester-hour program of graduate study. Other students must complete a preliminary program of business studies, which may require up to an additional 31 hours of study.

Applicants may be admitted for the fall semester, the spring semester, or the summer semester. Normally an applicant who presents a completed application, including an acceptable Graduate Management Admission Test (GMAT) score, official transcript of all previous academic work, letters of recommendation, and other required materials, at least one month prior to the beginning of the semester can be considered for admission.

The undergraduate prerequisite courses for students lacking a thorough undergraduate preparation include Accounting I & II, Calculus, Microeconomics, Business Law, Introduction to Computers, Business Statistics, Business Finance, Marketing, and Principles of Management. At the graduate level, there are required courses in accounting, business policy, finance,

marketing, management, economics, quantitative methods, and management information systems. In addition to these graduate courses, the candidate will take no less than three elective courses. The student may use these three elective courses to develop a specialization within the program or pursue a more general curriculum.

The program is offered on both a part-time and full-time basis. Classes are offered both day and evening. The summer session consists of a pre-, main, and postsession in which students may take up to a full semester of work.

In the course of instruction, lecture, case method, computer simulations, planned projects, and field trips are used. In the Indiana University of Pennsylvania program, the student develops proficiency in various types of managerial skills. These include analysis of problems by means of models provided by mathematics, accounting, economics, and behavioral sciences; use of various quantitative tools; understanding of the various contexts of business activities including processes and institutions; organizational change and established patterns of behavior; understanding of the various contexts of business, such as the legal, social, and ethical environments; and ability to synthesize and act on conclusions at a policy-making level.

ADMISSION

Admission into the program is based upon several criteria that include the following:
- undergraduate record,
- Graduate Management Admission Test (GMAT) results,
- responsibility and accountability in professional work,
- motivation and ability to succeed in the M.B.A. program,
- a score of 500 or higher on the Test of English as a Foreign Language (TOEFL) for non-native speakers of English.

University of Pennsylvania, like many other business schools, uses a formula that combines the student's undergraduate grade-point average and his or her GMAT score. A somewhat lower than average score on one of these criteria could be offset by a higher than average score on the other.

EXPENSES

Tuition for full-time graduate students (9 to 15 semester hours) is $800 per semester. Part-time tuition is $89 per semester hour. Graduate students taking undergraduate courses pay $68 per semester hour to a maximum of $800. An application fee of $10 must accompany the application form.

While the university does not have specific graduate dormitories, there is a great deal of off-campus housing, both apartments and privately run dormitories, available for the use of graduate students. For details and listings, please contact Residence Life, Clark Hall.

FINANCIAL ASSISTANCE

Contact the Financial Aid Office for information concerning scholarships and loans. A limited number of graduate assistantships are available, typically paying $3,000 for the academic year, plus a full tuition remission for the full calendar year. Contact the Director of Graduate Programs, School of Business, for information on assistantships. These assistantships are usually awarded in early spring; however, there may be openings at other times throughout the academic year.

PLACEMENT

The Office of Career Services, 302 Pratt Hall, is open to all IUP graduate students and alumni. Students and classes are invited to use the facilities and professional staff for assistance in career planning and development.

CORRESPONDENCE

For further information, contact
Director of Graduate Programs
School of Business
Indiana University of Pennsylvania
Indiana, Pennsylvania 15705
Telephone: 412-357-2520

INDIANA UNIVERSITY—PURDUE UNIVERSITY AT FORT WAYNE
FORT WAYNE, INDIANA

The Division of Business and Economics initiated the Master of Science in Business Administration (M.S.B.A.) degree program in 1968. The program is designed for individuals who are employed in positions of responsibility in business as well as public organizations and who wish to pursue a graduate education concurrently with their employment. To service this type of clientele, all graduate courses are offered in the evening.

The M.S.B.A. program provides a professional education in business for students who possess the baccalaureate degree in any discipline. For most students, the M.S.B.A. is a terminal professional degree designed to enhance their performance in present and future managerial positions. Increasingly, individuals employed in nonbusiness fields have utilized the program to broaden their academic training in order to enhance their prospects for a career in business.

Within a typical semester, there are more than 200 students taking classes with the average course load being approximately five hours. Slightly in excess of 20 percent of the students in the program are women. The students enrolled in the program come from a broad range of academic backgrounds and from a very diverse group of companies. The teaching staff consists of 31 full-time faculty members.

PROGRAM OF STUDY
The M.S.B.A. program of study is divided into three sections. Students must complete all courses listed in Sections I and II of the program or have received prior academic credit.

Sections I and II contain courses presenting candidates with a broad foundation in theory, tools, and techniques as required for competent managerial decision making. Section III of the program provides an opportunity for the candidate to select at least 15 hours of course work that apply to career goals, objectives, or personal interests.

The M.S.B.A. program requires completion of 54 graduate credit hours for the candidate having no applicable waivers. A minimum of 39 hours is required of students who receive 15 hours or more of waivers. Distribution of hours is as follows:

Section I: 21 hours
  Sequence A—12 hours
  Sequence B—9 hours

Section II: 18 hours
  Sequence C—15 hours
  Sequence D—3 hours
Section III: 15 hours
  Sequences E, F, and G

If a student has completed course work encompassing material included in Sections I and II of the program, certain waivers may be granted. The student will be notified as to waivers granted when the application for admission is formally approved. In cases where the number of waivers exceeds 15 hours, additional elective credit beyond the 15 hours specified in Section III will be used to fulfill the 39 hours required for the completion of the program.

The minimum passing grade for any course taken for graduate credit is C. An accumulative index of 3.0 (4.0 = A) or higher in graduate work must be earned for continuation in good standing and graduation.

ADMISSION
Admission to the M.S.B.A. program is limited to students of demonstrated aptitude, ability, and scholarship. Every applicant is required to complete the Graduate Management Admission Test (GMAT). The admission decision is based upon a composite evaluation of the applicant's undergraduate academic performance, as measured by the cumulative grade-point average and the scores earned on the GMAT.

A committee of faculty members in the Division of Business and Economics assists the Director of Graduate Studies in Business in the making of admission decisions. Admission decisions will be made by August 1, December 15, and April 15 on applications submitted by the July 1, November 15, and March 15 deadlines, respectively.

Candidates may enter the program at the beginning of the fall, spring, or summer semesters. A completed application and all supporting documents must be submitted by the established deadline date. If the GMAT scores are not available by the deadline, the scores from the test period which immediately follows will automatically be incorporated into the admission file when received. An official transcript for each college attended is required. A limited number of graduate assistantships are available to qualified applicants.

EXPENSES
An admission fee of $20 is required of all new applicants for admission to Indiana University. Those who have previously attended Indiana University as regularly admitted students will not be required to pay this fee. Tuition fees are assessed at the current rate of $59.00 per credit hour of enrollment in graduate courses. Students whose residence is located outside Indiana must pay $132.50 per credit hour. Applicants to the M.S.B.A. program, who have recently moved into the Fort Wayne area, will be granted resident status if it can be established that their move was a condition of employment with their present employer.

PLACEMENT
A placement office is available and may be used by the M.S.B.A. degree candidates who are seeking initial placement or by alumni considering a job change.

CORRESPONDENCE
For further information and application forms, address
  Director of Graduate Studies in
    Business
  Indiana University—Purdue University
    at Fort Wayne
  Neff Hall, Suite 340
  2101 Coliseum Boulevard East
  Fort Wayne, Indiana 46805

INSEAD—
The European Institute of Business Administration
FONTAINEBLEAU, FRANCE

INSEAD—the European Institute of Business Administration—was founded in 1958 by a group of European business leaders supported by the Paris Chamber of Commerce and inspired by Professor Georges Doriot from Harvard. It was founded to answer the growing management education needs of the European business community at a time when a new Europe was being built.

PROGRAM OF STUDY
Among the large range of programs now offered by INSEAD, the Master of Business Administration (M.B.A.) program remains the most important with over 300 participants enrolling each year.

The M.B.A. candidate who chooses INSEAD will do so for three reasons:
- because its degree is highly regarded around the world;
- because the M.B.A. program lasts just one year; and
- because INSEAD is an international and specifically European business school in which the learning environment encourages the participants to develop an awareness of the deep changes affecting business decisions in Europe and around the world.

INSEAD's teaching staff come from more than 15 countries and the M.B.A. participants from 30. From this diversity of attitudes, values, and knowledge springs confrontation, which is the substance on which the self-examination and change of attitude of each participant are founded. From the outset, students form work groups of about six people, selected to maximize the variety of national, educational, and professional backgrounds within each group. This is their first encounter with the continuing feature that is unique to INSEAD: the need to work with and learn from individuals having widely different backgrounds.

The course is divided into five periods. Each ends with written examinations which are graded; grades are also given for individual and group assignments and for classroom participation. Maintaining a satisfactory average grade is essential to graduation.

Initially, emphasis is on the compulsory courses: accounting, computing, organizational behavior, statistics, marketing, finance, planning and control, operations research, and business policy as well as an INSEAD speciality, the European business environment. Later in the year students choose from a wide range of optional courses. INSEAD's aim is to concentrate on real current management problems. Teaching, at one time largely based on the case method, has in recent years become more flexible and varied. Lectures, audiovisual programs, simulation techniques, interactive computer terminals, closed-circuit TV, and language laboratories are all used, and students are required to prepare assignments and presentations.

ADMISSION
Candidates for the M.B.A. program normally have the following qualifications:
- They hold a university degree or professional qualification. Candidates without a degree can be admitted if they have at least five years' experience that has led to a position of responsibility.
- They have two or three years' professional or business experience. Participants who have little or no practical experience must have an outstanding academic record and be unusually mature.
- They must have fulfilled all military obligations.
- They are fluent in English and French. A knowledge of German is an advantage.
Applications from candidates who do not speak German are considered in the normal way; if accepted, they will be asked to gain a working knowledge of German during the year. Applicants are normally between 24 and 31 years old.

Deadline for applying is March 1 for mid-September entry and July 1 for mid-January entry.

EXPENSES
For the academic year 1985-1986, the tuition fees, including books, were FF 83,000. Residence and food amounted to approximately FF 45,000.

FINANCIAL ASSISTANCE
No potential participant with a reasonable future earning capacity should be denied coming to INSEAD for financial reasons. There are three kinds of financial aid:
- scholarships—a limited number available from various sources;
- bank loans, which are the major source of finance for participants;
- INSEAD loans—administered directly by INSEAD as a lender of last resort and requiring a French resident guarantor.

PLACEMENT
INSEAD has a placement office to help its M.B.A. graduates, and each year over 250 organizations from throughout the world come to recruit in Fontainebleau.

CORRESPONDENCE
For all further information, write to
INSEAD
Admission Office
Boulevard de Constance
F-77305 Fontainebleau Cedex, France
Telephone: 6/072 4000

INSTITUT PENGEMBANGAN MANAJEMEN INDONESIA
(The Indonesian Institute for Management Development)
JAKARTA, INDONESIA

Institut Pengembangan Manajemen Indonesia or Indonesian Institute for Management Development (IPMI) was established in 1982 as an independent, nonprofit institution devoted to education and research in management. The institute is maintained by the Indonesian Foundation for Management Development. The objective of the foundation is to further the advancement of management education and performance in Indonesia by providing a high-quality, practitioner-oriented education in Indonesia.

The foundation has two external advisory bodies:

● a Board of Counselors consisting of leading Indonesian and foreign professionals representing government and business, business education, and professional management associations; and

● an International Advisory Committee consisting of four prominent professors from overseas graduate business schools.

PROGRAM OF STUDY

The institute's M.B.A. program is designed for a one-year period. Many M.B.A. programs are two years in length, but the two-year concept has been successfully adapted to one year, notably at Europe's well-known business schools: IMEDE in Switzerland and INSEAD in France. IPMI is unique in being the only Indonesian education institution using English as the medium of instruction.

The institute's M.B.A. program is designed to develop in the student an analytical framework for understanding and assessing management problems and opportunities, with special emphasis on situations likely to be found in Indonesia and other developing countries in the Asia-Pacific region.

The complete program will be given in three terms:

● Term I is concerned with techniques, tools, and concepts for analyses. Courses given in Term I are Management Accounting and Control, Quantitative Analysis, Organizational Behavior, Analysis and Presentation of Management Problems, and Computer Familiarization.

● Term II focuses on basic functional areas of business. Courses given in this term are Financial Management, Marketing Management, Production and Operations Management, and Group Field Project.

● Term III treats the business firm as a whole. Courses given in this term are Business Policy, Business Environment Analysis, Simulation Exercise, and Group Field Project.

The institute's teaching relies heavily on the case study method. This method emphasizes active class discussion of an actual business situation.

The use of the case method in IPMI's M.B.A. program is influenced primarily by the Harvard-style M.B.A. program. This M.B.A. program has the greatest international prestige and has been adopted at such leading business schools as INSEAD in France, IMEDE in Switzerland, and AIM in the Philippines.

ADMISSION

Applications to the M.B.A. program are invited from men and women from Indonesia and other countries who have one of the following qualifications:

● a bachelor's degree from outside Indonesia or Sarjana plus two years of work experience or

● Sarjana Muda plus four years of work experience.

In addition, all applicants are required to submit to IPMI the results of the Graduate Management Admission Test (GMAT) and the Test of English as a Foreign Language (TOEFL).

Applicants are judged on past achievements and motivations, and future promise. In looking at the past and future, attention is given to academic performance, business experience, indications of leadership ability, and personal objectives.

EXPENSES

For the academic year 1985-86, tuition fees were $8,500 for individual applicants and $10,500 for company-sponsored applicants. Included in the tuition fees are all costs for case materials and board (lunch and dinner). The above fees are subject to change without notice.

FINANCIAL ASSISTANCE

For nonsponsored individuals accepted to the program, student loans and a limited number of scholarships are available.

PLACEMENT

Senior faculty, all of whom have had management experience, assist students in identifying employment opportunities.

CORRESPONDENCE

For further information or to request an application for admission, please write or call

Mrs. Minky Lesmana
Assistant to the Director
 for External Affairs
IPMI Building, 3rd floor
Jalan Taman Kemang I
P.O. Box 592/KBY
Jakarta 12730
Indonesia
Telephone: 793480
Telex: 47319 FINAS IA

INTERNATIONAL MANAGEMENT INSTITUTE (IMI)

GENEVA, SWITZERLAND

Located in Geneva, Switzerland, the International Management Institute (formerly CEI) is an independent educational institute associated with the University of Geneva. Since its founding in 1946, IMI has contributed to improving management effectiveness of corporations and other organizations throughout the world. This mission is accomplished through programs of teaching and research into the most effective ways of management across national boundaries and in widely differing political, economic, and cultural settings.

A milestone in the history of the nine-month program was reached in 1956 when it received the patronage and endorsement of the University of Geneva. The Master of Business Administration (M.B.A.) degree awarded to those who successfully complete the program is signed jointly by IMI and the University of Geneva.

In addition to the M.B.A. program, IMI holds annually in Geneva a variety of postexperience programs for managers and executives at different levels of responsibility and in different functions. Companies, government agencies, and international organizations from some 100 nations have sent over 10,000 managers and officials to IMI's programs.

PROGRAM OF STUDY
The M.B.A. program at IMI differs from other management courses throughout the world in the following ways:
- The curriculum is designed to prepare managers for successful careers in international management. The IMI M.B.A. program examines those concepts and skills that have their roots in particular socio-political settings as well as those that are considered universally applicable.
- The program includes industry study trips. During these trips the students visit ministries and industrial companies to discuss economic, cultural, social, and administrative problems. Industry study trips have recently been hosted by China, Singapore, Poland, the USSR, Ireland, the UK, France, Germany, and India.
- The international character is further reflected in the composition of the permanent faculty represented by 12 nationalities. The participants themselves are selected from all continents: each group averages 15 to 20 nationalities.
- The IMI M.B.A. ends with a five-week consulting project in which participants are able to put into practice some of the managerial know-how they have acquired during the course. Participants

go out in groups of three to five to work in the field for a client—usually a European company or government agency.
- It requires previous experience. The IMI's M.B.A. program gives preference to applicants with significant business experience. Thus the participant body brings with it practical exposure that can be shared and used to improve managerial effectiveness. In recent years one third of the participants have been sponsored by their companies and organizations.
- It applies a variety of teaching methods. Rather than using just one educational methodology, IMI has chosen to adapt its teaching techniques to the objectives of each educational event. A broad range of teaching and learning experience is used—to increase knowledge, to develop skills, and to re-examine attitudes.
- It maintains an optimal class size. The IMI accepts approximately 50 M.B.A. candidates each year. The group is small enough to become a cohesive unit with close interaction among participants and large enough to encompass a variety of backgrounds, nationalities, and personalities.
- It has a cordial atmosphere. IMI's M.B.A. program takes place in an agreeable, pleasant atmosphere. Students can meet participants in the programs for senior executives, which are run throughout the year.
- It offers a modular format. It is possible, under certain circumstances, to take the program's first or second module separately.

ADMISSION
IMI's M.B.A. program is designed for men and women with a previous university degree who
- have had at least three years of practical experience in industrial or business enterprises, in government service, or other fields;
- have proven their potential for further growth; and
- are expected to assume greater managerial responsibilities in the future, especially in international management.

EXPENSES
The tuition fee for the complete M.B.A. program is Swiss Francs 32,000. This amount covers the tuition costs as well as all books and teaching materials, the cost of industry study trips and, depending on the client out-of-pocket expenses for the

management consulting projects, travel to the location at which the consulting project is carried out. It does not cover living expenses in Geneva.

Where a participant enrolls for only a single module, the fees are Swiss Francs 18,000 for Module I and Swiss Francs 22,000 for Module II.

FINANCIAL ASSISTANCE
Although IMI itself does not provide any financial aid, various means of financing are available. In many cases bank or government loans, at preferential rates, may be procured in the country of origin. Scholarships are difficult to obtain and for the most part these are granted by national organizations to citizens of their country. IMI can provide limited information on possible sources of financing, but financing the M.B.A. studies from external sources depends on the initiative of the individual candidate.

Participants who are financing their own stay at IMI-Geneva may qualify for a bank loan.

CORRESPONDENCE
For further information, please write to
M.B.A. Program Administrator
International Management Institute
4 chemin de Conches
1231 Conches/Geneva
Switzerland
Telephone: 022-47.11.33
Telex: 427452

Jackson State University's School of Business and Economics was established in September 1972. The Master in Business Administration (M.B.A.) program was initiated at the same time. Jackson State University is a state-supported university offering degree programs through the master's level.

PROGRAM OF STUDY

The M.B.A. degree program is primarily a general business program stressing the quantitative aspects of management decision making. All students are required to complete courses in mathematical analysis, statistics, and computer applications in management, which constitute the quantitative core of the M.B.A. degree program.

Students are required to complete a core of 9 three-credit courses; each student may elect three courses either within the area of business and economics or in any other approved field to supplement the core curriculum.

Completion of the M.B.A. degree program requires a total of 36 semester hours of course work and completion of the Graduate Written Comprehensive Examination in Business.

Track I

Four-Semester Program   Sequence Credits

Semester I
MGNT 502: Human Relations and
   Organizational Behavior 3
MGNT 516: Statistics for Business
   Decisions 3
MKT 530: Managerial Marketing 3
ACCT 540: Managerial Accounting..... 3
Total 12

Semester II
MGNT 511: Computer Application
   in Management 3
ECO 511/512: Macro or Micro-
   economic Theory................. 3
FNGB 515: Special Problems in
   Business Finance 3
Elective: 3
Total 12

Semester III
MGNT 560: Seminar in Business
   Policy 3
Elective: 3
Total 6

Semester IV
FNGB 561: Business Research Project... 3
Elective: 3
Total 6

ADMISSION

Applicants for admission to the M.B.A. program must

- submit a score on the Graduate Management Admission Test (GMAT),
- have completed requirements for a bachelor's degree in a field of business or economics or complete remedial course work at the undergraduate level in business,
- file an application for admission with the Graduate School including official copies of all transcripts,
- complete and pass the English Competence Examination administered on Jackson State University campus each semester, and
- submit three letters of recommendation to the Graduate School with the application for admission.

Additional admission requirements include

- a baccalaureate-level degree in a business-related field—if the baccalaureate-level degree is in any other field, the person would be required to take the following courses and obtain at least a B average before being admitted to the M.B.A. program:

	Credit Hours
Accounting 211 and 212	6
Economics 211 and 212	6
Business Finance 320	3
Business Statistics 354/355	6
General Management 330	3
Principles of Marketing 351........	3
Business Communication 325	3
Total	30

- undergraduate grade-point average and performance on the Graduate Management Admission Test—a minimum of 3.00 during the last two years of undergraduate study or an overall grade-point average of 2.50 and a minimum GMAT score of 300.

EXPENSES

Tuition for the 1985-86 academic year was $67 per credit hour, plus an additional fee of $588 per semester for out-of-state students. While nine hours is a full load, students on some types of financial assistance (either graduate work study or graduate assistantship) are required to take a minimum of 12 semester hours. Housing is available for graduate students.

FINANCIAL ASSISTANCE

Graduate assistantships and graduate work-study positions are available for M.B.A. degree students who intend to carry a full course load in the program each semester. These awards are granted on the basis of demonstrated academic excellence at the undergraduate level and financial need. Each award carries with it the responsibility to work under the Department of Business Administration in a research or classroom assistance capacity.

PLACEMENT

Placement of M.B.A. degree recipients from Jackson State University is performed as a dual function by the Business Administration Department and the Placement Office housed on the university campus.

CORRESPONDENCE

Inquiries should be addressed to
   Dr. John Wade
   M.B.A. Program Director and
   Administrative Assistant to the
     Dean (SOBE)
   Jackson State University
   Jackson, Mississippi 39217
    or
   Dr. Leslie McLemore
   Dean of the Graduate School
   Jackson State University
   Jackson, Mississippi 39217

Jacksonville University, founded in 1934, is a private, independent, fully accredited educational institution that offers graduate programs in business and education. The campus consists of 273 acres on the St. Johns River, 10 minutes from downtown Jacksonville and 20 minutes from the beaches. The school consists of 26 modern, air-conditioned buildings, including 8 residence halls, and a library housing 285,085 volumes. Facilities also include a heated outdoor pool and playing fields for soccer, softball, baseball, tennis, racquetball, and volleyball. Students also have use of a boathouse, dock, and a nine-hole golf course.

PROGRAM OF STUDY

The Graduate School of Business Administration offers the Master of Business Administration (M.B.A.) degree, with concentrations in health care, management, marketing, and a combined management/marketing concentration. The M.B.A. program seeks to promote the growth of managers and facilitate the attainment of executive-level positions in business, industry, and government. The 30-semester-hour program consists of 21 semester hours of core requirements and 9 semester hours in the area of concentration. Classes are held one night a week, and the program can usually be completed in four semesters of full-time study or approximately 30 months of part-time study. The program is designed for individuals who have completed undergraduate degrees in either business or nonbusiness areas. An 18-month executive M.B.A. program is also offered on weekends.

ADMISSION

Admission to the M.B.A. program is based upon undergraduate grade-point average, Graduate Management Admission Test (GMAT) scores, letters of recommendation, professional experience, and a personal interview. All non-native English speaking students are required to submit Test of English as a Foreign Language (TOEFL) scores; students in this category must attain a score of 550 or greater. M.B.A. students can enter in the fall, winter, or summer. A completed application package must be available for evaluation 30 days prior to the start of the desired semester.

EXPENSES

Tuition and general fees for M.B.A. program full-time students are $1,480 per semester. Tuition is based on a $160 per semester hour rate; this does not include books.

FINANCIAL ASSISTANCE

The university offers a limited amount of financial aid for students. The financial aid program is administered in accordance with the nationally established policy of meeting demonstrated need. Students must be accepted by the university before financial assistance may be awarded. Assistance in obtaining veterans' benefits is available.

PLACEMENT

A career placement service is available. Representatives from various employers visit the campus at announced intervals to interview graduating students. The Director of Placement provides assistance regarding resumes, counseling, and interviews. The Placement Office also maintains an up-to-date file of off-campus, part-time jobs, as well as a list of career positions available.

CORRESPONDENCE

For further information or to request an application for admission, please write or call

Director, The M.B.A. Program
College of Business
Jacksonville University
Jacksonville, Florida 32211
Telephone: 904-744-3950, extension 4431

JAMES MADISON UNIVERSITY

HARRISONBURG, VIRGINIA

James Madison University is a state-supported, coeducational university of 9,400 students located in the beautiful Shenandoah Valley of Virginia. Harrisonburg, Virginia, is a town of 26,000 in a rural setting. The region is alive with history and unrivaled in natural beauty. Three major metropolitan areas, Washington, D.C., Richmond, and Roanoke, are within a two-hour drive of the campus.

PROGRAMS OF STUDY

James Madison University offers programs leading to the Master of Business Administration (M.B.A.) and Master of Science in Accounting (M.S.A.) degrees.

The Master of Business Administration is an evening program (30-57 credits) designed to meet the career development and advancement objectives of both full-time and part-time students. M.B.A. program requirements are in two phases. Applicants may be exempted from any or all of the nine Phase A courses by appropriate undergraduate preparation in business and economics, or by exemption tests. No Phase A course may be used as an elective in Phase B.

Semester Hours
Phase A..................... 27
ECON 524 Economic Analysis
IDS 506 Quantitative Analysis I
IDS 507 Quantitative Analysis II
ACTG 515 Financial Accounting
MKTG 574 Marketing Analysis
FIN 555 Financial Management
BLAW 509 Legal and Social Environment
of Business
IDS 510 Computers in Management
MGT 512 Management of Organizations
Semester Hours
Phase B..................... 30
MKTG 674 Marketing Management
FIN 655 Corporation Finance
ACTG 673 Managerial Accounting
IDS 605 Operations Analysis
MGT 690 Business Policy
One economics course selected from the following:
ECON 620 Macro Theory and Economic Policy
ECON 624 Managerial Economics
ECON 650 Economics of the Firm

Twelve additional credits of business and economics electives (excluding Phase A courses) or six credits thesis and six credits electives are required. These 12

hours of electives may be chosen in a particular field of study (accounting, economics, finance, management, or marketing) and thereby achieve a concentration in this field.

The primary purpose of the Master of Science in Accounting program (33 credits) is to promote the self-development of professional accountants in business, industry, and government.

M.S.A. program requirements consist of any required prerequisites and the course work of the program itself. Admission is limited to individuals possessing a baccalaureate degree in business or economics with a concentration or major in accounting (or the equivalent through prerequisite courses taken or exemption tests.)

The course work for the M.S.A. program consists of a common core and electives with a thesis option.

Semester Hours
M.S.A. Core Requirements..... 15
IDS 507 Quantitative Analysis II
ECON 624 Managerial Economics
FIN 655 Corporation Finance
ACTG 675 Accounting Theory
ACTG 694 Accounting Systems
Electives/Thesis Requirements .. 18

Eighteen additional credits at the graduate level are required. Of these, 12 must be chosen from course offerings in accounting or 6 credits for a thesis and 6 credits in accounting electives. The remaining 6 credits may be chosen from among any business and economics electives (or electives from other fields of study with approval of an adviser).

ADMISSION

In general, admission is based upon a combination of the Graduate Management Admission Test (GMAT) score and undergraduate grades as suggested by the American Assembly of Collegiate Schools of Business (AACSB). Each applicant is reviewed individually, however, and consideration will be given for employment experience, motivation, and personal objectives. A personal interview is not required, but applicants with particular questions are encouraged to visit the school. No specific undergraduate courses are required.

Applications are processed on a continuous basis, and students may enter the program in September, May, or January. There is no deadline for applications. Students who have Phase A courses waived may complete the degree requirements in 12 months of full-time study.

EXPENSES

Tuition for the 1985-86 academic year was $80 a credit hour for Virginia residents and $150 a credit hour for nonresidents. While 9 hours is a full load, students who desire to finish their program as rapidly as possible may take 12 hours a semester. No campus housing is available for graduate students, but housing is readily available in the community. A minimum budget, excluding tuition, is estimated at $375-$425 a month.

FINANCIAL ASSISTANCE

The school has available a limited number of graduate assistantships for students. Regular federal and state loan programs are also available. Applicants requiring more information should write the Office of Financial Aid.

PLACEMENT

A placement office is available to aid students. Numerous private and governmental organizations recruit regularly on campus.

CORRESPONDENCE

For additional information, write
    Director, M.B.A. Program
    College of Business
    James Madison University
    Harrisonburg, Virginia 22807

John Carroll University celebrates 100 years of service in 1986. One of 28 colleges and universities operated in the United States by the Society of Jesus, it was founded as St. Ignatius College in 1886. It has been in continuous operation as a degree-granting institution since that time. In 1923 the college was renamed John Carroll University, after the first arch-bishop of the Catholic Church in the United States. In 1935 it was moved from its original location on the West Side of Cleveland to its present site in University Heights, a suburb 10 miles east of down-town Cleveland.

To provide professional training for stu-dents aspiring to positions of responsibil-ity in the business world, a Department of Business Administration was established in 1934 in the College of Arts and Sci-ences. This department was expanded in 1945 into the School of Business.

With other units of the university, the School of Business seeks to cultivate in its students those qualities of intellect and will that develop useful, moral citizens, and to provide professional education for admin-istration in business and economic affairs.

At John Carroll University, the empha-sis is on excellent teaching. The graduate faculty are also active in research and pro-fessional activities. Classes are small, and there is ample opportunity to interact with the faculty and with classmates who bring with them a wide variety of business expe-rience. The university boasts a fine library, an excellent computer center, and a newly constructed recreation complex. In addi-tion, the School of Business has recently established a microcomputer laboratory for use in classes and for faculty research.

PROGRAM OF STUDY
A master's program in business, leading to the degree, Master of Business Adminis-tration (M.B.A.), is offered by the School of Business. The purpose of the program is to educate men and women for com-petent and responsible execution of man-agerial duties; its primary aim is to develop the generalist manager. The pro-gram is designed specifically for those who are presently employed and who wish to obtain an advanced degree on a part-time basis, without interruption of work.

Students whose undergraduate degree is in an area other than business are required to complete 24 semester hours of basic business courses. These are then followed by 36 semester hours of advanced courses. The student with an undergraduate degree in business may be able to complete the program with a minimum of 36 hours.

The basic courses cover the following areas: accounting, economics, statistics, mathematics, computers, finance, market-ing, and business law.

The advanced courses consist of Man-agerial Accounting; Human Resource Management; Quantitative Methods for Management Decision Making, Organiza-tional Behavior, Production/Operations Management; Problems in Financial Man-agement; Managerial Economics; Money, Income, and Government Policies; Prob-lems in Marketing Management; Social Issues and Managerial Decision Making; Corporate Strategy and Long-Range Plan-ning; and a choice of one of four interna-tional business courses.

Classes are held in the evenings. The program may be completed in a minimum of 24 months.

ADMISSION
The M.B.A. program is open to men and women graduates of any accredited uni-versity, regardless of undergraduate major, who show high promise of success in grad-uate work. Students may apply for admis-sion for the fall (September) or spring (January) semesters or the summer session (June). All applicants must submit official transcripts from all colleges or universities attended and the Graduate Management Admission Test (GMAT) score. The pri-mary criterion for admission is the combi-nation of GMAT score and undergraduate grade-point average. The applicant must have a total of at least 950 points based on the formula: GMAT score plus 200 times the undergraduate grade-point average.

In addition, before beginning advanced courses, the student must submit verifica-tion of at least two years of postbaccalau-reate work experience.

EXPENSES
Tuition and fees include the following:

Application fee	$ 20
Tuition	205
Degree evaluation and graduation fee	50

CORRESPONDENCE
For further information on the M.B.A. program at John Carroll University, write

Director, M.B.A. Program
School of Business
John Carroll University
University Heights, Ohio 44118

One of the nation's original land-grant universities, Kansas State University (KSU) was established under the Morrill Act on February 16, 1863. Current enrollment is about 17,500 students. The 668-acre main campus is in Manhattan, Kansas, situated among the gently rolling Flint Hills of northeastern Kansas, 125 miles west of Kansas City via Interstate 70.

PROGRAM OF STUDY

The Master of Business Administration (M.B.A.) program at Kansas State University is designed to provide professional managerial education to individuals who wish to pursue administrative careers in both the private and public sectors. The 33-hour program is accredited by the American Assembly of Collegiate Schools of Business (AACSB). It may be entered in any semester or the summer session and may be completed at a very full pace in two regular semesters and a summer session or in three regular semesters. Part-time students may progress through the program in an orderly, logical sequence taking one, two, three, or four courses per semester. Evening courses are conducted during fall and spring semesters to accommodate students who work full time, making degree completion possible in three to six years, depending on the academic pace undertaken.

Before beginning the M.B.A. curriculum, students without prior or complete business training in these areas must acquire a basic foundation in the following through specified undergraduate and graduate course work: accounting, statistics, computer science, mathematics, economics, finance, marketing, and management. This foundation course work may be taken after admission to the M.B.A. program.

M.B.A. Curriculum (33 hours)
- Analytical base (12 hours): Accounting Controls for Business, Applied Linear Statistical Models, Managerial Economics, and Advanced Management Information Systems;
- Business core (12 hours): Business Operations Analysis, Financial Controls for Business, Advanced Marketing Management, and Behavioral Management Theory;
- Capstone (6 hours): Administrative Strategy and Legal and Social Environment of Business;

- Graduate elective (3 hours): any graduate-level course approved by student's supervisory committee;
- Comprehensive examination in final semester.

ADMISSION

Admission is granted to students showing high promise of success in postgraduate business study. Following appraisal of prior scholastic performance, employment experience, and performance on the Graduate Management Admission Test (GMAT), the Graduate Studies Coordinator makes the admission recommendation to the Graduate School for the final review.

Admission with full standing requires that the applicant meet the following requirements of the Graduate School:
- a bachelor's degree from an approved institution,
- adequate undergraduate preparation for the intended field of study (provisional admission may be granted to applicants who have subject matter deficiencies in undergraduate preparation),
- an undergraduate grade average of 3.0 or above for the junior and senior years, and
- for international students, a score of at least 550 on the Test of English as a Foreign Language (TOEFL).

EXPENSES

Expenses for graduate study at Kansas State University are largely dependent on the student's life-style; however, general guidelines would include the following:

Per semester	In-state	Out-of-state
Tuition & fees	$ 685.50*	$1,587.50*
Room & board	990.00*	990.00*
Books & supplies	200.00	200.00
Total	$1,875.50	$2,777.50

*Subject to change for fall semester, 1986.

FINANCIAL ASSISTANCE

Aid is available through four sources: scholarships, loans, graduate assistantships, and fellowships. The KSU Office of Student Financial Assistance receives applications for loans and scholarships. The College of Business Administration receives applications for graduate assistantships and fellowships. Stipends vary with the work responsibilities of the individuals selected. A College Work-Study Program is also available to graduate students who meet CWSP requirements.

PLACEMENT

The University Career Planning and Placement Center assists graduates in obtaining suitable positions in business, industry, and government. This office provides assistance in arranging interviews and allows continuous contact with graduates throughout their careers. The Office of Career Planning and Placement maintains active contact with a large number of public accounting firms, industrial firms, and government agencies.

CORRESPONDENCE

For further information or to request an application for admission, please write or call
Graduate Studies Coordinator
College of Business Administration
Calvin Hall
Kansas State University
Manhattan, Kansas 66506
Telephone: 913-532-6180

KELLER GRADUATE SCHOOL OF MANAGEMENT

CHICAGO, ILLINOIS

Keller Graduate School of Management is a private institution located in downtown Chicago, at four Chicago suburban locations, and in Milwaukee, Wisconsin. Keller Graduate School of Management offers an accelerated practitioner-oriented program leading to the Master of Business Administration degree (M.B.A.). Emphasis is placed on practical, usable skills. Courses are taught by practicing business executives who combine management experience with a commitment to excellence in teaching.

PROGRAM OF STUDY

The objective of the program is to develop in its students a high degree of competence in the application of technical business skills and sound business judgment to the solution of business operating problems. The program prepares its graduates to contribute more effectively to the activities of their employer's organization by focusing upon functional business skills required to plan, analyze, and control company activities.

Traditional teaching methods, such as lectures and seminars, provide an initial exposure to basic business management concepts. Practice in analysis and decision making is obtained by selective use throughout the program of case analysis and directed class discussion sessions.

Graduation from the M.B.A. program requires successful completion of 16 courses. These include eight core courses: Accounting I and II, Financial Analysis and Control, Corporate Finance, Marketing Management, Management Applications of Electronic Data Processing, Managerial Statistics, and Business Economics. In addition to the core courses, students must successfully complete eight advanced courses. Of these eight, one must be an advanced accounting course and one must be the business planning seminar.

The business planning seminar serves as an integrating exercise for the curriculum. In the seminar, students prepare a comprehensive proposal for an entirely new business entity, or for a new venture within an existing company.

In addition to the flexible regular program, which is available in day, evening, and weekend formats, Keller Graduate School offers the internship M.B.A. program. This program specifically addresses the needs of recent college graduates or others exploring career alternatives.

The internship M.B.A. program offers college graduates an intensive one-year educational experience that combines course work leading to the M.B.A. degree and 13 weeks of internship experience with Chicago area business firms. Tuition costs are partially underwritten by participating firms. The purpose of the program is to provide students with both a high quality management education and the experience needed to make intelligent career decisions.

In addition to course work and the internships, students are involved in a program of activities designed to assist them in achieving an informed and realistic approach to their career planning. To this end, students meet informally with executives representing a variety of firms and job categories and participate in group career-planning sessions designed to hone their skills in resume preparation, job searching, and interviewing.

ADMISSION

Admission to the program is open to qualified men and women who hold a bachelor's degree in any field or discipline. The institution seeks applicants who can demonstrate both the motivation and the ability to succeed in a business career. Thus, a personal interview is required of each candidate. Consideration is also given to previous academic performance, scores on the Graduate Management Admission Test (GMAT), and work experience (if any).

Keller Graduate School of Management offers five 10-week academic terms per year. Except in the case of the internship M.B.A. program, which begins in the fall term, students are admitted prior to the beginning of any term. This arrangement allows students to commence their studies less than 10 weeks after submitting their applications.

EXPENSES

Tuition for the 1985-86 academic year was $525 per course. There is no additional charge for out-of-state students.

Tuition costs for the internship M.B.A. program are partially underwritten by participating corporations. Students pay regular tuition for the first 12 courses; however, tuition for the last 4 courses is paid by sponsoring corporations, and participants receive a monthly stipend of $250 that will continue through the completion of the program. This reduces the students' net cash outlay by $3,850.

FINANCIAL ASSISTANCE

Financial aid is available for qualified students. Interested applicants should write the Dean of Students at Keller Graduate School.

PLACEMENT

The school maintains an active placement office to serve the needs of its current students and alumni. Each year the office receives numerous inquiries and opportunities for its graduates in a wide range of business areas. The placement staff works closely with each student in the development and implementation of career goals.

CORRESPONDENCE

For additional information, please write or call

Director of Admissions
Keller Graduate School of Management
10 South Riverside Plaza
Chicago, Illinois 60606
Telephone: 312-454-0880

Kent State University, founded in 1910, is the largest state university in northeastern Ohio. The proximity of the university to one of the most highly industrialized areas of the nation provides students with a tremendous opportunity for interaction with the business community as well as easy access to transportation and cultural facilities. More than 19,000 students attend the university's main campus, and approximately 7,000 attend one of the off-campus university centers. More than 3,000 undergraduate and 600 graduate students are enrolled in the College of Business Administration.

PROGRAMS OF STUDY

The Graduate School of Business Administration offers the following degree programs: Master of Business Administration (M.B.A.), Master of Public Administration, Master of Science in Accounting, Master of Arts in economics, and Doctor of Business Administration (D.B.A.).

The Master of Business Administration program seeks to promote the self-development of potential executives for business, industry, and government and to prepare graduates for doctoral study. The 52 hours of course work are normally completed in four semesters of full-time study or three to five years of part-time study. The hour requirement is increased for those without the necessary foundation courses. These courses total 12 hours and may be taken at Kent State the summer prior to starting the program or at another school accredited by the American Assembly of Collegiate Schools of Business (AACSB).

The full-time M.B.A. program has a field study requirement during the middle summer. This unique feature of the Kent State program gives students practical business experience. The program also has a heavy emphasis on management information systems and international business.

The Master of Science in accounting provides a higher degree of specialization in accounting than is possible in the M.B.A. program. The one-year full-time program for students with undergraduate degrees in accounting is designed primarily for those who plan careers in public or industrial accounting.

The Doctor of Business Administration program is designed primarily for students who plan careers in university teaching and research. Admission is limited to highly qualified candidates who show outstanding potential for doctoral study and for later professional achievement. Most successful applicants have completed the master's degree, but outstanding baccalaureate degree holders are also considered.

D.B.A. fields of specialization offered include accounting, finance, marketing, organization and administration, economics, decision science, international business, and information systems. Each D.B.A. program also requires study in economic theory and quantitative methods. The D.B.A. degree will require a minimum of three years of full-time study beyond the baccalaureate degree.

ADMISSION

Admission criteria for master's degree applicants are the same for full-time and part-time evening students. Factors considered include undergraduate academic performance (minimum cumulative grade-point average of 2.75), scores on the Graduate Management Admission Test (GMAT), letters of recommendation, and professional experience. Applicants to the full-time program must also answer several essays. Admission is competitive.

Admission to the doctoral program requires superior performance on the above criteria. Personal interviews are encouraged.

Admission criteria for international students are identical to those of domestic students with the additional criterion of adequate performance on the Test of English as a Foreign Language (TOEFL).

Students may enter the full-time M.B.A. program in June or September depending upon their fulfillment of the foundation course requirements. Applicants to the other programs may apply for any semester but must be aware of application deadlines.

EXPENSES

Fees per academic semester for full-time students:

Residents of Ohio $1,090
Nonresidents of Ohio 1,790

Part-time students are charged $101 per credit hour for residents of Ohio and $161 per credit hour for nonresidents.

The university maintains on-campus furnished apartments for married students and a graduate dormitory for unmarried students. Information about housing may be obtained from the Office of Student Residence Life.

FINANCIAL ASSISTANCE

Graduate assistantships include a waiver of the instructional fee and resident fee, in addition to the basic stipend. Graduate assistants pay the general services fees.

Stipends for master's candidates range from $2,000 to $4,000. Appointments may be renewed after a year of outstanding work. Stipends for D.B.A. students range from $4,000 to $6,000 per academic year.

Graduate students are also eligible for appointment to counseling staffs of residence halls. Stipends include room and board and fee privileges. Information may be obtained from the Office of Vice President for Student Affairs. Part-time employment for students is also available.

A very limited amount of financial aid is available to international students.

PLACEMENT

The University Career Planning and Placement Center assists graduates in obtaining full-time employment. Hundreds of companies, including most major national corporations, conduct interviews on the campus each year. In addition, faculty members often assist in placing graduates with leading area and national firms.

CORRESPONDENCE

For further information, please write or call

Director
Graduate School of Business
  Management
Kent State University
Kent, Ohio 44242
Telephone: 216-672-2282

Kingston Polytechnic was formed in 1970 by the amalgamation of three colleges, one of which was founded nearly a century ago. Currently the Polytechnic has 5,219 full-time students and 1,172 part-time on its four sites in the historic Royal Borough of Kingston upon Thames, five miles southwest of Central London.

The part-time M.B.A. program is based at Kingston Regional Management Centre (KRMC). This is one of 12 Regional Management Centres in England and Wales that were designated by the United Kingdom Department of Education and Science in 1971 as a focal point in the public Further and Higher Education sector for management education. Kingston RMC operates in the London and South East Region. Its purposes include the provision of short courses and consultancy to meet the needs of industrial, commercial, and public service organizations.

Kingston RMC is located at the Polytechnic's Gipsy Hill Centre, on Kingston Hill. This is a wooded site, close to Richmond Park and Wimbledon Common. On the campus is a new library, which has special provision for management education. In addition, candidates have access to—and will be expected to use—the Polytechnic's extensive computer facilities. These include eight VAX machines linked via several local area networks. There are over 400 terminals that are supported in this way and additional peripheral devices, as well as a substantial library of software.

The M.B.A. program is supported at KRMC within the Polytechnic's Faculty of Business and Administration. The Faculty runs a range of highly regarded programs at the undergraduate and postgraduate levels in business, management, and the social services. Teaching staff within the Faculty number 108; 1,186 full-time and 615 part-time students attend.

PROGRAM OF STUDY

The Kingston M.B.A., a two-and-a-half-year program, is offered on a part-time basis for a carefully selected group of 25 to 30 people. Able candidates, with diverse academic backgrounds and specialisms, ranging from engineering to accountancy, are enabled to study the full range of business disciplines, while maintaining their work experience. The program is designed to enable them to view organizational practice from a corporate perspective, built on the foundation of a unified body of knowledge. Motivations for attending a course of this kind are varied, so the latter part of the program offers a choice of study. There is a wide range of subjects, from which the candidate may elect either to specialize in a particular business function (for example, by choosing all the marketing electives), or may opt for specific related topics, such as public finance or state enterprise and public sector management. It is in this part of the course that the candidate will attend a residential module or project methodology to prepare him or her for the project. This is seen as a critical part of the study, leading to the award of the M.B.A. degree. If appropriate, the project will be specifically related to the candidate's organization. The project methodology course is then taught during the time allocated for the project, and candidates are supervised by staff who have considerable experience in this area.

The Kingston M.B.A. is based on two 16-week semesters, rather than three 12-week terms per year. This system integrates well with a course credit assessment procedure, since absences from the course due to work commitments can be phased so that the candidate can accumulate credits from courses attended and, after a break, resume at the next appropriate course. All the semesters bridge standard academic vacations, giving the candidate a "breathing space" within each phase of the course.

ADMISSION

Applicants for the course will typically have a good honors degree or a professional qualification. They will be expected to have had substantial work experience. All will be required to take the Graduate Management Admission Test (GMAT). Candidates wishing to apply for the course are asked to complete an application form and provide two references. Some applicants will be invited to take part in a half-day selection session.

EXPENSES

Tuition fees in March 1986 were £869 per year. To this cost, candidates must add the cost of books and other general living expenses, £120 accommodation fee for a four-day residential module each year, the GMAT test fee, and a £20 application fee.

FINANCIAL ASSISTANCE

There are a limited number of bursaries available, which will cover part of the tuition fee.

PLACEMENT

Counseling is available.

CORRESPONDENCE

To obtain more information, write to
  The Course Director
  Part-Time Master in Business
    Administration Programme
  Kingston Polytechnic
  Gipsy Hill Centre, Kingston Hill
  Kingston upon Thames, Surrey,
    England KT2 7LB
  Telephone: 01-549-1141

Kutztown University, founded in 1866, is one of 14 universities in the State System of Higher Education. Located in east-central Pennsylvania between Allentown and Reading, the university is also convenient to Philadelphia and New York City. Approximately 5,500 undergraduate and 540 graduate students are enrolled.

The College of Graduate Studies' basic commitment is to students matriculated in programs and courses designed to increase academic and professional competence. Schedules are designed primarily to accommodate students who can attend class in the late afternoons, evenings, and Saturday mornings. Most first- and second-semester courses are offered one evening per week. Although most students attend part time because they have other responsibilities that prevent them from taking a full schedule, about 45 full-time graduate students usually enroll each semester.

The Rohrbach Library houses a collection of more than 333,000 volumes of books and periodicals, subscriptions to over 2,000 periodicals and newspapers, and 900,000 microform units, including the Congressional Information Service Microfiche Library and the Library of American Civilization. These holdings include approximately 14,000 titles in accounting, management, marketing, and general business subjects with subscriptions to 200 business periodicals.

The Computer Center houses a Burroughs A-9 computer system with keyboard terminals across the campus which support administration and academia. The Audio-Visual Communications Center, located on the ground floor of Rohrbach Library, has in its collection over 15,000 pieces of nonprint materials, which include 16mm films, 35mm filmstrips, records, cassette tapes, and over 250 pieces of microcomputer software. Also housed in the AV Center are over 40 Apple II-e and II-e+ microcomputers for student use. In addition, the spring of 1987 will see the addition of a microcomputer lab specifically for business students. It will be comprised of various business application software and over 25 IBM PC microcomputers.

PROGRAM OF STUDY

The Master of Business Administration (M.B.A.) program is intended for persons seeking or holding managerial positions in private and public businesses and institutions. The curriculum assumes that students will have achieved an understanding of the common body of knowledge found in foundation courses that make up a comprehensive undergraduate business administration program before beginning specific graduate course work.

The purpose of the program is then to provide (1) a breadth of understanding of the functional areas of business; (2) the concepts, strategies, processes, and skills that upper-level managers use in decision making, and (3) a sense of responsibility to society and a commitment to ethical action.

The program consists of 36 semester hours in exclusively graduate courses (500-level). The prescribed courses account for 30 semester hours and the remaining 6 semester hours are in elective courses.

A graduate student having completed at least 24 semester hours in foundation courses as defined above and having been granted regular admission to the M.B.A. program may enroll in graduate-level courses for which the specific prerequisite foundation courses have been completed.

There is no specific requirement for the M.B.A. program; however, all requirements for the degree must be completed within six years commencing with enrollment in the first 500-level course.

ADMISSION

A bachelor's degree from an accredited college or institution is required for persons to be considered for admission to the program. Admission will be granted only to applicants showing high promise of success as revealed by a combination of performance on the Graduate Management Admission Test (GMAT) and the undergraduate grade-point average. In some instances a record of relevant employment in ascending levels of responsibility may offset a marginal performance in one of the two primary factors.

Admission criteria for international students are identical to those for domestic students with the additional criterion of adequate performance on the Test of English as a Foreign Language (TOEFL).

The dates by which an applicant must have a complete application on file in the Graduate Dean's Office are July 1 for admission to the fall semester and November 1 for admission to the spring semester.

EXPENSES

Fees, per academic semester, are $800 for full-time students (9 or 12 semester hours) and $89 per credit for part-time students (less than 9 semester hours). There is no additional fee for nonresidents. Fees are subject to change without prior notice.

FINANCIAL ASSISTANCE

Financial assistance is limited to 15 graduate assistantships which include a stipend for the year and remission of fees. Students may apply for a Guaranteed Student Loan by obtaining an application from their bank.

PLACEMENT

The University Career Planning and Placement Center assists graduates in obtaining full-time employment. Many companies interview on campus each year. Faculty often assist in placing graduates with local and national firms.

CORRESPONDENCE

For further information or to request an application for admission, please write or call

Dean, College of Graduate Studies
Kutztown University
Kutztown, Pennsylvania 19530
Telephone: 215-683-4200

LAKE FOREST
GRADUATE SCHOOL OF MANAGEMENT
LAKE FOREST, ILLINOIS

The Lake Forest Graduate School of Management is a private nonprofit independent institution located on the campus of Lake Forest College. The school, founded in 1946 as a cooperative venture of the industrial and academic communities, is supported by 270 companies and other organizations in the north and northwest suburban Chicago areas. Students come primarily from the middle management of these organizations. Two master's degree programs are offered: a Master of Business Administration (M.B.A.) and a Master of Science in Management (M.S.M.). The school also offers a noncredit management development program. The programs, held on weekday evenings and Saturdays, are designed to raise the performance level of managers and better equip them to advance to higher levels. The school is accredited at the master's level by the North Central Association and the Illinois State Board of Higher Education.

PROGRAMS OF STUDY
The master's degree programs are designed to present the most up-to-date techniques and knowledge, covering the broad range of the managerial spectrum. The material is presented in a practical and pragmatic manner so that the students can readily apply their learning experiences to their current jobs. All the faculty have actual managerial experience, and all currently hold jobs or are consultants in industry. Direct feedback from the students at the end of each course—on the instructor, materials, teaching methods, and specific elements of the course content—is used to assure constant relevancy and maximum faculty standards.

The courses are designed to develop and heighten the students' analytical and decision-making abilities. Accordingly, classes are of an informal, seminar nature, with heavy emphasis on student participation. Instructional methods vary widely; case study, role playing, small team work, simulation, business games, films, and field research are used frequently. Whenever practical, discussions and outside projects are directly related to, and sometimes conducted in, the students' companies.

The curriculum for the M.B.A. program for general management is more quantitatively oriented, while the M.S.M. program emphasizes the behavioral sciences. Both programs stress management and have no majors, thesis, or comprehensive examination requirements.

The M.B.A. carries four quarter hours credit and is composed of 16 courses. Classes normally meet one evening per week or on Saturday. The academic year runs from September through June and is made up of four quarters, each 10 weeks long. Depending on the individual course load, a candidate can complete the program in two years by taking two courses per term or in four years by taking one course per term. New classes begin in September, November, January, and April. The Master of Science in Management program is completed in two years by taking courses conducted on Saturdays from September through June. A student can also enter the program in February.

The programs are designed to serve part-time students, virtually all of whom are working full time for companies and other organizations in the area. There are no dormitory facilities.

ADMISSION
Applications for admission from all types of individuals are considered. Preference is given to experienced, qualified employees who are recommended by area organizations and who meet the standards set for admission by the school. Applicants normally are expected to have college degrees and to meet minimum skill-level requirements in quantitative areas. Admission is based heavily on motivation—typically very high among Lake Forest Graduate School of Management students—and on past work experience and potential for growth, rather than solely on formal prerequisites. Thus, college nongraduates, especially those who have several years' management experience, can be considered for admission. If necessary, special students can be admitted on a probationary basis until they have completed prerequisite or workshop skill courses and/or have demonstrated ability to meet the school's educational standards. The median student age is 34; ages range from 24-61. The minimum standard for work experience is four years for the M.B.A. program; three years for the M.S.M. Incoming students normally average 9-10 years.

All applicants must take the Graduate Management Admission Test (GMAT), submit three letters of personal recommendation, and forward official transcripts of previous educational records in support of the application.

EXPENSES
The tuition in 1985-86 was $675 per course, including all books and other materials. There are no other fees.

FINANCIAL ASSISTANCE
The Lake Forest Graduate School of Management does not provide any financial assistance; however, student loans are available from local banks through the Illinois Guaranteed Student Loan program.

CORRESPONDENCE
For information, write or call
  Director of Admissions
  Lake Forest Graduate School
    of Management
  Lake Forest, Illinois 60045
  Telephone: 312-234-5005

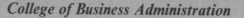

Lamar University, a state-supported institution, is located in Beaumont, Texas, one of the world's largest petrochemical centers. Beaumont is one of the fastest growing and most progressive cities in the Sunbelt. The city offers private and public schools, churches, museums, shopping districts, and wide ranges of leisure activities to serve a city of 130,000 and metropolis of 375,000. A civic center, convention center, and coliseum draw professional entertainers and a wide variety of business, social, and professional groups to the city. Beaumont is convenient to major recreational facilities of Southeast Texas, including the Gulf of Mexico, large lakes, and the Big Thicket National Forest.

Lamar University was established in 1923. Since then, enrollment has increased to more than 15,700 students, and the curriculum has been expanded to include many areas of study. Graduate work began in the academic year of 1960-61. Lamar University is fully accredited by the Association of Texas Colleges and Universities and by the Southern Association of Colleges and Schools. The College of Graduate Studies is a member of the Council of Graduate Schools in the United States.

PROGRAM OF STUDY

The College of Business offers a program of study leading to the Master of Business Administration degree (M.B.A.). The objective of the M.B.A. program at Lamar University is to provide intensive, rigorous training to produce managerial professionals with a thorough understanding of the economic, legal, and ethical environment of public and private sector organizations and the capability of applying analytical, problem-solving skills to a broad range of decision situations that may arise within one or a combination of functional areas within the organization.

Students must complete all course work applied toward the M.B.A. within a period of six years from the date of the first graduate course taken. The program is a two-year M.B.A., with first-year courses designed for students without appropriate academic training in business disciplines. If a thesis is written, 30 hours of second-year M.B.A. courses are required under College of Business degree requirements, plus any first-year M.B.A. courses required. If a thesis is not written, 36 hours of second-year M.B.A. courses under College of Business degree requirements, plus any first-year M.B.A. courses,

must be completed. The number of hours required may vary somewhat for those students with greater undergraduate business backgrounds.

ADMISSION

Admission criteria for master's degree applicants are the same for full-time and part-time students. The factors considered include undergraduate academic performance and scores on the Graduate Management Admission Test (GMAT). The applicant's undergraduate grade-point average and GMAT scores must equal or exceed the minimum standards. At least one of the following two standards must be met by students: (1) 200 times the overall undergraduate grade-point average (4.0 system) plus the GMAT score equaling a total of at least 950 points, or (2) 200 times the grade-point average (4.0 system) of the last 60 hours of undergraduate work, plus the GMAT score equaling a total of at least 1000 points. Students admitted on an unconditional basis must make a minimum score of 450 on the GMAT regardless of grade-point average. Students who make 400-450 and the 950 or 1000 total points will be admitted conditionally pending satisfactory completion of nine hours of graduate business courses with a B (3.0) average. A student who makes less than 400 on the GMAT will not be admitted regardless of grade-point average.

Admission criteria for international students are identical to those of domestic students with an additional criterion of a score over 500 on the Test of English as a Foreign Language (TOEFL).

EXPENSES

Hours	Total In-State Fees	Total Out-of-State Fees
3	$185	$ 445
6	223	843
9	266	1,238
12	323	1,619

FINANCIAL ASSISTANCE

Financial assistance in the form of loans, grants, and scholarships is available for a number of qualified students. Fellowships and assistantships are awarded only to those who meet all admission requirements to a graduate degree program, including satisfactory GMAT scores.

Stipends for master's candidates range from $800 to $4,500 for nine months in the form of teaching fellowships, assistantships, and scholarships.

PLACEMENT

The Placement Center, a centralized operation responsible for placement activities for all colleges of the university, is located in the College of Business Building. The center keeps updated information on career fields and job areas, employers, and the kind of employees being sought. Interviews are scheduled regularly with companies, governmental agencies, schools, and other employers.

CORRESPONDENCE

For further information or to request an application for admission, please write or call

Dr. Robert A. Swerdlow
Coordinator of Graduate Studies
College of Business
Lamar University
Beaumont, Texas 77710
Telephone: 409-880-8604

LA ROCHE COLLEGE

PITTSBURGH, PENNSYLVANIA

The Human Resources Management (HRM) degree at La Roche College offers students a professional program combining concepts and theory in human resources management with the development of specific skills in the field. The HRM program is an innovative graduate business degree providing a balance of the qualitative, as well as quantitative, approaches to contemporary issues in management. Students who graduate with the HRM degree are qualified to assume professional positions in personnel administration, organizational development, training, and general management in a variety of settings. The program also serves as a foundation for doctoral studies.

PROGRAM OF STUDY

The master's program is designed for the working person. Classes are offered on the North Hills campus in the evening, and students may attend on a full- or part-time basis. Students can complete the program in as little as two years, but may take up to six years to do so. The graduate studies program operates on a 10-month schedule, divided into fall, spring, and summer sessions.

The Master of Science degree in human resources management consists of 42 credits, 27 of which form a core curriculum and lay the foundation for 15 credits in a specialty area of HRM. Students choose one of two areas of concentration in this program:

● Human Resources Administration— Objectives are to acquire greater knowledge in the management of the employee in the workplace including hiring, compensation management, EEO and affirmative action, labor relations, and collective bargaining; also, to develop skills in recruitment, interviewing, orientation, salary survey, grievance mediation, labor-management dispute settlement, application of the law, management of a wage, salary and benefits program, and bargaining and negotiation.

● Human Resources Development— Objectives are to acquire greater knowledge regarding employee motivation and enrichment, and organizational design, needs and change; also, to develop skills in administering training programs and in designing programs, including needs analysis and evaluation, organizational change activities including needs assessment, intervention strategies and evaluation, and organizational development strategies.

ADMISSION

The following items are required for admission: a bachelor's degree from a regionally accredited institution or proof of equivalent education at a foreign institution, at least a 2.7 grade-point average in upper-division course work (junior and senior college level), an acceptable score on the Graduate Management Admission Test (GMAT), two letters of recommendation from employers and/or professors, an essay explaining the reasons for applying to the Human Resources Management Program, a resume of work experience, and acceptance by the Graduate Admissions Committee. Prerequisite course work consists of six credits of psychology and three credits of statistics. Students lacking these prerequisite courses may be admitted to the program, and these courses may be taken at the beginning of graduate course work.

EXPENSES

Tuition, per semester credit hour . . . $170
Application fee. 25
Change of course fee
 (after registration week) 25
Graduation fee. 55
Transcripts (after the first). 2
Tuition and fees are payable in advance and are subject to change without notice.

FINANCIAL ASSISTANCE

Government loans are available; information may be obtained and arrangements made through the Office of Financial Aid. In addition, a payment plan is available through the business office for those students who wish to pay tuition over the course of the semester.

PLACEMENT

The Career Development Center provides a full range of services.

CORRESPONDENCE

For additional information, please write or call
 Director of Graduate Admissions
 La Roche College
 9000 Babcock Boulevard
 Pittsburgh, Pennsylvania 15237
 Telephone: 421-931-7380

LA SALLE UNIVERSITY

PHILADELPHIA, PENNSYLVANIA

La Salle University is a private independent institution located near the northern perimeter of Philadelphia. Founded in 1863 by the Christian Brothers, the university currently has in excess of 6,000 students enrolled in its undergraduate and graduate divisions. The university began offering programs in business administration in 1928; a separate School of Business Administration was organized in 1955. Over 3,000 students are presently registered in business administration programs.

PROGRAM OF STUDY
La Salle's M.B.A. program addresses itself to the recent graduate from college or the professional with years of work experience. It offers the flexibility that allows the student to earn the M.B.A. degree on either a part-time or full-time basis. Quality programs have always been the hallmark of La Salle; the M.B.A. program continues in that tradition. The tradition of La Salle addresses the needs of the individual student. What this means is convenience of flexible course scheduling in four locations in the Delaware Valley, an average class size of less than 20, and access to personal counseling. Classes are scheduled in the evening, late afternoon, and on Saturday.

La Salle's M.B.A. program, begun in 1976, now has over 800 graduates, with a current enrollment of over 900 students. The program is geared to students from either a business or nonbusiness undergraduate background. Students need not take undergraduate prerequisite courses as a requirement for admission. A student could be required to complete anywhere from 36 (minimum) to 57 (maximum) credits to satisfy degree requirements. In other words, there are 21 credits of basic or foundation graduate courses for the student from the nonbusiness background. Any or all of these 21 credits could be waived for the student showing proficiency in these areas.

The La Salle M.B.A. student may elect professional specialization in the following areas: accounting, finance, health care administration, human resource management, management, management science, marketing, and taxation.

The program, designed to meet the needs of the full- and part-time student, is based upon three premises:
- Each student is unique in terms of his or her academic background and professional experience; current goals, motivations, and employment circumstances; and time and place constraints on availability for attendance.
- A program should stress direct relevance to one's professional development and employment circumstances.
- The program should have a flexible structure to respond to each individual's uniqueness and needs.

Within the curriculum standards of the American Assembly of Collegiate Schools of Business (AACSB), students are encouraged to tailor the program specifics to their own needs. Individualization is achieved through the implementation of two program principles:

(1) Program flexibility permits student individualization of graduate education. This allows the student to build upon previous academic background and managerial experience and to tailor the program to maximize his or her individual professional development. Program flexibility provides a series of choices involving learning methodology and course sequencing by which the student individualizes his or her own program of professional development.

(2) The student builds upon his or her previous academic and professional experience rather than repeating it. The program recognizes that each person has a unique academic background and set of professional experiences.

ADMISSION
Every applicant is encouraged to visit the campus and discuss the program as well as his or her background and career goals with an M.B.A. adviser. Each applicant should possess a baccalaureate degree from an accredited college or university and should submit a completed application form, an official undergraduate transcript, and an official report of score achieved on the Graduate Management Admission Test (GMAT).

EXPENSES
Application fee. . . . . $ 20
Tuition, per credit hour 192

PLACEMENT
La Salle has an active Placement Office with an established reputation in the Delaware Valley area. The office provides a variety of employment-related services including counseling in career choice, resume writing, and job interviewing techniques in addition to placement interviews. Over 100 firms conduct campus interviews each year.

CORRESPONDENCE
For further information, please call or write
M.B.A. Program Director
M.B.A. Program
La Salle College
Philadelphia, Pennsylvania 19141
Telephone: 215-951-1057

LEHIGH UNIVERSITY

BETHLEHEM, PENNSYLVANIA

Situated on an attractive wooded campus, Lehigh is a private university with an enrollment of 6,200, of whom approximately 2,000 are graduate students. Bethlehem, Pennsylvania, is a heterogeneous community of some 80,000 people located 90 miles west of New York City, 60 miles north of Philadelphia, and 35 miles south of the Pocono Mountains, a summer and winter resort area. Most graduate students live off campus in apartments or rooms. Inquiries on the limited number of university apartments should be directed to Residence Operations, Rathbone Hall #63.

The student body of the College of Business and Economics consists of approximately 840 undergraduate and 400 graduate students. The graduate students include 360 M.B.A. students (60 are full-time and 300 are part-time), 15 M.A. or M.S. students, and 25 doctoral students.

The profile of a recent M.B.A. class is as follows: male, 67 percent; female, 33 percent; Graduate Management Admission Test (GMAT) mean score 540; undergraduate cumulative average, 3.1; undergraduate majors—business and economics, 48 percent, engineering and physical sciences, 31 percent, arts and science, 15 percent, other, 6 percent; married, 52 percent; single, 48 percent; average age of full-time students, 24 years; 90 percent of students were from New Jersey, New York, or Pennsylvania, 5 percent from other states, and 5 percent from foreign countries.

The College of Business and Economics is housed in Drown Hall, which is centrally located on the Lehigh campus. The college has three academic departments: Accounting and Law, Economics, and Management, Finance and Marketing. The undergraduate and graduate business programs have been accredited by the American Assembly of Collegiate Schools of Business (AACSB).

The library's policy of open access to its general collection furnishes Lehigh students with maximum opportunity to explore the literature in their field of study. Gothic-styled Linderman Library contains approximately 850,000 volumes in the humanities and social sciences, including business and economics. Computing facilities are excellent and include the Arthur Andersen & Co. Computing Laboratory in which there are 16 remote terminals and two on-line printers connected to Lehigh's Computing Center. The laboratory, located in Drown Hall, is open 75 hours per week.

PROGRAMS OF STUDY

The M.B.A. program is designed to give candidates conceptual, analytical, and operational knowledge of decision-making processes in the management of human and physical resources. It seeks to promote the self-development of current and potential managers for business, industry, government, and not-for-profit organizations. The program is designed for men and women who hold baccalaureate degrees in a wide range of disciplines as well as in business and economics. The degree can normally be completed in one to two academic years for full-time students and three to four years for part-time students.

The M.A. and M.S. degrees are offered to students interested in pursuing graduate work in economics or in economics and business. A minimum of 30 semester hours of course work is required. The M.S. degree emphasizes development of statistical and quantitative skills.

The M.S. in management science program is directed toward integrating the scientific method with the functional aspects of organizations by investigating the application of quantitative methodology and systems analysis in the context of such areas as accounting, finance, marketing, production, and public service. A minimum of 30 semester hours of course work is required.

The Ph.D. program is designed to nurture intellectual growth so that the student may independently pursue personal and professional goals in teaching and/or research.

ADMISSION

Broad admission standards, but not strict cutoff points, are B− or above cumulative undergraduate average, B or above in senior year, 500 or above score on the Graduate Management Admission Test (GMAT), and a review of letters of recommendation, work experience, and a written statement indicating the candidate's educational career objectives. Approximately 60 percent of applicants are accepted. Candidates may be admitted to commence study in August, January, May, or July; August is the preferred starting date.

EXPENSES

Full-time students paid $9,550 in tuition for the academic year starting in September 1985. Part-time students taking less than 12 semester hours paid $400 per semester credit hour. An increase of approximately $1,000 per year for full-time students should be anticipated. Other living costs for a single person are estimated at $5,000-$5,600 for the academic year.

FINANCIAL ASSISTANCE

Fifteen teaching or graduate assistants are appointed each year. These half-time appointments will carry an estimated stipend of $6,700-$6,900 for the academic year in addition to tuition allowance. A limited number of scholarships (tax-free) and fellowships are available at the college and university levels. Unionbank Research Fellows are selected by individual faculty members to work on faculty research projects at the rate of $6 per hour. Tuition loans may also be obtained through the financial aid office. The deadline for filing financial aid applications is February 1.

PLACEMENT

Normally, representatives of some 300 companies of all descriptions interview undergraduate and graduate students. The average starting salaries for full-time M.B.A. graduates in 1985 was $28,500. A 1976 study by Standard and Poor's ranked Lehigh as an institution fifth in the country in the portion of its alumni who are officers or directors of corporations.

CORRESPONDENCE

For further information, please write or call

Graduate Admissions Office
Whitaker Laboratory #5
Lehigh University
Bethlehem, Pennsylvania 18015
Telephone: 215-861-4500

The Lewis University Graduate School of Management serves 600 students from the Chicago metropolitan area through programs at Oak Brook and Romeoville and extension classes at four suburban locations (Orland Park, Schaumburg, Naperville, and Oglesby, Illinois.)

Lewis University was founded over 50 years ago to serve the higher educational needs of the Chicago metropolitan area. The university is a private, coeducational school located 30 miles southwest of downtown Chicago within the greater metropolitan area. Over 3,000 students, many of whom are adults, are pursuing degrees in 33 undergraduate and 4 graduate programs.

The Master of Business Administration (M.B.A.) program has grown in prominence due to its carefully designed curriculum and excellent teaching. What has been characteristic of the school is the close personal relationship between faculty and students and the careful balance maintained between theory and application. Courses are offered both evenings and Saturdays to facilitate the needs of the working adult student.

PROGRAM OF STUDY

The M.B.A. is an advanced professional degree in management designed to prepare students professionally for responsible careers as generalist managers. The breadth of instructional material presented through class lecture, seminars, and case analysis provides the prospective graduate with a diversification of administrative competencies which can be applied in public, private, or nonprofit organizations. The program is open to those who have a bachelor's degree in either business or nonbusiness subject areas. The curriculum is composed of four phases consisting of 36 to 54 semester hours. Generally, students with a baccalaureate in business administration will begin at the phase II level. All other degree-track M.B.A. candidates will have their records evaluated for successful completion of phase I course equivalents from previously attended colleges or universities. Students will be required to maintain a 3.0 average based on a 4-point system.

Phase I (Foundation)   *Semester Hours*
ACCT. 501: Survey of Accounting. . . . 3
ECON. 502: Business Economics. 3
MGSC. 504: Quantitative Methods
   and Statistical Influence 3
MGSC. 506: Information Systems
   and Data Processing 3
BSAD. 508: Administrative Theory . . . 3

BSAD. 510: Survey of Marketing 3
FIN. 512: Financing the Business
   Enterprise 3

Phase II (Core)
ECON. 554: Managerial Economics . . 3
ACCT. 550: Managerial Accounting . . 3
BSAD. 611: Effective Business
   Communications 3
BSAD. 568: Marketing Policies and
   Problems. 3
BSAD. 620: Business Policy 3
BSAD. 601: Legal and Social
   Foundations for Business 3
FIN. 652: Managerial Finance 3

Phase III (Functional Area Courses) 9 credit hours—Finance, Human Resources, Marketing, Operations Management.

Phase IV (Elective Courses) 6 credit hours—Elective courses or M.B.A. Executive Seminars fulfill this requirement.

ADMISSION

Admission to the degree program is granted to graduates of regionally or nationally accredited colleges and universities who show high promise of success in graduate business study. Criteria used for admission include the candidate's performance on the Graduate Management Admission Test (GMAT), undergraduate grades, letters of recommendation, and seriousness of intent for graduate studies.

Students can also be admitted on an at-large basis. They must have had a cumulative undergraduate grade-point average of at least 2.7 on a 4.0 scale. Applicants whose native language is not English are required to submit a score on the Test of English as a Foreign Language (TOEFL).

Qualified candidates may enter the program at the beginning of any semester.

EXPENSES

Tuition for M.B.A. students is $176 per credit hour.

FINANCIAL ASSISTANCE

A limited amount of financial assistance is awarded in the form of scholarships, loans, V.A. benefits, graduate assistantships, and work/study arrangements. The majority of current students are employed by businesses and industries within commuting distance of the university. These students generally receive financial aid through their companies.

PLACEMENT

The university maintains an active placement office. Services of the placement office are available to students and graduates. Requests for personnel are received from all types of businesses, financial institutions, and government agencies. Numerous employer representatives come to the campus for interviews.

CORRESPONDENCE

For further information, please write or call
   Director
   Graduate School of Management
   Lewis University
   Romeoville, Illinois 60441
   Telephone: 815-838-0500, extension 381
            312-242-0015, extension 381

LOMA LINDA UNIVERSITY

RIVERSIDE, CALIFORNIA

Loma Linda University is a Seventh-day Adventist institution located in inland southern California, with a strong international flavor. Though the primary emphasis is on medicine and health-related sciences, business training constitutes the second largest program. The university's graduate program is intended to provide practical and theoretical knowledge to its students that would prepare them to assume leadership roles in business and nonprofit institutions worldwide. Accordingly, the university aims to provide education that is comprehensive and integrative, including for every student (1) a mature understanding of oneself as a person in relation to God and to other persons; (2) an awareness and appreciation of the nature of ultimate reality, of the created universe, and of human existence; (3) a mastery of the basic knowledge and skills necessary for professional success or for advanced study in a particular discipline or vocation; (4) a commitment to personal integrity and generous service; (5) an attitude of continuing curiosity and inquiry, and a sense of the excitement of discovery; and (6) a life-style that facilitates the maximum usefulness of a person's abilities. The teaching approach combines lectures, case studies, computer simulations, and individual research projects. Small classes assure the student constant interaction with the faculty and give plenty of opportunity for exchange among the students.

PROGRAM OF STUDY

The Master of Business Administration (M.B.A.) program is intended for persons pursuing administrative careers. It is designed to enhance and develop the knowledge and skills of those interested in nonprofit as well as commercial organizations. Three areas of concentration are provided: marketing, human resources, and financial management. Each area of concentration consists of three courses (12 quarter units) in addition to core courses. All students in the M.B.A. program complete one graduate-level course in religion.

ADMISSION

Intellectual capacity and ability appropriate to admission are judged from transcripts, record of experience, recommendations, and the applicant's score on the Graduate Management Admission Test (GMAT). Admission is considered on the basis of (1) either a grade-point average (GPA) of 2.75 (on a 4.0 scale) and a GMAT score of 500 or better; or a combination of GPA or GMAT of 1,100 or better, calculated as GPA × 200 + GMAT; (2) acceptable academic, employer, and character recommendations; possession of a baccalaureate degree from an accredited college or university; and, for applicants whose native language is other than English, a score of 92 or above on the Michigan Test of English Language Proficiency (MTELP).

EXPENSES

Costs are estimated for the 1985-86 academic year. Tuition and fee assessments are subject to change without notice.

Tuition and fees	
($172 per unit)	$ 6,150
Room and board	3,771
Books and supplies	360
Personal expenses	1,134
Transportation	675
Total	$12,090

Students will incur additional tuition, living expenses, etc. for the summer session.

FINANCIAL ASSISTANCE

University fellowships are awarded annually to students of outstanding performance and promise. University fellowships carry stipends and remission of tuition. Partial- or full-tuition waivers are recommended by program chairmen and coordinators for students of demonstrated achievement.

PLACEMENT

A placement director and the senior faculty work with the students to identify employment opportunities. Nearly 100 firms conduct on-campus interviews of Loma Linda University students annually. Graduates are employed throughout the United States and abroad.

CORRESPONDENCE

For further information or to request an application for admission, please write or call

Dr. Ignatius Yacoub, Chairman
Department of Business and Economics
Loma Linda University
Riverside, California 92515-8247
Telephone: 714-785-2060

LONDON BUSINESS SCHOOL

LONDON, ENGLAND

The London Business School is an autonomous institution within the framework of the University of London. The formal title is the London Graduate School of Business Studies. The school offers programs leading to the University of London master's and Ph.D. degrees and a wide range of postexperience courses for executives, including a nine-month Sloan Fellowship Program. The school is located in magnificent Nash Terrace overlooking Regent's Park in central London and combines an original classical facade with modern facilities.

PROGRAMS OF STUDY

The master's program is offered on both a full-time (21 months) and a part-time (3 years) basis. It is a general management program and is equivalent to two-year M.B.A. programs from leading schools in the United States. Approximately 100 full-time and 60 part-time master's students are accepted each year. The program consists of core courses that focus on the disciplines and language of management and cover the concepts and tools used in the main functional activities of organizations. The core courses are built on by a wide range of elective courses that offer the opportunity to explore areas of particular interest in greater detail and allow for some specialization. Approximately 50 elective courses are offered during the program. Project work forms an integral part of the program for all students. Full-time students undertake projects sponsored by external clients in both their first and second year of the program. This experience provides students with excellent opportunities for working in a different area or type of organization than they have previously experienced and can be of great help to participants in testing out and clarifying their future employment intentions. Part-time students undertake two major group projects during the program, one based in the United Kingdom (U.K.) and one overseas.

The program reflects the international nature of the school, not only in the courses offered, but in the mix of participants. In addition, a number of students are able to spend one term studying at an overseas business school, and exchange arrangements exist with business schools in the U.S.A., Canada, and Continental Europe.

Each student is graded individually for the courses taken throughout the program, and progress can be monitored on a regular basis. The award of the master's degree is based on an overall assessment of the grades achieved during the program, together with the marks from the final examination, which consists of four written papers.

The Ph.D. program is intended for those wishing to engage in research in the field of business studies. To obtain their doctorate, candidates must demonstrate competence and basic knowledge both in the functional areas of business and their chosen field of concentration. The thesis must be in some area related to the theory and practice of management. The program is full time.

The London Sloan Fellowship Program is an intensive nine-month general management and career development program for experienced people, typically in their mid-thirties, who are in the process of making a major career advance.

ADMISSION

The minimum academic qualification for admission to the master's program is an honors degree in any subject from a recognized university or an equivalent professional qualification. In addition, candidates would normally be expected to have at least three years practical managerial or professional work experience. In selecting students, particular attention is paid to intellectual ability and general fitness to pursue a successful career in management. Those wishing to apply for admission must complete the standard application form, provide two references, and obtain a satisfactory score on the Graduate Management Admission Test (GMAT). Those short-listed will be interviewed.

EXPENSES

For those attending the full-time option who do not qualify as ordinarily resident in the U.K. or European Economic Community (E.E.C.), tuition fees for the academic year 1985-86 were £4,500. For U.K. and E.E.C. residents the fees were £1,600 for 1985-86. For the part-time option, the fees were £1,400 per year.

Additional expenditure for those attending the full-time option, including expenses, accommodation, board and books is likely to amount to about £3,800 per year, or less than £3,300 for those occupying low-cost accommodations at the school.

FINANCIAL ASSISTANCE

All United Kingdom residents on the full-time option are eligible to apply for U.K. government funding and for low-interest bank loans. The London Business School also has a limited number of scholarships available to full-time students. There are no grants or scholarships currently available to part-time students, but low-interest bank loans may be available to cover tuition fees.

PLACEMENT

Career advice and counseling is provided for full-time students. The school has its own appointments' officer and is in close touch with over 1,000 British and foreign companies about the employment of graduates.

CORRESPONDENCE

To obtain a program brochure, please write to the Registrar of the appropriate program at
  The London Business School
  Sussex Place
  Regent's Park
  London NWI 4SA
  England

Founded in 1975, and celebrating its 10th anniversary year, the Westchester Campus is one of six regional campuses of Long Island University (LIU). Housed at the Mercy College campus in Dobbs Ferry, New York, and conveniently located on Route 9, LIU/Westchester offers ample parking and a pleasant environment, including excellent recreational and library facilities, as well as a panoramic view of the Hudson River. The location is convenient to Connecticut and Westchester residents and accessible to public transportation. One thousand students attend LIU/Westchester.

A basic philosophy of the graduate program leading to the Master of Business Administration degree is to provide an insight into the broadest spectrum of administrative activity, in the expectation that graduates will be generalists in the field of administration rather than specialists in specific functional areas. The program aims to facilitate the student's development as an executive in the public or private sector; to emphasize the understanding of enterprise as a whole, not a series of separate functions; to stress basic concepts and methods of thinking rather than limited functional training; and to lay a firm foundation for life-long learning, essential to successful leadership. The faculty consists of professionals currently working in their respective fields. The program is scheduled on a trimester plan.

The university is accredited by the Middle States Association of Colleges and Schools, is a member of the College Board, the Association of American Colleges, and the Middle Atlantic Association of Colleges of Business Administration. Graduate and professional accrediting agencies recognize the university's degrees.

PROGRAMS OF STUDY

Students may pursue the Master of Business Administration (M.B.A.) program; the M.B.A.-C.P.A. preparation program; joint degree programs in M.B.A./Master of Science in community health, M.B.A./Master of Science in pharmaceutical administration; and a graduate business certificate program. For Master of Business Administration graduates, LIU provides the opportunity to acquire new skills or to expand their current expertise in a specific area of business through the Post Master's Certificate in Business Administration.

The M.B.A. program requires between 33 and 57 credit hours of work, depending upon the student's prior preparation. Eight introductory core courses provide a foundation for candidates who have not pursued an undergraduate business concentration. These courses are waived according to the prior academic preparation. Students choose five out of a possible nine courses in advanced core preparation in computers, economics, management, finance, quantitative methods, and government and business. Finally, four courses of advanced graduate course work are required in the form of a concentration. Students may concentrate in one of the following areas: marketing, management, computer science, international business, accounting/taxation/law, or quantitative analysis. An innovative selection of capstone courses and a seminar complete the M.B.A. program; students may choose to pursue a thesis seminar, independent study, or venture capital game. The program can be completed in two years on a full-time basis or three to five years part-time.

ADMISSION

Graduates who hold a baccalaureate degree from an accredited college or university, have above average grade-point averages, and acceptable scores on the Graduate Management Admission Test (GMAT) are eligible to apply for admission. A background in business is not required, and students with liberal arts, engineering, natural science, social science, or educational backgrounds are welcome to apply. In deciding upon an application, the Admissions Committee considers occupational history, career goals, educational attainments, letters of recommendation, and GMAT score. Admission occurs for each trimester. Interviews are encouraged.

EXPENSES

Tuition is $190 per credit hour. In addition, there is a $20 application fee. Students may pursue their degree either on a full- or part-time basis. The courses are offered on a trimester basis, in the evening, and on the weekend, for the convenience of the working person.

FINANCIAL ASSISTANCE

A number of assistantships and scholarships, financed by the university, are offered to outstanding candidates. In addition, government assistance and loans are available.

PLACEMENT

Career Planning offices at Mercy College and at LIU's Brooklyn campus are available to students and graduates to assist in formulating and implementing career plans. Because classes are kept small, faculty are often very helpful in assisting students to develop plans and contacts.

CORRESPONDENCE

For further information or to request an application for admission, write or call

Office of Graduate Admissions
Long Island University
Westchester Campus at Mercy College
555 Broadway
Dobbs Ferry, New York 10522
Telephone: 914-693-8206
   (direct line, 24 hours)

LOUISIANA STATE UNIVERSITY IN BATON ROUGE
BATON ROUGE, LOUISIANA

Louisiana State University, founded in 1860, is the major public institution of higher learning in Louisiana. Located in Baton Rouge, a petrochemical, business, and trade center of 350,000 people, the campus enrolls close to 30,000 students. The university is coeducational and offers master's degrees in 75 fields and doctoral degrees in 45 major fields as well as a complete undergraduate program.

The College of Business Administration, Baton Rouge campus, is internationally recognized as one of the outstanding schools of business. It was organized in 1928 and in 1931 its undergraduate program was accredited by the American Assembly of Collegiate Schools of Business (AACSB). In 1963, its Master of Business Administration (M.B.A.) program was among the first to be accredited by the AACSB. The graduate programs of the college currently enroll approximately 500 students.

The university operates on the semester system with a nine-week summer semester. Admission to the M.B.A. program occurs only in fall semester; students may enter all other programs in any semester. Graduate students may attend full time or part time, and some evening courses are available.

PROGRAMS OF STUDY
In addition to the college-wide M.B.A. program, the departments of accounting, economics, finance, management, marketing, and quantitative business analysis offer curricula leading to the Master of Science (M.S.). The department of Economics offers a program leading to the Master of Arts degree. The college also sponsors a joint program in conjunction with the department of Political Science leading to the Master of Public Administration (M.P.A.) degree.

The M.B.A. program is specially designed to provide professional graduate education in business administration for those who have completed their undergraduate degrees in arts and sciences or in specializations such as engineering, geology, chemistry, physics, and agriculture, as well as students with degrees in business administration.

New developments in business education in the areas of management information systems, organization theory, quantitative methods, and the behavioral sciences are incorporated into the program. A degree of specialization is possible through concentrating electives. Normal program length is 54 semester hours; up to 6 hours may be waived on the basis of previous course work taken at AACSB-accredited institutions. Students without undergraduate degrees in business may be required to take up to 9 hours of pre-program course work prior to admission.

M.S. programs are offered in accounting, economics, finance, management, marketing, and quantitative business analysis. Both thesis (30 semester hours) and nonthesis (36 hours) options are available. Students without educational backgrounds in business administration must also complete studies in the common body of knowledge in business administration.

The college offers three doctoral programs. A Ph.D. in business administration program is offered jointly by the departments of finance, management, marketing, and quantitative methods. Doctor of Philosophy programs are offered in economics and in accounting. Specific requirements for each of the doctoral programs will be supplied upon written request.

ADMISSION
Admission information for all graduate programs may be obtained by writing to the Associate Dean for Graduate Studies. In general, admission to master's programs requires a minimal 3.00 grade-point average and a score above 500 on the Graduate Management Admission Test (GMAT). Admission to the doctoral program is normally limited to students whose records indicate the highest academic achievement and strong capacity for graduate study. All applicants should take the GMAT prior to submitting the admission application. Foreign students must submit scores from the Test of English as a Foreign Language (TOEFL) above 550 to be considered for admission.

EXPENSES
Current tuition and fees for full-time graduate students who are Louisiana residents total $630 per semester. Non-residents pay an additional $1,000 per semester. Summer session fees are proportionally lower. Costs of food and housing on or off campus are moderate. Students are not required to live on campus. Additional housing information may be secured from the Director of Housing.

FINANCIAL ASSISTANCE
The Office of Graduate Studies annually awards a large number of graduate assistantships to new M.B.A. students with high academic promise. In addition, a number of graduate assistantships are available to students in all departments. Graduate assistants are exempted from the nonresident tuition fee and certain other fees. Thirty Alumni Foundation Fellowships are awarded annually to outstanding Ph.D. students; these fellowships carry an annual stipend of $10,000 and are renewable up to four years. Information on assistantships and doctoral fellowships may be obtained by writing to the Office of Graduate Studies.

The university also has available a large number of federal and state, private, and L.S.U. loan funds. These funds and other part-time work available will make it possible for any worthy student to attend the university regardless of his or her financial circumstances. Loan applications should be sent to the Student Aid Office.

PLACEMENT
The departments of business and engineering jointly operate a placement service. The student is assured of assistance in finding the very best job opportunity available in industry, business, or teaching. Many national firms interview on campus.

CORRESPONDENCE
For information, write to
Associate Dean for Graduate Studies
College of Business Administration
Louisiana State University in
Baton Rouge
Baton Rouge, Louisiana 70803
Telephone: 504-388-8867

Louisiana State University in Shreveport (LSUS) initiated classes in 1967 as a separate campus within the Louisiana State University System, and enrollment has continually expanded since that time. The College of Business Administration, in which the Master of Business Administration (M.B.A.) program is housed, has over 1,300 students. A new building to house the college was completed during the 1980-81 academic year. Being located in an urban area that has a very diversified base, the college offers many opportunities to the graduates of the M.B.A. program and attracts a conscientious M.B.A. student body who have varied backgrounds and experiences. Over 35 percent of the M.B.A. students have undergraduate degrees from institutions outside Louisiana, and over 60 percent have an undergraduate degree in a nonbusiness discipline.

The M.B.A. program concentrates on the decision-making processes and their impacts as a means of exposing students to the responsibilities encountered by top-level management. Since a high proportion of the M.B.A. students are employed full time in career-oriented positions, there is ample attention given to current management practices and issues.

PROGRAM OF STUDY
The M.B.A. program is designed to prepare men and women for top-level managerial positions and for the responsibilities related to those positions. Approximately 40 percent of the M.B.A. students at LSUS are women.

The M.B.A. program consists of the foundation course component and the graduate course component. The foundation component must be completed by students who possess an undergraduate degree in a nonbusiness discipline. For students having an undergraduate degree from an accredited college of business, the graduate component may be completed in one calendar year if no additional foundation course work is needed.

The foundation component of the M.B.A. program consists of 30 semester credit hours in such courses as accounting, business statistics, micro- and macroeconomics, organization theory and behavior, business finance, principles of marketing, and the legal environment of business. The graduate component of the M.B.A. program consists of 33 semester credit hours that encompass course work in each of the major disciplinary areas in business administration. Of the total graduate-level requirement, 24 credit hours are required courses and 9 credit hours are elective courses. Both the foundation and graduate components of the M.B.A. program are designed to expose the student to the various business disciplines and to interrelationships among those disciplines. The M.B.A. program is structured to allow the student to earn credit in a variety of courses covering several of the disciplines in business.

The M.B.A. program requires no thesis as the research element of the program is incorporated into the required course work. A full complement of courses is scheduled each semester to accommodate both the full-time and part-time students in day and evening classes. All graduate-level course work is offered exclusively in the evening program.

ADMISSION
Admission to the M.B.A. program is based on the student's score on the Graduate Management Admission Test (GMAT) and undergraduate grade-point average. Students must submit a completed application for admission to graduate study and two official copies of undergraduate transcripts to the LSUS Office of Admissions in the semester prior to the semester of entry. All students must submit a score on the GMAT and meet all other requirements for unconditional admission prior to the semester in which they take their first course work for graduate credit. International students must submit scores of at least 550 on the Test of English as a Foreign Language (TOEFL) and 450 on the Graduate Management Admission Test (GMAT) to be considered for admission. An international applicant must submit a completed application and data sheet, a $10 nonrefundable application fee, and all required records at least 90 days prior to his or her anticipated registration date. An international student must submit a signed financial statement showing the sources and amount of money in U.S. dollars available for each year of study in the United States. A student who has attended institutions outside the United States should submit completed academic reports translated into English and certified as true and correct copies.

EXPENSES
Approximate expenses for the 1985-86 academic year (two semesters and summer term):

	Full-time Students	Part-time Students
Tuition (Louisiana residents)	$1,225	$ 800
Tuition (out-of-state residents)	2,760	1,525
Books and supplies	300	200
Total (Louisiana residents)	$1,525	$1,000
Total (out-of-state residents)	$3,060	$1,725

There is no on-campus housing available at Louisiana State University in Shreveport.

FINANCIAL ASSISTANCE
The financial aid program of the university includes elements of most loan programs and other forms of financial aid. Inquiries about financial aid should be addressed to Financial Aid Office, LSUS, 8515 Youree Drive, Shreveport, Louisiana 71115.

PLACEMENT
The university maintains an active program for the placement of its graduates through an organized Placement Office. Students may also make use of that office's services in locating part-time employment opportunities.

CORRESPONDENCE
For additional information concerning the M.B.A. program at Louisiana State University, please write
Office of the Dean
College of Business Administration
Louisiana State University in Shreveport
8515 Youree Drive
Shreveport, Louisiana 71115
Telephone: 318-797-5383

LOUISIANA TECH UNIVERSITY

RUSTON, LOUISIANA

Louisiana Tech University, founded in 1894, has an enrollment of approximately 10,700. Located at Ruston among the rolling hills of north Louisiana, it is favored with a mild climate and is accessible to the larger cities of Shreveport and Monroe via Interstate 20.

The undergraduate and master's programs offered by the College of Administration and Business are accredited by the American Assembly of Collegiate Schools of Business (AACSB). The college offers the Master of Business Administration (M.B.A.), the Doctor of Business Administration (D.B.A.), and the Master of Professional Accountancy (M.P.A.) degrees. The college operates on a quarter calendar. Students may enter the M.B.A., D.B.A., and M.P.A. programs at the beginning of any quarter. Applications should be received two weeks prior to the opening of the quarter. Scores on the Graduate Management Admission Test (GMAT) are required of all applicants for graduate admission.

PROGRAMS OF STUDY

In a rapidly changing business society there is an expanding need for professional training in business at the graduate level. A principal purpose of the graduate programs in business and/or economics at Louisiana Tech University is to provide the professional training that will benefit those individuals who seek responsible positions in business, government, or educational institutions.

The M.B.A. program provides the student with training in management and administration, as well as the opportunity to specialize in one of several subject areas. The specialties available are accounting, business education, economics, finance, management, marketing, and quantitative analysis. Those students who do not specialize take 12 elective hours (see below) in any of the areas of specialization. The degree program may be built on a bachelor's degree in business or on a bachelor's degree in other areas such as engineering, arts, and sciences. Time required for completion will vary from one to two years, depending on the amount of work in certain business subjects included in the academic background.

The M.B.A. program comprises 33 semester hours, including 12 hours of electives in the area of specialization. The three-credit core courses required of everyone are accounting analysis for decision making, administrative policy, directed research and readings, introduction to management science, financial management, marketing management, and managerial economics.

The Doctor of Business Administration degree program is intended for unusually qualified students who are interested in careers in university teaching and research, or in high-level staff positions in business or government. The program requires the development of a major and two minor fields, and a research dissertation.

The M.P.A. program is designed to prepare accountants so that they may begin professional careers with a minimum of on-the-job training, may more readily pass the C.P.A. examination, and may hold responsible accounting and management positions.

ADMISSION

For the M.B.A. and M.P.A. programs, any person who holds a bachelor's degree from an accredited college or university may be considered for admission regardless of the undergraduate field of study. Each applicant's complete set of credentials, including grade-point average, trend of grades, score on the GMAT, and, if available, rank in graduating class, is used in making admissions decisions.

Doctoral applications for admission will be reviewed by the Doctoral Admissions Committee. Specific criteria considered are scores on the GMAT, undergraduate and graduate grades, letters of recommendation, oral interview, and other items comprising the overall application. Additionally, international students must submit a satisfactory score on the Test of English as a Foreign Language (TOEFL) and provide a financial statement.

EXPENSES

For full-time graduate students, tuition and fees total approximately $382 per quarter. The nonresident pays an additional tuition charge. Housing and food both on and off campus are considered to be relatively inexpensive.

FINANCIAL ASSISTANCE

Financial aid exists in the form of loans, graduate assistantships, part-time instructorships, and miscellaneous part-time jobs on the campus. A limited number of graduate assistantships are available each year to students of high academic accomplishment. The stipend for graduate assistants is normally $4,000 per year. The graduate student who holds an assistantship is expected to carry a reduced classwork load that will vary depending on the individual's scholastic record and the amount of work required by the assistantship. Teaching assistantships are awarded mainly to doctoral students. Salaries paid for these part-time assignments normally amount to $5,800. Loans are available through the Student Financial Aid Program and the National Direct Student Loan Program.

PLACEMENT

The university maintains an excellent placement bureau. The services of the bureau are available to students on campus and to graduates seeking new positions. Requests for personnel are received from all types of businesses, financial institutions, government agencies, and educational institutions. Numerous employer representatives come to the campus for interviews.

CORRESPONDENCE

For further information on the graduate programs in business offered at Louisiana Tech, write or call

Director of the Graduate Division
College of Administration and Business
Box 10318
Louisiana Tech University
Ruston, Louisiana 71272
Telephone: 318-257-4528

Loyola College's graduate business programs provide training in the analytical and quantitative skills necessary for success in business. Ninety-five percent of its 900 graduate students in business maintain their employment while pursuing study, and the college regards the professional character of its student body as a great asset. Founded in 1852, Loyola began its M.B.A. program in 1967, and its executive M.B.A. program in 1973. The college is accredited by the Middle States Association of Colleges and Secondary Schools and is a member of the American Assembly of Collegiate Schools of Business (AACSB).

PROGRAMS OF STUDY
Loyola offers the Master of Business Administration (M.B.A.), the Master of Science in Finance (M.S.F.), and the Master of Professional Accountancy (M.P.A.) for both full-time and part-time students. Courses are offered at the college's centers in the Baltimore suburbs of Columbia and Hunt Valley as well as at the main campus. Classes meet in the late afternoons and evenings on Monday through Thursday.

The M.B.A. program at Loyola gives a broad education in management problems and analytical methods. Concentrations are available in accounting, economics, finance, management, decision science, and marketing. The course of study for the M.B.A. degree is 10 courses (30 credits); students take 8 core courses and 2 concentration courses. The program stresses applications and utilizes a variety of teaching methods including case method, lecture and discussion, and the experiential approach.

The programs of study in the M.S.F. and M.P.A. are more specialized than the M.B.A., with core courses and electives in finance and accounting, respectively. Both programs require 10 graduate-level courses. The M.P.A. program prepares nonaccountants to work in the field and allows practicing accountants to strengthen their background. The M.P.A. program meets the Maryland requirement for taking the C.P.A. exam.

In addition to the 10 courses for each of these graduate business programs (30 credits), foundation courses comparable to the professional core in the undergraduate curriculum of the School of Business and Management are available. All or some of these courses may be waived for students who present evidence of satisfactory equivalent preparation. Courses for which waivers are not granted may be completed subsequent to admission into the graduate program in not more than 10 courses.

For those with significant work experience and responsibility, Loyola offers an executive M.B.A. program at its Baltimore and Columbia centers. This program has a limited enrollment and meets on alternate Fridays and Saturdays for two years, summer excepted. For emerging executives, Loyola offers a graduate fellows M.B.A. program. Fellows classes meet on Saturdays only, over three years, summer excepted. This program stresses preparation for advancement to positions of significant responsibility.

ADMISSION
An applicant to the graduate business programs must hold a bachelor's degree from an accredited institution. The admission decision is based primarily on Graduate Management Admission Test (GMAT) score, undergraduate record, and professional accomplishment. Most applicants have at least 500 on the GMAT and a 3.00 undergraduate grade-point average. For a recent entering class the average GMAT score was 530 and 3.24 the average grade-point average.

Applicants should submit the completed application, official transcripts of all previous college-level work, the GMAT results, and a personal essay detailing academic and professional experience. Admission is on a rolling basis; new graduate business students are admitted to all terms. All application materials should be sent to the Graduate Admission Office by July 20 for the fall session, December 20 for the spring session, and April 20 for the summer sessions. There is a $25 nonrefundable application fee.

EXPENSES
Tuition for the M.B.A., M.P.A. and M.S.F. programs is $160 per credit hour, and books average $40 per course. For the XMBA, tuition is $6,500 per year and covers all academic costs. Fellows tuition is $4,000 per year.

FINANCIAL ASSISTANCE
Graduate assistantships are available and should be applied for through the office of Graduate Programs in Management.

PLACEMENT
Students looking for employment can use the Placement Office (190 companies recruited on campus in 1984-85), and they may attend career seminars for M.B.A. students (business representatives participate and meet students informally). Many students find positions due to encounters with fellow students who are working professionals.

CORRESPONDENCE
For further information, write or call
  Dean
  Graduate Programs in Management
  Loyola College
  4501 North Charles Street
  Baltimore, Maryland 21210
  Telephone: 301-532-5067

Loyola Marymount University emerged from the merger of Loyola University of Los Angeles and Marymount College, which took place in 1973. The university has a student body of approximately 2,400 men and 2,200 women. Located in Westchester, about one-half mile from the Pacific Ocean, it enjoys a delightful, smog-free climate.

PROGRAMS OF STUDY

The university has two undergraduate programs in business administration: one leads to the Bachelor of Business Administration degree in the fields of management, marketing, industrial relations, production management, management science, and finance; the other to the Bachelor of Science in Accounting degree. Both undergraduate programs are full-time day programs. The university offers a Master of Business Administration (M.B.A.) program that holds evening classes only and is aimed at serving employed professionals in the southern California area.

The first year or core of the M.B.A. program consists of nine courses in the legal environment of business, management and organizational behavior, business economics, financial management, managerial accounting, statistics, marketing, operations analysis and strategy. The advanced curriculum or second year of the M.B.A. program avails the student the opportunity to major in one of seven areas of emphasis by taking three elective courses in that field. These areas of emphasis are management and organizational behavior, marketing management, information and decision sciences, human resource management, financial decision systems, international business systems, and entrepreneurship. Breadth is provided through five electives taken from three additional fields. An integrative elective provides a capstone learning experience. The methods of instruction lay heavy stress on lecture and discussion, case analysis, computer games, problem seeking and solving, readings, group study, and other methods designed to bring a positive transfer from the educational experience to the uncertainties of the real world. Particular emphasis is given to the manager's role in a world where scarcity of resources, allocations, and international political and governmental constraints loom large in planning and decision making.

ADMISSION

Admission to the M.B.A. program is open to qualified men and women who hold a bachelor's degree in any field or discipline. Criteria for acceptance are highly competitive and are aimed at determining the capability and potential capacity of the applicant as a manager. Primary consideration is given to undergraduate grade-point average and scores on the Graduate Management Admission Test (GMAT). Letters of recommendation are sometimes requested but are not weighted as heavily. All admitted candidates are encouraged to discuss their application with the Program Director who develops an individualized program of studies for each student. Students normally start in the fall semester but may also start in the spring. Full-credit courses are run in the summer, giving the student the opportunity to speed up his or her program or lighten his or her load during the regular academic year. It is possible for the very able and highly motivated student to complete the work for the M.B.A. in three years of evening classes. Students who have a recent bachelor's degree in business administration may have some, or even all, first-year courses waived, or may be given the opportunity to establish competence through examination.

Representative faculty in the M.B.A. program combine years of business or consulting experience with doctorates from the nation's leading Ph.D. and D.B.A. programs.

EXPENSES

Tuition in the M.B.A. program for the academic year 1985-86 was $723 per course. The student may elect to take one, two, three, or four courses.

Other expenses vary with individual needs and capabilities. All M.B.A. students pay a flat $25 per semester M.B.A. Student Association fee.

FINANCIAL ASSISTANCE

The university maintains an Office of Financial Aid with a full-time director and staff to assist those students who require financial aid to pursue their education at Loyola Marymount University. Scholarships, grants, loans, and campus employment exist. But since the assumption is that most graduate students will be employed full time, scholarship aid is available only in unusual circumstances.

CORRESPONDENCE

For further information, please write or call

Dr. H. Daniel Stage, Associate Dean
Graduate Program in Business
  Administration
College of Business Administration
Loyola Marymount University
Loyola Boulevard at West 80th Street
Los Angeles, California 90045
Telephone: 213-642-2848

Loyola University is a private, coeducational institution, founded in 1912 as a result of a merger of the College of Immaculate Conception, founded in 1849, and Loyola College, established in 1904. It is owned and operated by the Society of Jesus.

The campus is located in the university section of New Orleans, opposite Audubon Park, which is noted for its golf course and zoological park. Streetcar and bus service on both sides of the campus lead directly to the central city, with its cosmopolitan atmosphere and French Quarter. Swimming, fishing, and hunting are readily accessible. Professional sports are played in the new Superdome. The Sugar Bowl games and the Mardi Gras are also held in New Orleans.

The university is composed of the College of Business Administration, the College of Arts and Sciences, the City College, the College of Music, and the School of Law. Current enrollment is approximately 4,950, 250 of whom are Master of Business Administration (M.B.A.) students. The great majority of M.B.A. students attend part time. They have earned their baccalaureate degrees from institutions throughout the United States as well as from institutions in several foreign countries.

The College of Business Administration houses a modern computer laboratory linked to the university's Hewlett-Packard 3000 and VAX-11/750 computers. In addition, two microcomputer laboratories are located conveniently on campus. Loyola has tie-ins with other sophisticated computer facilities in the city. Students have access to the Loyola University library containing 250,000 volumes and to other nearby library facilities. Graduate students who are unable to commute may live in university housing or find rooms and apartments in the residential area surrounding the campus.

PROGRAMS OF STUDY

The College of Business Administration offers an evening program leading to the Master of Business Administration. The principal objective of the M.B.A. program is to prepare graduates for advancement to the high-level management positions in both the private and public sectors of the nation's economy.

Applicants holding degrees from institutions accredited by the American Assembly of Collegiate Schools of Business (AACSB) may usually enter directly into the 30-hour program of graduate work; all other students must complete courses from the required undergraduate business core curriculum. Credit will be granted for courses taken in any recognized baccalaureate degree program.

A Juris Doctor (J.D.)/M.B.A. program is also available. Designed for those students seeking advanced education in business administration in addition to an education in law, this program enables students to meet the requirements for both the Juris Doctor and Master of Business Administration degrees with a total of 102 semester credit hours. In order to be eligible for the J.D./M.B.A. program, students must have applied and been admitted to both the School of Law and the Master of Business Administration program at Loyola and must have completed all of the foundation course requirements for the M.B.A. program.

The graduate management programs are accredited by the AACSB.

ADMISSION

Admission to the M.B.A. program is based upon an undergraduate grade-point average of 2.5 or higher and an acceptable score (usually 450 or higher) on the Graduate Management Admission Test (GMAT). International students must also submit scores of 550 or higher on the Test of English as a Foreign Language (TOEFL) or provide certification of competence in the use of the English language.

EXPENSES

Tuition for graduate students is based on the number of semester hours taken. Current tuition is $182 per hour. Other university fees are also paid by graduate students. Students may live off campus or may apply for university housing. The latter is quite limited, and application should be made early in the year.

FINANCIAL ASSISTANCE

A limited amount of aid, mostly in the form of assistantships, is available for graduate study. Students interested in financial assistance should write directly to the Financial Aid Office, Box 206, Loyola University, New Orleans, Louisiana 70118.

CORRESPONDENCE

For further information, write or call
Graduate Coordinator
College of Business Administration
Loyola University
New Orleans, Louisiana 70118
Telephone: 504-865-2549

Loyola University, Chicago's oldest institution of higher learning, was founded in 1870. The Graduate School of Business is located at 820 North Michigan Avenue, near the John Hancock Building.

PROGRAM OF STUDY

The Graduate School of Business at Loyola provides professional education for executive positions through courses leading to the Master of Business Administration (M.B.A.) degree. Loyola places emphasis on basic disciplines and skills rather than specialized operational techniques, stressing the role of business in society and the responsibility of business leaders to society. A student equipped with the basic knowledge to deal effectively with the rapidly changing environment will find business a rewarding career.

The Graduate School of Business at Loyola is a program of study consisting of full- and part-time students. The faculty, curriculum, and administration of the school are geared exclusively to the M.B.A. degree. This specialization of study produces students with a professional, terminal degree in management skills. Over 950 students are currently enrolled. The school operates on the quarter system, with 10 weeks per quarter. Classes meet once each week of the quarter. Students may enter at the beginning of the autumn, winter, spring, or summer quarter.

The course requirements are as follows:
• Curriculum A for nonbusiness administration undergraduate majors consists of 16 courses.
GB 400 Accounting for Business
        Decisions
GB 401 Financial Analysis for Decision
        Making
GB 410 Psychology and Sociology for
        Business
GB 420 Managerial Economics
GB 421 Business Fluctuations
GB 430 Business Organization and
        Policies
GB 440 *or* GB 441 Public Policies toward
        Business *or* Social Responsibili-
        ties of Business
GB 450 Financial Management
GB 460 Marketing Management
GB 470 Management
GB 480 Operations Management and
        Management Science

GB 490 *or* GB 492 Mathematics for
        Management Computers and
        Systems
GB 491 Managerial Statistics

Three courses in field of specialization or three electives
• Curriculum B for business administration undergraduate major consists of 12 courses. Depending on the undergraduate major and courses taken, four of the following may be waived: GB 400, GB 420, GB 440 or GB 441, GB 450, GB 460, and GB 490.

The fields of specialization are accounting, financial management, marketing management, personnel management, production management, and quantitative methods and computers.

ADMISSION

All applicants to the M.B.A. program must possess a bachelor's degree from an accredited institution and must take the Graduate Management Admission Test (GMAT). There are no specific undergraduate course requirements; all students, regardless of undergraduate major, begin with graduate course work.

Students are admitted to the school as candidates for the degree of Master of Business Administration on the basis of interest, aptitude, and capacity for business study as indicated by previous academic record, scores on the GMAT, letters from faculty members and employers, and pertinent information from the student's application.

Advisers are available both day and evening to assist applicants and students in guidance, orientation, and program planning.

EXPENSES

The tuition for each course in the Graduate School of Business is $680. The University Housing Bureau maintains a file of available housing for both single and married graduate students. Information may be obtained from the Housing Office, Graduate Student Housing, 6525 North Sheridan, Chicago, Illinois 60626.

FINANCIAL ASSISTANCE

Scholarships, loans, a limited number of research assistantships, and a wide variety of part-time, professional employment opportunities are available.

PLACEMENT

Representatives of many companies, institutions, and government agencies visit the Placement Office each year. The demand for M.B.A. graduates for these opportunities continues to exceed the supply. The facilities are also available for alumni placement.

CORRESPONDENCE

For further information or to request an application for admission, write or call
    The Director of Admissions
    The Graduate School of Business
    Loyola University
    820 North Michigan Avenue
    Chicago, Illinois 60611
    Telephone: 312-670-3140

The graduate program in business administration was begun in 1967 with an objective to develop "line managers" by offering an area of concentration in management control based on the "case-study" method of instruction. The part-time program consists of 48 hours of course work in the area of management accounting, finance, economics, marketing, human relations, statistics, and business policy. The candidate may elect to do original research leading to a thesis, for which he or she will receive six hours of credit in lieu of six hours of course work.

PROGRAMS OF STUDY

The objective of the Master of Business Administration (M.B.A.) program is to develop practicing managers with a generalist viewpoint. The development of skills in problem solving, opportunity analysis, and communication to reach and execute effective management decisions is a major purpose of the program. In support of the objective, material is offered in each of the fundamental functional areas of business: marketing, accounting, finance and operations. These offerings are supported by background and technique courses in quantitative methods, economics, organizational behavior, legal environment, and analysis and communication. The integration of general management concepts is achieved through the use of cases and experiential exercises. The program culminates with a policy course that requires the student to draw upon and utilize the concepts and techniques acquired to address a variety of problems in a total business context.

The Master of Administration (M.Ad.) in industrial management is designed to prepare the student for administrative roles in the acquisition and utilization of the resources necessary to produce and deliver the products demanded by a firm's customers. The field deals with human, financial, and material resources. Study is oriented toward understanding the nature of each of the resources and the methodologies useful in its management. Topics studied include accounting principles, job costs, process costs, standard costs, capital budgets, expense budgets, production planning and control, inventory management, and other analytical techniques applicable to the management of production operations. The human dimension is carefully considered in topics dealing with motivation, direction, control and labor relations.

The Master of Administration (M.Ad.) in personnel management is a program designed to prepare the student to effectively fulfill the responsibilities of administration in numerous positions throughout a variety of enterprises. The role of personnel management has experienced a rapid rise in importance in recent years. The influences of the labor movement, legislation, court decisions, consumerism, and internationalism have increased the level of concentration on the problems of human resources in all forms of enterprise. This is reflected in the professional status of the personnel management function and in the administrative activities of other managerial functions. While the principal concentration of the program is personnel management, a skillful selection of electives can give the student added strength in a second function. The combination of courses required in this program will equip the student both theoretically and practically to meet the needs of administrative management in contemporary society.

ADMISSION

Applicants are not required to have an undergraduate degree in business management or accounting, and previous business-related courses are not required for admission to the programs. Applicants are required to hold a bachelor's degree from an institution accredited by a regional accrediting association, and an official transcript is required. The admission decision is based on the committee's evaluation of the following: previous academic work, letters of recommendation, and test scores. Applicants for the M.B.A. are required to take the Graduate Management Admission Test (GMAT), and M.Ad. applicants may submit either the GMAT or Graduate Record Examinations (GRE) scores. All international applicants must submit Test of English as a Foreign Language (TOEFL) scores and all application materials including appropriate test scores (GMAT or GRE) at least three months prior to the beginning of the term or semester for which admission is sought.

EXPENSES

Costs are estimated for the 1985-86 academic year. Tuition is based on cost per credit hour, and is subject to change without notice ($105 per hour.) Room and board for those students who may wish to live in the dormitories is $3,200 from September to May.

FINANCIAL ASSISTANCE

Financial aid is available to graduate students taking at least six credit hours per semester. Aid is limited generally to National Direct Student Loans, Guaranteed Student Loans, and College Work-Study placement opportunities. Resident assistantships are sometimes available for students desiring to serve in residence halls. Virginia residents enrolled in a graduate degree program on a full-time basis (nine credit hours per semester) are eligible to apply for the Virginia Tuition Assistance Grant program, which amounted to $1,000 for the 1985-86 academic year.

CORRESPONDENCE

For further information or to request an application for admission, please write or call

Dean Kamal M. Abouzeid
School of Business
Lynchburg College
Lynchburg, Virginia 24501
Telephone: 804-522-8257

The Madonna College Master of Science in Administration (M.S.A.) program prepares professionals for key management roles in private and public, profit and nonprofit organizations by focusing on the effective management of human and fiscal resources. Designed for the part-time student with a full-time work commitment, the program schedules courses in late afternoons and evenings and on weekends. Balancing theory and practical application, the program takes an issues management and future studies orientation, emphasizes ethical decision making, and maintains a strong research component. Graduates are prepared to accept the responsibilities of middle- and top-level management roles in such diverse contexts as business, industry, health care, human services, and government.

Located in the western perimeter of metropolitan Detroit, Madonna College draws on the business, educational, scientific, and cultural resources available in the Detroit-Ann Arbor areas. Primarily a commuter campus, the college provides ample free parking and easy access to major freeways and state highways.

PROGRAMS OF STUDY
The Master of Science in Administration (M.S.A.) program currently offers two specialties: business administration and nursing administration. Interdisciplinary in nature, the program entails 36 semester hours of course work, which includes a 15-semester-hour core in generic management courses. Beyond the core, students complete 21 semester hours in the specialty area, including 9 semester hours in research. Candidates for the M.S.A. are required to write and publish a master's thesis on an aspect of management in the student's career field.

The business administration students create an individual plan of study that builds on the management core. Options include course work in information systems, communications, finance, economics, and marketing. Students can also select short term workshop courses on specific topics such as strategic planning, product and service costing, international business, and SPSS-X programming.

Nursing administration students complement the management core with nursing theory and practice, along with course work in nursing administration and a practicum. This interdisciplinary approach provides the nurse administrator with the business background needed to effectively manage a nursing unit while also developing the student as a professional nurse.

ADMISSION
Madonna College welcomes applications from qualified individuals who seek professional education in management. Applicants need not possess an undergraduate degree in business or have completed business-related course work to be admitted to the program. Admission is granted three times per year, prior to the beginning of each semester: fall, winter, and spring/summer. The following admission materials must be submitted before the applicant's file is reviewed by the specialty department: completed application form, transcripts of prior academic work, test scores, and two letters of recommendation. Additionally, applicants are scheduled for an admission interview and the results are submitted to the admissions committee. Work experience, maturity, and motivation are major factors in determining the admissibility of applicants. All students granted regular admission to the program have had at least one year of full-time work experience.

Foreign students who are not native speakers of English are required to submit Test of English as a Foreign Language (TOEFL) scores. Nursing administration students must meet separate admissions criteria as determined by that specialty department.

EXPENSES
Tuition for 1985-86 was $120 per semester hour. A registration fee of $10 is charged each semester. A one-time thesis fee of $80 covers binding and publishing the master's thesis. The cost of books and supplies totals approximately $150-$250 per year for part-time students. Some courses carry special fees.

The college does not designate dormitory rooms for graduate students, but off-campus housing is available in the surrounding suburbs at reasonable rates.

FINANCIAL ASSISTANCE
Financial aid for graduate students is limited, for the most part, to loans and/or work. Some scholarships are available through external sources. All financial aid is coordinated through the Financial Aid Office.

PLACEMENT
Since most of the M.S.A. students are currently employed full time, a special placement program has not been developed for graduate students. Graduates may utilize the services of the Madonna College Career Resource Center, which conducts classes, maintains employer contacts, and provides students with information about job interviews.

CORRESPONDENCE
A graduate bulletin and application materials may be requested from
Director of Graduate Studies
Madonna College
36600 Schoolcraft Road
Livonia, Michigan 48150
Telephone: 313-591-5049

Maharishi International University (MIU) offers undergraduate, master's, and doctoral degree programs, including 13 undergraduate majors in art, biology, business administration, chemistry, computer science, education, electronic engineering, government, literature, mathematics, natural law, physics, and psychology; master's programs in business administration, education, higher education administration, computer science, professional writing, fine arts, and the science of creative intelligence; and doctoral programs in the neuroscience of human consciousness, psychology, physiology, and physics. MIU is accredited by the North Central Association of Colleges and Schools.

The speciality of the teaching procedure at MIU is that all the parts of knowledge are taught in terms of the wholeness of knowledge for that discipline, which in turn is connected to the pure intelligence of the student. Maharishi International University is the first university in the world to offer an integrated system of education that provides not only all the traditional knowledge of the physical sciences, social sciences, and humanities, but also the knowledge and experience of the Maharishi Technology of the Unified Field, which includes the Transcendental Meditation and TM-Sidhi program to help unfold the inner genius of every student.

The unified field, as recently glimpsed by modern physics and uncovered in Vedic Science, is the self-referral, infinitely dynamic, and self-sufficient source of creation from which nature organizes all activity in a completely automatic manner without mistakes. Through the Transcendental Meditation technique, the student directly experiences pure intelligence, which is found to be identical to the unified field, and through the TM-Sidhi program, a more advanced practice, the student learns to think and act from the level of the unified field. Therefore, as a student studies at MIU, he or she gains automatically in the total potential of nature law and begins to live a life in harmony with all the laws of nature, a life free from mistakes and problems. In this way, the unified field of the laws of nature, the fountainhead of all the organizing power of nature, becomes lively in the student.

PROGRAMS OF STUDY

The Department of Management and Public Affairs offers an undergraduate degree in business administration and in government and a full-time Master of Business Administration (M.B.A.) program. An executive M.B.A. program allows students to complete a master's degree in about two and a half years of weekend classes.

The M.B.A. program at MIU trains students for the highest level of corporate and entrepreneurial success with a full range of essential courses in such areas as marketing, finance, accounting, operations management, economics, management, decision science, policy, organization behavior, and informations systems. Elective specializations are offered in marketing, finance, management, management information systems, and public sector management. An elective concentration in accounting is also available. All courses are taught on the block system, with students taking just one course at a time in an executive-style atmosphere that combines lecture, case discussion, research, group projects, and consulting to produce an integrated and fulfilling learning experience.

Most importantly and uniquely, by utilizing the Maharishi Technology of the Unified Field, the M.B.A. program at MIU helps to develop in its students that supreme level of efficiency and organizing skill with which nature manages the infinitely diverse and complex universe. This is what enables students to perfect their administrative skill and excellence and what distinguishes the graduates of MIU from those of any other university in the world.

ADMISSION

Students wishing to enter the Master of Business Administration program are expected to have completed a four-year undergraduate program with a grade-point average of 3.0 or better and to place well on the Graduate Management Admission Test (GMAT). M.B.A. students are not required to have had prior business experience before entering the program.

For the undergraduate programs, MIU courses are open to all students with a high school diploma or equivalent level based on evaluation of their application for admission and personal and academic recommendations.

The Test of English as a Foreign Language (TOEFL) is required for students from non-English-speaking nations.

EXPENSES

The costs for attending the 44-week 1985-86 academic year at MIU were as follows:

	Graduate	Undergraduate
Tuition	$6,640	$5,920
Fees	140	140
Room and board (single room)	2,696	2,696
	$9,476	$8,756

FINANCIAL ASSISTANCE

All MIU applicants are encouraged to apply for scholarship or financial aid regardless of income level. In recent years, 85 percent of all MIU students received some form of financial assistance. Among those students, 97 percent received the full amount of aid they needed. Extensive scholarships for international students are available.

PLACEMENT

The MIU Career Planning Office offers full services in helping graduates and undergraduates identify and place in institutions of their choice. Internships during the M.B.A. program help students explore career interests and prospective employers.

CORRESPONDENCE

For further information and application materials please write or call
Office of Admissions
Maharishi International University
Fairfield, Iowa 52556
Telephone: 515-472-1166

Manhattan College, a private independent college in the suburban Riverdale section of New York City, was founded in 1853. The college offers programs in five schools: arts and sciences, business, engineering, teacher preparation, and general studies. Manhattan College has offered a distinctive program of higher education for business for more than 50 years.

PROGRAM OF STUDY
The educational objectives of the Master of Business Administration (M.B.A.) program are
- to develop professional managers and prepare prospective managers to function actively in positions of broad administrative responsibility in business, government, education, health, and other complex organizations;
- to impart a knowledge and understanding of the process of professional management and of the environments in which managers function;
- to give students the opportunity to develop a functional specialization in accordance with their talents and interests;
- to prepare students for doctoral study leading to careers in teaching and research; and
- to enable students to pursue graduate work in a nontraditional, independent study mode of learning.

Since the program seeks to develop managers in the broad context as well as functional specialists, it is intended for those who are already in management positions as well as those who are aspiring to management positions. Its advanced core is structured around the following areas of competence requisite for the development of effective professional managers:
- organizational environments—the interaction between the organization and the economic, social, political, and legal environments in which it operates;
- organizational dynamics—the behavioral dynamics of people at work (the vehicle of change is used to give the student insight into the nature and workings of human organizations);
- management analysis and decision systems—the application of the latest quantitative techniques to decision making;
- management operating and control systems—the interrelationship of the functions of the organization from a systems perspective (accounting, marketing, and financial systems);

- management planning and policy making—all areas of competence come into focus in planning and policy making. In this area, the student may examine the process of management in a particular type of organization, that is, business, government, health, or other not-for-profit institutions.

For each area of competence there are corresponding prerequisites. The student must complete the prerequisites before taking graduate courses in a particular area. However, all prerequisites need not be completed before moving into graduate work.

The program offers concentrations in the following fields: accounting, finance, international business, management, management information systems, and marketing. The degree awarded is the Master of Business Administration.

The M.B.A. program is a nontraditional, part-time program offering the student the option of individualization and partial externalization. All graduate and prerequisite courses are modular in design. Each course is divided into several modules having distinct objects and methodology, allowing the student maximum flexibility and convenience. The program offers the following options:
- a student may decide to take all the modules, or an entire graduate course, on campus in traditional classes, most of which are held each Saturday morning;
- a student may opt to take certain modules of a graduate course through independent study and attend classes for certain other modules (Students who opt for this partial externalization are required to meet only four class sessions in each semester. They are also permitted to attend any session of the regularly scheduled course);
- a student may take any undergraduate prerequisite course under the direction of a faculty member following a well-defined program of independent study, without attending classes.

The capstone of the program is the independent master's project. This is a professional activity involving an in-depth examination and analysis, under faculty guidance, of a real-world organizational problem related to the student's field of interest. Students have the option of taking courses in lieu of the project.

Graduate courses are offered three semesters each academic year, from early September through early August. A student typically takes three to six graduate credits per semester and may complete the graduate course work in two years.

ADMISSION
An individual holding a bachelor's degree from an accredited college or university will be considered for admission if performance on the Graduate Management Admission Test (GMAT) and performance at the undergraduate level—as measured by grade-point average and rank-in-class—are satisfactory.

EXPENSES
Tuition:
Advanced courses, per credit	$215
Prerequisites, on-campus, per credit	155
Prerequisites, independent study, per credit	125

Fees:
Application fee, nonrefundable	20
Registration, per semester	25

CORRESPONDENCE
For further information, write or call
Acting Dean Faraj Abdulahad
School of Business
    or
Dr. Herbert E. Wheeler
Director, M.B.A. Program
Manhattan College
Riverdale, New York 10471
Telephone: 212-920-0222

Mankato State University is located in Mankato, Minnesota, 80 miles south of Minneapolis, St. Paul, in the beautiful Minnesota River Valley—the Valley of the Jolly Green Giant. The university was established in 1866, with the College of Business being authorized in 1947. The first graduate work in the College of Business began in 1953.

Total enrollment is approximately 10,000 students in six colleges and one school. Dormitories are maintained for both men and women students, and excellent off-campus housing is available.

PROGRAMS OF STUDY

The College of Business has as its purpose the promoting and improving of collegiate education for business. The Master of Business Administration (M.B.A.) provides a broad study of the interrelated areas of business administration to prepare candidates for careers in management.

The M.B.A. program consists of a core of required courses:

	Quarter Hours
Techniques of Research	4
Statistical Analysis for Business	4
Accounting for Management Decisions	4
Business Policies	4
Economic Analysis	4
Financial Management	4
Organizational Administration	4
Marketing Analysis	4

The balance of the program will be planned by the student and a committee in relation to the student's career objectives.

The Master of Arts in economics is a specialized program providing preparation for research positions in business, college and university teaching, or additional graduate study.

All candidates for these degrees must complete, either as undergraduate or graduate students, basic instruction in each of the following areas: accounting, economic theory, statistics, management, marketing, finance, data processing, and business law.

A minimum of 45 quarter hours is required for the master's program with a thesis; a minimum of 51 quarter hours is required under the alternate plan. Candidates may elect either the thesis or the alternate plan program. The program will vary in length from one to two calendar years for the full-time student, depending upon the academic background of the candidate. Programs are offered on campus and off campus, both in day and evening offerings.

Concentrations may be included in the student's program by selecting four or five elective courses from the same area. Popular areas of concentration are accounting, economics, finance, international business, management, marketing, real estate and insurance.

ADMISSION

Applicants for admission must be graduates of accredited colleges and universities. A completed application blank and transcripts of all college-level work should be forwarded to the Dean of Graduate Studies. Acceptance is based upon the applicant's previous college record and scores on the Graduate Management Admission Test (GMAT) or, for economics, the Graduate Record Examinations (GRE). Consideration is given to all aspects of the student's record in determining final admission.

Applicants whose native language is not English must also submit a score on the Test of English as a Foreign Language (TOEFL).

Acceptance for enrollment in courses by the Graduate School does not constitute entrance into the graduate program; formal admission is based upon satisfactory performance on the GMAT and satisfactory undergraduate academic achievement. Upon receiving acceptance, the student may enter the program at the beginning of the next quarter.

EXPENSES

All students are required to pay a matriculation fee of $10 at the time the application blank is submitted.*

*Per quarter estimates***	*In-state*	*Out-of-state*
Tuition and fees	$ 600	$1,100
Room and board	1,700	1,700
Books and supplies	150	150
Average total	$2,450	$2,950

*Subject to change
**Estimates based on 12 graduate credits per quarter

FINANCIAL ASSISTANCE

A limited number of graduate assistantships are ordinarily available which carry stipends ranging from $2,500 to $5,000, depending upon the type of assignment. Applications for assistantships for the fall quarter should be submitted by April 15, although late applications will be considered as vacancies occur.

Student loans of various amounts are available. Students interested in loans should write to the Financial Aids Office.

PLACEMENT

The Center for Career Development and Placement provides placement services for all graduates of the College of Business. A fee of $25 is charged annually for active registrants.

CORRESPONDENCE

For further information, write or call
M.B.A. Director, College of Business
Mankato State University
Mankato, Minnesota 56001
Telephone: 507-389-5426

Marist is a private, nonsectarian, liberal arts college for men and women, located 70 miles north of New York City on the east bank of the Hudson River in Poughkeepsie, New York. Undergraduate enrollment is about 2,400 full-time students; there are about 500 graduate students, most of them attending part time. Approximately 250 students are enrolled in the Master of Business Administration (M.B.A.) and Master of Public Administration (M.P.A.) programs.

Founded in 1929, the college occupies a 100-acre campus of modern buildings. It is accredited by the Middle States Association of Colleges and Secondary Schools, approved for veterans' education, and accredited for the training of foreign students. Pertinent memberships include the Middle Atlantic Association of Colleges of Business Administration and the American Assembly of Collegiate Schools of Business (AACSB).

PROGRAMS OF STUDY
The purpose of the Marist College M.B.A. and M.P.A. programs is to provide preparation for the student who aspires to a responsible position in management. Although the quantitative aspects of the management sciences are included in the program, emphasis is on the behavioral influences affecting the successful operation of modern organizations. Specifically, the program objectives are
- to ensure an understanding of the basic functions of management and to provide the opportunity for intensive study in selected fields,
- to develop in students the necessary ability of rapid and incisive decision making in a constantly changing management environment,
- to familiarize students with the relationships existing between organizations and their environment,
- to instill in the future executive an awareness of his or her role with regard to effective and humane allocation of the world's natural and human resources,
- to establish a foundation for continued self-education.

In keeping with these objectives, graduate courses are taught by a largely full-time faculty representing a broad spectrum of management experience. Both programs are structured to accommodate all bachelor's degree holders, regardless of major. All courses are scheduled in the evening to make them available to part-time and full-time students. A minimum of 36 credits must be completed at Marist with a cumulative index of 3.0 or better. A terminal seminar provides a mechanism for integrating prior course knowledge; thus, no thesis or comprehensive examination is required.

The M.B.A. program offers concentrations in human resources management, accounting/finance, and information systems. A total of 60 credits is required for this degree, but candidates with prior related academic experience may have up to 24 credits waived.

The M.P.A. program reflects a dual orientation of public administration issues at both the conceptual and practical levels. Concentrations are offered in public management, criminal justice, and health services administration. Thirty-six credits at the graduate level are required, and depending on background, prerequisites may be specified.

ADMISSION
The overall scholastic record and potential of the applicant for admission is more important than prior preparation in the area of management. The Admissions Committee is concerned with the interest, aptitude, and capacity for management study. Prerequisites may be required of some applicants.

Any student planning to enroll in the graduate programs must
- hold a baccalaureate degree from an accredited college or university,
- complete the program application form,
- provide official transcripts of all undergraduate and graduate academic records,
- achieve acceptable scores on the Graduate Management Admission Test (GMAT).
Students are accepted in all semesters— fall, spring, and summer.

Application deadlines are July 15, December 15, and May 1 for the above semesters. Students will be notified of the admission decision no later than two weeks prior to the start of the semester.

International students must provide official or certified copies in English of all their transcripts. The Test of English as a Foreign Language (TOEFL) is required for students from non-English-speaking countries.

EXPENSES
Expenses are as follows:

Application fee	$ 25
Tuition, per credit hour	200
Matriculation fee	30
Registration fee, per semester	15
Degree fee	30
Room and board, per semester	$1,780

FINANCIAL ASSISTANCE
The Office of Financial Aid at the college advises students on the availability of scholarships, grants, loans, tuition aid plans, and part-time employment, as well as on the procedures and qualifications to apply for such assistance.

There are a number of graduate assistantships available; these carry stipends of a minimum of $1,500 for an academic year.

PLACEMENT
All facilities of the college's placement office are available to M.B.A. and M.P.A. candidates and alumni.

CORRESPONDENCE
For applications and information, write or call
Director of Graduate Admissions
Marist College
Poughkeepsie, New York 12601
Telephone: 914-471-3240

Chartered in 1864, Marquette University comprises a group of 13 colleges, schools, and programs of higher education in business administration, dental hygiene, dentistry, education, engineering, graduate studies, journalism, law, liberal arts, medical technology, nursing, physical therapy, and speech. Conducted by the Jesuit order, Marquette University is closely identified with the business and cultural community.

The total enrollment of the university is in excess of 11,000 and that of the College of Business Administration is about 2,100 with about 450 studying at the graduate level. The College of Business has been a member of the American Assembly of Collegiate Schools of Business (AACSB) since 1928; its graduate program was first accredited in 1963.

PROGRAMS OF STUDY

The Master of Business Administration (M.B.A.) program offered by the College of Business Administration is administered by the Graduate School of Marquette University. The primary objective of the M.B.A. program at Marquette University is to provide the student with a broad professional education in preparation for responsible managerial positions in business, industry, or education.

Both part-time and full-time students are admitted. The program has been attractive and beneficial, not only to business undergraduates, but fully as much to graduates of engineering and liberal arts colleges. Because many of the students are engaged in full-time positions, the graduate courses are offered in the late afternoon and evening.

If the foundation course requirements have been met, a full-time student may complete the M.B.A. program in one calendar year and a part-time student in a minimum of two years. Since the university operates on a semester plan, new students may enter the M.B.A. program in August or January, as well as in May for the summer session.

The M.B.A. program is structured as follows:
- foundation courses—9 courses, 27 hours (these courses may be waived with proper undergraduate preparation);
- core courses—8 courses, 24 hours;
- core elective—1 course, 3 hours chosen from several alternatives in the area of systems or operations management;

- free electives—2 courses, 6 hours;
- total program—20 courses, 60 hours.

Electives can be chosen in the areas of accounting, economics, entrepreneurship, finance, human resources, marketing, or operations management. Students may opt for elective course work from another area within the university for which they are qualified.

The College of Business also offers a Master of Accounting Science degree (M.A.S.). The primary purpose of the M.A.S. program is to provide a fifth year of advanced professional study in both accounting and business related areas for the undergraduate accounting major or equivalent. The program is designed to enhance the preparation of the candidate for employment in the public, private, or governmental sectors. In addition, the program would prepare the student for initial employment as an accounting instructor and for additional study of accounting and/or business at the doctoral level.

The M.A.S. program requires 30 semester hours of specifically designated graduate courses in business and accounting. Undergraduate preparation in accounting and business is required prior to enrolling in the graduate-level courses.

In addition, the Master of Arts degree in Applied Economics (M.A.A.E.) is designed for students seeking careers in business or government as staff economists, economic and financial analysts, economic researchers, and managers. The program combines training in economic theory and quantitative methods with an appreciation for and familiarity with practical problems confronting business firms and government agencies.

The program consists of 30 hours of graduate work plus a noncredit master's essay. The student can select one of three areas of specialization: business economics, financial economics, or public policy economics.

ADMISSION

Applicants to the M.B.A. program at Marquette are judged on an individual basis. The admission process seeks to determine the applicant's potential for successful completion of the program. Required for admission are a completed application, official transcripts indicating a bachelor's degree from a regionally accredited college or university as well as

transcripts from any other course work attempted, and results of the Graduate Management Admission Test (GMAT). International students are also required to submit results of the Test of English as a Foreign Language (TOEFL) and three letters of recommendation. Any student may submit additional supporting materials (letters of recommendation, resume, statement of purpose) if they wish. All application materials should be sent directly to the Marquette University Graduate School.

EXPENSES

The tuition fees for the 1985-86 academic year were based on a rate of $202 per semester hour. Living expenses vary greatly, depending upon whether a student maintains a family residence in the Milwaukee area or seeks single accommodations. For more information the student can contact the Office of Residence Life at Marquette.

FINANCIAL ASSISTANCE

Financial aid through tuition scholarships and graduate assistantships is available. Inquiries about such support should be addressed to the Dean of the Graduate School.

CORRESPONDENCE

Further information may be obtained by writing to or calling
Director of the M.B.A. Program
Marquette University
Milwaukee, Wisconsin 53233
Telephone: 414-224-7145

Founded in 1837, Marshall University is located in Huntington, West Virginia, a city of 75,000 people in the beautiful Ohio River Valley. The university is a coeducational state institution with an enrollment of more than 11,000.

The College of Business, with an enrollment of more than 2,000 majors, is organized into the following areas of study: accounting, economics, computer information science, management, marketing, finance, and graduate studies.

PROGRAM OF STUDY

Marshall University offers a unique experience to qualified candidates for the Master of Business Administration (M.B.A.) program, which recognizes the interdisciplinary nature of the executive function. Its purpose is to provide a strong professional preparation and foundation. The program emphasizes the development of a broad fundamental framework with exercises in managerial problem solving and decision making but still with a degree of specialization if desired. Individual programs of study are prepared to achieve the candidate's professional objectives.

To accomplish these purposes, the curriculum may include 32 semester hours of preparatory studies to assist the student whose undergraduate degree is in a non-business academic area; a base of functional studies in the various areas of business and their interrelationships; and a selection of courses in the candidate's area of specialization. Areas of specialization include accounting, finance, management, and marketing. Students whose undergraduate major is not in business administration and those who received the baccalaureate degree from a college or university not accredited by a regional accrediting association within the U.S. will be required to complete 32 hours of preparatory studies.

The program may be completed in three semesters on a full-time basis if the candidate has the necessary preparatory courses. Nine semester hours of graduate credit are considered to be a full-time semester class load. Courses are scheduled primarily in late afternoons and evenings throughout the year including summers.

The requirements for the Master of Business Administration degree are as follows:

- Each candidate must complete a minimum of 36 semester hours of graduate study. He or she must exhibit competence in the functional studies and in an area of specialization by satisfactory completion of designated courses with a minimum quality-point average of 3.0 (4.0 = A).
- Each candidate must pass a comprehensive, written examination. The examinations will normally be given each semester.
- The candidate must complete the program within five years of admission to the Graduate School.

ADMISSION

The Master of Business Administration program at Marshall University provides for the development of professional leaders in business and industry. The program is a demanding one requiring outstanding aptitude, ability, and scholarship of its candidates. Many factors in addition to undergraduate academic performance are considered in the standards established for admission. Undergraduate preparation in business administration is not a prerequisite for admission.

Each applicant is required to submit scores on the Graduate Management Admission Test (GMAT). These scores must be submitted before enrolling in the M.B.A. program.

Each application with accompanying transcripts, GMAT scores, and other documents will be considered carefully. Every effort will be made to select those applicants who can successfully complete the program and meet the demands that will be imposed upon them.

The application and all supporting documents must be sent to the Director of Admissions, Graduate School, at least 30 days prior to the opening of the term of enrollment. The Master of Business Administration program of Marshall University is subject to the requirements of Executive Order 11246 and participates as an affirmative action employer. All interested people are encouraged to apply.

EXPENSES

Fees are subject to change without notice.

Tuition, per semester
Full time (nine graduate semester hours)
  Resident student .... $ 575
  Nonresident student 1,600
Part time
  Resident student
    (three-hour course) 190
  Nonresident student
    (three-hour course) 531

Housing
  Married
    Efficiency apartment,
      per month.............. 160
    One-bedroom apartment,
      per month............. 160-280
    Two-bedroom apartment,
      per month.............. 290
  Single
    Dormitory fee,
      per semester 1,340-1,550

PLACEMENT

The Office of Career Planning and Placement is maintained as a service to students and alumni. Many national, regional, and local business firms make regular recruiting trips to the campus in search of business administration graduates.

CORRESPONDENCE

Address inquiries to
  Director, Graduate Business Programs
  College of Business
  Marshall University
  Huntington, West Virginia 25701

Marymount College of Virginia is the only independent, residential college in northern Virginia. Governed by a Board of Directors of business and professional men and women, the college is accredited by the Southern Association of Colleges and Schools, the State Council for Higher Education in Virginia, and by individual professional accrediting agencies. Founded in 1950 by an international Roman Catholic educational order, the Religious of the Sacred Heart of Mary, the college is located in a residential section of Arlington, just five minutes by car from Washington, D.C. Bus and subway transportation also provide easy access from the 17-acre campus to the nation's capital. The student population of more than 2,000 includes undergraduates, as well as graduate students in education and in business. On-campus research facilities include the College Academic Center, which houses Ireton Library, the Learning Laboratory and Audiovisual Center, and the Academic Computer Center. The rich and varied resources of the specialized government libraries are close at hand. Graduate courses are coeducational and linked to the principal belief of the college that true education involves the whole person in a lifelong process. The M.B.A. program is offered on campus, at the Pentagon, and at several high technology industrial sites in northern Virginia.

PROGRAM OF STUDY
The required 45 graduate credits consist of a 9-credit-hour core program, 21 credit hours of M.B.A. requisites, 12 hours of electives, and a 3-credit-hour capstone course. Core program courses may be waived for M.B.A. candidates who have an undergraduate degree in business administration or equivalent. The residual program is 36 semester hours.

ADMISSION
Admission to the Master of Business Administration degree program is based on prior academic record, transcripts of postsecondary work, scores on the Graduate Management Admission Test (GMAT), two letters of reference from educators or employers, and evaluation of life experience. The college has continuous admission for courses, which begin in the fall, spring, or summer semesters.

EXPENSES
Nonrefundable application fee is $20. Tuition for graduate courses is $180 per credit hour. Limited campus housing is available for women at $1,730 per semester, including board. (Rates subject to change.)

FINANCIAL ASSISTANCE
A few service assistantships are awarded to graduate students assigned to an academic division or an administrative office. The college also offers appointments as residence hall supervisors to women graduate students. Under the National Direct Student Loan program, a graduate student may borrow, if needed, as much as $2,500 per year, to a maximum of $10,000. The Guaranteed Student Loan Program is a federally supported program through which students may borrow up to $5,000 per academic year. The College Work-Study Program and campus employment are also available. The Virginia Education Loan Authority provides a source of loans to eligible students who are unable to secure loans from private lenders. To apply for financial aid, the graduate student must file the Graduate and Professional School Financial Aid Service application (GAPSFAS) with the College Scholarship Service, as well as the Marymount Financial Aid application. Cooperative arrangements are maintained with business employers of students for provision of tuition assistance. Necessary applications may be obtained from the Director of Financial Aid at the college. Students who apply for financial aid less than six weeks before the beginning of a semester may not receive notification of eligibility in sufficient time to have funds for tuition payment and for registration for classes.

PLACEMENT
The Graduate Placement Office invites representatives of local and national firms to recruit on campus and share their current opportunities for placement. The Center for Counseling and Career Planning offers a credential file service to all current students and alumni.

CORRESPONDENCE
For further information, contact
Dr. Richard H. Ross
Dean, School of Business
 Administration
Marymount College of Virginia
2807 North Glebe Road
Arlington, Virginia 22207
Telephone: 703-522-5600, extension 294

MARYVILLE COLLEGE—ST. LOUIS

ST. LOUIS, MISSOURI

Maryville College—St. Louis, founded in 1872, is one of the oldest institutions of higher education in St. Louis. It has fostered a tradition of academic excellence for over a century. The college offers a diversity of programs in career-oriented liberal arts study leading to associate, baccalaureate, and master's degrees. Maryville is an innovative, private institution responsive to changing individual and societal needs.

The college has the auxiliary mission of directing the design and development of the Maryville Center—an educational, cultural, corporate, research, recreational, and service center centrally located in the metropolitan community amidst the natural environment of the 290-acre Maryville campus.

Maryville College—St. Louis is accredited by the North Central Association of Colleges and Secondary Schools.

PROGRAM OF STUDY
The Master of Science in management program is a 30-credit-hour program, which can be completed in 16 months. It is designed to meet the unique needs of the working professional by allowing the student to directly link newly acquired knowledge with present planned work activities. The person's current job serves as a laboratory in which to examine concepts presented in the classroom. A major part of this type of program is the construction of a research project that enables the individual to apply management theory to a problem in the field. This research project, which continues throughout the program, serves as a catalyst to blend academic study with real work experience.

Each group of students meets once a week for four hours on Monday nights and remains together for the entire program (four semesters). Students who wish to take a part-time load (3-5 hours) may do so but will not remain with one group. Each semester is divided into two terms of eight weeks each. A three-hour course is completed in eight consecutive weeks and is then followed by a second three-hour course. Also, during three of the four semesters, students will complete a two-hour research seminar focusing on his or her research project. This seminar will meet approximately four times during the semester at times mutually agreeable to the students and the instructor.

The program emphasizes a balanced approach to the graduate study of management by giving students course work in the major areas of business (for example, finance, accounting, information resource management) as well as an opportunity to develop a concentration in organizational management, marketing, or health care management.

ADMISSION
No prerequisite courses are required for admission; however, for students who have no educational and/or work experience in business, compensatory work will be advised, especially in the areas of accounting, finance, and economics. Applicants are required to submit a completed application form; official transcripts from all undergraduate colleges and universities attended, including the institution that granted the undergraduate degree; a letter describing reasons for pursuing a graduate degree and qualifications for graduate study; and official Graduate Management Admission Test (GMAT) scores. Foreign applicants must also submit official Test of English as a Foreign Language (TOEFL) scores. The admission decision is based on an evaluation of the aforementioned application materials. Since the program is designed for working professionals, the majority of the students have several years of full-time work experience.

EXPENSES
Costs are estimated for the 1986-87 academic year. Tuition is subject to change without notice. All of the students to date are commuters from St. Louis and the surrounding areas.

Missouri residents/Out-of-State Residents

Tuition	$3,960
Books and supplies	300
Total	$4,260

FINANCIAL ASSISTANCE
Guaranteed Student Loans are available through banks and other lending institutions. A separate application from the Financial Aid Office is needed to obtain these loans.

PLACEMENT
A placement director is available to work with students to identify employment opportunities.

CORRESPONDENCE
For more information, please write or call
Coordinator of the Master of Science in Management Program
Graduate Management Division
Maryville College—St. Louis
13550 Conway Road
St. Louis, Missouri 63141
Telephone: 314-576-9317

Marywood College is a private, Catholic, liberal arts college located in northeastern Pennsylvania. It was established in 1915 by the Sisters, Servants of the Immaculate Heart of Mary, whose aim is to provide an education toward the self-development of a fully human person. The Graduate School offers two programs in business and managerial science: the Master of Business Administration (M.B.A.) and the Master of Science (M.S.) in managerial science. The programs are both accredited by the Middle States Association.

PROGRAMS OF STUDY
The Master of Business Administration degree provides the student with a common body of knowledge in business administration via the required core courses for the degree. Students seeking admission to this degree program must hold a bachelor's degree in a business-related field from a four-year college or university. Students must take 33 semester credit hours of graduate-level courses. No bi-level courses are acceptable as part of this degree program.

The Master of Science in managerial science degree program is designed to prepare candidates for career advancement and provide graduate students with an area of specialization in business and/or managerial science. Students seeking admission to this degree program must hold a bachelor's degree from a four-year accredited college or university. The bachelor's degree can be in any field. Selected courses in business managerial science must be taken to ensure that the student has a substantial understanding of managerial processes. Thereafter, the student must complete required courses in the chosen area of concentration.

In the M.B.A. program, core courses include Management Information Systems, Organizational Behavior and Development, Operation Analysis and Management (Quantitative Methods), Legal Aspects of the Administrative Management Process, Financial Planning and Management, and Research Methodology, including a Professional Contribution Proposal.

Each candidate for the M.B.A. degree must select an area of concentration within the business program. The following areas are available: finance and investments, information system technology, industrial management, international business, and health services administration.

In the managerial science degree, each candidate must select an area of concentration. Each area of concentration has a set of prerequisite courses and core course requirements. The available areas are finance and investment, information system technology, and industrial management.

ADMISSION
Applicants to either the M.B.A. or the M.S. degree program must submit to the graduate school the application forms, a $20 nonrefundable application fee, an official transcript of undergraduate work, two recommendation forms, and the scores attained on the Graduate Management Admission Test (GMAT). Students admitted into either of the degree programs may transfer up to nine graduate credit hours of business courses with a B average, subject to the approval of the department chairman or the graduate business committee.

In the M.B.A. program, graduates of accredited four-year colleges with an undergraduate core in business are eligible for admission. Students applying for admission to this program will be required to have a minimum of 21 to 30 undergraduate business credits, depending upon their background. These credits will include economics, marketing, computer programming, accounting, finance, business law, statistics, and management.

In the M.S. program, students enrolling must hold an undergraduate degree from an accredited four-year college or university. All major fields are eligible for admission to this degree program. Prerequisites related to the student's selected area of concentration are provided at Marywood College to accommodate the diverse majors admitted to the graduate program. The M.S. degree requires 33 to 48 semester hours, depending on the student's background.

EXPENSES
Tuition cost per graduate credit hour is $130.

FINANCIAL ASSISTANCE
Two graduate scholarships are available for business students who intend to pursue graduate work in any of the business areas offered. These are the Irenee DuPont Scholarship and the John Timko, Jr.

Scholarship. Financial assistance is also available to qualified students. Those who are interested may write to the Financial Aid Office, Marywood College, for application forms.

PLACEMENT
The Career Services Office has a fully qualified staff to assist students in meeting with representatives of multinational corporations on campus during the year.

CORRESPONDENCE
For further information, write
  S.P. Dagher, Ph.D., Head
  Business and Managerial Science
    Programs
  Marywood College
  Scranton, Pennsylvania 18509

The Sloan School of Management grew out of courses in administration and management that were first offered to undergraduate engineering students at Massachusetts Institute of Technology (MIT) in 1914. The scope and depth of this educational effort have grown steadily in response to advances in the theory and practice of management and its importance to society. Today, the school awards the degrees of Bachelor of Science in management science, Master of Science in management, and Doctor of Philosophy, and offers several executive education programs. The school also participates with MIT's School of Engineering in a 12-month master's degree program in the management of technology. All degree programs are full-time.

The school's enrollment is purposely small in order to maintain an environment that emphasizes frequent interaction among students and faculty. There are approximately 95 undergraduates, 400 master's students, 80 doctoral students, 55 Sloan Fellows, and 50 Senior Executives. The school's full-time, tenure-track faculty numbers over 80.

As an integral part of MIT, the Sloan School offers many advantages to its students. Within the smaller Sloan community a collegial and supportive atmosphere exists, encouraging cooperation among students. Numerous student-managed clubs sponsor activities ranging from talks by outside speakers to purely social events.

PROGRAMS OF STUDY
The two-year Sloan master's program, which commences in September, offers a comprehensive education in general management as well as the opportunity to develop competence in particular areas of interest. Through core and elective subjects, business communication workshops, group projects, and computer-based management games, students acquire the conceptual and analytical abilities they need for decision making at the executive level in both private and public sector organizations. The thesis provides an opportunity for intensive study of a problem of particular interest.

The Ph.D. program, which also begins in September, prepares students having strong scholarly interests for academic careers and other positions requiring advanced research capabilities. The initial phase offers experience with analytical tools in the disciplines underlying management; the second centers on preliminary research in the applied field of the student's choice; and the last consists of teaching and major research.

Areas of concentration available in both programs are accounting, planning, and control; applied economics; corporate strategy, policy, and planning; finance; health care management; human resource management; industrial relations; international management; management information systems; marketing; operations management; operations research and statistics; organization studies; system dynamics; and technological innovation. Other concentrations may be arranged, and most core requirements may be waived on the basis of examination results or prior study.

ADMISSION
The Sloan School welcomes applications from college graduates in all major fields, although applicants must have completed two semesters each of calculus and economic theory, including both micro- and macroeconomics, prior to enrollment. In addition, one year of full-time, postgraduate work experience is required of international applicants. All applicants must take the Graduate Management Admission Test (GMAT) by January in the year of application, and those whose native language is not English must also take the Test of English as a Foreign Language (TOEFL) by January. Interviews are not required, but information sessions may be arranged on request.

Applications should be submitted by January 3 for the guaranteed admission and early notification options in the master's program, January 24 for the doctoral program, and February 3 for the regular admission option in the master's program. Admission targets each year are 200 entering master's students and 20 entering doctoral students. Admission decisions are made by the first week in April.

EXPENSES
Tuition in the 1985-86 academic year was $11,200. The additional costs of housing, food, hospitalization insurance, books, and personal items brought the estimated total expenses to about $19,900 for a single student. Tuition and fees may be paid in monthly installments.

FINANCIAL ASSISTANCE
U.S. students lacking sufficient personal resources may apply for loans through MIT's Student Financial Aid Office. Entering doctoral candidates are considered for Sloan School fellowships and part-time research and teaching assistantships. Second-year master's students are also eligible for assistantships and a small number of merit scholarships.

Minority master's applicants are encouraged to apply for Johnson & Johnson Leadership Awards. Minority students are also considered for special school and institute scholarships.

PLACEMENT
Sloan's Placement Office serves its students by providing career counseling and coordinating job announcements. About 150 organizations visit the school annually to interview for permanent and summer positions, and several hundred others send job descriptions. Competition for Sloan graduates is intense, with most students receiving several offers of diverse, challenging positions. Average starting salaries are consistently among the highest of graduates of the nation's business schools.

CORRESPONDENCE
For further information, write or call
   Master's Program (or Ph.D. Program)
      Office
   Sloan School of Management
   Massachusetts Institute of Technology
   50 Memorial Drive, E52-112
   Cambridge, Massachusetts 02139
   Telephone: 617-253-3730

The Royal Charter of McGill University was granted by King George IV in 1821. Located in the heart of the island metropolis of Montreal, McGill University has a unique, bilingual, multicultural environment. The quality of its graduate teaching and research has always drawn students from around the world.

Teaching of management began in 1906 with a Bachelor of Commerce degree. Now the Faculty of Management offers a variety of graduate and undergraduate courses. Full-time enrollment in the Master of Business Administration (M.B.A.) program is 250, and part-time (evening) enrollment is 300.

The faculty library, located in the new Samuel Bronfman Building, serves a wide community. Students also have full access to most of the two million volumes provided by the University Library System.

PROGRAM OF STUDY

The M.B.A. program demonstrates how analytical techniques developing from the management sciences, the behavioral sciences, economics, and computer sciences can be applied to help solve the functional problems of business encountered in marketing, finance, accounting, policy, industrial relations, and international business. The subject matter of each course has been critically examined from the point of view of both functional and academic relevance in the light of the needs of tomorrow's business.

The primary objective of the M.B.A. program is to help the student acquire the necessary knowledge and skills to analyze and solve complex organizational problems including change in business, government, and other institutions. The major portion of the first year is devoted to basic concepts and theories and to mastering analytical techniques in both core and functional courses. However, the program is also designed to enhance managerial skills. The design of the second year permits the student to clarify his or her learning goals and to select learning methods (thesis, electives, projects) that contribute to the achievement of his or her objectives.

ADMISSION

Requirements for admission include
 • an undergraduate degree from an accredited college or university with a grade-point average of at least 3.0 out of a possible 4.0, and

 • the Graduate Management Admission Test (GMAT) and the Test of English as a Foreign Language (TOEFL), where applicable.

The program commences in September and ends in April for full-time students. Applications must be submitted by June 1. The part-time program starts in September and January. Applicants are advised of the admissions decision as soon as all supporting documents and test scores are received. A personal interview is not mandatory although it may be requested by the Director. Students are encouraged to gain some work experience prior to entering the program.

Advanced standing is granted for graduate work in business and related areas completed after earning a bachelor's degree. Credit for no more than five half-courses may be granted. Students who have completed undergraduate courses equivalent to core courses may apply for exemptions. Exemption permits the substitution of an elective for the required course but does not reduce the degree requirements.

The first year of the program consists of the following core courses: Business Communications, Basic Management Statistics, Introduction to Modeling Methods in Management, Finance I, Accounting, Managerial Economics, Macroeconomics, Marketing, Computer Science, Behavioral Science, and Introduction to International Business or Industrial Relations.

The second year consists of two core courses, Management Policy and Skill Development, and a choice of either eight half-course electives or six half-course electives and a research paper. Students are encouraged to follow one of 17 concentrations.

Since September 1972, the Faculty of Management has offered the M.B.A. degree for part-time students. Courses and standards are the same as for the full-time program. The part-time program permits students to work full time and obtain the M.B.A. in a minimum of four years. Part-time students may transfer into the full-time program after completion of all 10 of the first-year courses.

EXPENSES

Costs listed were in effect for the 1985-86 academic year. Tuition is in Canadian dollars and is subject to change without notice.

	Canadian Student	Student Visa
Tuition	$ 764	$ 6,940
Residence (8 months)	3,309	3,309
Books and supplies	500	500
Total	$4,573	$10,749

FINANCIAL ASSISTANCE

Graduate fellowships and scholarships are available through the Faculty of Graduate Studies, Fellowships Office, 853 Sherbrooke St. W., Montreal, Quebec, H3A 2T5, Canada. Application deadline is February 1. Awards are available through the M.B.A. program on the basis of academic merit. No application is necessary. Limited assistantships are awarded after September registration. Students are advised to apply to as many outside sources as possible.

PLACEMENT

The M.B.A. program has its own Placement Office geared specifically to the needs of prospective employers of M.B.A. students and to the needs of the students themselves. The office is in contact with organizations hiring M.B.A. graduates and arranges scheduled interviews with interested employers on campus and on the employer's premises. A referral service is available through the office for part-time students and alumni seeking a change in employment.

CORRESPONDENCE

For information on the program, write or call
 Admissions Office
 M.B.A. Program
 Faculty of Management
 McGill University
 1001 Sherbrooke Street West
 Montreal, Quebec, Canada H3A 1G5
 Telephone: 514-392-4336

McMaster University, founded in 1887, is located in the industrial center of southern Ontario. Greater Hamilton has a population of approximately one-half million and is located approximately halfway between Toronto and Niagara Falls, at the head of Lake Ontario. McMaster's unique location offers the business student opportunities to interact with the industrial and financial communities via student visits to nearby commercial facilities, research projects into the problems of both large and small companies in the area, and seminars in which executives visit the university.

A program of graduate study in business was first offered at the university in 1952. The Faculty of Business now administers the Master of Business Administration (M.B.A.) program, the B.Com. programs, the Ph.D. (management science/systems) program, and, in conjunction with the Faculty of Engineering, the undergraduate engineering and management program. In 1985-86, M.B.A. enrollment totaled approximately 490 students, of whom 210 were full-time or cooperative students.

PROGRAM OF STUDY
The graduate program in business leads to a Master of Business Administration degree. It is a professional course for university graduates who seek preparation for careers in business management, administration, and teaching. The course of study is designed to develop the knowledge, skills, and attitudes essential for the management of business and administrative affairs in today's complex setting. The curriculum provides intensive preparation in major fields of relevant knowledge. To achieve a balance between intellectual stimulation and practical application, it employs a blend of lecturers, case studies, seminars, field trips, group projects, independent research, and business simulation sessions.

The program is organized on the trimester system. To suit the particular needs of each student, considerable flexibility has been built into the program. Hence, the degree can be obtained either through the full-time or evening program. In September 1973, a cooperative work/study program was instituted, permitting students to alternate terms of study and work. This option is available only to Canadian citizens or landed immigrants.

In order to meet graduation requirements, the student must complete 20 credits (half-courses). These courses are organized into three categories: tool core courses (accounting, business economics, human relations, quantitative analysis, statistical analysis), area (or functional) core courses, and elective stream courses. In addition to a general program, specialization streams are available in accounting, finance, international business, marketing, personnel and human resource management, labor relations, information systems, management science, logistics/production/operations, and health services management.

Advanced standing may be granted for certain courses where the student can demonstrate a satisfactory level of competence either through having completed an equivalent undergraduate course with B standing or better, or by means of a waiver examination.

The normal time for completion of the full program is two years for full-time study, two years and four months for the cooperative option, and three to eight years for part-time study.

ADMISSION
Admission to the program leading to the degree of Master of Business Administration at McMaster is open to graduates of accredited colleges and universities. It is not necessary that the undergraduate degree program contain courses in business administration, although all candidates must display proficiency in calculus and linear algebra prior to admission. Admission is determined on the basis of demonstration of sound scholarship and aptitude for graduate study in business. In general, a student must have obtained at least a second-class standing in the last two years of his or her undergraduate work. In addition, applicants are required to take the Graduate Management Admission Test (GMAT). All students must be fluent in English.

EXPENSES
The cost of one academic year at the Faculty of Business is approximately as follows:

	Single
Tuition	$1,272
Living expenses	7,000
Books and supplies	500
Total	$8,772

Note: Candidates on a student visa will be assessed tuition fees of approximately $5,144 per academic year (two terms). Places for visa students are limited.

FINANCIAL ASSISTANCE
The various forms of financial aid include fellowships, scholarships, assistantships, and government aid programs. Due to the intensity of the program it is recommended that full-time students not rely on part-time employment for assistance. Further details on financial aid are included in the yearly calendar.

PLACEMENT
The Canada Manpower Centre has made available a Student Placement Office that cooperates with the Faculty of Business to assist students in finding suitable employment after graduation. Representatives of many companies visit the campus annually to interview students.

CORRESPONDENCE
For further information or to request an application for admission, write to
Director of Graduate Admissions
Faculty of Business
McMaster University
Hamilton, Ontario, Canada L8S 4M4

McNeese State University is located in southwest Louisiana in a spectacular setting of pine forests, rivers, lakes, grain fields, and the oil rich gulf coast. The university was established in 1939 and has an enrollment of over 7,800 with approximately 1,600 students in the College of Business. Preparing for accreditation by the American Assembly of Collegiate Schools of Business (AACSB), the College of Business is housed in the Southwest Louisiana Business and Economics Center, a new air-conditioned, four-story building that includes a large conference center, computer and stat lab facilities, several special purpose tiered classrooms, and a new IBM 4341 computing system for use by business students. The university offers a high-tech, highly industrialized petrochemical educational environment, which is conducive to research, consulting, and study in business. The university is located on I-10, within a two-hour drive from both Houston and Baton Rouge.

PROGRAM OF STUDY

The program leading to the Master of Business Administration (M.B.A.) degree is structured to provide a practical, problem-solving and solution-oriented program, designed specifically for the practicing manager. Providing a basic analytical tool kit for management, developing cognitive and noncognitive skills in using these tools, advancing the ability to make and carry out decisions, developing a basis for dealing effectively with people, and instilling a thorough understanding of the overall economic, political, and social environment are the aims of the M.B.A. program. It provides graduate study for students with undergraduate backgrounds in all fields of study. The M.B.A. program is available on both a full- and part-time basis; however, it is offered primarily in the evening.

The program leading to the M.B.A. requires the completion of 36 semester hours, of which 27 hours are basic core courses in accounting, quantitative analysis, managerial report writing, business administration, information systems, economics, finance, management and organizational behavior, marketing, and top management strategy and policy. An additional nine hours of electives must also be completed; however, a thesis (not required) may be substituted for the six hours of electives. All students must pass a comprehensive written final examination.

To prepare students with nonbusiness backgrounds, the College of Business offers 24 semester hours of foundation courses that must be successfully completed as prerequisites; however, students with previously approved academic training (undergraduate equivalent courses) may have some or all of the foundation courses waived.

For full-time students, the program generally takes two years, except for those who have received a waiver because of equivalent foundation courses taken at the undergraduate level. For these students, the M.B.A. program can be completed in one year. All foundation and M.B.A. curriculum courses are offered every 12 months.

ADMISSION

All correspondence concerning admissions should be directed to the Admissions Counselor in the Registrar's Office. An applicant for admission to the Graduate School must (1) satisfy all general admissions requirements of the university, (2) hold a bachelor's degree from an accredited institution, (3) submit to the registrar's office a complete and official transcript of work completed at each institution attended, and (4) submit the results of the Graduate Management Admission Test (GMAT).

Admission to the Graduate School does not imply admission to the M.B.A. program. In addition to the general requirements for admission to the Graduate School, applicants for admission to the M.B.A. program will meet one of the following requirements: (1) a total of at least 950 points based on the formula: 200 times the overall undergraduate grade-point average plus the GMAT score; or (2) at least 1,000 points based on the formula: 200 times the upper division grade-point average plus the GMAT score.

A student who fails to satisfy one of the above criteria will be classified as a nondegree (special) student until he or she meets the above formula. A nondegree student may take undergraduate prerequisites (equivalent courses) to make up deficiencies.

Foreign students must submit a score of at least 450 on the Test of English as a Foreign Language (TOEFL).

EXPENSES

	Fall or Spring Semesters
Registration and tuition fee*	
3 semester hours	$145.50
6 semester hours	250.50
9 or more semester hours	507.00
Nonresident fee*	
3 semester hours	none
6 semester hours	220.00
9 or more semester hours	440.00

*Fees subject to change without notice.

One half of the in-state and all of the out-of-state tuition fee is waived for students with graduate assistantships.

FINANCIAL ASSISTANCE

Three types of graduate assistantships are available for students enrolled in the M.B.A. program—teaching, research, and computer. The stipends for the M.B.A. graduate assistantships are $2,000 for one semester together with a waiver of one half of the in-state and all of the out-of-state tuition. Part-time employment and student loans through the university are also available to graduate students. Applications for financial assistance will be accepted throughout the school year.

PLACEMENT

McNeese State maintains a placement office that provides career counseling and guidance to both graduate and undergraduate students. This office aids in locating positions and arranging for interviews with the numerous employers who annually contact it.

CORRESPONDENCE

For further information, write to
    Registrar's Office
    McNeese State University
    Lake Charles, Louisiana 70609

Memorial University of Newfoundland (MUN), formerly Memorial College, dating back to 1925, is situated on a spacious modern campus in North America's oldest city, St. John's. The university has a student body of approximately 10,000 engaged in a full range of study and programs at the bachelor's, master's, and doctorate levels.

The commerce program was begun in the early 1960s. The school, a pioneer in the field of cooperative business education in Canada at the undergraduate level, has an enrollment of approximately 620 undergraduate students and another 100 graduate students in the Master of Business Administration (M.B.A.) program, which was established in 1978. The school's stature and importance in management education is recognized throughout Canada.

PROGRAM OF STUDY
The M.B.A. program at MUN is designed to develop well-rounded management decision makers who are both cognizant of their operating environment and well equipped with a broad knowledge of all areas of management.

Fundamental to the objective of the program is an understanding of and training in a common core of knowledge and skills required in managing all types of organizations: small and large, profit and not-for-profit. The first year consists of 12 courses arranged to examine the fundamentals of the functional areas of management (marketing, accounting, organizational behavior, and operations management) and statistics and economics.

Year two of the program builds upon the foundation established in year one, through a series of three compulsory, integrative courses combined with seven elective courses that allow the student advanced study and research in an area or areas of personal interest. Integrative second-year courses include management strategy and policy, research in management, social responsibilities of management, and decision making. The seven elective courses may be chosen from a selection of courses offered by the school, courses from other graduate programs within the university, or a research project, which may be assigned up to three course credits. Business school elective courses include small business, natural resource management, business and taxation law, management of nonprofit organiza-tions, and advanced courses in functional areas. The aim of the second year is to encourage the application of conceptual knowledge and analytical skills to management practice.

The program is available both on a full-time and a part-time basis. The educational approach will vary according to the content and objectives of each course; the format will vary from conventional lectures and case studies to simulations and research projects. A close student-faculty relationship is possible because of a limited enrollment and the assignment of a faculty adviser to each student.

ADMISSION
Admission is limited and competitive. To be considered for admission to the Master of Business Administration program, an applicant will normally hold at least a bachelor's degree in any discipline with a minimum B standing. Students who have completed an undergraduate degree in business with high academic standing may be exempted from certain first-year courses.

Applicants who do not possess a bachelor's degree, but who have a high level of professional training or significant employment experience may be considered for admission. All applicants must complete the Graduate Management Admission Test (GMAT) and achieve a satisfactory score.

An applicant whose native language is not English, or who received undergraduate instruction in a language other than English, is required to supply a certificate of proficiency in English.

Applicants with relevant employment experience will normally receive preference during evaluation of applications. Students applying for admission in September should submit their applications no later than May 31.

EXPENSES
There is a program fee of $1,944 for the master's degree. Student organization fees are $21 per year. Costs are estimated for the 1985-86 academic year as follows:

	Part-time	Full-time
Tuition and fees	$648	$800
Board (12 months)		950
Books and supplies	400	400

Full-time students from outside Canada must purchase health insurance at $325 for a single student and $650 for a married student. (Note that amounts are in Canadian dollars.)

FINANCIAL ASSISTANCE
A limited number of university and Provincial Government fellowships are available to students engaged in full-time study. Students may also supplement their finances with bursaries in varying amounts and by remuneration for extra duties performed for the school. Foreign applicants are advised that financial assistance is limited and work permits are difficult to secure. Such applicants are expected to have sufficient financial resources to support themselves during their period of study.

PLACEMENT
The Canada Manpower Centre has an office on campus for assistance in placing graduates. Both local and national companies actively recruit on campus.

CORRESPONDENCE
For additional information, please write to
Associate Dean, M.B.A. Program
Faculty of Business Administration
Memorial University of Newfoundland
St. John's, Newfoundland,
Canada A1B 3X5

MEMPHIS STATE UNIVERSITY

MEMPHIS, TENNESSEE

The Fogelman College of Business and Economics at Memphis State University (MSU) is one of the fastest growing centers of business study in the South. Located in Memphis, a metropolitan center of over one million people and the hub of the mid-South area, MSU offers the business student advanced learning and a wealth of potential material for research and study. Memphis State maintains extensive facilities for business research, including the Bureau of Business and Economic Research, the Center for Manpower Studies, and the Public Sector Employee-Employer Relations Center, which aid Memphis area businesses and governmental agencies in many ways through the collection, analysis, and interpretation of business data.

The university has approximately 22,000 students, of whom 3,000 are graduate students. Approximately 475 students are currently admitted to graduate programs in business and economics.

PROGRAMS OF STUDY

The Master of Business Administration (M.B.A.) degree is open to those who have a bachelor's degree in the arts, science, engineering, law, or to those who are changing their area of concentration in business. The program is designed to provide for professional practice in the field of business and in the field of business education and research. A foundation is provided for continued growth in any business endeavor or activity. Students in the M.B.A. program may emphasize one of the following areas of study: accountancy, economics, finance, management, management information systems, management science, marketing, and executive. A joint M.B.A./Juris Doctor (J.D.) program is also available.

The program consists of two groups of courses, core I and core II. There are eight areas in core I that may be waived if the student has completed equivalent course work in these fields. These areas include accounting, finance, economics, law, statistics, management, management information systems, and marketing. The core II courses required of all M.B.A. candidates include proseminar in economics, quantitative methods for business decisions, cases and problems in decision making, analysis and control of business, marketing structure and administration, seminar in business policy; and one of the following: research methodology, business and economics research, executive communications.

The remaining four courses may be used by the student in areas of interest. However, no more than five courses may be taken in any one area, and nine of the courses included in the student's program must be in courses open only to graduate students.

A thesis is not required for the M.B.A. degree; however, a final comprehensive examination, oral and/or written, is required of all students.

Students with adequate preparation in business administration may complete the program in a minimum of three semesters (one calendar year). Five semesters are normally required of students who have no undergraduate work in business. All requirements for the degree must be completed within six years from the date of the candidate's original registration for graduate courses.

The Master of Science (M.S.) degree is available to students desiring a higher degree of specialization than is possible under the M.B.A. program. Students may obtain the M.S. degree in accountancy, finance, management, management information systems, marketing, or taxation.

The Master of Arts degree is available to students who desire a high degree of specialization in the field of economics.

The Doctor of Business Administration (D.B.A.) degree is designed to include a pragmatic, interdisciplinary preparation for careers in college and university teaching, research, and administration, and for careers in business or other organizations where the desirable educational background is doctoral-level study.

ADMISSION

Admission to a degree program is granted to graduates of accredited colleges and universities who show high promise of success in graduate business study. Criteria used for admission include the candidate's score on the Graduate Management Admission Test (GMAT), undergraduate grade averages and the trend of the grades during undergraduate work. Applicants whose native language is not English must also present a score on the Test of English as a Foreign Language (TOEFL).

Qualified candidates may enter the program at the beginning of any semester. To assure proper evaluation, application credentials should be received at least 60 days prior to the beginning of the semester in which the candidate wishes to enroll.

EXPENSES

The fees for students in graduate study are as follows:

	Full-time	Part-time
Resident	$ 613	$ 59 per sem. hour
Nonresident	1,687	153 per sem. hour

Housing is available for students at varying costs, depending on facilities chosen. Contact the Office of Resident Housing for further information on housing.

FINANCIAL ASSISTANCE

Graduate assistantships are available to full-time graduate students. For a stipend ranging from $3,760 for master's candidates to $7,000 for doctoral candidates, and $1,062 per academic year for tuition, students are expected to provide part-time assistance in course preparation and research. Scholarships, residence hall assistantships, and loans are also available.

PLACEMENT

The university placement office assists students in seeking employment on a part-time or a full-time basis. On-campus interviews are scheduled from October through May, and an active file of employment opportunities is maintained for students and alumni who wish to change positions.

CORRESPONDENCE

For further information, write to
  Director of Graduate Studies
  Fogelman College of Business
    and Economics
  Memphis State University
  Memphis, Tennessee 38152

Mercer University, founded in 1833, is composed of seven coeducational schools: the College of Liberal Arts, the Walter F. George School of Law, and the School of Medicine in Macon; and the School of Pharmacy, School of Nursing, College of Arts and Science, and the School of Business and Economics in Atlanta. Mercer University Atlanta's School of Business and Economics, originally a division of Atlanta Baptist College (founded in 1964 and incorporated as a part of Mercer University in 1972) attained its present status as a school effective July 1, 1983. The School of Business and Economics is accredited by the Southern Association of Colleges and Schools. Its facilities are centered on 475 wooded acres located in the northeastern, most rapidly developing, section of metropolitan Atlanta. Mercer University Atlanta is an equal opportunity employment/education institution.

PROGRAM OF STUDY

The Master of Business Administration (M.B.A.) degree at Mercer University Atlanta is a professional degree for qualified students interested in the management of human, material, and financial resources in business, government, and nonprofit organizations. The program is tailored to meet the needs of individuals already employed as managers or administrators, along with those interested in embarking on a management career.

Taught by an experienced faculty with strong academic credentials and professional experience in business and other fields, the courses are strengthened by a new library facility. A nonthesis program, the M.B.A. course of study is open to individuals who have successfully completed a baccalaureate degree in any discipline or field of study.

Individuals with a nonbusiness undergraduate degree can remove course deficiencies by extended study of up to 35 quarter hours of prerequisite courses or appropriate equivalents. A student admitted into the second level of the program must complete 13 courses (65 quarter hours): 9 in the core program, 3 in an area of concentration (accounting, economics-finance, management, marketing, management information systems, taxation and pharmacy), and a capstone case study seminar.

Primarily, the program is designed for individuals employed during the day. Therefore, each course in the program is scheduled for one night per week, Monday through Friday, or on Saturday mornings.

ADMISSION

Admission is open to any student with a baccalaureate degree, regardless of the discipline, from an accredited college or university. In evaluating a student's application, primary emphasis is given to the student's undergraduate grade-point average and the score on the Graduate Management Admission Test (GMAT). However, the applicant's progress in his or her employment and other evidence of probable success in the graduate study of business are also considered. All M.B.A. applicants must take the Graduate Management Admission Test (GMAT). International students, in addition to the application and fee, must submit an official translation of their undergraduate transcript, a GMAT score, and proof of graduate-level English proficiency. A score from the Test of English as a Foreign Language (TOEFL) will suffice for overseas students' preliminary evaluation, but each student for whom English is not the native language must arrange to take the English Proficiency Test at Georgia State University as soon as he or she arrives in Atlanta. No international student will be considered for admission unless his or her file is complete.

It should also be noted that no financial assistance is available to any graduate students, including internationals. Moreover, inasmuch as Mercer University Atlanta is a commuter university, there are no living accommodations on campus. Finally, it is estimated that attending Mercer University Atlanta (tuition plus living expenses) requires expenditures that will approximate $10,000 to $12,000 per year.

EXPENSES

The application for admission must be accompanied by a $10 nonrefundable fee. Tuition during the 1985-86 academic year was $110 per credit hour for Level II courses and $100 per credit hour for Level I, prerequisite courses.

CORRESPONDENCE

Address inquiries concerning the M.B.A. program to

Director, M.B.A. Program
School of Business and Economics
Mercer University Atlanta
3001 Mercer University Drive
Atlanta, Georgia 30341
Telephone: 404-451-0331, extension 160

MERCER UNIVERSITY / MACON

MACON, GEORGIA

Mercer University, founded in 1833, is a private, church-related (Baptist) institution of higher learning that strives for academic excellence and scholarly discipline in the fields of liberal learning and professional knowledge. It is composed of seven schools offering degrees in the liberal arts, business, law, medicine, pharmacy, and nursing. Total university enrollment exceeds 5,000. The School of Business and Economics in Macon, Georgia, has an enrollment of approximately 220 full-time junior and senior students in its upper-division-level Bachelor of Business Administration program, and approximately 60 students pursuing the Master of Business Administration (M.B.A.) degree, the majority of whom attend on a part-time basis. Macon, Georgia, a city of approximately 150,000 population in a growing metropolitan area of 250,000, is located 85 miles south of Atlanta and 190 miles north of the Atlantic coast.

PROGRAMS OF STUDY

The principal objective of the M.B.A. program is to produce excellent general managers. Faculty members hold graduate degrees from such institutions as Harvard, Columbia, Michigan State, Vanderbilt, University of Georgia, Georgia State University, University of Alabama, and the University of Mississippi. All faculty teaching graduate courses hold doctoral degrees, have many years of teaching experience, and do regular consulting in the business world. Each member has had substantial experience at some point in his or her career as a full-time practitioner in the market place. No part-time faculty teach graduate courses.

Average enrollment per class is 13; the range is from 7 to 23. Personal attention and advisement are an important part of the program.

All courses are taught at night and are offered four quarters per year: fall, winter, spring, and summer. Usually a student may enter in any quarter. Although most students attend on a part-time basis while continuing in their careers, a number of students do attend on a full-time basis.

The graduate curriculum consists of 12 courses (60 quarter hours), divided between a required core of 8 courses and a 4-course concentration. Concentrations in finance, management/marketing, and general business are offered. Prior to enrolling in graduate courses, students should have successfully completed nine prerequisite foundation courses: Introductory Financial Accounting, Principles of Macroeconomics, Introductory Statistics, Calculus, Computer Science, Principles of Finance, Principles of Management, Principles of Marketing, and Business Law. These courses may have been taken previously at the undergraduate level or they may be taken upon entry into Mercer's program. Up to 10 quarter hours of graduate credit may be transferred from another M.B.A. program.

A joint M.B.A.-J.D. degree program is offered in cooperation with Mercer's Walter F. George School of Law. Most students can earn both degrees within four years, whereas separate matriculation normally would require five years. Students must file separate applications with each school and be admitted by both.

ADMISSION

Admission requires that an individual have earned a bachelor's degree from an accredited college or university in any major field. The Graduate Management Admission Test (GMAT) must be taken, and official transcripts from all previous colleges and universities attended must be submitted. A combination of a satisfactory GMAT score and overall grade-point average at the bachelor's level is required. Students from countries other than the United States for whom English is not the major language are required to score approximately 550 on the Test of English as a Foreign Language (TOEFL).

EXPENSES

In 1985-86, tuition and fees were $615 for one course, $1,179 for two courses, and $1,743 for three courses. These costs are subject to revision. One course per quarter constitutes part-time study; either two or three courses per quarter constitute full-time study. Housing and other living expenses are in addition to tuition. A limited number of university-owned rooms and apartments are available, as is a student cafeteria.

FINANCIAL ASSISTANCE

No scholarship or assistantship funds are available currently. University officials cooperate in completing required forms for various private and government-guaranteed loan programs; however, such arrangements must be initiated and completed by the student.

PLACEMENT

The university operates a Placement Office for providing assistance to students seeking full-time, permanent employment upon graduation.

CORRESPONDENCE

For further information and application forms, please contact
  Dean
  School of Business and Economics
  Mercer University
  1400 Coleman Avenue
  Macon, Georgia 31207
  Telephone: 912-744-2832

MEREDITH COLLEGE

RALEIGH, NORTH CAROLINA

Meredith College, with a rich heritage as an undergraduate institution for women, initiated its M.B.A. program in August 1983. The first graduates completed requirements for their degrees in August 1985.

The college is located on a 225-acre campus in Raleigh, a focal point of the Research Triangle Park, which has research facilities for major corporations in the United States. The location offers proximity to outstanding universities and affords students and faculty members academic privileges, cultural opportunities, and social activities.

M.B.A. students may attend classes for three semesters during the calendar year. Classes are held at convenient times for working women.

PROGRAM OF STUDY
The primary purpose of the Meredith M.B.A. program is to provide students with business knowledge and managerial skills that are essential for successful functioning in business, industry, and government. The program offers advanced study for women who are currently in management or administrative positions or who aspire to such positions.

The specific objectives of the program are
- to improve analytical, problem-solving, communication, and decision-making skills;
- to integrate business experience with current theories of management and to explore new business concepts in marketing, accounting, and economics;
- to analyze alternative solutions to business problems involving social, legal, economic, political, and ethical factors; and
- to develop techniques for meeting the challenges of management innovations, changing technology, and modern computers.

Candidates for the M.B.A. degree must successfully complete a minimum of 36 hours of graduate courses. Candidates who have completed all prerequisites may fulfill degree requirements in two years. They must complete requirements within six years.

Students who have not fulfilled prerequisite requirements must complete the 18 hours of undergraduate courses in economics, accounting, and mathematics in order to enroll in specified courses.

ADMISSION
Students with an interest in business who have baccalaureate degrees and who present other indications of potential success in graduate study may apply.

An applicant must submit the following documents: official transcripts from each college or university attended, application form, scores on the Graduate Management Admission Test (GMAT), two letters of recommendation from people with knowledge of the applicant's work or ability, and a statement of business work experience. Applicants should schedule interviews with the head of the department or the director of the M.B.A. program.

EXPENSES
Tuition charges for 1985-86 were $140 per credit hour. A person taking two courses for three semester during the year pays $2,520.

FINANCIAL ASSISTANCE
The Scholarships and Financial Assistance Office supplies information relative to financial assistance and assists graduate students in applying for federally insured loans through the College Foundation, Inc., Raleigh, N.C.

The Shearon Harris Scholarship Fund awards scholarships annually to two M.B.A. students. The fund was established by the Harris family to perpetuate the interest of Mr. Harris, former Chairman of the Meredith College Board of Trustees, in Meredith students.

PLACEMENT
The facilities of the Career Services and Placement Office are available to M.B.A. students. The director and her staff render services to students in discussing career plans, building a personnel file, and scheduling interviews with campus recruiters.

CORRESPONDENCE
For further information, write or call
Office of the Registrar
Meredith College
3800 Hillsborough Street
Raleigh, North Carolina 27607-5298
Telephone: 919-829-8593

Metropolitan State University (Metro U) was established by the Minnesota State Legislature in 1971 as the seventh member of the State University System. As an innovative university with a commitment to excellence, Metro U has acquired a national and international reputation for its successful approach to nontraditional higher education. The Metro U Master of Management and Administration (M.M.A.) program enables students to pursue their professional education while maintaining their ongoing responsibilities to family, work, and community. Metro U does not have a traditional campus. Instead, M.M.A. classes are held in the executive training facilities and conference rooms of corporations in the Twin Cities metropolitan area. Metropolitan State University is fully accredited by the North Central Association of Colleges and Schools.

PROGRAM OF STUDY

The Metropolitan State University Master of Management and Administration program has been structured to meet the academic needs of career-oriented, working adults in business, public, and nonprofit organizations who seek further management education that can fit into their demanding schedules. It provides for
- part-time enrollment,
- flexible scheduling,
- personalized attention,
- evening and weekend course work,
- financial assistance,
- individualized degree plans; and
- reasonable cost.

Several forms of study may be combined in order to permit flexible scheduling and different approaches to learning. These include Metro U course work, course work at another accredited institution, assessment of prior learning, independent study, internships, and seminars/workshops. The M.M.A. program is composed of three phases. Phase I includes seven required competences. Phase II consists of five individually designed competences, wherein degree plans are tailored to individual student needs. These competences are developed with the guidance of an adviser. In Phase III students participate in the Seminar in Management Directions. Students also complete and present their master's paper in Phase III.

M.M.A. Program Outline/Content Summary

Phase I

Admission
Core Competences:
Managerial Communications
Management Information Systems
Management and Organizational Behavior
Marketing Management
Managerial Accounting
Managerial Finance
Professional Development for Managers

Phase II

Five Individually Designed Competences

Phase III

Seminar in Management Directions
Presentation of Master's Paper
Graduation

Each student also writes a major professional paper as part of his or her program of study. This paper focuses on a significant problem in the student's main area of interest and its resolution. A core resident faculty of professional educators is complemented by community faculty. These are persons who have appropriate academic training and are expert practitioners with extensive professional experience in various aspects of management. Learning is optimized by keeping class size small, utilizing various teaching methods, and providing a balance of theory and practical applications.

It is possible for a student to complete the program in two years. The time limit for completion is five years.

ADMISSION

Persons who have a bachelor's degree in any field are eligible to apply for admission to the M.M.A. program; however, the following five undergraduate competences in the business area are required: macro- and microeconomics, financial accounting I and II, and statistics.

Required of all applicants are the following:
- a bachelor's degree from an accredited institution,
- a completed application for admission,
- Graduate Management Admission Test (GMAT) scores,
- official undergraduate transcripts and transcripts of any graduate work completed,
- a typed paper discussing "Why the Master of Management and Administration Degree Would Help Me Achieve My Professional Goals," and
- two letters of reference.

Admission is open each of the four academic quarters, and there are no specific deadlines for application.

EXPENSES

There is a $10 nonrefundable application fee. As of fall 1985, the Minnesota resident tuition was $157 per competence.

FINANCIAL ASSISTANCE

Various forms of financial aid are available to M.M.A. students. Requests for financial aid and/or veteran's benefits information should be directed to the Director of Financial Aid at the address below.

CORRESPONDENCE

For more information, please write or call
Graduate Program Director
Metropolitan State University
Suite 238, Metro Square
121 Seventh Place East
St. Paul, Minnesota 55101-2189
Telephone: 612-297-4399

Miami University was founded in 1809 as a state-supported university. The School of Business Administration began to operate as a distinct unit of the university in 1927. The Master of Business Administration (M.B.A.) degree was authorized in 1948. The Master of Accountancy (M.Acc.) program was authorized in 1980.

The university campus, consisting of 700 wooded acres, is located near the commercial and industrial area known as the Miami Valley. The many industries located in the valley provide numerous opportunities for direct contact with the business world.

PROGRAMS OF STUDY
The basic objective of the Master of Business Administration program is to provide for the professional development of those persons who wish to achieve responsible positions in business and government and to prepare graduates for doctoral study. The program is designed to impart a knowledge of basic business functions, to develop decision-making abilities, and to give a better understanding of the internal and external effects of economic forces on the management of business enterprise. While an area of concentration is required (finance, management, marketing management, or decision science), the emphasis of the program is on breadth.

The M.B.A. degree may be based on the Bachelor of Science in business degree or on a bachelor's degree in a nonbusiness discipline. In the former case students may complete the degree in a calendar year; in the latter case four semesters would be required to complete the degree requirements. Part-time study is possible.

The total hour requirement is 36 hours. No credit hours earned in survey courses or in undergraduate courses in areas in which the candidate lacks adequate undergraduate training may be counted toward the degree.

A thesis is optional. At the end of the program the candidate is required to pass a written comprehensive examination in the major field of specialization.

The Master of Accountancy program prepares students for professional careers in institutional, managerial, and public accountancy. The program has been developed along the guidelines provided by the Council of the American Institute of Certified Public Accountants in cooperation with other professional accounting organizations representing the various areas of accountancy specializations. This program requires one year (33 semester hours) of study beyond the baccalaureate degree provided the prerequisite courses have been successfully completed. The program is available to students with an undergraduate concentration in accountancy as well as students with no accounting background.

Admission requirements for both programs include a bachelor's degree from an accredited college or university, a cumulative grade-point average of at least 2.5 (4.0 scale), and an acceptable score on the Graduate Management Admission Test (GMAT).

Foreign students whose native language is not English must furnish an acceptable score on the Test of English as a Foreign Language (TOEFL).

EXPENSES
For full-time students, each semester:

Instruction fee	$1,065
General fee	248
Total	$1,313*

For students carrying fewer than 12 credit hours in a given semester:

Instruction and general fees, per credit hour

Ohio residents	$110
Others	193

*Plus tuition of $1,250 per semester for residents of states other than Ohio. Fees are subject to change.

FINANCIAL ASSISTANCE
To receive an appointment as a graduate assistant, a student must be accepted for admission to a degree program in the Graduate School with regular standing.

Graduate assistantships involve academic duties equivalent to those of a one-quarter-time member of the academic staff. Depending on the needs of a department, a graduate assistant may be assigned various duties or asked to assist in faculty research. In 1985-86 the stipend for two semesters was at least $1,785. Graduate assistants receive a waiver of the instruction fee and the out-of-state tuition fees. They may also have the instruction and tuition fees waived for the summer term preceding or following the year of appointment. Summer fellowships of up to $1,000 are also available. Graduate fellowships of up to $2,500 are available to some M.Acc. students.

Graduate grants-in-aid are available each year to able students who are seriously in need of financial assistance and who have strong academic records. These grants are designed for students entering upon or engaged in continuous full-time study leading to a degree. A graduate grant-in-aid offers remission of the instruction fee and out-of-state tuition fee but carries no cash stipend. Each grant is awarded for a specific period of one or more semesters or one six-week summer term. Continuance or renewal of a grant is dependent upon satisfactory progress toward a degree. Applications for graduate assistantships, fellowships, and grants-in-aid should be on file by March 1.

PLACEMENT
Each year, representatives of approximately 400 business organizations visit the campus to conduct employment interviews with prospective graduates. The director and staff of the Career Planning and Placement Service attempt to place every graduate in a suitable position. A referral service is maintained for alumni.

CORRESPONDENCE
For further information or to request an application for admission, write or call

Director of Graduate Studies
School of Business Administration
Miami University
Oxford, Ohio 45056
Telephone: 513-529-6643

Michigan State University is located in East Lansing, four miles east of the state capital. It has an enrollment of approximately 40,000 students. The Graduate School of Business Administration and the College of Business, the largest degree-granting unit on the campus, have a combined enrollment of 6,300 undergraduate and 800 graduate students. The faculty of the business school numbers approximately 136.

The school is housed in Eppley Center, a modern, fully integrated facility that provides an appropriate academic environment for graduate study. Owen Hall, a dormitory for the exclusive use of graduate students, is adjacent to the business school. Modern, completely furnished, one- and two-bedroom apartments for married students are available on the campus at reasonable rates.

PROGRAMS OF STUDY

The Master of Business Administration (M.B.A.) degree program is designed for the education of professional executives in business. While allowing for a functional concentration, the curriculum has been developed to provide breadth rather than narrow specialization. It is structured to accommodate students with or without an undergraduate degree in business administration.

The M.B.A. program requires 56 term or quarter hours of graduate course work including a core of 28 credits, 2 free electives, and a major area of concentration selected by the student from accounting, finance, economics, food systems economics and management, marketing, personnel and organization behavior, materials and logistics management, management science, and hotel, restaurant, and institutional management. The 56-hour program can be completed in about 15 months.

Additional course work is required of the student who has not completed certain prerequisite business-related subjects. An applicant with an undergraduate degree in business administration will probably have completed most of these precore requirements. They include courses in mathematics, statistics, computers, business law, accounting, finance, marketing, and intermediate microeconomics. A student may enter any one of the four terms during the year, but September is strongly recommended, particularly for foreign students.

The Ph.D. program requires satisfactory completion of comprehensive preliminary written examinations in three subject-matter areas, a program of research-related course work (or a reading knowledge of two foreign languages, or one language and an appropriate program of research related course work), a program of course work in economics, and a research dissertation. The three subject-matter areas requiring written examinations include a major functional field in business and two minor areas in business or related fields.

ADMISSION

In order to be admitted to the M.B.A. program an applicant must have a baccalaureate degree from an accredited institution, an academic record showing a B average or better for the junior and senior years of undergraduate study, and letters of recommendation from former classroom instructors and/or employers. Candidates should present a strong score on the Graduate Management Admission Test (GMAT).

In order to be admitted to one of the doctoral programs an applicant must have a prior academic record of significantly high scholarship, a strong GMAT score, and other evidence to indicate the probability of success. The admission decision is made by a faculty committee in the department that offers the applicant's chosen major. Majors include accounting, finance, marketing, transportation-distribution, management, organization, management science, production, and personnel-human relations.

EXPENSES
Subject to change
Tuition
  Michigan residents,
      per credit. . . . . $ 61.00
  Out-of-state residents,
      per credit. 126.00
Miscellaneous fees, per term 25.00
Room, graduate dormitory,
    per term including $155 food
    allowance (double). 626.50
                      (single). 738.50
Books and incidentals, per term . . 450.00

FINANCIAL ASSISTANCE

Graduate assistantships and fellowships are reserved primarily for doctoral students. In a limited number of cases, highly qualified M.B.A. students receive financial support. Graduate assistantships are administered by the chairperson of the student's major department, and interested applicants should correspond directly with that person.

Information on scholarships and need-based grants and loans is available from the Office of Admissions and Scholarships and the Office of Financial Aids. Special funding is available for qualified minority students. Placement Services and the Personnel Office assist students and their spouses in finding employment in the university and the local community.

PLACEMENT

Michigan State University maintains the largest centralized placement facility of any university in the country. Hundreds of the nation's leading employers visit, or are in active contact with, the Placement Bureau each academic year. The faculty maintains contact with deans and department heads at other institutions who may be interested in doctoral candidates as prospective employees.

CORRESPONDENCE

For further information or to request an application for admission, please write or call
  Director, M.B.A. Program
  215 Eppley Center
  Michigan State University
  East Lansing, Michigan 48824-1121
  Telephone: 517-355-7604

Michigan Technological University is an independent unit in Michigan's state-supported system of higher education. It was founded in 1885 as a mining school and has since distinguished itself in engineering, science, forestry, and business. The undergraduate enrollment is approximately 7,500. Full-time students in the Graduate School number about 350. The School of Business and Engineering Administration is accredited by the North Central Association of Colleges and Schools and is a member of the American Assembly of Collegiate Schools of Business (AACSB). It has 600 undergraduate and 40 graduate students served by a faculty of 29. Michigan Tech's main campus stretches for about a mile along Portage Lake in the city of Houghton, 550 miles northwest of Detroit and 450 miles north of Chicago on Michigan's Keweenaw Peninsula.

PROGRAMS OF STUDY

The Master of Science in operations management degree program is designed for persons with academic backgrounds in engineering, natural science, computer science, management science, or other appropriate fields who are, or expect to be, involved in the areas of materials management, production planning and shop floor control, logistics management, quality control and assurance, and the management of operations. The central focus of the field of operations management is on solving the managerial problems associated with controlling flows of materials and resources in manufacturing, distribution, and service organizations. This field integrates mathematics, statistics, and evolving concepts to improve the functioning of an organization. The focus of the program is on real-world problem solving using a rigorous core of analytical techniques drawn from several disciplines.

Operations Management Core	*Credits*
BA501 Managerial Economics and Finance	4
BA512 Operations and Production Management	4
BA513 Advanced Operations and Production Mgt.	4
BA514 Quality Assurance and Mgt.	3
BA517 Management System Dynamics	4
BA518 Business Logistics Management	3
BA594 Seminar in Operations Management	4
	26
Electives from business, engineering, mathematics and computer science	18
Thesis or project	10
	54

Students generally complete their course work during 12 months of full-time study on campus and complete their thesis or project under faculty guidance at an off-campus location such as the student's place of employment or internship site.

The Master of Science in mineral economics degree program is designed to prepare an individual for a career in planning mineral development, forecasting mineral market conditions, or financial analysis of mineral projects. An undergraduate degree in a field related to mineral engineering or mineral science such as mining engineering, metallurgy, or geology is an appropriate background.

ADMISSION

Acceptance to the programs will be determined on a competitive basis by the Graduate Committee. Applicants normally must meet the following standards:
● have an appropriate undergraduate degree;
● have an undergraduate grade-point average of 2.7 or better on a 4-point scale;
● have completed at least one college-level course in calculus;
● have scored 470 or higher on the Graduate Management Admission Test (GMAT).

Foreign applicants must also submit scores on the Test of English as a Foreign Language (TOEFL). New students normally start during the fall quarter.

EXPENSES

Expenses for four quarters are as follows:
Tuition
 Michigan resident $2,396
 Non-Michigan resident 5,264
Books and supplies 600
Board and room 3,387

FINANCIAL ASSISTANCE

Several graduate assistantships are available to students with special skills in computer programming or statistics; these pay $1,900 per quarter plus tuition. A limited number of smaller stipends are also available. Financial aid decisions are generally not made until August.

PLACEMENT

The Placement Office annually arranges for more than 300 companies to visit the university.

CORRESPONDENCE

For further information, write or call
 Dr. Paul A. Nelson
 Graduate Program Director
 School of Business and Engineering
  Administration
 Michigan Technological University
 Houghton, Michigan 49931
 Telephone: 906-487-2809 or 487-2669

Middle Tennessee State University (MTSU), established in 1911, has an enrollment in excess of 10,000 students, of whom more than 1,700 are at the graduate level. The campus is located 30 miles southeast of Nashville on I-24 and is noted for its beautiful landscape. There are 81 major buildings on 500 spacious acres.

The Andrew Todd Library houses 800,000 volumes and features a Tennessee Collection and the collected papers of former Senator Albert Gore, an MTSU graduate. Access to the computer, a Honeywell DPS-8/49D, can be either through remote terminals located in the Business School's computer lab or through batch processing at the computer center. The school's lab is also equipped with a variety of microcomputers. The Business and Economic Research Center is available to graduate business students and publishes a monograph series, a reprint series, and the bimonthly journal, *Tennessee Business and Economic Review*.

PROGRAMS OF STUDY
Generally, the objective of the programs is to provide a strong curriculum for the professional education of students, preparing them for positions in business organizations, government, and academic institutions.

The Master of Business Administration (M.B.A.) degree may be based on a bachelor's degree in the arts, science, engineering, or business. Approximately 45 percent of the school's graduate business students have a nonbusiness undergraduate degree. Completion of the program normally takes from one to two calendar years of full-time study, depending upon the background of the individual. The program may be completed at night by part-time students over a longer period of time. The curriculum is designed to recognize the need for an understanding of subject matter that meets the varied demands of individual students. Of the 36 graduate semester hours for the M.B.A., 24 are required courses and 12 are electives. The electives may be divided among the areas of accounting, marketing, management, economics, finance, or information systems. A thesis is not required.

The Master of Science degree in accounting and information systems permits an emphasis in either accounting or information systems. In this 30-semester-hour program, the accounting emphasis requires 15 hours in accounting and 6

hours in information systems; the information systems emphasis requires 15 hours in information systems and 6 hours in accounting.

The School of Business also offers course work for a Master of Arts degree with options in economics or industrial relations, and the Doctor of Arts with a major in economics and a minor in finance, management, marketing, accounting, information systems, or business administration.

ADMISSION
An application for admission to graduate studies in business and a recent Graduate Management Admission Test (GMAT) score should be submitted at least three weeks before the desired entry date. Students with a 3.0 or higher grade-point average (GPA) who have not submitted a GMAT score may be admitted on a conditional basis for one semester but must take the test at the first available administration. Students admitted conditionally must complete all requirements for unconditional admission (acceptable GMAT score and transcripts) before the close of the first semester.

When the combination of measures used is the GMAT score and grade-point average, the student should meet one of the following formula scores: (1) undergraduate GPA $\times$ 200 + GMAT score = or > 950 (2) upper-division GPA $\times$ 200 + GMAT score = or > 1,000. Foreign students are required to score at least 550 on the Test of English as a Foreign Language (TOEFL). All students must demonstrate ability to communicate effectively in English.

Students are admitted for the fall term beginning in late August, the spring term beginning in early January, or summer terms beginning in early May, June, and July. Applicants should request official transcripts from all colleges previously attended to be sent directly to the Office of Admissions.

EXPENSES
Expenses are for the 1985-86 academic year and are subject to change by the State Board of Regents.

Full-time per semester	In-state	Out-of-state
Tuition	$599	$1,673
Room (approximately)	500	500
Books and supplies (estimate)	140	140
Meals (daily estimate)	7	7

Tuition for part-time students is $59 per semester hour for Tennessee residents and $153 per semester hour for nonresidents.

FINANCIAL ASSISTANCE
A limited number of graduate teaching assistantships, graduate research assistantships, and doctoral fellowships are available. Applications and information may be obtained from the Director of Graduate Business Studies at the address below. An individual is expected to be in good standing, that is, having met the requirements for admission to graduate school (including successful test scores), and having a cumulative grade-point average of 3.0 or higher.

PLACEMENT
The university maintains a student placement office which is visited by more than 160 businesses and governmental employers each year.

CORRESPONDENCE
For further information concerning the programs of study offered by the School of Business, write

Dr. E. Dwight Bullard, Assistant Dean and Director of Graduate Studies
School of Business
Middle Tennessee State University
Murfreesboro, Tennessee 37132
Telephone: 615-898-2964

Millsaps College, founded February 21, 1890, is one of the youngest colleges supported by the United Methodist Church. A liberal arts college designed to train students for responsible citizenship and well-balanced lives, Millsaps also offers a Master of Business Administration (M.B.A.) program to meet the needs of the business and nonprofit communities of Jackson, the state capital. Both evening and day classes are available, and sufficient course work is offered every semester to allow full-time graduate students some flexibility in planning a curriculum of study.

PROGRAM OF STUDY

The Millsaps program is designed to develop in its students those qualities that reflect the needs of organizations for broadly educated managers who are adaptable to new environments and have a high degree of analytical skills.

The M.B.A. degree will require the equivalent of 51 semester hours of study in accounting, economics, finance, management, marketing, operations, and policy. Up to 21 of these hours are prerequisite and foundation in nature and subject to waiver on the basis of prior undergraduate or graduate work judged to be equivalent in content. A portion of the advanced course component may possibly be satisfied by transfer of equivalent graduate credit. However, at least 30 hours of graduate credit must be taken at Millsaps College. Students should complete most of the foundation course work before attempting advanced study.

Graduate Foundation Courses	Course Number	Credits
Survey of Accounting	580	3
Survey of Economics	500	3
Survey of Management	533	3
Survey of Operations Management	534	3
Survey of Finance	562	3
Survey of Marketing	521	3
Legal Environment of Business	520	3
Statistical and Computer Analysis	575	3
		24

The advanced component of the M.B.A. program is divided between core or required courses and elective courses. Electives are offered in accounting, economics, finance, management, marketing, policy, and quantitative management. No thesis is required.

Core and Elective Courses	Course Number	Credits
Managerial Analysis and Forecasting	601	3
Business Policy in the Global Economy	699	3
Total required		6
Core and elective Courses		24
Total hours		30

ADMISSION

Students may be admitted to the program and commence course work at the beginning of any semester: fall, spring, or summer. The procedure for being admitted to degree candidacy calls for

- submission of a completed application for admission to the program and the $20 application fee,
- submission of an official copy of the undergraduate transcript (sent directly by the institution to Millsaps College) which certifies the applicant has received the baccalaureate degree and other transcripts necessary to provide a complete review of prior academic work,
- submission of an official score on the Graduate Management Admission Test (GMAT) directly from Educational Testing Service, and
- an interview with the Dean of the School of Management is advisable.

Students must be admitted to the program before taking graduate-level course work at Millsaps, unless their undergraduate grade-point average is 3.0 (A = 4.0) or higher. Students with grade-point averages of 3.0 or higher may take graduate course work but must complete the admission process during their first semester. Undergraduate prerequisites may be taken before the student is admitted to the graduate program regardless of his or her grade-point average.

To be admitted to the M.B.A. program, applicants must demonstrate an aptitude for graduate study. The results of the GMAT and the applicant's previous college record will be the primary determining factors in making the admission decision.

Entering graduate students from countries other than the United States for whom English is not the major language are required to demonstrate high-level competence in the use of the English language by scoring at least 550 on the Test of English as a Foreign Language (TOEFL).

Foreign students coming to Millsaps College after completing a baccalaureate degree from a regionally accredited American college or university may have this requirement waived if satisfactory English grades were obtained in the student's undergraduate program.

EXPENSES

Basic expenses for full-time study at Millsaps are approximately $4,450 per semester. The part-time tuition rate is $190 per semester hour. Tuition and fees are subject to revision by action of the Board of Trustees.

FINANCIAL ASSISTANCE

Since most of the M.B.A. students at Millsaps work for businesses that have employee tuition assistance plans, only a limited financial aid program is available. Students enrolled for six or more hours during a semester are eligible for any of the many federal student aid programs. Limited scholarships are available for women and minority students with excellent admission credentials. A limited number of assistantships are also available for full-time students.

CORRESPONDENCE

For further information or to request an application for admission, please contact
Dr. Jerry D. Whitt, Dean
School of Management
Millsaps College
Jackson, Mississippi 39210
Telephone: 601-354-5201

School of Business Administration

MISSISSIPPI COLLEGE

CLINTON, MISSISSIPPI

Mississippi College, chartered by the legislature in 1826, is the oldest institution of higher learning in the State of Mississippi. The Division of Business and Economics, organized in 1959, became the School of Business Administration in 1975.

PROGRAM OF STUDY

The M.B.A. program offered by the School of Business Administration is designed primarily for people who work full time but desire graduate study on a part-time basis. The required courses are offered only in the evening, meeting once a week, Monday through Thursday from 7:00 p.m. to 9:30 p.m. Graduate study began with the M.B.A. program in 1967. The objective of this program is to offer professional training for the person who is already in a managerial capacity or who plans to embark on a career in management. The program is general and does not provide for concentration in any specific subject-matter area.

The curriculum consists of 30 semester hours of graduate study for the student who has an undergraduate major in economics and business administration or who has completed at least 24 hours of undergraduate study in these fields. The specific course requirements are listed under the "Admission" section.

Although any student who has a good academic record and holds a baccalaureate degree from an accredited four-year college or university may apply for admission, those who have no undergraduate foundation in economics or business may be required to take at least 54 semester hours for completion of the program. These courses would include the 24 semester hours of undergraduate economics and business subjects listed below under "Admission" plus the 30 semester hours of graduate study required of all graduate candidates.

Students are expected to complete the economics, accounting, and finance courses in the graduate core before proceeding further. The part-time nature of the program limits the academic load to six hours a semester.

Students in the M.B.A. program complete a graduate core that is intended to provide a knowledge of principles underlying the operations of business and public

enterprise. These courses constitute the foundation upon which the more advanced aspects of the program are built.

Graduate Core

ECO 531, Production Economics I (Microeconomics)	3
ECO 532, Production Economics II (Macroeconomics)	3
ACC 501, Accounting Policies	3
FIN 541, Financial Management	3
	12

Additional Courses Required for the M.B.A. Degree

MKT 581, Market Analysis	3
GBU 551, Human Relations in Business	3
MGT 571, Advanced Principles of Management I	3
MGT 572, Advanced Principles of Management II	3
Six semester hours of general business electives	6
	18
Total graduate hours	30

ADMISSION

Admission to the M.B.A. program is based on the combination of an applicant's previous academic record, score on the Graduate Management Admission Test (GMAT), and work experience. The basic requirements for admission are a bachelor's degree from an accredited college or university, an undergraduate record that indicates the ability to pursue the M.B.A. program, and a satisfactory score on the GMAT. For regular admission, applicants should score a total of 950 or more based on the formula: 200 × the undergraduate grade-point average (4.0 system) + the GMAT score. Students who have not taken the GMAT must take it the first time it is offered after an application for the M.B.A. program has been made. The test is administered three times a year at Mississippi College. Applications for the test may be obtained at the Graduate Office, the School of Business, or from Educational Testing Service.

The Graduate Program in Business Administration builds on a core of undergraduate courses normally taught in schools of business:

	Semester Hours
Accounting	6
Economics	6
Finance	3
Management	3
Marketing	3
Statistics	3
Total	24

EXPENSES

Tuition for 1985-86 was $110 per semester hour with a fixed registration fee of $24.

CORRESPONDENCE

To obtain further information or to request an application for admission, interested applicants should write

Dr. Gerald Lee, Dean
School of Business Administration
Mississippi College
Clinton, Mississippi 39058
or
Dr. Edward McMillan, Dean
Graduate School
Mississippi College
Clinton, Mississippi 39058

Mississippi State University was founded as a land-grant institution in 1878. The College of Business and Industry, organized in 1915, is one of the oldest in the South. The organizational structure of the college includes the School of Accountancy and the Departments of Business Information Systems and Quantitative Analysis, Economics, Finance, Management, and Marketing. The college also encompasses the Division of Research and the Division of Business Services. Both the undergraduate and graduate programs are accredited by the American Assembly of Collegiate Schools of Business (AACSB).

PROGRAMS OF STUDY

The Master of Business Administration (M.B.A.) is an advanced professional degree in administration. While some concentration in a particular functional area is permitted, breadth in the educational experience is the essential characteristic of the degree. There is no thesis required, but 30 graduate hours, 24 of which must be in courses reserved strictly for graduate students, are required beyond any prerequisite undergraduate courses the student may lack. The graduate study consists of nine semester hours of electives plus a compulsory core including Advanced Accounting Analysis for Decision Making, Business Statistics and Data Processing, Managerial Economics or Economic Analysis I (microeconomics), Economic Analysis II (macroeconomics), Financial Policies, Management Policies, and Marketing Policies.

Thirty hours beyond the prerequisite undergraduate courses are required for the M.S. degree in business administration, including six hours of thesis credit. A major in business information systems and quantitative analysis must be completed, and a minor, either inside or outside the college, is required. The M.S. degree permits a higher degree of specialization in information systems and/or quantitative analysis.

Forty-five hours of accounting credit are required in the combined undergraduate and graduate programs for the M.P.A. degree. The core of graduate credit courses consists of 12 hours elected from the last 7 courses listed in the M.B.A. core above, one of which must be an economics course. All B.P.A. requirements must be fulfilled.

All graduate programs require the following undergraduate prerequisite courses: principles of accounting—six hours, principles of economics—six hours, business law—three hours, business statistics—three hours, business finance—three hours, money and banking—three hours, principles of management—three hours, principles of marketing—three hours, and electronic information systems—three hours.

The successful completion of the Doctor of Business Administration (D.B.A.) degree program will necessitate a reasonable competence in the quantitative area of business. A minimum of 60 hours of course work beyond the baccalaureate degree is required (30 beyond a master's degree in business), as well as a research dissertation. No foreign language is required.

The D.B.A. curriculum consists of one designated 18-hour major field, two 12-hour minor fields, and 6 hours in each of three remaining fields for the total of 60 hours (minimum) beyond the baccalaureate degree. Concentrations are offered in six fields: accounting, business information systems and quantitative analysis, economics, finance, management, and marketing. A minimum of 30 hours must be taken in the program at Mississippi State.

With the approval of the major department, a student may elect one of the minor fields from an area outside the College of Business and Industry. In such cases, the so-called remaining fields in business increase in number from three to four and a minimum of 6 hours must be completed in each, which increases overall hour requirements to a minimum of 66 beyond the baccalaureate degree.

Written comprehensive examinations must be passed in the major field and in each of the two minor fields.

ADMISSION

Regular admission to all degree programs requires a 2.50/4.00 grade-point average on all undergraduate work or a 2.75/4.00 grade-point average on the last two years of baccalaureate work, a baccalaureate degree from an accredited four-year institution, and a minimum total score of 450 on the Graduate Management Admission Test (GMAT). When students are deficient in any of the criteria cited, they may nevertheless be considered for admission if they exceed the minimum required in the

other criterion in accordance with standards cited by the American Assembly of Collegiate Schools of Business (AACSB).

Admission to the doctoral program requires a GMAT score of 500 and cumulative undergraduate quality-point average of 2.75/4.00, plus a minimum quality-point average of 3.25/4.00 on all prior graduate work, with prior graduate hours in business and economics including no more than 20 percent below the grade of B. Consideration will be given to an applicant who is deficient in not more than one of the specifications cited above. Satisfactory English proficiency is required of all foreign applicants.

EXPENSES

Annual expenses (subject to change) for regular course loads:

In-state students	$1,301
Out-of-state students	2,483
Dormitory rooms or apartments, per semester	450

FINANCIAL ASSISTANCE

A number of graduate assistantships are available at both the master's and doctoral levels. The normal stipend for a master's level assistant is $2,700 for nine months. At the doctoral level, teaching (six hours per semester) and research assistantships carry stipends of $6,475 for nine months. Out-of-state tuition is waived for recipients of graduate assistantships.

CORRESPONDENCE

For further information, write to
Director
Division of Graduate Studies in
Business
College of Business and Industry
Mississippi State University
P.O. Box 5288
Mississippi State, Mississippi 39762

Founded in 1933, Monmouth College has offered graduate work at the master's level since 1967. Total college enrollment is approximately 4,000 students. Many students live on campus, but a significant number are part-time or full-time commuters. This diversity in the student body, as well as the wide range of available programs, makes Monmouth College a heterogeneous and dynamic institution.

Approximately 30 percent of the undergraduate and 60 percent of the graduate students at Monmouth major in business administration. The graduate component is made up primarily of part-time students who are employed in a variety of industrial, financial, and research organizations. The School of Business Administration accommodates business administration undergraduates as well as students who majored in other subjects.

The location of the college is ideal for business students. West Long Branch, New Jersey, is only a mile from the Atlantic Ocean in a growing shore area rich in employment and recreational opportunities. Only 50 miles from New York City and 75 miles from Philadelphia, the college is beautifully situated on 120 acres. Several large estates combine with attractive new buildings to form a campus valued at more than $40,000,000.

PROGRAM OF STUDY
Classes are usually held in the evening and meet once a week for three credits. Requirements for the Master of Business Administration (M.B.A.) degree vary from 39-60 credits, as explained below. On approval by the Dean, students may transfer credits from other graduate schools provided that a minimum of 24 credits from the required or elective core of courses are completed in residence at Monmouth College. Although it is possible to take three or four courses during a semester, most students take one or two courses. The average class size ranges from about 20 to 30; seldom are classes larger than 40; most students have several courses in which enrollment is as small as 15. The case study method is used in some courses.

The seven courses listed below, offered at the graduate level, are for students who have not completed the basic business common body of knowledge. They are prerequisite to all remaining courses but may be waived for acceptable equivalent courses taken either in an undergraduate or graduate program. Students for whom all seven courses are waived need complete only 39 credits.

BM 500 Introduction to Quantitative Analysis for Business Decisions
BE 501 Economics for Management
BA 503 Financial Accounting
BM 504 Computer and Information Systems
BM 505 Business Statistics
BF 507 Financial Institutions and Markets
BM 511 Management Theory and Practices

Courses required of all students are the following:
BM 513 Production and Operations Management
BM 514 Social Responsibility of Business
BM 516 Organizational Behavior
BF 521 Financial Management
BK 531 Marketing Management
BA 541 Managerial Accounting
BE 561 Managerial Economics OR
BE 571 Economic Policy in Society
BM 590 Business Policy

In addition to the required courses, students choose five electives (15 credits), guided by an adviser. Electives may be in concentrations such as accounting, acquisition and contracts, economics, finance, management information systems, marketing, or management.

ADMISSION
A candidate for the M.B.A. program is required to have obtained a baccalaureate degree from an accredited institution with an acceptable undergraduate scholastic average and to complete the Graduate Management Admission Test (GMAT). A weighted combination of the baccalaureate scholastic average and the GMAT is used for admission selection.

Students are admitted for the fall term beginning in September, the winter term in January, or the short (three-week and six-week) summer sessions during June, July, and August. Applications should be received at least three weeks prior to the beginning of a term.

EXPENSES
Tuition, per credit hour $195
Application fee 25
Comprehensive fee
   Less than nine credits 55
   Nine credits or more 110

FINANCIAL ASSISTANCE
Some students may be eligible for certain guaranteed student loans.

PLACEMENT
The college maintains its own Placement Office, visited annually by representatives of companies chiefly in the metropolitan area. The Placement Office also keeps interested alumni informed of employment opportunities for experienced personnel.

CORRESPONDENCE
For further information, write or call
   Graduate Admissions
   Monmouth College
   West Long Branch, New Jersey 07764
   Telephone: 201-571-3452

Established in 1908, Montclair is a coeducational, four-year college of liberal arts, sciences, professional, and graduate programs. The 200-acre campus is located 14 miles west of New York City in the relaxed and comfortable suburban atmosphere of Upper Montclair, New Jersey. Cultural opportunities abound within the area. The college also has convenient transportation links to the cultural amenities of New York City and its adjacent communities.

The college is accredited by the Middle States Association of Colleges and Secondary Schools and by the National Council for the Accreditation of Teacher Education. Among numerous other associations, Montclair is a member of The Council of Graduate Schools in the United States. Over 95 percent of the M.B.A. classes at Montclair are taught by faculty with doctoral or other appropriate terminal degrees. Both full-time and part-time students are welcome. The courses are offered primarily in the evening.

PROGRAM OF STUDY

The goal of the Montclair M.B.A. is to prepare management generalists who have the knowledge, techniques, and attitudes to analyze complex issues, establish logical goals, evaluate alternatives, form reasoned judgments, and effectively implement chosen options. While the development of analytical capacities is critical, the program's structure emphasizes the development of capacities that are tempered by a concerned awareness of obligations to the greater social environment.

The curriculum stresses the theoretical foundations of management-oriented disciplines, practical applications of research findings, and current managerial practices. This blend of theory and prevalent practice builds a strong foundation for immediate application as well as postgraduate professional growth.

The curriculum consists of 63 semester hours, of which 30 are devoted to a common body of knowledge, 27 are elected from advanced courses, and 6 are allocated to integrating courses. Within the 27 semester hours of advanced courses, to meet particular needs and interests, students may develop an area of specialization or choose to develop a general program without a specialization. A graduate cooperative education opportunity is also available.

Through prior academic experience, challenge examinations, nonacademic experience and/or graduate-level transfer credits, the 63 semester hour M.B.A. requirement may be reduced to 30 semester hours.

ADMISSION

The school invites applications from persons with baccalaureate or postbaccalaureate degrees. Because the program administrators actively seek a diverse student body, all previous academic majors are considered for admission. Admission to the M.B.A. program is very competitive.

Candidates are required to submit: two official copies of the transcript from each college and/or university attended, scores from the Graduate Management Admission Test (GMAT), a statement of professional objectives, two letters of recommendation from persons qualified to evaluate the applicant's promise of academic achievement and professional growth potential, and a nonrefundable fee of $10. Foreign students are required to submit their Test of English as a Foreign Language (TOEFL) scores. Applications may be submitted at any time of the year.

EXPENSES

Montclair's graduate tuition is exceptionally attractive. The current New Jersey resident tuition rate is $74 per semester hour ($222 per standard three-credit course). The nonresident tuition rate is $94 per semester hour. Miscellaneous service fees are approximately $55 per semester and are the same for both residents and nonresidents.

FINANCIAL ASSISTANCE

Graduate assistantships are available. Duties vary according to departmental needs and require 15 hours of service per week. Each assistant receives a stipend of $3,100. The tuition and fee charge for assistants is only $25 per semester. New Jersey State Guaranteed Student Loans and the PLUS program are available to citizens and permanent residents of the United States. A list of participating lending institutions may be obtained by calling the New Jersey Higher Education Assistance Authority (609-984-7070). The National Direct Student Loan program is also available through the college. Persons who come from economically disadvantaged backgrounds and have resided in New Jersey for 12 months prior to their application may be eligible for New

Jersey's Educational Opportunity Fund Graduate Grant (EOF). Montclair also participates in veterans' benefits programs and the College Work-Study program. Further information on all of the above may be obtained from Montclair's Graduate Studies Office (201-893-5147).

PLACEMENT

The Career Service Office provides resources, information and counseling for students and alumni seeking aid in finding satisfying careers. The office organizes seminars on resume writing, interview techniques, and job search strategies. It also provides a career library, listings of full-time and part-time job openings, computerized job-matching systems, a computerized interactive guidance system, an alumni career information network, and of course, on-campus recruitment by national, regional, and state organizations.

CORRESPONDENCE

For further information, write or call
Dr. Harold D. Flint, M.B.A. Director
School of Business Administration
Montclair State College
Upper Montclair, New Jersey 07043
Telephone: 201-893-4306

For 30 years the Monterey Institute of International Studies has been preparing professionals for international careers in business, education, and government. The program in business administration is one of several master's degree programs that combine professional skills, language abilities, cross-cultural understanding, and knowledge of international politics and economics. The Monterey Institute is private and accredited by the Western Association of Schools and Colleges. It is located 120 miles south of San Francisco in beautiful Monterey, a small but cosmopolitan community that is rich in history and culture. The institute has access to the educational resources of the Monterey Peninsula area, which includes several specialized libraries.

PROGRAM OF STUDY
The Master of Business Administration (M.B.A.) in international management develops the knowledge, skills, and commitments necessary to meet the challenges of a changing international environment. The goal of the program is to generate professional excellence and organizational productivity for graduates who can creatively use the most effective principles of management. The course sequences have been designed to cover the basic business skills in the first year: marketing, decision sciences, organizational behavior and development, accounting and finance, economics, and effective intercultural communications. The first semester also includes an introductory course in international business. In addition, students must acquire the capacity to speak a second language and understand political and economic conditions of other countries. These courses are taken from the Language and the International Policy Studies divisions and lead to a high cross-cultural sensitivity.

The second year of the M.B.A. program integrates management skills and international policy studies through a group project. Students develop a comprehensive business plan for establishing an entrepreneurial international business enterprise. This yearlong project is part of the general format used to stimulate actual working organizational environments in which teams work on projects to achieve a defined group of objectives. Understanding the group dynamics of these processes is central to the program. Advanced electives taken in the second year include a set of international content courses that cut

across various discipline sequences, including money and banking, finance, accounting, marketing (including consumer behavior and market research), market communications, industrial marketing, and trade management.

Other curricular innovations include integrated course work; emphasis on foreign language fluency; study of economic, political, and cultural contexts; application of state-of-the-art business techniques to practice decision-making problems; and a focus on increasing the student's capacity to use the knowledge gained for decision making. The institute goes beyond just "teaching" to create a learning environment. Students from distinct undergraduate backgrounds and having broad experience in foreign cultures participate in project groups to simulate complex organization settings in today's interdependent world. In short, students are prepared to operate creatively and effectively in the international management environment of the 1980s and beyond. The institute also works with students to set up summer internships abroad to enhance the international management skills building process.

The program is full-time for 2 nine-month academic years (64 semester units). Because of the careful design and highly integrated nature of the program, entry is limited to fall semester each year.

ADMISSION
M.B.A. students are mature (average age 25), self-motivated, and have broad experience. Many have lived overseas. Many are building professional careers on liberal arts undergraduate backgrounds. They come from 20 countries, approximately 20 percent being from outside the U.S.

Specific admission requirements are a minimum undergraduate grade-point average of 3.0 on a 4-point scale and at least two years (or equivalent) of college-level language study. Students are required to submit score reports from the Graduate Management Admission Test (GMAT). In addition, students who are not native speakers of English must achieve a score of 550 or above on the Test of English as a Foreign Language (TOEFL). Students who do not meet the language requirement are encouraged to attend the institute's intensive summer language program.

EXPENSES
Tuition at the institute is $6,250 per year. Students are responsible for their own housing for which there is a wide range of choices.

FINANCIAL ASSISTANCE
The Monterey Institute makes an effort to provide financial aid to students on the basis of need. Aid is usually awarded in a combination of grants, loans, and work opportunities. In addition to offering the full range of federally funded student aid programs, the institute awards special scholarships. Scholarships are available for former members of the Peace Corps, American Field Service, and Experiment in International Living, and for alumni from the Year Abroad Program of the State University of New York, the University of California, and the California state system.

PLACEMENT
The Monterey Institute has placed its graduates in major companies in the United States and throughout the world. The process begins with a series of career development seminars designed to help students set goals, identify opportunities, and prepare for the job market. Contacts are then made with potential employers. Some employers visit the campus, while others prefer that students be sent to them. The institute helps arrange interviews in both cases. A list of institute alumni placements is available.

CORRESPONDENCE
For further information, write or call
Director of Admissions
Monterey Institute of International Studies
425 Van Buren Street
P.O. Box 1978
Monterey, California 93940
Telephone: 408-649-3113
Outside California, use 800-824-7235

Morehead State University is located in Morehead, Rowan County, Kentucky. For more than 60 years, the university has served the people of Kentucky and the nation. The programs at Morehead are structured to meet the needs of the individuals and the communities of eastern Kentucky.

The School of Business and Economics at Morehead State was formed in 1972. The Master of Business Administration (M.B.A.) program was established in 1973. The program has grown steadily since its inception.

PROGRAM OF STUDY

The M.B.A. program at Morehead State provides an opportunity for the student to obtain competence in general business management, including the areas of economics, accounting, finance, marketing, and management. No specific areas of specialization are offered, although students may tailor their courses of study through the choice of electives. The program requires a minimum of 30 semester hours, which may be met either through full-time or part-time study. Required courses include the following:

	Hours
Accounting Analysis for Decision Making	3
Managerial Economics	3
Financial Management	3
Organizational Theory	3
Marketing Administration	3
Quantitative Business Analysis	3
Business Policy and Strategy	3
Approved electives in economics and business administration	9

ADMISSION

Applicants should be graduates of accredited four-year institutions, but a degree in business is not required. Students must submit the scores of the Graduate Management Admission Test (GMAT) prior to admission to the M.B.A. program. Foreign students must submit the scores of the Test of English as a Foreign Language (TOEFL).

To be fully admitted, applicants must have earned a baccalaureate degree with no less than a 2.5 (4.0 overall) grade-point average and grades of C or better in the business core prerequisites. Applicants who have not completed a business core may need to complete these prerequisites before being fully admitted to the M.B.A. program. The following prerequisites may be satisfied through graduate survey courses:

Prerequisites	*Hours*
Principles of Accounting	6
Principles of Economics	6
Principles of Management	3
Principles of Marketing	3
Business Finance	3
Quantitative Analysis (Statistics and Calculus)	6
Introduction to Computers	3
Production Management	3
Legal Environment of Business	3
Graduate Equivalent Courses	
ACCT 600 Survey of Accounting	3
ECON 604 Survey of Economics	3
MNGT 600 Survey of Marketing and Management	3
MNGT 601 Survey of Business Law	3
MNGT 602 Survey of Quantitative Analysis	3
DATA 600 Survey of Data Processing and Production Management	3
FIN 601 Survey of Finance	3

EXPENSES

Tuition, per semester:

Full-time resident of Kentucky	$ 516
Full-time nonresident of Kentucky	1,489
Part-time resident, per hour	58
Part-time nonresident, per hour	166
Housing	
Single students, per semester	385
Married students, per semester	600

FINANCIAL ASSISTANCE

A limited number of teaching and research assistantships offering a stipend of $3,000 per year (nine months) are available to fully admitted full-time graduate students. Applications are available from the Dean of Graduate Programs, Morehead State University.

PLACEMENT

The university maintains a job placement center to assist in the job finding process. Information can be obtained from the Director of Placement Services, Morehead State University.

CORRESPONDENCE

Correspondence concerning the M.B.A. program should be addressed to

MBA Coordinator
UPO 741
Morehead State University
Morehead, Kentucky 40351
Telephone: 606-783-2183

Graduate Program of Business

MOUNT SAINT MARY'S COLLEGE

EMMITSBURG, MARYLAND

Mount Saint Mary's College is a private, liberal arts college for men and women, located 2 miles south of Emmitsburg, Maryland, on U.S. Highway 15 approximately 12 miles south of the famed battlefields of Gettysburg, Pennsylvania. The college is within easy commuting distance of Washington, D.C. to the south, Baltimore to the east, and Harrisburg to the north. Enrollment of undergraduates is about 1,400, and there are approximately 200 students enrolled in the Master of Business Administration (M.B.A.) program. Most M.B.A. students attend part time. All classes are offered in the evening.

The college, founded in 1808, has a campus that comprises nearly 1,400 acres. The Department of Business and Economics is located in the Knott Academic Center, which was opened in 1975. A newly formed Computer Center opened in 1982. The modern library contains approximately 150,000 volumes and 850 journals and periodicals.

PROGRAM OF STUDY

The purpose of the Master of Business Administration program is to provide a broad education designed to prepare individuals for professional and managerial positions with decision-making responsibilities. The program, introduced in 1975, emphasizes the systems approach to management, and an interdisciplinary approach to the administration of the firm is employed. The M.B.A. program is accredited by the Middle States Association of Colleges and Secondary Schools and the State Department of Education in Maryland. The program is a member of the American Assembly of Collegiate Schools of Business (AACSB) and the Middle Atlantic Association of Colleges of Business Administration (MAACBA); it has been approved by the Maryland State Board for Higher Education and the Veterans Administration.

All students are required to have the following undergraduate prerequisite courses: six credits in principles of accounting, three credits in principles of economics, and three credits in statistics. All students are required to complete a 37-credit program. Each student is required to satisfy core requirements, select six credits in one area of concentration, and complete 4 credits in MBA 599, Independent Research. The program offers four areas of concentration: accounting, economics, management, and personnel and industrial relations.

A candidate must pass all course requirements with a cumulative grade-point average of at least 3.0 on a 4.0 system. A student will be admitted to candidacy after he or she has completed 12 credits with a cumulative grade-point average of 3.0 or better. All requirements for the degree should be completed within five years. Time extensions may be granted by the Dean.

The Graduate Program of Business currently offers M.B.A. degree courses at the Mount campus and at the following Maryland sites: Frederick, Hagerstown, and Germantown. Students may take no more than 12 credits at any one off-campus site.

ADMISSION

Admission is open to qualified students who hold the baccalaureate degree from an accredited college or university. No specific undergraduate courses are required for admission, but all applicants are required to submit scores on the Graduate Management Admission Test (GMAT).

Each applicant for admission to the program will be evaluated on his or her overall qualifications. The applicant will be judged by (1) the AACSB guidelines referring to an acceptable combination of undergraduate grade-point average and the GMAT score; (2) letters of recommendation submitted in his or her behalf; (3) managerial and executive potential as evidenced by undergraduate activities, military service experience, and/or professional managerial experience; and (4) a personal statement of career objectives. For those students having English as their second language, a Test of English as a Foreign Language (TOEFL) score of 550 or better is required.

EXPENSES

Application fee................ $ 20
Tuition, per credit hour......... 125
Books and supplies, per course... 25-35

FINANCIAL ASSISTANCE

A limited number of graduate assistantships are available for full-time students. Loans through commercial and governmental (GSL) sources are available.

PLACEMENT

The facilities of the Career Development Office are available to assist students and alumni in job selection.

CORRESPONDENCE

For further information, write or call
 Dean, Graduate Program of Business
 Mount Saint Mary's College
 Emmitsburg, Maryland 21727
 Telephone: 301-447-6122, extension 414

Murray State University, founded in 1922, is located in Murray, a city of 16,000 in western Kentucky. The campus is situated 15 miles from Kentucky Lake, Barkley Lake, and the 170,000-acre Land-between-the-Lakes National Recreation and Wildlife Area. Having an enrollment of 7,600 students, the university is organized into six academic colleges, one of which is the College of Business and Public Affairs. The Master of Business Administration (M.B.A.) program is accredited by the American Assembly of Collegiate Schools of Business (AACSB).

Offices and classrooms of the College of Business and Public Affairs are found in two modern, air-conditioned buildings located near the center of the campus. Computer facilities located in these buildings include a large Student Microcomputer Laboratory containing IBM Personal Computers, a Word Processing Center, and the university's main computer, an IBM 4341-2. The university's libraries contain 700,000 items of resource material and retain over 350,000 bound volumes. The business collection includes 80,000 volumes and 400 periodical subscriptions.

The average age of full-time students is 27.6 and for part-time students, 30.6. Minority students constitute 22 percent of the full-time students and 8 percent of all students. Approximately 75 percent of the students are married and 80 percent have had full-time work experience. Fifty-nine percent of the full-time and 94 percent of the part-time students are Kentucky residents. M.B.A. graduates have earned their undergraduate degrees from 128 universities in 48 states and 10 foreign countries. M.B.A. candidates have had over 30 different undergraduate majors, the most frequent being in the fields of business, science, and engineering.

All but one of the 33 graduate faculty hold a doctoral degree. All graduate classes are taught by graduate faculty, and the average class size for fall 1985 was 16. The faculty are most strongly interested in teaching, but research and service are also emphasized. Since 1967 the faculty has published the journal, *Business and Public Affairs*.

PROGRAM OF STUDY

The objective of the M.B.A. program is to enhance the candidate's ability to develop creative leadership traits in an increasingly complex, dynamic, quantitative, and social business community. M.B.A. requirements include 30 hours of foundation, or upper-class undergraduate, course work and 30 hours of graduate work. A candidate who has previously completed a foundation course, or its equivalent, will be awarded credit for such work.

The purpose of the graduate portion of the program is to develop advanced understanding and integration of concepts that can be used to plan and control a business organization. The graduate portion is made up of 21 hours of required courses over a broad spectrum of course work and 9 hours of electives. A candidate can use electives to develop a concentration or to broaden horizons.

ADMISSION

An applicant must submit a completed "Application for Graduate Admission," a "History of Prior Work Experience," and official transcripts of all undergraduate work showing completion or pending completion of a baccalaureate degree from an accredited college or university. He or she must also request that an official Graduate Management Admission Test (GMAT) report be sent to Murray State University. The MSU admission formula is 200 × undergraduate grade-point average + GMAT score + work experience (one point per month for relevant experience after graduation, up to 50 points). An applicant will be accepted if his or her formula score is 1,000 or more. An optional formula incorporating the grade-point average for the last 60 hours of course work may be applied. A few applicants (three to five per year) who are denied regular admission are granted special admission. Students who have a 2.5 grade-point average and have not taken the GMAT may enroll in foundation courses only.

A foreign applicant must also submit a medical examination report and a financial report. In addition, a foreign applicant who did not graduate from an undergraduate institution where English is the language of instruction must submit an official report on the Test of English as a Foreign Language (TOEFL). There is a $20 application fee.

EXPENSES

In 1985-86, fees and expenses per semester for a full-time graduate student were

Tuition and fees, Kentucky resident	$ 516
Tuition and fees, nonresident, border counties	616
Tuition and fees, nonresident	1,489
Dormitory (double occupancy)	370
Cafeteria (21 meals per week)	535
Books, supplies, personal	800

Part-time fees and expenses are $57 per credit hour for Kentucky residents, $68 per credit hour for border county residents, and $165 per credit hour for non-residents.

FINANCIAL ASSISTANCE

In addition to graduate research and teaching assistantships, a variety of assistance is available including student loan programs, federal work-study, and a university-sponsored Student Employment Program. Graduate assistants pay in-state fees.

PLACEMENT

An active placement service is maintained by both the university and the college. A number of well-known international firms and smaller regional firms regularly interview candidates on campus.

CORRESPONDENCE

Inquiries concerning the M.B.A. program at Murray State should be addressed to

Assistant Dean for Graduate Studies
College of Business and Public Affairs
Murray State University
Murray, Kentucky 42071

The National University of Singapore (NUS) was formed in August 1980 by a merger of the University of Singapore and Nanyang University. The School of Postgraduate Management Studies was formed to administer the new Master of Business Administration (M.B.A.) and diploma programs. Forty students were admitted as part-time M.B.A. students in the 1980 academic session. The number of students admitted has been increasing steadily over the years.

Today there are about 300 students, the majority of whom attend part time. A daytime program was also started for full-time students for the first time in 1985. Almost all M.B.A. students are Singaporean, but there are some Malaysians, Americans, Filipinos, Japanese, and other nationals working in Singapore.

PROGRAM OF STUDY
The school is located in new buildings at Kent Ridge campus of NUS. The philosophy of the school has remained the same since its inception, namely, to provide solid training in basic disciplines and case study in electives to equip those having a basic degree with the confidence needed to work as middle- and senior-level managers in a rapidly changing world.

The Master of Business Administration program calls for six core courses, six functional area courses, one business policy course and four electives, plus an advanced study project. Students may specialize in one of the following fields: finance, organizational behavior, marketing, business policy and international business, public management, or decision sciences. Exemption for up to two courses can be given for core courses on the basis of previous work done or an exemption test. No exemption can be given for functional area courses. The advanced study project, equivalent to work for one course, is a report on a case or inquiry into a problem or field research, such as a survey or library research. A unique feature of the program is this advanced study project requirement as well as an oral comprehensive examination. Each student must be prepared to answer questions related to their advanced study projects. The advanced study project should preferably be in the field of specialization.

The School of Postgraduate Management Studies (SPMS) draws its teaching staff from the Faculty of Accountancy and Business Administration (FABA) which includes the School of Accountancy and the School of Management. FABA has more than 200 academic staff teaching 3,000 undergraduates. Most of the staff hold doctoral degrees from universities in the United States, Canada, the United Kingdom, and Australia. The teaching staff are themselves divided into nine functional groups: marketing, finance and economics, organizational behavior, decision sciences, business policy and international business, financial accounting, cost and management accounting, auditing and systems, and legal studies and taxation.

Teaching methods incorporate the use of lectures, seminars, case studies, and projects. The language of instruction is English.

ADMISSION
A first degree is required as well as two years of working experience, which for Singaporeans can include their period of officer training in national service. An interview is normally necessary as well as an acceptable score on the Graduate Management Admission Test (GMAT). One admission exercise is done every year in July, the closing date for applications being the end of February. Candidates should have a knowledge of calculus and be proficient in English. Foreign candidates can apply for admission to the full-time program only.

EXPENSES
Tuition fees for Singapore citizens and permanent residents of Singapore:
Full-time, irrespective of the number of courses offered, per term $1,500
Part-time, per course   600
Tuition fees for other candidates:
Full-time, regardless of the number of courses offered, per term . .   2,250
Part-time, per course   900
Examination fee   150
Registration fee, payable once . .   50

CORRESPONDENCE
For further information, write to
Director
School of Postgraduate
  Management Studies
National University of Singapore
Kent Ridge
Singapore 0511
Republic of Singapore

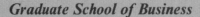

New Hampshire College offers advanced academic programs in the day and evening for persons who have completed undergraduate studies in business and related disciplines. The programs are offered in New Hampshire at centers in Hooksett, Concord, Keene, Nashua, Portsmouth, and Salem; in Maine at Brunswick; and in Puerto Rico. Enrollment has grown since the programs began in 1974 to more than 1,500 students. Approximately 200 students are enrolled in the full-time day program at the Hooksett, New Hampshire, headquarters of the Graduate School.

Courses in the graduate programs are taught by full-time graduate faculty members, full-time undergraduate faculty members, and a number of business and professional persons, selected as adjunct instructors on the basis of their managerial and technical experience as well as educational background. These adjunct instructors reinforce an ongoing interchange of theoretical knowledge and applied skills.

Graduate students have access to one of the most extensive business libraries in northern New England, and to a continually expanding array of state-of-the-art computational facilities; the satellite centers are also served by these facilities through remote access and through microprocessing equipment.

PROGRAMS OF STUDY

The Graduate School of Business offers a basic program in administration leading to the degree of Master of Business Administration (M.B.A.), which may be completed in a year's time. Students may also elect to pursue an M.B.A. degree with an advanced certificate in accounting, decision support systems, finance, international business, personnel administration/industrial relations, or marketing, each of which is normally an 18-month program of full-time study. The Graduate School also offers programs leading to the degree of Master of Science (M.S.) in accounting and in business education. The M.S. in accounting prepares students for careers as certified public accountants and may be completed in 18 months. All of these programs share a common core of courses; thesis and internship options are available in selected programs.

The degree programs are offered on a schedule of four 12-week terms annually, starting in September, December, March, and June; the M.S. in business education is offered on a schedule of two 16-week terms starting in September and March, and a special 4-week summer term. Students usually can enter the program in any of the four 12-week terms; day students are encouraged to enter in either September or March for the M.S. in accounting program.

All M.B.A. and M.S. degree options are offered in both the day and evening at Hooksett; the basic program in administration (M.B.A.) is available at all other centers in the evening. Advanced certificate options, as well as Saturday classes, are offered at specified centers.

ADMISSION

Applicants to the Graduate School must possess a bachelor's degree or higher from an accredited institution. An overall grade-point average of 2.5, or 2.7 for the latter half of the applicant's undergraduate work, is required for unconditional admission. Students must submit results of the Graduate Management Admission Test (GMAT). The exam is used for advising purposes only.

In addition, applicants for the M.B.A. and M.S. in accounting programs must satisfy specific background preparation in accounting, economics, and mathematics (six credits each), and in business organization, statistics, data processing, marketing, and business law (three credits each). Students lacking in these areas must complete background courses offered by the Graduate School as a part of their program, or satisfy the requirement through the College-Level Examination Program (CLEP) or, in some cases, by related work experience.

International students should submit scores from the Test of English as a Foreign Language (TOEFL) or other proof of English proficiency and an official transcript of their undergraduate record in the language of issue with a certified translation, if not issued in English.

A maximum of two graduate courses may be accepted in transfer from an accredited institution.

EXPENSES

Full-time day tuition is $8,662 per year, payable semiannually. Limited on-campus housing is available for single or unaccompanied graduate students, at a cost of $2,400 per year. Additional nonpersonal expenses are estimated at $700 per year. Evening tuition is charged on a per-course basis.

PLACEMENT

Students and alumni of the Graduate School may make use of the college's placement office and its services. Information on current openings in the private and public sectors is available through the office, which also participates in semiannual job fairs attended by recruiters from a wide range of companies, governmental agencies, and other organizations.

CORRESPONDENCE

Inquiries and requests for application materials and other information may be directed to

Assistant Dean, Graduate School
of Business
New Hampshire College
2500 River Road
Manchester, New Hampshire 03104-1394
Telephone: 603-485-8415 or 603-668-2211

New Mexico Highlands University was founded in 1893 as a liberal arts university, and today, as a state-supported school, continues its commitment to seeking the fullest personal and educational growth of both students and faculty. The university is located in Las Vegas, New Mexico, in the foothills of the Sangre de Cristo mountains within an hour's drive of the historic capital city of Sante Fe, and numerous ski and recreational areas. The university functions in an area rich in the cultural history of the American Indian, Spanish, and Anglo communities. A major goal of the university is to create an atmosphere conducive to intercultural exchange and learning.

New Mexico Highlands University is accredited for both undergraduate and graduate work through the master's degree by the North Central Association of Colleges and Schools and is a member of the American Assembly of Collegiate Schools of Business (AACSB). At the graduate level, the school offers Master of Business Administration (M.B.A.) degrees. The Business and Economics Department currently enrolls 450 undergraduate and 35 graduate students at the Las Vegas campus and 120 graduate students at the Kirtland Air Force Base Extension Center in Albuquerque. Total university enrollment is 2,220 graduate and undergraduate students on the Las Vegas campus.

PROGRAM OF STUDY
The Master of Business Administration degree is designed to provide a professional foundation for careers in business or public service. Emphasis is placed on developing tomorrow's managers for business and government and preparing graduate students for doctoral study. The nature of the business system is studied as a whole to prepare students to recognize, analyze, and solve problems inherent in organizations of varying size and complexity.

The curriculum is divided into a core of eight required courses and a series of elective courses. A total of 32 semester hours is required. There is no foreign language requirement. Core courses cover marketing management, finance, economics, quantitative business methods, accounting, research methods, and legal environments.

The International Bilingual Master of Business Administration degree program is a fully integrated multinational Master of Business Administration. It combines a broad-based program of functional expertise and management skills of business administration with a specialization in international business.

The resources of New Mexico Highlands University and the Polytechnic University of Madrid are brought together to provide an intensive curriculum in international business established in the rich multicultural settings that already exist on both campuses. The broad-based M.B.A. core segment of the curriculum is covered at New Mexico Highlands University. The international business segment of the curriculum is provided by the Polytechnic University of Madrid.

Students will be required to spend one year on the Highlands campus and one year on the Madrid campus to attain a minimum of 54 semester hours. Students must be proficient in Spanish before completing the program.

Students with degrees in nonbusiness subjects are welcome and encouraged to apply, although up to a year of additional course work in the business common body of knowledge may be required for either degree.

ADMISSION
Applicants must possess a baccalaureate degree from an accredited university or college. Satisfactory undergraduate grade-point average and performance on the Graduate Management Admission Test (GMAT) are prerequisites for regular graduate status. Students whose native language is not English must achieve a score of at least 520 on the Test of English as a Foreign Language (TOEFL) before they may be admitted.

Students may enter the master's programs in fall or spring semesters. Completed application forms and transcripts of all college work must be submitted to the Office of Admissions at least 30 days prior to matriculation. Application forms are available through the Admissions Office.

EXPENSES
Estimated costs per semester:

	Resident	Nonresident
Tuition and fees	$299.40	$1,151.40
Room and board, on campus (double occupancy, 20 meals per week)	924.00	924.00
Books	150.00	150.00

On-campus apartments are available for married students, and some off-campus housing is available.

FINANCIAL ASSISTANCE
A limited number of scholarships and assistantships (full-time) are available. Information concerning other financial assistance available may be obtained from the Financial Aids Office. The university does not discriminate on the basis of sex, handicap, race, color, religion, marital status, or national or ethnic origin in its programs and policies.

PLACEMENT
The university maintains its own Placement Office, visited annually by representatives from a variety of companies and government agencies. The Placement Office offers its services to interested alumni.

CORRESPONDENCE
For further information, please write to
Director of Admissions
New Mexico Highlands University
Las Vegas, New Mexico 87701
Telephone: 505-425-7511, extension 593

NEW MEXICO STATE UNIVERSITY

LAS CRUCES, NEW MEXICO

New Mexico State University, founded in 1888 as the state's land-grant institution, is located in the Rio Grande Valley in the south-central portion of the state. Within 45 miles and to the south is the urban area including the border cities of El Paso, Texas, and Juarez, Mexico. The proximity of Mexico provides an excellent opportunity for intercultural relations. In the commuting area are major federal research and military facilities. The main campus consists of 6,250 acres of land and over 80 buildings valued at $150 million. Guthrie Hall, the home of the College of Business Administration and Economics, was completed in 1968; it provides a very functional and attractive facility for the graduate program. The following degrees are offered by the college: Master of Business Administration (M.B.A.), Master of Accountancy, Master of Arts in economics, Bachelor of Accountancy, Bachelor of Arts in economics, and Bachelor of Business Administration. Baccalaureate and M.B.A. programs are accredited by the American Assembly of Collegiate Schools of Business (AACSB).

PROGRAM OF STUDY
The M.B.A. program is a professional, 55-credit program designed to provide the student with a broad orientation in the fields of management and administration. Students completing the program are prepared for administrative or management positions in all types of organizations, both private and governmental. In addition to the breadth of coverage in the program, students may select a specific field of six to nine semester credits in which they can develop some degree of specialization. Options are offered in accounting, economics, finance, management, and marketing. Minors of an interdisciplinary nature are available in other departments of the university (for example, computer science, industrial engineering, mathematics, psychology, sociology). Frequently these opportunities are used by students to update their undergraduate areas of specialization.

Prior preparation of students will vary widely, but it is emphasized that a baccalaureate degree in business administration is not required. For students with adequate preparation in business administration, however, up to 25 semester credits may be waived, provided that the courses upon which waivers are claimed have been taken within seven years of enrollment in the program.

Although it is not a stated requirement, competency in mathematics, communication skills, and computer programming is essential.

ADMISSION
Applicants holding a baccalaureate degree from any recognized college or university may apply for admission to the Graduate School. Admission requirements of the Graduate School must be met before the applicant may be admitted to the M.B.A. program. To be granted regular admission in the Graduate School the applicant must have a 3.0 grade-point average (out of a possible 4.0) either overall or for the last half of undergraduate work. For students who do not meet this requirement, provisional or unclassified admission is available. In addition to the Graduate School requirements, admission to the M.B.A. program must be obtained. All applicants must submit acceptable scores on the Graduate Management Admission Test (GMAT) at least one month prior to the student's first enrollment. Other indicators of potential may also be used: interviews, evaluation of work experience, and letters of reference from former professors.

EXPENSES
Costs for 1985-86 were as follows*:

Per semester	New Mexico Resident	Nonresident
Full time (12 or more credits)	$460.00	$1,533.00
Part time (11 or fewer credits), per credit	38.25	127.75
Summer sessions only Per credit for up to 6 tuition credits	38.25	38.25

*These costs may be subject to change without notice should conditions require.

FINANCIAL ASSISTANCE
Graduate assistantships are available to applicants eligible for regular admission who have a Bachelor of Business Administration or similar degree. Other financial assistance is available through the Office of Financial Aids. Employment on campus or in the community is generally available.

PLACEMENT
The University Placement Office services the College of Business Administration and Economics. Several hundred firms and agencies interview on campus.

CORRESPONDENCE
Inquiries concerning the program of study offered by New Mexico State University should be addressed to
  Director
  M.B.A. Program
  College of Business Administration
    and Economics
  New Mexico State University
  Box 3AD
  Las Cruces, New Mexico 88003
  Telephone: 505-646-2821

NEW SOUTH WALES INSTITUTE OF TECHNOLOGY

SYDNEY, NEW SOUTH WALES, AUSTRALIA

The New South Wales Institute of Technology was established to provide a wide range of courses for those entering or already employed in industry, government, and technological fields. The various courses offered by the institute are provided through seven faculties, of which the Faculty of Business is the largest. The institute's student body is composed of some 9,000 students including 8,300 undergraduates and 700 graduates. Approximately one third of these students are in the Faculty of Business, where there are 2,000 undergraduate and 500 graduate students; 75 percent of the students follow a part-time attendance pattern, and the remaining 25 percent are full-time students.

The institute's campuses are conveniently located in the heart of Sydney's business community. The Faculty of Business includes four schools: Business and Public Administration, Finance, Economics, and Marketing. The total academic establishment of the faculty is 84.5, with a full-time staff of 68. In excess of 100 well-qualified and experienced people from business, government, and the academic world make up the faculty's part-time teaching staff.

PROGRAMS OF STUDY

The Faculty of Business offers its students an undergraduate, a graduate, and a continuing management education program. The undergraduate program, the Bachelor of Business (B.Bus.) course, offers majors in accounting, business administration, marketing, and public administration. A number of submajors are also available to provide breadth and some additional depth to candidates for the degree. Examples of these include organization and management, operations management, and distribution management.

The faculty's graduate program comprises two-year, part-time graduate diplomas in accounting and finance, administration, employment relations, internal auditing, marketing, and public sector management; a Master of Business (by research and thesis); and the Master of Business Administration (M.B.A.), which includes an option in public sector management.

The continuing management education program comprises postexperience extension courses, seminars, conferences, and tailor-made courses.

The M.B.A., introduced in 1981, has grown out of the faculty's Graduate Diploma in Administration; it is a fully part-time degree, with attendance required two nights a week for four years. There are 12 core subjects, followed by a specialty strand composed of 3 subjects, and a related report, which is developed during the final year. The course also allows for an element of specialization by way of the fourth-year specialty strand. Depending on class viability, specialty strands in accounting and finance, employment relations, finance, marketing, management, and international business are offered. Additionally, students may negotiate tailor-made specialty strands to more closely meet personal development and career needs. The prospect of incorporating an overseas exchange element in the fourth year is under consideration. An exchange scheme already operates at the undergraduate level with the School of Business at Oregon State University.

ADMISSION

Applications for admission to the M.B.A. program open in August, and the final selection committee meets in December. There is a quota of 60 places, and competition for the course is high. Applicants must possess an undergraduate degree, have a minimum of four years' work experience in a managerial capacity, and have taken the Graduate Management Admission Test (GMAT). References and other documents of support should form part of the application.

Applicants for the course who are relying for admission on qualifications gained in countries where English is not the spoken language are advised to make early arrangements to take the Test of English as a Foreign Language (TOEFL) and, where appropriate, should consult Australian consular authorities regarding visa requirements. To determine the academic standing of their degrees, such applicants should also write directly to the Committee on Overseas Qualifications, P.O. Box 1407, Canberra City, 2601, Australia and include documentation of the ensuing correspondence with the committee together with their applications.

Applicants are advised of the outcome of their applications early in January. The course commences in mid-February.

EXPENSES

No tuition fees are charged by the institute but overseas students are charged a fee of approximately $2,500 by the Australian Government. Student Union fees are approximately $120 in the first year.

FINANCIAL ASSISTANCE

No financial assistance is available.

PLACEMENT

The faculty maintains a Careers Office. Campus interviews are arranged, and continual contacts are made with employing organizations.

CORRESPONDENCE

For further information or to request an application for admission, please write or call

The Director, M.B.A. Course
Faculty of Business
New South Wales Institute of
   Technology
P.O. Box 123
BROADWAY 2007
Australia
Telephone: (02) 20930

The New York Institute of Technology is a privately supported, nonsectarian, coeducational institution offering career-oriented education in the technologies, science, business, the fine arts, and the communication arts. The college is known for its innovations in educational technology and for the development of management systems for education—areas that have received liberal support from government and foundations in the form of grants to the Learning, Management, and Resources Center and the Advanced Systems Laboratory at the institute.

The college maintains an urban and suburban campus. The Metropolitan Center on West 61 Street in Manhattan is convenient to the heart of business enterprise in New York City. The Old Westbury campus in Nassau County occupies more than 700 acres of woodland and rolling fields and includes several estate facilities that are currently being converted for use as a management conference center. Each campus of the college has its own library. Students of the Division of Business and Management have access to an IBM 1620 and a Xerox Sigma computer facility, and computer applications are stressed throughout the program.

PROGRAM OF STUDY
Education for management must increasingly take new directions in a complex industrial society in which change is the only constant. The idea that there is a "business world" separate and distinct from all other communities is an anachronistic residue of the old economics. The modern corporation in all its conglomerate forms has become one of the institutional pillars of American society. Management personnel must be sensitive to the world around them and relate technological progress to the integrated needs of business and society. The Master of Business Administration (M.B.A.) program in management at the New York Institute of Technology is built on these awarenesses.

The M.B.A. program is designed to appeal especially to those who are holding full-time jobs while pursuing postgraduate study. Classes are scheduled to meet on weeknights and on Saturdays. The program operates on a trimester basis. Students whose undergraduate major was not in business and who lack the prerequisites for admission to this program will be permitted to enroll in the program while preparing for proficiency examinations. These examinations will be based on an independent-study program designed to make up the requirements for entrance into the program.

Thirty-six to 42 graduate credits are required for the M.B.A. degree. A maximum of nine credits of graduate course work earned at other institutions may be applied toward the M.B.A. degree.

ADMISSION
Admission requirements for matriculation in the M.B.A. program are
- the baccalaureate degree from an accredited college;
- the intellectual capacity and motivation to pursue graduate work, as determined by a review of the transcript of undergraduate work;
- the completion of certain undergraduate courses in business or certification of competency in these areas by means of a proficiency examination; and
- satisfactory performance on the Graduate Management Admission Test (GMAT), which is required of all applicants.

Applications for admission are accepted on a continuous basis for each of the three trisemesters.

EXPENSES
Tuition, per credit hour	$145
Application fee (not refundable)	15
Graduation fee	30

The cost of books and materials may be anticipated at about $150 to $250 per year.

FINANCIAL ASSISTANCE
Financial aid is available to full-time M.B.A. students through loans and government-sponsored financial aid programs. Inquiries should be directed to the Veteran's Affairs Counselor in the Office of Financial Aid.

PLACEMENT
The Placement Office, in the Division of Student Services, helps students obtain full- and part-time positions. A number of business firms recruit graduates on campus.

CORRESPONDENCE
Programs are available in New York, Old Westbury, and Central Islip, New York; and Crystal City, Virginia. Application forms and additional information may be obtained from

Dr. Marvin Weiss
Associate Director
Center for Business and Economics
New York Institute of Technology
1855 Broadway
New York, New York 10023
Telephone: 212-399-8329

New York University (NYU) Graduate School of Business Administration (GBA) is located in the heart of New York's business and financial district. Situated in the Wall Street area between the World Trade Center and the American Stock Exchange, the school plays a key role in training managers for the domestic and international arena. Faculty members are not only authorities in their academic fields but also professionals with considerable practical experience. In addition, experts from government and business offer advanced courses in their fields on an adjunct basis. Offering both full-time and part-time study, NYU GBA draws its students from the business community as well as from undergraduate institutions in the United States and 73 foreign countries. More than 1,100 full-time and 3,100 part-time students pursue a curriculum noted for its breadth and diversity. The resulting educational experience is a unique opportunity for advanced management study in the world's major commercial center.

PROGRAMS OF STUDY
The Master of Business Administration (M.B.A.) curriculum is designed to integrate the various aspects of business administration as study progresses from the theoretical to the practical. The program is divided into six levels, or tiers. Tiers I and II provide a foundation for advanced study and give students an opportunity to sample courses in all fields before choosing a major from among eight functional areas of concentration. In addition to courses in the major, students take several electives, which may be concentrated in a second area or distributed among the specializations. Tiers III and IV consist of the major and elective courses. Tier V comprises two half-term courses examining the legal and social context of business. Tier VI is a one- or two-semester final project that enables students to culminate their research and study in an actual field experience.

Study at GBA is on a full-time or part-time basis. Full-time students generally complete the M.B.A. program in four semesters, while evening students take from three and one-half to five years to finish their degree requirements. Students who have had prior academic work in business may be granted exemptions from Tier I and Tier II courses, substituting advanced electives in their place.

In addition to the M.B.A., special programs of study are also offered: Master of Science (M.S.) in accounting, M.S. in quantitative analysis, Juris Doctor (J.D.)/ M.B.A., Master of Arts (M.A.) journalism/M.B.A., M.A. politics/ M.B.A., and M.A. French studies/M.B.A. The doctoral program is designed to prepare students for careers in teaching and research as well as for key positions in industry and government. Students take a sequence of advanced courses in economics, quantitative analysis, and behavioral science and then proceed to advanced study in two other fields.

NYU also offers two M.B.A. programs for individuals who are being sponsored by their companies. One is the executive M.B.A. program for middle managers. The other is the M.B.A. program for financial personnel for junior-level personnel in financial institutions. For additional information, please contact Professor Norman Berman, 100 Trinity Place.

ADMISSION
Admission is open to all qualified men and women who hold the bachelor's degree from an accredited undergraduate institution. No specific majors or course prerequisites are required or preferred. Applicants are evaluated on the basis of previous academic work, meaningful employment experience, motivation for graduate study, and potential for a career in management. In addition to all other requirements, international students are strongly urged to submit scores from the Test of English as a Foreign Language (TOEFL). The school also requires that all international applicants submit a Declaration of Financial Evidence to show adequate funding to complete the degree.

The application deadline is April 15 for the fall semester, October 15 for the spring semester, and March 15 for the summer semester. For the doctoral program applications should be submitted prior to April 1 for the summer and fall semesters and November 1 for the spring semester.

EXPENSES
The tuition (1985-1986) was $5,154 per semester for full-time students (those registered for 16-21 points). Part-time students pay $444 for the first point and $314 for each subsequent point. Books and supplies are estimated at $400 a year. The off-campus budget (including room and board, transportation, and personal expenses) is estimated to be $7,465 per year.

For information on university-owned housing, contact the Housing Coordinator, 921 Nichols Hall, 100 Trinity Place, New York, New York 10006.

FINANCIAL ASSISTANCE
The school makes every effort to provide financial assistance to qualified full-time M.B.A. and Ph.D. candidates who would otherwise be unable to attend. A large number of fellowships, scholarships, assistantships, and loans are available, both for first-year and advanced graduate students. The financial aid application deadline is January 31. Students who are applying for financial assistance are required to submit both their application for admission and their application for financial aid prior to this date.

PLACEMENT
Since GBA is located near many of the nation's leading corporations and financial institutions, the school maintains a close relationship with the business community. As demonstrated by figures compiled for the 1985 graduating class, over 200 companies recruited on campus conducting 5,234 individual interviews. In addition, the Office of Career Development publishes *Profiles,* a resume book that is made available to over 350 companies in this country and around the world.

CORRESPONDENCE
Inquiries should be addressed to
  Director of Admissions and
    Financial Aid
  New York University
  Graduate School of Business
    Administration
  100 Trinity Place
  New York, New York 10006
  Telephone: 212-285-6250

New York University (NYU) was founded in 1831 and its Graduate School of Business Administration has been in the Wall Street area of lower Manhattan for more than 60 years. NYU's part-time, evening M.B.A. program in Westchester was established in 1977 on the campus of Manhattanville College. A complete graduate business education is provided in a suburban locale on the New York/Connecticut border for professionals working and living in nearby communities. Over 200 students from 96 companies are enrolled in the M.B.A. program. The school's programs are accredited by the American Assembly of Collegiate Schools of Business (AACSB).

The Graduate School of Business Administration (GBA) is committed to ensuring the quality and productivity of its faculty and the soundness of its educational programs in order to continue to offer students exceptional opportunities for study and individual development. The yardsticks of others are a measure of the school's achievements over the years:

● A recent Standard & Poor's survey shows New York University as the second largest source of graduate education for senior executives of major companies in the country.

● New York University was the number one graduate school attended by top women managers and the number two graduate school attended by top male managers according to a recent survey of senior managers published in a book called *Instant MBA*.

● GBA's finance area is ranked number one in the nation by the *Journal of Finance*.

● GBA's international business program is ranked number one in the nation by the Academy of International Business.

● A study by the executive search firm of Heidrick & Struggles, Inc. ranked GBA as the second largest source of M.B.A. degrees held by chief financial officers of leading U.S. corporations.

PROGRAM OF STUDY

The M.B.A. program prepares individuals for executive management and specialist positions in business and related fields. It provides knowledge of the internal operations of business firms, focusing on the economic, social, and legal context in which business operates. The program in Westchester culminates with the Management Decision Laboratory, a special intensive course that combines academic theory with practical experience in a simulated company. The same faculty teach at the Westchester campus as teach in Manhattan.

The M.B.A. program is designed to enable students:

● to develop the conceptual and analytical skills needed for reaching decisions and making judgments;

● to appraise situations from broad as well as specific business viewpoints;

● to consider broader social issues in management-business ethics, human resources, external economic factors, and legal and political concerns;

● to evaluate business firms and other organizations from an external as well as an internal viewpoint.

The degree program may be completed in three years of part-time study or may be spread over four or five years.

ADMISSION

Admission is open to all qualified men and women who hold a bachelor's degree from an accredited undergraduate institution. No special majors or course prerequisites are required or preferred. Applicants are evaluated on the basis of previous academic work, the nature and extent of previous work experience, motivation for graduate study, and potential for a career in management.

The application deadline is June 1 for the fall semester; students can enter the M.B.A. program only in the fall.

EXPENSES

The tuition (1985-86) for part-time students was $430 for the first point and $300 for each subsequent point.

FINANCIAL ASSISTANCE

Government Guaranteed Student Loans are the only form of assistance available to part-time students, other than employers' tuition reimbursement programs.

PLACEMENT

Students have the complete services of the Office of Career Development available to them at the Manhattan location of the New York University Graduate School of Business Administration. These services include on-campus recruitment; inclusion in *Profiles,* a resume book that is made available to 600 companies in this country and around the world; workshops; and speakers.

In addition, the Westchester program has on-site career workshops and, during the spring term, a career counselor is available for individual appointments. A book of currently available positions is maintained for student use.

CORRESPONDENCE

Inquiries should be directed to
Director, M.B.A. Program
New York University
    at Manhattanville College
Purchase Street, Route 120
Purchase, New York 10577

NIAGARA UNIVERSITY

NIAGARA UNIVERSITY, NEW YORK

Niagara University, founded in 1856, was granted its first charter on April 20, 1863, by the New York State Legislature. It was chartered by the Regents of the University of the State of New York in 1883 and is accredited by the Middle States Association of Colleges and Schools. One of four divisions of the university, the College of Business Administration, with approximately 1,000 students, offers programs in accounting, economics, finance, labor relations, and marketing, leading to the Bachelor of Business Administration (B.B.A.) and Bachelor of Science (B.S.) degrees. The Master of Business Administration (M.B.A.) program was approved by the New York State Board of Regents in November 1980. Graduate business courses were offered for the first time in January 1981.

The university, consisting of 25 buildings on its main campus, is uniquely situated on the lower Niagara River, 20 miles from Buffalo and 75 miles from Toronto, adjacent to the Niagara River and only four miles from the brink of the mighty falls. It is the terminus of three international bridges between the United States and Canada and is adjacent to the Robert Moses Power Plant, one of the largest hydroelectric plants in the world.

PROGRAM OF STUDY

The M.B.A. curriculum is professional in nature, offering both theoretical and application-oriented courses. The objective of the program is to educate forward looking managers in business, industry, government, and education. The program is of a general nature rather than focused on areas of specialization. The 48-semester-hour program is open to holders of any baccalaureate degree from a recognized college or university and offered principally to persons employed full time. Hence, all courses are scheduled in the evening, one night a week, Monday through Thursday. In effect, it is a part-time program but is adaptable to full-time study.

The 16 courses of the program are MBA 500, Financial Accounting; MBE 530, Economic Analysis; MBQ 500, Quantitative Management; MBQ 510, Quantitative Methods; MBQ 520, Advanced Quantitative Methods; MBC 545, Communications for Executives; MBM 570, Management and the Behavioral Sciences; MBA 520, Managerial Accounting; MBE 540, Economic Policy; MBI 560, Industrial and Labor Relations; MBF 550, Financial Management; MBR 665, Moral and Ethical Aspects of Corporations and Society; MBO 620, Production and Operations Management; MBK 580, Marketing Management; MBS 590, Management Information Systems; and MBP 680, Business Research, Strategy, and Planning.

The program brings together students with varied educational and occupational backgrounds. The richness of these divergent backgrounds is tapped in a number of courses in which case studies are used. The importance of effective communicative skills is emphasized throughout the curriculum. One course is devoted to solely communicative skills.

The program provides the tools required of top managers but also those tools required in the management of daily operations. This balance is achieved through the use of cases and a strong applications orientation.

ADMISSION

Each applicant must submit (1) a completed application form, (2) Graduate Management Admission Test (GMAT) scores, (3) official transcripts of all prior college work, (4) two letters of recommendation, and (5) other information that the Admissions Committee may require, such as an acceptable score on the Test of English as a Foreign Language (TOEFL).

Other factors are considered as well, such as the position a person holds in business and if increasing responsibility has been undertaken. Each application merits individual consideration.

EXPENSES

Tuition, per semester hour....... $180
Application fee (nonrefundable).. 25
Registration fee, per semester.... 10
MBA Association fee, per year... 10

FINANCIAL ASSISTANCE

Scholarships, assistantships, and loans are available as well as positions in undergraduate dormitories for those attending full time. Students interested in positions as Resident Directors or Resident Assistants should contact the Dean of Women or Dean of Men, as appropriate. Financial assistance should be requested from the Financial Aid Office as well as the M.B.A. Office.

PLACEMENT

The Office of Career Planning and Placement assists graduating students and alumni in obtaining career employment, counsels students and alumni on career opportunities, provides current occupational information, and assists students in securing part-time employment.

CORRESPONDENCE

Inquiries should be addressed to
M.B.A. Director
College of Business Administration
Niagara University
Niagara University, New York 14109

Nicholls State University, established in 1948, is located in Thibodaux, Louisiana, 60 miles from New Orleans and 65 miles from Baton Rouge. The area is rich in French cultural heritage and known for its hospitality and fine cuisine.

The university, housed on a spacious and beautiful campus, is the home of Ellender Memorial Library. Faculty credentials and experience, modern facilities, and a commitment to academic excellence combine to offer excellent educational opportunities to its 7,000 students. The undergraduate business programs are accredited by the American Assembly of Collegiate Schools of Business (AACSB). The College of Business Administration operates its own computer, the Cenac Center.

PROGRAM OF STUDY

The M.B.A. program is professional in nature, offering both theoretical and application-oriented courses. It is formulated for students with undergraduate backgrounds in all fields of study. The objective of the program is to prepare qualified and motivated persons to meet the management challenges of business, industry, and government. The program, composed of 24 semester credit hours of required courses and 9 semester credit hours of electives, is of a general nature rather than focused on areas of specialization. However, various areas of concentration in business may be achieved through the elective segment of the program. A student may elect to write a thesis, which reduces the elective credit hours to three.

Graduate courses are scheduled in the evening, Monday through Thursday, as are the undergraduate foundation courses.

ADMISSION

Admission to the Graduate School is open to qualified students who hold a bachelor's degree from an accredited institution. Emphasis is placed more on proven scholarship and academic promise than on the applicant's undergraduate program. Admission to the Graduate School does not imply admission to the M.B.A. degree program.

To be admitted to the M.B.A. program a student must 1) be admitted to the Graduate School, 2) submit Graduate Management Admission Test (GMAT) scores, and 3) score at least 1000 on the formula (200 × the grade-point average over last 60 undergraduate hours + GMAT score = 1000).

A student who fails to satisfy the 1000 formula score shall be classified as pre-M.B.A. until the criterion is met. A student classified as pre-M.B.A. cannot take any course for graduate credit, but may take undergraduate foundation courses as needed. Students whose native language is other than English must take the Test of English as a Foreign Language (TOEFL) and score at least 500 on the total and 55 in listening comprehension.

Students are admitted for the fall semester beginning in late August, the spring semester beginning in early January, or the summer session beginning in early June. Deadlines for application are July 1 for the fall semester, November 1 for the spring semester, and April 1 for the summer session.

EXPENSES

Tuition fees for Louisiana residents range from $113 for three hours or less to $494.75 for nine or more hours during fall and spring semesters, and $112 for three hours or less to $313.25 for six or more hours in the summer. A fee ranging from $147 to $440 for the fall and spring semesters and $147 to $270 for the summer is charged nonresident students. Room and board fees are $910 per semester for fall and spring and $500 for the summer. All fees are subject to change without notice.

FINANCIAL ASSISTANCE

A limited number of assistantships and loans are available to students who qualify. The assistantships pay tuition and carry stipends of $4000 for a nine-month period. Part-time employment is also available on campus.

PLACEMENT

Graduate students are invited to use the services of the Placement Office at Nicholls, which arranges interviews with the numerous employers who annually contact them.

CORRESPONDENCE

For additional information, write to
Director
Graduate Studies in Business
Nicholls State University
P.O. Box 2010
Thibodaux, Louisiana 70310

NICHOLS COLLEGE

DUDLEY, UXBRIDGE, AND WESTBOROUGH, MASSACHUSETTS

Nichols College is a private, nonsectarian institution located in the town of Dudley, Massachusetts. Its 200-acre campus situated in a New England country setting is within easy driving distance of several important metropolitan centers. The college traces its history back to 1815 when Amasa Nichols, a Dudley industrialist, founded Nichols Academy on the site of the present campus. The college was granted accreditation by the New England Association of Colleges and Secondary Schools in 1965. It received authorization to grant the degree of Master of Business Administration (M.B.A.) in 1974. Nichols presently has an enrollment of over 800 undergraduate and 250 graduate students. The Nichols M.B.A. program is now offered at three convenient locations in central Massachusetts: Dudley, Uxbridge, and Westborough.

PROGRAM OF STUDY

The Master of Business Administration curriculum is designed to provide the student with an understanding of the economic, behavioral, and quantitative aspects of the practice of business administration and a knowledge of the concepts and techniques involved in the various functional areas of business. The program stresses the student's development of decision-making skills, an analytical approach to management problems, and an appreciation of the interfaces between technology and people in complex organizations. The curriculum is equally applicable to individuals preparing for first management positions and managers preparing for senior functional or general management posts. Emphasis is placed on creating a capacity to continue learning from work experience. The M.B.A. curriculum provides a three-level program of study designed to be responsive to the student's prior academic training and his or her career objectives. Level I consists of eight foundation courses in economics, computer principles, legal environment, marketing, finance, statistics, management, and accounting. Six advanced courses required of all students at Level II cover managerial aspects of accounting, economics, policy formulation, and administrative practice. Level III provides a wide diversity of advanced electives. Students with sufficient previous background in foundation areas may be exempted from some or all Level I courses. All M.B.A. students must complete a minimum of 10 graduate-level courses (30 credits) unless transfer credit is awarded.

ADMISSION

Nichols College will consider for admission all students holding a baccalaureate degree from an accredited institution who show promise for success in graduate studies. Women and men from all undergraduate majors are welcome.

Generally, prospective candidates for the M.B.A. degree must provide the school with (1) an application form, (2) official transcripts for all undergraduate and graduate work attempted, (3) two letters of recommendation, and (4) Graduate Management Admission Test (GMAT) scores. There is a $25 application fee. Students are accepted on a provisional basis pending receipt of GMAT scores and/or official transcripts. Provisional students may take up to six credit hours of foundation-level graduate courses.

The normal formula used to calculate the student's potential for graduate study is as follows: grade-point average (4.0 system) in undergraduate work × 200 + GMAT score must equal 950 or above, or last 60 semester hours of undergraduate work (4.0 system) + GMAT score must equal 1,000 or above. In special cases, students who have demonstrated the maturity and ability to overcome weak past academic performance may be allowed to attend on a probationary basis.

An applicant may file for special nondegree status if he or she desires to take one or more specific graduate-level courses but does not plan to follow a graduate-degree program. Admission will be granted if the required documents indicate that the applicant possesses the necessary background for the desired courses. If an applicant originally admitted as a special, nondegree student should be changed to degree status at a later date, he or she will be permitted to transfer a maximum of six credit hours of academic work earned in special status.

EXPENSES

A tuition fee is charged each semester at the rate of $425 per course at the Dudley campus and $500 per course at the Westborough campus. Fees are payable not later than the time of registration unless otherwise specified. Fees and tuition are subject to change without notice. The school year is divided into two 14-week semesters and one summer session. Presently, most students are commuters who have full-time occupations.

PLACEMENT

Nichols College maintains a placement office that provides career counseling and guidance to both graduate and undergraduate students.

CORRESPONDENCE

For further information, write or call
Director, M.B.A. Program
Nichols College
Dudley, Massachusetts 01570-5000
Telephone: 617-943-1560

NIJENRODE,
THE NETHERLANDS SCHOOL OF BUSINESS

BREUKELEN, THE NETHERLANDS

Nijenrode, The Netherlands School of Business, was founded just after the Second World War by leading enterprises, who realized that international orientation was essential for helping to rebuild Dutch society and business. At the beginning Nijenrode focused its attention on the Anglo-Saxon countries. This explains why its main course leads to the equivalent of a Bachelor of Business Administration degree. Nijenrode also offers a specially designed program for graduates of technical and agricultural colleges, the Commercial Technical Program. The International Business Program is a one-year course taught in English for junior-year students of American business schools.

The graduate program leading to the Master of Business Administration (M.B.A.) degree was inaugurated in September 1982 and was first taught in English in September 1985.

Nijenrode is situated on a campus of 120 acres, located about 12 miles south of Amsterdam. The administrative center of the school is housed in a magnificent castle the origins of which go back to the thirteenth century. Students are accommodated in modern, well-equipped apartments.

PROGRAM OF STUDY

Nijenrode offers a one-year M.B.A. program for full-time students. The program is designed to prepare students for responsible positions, and, in view of this objective, aims to educate general managers rather than specialists.

As in most Dutch academic institutions, the study program is based on 1,680 hours, which are usually divided into 40 hours per week, 42 weeks per year. The study year is divided into three terms, 12 weeks each. Two extra exam weeks are added. The third term and the last two weeks of the first and second term are reserved for preparation of the end-of-study assignment.

In the end-of-study assignment the student has the chance to display his or her business capabilities. The assignment consists of three parts:
- a period of practical research in a company,
- preparation of a paper on the basis of this research, and
- an interview before a committee during which the student defends the findings.

The three preparation periods preceding the assignment are intended to allow the student to set up a reasonable problem for investigation and to determine the research strategy necessary.

The program provides work in the following areas: organizational studies, management and organization of multinationals, business and society, industrial society, financial management, management accounting, financial accounting and financial statement analysis, and currency management. A block of two weeks is kept clear to allow for a synthesis of the elements so far taught. This integration block is arranged through coordination between different departments. The departments of Applied Linguistics and Physical Education, whose very names denote their nature, add to the distinctive nature of the program.

ADMISSION

The M.B.A. degree program serves students having a bachelor's degree in business administration. Applicants are carefully evaluated in five areas:
- previous academic performance;
- completion of the Bachelor of Business Administration degree;
- test scores on the Graduate Management Admission Test (GMAT);
- work experience, extracurricular activities, and motivation; and
- Test of English as a Foreign Language (TOEFL) when appropriate.

Applications should be filed approximately seven months before the beginning of the September term, in accordance with the instructions that accompany the application form. Late applications are accepted on a space-available basis.

EXPENSES

Estimated total expenses are $5,000. This includes room and board, books and supplies, student services, and other facilities.

CORRESPONDENCE

For further information or to request an application for admission, please write or call

Nijenrode, The Netherlands School
  of Business
Att: M.B.A. Secretary
Straatweg 25
3621 BG BREUKELEN
The Netherlands
Telephone: (0) 3462-61044

NORFOLK STATE UNIVERSITY

NORFOLK, VIRGINIA

Founded in 1935, Norfolk State University is a state-supported coeducational institution located near the heart of Norfolk, Virginia. An integral part of Norfolk's renaissance, the spacious 110-acre campus consists of 30 modern buildings and provides students with easy access to all of the professional, cultural, and recreational opportunities that a large metropolitan area has to offer.

Students are offered a variety of activities, cultural events, and social events on campus as well. They can find billiards, tennis, bowling, swimming in an olympic-size pool, film series, art exhibits, dances, concerts, recitals, and public seminars featuring nationally prominent figures all on campus.

NSU's varsity teams have gained national reputation. Men's teams include football, basketball, baseball, cross-country, track, and wrestling. Women's teams include volleyball, softball, basketball, and track. The teams compete in the Central Intercollegiate Athletic Association Conference and the National Collegiate Athletic Association. Intramural sports include football, softball, basketball, archery, tennis, billiards, and cards—all with tournaments during the year.

Enrollment at the university is approximately 6,600 undergraduates and 800 graduate students, many of whom are from other states or nations. The School of Business has an enrollment of approximately 1,400 undergraduates and a faculty of 47 full-time teachers and administrators. The graduate program was organized and formally initiated in September 1980.

The School of Business is housed in Brown Hall, a remodeled facility providing air-conditioned classrooms and study carrels for graduate students. Also contained in Brown Hall is a modern research facility including access to a HP3000 computer main frame, a microcomputer classroom with 25 personal computers, and a computer work room with another 25 personal computers.

PROGRAM OF STUDY

The School of Business at Norfolk State University offers a two-year program leading to the degree of Master of Science in Business Administration (M.S.B.A.). While the M.S.B.A. qualifies the graduate for a career in general management, students may choose certain electives to prepare themselves for entry-level positions in specific functional areas. The objective of the program is to produce graduates who will be well-prepared functional managers capable of making informed decisions from a general management perspective.

To enter the graduate program, students are required to have adequate preparation in accounting, economics, finance, management, marketing, statistics, and legal environment of business. Students unable to provide evidence of such work must complete 27 hours of undergraduate course work in the areas listed before they may be permitted to undertake graduate course work.

The M.S.B.A. program at Norfolk State University is a 39-semester-hour program. The curriculum consists of a core of 21 graduate credit hours, 12 credit hours in a management emphasis, and 6 credit hours of electives in an area of specialization. The program is open to both full-time and part-time students.

The M.S.B.A. degree program is developed to prepare graduates to compete successfully in all domains of business, including the nonprofit and public sectors. Instructional leadership in business and the application of research as a means of attaining business ends are outcomes for which the program is designed.

ADMISSION

Entrance to the M.S.B.A. program is open to all qualified students who show promise of success in studying business. For regular admission to the program a student must have a 2.5 (on a 4-point scale) cumulative grade-point average and attain a score of at least 950 when the following formula is applied: (200 × grade-point average) + score on the Graduate Management Admission Test (GMAT). Students may transfer a maximum of six semester credit hours of graduate course work from an approved institution.

EXPENSES

For the 1985-86 academic year the following tuition and fees schedule existed:

	Resident	Nonresident
Full-time tuition and fees, per semester	$710	$1,145
Tuition and fees for less than nine semester hours, per semester hour	79	128
Application fee	20	20

FINANCIAL ASSISTANCE

Scholarships, fellowships, graduate assistantships, work-study grants, and loans are available. For further information contact the Director of Financial Aid, Norfolk State University, Norfolk, Virginia 23504.

PLACEMENT

The full services of the Career Planning and Placement Center are available to graduate business students. Individual counseling and assistance in placement are provided.

CORRESPONDENCE

For further information or to request an application for admission, please write or call

Dean, School of Business
Norfolk State University
2401 Corprew Avenue
Norfolk, Virginia 23504
Telephone: 804-623-8920

NORTH CAROLINA CENTRAL UNIVERSITY

DURHAM, NORTH CAROLINA

North Carolina Central University, chartered in 1909 as a private institution, first opened to students in July 1910. In 1923, it became the first state-supported liberal arts college for Black students in the United States. In July 1972, the university became one of the constituent institutions of the University of North Carolina system. Over the years, the institution has evolved into a multipurpose urban university with a cosmopolitan student body and more than 300 faculty members. In addition to the School of Business, the university has an undergraduate school of arts and sciences, a graduate school of arts and sciences, a school of library science, and a school of law.

There are approximately 1,000 graduate and professional students among the more than 4,500 students on campus. Approximately 600 students come from out of state; 60 percent are women; and about 22 percent are part-time students. During the 1985 commencement exercise, 220 graduate and professional degrees were conferred.

Durham, a city of over 100,000 people, is located in the eastern Piedmont region of North Carolina. Durham County is the site of the renowned Research Triangle Park, the research home for many multinational firms and government agencies. The city has mild winters. It has a variety of cultural, educational, and medical institutions and an active art, music, and theatrical life.

The James F. Shepard Memorial Library and other components of the campus library system provide approximately 480,000 cataloged books and bound serials, 60,000 serials, 100,000 microfilms, 35,000 audiovisual and nonprint materials, 35,000 pamphlets, and 98,000 federal documents.

The computer resources are available to faculty and students in three phases:

(1) The School of Business Computer Center serves the academic needs of the School of Business. A new digital (DEC) VAX 11/750 computer has been installed with three megabytes of memory with random access devices that provide 400 million bytes of fixed disks on-line storage and 30 terminals. COBOL and BASIC languages are used in the system.

(2) A number of microcomputers, such as Apple, Texas Instruments, Eagle, and IBM PCs, are available in a microcomputer lab for instruction and research.

(3) An Academic Computer Center serves the entire university including the School of Business. This center has the following facilities: 20 terminals connected to Triangle University Computing Center (TUCC) at Research Triangle Park, North Carolina, a Data General Eclipse MV/4000 super mini operating system, and eight display terminals to the Data General Eclipse. Languages on the Data General Eclipse are COBOL, BASIC, PL/I, FORTRAN, C, and ASSEMBLER. Software includes SAS, SPSS, and a database management system.

PROGRAM OF STUDY

The School of Business at North Carolina Central University offers a graduate program leading to the Master of Business Administration (M.B.A.) in business administration. The M.B.A. program seeks to provide students with the educational base for positions of leadership in business, industry, and government. While limited opportunities exist for specialization, program emphasis has been placed on managerial breadth. Classes are structured in such a way that students are given many opportunities to engage in problem definition, problem analysis, and problem solution or amelioration. The M.B.A. program consists of three components: 30 semester hours of foundation courses that may be waived depending on the student's educational background, 33 semester hours of graduate management core courses, and 6 hours of graduate electives.

ADMISSION

All admission credentials must be received 45 days before the beginning of the term in which the applicant wishes to enroll. The following items are required: a completed application form, two letters of recommendation, an official Graduate Management Admission Test (GMAT) score, official transcript(s) mailed from the college or university directly to the School of Business, and a $15 application fee.

EXPENSES

Total full-time fees for two semesters are $765 for state residents and $3,323 for out-of-state residents. Fees for part-time students are prorated. The application fee is $15.

Double-room accommodation rates on campus, including board and laundry, are $2,006 per year. Most graduate students live off campus, where costs vary depending on the type of accommodation. Board on campus is available to all students at a cost of $1,011 per year. Graduate students may elect room and laundry only at a yearly cost of $995.

FINANCIAL ASSISTANCE

Financial assistance may be secured through graduate teaching and research assistantships. Graduate students may seek positions as graduate residence assistants. Federal loans and work-study programs, administered by the Director of Financial Aid, are available for qualified students.

CORRESPONDENCE

For further information, please write
   Associate Dean of Graduate Programs
   School of Business
   P.O. Box 19742
   North Carolina Central University
   Durham, North Carolina 27707

North Texas State University, established in 1890, is a coeducational, state-controlled institution with a current enrollment in excess of 20,000 students. The university buildings and grounds are located on approximately 415 acres in a suburban area 35 miles northwest of Dallas. The physical plant contains 75 buildings.

The University Libraries house over 1,465,000 cataloged volumes of printed books, periodicals, documents, and microformats located in three separate facilities at the heart of the campus. The libraries can provide access to the bibliographic resources of area colleges and universities, and provide a variety of computerized services, including inter-library loan, bibliographic database searching and shared cataloging.

Students receive services in psychological counseling, career counseling, and placement.

The College of Business Administration offers courses leading to the degrees of Master of Business Administration (M.B.A.), Master of Science with a major in accounting, and Doctor of Philosophy. Both the undergraduate and the graduate programs are accredited by the American Assembly of Collegiate Schools of Business (AACSB).

PROGRAMS OF STUDY

The complexities of the economic, social, and scientific world of today are increasing the demand of the business community for students with advanced business degrees. The overall objective of the graduate program leading to the Master of Business Administration degree is to prepare its graduates to serve effectively in the business world or in the business aspects of government or other agencies. The specific objectives are as follows:

• to provide the candidate with the theory, principles, and knowledge required for effective management of modern business;

• to develop an appreciation of the role and responsibilities of business leaders in the social and economic order;

• to foster the techniques of basing decision and action on careful analysis of pertinent data.

A bachelor's degree from an accredited institution and admission to the Graduate School of the university are needed for graduate standing. The Master of Business Administration degree program requires, as a minimum background, the equivalent of the Common Body of Knowledge in Business Administration. Students may have acquired this background in their undergraduate programs by the completion of courses equivalent in content to the business foundation requirements for the bachelor's degree in business administration at North Texas State University.

The Master of Business Administration degree requires a minimum of 36 semester hours of graduate credit with an average grade of B.

ADMISSION

In the determination of an applicant's eligibility for admission, the following measures are of critical importance:

• overall undergraduate grade-point average and grade-point average on approximately the last 60 semester hours (the academic record must meet minimum requirements of the Graduate School),

• a satisfactory score on the Graduate Management Admission Test (GMAT) (specific requirements may be obtained from the Graduate Studies office of the College of Business Administration),

• a score of 550 on the Test of English as a Foreign Language (TOEFL) for students whose native language is not English.

Students are admitted to the M.B.A. program for fall, spring, or summer semesters.

EXPENSES

The following is an estimate of the expenses for a single student per semester for 12 credit hours:

Tuition and fees
Texas resident............. $ 329
Nonresident 1,625
Room and board.......... 950-1,200
Books and supplies 150-200

FINANCIAL ASSISTANCE

A limited number of teaching fellowships are available to master's degree candidates during the fall and spring semesters. Remuneration varies, depending upon qualifications of the graduate student and the nature of the assignment. Application should be made to the chair of the department in which the student is seeking a teaching fellowship.

CORRESPONDENCE

Inquiries should be addressed to
Director of Graduate Studies
College of Business Administration
P.O. Box 13677, NTSU
Denton, Texas 76203-3677
Telephone: 817-565-3030

Northeast Louisiana University is a state university located in Monroe, Louisiana, a metropolitan area with a population of more than 120,000. The university was established in 1932 and has an enrollment of over 11,000 (2,980 part-time), with approximately 2,016 (380 part-time) students in the College of Business Administration. The bachelor's and master's programs of the college are accredited by the American Assembly of Collegiate Schools of Business (AACSB). The College of Business Administration is housed in a new air-conditioned structure with modern teaching and research facilities, including an IBM 4341 computer and other statistical equipment for use by business administration students. Monroe offers a business and industrial environment that is conducive to research and study in business. Both the Bureau of Business Research and the Center for Professional Development at the university offer opportunities for community research and managerial involvement.

PROGRAM OF STUDY

The Master of Business Administration (M.B.A.) degree at Northeast is designed to give present and future business managers the flexibility and perspective demanded by the challenge of their careers and to provide a proper background for those who plan to pursue more advanced degrees. General preparation for business decision making and leadership is stressed in the program, together with an opportunity to develop an area of concentration. Analytical processes and problem-solving techniques are emphasized.

To enter the M.B.A. program, students are required to have adequate preparation in accounting, economics, finance, management, marketing, statistics, computer programming, and the legal environment of business. Students who have not satisfied these background requirements must either complete 30 hours of undergraduate courses in business administration or pass credit examinations. Most students who have an undergraduate degree in business will be able to satisfy these requirements.

The M.B.A. program at Northeast is a 33-semester-hour program with 24 hours of core courses and 9 hours of electives in the field of business administration. The nine hours are usually used in an area of specialization. At present core courses include three semester hours of each of the following: managerial accounting, quantitative methods, business research, survey and analysis in economics, seminar in finance, seminar in management, seminar in management policy, and seminar in marketing strategy. The program is available both full and part time.

ADMISSION

Admissions to Graduate School are under the direction of the Registrar. All correspondence concerning admissions should be directed to the Admissions Office.

An applicant for admission to the Graduate School must (1) satisfy all general admission requirements of the university, including the filing of a physical examination form, (2) hold a bachelor's degree from a regionally accredited college or university, (3) submit to the Admissions Office a complete and official transcript of work completed at each college or university attended, and (4) submit the results of the Graduate Management Admission Test (GMAT).

An applicant may be admitted to the Graduate School with regular status if he or she has earned a baccalaureate degree from a regionally accredited institution with a grade-point average of 2.5 (on a 4.0 scale) for all undergraduate work pursued and has met undergraduate prerequisites.

Admission to the Master of Business Administration program is at the discretion of the Graduate Admissions Committee of the College of Business Administration and the Dean of the Graduate School. Applicants must (1) meet all of the general requirements for admission to the Graduate School, (2) submit a satisfactory Graduate Management Admission Test (GMAT) score, and (3) demonstrate high promise of success in postgraduate business study. Additionally, international students must submit a satisfactory score on the Test of English as a Foreign Language (TOEFL).

EXPENSES

Regular semester
General registration fee
  (full time) $394*
Out-of-state student fee 340*
Summer sessions
General registration fee
  (full time) 134*
Out-of-state student fee 113*

---

*These fees are waived for persons with graduate assistantships.

FINANCIAL ASSISTANCE

Three types of graduate assistantships are available for students enrolled in the M.B.A. program: teaching, research, and laboratory. The stipends for the M.B.A. assistantships are $3,200-$4,400 for the nine-month academic year. Loans through the university are also available to graduate students. Applications for financial assistance will be accepted at any time; however, financial awards for the school year beginning in late August are generally granted in April.

PLACEMENT

Over 50 companies have actively recruited through the services of a full-time placement office in a year. Faculty members also assist in the placement of students. The university places top priority on securing challenging and rewarding employment for its graduates.

CORRESPONDENCE

For further information, write or call
  Associate Dean
  College of Business Administration
  Northeast Louisiana University
  Monroe, Louisiana 71209
  Telephone: 318-342-4190

NORTHEAST MISSOURI STATE UNIVERSITY

KIRKSVILLE, MISSOURI

Northeast Missouri State University (NMSU), located in Kirksville, Missouri, a community of approximately 17,000 people, was established in 1867 and has grown to become a multipurpose state university with an enrollment of about 6,400 students. In June 1985 Northeast Missouri State University was designated as the state's public liberal arts and sciences institution. Students now have an affordable alternative of a small select school with high academic standards. NMSU is accredited by the North Central Association of Colleges and Secondary Schools and several other accreditation boards and associations.

PROGRAMS OF STUDY

Two graduate accounting programs are offered at NMSU. The Master of Accountancy program is a 30-hour, one-year program designed for students who have a baccalaureate degree in accounting. The Master of Science (M.S.) in accounting program is a 60-hour, two-year program designed for students who have a baccalaureate degree in an area other than accounting. The M.S. program may be shorter for students with a baccalaureate degree in business administration. Both programs are designed to prepare graduates to enter the fields of public, private, and governmental accounting and accounting education. No thesis is required. The quality of any graduate program depends primarily on the quality, expertise, and dedication of the faculty and students. Students accepted into either of the graduate accounting programs will work closely with an exceptionally well-qualified faculty.

Graduate accounting students have the opportunity to take rigorous review courses for the C.P.A. examination and/or for the C.M.A. examination as a part of the graduate program.

NMSU's graduate and undergraduate accounting students ranked sixth and twelfth respectively in the nation on the percent passing all parts on the May 1984 Uniform C.P.A. Examination (Source: National Association of State Boards of Accountancy (NASBA) *Uniform C.P.A. Examination Statistical Nationwide Report*, May 1984).

ADMISSION

A student applying for admission into one of the graduate accounting programs must have a baccalaureate degree, be admitted to graduate studies, and be admitted to one of the accounting master's programs. The minimum requirement for consideration of admission is a combination of the Graduate Management Admission Test (GMAT) score and the overall or upper-division grade-point average (GPA) prior to graduate admission based on the following formulas: (1) at least 950 points as a result of 200 times the overall GPA plus the GMAT score or (2) at least 1,000 points as a result of 200 times the upper-division GPA plus the GMAT score. International students are required to submit acceptable scores on the Test of English as a Foreign Language (TOEFL) and to take the Michigan Test for English Language Proficiency and the Michigan Test of Aural Comprehension on campus.

EXPENSES

For graduate students enrolled in 12 semester hours, enrollment fees are approximately $530 for in-state students and $1,050 for out-of-state students on a semester basis. Enrollment fees for six semester hours for each five-week summer session are approximately $132 for in-state students and $264 for out-of-state students.

FINANCIAL ASSISTANCE

Several types of financial assistance are available. Graduate assistantships and part-time positions that require teaching, research, or other duties are available to students with outstanding credentials.

PLACEMENT

A centralized Career Planning and Placement Office assists graduates in obtaining career employment. Accounting faculty members are also involved in helping place students.

CORRESPONDENCE

For further information or to request an application for admission, write or call
Coordinator of Graduate Studies
   in Accounting
Division of Business
Northeast Missouri State University
Kirksville, Missouri 63501
Telephone: 816-785-4375 or
   816-785-4346

The Graduate School of Business Administration is one of nine graduate and professional schools within Northeastern University. Established in 1952, the Graduate School offers a variety of programs to meet the needs and schedules of graduate business students. For those interested in pursuing a Master of Business Administration (M.B.A.) degree on a full-time basis, the Graduate School offers two program alternatives: the cooperative education M.B.A. program or a two-year, full-time program. Individuals who wish to continue their full-time job responsibilities and complete an M.B.A. degree may consider the part-time, high-tech, or executive M.B.A. programs. The Master of Science (M.S.) in professional accounting is also offered as an intensive, full-time program specifically designed for liberal arts and other nonaccounting majors.

PROGRAMS OF STUDY

The M.B.A. program focuses upon the problem-solving and decision-making responsibilities of modern management and is aimed at providing broad-based preparation for careers in administration. Although the case method of study is used extensively, the different teaching methods employed are consonant with particular course objectives. All programs leading to the degree of Master of Business Administration have the same required courses in accounting, finance, marketing, management science, operations management, human resources, and business policy and also allow for individual specialization or broadening through elective courses.

The cooperative education M.B.A. program combines 15 months of academic study leading to an M.B.A. degree with a 6-month, paid work assignment. Co-op students are admitted as full-time M.B.A. candidates in January and June of each year. Work assignments, acquired with the assistance of the Graduate School staff, begin six months later.

The two-year, full-time program offers students the opportunity to pursue an M.B.A. degree by attending classes during the day and/or evening. Full-time M.B.A. students are eligible for graduate assistantships. Administrative and teaching assistants are expected to devote 20 hours per week to assigned duties for a stipend of $5,400 and full tuition remission for three academic quarters. Tuition assistantships are also available that include full tuition remission for 10 hours of work per week.

Part-time degree candidates may complete the M.B.A. program while continuing to develop their careers by pursuing one of two routes: the part-time program that takes three to four years to complete or the two-year, high technology program. In addition to core courses, the curriculum includes high technology courses that address the specific needs of managers in high technology companies. Classes meet one weekday evening and every other Saturday and include several residency weekends. The executive M.B.A. program, specially geared for middle and top management, offers an integrated curriculum relevant to students who continue to hold work positions while participating in this intensive 18-month program.

Residency periods or orientations are required of all M.B.A. students. These are designed either to acquaint students with the academic program, the faculty, and fellow students, or to discuss career development.

The College of Business Administration of Northeastern University offers a Master of Science degree in professional accounting for full-time students through the Graduate School of Professional Accounting. This concentrated 15-month program incorporates a 3-month internship with a national C.P.A. firm. New classes begin in mid-June.

ADMISSION

To be admitted for graduate work, applicants must have completed undergraduate work of high quality and obtained a bachelor's degree from an accredited institution of higher learning. The basic criteria considered in the admission procedure are undergraduate grades, Graduate Management Admission Test (GMAT) scores, previous graduate work, recommendations, essays, and job experience. An overall impression of strength, past success, and motivation to succeed in the Graduate School are desired in applicants for the program. Official transcripts and GMAT scores must be received before the deadlines in order for an application to be considered.

Application deadlines are as follows: June co-op—May 1, professional accounting—May 1, full time—May 1, high tech—August 1, executive—November 15, and January co-op—November 15. Deadlines for the part-time program vary. Please contact the Graduate School of Business Administration office for more information.

EXPENSES

An application fee of $30 is required. Tuition for all programs is $600 per course with the exception of the following programs: M.S. in professional accounting is $3,880 for each of four academic quarters, high tech is $750 per course, and executive M.B.A. is $24,200 for the whole program, books, and residencies inclusive. There are additional fees for health services, books, and so forth.

FINANCIAL ASSISTANCE

Graduate students are offered various alternatives for obtaining financial assistance through the Northeastern University Office of Financial Aid including work-study programs and various government loan programs.

PLACEMENT

A director of M.B.A. placement coordinates interviewing arrangements on campus with major companies. Graduate students and alumni may utilize this service.

CORRESPONDENCE

For further information, please write or call

Director, Graduate School of
 Business Administration
Northeastern University
205 Hayden Hall
Boston, Massachusetts 02115
Telephone: 617-437-2714

NORTHERN ARIZONA UNIVERSITY

FLAGSTAFF, ARIZONA

The Master of Business Administration (M.B.A.) program at Northern Arizona University was initiated in 1971 and is accredited by the American Assembly of Collegiate Schools of Business (AACSB). The program is designed to develop students for leadership positions in business and government and to prepare interested graduates for doctoral study. The program offers a thorough study of basic management and business functions and is intended to enhance the student's problem-solving and decision-making abilities. M.B.A. options are available with intensified studies in general management, management information systems, and wood products management. Enrollment averages about 30 students per class, which facilitates individual participation and close student-faculty interaction. Excellent hiking, camping, water recreation, and skiing facilities provide students with a unique contrast to the rigors of the classroom.

PROGRAM OF STUDY

The M.B.A. program is designed to provide one year of graduate-level study in business administration for students who have earned bachelor's degrees and completed foundation courses in the common body of knowledge in business. A student possessing a bachelor's degree in business administration from a college accredited by the AACSB is presumed to have completed all foundation courses. Students holding bachelor's degrees in other fields can complete all foundation courses in an additional year.

A student must complete 33 credit hours of course work at the graduate level for the M.B.A. degree, including 21 to 27 credit hours in the M.B.A. core program and 6 to 12 credit hours in the specific option area or electives. Substitutions and electives to the M.B.A. core program depend on the option chosen and are determined on an individual basis. The core program is as follows:

BA 600 Management Information
Systems 3
BA 601 Management Theory and
Analysis 3
BA 602 Managerial Economics 3
BA 603 Seminar in Marketing 3
BA 604 Quantitative Analysis—
Probabilistic 3
BA 605 Quantitative Analysis—
Deterministic 3
BA 606 Advanced Managerial
Accounting 3
BA 607 Financial Analysis for
Business Decisions 3
BA 613 Integrating Seminar 3

The program is designed so that a student who takes a normal course load of 12 credit hours a semester should complete the graduate-level course requirements in one calendar year—beginning in the summer or fall and finishing in the following spring or summer. There is no thesis requirement.

Eight units of graduate-level work may be accepted for transfer, provided the student has earned a grade of B or better in each course at an accredited institution.

Students in the M.B.A. program will be expected to maintain a grade-point average of B or better on all course work attempted. Failure to meet the minimum average by the end of a probationary semester will automatically terminate the student's standing as an M.B.A. graduate student.

ADMISSION

Applicants may be admitted as students with regular standing if they meet the following criteria:
 • hold a bachelor's degree from an accredited institution,
 • attain a composite formula score of 1,050 (or greater) according to the following formula: undergraduate grade-point average × 200 + Graduate Management Admission Test (GMAT) score with a 450 minimum GMAT.

Applicants who do not meet the above criteria may, at the discretion of the M.B.A. Admissions Committee, be admitted as graduate students with unclassified standing. For students so admitted a minimum of 3.0 (B) grade-point average for the first 12 units of work taken is necessary to remain in the program. The Graduate Committee may specify the minimum number of units to be carried by a special student.

Application forms plus an official transcript from each college attended and scores on the Graduate Management Admission Test should be forwarded to the M.B.A. Coordinator, College of Business Administration. Once this information is received, the student will be notified of his or her status.

EXPENSES
Approximate expenses for one calendar year:
 Tuition
  Arizona residents $1,136
  Out-of-state residents 3,692
  Room (single student) 1,000-1,500
  Meals (single student) 1,096
  Books and supplies 600
Information about university housing may be obtained from the Director of Housing.

FINANCIAL ASSISTANCE
A limited number of assistantships, fellowships, and scholarships are available to qualified students. These awards carry a stipend of $3,400 to $3,800 per academic year, a possible reduction in tuition and fees, and the opportunity to work hand in hand with the business community. Student loans are also available.

PLACEMENT
The office of Career Placement is available to M.B.A. candidates and alumni. Additionally the M.B.A. Director and the M.B.A. Student Association assist students in the placement effort through counseling, resume preparation, and employer contacts. Successful alumni of Northern Arizona University's M.B.A. program have also become a valuable resource for placement of M.B.A. candidates. Proximity to Phoenix, Tucson, and other centers of business and industry in the southwestern United States provides additional opportunities for employment interviews.

CORRESPONDENCE
For further information or to request an application for admission, write to
 Director, M.B.A. Program
 College of Business Administration
 Box 15066
 Northern Arizona University
 Flagstaff, Arizona 86011

Northern Illinois University in DeKalb, Illinois, is a state university strategically located to serve a large segment of the population in Illinois. The university, a major multipurpose institution committed to serving the educational needs of Illinois, is accredited in all of its degree programs by the North Central Association of Colleges and Secondary Schools. The undergraduate and graduate programs are accredited by the American Assembly of Collegiate Schools of Business (AACSB). Seventy-five faculty members, all with the earned doctorate, constitute the full-time graduate faculty in the College of Business and staff the courses of instruction offered through six departments. There are currently over 850 men and women enrolled.

PROGRAMS OF STUDY

The College of Business considers the satisfaction of the educational needs of students to be the primary goal of its endeavors. To help achieve this goal and to strengthen the effectiveness of teaching, the faculty is active in related service and research activities.

The proper use of analytical tools and management processes, skills in communication and social interaction, and competency in making and implementing decisions are the major thrusts of the instructional programs. The development of the student's capacity to pursue significant research undertakings and for growth in business careers is an important element in the total program.

The Master of Business Administration (M.B.A.) is offered by the College of Business as a nondepartmental degree. The Master of Science (M.S.) degree in finance, management, management information systems, and marketing, and the Master of Accounting Science are offered as departmental degrees. The Department of Business Education and Administrative Services offers the Master of Science in education and the Doctor of Education degree.

The M.B.A. program emphasizes the preparation of students for careers in business enterprises and other organizations such as public institutions, educational systems, and nonprofit organizations. An additional purpose of the program is to develop an understanding of research as it relates to business decision making.

Since a large number of students desiring graduate study in business do not have undergraduate preparation, the M.B.A. program varies in length with the upper limit at 54 graduate semester hours. Students with a bachelor's degree in business will usually have met all, or most, of the requirements of Phase One, while other students will have to take the maximum of 54 semester hours. Phase Two consists of 30 graduate semester hours of advanced work.

The aim of the Master of Science in business administration program is preparation for professional careers in the specialized areas of accountancy, finance, management, information systems, and marketing. The M.S. programs also aim to develop the capabilities of students to carry out in-depth research. A core of common knowledge in business, economics, and mathematics is also required of M.S. students. Phase One requirements are reduced with previous acceptable credit.

Current regulations of the Graduate School allow credit toward master's degrees in business for all applicable course work successfully completed through the NIU extension program. A list of centers approved for graduate extension work may be obtained from the Director of Extension, College of Continuing Education.

ADMISSION

Admission to the graduate programs in business is limited to those students who can demonstrate high promise of success in a graduate business degree program. The decision will be based primarily on the quality of prior academic achievement and on satisfactory scores (verbal, quantitative, and total) on the Graduate Management Admission Test (GMAT). Applicants must first satisfy the admission requirements of the Graduate School of the university. (To be admitted as graduate students, applicants must have obtained a bachelor's degree from a four-year accredited college or university, must have the approval of the department in which they plan to major, and must have a minimum 2.75 grade-point average, based on a 4.00 system, for the last two years of their undergraduate work.) If these requirements are satisfied, the applicant's credentials are reviewed for the purpose of applying the admission standards of the College of Business.

Application for the autumn semester should be submitted no later than June 1; for the spring semester, no later than November 1; and for the summer session, no later than April 1.

EXPENSES

Tuition and fees for full-time students:

Per semester	In state	Out of state
Tuition	$537.00	$1,611.00
Fees	210.12	210.12

FINANCIAL ASSISTANCE

Graduate teaching assistantships, graduate research assistantships, and graduate staff assistantships with stipends up to $4,950 for the academic year are available to qualified students. Fellowships are available to a limited number of outstanding students who meet the conditions established by the funding source.

Northern Illinois University participates in loan arrangements for students through national and state student loan programs. In addition, a number of campus foundations and loan funds are available to students.

PLACEMENT

Northern Illinois University maintains a placement office. Proximity to Chicago and industry in northern Illinois provides additional opportunities for employment interviews.

CORRESPONDENCE

For further information or to request an application for admission, please write to

Office of Graduate Studies in Business
Northern Illinois University
Room 120, Wirtz Hall
DeKalb, Illinois 60115

Northern Kentucky University (NKU) is the newest of Kentucky's eight state universities. The main campus is situated on 300 acres of rolling countryside along U.S. Highway 27 in Highland Heights, only seven miles southeast of Cincinnati, Ohio.

Greater Cincinnati has been named in *Advertising Age* as one of the top 10 metropolitan areas in the nation with a potentially excellent future for business activity and an outstanding quality of life. The M.B.A. program at Northern Kentucky University includes as its mandate the development of leadership for the region. The cultural and social advantages of greater Cincinnati, coupled with the economic potential and beauty of the northern Kentucky setting, enhance the excitement and opportunity of the institution. Recent completion of the region's interstate highways makes the campus accessible from any part of the area and only 10 minutes from major corporate headquarters in downtown Cincinnati.

The university has a modern, well-equipped library with an extensive collection of business, economics, and management texts, reference works, and periodicals. There are also several computer systems available for research activities.

PROGRAM OF STUDY
Great care has been taken to design the courses, curriculum, and program structure consistent with critical managerial needs. Design of the program was derived from, and continues to be developed in consultation with leaders of the business community of northern Kentucky and Cincinnati. As an example, emphasis on the development of each student's managerial, interpersonal, and communication skills is in response to needs voiced by senior executives. Experiential learning, case analysis, computer simulation, group project/presentations, and consulting assignments augment lectures and discussions in courses. Maintaining small class size is a priority consistent with these learning modes. The 36-hour (12-course) M.B.A. program is designed to provide practical and theoretical skills, values, processes, and concepts critical to success in middle- and upper-level management positions. The M.B.A. is a general degree, focusing on broad concepts of management; however, specialization is an option available through a choice of electives.

The program is designed to enhance students' development in the following areas:
- basic tools—mathematics, computerization, and business communication;
- problem analysis—using mathematical, accounting, economic, behavioral, and organizational models;
- environmental contexts—legal, social, and ethical;
- organizational structure and behavior—production operations, marketing, and finance;
- policy making—synthesis of data, decision making, and implementation.

Nearly all M.B.A. students work full time. They represent a diverse group of talented individuals from a variety of companies in the greater Cincinnati area. Many students are in major line and staff positions that suggest significant upward mobility. The program is especially well suited to the needs of these mature, working managers because courses are offered in the evening and on Saturday. Full-time students are welcome.

ADMISSION
Admission is restricted to students with a bachelor's degree from an accredited institution who meet the admission requirements established by the Graduate Council of NKU. Regular admission requires satisfaction of the following formula: [(200 × undergraduate grade-point average) + score on the Graduate Management Admission Test (GMAT)] > 950.

Application deadline for regular admission is 30 days prior to the beginning of classes. Students may enter in unclassified status through the first week of classes. Foreign students must submit a score of at least 550 on the Test of English as a Foreign Language (TOEFL).

EXPENSES
Tuition, per semester hour
Kentucky resident	$ 56
Nonresident	165

Tuition for full-time students (12 semester hours)
Kentucky resident	516
Nonresident	1,489
Cost of books and supplies per semester	150

Graduate Tuition Reciprocity: NKU and the University of Cincinnati have instituted a Graduate Program Reciprocity Agreement. For eligibility requirements and additional information, contact the Office of Admissions.

FINANCIAL ASSISTANCE
A limited number of graduate assistantships are available. The Office of Financial Aid also administers federal loan and aid programs. Assistantships are awarded on the basis of academic qualifications and appropriateness of professional goals to the position in question.

PLACEMENT
NKU has a Career Development Center which helps students identify employment opportunities. Fortune 500 companies interview on campus annually. The M.B.A. faculty has strong contacts with the business community of northern Kentucky/greater Cincinnati. This combination provides excellent potential for graduate student job placement, both nationally and locally.

CORRESPONDENCE
For further information, please write or call
M.B.A. Program Director
College of Business
Northern Kentucky University
Highland Heights, Kentucky 41076
Telephone: 606-572-6334

Northern Michigan University was established in 1899 as a state-supported institution. The university is located on the shores of Lake Superior in Marquette, a city of 25,000 inhabitants. The School of Business and Management offers a variety of programs to over 1,400 students.

PROGRAM OF STUDY

The primary objective of the Master of Business Administration (M.B.A.) program is to educate future middle and senior managers to deal with the basic problems of choice, complexity, and innovation in the ever-changing environment of business. The program is intended to develop skills to deal with these problems in a profit-oriented, free enterprise economy. Attention is therefore directed toward decision making, with the realization of the legal, social, political, and economic forces affecting business. This professional degree program is designed to serve students with backgrounds from a variety of academic disciplines. The program is divided into two phases. Phase one includes nine courses of prerequisite work. Areas covered by phase one courses are accounting, economics, finance, marketing, management, quantitative methods, mathematics, and statistics. Generally, a person having recently earned an undergraduate business degree will have met these requirements and will proceed directly to phase two, the M.B.A. core. The decision regarding the requirements of phase one courses will be made by the student's academic adviser in conjunction with the M.B.A. candidate.

The M.B.A. core, or phase two of the program, consists of 10 courses (31-32 credit hours). These courses are divided into three general groups. The first group emphasizes the analytical tools; the second focuses on applications of those tools to management decisions. The last group develops the student's ability to integrate all prior course material in solving comprehensive management problems. The courses making up the groups of the M.B.A. core are as follows:

Group I
  Managerial Accounting
  Managerial Economics
  Statistical Inference and Decision
    Making in Business
  Quantitative Systems Analysis

Group II
  Financial Analysis and Management
  Marketing Strategy
  Organizational Behavior and Human
    Performance
  One Elective

Group III
  Administrative Policy
  Business Ethics and Government Policy

The M.B.A. course offerings are structured so that a part-time student, taking six to eight credits (two courses) per semester, can complete the program in five semesters. All phase two core courses are offered in the evening.

ADMISSION

The M.B.A. program is open to qualified students who hold a bachelor's degree in any field from an accredited four-year college or university. The following admission requirements must be met: an undergraduate grade-point average of 2.5 (4.0 = A), an acceptable score on the Graduate Management Admission Test (GMAT), and in some cases two letters of recommendation and/or a personal interview. Application for admission to the fall semester must be completed by August 1. Application for the winter semester must be completed by December 15. Applicants from non-English-speaking countries must submit scores on the Test of English as a Foreign Language (TOEFL).

EXPENSES

Resident tuition,
  per credit hour . . . . $ 60.50
Nonresident tuition,
  per credit hour 106.00
The fees for room and board depend upon the type of living accommodations and the meal plan but range between $1,145.50 (one semester/10-meal plan) to $1,225.50.

FINANCIAL ASSISTANCE

Limited scholarships and graduate assistantships are available. Graduate assistantships carry a stipend of $4,000 for the year.

PLACEMENT

The university maintains a central Career Planning and Placement Service for graduates and alumni.

CORRESPONDENCE

For further information, write to
  Director of M.B.A. Program
  Northern Michigan University
  Marquette, Michigan 49855

Northwest Missouri State University was established in Maryville, Missouri, in 1905. Graduate work leading to a master's degree was offered for the first time in the summer session of 1955. The graduate program is accredited by the North Central Association of Colleges and Secondary Schools and the National Council for Accreditation of Teacher Education.

PROGRAM OF STUDY

The Master of Business Administration (M.B.A.) degree is offered by the School of Business. For those with an undergraduate degree in business from regionally or nationally accredited institutions, a total of 32 hours is required for the M.B.A. degree. Twenty-four of these hours are required, and eight hours are electives. Graduation requirements include an overall grade-point average of 3.0 plus successful completion of a four-hour comprehensive written examination, which is administered during the candidate's final academic term.

ADMISSION

An applicant must hold a bachelor's degree from an institution of higher learning accredited by the appropriate regional or national accrediting agency. A minimum grade-point average of 2.5 is required plus a satisfactory score on the Graduate Management Admission Test (GMAT).

Foreign students must score a minimum of 550 on the Test of English as a Foreign Language (TOEFL) and then take a written and oral test in English on arrival at Maryville. A low score on the local test in English will necessitate the student taking a reduced load plus a remedial English course.

Some students may be admitted to non-degree graduate study with the understanding that if the student decides to become a degree candidate, he or she must meet all admission requirements.

Students with degrees in fields other than business can be accepted for the M.B.A. program by completing the following prerequisites: economics, six hours; principles of marketing, three hours; statistics, three hours; principles of accounting, six hours; business law, three hours; fundamentals of business finance, three hours; and principles of management, three hours.

EXPENSES

Graduate incidental fees are charged on the following basis for each semester or summer session:
In-state
    $35 per credit hour, up to $560 for
    16 hours
Out-of-state*
    $65 per credit hour, up to $1,040 for
    16 hours

---

*Eligible, properly admitted nonresident graduate students may apply at registration for a nonresident graduate grant, which allows a $30 credit toward fees for each of the first six hours up to a maximum of $180. The grant certificate will be obtained from the Graduate Office.

FINANCIAL ASSISTANCE

Some assistantships ranging in value from $600 to $2,400 are available on a selective basis. Partial fee waivers are included. To be eligible the student must have a minimum of a 2.5 grade-point average on a 4-point scale. Application forms should be sent to the Graduate Office by April 1. Information about other financial assistance may be obtained by writing to the Student Financial Aids Office of the university.

PLACEMENT

Northwest Missouri State University provides placement assistance through the Placement Office. Many business, government, and public institutions regularly come to the campus to recruit graduates. The faculty members of the School of Business also work with graduates to aid in placement.

CORRESPONDENCE

For further information on the graduate program in business, write or call
    Dean of Graduate Studies
    Northwest Missouri State University
    Maryville, Missouri 64468
    Telephone: 816-562-1145
      or
    Director of Graduate Studies
    School of Business
    Northwest Missouri State University
    Maryville, Missouri 64468
    Telephone: 816-562-1277

A Department of Business was established at Northwestern State University of Louisiana in 1930 to offer undergraduate business programs. When this department became the College of Business in 1967, the Master of Business Administration (M.B.A.) program was added to existing baccalaureate programs in accounting, business administration, and economics. The present undergraduate enrollment in these three areas is over 1,000, while recent enrollments of graduate students seeking the M.B.A. degree have varied between 70 and 80.

PROGRAM OF STUDY

The purpose of Northwestern's M.B.A program is to provide educational preparation for persons currently employed or seeking careers as administrators. Recognizing that wherever there is a group activity utilizing resources there is a need for administration, the faculty has designed a graduate program that is suitable preparation for an administrative career in business, in the military, or in civic or institutional management. The faculty's teaching objectives, which are deemed to be consistent with the program's purpose, include achievement of a thorough knowledge of business and administrative functions, practice with quantitative and analytical tools of decision making, and development of oral and written communication skills.

A minimum of 30 semester hours of graduate work, including the areas of accounting, economics, finance, management, marketing, quantitative methods, and research methodology, is required. A thesis option or one of two nonthesis options may be elected. At the conclusion of the program students must pass a written comprehensive examination.

Students with a nonbusiness baccalaureate will be required to complete up to 27 semester hours of foundation courses in the above areas. This requirement may be met through course work, transfer credit, or proficiency testing utilizing the College-Level Examination Program (CLEP).

A full-time student with undergraduate preparation in business can complete the program in one and one-half years. A part-time evening program is also available on the main campus in Natchitoches, at Ft. Polk, and in the Alexandria/Pineville area. Because classes are small, students have ample opportunity to perform and develop through the seminar and case discussion format.

ADMISSION

Anyone who wishes to enroll in the Graduate School must file an application with the Dean of the Graduate School at least 30 days in advance of registration. Prior to, or at the time of, the submission of the application, the student must have two complete transcripts of his or her college record sent to the Dean of the Graduate School; in the event that a student has attended more than one college, transcripts must be sent from each college attended.

The criteria for regular status admission are 200 times overall grade-point average plus score on the Graduate Management Admission Test (GMAT) equals 950 or 200 times upper-division grade-point average plus GMAT score equals 1,000. A limited number of domestic students and all foreign students must present a minimum score of 550 on the Test of English as a Foreign Language (TOEFL).

EXPENSES

Per semester	In-state	Out-of-state	Foreign
Tuition	none	$ 440	$ 500
Fees	$ 450	450	450
Room and board	920	920	920
Books, etc.	300	300	300
Total	$1,670	$2,110	$2,170

Tuition for part-time students is $145 for the first one to three hours plus $35 for each additional hour.

Note: All fees and charges subject to change.

FINANCIAL ASSISTANCE

A small number of graduate teaching or research assistantships are awarded each year to students in the M.B.A. program. Student employment throughout the campus, which pays an hourly rate, is offered to students who qualify.

PLACEMENT

Personnel recruiters from private industry and government conduct job interviews in the university's placement bureau throughout the academic year.

CORRESPONDENCE

For further information or to request an application for admission, write to

Director of Graduate Studies
in Business
Department of Business Administration
and Economics
Northwestern State University
of Louisiana
Natchitoches, Louisiana 71497

The Kellogg School at Northwestern University provides an innovative program in which students prepare for careers in management. The emphasis is on management as a process applicable to any purposive organization, but specializations are available in business management, public and nonprofit management, hospital and health services management, and transportation management.

Students enrolling in the full-time master's degree program (enrollment, 850) or the Ph.D. program (enrollment, 75) will attend classes in Leverone Hall, on the Evanston campus. The 230-acre suburban campus on the shore of Lake Michigan is 12 miles north of downtown Chicago. The part-time evening managers' program (enrollment, 1,100) is located primarily on the Chicago campus.

PROGRAMS OF STUDY

The Master of Management (M.M.) degree program prepares men and women for positions of major executive responsibility. The program features

- widely varied pedagogical techniques including systems simulation, case studies, seminars, lectures, group and field projects, and computer-assisted learning;
- a flexible curriculum offering concentration of study in qualitative and quantitative disciplines;
- a full-time teaching faculty of 115 scholars, distinguished in their fields both as teachers and researchers;
- a location in a major metropolitan area which enables students to conduct research in the field (this complements the classroom education by providing actual experience with existing organizations).

The master's degree requires two academic years of study (23 courses, six quarters) for a full-time student. A one-year program (15 courses, four quarters) exists for those students who have been awarded a bachelor's degree by a school of business accredited by the American Assembly of Collegiate Schools of Business (AACSB).

The first year of the program includes a required core of work in computer methodology; accounting-information systems; quantitative methods; organization behavior; economic analysis; and the management of the financial, marketing, and production operations of organizations. The remainder of the first year and the second year are designed to integrate previous study and to complement it with opportunities to develop concentrations in one of the four institutional fields (business, health, public and nonprofit, transportation) and one or more of 12 functional areas. Electives may be taken in other university graduate programs. A thesis is not required.

The Kellogg School and the School of Law cooperate to provide a combined Master of Management-Juris Doctor (J.D.) program. The combined program provides the opportunity to complete both the M.M. and the J.D. degrees in a period of four years.

The doctoral program is designed for one who aspires to an academic career or a career as a research specialist in government or business. For information, contact the Director of the Doctoral Program at the address below.

A special master's degree program is available for middle-management executives sponsored by their companies. Details may be obtained from the Director of Executive Programs at the James L. Allen Center on the Evanston campus.

ADMISSION

Admission to the master's degree program is granted to students who appear well suited for management careers based on academic ability, intellectual capacity for graduate study in management, managerial talent, motivation, and personal characteristics. A candidate must hold a bachelor's degree or its equivalent from an accredited institution. Prior study in business or economics is not a requirement. A personal interview is expected of all applicants who are also encouraged to visit the campus. Students must submit results from the Graduate Management Admission Test (GMAT). About 95 percent of full-time students have one or more years of full-time work or military experience.

International students are required to file a certificate of financial responsibility in addition to the application for admission. Preliminary applications for foreign students are available through the address below.

The four-quarter program begins only in June; the six-quarter program only in September. Evening students may enter in January, April, June, or September.

EXPENSES

Expenses (1985-86 academic year) for a single six-quarter student:

Tuition	$11,295
Books and supplies	600
Room and board	5,050
Transportation	1,075
Personal	1,480
Total	$19,500

FINANCIAL ASSISTANCE

The school makes available to students over $5 million per year in the form of scholarships and loans. Over 70 percent of the Kellogg students receive financial aid. Minority scholarships are available to assist qualified minority students. Loans are generally available as needed. Applicants requesting aid must file a Graduate and Professional School Financial Aid Service (GAPSFAS) form.

PLACEMENT

The school operates an extensive placement service for M.M. and Ph.D. candidates and alumni. The office is visited annually by over 300 companies and institutions from all parts of the United States; many of them have international divisions.

CORRESPONDENCE

For further information or to request an application for admission, please write or call

Director of Admissions
J. L. Kellogg Graduate School
 of Management
Northwestern University
Evanston, Illinois 60201
Telephone: 312-491-3308

Nova University was chartered by the state of Florida in 1964 and commenced its educational activities in 1967. It is accredited by the Southern Association of Colleges and Schools. In 1970, the university joined in an educational consortium with New York Institute of Technology. Nova is a nonsectarian, nonprofit, racially nondiscriminatory institution. The university, recognized as an innovator in its field, is a leader in the administration and technology of offering external degree programs at the doctorate level to a national constituency. The Center for the Study of Administration is a member of the American Assembly of Collegiate Schools of Business (AACSB) and the National Association of Schools of Public Affairs and Administration.

PROGRAMS OF STUDY

The program for the Master of Business Administration (M.B.A.) and Master of Public Administration (M.P.A.) degrees with a general management curriculum consists of 40 graduate credits with a thesis option. It is a model program of study designed and operated for the mature person with industry experience; thus, redundancy of learning is minimized. Courses cover essential behavioral and quantitative areas needed for making sound decisions. The M.B.A. program stresses an innovative learning process.

There is also a Master of Science program in Human Resource Management (H.R.M.) with the learning design being a blend of traditional and behavioral management concepts including new ideas developed to meet the needs of organizational development and renewal. Nova's program makes both management and behavioral sciences available in a graduate degree so that both of these essential areas can be mastered by the nonbusiness major. The program covers theory and skills required to bring about a change in today's complex, dynamic environment.

Nova also offers its three master's programs in the corporate format. This means that the delivery of the programs will be on-site at a corporate location and all the members of the cluster will be employees of the contracting organization. The corporate program utilizes cluster coordinators who are also employees of the organization and who meet with the students between regular class sessions. These interim meetings ensure immediate application of course theories and concepts to specific corporate needs. All fees for the corporate program are the same as those of the regular programs.

The school calendar operates year round, and the average student enrolls for a block (two courses) which runs for three months. There are five weekend seminars for each course during each block. All courses represent three semester hours of graduate credit. Thus, the student is able to complete 24 credits of study a year by attending four blocks, and the average student is able to satisfy all course requirements in about one and a half years. Nova University will set up a local cluster whenever sufficient numbers make it feasible (30 students).

Nova also offers the Doctorate of Business Administration (D.B.A.) and Doctorate of Public Administration (D.P.A.) degree programs for practitioners, using the cluster format. These programs include classes in required locations around the United States and national seminars in Fort Lauderdale, Washington, D.C., and in conjunction with professional association meetings. The programs are oriented toward design making, problem solving, and strategic management in business, government, and industry. Course work can be completed in three years. Students are required to conduct research, write an applied dissertation, and publish at least one paper or research report.

ADMISSION

Admission requirements for M.B.A., M.P.A., and H.R.M. programs are as follows:
- a baccalaureate degree from an accredited college,
- three letters of reference (academic or business),
- a transcript of undergraduate record,
- the intellectual capacity and motivation to pursue graduate work as determined by credentials or interview,
- a completed application form and $30 fee,
- a satisfactory performance on the Graduate Management Admission Test (GMAT).

Admission requirements for the D.B.A. programs include the following:
- a master's degree from an accredited college;
- three letters of reference (academic or professional);
- official transcript of undergraduate and graduate work;
- intellectual capacity to pursue doctoral-level work;
- satisfaction of graduate course work in accounting/finance, economics, management/organizational theory, and statistics/quantitative methods;
- a score of 500+ on the GMAT;
- five years of management experience.

Students who do not meet all these requirements may be permitted to register as nonmatriculated or as conditional matriculants, gaining full matriculation upon satisfaction of all requirements.

EXPENSES

Tuition, per credit hour
(master's) $150
Tuition, per credit hour
(doctorate) 250
Application fee................. 30
Late registration fee........... 25
Graduation fee................ 20

FINANCIAL ASSISTANCE

Financial aid is available to full-time students primarily through the Federally Insured Student Loan Program. In addition, there are a limited number of graduate assistantships available each term that grant tuition in exchange for help in running tutorial sessions, grading for professors, or performing other support services. A special tuition consideration (one-half regular cost for second family member) is given when two or more members of the same immediate family are enrolled in the master's programs.

CORRESPONDENCE

For information, write to
Center for the Study of Administration
Nova University
3301 College Avenue
Fort Lauderdale, Florida 33314

Oakland University is located on a 1,600-acre estate adjacent to Rochester, Michigan, 23 miles north of the center of Detroit. Founded in 1959 as the result of a large private gift, Oakland is supported by the state of Michigan as an autonomous university.

The School of Economics and Management was established in 1969 and operates undergraduate programs in economics and business and the Master of Business Administration (M.B.A.) program.

PROGRAM OF STUDY
The Master of Business Administration program admits students with any undergraduate major but is designed for students who did not major in management or business. A typical entering class will contain students with undergraduate majors in the humanities, the social and natural sciences, engineering, computer science, the health sciences, and education, as well as management and business. The program stresses recognized common elements in management rather than concentrating on narrow traditional specialties. It is designed to educate students for managerial roles in either the private, public, or not-for-profit sectors of the economy. While learning to integrate the areas of economics, behavioral science, and quantitative methods with functional aspects of managerial problems, students are preparing for entry-level jobs. The program has a special emphasis on management information systems in all courses as well as the required courses on executive work stations, management information systems, and the management of information resources.

The program varies from 39 to 60 credits, depending on the student's prior preparation. The core program consists of 39 credits, which must be completed by all degree candidates. In addition, students may be required to take up to 21 credits of precore courses depending on their background in mathematics (including calculus), computer use, statistics, accounting, economics, business law, and organizational behavior. To register for the precore courses, the student must be admitted as a candidate for the M.B.A. degree.

All the M.B.A. courses are from 6:30 to 9:20 p.m. from Monday through Thursday. Part-time students may start the program in any term. Full-time students may start the program in the spring and fall terms. Full-time students can complete the 60-credit program in less than two calendar years taking four courses (12 credits) fall and winter semesters and two courses in a spring and a summer term. Part-time students can complete the 60-credit program in three years and four months taking two courses (6 credits) in the fall and winter semesters and one course in the spring and the summer terms. The "part-time" label should not mislead students about the workload or the commitment required. The program is highly structured with the student in the 60-credit program taking 16 of the 20 courses in lockstep with the other students who entered the program at the same time.

ADMISSION
Admission to the M.B.A. program is selective and depends on several elements, including scholarship and an ability to communicate effectively. A bachelor's degree or equivalent from an institution of recognized standing is required. The M.B.A. program assumes no academic preparation in management or business courses; however, students are expected to have college course work in algebra, economics, and computer programming. The primary criteria for admission to the program are the undergraduate grade-point averages of the applicants and their scores on the Graduate Management Admission Test (GMAT). In addition to using these criteria in making admission decisions, the Graduate Admission Committee may look at the work experience, postgraduate education, responses on the application, letters of recommendation (optional), and other evidence of the applicant's potential to succeed in the M.B.A. program. The applicants must also meet the general admission requirements for graduate study at Oakland University for the year in which they apply.

Applicants who wish to enter the precore program in the fall are advised to complete their applications before June 30. Applicants who wish to enter the program in the winter term should complete their applications before November 15, and those who plan to start the precore in the spring term should complete their applications by February 28.

EXPENSES
Tuition for residents of Michigan is $82 per credit hour. Nonresident tuition is $164 per credit hour. In addition to the tuition, students are assessed fees that range from $49.00 to $82.50 per term depending on the term and the number of credits taken. For the M.B.A. program the average cost per course for books and other supplies is $45. Although the M.B.A. students have access to the mainframe computer and an IBM Personal Computer lab, they are encouraged to acquire their own personal computer on which to complete their assignments. The cost of room and board in the dormitories for double room occupancy is $1,341 per semester. The rates for tuition, fees, books, and room and board quoted above are for the 1985-86 academic year. A limited amount of married student housing is available on the campus at $275 per month.

FINANCIAL ASSISTANCE
Graduate assistantships are available for well-qualified full-time students. Graduate assistants are normally assigned to work closely with individual faculty members on projects involving research, programmatic development efforts, or other projects of mutual interest. Normally, the graduate assistant is paid $3,600 for the academic year (fall and winter terms) and given 18 credits tuition remission for an average of 20 hours of work per week. Students interested in a graduate assistantship should contact the M.B.A. Office. Applications for graduate assistantships should be received before March 31 for the following fall term.

CORRESPONDENCE
For further information, please write or call

M.B.A. Office
413 Varner Hall
Oakland University
Rochester, Michigan 48063
Telephone: 313-370-3287

The Graduate School of Business Administration Zurich (GSBA–Zurich) OEKREAL Foundation located in Zurich and Winterthur, Switzerland, was established in 1968. GSBA–Zurich is now one of the leading graduate schools in business administration in the German-speaking part of Switzerland, especially in terms of the expertise of its teaching faculty and the wide range of course offerings. In particular, the newly developed case problem method entitled "Case Study of Gradually Increasing Complexity," is recognized as a specialty of the GSBA–Zurich faculty.

The Master of Business Administration (M.B.A.) degree is awarded to those who successfully complete the program requirements. As Zurich is the most important business center in Switzerland, the Graduate School of Business–Zurich offers an ideal training ground of Swiss management for aspiring upper-management executives of national and international companies.

PROGRAM OF STUDY
The M.B.A. program of GSBA–Zurich is primarily oriented toward persons with higher functional and managerial responsibilities within business organizations. This executive M.B.A. program provides students with tools, techniques, and conceptual insights to ensure that they will act decisively and positively in changing conditions of today's increasingly competitive business environment. GSBA–Zurich students are encouraged to expand their functional and business knowledge and skills while developing their awareness of professional and human challenges faced by contemporary business managers.

The executive M.B.A. program normally can be completed in four terms, which are divided into six to eight blocks of subject concentrations. Each block requires a three-month auto-didactic prerequisite study. Each block consists of two weeks of full-time student/faculty participation.

Educational instruction is accomplished through case studies, role playing, group discussions, team work, hearings, and lectures in a seminar environment. The seminars are conducted in German and English, reflecting the international dimension of the GSBA–Zurich M.B.A. program.

The curriculum offers a modular format. Given specified prerequisite accomplishments, it is possible for qualified students to enter the program at different seminar levels. The M.B.A. program participants progress through a sequence of block modules covering the following subject areas: international management, marketing management, personnel management, production and operations management, research and development management, financial management and controlling (MIS).

Each additional module of the different functional disciplines contributes to the growing body of knowledge as the participants continue to work in small study groups. The variety of experiences, backgrounds, and personalities combined in these study groups enable the participants to explore different dimensions of business-related problems.

Each module is completed with a block examination consisting of a team examination, individual examination, and a consulting situation simulation where the participants must present and defend their solutions to case related business problems in front of their fellow participants and the examining faculty.

As a final requirement in the M.B.A. program, each candidate is requested to elaborate a thesis relating to a selected problem area in a company of the candidate's choice. The thesis is executed as a formal and comprehensive project report. Included in the project are such topic areas as analysis of the business project and/or problem, analysis of current socioeconomic situations, evaluation profile of the business, problem solution(s), and recommendations. The thesis and oral defense are evaluated by expert faculty of the GSBA–Zurich.

ADMISSION
Candidates for the M.B.A. program must submit proof of these entrance qualifications:
- five years of experience in higher management position and a minimum age of 30 years;
- completed studies at American, Swiss, or other universities, or completed studies at higher technical schools together with equivalent additional education;
- a score of at least 550 on the Test of English as a Foreign Language (TOEFL);
- a score of at least 550 on the Graduate Management Admission Test (GMAT).

EXPENSES
The tuition fee for the complete M.B.A. program is Swiss Francs 19,800—payable within 30 days of admission, or on the installment plan: 6 × Sfr.4,000. The tuition fee covers books and teaching materials as well as examination fees. It does not cover fees for entrance tests (TOEFL, GMAT).

FINANCIAL ASSISTANCE
Participants are expected to secure their own sources of financing; however, to cover tuition fees and living expenses, students may qualify for a loan available at nominal interest rates.

PLACEMENT
The school provides placement service to assist non-sponsored participants in their search for employment.

CORRESPONDENCE
For further information, or to request application forms for admission, please write or call
The Graduate School of Business Administration Zurich
OEKREAL Foundation
Bahnhofstrasse/Schutzengasse
4 CH-8001
Zurich, Switzerland
Telephone: 01-211 60 68

Since its founding in 1870, the Ohio State University has upheld a tradition of excellence in teaching, research, and public service. Widely recognized as a leader among the world's major centers of learning, the university offers programs in more than 200 fields in 17 colleges. The Graduate School enrolls nearly 10,000 students in 116 master's and 86 doctoral degree programs. Nearly 3,000 students are enrolled in the professional schools of dentistry, law, medicine, optometry, and veterinary medicine.

The neighborly, small-school atmosphere of the College of Administrative Science helps ensure that the university's size never becomes overwhelming, and it encourages lively intellectual and social give-and-take between students and faculty members.

The college enrolls approximately 110 new full-time students and 55 part-time students in the M.B.A. programs each year and about 15 in the Ph.D. programs. About 30 to 40 percent of the students have an undergraduate degree in business. The majority of the students hold degrees in engineering, science, social science, and the humanities. Although about 40 percent of the students enroll directly following completion of their undergraduate degree, full-time students have, on the average, two years of work experience. Typically, 30 percent of the students are women, 15 percent are international, and 7 percent are American members of minority groups.

PROGRAMS OF STUDY
The Master of Business Administration (M.B.A.) program provides a tightly integrated learning experience based on the foundation tools of business management. There are no prerequisites for the full-time M.B.A. program. However, students are strongly encouraged to have basic knowledge in quantitative analysis, economics, and accounting before entering the program. All students must take the prescribed course of study; course waivers or substitutions in the program are not permitted. The structured 20-month program has a core of 18 required courses and 6 elective courses. Areas of emphasis are available in accounting, finance, human resources management, international business, management information systems, marketing, operations and logistics management, real estate, and insurance and risk. With permission, one may develop an individual area of emphasis, such as health service administration. Dual-degree pro-

grams are available with the College of Law (M.B.A./J.D.) and with the master's degree program in city and regional planning (M.B.A./M.C.R.P.). In addition, a part-time course of study known as the weekend M.B.A. program is offered on Saturdays. Unlike the full-time M.B.A. program, some prerequisites are necessary.

The Ph.D. program in business administration prepares students of exceptional promise so that they may be fully qualified to contribute to progress and understanding in the field of business, primarily through teaching and research. There is no language requirement. Major areas are finance, insurance, international business, logistics, industrial relations, marketing, organizational behavior, production and operations management, quantitative methods, and real estate and urban analysis. There are also Ph.D. programs in accounting and management information systems and in labor and human resources.

ADMISSION
Applicants for admission must hold a bachelor's degree from a regionally accredited institution. Factors considered in admissions decisions include undergraduate grades, scores on the Graduate Management Admission Test (GMAT), nature and length of work experience, and evidence of maturity and motivation. Admissions decisions are made on a rolling basis as each applicant's file is completed. To compete for a University Fellowship, one's file must be complete by February 1.

EXPENSES
Per quarter	In-state	Out-of-state
Tuition	$ 746	$1,796
Room and board	990	990
Books and supplies	133	133
Total	$1,869	$2,819

All fees and costs are subject to change.

FINANCIAL ASSISTANCE
Three kinds of financial aid—fellowships, assistantships, and loans—are generally available to U.S. applicants to the full-time M.B.A. program. The merit-based fellowships and assistantships are available only to exceptionally strong applicants. International applicants to the M.B.A. program are not considered for financial aid. Ph.D. students may also apply for teaching and research assistantships, which provide a monthly stipend and a tuition waiver.

PLACEMENT
The resources of the Administrative Science Career Counseling and Placement Office are available to all students. Representatives of over 200 companies visit the campus annually to interview students in business, and the office helps plan individual interviews and employment campaigns.

CORRESPONDENCE
M.B.A. Programs
College of Administrative Science
112 Hagerty Hall
Ohio State University
1775 College Road
Columbus, Ohio 43210-1309
Telephone: 614-422-8511
    or
Ph.D. Programs
College of Administrative Science
163 Hagerty Hall
Ohio State University
1775 College Road
Columbus, Ohio 43210-1309
Telephone: 614-422-0335

Consistent with its character and history as a pioneer educational institution, Ohio University inaugurated courses in business administration in 1893, at a time when few colleges and universities offered instruction in this area. The College of Business Administration was established in 1936; in 1950 its bachelor's degree program was accredited by the American Assembly of Collegiate Schools of Business (AACSB). The college is staffed by 43 full-time graduate faculty members, most of whom have substantial experience in business or government organizations. Approximately 100 students are enrolled in the Master of Business Administration (M.B.A.) program on a full-time or part-time basis. The average class size in advanced courses is 35.

PROGRAM OF STUDY
The Ohio University Master of Business Administration program is broad in nature and aimed at developing competence in overall management and administration. A highly integrated program that builds on a foundation of basic business knowledge, it emphasizes the mastery of advanced concepts and the application of these concepts to problem solving and decision making in business and other administrative organizations.

The Master of Business Administration program has two phases. Phase I consists of foundation courses aimed at the development of basic background knowledge in business and administration. Phase I requires course preparation in economics, accounting, marketing, finance, law, management, production, calculus, statistics, and computer science. A student who has received a bachelor's degree in business administration will normally have completed most of these courses as a part of the undergraduate work. A student with a nonbusiness undergraduate degree will receive waivers of Phase I courses to the extent that he or she has completed them satisfactorily as part of an undergraduate program.

Phase II helps the student develop a mastery of advanced concepts and provides opportunity for practical application of the concepts through course work, individual study projects, and the master's seminar. Phase II of the Master of Business Administration program consists of 48 quarter hours. All students are required to take the following courses: the master's seminar, a yearlong case course, offering opportunities to practice problem analysis, decision making, leadership, communication, and other managerial skills; managerial competencies, in which students assess their leadership skills and work to improve them through exercises and feedback; international business; human resource management; information systems; and a two-course concentration in finance, international business, marketing, or production.

ADMISSION
Admission to the program is on a competitive basis. Factors considered include the undergraduate grade-point average, scores on the Graduate Management Admission Test (GMAT), work experience, and recommendations. Preference is given to applicants who have an undergraduate grade-point average of 3.00 or better and a GMAT score of 500 or better. In addition, applicants whose first language is not English must submit scores on the Test of English as a Foreign Language (TOEFL). Admission to Phase II of the program is limited to the fall quarter. Students may, however, be admitted to take Phase I courses during any quarter.

EXPENSES
The comprehensive fee for 9 to 18 hours inclusive is $730 for residents of Ohio and $1,397 for nonresidents. Both university and private housing are available for graduate students. University apartments for married students are available at monthly rentals ranging from $249 for one bedroom, furnished, to $366 for two bedrooms, furnished.

FINANCIAL ASSISTANCE
Approximately 30 graduate associateships are available to qualified students in the College of Business Administration. Graduate associateships provide a stipend of $4,100 for the academic year and waiver of all fees, resident and nonresident, for three quarters plus two summers; however, the student must pay an incidental fee of $140 each quarter. The graduate associate is required to work approximately 15 hours weekly and take at least 9 academic hours a quarter.

University tuition scholarships are also available to graduate students. Special tuition scholarships are available for qualified minority applicants. These scholarships require full-time study. Other forms of financial aid, such as fellowships and loans, are also available. Students who want to be considered for scholarship and/or associateship aid should have all required materials in by March 1.

PLACEMENT
Ohio University maintains a full-time, fully staffed Placement Bureau. Annually, 500 organizations come to Ohio University to recruit students for future jobs. In addition, the faculty of the college and the Director of Graduate Programs work closely with the students to help them define career objectives, identify opportunities, and select initial jobs that are consistent with their career objectives.

CORRESPONDENCE
For applications and additional information, write
  Director of Graduate Programs
  College of Business Administration
  Ohio University
  Athens, Ohio 45701
  Telephone: 614-594-5078

The Oklahoma City University (OCU) School of Management and Business Sciences emphasizes the private enterprise concept; the importance of business disciplines in society; and the moral, ethical, and social responsibilities of business and its leaders. The graduate degree programs provide professional education for executive positions in business, industry, government, and the nonprofit service sector. The Master of Business Administration (M.B.A.) program focuses on the study of advanced and germane management disciplines of middle- and upper-level executives. In the Master of Science in Accounting (M.S.A.) program, prime attention is given to developing problem-solving and analytical skills, oriented toward people as well as production and resulting in sound financial decision making.

PROGRAMS OF STUDY

The M.B.A. and M.S.A. programs are offered on the OCU campus during 16-week semesters in the fall and spring. Courses are also taught during two summer sessions, each lasting six weeks. For students who have completed the preparatory courses, it is possible to finish the M.B.A. or M.S.A. graduate program in 12 months. The M.B.A. program on campus has been designed so that students may select one of several tracks or emphasis areas: arts/public service management, finance, information systems management, Juris Doctor/M.B.A., management, and marketing/advertising. Additionally, a management M.B.A. program is offered at off-campus locations where sufficient students are concentrated. Presently, off-campus programs are conducted at Lawton, Shawnee, downtown Oklahoma City, and Oklahoma Memorial Hospital. The off-campus programs are developed so that courses can be completed in 10-week semesters. Students who have finished the preparatory courses may graduate in 50 weeks. Those who have not finished the preparatory courses may graduate in 70 or 80 weeks.

ADMISSION

Formal application for admission to a graduate program must be made on the official application form, obtainable upon request from the Graduate Admissions Office. Early application is encouraged. Official transcripts of all previous college or university work should be requested and sent directly to the Graduate Admissions Office. Graduate study is not merely an extension of undergraduate study. It requires a substantially higher level of scholarship, ability, and motivation; and places a much greater emphasis upon research, creativity, and individual effort. Consequently, admission into the program will be based upon the Graduate Management Admission Test (GMAT) score, past academic achievement, the trend and areas of academic achievement, vocational progress and development, civic and professional activities, as well as education and training in colleges or universities, company programs, or the military. Demonstrated ability and potential, indicating a strong likelihood of success in the graduate program, will also be considered. All of these factors will be evaluated collectively in order to determine the admission status of each applicant. Upon admission each student will be assigned an adviser who will guide the student through his or her program of study. The minimum requirement for admission to the School of Management and Business Sciences graduate program is a baccalaureate degree from an accredited college or university. In addition, international students must present a score of 550 on the Test of English as a Foreign Language (TOEFL) or an equivalent test, prior to being considered for admission. Students will be admitted to study for only one graduate degree at a time. Those wishing to apply for a second graduate degree must make application again, following the admission procedure outlined above. Courses completed in pursuit of one graduate degree will not be allowed as credit toward another graduate degree. A maximum of six semester hours of study completed for graduate credit at another accredited college or university, with a grade of B or better, may be substituted for equivalent courses required in the Master of Business Administration core or track. Accordingly, a maximum of six semester hours of study, with a grade of B or better, may be substituted for equivalent courses required in the Master of Science in Accounting program.

EXPENSES

Costs are estimated on the 1985-86 academic year. Tuition and fee assessments are subject to change without notice.

Tuition, per credit hour $139
Books and supplies 175

FINANCIAL ASSISTANCE

There are several graduate assistantships (nonteaching) available to students. Also, Guaranteed Student Loans, National Direct Student Loans, and Work Study are available. Financial aid applications must be submitted by March 1. Resident hall counselor positions are available.

PLACEMENT

Placement services are available to students; local businesses employ many OCU students who attend classes during the evening hours.

CORRESPONDENCE

For further information, write to
   Office of Graduate Admissions
   Oklahoma City University
   2501 North Blackwelder
   Oklahoma City, Oklahoma 73106

Graduate education in business administration is an integral part of the Graduate College at Oklahoma State University (OSU) but is primarily under the direction of the College of Business Administration. Approximately 400 students are currently enrolled in graduate programs at the College of Business Administration. The university has approximately 22,000 full-time resident students; about 3,400 of these are graduate students.

PROGRAMS OF STUDY

The Master of Business Administration (M.B.A.) program is designed to provide the ability to manage the contemporary organization with its increasing complexity. The program provides breadth and depth in managerial thought, analytical skills, and administrative communication. It is a comprehensive yet flexible program consisting of 48 semester hours of course work. The teaching methods within the program include a variety of approaches such as lectures, case analysis, application of quantitative methods, field projects, and a major research report. Fifteen of the 48 hours may be taken in elective courses. Normally these will be taken in the areas of finance, management, or marketing, and the student has the option of diversifying his or her courses among these areas or concentrating them in a single area. In addition, under certain special circumstances, a student may take the elective hours as a block in other approved areas such as accounting, statistics, or computer science.

The academic year at OSU is divided into two semesters, beginning in August and January, and one eight-week summer term beginning in June. Students may enter the M.B.A. program at the beginning of any semester or term. The time requirement for completion of the program varies from four to five semesters.

The Master of Science degree in accounting requires at least 32 semester hours of work beyond the baccalaureate degree. The study program usually includes 21 semester hours of graduate courses in areas such as accounting theory, cost-managerial accounting, auditing, financial accounting, and taxes; 9 hours in other courses such as financial controls, computer science, operations research, business law, administrative policies, and economics; and 2 semester hours of credit earned by writing a scholarly report or by taking an additional course.

The Ph.D. program in business is designed to prepare students jointly for university teaching and academic research. The student will select a major from accounting, finance, marketing, or management. In addition, he or she will select two minor areas, one of which must be from the College of Business Administration. A nine-hour quantitative tool is also required.

This summary does not describe the requirements for the Master of Science in business education, distributive education, and economics, nor does it cover the requirements for the Ed.D. in business education and the Ph.D. in economics. For information on these programs and for more detailed material on the programs described, write to the Dean, College of Business Administration.

ADMISSION

Outstanding students with undergraduate degrees in any field of study may be admitted. Applications are evaluated on the basis of the applicant's indicated potential for successful graduate study through the undergraduate grade-point average, scores on the Graduate Management Admission Test (or the General Test of the Graduate Record Examinations for the M.S. in accounting), and prior extracurricular achievements.

EXPENSES

Tuition per credit hour is $27.30 for residents and $97.30 for nonresidents. The average unmarried resident student requires approximately $4,200 per academic year for fees, books, room and board, and miscellaneous expenses.

Married students can obtain university housing if their applications are received in sufficient time. Excellent facilities are available at a rate of $230 to $290 a month for a two-bedroom furnished apartment with bills paid. Inquiries should be made directly to Family Housing.

FINANCIAL ASSISTANCE

There are a number of quarter-time assistantships available for the master's program that pay $225 a month and require a maximum of 10 hours of work a week. Assistantships for doctoral candidates are also available and pay $660 per month for one-half time. Out-of-state fees are waived for graduate assistants. Assistantship applications are accepted at any time. A limited number of tuition fellowships are also available.

Student loans of various amounts are available at nominal interest rates. The terms of the loan are tailored to the applicant's circumstances. Students desiring additional information should write to the Student Loan Office.

PLACEMENT

The College of Business Administration maintains an excellent placement service and also cooperates with the university placement service. Representatives from companies throughout the United States annually recruit on campus.

CORRESPONDENCE

For further information, write or call
  Dean
  College of Business Administration
  Oklahoma State University
  Stillwater, Oklahoma 74078
  Telephone: 405-624-5064

Old Dominion University, founded in 1930, is a coeducational, state-supported institution located in a metropolitan area of about one million people. The university enrolls approximately 15,500 students, of whom about 2,000 are in the School of Business Administration. The administrative structure is organized around schools of arts and letters, sciences and health professions, business administration, education, and engineering.

The school is housed in a modern facility containing classrooms, seminar rooms, computer terminals, offices, a lecture hall, and faculty lounge. The school offers a Bachelor of Arts degree in economics; a Bachelor of Science degree with concentrations in accounting, economics, finance, management information systems, management, and marketing; a Master of Business Administration (M.B.A.) degree; and a Master of Arts degree in economics.

PROGRAM OF STUDY

The M.B.A. program is designed to present a broad but thorough insight into the basic problems of management and promotes, through graduate-level study, the self-development of executives for business, government, and industry. Case problems and independent research projects, along with oral and written presentations of findings, are used as vehicles in developing an integrated approach to the concept of management.

The program is designed to accommodate both full-time and part-time students. Most of the courses are offered in the late afternoon or evening. Courses are also offered every semester at off-campus locations.

The curriculum consists of a maximum of 20 courses and is divided into three modules: foundation (ten courses), breadth (six courses), and concentration/generalization (four courses).

The foundation module requires each student to take 10 courses that cover the common body of knowledge as specified by the American Assembly of Collegiate Schools of Business (AACSB). Students demonstrating sufficient knowledge in the area of a foundation course may request a waiver for both the course and its associated hours. These courses are accounting, computer-based information systems, finance, macroeconomics, management,

marketing, microeconomics, operations and production management, quantitative methods, and statistics.

The breadth module requires the student to (1) take five courses selected from the following six departments: accounting, economics, finance, management, management information systems, and marketing and (2) take the capstone course in business policy. No more than one course may be taken in any one area. Students concentrating in any of these areas may not select a course from the area of concentration to satisfy the breadth module's requirements.

The concentration/generalization module provides the ability for a student to either focus on an area of specialization or acquire a broader and more general background. This module consists of four courses. The selection of the courses is with the advice of the concentration/generalization area coordinator and the graduate program director. The student seeking a generalist degree is required to take at least one course in the area excluded within the breadth module.

ADMISSION

Prospective students may apply for entrance into the program during any semester. Criteria used for admission include the candidate's score on the Graduate Management Admission Test (GMAT), undergraduate grade averages, the trend of the grades during undergraduate work, letters of reference, and work experience.

To apply for admission, students should submit to the Admissions Office application forms for graduate study in business, official transcripts of all previous college work, a letter of recommendation, and scores on the Graduate Management Admission Test (GMAT). Applicants whose native language is not English are also required to submit an acceptable score on the Test of English as a Foreign Language (TOEFL).

EXPENSES

Expenses are as follows:

Application fee, nonrecurring . . . . . $ 20
Resident of Virginia, per hour 80
Nonresident of Virginia, per hour . 174
Student health service fee,
  per semester 23
Graduate diploma fee,
  nonrecurring. 20

For information on housing available to graduate students, write Housing Office, Old Dominion University, Norfolk, Virginia 23508.

FINANCIAL ASSISTANCE

Applicants for the graduate programs may compete for institution-wide university fellowships, with stipends of $5,000 for one academic year. Awards are made to outstanding entering full-time students. In order to be considered for an award, an applicant must have all admission credentials in the Admissions Office by February 15. Part-time employment as a teaching or research assistant in the School of Business is also available. Stipends are $4,500 per year and admission credentials must be in the Admissions Office by March 15 to be considered for a position.

PLACEMENT

The university's Career Planning and Placement Office makes its placement services available to graduate students. Employment interviews may be arranged with representatives of firms visiting the campus.

CORRESPONDENCE

For further information concerning the M.B.A. program, please write or call
  School of Business Graduate Division
  Old Dominion University
  Norfolk, Virginia 23508
  Telephone: 804-440-3585

ORAL ROBERTS UNIVERSITY

TULSA, OKLAHOMA

Oral Roberts University (ORU) is a private, nonsectarian, liberal arts and sciences institution in suburban Tulsa, Oklahoma. ORU has 4,600 students who come from every state and 40 foreign countries, and represent every race and more than 40 denominations. ORU is committed to a philosophy of education for the whole person—body, mind, and spirit.

Founded in 1963 with the first class in 1965, the university campus is valued at more than $150 million with 22 major buildings. ORU offers 62 majors on the undergraduate level and has graduate and professional programs in medicine, nursing, education, and theology as well as business. The School of Business opened in 1975 and in 1984-85 had 141 full- and part-time students.

The university is fully accredited on the baccalaureate, master's, and first professional degree levels by the North Central Association of Colleges and Schools. There are more than 350 faculty members. Its founder and president is evangelist and educator Oral Roberts.

The university has constructed the City of Faith, a $250 million medical and research center adjacent to the campus. This complex is used for continuing education, research, health care, and medical student education.

PROGRAM OF STUDY

The principal objectives of the ORU School of Business are to provide leadership on all levels of business activity, personal, corporate, and public; to emphasize management strategy and techniques, organizational behavior, communication, motivation, management by objectives, and long-range planning; and to place special emphasis on business ethics. The Master of Business Administration (M.B.A.) degree requires a minimum of 39 semester hours of graduate course work for students with a business background. M.B.A. students without previous academic training in business must pass proficiency exams or take nine courses to compensate for the deficiency in undergraduate preparation. These background courses are Principles of Economics I, Fundamentals of Accounting I and II, Business Law I or II, Principles of Marketing, Financial Management, Elementary Statistics, Principles of Management, and Introduction to Business Computing. Full-time students should be able to complete the M.B.A. program in three semesters (with adequate background) or four semesters (without

background). Course work must be completed within five years of matriculation with a 3.0 grade-point average.

A core of 17 semester hours is required of all students: Management, Organization Theory (modular); Managerial Accounting and Control (modular); Financial Management (modular); Marketing Management (modular); Ethics of Business, Government, and Society; and Cross-Pollination.

The modular courses are taught by teams of faculty members from the accounting, finance, management, and marketing disciplines.

A health care administration program is administered by the School of Business, with faculty members from the ORU business school and adjunct instruction from the health care professions. Courses such as Introduction to Health Care, Health Care Policy and Planning, Health Care Administration, and Health Care Marketing examine the structure of health service organizations, resource allocation, political consideration, state and national health agencies, and regional and local health departments.

ORU has a cross-pollination emphasis that puts professional students together in a series of academic and nonacademic experiences to enlarge each student's understanding of human problems and needs, other professional perspectives, and ways in which professionals might work together.

ADMISSION

Prospective students must meet all of the undergraduate admission requirements governing entrance to ORU and have completed a baccalaureate degree from an accredited institution. Grade-point average, scores from the Graduate Management Admission Test (GMAT), and work experience are evaluated. Up to nine hours of transfer credit can be granted upon careful evaluation.

EXPENSES

Expenses for the 1985-86 academic year were

Tuition, per semester hour.	$155
Books (estimate for the year)	400

Married students are housed in university-owned apartments that rent for $289-$319 per month, two bedroom, unfurnished; or $247 per month, one bedroom, unfurnished. Single students' apartments rent for $165 per month, per student, two bedroom, unfurnished; or $175 per month, per student, furnished.

FINANCIAL ASSISTANCE

Sources of financial aid include teaching and research assistantships and fellowships, various types of university grants, and federal loans. Financial awards for qualified students, excluding loans, range from $1,000 to $6,600 a year. All applications for financial aid should be filed with the ORU Financial Aid Office.

PLACEMENT

ORU's Career Planning and Placement Office assists all students, including M.B.A.s and alumni. More than 25 national corporations and companies visit the campus each year seeking qualified candidates.

CORRESPONDENCE

Inquiries concerning the M.B.A. program offered at Oral Roberts University should be directed to

Graduate Business Admissions
Oral Roberts University
7777 South Lewis Avenue
Tulsa, Oklahoma 74171
Telephone: 918-495-6509

Oregon State University, founded in 1868 as the state's land-grant institution, is located in western Oregon in the heart of the Willamette Valley. This location affords ready access to the Portland metropolitan areas, as well as to the various recreation areas of the Cascades and Pacific Ocean coastline. Approximately 15,000 students are enrolled in the university's degree programs. The College of Business offers both undergraduate and master's degree programs in business administration; about 100 students are enrolled in the graduate program.

PROGRAM OF STUDY
The purpose of the Master of Business Administration (M.B.A.) program is to provide a professional education that will enable qualified individuals to develop, with experience, into competent and responsible executives in business, industry, and government. The major objective of the M.B.A. program is to provide graduates with a sound professional preparation for responsible career positions in business and other enterprises where managerial skills are needed. The curriculum emphasizes the achievement of a broad understanding of all phases of business, together with the development of the decision skills required of the modern manager. The M.B.A. electives can be used to develop areas of special interest, including graduate professional courses taken outside the college.

The M.B.A. degree program consists of 45 quarter hours, including 33 hours of specific graduate courses that provide broad preparation for management and 12 hours of elective courses. A qualified candidate can complete the program in one calendar year.

Course	Quarter Credits
Management and Organization Theories	3
Behavior in Business Organizations	3
Marketing Management	3
Financial Management	3
Operations Management	3
Business in its Environment	3
Administrative Accounting	3
Business Conditions Analysis	3
Computer-Assisted Management	3
Deterministic Models for Business Analysis or Decision Analysis	3
Business Policy Formulation	3
Approved electives	12

If the individual has not had training in business subjects, the program includes prerequisite courses and becomes about 76 quarter hours. The extended program should take six quarters to complete. M.B.A. candidates are required to successfully complete a final written comprehensive examination as part of the requirements for the degree.

In order to enroll in a graduate-level business course, a student must be a classified graduate student and successfully complete the prerequisite applicable to the course. Included in the prerequisite requirements are courses in economics, calculus, statistics, management and organizational behavior, accounting, computer programming, finance, operations management, and marketing. Preparation in college algebra and computer programming is strongly recommended prior to admission to the program. If this preparation has not been accomplished, there may be problems in scheduling certain classes and in completing the program in six quarters or less.

ADMISSION
The M.B.A. program is open to qualified men and women who hold undergraduate degrees from accredited universities or colleges. Admission is granted to those individuals who show high promise of success in the program.

The Graduate Management Admission Test (GMAT) score and the undergraduate grade-point average are the primary criteria used in the admission decision. Foreign applicants whose native language is not English are required to take the Test of English as a Foreign Language (TOEFL). A minimum score of 550 is required.

No prior course work in economics or business is required for admission. A course in college-level algebra is, however, required for admission to the program.

Candidates may enter the M.B.A. program in any quarter (including summer), but because of the sequencing of certain courses, it is advantageous to enter during the fall quarter. Those who have completed the prerequisites to all 500-level courses and who enter during the fall can expect to graduate in one calendar year.

Application for admission should be made no later than one month before the registration date of the quarter of entrance. Under certain circumstances, applications are accepted after this deadline.

EXPENSES
Graduate tuition for 1985-86 was $710 per quarter for resident graduate students and $1,139 per quarter for nonresident graduate students. Tuition and fees are subject to change. The approximate living costs for graduate students for the 1985-86 academic year (including board and room) were $4,000.

FINANCIAL ASSISTANCE
Information regarding loans and the federally sponsored College Work-Study Program is available from the OSU Office of Financial Aid.

PLACEMENT
Graduates of OSU's M.B.A. program hold a wide range of responsible positions in various businesses, educational institutions, health care organizations, labor unions, and foundations. The College of Business, in conjunction with the Careers Planning and Placement Center, maintains files to assist students and alumni in defining career objectives, exploring alternative career paths, and obtaining satisfying employment. About 250 firms and organizations from across the nation interview on campus annually.

CORRESPONDENCE
For further information, write or call
Director of Graduate Business Programs
College of Business
Oregon State University
Corvallis, Oregon 97331
Telephone: 503-754-3490

The School of Business Administration, established in 1960, offers the oldest evening Master of Business Administration (M.B.A.) program in the Pacific Northwest. The Bachelor of Business Administration, the M.B.A., and the accounting programs are accredited by the American Assembly of Collegiate Schools of Business (AACSB).

Pacific Lutheran University (PLU), founded in 1890, is located on a picturesque 126 acres in a suburban section of Tacoma, Washington. The Pacific Northwest is abundant with natural scenic beauty. Puget Sound, the Pacific Ocean, rivers, lakes, and mountain streams attract fishermen, boaters, swimmers, and scuba divers. Mount Rainier, visible from many places on campus, dominates the Cascade range. The Cascades, as well as the Olympic mountain range to the west, offer countless recreational opportunities for skiers, campers, and hikers.

The 2,700 full-time and 800 part-time students represent most of the 50 states and some 20 foreign countries.

PROGRAM OF STUDY

The purpose of the evening Master of Business Administration program is to nurture, through education, the professional development of line managers with broad administrative capabilities. Since the great majority of PLU M.B.A. students are employed full time in industry, government, or nonprofit institutions, there exists ample opportunity for intellectual interchange with working professionals. The graduate-level business courses are taught by full-time, doctorally qualified faculty who are active in both research and consulting.

The Master of Business Administration curriculum consists of 14 courses (54 semester hours), of which 24 semester hours must be taken at Pacific Lutheran University. The general structure of the program is as follows:

Preparatory Core
Fundamentals of Accounting
and Finance
Fundamentals of Marketing and
Management
Applied Statistical Analysis
Management Use of Computers

Analytical Techniques and Managerial Environment
Economic Analysis and Policy
Decisions

Quantitative Methods
Accounting Information and Control
Organizational Behavior and
Environment

Management of Business Functions
Operations Management and
Systems Seminar
Financial Management Seminar
Marketing Management Seminar
Business Strategy and Policy

Specialization/Research Alternatives
Alternative 1: completion of two graduate elective courses *or*
Alternative 2: completion of requirements for a concentration in management information systems
Alternative 3: completion of research colloquium and formal thesis or case study.

Students who have met the preparatory core requirements can finish the evening master's program in 15 months of full-time study or in two-and-a-half years of part-time study. Since the graduate-level courses are offered in the evening, some students choose to begin the program on a full-time basis and then start or continue a management career in the Seattle-Tacoma metropolitan area. The M.B.A. degree requirements would then be completed on a part-time basis.

ADMISSION

Admission to the Master of Business Administration program is based upon sound scholarship and promise of development rather than on the precise content of an applicant's undergraduate degree. The admission criteria include total overall undergraduate grade-point average, scores on the Graduate Management Admission Test (GMAT), and letters of recommendation. Once accepted, candidates are expected to maintain a 3.0 grade-point average in all graduate-level work. Students from non-English-speaking countries must also submit scores from the Test of English as a Foreign Language (TOEFL).

Students are admitted for the fall semester beginning in early September, the spring semester beginning in early February, or the summer semester beginning in early June. Summer courses are offered each year. Applications for fall, spring, and summer should be complete by July 15, November 15, and February 15, respectively.

EXPENSES

Tuition for full-time and part-time students is $198 per semester hour (1985-86).

FINANCIAL ASSISTANCE

Limited aid is available in terms of loans, scholarships, and one graduate assistantship position a year.

PLACEMENT

The university maintains its own Career Services Office, which is visited regularly by representatives of industry and government agencies. The office also maintains contact with private executive search and placement agencies.

CORRESPONDENCE

For further information or to request an application for admission, please write or call

Director, M.B.A. Program
School of Business Administration
Pacific Lutheran University
Tacoma, Washington 98447
Telephone: 206-535-7250

PACIFIC STATES UNIVERSITY

LOS ANGELES, CALIFORNIA

Pacific States University is a private, non-profit institution located in southern California. Founded in 1928, it is engaged in training the professionals, both men and women, for leadership positions in commerce and industry. The College of Business Administration offers programs leading to a Master of Business Administration (M.B.A.) degree in industrial management, Master of Business Administration degree in accounting, Master of Business Administration degree in international business, and Master of Business Administration degree in international finance and economics. The College of Business Administration is equipped with an outstanding faculty, computer center, seminar and conference rooms, offices, and library. The library and research facilities are open for students and faculty. The university has campuses in Los Angeles, California, and London, England.

PROGRAMS OF STUDY

The objective of the Master of Business Administration program is to prepare men and women for management positions in a rapidly changing business world. The program stresses flexibility and performance with concentration on modern (developing) management techniques and decision making, using analytical and quantitative methods. The program is comprehensive and demanding, requiring the completion of 45 units plus a research project or thesis. The university is firm in the belief that master's courses should be taught by successful industrialists and businessmen.

The Master of Business Administration in accounting is designed to provide individuals with the necessary preparation required to enter and advance in the various fields of specialization in the accounting profession. The degree of Master of Business Administration in accounting is conferred after satisfactory completion of 36 units.

The M.B.A. accounting courses are Advanced Accounting 1, Advanced Accounting 2, Advanced Accounting Theory, Auditing 2, Income Tax 2, Government Regulations in Business, CPA Review, Controllership, Budgetary Accounting, Internal Auditing, Governmental Accounting, Computer in Accounting, Seminar in Accounting, International Accounting, and Advanced Tax Planning.

The M.B.A. industrial management courses are Marketing, Management, Managerial Accounting, Controllership, Contract Law, Industrial Management, Quality Control, Managerial Psychology, Organizational Behavior, Computer Technology, Negotiable Instruments, Physical Supply and Distribution, Operations Analysis, Logistics and Customer Support, and two options.

The international section of the curriculum arises from a popular demand to establish a posture that speaks to the expanding world of international trade and business activity. Courses are designed to meet specialized requirements in the areas of marketing, business economics and finance, and general business. Each area is directed towards international case studies and problem solving.

The university stresses in all its programs the pragmatic professional approach. Pacific States University has been oriented to the closer student-faculty relationship and will continue the tradition. Graduates of Pacific States University are well received in the commercial world, and the university is proud of its alumni.

ADMISSION

Applicants are required to have a bachelor's degree from an approved university or its equivalent. The Graduate Committee evaluates individuals not only upon past academic performance but also on professional experience and, perhaps most important, on potential. Many international students apply for these programs and are welcome.

Scores from the Graduate Management Admission Test (GMAT) are required of all candidates for admission. The highest scoring student is awarded a $400 cash scholarship, and $100 is awarded to all students receiving all As in a trimester. Applications should be received at least 30 days prior to the starting date of the trimester.

EXPENSES

Tuition, per unit $100
Special examinations 25
Graduation fee 70
Application fee
(payable only once) 20
Late registration fee
(No registration accepted
after second week without
approval of the Department
Chairman) 50
Foreign student fee
(payable only once) 35

CORRESPONDENCE

For further information, write or call
Graduate Committee
College of Business Administration
Pacific States University
1516 South Western Avenue
Los Angeles, California 90006
Telephone: 213-731-2383

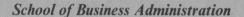

Pan American University, located in the semitropical lower Rio Grande Valley at the southern tip of Texas, opened its doors in September 1927 as Edinburg Junior College and continued as a junior college until 1952. At that time, the institution became a four-year, locally supported college and in September 1965 became a fully state-supported senior institution. The Graduate School at Pan American University first started accepting students in 1971, and enrollment has grown to almost 1,000 students.

The proximity of Pan American University to the heavily populated northern Mexico border area creates a bilingual, bicultural environment that influences all the programs of the university. The environmental effects are reflected in the architectural style of the multimillion-dollar university campus, which has been completed virtually within the past 12 years.

The undergraduate and graduate business school programs are accredited by the American Assembly of Collegiate Schools of Business (AACSB).

PROGRAM OF STUDY

The Master of Business Administration (M.B.A.) degree at Pan American University is designed primarily for people in administrative positions in business and other enterprises who wish to enhance their career opportunities. The program will assist these people by broadening their knowledge of the general field of business administration and by intensifying their knowledge of one or more specific areas within the field.

The program is also designed for students who wish to acquire broader and more intensive knowledge of management and administration in organizations of all kinds. Persons who wish a career in the teaching of business subjects or in business research will benefit from this training as well.

Training in this program will stress greater understanding of the interdependent nature of our society and interactions between the private, profit-oriented section and agencies of the public sector of the economy. Emphasis will also be placed on the importance of decision-making skills necessary for successful pursuit of careers in administrative positions in public or private organizations.

The M.B.A. requires 36 hours, 30 of which must be in courses open only to graduate students. In addition to fulfilling general requirements for a master's degree specified by the Pan American University Graduate School, candidates for the M.B.A. will be required to complete successfully a core of 27 semester hours. The student will select the remaining nine semester hours from approved graduate offerings of the university. Six hours may be taken from offerings outside the School of Business Administration with the approval of the Director of Graduate Studies in the School of Business Administration. A student may elect to write a thesis in lieu of six hours of graduate elective course work; however, each M.B.A. candidate, regardless of the option selected, must successfully pass a written comprehensive examination over the core curriculum.

ADMISSION

In order to be admitted unconditionally to the M.B.A. program, the student must meet all requirements of the University Admissions Office as well as providing the Director of Graduate Studies in the School of Business Administration with the following: (1) an official Graduate Management Admission Test (GMAT) score, (2) official transcripts indicating completion of M.B.A. prerequisite courses, and (3) admission points of 1,000 or more based on the formula of 200 times the undergraduate grade-point average plus the GMAT score. Grade-point average is calculated on the last 60 hours of undergraduate courses completed.

Foreign students from countries whose native language is not English will be expected to take the Test of English as a Foreign Language (TOEFL). Students scoring below 540 on the TOEFL will be denied admission, while those scoring between 540 and 560, but otherwise meeting M.B.A. admission requirements, will be required to take prescribed courses in English.

Further information on the Test of English as a Foreign Language and the Graduate Management Admission Test may be obtained by contacting Educational Testing Service, Princeton, New Jersey 08541 or Office of Career Planning, Placement and Testing Center, Pan American University, Edinburg, Texas 78539.

EXPENSES

Estimated expenses for a single student enrolled in nine semester hours of graduate course work:

Texas residents	$ 207
Nonresidents	1,179
Room and board	1,440
Books and supplies	200

FINANCIAL ASSISTANCE

Financial assistance is available through a limited number of graduate teaching and research assistantships. The assistantship pay is in excess of $5,000 for the nine-month academic year. In addition, a scholarship program is also available. Scholarship and assistantship recipients are exempt from nonresident tuition.

PLACEMENT

An active Placement Bureau is maintained for all students and alumni of Pan American University.

CORRESPONDENCE

Inquiries should be addressed to
Director of Graduate Studies in Business
School of Business Administration
Pan American University
Edinburg, Texas 78539
Telephone: 512-381-3311

THE PENNSYLVANIA STATE UNIVERSITY

UNIVERSITY PARK, PENNSYLVANIA

The Pennsylvania State University at University Park is located in the borough of State College in the center of the state. The location provides excellent recreational facilities while the university and surrounding communities support numerous cultural activities. University Park is located close to centers of business and government such as Pittsburgh, Philadelphia, New York City, and Washington, D.C., offering students opportunities to devote themselves to studies and cocurricular activities. While University Park Campus is a major center of graduate and undergraduate studies, the College of Business Administration supports a relatively small graduate program of about 450 students, allowing a high degree of student/faculty interaction.

PROGRAMS OF STUDY

The Master of Business Administration (M.B.A.) is a professional degree designed to prepare individuals for managerial positions in business, government, and nonprofit institutions. The curriculum blends technical rigor, managerial theory, and integrative learning experiences through case studies and other teaching methods. A managerial communications course is fully integrated into the program. The program consists of two distinct portions: (1) preprogram competency expectations in accounting, economics, mathematics, and statistics and (2) 54 credits of graduate courses and an optional professional paper. Individuals who did not have quantitative preparation in their undergraduate programs can develop the required minimum level of competency through self-teaching guides or formal course work at an accredited institution. This competency must be developed before graduate study can begin.

Work on the M.B.A. degree may be started in the fall semester only. The time required to complete the program, based on full-time study, is 21 months. The student body is divided into sections of approximately 40 students, proceeding through the same core classes each semester. The college also offers study/internship programs in France, Germany, and Peru.

The Master of Science (M.S.) in business administration program is highly flexible and designed for advanced study in a specialized field. The M.S. program is directed toward the development of competency within a defined area of management. Fields such as accounting, business logistics, finance, marketing, personnel management/human resources, management information systems, and management science are examples of career opportunities requiring specialized knowledge and skill, including research. Preparatory work consists of 33 credits; the degree program consists of 30 credit hours and a thesis or research paper. Excepting preparatory work, program completion takes two semesters of full-time study.

The Doctor of Philosophy (Ph.D.) in business administration program offers advanced graduate education for students contemplating careers in academic teaching and research and for research in nonuniversity settings. The faculty of the college views the Ph.D. as evidencing scholarship at the highest level.

ADMISSION

Applicants must hold baccalaureate degrees from accredited institutions. Candidates must submit Graduate Management Admission Test (GMAT) scores. Criteria for evaluating applicants include professional and academic accomplishments, GMAT scores, recommendations, and personal data from application forms that provide indications of future academic and professional accomplishment. M.S. and Ph.D. candidates may begin either the fall or spring semesters. Individuals of all undergraduate disciplines are encouraged to apply.

Applications from international students are welcome; however, a preliminary application must be submitted. For a preliminary application, please contact the Graduate Programs in Business Office. A minimum score of 550 on the Test of English as a Foreign Language (TOEFL) is required.

EXPENSES

Students may use the following general guide in planning for their academic year expenses (two 15-week semesters).
Tuition for the academic year:

Pennsylvania residents	$2,942
Out-of-state residents	5,880
Room and board	2,790
Books/supplies and personal	2,700

FINANCIAL ASSISTANCE

A limited number of quarter-time and half-time graduate assistantships are available with stipends ranging from $2,610 to $5,860 per academic year plus a grant-in-aid which covers tuition. Other aid includes fellowships, scholarships, tuition grants-in-aid, and loans. For detailed information, applicants may write to the Graduate School Fellowships and Awards Office, 320 Kern Building, University Park, Pennsylvania 16802.

PLACEMENT

Over 160 firms visit Penn State annually to interview 160 M.B.A. candidates. Placement services are available through the Graduate Programs Office and the University Placement Center. The reputation of the university, coupled with its proximity to the business centers of the Northeast, has resulted in the large numbers of recruiters from business, government, and education seeking prospective employees at University Park.

CORRESPONDENCE

For further information, please write or call

Graduate Programs in Business
  Administration
106 Business Administration Building
The Pennsylvania State University
University Park, Pennsylvania 16802
Telephone: 814-863-0474

The Pennsylvania State University is the land-grant institution of the Commonwealth of Pennsylvania. The Capitol Campus was established in 1966 as an upper-division undergraduate and graduate center. Located on approximately 215 acres 10 miles southeast of Harrisburg, Capitol Campus is within commuting distance of York, Lancaster, Hershey, and Reading. The fall 1985 enrollment included 1,713 undergraduates and 750 graduate students. There were 246 students pursuing studies in the Master of Business Administration (M.B.A.) program.

PROGRAM OF STUDY

The Master of Business Administration, a professionally oriented degree program, is intended for persons seeking or holding management positions in business firms, or in engineering, scientific, technical, or health care organizations. The goals of the program are to develop competence in decision making, skill in interpersonal and group relations, the ability to integrate and interrelate the various functions of the firm, a sense of responsibility to society, and a commitment to ethical action within and outside the firm. The degree may be earned through full- or part-time study. All graduate classes are held after 5:30 p.m.

The degree program includes foundation, prescribed, and elective courses. The foundation courses may be satisfied by prior course work or by taking the following courses at Capitol Campus:

BUS	491 Managerial Statistics
BUS	492 Management Science
ECNMS	310 Microeconomic Analysis
ECNMS	311 Macroeconomic Analysis
FINAN	492 Business Finance
MNGMT	491 Management Information Systems
MRKT	370 Marketing Principles
P ACC	491 Accelerated Elementary Accounting

After the foundation courses, the student must take 30 credits in prescribed courses, as follows:

BUS	552 Advanced Managerial Statistics
BUS	554 Master's Project
BUS	584 Business and Society
BUS	588 Business Policy Formulation
ECNMS	510 Managerial Economics
FINAN	530 Advanced Financial Management
MNGMT	510 Organizational Behavior
MNGMT	522 Operations Management
MRKT	570 Advanced Marketing Management
P ACC	540 Managerial Accounting

Nine credits of electives are also required. No more than six credits may be in a single discipline, that is, marketing, finance, management, etc. Research competence is demonstrated by completion of a professional paper.

ADMISSION

An applicant must present a baccalaureate degree from an accredited institution in any field. Admission decisions are based on an applicant's junior-senior cumulative grade-point average, Graduate Management Admission Test (GMAT) score, postgraduate work experience, and the degree of fit between the objectives of the student and those of the program. The best qualified applicants will be accepted up to the number of spaces that are available for new students. Applicants whose original language is not English are required to submit a 550 score on the Test of English as a Foreign Language (TOEFL). The GMAT + TOEFL scores must be submitted before the applicant is considered for admission.

Admission is open each semester of the academic year. Deadlines for applying are established to allow time for processing the application after all required information is available for consideration.

EXPENSES

Tuition for Pennsylvania residents is $115 per credit (11 or fewer credits) or $1,380 per semester (12 or more credits) for full-time study. Tuition for out-of-state students is $231 per credit (11 or fewer credits) or $2,772 per semester (12 or more credits) for full-time study. Residence charge is $390 to $825 per semester, and family housing is available at $275 to $335 per month. All charges are subject to change.

FINANCIAL ASSISTANCE

Limited financial assistance is available. Inquiries should be addressed to Financial Aid Office, Capitol Campus, Middletown, Pennsylvania 17057.

PLACEMENT

Placement assistance is available through the Campus Placement Center.

CORRESPONDENCE

For further information or to request an application for admission, please write or call

Admissions Office
Master of Business Administration Program
The Pennsylvania State University
The Capitol Campus
Middletown, Pennsylvania 17057
Telephone: 717-948-6200

PFEIFFER COLLEGE

CHARLOTTE, NORTH CAROLINA

Pfeiffer College, for its first 100 years, was a private, undergraduate, liberal arts institution. In 1985, the first graduate program, the Master of Business Administration (M.B.A.), was offered. Pfeiffer College's main campus is located in Misenheimer, North Carolina, which is about 40 miles northeast of Charlotte. The Charlotte campus, located in Myers Park on the periphery of downtown Charlotte, houses the M.B.A. program. The typical M.B.A. student is between 28 and 35 years of age and has a full-time job as an executive in the Charlotte area.

Pfeiffer College offers a Master of Business Administration (M.B.A.) program that is case oriented. The program stresses the basics in reading, writing, computer, and quantitative skills and has as its goal to graduate literate business managers who are comfortable using the most current management technology available.

PROGRAM OF STUDY
The executive Master in Business Administration program is a 24-month (36-credit-hour) program with all classes being offered in the evening. In order to complete the program in 24 months, individuals must enroll in two courses in both the fall and spring semesters and one course in each of the two summer sessions, for a total of six courses per year. With its case study approach, this program is attractive to those with or without undergraduate business degrees who are pursuing a career in business management.

ADMISSION
Pfeiffer requires an undergraduate grade-point average of 2.75, a Graduate Management Admission Test (GMAT) score of 425, three letters of recommendation, and at least two years of full-time work experience. Those candidates for admission who do not meet these requirements may be admitted on a probationary basis. The following undergraduate courses are prerequisites to entering the M.B.A. program: Principles of Accounting I and II, Principles of Economics I and II, Business Statistics, and Financial Management.

EXPENSES
Tuition and fees are subject to change without notice. The 1985-86 academic year costs are as follows:

	One course, per semester	Two courses, per semester
Tuition	$1,125	$2,250
Books	150	300
Totals	$1,275	$2,550

CORRESPONDENCE
For further information or to request an application for admission, please write or call

M.B.A. Coordinator
Pfeiffer College—Charlotte
1416 East Morehead Street
Charlotte, North Carolina 28204
Telephone: 704-333-1422

PHILADELPHIA COLLEGE
OF TEXTILES AND SCIENCE
PHILADELPHIA, PENNSYLVANIA

The Philadelphia College of Textiles and Science (PCT&S) is a private, coeducational institution with a unique 100-year history of leadership and growth.

The primary objective of the PCT&S Master of Business Administration (M.B.A.) program is to provide, within a small college environment, a quality professional graduate degree program that meets the needs of students and the standards of the business community. To this end, it emphasizes clearly defined instructional methods and a curriculum that reflects the growing sophistication of this field.

The program is designed with the understanding that the M.B.A. degree is a professional management degree. PCT&S offers a rigorous program that will challenge students and give them the tools and skills needed to assume positions of leadership and responsibility.

PROGRAM OF STUDY
The M.B.A. program is designed for individuals with practical business experience who recognize the need for more advanced knowledge and skills. The program should be thought of as a major step in the continuing process of self-development.

In order to permit students to attend classes with a minimum of conflict with their full-time jobs, classes are held in the late afternoon and evenings, with one class meeting scheduled each week during the fall and spring semesters. Classes are also offered during the summer semesters.

Learning occurs through several processes. The various courses in the M.B.A. curriculum employ differing teaching approaches: lectures, seminars, cases, behavioral experiments, and projects. Every effort is made to match the method with the course objectives and content.

Since all learning does not take place in the classroom, a feature of the program is the opportunity for students to fulfill some degree requirements by doing independent study. Based on the student's academic record, background, and work experience, the M.B.A. Director may permit the student to register for a course on an independent basis. This aspect of the program can benefit the student in two ways. First, it allows the student to demonstrate proficiency and to earn credit for relevant work experience. (No graduate credit will be awarded solely on the basis of work experience; proficiency must be demonstrated.)

Second, since independent study does not require classroom attendance, students can elect independent study during a semester in which their work schedule or traveling would prevent them from attending class.

The M.B.A. program consists of the following 10 courses (30 credits): Applied Economic Theory, Managerial Economics, Information Systems, Managerial Marketing, Managerial Accounting, Financial Decision Making, Management and Organizational Development, Operations Management, Quantitative Analysis, Seminar and Business Policy. Three elective courses (nine credits) are also required of all M.B.A. students.

While the M.B.A. program does not require a concentration in a subspeciality area, the objective of the three elective courses is to provide the student with the opportunity to pursue a more in-depth study of business functions and management processes. Elective options include accounting, management, marketing, finance, retailing, health care administration, computer applications, international business, and textiles/apparel. Graduate students pursuing a career in the textile field are encouraged to take electives in courses related specifically to the textile and apparel industries.

ADMISSION
Admission is open to qualified students who hold a bachelor's degree in any field from an accredited college or university. Admission is competitive among the applicants applying each semester.

Each applicant is considered on an individual basis. Generally, in making its decisions, the Admissions Committee is guided by the applicant's (1) academic potential as evidenced by undergraduate academic records and scores on the Graduate Management Admission Test (GMAT); (2) management potential as evidenced by job experience, extracurricular activities, and/ or military service; (3) recommendations from professors and supervisors; and (4) personal statement of career objectives and motivation for seeking the M.B.A. degree. International students must also provide scores from the Test of English as a Foreign Language (TOEFL).

EXPENSES
Tuition is $195 per graduate credit. The application fee is $20.

CORRESPONDENCE
For futher information, write or call
Jeffrey B. Berlin, Ph.D.
Director of Graduate Admissions
Philadelphia College of Textiles & Science
School House Lane and Henry Avenue
Philadelphia, Pennsylvania 19144
Telephone: 215-951-2800

Gladys A. Kelce School of Business and Economics

PITTSBURG STATE UNIVERSITY

PITTSBURG, KANSAS

The Gladys A. Kelce School of Business and Economics at Pittsburg State University is located in southeast Kansas within 150 miles of each of the following metropolitan areas: Kansas City, Missouri; Wichita, Kansas; and Tulsa, Oklahoma. The faculty is almost exclusively full time and emphasizes teaching and applied research.

PROGRAM OF STUDY

The Master of Business Administration (M.B.A.) degree is a two-year graduate professional program designed to prepare future business executives. The course requirements for the M.B.A. degree consist of a minimum of 33 hours and a maximum of 60 hours. The 27 semester hours of foundation courses may be waived if appropriate undergraduate courses have been taken. None of the decision and strategy, integrating, or elective courses may be waived. The course requirements for the degree are stated below:

Foundation Courses—Common Body of Knowledge

Behavioral Aspects of Management 801	3
Managerial Finance 802	3
Marketing for Management Decision 803	3
Legal and Social Environment of Business 804	3
Economic Analysis 805	3
Statistical Methods for Management 806	3
Financial Accounting 807	3
Management Information Systems 809	3
Production Management 811	3
Total Foundations	27

Decision, Strategy, and Integrating Courses

Administrative Decision and Control 914	3
Managerial Forecasting and Resource Allocation 926	3
Business, Government, and Society 930	3
Operating in the International Environment 931	3
Financial Strategy 936	3
Marketing Strategy 939	3
Management Strategy and Administration 995	3
	21

Specialization Courses—Electives
Students select 12 hours in one of the following:

Accounting, Economics, General Administration	12
Total beyond foundations	33

A maximum of nine hours of transfer credit from an accredited graduate institution may be applied to the program of study.

ADMISSION

Admission is open to all qualified individuals who hold a bachelor's degree from an accredited undergraduate institution. Approximately 40 percent of those admitted to the M.B.A. program do not have undergraduate business degrees, and approximately 50 percent of the admissions have been women and minorities. The program has an enrollment limited to 80 full-time and part-time students. The Graduate Management Admission Test (GMAT) is required of all applicants. Applications are processed as they are received. For the 1986-87 academic year applications and official transcripts should be submitted to the graduate office no later than July 15 for the fall semester, December 15 for the spring semester, and May 1 for the summer session. Applications for assistantships and other forms of financial aid should normally be submitted prior to March 1. Unconditional admission requires a student to attain a minimum of 1,050 based on the formula: (200 × grade-point average) + GMAT score. A minimum score of 575 on the Test of English as a Foreign Language (TOEFL) must be submitted by a student whose native language is not English.

EXPENSES

The state of Kansas does not charge tuition. Full-time student fees for the 1985-86 academic year were $574 per semester for residents of Kansas and $1,162 per semester for nonresidents. Part-time students (maximum of six semester hours) paid $34.00 per semester hour if they were Kansas residents and $73.25 per semester hour if they were nonresidents. A minimum budget for a single student, including fees, was approximately $5,510 for the academic year. A married student required a minimum of $6,928 for nine months.

Residence halls with private rooms are available for single graduate students. University-owned married student housing is available. There is normally a good supply of off-campus housing for single students and a reasonable supply of off-campus housing for married students. Information about campus-owned housing is available from the Director of Student Services, Russ Hall, Pittsburg State University, Pittsburg, Kansas 66762.

FINANCIAL ASSISTANCE

Teaching and research assistantships are awarded to full-time highly qualified M.B.A. candidates on a competitive basis. Loans are available to qualified students to assist with fees and living expenses. Information regarding student loans can be obtained from the Office of Student Financial Aids, Russ Hall, Pittsburg State University, Pittsburg, Kansas 66762.

PLACEMENT

Because the university has controlled admissions to the M.B.A. program and because of a good working relationship with businesses in surrounding metropolitan areas, the institution has an excellent record of placement of its M.B.A. candidates. The Placement Office provides considerable assistance to M.B.A. students, and a large number of firms visit the institution to recruit M.B.A. students each year.

CORRESPONDENCE

Further information concerning the M.B.A. program at Pittsburg State University can be obtained from
Ronald G. Wood
M.B.A. Program Director
School of Business
Pittsburg State University
Pittsburg, Kansas 66762
Telephone: 316-231-7000, extension 4598

PLYMOUTH STATE COLLEGE

PLYMOUTH, NEW HAMPSHIRE

Plymouth State College is located in north central New Hampshire, where it shares the beauty of the lakes and mountains with the 5,000 inhabitants of the town of Plymouth. The college, founded in 1871, now enrolls 3,200 students and offers programs leading to associate, bachelor's, and master's degrees. Living accommodations for both single and married students are available on campus.

PROGRAM OF STUDY

Many businesses are seeking personnel who have practical business training and experience beyond the bachelor's degree level. These firms want persons with a sound grasp of applied business theory. To meet this need, Plymouth State College has developed both a one-year and a two-year Master of Business Administration (M.B.A.) degree program.

The M.B.A. at Plymouth is a unique educational experience. Its objective is to extend and expand the candidate's awareness of applied business techniques and to improve an individual's business potential. This is accomplished by focusing the curriculum on applied concepts developed through theoretical and substantive courses. Working with faculty who have had experience in business, industry, and government, students can tailor their own programs by selecting courses from a wide variety of business-related electives.

In addition to the Plymouth campus, the M.B.A. program is also offered at five off-campus centers: Keene, Manchester, Hanover, Conway and Portsmouth, New Hampshire. Plymouth's M.B.A. program consists of 36 graduate semester hours. Students can earn the degree by attending classes full time during the college's regular fall and spring semesters and the January winterim. Part-time students have up to five years to complete the program, or they may, through intensive evening study, complete the M.B.A. in two years. The flexibility of Plymouth's M.B.A. allows students to design their curricula to meet their own interests and needs.

For students whose previous experience lies in areas outside of business, an M.B.A. "preparation core" will prepare them to earn the degree. Proficiencies in the following substantive course material must be demonstrated prior to final acceptance into the M.B.A. program: macro-

and microeconomics, statistics, financial accounting, managerial control, organizational behavior, and computer literacy.

These proficiencies would normally be satisfied by taking the appropriate college courses but may be waived by the demonstration of an equivalent proficiency to the department and the Director of Graduate Studies. All members of Plymouth's graduate business faculty have worked successfully in business, industry, or government. The full-time staff includes four Certified Public Accountants, four attorneys, five economists, a former company controller, and a former company president. The faculty have experience in accounting, marketing, production, wholesaling, transportation, labor relations, small business management, and computer applications. To remain abreast of current issues, many work as consultants to a variety of businesses. This practical experience, blended with their role as educators, adds a vital ingredient to a realistic and pragmatic M.B.A. program.

The requirements for completion of the program are as follows:
• completion of 36 graduate hours of study with a 3.0 (B) cumulative average (9 credits may be transferred or applied to the program as long as they were achieved less than five years before the time of acceptance),
• filing of an approved program contract in the Office of Graduate Studies by the end of the first semester of graduate work, and
• completion of the program within five academic years from the time of acceptance.

ADMISSION

Students applying to the Plymouth M.B.A. program are required to have a bachelor's degree. Actual business experience is also a prime consideration. The applicant must meet one of the following sets of criteria:
• a bachelor's degree in business administration with a 2.5 cumulative average (A = 4.0) and an acceptable score on the Graduate Management Admission Test (GMAT) or
• a bachelor's degree with a 2.5 cumulative average (A = 4.0), an acceptable score on the GMAT, and course work (or demonstrated competencies) in accounting, economics, management, statistics, and computer literacy.

A completed application, three letters of recommendation, and official copies of transcripts (undergraduate and graduate) are also required. An interview is encouraged. Students are admitted to the M.B.A. program at any time and may begin their program cycle in September, January, February, or July.

EXPENSES

Assuming that a candidate wishes to attend full time, completing the program in one year, estimated cost (based on 1985-86 figures) is as follows:

	N.H. residents	Non-residents
Tuition (36 hours)	$3,500	$ 7,000
Room and board	3,200	5,400
Textbooks and supplies	500	500
Miscellaneous fees	500	500
Total M.B.A. program	$7,700	$13,400
Part-time tuition per credit	$ 83	$ 176
Off-campus centers/course	$ 325	$ 325

FINANCIAL ASSISTANCE

Two graduate scholarships are available to full-time graduate students. A limited number of graduate assistantships are also available. Financial aid requests should be received by March 1.

PLACEMENT

Placement services are available for M.B.A. students through Plymouth State College and through the New Hampshire College and University Consortium.

CORRESPONDENCE

Please address inquiries to
Director of Graduate Studies
Plymouth State College
Plymouth, New Hampshire 03264
Telephone: 603-536-1550, extension 227

Polytechnic University, a coeducational, private, nonsectarian, technological university, was formed in 1973 by the merger of the Polytechnic Institute of Brooklyn with the New York University School of Engineering and Science. Today, Polytechnic is the largest technological university in the metropolitan area. Of the 5,256 students at the Polytechnic, 2,763 are in graduate programs.

In 1983, the Polytechnic was selected as the New York State Center for Advanced Technology in Telecommunications. A new degree, the Master of Science (M.S.) in telecommunications management, was introduced in fall 1984.

The New York City campus of Polytechnic is located near Brooklyn Heights, a fine residential area, the Brooklyn Civic Center, and the downtown shopping area. It is just 5 minutes from Wall Street and 15 minutes from midtown Manhattan by subway. It is part of, and contributes to, the unmatched educational, cultural, and professional opportunities of New York City. The campus in Farmingdale is in the heart of the industrial and business area of Long Island, New York. There is also a graduate campus in White Plains (Westchester County) New York.

PROGRAMS OF STUDY
The Master of Science in management program is designed for students who have earned a bachelor's degree in engineering, behavioral or physical science, the arts, business, or public administration. The goal is to develop competence in planning and decision making, and in the selection, allocation and direction of human, financial, and physical resources. Degree requirements, which consist of a maximum of 48 units at an overall B average performance, may be reduced by waivers of some core courses and/or evaluated transfer graduate course units (not more than nine).

The core courses listed below provide an intensive introduction to the basic disciplines of professional management. The adviser may waive corresponding courses on proof of competence.

		Units
MG 600	Management Process. . . .	3
MG 601	Organizational Behavior .	3
MG 636	Computers in Management	3
MG 650	Economic Environment of Management.	3
MG 700	Managerial Accounting. .	3
MG 702	Statistical Analysis.	3
MG 751	Managerial Finance.	3
MG 851	Marketing Management .	3

Four courses may be chosen in one of the following areas to form a concentration: Accounting and Control, Computer Applications, Construction Management, Economics and Finance, Energy Management, General Management, Human Resources, Management Science, Public Policy, Technology Management, and Transportation Management. The integrative course and project (taken in the last term) is MG 970 Business Policy, which carries three units. Two or more graduate courses chosen as free electives from those offered by any Polytechnic department bring the total number of courses to the required minimum.

The program is offered on both full-time and part-time bases. Most courses are given in the evening and late afternoon. All requirements for the M.S. degree must be completed within five years; full-time students can complete their work in two or three semesters.

The division also offers M.S. programs in economic systems and organizational behavior.

Certificates may be earned in 15 specialized areas in management and other program areas, for specified groups of five graduate courses; these courses may be the same ones used to satisfy the M.S. requirements.

ADMISSION
All applicants for the M.S. in management must have a bachelor's degree from an accredited school and must take the Graduate Management Admission Test (GMAT). Students who show potential for advanced study, but have an undergraduate average below B, may be admitted with nondegree status; satisfactory performance at the Polytechnic will permit degree status later.

Application deadlines are July 1 for fall registration, December 1 for spring, and May 1 for summer, although late admission may be possible. The deadline for financial aid applications is March 15.

Foreign applicants must provide scores from the Test of English as a Foreign Language (TOEFL).

EXPENSES
Full-time students' tuition,
    per semester $4,300
Part-time students' tuition,
    per unit 295
Dormitory facilities are maintained in a nearby college and in the Residence Hall on the 25-acre campus in Farmingdale, Long Island. Room rates are $730 per semester. Rooms can also be rented near both campuses, and both campuses have cafeterias. Total living costs average $500 per month.

FINANCIAL ASSISTANCE
Tuition aid in the form of partial scholarships, loans, and work-study may be available for some students who are not reimbursed by employers.

PLACEMENT
The Career Services Office hosts hundreds of recruiters from industry, business, and government to interview students for employment and sponsors career days and seminars. These services continue to be available to students after graduation.

CORRESPONDENCE
For further information on the programs offered by the Polytechnic University, telephone 718-643-7170 or write
    Dean of Management
    Polytechnic University
    333 Jay Street
    Brooklyn, New York 11201

Portland State University was founded as a degree-granting institution in 1955. Undergraduate and graduate degrees are offered in most academic disciplines. Ph.D. degrees are offered in environmental sciences, systems science-business administration, and urban studies. Portland State has an enrollment of 15,000 and is located in Portland, Oregon, a city in a metropolitan area including more than 1,000,000 people. The campus is situated only a few blocks from the core of downtown Portland. A new School of Business Administration building is under construction (with a planned August 1987 occupancy).

The School of Business Administration was established in 1961 and enrolls approximately 3,500 undergraduate and 500 graduate students per term. Both the bachelor's and the master's degree in business administration, which was introduced in 1967, are accredited by the American Assembly of Collegiate Schools of Business (AACSB).

PROGRAM OF STUDY
The Portland State University M.B.A. program prepares individuals for management of profit and nonprofit institutions. Through a carefully designed program of study, students acquire the creativity, perspective, and analytical skills necessary to meet the challenges of a rapidly changing world.

The M.B.A. curriculum seeks to develop in students the creativity and initiative to work effectively in a dynamic, complex, and competitive world. It exposes students to the broad theoretical concepts and principles that provide an overview of management thought and practice. It emphasizes the practical tools necessary to identify, analyze, and solve long-term organizational problems. Students polish their oral and written communication skills. They develop technical knowledge, breadth, and depth of understanding, and an ability to work with and direct people to achieve organizational goals.

A variety of electives supplements the required courses so that students may focus their learning in a particular area of business. Most students concentrate in one of four major business areas: accounting, finance and law, management, and marketing. The curriculum provides students with the opportunity to develop academic and research skills as well as to gain practical experience through internships and practicums in the business community.

Portland State's M.B.A. program consists of 72 quarter credits of graduate work (equivalent to 48 semester credits). There are no prerequisite courses required for entrance into the program. By waiver or examination the program may be reduced to a minimum of 57 quarter credits.

ADMISSION
Graduates of accredited colleges and universities are eligible to apply for admission. Acceptance is based upon the applicant's previous college record and scores on the Graduate Management Admission Test (GMAT) in accordance with the following requirements:
- an undergraduate cumulative grade-point average of 2.75 or better, *or* an upper-division grade-point average of 3.0 or better *or* a graduate grade-point average of 3.0 or better (must include 15 or more credits);
- a GMAT score of 450 or better;
- a TOEFL score of 550 or better, if a student's native language is not English (even for those who have graduated from a U.S. college or university).

A limited number of applications will be considered as exceptions each quarter. Information regarding the criteria for these admissions is available on request.

EXPENSES
Regular fees and tuition for Oregon residents in graduate studies total $717 a term. Students holding graduate or research assistantships that involve teaching or research duties pay a special reduced fee of $95 a term. Fees and tuition for nonresident students enrolled in graduate programs total $1,108 a term. Part-time students pay proportionately less.

FINANCIAL ASSISTANCE
Assistantships are available in the departments of Accounting, Finance/Law, Management, and Marketing. Stipends range from $3,510 to $6,174 per academic year. Eligibility for graduate assistantships is limited to full-time students who have been admitted and accepted by a department and who meet the minimum university requirements for regular degree status. A few graduate student scholarships are available directly from departments.

Long-term loans are available under the Guaranteed Loan Program and the National Direct Student Loan Program. Part-time jobs are also available in the College Work-Study Program. Application for loans and work-study is made through the Director of Financial Aids.

PLACEMENT
The university maintains a centralized placement office to assist graduate students and alumni seeking professional placement. Graduate students who need part-time work or employment following graduation are encouraged to establish a file with the Placement Service.

CORRESPONDENCE
For further information, please write or call
M.B.A. Program
School of Business Administration
Portland State University
P.O. Box 751
Portland, Oregon 97207
Telephone: 503-229-3712

Providence College, which is primarily a four-year college of liberal arts and sciences, also offers a limited number of graduate programs leading to advanced degrees. It is conducted under the auspices of the Order of Preachers of the Province of St. Joseph, commonly known as the Dominicans. The college was founded in 1917, under an Act of Incorporation approved by the General Assembly of the State of Rhode Island.

It is the policy of Providence College not to discriminate on the basis of age, sex, race, handicap, marital status, religion, national origin, color, or political affiliation. A coeducational, equal-opportunity institution, the college is accredited by the New England Association of Colleges and Secondary Schools.

Situated on a 99-acre campus in the city of Providence, Rhode Island, Providence College enjoys the advantages of an atmosphere far removed from the traffic and commerce of the metropolitan area, but it also provides easy access to the many cultural attractions of a city which is not only the capital of an historic state but also the center of a variety of institutions of higher learning.

PROGRAM OF STUDY

The Master of Business Administration (M.B.A.) program is management-oriented. It provides knowledge useful to junior-level business executives as well as to others who seek an advanced degree before entering the business community. Some courses deal with tools useful to managers. Others are concerned with various business functions. There is a quantitative emphasis in many of the courses and computer applications in others. All students follow the same basic program of studies. Courses are offered in the evening only.

If a student comes into the program with all the necessary undergraduate prerequisites, the M.B.A. degree can be earned by successfully completing 12 graduate courses (36 credits). Eight of these graduate courses are required (one each in the areas of accounting, computer systems, operations research, human resource management, marketing, finance, and a capstone seminar course), and the other four are electives. The undergraduate prerequisite courses are in the areas of accounting, mathematics, economics, quantitative methods, finance, and computer science and would normally total 36 credits. Graduate-level foundation courses are offered in accounting, mathematics, statistics, economics, and finance. These courses permit a student to accomplish six semester hours of undergraduate prerequisite work by taking one three-semester-hour, graduate-level course.

A student will be required to maintain a B average in his or her graduate courses in order to complete the program successfully. There is no language or thesis requirement; however, a thesis can be opted, and, if it is, two of the elective courses will be waived.

ADMISSION

Admission to the graduate program is open to qualified holders of bachelor's degrees in any field from accredited undergraduate institutions. In addition, all applicants are required to take the Graduate Management Admission Test (GMAT). Two letters of recommendation should also be requested by the candidate from former teachers or employers who have had the opportunity to evaluate the student's potential for graduate studies. At the discretion of the program director, an interview with the candidate will be arranged.

EXPENSES

Tuition for graduate courses is $85 per credit. Where a particular course makes use of the computer to a great extent, a laboratory fee will be charged. There are no housing facilities available to graduate students.

FINANCIAL ASSISTANCE

At this time, there is no financial assistance available to graduate students.

PLACEMENT

The services of the College Placement Office are available to all graduate students. Local, regional, and national firms visit the campus to interview those seeking positions. The college maintains what amounts to a lifetime placement service.

CORRESPONDENCE

For further information, please write or call

Director, M.B.A. Program
Providence College
Providence, Rhode Island 02918
Telephone: 401-865-2332

Krannert Graduate School of Management
PURDUE UNIVERSITY
WEST LAFAYETTE, INDIANA

The Krannert Graduate School of Management at Purdue University offers graduate programs dedicated to providing the practical and theoretical skills necessary for its graduates to assume challenging managerial roles. Since its inception, the school has built upon its special strength—superior management education for students with quantitative and technical backgrounds. By combining the use of case studies, interactive computing, and research projects and lectures, the Krannert graduate programs prepare graduates of the highest caliber for the nation's businesses, industries, academic institutions, and government.

PROGRAMS OF STUDY
The Master of Science in Industrial Administration (M.S.I.A.) program is a unique 11-month program which integrates all of the functional areas of management. The program is highly structured, with all students enrolled in essentially identical core course sequences each semester. Consisting of 49 credit hours to be completed over an 11-month period, the M.S.I.A. program imposes a heavy workload that requires a high degree of discipline and commitment on the part of the student. Because of the heavily quantitative and intensive nature of the program, it is particularly attractive to individuals with engineering or science backgrounds.

The Master of Science (M.S.) in management program, consisting of 61 credit hours which can be completed in 18 months or two years, also requires core courses in the functional areas of management. The elective credit hours comprise an option area and can be structured to include one of several concentrations compatible with the student's background and interests. The option areas include the following specializations: accounting, finance, management information systems, management science-quantitative methods, organizational behavior and human resource management, marketing, operations management, and strategic management. Students enrolled in the M.S. program are encouraged to participate in the Krannert internship program during the summer between their first and second years. Summer internship opportunities are available with large corporations throughout the country.

The Master of Science (M.S.) in human resource management curriculum provides professional training for careers in personnel administration, labor relations, recruitment and staffing, training and development, compensation, and other aspects of human resource management. The program consists of 55 credit hours and is normally completed in two years. In addition to a core of courses in the traditional areas of human resource management, the program includes a research methodology sequence; an interdisciplinary component of courses in economics, behavioral sciences, communication, and organizational behavior; and a management core of courses in accounting, marketing, finance, and strategic management. This program emphasizes strategic and analytical thinking, focusing on human resource management in a business context. Corporate summer internships are available.

The doctoral (Ph.D.) programs offer a unique opportunity to blend professional graduate study in management with rigorous advanced study of research-oriented disciplines. Formal research and teaching relevant to the student's area of specialization are a part of each doctoral program. The Ph.D. programs provide an outstanding educational base for teaching and research in economics, management, and organizational behavior/human resource management.

ADMISSION
The Krannert School seeks highly qualified applicants for the master's and doctoral programs. Neither an undergraduate degree in management nor previous business-related courses are required for admission to the programs. The admission decision is based on an evaluation of all application materials submitted by the individual. Previous academic records, prior work experiences, recommendations, test scores, and evidence of maturity and motivation are among the factors assessed during the admission process. All applicants are required to submit official Graduate Management Admission Test (GMAT) scores. Foreign applicants are also required to submit official Test of English as a Foreign Language (TOEFL) scores. Over two thirds of the master's students have at least one year of full-time work or military experience.

EXPENSES
Costs are estimated for the 1985-86 academic year. Tuition and fee assessments are subject to change without notice.

	Indiana Resident	Out-of-state Resident
Tuition and fees	$1,629	$ 4,835
Room and board	5,200	5,200
Books and supplies	500	500
Total	$7,329	$10,535

M.S.I.A. students will incur additional tuition and living expenses for the summer session.

FINANCIAL ASSISTANCE
The Krannert Graduate School is able to award cash fellowships ranging from about $500 to $5,000 to outstanding applicants. A limited number of teaching and research assistantships are awarded to qualified M.S. students. Assistantships include tuition and fee remission and a monthly stipend. Information about assistantships and fellowships is included on the application for admission. Financial aid applications must be submitted no later than March 1.

Students may be eligible to hold residence hall counselorships. Counselors supervise groups of from 50 to 175 students. These positions provide room and board as well as tuition and fee remission. For further information, write Director of Residence Halls, Purdue University.

PLACEMENT
A placement director and the senior faculty work with the students to identify employment opportunities. Nearly 150 firms conduct on-campus interviews of Krannert master's students annually. Over 75 percent are Fortune 500 Industrials and many of the others are major banks, accounting firms, and utilities. Graduates accept positions throughout the U.S. and abroad and consistently receive starting salaries well above the national average.

CORRESPONDENCE
For further information or to request an application for admission, please write or call
Associate Director of
    Professional Master's Programs
Krannert Graduate School
    of Management
Purdue University
West Lafayette, Indiana 47907
Telephone: 317-494-4365

The Calumet campus section of the Graduate School of Management offers graduate work leading to a Master of Science degree with a major in management. Graduate courses are offered in the evening hours so that the degree can be completed exclusively at night.

The objective of the program is to help students prepare for positions of major responsibility in American industry. The program is designed to help those with undergraduate training in engineering, mathematics, science, humanities, or business. The curriculum provides an opportunity for the student to gain an understanding of and develop some useful managerial skills in each of the major functional areas of industrial management. One of the major purposes of each course is to help students acquire increased managerial competence and breadth in administrative decision making.

PROGRAM OF STUDY

The Master of Science in management program consists of the following:

Core Requirement I   *Hours*
Two courses in differential and integral calculus (This requirement may be satisfied by prior undergraduate work.) 6
Two courses in quantitative methods 6
Core Requirement II
Managerial Accounting and Financial Management, Marketing, and Production 15
Core Requirement III
Behavioral Science and Industrial Relations. 3
Core Requirement IV
Economics 3
Core Requirement V
Business Policy. 3
Core Requirement VI
Legal and Social Environment of Business 3
Elective 9
Total semester hours 48

The following graduate courses are offered by the Graduate School of Management:

513 Economic Theory
522 Public Finance and Taxation
523 State and Local Finance
525 Government and the Economy
530 Money and Finance
534 International Trade Theory
535 Current World Economic Problems
560 Economics of Health
585 U.S. and World Economics in Recent Times
503 Accounting Problems
504 Tax Accounting
505 Management Accounting II
506 Auditing
512 Financial Institutions and Markets
516 Investment Management
590A Accounting Theory
553 Labor Law I
583 Small Business Management
600 Financial Control I
601 Financial Control II
611 Financial Management
584 New Enterprises
620 Marketing Management
630 Legal and Social Foundations of Management
631 The Personnel Function
632 Collective Bargaining
636 Government and Industrial Relations
650 Topics in Strategic Management
660 Operations Management
661 Management of Operating Systems
670 Quantitative Methods I
671 Quantitative Methods II

ADMISSION

Candidates are expected to have a bachelor's degree from an accredited college or university, and all must take the Graduate Management Admission Test (GMAT).

In evaluating applications, the school is concerned primarily with an individual's capacity for management responsibility. Demonstration of intellectual capacity is a prime consideration; however, close attention is also given to indications of personal development that may have a bearing on the individual's prospects for career success in industry. The evaluation is based upon a detailed review of the written application, academic transcripts, letters of evaluation from former instructors and others who are qualified to evaluate the applicant's capacity for graduate study, and scores on the Graduate Management Admission Test.

A minimum prerequisite for the degree is a full year of calculus—including at least one semester of differential calculus and one semester of integral calculus. Students not satisfying the calculus prerequisite must complete 48 semester hours of course work. Students satisfying the calculus prerequisite must complete 42 semester hours of course work. There is no foreign language requirement, but basic English proficiency must be shown by credit or test.

EXPENSES

Fees are paid at the time of registration each semester and are subject to change by action of the trustees. Indiana residents pay $58.75 per graduate credit hour and nonresidents, $133.50 per graduate credit hour.

CORRESPONDENCE

For further information, write or call
Director, Master of Science in Management
Purdue University Calumet
Hammond, Indiana 46323
Telephone: 219-844-0520, extension 388

Queens College is a 130-year-old, private liberal arts college located near the heart of the largest city in the Carolinas. The city is a banking center for the Southeast and the headquarters for many large national and international companies. The Master of Business Administration (M.B.A.) program has over 250 students who are either taking prerequisites or have been admitted.

Students have the advantage of an urban setting and ready access to the resources and outstanding leaders of the business and corporate community, as well as a low student-faculty ratio and instruction from full-time resident faculty. The program also benefits from supplemental input by "Distinguished Executive Lecturers"—selected prominent business leaders from major national and international corporations who share their time, energy, and expertise with Queens M.B.A. students. The Queens M.B.A. student is thus offered a unique blend of the theoretical and practical perspectives.

PROGRAM OF STUDY

The Master of Business Administration at Queens College is a strong and distinctive program that prepares men and women for leadership positions in business and industry. The program is geared to equip the graduate with the essentials necessary for dealing with the major management challenges of the eighties and beyond. There is emphasis not only on skills and knowledge of the basic areas of business and management but also on the major role of changing technologies, the effects of increasing governmental regulation of business, and the impact of ethical and environmental considerations upon business policy.

The content of the Queens College M.B.A. program begins with preparatory or prerequisite undergraduate courses. The student must show adequate preparation in economics, accounting, statistics, mathematics, information systems, corporate finance, marketing, and management.

The graduate course requirements include a total of 11 three-hour graduate courses (33 hours): 9 required courses and 2 electives. Business Policy and Society is the capstone course, which is taken as the last course in the 11-course sequence. This course includes a comprehensive project designed to encourage a synthesis of material included in the entire M.B.A. course sequence.

The Queens M.B.A. program is structured to ensure standardization of exposure to specific areas, techniques, experience, and information that is pertinent to a successful career in management. Course instruction is a combination of approaches, including the case study method, the traditional lecture format, simulations, and seminars. The variety and depth of educational and work experience the students bring to the program adds excitement and stimulation to the learning experience.

Blumenthal Fellowships, funded by the Blumenthal Foundation, are available to outstanding applicants of proven academic achievement and potential. Awards are based on undergraduate quality-point average, score on the Graduate Management Admission Test (GMAT), and an interview.

The Blumenthal Conference on Business Ethics is held annually in the North Carolina mountains. The Blumenthal Fellows join with speakers of national reputation as well as leaders in the regional business community. The conference provides a unique opportunity to explore and debate current issues impacting business and society.

ADMISSION

The M.B.A. program at Queens seeks students who represent outstanding promise for graduate work. Because the student body is the college's most important resource, careful attention is given to each student. Each applicant is considered on the basis of his or her individual achievements and merits.

For admission to the M.B.A. program, a student should have a baccalaureate degree from an accredited institution, demonstrate a strong academic undergraduate record, show aptitude on the Graduate Management Admission Test (GMAT), and evidence maturity and motivation for pursuing graduate-level work.

The Graduate School at Queens operates on a continuous admissions procedure, announcing admissions decisions as soon as a file is completed and processed by the Graduate School Admissions Committee.

EXPENSES

The following fees were established for the Graduate School for the fiscal year 1985-86:

Tuition, per credit hour	$130
Application fee, nonrefundable	20
Registration fee, nonrefundable	7
Transcript fee, if necessary	2

FINANCIAL ASSISTANCE

The Graduate School at Queens will make every effort to meet the demonstrated need of a student for financial aid. A student must be enrolled on a half-time basis or more in order to be eligible for student financial aid. A deferred payment plan is also available.

PLACEMENT

The Queens Career Center provides various placement and counseling services to Queens graduate students on a fee basis. The Career Center offers individual and group career/life-planning services, testing service, and workshops on topics such as managing a career, how to organize a job search, assertiveness training, and self-awareness.

CORRESPONDENCE

For additional information, please write or call

Graduate Admissions
Queens College
1900 Selwyn Avenue
Charlotte, North Carolina 28274
Telephone: 704-337-2313

In 1919, the School of Commerce of Queen's University at Kingston, Canada, was established within the Department of Political Economy. In 1963 the School of Business was formed as a separate entity. The school offers a four-year undergraduate program in commerce leading to the Bachelor of Commerce degree, a two-year graduate program in business administration leading to the Master of Business Administration (M.B.A.) degree, and a Doctor of Philosophy (Ph.D.) program in management. Enrollment approximates 750 undergraduates, 25 graduates, 250 postgraduates; the faculty includes 50 full-time instructors.

PROGRAMS OF STUDY

The goal of the M.B.A. curriculum is to produce graduates capable of identifying and solving problems within complex organizations. Qualification for the degree requires full-time attendance for two academic sessions. Each session is composed of two terms. The fall term runs from September to December and the winter term from January to April.

The curriculum of the first year is designed to enable the student to acquire a solid grasp of the modern tools and techniques available for decision makers as well as a background in the functional areas of organizations. The fall term emphasizes the major disciplines of economics, behavioral science, computing, and quantitative methods as foundations for decision making in complex organizations. In addition, the functional field of marketing in the first term allows the student to apply the theoretical concepts of the other first term courses. Along with macroeconomics in the second term, the functional courses (managerial accounting, finance, production, manpower, and operations research) are introduced.

The second year of the program offers a large degree of flexibility and free choice so that the student may study more intensively in one or more of the major decision areas of the organization. In addition, during this year the student is required to examine critically the whole organization as an integrated system.

The Ph.D. program in management prepares candidates for careers in education, research, government, and industry. Concentrations are available in the various functional fields of management, as well as in the supporting disciplines of management science, economics, and organizational behavior. Candidates are encouraged to blend advanced study in a functional field with the rigor of the supporting disciplines. Early involvement in research facilitates the preparation of a thesis proposal, and ultimately the defense of the thesis. Faculty advisers help with the development of individual programs of study to suit the candidates' interests. For further information, please contact the Chairman of the Ph.D. Program in Management.

ADMISSION

To be considered for admission to the M.B.A. program, a candidate must hold an undergraduate degree in arts, science, or engineering from an accredited university recognized by the Senate of Queen's University. Candidates must arrange to provide the Admissions Committee with an official academic transcript of the undergraduate program. All candidates must arrange to take the Graduate Management Admission Test (GMAT). Foreign students are required also to take the Test of English as a Foreign Language (TOEFL) or the ELI Test (Michigan). Foreign students should arrange to take these tests no later than January for the new session following in September.

Applications from all candidates may be filed up to June 1. The Admissions Committee resumes sittings in January. Offers of admission, along with offers of awards, will be made as early as possible. Normally all spaces are filled by mid-June.

EXPENSES

Graduate fees, 1986-87, for a single student:

Tuition (Canadian citizen or exempt foreign student)	$1,300*
Student interest, faculty society fees	185
Textbook allowance	600
Personal and living costs (33 weeks)	3,432
Ontario hospital insurance	216
Miscellaneous	300
Total	$6,033
*Foreign students on student visa	$7,385

For information on accommodations, please contact the Office of Residence Admissions, Brockington House, or the Office of Apartment and Housing Service, 86 Queen's Crescent, Queen's University.

FINANCIAL ASSISTANCE

Entrance scholarship and fellowship awards are offered in open academic competition. Awards are based primarily on academic achievement, aptitude for graduate study in business, and breadth of interests. Graduate assistantships are not offered to candidates on admission. A substantial number of term teaching assistantships are offered to registered students.

PLACEMENT

The university provides a full-time Career Planning and Placement Service, and the school provides additional counseling services.

CORRESPONDENCE

For further information, please write or call

Assistant Chairman, (M.B.A. Program)
School of Business
Queen's University at Kingston
Kingston, Ontario, Canada K7L 3N6
Telephone: 613-547-3234

REGIS COLLEGE

DENVER AND COLORADO SPRINGS, COLORADO

Regis College is a private, coeducational institution founded in 1877. It is operated under the sponsorship of the Society of Jesus (Jesuit), a religious order of the Catholic Church. The college is accredited by the North Central Association of Colleges and Secondary Schools and holds memberships in the Association of Jesuit Colleges and Universities, the Association of American Colleges, the American Council on Education, and several other academic associations.

The Regis College main campus is located in Denver, the financial, industrial, professional, and cultural center of the vast Rocky Mountain region. The Regis College southern campus is located in Colorado Springs, the "high technology" center of the Rocky Mountains.

PROGRAM OF STUDY

Given extensive input from the business community, the Regis M.B.A. program, which has business values and ethics at its core, is designed for working professionals who show high achievement, focused ambition, and potential for professional vision and advancement. These qualities constitute a unique program in the Rocky Mountain area. By constant involvement with the business community, particularly through the M.B.A. Advisory Council, a group of prominent business executives, the Regis program will ever be renewed and always serving the contemporary needs of those seeking advancement in business through education.

The curriculum consists of 30 semester hours of course work. Six courses constitute the core, with four electives required to complete the degree. Majors are available in finance and accounting, information systems, and management of technology. Elective courses are designed to accommodate the individual needs and interests of the students. A maximum of six semester hours of appropriate graduate-level course work may be transferred to Regis with approval of the M.B.A. Director.

The following graduate fundamentals courses are required of those students who have not previously completed studies in the respective areas: Management and Business Communications, Financial Accounting, Management Accounting, Economics, Business Finance, Business Statistics, Marketing, and Introduction to Computer Science.

The Regis M.B.A. program is designed to accommodate the working adult with evening classes throughout the calendar year. The time needed to complete the degree depends on the student's previous education and the pace at which courses are taken. A full-time student is one who takes two courses each semester. Courses are offered throughout the calendar year.

The Regis M.B.A. faculty is composed of full-time college professors as well as specially recruited professionals from the area business and financial community. Those who teach in the program are selected on the basis of their academic background, significant teaching competence, and practical expertise in either profit-oriented or not-for-profit organizations.

ADMISSION

To be admitted to the program, an applicant must have (1) a bachelor's degree from an accredited institution in any field of study; (2) official transcript(s) from all colleges or universities previously attended; (3) three letters of recommendation, one of which should be from the present employer or supervisor, appraising the applicant's ability to pursue graduate studies successfully; (4) scores on the Graduate Management Admission Test (GMAT); and (5) a personal interview with the M.B.A. Director. The admission decision is not based on any one of the above in isolation; rather, it is made as a result of the review of each applicant's overall profile. Students may enter the program at the beginning of any academic term during the year.

EXPENSES

There is a one-time, nonrefundable application fee of $125, which includes the evaluation of all application materials and the interview with the M.B.A. Director provided to complete the applicant's acceptance into the program and to plan course selection in light of career goals. Tuition is $208 per semester hour. Tuition and fees are subject to change.

CORRESPONDENCE

For additional information, please write or call

M.B.A. Director
Regis College
West 50th and Lowell Boulevard
Denver, Colorado 80221
Telephone: 303-458-4080
or
M.B.A. Director
Regis College
2300 Robinson
Colorado Springs, Colorado 80904
Telephone: 303-634-3706

Located in Houston, home to over 1,000 corporations and the nation's fourth largest and fastest growing major city, Rice University occupies a beautiful 300-acre campus a few miles from center city. Established in 1912, the university currently enrolls 3,900 students in graduate and undergraduate studies in humanities, social sciences, natural sciences, engineering, architecture, music, and management.

The Jones Graduate School of Administration with its faculty in accounting, economics, marketing, finance, and international and public management upholds the well-earned reputation of the university for academic excellence and distinguished teaching and research.

PROGRAMS OF STUDY

The Jones School offers the degrees of Master of Business Administration (M.B.A.), Master of Accounting (M.Acco.), and Doctor of Philosophy (Ph.D.) in accounting. Both master's degree programs have a common first-year curriculum. First-year students take courses in financial and managerial accounting, micro- and macroeconomics, finance, marketing, law, statistics, quantitative methods, and organization theory. Also included is training in effective communication.

After the first year, students select a degree program and an area of concentration within that program. Each program requires two years of study and completion of 64 credit hours.

The M.B.A. curriculum is unique and innovative in concept. The program prepares students to advance to senior-level management positions. Merging the traditional concerns of business administration with those of public administration and international management, the curriculum gives students a broad managerial perspective with cross-training in both corporate and public management. First-year course work balances quantitative and analytical methods with theoretical perspectives while integrating case materials. In the second year the case study method is emphasized. Students also acquire specialized preparation by selecting a concentration. Concentrations include accounting, entrepreneurship, finance, international management, managerial accounting and information systems, marketing, and public/nonprofit management. By special

arrangement with other university departments, concentrations are also available in operations research and organizational behavior.

The M.Acco. program prepares students for professional careers in public accounting or senior-level financial and managerial positions in business, government, and nonprofit organizations. Instruction is in the context of the planning and control of organizations; the program's goal is to educate individuals for positions requiring technical proficiency and management skill. The M.Acco. program is structured around course work in six areas: financial accounting, managerial accounting, information systems, economics and finance, quantitative methods, and accounting theory. Concentrations include auditing, financial reporting, managerial accounting and information systems, and taxation. Both degree programs provide for elective courses.

The Ph.D. program in accounting is designed for those who are interested in teaching and research careers in accounting.

ADMISSION

Admission is offered once a year for entrance in the fall semester. The programs are full-time. No evening, summer, or part-time programs are offered. Entering classes are no larger than 100 students and high standards are set to ensure small class size, an interpersonal environment, and the highest quality instruction. Primary consideration is given to applicants with a strong undergraduate record, excellent interpersonal skills, work experience, and an aptitude for graduate management education. Transcripts of all undergraduate and graduate work, results of the Graduate Management Admission Test (GMAT), and three confidential evaluations must be submitted. For foreign students the Test of English as a Foreign Language (TOEFL) is also required. The application deadline is April 1. There is no application fee.

No specific undergraduate major is desired or preferred; no prerequisite courses are required for admission.

EXPENSES

Tuition for 1985-86 was $4,100; also, a student should budget $7,000-$8,000 a year for room and board, books, transportation, and personal expenses. There are also fees for health service and student association membership. Tuition and fees are subject to change without notice.

FINANCIAL ASSISTANCE

The Jones School financially assists as many students as possible through a program of scholarships, grants, and loans. Full- or partial-tuition scholarships are awarded primarily on the basis of academic merit with some consideration given to financial need. All other financial assistance is awarded for demonstrated financial need and governed by the availability of funds. Deadline for applying for financial assistance is April 1.

PLACEMENT

The Jones Graduate School Placement Office provides assistance to students in securing both summer internships and permanent employment following graduation. Assistance is provided in the areas of career counseling, resume preparation, and interviewing techniques. Many corporations, private firms, and government agencies have employed graduates of the school.

CORRESPONDENCE

For further information or to request an application for admission, please write or call
Rice University
Jesse H. Jones Graduate School
of Administration (Admissions)
P.O. Box 1892
Houston, Texas 77251
Telephone: 713-527-4918

Rider College is a private, coeducational, nonsectarian institution of higher learning which was founded in 1865 as the Trenton Business College. It is now located on a 333-acre suburban campus on Route 206 between Trenton and Princeton. Rider's well-balanced academic program is offered through four schools: the School of Business Administration, the School of Education, the School of Liberal Arts and Science, and the School for Continuing Studies.

Rider College has granted degrees in accounting and commerce since 1922. The School of Business Administration was established in 1962 and has an enrollment of approximately 2,000 full-time undergraduates. The graduate program leading to the degree of Master of Business Administration (M.B.A.) was started in 1967 and currently enrolls over 450 part-time students. This graduate program offers only evening courses designed primarily to meet the needs of part-time students; however, a student may pursue graduate studies on a full-time basis by attending classes three or four evenings a week.

PROGRAM OF STUDY

The basic purpose of Rider's M.B.A. program is to prepare individuals for responsible managerial positions in an increasingly complex and demanding economic society. Therefore, this program emphasizes the development of managerial generalists rather than specialists in any one field of business administration. This is achieved (1) by an emphasis on the ability to communicate effectively; (2) by requiring an adequate knowledge of such basic tool subjects as mathematics, statistics, and business-research methods; (3) by requiring the study of the major functional areas of business administration and by providing some opportunity to concentrate in one of these areas; (4) by emphasizing the development of a problem-solving and decision-making capacity; and (5) by fostering an understanding of the social responsibilities of business as well as development of a social conscience.

Ordinarily, students admitted to the M.B.A. program must complete a total of 57 semester hours of graduate course work with an average grade of B or better. The specific courses required are listed below.

Foundation courses (33 semester hours)
Fundamentals of Accounting, Economic Analysis, Mathematics for Business Decisions, Foundations of Statistical Analysis,

Information Systems, Financial Management, Marketing Management, Management Theory and Application, Business and Its Environment, Production and Operations Management, and Administrative Policy and Decision Making.

Core courses (18 semester hours)
Managerial Accounting, Managerial Economics, Problems in Finance, Problems in Marketing Management, Strategic Planning and Policy, and Advanced Organizational Theory or Personnel: A Behavioral Approach.

Electives (6 to 12 semester hours)
Decision Support Systems, Operations Research, Analysis of Business Conditions and Forecasting, Securities Analysis, International Business Economics, Labor Relations and Collective Bargaining, Statistical Methods, Consumer Behavior, Financial Market Operations, Financial Reporting, Federal Income Taxes, Computer Based Accounting and Control, International Financial Management, Power and Politics in Organizations, Organization Development and Effectiveness, Selected Topics in Marketing, and International Marketing Management.

One or more of the foundation courses may be waived at the discretion of the department responsible for the course. For every course that is waived, the 57-semester-hour graduation requirement will be reduced by 3 semester hours, but in no event will a student be graduated with less than 30 semester hours.

In order to receive a course waiver, a student must demonstrate proficiency with respect to the subject matter involved. Such proficiency may be demonstrated by appropriate graduate and undergraduate courses taken during the preceding six years or by successfully passing a proficiency examination.

ADMISSION

No decision is made with respect to an application for admission to the graduate program of the School of Business Administration until all required credentials have been submitted. These must include a completed application form, a $25 application fee, official notification by Educational Testing Service as to the score achieved on the Graduate Management Admission Test (GMAT), and an official transcript from every institution of higher learning attended. In order to be admitted to the

program, an applicant must show evidence that he or she has earned a bachelor's degree from an accredited institution of higher learning and has the potential for performing satisfactorily at the graduate level. The primary criteria used by the Admissions Committee in making such a judgment are the undergraduate grade-point average and the score achieved on the Graduate Management Admission Test.

The deadline for the submission of all required credentials by an applicant for admission is August 1 for the fall semester, December 1 for the spring semester, and May 1 for the summer session.

EXPENSES

Tuition for graduate courses in business administration (1985-86 academic year) is $528 per course.

PLACEMENT

Rider College maintains an active Placement Bureau to aid graduate students seeking positions in business and industry.

CORRESPONDENCE

For further information, please write or call
Associate Dean
School of Business Administration
Rider College
2083 Lawrenceville Road
Lawrenceville, New Jersey 08648-3099
Telephone: 609-896-5127

RIVIER COLLEGE

NASHUA, NEW HAMPSHIRE

Rivier College is a fully accredited liberal arts college located on a 44-acre campus some 35 miles northwest of Boston. All five graduate programs are coeducational; undergraduate full-time programs are for women; undergraduate part-time programs are coeducational. Over 20 undergraduate areas of study are offered. In addition to the Master of Business Administration (M.B.A.) program, the graduate division offers master's degrees in biology, education, English, and computer science. Founded in 1933 by the Sisters of the Presentation of Mary, Rivier is the only four-year and graduate institution in the greater Nashua area. The enrollment for the past four years has topped the 2,000 mark, and the college carefully guards its policies of nondiscrimination.

PROGRAM OF STUDY

The master's program in business administration at Rivier College is geared for men and women who wish to get an M.B.A. degree on a part-time basis. Courses are conveniently scheduled for late afternoons, evenings, and Saturday mornings for students who work full time. There are currently over 580 students in the M.B.A. program. The program is designed for both undergraduate majors in business and applicants with a good academic record in an undergraduate discipline other than business. The applicant's entire educational background, relevant experience, and professional aims are considered in the admission process. Because previous work in mathematics, economics, management, and the behavioral sciences are of particular relevance to graduate study in business administration, the M.B.A. program is designed in such a way that the nonbusiness undergraduate major can fulfill these undergraduate prerequisites at the graduate level.

The courses of study offered in the Rivier M.B.A. program emphasize management among the various functional areas of the business world. As with other disciplines, experience has shown that early specialization tends to limit career potential. The program offers the student thorough training and basic instruction in the related areas of finance, marketing, and analysis. Through election options the student gains exposure to, or explores, one of these functional areas in greater depth.

Overall, the program is aimed at broad training rather than intensive specialization. It consists of 36 to 45 semester hours, of which a maximum of 9 semester hours may be in foundation courses. The latter permit the nonbusiness undergraduate major to fulfill undergraduate prerequisites at the graduate level. The areas included in the foundation courses are economics, accounting, and management. The graduate courses integrate operational, analytical, and professional disciplines with a view to developing the sort of understanding, appreciation, and workable knowledge required of the business executive.

The length of time needed to complete the requirements for an M.B.A. depends on the student's academic background and on the number of courses taken each year. The maximum course load for the graduate student employed full time is two courses each in the fall and spring semesters and one or two courses in the summer session. This schedule will permit the student to complete degree requirements in two and one-half to three years of part-time study. At both Nashua and Windham locations, there are 50 course offerings in the fall and spring semesters and 20 courses in the summer session. The maximum time allotted for a student to complete his or her degree requirements under normal conditions is six years.

ADMISSION

Basic requirements for admission include the following: (1) the applicant must file a completed application form (to be admitted a student must have received a bachelor's degree from an accredited institution); (2) the applicant must supply official transcripts of all college and university study, both undergraduate and graduate; (3) in addition to fulfilling the academic requirements, the applicant for admission to the M.B.A. program must take the Graduate Management Admission Test (GMAT); (4) a personal interview with the prospective student may be required when deemed necessary by the chairman of the department.

EXPENSES

Expenses are as follows:
Application fee	$ 25
Tuition, per semester hour of credit	142
Scheduled registration fee, per semester	10
Graduation fee	30

CORRESPONDENCE

For additional information, write to
Chairman
Master's Program in Business
Administration
Rivier College
Nashua, New Hampshire 03060

ROBERT MORRIS COLLEGE

CORAOPOLIS, PENNSYLVANIA

Founded in 1921, Robert Morris College is an independent, nonprofit, coeducational institution specializing in business administration programs. The main college campus is located a mile from the Greater Pittsburgh International Airport and 15 miles west of the city of Pittsburgh. The college also owns and operates the Pittsburgh Center, an eight-story educational facility in downtown Pittsburgh. In September 1984, 5,708 students were studying at the two locations of the college. Of that total, 5,115 were attending undergraduate classes and 593 were enrolled in graduate courses. Fall 1984 full-time equivalent enrollment was 4,095. Females make up 55 percent of all students.

PROGRAMS OF STUDY
The Master of Science (M.S.) degree program is designed to meet the needs of employed adults and is directed at these types of professionals:
- those who are in business enterprises in a variety of job titles whose advancement and personal satisfaction depend considerably upon the development of competencies in administration for business, government, and industry not acquired in an undergraduate education;
- those who are engaged in teaching business concepts and studies to others in a variety of public, private, and corporate educational institutions whose knowledge, instructional, and communications skills to a large extent determine the success with which learning takes place;
- those who are engaged in service to individual, organizational, and business clients needing direction, advice, and assistance in complying with complex tax regulations and laws at local, state, federal, and international levels.

Distinct curricular "tracks" are available in business administration, business education, and taxation. Students in business administration may choose from concentrations in accounting, computer information systems, management, or sport management. Courses are offered in late afternoons and evenings in six- and nine-week terms. A thesis is not required.

The program in business administration can accommodate individuals with diverse baccalaureate degrees. The core I portion consists of basic courses that are prerequisites to the advanced courses in core II and core III. The core I classification represents the "common body of knowledge" typically associated with baccalaureate

degree programs in business. Students having appropriate undergraduate preparation may have core I courses waived. Advanced business subjects make up the core II category while courses within the optional concentration areas are designated core III. Program objectives are designed to provide the individual with
- broad decision-making skills in complex organizations;
- competencies in using basic management tools, communicating effectively, applying quantitative methods, and improving information systems;
- an understanding of the legal, social, and economic environment within which organizations function;
- competence in dealing with typical business functional disciplines including accounting, finance, management, and marketing.

The program format in business education features student design of a personal curriculum in consultation with a faculty adviser. The student must choose at least two courses from each of three clusters identified as (1) the learning environment, (2) improvement of instruction, and (3) development for business and education. Nearly half of the student's program consists of electives taken from business education and business administration offerings. Such flexibility is an intentional feature of the program.

The program in taxation is almost evenly divided between foundational and specialized applications of tax law. All students complete an eight-course sequence in foundations of taxation. They complete the program by electing courses from seven specialized tax areas. This flexibility permits the student to build upon previous educational and employment experience and to tailor the program of professional development to its maximum.

ADMISSION
All applicants should possess a baccalaureate degree from an accredited college or university and should submit a completed application form, an official undergraduate transcript, an acceptable score on the Graduate Management Admission Test (GMAT), and a nonrefundable application fee of $25. International students should submit acceptable scores from the Test of English as a Foreign Language (TOEFL).

EXPENSES
Tuition, per credit hour $136
Application fee 25

FINANCIAL ASSISTANCE
Students interested in obtaining information concerning student aid, loans, and veterans' benefits should contact the Financial Aid Office, Robert Morris College.

PLACEMENT
Robert Morris College has an active placement bureau. All services of the placement bureau are available to M.S. candidates and alumni.

CORRESPONDENCE
For further information, write or call
Graduate Admissions Office
Robert Morris College
Narrows Run Road
Coraopolis, Pennsylvania 15108
Telephone: 412-262-8404 or
412-227-6876

Rochester Institute of Technology (RIT) is a privately endowed, coeducational, non-sectarian school. Established in 1829, RIT is one of the pioneers in the cooperative work-study plan that provides students with alternate periods of classroom study and work experience related to the academic program. The institute's graduates are in high demand due to this unique program.

The College of Business maintains membership in the Middle Atlantic Association of Colleges of Business Administration and the American Assembly of Collegiate Schools of Business (AACSB). Located on RIT's new 1,300-acre campus on the edge of Rochester, the College of Business is the largest of the institute's nine colleges. The Rochester community provides ample opportunity for a rewarding living-learning experience. Serving the College of Business is the Wallace Memorial Library, one of the finest specialized libraries of its kind in the country. The computer capability of the College of Business, including time-sharing mainframe facilities and a separate IBM personal computer lab, are utilized throughout the management program.

PROGRAMS OF STUDY

The College of Business offers the Master of Business Administration (M.B.A.) with option areas in corporate accounting, public accounting, finance, marketing, management, and personnel/human resources. The program provides a balanced exposure to the quantitative and qualitative aspects of management. The applied dimension of solving real problems in actual companies and the theoretical underpinnings of decision making are both emphasized in the M.B.A. course work.

The program requires 80 quarter-credit hours or 20 courses (up to 20 hours may be waived given the appropriate background). All students receive a thorough grounding in the foundations, take courses covering functional areas, and choose a specific option area in which to concentrate their studies. Students are provided the opportunity to benefit from RIT's other outstanding technological programs through free electives.

The M.B.A. public accounting option is registered with the New York State Education Department and meets the requirements for the Uniform Certified Public Accounting Examination. Graduates may sit for the examination upon successful completion of the master's degree. The program also provides an appropriate education for the Certified Management Accountant Examination.

Full-time students desiring work experience may apply for a three- to six-month internship. Students accepted into the internship program will be eligible to interview for positions once they complete their first year of course work. RIT attempts to provide internships for all qualified students, but cannot guarantee that all students will be placed.

All graduate programs (options) are available on a full-time and part-time basis. Courses are offered on weekdays, evenings, and on Saturdays. Course requirements are the same for full-time and part-time students.

ADMISSION

Full admission will be granted to graduates of accredited baccalaureate degree programs who, in the opinion of the Graduate Admissions Committee of the College of Business, have demonstrated through their achievements in the undergraduate program and the results of the Graduate Management Admission Test (GMAT) the potential to successfully complete graduate management studies.

Foreign degrees or diplomas will be evaluated to determine their equivalency to an accredited bachelor degree program in the U.S. Foreign students must submit a Test of English as a Foreign Language (TOEFL) score along with the aforementioned application materials.

EXPENSES

Tuition for full-time students (12 or more credit hours) is $2,485 per quarter. Part-time tuition is $211 per quarter-credit hour. Married student apartments and townhouses are available on campus.

FINANCIAL ASSISTANCE

Scholarships, fellowships, and assistantships are available to deserving graduate students.

PLACEMENT

RIT provides a central placement office visited annually by representatives from approximately 450 companies from all parts of the country. The placement office works closely with members of the graduating class and maintains an interest in alumni. The placement rate for the 1984 academic year was 94 percent.

CORRESPONDENCE

For further information, write to
Chairman
Graduate Business Programs
Rochester Institute of Technology
One Lomb Memorial Drive
Rochester, New York 14623
Telephone: 716-475-2256

Rockhurst, Kansas City's Jesuit College, received its corporate charter in 1910. It is the largest private college in the surrounding four-state area and presently enrolls over 700 Master of Business Administration (M.B.A.) students in addition to more than 3,000 day and evening undergraduate students. Rockhurst is one of the 28 Jesuit colleges and universities in the United States. The Jesuits have been noted for an educational system of excellence and a tradition that started over 400 years ago.

The program has been designed for men and women who want to complete an M.B.A. while continuing their careers. All courses are offered one night per week with some offerings also given on Saturday mornings.

PROGRAM OF STUDY

The curriculum and the philosophy of the Rockhurst M.B.A. program is clearly pragmatic in approach and designed to develop professionals with broad-based fundamental capabilities. Use of live business cases from the Kansas City area and region provides hands-on decision-making opportunities for M.B.A. students. In addition to the regular M.B.A. track, a two-year weekend option—the Rockhurst Executive Fellows—provides an M.B.A. curriculum specifically tailored to the needs of experienced, senior, mid-career managers and executives.

The degree, Master of Business Administration, is awarded upon completion of a graduate program that enables successful candidates to demonstrate knowledge of the various functions of business organizations and synthesizes that knowledge into the practice of management. Students are expected to achieve an understanding of the function of the executive and to develop a high degree of professional competence in transferring knowledge to practical work situations.

To achieve these objectives the Rockhurst M.B.A. student completes a 36-hour program. In this program, nine required courses of three hours each form a broad core curriculum encompassing the major facets of business administration. Specifically, the core includes business communications (should be taken early as it is a tool course for other M.B.A. courses), managerial economics, marketing, corporate social responsibility, managerial accounting, operations management, administrative processes of management, financial management, and business policy.

In addition to the core requirements, each candidate is expected to develop an area of specialization by concentrating at least six hours in a specific field of study. Presently a candidate may elect a concentration from the following areas: accounting, finance, marketing, general management, human resources management, and purchasing materials management.

Recognizing that all men and women who desire an M.B.A. degree do not possess the undergraduate business background required for the above program, Rockhurst College has designed five accelerated graduate-level courses in economics, accounting, finance, quantitative techniques, and computer concepts and applications. The requirement for an undergraduate management and marketing course may be satisfied by taking a CLEP examination or an examination prepared by the graduate business program for each of these subject areas.

In accordance with the more usual practice today, there is no modern language required for graduation, and there is no master's thesis requirement. The Business Policy course, BA 381, ties all the courses and material together and uses live cases extensively.

Transfer credit may be allowed for certain graduate courses taken in other accredited graduate business programs. The director of the M.B.A. program will determine the transferability of credits at the time of admission.

ADMISSION

Admission will be open to all qualified men and women who hold a bachelor's degree in any field of study. Acceptance for admission will normally be based on (1) undergraduate grade-point average, (2) professional development and/or business experience, and (3) the Graduate Management Admission Test (GMAT). The goal of Rockhurst College's admission policy is the selection of those candidates who indicate the greatest potential for academic achievement. Students may enter the program in the fall, spring, or summer terms. The program can be completed on a part-time basis in two to four years.

EXPENSES

Tuition for courses is based on a semester-hour cost of $165 per hour. There is a one-time matriculation fee of $20.

FINANCIAL ASSISTANCE

Guaranteed student loans are available through most area banks. Also, many of the major Kansas City employers provide tuition assistance to their employees.

PLACEMENT

Rockhurst College's Career Center assists students with career planning. The Career Center also coordinates interviews with the large business and governmental agencies.

CORRESPONDENCE

For further information, write or call
  Director, Graduate Business Program
  Rockhurst College
  5225 Troost Avenue
  Kansas City, Missouri 64110
  Telephone: 816-926-4090

The Roy E. Crummer Graduate School of Business is the only graduate or professional school on the campus of Rollins College, which is noted for its high-quality liberal arts programs. The Crummer School offers the Master of Business Administration (M.B.A.) degree specifically designed for the student who has not studied management or business on the undergraduate level. Those students who have done undergraduate work in management, however, may be able to enter the program with advanced standing.

The Crummer School's main emphasis is on maintaining a quality program with small classes, high faculty-student interaction, extensive computer usage, and personal attention emphasizing both written and oral communications skills. The Crummer School has a nationally recognized faculty with an outstanding publication record and excellent teaching skills. In order to assure that each faculty member possesses the proper teaching abilities, the school only hires associate or full professors. Therefore, all members of the faculty have been recognized for their teaching abilities at other institutions before coming to Crummer. The Crummer mission, however, is not only to teach theory, but also to teach the implementation of theory. Most academic institutions assess scholarly performance based on publications appearing in prestigious journals. In using this criterion, the Crummer faculty is impressive. The 12-member faculty has written a total of 23 textbooks, which is an average of 1.9 books per person. This is a record that is not matched by any other school in the country.

The Crummer School is one of 216 schools accredited at the master's level by the American Assembly of Collegiate Schools of Business (AACSB), and one of only 16 that are accredited as a separate graduate school of business.

PROGRAM OF STUDY
The Roy E. Crummer School of Business is one of few collegiate schools of business to devote its efforts solely to graduate education. The faculty and administration believe that the best education for management consists of a broad-based undergraduate program in the arts or sciences coupled with a full two-year M.B.A. program. It is on the undergraduate level that students should learn the fundamentals that give them the abilities to communicate and make ethical judgments, and it is

the graduate level at which they should learn the skills that are necessary to make decisions concerning the management of an organization.

The Crummer School requires the student to do more than memorize technical material. In core courses that introduce the subjects, the textbook is meant to be a resource that should be used as an encyclopedia. Thus, the learning of textual material is not the goal of the course; it is only an intermediate step. The goal is to apply the portion of the material that is appropriate for the particular problem being solved. It is important to note that the school is not trying to substitute practicality for academic theory. Rather, the school is trying to supplement theory with the ability to implement it.

The Crummer School offers a 56-credit-hour program which includes 8 credits of intensive prerequisite courses. For those students who have done undergraduate work in business, four of the eight intensive courses may be waived.

Intensive Courses
   Case Analysis and Presentation
   Legal Environment of Business
   Ethical and Social Issues of Business
   Concepts of Management
   Concepts of Microeconomics
   Concepts of Macroeconomics
   Concepts of Mathematics
   Concepts of Computers
Integrating Courses
   Management Game
   Management Policy
Required Core Courses
   Financial Accounting
   Managerial Accounting
   Managerial Economics
   Quantitative Methods
   Operations Management
   Organizational Behavior
   Marketing Management
   Financial Management
Electives
   six courses with a maximum of three in
   any one area of specialization

ADMISSION
Admission to the M.B.A. program of the Crummer School is selective and based upon academic potential as demonstrated by undergraduate work completed at a regionally accredited college or university and performance on the Graduate Management Admission Test (GMAT). Other pertinent information that would influence

a positive decision includes recommendations, awards, work experience, and positions held in various social and school-related organizations.

EXPENSES
Tuition for 1985-86 (subject to modification)
   1-8 credits, per credit . . . . $ 168
   9-12 credits, per term   2,890

FINANCIAL ASSISTANCE
In addition to student loans, which are available to all students who have financial need, scholarships are awarded to full-time students on the basis of merit. These scholarships and graduate assistantships have a total value ranging from $5,000 to $9,000 and are used to help defray the cost of tuition. Merit-based financial aid is available to approximately one third of the entering class of full-time students.

PLACEMENT
The Crummer School offers a career planning and placement service to all full-time M.B.A. students. Career workshops and corporate speakers series are important components of the two-year M.B.A. program. The job market is competitive for even the most qualified M.B.A. degree holders, and the school feels it is imperative that all full-time students begin preparation for the job search process as soon as they enroll. The Crummer School offers programs to assist the student in all areas of career planning and conducting a successful job search.

CORRESPONDENCE
For further information, write or call
   Office of Admissions and Registration
   Crummer Graduate School of Business
   Rollins College
   Winter Park, Florida 32789-4499
   Telephone: 305-646-2405

Rosary College traces its origin to 1848 in Wisconsin. The college moved to River Forest when it was incorporated as Rosary College in 1918. The River Forest campus is a 30-acre wooded site adjacent to a forest preserve that is easily accessible by car, bus, and train. The campus is approximately 20 minutes from downtown Chicago. M.B.A. classes are also offered in Northbrook, Illinois. The college is accredited as a master's degree-granting institution by the North Central Association of Colleges and Secondary Schools.

The Graduate School of Business was created to provide professional preparation for people who are interested either in entering the business and management professions or in preparing for advancement within the profession. The school also aims to serve the continuing education needs of the business and management professional. The faculty has been chosen to create a body that has a blend of teaching, research, scholarship, and real-world experience. It also reflects a broad interdisciplinary approach to business education. The school makes use of a dual track system to accommodate not only those persons whose undergraduate work was in business or accounting but also the needs of liberal arts and other graduates.

The school offers part-time evening programs leading to the degrees of Master of Business Administration (M.B.A.) and Master of Science in Accounting (M.S.A.). The school also offers a weekend M.B.A. program. The M.B.A. degree provides for concentrations in accounting, finance, health care administration, management information systems, marketing, public administration, human resource management, and international business. The programs are offered on a semester basis. Students may enter the programs at the beginning of the fall, spring, or summer term. The school also offers several joint degree programs: one with the John Marshall Law School, one with Rosary's Graduate School of Library and Information Science, and one with Rosary's undergraduate college.

PROGRAMS OF STUDY

The Master of Business Administration degree program is designed to provide the college graduate with the necessary techniques and theoretical background needed by managers of businesses and organizations. The objectives of the M.B.A. program are:

- to provide qualified persons with the skills of the professional manager,
- to provide the breadth of insight that can only come from in-depth study of the business disciplines,
- to give a humanistic dimension to the education of business and organizational managers, and
- to encourage research and scholarship in the problems of modern management.

Candidates for the Rosary College M.B.A. will need from 11 to 15 courses depending on their undergraduate preparation. Candidates with undergraduate preparation in computer science, statistics, economics, and accounting will normally need 11 courses. All courses carry three semester hours of credit. The degree of Master of Business Administration will be conferred upon candidates who have met the following program requirements:

- completion of a minimum of 33 hours of graduate credit,
- attainment of a minimum grade-point average of 3.0, and
- satisfactory completion of certain required courses.

A candidate for the M.S.A. degree will normally need 15 courses to complete the degree. Depending upon the candidate's undergraduate preparation, one or more of the foundation courses may be waived. A minimum of 11 courses will be required for the degree.

The degree of Master of Science in Accounting is conferred upon candidates who have met the following requirements:

- completion of a minimum of 33 hours of graduate credit with a minimum of 24 hours completed in the M.S.A. program,
- attainment of a minimum grade-point average of 3.0, and
- satisfactory completion of certain required courses.

ADMISSION

Admission to the Graduate School of Business is open to those who hold a bachelor's degree in any field from an accredited institution. No prior business courses are required. The Committee on Admissions bases its decision on the applicant's total academic record, scores on the Graduate Management Admission Test (GMAT), three references from the applicant's professors and/or supervisors, and pertinent information from the applicant's application.

EXPENSES

Tuition is $510 per course. Each course carries three semester hours of credit. Application fee is $15, and there is a one-time matriculation fee of $10.

FINANCIAL ASSISTANCE

Several assistantships are awarded to students who wish to combine professional study with work experience in the Graduate School. The assistantships allow tuition waivers for one or more courses depending on the background of the applicant and the needs of the Graduate School.

PLACEMENT

The college maintains a placement office whose services are available to all students enrolled in the Graduate School of Business.

CORRESPONDENCE

Prospective applicants may write or call
Admissions
Graduate School of Business
Rosary College
River Forest, Illinois 60305
Telephone: 312-366-2490, extension 210

Russell Sage was founded in Troy in 1916. Today it is a multi-campus, comprehensive college that has pioneered in meeting the needs of working adults who have decided to go beyond the bachelor's degree. In 1950, the college opened its first master's degree program.

Schedules at Russell Sage are flexible, and courses are planned for late afternoons, evenings, and weekends. They are directed at mature individuals who have worked—either inside or outside the home—and who have gained insights through their experience.

PROGRAM OF STUDY

The Russell Sage M.B.A. program is designed to develop managers with the capacity for moving into high-level positions in business, industry, government, and the nonprofit sector; it is specially tailored for the person already in the workplace.

The M.B.A. program at Sage is systems based and behaviorally oriented. It is designed to educate the manager to view the whole organization as a system that is composed of interdependent subsystems: structural, human, financial, marketing, and economic. When combined with prior business experience, the program will develop managers prepared to make decisions in the context of the welfare of the total organization.

The Russell Sage M.B.A. requires a minimum of 45 semester hours of graduate course work if all prerequisites have been completed prior to entry into the program. Without previous completion of prerequisites, the program will require up to 54 semester hours of graduate course work. Waivers may be granted for certain required courses beyond the prerequisites if the student has taken undergraduate courses that are clearly their equivalents, but for each course waived in this manner the student must pass an equivalency examination. No waiver can be granted for courses in the systems core. A limited number of graduate credits may be transferred from other institutions, but, after waivers and transfers, a minimum of 36 credits must be completed at Russell Sage College.

Undergraduate prerequisites include Principles of Accounting (six credits), Introduction to Macroeconomics (three credits), Introduction to Microeconomics (three credits), Statistics (three credits),

and Calculus (three credits). Those who have not taken the undergraduate prerequisites may complete this requirement by taking nine semester hours of graduate prerequisite courses.

Following completion of the prerequisites, the student must complete the core competencies (15 credit hours), the systems core (15 credit hours), and, by advisement, a specialization in one of the three following areas: finance, management, or human resources (12 credit hours). The final program requirements are a Seminar in Policy Analysis and Formation (three credit hours), a noncredit lecture series on "Business and Society," and a comprehensive examination covering all areas of course work.

ADMISSION

A matriculated degree-seeking graduate student is an applicant officially admitted by the Graduate Studies Committee upon recommendation from the Dean of Graduate Studies and the Director of the M.B.A. Program.

Admission as a degree-seeking student takes one of two forms: regular status and provisional.

Applicants who meet all requirements for admission to the graduate program are matriculated as regular degree-seeking graduate students. The requirements for regular admission are as follows:
• baccalaureate degree from an accredited four-year college with at least a 2.75 average on a 4.00 scale or, if the average is below 2.75, completion of nine hours of graduate work approved by the program director with at least a 3.00 average,
• satisfactory recommendations,
• acceptable Graduate Management Admission Test (GMAT) scores,
• satisfactory written statement of personal and professional goals, and
• personal interview with M.B.A. Program Director.

Students who do not fully meet the requirements for admission to the degree program may be admitted on a provisional basis if program faculty feel that the student has potential for success in the program.

EXPENSES

Tuition is $150 per credit hour. The application fee is $20. There is a one-time registration fee of $5.

FINANCIAL ASSISTANCE

Russell Sage College administers a number of student assistance programs and participates in most aid programs administered by state and federal agencies. For some special graduate student aid programs, availability of funds each year depends on adequate federal funding.

PLACEMENT

Russell Sage is justifiably proud of its career planning and placement services, and all graduate students are welcome to take advantage of these fine resources. Counseling is offered on a one-to-one basis at both the Albany and Troy campuses.

In addition to counseling, students can delve for information in an extensive career resource library housed in the Career Development Center in Troy and in the Albany library. Moreover, throughout the academic year, workshops focusing on career issues and job hunting are held on both campuses. Graduate students also are welcome to participate in the on-campus employer recruiting program, and they are encouraged to establish a credential/placement file at no charge.

CORRESPONDENCE

For further information, please write or call
   Director
   M.B.A. Program
   Russell Sage College
   140 New Scotland Avenue
   Albany, New York 12208
   Telephone: 518-445-1763

The Graduate School of Management is one of 11 professional schools in Rutgers, The State University of New Jersey. With over 47,000 students on three campuses in Newark, New Brunswick, and Camden, the university is one of the major state educational systems in the nation. Rutgers is also situated at the center of one of the most impressive academic and corporate communities. In addition to the Graduate School of Management, other professional schools within Rutgers include law, criminal justice, psychology, performing and fine arts, environmental studies, pharmacy, engineering, and social work. Over 250 of the nation's largest companies have corporate offices located within a 60-mile radius of the university.

Programs offered by the Graduate School of Management include a Master of Business Administration (M.B.A.) in management and professional accounting, an executive M.B.A. and a Doctor of Philosophy (Ph.D.) in management. The school's master's program, which has been accredited by the American Assembly of Collegiate Schools of Business (AACSB) since 1941, is dedicated to graduating productive, principled, and skilled professionals whose commitment to excellence will endure throughout their careers. Designed to equip future executives to plan for decision making and manage resources with maximum effectiveness, as well as to motivate individuals to their full potential, the Rutgers M.B.A. programs combine the teaching of tools, concepts, and theories with the opportunity to test these tools and theories in the field.

Unique features of the school are its internationally known New Jersey Small Business Development Center, the Rutgers Minority Investment Company run by students and faculty, and the Rutgers University Technical Assistance Program. These small business activities attract research projects for faculty and students and provide students with applied experience and internships.

PROGRAMS OF STUDY
The M.B.A. program in management is a 61-credit degree with required core courses in accounting, international business, economics, finance, government-business interface, management, marketing, production, quantitative methods, and a six-month management consultancy. At the elective level, students may specialize in areas of career interest.

The 63-credit M.B.A. in professional accounting program prepares students for careers in public accounting. The program accepts only students with nonbusiness undergraduate degrees and less than nine semester hours of accounting.

The Ph.D. in management offers the serious management student opportunities for study and research in economics, finance, organization behavior, operations management, and computer technology. The program is aimed at the student who is planning to teach or specialize in management research in industry.

The executive M.B.A., a 52-credit program, is designed for company-sponsored, experienced managers who wish to pursue the degree at a full-time pace while continuing their careers. It can be completed in four terms.

The school operates on a trimester calendar. Full-time students are admitted to the professional accounting program in June and to the full-time management program in September. Part-time students are admitted in September and February. The full-time program may be completed in 15 months; the part-time program in three-and-one-half years. Classes are held on the Newark and New Brunswick campuses.

ADMISSION
Candidates for admission should hold a baccalaureate degree from an accredited institution. Previous academic work, Graduate Management Admission Test (GMAT) score, recommendation by an academic adviser or employer, and a potential for success in the field of management are criteria considered for admission. A personal interview is not required for the program in management; however, the faculty committee on admissions may request an interview. A personal interview is required of all applicants to the program in professional accounting. Foreign applicants are required to submit the Test of English as a Foreign Language (TOEFL) results as well as evidence of financial support.

EXPENSES

Full-time students:	*New Jersey* Residents	Nonresidents
Tuition, per trimester	$1,506.00	$2,240.00
Fees, per trimester	95.25	95.25
Part-time students:		
Tuition, Per trimester	128.00	187.00
Fees, per trimester	26.50	26.50

On-campus housing is available, as well as accommodations in Newark, New Brunswick, and the surrounding towns. Total academic and nonacademic expenses for a single independent student approximate $4,150 per trimester. Expenses for a dependent or married student vary.

FINANCIAL ASSISTANCE
Support is available in the form of state and federal aid for grants, college work-study, student loans, and scholarship assistance. The school cannot guarantee assistance but will make every effort to meet students' needs.

PLACEMENT
The Graduate School of Management's placement office provides workshops on career options, resume writing, and interviewing techniques as well as individualized counseling for students. Last year 204 companies, representing banking, insurance, investments, mortgages, management consultancy, marketing and marketing research, information systems, retailing, telecommunications and broadcasting, and governmental agencies and commissions, recruited on campus for 574 positions. Nine large international accounting firms routinely recruit at the school for graduates of the program in professional accounting.

CORRESPONDENCE
For further information, please call or write

Assistant Dean, Admissions
Rutgers Graduate School of
  Management
92 New Street
Newark, New Jersey 07102
Telephone: 201-648-5275

The Faculty of Business Studies in Camden is an important unit of Rutgers, The State University, which was founded in 1766 as Queens College. Rutgers—Camden is located directly across the Delaware River from Philadelphia in the transportation hub of southern New Jersey.

PROGRAM OF STUDY

The Master of Business Administration (M.B.A.) program offered by the Faculty of Business Studies through the Graduate School in Camden is designed to provide students with a broad professional education that will prepare them for the increasingly complex demands of management. Fifty-four credits are required for graduation. The program includes both core courses offering a common body of knowledge and elective courses of specialized study.

The program is offered in the evening, and the typical student should complete the program in six semesters. Required prerequisite undergraduate courses are introductory courses in accounting, economics, statistics, and calculus. Prospective students must also take the Graduate Management Admission Test (GMAT). Although applications will be reviewed even though the prerequisite courses and the GMAT have not been completed, these requirements must be satisfactorily met before the acceptance of the student into the program on a matriculated basis.

The core program, based on the premise that there is a common body of knowledge called upon for managerial decisions, must be taken by all students. In addition, elective courses may be selected by students who have taken the appropriate prerequisite courses. There are 8 core courses plus 10 elective courses. Management Policy, which is a core course, is taken as the capstone integrating course in the student's final semester. In addition, there is the opportunity for students to design directed study courses with the approval and supervision of an instructor in the M.B.A. program.

ADMISSION

Applicants are admitted in September (application deadline August 1) and January (application deadline December 1). Applications received after these dates will be acted upon at the discretion of the Admissions Committee only if time permits adequate review of credentials and when it has been determined that space is still available for additional students.

Application forms may be obtained by writing to the Graduate Admissions Office, Rutgers University, Camden, New Jersey 08102.

EXPENSES

Tuition as of September 1985 was $126.00 a credit hour for New Jersey residents and $187.00 a credit hour for out-of-state students; this may be subject to change. Each application is to be accompanied by a nonrefundable application fee of $20.00 payable only by check or money order to Rutgers University. A student fee of $24.25 is payable each semester.

PLACEMENT

Facilities of the Rutgers—Camden Placement Office are available to students. A number of business and professional firms, government agencies, not-for-profit organizations, and academic institutions recruit on the Camden campus each year.

CORRESPONDENCE

For further information on the M.B.A. program at Rutgers—Camden, write or call

Director
Graduate and Professional Admissions
Rutgers University
Camden, New Jersey 08102
Telephone: 609-757-6102

Sacred Heart University, founded in 1963, is located in suburban Fairfield on a 62-acre campus, which offers a full range of facilities including a computer center. The cafeteria and bookstore serve students during the day and evening sessions, and the student lounge offers a working atmosphere for group conferences as well as individual studies. There are well-lighted and patrolled parking lots containing 1,200 parking spaces on the campus.

PROGRAM OF STUDY
The Master of Business Administration (M.B.A.) program is designed to prepare men and women for positions of administrative responsibility in business, as well as nonprofit and governmental institutions, while bringing students to a full realization of the ethical and social responsibilities inherent in the managerial role.

Students receive a broad understanding of business and organizational problems, a sound knowledge of effective methods of solving these problems, the analytical skills necessary for recognizing problems and implementing solutions, and an appreciation of the place and the responsibility of the business person and the administrator in society. A fundamental philosophical context of the program is the consideration of ethics in the functioning of the business enterprise.

The program is based on a core of courses that examines the functions of the executive and the environment of the administrator. Beyond the core, students may pursue, in some depth, a number of particular fields in business administration and economics. Candidates will be required to participate in the university's annual program on ethical issues in business life.

The majority of classes are conducted in the evening with some Saturday sessions. This enables employed men and women to earn an advanced degree and makes available to the program faculty members who not only possess excellent academic credentials but also have pragmatic administrative experience to bring to the classroom.

A total of 57 credit hours of graduate course work is required for the M.B.A. degree with a quality-point average of 3.0 preferred. Depending on undergraduate preparation, students can reduce the number of credit hours by as many as 21. The M.B.A. program operates on a trimester basis, which allows candidates who have all undergraduate preparation completed the opportunity to earn an M.B.A. in two years. Despite the number of transfer credits and waivers for which a student may be eligible, an absolute minimum of 30 credit hours must be taken at Sacred Heart University, and these credit hours must be the last 30 prior to receiving the degree.

Six credit hours per semester are considered the maximum work load for the individual employed full time. Anyone wishing to take more than six credits must receive permission from the M.B.A. Program Director. A candidate must complete all courses no later than six years after matriculation.

With the approval of the adviser, a thesis may be substituted for six semester hours of elective credit.

ADMISSION
An applicant must hold a baccalaureate degree from an accredited institution. An application and official transcripts from all undergraduate and graduate institutions previously attended must be sent directly to the M.B.A. Program Director. Letters of recommendation are necessary from two persons who have knowledge of the candidate's academic and business accomplishments. In some instances a personal interview may be requested.

Applicants must take the Graduate Management Admission Test (GMAT). Foreign applicants are also required to take the Test of English as a Foreign Language (TOEFL). Information regarding both these examinations may be obtained by writing directly to Educational Testing Service, Princeton, New Jersey 08541. (Sacred Heart's ETS code number is 3780.)

To achieve full matriculation status, admissions materials should be received no later than three weeks prior to the beginning of the candidate's first term. The M.B.A. Admissions Committee will consider applications received after this time on a provisional basis.

EXPENSES
Expenses are as follows:

Tuition, per semester hour	$151
Application fee, nonrefundable	20
Graduation fee	45
Registration fee	10

FINANCIAL ASSISTANCE
At this time the financial assistance available to graduate students is provided through private banking sources. Inquiries may be made to the Director of Financial Aid.

PLACEMENT
The services of the university's placement office are available to all graduate students seeking full-time professional employment as well as part-time work opportunities.

CORRESPONDENCE
For applications and information, please write or call
Program Director—M.B.A.
Sacred Heart University
P.O. Box 6460
Bridgeport, Connecticut 06606
Telephone: 203-371-7850

SAGINAW VALLEY STATE COLLEGE

UNIVERSITY CENTER, MICHIGAN

PROGRAM OF STUDY

The Master of Business Administration (M.B.A.) program at Saginaw Valley State College (SVSC) consists of 60 graduate credit hours of foundation, core, and elective courses. Students with prior course work in business and economics may be able to enter with advanced standing and reduce this 60-hour maximum requirement to as low as 36 credit hours of graduate course work. A minimum of 24 credit hours above the foundation level (including Mgt. 690 and Mgt. 695) must be taken at Saginaw Valley State College.

Elective hours may be spread over several areas or concentrated. If a student elects to concentrate his or her studies in a specific field (for example, accounting, economics, finance, management, or marketing), a minimum of nine credit hours beyond the core must be completed in the area of concentration.

Foundation Courses	*Hours*
Accounting 511: Financial Accounting	3
Economics 522: Economic Analysis	3
Finance 504: Managerial Finance	3
Law 508: Law of Contracts and Business Organizations	3
Management 521: Organization and Administration	3
Marketing 531: Marketing Systems	3
Economics 536: Statistical Analysis	3
Management 525: Computer Programming	3

Business and Management Core	
Accounting 612: Accounting for Management Decisions	3
Economics 622: Microeconomic Analysis	3
Finance 604: Financial Planning and Control	3
Management 621: Organizational Behavior	3
Management 690: Social Environment of Business	3
Management 695: Executive Policies and Planning	3
Marketing 631: Marketing Administration	3
Quantitative Methods 620: Quantitative Analysis for Decision Making	3

Electives	
(including optional three-credit-hour thesis)	12
Maximum credit hours required	60
Less hours subject to elimination if candidate qualifies for entrance with advanced standing	24
Minimum credit hours required	36

A cumulative grade-point average of at least 3.0 in all work applicable to the degree is required for graduation. Courses in which a grade below C is received cannot be counted toward satisfaction of degree requirements. If the cumulative grade-point average falls below 3.0 at any time after accumulation of 12 credit hours at SVSC, circumstances of the individual case will be examined, and the student may be dismissed from the program.

ADMISSION

Students who have earned an undergraduate degree at an accredited college and who demonstrate the maturity and intellectual ability to participate in a rigorous academic program may be admitted to the program for the degree of Master of Business Administration at Saginaw Valley State College. There are no prescribed undergraduate prerequisite courses that must be completed prior to admission to the M.B.A. program. Factors considered in evaluating the applicant's potential for success in graduate business study include

- previous academic performance,
- score on Graduate Management Admission Test (GMAT),
- work experience, and
- professional achievements.

Normally an undergraduate grade-point average of 2.5 (4.0 scale) plus a better-than-average score on the Graduate Management Admission Test is required.

To ensure that there is no needless duplication of subject matter previously mastered, the student with prior course work may enter with advanced standing. Required foundation courses may be eliminated by waiver based upon substantially equivalent prior academic work, provided it has been completed within six years preceding the date of admission. The student may be requested to present course descriptions and course textbooks to facilitate this evaluation.

Graduate credits earned at another accredited institution are transferable only for appropriate graduate courses completed with a high quality of achievement (B or above) within six years preceding the date of admission to the M.B.A. program. A maximum of 12 graduate credits may be transferred. Such transfer credit must be requested in writing at the time of admission.

EXPENSES

Tuition and fees, as of fall 1985, were as follows:

Tuition (on- and off-campus courses)
Michigan residents, per credit hour	$ 72.50
Nonresidents, per credit hour	145.00

Fees
Facilities (on-campus courses), per credit hour	3.00
Athletic season pass, per semester (optional)	20.00
Matriculation fee for new students only	25.00

CORRESPONDENCE

For further information and application forms, contact

School of Business and Management
Saginaw Valley State College
University Center, Michigan 47810
Telephone: 517-790-4064

The Master of Business Administration (M.B.A) program at St. Ambrose College is built on the strengths of the two largest undergraduate departments at the college—(1) accounting and (2) economics and business administration. Programs in the areas of computer science, operations research, scientific management, and statistics also provide input for the M.B.A. program. Faculty members teaching graduate business programs also serve as faculty for certain undergraduate course offerings, but only graduate students attend St. Ambrose's graduate classes. The St. Ambrose College M.B.A. program is accredited by the North Central Association and approved for study by the Veterans Administration.

To support graduate business administration and management courses, St. Ambrose continues to increase its library holdings in the business and management area, already the strongest in the library. The college also utilizes interlibrary loan capabilities and computerized information retrieval services to further assist students in their study programs. St. Ambrose College's modern videotape facilities are available for graduate students in the Galvin Fine Arts and Communication Center. The college offers hands-on computer experience with its on-campus computer plus a major link with the University of Iowa's computer center.

PROGRAM OF STUDY
The objective of the St. Ambrose College M.B.A. program is to educate contemporary, efficient, and professional managers for positions in business, industry, and the nonprofit sector, initially in middle management, but ultimately for top-management roles. Exposure is given to companies of all sizes with primary emphasis on the types of firms operating in the Quad Cities area. As such, the Ambrose approach blends theory and application and is division-based in scope and professional (rather than research oriented) in thrust.

The M.B.A. program consists of 15 three-credit courses and takes approximately two years and eight months (part-time evenings) to complete. Each course/seminar meets one night a week for approximately 15 weeks during the fall and spring, two nights a week during the abbreviated summer semester. It is suggested that students register for two courses each fall, two each spring, and one each summer.

Classes are also offered on Saturdays each fall and spring semester. No Saturday classes are offered in the summer. Attending Saturday only, the program takes three and a half years to complete.

The St. Ambrose College M.B.A. program is open to any student holding a bachelor's degree, regardless of undergraduate major. Students falling below specific standards will be required to take remedial undergraduate work. A maximum of nine credits may be transferred from other approved graduate schools of business.

The St. Ambrose College M.B.A. program consists of the following 15 graduate-level courses, each earning three semester credits:
Part I: *Foundation Courses*
  Statistical Methods for Decision
    Making
  Financial Accounting
  Managerial Accounting
  Macroeconomic Analysis for Business
Part II: *Management Core Courses*
  Organizational Theory, Behavior and
    Communication
  Managerial Economics
  Legal and Social Environment of
    Business
  Dimensional Management Training
    Seminar
Part III: *Decision-Making Courses for*
Management
  Operations Management
  Financial Management
  Marketing Management
  Human Resources Management
Part IV: *Concentration Seminars* (two
elective seminars are required)
  Business Ethics Seminar
  Management Seminar I, II
  Finance Seminar I, II
  Marketing Seminar I, II
  Seminar for Nonprofit Organizations I
Part V: *Capstone Seminar*
  Policy Formation and Implementation

ADMISSION
The St. Ambrose admission decision considers (1) undergraduate grade-point average, (2) Graduate Management Admission Test (GMAT) score, (3) responsibility and accountability in professional work, and (4) motivation to take and complete a rigorous graduate-level program. Eligible students may begin studies in the fall, spring, or summer.

EXPENSES
Application fee, nonrefundable .... $ 25
Tuition, per semester credit hour ...   185
Fees, per semester credit hour......   3

As a cost guide, additional expenses for books, classroom materials, and lab fees are estimated at $30 for each course.

CORRESPONDENCE
For additional information and application forms, contact
  Dean
  Graduate School of Business
    Administration
  St. Ambrose College
  518 West Locust Street
  Davenport, Iowa 52803
  Telephone: 319-383-8760

The School of Business Administration offers a program of graduate study leading to a Master of Business Administration (M.B.A.) degree. Areas of concentration offered are accounting/finance, management/marketing, or an interdisciplinary program. In any track, the M.B.A. program is designed to develop a strong foundation for the professional practice of administration and for continued advancement in executive responsibilities. Most classes are small in size and structured to include both theoretical and applied techniques of the discipline. The learning experience is enhanced by the use of micro- and minicomputers as tools for effective decision making.

PROGRAM OF STUDY

The M.B.A. program is open to eligible students from all undergraduate majors. Exceptionally well-qualified students may complete the program in one year, (two semesters plus one or two summers). In the 54-credit (18-course) program, up to 24 credits (8 courses) may be waived based on previous academic experience as described below.

The full- or part-time student attends late afternoon or evening classes meeting once a week during the fall and spring semesters and two nights a week during each of two summer sessions. The program is divided into the following four parts.

The foundation courses (Part I) are designed to make certain that all applicants have a common background as well as some breadth in the concepts used in subsequent courses and in business. Students who have completed equivalent courses at the undergraduate level within the last five years with a grade of B or better may waive these courses. All other students may request to take a proficiency exam in any of these courses.

MATH 600	Mathematics for Management
MBA 601	Accounting Foundations
MBA 602	Macroeconomics
MBA 603	Microeconomics
MBA 604	Financial Foundations
MBA 605	Computer Applications in Business
MBA 608	Statistics

The business core (Part II) introduces functional areas of management to ensure a conceptual framework for the analysis of business problems and decisions. Students with undergraduate majors or minors that included courses from the following set may have some of these courses waived at the discretion of the M.B.A. director.

MBA 610	Financial Management
MBA 611	Legal Environment of Business
MBA 612	Marketing Management
MBA 613	Organizational Behavior
MBA 614	Quantitative Methods
MBA 615	Contemporary Accounting

The graduate electives or specialization (Part III) are designed to give an area of concentration in accounting/finance or management/marketing. Students who do not wish to select a program concentration may choose a set of electives from either track to meet their individual career goals.

Accounting/Finance (4 courses):

MBA 622	Federal Taxation
MBA 624	Production Management
MBA 626	Investments
MBA 628	Applied Economics
MBA 696/	Special Topics in Finance and Accounting/
MBA 699	Independent Study

Management/Marketing (4 courses):

MBA 624	Production Management
MBA 628	Applied Economics
MBA 632	Manpower and Conflict Management
MBA 636	Marketing Research
MBA 638	Consumer Behavior
MBA 698/	Special Topics in Management or Marketing/
MBA 699	Independent Study

Business Policy (Part IV) MBA 649 is the capstone course which integrates the entire program and is required of all students in their final year of study.

ADMISSION

In order to be admitted to the M.B.A. program, students must hold an undergraduate degree from an accredited college or university. The primary criteria for admission are the student's undergraduate academic record and the scores from the Graduate Management Admission Test (GMAT). In addition, students may support their application with appropriate letters of recommendation, work experience, and a personal interview.

EXPENSES

Costs are estimated for the 1986-87 academic year and are subject to change.

Tuition, per credit hour $160
Books and supplies, per year 400

An initial matriculation fee of $10 is also required. At present there are no graduate housing facilities on campus.

FINANCIAL ASSISTANCE

A limited number of graduate assistantships are available to students pursuing the M.B.A. degree on a full-time basis. The current stipend associated with graduate assistantships is $3,400 per academic year plus a nine-credit tuition waiver. There are also residence hall directorships available for which single graduate students are eligible to apply. Loans are available through the university and government agencies.

PLACEMENT

The student placement bureau arranges interviews with various companies, organizations, and agencies throughout the year. Graduate students are urged to pursue career opportunities through this service.

CORRESPONDENCE

For further information or to request an application for admission, please write or call

Director, M.B.A. Program
St. Bonaventure University
St. Bonaventure, New York 14778
Telephone: 716-375-2111

St. Cloud State University (SCSU) is situated on the banks of the Mississippi River in central Minnesota, about 65 miles northwest of Minneapolis and St. Paul. Approximately 12,000 students attend classes on campus. About 3,650 are registered in undergraduate College of Business programs; 110 students are enrolled in master's degree programs.

The undergraduate and master's programs offered by the College of Business are accredited by the American Assembly of Collegiate Schools of Business (AACSB). AACSB accreditation is the mark of a quality program and enhances the business program, faculty, and graduates.

The College of Business is organized into five departments: accounting, business education and office administration, management and finance, marketing and general business, and quantitative methods and information systems. An Office of Research, Development, and Community Service provides facilities and opportunities for research in business and related areas.

PROGRAMS OF STUDY
A Master of Business Administration (M.B.A.) program and Master of Science (M.S.) programs in accounting and in business education are offered. The Master of Business Administration program provides opportunity for advanced specialization in business management and the expansion of an educational foundation so necessary to rapid advancement in executive positions in business, industry, and government. The Master of Science in accounting program provides the additional academic preparation needed by professionals entering the field of public accounting. Financial accounting, auditing, tax, and management are included.

The Master of Science in business education program offers an individualized program of advanced study in business education or a related field.

ADMISSION
The Master of Business Administration program is open to qualified graduates having bachelor's degrees in a variety of fields from accredited four-year colleges and universities. The holder of a bachelor's degree in business administration may expect to spend one year to complete the 48-credit program. The student who has a bachelor's degree in another field may expect to spend two years.

Admission to the graduate programs is based on these factors: (1) a bachelor's degree from an accredited college or university, (2) performance on the Graduate Management Admission Test (GMAT), (3) undergraduate performance, and (4) evidence of aptitude for successful graduate business study. Each applicant who is accepted will be expected to have completed, or to complete, course study in basic foundation courses.

The following four-credit courses must be completed by all M.B.A. students: financial management policy, management of human resources, decision-making techniques, corporate financial reporting, managerial accounting, business economics, marketing plans and decision making, production and operations management, legal and social foundations of business, and corporate strategies.

In addition, with the adviser's approval, the candidate elects 12 quarter credits in a functional concentration: accounting, finance, management, marketing, quantitative methods and information systems, or economics.

M.S. in accounting students complete the equivalent of an undergraduate accounting major and 48 graduate-level credits, at least 24 of which are in accounting. Applicants for the M.S. in business education may choose one of the three program options.

All foreign students whose native language is other than English must take the Test of English as a Foreign Language (TOEFL) and request that the score be sent to the School of Graduate Studies. A score of 575 is required for admission to a graduate degree program. The TOEFL does not replace the GMAT. For information on the TOEFL, write to TOEFL, CN 6151, Princeton, NJ 08541-6151. For information on the GMAT, write to GMAT, CN 6101, Princeton, NJ 08541-6101. Foreign students are required to follow the same procedures for entrance into graduate school as all other applicants.

EXPENSES
Graduate resident tuition is $39.25 per quarter of credit. Nonresident graduate tuition is $68.80 per quarter of credit. Incidental fees are assessed to students on the basis of $4.40 per credit hour, with a maximum charge of $70.40 per quarter.

FINANCIAL ASSISTANCE
Graduate assistantships and work-study funds are available to qualified students. National Direct Student Loans and Guaranteed Student Loans can be obtained through the University Financial Aids office.

PLACEMENT
The M.B.A. graduate is in high demand by business and governmental enterprises. The St. Cloud and Twin Cities areas have numerous firms affording excellent placement oportunities. SCSU Career Planning and Placement Services provides individual assistance to identify students' career goals and develop placement contracts.

CORRESPONDENCE
For catalogs and applications, write the Dean, Graduate Studies. Specific questions about curriculum and academic counseling should be addressed to
Graduate Programs Coordinator
College of Business
St. Cloud State University
St. Cloud, Minnesota 56301
Telephone: 612-255-3212

St. John Fisher College is located in suburban Rochester, New York, in the midst of a dynamic business community. Founded in 1948 as a private, Catholic college for men under the direction of the Basilian Fathers, Fisher today is a coeducational, independent college of science, commerce, and the humanities. Offering courses in 26 majors, Fisher grants the bachelor of arts, sciences, and business administration degrees at the undergraduate level. In 1983 the Fisher Graduate School of Management opened with the distinctive "Action Analysis" program leading to the Master of Business Administration (M.B.A.) degree.

PROGRAM OF STUDY

St. John Fisher College's Action Analysis M.B.A. program serves to develop action skills and understanding. Action Analysis is an educational strategy designed to promote effective managerial action in response to the multitude of complex and routine problems encountered in organizational settings.. The learning process, experiential and interventionist in nature, is founded on the assumption that effective action requires a tri-part integration of conceptual, technical, and behavioral learnings that can be mastered and transferred to real-world situations.

Effective managerial action incorporates competencies in problem discovery and diagnosis, decision making, and implementation. Conceptual courses aid in problem identification by objectifying relationships among various components of an organization's operation. Students acquire a repertoire of diagnostic tools useful in determining the extent to which intervention is required in aspects of the organizational structure, task design, technology selection and utilization, interpersonal relationships and social interactions, or some combination thereof. Decision-making competencies are gained in courses where students confront real or simulated managerial dilemmas. Learning activities consist of analyzing one's reasoning process and clarifying undergirding values and assumptions. Applied skills are accrued through participation in a variety of action projects where students need to accommodate diverse points of view while preserving an atmosphere of cooperation and commitment. Students may choose to pursue either a 54-credit-hour general M.B.A. or a 60-credit-hour M.B.A. with a concentration. Both programs include three major elements: 14 core courses, 2 capstone courses, and advanced electives. The required courses are the following:

Core Courses
  MGT 500 – Perspectives in Management
  MGT 501 – Introduction to Computers
  MGT 502 – Introduction to Accounting
  MGT 503 – Rhetoric and Composition
  MGT 504 – Statistics
  MGT 505 – Organization Theory
  MGT 506 – Economic Principles for Management
  MGT 507 – Quantitative Methods for Managers
  MGT 508 – Corporate Financial Management
  MGT 509 – Management Information Systems
  MGT 510 – Introduction to Marketing
  MGT 511 – Human Resources Management
  MGT 512 – Operations Management
  MGT 513 – International Business
Capstone Courses
  MGT 520 – Environmental Analysis
  MGT 521 – Integrated Business Analysis

Students may be eligible for exemptions from core course requirements for up to 12 credit hours on the basis of prior course work or experience, or by virtue of their performance on proficiency examinations.

Students pursuing the general M.B.A. complete their program by taking any two advanced elective courses. Those wishing to receive the M.B.A. with a concentration must take four electives, all of which must be in the same functional area. Available concentrations are management information systems, marketing, finance, international business, accounting, human resource management, and industrial and labor relations (in cooperation with the Cornell University New York State School of Industrial and Labor Relations).

Directly related to the two capstone courses is a project. Students are expected to formulate a project of manageable size in any one of the areas of management, such as production and operations management, organization, personnel, M.I.S., finance, or marketing. Student research work will involve examination of theoretical issues of the project, identification of major factors and dimensions of the problem, collection, analysis and interpretation of data for improved decision making, and implementation in a management problem area of their own selection. Thus the project is intended to allow the student both to integrate his or her previous course work into a unified managerial approach and to gain valuable experience in a managerial setting.

St. John Fisher College's M.B.A. program is open to qualified students with a variety of undergraduate majors and can be pursued on either a full- or part-time basis.

ADMISSION

In judging applications, the Admissions Committee considers, among other things, undergraduate grade-point average, score on the Graduate Management Admission Test (GMAT), and letters of recommendation. Students may enter the program during the fall, spring, or summer sessions, and may enroll on a course-by-course basis for a limited time prior to matriculation. Students from other countries must submit scores on the Test of English as a Foreign Language (TOEFL). Several courses in the program require substantial quantitative skills. Those students who enter the program lacking such skills may develop them by taking a noncredit course in mathematics offered by the graduate school.

EXPENSES

Tuition (subject to change) is $225 per credit hour or $675 per three-credit hour course.

FINANCIAL ASSISTANCE

Several types of financial assistance are available to qualified students. Normally, awards are made on the basis of demonstrated financial need as well as academic achievement and promise.

PLACEMENT

Working in close cooperation with the Graduate School of Management, the Career Planning and Placement Office assists both students and alumni in preparing for a job search and in finding career employment.

CORRESPONDENCE

For further information, please write or call
  Director
  Graduate School of Management
  St. John Fisher College
  3690 East Avenue
  Rochester, New York 14618
  Telephone: 716-385-8079

St. John's University Graduate Division of the College of Business Administration offers complete programs leading to a Master of Business Administration degree at convenient locations in Queens and Staten Island. Both campuses are situated in close proximity to the business, financial, and cultural center of New York City. As a professional school, its goal is to serve the professions and society by advancing the education of current and potential executives in business, health care, and government organizations. Moreover, as economic and environmental changes affect organizations and society, the College of Business Administration is pledged to the development of innovative concepts and methodology in order to meet the educational requirements of professionals in private industry as well as nonprofit institutions.

PROGRAM OF STUDY

The Master of Business Administration (M.B.A.) degree requires the completion of a minimum of 39 credits taken either on a full- or part-time basis. These credits are equally divided into two parts: the core and the field of specialization. The core has a total of 15 credits. The specialization consists of at least 15 credits in the field of study selected by the M.B.A. candidate plus 9 credits of electives, or one general 3-credit elective plus a 6-credit thesis.

In addition to the credits in the core and in the field of specialization, a student who has not taken undergraduate business and economics courses may be required to complete up to 30 additional credits in the prerequisite area. These courses provide enrichment in fundamental business areas. The number of credits required in the prerequisite area is determined on an individual basis. The total degree requirements, therefore, consist of the core, the field of specialization, and prerequisite courses (where required). It is suggested that the student request a personal interview to outline his or her course requirements.

Fields of specialization offered in the M.B.A. program include public accounting (C.P.A.), controllership, taxation, economic theory, finance, executive management, marketing, and quantitative analysis. In addition, various options within these fields are available: international finance, bank administration, international management, industrial and labor relations, human resources management, marketing management, international

marketing, computer information systems for managers, operations research, and advanced statistics for managers.

ADMISSION

Admission to the M.B.A. program will be granted only to applicants holding a bachelor's degree from an accredited institution who show promise of success in graduate business studies. Among the criteria used for admission are performance on the Graduate Management Admission Test (GMAT), undergraduate grade-point average, undergraduate class rank, relevant work and leadership experience, and previous graduate study (if any). No previous undergraduate business preparation is required. Applications for admission may be obtained from the Office of the Dean of Admissions and Registrar, or the Graduate Division Office. Completed applications with all supporting credentials should be filed with the Office of the Dean of Admissions at least two months prior to the semester in which the student wishes to begin his or her program of studies. It is the student's responsibility to have official transcripts of all courses taken for the baccalaureate degree sent directly to the Office of the Dean of Admissions. Personal interviews are not mandatory, although prospective students are encouraged to visit the school and discuss the M.B.A. program with an adviser.

The university maintains a rolling admissions policy, and students may enter in the spring, fall, or summer semesters. Applicants with degrees from foreign universities and colleges may be admitted if such candidates have completed the equivalent of an American bachelor's degree. In addition to the official application form, they must submit authorized school records and notarized translations of these records as witness of their previous educational experience. Foreign students are required to submit GMAT scores as well as results of the Test of English as a Foreign Language (TOEFL). A foreign student wishing to be considered for acceptance must file an application and supporting credentials a minimum of 90 days prior to the semester for which he or she wishes to commence studying.

EXPENSES

The schedule of fees (subject to change) for 1985-86:

Tuition, per credit	$183
General fee, per semester (nonrefundable)	40
Application fee	20

FINANCIAL ASSISTANCE

Research assistantships providing for free tuition in addition to monthly stipends are available to qualified M.B.A. students. Appointees carry a program of graduate study commensurate with their assistantship schedule. These assistantships are contracted on a yearly basis. In addition, scholarships, awards, and loans financed by federal and state agencies are available.

PLACEMENT

The Graduate Division of the College of Business Administration, through its close association with the business community, makes every effort to obtain positions for both current students and alumni. The Placement and Career Development Center offers assistance in developing career goals and obtaining knowledge about various areas of specialization in the labor market. Arrangements are made for students to meet with corporate recruiters on campus.

CORRESPONDENCE

Inquiries should be directed to
Dr. John C. Alexion, Vice President for Business and Career Oriented Programs
Dr. Mary Maloney, Assistant Vice President for Business and Career Oriented Programs and Dean of the Graduate School of Business Administration
St. John's University
Graduate School of Business
Grand Central and Utopia Parkways
Jamaica, New York 11439
Telephone: 212-990-6161, extensions 6417 or 6418, *or*
Irene McCarthy, C.P.A., Associate Dean
300 Howard Avenue
Staten Island, New York 10301
Telephone: 212-447-4343, extension 317

Saint Joseph's University is the Jesuit university in Philadelphia. It is a private, Catholic, liberal arts institution for men and women which was founded in 1851 and chartered by the Commonwealth of Pennsylvania in the following year. Saint Joseph's was recognized as a university by the Secretary of Education of the State of Pennsylvania in 1978. Dedicated to liberal education, it teaches disciplined reasoning, effective communication, and a love of learning, while at the same time stressing a concern for the individual and for life values.

The university's physical plant, composed of eight major educational facilities and more than a score of student residences, straddles the western boundary of Philadelphia and the eastern boundary of its suburban Main Line community. It is convenient to reach by both automobile and public transportation. Undergraduate enrollment is 2,400 full-time day students and 2,175 evening students. Graduate enrollment is 1,500, of whom about 1,050 are in the Master of Business Administration (M.B.A.) program.

PROGRAM OF STUDY
The M.B.A. program is designed to prepare students for management positions in industry and not-for-profit enterprises. The program of studies is primarily concerned with analytical tools relevant to a broad range of managerial problems. Emphasis is placed on the ability to analyze problems, to identify alternatives, to make decisions, and to implement those decisions. The M.B.A. program can be viewed as advanced general management training complemented by specialization in one of eight areas which currently include accounting, banking, finance, administrative management, production management, marketing, information systems, and health administration. About two thirds of the course work is in the area of general management training, and the remaining one third is in the area of specialization.

The M.B.A. program consists of seven foundation, six core, three module or area of specialization, one elective, and one integrative or capstone course. Applicants may request a waiver of any of the foundation courses if they have taken equivalent courses in an accredited educational institution. These foundation courses consist of financial accounting, micro- and macroeconomics, business statistics, business mathematics, financial management,

introduction to computer systems, and management theory. The six core courses can be chosen from managerial accounting, management, marketing, managerial finance, managerial economics, quantitative analysis, information systems analysis, and a required course in business ethics. The remaining M.B.A. courses consist of three courses in an area of specialization, an elective, and an integrative or capstone course.

A post-M.B.A. certificate can be earned by taking four additional courses in another area of specialization different from that chosen for the M.B.A. degree.

At present, the M.B.A. program serves primarily the interests of individuals with full-time employment who desire part-time graduate study. Classes are held once a week Monday through Friday evenings and on Saturday mornings. Saint Joseph's University M.B.A. program is also offered at Albright College, Reading, Pennsylvania, and Ursinus College, Collegeville, Pennsylvania.

The faculty is composed of full-time members and adjunct faculty with primary interests in business, consulting, and governmental enterprises. Classes are held during the fall and spring semesters and during an eight-week summer session beginning in mid-May.

ADMISSION
All qualified students who hold a baccalaureate degree in any field from an accredited college or university or an equivalent degree from a foreign educational institution are invited to apply for admission. The M.B.A. program is open to graduates in liberal arts, science, business, and other fields.

Students are admitted for enrollment each year in September, January, and May. Preferred consideration for admission is given to those applicants whose admission packages are complete six weeks prior to the beginning of the term.

Requirements for the admission package are as follows:
• a completed application form accompanied by a $20 application fee and a cover letter containing information about past achievements, work experience, and future goals (work experience, however, is not a prerequisite to admission);

• possession of a baccalaureate degree from an accredited college or university as attested by an official transcript or transcripts;
• scores on the Graduate Management Admission Test (GMAT); and
• two letters of recommendation, one from an employer and one from a former professor (if there is no prior employment, both letters may come from professors). Foreign applicants whose native language is not English are required to take the Test of English as a Foreign Language (TOEFL).

EXPENSES
Tuition for 1985-1986 for the M.B.A. program was $184 per semester hour or $552 per three-credit course unit.

FINANCIAL ASSISTANCE
Requests for financial aid in the form of university and government grants and private and government loans should be directed to the Director of Financial Aid, Saint Joseph's University. Requests for information concerning veterans' benefits should be directed to the V.A. Programs Coordinator, Saint Joseph's University.

PLACEMENT
The university placement office is visited annually by the representatives of numerous profit-seeking and not-for-profit enterprises.

CORRESPONDENCE
For further information, please write or call
Graduate Business Office
Saint Joseph's University
5600 City Avenue
Philadelphia, Pennsylvania 19131
Telephone: 215-879-7666

The Saint Louis University School of Business and Administration offers programs of study leading to the degree of Master of Business Administration (M.B.A.), as well as specialized master's degrees in the fields of accounting, finance, and management sciences. In cooperation with the School of Law and the Department of Health Care Administration, joint degree programs are offered. Through the Graduate School of Saint Louis University, the School of Business and Administration provides programs leading to the degree of Doctor of Philosophy in business administration, Master of Arts in economics, and Doctor of Philosophy in economics.

PROGRAMS OF STUDY

The M.B.A. program is designed for students who have the aptitude and motivation to pursue the study of business at the graduate level. The program is structured with sufficient flexibility to serve qualified individuals who possess the baccalaureate degree in business administration, as well as those who hold degrees in nonbusiness fields. The program includes 27 hours of core requirements; 18 hours of advanced-level requirements, including one course each from the areas of accounting, economics, finance, management sciences–behavioral, management sciences–quantitative, and marketing; and 12 hours of graduate electives which may be taken in accounting, economics, finance, international business, management sciences–behavioral, management sciences–quantitative, marketing, or personnel and industrial relations. Proficiency in calculus is also required. The student who has an undergraduate degree in business or who has completed considerable undergraduate work in business may have up to 27 hours of the core requirements waived.

Specialized master's degree programs are offered in the areas of accounting, finance, and management sciences for those students who wish to pursue in-depth study in one of these fields. Applicants are expected to meet the same admissions criteria as those applying to the M.B.A. program.

The joint programs leading to the combined degrees of Juris Doctor/Master of Business Administration, Juris Doctor/Specialized Master's, and Master of Health Administration/Master of Business Administration are integrated in such a way as to allow the student to complete both degrees

in less time than would be required to complete each degree separately.

The School of Business and Administration provides a program leading to the degree of Doctor of Philosophy in business administration. Applicants are expected to possess the Master of Business Administration or its equivalent with evidence of sufficient breadth of study in business areas and a high level of academic performance. The program permits concentration of study in a major and a minor field. The major field will be chosen from the academic disciplines of accounting, economics, finance, international business, management sciences (behavioral or quantitative), or marketing. The minor area will be selected either from another area of business or from a related field. In addition, all students must satisfactorily complete graduate course work in both economics and statistics. Upon completion of the course program, the student must pass written and oral examinations relating to the major and minor areas of study. Finally, a sufficient level of scholarly ability must be demonstrated in a dissertation.

The Master of Arts in economics program requires 30 semester hours exclusive of the thesis. Proficiency in a foreign language, statistics, or a related field is required.

An applicant to the Doctor of Philosophy in economics program is expected to possess an undergraduate degree in economics or its equivalent, evidencing sufficient academic ability to pursue advanced study. The candidate for the degree must demonstrate proficiency by written examination in economic theory and the history of economic thought. Written examinations must also be taken in three of the following areas: econometrics, public finance, monetary economics, labor economics and industrial relations, economic development, international economics, and urban economics. Proficiency is required in one foreign language, mathematics, statistics, or a related area. An oral examination precedes the doctoral dissertation.

ADMISSION

The applicant for admission to graduate study in business must possess the appropriate degree (or its equivalent) for the specific program of interest. The degree must be from a recognized college or university, and the applicant's scholastic record must evidence a satisfactory level of

achievement at that university. Satisfactory scores on the Graduate Management Admission Test (GMAT) are required prior to acceptance for all programs except the Master of Arts and the Doctor of Philosophy in economics, for which the GMAT or the Graduate Record Examinations are required (Advanced Test in Economics only). Both the Graduate Management Admission Test and the Law School Admission Test are required for entrance to the Juris Doctor/Master of Business Administration degree program.

EXPENSES

Tuition, per credit hour $230
Application fee, not refundable . . 25

FINANCIAL ASSISTANCE

Graduate assistantships, fellowships, and scholarships are available to a select number of students each year. In addition, a limited number of grants and loans are available through the Director of Financial Aid.

PLACEMENT

The Career Development and Counseling Center is a service facility provided free for students and alumni in order to assist them in acquiring suitable employment.

CORRESPONDENCE

Prospective applicants may address correspondence to
Graduate Studies in Business
School of Business and Administration
Saint Louis University
3674 Lindell Boulevard
St. Louis, Missouri 63108
Telephone: 314-658-3801

Saint Martin's College, established in 1895 by the monks of the Order of Saint Benedict, is an intimate liberal arts college located in western Washington at the southern tip of Puget Sound, adjacent to the capital city of Washington. Less than two hours from either Portland, Oregon, or Seattle, Washington, this proximity to both Pacific Northwest population centers offers the student access to diverse cultural and business activities. The college enrollment is less than 1,000, with the graduate programs limited to 60 students.

PROGRAMS OF STUDY

Graduate studies in management at Saint Martin's can lead to either a Master of Business Administration (M.B.A.) or Master of Engineering Management (M.E.M.). The Master of Business Administration program is designed to prepare the student for management responsibilities, as opposed to specialized technical skills. The emphasis is on the total administrative system and developing a capacity for understanding the interrelationships in modern organizations whether public or private. The program is 30-54 semester hours, depending upon the student's prior educational background and/or work experience. The minimum program can normally be completed in one calendar year of study (four graduate terms) for the full-time student or two years on a part-time basis. All course work is offered in the evening so that it is possible to coordinate the study with an existing working career. Development of expertise in elective functional areas of management by coordination of two elective courses and a research project is encouraged.

The Master of Engineering Management is tailored to prepare engineering and science graduates for management-oriented careers in the field of engineering. The program stresses the interrelationships of the management and engineering efforts required for planning, design, construction, and operation of facilities and systems. The program requires 36 semester hours of study including a research project.

ADMISSION

Admission criteria for the M.B.A. program are identical for full-or part-time students, that is: (1) an undergraduate degree in any field from an accredited college or university, (2) completion of the Graduate Management Admission Test (GMAT), and (3) a total of at least 1,000 based on the formula $200 \times$ grade-point average + GMAT score. Grade-point average is measured in the last 60 semester hours (or equivalent) on a A=4.0 basis. Admission criteria for the M.E.M. program include (1) an undergraduate degree in engineering, mathematics, or natural sciences, (2) a grade-point average of at least 2.6, (3) successful completion of engineering license examinations, and (4) letters of recommendation from registered engineers.

Students may enter either program at any semester. Students with deficiencies in any area are encouraged to discuss their unique circumstances with the graduate office.

EXPENSES

Fees range from $178-$200 per semester credit hour, depending upon the course. Dormitory housing is available on campus, and the local community offers a wide range of housing alternatives and prices for both single and married students.

FINANCIAL ASSISTANCE

Graduate students are eligible for a variety of financial assistance as well as on-campus employment. Concerned students should contact the Office of Financial Aid directly.

PLACEMENT

The college maintains a career planning and placement center to assist students in obtaining either full- or part-time employment.

CORRESPONDENCE

For further information or to request an application for admission, please call or write
Dr. Gary Ray
Graduate Studies in Management
Saint Martin's College
Lacey, Washington 98503
Telephone: 206-491-4700, extension 339

The Graduate School of Business was established by Saint Mary's College in 1975 after more than a century of providing undergraduate education in business. The school is located on a spacious, 450-acre suburban campus of exceptional beauty, one-half hour from San Francisco and Berkeley. The academic year consists of four terms, with classes beginning in October, January, April, and July. Almost all classes are offered in the evening. The student body consists of approximately 250 students, most of whom study part time while working in industry. Depending upon the academic program and the previous preparation of the student, the average time for completion of degrees is approximately two years.

PROGRAMS OF STUDY

Two programs are offered that lead to the Master of Business Administration (M.B.A.) degree. An executive M.B.A. program, which requires 21 months of study in seven quarters, is designed for working managers who have had at least five years of business experience. Students enter with a class and proceed as a cohort through the program. Most courses are required, but students complete their curriculum with three electives.

The other program leading to an M.B.A. degree does not require business experience of its students; it consists of foundation courses (some or all of which may be waived on the basis of previous business education), core or common body of knowledge courses, and concentration courses in three management areas: human resources, finance, and marketing.

A Master of Science program in international business is also offered. One version of this program is designed for full-time students and can be completed in one year. There are 12 required courses, the first of which are offered in October of each year. A part-time version of this program offered to evening students is completed in 18 months, with classes also beginning in October.

ADMISSION

Requirements for admission are as follows:

M.B.A. Program
- possession of a baccalaureate degree from an accredited institution
- scores on the Graduate Management Admission Test (GMAT)

Executive M.B.A. Program
- possession of a baccalaureate degree from an accredited institution
- at least five years of management experience
- personal interview with admissions panel
- optional GMAT score

M.S. in International Business
- possession of a baccalaureate degree
- optional GMAT score

Graduates of foreign universities where the language of instruction was not English must submit the results of the Test of English as a Foreign Language (TOEFL).

Admission to all programs is done on a rolling basis, but students are encouraged to complete their applications at least one month prior to the quarter for which they are applying.

EXPENSES

Tuition for the 1985-86 year was $150 per quarter unit. There are incidental laboratory and materials fees during some quarters, together with an initial application fee of $30. All students are responsible for their own living expenses. There are no residence facilities for graduate students on campus.

The following estimated costs do not include living expenses. The annual costs shown assume the student is taking two courses per quarter and attending all four quarters of the academic year. Total costs reflect the maximum tuition cost of each program at 1985-1986 rates, which are subject to change without notice.

	Annual	Total
M.B.A. Program	$4,800	$10,800
Executive M.B.A. Program	4,800	8,400
M.S. in International Business	3,600	5,400

FINANCIAL ASSISTANCE

Student loans are available to qualified students through local banks. Very limited scholarship aid is available to students of special need and merit.

PLACEMENT

The Career Planning and Placement Center assists students and alumni by providing counseling, workshops, job listings, and job search support.

CORRESPONDENCE

For further information, write or call
Graduate School of Business
Saint Mary's College
P.O. Box M
Moraga, California 94575
Telephone: 415-376-3840

Saint Mary's is a residential coeducational university characterized by a personalized student-centered education and easy rapport among students, faculty, and administration. It had its beginnings in 1802 and was originally a church-related institution. It is now a public, nondenominational university directed by a Board of Governors whose 30 members represent students, faculty, administration, and the outside community. An attractive 30-acre campus, surrounded by lush parkland and one of the city of Halifax's most desirable residential areas, Saint Mary's provides the most modern academic, recreational, and residential facilities. The Faculty of Commerce, with an enrollment of over 1,600 students, is widely recognized for the quality of its programs and has one of the largest commerce/business enrollments in Canada. The 55-member faculty has both industrial and teaching experience in leading business schools in Canada and the United States.

PROGRAM OF STUDY

The primary objective of the Master of Business Administration (M.B.A.) program is to provide an intellectual and social environment in which each student can discover how to develop his or her potential for effective management. Business and government are increasingly demanding that professional administrators possess both specialist competence as a prerequisite for middle management employment and generalist competence for those who seek more senior management positions. The program is designed to help achieve the following:

- to satisfy the short-term educational needs of the students by providing "specialist" concepts and techniques applicable to a particular line or staff area (this part of the program provides a functional identity which can be exploited during the early years of an individual's career to acquire middle management experience) and
- to satisfy the longer term educational needs of the student by providing "generalist" concepts in anticipation of his or her potential to succeed in more general and senior management positions later.

The courses are neither "discipline" nor "case" oriented but embrace combinations of lectures, case discussions, seminars, and assignments according to the requirements of individual subjects. Attention throughout the program is focused on both the practical and academic aspects of the materials covered. More importantly, the faculty believes that management education is essentially a process of personal development which must be "student centered." Therefore, immediately on entering the program, each student is assigned a personal adviser who will be available to provide advice and help to students throughout their studies. This adviser will, on request, do all he or she can to help facilitate the students' academic and management development as they pass through the program.

ADMISSION

Admission to the program is open to students holding a bachelor's degree from a recognized university, whose scholarly records indicate that they are capable of studying management and administration at the graduate level, and who obtain satisfactory scores on the Graduate Management Admission Test (GMAT). Overseas students whose native language is not English are also required to take the Test of English as a Foreign Language (TOEFL) or an equivalent test. Students wishing to enter the program in September should submit a completed application by May 30.

EXPENSES

A distinct feature of the campus is its award-winning residence complex comprising high-rise "coed" apartment buildings. These are linked together and serviced by cafeteria, shops, recreational facilities, and underground parking. Accommodations vary from single rooms to suites designed to accommodate six students. Private accommodations nearby are also available. The fee for the M.B.A. program is approximately $1,500 per academic year for full-time students and $290 per course for part-time students.

There is an additional $1,700 annual fee for non-Canadian residents.

FINANCIAL ASSISTANCE

Financial aid is available through university scholarships, assistantships, and Canada Student Loans. Part-time student jobs are also available in the Halifax—Dartmouth metropolitan area.

PLACEMENT

The university offers placement services to graduating M.B.A. students in cooperation with the Canada manpower office on campus.

CORRESPONDENCE

For further information concerning the M.B.A. program, please write or call
Director of Admissions
Saint Mary's University
Halifax, Nova Scotia B3H 3C3 Canada
Telephone: 902-429-9780, extension 2110

The origins of St. Mary's University go back to 1852—just 16 years after the fall of the Alamo. The first classes were conducted in temporary quarters on Military Plaza. The following year a permanent site was selected on a bend of the San Antonio River. By 1894, as the school expanded, a new campus was built in Woodlawn Hills northwest of the city on a site of 130 acres. The university is comprised of the School of Humanities and Social Sciences; School of Science, Engineering, and Technology; the School of Business and Administration; the School of Law; and the Graduate School.

Programs of study in business administration have been offered since 1923. The graduate division was established in 1959. Approximately 150 students are enrolled in the Master of Business Administration (M.B.A.) program. Graduate courses are held in the evening. The degree of Master of Science in public administration is offered for applicants interested in the management of nonprofit or government institutions.

PROGRAM OF STUDY

Enterprises require the effective coordination and administration of human ingenuity and material resources in achieving their objectives. The course content and sequence of the Master of Business Administration (M.B.A.) program at St. Mary's University is designed to develop competent individuals for responsible performance and leadership in business, professional organizations, institutions, government, education, and research.

The integrating concept that gives the degree its character is found in the composite of these administrative functions:

(1) environmental analysis, goal and policy formulation, and decision making;

(2) organization, motivation, and operations;

(3) evaluation and recommendation, and control.

These functional objectives, pursued within the framework of the finest human and social considerations, focus the student motivation, determine the course content, unify the curriculum, dictate the instructional methodology, and define the faculty orientation.

The program of studies, emphasizing preparation for a general management career, provides a broad and humanistic background encompassing a judicious degree of concentration.

Students may elect a thesis or nonthesis option. The thesis option requires 33-36 semester hours or 11-12 courses, depending upon the student's background. The schedule of courses is arranged in consultation with the graduate adviser. Candidates write a thesis under the direction of a supervising professor and two readers. Candidates must also pass an oral comprehensive examination covering their thesis and graduate studies.

The nonthesis option requires 36 semester hours or 12 courses. The schedule of courses is arranged in consultation with the graduate adviser. No thesis is required for this program. Candidates are required to pass a written examination covering their graduate studies.

ADMISSION

Generally, admission is granted only to those with high promise of success in postgraduate business study. An applicant may show high promise by previous schooling and testing, which results in a minimum total of 950 points based upon the formula: 200 times the grade-point average (GPA) plus the Graduate Management Admission Test (GMAT) score; *or* 1,000 points based upon the formula: 200 times the upper-division GPA plus the GMAT score.

Generally, students who are enrolled as special, provisional, conditional, or regular must meet the 950/1,000 standard at the time of enrollment.

EXPENSES

Tuition for graduate courses in the M.B.A. program is $168 per semester hour.

FINANCIAL ASSISTANCE

Some assistantships for graduate study are offered. These appointments are made to superior students who have demonstrated high performance. Stipends are $2,000 for the academic year. The assistantships carry with them a service requirement. Loans are available. Because of the provisions on scholarship funds and the difficulties of repaying loans, students from other countries should be prepared to meet their own expenses from private or government sources. Grants are available for out-of-state residents.

PLACEMENT

Graduate students are invited to use the facilities of the Placement Office. This office aids in locating positions and arranges for interviews with the several hundred employers who annually contact the Placement Office.

The M.B.A. is a broad program that enables the student to become the chief executive officer of the organization. It does not matter if he or she does not become the chief. The important thing is that one analyzes problems and solutions from a broad organizational perspective rather than some narrow functional area. This might be called the presidential view. M.B.A. graduates may expect job opportunities in varied functional areas at virtually all organizational levels, depending upon interest, experience, and other qualifications.

CORRESPONDENCE

For further information, write or call
   Ronald D. Merrell, Ph.D.
   Dean of Graduate School
   St. Mary's University
   San Antonio, Texas 78284
   Telephone: 512-436-3101

St. Thomas University, (formerly Biscayne College), is a Catholic, coeducational, liberal arts institution. Its history is traced to Villanova University in Havana, Cuba, which was run by the Order of St. Augustine from 1939 until 1961 when the order came to Miami and opened Biscayne College. Diversified programs and a student body of 3,000 representing all races, ages, and faiths reflect the university's commitment of Judeo-Christian values and to the international community it serves.

Located in the heart of southeastern Florida, St. Thomas offers students access to numerous opportunities for direct contact with top corporations. The Miami-Ft. Lauderdale metroplex represents one of the fastest growing population sectors in the United States and serves as home base for both domestic and international operations of major private and public sector firms.

St. Thomas University is accredited by the Southern Association of Colleges and Schools as a four-year, degree-granting university and is also approved by the Southern Association to offer master's level programs.

PROGRAMS OF STUDY

The Graduate School at St. Thomas offers programs leading to the following degrees: Master of Business Administration (M.B.A.), Master of Science (M.S.) in management information systems and in management, and Master of Accounting (M.Acc.).

The M.B.A. program is designed to provide executive management training. The objective is to develop potential managers who not only have the knowledge necessary for today's rapidly changing, unpredictable business environment, but who also have the skills to apply and utilize this knowledge on an appropriate contingency basis.

The core courses, representative of the many disciplines necessary for success in the business world, include the following:

MAN 510–Management Ethics
BUS 670–Advanced Operations
    Management
BUS 673–Management Writing and
    Reporting

MAN 700–Organizational Behavior
    OR
MAN 703–Human Resource
    Management
BUS 704–Policy, Planning, and
    Strategy Systems
BUS 705–Advanced Information
    Systems

The three available areas of specialization (management, international business, or health management) each require an additional 18 hours including both required courses and a wide range of advanced electives concentrated in the area of specialization.

In addition to the M.B.A., a special program of study is offered leading to the degree of Master of Accounting. The Master of Accounting degree program is designed for those currently in, or planning to enter responsible professional or management positions in accounting. This would include business and government as well as independent accounting firms. The degree provides a significant core of advanced accounting courses, a broadening base of management courses, and the opportunity to pursue a special interest through two electives. The Master of Accounting degree program requires 36 credits.

Courses for both the M.B.A. and the Master of Accounting degree are offered only during evening hours and on Saturday mornings, enabling the student to work full or part time while pursuing course work.

ADMISSION

Admission is open to all qualified men and women who hold a bachelor's degree from an accredited undergraduate institution. To qualify for the M.B.A. program, the bachelor's degree should generally be in business, although nonbusiness majors are encouraged to apply. Additionally, all applicants need a minimum of 15 semester hours in business (accounting, finance, economics, business statistics) at the undergraduate level. Satisfactory grade-point average and Graduate Management Admission Test (GMAT) scores are also required of all applicants.

To apply for the M.B.A. and Master of Accounting programs, students must submit
  ● a completed application form,
  ● official transcripts of all prior college work,
  ● two letters of recommendation, and
  ● other information that the Admissions Committee may require, such as, in the case of students for whom English is not the native language, an acceptable score on the Test of English as a Foreign Language (TOEFL).

EXPENSES

Current (September 1985) expenses include the following:

Tuition, per semester hour....... $160
Application fee (nonrefundable).. 25
Student fee, per semester
  (approximately) 40

Certain special fees, such as late registration fee, computer lab fee, change of course and unauthorized withdrawal fees may also be applicable. All charges are subject to change without notice.

FINANCIAL ASSISTANCE

Loans are available through the National Direct Student Loan and Guaranteed Student Loan Programs. In addition, a limited number of graduate assistantships and scholarships are also available. Financial assistance should be requested through the office of the Dean of the Graduate School no later than two months before the semester of entrance.

CORRESPONDENCE

Inquiries should be addressed to
  The Graduate School
  St. Thomas University
  16400 N.W. 32nd Avenue
  Miami, Florida 33054
  Telephone: 305-625-6000, extension 167

SAINT XAVIER COLLEGE

CHICAGO, ILLINOIS

Saint Xavier College is a coeducational school for commuter and resident students located on the southwest side of Chicago. The college was founded by the Sisters of Mercy and chartered in 1847. The Graham School of Management Master of Business Administration (M.B.A.) program is accredited by the North Central Association of Colleges and Secondary Schools; the school holds membership in the American Assembly of Collegiate Schools of Business (AACSB).

PROGRAM OF STUDY

The Graham School of Management M.B.A. program prepares students for advanced managerial responsibilities within the broad context of liberal education.

Students who majored in business administration as undergraduates can complete the M.B.A. in an accelerated period of time by completing the following 36 graduate semester hours:

Common Management/
Administration Core   21 Hours
  Managerial Economics
  Managerial Accounting
  Managerial Finance
  Information Systems Technology
  Advanced Management
  Managerial Statistics
  Government/Business/Society
Students may choose any one of the following tracks as their area of subspecialization: management, marketing, or international business.

Subspecialization   9 Hours
  In addition, students may choose two courses as electives.

Electives   6 Hours

The degree requirements for the student who does not possess an undergraduate degree in business are 54 semester hours, which include the above 36 hours plus the following 18 semester hours:

Foundation Core   18 Hours
  Principles of Economics (Macro)
  Principles of Accounting I
  Business Statistics or Management Science
  Organizational Behavior and Management
  Marketing
  Finance

The Graham School of Management M.B.A. program, designed to accommodate the working adult, offers evening and weekend classes throughout the year. The faculty is composed of 90 percent full-time college professors with Ph.D. or J.D. degrees as well as specially recruited professionals from the Chicago business and financial community. Their selection was made on the basis of their academic background, significant teaching competence, and practical expertise in either profit-oriented or not-for-profit organizations.

All graduate courses attempt to combine theory, case analysis, and student research. Whenever possible, each course utilizes three instructional methods: the presentation of lectures, the analysis of case studies, and the participation of students in discussion and presentation of their research. Case studies and term papers focus primarily on analysis of actual business problems.

ADMISSION

Applicants to the M.B.A. program must meet the following requirements: (1) graduation from an accredited college, (2) acceptable score on the Graduate Management Admission Test (GMAT), (3) two years of work experience or equivalent, and (4) two letters of recommendation. Admission criteria for international students are identical to those of domestic students with the additional criterion of adequate performance on the Test of English as a Foreign Language (TOEFL).

EXPENSES

There is an initial nonrefundable application fee of $20. Tuition charges for graduate courses are $187 per credit hour, while charges for undergraduate courses are $174 per credit hour.

FINANCIAL ASSISTANCE

Student loans and grants are available to M.B.A. students through the Saint Xavier College Financial Aid Office.

PLACEMENT

Saint Xavier College maintains a placement office; services are available to all students enrolled at the college or to alumni. In addition, the college is located in one of the largest business centers of the world, which provides different and varied employment opportunities.

CORRESPONDENCE

For further information or to request an application for admission, please write or call
  Graduate Admission Office
  Saint Xavier College
  3700 West 103rd Street
  Chicago, Illinois 60655
  Telephone: 312-779-3300, extension 286

SALEM STATE COLLEGE

SALEM, MASSACHUSETTS

The master's degree program in the Department of Business Administration was initiated at Salem State College in the fall of 1982—the first such program within the Massachusetts State College system. Salem State's part-time Master in Business Administration program (M.B.A.) has been uniquely developed to serve students and to assume a significant role in assisting the North Shore business community. Its library resources, computer capabilities, and faculty combine to provide a highly competitive quality program.

PROGRAM OF STUDY

Dedicated to the philosophy of rigorous training in specific business disciplines and management techniques, the M.B.A. program emphasizes the general management function. No single method of teaching dominates the learning approach, which blends teaching methods ranging from casework, small group seminars, lectures, computer simulations, management decision games, role playing, and student projects.

Of 60 credit hours of course work required for the M.B.A. degree, a minimum of 48 must be earned in business graduate courses taken at Salem State College. Since most graduate students in the M.B.A. program are employed full time, they are permitted to take a maximum of two courses per semester. Students not employed full time, and/or the principal part thereof, may pursue a program of 12 semester hours, the equivalent of full-time study.

All requirements for the degree must be completed within six years from the date of the student's acceptance. No graduate course taken for the degree may be more than six years old at the time degree requirements are completed.

ADMISSION

Applicants must have (1) a satisfactory cumulative grade-point average at the undergraduate level, (2) a baccalaureate degree in any field of specialization from an accredited institution, and (3) satisfactory performance on the Graduate Management Admission Test (GMAT). Other admission criteria include three letters of recommendation substantiating undergraduate/graduate achievement and professional job performance and competence, a personal interview, and a resume reflecting business, management, and work experience.

Admission criteria for international students are identical to those of domestic students with the additional criterion of satisfactory performance on the Test of English as a Foreign Language (TOEFL).

All application materials are due July 1 for September admission and November 1 for January admission. All admission requirements must be satisfied by the deadline before an applicant will be considered.

EXPENSES

Tuition for Massachusetts residents:
  $75 per graduate credit hour
Tuition for nonresidents of Massachusetts:
  $95 per graduate credit hour
Fees:

Application fee (nonrefundable)...	$25
Registration fee	10
Laboratory fee	15
Library fee	5
Physical education facility fee.....	5
Placement fee (one time only).....	5
Late registration fee............	10
Change of course fee	2

  (changes after initial registration)
Please note: Fees are subject to change and are not refundable unless a course is canceled by the college. Please consult the Graduate and Continuing Education credit brochure for current semester fees.

FINANCIAL ASSISTANCE

Limited aid is available in terms of loans, scholarships, and one graduate assistantship position each year.

PLACEMENT

Services of the College Placement Office are available to all graduate students. Representatives of many regional and national firms visit the campus for interviews.

CORRESPONDENCE

For information and application materials, write or call
  Director
  M.B.A. Program
  Division of Graduate and Continuing
    Education
  Salem State College
  Salem, Massachusetts 01970
  Telephone: 617-745-0556

The Master of Business Administration (M.B.A.) program at Salisbury State College is broad in nature and aimed at general competence for overall management. It is structured to foster an understanding of each functional area of management and to provide both the behavioral and empirical skills necessary for success. Lectures, research projects, case studies, and various computer applications are among the techniques used to prepare students for today's fast-paced business environment. Both the faculty and the student body are of high quality. Salisbury State College is an accredited four-year, comprehensive college offering 35 distinct undergraduate and graduate degree programs in a friendly atmosphere that encourages close relationships between faculty and students. Excellent facilities are available to support the graduate program in business.

PROGRAM OF STUDY

The Master of Business Administration is a 30-semester-hour, graduate professional degree program designed to develop analytical and professional abilities in management. The highly structured program presents a broad but thorough perspective of the management process, the environment of management, and the functional management areas of accounting, finance, and marketing. Provisional admission may be granted to applicants who have not yet completed the required core of undergraduate courses. Graduate survey courses are available to provisional students.

Full-time students will normally complete degree requirements in three semesters; part-time students in five semesters. The program is scheduled to encourage the participation of part-time students, particularly those active in management who desire a solid basis for future professional growth in the public or private sectors of society.

The core of undergraduate courses required for admission to the M.B.A. degree program includes the following: Accounting I, Accounting II, Microeconomics, Macroeconomics, Corporate Finance, Principles of Management, Principles of Marketing, Quantitative Methods, and Intermediate Business Statistics. These requirements may be completed through nine undergraduate courses or the six graduate survey courses offered by the School of Business. In addition to the above prerequisite courses, students must have a course in introductory statistics,

computer programming, and either finite mathematics, applied calculus, or an equivalent college-level mathematics course.

To receive the M.B.A. degree, candidates must complete an approved program of 30 semester hours of upper-level course work with a cumulative grade-point average of at least 3.0 and no grade lower than C. Of the 30 semester hours, 21 are required, while the remaining 9 are elective (that is, electives within the M.B.A. program) and may be used for individualizing the student's program. A typical program would include the following: Organizational Theory, Economic Environment of the Organization, Managerial Accounting, Corporate Financial Management, Managerial Decision Making, Research Methodology, Organizational Behavior Seminar, External Environment of the Organization, Marketing Strategy, and Corporate Strategic Planning and Policy. There is no thesis requirement.

ADMISSION

The M.B.A. program seeks students from all academic areas. Graduate survey/leveling courses are available for individuals without undergraduate training in business.

Requirements for admission include the following:
• a bachelor's degree from an accredited university or college,
• satisfactory results on the Graduate Management Admission Test (GMAT),
• submission of official transcripts from all universities and colleges attended,
• two letters of recommendation, and
• a resume including a statement of career goals and reasons for pursuing the Master of Business Administration degree.

Admission standards recommended by the American Assembly of Collegiate Schools of Business (AACSB) are employed. These standards include an evaluation of the applicant's undergraduate grade-point average and GMAT score in addition to other criteria.

EXPENSES

The following costs (1985-86) are estimated. Tuition for graduate students classified as Maryland residents is $70 per semester hour. For out-of-state graduate students, tuition is $74 per semester hour. Additional fees are $18 per semester for in-state students and $33 for out-of-state

students. Textbook cost per course averages $50. Room and board in the Salisbury area is approximately $1,500 per semester, depending on accommodations.

The approximate total cost for a full-time student with a 12-credit load is $2,558 for residents and $2,621 for nonresidents per semester.

FINANCIAL ASSISTANCE

The School of Business awards a number of graduate assistantships to qualifying applicants. These include remission of tuition plus a stipend.

PLACEMENT

The Dean of the School of Business and the senior faculty work closely with students to identify employment opportunities and place students in appropriate professional positions. In addition, the college-wide Career Planning and Placement Office provides substantial assistance including on-campus recruiting.

CORRESPONDENCE

For further information, please write or call
  Director of Graduate Studies
  School of Business
  Salisbury State College
  Salisbury, Maryland 21801

SAMFORD UNIVERSITY

BIRMINGHAM, ALABAMA

Samford University, located at Birmingham, Alabama, was founded in 1842 and operated as Howard College until 1965 when it assumed university status. The Master of Business Administration (M.B.A.) program, which was instituted in June 1965, is designed for and primarily limited to persons pursuing full-time careers in business, government, and industry. The approximate annual enrollment of the M.B.A. program is 200. This permits a close relationship between students and faculty.

The purpose of the M.B.A. program is to prepare individuals for increasing responsibilities in management. Emphasis is placed on giving students a broad understanding of business management and the environment in which it operates. Such an educational background is becoming increasingly essential for persons who aspire to positions of leadership in a dynamic economy.

Students holding full-time positions in business will not be permitted to take more than six semester hours in a regular semester and three semester hours in a summer term without special permission. All required courses will meet in the evening on the Samford campus.

PROGRAMS OF STUDY

The M.B.A. program at Samford is designed for two distinct groups. Students having undergraduate degrees in business administration or economics could complete the M.B.A. program by taking 30 semester hours of work as outlined by the School of Business. Students having undergraduate degrees in fields other than business administration or economics would normally be required to take 60 semester hours of course work. Fewer hours would be required for students who have had some of the basic undergraduate core courses listed under prerequisites.

Undergraduate Prerequisites	*Hours*
Principles of Accounting	6
Principles of Economics	6
Statistics	3
Business Finance	3
Marketing	3
Management	3
Basic Computer Course	3
Total	27

Course Requirements	*Hours*
BA 501 Managerial Economics	3
BA 502 Business Conditions	3
BA 505 Public Policy and Business Ethics	3
BA 510 Managerial Accounting	3
BA 520 Financial Administration or BA 421 Advanced Business Finance	3
BA 545 Management Theory and Practice	3
BA 550 Marketing Administration or BA 451 Advanced Marketing	3
BA 441 Production Management, BA 442 Labor Relations, BA 443 Management of Human Resources, BA 445 Organizational Behavior, or BA 446 Entrepreneurship	3
BA 549 Business Policy	3
BA 570 Quantitative Methods	3
Total	30

Each student must complete at least five 500-level courses and will be required to demonstrate the ability to write effectively and/or conduct research. This requirement will be met by the writing of term papers and reports in most courses.

The School of Business and the Cumberland School of Law of Samford University offer a combination degree program leading concurrently to a Master of Business Administration degree and a law degree (J.D.). The combination-degree student must meet the admission and graduation requirements of both schools. Admission to one school does not constitute automatic admission to the other. A statement of admission standards for each degree is available in the office of the dean of each school. In each program six hours of work done toward one degree will count toward the other. A student will be required to complete 82 semester hours of law courses (rather than the normal 88 hours) and 24 hours (rather than the normal 30 hours) in the M.B.A. program.

CORRESPONDENCE

For additional information, write to
Dr. William D. Geer, Dean
School of Business
Samford University
Birmingham, Alabama 35209
Telephone: 205-870-2935

For application, write to
Dr. Lee N. Allen, Dean
School of Graduate Studies
Samford University
Birmingham, Alabama 35209
Telephone: 205-870-2842

San Diego State University is the southernmost link in the California State University and Colleges system. The community of San Diego, where the university is located, is one of the major metropolitan business and residential areas in the United States. In addition, San Diego's recreational opportunities and outstanding climate make it an extremely desirable place in which to work and play.

The College of Business Administration, with over 6,000 undergraduate students and 900 graduate students, has long prided itself on the depth and breadth of its offerings. Both the graduate and the undergraduate programs are accredited by the American Assembly of Collegiate Schools of Business (AACSB). The Master of Science (M.S.) in accountancy has been separately accredited by the AACSB.

PROGRAMS OF STUDY

The Master of Business Administration (M.B.A.) program is designed for students holding undergraduate degrees in any field, including business, who are seeking a degree with broad managerial emphasis. Between 30 and 60 units are required, depending on previous academic background. Students may work for an M.B.A. on either a full-time or part-time basis.

M.B.A. students must meet the following requirements:
- complete up to 36 units in the following core courses for which acceptable equivalents have not been completed—financial and managerial accounting (6 units), organizational theory and behavior (6), quantitative methods (6), marketing (3), law for business executives (3), finance (3), computer programming and systems analysis (3), and economics (6);
- complete 6 units in two required courses—research and reporting (3) and policy formulation (3);
- complete at least 21 units in a combination of specialization and elective categories (specializations available include finance, information systems, international business, management, management science, marketing, personnel and industrial relations, production and operations management, and real estate);
- complete a thesis for 3 units or pass a comprehensive exam.

The M.S. program affords additional education in business for students who have undergraduate degrees in business administration or closely related fields. Students may work for the M.S. on either a full-time or part-time basis. Concentrations in the M.S. program are the same as those in the M.B.A. program, with the addition of financial services. M.S. students must complete a 30-unit program as individually developed. The M.S. in accountancy programs are for students interested in careers in accounting. Specializations are available in financial accounting, managerial accounting, or taxation. With the equivalent of a bachelor's degree in accounting, the student must complete a 30-unit program as individually developed.

ADMISSION

Classified graduate standing is required for admission to any graduate program. Classified graduate standing is granted to students who hold an acceptable baccalaureate degree and who demonstrate their ability for graduate study by their undergraduate grade-point average and by earning an acceptable score on the Graduate Management Admission Test (GMAT). There are no specific prerequisite courses for admission.

Applications for admission to the university should be filed with the Admission Office beginning in the previous November for the fall semester and in August for the spring semester.

EXPENSES

Registration fees (subject to annual revision) are $330.50 per semester for course loads of 6.1 or more units. California residents do not pay tuition. Nonresident and foreign students must pay tuition of $126.00 per unit. There are no provisions for waiving this tuition. Total expenses would depend upon individual needs. Campus residence halls, as well as apartments and other rentals, are available.

FINANCIAL ASSISTANCE

Graduate students may obtain financial assistance through one of the grant or loan programs in operation at the university. Graduate teaching and nonteaching assistantships in the College of Business Administration are available to a limited number of qualified students.

PLACEMENT

The Placement Center serves students seeking part-time or career employment. Over 1,000 business firms, government agencies, and school districts actively recruit through the Placement Center each year.

CORRESPONDENCE

For further information, please write or call

Associate Dean for Graduate Study
College of Business Administration
San Diego State University
San Diego, California 92182
Telephone: 619-265-6479

San Francisco State University is one of the 19 institutions in the California State University and Colleges system. The university is a multipurpose, coeducational institution of more than 24,000 students, of whom more than 7,000 are enrolled in postbaccalaureate study.

Seventy percent of the entering graduate students hold bachelor's degrees in subjects other than business, most having matriculated in humanities, social science, engineering, natural sciences, or economics. Most have two to five years of work experience.

In order to meet student needs, the full range of graduate courses is offered during the evening. There is no separation of day and evening programs. Regular full-time faculty teach at all times of the day. Over half of the graduate students work, many on a full-time basis.

Of particular note are (1) a special program in which carefully selected graduate students complete a portion of their program at Boeki Kenshu Center in Japan; (2) the U.S.-Japan Institute, which conducts a number of programs with the business community; (3) the Center for World Business which, with the financial support of major firms in the Bay Area, provides advanced study in various phases of world business; (4) the Retail Management Center; and (5) the Pension Research Institute.

PROGRAMS OF STUDY

The School of Business offers two degrees at the graduate level—Master of Business Administration (M.B.A.) and the Master of Science in Business Administration (M.S.B.A.). The M.B.A. is a broad-based degree with limited specializations in human resources management, productivity improvement, information systems management, finance, marketing, management, operations research, transportation, and international business. The M.S.B.A. allows greater specialization in the above areas and in accounting.

The Master of Business Administration program is structured as a broad preparation for managerial careers in business. Selected management seminars and a research project are specified. The remaining 12 semester hours for specialization may be selected by the student with the approval of the major adviser.

The Master of Science in Business Administration program is designed for those who desire specialization, unusual breadth, or interdisciplinary study involving other schools on campus.

Both the M.B.A. and the M.S.B.A. programs are open to students who have completed undergraduate majors in any field. Entering students should have knowledge of basic business mathematics and statistics. This knowledge may be demonstrated in examinations given at the beginning of the semester or developed through course work.

Each program consists of two parts: (1) a set of foundation courses that provide knowledge equivalent to that which would be gained in an undergraduate business program; (2) a set of 10 program courses, which are three semester units each. For students with little or no background in business studies eight or nine foundation courses of three semester units each will be required. If recent work in business subjects has been completed with acceptable grades at accredited institutions, waivers for the prerequisite courses are granted on a course-by-course basis.

The total program for the M.B.A. will normally require 30 to 54 semester units of work and the M.S.B.A. will normally require 30 to 57 semester units of work, assuming basic knowledge of mathematics, statistics, and basic economics.

It is possible to take all of the courses required for the degree after 6 p.m.

ADMISSION

Requirements for admission include a baccalaureate degree from an accredited college or university with an acceptable grade average, acceptable scores on the Graduate Management Admission Test (GMAT), and a letter of intent that relates past achievements and career goals to the program desired. The School of Business requires an entry index of 1,100, based on a combination of the last 60 semester units or 90 quarter units and the GMAT test score. The index is computed as 200 times the last-60-unit grade-point average (based on A = 4) plus the GMAT score. Normally the minimum acceptable GMAT score is 450. In cases of exceptions to the minimum entry index, the selection committee will consider evidence of unusual motivation, career maturity, and past success.

Application periods are from November 1 of the prior year to July 1 for fall semester admission, and from August to December 1 of the prior year for spring semester. Applications from foreign students are accepted only in November of each year and only for the fall semester. A score of 550 on the Test of English as a Foreign Language (TOEFL) is required for foreign students.

EXPENSES

Graduate students may enroll in as few as 3 to as many as 15 credit hours each semester. Enrollment fees currently range from $216 to $336 per semester. In addition, out-of-state tuition fee is $126 per unit. Summer sessions are supported by student fees of $70 per unit for all students.

On-campus dormitory facilities are available for students; room rates range from $550 to $600 per semester plus dining privileges at moderate rates. Living accommodations in off-campus facilities range upward from $1,500 to $3,000 per calendar year for room and meals. The Housing Office helps students find suitable housing.

FINANCIAL ASSISTANCE

The school has a limited number of graduate equity fellowships and graduate assistantships, usually available only to continuing students. The chairman of the appropriate department will provide further information. Other types of financial aids are available.

PLACEMENT

A placement service is available to students and graduates of the university. Assistance is given in obtaining full-time, part-time, and summer positions. The San Francisco area offers excellent opportunities for student employment.

CORRESPONDENCE

For further information, please write or call

Director of Graduate Studies
School of Business
San Francisco State University
1600 Holloway Avenue
San Francisco, California 94132
Telephone: 415-469-1279

Founded in 1857, San Jose State University (SJSU) is one of three major universities located in "Silicon Valley"; it is the only public one in the area. In the immediate vicinity of its downtown campus location are the headquarters and professional staff facilities of many major high technology companies. The area is one of the two most technically diverse locations in the U.S. and has served as a model of innovation and technology around the world. The business and engineering schools especially have benefited from this proximity, and they have both been able to establish cooperative ventures and receive major donations of equipment and support from companies like AT&T, IBM, DEC, H-P, and Intel.

SJSU admission standards for the Master of Business Administration (M.B.A.) program exceed those required by the American Assembly of Collegiate Schools of Business (AACSB), and SJSU is one of fewer than 200 business schools accredited both by AACSB and a regional accrediting body (WASC). Being a California public institution, SJSU offers a program that is a tremendous value in M.B.A. education for state residents.

The Graduate Program has grown to over 500 students on-campus and to over 200 students in its accelerated off-campus program. By 1990 the school expects to have 1,000 enrolled. Off-campus courses are offered in an eight-week format in typical corporate locations in Sunnyvale, Santa Clara, and Cupertino. Past corporate hosts have included AT&T, Applied Technology, Tandem Computers, and the San Jose Mercury News.

PROGRAM OF STUDY

The M.B.A. program is structured to develop advanced skills in its students in the areas of accounting, marketing, organizational behavior, quantitative business methods, finance, operations management, and strategy. Functional specializations have been developed in taxation and in marketing; a third in human resources management should be in place for the 1986-87 academic year.

Students admitted into the program with a partial academic background in business or no background will be required to complete from one to eight graduate-level M.B.A. foundation courses. The courses assume that this will be the student's first introduction to the subjects and prepares them for success in the advanced management series of 10 courses (7 required, 3 elective). The foundation sequence consists of courses that cover economics and business law, business communication research, accounting fundamentals, marketing, data processing, organizational behavior, quantitative business methods, and corporate finance. The final graduation requirement consists of a three-part comprehensive examination administered during the last semester in conjunction with the business policy and strategy course. The examination is interdisciplinary.

ADMISSION

The school accepts all applicants that meet the three basic criteria: a bachelor's degree from an accredited four-year college or university, a grade-point average of 3.0 minimum in all upper-division undergraduate and all graduate work (work at a junior college is not computed in this average), and a score of 500 or better on the Graduate Management Admission Test (GMAT) with both verbal and quantitative subscores above the 50th percentile. International students (those without a bachelor's degree from a U.S. institution) are also required to submit scores of 550 minimum on the Test of English as a Foreign Language (TOEFL).

Applicants to the on-campus program must submit applications, fees, scores, and transcripts to the Admissions and Records Office in time to allow two to three months processing before the spring (January) or fall (August) semesters. International students are required to submit material six months in advance.

Admission to the accelerated off-campus program requires all applications, fees, scores, and transcripts be submitted directly to the Graduate Programs Office—School of Business BT250 one to two months prior to any of the 6 eight-week sessions per year. Admission to either program qualifies the student to register in either or both on- and off-campus programs, and courses may be mixed from both to complete graduation requirements.

Recommendations and lengthy personal essays are not required for admission. Personal interviews in unusual or marginal situations are infrequently requested. Graduate Advisors are available in person, or by phone, to assist students with questions about admissions and the program of study. Campus tours are sponsored by the university.

EXPENSES

Fall 1985 figures

Application fee	$ 39.00
Aggregate semester fees	
0.1 units to 6.0 units	243.50
6.1 units or more	363.50
Nonresident tuition, each unit	120.00
Off-campus M.B.A. classes for residents and nonresidents, total charges per course	450.00

The Student Housing Office, SJSU at 408-277-2126 can assist students with questions about housing.

FINANCIAL ASSISTANCE

Students may contact the Financial Aids Office at 408-277-2975 for information on financial assistance.

PLACEMENT

For placement information, students should contact Career Planning and Placement at 408-277-2272.

CORRESPONDENCE

For M.B.A. advising, GMAT bulletins, applications, and the SJSU M.B.A. brochure, call or write

Graduate Programs
School of Business—BT250
San Jose State University
One Washington Square
San Jose, California 95192-0162
Telephone: 408-277-2308

Sangamon State University is unique in that it offers only graduate degrees and upper-division (junior and senior) undergraduate course work. The students in general, and the Master of Business Administration (M.B.A.) students in particular, are older than the national norm and usually have several years of work experience prior to enrolling.

The academic programs and the instructional modes are designed for a mature, experienced student. Class sizes are small, which permits discussions that draw on the real-world experiences of students.

Most M.B.A. classes are taught by full-time faculty who teach primarily graduate business courses. Some specialized electives are taught by part-time practitioners. Most full-time faculty have held responsible positions in business or government.

The university is located in Springfield, the capital of Illinois, one mile from I-55 which connects St. Louis (two hours) and Chicago (four hours). AMTRAK and air service is also available.

The university offers 22 graduate and 21 undergraduate major programs.

PROGRAM OF STUDY
The M.B.A. program is particularly well adapted to students who have undergraduate degrees in fields other than business, and have several years of work experience of any type.

The maturity and practical experience of M.B.A. students allows those with non-business backgrounds to begin taking graduate-level course work after completing three prerequisite courses (accounting, economics, and statistics). Students who have undergraduate degrees in business start directly with graduate courses.

The M.B.A. requires the successful completion of 12 courses (4 credits each) for a total of 48 credit hours. Students may attend part time or full time. Classes are offered in the evenings and on weekends. Required core courses are generally offered each semester so that students can enter the program at any time. No thesis is required.

A typical full-time schedule is four courses per semester, generally taken by attending some combination of evening and weekend classes. Part-time students generally take two courses per semester. Some, but not all, courses are offered in the summer.

Four of the 12 courses are electives that can be taken within the Business Administration Program, or in some other program of the university with the permission of the student's adviser.

Related programs include master's degrees in public administration, accountancy, economics, management information systems, health care administration, and community arts management. For students interested in governmental service, the university has an internship program with the Illinois state government for which eight credit hours of elective credit may be granted.

ADMISSION
The packet of enrollment information, available on request, includes an application for admission to the university as a whole (which is automatic for holders of bachelor's degrees from accredited universities) and a second application for admittance to the M.B.A. program.

A formula that weights undergraduate grades and scores on the Graduate Management Admission Test (GMAT) is used by the faculty in screening applicants; however, the final admission decision is made on the basis of the total configuration of qualifications. The M.B.A. faculty, all of whom were undergraduate students at one time, understand that undergraduate grades may not indicate an applicant's full potential. They are also aware that applicants who have been out of college for some time or who have undergraduate degrees in fields unrelated to business may not do well on a standardized test such as the GMAT.

Students who have been admitted to the university but have not as yet taken the GMAT may take all the prerequisites and 12 credit hours of graduate work while awaiting the GMAT scores and admission to the M.B.A. program. Admission to the university and the taking of some graduate courses does not necessarily mean subsequent admission to the Business Administration Program. The application for admission to the M.B.A. program will be acted on by the M.B.A. faculty when the following have been received: (1) admission to the university, (2) application for admission to the M.B.A. program, and (3) GMAT scores.

Students may begin course work in the fall semester beginning in late August, the spring semester beginning in mid-January, or the summer session beginning in June. Applications for admission are accepted year-round.

EXPENSES
Cost estimates are based on the 1985-86 academic year and are subject to change.

	Illinois Resident	Out-of-State
Full-time tuition and fees	$561.00	$1,599.00
Part-time, per credit hour	43.25	129.75

Most graduate students live in off-campus housing, which is readily available.

FINANCIAL ASSISTANCE
Assistance is available in the form of grants, tuition waivers, assistantships, scholarships, loans, part-time employment, and veterans' benefits.

PLACEMENT
The Career Services and Placement Office assists students in implementing life/career plans through job or educational placement.

CORRESPONDENCE
For further information, please write or call
  Director of Admissions
  MBA Program, L-109
  Sangamon State University
  Springfield, Illinois 62708
  Telephone: 217-786-6780
  (Toll free in Illinois, 800-252-8533)

Leavey School of Business and Administration

SANTA CLARA UNIVERSITY

SANTA CLARA, CALIFORNIA

Santa Clara University is located 46 miles from San Francisco near the southern tip of the San Francisco Bay in an area that is rich in opportunities for learning. The campus is situated in Silicon Valley, one of the nation's great concentrations of high-technology industry and of professional and scientific activity. The cultural and entertainment centers of San Francisco, Berkeley, Oakland, and Marin County are within one hour's travel by bus, train, or car. In the opposite direction, about 30 minutes away, are the beaches of Santa Cruz on the Pacific Ocean, and less than two hours' drive away is the world-famous Monterey Peninsula.

PROGRAM OF STUDY

The Board of Trustees established the School of Business and Administration as an integral part of Santa Clara University in 1926. The four-year bachelor's curriculum was approved in 1927. The Master of Business Administration (M.B.A.) program was established in 1958 and received accreditation by the American Assembly of Collegiate Schools of Business (AACSB) in 1963, one of the first M.B.A. programs nationwide to be so recognized. There are six departments within the school—accounting, economics, finance, management, marketing, and decision and information sciences—and the Institute of Agribusiness.

The Leavey School of Business and Administration correlates the general educational aims of the university with preparation in meeting the general and specific problems of industry, commerce, and institutions of various types. The specific aims are to supply professional training for those who are aiming at responsible positions in corporations, in their own businesses, in professional organizations serving business, or in government agencies.

To assist students in developing the attributes of business leadership, the graduate program leading to the M.B.A. degree stresses the significance of the orientation of business to a dynamic society and the problems of control of the increasingly complex aspects of the economy. The curriculum is focused on the problems of business, but is intended to be broad and general rather than vocational.

Graduate courses are offered during three quarters and one summer session each year, starting in September, January, March, and June. All classes are scheduled during the late afternoon and evening periods to allow graduate students employed during the day to complete the requirements for the M.B.A. degree.

ADMISSION

Requirements for admission recognize differences among candidates in educational background and experience. The M.B.A. program can be built upon undergraduate work in engineering, business, arts and sciences, and other areas. A candidate for admission must have a bachelor's degree from an institution of accepted standing.

Entering students are admitted each quarter, including summer. Application forms and instructions are available from the M.B.A. Admissions Committee. The applicant must complete and submit all items requested in the application package. These include (1) two copies of the application form, (2) two confidential letters of recommendation forms, (3) two official transcripts from each institution attended, (4) Graduate Management Admission Test (GMAT) score, (5) Test of English as a Foreign Language (TOEFL) score (if applicable), and (6) a $25 application fee ($31 for international students).

All application materials must be assembled and submitted (except GMAT and TOEFL scores) in one package. This allows greater control over the admission package and reduces the chance of materials being lost or delayed. Applications will not be considered until all materials are received.

EXPENSES

Tuition for 1985-86 was $176 per quarter unit. There is a $5 registration fee payable each quarter.

FINANCIAL ASSISTANCE

Financial assistance is awarded on the basis of academic record and financial need. It is available in the form of scholarships, loans, deferred-payment plans, and jobs, including work-study. The school offers a limited number of scholarships to outstanding graduate students. In selecting students to receive financial aid, evidence of financial need is required. Because scholarships and grants are limited, many students applying for aid find the most advantageous method of financing their

education is through a loan program. Among those available to students are the National Direct Student Loan Program and Federally Insured Student Loans. It is also possible for graduate students who are residents of California to apply to the California State Scholarship and Loan Commission for graduate fellowships. Application forms and further information may be obtained from the Office of Financial Aids.

PLACEMENT

The university maintains a placement service which serves students who are interested in obtaining part-time employment during their school program and full-time employment upon graduation.

CORRESPONDENCE

Requests for information should be addressed to
Director of Graduate Education
Leavey School of Business and Administration
Santa Clara University
Santa Clara, California 95053

SAVANNAH STATE COLLEGE

SAVANNAH, GEORGIA

Savannah State College, a unit of the university system of Georgia, was founded in 1890 by an Act of the General Assembly of the state of Georgia in conjunction with the state university system. The Master of Business Administration (M.B.A.) program, established in 1972 as a joint program of Armstrong and Savannah State Colleges, became an integral part of the School of Business at Savannah State College. The graduate program in business administration, the School of Business, and Savannah State College are accredited by the Southern Association of Colleges and Schools, characterized by a multiracial, coeducational balance of students and faculty, and committed to an academic program of excellence.

PROGRAM OF STUDY

The Master of Business Administration program at Savannah State College is committed to providing the candidate with a professional educational foundation requisite for a leadership role in business. Faculty and staff offer courses of study, seminars, and related experiences to meet this objective. In particular, directed student research in community service projects of a business nature is encouraged to enhance this phase of development.

The M.B.A. curriculum has been designed to provide latitude rather than specialization and is structured to accommodate students with or without an undergraduate degree in business administration. Graduate requirements consist of 12 courses (60 quarter hours), 9 of a core nature and 3 electives, which may be completed in evening classes within four academic quarters (one calendar year). A two-year academic planning schedule is available to enhance timely completion of the program. A thesis is not required for the M.B.A. degree; however, a comprehensive oral examination is required of all candidates.

Six courses, recognized as a "common body of knowledge" in business, are prerequisite to the M.B.A. program. M.B.A. applicants may satisfy this 30 hours of requirements through the College-Level Examination Program (CLEP) and/or correspondence study as well as by actual class attendance. The prerequisite courses include elementary statistics, introductory economics, accounting principles, business finance, introduction to management, and introduction to marketing.

ADMISSION

For admission to the M.B.A. program, applicants must have earned a baccalaureate degree with an acceptable record from an accredited institution. Additionally candidates must present two letters of recommendation from classroom instructors and/or employers and satisfactory scores on the Graduate Management Admission Test (GMAT).

EXPENSES

Fee schedule for fall quarter, 1985

	Resident Day	Nonresident Day
Matriculation....	$320	$ 320
Nonresident tuition........		640
Health fee.......	30	30
Student activity fee...........	20	20
Athletic fee......	38	38
Totals	$408	$1,048

Boarding students' expenses will also include $230 for room and $290 for board per quarter.

The college reserves the right to make changes in its fees at the beginning of any quarter and without prior notice.

FINANCIAL ASSISTANCE

A limited number of scholarships and work assistantships are available to qualified students.

PLACEMENT

Graduate students in the School of Business Administration at Savannah State College are assisted with job placement both by the campus placement office and by the faculty and administration.

CORRESPONDENCE

For further information, please write or call

Coordinator, M.B.A. Program
School of Business
Savannah State College
Savannah, Georgia 31404
Telephone: 912-356-2255

Seattle Pacific University, founded in 1891, is a Christian liberal arts university located in the heart of the Pacific Northwest. Some 2,800 students choose from an innovative curriculum that offers 52 undergraduate majors and 30 graduate areas of specialization. Seattle Pacific's location provides tremendous opportunity for practical internships as well as classroom studies. The School of Business at Seattle Pacific offers undergraduate majors in accounting, economics, finance, management, and marketing.

PROGRAM OF STUDY
The Graduate School of Business at Seattle Pacific University offers a program leading to a Master of Business Administration (M.B.A.). Students seeking admission to the school should have two full years of working experience or the equivalent, as determined by the Faculty Admissions Committee prior to entering. It is assumed that applicants to this program seriously seek a graduate education in business administration and the attainment of the M.B.A. degree.

The curriculum of the school is designed to teach the practice of business administration and presumes a general understanding of the basic functions of business in a free enterprise society. The intent is to teach the application of principles far more than the theoretical foundations of such business principles.

The time schedule of classes is specifically designed to allow for and encourage participation by students who have full- or part-time regular employment. It is anticipated that a student with full-time employment could successfully complete the program in 12 academic quarters. The faculty includes both full-time and part-time members. Full-time faculty are appreciative of the work demands of those who are employed both full and part time and make every effort to accommodate the time requirements of such students by arranging meetings to correspond with student availability.

The intent of the graduate business program at Seattle Pacific University is to assist its students to develop the ability to significantly improve their performance on their jobs, in their personal lives, and as contributing members of their community and country.

ADMISSION
Students applying for admission to the Master of Business Administration program in the School of Business and Economics must fulfill the requirements for admission to the university as outlined in the university catalog.

After admission to the university, the student must then apply for admission to the School of Business M.B.A. program. Admission to the university does not imply admission to the School of Business.

The School of Business and Economics will require, in addition to the general requirements of the university, M.B.A. candidates to have a baccalaureate degree from institutions accredited by a Council on Postsecondary Accreditation (COPA) recognized institutional accrediting agency. Only students showing high promise of success in postbaccalaureate study will be admitted. This criteria will be determined by a combination of the following:

● the candidate will demonstrate competency by completing the Graduate Management Admission Test (GMAT) with a score of 450 or higher;
● the candidate will have a grade-point average sufficient that, when combined with the GMAT score, totals 1,050 points. (the formula used for computing this point total will be the GMAT score plus 200 times the applicant's undergraduate grade-point average);
● the applicant will also demonstrate a record of appropriate employment at increasing levels of responsibility with letters of recommendation from an immediate supervisor and from a manager one level above the immediate supervisor. The letters will indicate the writer's evaluation of the applicant's success in the M.B.A. program.

Seattle Pacific University is an academic, social, and religious community with expectations that serve as guidelines for attendance. These expectations include a standard of personal health, moral integrity, social consciousness, and concern for others. It is expected that all graduate students will abstain from the use of alcohol and tobacco while on campus.

International students must provide a confidential financial statement and scores on the Test of English as a Foreign Language (TOEFL) in addition to the requirements listed above.

EXPENSES
Seattle Pacific University's academic programs operate on the quarter system. All fees are figured on three quarters per academic year. Cost for the 1985-86 school year was $150 per credit.

FINANCIAL ASSISTANCE
Financial Aid is limited for graduate students. All interested students should contact the Financial Aid Office, Seattle Pacific University, Seattle, Washington 98119 (Telephone 206-281-2046).

PLACEMENT
Assistance is offered to students in obtaining full-time and/or part-time employment. Seattle Pacific's Office of Career Planning and Placement provides counseling, placement examinations, and information concerning corporations and companies conducting interviews on campus.

CORRESPONDENCE
For further information or to request an application for admission, please contact
Director of Admissions
Master of Business Administration
   Program
Seattle Pacific University
Seattle, Washington 98119
Telephone: 206-281-2265

The Master of Business Administration (M.B.A.) program at Seattle University was established in 1967 in response to the growing number of individuals desiring graduate studies in the field of business administration. The program is accredited by the American Assembly of Collegiate Schools of Business (AACSB) and is designed for students who have demonstrated the potential for responsible leadership necessary to deal decisively with the complex, dynamic environment within which business functions. Graduate students at Seattle University are exposed to a highly qualified and experienced full-time faculty. The emphasis of studies is on a broad spectrum of administration, and the program is designed to offer an interdisciplinary view of business. Vocational and professional training is not the aim. The principal objective of the program is to develop those managerial talents related to the fundamentals of business and economics. Since the majority of the students are employed full time and therefore taking less than three courses per quarter, classes are conducted only in the evening.

PROGRAM OF STUDY

The Master of Business Administration may follow a bachelor's degree in the arts, science, engineering, education, general studies, or business. The M.B.A. program offers four areas of concentration: behavioral, environmental, functional, and operations and systems. In order to complete the program, a student must progress through four phases of study. Foundation courses may be required as additional background and to provide an academic platform for those entering without sufficient introduction to the fundamentals of business administration. Although all of the foundation courses are graduate level, they do not count toward the 15 courses (45 credit hours) required for the M.B.A. degree.

ADMISSION

A candidate for admission must have a bachelor's degree from an accredited institution. Admission to the M.B.A. program is granted only to those applicants who demonstrate the qualifications for successful completion of the requirements. A serious intent is imperative. Criteria for admission give recognition to the differences in educational background and experience of individual candidates. The M.B.A. program is designed to satisfy the measures of quality that the American Assembly of Collegiate Schools of Business uses in the accreditation of graduate study in business.

The following criteria are relevant:
● the applicant's grade-point average and the trend of grades during undergraduate studies, specifically, the last two academic years;
● the applicant's rank in the graduating class;
● the applicant's potential as measured by conscientious letters of recommendation;
● the applicant's performance on the Graduate Management Admission Test (GMAT);
● the applicant's business and professional performance;
● the applicant's previous graduate study in an accredited school of business.

The M.B.A. program is conducted on the quarter system. There are four quarters in each year: fall, winter, spring, and an optional summer quarter. Students are admitted for any of the four quarters during the year, and applications should be submitted at least 30 days before the beginning of the quarter of first enrollment.

EXPENSES

Expenses for 1985-86 were as follows:
Application fee
  (nonrefundable) . . . . $ 15
Matriculation fee
  (one time only) 45
Each quarter credit hour 174

FINANCIAL ASSISTANCE

The M.B.A. program is designed for the graduate student whose obligations prohibit a full-time day commitment. In order to meet the needs of this type of student, many Pacific Northwest companies reimburse the mature, serious-minded student for tuition and fees incurred at Seattle University. The university has several types of student loans available. For information, write Director of Financial Aid, Seattle University, Seattle, Washington 98122.

CORRESPONDENCE

For further information, please write or call
  Admissions Officer
  Graduate Business Program
  Albers School of Business
  Seattle University
  Seattle, Washington 98122
  Telephone: 206-626-5455

W. Paul Stillman School of Business

SETON HALL UNIVERSITY

SOUTH ORANGE, NEW JERSEY

Seton Hall University, located in South Orange, New Jersey, approximately 15 miles from New York City, is the largest Catholic diocesan university in the United States. The university, founded in 1856, has been located on a 56-acre campus in South Orange since 1860. Its proximity to New York City, the nation's business capital, and its ideal location within the business and industrial complex of northern New Jersey allow students to supplement their formal education through activities outside the classroom.

The W. Paul Stillman School of Business, founded in 1951, has an enrollment of 900 Master of Business Administration (M.B.A.) degree candidates and 200 Master of Science (M.S.) in taxation candidates. The academic year for students enrolled in the graduate school is composed of two semesters and a summer session. The program may be completed on either a full-time or part-time basis.

PROGRAMS OF STUDY
All programs at the W. Paul Stillman School of Business are accredited by the American Assembly of Collegiate Schools of Business (AACSB). The M.B.A. curriculum is designed to provide a strong foundation in the disciplines of economics and the behavioral and quantitative sciences. The first three levels (30 credits total) provide the base from which each student can select a specialization. Individuals may receive credit for those courses in the first three levels for which evidence is shown of prior academic performance from accredited institutions and/or successful completion of challenge examinations administered by the School of Business. At the fourth level, each student is required to complete 12 credits in his or her chosen specialization. Students wishing to specialize in accounting must complete 15 credits in that area. Currently, the specializations include accounting, economics, finance, information systems, management and industrial relations, marketing, and quantitative analysis. The remaining 15 credits are electives selected from a field in the M.B.A. curriculum other than the student's field of specialization. Electives are limited to six credits in any single field. A thesis (optional) can be used to satisfy six hours of elective credit. The fifth level is Business Policy, the capstone of the program, integrating all of the knowledge gained in previous courses. In order to complete the program a student is required to take a minimum of 30 hours, with a maximum of 60 hours.

The W. Paul Stillman School of Business and the School of Law offer a program leading to the degrees of Master of Business Administration (M.B.A.) and Juris Doctor (J.D.). The curriculum can be completed in four years rather than the normal five years through the use of courses acceptable as joint credits. The J.D. degree consists of 84 credits. A maximum of 12 credits may be applied to both degree requirements. Students interested in entering the joint program must follow the separate application procedures of each school. It is suggested that applications be submitted to both schools simultaneously in order to facilitate the decision-making process. For further information about the joint program, contact the schools of business and law.

The Master of Science in taxation program provides a comprehensive background for professional careers in the field of taxation, primarily in industry and public accounting. Completion of the M.S. degree requires 12 semester hours of required courses and 18 credit hours of elective courses. Prerequisite courses or their equivalent are required of all M.S. candidates before enrollment in tax courses. Individuals may receive credit for prerequisite course work if evidence is shown of prior academic performance and/or successful completion of challenge examinations administered by the School of Business. Candidates for the Master of Science in taxation must fulfill all degree requirements within five years.

ADMISSION
Admission to the M.B.A. and M.S. programs is open to holders of baccalaureate degrees from accredited colleges or universities. Applicants must submit (1) a completed application form with a nonrefundable $30 application fee; (2) one official copy of each transcript from all colleges and universities attended—undergraduate, graduate, and professional; (3) score on the Graduate Management Admission Test (GMAT); and (4) three letters of reference from individuals concerning the applicant's work experience and academic performance. Foreign applicants are also required to submit official Test of English as a Foreign Language (TOEFL) scores. Applications must be submitted no later than April 1 for the fall semester, August 1 for the spring semester, and February 1

for the summer session. The school does not expect to admit an applicant whose grade-point average is below 2.75 (on a 4.0 scale) and whose GMAT score is below 500.

EXPENSES
Tuition for graduate courses in the M.B.A. program was $201 per credit hour for the 1985-86 academic year.

FINANCIAL ASSISTANCE
The W. Paul Stillman School of Business offers graduate assistantships each year for students interested in pursuing a degree in business on a full-time basis. A graduate assistant is assigned 20 hours of work per week and receives a stipend of $3,500 for a nine-month period. In addition, the assistant receives remission of tuition, but not of fees, for 12 credit hours per semester. Information regarding other available forms of financial aid may be obtained from the Office of Financial Aid.

PLACEMENT
Prospective graduates of the W. Paul Stillman School of Business are assisted by the Student Development Center in finding suitable positions. More than a hundred leading companies recruit regularly on campus.

CORRESPONDENCE
For further information, contact
  Office of Student Advisement
  W. Paul Stillman School of Business
  Seton Hall University
  400 South Orange Avenue
  South Orange, New Jersey 07079
  Telephone: 201-761-9222

The Master of Business Administration program at Shenandoah College provides upward mobility for individuals with career aspirations in professional and managerial positions in both profit-making and nonprofit institutions. Persons currently employed in any field may take advantage of the program to strengthen their managerial and business skills, acquire degrees, and further their professional advancement.

Shenandoah's business program accepts full- or part-time students. Course schedules generally permit a student to meet the employer's requirements for travel, shift work, or changes in work assignments.

The program uses many methods, including lectures, seminars, field studies, workshops, and case studies. Class discussions, written reports, staff studies, and oral presentations utilizing TV and other audiovisual aids sharpen analytical judgment and develop communication skills. Students are exposed to practical experiences that enrich their understanding of theories and concepts explored in the classroom.

Shenandoah College and Conservatory is accredited by the Southern Association of Colleges and Schools. The college is a private, coeducational institution located in historic Winchester, Virginia, at the intersection of US Rt. 50 and Interstate 81, 75 miles west of Washington, D.C., in the beautiful Shenandoah Valley.

PROGRAM OF STUDY
The Master of Business Administration (M.B.A.) degree program is for the individual who possesses a bachelor's degree in any field and wishes to pursue advanced studies in business administration. The M.B.A. program consists of a minimum of 36 graduate semester credit hours for the holder of a bachelor of business degree and 45 graduate semester credit hours for the holder of a nonbusiness bachelor's degree. Communication and writing skills are stressed throughout the entire M.B.A. program.

The Byrd School of Business is assisted by the Business/Management Advisory Committee, which is composed of 25 local business and industrial leaders. This group, formed in 1979, meets periodically during the school year and advises the administration in matters ranging from curriculum to public relations. As a sample of one of the contributions of this group, new courses are being offered in Superior-Subordinate Relationships and

Business Written and Oral Presentations. Close interaction between the school and the business community is an ongoing activity at Shenandoah.

Some of the business classes take field trips to local industrial plants for first-hand observation of managerial practices. Plant managers and industrial relations officers brief the students on the company's organizational structures, training programs, and other pertinent concepts of their managerial philosophies. On occasion, students employed by local industry assist in arranging tours of the manufacturing sites.

The Honorable Harry F. Byrd, Jr., upon his retirement from the United States Senate in 1983, accepted an appointment as Distinguished Professor of Business. In that same year, the Byrd Distinguished Lecture Series was established to provide a forum for the presentation, consideration, and discussion of critical issues on the national scene. Noted speakers are invited to present their views on topics of timely importance in national and international issues and events.

Because of Senator Byrd's long and dedicated political career, his success as a businessman, and the outstanding reputation he and his family have built for integrity, honesty, and sound business-like management of government, the Board of Trustees of Shenandoah College asked his permission to name its School of Business in his honor. In June 1984, the Board of Trustees voted unanimously to create the Byrd School of Business and to authorize a $1.5 million campaign to construct a building and enlarge the endowment for the business programs.

ADMISSION
Prospective graduate students may make application on forms requested from the Admissions Office. Admissions requirements include the following:
- an official transcript of all undergraduate work,
- an undergraduate grade-point average of 2.50 on a 4.00 scale, and
- two letters of recommendation.

EXPENSES
Graduate students pay tuition at a rate of $170 per credit. A Virginia Tuition Assistance Grant, set at $1,000 per year for 1985-86, is available to Virginia residents attending Shenandoah College. The 1985-86 academic year was the first time this grant was available to full-time graduate students. The $1,000 grant is based upon state residence and is not influenced by need. As a grant it need not be repaid, and it can be applied for through a simple one-page application form obtained at the college's Financial Aid Office.

FINANCIAL ASSISTANCE
Financial aid is available in various forms, including graduate assistantships, fellowships, and scholarships. Shenandoah has kept its tuition competitive and has enlarged its scholarship budget to make a quality education possible for every student who meets the entrance requirements.

CORRESPONDENCE
For further information, contact
Director of Admissions
Shenandoah College and Conservatory
Winchester, Virginia 22601
Telephone: 703-665-4500

Shippensburg University is located in the beautiful Cumberland Valley in the community of Shippensburg, a town of approximately 7,000 residents. The town and campus are 40 miles southwest of Harrisburg and 100 miles northwest of Baltimore and Washington, D.C.

Founded in 1871, Shippensburg University is one of 14 state-owned institutions of higher education in Pennsylvania. Shippensburg University is fully accredited by the Middle States Association of Colleges and Secondary Schools. The university welcomes students from all racial, religious, national, and socioeconomic backgrounds.

The academic year for graduate work leading to the Master of Business Administration (M.B.A.) degree includes two semesters and two summer sessions. The first semester begins in early September and ends just before the Christmas holidays. The second semester begins in mid-January and ends in early May. There are 2 six-week summer sessions. The program is planned for full-time or part-time students. Students with the appropriate academic background can earn their M.B.A. degree in one academic year.

PROGRAM OF STUDY

The M.B.A. program seeks to provide students with a broad range of advanced skills and knowledge in all the business disciplines, with an emphasis on decision and policy making, ultimately preparing students for management positions in business and government. Much of the course work focuses on the quantitative aspects of business. Therefore, it is recommended that students be well prepared in this area before commencing the M.B.A. program.

The M.B.A. program consists of 30 credits of foundation courses, 24 credits of core courses, and 6 credits of electives. Foundation courses may be waived depending upon the academic background of the student. A student who either completed a foundation course more than seven years before enrollment in the M.B.A. program or received a C or less in a foundation course, may be required to retake the course or pass a proficiency test in order to ensure adequate preparation for the core courses. The following foundation courses, or their equivalents, are required: Economic Analysis, Survey of Accounting, Finance, Math of Management, Quantitative Management Methods and Statistics, Production Management,

Introduction to Information Technology, Studies in Management, Studies in Marketing Management, and Business and Society.

A student who has satisfactorily met all the foundation course requirements will have a 30-credit degree program, consisting of 24 credits in core courses and 6 credits of electives. A minimum of 30 credits, with a maximum of 60 credits, is required to complete the M.B.A. program. The core curriculum includes Accounting for Management Control, Managerial Finance, Behavioral Factors in Management, Quantitative Analysis for Business, Managerial Economics, Consumer and Buyer Behavior, Management Applications of Multivariate Statistical Analysis, and Management Policy Formulation. Electives can be chosen from specialized fields such as accounting, data processing/information systems, finance, management, management science, or marketing.

ADMISSION

Applicants for admission to the M.B.A. program must submit (1) a completed application form with a $15 application fee, (2) transcripts of all college-level work showing the satisfactory completion of a bachelor's degree, and (3) scores on the Graduate Management Admission Test (GMAT). Applications must be filed prior to the opening of the semester for which admission is sought. Foreign students are required to take the Test of English as a Foreign Language (TOEFL) and present an affidavit of financial support.

EXPENSES

Graduate tuition is $800 per semester or $89 per credit for residents of Pennsylvania and $891 per semester or $99 per credit for nonresidents. Board is available for $380 per semester.

On-campus housing is not available for graduate students during the regular academic year. However, rooms and apartments are available within walking distance of the campus, starting at about $100 per month. Both room and board are available for the summer sessions; the cost is approximately $350 per six-week session.

FINANCIAL ASSISTANCE

Graduate assistantships are offered on a competitive basis to well-qualified graduate students who have been admitted to the M.B.A. degree program on the main campus. Graduate assistant appointments (full-time) during the nine-month academic year provide full tuition remission and a $2,705 stipend. Full-time graduate assistants are required to enroll for at least 9 hours of graduate credit each semester and work 20 hours each week. Some half-time assistantship positions are available during the academic year and offer a stipend of $1,352.50 with full tuition remission; half-time graduate assistants are required to enroll for at least 6 hours of graduate credit each semester and work 10 hours each week. Graduate assistants are assigned to individual areas of responsibility, according to the needs of the College of Business.

Tuition-free scholarship and work contracts are available. There are special stipends for minority students. Tuition may not be paid in installments. Students may apply for a Guaranteed Student Loan by obtaining an application from their bank. Students interested in information concerning additional sources of financial assistance should consult the university's Director of Financial Aid.

PLACEMENT

An active Placement Office is maintained for students in the M.B.A. program and for alumni.

CORRESPONDENCE

Inquiries and application requests may be directed to

Director of Academic Programs
College of Business
Shippensburg University
Shippensburg, Pennsylvania 17257
Telephone: 717-532-1237

Established in 1974, the Simmons College Graduate School of Management (GSM) offers a rigorous, intense educational program designed for capable women who want to change the direction of their working lives. The curriculum emphasizes functional and quantitative skills, and leads to the Master of Business Administration (M.B.A.) degree. Founded by Margaret Hennig and Anne Jardim, authors of the highly acclaimed book, *The Managerial Women,* the GSM's behavioral courses help women to work effectively in an organizational structure.

PROGRAM OF STUDY
The GSM program of study is usually completed in one year by full-time students, and in two or three years by part-time students. The curriculum is distinguished by a number of features not found elsewhere, including the following:
- the opportunity for nontraditional students—those women who do not hold a bachelor's degree, but who have demonstrated exceptional promise in work experience—to obtain a master's degree, as well as for traditional postbaccalaureate students to do so;
- a learning pace, including pre-program courses, expressly designed to maximize women students' ability to deal with heavily quantitative material as they progress toward the degree;
- an emphasis on group process and group problem solving that is tied to completing specific consulting projects for corporations and other organizations;
- the strong component of behavioral courses based on the research of Deans Hennig and Jardim, designed to help women understand and work effectively in the organizational environment.

The program of study consists of the following courses:
- *Functional*—Economic Analysis for Managers, Quantitative Analysis for Managers, Financial Accounting, Accounting for Control, Finance, Financial Analysis for Decision Making, Marketing Management, Market Research, Strategic Management, Operations Management, Introduction to Information Technology, Computer Resource Management;
- *Behavioral*—Organizational Structure, Management of Human Resources, Management and Behavior;
- *Integrative*—The Middle Manager: Issues and Problems, Leadership in Management: Policy, Personality, Strategy, and Career Planning and Development.

A six-week internship or independent study project is required of each student.

The year of full-time study, beginning in September and ending in August, comprises three semesters during each of which the student takes approximately six courses. Part-time study may be completed in two or three years, with all courses meeting in the evening.

ADMISSION
The Committee on Admissions attempts to assess potential for academic success in a highly quantitative program of study and professional success thereafter. Applicants must have at least two years of work experience; most hold the baccalaureate degree or higher. However, nontraditional applicants who do not hold the bachelor's degree, but can present a record of relevant professional achievement, may also be considered. Although no specific preparation is mandated, the program presupposes a working knowledge of intermediate college algebra. Applications are evaluated after the following documents are received: scores on the Graduate Management Admission Test (GMAT), three letters of recommendation, and transcripts for all course work beyond high school. Both full-time and part-time students may begin the program only in September. A rolling admission system is followed; however, students must submit applications by March 31. Inquiries regarding admissions should be sent to: Director of Admissions, Simmons College Graduate School of Management, 409 Commonwealth Avenue, Boston, Massachusetts 02215 (617-536-8289).

EXPENSES
Expenses for 1985-86 were as follows:

Application fee, nonrefundable	$ 30
Tuition deposit, applicable to tuition but nonrefundable	100
Tuition for the 45-hour program ($290 per credit hour)	13,050
Books and supplies (approximate)	900
Student activity fee ($20 per semester)	60
Total cost	$14,140

The tuition covers eleven and a half months or the equivalent of three semesters of full-time work.

FINANCIAL ASSISTANCE
The program participates in federal student loan plans, administers its own loan fund, and has some scholarship money available. Requests for information about financial aid should be directed to the Student Financial Aid Office, Simmons College, 300 The Fenway, Boston, Massachusetts 02115 (617-738-2138).

PLACEMENT
The GSM Placement Office offers a variety of services to assist graduates in locating appropriate job opportunities. Starting salaries for Simmons graduates are consistently well above the national average.

CORRESPONDENCE
For further information, please write
Simmons College
Graduate School of Management
409 Commonwealth Avenue
Boston, Massachusetts 02215

SIMON FRASER UNIVERSITY

BURNABY, BRITISH COLUMBIA, CANADA

Simon Fraser University opened in September 1965 with an entering class of 2,500 students. Approximately 12,000 students are currently enrolled in undergraduate and graduate programs. The campus setting atop Burnaby Mountain provides magnificent views of the city, the mountains, and the Vancouver Harbor.

The Faculty of Business Administration, established as a separate unit in 1982, now includes 46 faculty and more than 2,200 students. The Bachelor of Business Administration degree and two programs leading to the Master of Business Administration (M.B.A.) degree (day-time M.B.A. and executive M.B.A.) are offered. In addition, a joint Doctor of Philosophy (Ph.D.) degree in economics and business administration is offered.

PROGRAM OF STUDY

The innovative M.B.A. program, which commenced in September 1984, is designed for students who already have a first degree in business administration or commerce and who desire to specialize in some functional area of business. The program is intended to provide the graduate with a capacity for dealing with complex, strategic issues in an uncertain and dynamic environment, exceptional proficiency in at least one of the available fields of concentration, and competency in an additional supporting field. The graduate can expect to have acquired expertise in technical skills within specific functional areas as well as in research and investigative techniques. Students are encouraged to develop joint programs with areas such as resource management, economics, computing science, criminology, and engineering science.

M.B.A. program requirements include components of course work and written research under one of two available options: the project option or the thesis option. In addition, the student must choose a field of concentration, that is, *one* of accounting and management information systems, business, government and society, finance, management science, marketing or organizational behavior, and a supporting field. The student is also required to take course work in research.

The executive M.B.A. program, established in 1968, offers the M.B.A. degree in three years of evening instruction for experienced executives in the Vancouver area. The objective of the program is to provide a strong multidisciplinary education in administration. In addition to the division of some courses into functional areas, the program examines organizations as operating systems and focuses the subject matter by examining processes that cut across these functional areas. Moreover, students examine the interrelationship between the organization and its environment. Analytic and behavioral approaches receive equal emphasis in the general management perspective taken by the program.

In order to enter in good standing into the executive M.B.A. program, a student must demonstrate a working knowledge of elementary calculus, probability and statistics, and microeconomic principles. Twelve courses are subsequently taken over six semesters (excluding summer semesters). Nine of these courses are required and three are elective.

ADMISSION

Admission requirements for the M.B.A. program include a bachelor's degree in business with a minimum of 3.0 grade-point average (B), acceptable scores on the Graduate Management Admission Test (GMAT), strong letters of reference, balance in the instructional areas of the program, and acceptable Test of English as a Foreign Language (TOEFL) scores for those whose native language is not English. The maximum of students admitted in any one year is expected to be 30; therefore, admission will be highly competitive. Although the majority of students enter in the fall semester, students may be admitted in any semester.

Admission to the executive M.B.A. program is restricted to experienced executives. With the exception of a few outstanding executives who qualify without possessing a bachelor's degree, a degree in any discipline with a good second-class (B) standing is required. Referee's comments, career patterns, and scores on the GMAT are also considered. Students are admitted only in September each year. Applications must be submitted no later than April 1 for admission the following September.

EXPENSES

For the academic year 1984-85 costs were as follows:

Tuition fees, per semester $1,043
Student activity fee,
   per semester 26
Athletic recreation fee,
   per semester 9

During non-course-work semesters (that is, during writing of the research project or thesis), a registration fee of $129 is charged.

These fees cover tuition, books, instructional materials, student activity fees, and dinner on class meeting nights. There are additional fees for classes required for removal of deficiencies prior to admission to the program. A nonrefundable fee of $5 is charged at the time of initial application.

FINANCIAL ASSISTANCE

A limited number of teaching assistantships are available to selected qualified graduate students in the M.B.A. program. In addition, research assistant positions may be available, and there are other university scholarships and awards available to graduate students.

Normally, students enrolled in the executive M.B.A. program are employed full time during the program; therefore, no financial assistance is available. However, many firms provide assistance to their employees in the form of grants or tuition reimbursements.

CORRESPONDENCE

For further information, write to
   The Director, Graduate Programs
   Faculty of Business Administration
   Simon Fraser University
   Burnaby, British Columbia V5A 1S6,
   Canada

Sonoma State University, one of the 19 campuses of the California State University System, is located in Sonoma County 40 miles north of San Francisco. The campus is set amidst the scenic hills and countryside adjacent to the San Francisco Bay Area. It borders on the renowned Napa Valley and is a half-hour from the spectacular northern California beaches.

The university was founded in 1960 and currently has some 5,500 students enrolled. The School of Business and Economics has a faculty of 30 and over 1,000 students. It offers a Bachelor of Arts as well as a Master of Arts (M.A.) in management. The Department of Management also offers a joint program with the Psychology Department in organizational development.

Sonoma State University has a wide range of resources available to students. Among these services are a Career Development Center, an Office of Veterans Affairs, an Equal Opportunity Program for minority students, and an Office for Students with Disabilities. For foreign students there is a range of special services including the Sonoma State American Language Institute which offers a continual series of classes at the beginning, intermediate, and advanced levels for students who are not native speakers of English.

In addition to these services, the university has an outstanding library which has computer listings and access to the resources of all other libraries of the California State Universities as well as the University of California. The university's computer services include CYBER and PDP. In addition, there are two laboratories with Apple and IBM personal computers for student use.

PROGRAM OF STUDY

The primary objective of the graduate program in management is to prepare graduates for positions of leadership in the private sector, government service, and the community. Through a structured program of study, students receive training in all aspects of management requisite to prepare them to deal with the complex environment and strategic issues they will face upon graduation. The graduate will have gained proficiency in core courses in management theory, finance, marketing, operations management, and organizational behavior. In addition, the graduate will have mastered one area of concentration and applied his or her research and analytical skills to a variety of practical management issues. It is important to note that since many of the graduate students enter the program with prior work experience there is much learning that takes place from other students.

For students who enter the program without a previous degree in management or business administration, a series of basic core courses is offered. The prerequisite core includes courses in managerial economics, statistics, management theory and organizational behavior, managerial finance, operations management, the legal environment of management, human resource management, and accounting. Those with prior course work in any of these areas may be exempted from retaking those courses. The fields of concentration in the graduate program include international business, marketing, finance, human systems management, and management theory. Students are encouraged to take courses in related fields such as economics, computer science, psychology, and environmental studies.

The M.A. requires 30 units of course work plus a thesis, project, or comprehensive examination. A total of 21 units must be taken in residence while up to nine units may be transferred from postgraduate studies at another institution subject to departmental approval. A minimum of 18 units must be taken from courses within the School of Business and Economics. At least 20 units must be graduate courses, while up to 10 units may be selected from the undergraduate upper-division curriculum. The student's field of concentration will include a minimum of 14 units. Courses are four units with the exception of directed thesis research, internships, and special studies.

Students may elect to complete the program with a thesis, creative project, or comprehensive examination in their field of concentration. A full range of courses is available in the evening to accommodate the executive or working student. The minimum time required to complete the program for a full-time student is one year, but in practice since the majority of students are employed, two years or more may be required for completion.

In 1985, 66 new students entered the M.A. program, 10 were graduated, and at the end of the year 106 were enrolled.

ADMISSION

Admission to Sonoma State University in postbaccalaureate standing requires a minimum grade-point average of 2.50 (3.00 for foreign students) in the last 60 units attempted. Admission to the M.A. program in management is based on evidence that the student shows high promise of success in the program. Specific indicators of high promise considered are: (1) candidate's performance on the Graduate Management Admission Test (GMAT), (2) upper-division grade-point average prior to master's admission, and (3) a record of appropriate employment at increasing levels of responsibility. When using indicators (1) and (2) above, candidates showing high promise are defined as those obtaining a total of at least 1,000 points based on the formula: 200 times the upper-division grade-point average plus the GMAT total score. Supplementary evidence that a satisfactory level of scholastic competence will be maintained will be considered by the department screening committee. Foreign students must have a minimum score of 550 on the Test of English as a Foreign Language (TOEFL)..

Prerequisite course work is required in the fields of management theory or systems theory, managerial statistics, and in four of the following seven fields: accounting; legal, social, and economic environment of management; finance; marketing; quantitative methods; human resources and organizational behavior; organizational communication; and management information systems.

EXPENSES

For the academic year 1986-87, fees are as follows: residents of California, 0-6.0 units at $222.50; 6.1+ units at $342.50. Nonresidents of California pay $126 per unit in addition to registration fees. Summer session cost per resident unit is $71. Fees are subject to change.

FINANCIAL ASSISTANCE

A limited number of scholarships and loans are available to students. In addition, work-study and internships are available to qualifying students. Applications and information may be obtained by writing to the Financial Aid Office.

CORRESPONDENCE

For further details, contact
Graduate Coordinator
School of Business and Economics
Department of Management
Sonoma State University
Rohnert Park, California 94928

Southeast Missouri State University was established in 1873 in Cape Girardeau, Missouri. The city is along Interstate Highway I-55 in the Mississippi River Valley adjacent to the Ozark Mountains. The university serves approximately 35 counties in southeast Missouri including St. Louis county. The university serves both full- and part-time students. All Master of Business Administration (M.B.A.) courses designated for graduate students are offered only in the evening during the academic year. Courses which may be taken by both graduate and undergraduate students are offered during the day and in the evening.

PROGRAM OF STUDY

The Master of Business Administration degree program is designed to serve any undergraduate major. M.B.A. students must complete the following prerequisites as part of their plan of study before enrolling in 500- or 600-level courses. Students must have received a grade of C or better in undergraduate prerequisite courses or have received a grade of B or better in 500-level prerequisite courses.

Prerequisites for M.B.A.		*Credit Hours*
AC 500	Foundations of Financial and Managerial Accounting	3
EC 500	Foundations of Economics (Macro and Micro)	3
MG 500	Foundations of Management (Principles and Operations)	3
MK 500	Foundations of Marketing (Marketing and Consumer Behavior)	3
BE 252	Business Correspondence and Reports	3
FI 361	Corporation Finance	3
	Statistical Competency (Bus. Statistics)	
	Computer Competency*	
	Mathematical Competency (College Algebra)	

*CS 601 Computerized Information Systems will satisfy this competency and could be used as a graduate elective.

Other requirements include the following graduate courses:

M.B.A. Core		*Credit Hours*
AC 539	Managerial Accounting Strategies	3
EC 560	Managerial Economics	3
FI 660	Financial Management Strategies	3
MG 650	Organization Behavior	3
MG 658	Decision Systems for Operations Management	3
MK 640	Marketing Strategy	3
BA 610	Research Methods in Business Administration	3
BA 690	Studies in Business Policy Application	3
		24
Business Electives**		8
		32

**Students may take one 3-credit hour course from an area other than business if approved by the M.B.A. coordinator.

M.B.A. students must complete 32 hours of graduate courses, maintain a 3.0 grade-point average, and pass a written comprehensive examination. An M.B.A. research paper or creative project must be completed in conjunction with one of the 600-level courses taken as part of the M.B.A. program.

ADMISSION

Applicants who wish to enroll in the M.B.A. program must be admitted to graduate studies and have a baccalaureate degree or the equivalent from an accredited institution. Applicants must show potential for continued success as graduate students in business studies.

Major criteria used by the M.B.A. Admissions and Advisory Committee in evaluating applicants are as follows: (1) undergraduate grade-point average, (2) undergraduate grade-point average in last 60 hours, (3) score on the Graduate Management Admission Test (GMAT), and (4) employment and academic references (when requested).

Additional criteria used to evaluate international students will include the score on the Test of English as a Foreign Language (TOEFL). International students must also submit an Official Statement of Finances.

EXPENSES

Transcript evaluation fee	$10
Registration (per semester hour for resident students, maximum of $510)	73
Registration (per semester hour for nonresident students, maximum of $1,000)	143
On-campus, single student housing (per semester, estimate)	825-850

These expenses are subject to change each semester.

FINANCIAL ASSISTANCE

A limited number of assistantships and fellowships are available to highly qualified full-time students.

PLACEMENT

The facilities of the Office of Career Services are available to assist students and alumni in job selection.

CORRESPONDENCE

For further information on the M.B.A. program at Southeast Missouri State University, write or call

Dean of the College of Business and Public Administration
or
Coordinator of the M.B.A. Program
College of Business and Public Administration
Southeast Missouri State University
Cape Girardeau, Missouri
Telephone: 314-651-2112 or 314-651-2547

SOUTHEASTERN LOUISIANA UNIVERSITY

HAMMOND, LOUISIANA

Southeastern Louisiana University is located in Hammond, Louisiana, which has a population of approximately 20,000. Hammond is the largest city in Tangipahoa Parish (county) situated in southeastern Louisiana. Located at the junction of Interstate Highways I-55 and I-12, the university draws approximately 97 percent of its enrollment from an area within an 80-mile radius of Hammond. This drawing area includes all of both Baton Rouge and New Orleans.

PROGRAM OF STUDY

The Master of Business Administration (M.B.A.) is a professional degree that is offered as an interdisciplinary program by the various departments of the College of Business. The major objective of the graduate program in business administration is to prepare students to assume positions of leadership and responsibility in management by providing (1) a common body of knowledge that is applicable to the management of private, public and nonprofit organizations; (2) skills in the ability to identify problems, obtain relevant information, analyze alternative solutions, and implement chosen solutions; (3) experience at integrating the concepts and techniques from the various functional areas of business and applying them to organization-wide management problems; and (4) an understanding of the problems and opportunities afforded by the various environmental forces confronting management in all types of organizations.

Graduate-level requirements for the M.B.A. degree include the completion of 33 semester hours of graduate work with a B average. Degree candidates may not have earned more than six semester hours with a grade of C and no grade below C will be accepted for graduate credit. Specific course requirements are Accounting for Business Decisions, Managerial Economics, Financial Policies, Statistical Methods in Business and Economics, Organizational Theory and Behavior, Business Policy and Strategy, Information Systems Analysis and Design, and Marketing Administration. Approved graduate electives are selected from the fields of accounting, economics, finance, management, and marketing.

In addition to meeting requirements for admission into the M.B.A. program, students must have credit for, or will be required to take, the following undergraduate courses: (1) principles of accounting (six hours), (2) principles of economics (six hours), (3) the legal environment of business, (4) business finance, (5) business statistics, (6) production management, (7) management of organizations, and (8) principles of marketing. Students lacking no more than six semester hours of these prerequisite courses may also enroll in graduate-level courses while satisfying these undergraduate deficiencies. However, no student will be permitted to schedule graduate courses in any one of these subject areas until the appropriate prerequisite course(s) have been completed.

ADMISSION

Admission is open to qualified students who hold the baccalaureate degree from an accredited college or university. All applicants are required to submit scores on the Graduate Management Admission Test (GMAT) prior to being admitted to the M.B.A. program. In addition to the general requirements for admission to the Graduate School, applicants for admission to the Master of Business Administration program must meet one of the following requirements: have at least 950 points based on the formula of 200 × the overall undergraduate grade-point average + the GMAT score or have at least 1,000 points based on the formula of 200 × the junior/senior grade-point average + the GMAT score. Foreign students must present a score of at least 500 on the Test of English as a Foreign Language (TOEFL).

EXPENSES

Application fee (U.S. students)...	$ 5
Application fee (out-of-country students)	15
Registration fee, per semester hour...........	45
Nonresident fee, per semester hour...........	40
International student fee, per semester	60
Room rent with meals (seven-day plan)............	910

FINANCIAL ASSISTANCE

A limited number of scholarships and assistantships are available for full-time graduate students. Loans through commercial and governmental sources are also available.

PLACEMENT

The facilities of the College Placement Office are available to assist students and alumni in job selection.

CORRESPONDENCE

For further information on the M.B.A. program at Southeastern Louisiana University, write or call

Director of M.B.A. Program
Southeastern Louisiana University
Hammond, Louisiana 70402
Telephone: 504-549-2146

PROGRAM OF STUDY

The program leading to a master's degree in business administration at Southeastern Massachusetts University (SMU) is designed for students with three things in common: a bachelor's degree, the drive to learn more, and a need for practical business management skills.

Now in its second decade, the program has more than fulfilled its promise. One measure of its quality is the number of businesses that are willing to pay the cost of having their employees attend. As for the students, they are turning out to be just the people for whom the program was planned—males and females with diverse backgrounds, but with a common need for more management skills.

Although it is impossible to single out a "typical" student, there are some similar themes running through most of the students' careers. Several, for example, are engineers who find that they are now being asked to do more managing than engineering. Others have simply outstripped their old credentials; they even may be working in positions for which, under current standards, they couldn't be hired.

Designed with students such as these in mind, the program has several key features:

- classes are offered at a time when the working professional can best take advantage of them;
- the program is general enough to suit a broad range of needs, yet provides specific options;
- emphasis is placed on broad but practical applications.

Classes are given in the late afternoon (4-7 p.m.) and evening (6:30-9:30 or 7-10 p.m.) Monday through Thursday.

A generalist program is offered, but students can specialize in any of four subject areas through the elective portion of the program: marketing, management, human resources, and accounting and finance.

Throughout the program, emphasis is placed on the integration and synthesis of course material in terms of its applications to business policy decisions and administrative action. Written and oral expression, the handling of interpersonal relations, and the ability to design and carry out projects are stressed—with increasing emphasis on computer use.

All of this is presented in a modern educational environment on SMU's 710-acre North Dartmouth campus. The campus is a relatively short commute by major highways from nearly anywhere in southeastern Massachusetts. Students will find traffic generally light and parking accommodations more than adequate. Classroom activities are supported by complete computer facilities including access to a mainframe, super-mini, and various microcomputers as well as a 300,000-volume library with many individual study stations.

ADMISSION

Admission to the M.B.A. program is open to all qualified men and women who hold a bachelor's degree from an accredited undergraduate institution. A number of factors are considered in evaluating applications: the applicant's intellectual development as evidenced by previous academic work, the score on the Graduate Management Admission Test (GMAT), extracurricular activities, employment experience, references, and the applicant's comprehensive statement of objectives (required as part of the application).

Completed applications, GMAT score, transcripts, and reference forms should be submitted no later than April 15 for the fall semester and by August 15 for the spring semester. Applications received after these dates may not be processed before the beginning of classes.

Courses customarily meet one evening a week for two and three-quarter hours per session. Depending on foundation course preparation, a student taking two graduate courses per semester (considered to be a full load) during the academic year (from September to May) will be able to complete the required work for the M.B.A. in three years. Someone working full time should discuss taking more than two courses per semester with the program adviser before enrolling in the extra course(s).

EXPENSES

Graduate tuition, per credit hour . . $75
Registration fee 10
Student fee, per credit hour
  (maximum of $20 per
  semester) 3
Library fee, per credit hour
  (maximum of $15 per
  semester) 1

These figures may vary as time goes on. For current rates, please refer to the appropriate Division of Continuing Studies Course Announcement Bulletin.

CORRESPONDENCE

For additional information on the M.B.A. program at Southeastern Massachusetts University, write or call
  Dean Richard J. Ward
  College of Business and Industry *or*
  Richard D. Legault, Coordinator
    M.B.A. Program *or*
  Sandra White, Assistant to the Dean
  Division of Continuing Studies
  Southeastern Massachusetts University
  Old Westport Road
  North Dartmouth, Massachusetts 02747
  Telephone: 617-999-8000

Southeastern University's roots go back to 1879, when the Washington Young Christian Association (YMCA) first sponsored formal programs of study, including business courses. The university is chartered by the Congress of the United States and accredited by the Commission of Higher Education of the Middle States Association of Colleges and Schools. A primary objective of Southeastern is to provide an educational opportunity to responsible working individuals at a reasonable cost and at times convenient to their schedules. As an integral part of the Washington community, Southeastern has a working relationship with the federal government in a truly literal sense. Many faculty members hold federal appointments, while many students are government employees. Similarly, the university is linked to business establishments, law firms, and financial institutions in the community.

PROGRAMS OF STUDY

Southeastern University's Graduate School offers master's degree programs in seven principal areas: accounting, business administration, economics, finance, marketing, public administration, and taxation. The Master of Business Administration (M.B.A.) degree program offers specializations in the following areas: management, labor relations, international management, and productivity and acquisition management. The Master of Public Administration program offers concentrations in the following areas: government administration, health administration, and productivity and acquisition management. Although the majority of graduate courses are offered on weekends, some are available on weekdays.

The master's degree requires the completion of 36 credit hours. A maximum of nine credit hours may be applied towards the degree through transfer credit. A student must successfully complete a comprehensive exam during the final term or may elect to take nine additional hours of course work.

The university operates on a trimester system, which allows a student to continue taking a full-time load in the summer. A full-time graduate student at Southeastern must carry nine hours of credit per trimester and could expect to complete the program at the end of four trimesters.

There are 35 graduate faculty members, most of whom are adjunct faculty. For the most part, members of the faculty are outstanding professionals who work full time at the disciplines in which they teach.

ADMISSION

All applicants for admission to the Graduate School must hold an earned baccalaureate degree from an accredited college or university or an equivalent degree from a foreign university. Upon acceptance, applicants are assigned to one of the following categories: degree candidate, provisional student, or nondegree student. Degree candidates should have taken an undergraduate major in business administration, public administration, or a related field and maintained a minimum grade-point average of 3.0 in their undergraduate degree work. Other factors considered include undergraduate academic performance and scores on the Graduate Management Admission Test (GMAT).

Applicants will be classified as provisional students if they (1) do not meet minimum academic standards for admission [for example, low or no scores on the Test of English as a Foreign Language (TOEFL), low grade-point average, low or no scores on the Graduate Management Admission Test (GMAT) and/or lack of required prerequisite courses], but offer potential with "developmental" work, or (2) if they submit incomplete or unofficial documents at the time of application. A transfer to degree candidacy can occur after completion of nine credit hours at Southeastern University with a cumulative average of 3.0 or better. Students may also be placed in a provisional status if they lack a sufficient business-related background or if they demonstrate low proficiency in English. Transfer to degree status may take place after the successful completion of developmental or background course work. Applicants who are classified as special students will be allowed to take courses with the understanding that credit will not be applied toward a graduate degree at the time.

Nondegree students must submit an application and fee, although they do not have to file any supporting documents until they apply for a change of degree status. Students seeking degree candidacy who do not submit official transcripts may be admitted as nondegree students until official documents are received.

All applicants must submit a $25 application fee (nonrefundable) with the application. Official transcripts and GMAT scores should be sent directly to the Admissions Office. Admission criteria for international students are identical to that of domestic students with the additional criterion of adequate TOEFL performance. Applications are accepted for any of the three trimesters (fall, winter, or summer). After the receipt of all necessary documents, applicants are informed of the admission decision within two to three weeks.

EXPENSES

Tuition for graduate students is $150 per trimester hour ($450 per course). A $75 university fee is also charged at each registration. Books and supplies are estimated at $120 per semester. The university has no housing for graduate students; however, the Office of Student Services maintains a housing referral service.

FINANCIAL ASSISTANCE

Many individuals with high potential for success as students lack the personal financial resources to attend college. Realizing the important role of economics in a college education, Southeastern University has traditionally kept its tuition moderate and has made an effort to help students achieve their educational goals regardless of their economic status.

CORRESPONDENCE

For further information, please write
Director of Graduate Admissions
Southeastern University
501 I Street S.W.
Washington, DC 20024

College of Business and Administration

SOUTHERN ILLINOIS UNIVERSITY AT CARBONDALE

CARBONDALE, ILLINOIS

The College of Business and Administration at Southern Illinois University (SIU) is one of the nation's best-kept educational secrets. Located on a spacious, wooded campus, the college's 60-plus faculty include individuals who are recognized as outstanding scholars, teachers, and consultants. Over 30 of these have been selected as members of the graduate faculty to teach in the three graduate programs, which are accredited by the American Assembly of Collegiate Schools of Business (AACSB). To maintain the high quality and personal nature of these programs, total graduate enrollment is limited to a select group of 190 individuals who show high promise for successful careers. Most graduate courses do not exceed class size of 30, resulting in a close working relationship between members of the class and the graduate faculty. This personal attention produces graduates who have become leaders in business, government, and educational organizations, both in the U.S. and abroad.

Carbondale, a community cited in *The Best Small Towns in America,* is the economic center of southern Illinois. Located 100 miles southeast of St. Louis, Carbondale offers the advantages of a traditional "college town." Business and industry are also nearby, including plants operated by Norge Division of Magic Chef, Olin Corporation, and Phelps Dodge.

PROGRAMS OF STUDY

The College of Business and Administration offers programs leading to the Master of Business Administration (M.B.A.), Master of Accountancy (M.Acc.), and Doctor of Business Administration (D.B.A.) degrees. In addition, concurrent programs are offered, in conjunction with the School of Law, leading to Juris Doctor (J.D.)/M.B.A. or J.D./M.Acc. degrees. All programs are fully accredited.

The M.B.A. program has as its basic objective the development of professional managers and executives to serve the needs of business, government, and other organizations. A minimum of 36 semester hours of course work are required, including 27 hours of core business courses and 9 hours of electives. The M.B.A. program offers students the option of either pursuing a general education or specializing in courses offered by the Departments of Accountancy, Finance, Management, and Marketing or other departments of the university.

The objective of the M.Acc. program is to prepare students for careers as professional accountants in financial institutions, government, industry, nonprofit organizations, and public practice. At least 30 semester hours in accounting are required, and at least 15 of these must be at an advanced level. In addition, students must take courses covering each of the following areas: financial accounting and accounting theory, management accounting, management information and computer systems, financial and operational auditing, and taxation. Students may specialize in areas including, but not limited to, management advisory services, auditing, controllership, information systems, and not-for-profit accounting.

The D.B.A. program is designed to prepare individuals for faculty research and teaching positions in academic institutions and for high-level administrative or staff positions in business, government, and other organizations. Specific course work is planned through consultations between the student and an advisory committee of college faculty members, with the goal of serving each student's career objectives. Major D.B.A. concentrations are offered in accountancy, finance, management, and marketing.

ADMISSION

Admissions are granted on a rolling basis for any semester. Decisions are based on an assessment of the applicant's potential for success in graduate study and in a career afterward. This assessment is made by careful examination of undergraduate grades, scores on the Graduate Management Admission Test (GMAT), previous work experience, letters of recommendation, and personal essays. Applicants from countries where English is not the native language, whose undergraduate degree was not awarded by an accredited U.S. institution, must earn at least 550 on the Test of English as a Foreign Language (TOEFL).

EXPENSES

At the present time, tuition and fees for Illinois resident graduate students amount to approximately $762 per semester. Non-Illinois residents pay approximately $1,770.

The average cost of room and board in university residence halls is $2,224 per academic year. One- to three-bedroom apartments are available in university housing with rents varying from $224 to $306 per month, including utilities. Off-campus housing varies widely in price and quality.

FINANCIAL ASSISTANCE

Many graduate assistantships and some fellowships are available to qualified students on a competitive basis. In 1985-86, fellowships carry a stipend of $520 per month and tuition remission. Assistantships provide a stipend of $550 per month and tuition remission in exchange for 20 hours of work per week. This work consists of assisting faculty with teaching and research or providing administrative assistance. The university also offers various forms of tuition scholarships and student work programs.

PLACEMENT

Graduate students are assisted in placement both by the SIU Career Planning and Placement Center and by the faculty and administration of the College of Business and Administration.

CORRESPONDENCE

For further information or to request an application for admission, please write or call

Graduate Programs
College of Business and Administration
Southern Illinois University
Carbondale, Illinois 62901
Telephone: 618-536-4431

Southern Illinois University—Edwardsville, a 2,600-acre campus, is located on the Illinois side on bluffs overlooking the Mississippi River Basin, 17 miles northwest of downtown St. Louis. The university has an enrollment of more than 10,000, with over 2,000 graduate students. Master's level work is offered in some 35 fields, and doctoral-level work is offered in the School of Education. The library holdings exceed 800,000 volumes and continue to expand. The campus has received national acclaim for its outstanding aesthetic and functional qualities.

PROGRAM OF STUDY
The Master of Business Administration (M.B.A.) degree program provides an educational foundation upon which careers in management may be developed. The program has been designed with the management "generalist" in mind. The "generalist" approach is based upon the educational philosophy and experience that graduate business education can best serve the student's professional interests if it develops awareness, understanding, and competence to deal with the problems faced by line managers. Through graduate business study, candidates become knowledgeable in the disciplines underlying business operations and view business organizations as integrated systems. Attention is directed toward the management of human resources in the business firm and the economic, political, social, and international forces shaping the firm's external environment.

The program is designed to accommodate the student who is employed full time. Course offerings are scheduled during the 12 months so that a student may take one or two courses per quarter. It is expected that each foundation and core course will be offered at least once each year in one of the following formats: day, evening, or weekend.

The Master of Business Administration degree program requires a minimum of 48 quarter hours of graduate-level courses plus, when necessary, any courses needed to make up deficiencies in the student's educational background. Deficiencies are determined on an individual basis. Normally, such work will not exceed 32 quarter hours.

The program is designed to:
- prepare professional managers and executives for present and future administrative roles,
- facilitate the education of individuals employed full time who wish to earn the M.B.A. degree as part-time students,
- provide a broad-based administrative core with the option to select electives beyond the core in the respective business disciplines.

The foundation courses are designed to provide the student who is missing basic business courses with the opportunity to prepare for graduate-level work. Students may be given waivers in the foundation courses on the basis of undergraduate course work or proficiency examinations.

The program of study has been designed for the individual who desires to continue his or her professional development through graduate study. Proven educational innovations are combined with currently accepted administrative practices to offer an unusual approach to continuing graduate study in business. Courses in the core are Managerial Accounting, Managerial Economics, Financial Management, Corporate Policy Formulation and Administration, Advanced Organizational Behavior, Marketing Management and Policy, and Operations Management.

Electives provide the student with the opportunity to study at least two areas in some depth. Students must take 20 hours of elective courses with not more than four courses in one area. Electives are available in all business and economic specialties. A comprehensive examination is required.

ADMISSION
An M.B.A. degree policy committee supervises admission to the program. Admission requirements of the Graduate School are to be met, and all applicants to the program must take the Graduate Management Admission Test (GMAT). In making decisions, the policy committee is guided by the American Assembly of Collegiate Schools of Business (AACSB) standards. To be admitted to the program, applicant's scores on the following formula must exceed 950: 200 × undergraduate grade-point average (A = 4.0) + GMAT; the GMAT score must be equal to or greater than 400; and verbal and quantitative scores must exceed 20.

EXPENSES

Quarter Hours	4	6-11	12-18	19 & over
Tuition				
Illinois resident	$117.20	$234.85	$ 352.30	$ 381.60
Out-of-state resident	351.60	$704.55	$1,056.90	1,144.80
Fees	53.20	72.75	82.25	95.55
Total Illinois resident	$170.40	$307.60	$ 434.55	$ 477.15
Total Out-of-state resident	$404.80	$777.30	$1,139.15	$1,240.35

Information about housing may be obtained from the University Housing Office.

FINANCIAL ASSISTANCE
Financial assistance, fellowships, and graduate assistantships are also available and are awarded by analysis of individual case applications.

PLACEMENT
Placement assistance is offered to students through the university placement services.

CORRESPONDENCE
For further information or to request an application for admission, write to
Dean
School of Business
Southern Illinois University—
Edwardsville
Box 1051
Edwardsville, Illinois 62026

The Edwin L. Cox School of Business at Southern Methodist University (SMU) offers a unique one-year, three-trimester program for full-time students. Also offered is a three-year, part-time program for those who wish to continue working while pursuing their M.B.A. degree. Dual degrees are offered in law/business, arts administration/business, and engineering/business.

The school is located in University Park, a municipality that is centrally located in Dallas. The SMU campus is only five miles from the center of downtown Dallas. The Dallas/Fort Worth metroplex is one of the fastest growing areas in the United States and offers M.B.A. students a Sunbelt location plus a vital evolving relationship with the business community.

PROGRAMS OF STUDY

The philosophy of the school is to emphasize the development of an administrative perspective as well as of general management skills. Through a program that encompasses both academic study and exploration in the business community, the school trains broadly educated general managers who have the ability to make strategic planning and tactical operating decisions in a business environment.

The full-time program requires one calendar year of study, from August to August. Each student takes 30 credit hours of required courses and 18 credit hours of elective courses, for a total of 48 credit hours. Core courses are required in accounting, management science and computers, economics, finance, marketing, individual and organizational behavior, operations management, the legal environment of business, and management of the total enterprise.

The three-year part-time program is designed for students who wish to continue working while pursuing their M.B.A. degree. Classes meet on weekday evenings and Saturday mornings. The degree requirements are the same as those for the full-time program.

During the M.B.A. program, the student is given the opportunity to compress a concentrated learning experience into a short period of time. The core courses

comprise a well-integrated curriculum of fundamental business subject areas. Subsequently, the student, through his or her own initiative, plans a program of elective courses to suit individual career goals.

A variety of teaching methods are used including the case method, lectures, discussion, and independent and group projects.

The M.B.A. program is staffed by 69 full-time faculty members with a strong commitment to teaching and research. Endowed chairs are held by distinguished scholars in financial management, real estate, organizational behavior and administration, accounting, and management information systems.

A two-year executive M.B.A. program is offered for middle management and senior executives sponsored by their firms. Information may be obtained from the Director of Executive Programs.

ADMISSION

The Admissions Committee seeks to measure the applicant's potential for a professional career in business or management and for academic success in the M.B.A. program. A candidate must hold a bachelor's degree or its equivalent from an accredited institution. Each applicant is required to submit a typewritten application, transcripts from all colleges and universities attended, two recommendations, and scores from the Graduate Management Admission Test (GMAT).

International students must also submit scores from the Test of English as a Foreign Language (TOEFL) and a certificate of financial responsibility. Preliminary applications for foreign students are available through the address below.

The full-time program begins in August only. Part-time students may enter in August or January.

EXPENSES

Estimated expenses for a single student for the entire one-year program (1985-86 academic year):

Tuition	$13,150
General student fees	1,250
Living expenses	7,820
Books	680
	$22,900

FINANCIAL ASSISTANCE

Scholarships and assistantships are awarded by the Cox School of Business to students selected on the basis of demonstrated academic achievement and managerial promise. Need-based assistance, such as loans and grants, are available through the university Office of Financial Aid. Students should apply before March 1 to be eligible for M.B.A. scholarships and priority need-based financial assistance.

PLACEMENT

The unique relationship of SMU with the Dallas business community is invaluable in the job search and in career counseling. Establishing contacts with business representatives and key executives is an unlimited source of career information and provides an opportunity to nurture contacts the student might otherwise never have been able to make. Each year companies and organizations interview M.B.A. candidates through the SMU Career Center. Other companies list openings by mail and telephone. These companies represent a variety of industries, fields, and opportunities throughout the country.

CORRESPONDENCE

For further information on the programs of study offered at SMU, please write or call

Director of Graduate Admissions
Edwin L. Cox School of Business
Room 32-G
Southern Methodist University
Dallas, Texas 75275
Telephone: 214-692-2630

Southern Oregon State College (SOSC) is located in Ashland within convenient walking distance of the city's center. Ashland, with a population exceeding 14,000, has a campus covering 175 acres in the foothills of the Siskiyou Mountains at the southern end of the Rogue River Valley. The Division of Business of Southern Oregon State College was formed in 1963. Since that time, the school has maintained a rapid growth, and today approximately 900 students major in business administration. In 1977, the legislature of the State of Oregon authorized SOSC to offer a Master of Science in Business Administration (M.S.B.A.).

PROGRAM OF STUDY
The Master of Science in Business Administration degree is designed for both those who hold a degree in business as well as for those who hold a baccalaureate degree in another discipline. The program is designed to provide advanced study for the business man or woman and/or give professional people an opportunity for growth in current areas of business and management. The degree is specifically designed to allow the candidate an opportunity to broaden horizons and to specialize in a specific area of interest, for example, accounting, management, or marketing.

The M.S.B.A. degree requires 45 term hours in three phases: (1) a 15-hour core consisting of Administrative Accounting; Business, Society, and Policy; Management of Human Resources; Statistical Applications for Management; and Business Research; (2) 15 term hours of graduate business electives in the student's selected area of interest; and (3) 15 term hours of electives, 6 of which must be in graduate economics and the remaining 9 of the student's choice.

The M.S.B.A. degree may be earned through full- or part-time study or a combination of both. The student has a seven-year period in which to complete the 45 hours of course work. A comprehensive written examination is a requirement of the M.S.B.A. degree. There is no thesis or foreign language requirement. The program may be started during the fall, winter, spring, or summer term.

ADMISSION
The school welcomes applications from men and women who will have received the baccalaureate degree from an accredited college or university. The applicant must have earned above-average grades and obtain an acceptable score on the Graduate Management Admission Test (GMAT).

EXPENSES
Graduate tuition, per term, for 1985-86 was as follows:
Residents, full-time
  (9 to 16 hours) .... $ 718
Nonresidents, full-time
  (9 to 16 hours) 1,147
Tuition for part-time students is based on a sliding scale; complete information may be obtained from the Registrar's office.

FINANCIAL ASSISTANCE
Graduate assistantships are available to applicants eligible for regular admission who have a B.B.A. or similar degree. A resume and two letters of recommendation are needed, and applicants should have all papers filed by March 15 for consideration for the following year. Other financial assistance is available through the Office of Financial Aids.

PLACEMENT
An active Placement Bureau is maintained for all students and alumni of Southern Oregon State College.

CORRESPONDENCE
For further information, write or call
  Coordinator of Graduate Studies in
    Business
  School of Business
  Southern Oregon State College
  Ashland, Oregon 97520
  Telephone: 503-482-6484

SOUTHWEST MISSOURI STATE UNIVERSITY
SPRINGFIELD, MISSOURI

Established as the Missouri State Normal School, Fourth District, by legislative statute in 1905, Southwest Missouri State University (SMSU) has evolved into a multipurpose institution of higher education. SMSU, the largest of the five regional state universities, is located in Springfield, the third largest city in Missouri, with a metropolitan population of over 200,000. The compact, attractive Springfield campus encompasses 121 acres, serves over 16,000 students, and employs over 1,200 full-time faculty and staff. The College of Business Administration, one of six colleges at SMSU, has an enrollment of approximately 3,200 undergraduate and 120 graduate students.

PROGRAMS OF STUDY
The College of Business Administration at SMSU seeks to acquaint students with a broad understanding of the total business environment. Graduate programs are designed to prepare the student for a managerial, professional, or administrative career in business, government, education, and not-for-profit institutions.

The College of Business Administration offers graduate courses through the Departments of Accounting (ACC), Finance and General Business (FGB), Computer Information Systems (CIS), Management (MGT), Marketing (MKT), and Office Administration and Business Education (OBE). The Department of Office Administration and Business Education offers the Master of Science in Education (M.S. in Ed.) degree—directed primarily toward the teaching of business subjects at the secondary school level.

The Master of Business Administration (M.B.A.) degree is a business school degree with courses taken in various departments. The program is specifically designed for students who hold undergraduate degrees in arts, science, engineering, and law, as well as for students who hold baccalaureate degrees in business administration. The program is designed to provide the background knowledge necessary for professional practice in the field of business. Students with an undergraduate degree in areas other than business administration must complete 28-31 prerequisite hours in the following areas: accounting, economics, statistics, computer information systems, finance, law, management, marketing, and operations management. Students

with appropriate prior academic preparation in business and economics may complete the program in one calendar year.

The M.B.A. degree requires 33 semester hours plus any prerequisite requirements. All students are required to complete a 21-hour core distributed in the following areas: managerial finance, managerial accounting, economic analysis, organization theory and behavior, advanced marketing theory and problems, quantitative methods for business decisions, and business strategy and policy. For the remaining hours, students may concentrate in an area of their special interest—economics, data processing, finance, management, marketing, or office administration. A written comprehensive examination over the core requirement and the student's area of concentration is given during the student's final semester.

The Master of Arts (M.A.) in accounting program offers a concentrated course of study in the technical aspects of accounting and is designed to fulfill the needs of professional accountants. Of the minimum of 33 hours required for the degree, 24 must be completed in accounting courses determined by the program.

ADMISSION
Admission to the M.B.A. or the M.A. in accounting program is granted to graduates of accredited colleges and universities who fulfill the following provisions:
- the student must have received a bachelor's or master's degree from a regionally accredited college or university;
- the student must have attained an undergraduate grade-point average of at least 2.75 for the last 60 hours of academic work and have achieved a satisfactory score on the Graduate Management Admission Test (GMAT).

Students who do not meet the minimum grade-point average but who have a record of satisfactory business experience or a strong performance on the GMAT will be considered for probationary admission.

Applicants from foreign countries whose native language is not English are required to submit scores on the Test of English as a Foreign Language (TOEFL). Normally, TOEFL scores of 550 or higher are required for admission.

Qualified applicants may enter the program at the beginning of any semester; however, applicants are encouraged to apply well in advance of the graduate school deadline.

EXPENSES
Semester expenses for tuition and incidental fees for full-time students are $612 for in-state students and $1,224 for out-of-state students. University housing, as well as private apartments and households, are available. Room and board in university housing ranges from $900 to $970 per semester for single students. Off-campus housing will vary from $300 to $1,200 per semester depending on size and location.

FINANCIAL ASSISTANCE
A limited number of assistantships are available. A stipend of $4,750 per academic year and a waiver of tuition and fees normally accompanies each assistantship. Loans, part-time employment, and some cooperative education placements are available.

PLACEMENT
Services of a full-time Placement Office are available to graduate students. Several hundred companies and governmental agencies conduct on-campus interviews each semester. Graduates have found a wide variety of placements in all areas of the United States.

CORRESPONDENCE
For further information, write or call
Director of Graduate Studies
College of Business Administration
Southwest Missouri State University
Springfield, Missouri 65804
Telephone: 417-836-5373

Southwest Texas State University (SWT), established in 1899, has grown from a two-year normal school to a multipurpose university with an enrollment of more than 18,000. Located at the foot of the Texas Hill Country, Southwest Texas State University enjoys a setting that is unique among Texas universities. The beauty of the crystal clear San Marcos River and many sprawling cypress and pecan trees on the campus add to the charm of this picturesque locale. Although major metropolitan centers are not far away, San Marcos has managed to retain the charm of a smaller community, and Southwest Texas State University still has a real university atmosphere—a place where faculty and students take the processes of teaching and learning seriously.

PROGRAM OF STUDY
The School of Business at SWT offers the Master of Business Administration (M.B.A.) degree program. The M.B.A. program emphasizes tools and knowledge needed for professional success. The curriculum provides generalized training and development of each individual rather than confining students to narrow specializations. The M.B.A. degree is designed to provide an integrated framework of course material logically sequenced through three distinct program phases: core, electives, and a capstone course.

The M.B.A. degree may be earned under either a thesis or nonthesis plan. Under the thesis plan, the student must satisfy the common body of knowledge (background courses), plus 30 semester hours of graduate-level courses. Under the nonthesis plan, the student must satisfy the common body of knowledge, plus 36 hours of graduate-level courses. A comprehensive examination covering the M.B.A. core areas is required. A core of 24 graduate hours must be completed under either program.

Graduate-level M.B.A. courses meet once per week on the campus in the evening for three hours. A limited number of core courses and electives are offered in the summer during the day. Full-time students normally complete the 12-course graduate sequence in one calendar year. Part-time students normally take two courses per semester with the summers off. If the normal part-time sequence is followed, the graduate curriculum can be completed in three years.

ADMISSION
Applicants to the M.B.A. program must achieve a satisfactory admission index as determined by a combination of the applicant's Graduate Management Admission Test (GMAT) and the overall or upper-division (last 60 hours) grade-point average of the baccalaureate degree. Applicants not submitting a GMAT score, but possessing an overall 3.00 grade-point average or an upper-division grade-point average of 3.25, may be admitted for one semester only, during which time they must submit a GMAT score that in combination with the grade-point average meets the minimum admission index requirements. International students are also required to demonstrate adequate performance on the Test of English as a Foreign Language (TOEFL) and, in some cases, the Test of Spoken English (TSE).

Application materials should be submitted no later than the following deadlines in order to ensure processing for the desired semester: July 15 for fall semester admission, December 1 for spring semester admission, April 15 for first summer session admission, and June 1 for second summer session admission. An application form and Graduate Bulletin may be obtained by writing to the Dean of Graduate Studies and Research.

EXPENSES
Texas resident tuition (up to 12 semester hours)	$144
Nonresident tuition, per semester hour	120
Fees, per semester	191

Tuition and fees are subject to change.

FINANCIAL ASSISTANCE
The Office of Student Financial Assistance awards aid on the basis of financial need, starting with the highest need factors and awarding aid until funds are depleted. Meeting the application priority dates is important as there is a limited amount of aid to be distributed to students, and those applications completed by priority dates will be considered first. Applications and all required documentation must be on file by the following priority application dates: May 1 for fall semester, October 15 for spring semester, and March 15 for summer. These are "priority dates" and not deadlines. However, if a student applies and/or completes the financial aid records after these dates, he or she faces the increased possibility that funds will not be available. More information can be obtained by contacting the Director of Student Financial Assistance.

PLACEMENT
Employment information and services are available through the Center for Counseling and Placement. A job placement file will be prepared for any student who requests it. The office also assists graduating students and alumni in finding employment, posts notices of job openings, and arranges on-campus interviews for employer representatives.

CORRESPONDENCE
For further information, please contact
Director of the M.B.A. Program
School of Business
Southwest Texas State University
San Marcos, Texas 78666

Stanford University's Graduate School of Business (GSB), located on the Stanford campus 35 miles south of San Francisco, offers a two-year, full-time Master of Business Administration (M.B.A.) degree program. Within the M.B.A. program are special options in public management and health care administration as well as a four-year M.B.A./Juris Doctor degree program in cooperation with the School of Law. The Graduate School of Business does not offer part-time, evening, or summer M.B.A. programs. All admitted students enter in fall quarter only.

Stanford also offers a Doctor of Philosophy program and a nine-month Master of Science in Management degree program (Stanford Sloan Program, which is limited to 42 fully sponsored executives from industry and the public sector, from the U.S. and abroad). In addition, during the summer a variety of general and specialized executive management programs are offered.

PROGRAM OF STUDY

The Stanford M.B.A. program seeks to prepare students for senior-level general management careers in business and other organizations. Its concentration is clearly future oriented; through its curriculum and faculty research, the program seeks to anticipate the roles of managers 10 to 30 years ahead while developing the decision-making approaches necessary to manage in a rapidly changing environment.

The school is committed to providing each student with the primary foundations of management. These are the ability to analyze problems, to weigh alternatives and make decisions, and to implement these decisions. One hundred and eight quarter units (27 courses) are required for graduation. The 13-course core curriculum provides a set of analytical tools sufficiently fundamental to be relevant to a broad range of management problems.

The first-year core is designed to develop understanding and competence in four broad areas. The first, the internal or organizational environment of the firm, is concerned with human behavior and the way in which people function in different organizational structures and situations. A second area focuses on the external environment of the firm, the economy, and society. In the third area, students are introduced to the functional areas of accounting, finance, marketing, and operations. Finally, a fourth area is devoted to developing skills in the application of quantitative techniques to management problems, including computer and general information systems.

The first year is intensive and structured; however, required courses are complemented with three electives. Also, all core courses may be exempted by examination; the exempted course is replaced by any advanced course offered within the school.

The second year of the program provides students with the opportunity to choose from a broad range of courses in areas of management of particular interest. Seven faculty groups (accounting, decision sciences, economic analysis and policy, finance, marketing, organizational behavior, and strategic management) offer courses. Up to 16 units (four courses) may be taken in other departments of the university. Students are encouraged to take courses in any and all areas applicable to future career aspirations.

ADMISSION

The task of the Committee of Admissions is to select, from an applicant pool of approximately 5,000 candidates, the 318 students who evidence both a strong academic background and the potential for success as professional managers. The GSB encourages applications from qualified U.S. and international candidates. Admission is competitive and only a portion of the qualified applicants, whether from the U.S. or abroad, can be accepted. Applications are evaluated in relation to the overall applicant pool in a given year.

A completed application includes selected biographical data, employment history, responses to a series of essay questions, three recommendations written by persons of the applicant's own choosing, academic transcripts, application fee, and results of the Graduate Management Admission Test (GMAT). Applicants whose native language is not English or who have not completed their university study in a U.S. institution must also submit results from the Test of English as a Foreign Language (TOEFL).

From the application, the committee derives information about, but not limited to, such issues as the candidate's demonstrated motivation, academic aptitude, communicative and interpersonal skills, maturity, achievement orientation, capacity to command the respect of others, energy level, and ability to exploit opportunities and resources.

EXPENSES

A budget for the the nine-month 1985-86 academic year for a single student was $19,860 and for a married couple without children, $25,950. These figures include tuition ($11,100) and living expenses and will increase for the academic year 1986-87.

FINANCIAL ASSISTANCE

The M.B.A. program has a limited fellowship program. Loans are available from government, Stanford, and private sources for citizens and permanent residents of the United States and Canada. Repayment schedules vary from 5 to 15 years, beginning one to six months after graduation; some accrue interest during the in-school period.

CORRESPONDENCE

For M.B.A. details, write
 Office of M.B.A. Admissions
 Graduate School of Business
 Stanford University
 Stanford, California 94305
 Telephone: 415-723-2766
For Ph.D. details, write
 Office of the Doctoral Program
 Graduate School of Business
 Stanford University
 Stanford, California 94305

STATE UNIVERSITY OF NEW YORK AT ALBANY
ALBANY, NEW YORK

The State University of New York (SUNY) at Albany is a major university center providing academic programs from the bachelor's through the doctoral level in many areas of the arts and sciences and in several professional schools. The main campus is located on a 350-acre site and includes a strikingly modern complex of buildings designed by Edward Durell Stone, one of the world's foremost architects.

PROGRAMS OF STUDY
Graduate study in the School of Business stresses abiding principles rather than present expedience, sharpened analytic powers rather than the accumulation of information, and broad development rather than narrow specialization. The school's programs have many innovative aspects and feature relatively small classes, close student/faculty contact, and requirements tailored to individual student needs. Graduate degrees offered include a Master of Business Administration (M.B.A.) and a Master of Science (M.S.) in accounting, both of which are available for full- or part-time students.

The M.B.A. program provides a comprehensive education in business administration for holders of bachelor's degrees in arts and sciences, engineering, or professional areas. In the first semester, coverage of the disciplines of mathematics, statistics, economics, behavioral science, and accounting is achieved in a modular format which allows each student to adapt the program to his or her special needs. The second semester introduces concepts and methodologies from the functional areas of operations management, marketing, finance, and human resource management and begins the development of an integrative view of the management process. Team teaching, a business game, and group projects are used extensively.

The second year of the M.B.A. program builds skill in depth in one area on the firm foundation of the first year. The principal educational vehicle is the subprogram, which includes intensive course work taught in small groups and a major faculty/student team project conducted in a major corporation. Subprograms currently available include marketing, finance, human resource management/ human resource information systems, management information systems, and operations management. The second-year program also includes course work in business policy and the social, legal, and political environment of business.

The field projects with major corporations, a dynamic, young faculty deeply committed to program development and innovation, and small classes with ample opportunity for interaction with the faculty and fellow students are major features of the SUNY-Albany M.B.A. program. The close contact with companies, which is a required aspect of the M.B.A. program, has proven to be an excellent vehicle for job placement.

The Master of Science program in accounting is available in two versions—a 30-hour program for students with an undergraduate degree in accounting or business administration and a two-year program for students without prior training in accounting.

The newly developed two-year accounting program is designed to prepare bachelor's degree holders in such nonbusiness areas as arts and sciences or engineering for a career in accounting, one of the fastest growing professions. Courses in the program are compact and efficient. Requirements in economics, statistics, and finance are coordinated with the M.B.A. degree.

Students entering the 30-hour program in accounting must hold a bachelor's degree in accounting or business administration which includes at least 21 hours of accounting; 6 hours each of business law, finance, and economics; and 3 hours of statistics. Deficiencies may be made up by taking work beyond the 30-hour program requirement.

Both accounting programs are registered with the New York State Education Department. Successful completion of either program reduces the experience requirement for the C.P.A. certificate by one year.

ADMISSION
Full-time students are admitted only at the start of the academic year in September. Part-time students may enter in September, January, or June. The school seeks candidates whose undergraduate record, scores on the Graduate Management Admission Test (GMAT), recommendations, and experience indicate a commitment and clarity of purpose that will likely predict success in the mature environment of a graduate program. The real-world focus of the school's programs causes the admissions committee to place important emphasis on the personal qualities conducive to effective business performance. International students must apply through the centralized foreign student admissions office of the university.

EXPENSES
The following is a schedule of estimated expenses for full-time graduate students for the academic year:

	New York State Resident	Out-of-state
Tuition and other fees	$2,160	$3,180
Books (approximate)	400	400
Room (double occupancy) and board (except lunches)	2,150	2,150
Health and accident insurance	111	111
	$4,821	$5,841

FINANCIAL ASSISTANCE
A number of assistantships are available to academically qualified students. Full appointments carry cash stipends of $4,100 and include a full tuition waiver. Partial assistantships carry stipends of $4,100 and include a waiver of half of the tuition.

CORRESPONDENCE
For further information or to request an application for admission, please write or call
Office of the Dean
School of Business
State University of New York at Albany
1400 Washington Avenue
Albany, New York 12222
Telephone: 518-442-3955

In September 1962 the University of Buffalo merged with the State University of New York, giving added impetus to its development as one of the leading academic institutions in the nation. Total enrollment is in excess of 26,000 students. The School of Management was founded in 1927; graduate programs were established in 1935.

PROGRAMS OF STUDY

The Master of Business Administration (M.B.A.) program is so designed that a student begins study in the fall semester. It is possible for some students to start their program in the spring semester. Students accepted for the fall semester may commence their course work in the summer session. A part-time evening M.B.A. program is available. The M.B.A. prerequisites include a bachelor's degree from an accredited institution, with an undergraduate average indicating ability to progress beyond the bachelor's level, satisfactory performance on the Graduate Management Admission Test (GMAT), and two letters of recommendation. In addition, those applying for the evening program must have completed at least one year of relevant work experience at the time of admission and three years by the completion of the program.

The School of Management day M.B.A. curriculum is divided into two tracks: business and public. All students in the program complete core courses relating to fundamental disciplines essential to management. The next level introduces basic courses in either the business or public area, depending on the student's interest. Electives are then chosen in an option, concentration, or selectively.

At present, there are eight options in the M.B.A. program. They are (1) financial planning and control, which provides preparation for careers requiring in-depth knowledge of corporate accounting and finance as applied to planning and control functions; (2) health care systems management, which develops skills in applying quantitative and behavioral techniques to the management of health care delivery systems; (3) human resources management, an option designed for those who wish to assume a career role in the professional personnel-manpower development field; (4) managerial economics and policy, which prepares a student to serve as an applied economist and policy analyst in either the public or private sector; (5)

management information systems, which is designed to provide the skills necessary to function in an entry-level position within either an MIS group or a functional user area in the public or private sector; (6) marketing management, an option which provides sufficient training for entry-level line and staff jobs in marketing, and a broad enough perspective on all operational areas in marketing to prepare students for managerial careers; (7) professional accounting, which is designed for those students interested in meeting the educational requirements for the C.P.A. examination in New York; (8) management science, offered for those students with a background in mathematics who wish to utilize quantitative methods in solving complex business and not-for-profit sector problems. Students may also concentrate in the more traditional areas (management policy, operations analysis, etc.). The public management track will prepare students for public sector management careers.

The school has several dual graduate degree programs with other units of the university; for example, the Law School, School of Architecture, and the Department of Geography. Applicants interested in dual graduate degree programs are advised to contact both schools involved.

Students presenting courses in business administration and economics or other relevant areas may request that these courses be evaluated for partial fulfillment of the M.B.A. program. The minimum residency requirement for the M.B.A. degree is 30 credit hours.

Programs leading to the Doctor of Philosophy (Ph.D.) degree in management are offered in each of the departments of the School of Management. A master's degree is not a prerequisite for admission. The requirements for the Ph.D. are not stated to be a specific number of credit hours. The equivalent of four academic years of full-time study beyond a baccalaureate completed in a related area is the normal standard. A doctoral dissertation is required.

Candidates for the degree of Doctor of Philosophy in management select an area of concentration from among the following fields of study: accounting, managerial economics and policy, finance, human resources, management science, management systems, marketing, and organiza-

tion. Supporting fields of study are to be selected from the above and from offerings of other departments.

EXPENSES
Tuition and fees for full-time graduate students are $2,150 for New York State residents and $3,735 for out-of-state students per year.

FINANCIAL ASSISTANCE
The Helen Crosby Scholarships were established in 1926 and are awarded on a one-time basis to four new students with outstanding credentials. Each fellowship carries a modest stipend.

Minority fellowships are awarded by Carborundum (SOHIO), Marine Midland Bank, and Westwood Pharmaceuticals, Inc. A Graduate and Professional Opportunity Program fellowship is also available.

Research assistantships and part-time instructorships are available to Ph.D. candidates in management. Appointments carry cash stipends up to $7,298 per academic year, plus a waiver of all tuition, excluding the university fee.

The student is advised to contact the Regents Examination and Scholarship Center, 99 Washington Avenue, Albany, New York 12214 for information on types of assistance that may be available for New York State residents.

PLACEMENT
The school has an Office of Career Development Services that offers specific counseling and placement activities designed to enhance the student's career search. Also, the facilities and services of the university's Career Planning Office are available to management students.

CORRESPONDENCE
Please write to
Mrs. Arlene R. Bergwall
Director of Student Affairs (M.B.A.)
Dr. Lawrence D. Brown,
Ph.D. Program Chairman
School of Management, Jacobs Management Center
State University of New York at Buffalo
Buffalo, New York 14260

STATE UNIVERSITY OF NEW YORK
MARITIME COLLEGE
FORT SCHUYLER, BRONX, NEW YORK

The Graduate Study Program of the State University of New York (SUNY) Maritime College was established in 1968 to offer instruction leading to the Master of Science (M.S.) degree in transportation management. As a specialized unit within the State University of New York, the Maritime College seeks to serve the needs of the transportation community within its fields of expertise. The program is highly specialized, and the student body now numbers over 200 men and women.

PROGRAM OF STUDY
The program provides graduate-level education in the field of transportation management through
- developing in the student a pattern of original and creative thought,
- developing skill in analyzing and solving problems,
- identifying the vital issues confronting the transportation industry.

As implemented, the program serves full- and part-time, primarily evening, students.

The Master of Science degree in transportation management may be based on a bachelor's degree in the arts, science, engineering, or business. The program consists of 18 credits in management core courses, 18 credits of transportation business/management, economics, systems and logistics and/or marine insurance and maritime law electives, and 3 credits of thesis seminar for a minimum total of 39 credits. On a rotating basis, 75 credits of electives are offered.

Prerequisite courses in accounting, quantitative analysis, economics, business law, and information systems, not applicable to the degree requirements, will be waived when justified and appropriate to avoid repetition of completed work at the undergraduate level in an accredited institution.

A maximum of nine credits completed at another institution may be accepted toward the degree. Such courses with a minimum grade of B must have been taken at the graduate level in an institution accredited and authorized to grant graduate degrees. Each candidate must satisfactorily complete a graduate research seminar and an acceptable thesis in a field of specialization.

Independent study is emphasized. Graduate students have the ability to enrich their educational experience and career opportunities because classes are held in view of one of the world's finest and busiest ports. The Port of New York and New Jersey contains a comprehensive cross section of both traditional and sophisticated transportation modes. In Manhattan and Brooklyn, docks transfer thousands of tons of break-bulk cargo, while the port container terminals include the most modern maritime techniques and electronics in the industry today.

Adjacent to the campus are numerous additional examples of transportation management in action, via international airports, transcontinental railroads, pipelines, truck terminals, inland waterway vessels, and extensive public mass transportation systems.

Weekly evening tutorial meetings are held in lower Manhattan at the New York State Office Building, 270 Broadway. At approximately monthly intervals throughout the semester, students meet at the college at Fort Schuyler. At these meetings lectures by the instructor and guests supplementing the syllabus will be given, examinations held, and demonstrations conducted.

ADMISSION
Admission is based on evidence of sound scholarship and mature motivation. All candidates are required to take the Graduate Management Admission Test (GMAT) and achieve a score acceptable to the Maritime College. Evaluation of undergraduate transcripts is also involved. Work experience is considered closely.

While admission to the program allows students to attend classes, a student wishing to receive the M.S. degree must achieve matriculation status. Matriculation is achieved when the student obtains 950 points based on the following formula: the cumulative grade average of the first 12 credits completed at Maritime multiplied by 200 plus the total Graduate Management Admission Test score.

Students are admitted for the fall term in late August, for the winter term in January, and for the summer term in late May.

EXPENSES
Tuition, per credit

Part-time, in-state	$ 90.00
Part-time, out-of-state	156.00
Full-time, in-state	1,075.00
Full-time, out-of-state	1,867.50

CORRESPONDENCE
For further information, please write or call
> Graduate Study Program
> SUNY Maritime College
> Fort Schuyler, Bronx, New York 10465
> Telephone: 212-409-7285

Stephen F. Austin State University is located in Nacogdoches, Texas, a city of 30,000 in the heavily forested section of east Texas. Total enrollment of the university is approximately 12,500; about 35 percent of the students are enrolled in graduate or undergraduate programs in business or economics. In an impressive setting of pine trees and natural beauty, the university has some 20 major instructional buildings and 19 dormitories.

PROGRAM OF STUDY

The Master of Business Administration (M.B.A.) degree is obtained through a broad field program that requires a core of graduate business courses. In addition to the core requirements, the student is encouraged to develop professionally through a diverse exposure to the business disciplines.

An emphasis is also offered in international management. The program allows the student to develop knowledge of the social, political, and managerial aspects of business in a multinational environment.

The M.B.A. program consists of four parts. Parts I and II are the core requirements. Part I of the program, the common body of business knowledge, is 24 semester hours in length. This part includes the following courses: Acc 501—Financial Accounting, MGM 502—Quantitative Analysis, CSC 501—Introduction to Computers and Information Processing, MGM 512—Seminar in Management, ECO 515—Managerial Economics, MGM 571—Production/Operations Management Seminar, FIN 504—Seminar in Finance, and MKT 578—Seminar in Marketing.

A student with a baccalaureate degree in business administration from an accredited school may waive a maximum of 18 hours of the Part I requirements. The waiver, if any, is made by the graduate adviser in business and the head of the department responsible for the course.

Part II of the M.B.A. program is the required core and will be assigned to each person seeking the M.B.A. degree. The courses in Part II include ACC 511—Accounting for Management, MKT 513—Marketing Management, FIN 514—Financial Management, MGM 517—Administrative Policy, and ADS 537—Legal and Social Environment of Business. The total hours for Part II are 15.

Part III of the M.B.A. program is provided to allow the student to develop an in-depth knowledge of a particular functional area. The student will, with the assistance of the adviser, select a minimum of nine semester hours of 500-level electives from any area or combination of areas in the School of Business.

Part IV of the program is six hours of free electives.

ADMISSION

Entrance to the M.B.A. program is open to students having any baccalaureate degree. It is not necessary to have any previous business courses in order to be admitted.

Students seeking admission to the M.B.A. program must present a satisfactory score on the Graduate Management Admission Test (GMAT). Students should take this test sufficiently early so that the scores may be received by the university before the date of admission. In order to be admitted, a person must have an acceptable combination of grade-point average (GPA) and test scores on the Graduate Management Admission Test. A candidate will be admitted based upon one of the following formulas: 1. (overall GPA $\times$ 200) + GMAT = 950 *or* 2. (upper-division GPA $\times$ 200) + GMAT = 1,000.

Persons meeting either of these criteria may be granted admission to the program. Persons not having these will be denied admission to the M.B.A. program. No one will be admitted without a GMAT score.

EXPENSES

All Texas resident students attending the university during the regular semester will pay a $100 tuition fee for 1 to 8 semester hours plus approximately $12 per semester hour in excess of 8. All non-Texas resident students will pay a registration fee of $120 per hour. All full-time students will also pay a student service fee of $7.50 per semester hour and a general fee of $6.00 per hour.

During each term of the summer session full-time Texas resident students will pay a $50 tuition fee, and nonresident students will pay a tuition fee of $120 per hour. All students will pay a student service fee of approximately $7.50 per semester hour and a general fee of $6.00 per hour.

The cost of room and board in college dormitories ranges from $1,122 to $1,310 per semester and approximately $475 per summer term of six weeks. All dormitories are air-conditioned.

FINANCIAL ASSISTANCE

Loans, work-study arrangements, and assistantships are available to qualified students.

PLACEMENT

Stephen F. Austin State University maintains an active Placement Office to assist students and former students seeking employment. The Placement Office does not control jobs but serves as the liaison between those interested in employment and business, industry, public schools, and colleges seeking employees.

A completed placement folder consisting of personal data, transcripts, and references is maintained as a permanent record. Folders are sent to prospective employers at the student's request.

CORRESPONDENCE

Inquiries should be addressed to
Dr. Marlin C. Young
M.B.A. Adviser
Stephen F. Austin State University
Post Office Box 13004-SFA Station
Nacogdoches, Texas 75962
Telephone: 409-569-3101

STETSON UNIVERSITY

DeLAND, FLORIDA

John B. Stetson University, founded in 1883, is the oldest institution of higher education in the state of Florida. The university has long recognized the importance of business studies, continuously offering a business curriculum since 1885—longer than any university in Florida. Stetson's many business alumni hold executive positions in business throughout Florida and the nation.

Stetson is primarily concerned with creating an effective learning situation in the classroom. The university maintains a low student-faculty ratio to assure strong student-faculty interaction in the classroom and the capacity to deal with students individually.

Davis Hall, the site of the School of Business Administration, is a modern classroom and faculty office building well suited to effective teaching. The university's various libraries house more than 400,000 cataloged items, including a strong business collection. The university has recently installed a new computer for academic purposes only, providing both students and faculty ample capacity and facilities for research and study.

The university is located in central Florida, the state's fastest growing area, convenient to transportation, attractions, and recreation. The location offers a gentle climate and attracts a varied student body and a faculty of high quality. The university is fully accredited by the Southern Association of Colleges and Schools as well as a variety of professional and specialized accrediting agencies.

PROGRAM OF STUDY
The Master of Business Administration (M.B.A.) program is designed to provide graduates broad competence in administration and managerial decision making. The program is clearly structured, requiring a maximum of 60 hours of course work.

The course of study is divided into two broad areas—the business foundation and the advanced-level courses.

Business Foundation	*Semester hours*
Microeconomics	3
Production and Operations Management	3
Business Statistics	3
Principles of Accounting	6
Principles of Management	3
Principles of Marketing	3
Introduction to the Computer	3
Business and Society	3
Business Finance	3

The courses in the business foundation are designed to provide the students with the basic concepts and techniques needed in the advanced-level courses. Thus, the foundation work must be completed before advanced-level work is attempted. If students have had prior academic work in business, those courses already completed may be waived.

Advanced-Level Courses		*Semester hours*
Atg 510	Managerial Accounting	3
Atg 515	Advanced Financial Accounting	3
Fin 503	International Business and Finance	3
Fin 511	Advanced Financial Management	3
Qm 507	Operations Research	3
Mgt 509	Business and Its Environment	3
Mgt 519	Organizational Theory	3
Mkt 516	Marketing Management	3
Mgt 599	Administrative Policies	3
IS 591	Computer Based Information Systems	3

The advanced-level courses present a structured program that offers students the opportunity to develop professional-level capabilities across a broad range of functional and technical areas. In addition to the M.B.A. program, Stetson offers the Master of Accountancy. This program is designed for students who have completed an undergraduate degree program in accounting.

ADMISSION
Graduates of accredited universities who have received a baccalaureate degree are eligible to apply for admission to Stetson's M.B.A. program. The undergraduate degree need not be in business administration. The course of study is specifically designed to accommodate the nonbusiness as well as the business degree holder. Indeed, combining the M.B.A. with a non-business undergraduate degree is considered outstanding career preparation in many fields.

Application requires official transcripts of all undergraduate work, scores from the Graduate Management Admission Test (GMAT), and letters of recommendation. International students must also provide upon application, evidence of a score of not less than 550 on the Test of English as a Foreign Language (TOEFL). Application materials must be submitted to the director of the M.B.A. program 30 days prior to the beginning of a term to ensure consideration for that term. Students may apply for admission for the fall, spring, or summer terms.

Applications will be evaluated by the Graduate Committee of the School of Business. Acceptance is based on undergraduate academic performance, GMAT score, and evidence of leadership and experience.

Stetson University does not discriminate on the basis of race, color, physical handicap, national and ethnic origin, or sex in its admission or educational policies.

EXPENSES
Charges for graduate course work at Stetson are $120 per semester hour.

FINANCIAL ASSISTANCE
Stetson offers a full range of financial aid programs including scholarships, grants, loans, and student employment. Application for assistance should be made through the Financial Aid Office. No special financial aid is available at this time for foreign students.

PLACEMENT
The Office of Career Planning and Placement, staffed by full-time professional counselors, assists students in evaluating career opportunities and locating employment.

CORRESPONDENCE
For further information, write or call
Office of Graduate Business Programs
Stetson University
Box 8398
DeLand, Florida 32720
Telephone: 904-734-4121, extension 635

The Department of Management at Stevens offers a curriculum that shows how the analytical methods of management apply to the complex problems of modern organizations. In the department's view, dealing properly with these problems calls for informed consideration of their quantitative, economic, and behavioral aspects. The curriculum stresses the balance and interaction that must be maintained among these three approaches, and the disciplines behind them, for effective management action; and it integrates the different concepts and methodologies inherent in each discipline in the handling of real-world situations.

The department enrolls some 250 primarily part-time students in its master's programs and grants approximately 60 degrees a year. About 14 students are engaged in doctoral work. At the undergraduate level the department has close relations with students in the engineering and science curricula, playing a central role in the school's recently adopted systems, planning, and management program. The permanent faculty of 15 is organized along disciplinary lines, including core groups in operations research, management economics, and behavioral science.

The programs are particularly well suited for working managers in the metropolitan New York-New Jersey area who want to upgrade their management skills through a concentrated evening program and for psychology majors seeking a graduate program that emphasizes industrial applications.

PROGRAMS OF STUDY
The department offers the following four degrees:

• Master of Management Science, a predominantly evening program, is designed to develop professionals in management science through emphasis on the basic disciplines underlying the management process. The program consists of a group of core courses in operations research, management economics, and behavioral science (six to eight) and a group of electives in application areas. Well-developed concentrations exist in management information systems and business economics. Thirteen courses are required for a degree.

• Master of Science (Management) is a program concerned with the tools for the effective and efficient utilization of human resources. The orientation is basically an emphasis on practical approaches but with some understanding of their theoretical underpinnings. At least two years of practical experience are expected for admission. Twelve courses are required for the degree.

• Master of Science (Applied Psychology) is a professionally oriented program for students who want to practice psychology in industry. Two concentrations are available, one in human performance, the other in industrial/organizational psychology. Each program includes a group of core courses in methodology, theory, and application together with a group of specialized courses and electives. Twelve courses (thesis optional) are required for a degree.

• Doctor of Philosophy is a research program requiring at least one year of residence. Two concentrations are available, one in management systems, the other in applied psychology. Each is built on the appropriate master's degree.

The department conducts various applied research programs in management information systems, expert systems, business economics, human performance, and human resource development. The latter programs incorporate the systems approach to such problems as manpower evaluation, police selection, discrimination in employment, and employee motivation.

ADMISSION
Applications are presently being accepted for the fall, spring, or summer terms. Standards include a college degree with above-average performance and ability to do graduate work. Undergraduate preparation normally should include courses in calculus, probability, economics, psychology, and computer programming, depending on the student's area of study.

EXPENSES
Tuition for graduate students is at the rate of $310 a credit (two and one-half credits per course).

FINANCIAL ASSISTANCE
Both research and teaching assistantships in limited numbers are available for qualified students.

PLACEMENT
The resources of the Stevens placement office run by the Alumni Association are available to graduates of the program. In addition, a number of companies apply to the department directly for referrals.

CORRESPONDENCE
For further information, write to
Graduate Admissions Office
Stevens Institute of Technology
Castle Point
Hoboken, New Jersey 07030

Suffolk University, founded in 1906, is located in Boston on historic Beacon Hill adjacent to the Massachusetts State House. The university is accredited by the New England Association of Colleges and Secondary Schools and the National Association of Schools of Public Affairs and Administration.

Presently, 67 full-time students and 857 part-time students are enrolled in the Master of Business Administration (M.B.A.) program. For students interested in federal, state, or local government service, the School of Management offers a Master of Public Administration (M.P.A.) program which enrolls 36 full-time and 142 part-time students.

Graduate student research opportunities abound in the numerous university and public libraries in the greater Boston area. In addition, Suffolk University's proximity to the downtown Boston business district and the Route 128 industrial complex provides students with opportunities to observe practical business in a dynamic setting. For students whose interests lie in the area of government administration, Boston's Government Center and the Massachusetts State House are a one-minute walk from the campus. The university's urban location thus provides the graduate student with a myriad of opportunities for part-time employment while in school and career placement upon graduation. In addition, Boston's world famous educational and cultural institutions provide a stimulating setting in which to pursue graduate studies.

PROGRAMS OF STUDY
The objective of the School of Management is to provide broad management education with the limited opportunity to concentrate in a functional area such as accounting, computer information systems, finance, marketing, management, or general business. In achieving this objective, a variety of teaching methods are employed including case studies, computer-based business games, role playing, and "live" case studies. The M.B.A. and M.P.A. programs are conducted in the day, the evening, and on Saturday. Sessions are conducted in the fall, spring, and summer. Most students with appropriate preparation can complete the M.B.A. program in one year of full-time study or two years of part-time evening work. The intent of the M.B.A. and M.P.A. programs is to provide men and women with the broadly based analytical and decision-making abilities that are necessary to assume managerial positions in business, government, or other nonprofit sectors of society.

The M.B.A. program is open to students with an undergraduate concentration in business or economics, as well as to those who present an undergraduate degree in other areas. Those students with an extensive background in business, accounting, or economics can complete the program with 30 semester credit hours as follows: Organizational Dynamics and the Management Process, Strategic Marketing, Management of the Production Process, Capital Management, Statistical Analysis for Managers, Managing in the External Environment, Business Policy, and four graduate electives. Advanced graduate electives are available in computer information systems, financial and management analysis, organizational development, taxation, personnel and labor relations, and international business.

Students without an extensive background in business, accounting, or economics are required to take up to 30 hours of courses which have not previously been taken from among the following prerequisite core courses: Introduction to Computer Information Systems, Graduate Financial Accounting, Graduate Managerial Accounting, Managerial Principles, Marketing Principles, Quantitative Analysis, Managerial Economics, Business Law, and Managerial Finance.

The following graduate and postgraduate programs are also offered by the School of Management: executive M.B.A.–Saturday program for persons with five years' professional experience, executive M.P.A.–Saturday program; Advanced Professional Certificate program–post-M.B.A. study; M.P.A. program with a concentration in health administration; M.P.A./Juris Doctor (J.D.) program.

ADMISSION
All applicants for admission to the M.B.A. program must submit scores on the Graduate Management Admission Test (GMAT). Entering students must have an undergraduate degree from a recognized institution and should have a grade-point average of 2.5 or better. Admission to the M.B.A. and M.P.A. programs is on a rolling admission basis. Applications for the executive programs are required one month prior to the starting quarter.

EXPENSES
Tuition for full-time study in the M.B.A. program is $6,810 per year, part-time is $681 per three-credit course. Full-time study in the M.P.A. program is $6,600 and part-time study is $660 per three-credit course.

FINANCIAL ASSISTANCE
Graduate fellowships, teaching assistantships, and loan funds are available. Applications must be received no later than April 1 for fall and November 10 for spring. Opportunities for part-time employment are available in the Boston area.

PLACEMENT
The university placement office provides career counseling and placement services for students and alumni.

CORRESPONDENCE
For further information, please write or call

Director of Graduate Admissions
Suffolk University
8 Ashburton Place
Boston, Massachusetts 02108-9911
Telephone: 617-723-6834

SUL ROSS STATE UNIVERSITY

ALPINE, TEXAS

The Division of Business Administration is dedicated to thorough scholarship and selects its faculty not only for their ability to teach but also for their ability to contribute to the extension of knowledge in the field of business and economics. The division takes pride in the quality of its graduates and their career success.

The university is located in Alpine, designated in several environmental studies as one of the five best U.S. cities in which to live. The Big Bend Alpine country and climate is also an ideal environment for serious study.

PROGRAM OF STUDY

The Master of Business Administration (M.B.A.) program gives a student the opportunity to increase professional skills, status, and earning potential, in addition to growing toward greater personal fulfillment by integrating the theoretical and the practical aspects of business administration. Study can be pursued on a part-time or full-time basis. The Master of Business Administration degree may be attained either through a 30-hour program with a thesis or through a 36-hour program without a thesis. Such a program may be completed in a minimum of 12 months.

One basic course in each of the following areas is required of all students: research and reporting, management, marketing, finance, accounting, quantitative analysis, and managerial economics. This core curriculum is pursued early in the program so that each student has an opportunity to explore all of the subject areas within business before taking more specialized courses. In order that the student may be exposed to topics of current interest in business, several of the elective seminar topics are rotated and chosen by professors each semester. In this program the student is given the opportunity to develop leadership potential by practicing the whole range of management actions in the classroom and through on-site small business, industrial, and agricultural problem solving. The advantages of small classes and frequent student-professor contact make the learning process more enjoyable, personal, and fulfilling.

Majors are offered in accounting, agribusiness, international trade, and advanced management. The international trade program places special emphasis on Latin American and Asian trade.

ADMISSION

Applicants for the M.B.A. program at Sul Ross should have a baccalaureate degree from a recognized institution of higher learning. For full admission the student must have at least 12 semester hours of advanced courses in business administration and economics on the undergraduate level. In addition, the student must have a score of no less than 450 on the Graduate Management Admission Test (GMAT), an overall grade-point average of no less than 2.5 on a 4-point maximum system, and a grade-point average in business administration of no less than 3.0. A student may be granted admission on a conditional basis with a score of 350 on the GMAT, an overall grade-point average of 2.3, and a grade-point average in business administration courses of 2.5.

In addition to the above requirements, international students must obtain a score of 520 on the Test of English as a Foreign Language (TOEFL) or certification of achievement in an English Language Program. Upon admission to the M.B.A. program, international students must make a housing deposit of $75, which is refundable if the student does not enroll, and pay an application fee.

Students may enter the M.B.A. program in January, June, July, or September. All application procedures must be completed before full admission status is granted.

EXPENSES

Costs are estimated for the 1985-86 academic year (two semesters); tuition and fees are subject to change without notice.

	Texas Resident	Out-of-State or International
Tuition and fees	$ 652	$3,344
Room and board	2,340	2,340
Books and supplies	200	200
Total	$3,192	$5,884

Additional tuition and living expense will be incurred for the summer session. Married students may rent furnished cottages and apartments for as low as $160 per month.

FINANCIAL ASSISTANCE

Sul Ross offers a limited number of graduate assistantships which are awarded on the basis of merit. Limited loans are available to qualified students with insufficient resources to cover educational expenses. Application for financial assistance should accompany application for admission to the university. Interested students should submit applications for graduate assistantships by April 1 for consideration for the fall semester.

PLACEMENT

Sul Ross State University maintains a full-time placement service for students and alumni. The Placement Center invites companies and government agencies to interview students on campus. The office also provides a placement file to prospective employers at a student's request.

CORRESPONDENCE

For further information regarding the M.B.A. program, write or call
   Graduate Dean
   Sul Ross State University
   Alpine, Texas 79832
   Telephone: 915-837-8053

The School of Management has been offering graduate programs since 1947. The Crouse-Hinds School of Management Building, opened in 1983, contains classrooms of various sizes, computer terminal facilities, a graduate student lounge, the school's placement office, and offices for over 100 faculty and graduate assistants.

Enrollment numbers 300 full-time students, who represent 100 undergraduate colleges and universities. Women make up 33 percent of enrollment, and 60 percent of the students have prior full-time work experience.

PROGRAMS OF STUDY

The focus of the Master of Business Administration (M.B.A.) program is on providing students with an education in general management and the opportunity, should they wish, to develop a concentration in any of eight areas. Both qualitative and quantitative approaches to managerial decision making are presented to students in a relatively equal manner. Eleven required core courses and 9 elective courses are included in the 20-course, 60-credit curriculum.

"Flexibility" is the key to the Syracuse M.B.A. program. Students may (1) select a major from accounting, finance, international business, management information systems, marketing, operations management, personnel and industrial relations, or transportation; (2) develop their own "individualized" major if none of the above meets their interests; (3) enroll in elective courses offered elsewhere in the university, including the College of Law, the Newhouse School of Communications, the Maxwell School of Public Administration, the College of Engineering, the School of Computer Science, and the College of Arts and Sciences.

Further examples of the M.B.A. program's flexibility are that students may (1) be exempted from required courses if they have an adequate amount of undergraduate course work in the area—such exemption shortens the length of their program as it is not necessary to substitute an elective course for an exempted course, (2) attend classes in the summer thereby shortening the time period required to complete their program, and (3) participate in an optional corporate internship program and acquire corporate experience while enrolled in the program.

The M.B.A. program faculty is a talented and accomplished group of scholars who represent a broad range of academic and business experience. Through teaching in management development programs, consulting, and research activities they maintain a close association with the business world and are thus able to integrate practice with theory in the classroom.

Classes in the M.B.A. program are small with an average class size of about 30 students. The case method, computer games and simulations, as well as the traditional lecture/discussion approaches to teaching are used. The environment of the school is characterized by openness, friendliness, and cooperation among students, faculty, and administration.

Other graduate degree programs offered by the school include the Master of Science in accounting, Juris Doctor (J.D.)/M.B.A. and J.D./M.S. in accounting in cooperation with the College of Law, M.P.S. in media administration offered jointly with the S.I. Newhouse School of Communications, and a Doctor of Philosophy in business administration.

ADMISSION

Successful applicants will be those who show the greatest promise of satisfactorily completing the academic program and of achieving successful careers in management. Therefore, each applicant is evaluated individually based upon his or her background and qualifications. No specific undergraduate majors or courses are required or preferred for admission. Prior full-time work experience, although encouraged, is not mandatory. Personal evaluative interviews are strongly suggested to help assess the applicant's interests and background as well as maturity, motivation, and leadership ability. Academic achievements, performance on the Graduate Management Admission Test (GMAT), and recommendations are also considered.

Applications should be submitted by June 30 for fall admission, December 1 for spring admission, and May 1 for summer admission. Applications received after these dates will still be considered pending availability of space. Admitted applicants may defer their admission for up to two years.

EXPENSES

Tuition in the 1985-86 academic year was $229 per credit. For a normal course load of 30 credits per academic year, tuition was $6,870. Total costs, including living expenses and books, are estimated at $13,000 for nine months. University housing is available for single and married students. Off-campus housing is plentiful.

FINANCIAL ASSISTANCE

Over 20 percent of M.B.A. program students receive fellowships, assistantships, or scholarships. These are awarded on a competitive basis with prior academic achievement and GMAT performance the primary selection criteria. Fellowships carry a stipend of $6,175 and 30 credits remitted tuition; assistantships a stipend of $4,500 and 24 credits of remitted tuition; scholarships are for remitted tuition in amounts varying from 12 to 30 credits per year.

The National Direct Student Loan and College Work-Study employment programs are available to students who demonstrate financial need.

PLACEMENT

The school maintains its own placement office for students and alumni. It provides career and job counseling; assistance in resume preparation; practice interviewing, including video-taping; a computerized position referral system; hosting of numerous companies who recruit at the school; and preparation of an annual resume book distributed to over 500 companies. In 1985, graduates of the M.B.A. program averaged $30,000 in starting salary.

An optional internship program enables students to obtain corporate experience during the academic year with companies in the Syracuse area.

CORRESPONDENCE

For further information, please write or call

Jack Huebsch, Assistant Dean
School of Management
Syracuse University
Syracuse, New York 13210
Telephone: 315-423-3850

TEL AVIV UNIVERSITY

TEL AVIV, ISRAEL

The Faculty of Management—Leon Recanati Graduate School of Business Administration is the largest faculty in Israel where instruction and research are conducted in all areas pertaining to management. Located in the city of Tel Aviv, it is near the hub of Israel's business life. The faculty offers programs on both the undergraduate and graduate levels. Bachelor's degree programs include accounting and management. A very broad range of graduate programs is offered leading to a master's degree and a Doctor of Philosophy in business administration.

PROGRAMS OF STUDY

Studies of the Master of Business Administration (M.B.A.) degree include 34 semester units. (Each semester unit represents a 75-minute meeting once a week during one semester.) The curriculum is divided into four phases. Noncredit preparatory courses are required in introductory mathematics, statistics, economics, behavioral science, computers, and English. (An exemption exam is given.) Basic required courses provide knowledge and analytical tools in disciplinary studies. These include fundamentals of management, finance and accounting, marketing, production management, and quantitative methods. A minimum grade of 75 in this phase is required to continue studies toward the M.B.A. degree. Courses within a chosen concentration include required and elective courses, and advanced seminars. The concentrations offered are finance and accounting, banking, insurance, production management, marketing, international management, information systems, organizational behavior, and operations research. Two advanced required courses, business policy and the business game, conclude the curriculum. An individually tailored, accelerated program is available, as is a continuing studies program for M.B.A. graduates.

The Master of Management Science (M.Sc.) program trains management specialists in a specific field. This program is available in three areas: operations research, information systems, and organizational behavior. The program emphasizes the study of scientific methods in the solution of management problems. The curriculum is composed of 24 semester units of course work and seminars plus a thesis. In addition, a student may be required to take additional noncredit preparatory courses in some field, depending on academic background. The program endeavors to be as flexible as possible in order to make maximum use of the student's background and interests. The student will be required, however, to acquire advanced knowledge in some functional area of management, for example, marketing or finance.

The Master of Management in Health Systems, offered jointly with the Faculty of Medicine, prepares students for management positions in the health sector. The three-year, 36-semester-unit program includes noncredit preparatory, required and elective courses; a specialization, including a summer field project; and a thesis. The curriculum combines management theory, techniques and tools, and their application.

The Ph.D. program in business administration will consider candidates who have completed a master's degree that included a thesis. Doctoral students are required to spend at least two years in full-time residence at the university. For further information, contact the Chairperson of the Doctoral Program.

ADMISSION

Students may enroll three times a year; at the start of each new semester (October, February, and July). Applicants to the M.B.A. program must have a bachelor's degree from an accredited college or university with a minimum average grade of 70 in order to apply. Classes are conducted in Hebrew, and a knowledge of the language is necessary (Hebrew language courses are offered). Applicants are required to take the Graduate Management Admission Test (GMAT).

Applicants to the M.Sc. program will be considered if they have a bachelor's degree from an accredited college or university and a grade-point average of at least 80 or a B grade. Applicants to the information systems program are required to take the GMAT.

The programs in operations research and information systems admit students whose undergraduate degree is in mathematics, statistics, economics, engineering, and in certain cases, in other disciplines in the social or exact sciences.

The program in organizational behavior admits students whose undergraduate degree is in sociology, behavioral science, social work, education, or business administration.

The program in health systems management is open to applicants with an undergraduate average of 75 or an advanced degree, subject to the decision of a joint admissions committee.

EXPENSES

Approximate annual tuition (two semesters) is $1,100 for full-time students (subject to change). Summer semester tuition is charged per semester unit and will amount to not more than 50 percent of full-time tuition. On-campus housing is limited.

FINANCIAL ASSISTANCE

The school makes an effort to provide an opportunity for all students whose achievements prove their ability for advanced study in business administration. Candidates may apply for scholarships and grants.

CORRESPONDENCE

For further information, please write to
  Admissions Committee
  Faculty of Management—
    The Leon Recanati Graduate School
    of Business Administration
Tel Aviv University
P.O.B. 39010
Ramat Aviv, Tel Aviv 69978, Israel
Telephone: 03-420-521, 420-722

Temple University is part of the Pennsylvania Commonwealth System of Higher Education. Business courses were first offered at Temple in the year 1884, and the bachelor's and master's programs in the School of Business Administration are accredited by the American Assembly of Collegiate Schools of Business (AACSB). The university is located in Philadelphia, a major financial services center and corporate headquarters for a major number of American businesses. The Master of Business Administration (M.B.A.) program is offered at three campuses: Main, Ambler, and Center City.

Dormitory facilities and apartments for graduate men and women are available. Interested applicants should apply to the Director of Residence for information about accommodations.

PROGRAMS OF STUDY

The M.B.A. program of study, while providing for specialization in a selected field, is primarily concerned with the advanced study of broad business concepts and relationships. The purpose is to develop individuals who can assume leadership positions in business concerns, nonprofit institutions, and public administrative entities.

The fields in which the specialization may be taken are accounting, actuarial science, chemistry, economics, finance, health administration, industrial relations, computer and information sciences, risk management and insurance, international business administration, marketing, human resource administration, operations research, physical distribution, real estate and urban land studies, and statistics.

The degree requires the successful completion of 36 credits plus demonstration of proficiency in each of the subject-matter areas fundamental to business. These areas include accounting, management information systems, economics, finance, human resource administration, operations management, marketing, mathematical analysis, and statistics. Proficiency in an area may be demonstrated by passing a first-year graduate course in the subject, passing a special examination, or having a strong foundation in appropriate undergraduate courses.

Graduate courses are available in the late afternoon and evening for the convenience of students who are actively engaged in business. Selected graduate courses are available during the day for full-time or part-time students. The university uses the semester system, and applicants are accepted for the fall, spring, and summer semesters.

The school also offers a Master of Arts (M.A.) and Doctor of Philosophy (Ph.D.) in economics, M.A. and Ph.D. in computer and information sciences, Master of Science (M.S.) and Ph.D. in applied statistics, and M.S. and Ph.D. in business administration.

ADMISSION

Admission to the M.B.A. program is open to students who have a baccalaureate degree from a recognized college or university. No previous academic training in business is required; the program is open to graduates in science, liberal arts, education, engineering, or other fields. In evaluating an application for admission, primary emphasis will be given to the undergraduate record and scores on the Graduate Management Admission Test (GMAT). Students whose native language is not English must also submit scores on the Test of English as a Foreign Language (TOEFL). The applicant's intellectual development during the course of his or her academic career, extracurricular activities, employment experience, and evidence of motivation for graduate study will also be considered.

In order that requests for admission to the Graduate Division may be acted upon promptly, an applicant for the September semester is required to take the GMAT no later than January. Application, transcript, and test score must be submitted by April 15 for admission in September, by September 30 for January, and by March 15 for summer sessions.

EXPENSES

Tuition for graduate courses in the part-time M.B.A. program is $142 per credit hour for Pennsylvania residents and $179 per credit hour for others.

FINANCIAL ASSISTANCE

Graduate assistantships are offered each year from September to May. Assistantship awards carry a stipend of $5,000 for the academic year in addition to tuition remission. Graduate assistants will ordinarily assist faculty members in their research projects. Graduate assistants are expected to work 20 hours per week. Tuition remission scholarships are also available. (A larger number of assistantships and some fellowships are available for doctoral candidates.)

To be eligible for assistance, an applicant must take the Graduate Management Admission Test no later than January, and all other credentials must be received by the School of Business Administration no later than March 15. An application for assistance will be mailed upon request.

PLACEMENT

The M.B.A. placement program, coordinated by the Career Development Center prepares M.B.A. students for career planning and job placement. Services include placement counseling, job-finding seminars, weekly employment listings featuring M.B.A. vacancies nationwide, placement in summer internships, co-op programs and part-time jobs, the publication of an M.B.A. resume book sent to 300 major corporations, and an opportunity for on-campus interviews with over 250 leading business, industry, and government employers.

CORRESPONDENCE

For additional information, please write to
Director, M.B.A. Program
School of Business Administration
Room 1, Speakman Hall
Temple University
Philadelphia, Pennsylvania 19122
Telephone: 215-787-7672

The Master of Business Administration (M.B.A.) program of Tennessee State University was established in 1971 at the former University of Tennessee at Nashville to offer evening instruction leading to the M.B.A. degree. The Downtown Campus of Tennessee State University is located in the heart of Nashville, two blocks from the State Capitol. Enrollment is approximately 150 students at the present time.

PROGRAM OF STUDY

The primary purpose of the M.B.A. program is to provide professional training for working men and women who wish to improve their managerial abilities and rise to more responsible positions in business, government, and nonprofit organizations. While the program is designed to serve both full-time and part-time students, particular emphasis is placed on meeting the needs of working adults who can only pursue their graduate studies on a part-time basis in the evening. More concretely, the major objectives of the program are

• to promote the intellectual growth of the individual student by means of interdisciplinary training including behavioral as well as quantitative approaches;

• to develop student research skills necessary for dealing with the economic, political, and social aspects of administration;

• to provide the student with an adequate base for continuing self-education;

• to enhance the educational process through student and faculty involvement in community problems and potentials; and

• to develop competence in the administration of business, government, and service organizations and stimulate interest in improving the economic performance of these institutions.

Insofar as possible, the overall program of study for each student is designed to meet his or her educational needs. Students learn not only from class instruction but also from the interchange of experiences with fellow students and independent research, which—where possible—is related to the student's own employment sector. In addition to traditional lectures and seminars, methods of instruction include forums where business and government professionals with outstanding managerial experience are invited to discuss with the faculty and students some of the relevant and timely issues pertaining to their field of endeavor.

The M.B.A. program includes a core of required courses totaling 22 semester hours and 12 hours of electives that may be used to concentrate in a functional area of business. The specific functional areas of concentration available are accounting, economics, finance, general business, management, marketing, and real estate and urban development. This curriculum enables a working student, who has all the necessary undergraduate prerequisites, to complete the program in six semesters when taking courses on a half-time basis.

ADMISSION

A holder of the bachelor's degree from an accredited institution, regardless of undergraduate major, may be admitted to the program depending on undergraduate grade-point average and scores from the Graduate Management Admission Test (GMAT). If a student does not have the necessary undergraduate foundation in accounting, finance, management, marketing, statistics, economics, and mathematics, he or she will be admitted on a conditional admission status and be required to take selective prerequisite courses prior to gaining unconditional admission status.

Students may be admitted prior to the beginning of each semester, but students are advised to send their application, undergraduate transcripts, and GMAT scores to the Graduate School at least two months before the beginning of each semester. Foreign students must, in addition, present acceptable Test of English as a Foreign Language (TOEFL) scores and evidence of financial capability to support themselves.

EXPENSES

Per course hour	In-state	Out-of-state
Tuition and fees	$58	$156
Books and supplies	$11	$ 11
Total	$69	$167

FINANCIAL ASSISTANCE

A limited number of graduate fellowships and assistantships are available.

CORRESPONDENCE

For further information on the program in management offered at Tennessee State, please write or call

Dr. Tilden J. Curry
Acting Dean
School of Business
Tennessee State University
10th and Charlotte
Nashville, Tennessee 37203
Telephone: 615-251-1251

TENNESSEE TECHNOLOGICAL UNIVERSITY

COOKEVILLE, TENNESSEE

Tennessee Technological University, founded in 1916, is a coeducational, state-supported institution located on the eastern Highland Rim of Tennessee in Cookeville, a city of approximately 20,000. The area is particularly noted for its state parks, lakes, and natural beauty. The College of Business Administration was established in 1949. The university has an enrollment of approximately 8,000 students, of whom 1,300 are enrolled in the College of Business Administration.

PROGRAM OF STUDY

The Master of Business Administration (M.B.A.) degree is offered by the Division of M.B.A. Studies in the College of Business Administration. The purpose of the M.B.A. degree is to offer a professional program preparing men and women for high-level careers in business organizations. The course material is broad in scope in order to develop general managerial competence through extensive use of the case method and selected use of other pedagogies such as exercises, simulations, and research projects.

The unique qualities of the M.B.A. degree are reflected in the curriculum which is dedicated to the development of those managerial attributes important for men and women who seek responsible business management positions. The M.B.A. program is designed to meet the needs of nonbusiness as well as business undergraduate majors and experienced managers. The advanced M.B.A. program (core plus electives) consists of 60 quarter hours (12 five-credit-hour courses) and may be completed in four quarters of full-time work. Foundation courses (six subject areas with a total of 24 credit hours) are designed for students lacking specific business preparation in their previous academic programs. Such students will consult with the Division of M.B.A. Studies to determine the foundation course requirements (all or part) based on their individual backgrounds.

Those students without a business background will take part or all of the foundation offerings before entering the advanced M.B.A. core program. Following completion of the core portion of the M.B.A. program, the student will take elective courses in such areas as accounting and financial control, marketing, and operations management.

ADMISSION

Admission is open to qualified students who have a bachelor's degree from an accredited undergraduate institution. Previous enrollment in business courses is not required. Qualification is determined by undergraduate grade-point average and scores on the Graduate Management Admission Test (GMAT). Generally, students will be required to have a score of 950 points using the formula: 200 × grade-point average + the GMAT score. Employment experience and the motivation for enrollment in the program also will be considered. An interview with the M.B.A. Director in person or by long-distance telephone is required. Applications are processed on a continuous basis; however, enrollment in the core program is limited to classes beginning in the fall. Applications and all supporting credentials for the M.B.A. program should be submitted prior to July 28 for the fall quarter, November 29 for the winter quarter, February 27 for the spring quarter, and April 28 for the summer quarter.

EXPENSES

Tuition is $716 per quarter for full-time, out-of-state students and $409 for residents of the state of Tennessee. Double occupancy dormitory room rent is approximately $292, and estimated cost of meals in the school cafeteria is $375. Information on housing and board is available from the Director of Housing, Campus Box 5016, Tennessee Technological University.

FINANCIAL ASSISTANCE

A number of graduate assistantships are awarded to superior applicants each year. Half-time graduate assistants are required to work approximately 10 hours per week and receive $165 per month. They pay one half of regular tuition. Twenty-hour graduate assistants receive $330 per month and receive a complete waiver of tuition. Out-of-state tuition is waived for students receiving graduate assistantships. Scholarships are available through the College of Business Administration Foundation.

Application for this type of assistance should be submitted directly to the M.B.A. Office with admission applications. For other possible work-related assistance, applicants should contact the Director of Student Financial Aid, Campus Box 5076.

PLACEMENT

An active placement service is provided to help in securing positions for graduates of the university.

CORRESPONDENCE

Inquiries should be addressed to
  Director
  Division of M.B.A. Studies
  Tennessee Technological University
  Campus P.O. Box 5023
  Cookeville, Tennessee 38505

Texas A&M University is a dynamic, growing public institution of higher education. Current enrollment is approximately 35,000 students, with more than 5,000 pursuing graduate studies. Established in 1876 as a land-grant college and the state's first public institution of higher learning, Texas A&M today ranks among the nation's leading universities in academic achievement, enrollment of National Merit Scholars, research activity, and support by alumni and private sources.

The main campus of Texas A&M in College Station, Texas, is centrally located among the state's major metropolitan centers of Houston (95 miles), Dallas (180 miles), Austin (100 miles), and San Antonio (180 miles). College Station is one of the Southwest's fastest growing standard metropolitan statistical areas.

The College of Business Administration was established in 1968. In the 1985-86 year, 455 students pursued graduate degrees—351 in the master's programs and 104 in the doctoral program. The college is housed in a large, modern, six-story facility on campus.

PROGRAMS OF STUDY

The college offers graduate degree programs leading to the Master of Business Administration (M.B.A.), the Master of Science (M.S.), and the Doctor of Philosophy (Ph.D.) in business administration. The programs are accredited by the American Assembly of Collegiate Schools of Business (AACSB) at the baccalaureate and master's levels.

The M.B.A. degree program is designed to prepare men and women of all educational backgrounds for positions of leadership in a wide variety of organizations. Although the M.B.A. degree program is general in orientation, students may choose to take their electives in one or more academic areas: accounting, business computing science, finance, management, or marketing. The curriculum consists of 48 semester hours which includes 12 hours of elective course work. Students with business undergraduate degrees granted within the past two years may be able to omit certain foundation-level courses under the waiver conditions as defined by the M.B.A. Program Director.

It is required that all students have completed mathematics course work through calculus and one year of economics course work (micro/macro) prior to entering the M.B.A. program. Students may enter the

M.B.A. program in the fall or spring semesters. The full-time program may be completed in 18 to 24 months.

The Master of Science degree program is for those who wish to specialize in one of the following areas: accounting, business computing science, finance, management, or marketing. Students may select either a thesis or nonthesis option.

The Doctor of Philosophy in business administration degree program is intended to prepare qualified students to conduct research in business and other organizational environments, to communicate research findings, and to teach at the university level. The highly individualized program structure includes designation of an area of specialization in business, but offers freedom to utilize interdisciplinary course work in a supporting role. Major fields are offered in accounting, business analysis and research, finance, management, and marketing.

ADMISSION

Applicants to the master's programs must submit Graduate Management Admission Test (GMAT) scores, two official transcripts on all academic work, a resume, and three reference evaluation forms provided with the application. Most applicants admitted have a 3.0 or better (on a 4.0 scale) on their upper-division undergraduate degree work and have test scores in the 70th percentile or above. Superior international applicants are encouraged to apply. Selection is based upon a distinguished undergraduate record, competitive GMAT scores, and above-average scores on the Test of English as a Foreign Language (TOEFL).

Applications to the M.B.A. program should be submitted for the fall semester by the previous February 15 and for spring semester by the previous September 15. Applications received after these dates will be considered, but those completed before these dates will be given priority. Applicants to the M.S. and Ph.D. programs may apply for fall, spring, and summer entrance. Doctoral applicants may submit Graduate Record Examinations (GRE) scores in lieu of GMAT scores.

International applicants applying for M.S. and Ph.D. programs must meet the university's deadline dates of February 1 for summer and fall semesters and September 1 for the spring semester.

EXPENSES

The following fees are subject to change. An in-state graduate student registered for 12 semester credit hours would expect to pay $300 per regular semester in tuition and fees. An out-of-state or foreign student would expect to pay $1,600. Tuition and fees are slightly less for the two summer terms. Most graduate students live off campus.

FINANCIAL ASSISTANCE

Graduate teaching and research assistantships are available throughout the college. Stipends, which are subject to change, begin at $465 (master's) or $700 (doctoral) per month for 20 hours per week. (Out-of-state students who are half-time research or teaching assistants are eligible for in-state tuition.) Master's scholarships/fellowships are available on a competitive basis.

PLACEMENT

In 1984-85 more than 30,000 interviews were held by over 650 companies through the university's Career Planning and Placement Center. Annually the M.B.A. Association publishes a resume book which is distributed to regional and national employers. Salaries for Texas A&M's M.B.A. graduates are competitive with national averages.

CORRESPONDENCE

For further information or to request an application for admission, please write
Director
Master's Programs
Texas A&M University
College Station, Texas 77843

M.J. Neeley School of Business
TEXAS CHRISTIAN UNIVERSITY
FORT WORTH, TEXAS

The M.J. Neeley School of Business at Texas Christian University (TCU) is located in Fort Worth, Texas, an area that has been voted by management graduates from around the country as among the most desirable of all major business centers in which to locate. Joined to its neighbor, Dallas, the metropolitan area is the nation's fifth largest with a population of over 2.5 million. Texas, the nation's second fastest-growing state, has what has been termed "the best business climate in the country" with its moderate climate, rich natural resources, and low taxes.

TCU was founded in 1873. Its academic programs have earned the highest possible accreditations including recognition by the American Assembly of Collegiate Schools of Business (AACSB). It is a private, independent university with a total enrollment of 7,000. TCU is a member of the Southwest Athletic Conference and is best known for its programs in business, arts, science, and theology. Students and staff are selected solely on the basis of educational qualifications without regard to religion, race, sex, age, or handicap.

PROGRAMS OF STUDY
TCU offers both full-time and part-time programs of study. Approximately 150 students are enrolled in each program for a total enrollment of 300.

The length of the Master of Business Administration (M.B.A.) program will vary depending on the educational background and preparation of each candidate and the number of courses taken each semester. For students with no prior work in business administration, the program will ordinarily require two years of full-time graduate study. For a student with a very strong background in business, the program will require a minimum of 36 semester hours, which can ordinarily be completed in one full year of graduate study.

Two examples of the distinctive nature of the M.B.A. program are the Educational Investment Fund (EIF) and the Leadership Development Project—programs designed to give each M.B.A. candidate executive experience while he or she is earning academic credit. The Educational Investment Fund gives student real-world experience in the management of a portfolio of assets that is currently approaching $1,000,000. A *Business Week* article described the EIF as probably the largest of its kind among business schools

in the United States. Another innovative feature of the M.B.A. program at TCU is the Leadership Development Project. The project involves intensive leadership preparation through seminars, lectures, and briefings conducted by the coordinator. Students apply this classroom knowledge to real-world problems by preparing recommendations for action to top-level executives of the firms and organizations selected to participate.

ADMISSION
Admission is selective with approximately one of three applicants gaining admission. No specific undergraduate degree is given preference in the admission process. A variety of information is requested in order to develop a profile of each applicant. The profile is composed of five items: (1) a complete application, (2) a self-evaluation essay, (3) three reference reports, (4) transcripts from all educational institutions attended since high school, and (5) scores from the Graduate Management Admission Test (GMAT).

Applications are accepted for the fall semester which begins in August, for the spring semester which begins in January, and for the summer session which begins in May. Applicants are encouraged to apply early because admission is selective and the beginning class size is limited.

International students must complete a special application form. In addition, international students must submit scores from the Test of English as a Foreign Language (TOEFL). Another requirement is the submission of an affidavit of financial support certifying that the student will have sufficient funds to complete the total program. Financial aid is not available to assist international students.

EXPENSES
Estimated costs for a full-time student (for nine months) are as follows:

Tuition	$4,128
Room and board	3,600
Books and supplies	400
	$8,128

FINANCIAL ASSISTANCE
To assist qualified, full-time students who are U.S. citizens, TCU offers a full range of financial aid, including scholarships, assistantships, grants, and loans. Generous research assistantships—full tuition plus a $3,600 stipend—are available for superior students. Applications should be made on the Graduate and Professional School Financial Aid Service (GAPSFAS) form.

PLACEMENT
TCU offers a professionally staffed Career Planning and Placement Office that provides a full range of counseling and placement services. The Placement Office aids students with career planning and schedules visits by personnel officers from major firms in search of M.B.A. graduates.

CORRESPONDENCE
For more information and an application, contact
Dr. Tom F. Badgett, Assistant Dean
M.J. Neeley School of Business
P.O. Box 32868
Texas Christian University
Fort Worth, Texas 76129
Telephone: 817-921-7531
Toll free (within Texas): 800-828-8765
Toll free (outside of Texas): 800-828-8777

TEXAS SOUTHERN UNIVERSITY

HOUSTON, TEXAS

Texas Southern University, founded in 1947, is located in Houston, a city of over two million people. The university is in an urban setting and occupies a 70-acre site in the southeastern section, two miles from the downtown area. There are unlimited opportunities for students to enrich their studies by the use of museums, libraries, and other educational facilities in the city and at neighboring universities. More than 9,000 students attend the university. More than 1,500 undergraduate students and over 100 graduate students are enrolled in the Master of Business Administration (M.B.A.) program. The baccalaureate and master's programs are accredited by the American Assembly of Collegiate Schools of Business (AACSB).

PROGRAMS OF STUDY

The Master of Business Administration degree is conferred under one distinct program—general business administration. The M.B.A. program is open to qualified holders of a baccalaureate degree, regardless of undergraduate major field of study. The objective of the program is education in business administration. Emphasis is placed upon the development of analytical, leadership, and problem-solving skills and the ability to manage effectively the utilization of human and material resources. The program provides a strong foundation in the economic, social, and political forces that determine and shape the environment in which the management sciences must be applied. The objectives of the program are deemed to be most expeditiously attained through a balanced sequence of the quantitative, social sciences, and functional disciplines.

The M.B.A. program consists of two tracks: Track I, consisting of 30 semester hours, is designed for students with undergraduate degrees in business administration from regionally accredited institutions. Track II, consisting of 60 semester hours, is designed for students with undergraduate degrees in areas other than business administration from regionally accredited institutions. Students in this track are required to complete some 30 semester hours of business core courses in addition to the 30 semester hours of advanced work. However, depending on the type and number of business administration courses a student may have completed prior to admission, a student's M.B.A. program may be expected to vary from 30 to 60 semester hours.

The purpose of the Master of Professional Accounting (M.P.A.) program is to provide the necessary theoretical knowledge, specific skills and communicative ability essential for professional careers in C.P.A. firms, private industries, governmental and educational institutions. This program, unlike other master's programs in accounting, is designed to meet the requirements of the final year of five-year programs in professional schools of accountancy. Upon completion of the program, students are prepared to take the C.P.A. examination.

ADMISSION

Unconditional admission to the M.B.A. program requires acceptance by the Graduate School and compliance with one of the following requirements: (1) undergraduate grade-point average × 200 + Graduate Management Admission Test (GMAT) total score must equal at least 950 points, or (2) undergraduate grade-point average on the last 60 semester hours × 200 + the GMAT total score must equal at least 1,000 points.

For conditional admission, the student must have at least a 3.00 undergraduate grade-point average, or his or her undergraduate grade-point average for the last 60 hours of course work must be at least 3.25. Students admitted in this category will be required to meet the unconditional admission criteria by the end of their first semester of enrollment. Failure to do so will result in the student being dropped from the program.

In addition to other requirements, evidence of English proficiency is required for international students. Results of the Test of English as a Foreign Language (TOEFL) should be sent to the Graduate School by Educational Testing Service (ETS). TOEFL score should be at least 550. International students are required to submit an application fee of $50 in the form of a money order. This fee should accompany the application form.

Students may enter the M.B.A. program in any semester. Application deadlines are August 1 for September admission, December 1 for January admission, and May 1 for June admission.

EXPENSES

Fees per academic semester for full-time students:

Residents of Texas	$ 450
Nonresidents of Texas	2,444

Residential life/housing accommodations include three halls for women, two for men, and one apartment complex that houses graduate students, law students, and married couples only.

FINANCIAL ASSISTANCE

Graduate and teaching assistantships are available to qualified students. In addition, the university maintains student loan programs. A variety of opportunities exist for students to obtain employment on campus and in the city of Houston. Graduate assistants earn $357 per month. Out-of-state fees are waived for nonresident students who qualify for graduate assistantships.

PLACEMENT

The University Career Planning and Placement Center assists graduates in obtaining full-time employment. Hundreds of companies, including most major national corporations, conduct interviews on the campus each year.

CORRESPONDENCE

Inquiries concerning graduate study at Texas Southern should be addressed to
Director of Graduate Programs
School of Business
Texas Southern University
3100 Cleburne Avenue
Houston, Texas 77004
Telephone: 713-527-7780 or 527-7781

Texas Tech University is located in Lubbock, a growing city of 200,000 that is a business and service center for West Texas. The university complex includes six colleges, schools of law and medicine, and the graduate school. The spacious campus has an enrollment of 24,000 students.

The College of Business Administration enrolls 4,800 students in its graduate and undergraduate programs, which are recognized throughout the Sunbelt for academic excellence. At the graduate level, 350 master's and 70 doctoral students work closely with the graduate faculty in a stimulating and supportive environment. The 65 members of the business school graduate faculty make up one of the largest faculty resource bases in the country.

PROGRAMS OF STUDY
The Master of Business Administration (M.B.A.) degree at Texas Tech University is designed to provide a broad background in business administration, complemented by a well-developed managerial perspective and strong analytical skills. Core courses study the financial, managerial, marketing, and analytical functions of the firm, as well as economics and business policy. Electives are used to develop additional expertise in the student's major area(s) of interest. Students may expect to complete the M.B.A. in one to two years, depending on their previous backgrounds in business and the amount of basic studies or leveling course work required.

The M.B.A./Juris Doctor (J.D.) is offered in association with the School of Law, enabling students to earn both degrees in three to four years of full-time study.

The Master of Science (M.S.) in business administration degree is available for students who wish to concentrate their graduate study in one area of business. Areas of specialization for the M.S. are finance, banking, marketing, management information systems, business statistics, management science, production/operations management, and management. M.S. students take a majority of their course work in their area of specialization. Required quantitative courses and electives make up the balance of their programs. The M.S. degree may be completed in one to two years of graduate work, depending on the student's academic preparation in business.

The Master of Science in accounting degree is offered for students who wish to specialize their graduate study in accounting. Concentrations in taxation and general accounting are available. The graduate accounting programs may be completed in one to two and one-half years of study, depending on the student's background in business and accounting.

The Doctor of Business Administration (D.B.A.) degree prepares students for careers in teaching, continuing scholarly research and publication, and service to the university and business communities. Areas of specialization for the D.B.A. are accounting, finance, management, marketing, business statistics, management information systems, management science, and production/operations management.

Doctoral students are acquainted with the most advanced levels of learning in their area of specialization and two supporting fields. In addition, they become proficient in research methodology and in the use of quantitative and economic tools of analysis. Students who are successful at each step in the program should complete degree requirements for the D.B.A. in two to three years of full-time study beyond the master's degree. There is no foreign language requirement.

ADMISSION
Application may be made for the fall, spring, or summer terms. No specific undergraduate courses or majors are required as prerequisites for admission. However, students are expected to be able to write and speak effectively, and to possess a solid aptitude for mathematics. The admission decision is based primarily on the student's academic record, particularly in the last 60 hours of undergraduate work, and on his or her aptitude for graduate work as evidenced by scores on the Graduate Management Admission Test (GMAT). In addition, applicants to the Master of Science in accounting programs must have a minimum grade-point average of 3.0.

EXPENSES
Total tuition and fees for Texas residents are approximately $360 per semester; for non-Texas residents, approximately $1,600 per semester. These fees are based on a 12-hour course load.

FINANCIAL ASSISTANCE
Teaching and research assistantships are awarded on a competitive basis to students with outstanding academic credentials. To be considered, students need to submit completed applications by April 1 for the fall semester, or by November 1 for the limited number of positions that become available at mid-year. Additional forms of aid, primarily loan funds, are available through the university's Office of Student Financial Aid. Academic scholarships are available and qualify the student for in-state tuition rate.

PLACEMENT
The Career Planning and Placement Center coordinates an extensive program of corporate recruitment and provides career counseling services. In 1984-85, master's degree candidates had the opportunity to interview with approximately 275 major public and private firms. They averaged three job offers each, and accepted starting salaries competitive with and exceeding those of graduates of other leading business schools in the Southwest. Doctoral students were placed on the faculties of prestigious universities across the United States.

CORRESPONDENCE
For additional information on the programs of study offered by Texas Tech, please contact
Associate Dean for Graduate Programs
College of Business Administration
Texas Tech University
Box 4320
Lubbock, Texas 79409
Telephone: 806-742-3184

THOMAS COLLEGE

WATERVILLE, MAINE

Thomas College, one of the oldest independent colleges of management in the United States, was founded in 1894 as a nonsectarian, coeducational college dedicated to career education. The college is accredited by the New England Association of Schools and Colleges and authorized by the state of Maine to award the Master of Business Administration (M.B.A.) and Master of Science in Business (M.S.B.) degrees, as well as a variety of undergraduate degrees. The college serves approximately 1,100 full-time and part-time students. The 70-acre campus has been recognized as one of the most modern small college facilities in New England. Graduate programs are also offered at 15 Monument Square, Portland, Maine, and at International Paper Company in Jay, Maine.

The college maintains a VAX 11/750 computing system with extensive software as well as a microcomputer laboratory to support the instructional and research needs of students and faculty. The Marriner Library contains an extensive collection of business and related materials.

PROGRAMS OF STUDY

The primary objective of the Master of Business Administration program is to develop broad abilities rather than specific skills. In keeping with this objective, courses with a broad perspective are offered rather than courses of a highly technical and specialized nature.

Candidates for the M.B.A. program are generally expected to have a broad background in business and management. Candidates with undergraduate degrees in business, management, or related areas from accredited institutions of higher education with acceptable grade-point averages are presumed to have this background. Candidates without degrees in these areas or with deficient grade-point averages may be required to take additional graduate or undergraduate course work prior to full matriculation in the graduate program.

The Master of Science in Business program is a specialized, individually designed, graduate program whose purpose is to build upon an already established area of management expertise.

All candidates will be required to demonstrate competence in each of the following areas: accounting, economics, and quantitative methods. This may be achieved in any one of the following ways for each area: (1) completion of acceptable undergraduate course work with a grade of B or better; (2) successful completion of a noncredit, graduate-level course (AC50, EC50, MS50); and (3) satisfactory performance on examinations approved by the Graduate School. If a candidate is judged to be deficient in communications skills, he or she may be required to take MG57 as an elective.

ADMISSION

The Graduate School Admission Committee, composed of three members of the resident graduate faculty, decides upon the admissibility of each applicant based upon the following information:

(1) Certified copies of all the applicant's previous academic work must be forwarded by each institution attended to the Dean of the Graduate School at Thomas College. Copies in the possession of the candidate are not acceptable. A bachelor's degree from a regionally accredited college or university is required.

(2) Students who have completed acceptable graduate work at another graduate school must have official transcripts forwarded to the Dean of the Graduate School to ensure that proper transfer credit is awarded by the Graduate School Admission Committee.

(3) All applicants must submit the results of the Graduate Management Admission Test (GMAT). The Thomas College score report number is 3903 and should be indicated on the GMAT registration form.

(4) The recommendations for three persons attesting to the applicant's previous experience and potential, as both a graduate student and a professional manager, are required. The candidate should request that each reference write directly to the Dean of the Graduate School.

(5) Candidates who are graduates of foreign universities must submit their scores on the Test of English as a Foreign Language (TOEFL). These scores must be received 30 days before the start of the semester for which the student plans to enroll.

(6) Complete information must be provided on a Thomas College Graduate School Application form.

EXPENSES

Full-time tuition $2,781
Part-time tuition, per course 309
Application fee (not refundable) . . . 35
Thesis fee 125
Graduate Association fee,
   per trimester 5
Graduation fee 100

FINANCIAL ASSISTANCE

Graduate students may be eligible for Graduate School assistantships or Guaranteed Student Loans. For further information, please contact the Graduate School.

PLACEMENT

The Graduate School of Management has complete access to the college placement service. Representatives from both the business and nonprofit sectors throughout the United States annually recruit on campus.

CORRESPONDENCE

For further information, write or call the Dean of the Graduate School

   Thomas College
   West River Road
   Waterville, Maine 04901
   Telephone: 207-873-0771
    OR
   Thomas College
   15 Monument Square
   Portland, Maine 04101
   Telephone: 207-879-0685

Trenton State College was founded in 1855 and is now located in a wooded lake area north of Trenton, New Jersey. The college is a multipurpose institution with more than 7,500 students. The School of Business had over 1,000 majors during the 1984-85 academic year. The college has two semesters and a summer session each year. Graduate student enrollment is over 1,100 students.

PROGRAM OF STUDY

The School of Business offers a graduate program leading to the Master of Science (M.S.) in management. A minimum of 30 semester hours of advanced graduate courses is required of all students. This M.S. degree program prepares graduates for managerial positions in business, government, and nonprofit organizations. The program's goal is to prepare managers in problem solving, employing modern management skills and knowledge. Preparing specialists in specific disciplines or fields is secondary to preparing people to manage in a variety of situations.

The M.S. program in management consists of 10 courses (3 semester hours each) including 18 hours of required courses dealing with managerial tools, organizational dynamics, financial management, functional areas, business environment, and policy/decision making and 12 semester hours of electives with advisement. Students may elect courses in such related fields as political science, economics, psychology, sociology, mathematics, or other fields that are congruent with their managerial career goals.

Students who have had no undergraduate work in business or economics will find it necessary to complete foundation courses that are designed to provide preparation comparable to that found in the undergraduate curriculum in a school of business.

Some or all of the foundation courses may be waived for students who present satisfactory equivalent preparation. Ordinarily the foundation courses must be fulfilled before enrolling in an advanced graduate course that meets degree requirements. This includes courses in the core, elective, and related fields categories.

The minimum general requirements for the degree are a B average in the graduate courses with no more than two C grades and a passing grade on the comprehensive examination component.

ADMISSION

Admission to this program is highly competitive as a result of enrollment limitations. All applicants must have a bachelor's degree from an accredited college or university in the United States or proof of equivalent preparation at a foreign institution and must take the Graduate Management Admission Test (GMAT). Students must possess at least a 2.75 undergraduate grade-point average for the junior and senior year courses or a 2.50 minimum cumulative grade-point average for all undergraduate-level work.

Foreign applicants must also provide scores from the Test of English as a Foreign Language (TOEFL).

It is expected that not all qualified students can be accommodated; however, accepted students may begin course work in the fall or spring semester and in the summer session. Summer class offerings are available on a limited basis.

EXPENSES

New Jersey residents are charged tuition of $68 per semester hour; out-of-state students pay tuition of $86 per semester hour. Fees include a $10 application fee, a $6 per semester hour service fee, and a $3 per semester hour student center fee. These fees are subject to change.

Nearly all graduate students live off campus. The housing office on campus maintains a list of off-campus housing.

FINANCIAL ASSISTANCE

A limited number of graduate assistantships are available each semester with the greatest number granted for a 12-month period beginning with the fall semester. Certain loan funds and part-time employment opportunities are available to qualified persons.

PLACEMENT

The college's placement office is available to graduate students and alumni, including scheduled visits with representatives from businesses and government. The graduate supervisor and faculty of the M.S. program also assist students in seeking suitable employment.

CORRESPONDENCE

For further information and/or to request an application, please contact
Office of Admissions
Trenton State College, CN 550
Hillwood Lakes
Trenton, New Jersey 08625
Telephone: 609-771-2131

Trinity University, founded in 1869, is a privately supported, coeducational school with a current enrollment of about 3,000 students. The modern campus overlooks San Antonio, a city with a population of about 900,000. On a 107-acre tract, the university is located in one of the city's exclusive residential areas and is one of the most beautiful college campuses in North America.

Because Trinity is a relatively small school, the students benefit greatly from a close student-faculty relationship. The objective of graduate work at Trinity is to provide the student with every opportunity to achieve productive scholarship and professional competence in the area of specialization. The emphasis is upon the development of analytical thinking, independent and original research, and effective communication. Graduate work is offered in both the regular and the summer sessions and includes classes scheduled in the evening.

PROGRAM OF STUDY
The Department of Business offers work leading to the degree of Master of Business Administration (M.B.A.). Applicants for admission to candidacy for this degree should, in addition to satisfying all admission requirements of the Graduate School, either have completed, or complete as part of their graduate program, basic college courses in accounting, business law, economics, finance, management, marketing, calculus, and business statistics. The following series of courses has been designed to provide graduate students with a business background:

ACCT 380P Survey of Financial
          Accounting
BUSN 380P The Business Environment
ECON 380P Economic Analysis for
          Business
FNCE 380P Finance for the Business
          Enterprise
MGMT 380P Survey of Operations
          Management
MKTG 380P Survey of Marketing
          Administration
QUAN 380P Statistical Applications for
          Business

A candidate for the degree should complete at least 24 graduate hours in business administration and up to 12 graduate hours from supporting areas. The M.B.A. program, outlined below, requires 36 graduate hours for completion.

Core courses:
MGMT 380 Theory and Practice of
          Administration
MGMT 385 Managerial Economics
FNCE 387 Financial Analysis for
          Decision Making
ACCT 384 Managerial Accounting
MKTG 386 Marketing Analysis
QUAN 381 Statistical Research
BUSN 398 Business Policy and Strategy
Elective courses: 15 semester hours, including at least 9 semester hours of graduate business electives and up to 6 hours outside of business administration with the approval of the Department of Business.

Course work in business administration emphasizes administrative theory and processes and provides work in management, marketing, and finance. Individual programs are tailored to the objective of students in consultation with their graduate advisers. Depending on undergraduate preparation, full-time students will require one to two years to complete work for an M.B.A. degree.

ADMISSION
By its nature, Trinity is a highly personalized institution, and applicants admitted to the graduate school are carefully selected. Admission to the program of study leading to the M.B.A. degree is based upon undergraduate performance, scores on the Graduate Management Admission Test (GMAT), and other evidence that the candidate is capable of success in the program.

Full admission to the Graduate School requires a bachelor's degree from an accredited institution with a B average in the last 60 hours of undergraduate work, a B average in all work in business administration, and satisfactory GMAT scores. If a student holds a degree from an accredited college but does not have the required grade level in undergraduate work, he or she may, at the discretion of the Dean of the Division of Business and Administrative Studies, be admitted as a provisional student. Students should send an application to the Graduate Admissions Office and submit transcripts and scores on the Graduate Management Admission Test.

EXPENSES
Tuition for full-time graduate students was $3,120 per semester in fall 1985. Tuition for part-time graduate students was $260 per hour for the fall 1985 semester. Changes in tuition rates may occur.

FINANCIAL ASSISTANCE
Graduate assistantships are available for a limited number of students. These awards include tuition remission and a stipend for a nine-month period. A limited amount of scholarship aid is available, as well as National Direct Student Loans for qualified graduates pursuing a minimum of nine semester hours of work.

PLACEMENT
Trinity University's placement office provides assistance to students seeking part-time or full-time employment. Recruiting schedules include national and local businesses, governments, and institutions.

CORRESPONDENCE
For further information, please write or call
    Director of Graduate Studies
       in Business Administration
    Trinity University
    715 Stadium Drive
    San Antonio, Texas 78284
    Telephone: 512-736-7238

TROY STATE UNIVERSITY DOTHAN/FORT RUCKER

DOTHAN, ALABAMA

Troy State University Dothan/Fort Rucker is an integral part of the Troy State University System. Courses were first offered at Fort Rucker in 1951. In 1976, Troy State University Dothan/Fort Rucker opened its Houston Hall facility in Dothan, Alabama. Dothan is 50 miles south of the Troy Campus and within 90 miles of the beautiful Panama City, Florida, beaches.

The School of Business currently offers undergraduate degrees in accounting and business administration with areas of concentration in data processing, economics, management, and general business. Master's degrees are offered in personnel management and business administration.

PROGRAM OF STUDY

The Master of Business Administration (M.B.A.) program is designed to provide managerial knowledge and skills for those persons aspiring to positions with administrative responsibilities. Much of the expertise gained from the M.B.A. program is relevant to professional administration in governmental, educational, and other institutions, as well as in business organizations.

Specific M.B.A. program goals are
• to develop a high degree of competence in making decisions and initiating actions based on the theory and nature of business organizations and their environment,
• to develop skills in interpersonal and group relations within organizations,
• to develop a sense of the role of responsible professional management within the firm and society,
• to develop a competence in communication within organizations for motivating individuals and groups to undertake appropriate action,
• to develop the competence to integrate and interrelate in a decision-making sense the contributions of the business functions to the operation of the firm as a whole.

Oriented to a management point of view, the M.B.A. program seeks to instill in the student a broad knowledge of professional responsibilities. The program stresses that a combination of cooperative effort and respect for human values is basic to the successful administrator, that the business executive operates within a sphere greater than his or her particular enterprise, and that business decisions affect—and are affected by—the eco-

nomic, social, and political environment. Students learn that executives must act with a constant awareness of the social and ethical implications of business activity. Recognizing the diversity of interests of students, the program seeks to provide sufficient flexibility so as to enable specialization in various areas.

The Troy State University Dothan/Fort Rucker M.B.A. program consists of 60 quarter hours of which 50 hours are core courses required of all students and 10 hours are electives. A thesis may be substituted for 10 hours of electives. Upon approval of the graduate adviser, a maximum of 10 hours of graduate courses may be taken outside of business and economics in fields such as psychology, guidance and counseling, sociology, and mathematics, whenever graduate prerequisites can be met.

Core courses	Quarter hours
Business Research—610	5
Business Strategy—611	5
Business Seminar—612	5
Marketing Management—661	5
Managerial Finance—631	5
Decision Theory—641	5
Managerial Economics—651	5
Macroeconomics and Forecasting—652	5
Organization Theory—671	5
Managerial Accounting—691	5
Total core courses	50
Electives	10
Total degree requirements	60

ADMISSION

To be admitted to the M.B.A. program, a candidate must hold a baccalaureate degree from a regionally accredited institution and must show high promise of success as determined by (1) performance on the Graduate Management Admission Test (GMAT) and (2) undergraduate grade average.

The program is open to all students who qualify, regardless of undergraduate major. However, certain preparatory courses in economics, accounting, marketing, finance, management, statistics, and business law are required. Students who have received a bachelor's degree in business generally have fulfilled this requirement, but students may have to complete up to 40 quarter hours of preparatory work.

A special information and admission application packet is available for foreign students.

EXPENSES

Tuition of $32 per quarter hour is subject to change.

FINANCIAL ASSISTANCE

A limited number of scholarships and assistantships are available. The usual government scholarship loans are also available to qualified students.

PLACEMENT

The university maintains its own placement office, which is visited annually by representatives of leading companies. The placement office also keeps interested alumni informed of employment opportunities for experienced personnel.

CORRESPONDENCE

For further information, write or call
  Dean
  School of Business and Commerce
  Troy State University
    Dothan/Fort Rucker
  Dothan, Alabama 36303
  Telephone: 205-793-1445

The A. B. Freeman School of Business at Tulane University is firmly committed to a rigorous integrated program for business management. Founded in 1916, it is one of the oldest business schools in the United States. The school is fully accredited and is a charter member of the American Assembly of Collegiate Schools of Business (AACSB). Current enrollment in the M.B.A. program is 245 full-time students and 160 part-time students, with a full-time faculty of 37. The school is housed in a new six-story building with tiered and case classrooms, state-of-the-art computer facilities, and a fully equipped audiovisual center.

PROGRAMS OF STUDY

To educate the well-rounded, balanced manager, the Freeman School stresses an interdisciplinary approach to general management education. A theoretical foundation is provided in all functional areas, and students learn to solve applied problems with emphasis on analyzing problems, developing solutions, and implementing plans. Teaching techniques include lecture, case analysis, group projects, simulation games, video-tape sessions and field assignments. An informal work environment allows considerable interaction between students and faculty and fosters an atmosphere of support and cooperation among students.

The 60-hour curriculum is divided into core (required) and elective courses. The core courses, taken during the first year, include study in organizational behavior, economics, management science, accounting, finance, marketing, law, communications, and computers. The second year includes two required courses and eight electives appropriate to individual career interests. Two electives can be taken in other graduate divisions of Tulane, and a three-hour independent study can be completed. Students can choose to concentrate in a functional area or select electives to maintain breadth in the curriculum.

Transfer credits are not accepted; however, a student with prior academic work in the core set may be granted a course waiver by passing a qualifying examination on the subject matter. A course waiver reduces the total number of credit hours needed to earn the M.B.A. degree.

The evening part-time curriculum is identical to the full-time program and is taught by the same professors.

Tulane offers three joint degree programs in conjunction with other divisions of the university in the areas of law, health systems management, and environmental health sciences. Each program requires a separate application.

The school offers a number of in-house research facilities. The Center for Technology houses numerous microcomputers that are networked to one another and can access Tulane's DEC 2060 and IBM 3801 mainframe systems. The Communications Skills Center, which includes a closed-circuit television studio, monitoring facilities and other equipment, is an integral part of the M.B.A. program. The Freeman School library contains approximately 42,000 volumes and is the most modern, comprehensive business reference facility in the area.

ADMISSION

The school seeks students from all parts of the world and encourages applicants with bachelor's degrees in all major fields of study. Although work experience is not required, its value is recognized in terms of practical education.

A completed application includes official transcripts of all course work, scores on the Graduate Management Admission Test (GMAT), several short essays, and three letters of recommendation. International students must also submit scores on the Test of English as a Foreign Language (TOEFL) and a statement of adequate funding. An orientation program is required for all international students. The Admissions Committee carefully weighs academic and nonacademic data as indicators of the student's maturity, motivation, and ability. Because admission is competitive, completed applications for the fall and spring semesters should be submitted by May 31 and December 1, respectively. Interviews are encouraged.

EXPENSES

The cost for the 1985-86 academic year for an unmarried student was, approximately, as follows:

Tuition, fees, books, supplies	$ 9,480
Living expenses (off campus)	6,740
Total	$16,220

FINANCIAL ASSISTANCE

The Freeman School is strongly committed to making aid available to eligible students. Approximately one half of the entering class receives merit-based fellowship awards, which range from partial to full tuition waivers. Many students work as teaching or research assistants for professors. Need-based work/study jobs and federal loans are also available. Students may be considered for all types of aid.

PLACEMENT

The Freeman School's professional placement staff emphasizes individual career counseling, a comprehensive career development program, and strong connections to Tulane alumni. Approximately 100 corporate recruiters visit campus annually, and approximately 300 openings for internships and permanent jobs are listed with the placement office. Freeman graduates are employed nationwide and receive starting salaries above the national average.

CORRESPONDENCE

For further information or to request an application for admission, write or call
Director of Admissions
A. B. Freeman School of Business
Tulane University
New Orleans, Louisiana 70118
Telephone: 504-865-5410

UNION COLLEGE

SCHENECTADY, NEW YORK

The Institute of Administration and Management is part of Union College, founded in 1795 in Schenectady, New York. Union College has a strong tradition of leadership in the implementation of broad programs incorporating liberal arts, sciences, and engineering.

PROGRAMS OF STUDY

The general Master of Business Administration (M.B.A.) program is designed to prepare individuals from various undergraduate backgrounds for successful careers in business, government, and education. The curriculum emphasizes analysis of the interdependencies in large complex systems as a framework for managerial decision making. Rigorous academic study is combined with practical applications to provide a comprehensive, sophisticated view of the nature of management. The 18 courses are taken from such core areas as quantitative analysis, accounting-management control, behavioral science-organizational theory, business economics, financial management, and business policy. Electives can be taken from courses in international management, financial planning and control, and computer information systems.

The primary objective of the M.B.A. in accounting program is to prepare individuals with no prior business or accounting education to enter and successfully advance in the profession of public accounting. The program builds upon the analytical and communication skills acquired in undergraduate liberal arts or science courses. Upon completion of the program the student will have earned an M.B.A. degree and will have fulfilled the educational requirements needed to sit for the C.P.A. exam. The practical orientation of the program is emphasized by a required one-term internship with a national public accounting firm.

The M.B.A. in health systems administration program prepares students for professional administrative and managerial careers in public and private health service organizations. A relatively large number of graduates have entered careers with health care consulting firms. This two-year program requires 18 courses plus a 10-week residency in a health care institution or in one of the consulting firms. It is accredited by the Accrediting Commission on Education for Health Services Administration and has thus met the stringent criteria for graduate education in hospital and health services administration.

All M.B.A. programs take approximately two years of full-time study (or 18 courses) to complete. The M.B.A. in accounting requires an internship typically taken during the winter term of the first year. The M.B.A. in health systems administration residency is usually taken during the summer between the first and second year. A comprehensive examination completes the requirements.

All programs emphasize the use of computers as a tool. Students practice on the most advanced software and hardware generally available in business. The college possesses a great number of modern computing facilities. Management students also learn on a large number of the most widely used personal computers.

The Master of Science (M.S.) degree in industrial administration is designed primarily for the student with a degree in engineering or natural science and stresses the training of technical managers. This one-year curriculum draws upon the foundation of administrative theory, mathematics, behavioral science, and economics to develop strong analytical tools for complex problem solving.

The Master of Science degree program in operations research/applied statistics has been developed for students with a sound training in mathematics who desire a high level of competence in these fields.

Fifteen courses and a comprehensive examination are required for all Master of Science degrees. M.S. programs can be completed in one calendar year of full-time study.

The Doctor of Philosophy degree is awarded in administrative and engineering systems in cooperation with the Engineering Division; the program emphasizes a broad interdisciplinary approach to problem solving (behavioral science, engineering, operations research, statistics, economics, and management). Research and thesis, developed in close consultation with the faculty, are of greatest importance in this program. The program is intended for students of the highest academic promise who have an interest in research, teaching or careers as consultants in industry and health care organizations. This program typically will take the equivalent of three years of full-time study. There is a residency requirement of one year.

ADMISSION

Admission to all programs is open to graduates of accredited colleges and universities. The Graduate Management Admission Test (GMAT) is required of all applicants, and scores on the Test of English as a Foreign Language (TOEFL) are required of all foreign students. Union College operates on a trimester schedule and holds two summer sessions. Selection is based on academic ability and leadership potential. Admission criteria include scholarship as demonstrated by undergraduate or graduate work and commensurate scores on the GMAT.

EXPENSES

M.B.A. programs requiring 18 courses will amount to approximately $10,000; M.S. programs approximately $6,500; the Ph.D. program, about $12,000.

FINANCIAL ASSISTANCE

Scholarships, assistantships, and fellowships in various combinations of stipends and tuition waivers, are awarded in accordance with academic promise. Stipends may range from $1,500 to $2,700 per year. The Registrar's Office will aid students in securing state and federal loans.

CORRESPONDENCE

For further information, please write
Institute of Administration and
  Management
Union College
Schenectady, New York 12308
Telephone: 518-370-6237

The School of Business and Management at the United States International University offers three programs leading to the master's degree and the degree of Doctor of Business Administration (D.B.A.). All graduate courses are offered during evening hours and on weekends, in order to maintain the highest degree of flexibility in these programs, which are designed for working adults.

The university is located on 200 wooded acres within minutes of the Pacific Ocean and its beaches in San Diego. Students from over 79 countries blend their cultures and backgrounds to add significantly to the international focus—which is also enhanced by campuses in London, England; Mexico City; and Nairobi, Kenya. Students may transfer freely between campuses without loss from one international setting to another and thus deepen their understanding of world culture.

The school takes as its orientation that the faculty, staff, students, and administration are a community with a commitment to excellence in carrying out the educational mission. The emphasis is on close personal contact and a true educational dialogue. Four 10-week quarters and three intersessions are offered each year.

PROGRAMS OF STUDY
Three programs are offered leading to master's degrees. The Master of Science in Management and Organization Development (M.O.D.) program is designed for individuals already in management positions or those seeking more extensive knowledge of the human component in an organizational environment. It consists of nine courses (approximately one calendar year) emphasizing the human factor in work, the relationship between human performance and potential in different organizational environments, and various methods for bringing about organizational changes and reducing conflict to expand the human potential along with organizational productivity.

The Master of Business Administration (M.B.A.) program is primarily oriented toward individuals who have progressed beyond the entry-level positions in any organization to positions of expanded responsibility. The program can range between 12 courses and 18 courses: the 12-course, 60-quarter-unit program is designed for students with undergraduate degrees in business; the 18-course, 90-quarter-unit program is designed for students coming from nonbusiness disci-

plines. The specific courses required will be determined after a review of the applicant's undergraduate degree transcript.

The Master of International Business and Administration degree program is designed for individuals who seek a career in international business and management or already are in such a position and seek to advance their knowledge and potential to function more effectively in this environment. Courses cover each of the areas with which an international businessperson or manager must contend as well as an appreciation for cultural differences in seeking solutions to common management and business problems. Students have a choice within the curriculum to select an emphasis in international marketing or international finance and investment. The program can range between 12 courses and 18 courses: the 12-course, 60-quarter-unit program is designed for students with undergraduate degrees in business; the 18-course, 90-quarter-unit program is designed for students coming from non-business disciplines. The specific courses required will be determined after a review of the applicant's undergraduate degree transcript.

The Doctorate in Business Administration (D.B.A.) is designed to expand and enhance the student's potential within an international and interdisciplinary environment. The program's degree concentrations are designed to challenge the mid-career individual who possesses significant applied experience and wishes to broaden his or her perspective as it relates to business and management.

ADMISSION
The basic requirements for admission to a master's program will include a baccalaureate degree from an accredited college or university with a minimum grade-point average of 2.7 and an acceptable score on the Graduate Management Admission Test (GMAT). Criteria for admission to the D.B.A. program include the possession of a master's degree in business administration or a related business discipline from an accredited university with a minimum grade-point average of 3.5 and an acceptable score on the Graduate Management Admission Test (GMAT). Under certain conditions graduate units may be transferred into the D.B.A. program by permission of the dean. Determination of any transfer units will be made upon an analysis of the applicant's graduate tran-

script. Courses with grades below 3.0 (B) are not eligible for transfer credit in either program.

EXPENSES
Tuition, per quarter unit $140
Tuition, per course 700
Room and board, per quarter 1,090-1,290
Books and course materials/quarter. . 200

FINANCIAL ASSISTANCE
Financial aid is available to graduate students in the form of long-term educational loans and part-time employment through the College Work-Study Program (CWSP). Student loans are available year round through the Guaranteed Student Loan programs and the California Loans to Assist Student program (CLAS). Students should contact the U.S.I.U. Office of Financial Aid for specific information.

PLACEMENT
The university offers a placement service. Representatives of domestic and multinational organizations visit the campus regularly to interview qualified students.

CORRESPONDENCE
For further information, contact the Admission Office or
 Dean
 School of Business and Management
 United States International University
 10455 Pomerado Road
 San Diego, California 92131
 Telephone: 619-271-4300

UNITED STATES INTERNATIONAL UNIVERSITY—EUROPE

LONDON, ENGLAND

United States International University—Europe (USIU—E), an associate campus of United States International University of San Diego, California, is located in Bushey, Hertfordshire, in an idyllic setting 16 miles northwest of London. It is truly an international school: over 60 nationalities are represented in the student body of some 700 undergraduate and graduate students. The School of Business and Management, presently the largest discipline, contains approximately 442 students of whom 78 are enrolled in the graduate program.

United States International University—Europe (USIU—E) is accredited by the Western Association of Schools and Colleges (WASC), as are the other associate campuses in Nairobi and Mexico City. USIU—E is also a member of the Council of Graduate Schools of the United States and the Western Association of Graduate Schools. The School of Business and Management is a member of the American Assembly of Collegiate Schools of Business (AACSB).

The campus of 95 acres is composed of playing fields, lawns, and 32 major buildings dominated by the campus bell tower rising above the administrative block. Housing is available for single undergraduate and graduate students.

PROGRAMS OF STUDY

The Graduate School of Business and Management offers the following degree programs: Master of Science (M.S.) in management of human resources, Master of Science in business management, and the Master of Business Administration (M.B.A.). The M.S. in management of human resources is designed for individuals in management positions or aspiring to management positions, who are seeking more extensive knowledge of the human component in the organizational environment. The program focuses upon the organization of work environments, the relationship between human resources, and methods of organizational change that reduce conflict while expanding human potential and productivity.

The M.S. in business management is a general program designed for students who do not intend to pursue the two-year M.B.A. program. It provides a solid foundation in advanced issues in business and management. Students who complete the M.S. and then wish to obtain an M.B.A. degree as well will have 30 of the 45 units credited toward the 90-unit M.B.A. program for either M.S. program. The nine

courses (45 quarter units) required normally take one academic year of full-time study (three courses per quarter) or longer if fewer courses are taken per quarter.

The M.B.A. program is primarily oriented toward individuals who have progressed beyond the entry-level managerial position in an organization to a position with expanded responsibilities. It provides the student with a deeper and broader exposure to each of the functional areas and a more complete understanding of the human dimension in business and management.

The program has two tracks: Track I is for students who have completed a bachelor's degree in business administration with 45 upper-division units in the major or who have completed the M.S. in management of human resources or in business management at USIU—E. Such students may have up to six courses (30 units) of the 90 units required waived on the basis of course equivalencies. Track II is for students not meeting the aforementioned criteria and therefore requires 18 courses (90 units).

The Doctor of Business Administration (D.B.A.) program is designed to instill in managers a multidisciplinary global perspective, emphasizing practical abilities and experience as well as theory. Its focus encompasses social, psychological, economic, and political aspects in complementing the business and management phases. The program goal is to assist highly motivated, mature students become either competent strategic managers in a transnational world or career teachers or researchers.

ADMISSION

Admission criteria for master's degree applicants are the same for all three programs. Factors considered are undergraduate academic performance (minimum cumulative grade-point average of 2.70), scores on the Graduate Management Admission Test (GMAT) and letters of recommendation. In addition, for international students adequate performance on the Test of English as a Foreign Language (TOEFL) is required. Students may enter the programs at the beginning of any quarter.

For admission to the D.B.A. program a master's degree in business management or a related field with a grade-point average of 3.5 is required. The GMAT score must be submitted along with two letters of recommendation, attesting to a strong capacity for advanced graduate study.

EXPENSES

Fees per academic quarter for full-time students:

Tuition, per quarter (15 units). . . £1320
Tuition, per course (5 units) . . . . £ 440
Room and board, per quarter . . £ 650

All applicants for admission must pay a nonrefundable £25 evaluation fee at the time of application. All fees are subject to change.

FINANCIAL ASSISTANCE

Graduate students may be eligible for appointment to counseling staffs of residence halls. Stipends include room and board fees.

There are no academic fellowships currently available to international students. State and federal government grants to United States students are honored.

CORRESPONDENCE

For further information or to request an application for admission, please write or call

Director of Admissions
United States International University
10455 Pomerado Road
San Diego, California 92131
Telephone: 619-271-4300
    or
Director of Admissions
USIU—E
The Avenue, Bushey
Herts, WD2 2LN
England
Telephone: Watford 49067

The Faculte d'administration de l'Universite de Sherbrooke, established in 1955, became in 1965 the first French-speaking university to offer a cooperative Master of Business Administration (M.B.A.) program.

PROGRAMS OF STUDY

The goal of the M.B.A. program is to train individuals in management in order to help them realize their own career goals, to operate effectively within an organization, and to help society adapt to change.

The Universite de Sherbrooke was the first in Canada to offer a cooperative system for a graduate business program. In addition to four academic terms, students spend periods in industry where they relate the theory they have learned to practice. These jobs are carefully chosen so that each student gets the experience in the field which is the most interesting to him or her. The duration of the program is 24 months.

The Faculte d'administration also offers a Master of Science (M.Sc.) degree in systems analysis, finance, marketing, and human productivity management. The M.Sc. program aims toward the training of theorists in the management sciences, specialized in one or the other of the above mentioned fields. Most of the graduates opt for careers in business or teaching. Those who choose business will normally be called upon to act as counselors and very often participate in further training programs for executives. As to those who are looking for professorship, the training they will receive will prepare them to assume teaching positions or to pursue doctoral studies.

In order to prepare them for these careers, the training of the candidates revolves around the three following points:
• mastering the concepts, techniques, and tools in the chosen field of specialization;
• becoming familiarized with the techniques and the rigorous methodology of scientific research;
• initiating oneself with the most appropriate teaching methods in these fields.

The duration of the program is at least 16 months; however, the student may extend it to more in order to profit from and contribute to the academic environment. The maximum duration, however, is set at four years.

ADMISSION

The selection of students must conform to the objectives and characteristics of the program. Therefore, one of the roles of the Admission Committee is to examine each application in terms of the heterogeneity of the group to be formed. The majority of M.B.A. candidates already have a university degree in law, engineering, social sciences, pedagogy or pure sciences. All of the candidates have at least two years of practical experience. A number of persons who do not have a university degree but who do have a solid professional background are admitted to the program every year. The selection process consists of four steps: (1) each applicant must submit application forms, undergraduate grades, and three personal recommendations to the Director of the Program; (2) each applicant must submit scores on the Graduate Management Admission Test (GMAT); and (3) each applicant will be interviewed by the members of the Admissions Committee. All necessary credentials should be on file in the school by May 31. Forty-five students are enrolled each year in the M.B.A. program.

The recruiting of some 30 candidates admitted each year in the M.Sc. program is done mainly among Canadian and European universities and more specifically among the graduates who hold a bachelor's degree in administration or in economics who wish to pursue specialized training. The candidate interested in enrolling in this program must obtain, complete, and return to the Registrar's Office the forms needed to constitute a personal record.

EXPENSES

Tuition for the M.B.A. program is $365 per academic session. Costs during an academic session term are, at a minimum, the following: (1) food and lodging, $300 a month for a single person, $400 a month for a married couple; (2) $100 for books for each academic session; and (3) $50 per month for other expenses.

Tuition for the M.Sc. program is $315 per session. For the second year and the following one tuition is $25 per year. Food and lodging could be estimated at $300 per month for a single person, $400 per month for a married couple.

Tuition fee for foreign students is $2,307.50 for each academic session for the M.B.A. program and $2,257.50 for the M.Sc. program.

FINANCIAL ASSISTANCE

For M.B.A. students a plan for aid offers loans to pay tuition fees for the second, third, and fourth academic sessions. The criteria for the awarding of a loan are, first, academic success and, second, financial need. During their practical work sessions, students earn on the average more than $1,600 per month; therefore, it is possible for a student to cover a large part of the expenses during the program. For more information on scholarships, write to Madame Louise Bedard, Bureau de la Recherche et des Bourses, Pavillon Central, Universite de Sherbrooke, Sherbrooke, Quebec.

PLACEMENT

The university maintains a placement office. Many of the students stay on with the employers who offered them practical work sessions. The Coordination Service also aids in finding employment opportunities.

CORRESPONDENCE

For further information, write to
Directeur du Programme M.B.A. *or*
Directeur de Programme M.Sc.
Faculte d'administration
Universite de Sherbrooke
Sherbrooke, Quebec J1K 2R1
Canada
Telephone: 819-821-7330
Telex: 05-836149

University College Galway was founded in 1845 and became a constituent college of the National University of Ireland in 1908. Located in the city of Galway on the west coast of Ireland, the college offers undergraduate and postgraduate courses in the Faculties of Arts, Commerce, Science, Engineering, Medicine, and Law. Degrees are conferred by the National University of Ireland. The college has an academic staff of 250 professors and lecturers, and a student enrollment of 4,600. The academic year of the college commences in September and finishes in June.

PROGRAMS OF STUDY

The Faculty of Commerce offers undergraduate courses leading to the degree of Bachelor of Commerce. The Master of Business Administration (M.B.A.) program commenced in 1972, and more recently, a program of study leading to the degree of Master of Business Studies (M.B.S.) became available in the college. The Faculty of Commerce also offers courses leading to a postgraduate Diploma in Systems Analysis.

The M.B.A. program is offered on a part-time basis only, over two academic years. It is designed to prepare qualified and experienced people for wider responsibilities in the field of management or administration. The first year of the program consists of courses in business administration, quantitative analysis, accounting, finance, production, marketing, organizational psychology, and economics. The second year courses are designed to treat some of these subjects at a more advanced policy level, and to integrate that knowledge in the solution of business problems. The courses for the second year are business policy, management of new enterprise, business law, management accounting, financial analysis, production policy/quantitative analysis, marketing policy, and industrial relations. The emphasis is on classroom discussion, and particularly in the second year, on case studies. In addition to these course requirements, a dissertation must be submitted by degree candidates at the end of the second year.

The M.B.A. program is offered on a cyclical basis, with the admission of about 30 students every two years. The next cycle of the program will commence in September 1988. Applications for this cycle will be sought in January 1988.

The M.B.S. program is designed for the student with an honors undergraduate degree in business from a recognized university who wishes to specialize further within the business area. The student may concentrate in accounting/finance, marketing, or in management information systems. The normal duration of the program is one academic year of full-time study. A research dissertation in the chosen major subject area must be presented by candidates for the degree at the end of their period of study.

The Diploma in Systems Analysis is offered on a part-time basis over one academic year to students who hold a degree from a recognized institution, and who have not had substantial exposure to the computing/information systems area. The diploma course is significantly project oriented, and students are required to complete a number of management information systems projects during their period of study.

ADMISSION

To be eligible for admission to the M.B.A. program, applicants must hold a degree from a recognized university, and have at least three years of full-time business or administrative experience. Prior study of business subjects is not a requirement. The criteria used in the evaluation of applications include the quality of previous academic work, Graduate Management Admission Test (GMAT) scores, and evidence of maturity, motivation, and potential obtained from personal interviews and letters of recommendation. Acceptance is conditional on the applicant demonstrating a basic competence in certain core disciplines before commencing formal M.B.A. studies. For this purpose, preliminary courses are held in the college during the months of August and September immediately prior to the commencement of each cycle of the program.

EXPENSES

The following M.B.A. program expenses (subject to change) are based on the costs pertaining to the 1984-86 cycle of the M.B.A. program.

	E.E.C. Residents	Others
Tuition fees, per year	IR£1,256	IR£2,512
Application fee	20	20
Preliminary course fee	50	50
Books, etc., per year	500	500

(Note: IR£ = US$1.25 approx.)

CORRESPONDENCE

For additional information, write to
  The Academic Secretary
  University College
  Galway, Ireland

The University of Adelaide was established in 1874 and is the third oldest university in Australia. Today, over 9,000 students are enrolled in undergraduate and postgraduate courses offered through the faculties of Agricultural Science, Architecture and Planning, Arts, Dentistry, Economics, Engineering, Law, Mathematical Sciences, Medicine, Music, Science, and the Board of Environmental Studies. The main campus of the university is situated on North Terrace in the city of Adelaide, South Australia.

For the student, the university provides a wide range of services and facilities. These include a careers and counseling service, a network of course advisers, a university health service, student welfare support, and a physical education center.

In addition to their studies, students have the opportunity to participate in a wealth of cultural, social, and sporting activities on campus with over 60 clubs and societies to join.

PROGRAM OF STUDY

In 1963, the University of Adelaide admitted, for the first time, candidates to the course for the degree of Master of Business Management (M.B.M.). It thus became one of the first universities in Australia to offer a master's degree in management. The degree was given a new structure in 1976, and this structure has been further modified since then, but the basic objectives remain unchanged. The course is designed for well-qualified university graduates planning a career in senior management. Other persons who provide satisfactory evidence of their fitness to undertake work for the degree may be admitted to the course.

In 1982, in response to demands from graduates and current students, the university decided to change the name of the degree from M.B.M. to Master of Business Administration (M.B.A.). The change of name became effective in 1983, but the structure and content of the program remain unaltered.

The M.B.A. program, which is available on both a full-time and part-time basis, is designed to be completed in two years of full-time study or in approximately four years of part-time study.

Currently, approximately 130 students are enrolled in the program. These students are drawn from diverse backgrounds with previous tertiary studies, including engineering, science, arts, law, economics, architecture, and agricultural science. Employment experience prior to entry to the course is also extremely varied and includes employment by commercial and industrial enterprises, government and semi-government authorities, professional offices, and educational institutions.

The University of Adelaide adopts a multidisciplinary approach to management education. The compulsory core of the M.B.A. program is designed to ensure that graduates understand the basic concepts of economics, mathematics, statistics, accounting, finance, marketing, and behavioral science, which are relevant to management. Later in the course these concepts are applied to the analysis and solution of problems that arise in a wide range of managerial situations. The project work requirement similarly is designed to develop the student's ability to apply the various disciplinary concepts to specific management problems.

The course aims to educate potential managers in all areas of management rather than in specialist functional areas. At the same time it allows students a significant degree of choice in the second part of the course. The University of Adelaide takes the view that the program should be aimed at assisting the graduate in academic and personal development, rather than attempting to provide a standard set of management tools and techniques.

ADMISSION

Applications for admission are considered by a Selection Committee, which meets in the December prior to the start of the academic year in March of the following year. Admission is open to all qualified men and women who hold a bachelor's degree in any field from an approved undergraduate institution and who have worked for at least two years.

The Graduate Management Admission Test (GMAT) is required of all applicants. Applicants should take the test no later than October. Selection is based on the applicant's academic record, score on the GMAT, evaluation of referees' reports, and employment experience.

Applications for admission should be filed by October 31 and should be accompanied by official transcripts of previous academic studies. Applicants are advised of the result of their applications early in January.

EXPENSES

No tuition fees are currently made. Students are required to pay the prescribed statutory fees, which currently are approximately $200 p.a. for full-time students and a lesser rate for part-time students. Single students are advised to allow at least $130-$150 (Aust.) per week to meet the costs of board and lodging, clothing, and daily travel.

FINANCIAL ASSISTANCE

With the exception of a limited number of Commonwealth Postgraduate Course Awards, financial assistance is not available.

CORRESPONDENCE

For further information or to request an application for admission, write or call

Director
Graduate School of Management
University of Adelaide
Box 498, G.P.O.
Adelaide, S.A., 5001, Australia
Telephone: Adelaide (08) 228-5525

Buchtel College was established in 1870, becoming the municipal University of Akron in 1913. In 1967, the University of Akron became a state university and now enrolls more than 26,000 students.

The Department of Commerce began offering courses in 1919. In 1953 the College of Business Administration was established; current enrollment is 2,100 undergraduate and 500 graduate students. All master's programs are accredited by the American Assembly of Collegiate Schools of Business (AACSB). Graduate courses are offered only in the evening hours, as most of the graduate business students work full time. The graduate programs are designed to develop both the practical and theoretical skills necessary for graduates to assume challenging managerial roles. Graduate courses use case studies, interactive computing, research projects, and lectures to prepare graduates for business careers.

PROGRAMS OF STUDY

Programs leading to the degrees of Master of Business Administration (M.B.A.), Master of Science in Management (M.S.M.), Master of Science in Accounting (M.S.A.), and Master of Taxation (M.T.) are offered.

The M.B.A. program (36 semester credits) provides a broad general knowledge of the functional areas of business as well as concentration in one area (accounting, finance, international business, management, or marketing).

The M.S.M. (36 semester credits) and M.S.A. (30 semester credits) programs provide a limited exposure to the functional areas of business and a detailed concentration in management or accounting. Because of the heavily quantitative nature of the M.S.M. program, it is particularly suited to individuals with engineering or science backgrounds.

The Master of Taxation degree program (30 semester credits) is designed to meet the growing need for specialization in taxation. The taxation program is particularly attractive to students with accounting or law backgrounds.

All graduate degree programs may require "bridge-up" credits for students without undergraduate degrees in business.

ADMISSION

The University of Akron seeks qualified applicants for the master's programs. Neither an undergraduate degree in business nor previous business-related courses are required for admission to the programs. The admission decision is based on an evaluation of all application materials submitted by the individual. Previous academic records, prior work experiences, recommendations, test scores and evidence of maturity and motivation are among the factors assessed during the admission process. All applicants are required to submit official Graduate Management Admission Test (GMAT) scores.

To be eligible for consideration for admission to the graduate programs in the College of Business Administration (C.B.A.), the domestic applicant must meet one of the following two minimum requirements:

(1) hold a domestic baccalaureate degree from a regionally accredited college or university and have a total score of 1,000 or more points based upon the overall undergraduate grade-point average $(A = 4.0) \times 200 +$ the GMAT score, or

(2) hold a domestic baccalaureate degree from a regionally accredited college or university and have a total of 1,050 or more points based upon the junior-senior (last 64 semester or 96 quarter credits) grade-point average $\times 200 +$ the GMAT score.

Foreign applicants having a degree from outside the United States must have an academic standing of first or high second class, score 550 or above on the Test of English as a Foreign Language (TOEFL), and score at least 450 on the GMAT.

Offers of admission are normally limited to the most qualified of the eligible applicants as determined by the C.B.A. Graduate Admissions Committee. The Graduate Admissions Committee meets four times per year (approximately four weeks after each GMAT administration date) to evaluate all current applicants simultaneously. Therefore, all of the applicants' credentials (except the GMAT score for those taking it on the most recent test date) must be received at least four weeks before the Graduate Admissions Committee meets.

EXPENSES

A nonrefundable application fee of $25 is charged. Graduate tuition is $77 per semester credit for Ohio residents and $133 per credit for non-Ohio residents. Tuition and fees are subject to change without notice. Housing in the community is available at a variety of rates.

FINANCIAL ASSISTANCE

A limited number of graduate assistantships are available. Graduate assistantships provide a modest stipend of $4,500 per year, plus remission of tuition and fees. Graduate assistants are expected to assist in research or perform other duties for the university for approximately 20 hours per week and are expected to carry an academic load of 9 graduate credits per semester. Graduate assistantship applications should be on file by April 1 for the following academic year.

PLACEMENT

The University Placement Office assists students seeking employment. An active file of employment opportunities is maintained for students and alumni.

CORRESPONDENCE

For further information, write or call
Director, Graduate Programs
 in Business
College of Business Administration
University of Akron
Akron, Ohio 44325
Telephone: 216-375-7043

The University of Alabama's Graduate School of Business was established in 1919. The school began to offer the Doctor of Philosophy (Ph.D.) degree in business administration in 1950. Instruction leads to the Master of Business Administration (M.B.A.), the Executive M.B.A. degree (E.M.B.A.), Educational Specialist in Business Administration (Ed.S.), and the Ph.D. degrees.

Full-time enrollment in the M.B.A. program is currently 100; doctoral students number 109. There are 101 members of the Graduate School of Business Faculty.

PROGRAMS OF STUDY

The M.B.A. degree is currently the primary source of managerial talent for many organizations in both the public and private sector. Hundreds of organizations are seeking executives for the future from within the ranks of the nation's M.B.A. programs. The M.B.A. program at Alabama is designed to provide students with an educational experience that will give them access to the executive world of business, industry, and government.

The Alabama M.B.A. is a full-time, two-year program emphasizing the skills of decision making and communication. The program is intentionally small; only a limited number of highly qualified students are accepted each year. The program is called a "lock-step" program because students are admitted as a class in the fall only and stay together as a class for most of the two-year period.

The first year of study consists of 30 hours of course work (15 hours per semester) structured to introduce students to the functions of management as well as the analytical tools of decision making. The second year consists of 30 hours of course work, which emphasizes organizational strategy and an understanding of the organization's role in the environment and allows students to develop an area of concentration in one of the various business disciplines.

The lock-step M.B.A. program is specifically structured to allow M.B.A. students to gain practical experience and establish beneficial contacts in the business community through a summer internship program during the summer between their first and second years. Upon approval of the M.B.A. Committee, a student may receive three hours of elective credit within his or her area of concentration for the internship.

The Graduate School of Business and the School of Law at the University of Alabama offer a jointly administered program leading to the Master of Business Administration and Juris Doctor degrees. Candidates for admission to the joint program are expected to meet the admission requirements of both schools.

The Executive M.B.A. Program is a weekend program for full-time managers, specialists with technical backgrounds, entrepreneurs, and managers in the not-for-profit or private sector. It meets on alternate weekends over a 17-month period. It is equivalent to the full-time program offered to lock-step students, but tailored in time, scheduling, and emphasis to fit the needs and responsibilities of experienced executives.

All classes are held at North River Yacht Club, one of North America's most exclusive conference retreats.

The programs leading to the degree of Educational Specialist or Ph.D. in business administration are flexible and are based on the student's interests and education.

ADMISSION

Students are admitted to the school on the basis of aptitude and intellectual ability evidenced in their undergraduate record, letters of recommendation, and scores on the Graduate Management Admission Test (GMAT). Scores on the Test of English as a Foreign Language (TOEFL) are required of foreign applicants.

M.B.A. students enter in August only; E.M.B.A. students enter in January only. Applications should be filed at least three months prior to planned enrollment.

EXPENSES

Tuition and fees for 1985-86 were $1,206 for full-time, in-state students and $1,293 for out-of-state students for the academic year. E.M.B.A. tuition, meals, books and lodging amount to $13,250 for the entire program.

The average charge for room and board in university residence halls is approximately $2,500 per year. Private apartments are available at varying costs.

FINANCIAL ASSISTANCE

Students applying for financial aid through the Graduate School must be admitted to the University of Alabama and the Graduate School.

The Graduate School awards a limited number of Graduate Council Fellowships to students with outstanding academic records. In addition, several departmental assistantships are awarded by the various areas within the college. Further information can be obtained from the Financial Aids Advisor in the Office of the Graduate School, Room 102, Rose Administration Building or the M.B.A. Coordinator.

PLACEMENT

Graduate students in business may use the services of the University Career Planning Service. Approximately 300 organizations visit the campus to recruit University of Alabama students each year. Other services provided by the Career Planning Service include seminars on resume writing and interview skills as well as career planning counseling.

CORRESPONDENCE

For further information, please write or call

M.B.A. Coordinator
The University of Alabama
Graduate School of Business
P.O. Box J
University, Alabama 35486
Telephone: 205-348-6517

UNIVERSITY OF ALABAMA AT BIRMINGHAM

BIRMINGHAM, ALABAMA

The University of Alabama at Birmingham (UAB) was established by action of the Board of Trustees in 1966 and was accredited as an independent educational institution in 1970 by the Southern Association of Colleges and Schools.

The University of Alabama at Birmingham is an urban university located in the financial, commercial, and manufacturing center of the state. Enrollment in all units for the fall quarter of 1984 was approximately 14,200 students.

The School of Business is an integral part of University College with an enrollment of approximately 2,000 undergraduate and 350 graduate students. The school is accredited at both the undergraduate and graduate levels by the American Assembly of Collegiate Schools of Business (AACSB). The university operates on a modified quarter system with admission to the Master of Business Administration (M.B.A.) and Master of Accounting (M.Ac.) programs limited to the fall and spring quarters of each academic year.

PROGRAMS OF STUDY

The UAB School of Business offers a professional graduate program designed to acquaint students with all aspects of business activity while developing competency in management and organization.

The M.B.A. program is directed toward preparing graduate students, regardless of their undergraduate training, for leadership in business, industry, government, and social service. A maximum of 54 semester hours credit is required for the M.B.A. degree. However, undergraduates in business or other areas with course work in required functional areas may have certain core courses waived. The minimum requirement is 36 semester hours. Evening offerings ensure the availability of courses for students attending on a part-time basis.

The M.Ac. program provides specialized graduate-level instruction in accounting for students who plan to assume leadership roles in the production and use of accounting information in industry, public accounting, and not-for-profit organizations. The program is designed to build an entry level of professional competence and to lay the foundation for subsequent professional development or additional graduate study. A minimum of 33 semester hours is required for the degree. For students with baccalaureate degrees in fields other than accounting, the maximum may be as high as 66 semester hours.

The School of Business in cooperation with the School of Community and Allied Health also offers the Ph.D. in administration/health services. The program is designed to attract a small number of highly qualified students who wish to pursue full-time advanced studies in the conceptual, philosophical, and applied aspects of administration in the health career environment.

ADMISSION

Admission to the M.B.A. program is limited to holders of baccalaureate degrees from regionally accredited institutions. Students seeking admission to the program must have completed satisfactorily (C grade or above) an undergraduate calculus course or must remove the deficiency within the first 12 months of their enrollment in the program. In addition, applicants must present evidence including, but not limited to, admission test scores and undergraduate records indicating high promise of success.

The admission decision will be made as follows: (1) the students must present a minimum Graduate Management Admission Test (GMAT) score of 450; (2) they must also have at least 950 points based on the formula 200 × the undergraduate grade-point average (4.0 system) plus the GMAT score; or at least 1,000 points based on the formula 200 × the upper-division grade-point average plus the GMAT score. For fall or spring admission, all required information must be in the Graduate School six weeks prior to regular registration for the quarter in which the student seeks admission.

Admission to the M.Ac. program will be made on the same basis as the M.B.A. program.

EXPENSES

General fees for all in-state graduate students

Graduate School fees,
per semester hour........... $ 59
(Maximum of $490 per quarter)

General fees for all out-of-state graduate students

Graduate School fees,
per semester hour........... 108
(Maximum of $980 per quarter)

Student activity fee for
all students................. 15
Building fee 15

FINANCIAL ASSISTANCE

Assistantships, ranging to $1,500 per quarter, are available for qualified full-time graduate students. Graduate students also have the opportunity to earn funds by assisting individual faculty members on funded research projects.

CORRESPONDENCE

For further information on the M.B.A. and M.Ac. programs, write
Graduate Coordinator
Graduate School of Management
University of Alabama at Birmingham
Birmingham, Alabama 35294
Telephone: 205-934-8817

School of Administrative Science
THE UNIVERSITY OF ALABAMA IN HUNTSVILLE
HUNTSVILLE, ALABAMA

The University of Alabama in Huntsville was established to provide postbaccalaureate education in support of the needs of scientific and technological enterprises and the cultural and intellectual needs of a rapidly expanding region. The university has evolved into a major southeastern center of high technology and research complementing governmental and industrial activities in missile and aerospace research and development, space technology, computers and electronics, energy and environmental studies.

The university has a student enrollment of approximately 5,000. It is located in northwest Huntsville adjacent to the 1,300-acre Research Park and near the NASA Marshall Space Flight Center, the US Army Missile Material Readiness Command, and numerous high-technology firms. Huntsville, which has a metropolitan area population of approximately 300,000, is located in the Tennessee River Valley and surrounded on three sides by the Appalachian Mountain foothills.

The School of Administrative Science is committed to a standard of excellence in educating students who will enter business, industry, and government at all levels of responsibility. The school has over 1,000 undergraduate and 200 graduate students. A central premise of the school's mission is that the ever-increasing influence and importance of complex organizations require the development of competent and creative managers who understand the role of complex systems now and in the future.

PROGRAM OF STUDY
The Master of Administrative Science degree program provides entry-level and mid-career students with a broad understanding of managing complex organizations. The program is designed to create an awareness of the legal, social, and ethical environment in which public and private management tasks are accomplished. The quantitative and human aspects of organizational problem solving in a high-technology environment are emphasized as well as the communication, interpersonal, and negotiating skills essential to effective management. Entering students with no previous academic course work in business or management may be required to complete up to 21 hours of foundation course work in addition to the 36-hour degree program.

The degree program includes a core curriculum in management concepts, organizational theory, organizational behavior, managerial economics, and accounting, as well as quantitative methods.

In addition to the core curriculum, every student completes an option consisting of 15 semester hours. Options are available in management information systems, economics, educational administration, operations research, personnel and human resources management, product management, and project management. A student may also tailor an option to fit his or her individual career needs.

The program culminates with the capstone seminar, which is a study of administrative processes under conditions of uncertainty and involves doing integrative analysis and strategic policy determination at the overall management level.

ADMISSION
Admission to the graduate program is based on the student's aptitude, ability, achievement, work experience, and leadership qualities. Successful candidates have (1) strong analytical skills; (2) a strong background in mathematics, economics, the social and behavioral sciences, and communication skills; and (3) full-time work experience.

Unconditional admission requires a minimum score of 450 on the Graduate Management Admission Test (GMAT) and a minimum undergraduate grade-point average of 3.0. Students not meeting these standards may be admitted probationally if there is strong evidence of potential to successfully perform graduate work in the student's academic performance, GMAT score, and work experience.

Application may be made for admission during any term by submitting an application, two copies of transcripts, GMAT scores, and any additional information that may assist the admissions committee in its decision. Application should be made at least two months before the term. Applicants for whom English is not the native language must also submit Test of English as a Foreign Language (TOEFL) scores of at least 500.

EXPENSES
For Alabama residents tuition and fees for 1984-85 were approximately $1,200 per academic year for a full-time student. Nonresident graduate students paid approximately $2,200 per academic year. Reduced tuition rates applied to students taking less than six semester hours. A realistic budget (excluding tuition) for a single person is $4,925 per academic year. A couple should budget about $5,925 per academic year, adding approximately $1,500 per child.

FINANCIAL ASSISTANCE
The Graduate Program in Administrative Science provides a variety of financial assistance opportunities. Graduate research and teaching assistantships are available with academic year stipends ranging from $2,500 to $5,000. Individuals holding assistantships will receive partial or full tuition remission. Teaching and lab assistantships are available for students with a strong background in accounting, economics, or quantitative methods. Letters of application, including a resume, should be directed to the Graduate Program Coordinator.

A graduate cooperative education program involving alternating six-month periods of full-time work and academic study is available with placements in a wide range of area industries and governmental organizations.

Information about loans, grants-in-aid, and part-time work can be obtained from the Financial Aids Office.

PLACEMENT
The school provides career counseling and other opportunities through the Career Planning and Placement Office.

CORRESPONDENCE
For further information, write or call
Graduate Program Coordinator
School of Administrative Science
The University of Alabama in
Huntsville
Huntsville, Alabama 35899
Telephone: 205-895-6024

UNIVERSITY OF ALASKA, ANCHORAGE

ANCHORAGE, ALASKA

A major university campus of the University of Alaska (UAA) statewide system of higher education, the University of Alaska, Anchorage, became a four-year institution in 1977. UAA is accredited by the Commission on Colleges of the Northwest Association of Schools and Colleges. The university also has professional accreditation and certification in nursing, social work, engineering, and education.

UAA serves some 5,000 students in its undergraduate, graduate, and continuing education programs. Organized research units include the Alaska Center for International Business, Institute for Social and Economic Research, Center for Economic Education, Justice Center, Center for Alcohol and Addiction Studies, and the Center for High Latitude Health Research.

Served by public transportation, students enjoy ready access to theaters, restaurants, shopping, and housing. On-campus housing is available. Located on a scenic, wooded campus with a spectacular view of the snow-capped Chugach Mountains, UAA is only a short drive from the major recreational areas of the state.

The School of Business and Public Affairs is located in the state's commercial, financial, and cultural center. The proximity of the university to the city center allows the School of Business and Public Affairs faculty and students to work closely with business organizations and governmental agencies. Case studies, research, and off-campus education are facilitated by the willingness of the community to assist faculty and students in studying business and governmental institutions and activities.

PROGRAM OF STUDY

The Master of Business Administration (M.B.A.) is a professional degree offered through the School of Business and Public Administration. It is designed to prepare students to pursue meaningful and rewarding careers in management. The curriculum for the M.B.A. degree is management-oriented rather than highly specialized and emphasizes concepts that are relevant to both small and large firms and both the public and private sectors.

The M.B.A. degree is designed for the individual who wants to pursue a professional career in management or one of its subfields. The 30-credit-hour program consists of basic core courses (24 credit hours) and electives (6 credit hours).

After completing the basic core courses the student must pass a written comprehensive examination. No formal thesis is required for the program, but the integrative course at the end does require that the student develop and complete a practical project in general administration.

The content of the core courses assumes an undergraduate business background or equivalent level of knowledge. Thus the student entering the program is expected to have introductory-level knowledge of accounting, finance, marketing, organizational behavior, management, micro- and macroeconomics, elementary statistics, calculus, and computer programming. Students who are deficient in one or more of these areas are expected to make up these deficiencies by completing equivalent undergraduate courses.

It is possible to complete all requirements for the M.B.A. degree while employed full time. Most graduate classes are scheduled at night, and part-time students typically enroll in one or two classes per semester. A full-time student may complete the program in three semesters, depending on scheduling and other factors.

ADMISSION

Admission to the program is based on the formula: (undergraduate grade-point average) × 200 plus Graduate Management Admission Test (GMAT) score, to total at least 1,050 points. Transcripts of all college work are also required. Applications may be obtained from the Office of Admissions.

The fall semester extends from early September to mid-December, and the spring semester begins in mid-January and ends in early May. Applications for fall admission are accepted up to May 1 and for spring admission until October 1.

EXPENSES

Tuition, per semester
Resident .... $ 585*
Nonresident 1,215*
Fees 39*

---

*Subject to change.

After 1986, UAA will have campus housing. For information, write to the UAA Housing Department.

FINANCIAL ASSISTANCE

Inquiries concerning financial aid should be directed to the Financial Aid Office, which maintains information both on general university financial aid programs and those particularly applicable to graduate students. Information on part-time employment, both on campus and in the community, is available through the Office of Student Services.

PLACEMENT

The university Placement Office conducts an active recruiting service and maintains placement files for graduates. Numerous employers recruit on campus during both fall and spring semesters.

CORRESPONDENCE

For further information or to request an application for admission, please write
M.B.A. Program Director
University of Alaska, Anchorage
3210 Providence Drive
Anchorage, Alaska 99508

The University of Alberta is a publicly supported coeducational institution located about two miles from the business center of Edmonton, the capital of Alberta. Since its founding in 1906, it has had a record of rapid growth, especially during the last 20 years. During the 1984-85 year, there were more than 23,800 full-time students registered in degree and diploma programs of the university. Of these, approximately 2,500 were pursuing graduate programs. The full-time academic staff numbers about 1,580.

University research facilities include an extensive library system holding over 2,000,000 volumes, 500,000 documents, 15,000 periodical subscriptions, audiovisual aids, and a large collection of research materials in microfilm. The university has, for use of students and faculty, one of the larger computers in Canada. This facility provides excellent time-sharing capability for the more than 2,200 terminals distributed throughout the campus, as well as batch processing that commonly provides very fast turnabout time.

The Master of Business Administration (M.B.A.) program at the university was started in 1964. Since that time, its enrollment has grown to the present level of 130 full-time and 120 part-time students. The Master of Public Management (M.P.M.) program was started in September 1982. The Faculty of Business has a full-time academic staff of 72, plus a number of sessional lecturers. Undergraduate enrollment in the faculty is approximately 1,750 full-time students.

PROGRAMS OF STUDY

The Faculty of Business offers two programs of professional education for business and government leadership: the Master of Business Administration degree and the Master of Public Management degree. Both programs are designed for students with various educational backgrounds: liberal arts, engineering, science, education, business administration, and others. Normally requiring two academic years of study, each program is structured in two phases. The first consists of half-year core courses in the fundamental areas underlying administration and decision making. These core courses give all students a common comprehensive base upon which advanced elective courses are built. Some of the foundation courses in both programs are jointly core. This recognizes that some management skills and theories are equally applicable in both the public and private sectors. Students who have already developed competence in one or more of these core areas may satisfy the corresponding requirement(s) by satisfactory performance on wavier examination(s).

The core courses may be taken either on a normal full-time basis or on a part-time basis, that is, one or two courses at a time. To accommodate those students who want to do this part of the program on a part-time basis, the majority of courses are offered in evening sections as well as sections that meet during the usual school day.

The M.B.A. program is designed to develop the student's critical, analytical, problem-solving, and decision-making capabilities, and to give him or her both a sense of mission and a sense of confidence in his or her abilities. Following completion of the foundation courses, the student then moves to the second part of the program consisting of advanced elective courses that give him or her the chance to pursue areas of interest in depth, either with or without a master's thesis. The thesis option requires a minimum of six advanced half-year courses in addition to the thesis; the nonthesis option requires a minimum of eight advanced courses and an individual research paper written under the direction of a faculty supervisor.

The M.P.M. program is designed for those interested in management careers in the public sector. It focuses on both management theory and skills and on public issues, policy formulation, and implementation. After completion of the foundation courses, the student may follow one of two streams in the second part of the program: thesis or nonthesis. Both options require a two-course sequence in public management and policy, as well as an advanced seminar in each of accounting and finance in the public sector. In addition to these required courses, the nonthesis option also includes three elective courses, which may be selected from a wide range of choices within the faculty's curriculum or through other departments of the university, as well as a research paper. With the thesis option, a thesis would be written and one elective course would remain to be completed.

ADMISSION

Admission to the M.B.A. or M.P.M. program is open to students holding a baccalaureate degree who present satisfactory evidence of ability to pursue graduate study. This evidence takes the form of academic performance during their last two years of formal study, scores on the Graduate Management Admission Test (GMAT), letters of recommendation, and a brief statement of purpose in undertaking either graduate program. In some instances, a personal interview may be requested. In addition, students whose native language is not English must demonstrate proficiency in English to the satisfaction of the Associate Dean.

EXPENSES

Tuition and fees for the 1985-86 academic year were $1,188 or $1,722 for holders of student visas. Living expenses vary depending upon housing and miscellaneous expenses but may typically be $5,500 for an eight-month academic year.

FINANCIAL ASSISTANCE

The faculty has a number of teaching and research assistantships which pay from $6,352 to $6,898 per academic year (1985-86 rate) in exchange for 12 hours of work each week. Limited fellowships and scholarships are also awarded.

CORRESPONDENCE

For further information, write to
Associate Dean M.B.A./M.P.M.
  Programs
Faculty of Business
The University of Alberta
Edmonton, Alberta T6G 2R6, Canada

Established in 1885, the University of Arizona is a land-grant state university. In addition to 14 colleges, the university contains 38 divisions of research.

Located in Tucson, Arizona, one of the fastest growing cities of the Sun Belt, the university is surrounded by an energetic, diverse community located 60 miles north of the United States-Mexican border. In the forefront of the developing high-technology, service-oriented economy of the future, Tucson attracts thousands of newcomers and visitors annually.

PROGRAMS OF STUDY
The College of Business and Public Administration offers the following programs of study at the master's level: Master of Business Administration (M.B.A.), Master of Accounting, Master of Arts in economics, Master of Science in finance, Master of Science in management, Master of Science in management information systems, Master of Science in marketing, Master of Public Administration, and Master of Policy and Planning. Doctor of Philosophy (Ph.D.) programs are offered in business administration and economics.

The M.B.A. student receives thorough training in the basic disciplines of problem solving and decision making. A key aspect of the M.B.A. program is an emphasis on the acquisition, management, and use of information for decision making. To accomplish this, all courses in the program integrate the use of micro and mainframe computers into their pedagogy. Previous business courses are not required; however, it is recommended that undergraduate courses in finite mathematics and elements of calculus be completed prior to entering the program. The degree requires 57 semester hours of graduate credit, 13 comprehensive core courses, and 6 electives. The program has both a part-time and full-time component and offers specialization options in accounting, economics, finance, health services administration, management information systems, organizational behavior/personnel management, and marketing.

The Master of Science degrees in finance, management, and marketing require 30 semester hours of graduate credit, and undergraduate business courses are a prerequisite. The Master of Science in management information systems degree requires 38 semester hours of study, and some previous study of economics,

statistics, and introductory work in computers is necessary. The Master of Public Administration (M.P.A.) degree requires 51 semester hours of credit. Most of those who enter the M.P.A. program have no previous study of public administration. The Master of Public Planning and Policy degree requires 54 semester hours of credit and is designed for students interested in careers as planners.

The Ph.D. programs in business administration and economics are designed for outstanding students who wish to prepare for careers in teaching and research.

ADMISSION
Master's candidates should submit application material as follows:
- application for admission to the Graduate College;
- two sets of official transcripts of all undergraduate and graduate work (to be sent directly from the institution);
- Graduate Programs Supplemental Information form with accompanying essays;
- resume describing relevant experiences, responsibilities, and achievements;
- two letters of recommendation from persons able to provide verification and a specific description of outstanding achievements;
- scores on the Graduate Management Admission Test (GMAT).

These materials should be sent to Director, Graduate Professional Programs, College of Business and Public Administration, University of Arizona, Tucson, Arizona 85721.

Applications are accepted and processed throughout the year. Entry into the M.B.A. program is for the fall semester only. Other students may begin study in August, January, or either summer session. The committee evaluates past academic performance, scores from the GMAT, and potential for success as indicated by employment experience and recommendations.

Foreign residents should also provide scores from the Test of English as a Foreign Language (TOEFL), if their native language is not English, and certification that sufficient funds are available for financing the first year of study.

EXPENSES
For the academic year 1985-86 (two semesters), Arizona residents were charged $990 in registration fees. Nonresident students paid tuition and fees of $3,844 for the academic year. Charges are subject to change by the Board of Regents.

FINANCIAL ASSISTANCE
Graduate assistantships, out-of-state tuition waivers, and academic scholarships are available. Applicants should apply early for consideration. The University of Arizona Financial Aids Office also makes arrangements for National Direct Student Loans.

PLACEMENT
The college has a Graduate Professional Programs Placement Office to assist graduates in obtaining employment in their professional fields.

CORRESPONDENCE
For information on master's programs, write

> Director, Graduate Professional
>   Programs
> College of Business and Public
>   Administration
> University of Arizona
> Tucson, Arizona 85721

For information on Ph.D. programs, write
Dr. William B. Barrett
Associate Dean
College of Business and Public
    Administration
University of Arizona
Tucson, Arizona 85721

The College of Business Administration under the auspices of the Graduate School of the University of Arkansas offers programs leading to the Master of Business Administration (M.B.A.) and Doctor of Philosophy (Ph.D.) in business administration, Master of Science (M.S.) in accounting, and Master of Arts (M.A.) and Ph.D. in economics degrees. The organizational structure of the college includes six departments: accounting, economics, finance, management, marketing, and quantitative management science. Both the undergraduate and master's degree programs in business administration are accredited by the American Assembly of Collegiate Schools of Business (AACSB).

The campus location in the Ozark Mountains offers extensive outdoor recreational opportunities. A new $5-million College of Business Administration Building was occupied in 1977. With over 100,000 square feet of floor space, the building offers the most up-to-date facilities.

PROGRAMS OF STUDY
The M.B.A. program is designed to provide for graduates from diverse academic backgrounds a professional foundation for careers in business and related fields. Emphasis is placed on understanding the nature of the business and economic system as a whole in order to prepare students for their future responsibilities in recognizing, analyzing, and solving organizational problems. While a number of courses of specialized nature are offered, overall emphasis is placed on breadth and integration of knowledge. The program reflects the importance of each student acquiring sound general principles and decision-making techniques that will remain effective in a changing environment. The M.B.A. is designed as a two-year degree, although students who have completed a bachelor's degree in business administration and who have had sufficient instruction in accounting, economics, statistics, business law, finance, marketing, and management can normally complete the program within one year. The final 30 hours of the M.B.A. are an integrated core of 18 hours covering the areas of accounting, economics, finance, marketing, management, and quantitative management science, and 12 hours of approved electives. The program does not require a thesis.

The student may, if desired, use the program's elective hours to concentrate in a special field. Besides the traditional func-tional areas, a number of other special fields of concentration are available. Courses in these fields are taught by scholars drawn from various disciplines. Examples of fields available include international marketing, real estate and urban land economics, computer-based systems/management science, and manpower management.

The Master of Arts in economics is designed for holders of baccalaureate degrees in either economics or business. The program requires 24 hours of course work plus a thesis. The thesis, however, may be waived if the student presents six hours of additional course work in a research-related area. Assignment of specific courses is generally accomplished after consultation with the major adviser of the Department of Economics.

The Master of Science in accounting program is designed for individuals interested in careers in professional accounting. The degree program requires 30 hours of course work for students with a baccalaureate degree in accounting. Students without previous course work in business or economics can complete the course of study in two years. The degree program does not require a thesis.

The doctoral program is designed for those who wish to prepare for college and university teaching, although a thorough background is provided for those who wish to pursue professional careers in industry, government, or private consulting. Before being admitted to candidacy, applicants for the Ph.D. degree must meet both the general requirements of the Graduate School, as outlined in the *Graduate Bulletin,* and those of the Graduate Advisory Committee of the College of Business Administration.

ADMISSION
Admission to all degree programs, except the M.A. and Ph.D. in economics, requires an undergraduate grade-point average of at least 2.5 (4.0 = A), a baccalaureate degree from an accredited four-year institution, and acceptable scores on the Graduate Management Admission Test (GMAT). Students holding appropriate master's degrees are evaluated in accordance with standards established by the Graduate School and the College of Business Administration.

EXPENSES
Semester tuition expenses for regular course loads:

In-state students	$ 550
Out-of-state students	1,180

FINANCIAL ASSISTANCE
Graduate assistantships at the master's level are awarded on the basis of undergraduate grade-point averages, GMAT scores, and letters of reference. The normal stipends range from $1,700 to $3,000 for nine months. Recipients of graduate assistantships are expected to work up to 16 hours per week in a research- or academic-related area. At the doctoral level, teaching associateships (six hours per semester) carry a stipend of $6,250 for nine months. Appointment as a teaching associate is based on grade-point average, GMAT scores, letters of reference, and teaching competency. All tuition is waived for the fall and spring for recipients of teaching associateships.

PLACEMENT
The university maintains a central placement office visited annually by representatives of approximately 300 companies from all sections of the country. The Graduate Studies Office of the College of Business Administration maintains a placement service for graduates seeking teaching and/or administrative positions.

CORRESPONDENCE
For further information or to request an application for admission, please call or write

Associate Dean—Graduate Programs
College of Business Administration
  (BA 334)
University of Arkansas
Fayetteville, Arkansas 72701
Telephone: 501-575-2851

The Master of Business Administration (M.B.A.) degree is designed to meet the need for well-educated managers and specialists in business, industry, finance, government, and nonprofit organizations. It is a professional degree designed primarily for those who desire graduate education to complete academic preparation for their chosen careers in business. The M.B.A. degree is recognized for faculty positions at community colleges and for initial appointments at some four-year institutions.

Emphasis in the program is on the practice of administration. The basic objectives of the program include the provision of an understanding of the basic concepts underlying the administrative process, development of skills in the identification and solution of problems, and the recognition of and creative response to opportunities. Students are afforded an opportunity to increase their competence in the practice of management through study of modern quantitative and behavioral theories and methodologies.

PROGRAMS OF STUDY

The M.B.A. program consists of two series of courses: Level I and Level II. Level I presents in nine courses (27 credit hours) a foundation level of knowledge equivalent to the undergraduate business core. Although it is designed as a transitional program for nonbusiness degree holders, the transcripts of all incoming students are evaluated, on a course-by-course basis, to determine whether they have had equivalent courses. In most cases, a student with an undergraduate business degree from a program accredited by the American Assembly of Collegiate Schools of Business (AACSB) may have most if not all Level I courses waived.

Level II consists of nine required courses (27 credit hours) and three electives (9 credit hours). The M.B.A. degree, therefore, may be earned with a minimum of 36 credit hours. A concentration in management, finance, or marketing may be achieved by taking all nine credit hours of electives in that area.

The M.B.A. program is a nonthesis program, but students contemplating entering a doctoral program are encouraged to take a directed research course to obtain some of the formal research experience that a thesis would provide. However, no more than three credit hours of independent study or directed research courses may be counted toward the requirements of the M.B.A. program.

The college offers a joint program with the Law School for those aspiring to both the M.B.A. degree and the Juris Doctor (J.D.). Contact the Director of the M.B.A. program for details.

ADMISSION

To be considered for admission to the M.B.A. program, the student must have a bachelor's degree from an accredited institution of higher education and must take the Graduate Management Admission Test (GMAT). The undergraduate grade-point average is combined with the score on the GMAT to ascertain the student's eligibility for admission. Admission to the program requires admission to the Graduate School and a total of 1,050 points based on the formula: 200 times upper-division grade-point average plus the GMAT score. An applicant whose GMAT score is below 450 or whose grade-point average is less than 2.5 will not be granted admission. The college admits students in fall term only. Applications to the Graduate School must be received by May 31.

Credit for course work at another accredited college or university may be applied without limit toward the foundation (Level I) courses. A maximum of six semester hours of graduate credit may be transferred from approved graduate schools and applied to the Level II requirements of the program. It is assumed that entering students will have an elementary knowledge of the calculus.

EXPENSES

The registration fee is $55 per credit hour for Arkansas residents ($550 for full-time students). For out-of-state students, it is $118 per credit hour ($1,180 for full-time students).

FINANCIAL ASSISTANCE

A limited number of assistantships are available to well-qualified candidates. These require a 3.0 overall grade-point average and are awarded on the basis of undergraduate grade-point average and GMAT score. Assistants work 20 hours per week with professors in the college. The stipend is $5,100 for nine months and partial tuition remission.

CORRESPONDENCE

For further information, please write
Director of the M.B.A. Program
College of Business Administration
University of Arkansas at Little Rock
33rd and University Streets
Little Rock, Arkansas 72204
Telephone: 501-569-3356

The University of Baltimore, founded in 1925, is an upper-division, public institution, providing the third and fourth collegiate years, graduate programs and professional studies in law. Its curriculum has always been designed to prepare graduates for specific career fields. The university is accredited by the Middle States Association; its undergraduate business program is accredited by the American Assembly of Collegiate Schools of Business (AACSB).

The School of Business enrolls approximately 1,100 men and women at the graduate level, the majority of whom study part time. Classes are small, and no teaching is done by teaching assistants. Over 80 percent of the business faculty hold doctorates.

The University of Baltimore is an urban campus, which has taken advantage of its midtown location by developing strong links with the Baltimore business community for educational and job placement purposes. It has a consolidated campus, conveniently accessible to the surrounding region via major transportation routes.

PROGRAMS OF STUDY
The School of Business offers two major approaches to graduate studies, each resulting in the master's degree.

The Master of Business Administration (M.B.A.) curriculum has been designed for students with varied academic discipline backgrounds. Preparation in engineering, the arts or sciences, law, education, and other fields provides appropriate academic background for the M.B.A. program. The M.B.A. program includes such preparatory work as each student may be required to take, plus the basic 30-credit-hour program consisting of the functional and advanced-level specialization courses. Full-time students needing only the 30 hours of course work may complete the program in two semesters.

The M.B.A. program allows the student to select three electives from any of the graduate courses offered by the School of Business. Electives may be taken in accounting, economics, finance, international business, labor relations, management, management information systems, marketing, operations research/management science, personnel and industrial relations, and taxation. Students with prior professional studies may petition for six hours to apply toward their M.B.A. degree. The M.B.A. degree may be earned by taking day, evening, or weekend courses (Friday evening and Saturday morning) only or by mixing class selections.

The Master of Science (M.S.) degree is awarded to the student who completes any one of several specialized programs. These program curricula have been designed for students desiring to meet the increasing demands of a particular professional field. Programs offered that result in the award of the M.S. degree are accounting and business (with concentrations in economics, finance, international business, management, management information systems, marketing, operations research/management science, personnel and industrial relations, and production/operations management), economics, and taxation.

The School of Business, in concert with the School of Law, offers concurrent instruction leading to joint degree programs with the combination of Master of Business Administration/Juris Doctor (M.B.A./J.D.) and J.D./M.S. in taxation.

ADMISSION
The School of Business welcomes applications from all men and women holding baccalaureate degrees. The aim of the School of Business is to select those applicants who can successfully complete quality graduate study. To apply, students should submit the admission application, $25 fee, official transcripts, and the Graduate Management Admission Test (GMAT) score by July 15 for fall admission, December 1 for spring, or April 15 for summer. All international students are required to submit a 550 or higher score on the Test of English as a Foreign Language (TOEFL) and a score of 250 on the Test of Spoken English (TSE) prior to beginning their studies.

EXPENSES
Tuition and activity fees for graduate students in the current academic year total $88 per credit hour for graduate courses and $59 per credit hour for undergraduate courses. There are no out-of-state fees for graduate business studies.

CORRESPONDENCE
For further information, please write or call

Admissions Office
University of Baltimore
Charles Street at Mt. Royal
Baltimore, Maryland 21201
Telephone: 301-625-3348

UNIVERSITY OF BATH

BATH, UNITED KINGDOM

Bath is a historic and beautiful city with a modern university that is now one of the most popular in Britain. Bath combines the advantages of small size and varied entertainment with quick and easy access to larger cities such as London (just over one hour by train) and Bristol (10 minutes by train).

The University of Bath is a new university of 3,100 undergraduates, 600 graduate students, and a faculty of 300. The campus, one mile east of the city center, and some 600 feet above it on Claverton Down, is modern, self-contained, and occupies about 200 acres of playing fields, student accommodation, and academic buildings in a rural setting. The University Library is at the center of the campus complex and is open seven days a week.

The master's degree taught course in business administration is offered by the School of Management, which is on the main university campus, and is one of the largest schools in the university. The school offers an undergraduate Bachelor of Science (B.Sc.) in business administration, research degrees, and in-company programs, in addition to the master's degree taught course.

The school is one of the best known in the United Kingdom. The undergraduate degree has been named as the best program in the U.K. in various reports. The research program is well established with over 120 postgraduate research students. The taught master's degree is recognized by the U.K. Economic and Social Science Research Council, which annually funds some U.K. students for the degree. The whole school is proud of its close links with industry.

PROGRAMS OF STUDY
The Bath M.B.A. degree is different from a typical M.B.A. program in several ways; perhaps the most important differences are as follows:

(1) There is considerable emphasis on business policy and the strategic management of enterprises. Today it is important for all levels of management to be aware of the external environment, particularly in a world which is changing so rapidly. This emphasis will be of interest not only to students intending to achieve general management, but also to other staff, and to advisers, planners, consultants, and educators.

(2) There is a major team work exercise, the "Claverton Entrepreneurship Project" in which students act as a "venture group" setting up a completely new business as a subsidiary of "Claverton Enterprises." This is a most important exercise for integration. Directors of local companies role play as directors of the parent company.

(3) In the summer students do a major individual project, usually involving field-work interviewing, under the supervision of a member of staff. Students effectively have about four months for this; since there is considerable freedom of choice, students can normally select a project that is of potential use in their future career, or of use to their sponsoring organization, if any.

(4) The course has an international student body. In 1984-85 for example, although the largest single group was from the U.K., students from North America, Scandinavia, the European Economic Community, Hong Kong, and Singapore were also enrolled.

(5) The course is deliberately kept fairly small and somewhat elite. Although over 1,000 applications are received each year, only a maximum of 30 students are admitted.

(6) The location of Bath University is an advantage. Bath University has a high reputation, and many people feel Bath is the most beautiful city in Europe.

The course is a full-time, 12-month program starting on the first day of the academic year. The 1986-87 academic year starts October 6, 1986, and the academic year 1987-88 starts October 5, 1987.

The first two terms consist of six elements as follows: (1) Business Policy I (lectures/seminars), (2) Business Policy II (case study program), (3) Claverton Entrepreneurship project (this is supported by a course in Decision Analysis, covering the issues of working in teams), (4) Managerial Economics, (5) Financial Management and Control, and (6) Marketing Management.

Examinations are held at the end of the two terms of taught courses and contribute (together with course work and the Claverton Project) to the final marks.

During the first few weeks of the summer term, a series of "Summer Seminars" are run with a large degree of choice, which provide a lead into the major summer individual project. Students then complete their project by the end of September. The degree awarded is the Master of Science (M.Sc.) in business administration; it is also available part time over three years.

Applications are also being sought for the Master of Philosophy and Doctor of Philosophy programs. It is possible to read for these degrees on a full-time or part-time basis. Unlike the M.Sc. in business administration taught course, these degrees are undertaken primarily by research. Applicants must submit an outline for their proposed research topic area, which is then directed to an appropriate member of staff for consideration.

ADMISSION
Applicants should normally be graduates of an approved university or college. Nongraduates should have an approved full professional qualification (such as accountancy).

Work experience of three years or more is preferred but not essential. Students whose first language is not English should provide evidence of fluency in English. Applicants should supply GMAT test scores.

EXPENSES
Overseas student fees are £3,360 for 1985-86 and will broadly be adjusted for inflation in 1986-87 and 1987-88.

Accommodation is normally available on campus, but cannot be guaranteed for late applicants. Students should expect living expenses of about £3,500 or more a year, in addition to the fee.

CORRESPONDENCE
All applications should be addressed to
The Postgraduate Secretary
School of Management
The University of Bath
Claverton Down
BATH BA2 7AY
England

Management study at the University of Bridgeport focuses on leadership and control. Case study, theory, experiential learning, and gaming are used to integrate the tools of analysis and planning with the functions of leadership and control.

Founded in 1927, the University of Bridgeport is a private, nonsectarian, coeducational university enrolling 6,500 students in four colleges and a school of law; 2,200 are graduate students.

The history and location of the university have had significant influence on the Master of Business Administration (M.B.A.) program. Bridgeport, Connecticut's largest city, has 160,000 people and a very diverse industrial base including aerospace, consumer products, electronics, firearms, heavy castings, helicopters, and precious metals. Management study at the university grew initially to serve local and regional industry and expanded as the Bridgeport area became home to the second largest concentration of Fortune 500 corporation headquarters in the nation.

The university is near to the industrial, commercial, and cosmopolitan center of the city, but sequestered by an 86-acre campus and 200 acres of parkland on the shore of Long Island Sound.

Accreditation of degree programs has been given by the American Assembly of Collegiate Schools of Business (AACSB), the New England Association of Schools and Colleges, and the Connecticut Board of Higher Education.

PROGRAM OF STUDY

The M.B.A. degree is offered with concentrations in accounting, finance, general administration, international business, industrial relations, information systems, marketing, and operations research. Completion of degree requirements normally requires two years of full-time study or three to five years of part-time study. Accelerated study is available for qualified students with recently completed business degrees from accredited colleges. In accelerated study students can usually complete degree requirements in one year of full-time study.

M.B.A. study begins with analysis and evaluation of the tools for organization control and the environment for leadership action. This study includes the subjects of accounting, economics, and decision theory; the organization and management

of finance, production, and marketing; and social-environmental study of people in organizations and organizations in the greater society. This normally constitutes the first year of study.

Introductory subjects are integrated and expanded in the advanced courses of the second year, concurrent with in-depth study in the major concentration. Advanced courses provide breadth and integration of management study while expanding the students' knowledge and ability with analytic tools. Study in one of the eight concentration areas provides depth in a specific discipline for potential job entry or advancement.

ADMISSION

Students may begin classes full time or part time in September, January, or May.

Selection for admission is based on demonstrated intellectual capacity and personal experiences suggesting success in graduate study and leadership positions thereafter. Applicants must have a bachelor's degree or equivalent from a school appropriately accredited by the official agencies of the region or nation.

Students are admitted to M.B.A. study from any undergraduate background. No prerequisites are specified, but students are expected to be computer literate and to have studied at least one semester of differential and integral calculus. Introductory courses in these subjects may be specified for students without such background.

Four criteria are used to evaluate applicants for admission: undergraduate records (and/or previous graduate study), achievement on the Graduate Management Admission Test (GMAT), letters of recommendation, and the personal supporting statement on the application. For students whose native language is not English, the Test of English as a Foreign Language (TOEFL) is also required. If additional English language study is necessary, the university has one of the largest ELS centers for students of all nations.

EXPENSES

For 1985-86, tuition was $7,200 for the academic year. Tuition, room, and board (on or off campus), books and supplies, personal expenses, travel, and contingencies are estimated to be $12,150 for the academic year. Part-time students should consult the course schedule printed each semester for individual course rates.

FINANCIAL ASSISTANCE

Benton fellowships provide full tuition for selected students from each entering class. These are merit based, and recipients are normally expected to have at least a 650 GMAT score with an undergraduate average of 3.5 or higher on a 4-point scale. Graduate assistantships provide nine credits tuition remission and a stipend each semester for faculty assistance, primarily in research. Students applying for assistantships should do so on or before April 15. A limited amount of M.B.A. financial aid based on need is available through the Dean's Office. For additional sources students should contact the Office of Financial Aid at the university.

PLACEMENT

The Office of Career Planning and Placement schedules on-campus interviews with prospective employers and is available to assist students with career planning or the search for employment opportunities.

CORRESPONDENCE

For further information, write or call
  Director
  M.B.A. Program
  Graduate School of Business and
    Public Management
  University of Bridgeport
  Bridgeport, Connecticut 06601
  Telephone: 203-576-4363 or 576-4558

The Faculty of Commerce and Business Administration at the University of British Columbia offers various graduate programs in management: the Master of Business Administration (M.B.A.), Master of Science (M.Sc.), and the Doctor of Philosophy (Ph.D.). The excellence of the programs is determined by the quality of the teaching staff and the caliber of students that the school is able to attract. The faculty ranks among the most productive in terms of research and other scholarly contributions in North America, and the average Graduate Management Admission Test (GMAT) score of incoming students is above 600 (90th percentile). The beautiful campus of the University of British Columbia covers almost 1,000 acres and is surrounded by another 2,000 acres of undeveloped forest and ocean beach. In 1984-85, the student enrollment was about 34,000. Of this total, some 1,600 students were enrolled in the Faculty of Commerce and Business Administration undergraduate (B.Comm.) program and 500 were enrolled in the graduate programs.

PROGRAMS OF STUDY

The M.B.A. program aims to prepare students who have a variety of prior academic backgrounds for a higher level career in general management. The program stresses both the conceptual foundations of management and the practical application of modern management techniques. It generally is a two-year, intensive, full-time program of studies, with the academic year beginning in September and ending in April. The first year of the M.B.A. program covers a common required core that exposes the student to the basic foundation and functional areas of management. The second year provides wide latitude for electives and limited specialization. The broad range of advanced seminars, both in terms of topic areas and in terms of emphasis and teaching methodology, are a particular strength of the faculty. Fields of specialization within the Faculty of Commerce and Business Administration include accounting, finance, marketing, management information systems, management science and statistics, organizational behavior and industrial relations, policy, transportation, urban land economics, and international business. The M.B.A. program can also be completed on a part-time basis over a period of four years.

The M.Sc. program provides students who have specific career interests with an opportunity to specialize and do creative research in one management area. Students enrolled in this program often have a management related undergraduate degree and use their M.Sc. studies to develop specialized skills in a particular area such as accounting, industrial relations, management science, transportation, and urban land economics.

The M.Sc. program requires a minimum of 15 and a maximum of 33 units of course credits. The completion of a three-unit thesis is normally required as evidence of ability to perform scholarly research. The precise number of units required depends upon the level and extent of the individual candidate's preparation for his or her chosen field of study. The period of study required for the degree will vary accordingly.

The basic objective of the doctoral program is to prepare students for research and teaching positions. At the present time, doctoral candidates will be accepted for programs with specialization in accounting and management information systems, finance, management science, marketing and organizational behavior. A student may pursue a cross-field or interdisciplinary program and concentrate in such areas as transportation, urban land economics, international business, or policy analysis; or develop a program that crosses department or faculty boundaries. The program is strongly research-oriented, and special attention is given to each student in developing research creativity and productivity.

ADMISSION

To be eligible for admission to the Faculty of Graduate Studies, students applying from Canadian universities must generally have a four-year university degree and, in their final two years, have maintained at least a high second-class average, including at least six units of first-class marks. Students applying from other countries must, in their final two years, have obtained a grade-point average of at least 3.00 on a 4.00 scale or the equivalent from a recognized university. The Graduate Management Admission Test (GMAT) is required.

Applications for admission to the M.B.A. or M.Sc. program should be submitted to the Faculty of Graduate Studies before May 15 of the year for which admission is sought. Evaluation of an application is based on the candidate's undergraduate and/or graduate record, performance on the Graduate Management Admission Test, and other relevant experience.

EXPENSES

The tuition fee for the first year of the master's or doctoral program is $1,909.

FINANCIAL ASSISTANCE

Financial assistance is provided by a number of funding agencies and by the University of British Columbia for qualified scholars on a competitive basis. Candidates are under automatic consideration for financial aid upon acceptance.

PLACEMENT

The Faculty's placement service works in conjunction with the Canada Employment Center on campus to provide placement services, which include a pre-recruitment program, on-campus recruitment program, collection of placement resource materials, and placement/career counseling. Last year over 90 firms recruited master's graduates for permanent career opportunities as well as summer positions. In addition, Commerce Placement Services engages in a number of marketing activities to make contact with firms throughout Canada and internationally to add to the list of recruiters.

CORRESPONDENCE

For further information or to request an application for admission, please write or call

Director, M.B.A. Program
or
Director of Ph.D./M.Sc. Programs
Faculty of Commerce and Business Administration
University of British Columbia
Vancouver, British Columbia, V6T 1Y8 Canada
M.B.A. Program Telephone:
604-224-8422
Ph.D./M.Sc. Programs Telephone:
604-224-8366

Master of Business Administration, Faculty of Management

THE UNIVERSITY OF CALGARY

CALGARY, ALBERTA, CANADA

The University of Calgary is a publicly supported, coeducational institution located in one of Canada's fastest growing business and financial centers. During the 1983-84 academic year, there were approximately 20,000 students enrolled in 15 faculties.

The university library system contains over 1.2 million volumes and 1.5 million microforms, as well as over 1.3 million items in collections of government documents, architectural plans, maps, and air photos. About 13,800 serials are on current subscription.

Computing Services operates a number of systems including a Honeywell MULTICS computer, a CDC CYBER 175, a CDC 205 "Super" computer, and several types of minicomputers and terminals. These systems handle student and faculty processing both in the batch and time-sharing mode. Microcomputers are also available for student use.

PROGRAM OF STUDY

The purpose of the Master of Business Administration program is to prepare men and women with diverse academic and professional backgrounds for management careers in business and public organizations. The specific objectives of the program are to provide an opportunity for potential managers to develop

• the knowledge of theoretical concepts and analytical methods and the behavioral skills necessary to solve complex organizational problems,

• the capability of applying this knowledge and these skills in different types of organizations,

• an awareness of the critical role of entrepreneurship in all organizations—the revitalizing of existing organizations as well as the designing of new organizations,

• a sensitivity to value conflicts and issues of professional ethics at all levels of management.

Applicants who are admitted to the program will be expected to have adequate academic preparation in the following subject areas: economics, behavioral sciences, mathematics/statistics, computer science/data processing, and financial accounting. Applicants with inadequate preparation in one or more of these areas will be required to successfully complete specified prerequisite courses prior to enrolling in the core courses.

The M.B.A. degree may be earned by a courses-only option or by a thesis option. The course-based M.B.A. program requires successful completion of 14 half courses—in addition to any required foundation course(s)—plus a research project. A student may substitute an additional half course for the research project from selective offerings, subject to the approval of the student's adviser. A minimum of 10 half-credit courses plus the research project must be completed as a regular graduate student in the Faculty of Graduate Studies. The first phase of the program consists of the following core courses: management accounting, managerial finance, organizational management, operations management, marketing and distribution systems management, and management information systems.

The second phase of the program offers specialization in one of the following areas: accounting and information systems, entrepreneurship and new venture development, management of human resources, management of financial resources, management of public institutions, marketing and distribution systems, and production and operations management. Students who so desire may choose not to concentrate in any particular area. However, the selection of courses will be subject to their adviser's approval. While the program can be completed in two years of full-time study, part-time students are expected to complete the degree requirements in three or four years with a maximum of six years.

The thesis option is normally offered only to students who possess a Bachelor of Commerce degree or its equivalent and who wish to pursue a special research interest on a full-time basis. Requirements are satisfied by completion of a thesis and a course work program consisting of eight half-course equivalents. The full-time study period requirement is a minimum of two consecutive four-month terms of full-time study. Students will be expected to fulfill the research component during this time. All requirements must be completed within five calendar years from the time of first registration in the program.

ADMISSION

Applicants must hold a bachelor's degree or the equivalent from a recognized institution and present clear evidence of ability to pursue graduate study in management. The admissions committee considers academic performance during the last two years of previous university study, scores on the Graduate Management Admission Test (GMAT), letters of recommendation, and a personal statement outlining career goals and how the M.B.A. will help achieve those goals. Preference is given to applicants with full-time work experience who have demonstrated the potential for success as professional managers. Applicants whose native language is not English must also submit scores on the Test of English as a Foreign Language (TOEFL).

Completed applications and all supporting documents must be submitted before May 30 for September admission.

EXPENSES

Tuition, per semester course $134
General fees, per year 80

FINANCIAL ASSISTANCE

A limited number of research assistantships, scholarships, and fellowships are awarded competitively each year by the Faculty of Graduate Studies. In addition, the Faculty of Management awards a number of teaching assistantships that range from $3,750 to $4,400 per semester. Financial assistance is limited to full-time students.

CORRESPONDENCE

For further information, please write to
   M.B.A. Program, Faculty of
      Management
   The University of Calgary
   Calgary, AB Canada T2N 1N4

Oldest of the nine campuses of the University of California, the Berkeley campus is located at the foot of the wooded Berkeley Hills, which afford a panoramic view of the San Francisco Bay Area. The Graduate School of Business Administration on the Berkeley campus offers programs leading to the Master of Business Administration (M.B.A.), joint Master of Business Administration/Juris Doctor (M.B.A.-J.D.), Master of Business Administration/Master of Public Health (M.B.A./M.P.H.), and the Doctor of Philosophy (Ph.D.) degrees. Candidates are admitted to programs that emphasize scholarship and research made possible through a distinguished faculty, an excellent library, laboratory and computer facilities, and the many other advantages offered by one of the leading university campuses in the world. Within this academic environment, candidates for higher degrees in business administration at Berkeley study to prepare themselves for responsible positions as business leaders, researchers, and teachers. Current enrollment is about 500 full-time master's students, 250 part-time students (San Francisco program), and approximately 75 in the Ph.D. program. The school offers two semesters and an eight-week summer session. Students are expected to spend full time on their studies.

The school has research facilities in the Institute of Business and Economic Research, the Center for Research in Management, and the Institute of Industrial Relations. In addition, joint projects are undertaken under the auspices of other campus organizations such as the Survey Research Center, the Space Sciences Laboratory, the Institute of International Studies, and the Earl Warren Legal Institute. The school has its own time-shared DEC PDP 11/70 computer which supports instruction in scientific computing, database management, and word processing.

PROGRAMS OF STUDY

The M.B.A. degree, directed toward professional management, requires two years (four semesters) of study. Emphasis may be placed upon accounting; economic analysis and policy; finance; general management; international business; marketing; management science; organizational behavior and industrial relations; political, social, and legal environment; and real estate and urban land economics. However, students are not required to select an area of emphasis. An applied management project must be completed using methods and techniques gained from the M.B.A. curriculum.

The joint M.B.A.-J.D. program is offered under a cooperative arrangement between certain schools of law associated with the University of California and the Graduate School of Business Administration. Also offered is a joint program with the Graduate School of Public Health which allows completion of the Master of Business Administration/Master of Public Health degree in three years. Students in the joint programs must meet the admission requirements of both schools including standard admission tests and application forms. Further details may be obtained from the Graduate School of Business Administration.

The Ph.D. degree is designed for students of exceptional ability who plan careers in college or university teaching and research or high-level staff positions in business or government.

ADMISSION

Admission is limited to the fall semester of each year. Deadline for application materials and transcripts to be submitted is February 1 for admission and financial aid. The criteria employed for admission are as follows: the quality of the educational preparation, results from the Graduate Management Admission Test (GMAT), full-time work experience, and a general assessment of managerial potential. Foreign students compete for admission on the same basis as United States citizens, and non-English-speaking foreign students must submit results from the Test of English as a Foreign Language (TOEFL).

EXPENSES

For California residents, the semester fee is $703.25. Nonresident graduates pay $2,611.25 per semester and foreign students $2,691.00 a semester. Fees for the eight-week summer session run about $275.00 regardless of residency. (Fees are subject to change.)

FINANCIAL ASSISTANCE

All university financial aid is need based and is essentially limited to students showing evidence of financial need. Loans, grants, and work-study are the principal forms of aid administered through the University Financial Aid Office. Disad-vantaged students who are U.S. citizens are encouraged to apply for special financial assistance from the University Graduate Division. A limited number of teaching and research assistantships are available to highly qualified students through the school's departments and institutes. All students admitted to the school who are not U.S. citizens will be expected to make outside arrangements for the full course of their education.

PLACEMENT

Assistance in securing career employment is provided by the university's Placement Center and by the school. Major business, industrial, and government units send recruiting teams to the campus for interviews each year. A variety of other career planning and placement services are offered.

CORRESPONDENCE

Address all inquiries concerning the management programs offered by the University of California, Berkeley, to

Director of Admissions
Graduate School of Business
 Administration
University of California
350 Barrows Hall
Berkeley, California 94720

The Graduate School of Administration (GSA) of the University of California, Davis, prepares men and women of clear promise and ability for management careers in business, government, and non-profit enterprise. The school combines the principal components of traditional programs of business management and public policy analysis into an intensive two-year course of study leading to the Master of Administration degree.

The Davis Campus, the second oldest and third largest in the nine-campus University of California system, has an enrollment of 18,000 undergraduate and graduate students. It is located in the central valley about 20 miles from Sacramento, the state capital, and about 70 miles from San Francisco. The Graduate School of Administration admitted its first class in the fall of 1981. It seeks an entering class of 60 students in the fall of 1986 and a total enrollment of approximately 110.

Campus research facilities available to students of the GSA include a 1.5 million volume collection in the Shields Library and resources available in the campus computing center as well as in the GSA Information Systems Laboratory. In addition, close cooperation between the GSA and other departments on campus provides opportunities for study and research in the areas of economics, political science, sociology, psychology, computer science, applied mathematics, statistics, environmental science, engineering, agricultural science, and food science and technology.

PROGRAM OF STUDY

The two-year graduate program seeks to provide both entry-level and mid-career students with an understanding of management approaches to problem solving and an awareness of the environment within which public and private management decisions are made.

The program has a first-year core that emphasizes concepts and techniques appropriate to management in either the public or private sector so that students, no matter what their special interests, are prepared to function in either sphere. Courses in the core cover economic analysis, policy analysis, quantitative methods, accounting, budget and control, marketing and finance, organizational theory and behavior, and law. During the second year, students specialize in one of several concentrations including general management,

management science, finance and accounting, science and engineering management, agricultural management, and environmental and resources management, each with an emphasis in either the public or private sector. Joint degrees in law and management, and engineering management are also offered.

An internship during the summer after the first year and a problem-oriented, second-year seminar give the student contact with real management problems to which the concepts and methods learned in the first year can be applied.

ADMISSION

Admission is for the fall quarter only. Application materials may be obtained from the Graduate School of Administration and must be completed and returned, with all supporting documentation, by April 1. Applications for fellowships and scholarships must be filed by January 15.

A bachelor's degree and a firm interest in professional management are prerequisites for admission to the school. Although the program has no specific prerequisites, it is strongly recommended that the student have prior course work in microeconomics and statistics. The GSA draws students from diverse backgrounds, both in terms of professional experiences and undergraduate majors.

The criteria employed for admission are as follows: a transcript from an undergraduate program that presents clear evidence of an applicant's ability to pursue graduate study, results from the Graduate Management Admission Test (GMAT), professional work experience, letters of recommendation, and a personal statement that discusses career objectives and educational reasons for seeking admission to the program.

EXPENSES

For California residents, the quarterly fee is $439. Nonresident graduate students pay $1,711 per quarter. Fees are assessed by the university and are subject to change.

FINANCIAL ASSISTANCE

Financial assistance at the University of California, Davis, is awarded on the basis of either academic record or financial need, or both. Loans, grants, and work-study are the principal forms of aid administered through the university Financial Aid Office. A limited number of university fellowships, scholarships, and research and teaching assistantships are available through the GSA. Students from disadvantaged backgrounds may be eligible for university Graduate Opportunity Funds.

PLACEMENT

Assistance in securing career employment is provided by the university's Career Planning and Placement Center and by the school. Major business, industries, and government agencies recruit on campus each year.

CORRESPONDENCE

Inquiries concerning the programs of study offered by the GSA should be directed to
   Director of Admissions
   Graduate School of Administration
   Voorhies Hall
   University of California, Davis
   Davis, California 95616

UNIVERSITY OF CALIFORNIA, IRVINE

IRVINE, CALIFORNIA

The University of California, Irvine, campus is located approximately 40 miles from downtown Los Angeles in the center of Orange County, one of the nation's fastest growing regions. Now in its second decade, the Graduate School of Management (GSM) on the UC Irvine campus offers the Master of Business Administration (M.B.A.) degree. The school also offers the Doctor of Philosophy (Ph.D.) in administration.

The students are divided almost equally between those with prior work experience and those enrolling directly from their undergraduate program. The 280 students, of whom some 27 are studying for their Ph.D. degree, have diverse educational backgrounds, including engineering, social sciences, humanities, business administration and so forth. There are many opportunities for research, both with the individual faculty members and in such research units as the Institute of Transportation Studies and the Public Policy Research Organization. The research facilities available to the student in GSM include a research collection supplementing the more than one million volumes in the UC Irvine Library, a laboratory for experimental opportunities, and the considerable resources of the UC Irvine Computer Facility.

PROGRAMS OF STUDY

The GSM curriculum has evolved to reflect the generic philosophy of the school. The Tier I core courses, required of all master's degree students, consist of 10 courses that develop skills needed to select and use effectively the appropriate means, methods, and techniques for diagnosing and solving organizational problems, whether they are in business or the public sector, and to identify the significant concepts and phenomena associated with the study of the complex organizations. These bring to bear the relevant contributions of the core disciplines or interdisciplinary sources on the analysis of varied organizations and the administrative process.

All students pursuing the M.B.A. degree also must take the four Tier II business courses, which stress such concepts as corporate finance, business strategy, and marketing. The balance of the 23 courses is made up of electives, with the approval of the faculty adviser. No thesis is required for the above degree.

GSM offers advanced study leading to the Doctor of Philosophy in administration. The doctoral program is designed primarily to prepare individuals for careers in teaching and scholarly research at the university level. Because of its relatively small size, the GSM doctoral program is highly individualized with a minimum of structure. Only full-time students are currently admitted to the GSM doctoral program.

ADMISSION

Applicants for the master's degree program should complete all phases of the application process by June 1 for the fall quarter.

GSM employs the following criteria for admission decisions: a bachelor's degree or its equivalent from an institution of acceptable standing, results from the required Graduate Management Admission Test (GMAT), and three letters of recommendation. Course work in calculus and statistics with probability is required. It is recommended that students have prior courses in economics, psychology, sociology, political science, and other social sciences. For those not satisfying this requirement, but otherwise qualified, it is possible to fulfill the requirement by the end of the first quarter in residence. Approximately 40 percent of the students have current or previous work experience.

Admission to the doctoral program is usually in the fall quarter only, although exceptional applicants may be admitted in other quarters. Applicants should complete all phases of the application process by April 1. Required criteria for admission are previous academic excellence as evidenced by the bachelor's or master's degrees, three letters of recommendation from current or former professors, results from the GMAT, a previously prepared paper (research report, essay, case study) which may be indicative of the applicant's interests and capabilities, and a statement indicating areas of proposed study and interests. A prior master's degree is not required.

EXPENSES

Fees are assessed by the university at the proposed rate of $1,384.50 per year for residents of California. Nonresidents are subject to an additional out-of-state tuition fee of $3,816.00 per year. Fees are subject to change without notice.

FINANCIAL ASSISTANCE

The University Financial Aids Office and the Division of Graduate Studies and Research make available each year a limited number of fellowships, scholarships, and loans. In addition, the Career Planning and Placement Center maintains a listing of part-time positions available to students. Also available are a limited number of research assistantships with various research projects on campus. Since these are subject to the availability of funding, it is not possible to predict accessibility.

PLACEMENT

The University Placement Center and the Graduate School of Management assist in placing students through a series of planned recruiting visits by major business, industrial, and governmental units, a widely distributed resume booklet which is published yearly, and career days designed for GSM students.

CORRESPONDENCE

For further information, contact
Graduate School of Management
Social Science Tower
University of California, Irvine
Irvine, California 92717
Telephone: 714-856-7166

Established 50 years ago, the University of California, Los Angeles (UCLA) Graduate School of Management offers a two-year Master of Business Administration (M.B.A.) degree, an academic Master of Science (M.S.) program (offered only with specializations in business economics and operations research), and a Doctor of Philosophy (Ph.D.) program. In addition to the regular M.B.A. program, the school offers a four-year program leading to the M.B.A./Juris Doctor degrees and three-year joint programs coupling an M.B.A. degree with the Master of Science in computer science, Master of Arts (M.A.) in Latin American studies, Master of Library Science (M.L.S.), Master of Public Health (M.P.H.), and Master of Urban Planning (M.U.P.) degrees.

UCLA is located about 10 miles west of the heart of Los Angeles and 5 miles from the Pacific. Housed in its own facility, the Graduate School of Management offers the resources of a large university and the atmosphere of a smaller school where students enjoy close contact with the faculty and each other.

Of the 1,070 students currently enrolled in the school, 950 are in the M.B.A. program, 115 are in the Ph.D. program, and 5 are in the M.S. program. They represent 40 countries and 130 different undergraduate institutions. The school's full-time faculty number approximately 100.

PROGRAMS OF STUDY

The highly flexible M.B.A. program focuses on the development of broad managerial expertise and on thorough groundings in one, two, or three areas of study. The curriculum offers a balanced approach between the theoretical and the practical. There are four main components of the program: a set of activities called the nucleus, the management core, the area electives, and free electives. In the nucleus and management core segments, students develop competence related to general management. Through the area electives (drawn from 11 areas of study and 3 interdisciplinary areas) each student designs a program of study.

In the first year, students are divided into nucleus sections of approximately 25. The first-year nucleus course provides an environment in which students can experiment with different methods and styles of approaching managerial situations and problems. The second year consists of the management field study project where students integrate and apply their knowledge and skills in a professional setting outside the school. Working in teams under a faculty adviser, they conduct a thorough study of a management problem identified by a client, prepare a written report, and present their recommendations for implementing a solution to top management.

The management core consists of 12 courses on subjects essential to the practice of management. The core has three components: (1) management analysis (accounting, managerial computing, managerial economics, model building and statistics); (2) functional fields (finance, marketing, operations management, personnel management); and (3) management process (management of organizations and management policy). All students take at least 10 of the 12 core courses. Substitutes for specific management core requirements may be approved. This includes the possibility that studies completed prior to entering the M.B.A. program may satisfy the core requirements, but then the student must select additional area electives to complete 96 units of work in the program.

Area electives comprise approximately one third of the program. Students are encouraged to establish a general management perspective through a broad base of knowledge by choosing area electives that meet their specific academic and professional needs. There are over a dozen areas of the curriculum, including accounting information systems, behavioral and organizational science, business economics, computers and information systems, finance, human resource management and industrial relations, management science, organization and strategic studies, marketing, production and operations management, and urban land economics. Interdisciplinary programs of study are offered in arts management, international business and comparative management, and public not-for-profit management.

ADMISSION

A candidate for admission to any of the programs offered by the school must hold a bachelor's degree from a college or university of recognized standing. Although no specific undergraduate major is required, all admitted candidates must demonstrate a working knowledge of algebra and differential calculus before beginning their course work.

In evaluating applications for the M.B.A. program, consideration is given to the applicant's academic record, scores on the Graduate Management Admission Test (GMAT), and potential for management as evidenced by work experience and demonstrated leadership through community or extracurricular activities. A personal statement and two recommendations are also important components of the selection process. Students are admitted to begin the M.B.A. program in the fall quarter only. International students should submit their applications by February 15. Early application is strongly advised, and applications should be filed between October 15 and May 15.

EXPENSES

Personal expenses vary widely, but certain costs are predictable. For residents of California, registration and educational fees are $1,436 per year. Out-of-state residents pay an additional $3,816 tuition per year.

FINANCIAL ASSISTANCE

A limited number of fellowships, scholarships, and part-time positions are available. Students may also apply for need-based financial aid through the university.

PLACEMENT

Well-developed, university-wide and school placement services are available. Over two hundred firms from throughout the country visit the school each year.

CORRESPONDENCE

For further information, please write to
M.B.A. Admissions
UCLA Graduate School of
Management
405 Hilgard Avenue
Los Angeles, California 90024
Telephone: 213-825-8874

The University of California campus at Riverside (UCR) came into being in 1907 with the establishment of the Citrus Experiment Station. The Board of Regents declared UCR a general campus in 1959. Enrollment in the university is presently about 4,900; 30 percent of these are graduate students. Approximately 150 students are enrolled in the Graduate School of Management (GSM), 70 percent are full-time students and about 30 percent are career professionals pursuing their M.B.A. degree on a part-time basis.

The GSM emphasizes personal interaction among faculty and graduate students in its classes and advising. The school is small enough in size to provide individual attention to students and to individualize course selections toward career interests. The school has its own computing facility, which is being utilized for teaching, class demonstrations, theses research purposes, and as a tool for effective management decision making. The ratio of students to microcomputers and terminals is 3 to 1, which places GSM in the top group of business schools in the country on a per capita basis. The university library, which has over 1.2 million volumes and 14,000 serials, provides substantial literature and journals in management. The 1,200-acre Riverside campus of the University of California is conveniently located some 50 miles east of Los Angeles, within easy driving distance of most of the major cultural and recreational offerings in southern California.

PROGRAM OF STUDY
The Graduate School of Management offers a professional graduate program in management leading to the degree of Master of Business Administration (M.B.A.). The program is characterized by a tradition of academic excellence and an innovative student-centered curriculum. It is flexible in design in order to accommodate the unique requirements of both full-time students and career professionals. In addition to regularly scheduled course work during the day, sufficient sections of courses are offered in the evenings to permit career professionals to pursue the M.B.A. on a part-time basis. The program can be completed within two years by full-time students; between three and four years by part-time students. It is open to eligible students from all undergraduate majors. Basic accounting and differential and integral calculus are prerequisites to

the program. Qualified students who have not taken these prerequisite courses must meet the requirements during their first two quarters in residence.

The M.B.A. program consists of 23 courses (92 quarter units). In the first year, all students take 48 units in a common body of knowledge which consists of courses in statistical methods for management, microeconomics, macroeconomics, managerial accounting, organizational behavior, human resources management, management science, operations management, computer systems, financial management, marketing, and government-business relationships. Thereafter, students take a minimum of 36 units, selected from general and specialized electives, and complete a capstone course and a thesis.

Students may choose general management or concentrate in a specialized area. Program concentrations are offered in finance, with an emphasis on financial institutions, and in marketing, with a focus on strategic marketing. The financial institutions cluster of courses emphasizes developments in corporate financial management, financial markets, international finance, and cases in financial institutions. The strategic marketing cluster of courses stresses the advanced market research techniques oriented towards strategic product decisions, product management and development, advanced market modeling and simulation techniques, and international and industrial marketing strategy.

Students who elect the general management option select, with the assistance of a faculty adviser, a set of electives to meet their individual educational and career goals. In addition to courses in finance and marketing, electives are offered in areas such as accounting, human resources management, management science, and public management.

ADMISSION
Admission to the M.B.A. program is based on several criteria including the quality of previous academic work, scores on the Graduate Management Admission Test (GMAT), letters of recommendation, and potential for success in the program. In addition to the above requirements, foreign students must submit scores from the Test of English as a Foreign Language (TOEFL) and must score a minimum of 550. New students are admitted in the fall, winter, and spring quarters. Applications

for fall should be submitted by July 1, for winter by October 1, and for spring by January 1. Enrollment is limited; therefore, students are encouraged to apply early.

EXPENSES
Fees per quarter for graduate students are

Residents of California . . . . $ 448
Nonresidents of California 1,720

The university has two coeducational on-campus residence halls housing about 1,200 students, a modern apartment complex, and a student family housing complex consisting of 268 houses. Residence hall fees, which include room and board, are approximately $1,050 per quarter for double occupancy, which includes room and board. Student family housing is $189-$200 per month for unfurnished two-bedroom units. Off-campus housing ranges from $275 to $425 for one- and two-bedroom units.

FINANCIAL ASSISTANCE
A number of fellowships, which range in value up to $10,460 for one academic year, are awarded annually to full-time students. Teaching and research assistantships are also available. Loans, grants, work-study credits, and fee deferments are available through the Financial Aid Office.

PLACEMENT
In conjunction with the university Career Planning and Placement Office, an active program assists students in formulating and obtaining career objectives. A variety of services, including workshops, individual counseling, on-campus recruiting, a computer data bank of employer information, and a career information library, are available. The GSM also distributes an annual resume directory to hundreds of potential employers.

CORRESPONDENCE
For further information, write or call
Graduate School of Management
University of California
Riverside, California 92521
Telephone: 714-787-4551

The Graduate School of Business was formed in 1965 as part of the Faculty of Commerce of the University of Cape Town to provide advanced training in business administration leading to a Master of Business Administration (M.B.A.) degree or an Advanced Diploma in Business Administration.

PROGRAM OF STUDY

The Master of Business Administration program is designed to provide concentrated experience in the basic tools of business such as marketing, computers, organizational behavior, finance, and economics. The objective of the course is to develop the student's ability to deal with problems, to make decisions, to communicate them, and to support them. The school seeks to develop practical business men and women with the skills, attitudes, and knowledge that are the foundation for management responsibility.

Most of the program consists of participative training based on the case method of instruction in addition to formal lectures. This training stresses the learning process rather than the teaching process. The student, like the businessperson, grapples with combinations of facts, opinions, and ideas in an effort to understand problems, seek solutions, and make business decisions. In constant consultation with fellow students, instructors, and visiting businessmen, he or she acquires the skills, attitudes, and knowledge appropriate to the practical administrator. An extensive reading program is also required. The student is required to complete 14 core courses, 3 elective courses chosen from a range of business fields, and a technical report.

The four-term program of full-time study runs from the middle of February to early December. A part-time program is offered over two years. For the two-week period immediately preceding the start of both programs, a pre-M.B.A. course is conducted for students whose business academic background is weak in relation to course requirements.

A large number of executive courses are run by the school. These range from two-day seminars and three-week management development programs to a six-week construction management program.

ADMISSION

The M.B.A. program is open to a limited number of outstanding men and women. A degree from a recognized university in South Africa or abroad in engineering, science, arts, commerce, law, or social science or other degrees normally recognized by the University Senate, is a requirement for degree candidates. Chartered Accountants registered with the Public Accountants' and Auditors' Board of South Africa or of a similar body in other countries, as well as associate members or fellows of the Institute of Cost and Management Accountants, may also be accepted as degree candidates. No particular background, majors, or areas of concentration are required for admission. There is no rigid experience requirement, but members with some full-time employment experience usually derive more benefit from the program.

The M.B.A. program is also open to nondegree candidates possessing suitable professional qualifications and/or extensive business experience.

The Admission Board will evaluate each candidate on the basis of an application form, scores from the Graduate Management Admission Test (GMAT), an interview, and two references. Particular attention will be given to the candidate's leadership potential, motivation, maturity, GMAT scores, academic record, and work experience. The age range of candidates is usually between 25 and 35. Candidates whose qualifications do not meet requirements may be advised to complete additional studies or gain further experience before seeking admission.

Candidates should mail their application forms to the school as soon as possible. Selection of candidates will take place at the end of May, August, and November each year. All applicants who have successfully completed the admissions procedure by these dates will have their applications considered. Completed application forms from South African candidates must reach the Admissions Secretary at least one month before a selection date in order to ensure that admissions procedures are completed prior to the meeting of the Admissions Board. Foreign candidates are advised to submit their completed applications at least two months before a selection date to allow sufficient time for admission interviews to be arranged and interview reports returned.

Foreign candidates should apply for a study visa in good time (allow up to six months) through the nearest South African Embassy. Candidates who are put on a waiting list will have their applications reconsidered on the next selection date.

FINANCIAL ASSISTANCE

It is a basic policy of the school that no qualified candidate be prevented from attending for financial reasons, and bank loans (subject to exchange control regulations) are readily available to permanent residents of South Africa.

PLACEMENT

Each year the school arranges for executives from major South African companies to visit and interview successful members for employment. The GSB Placement Office publishes a comprehensive resume booklet on M.B.A. graduates seeking employment, which it distributes throughout southern Africa.

CORRESPONDENCE

For further information, write to
Director
Graduate School of Business
University of Cape Town
Private Bag, Rondebosch
7700, South Africa
Telephone: Cape Town 69-5382

PROGRAM OF STUDY

The Master of Business Administration (M.B.A.) program is a 30-hour program that integrates all of the functional areas of management. The program is highly structured: all students are enrolled in essentially identical core course sequences each semester. The program imposes a heavy workload that requires a high degree of discipline and commitment on the part of the student. By combining the use of case studies, interactive computing, and research projects and lectures, the M.B.A. program prepares graduates of the highest caliber for the nation's businesses, industries, academic institutions, and government.

ADMISSION

The University of Central Arkansas seeks highly qualified applicants for the Master of Business Administration program. Neither an undergraduate degree in management nor previous business-related courses are required for admission to the program. The admission decision is based on an evaluation of all application materials submitted by the individual. Previous academic records, prior work experiences, recommendations, test scores, and evidence of maturity and motivation are among the factors assessed during the admission process. All applicants are required to submit official Graduate Management Admission Test (GMAT) scores. A minimum grade-point average (GPA) of 2.5 and a minimum GMAT score of 350 are required plus a formula score of 950 (GPA $\times$ 200 + GMAT = 950). Foreign applicants are also required to submit official Test of English as a Foreign Language (TOEFL) scores. A minimum of 550 is required for admission to the university.

EXPENSES

Costs are estimated for the 1985-86 academic year. Tuition and fee assessments are subject to change without notice.

	Arkansas Resident	Out-of-State
Tuition and fees	$ 477	$ 870
Room and board	2,000	2,000
Books and supplies	500	500
Total	$2,977	$3,370

FINANCIAL ASSISTANCE

A limited number of graduate assistantships are available for qualified students in business administration. Stipends for graduate assistantships are $4,800.

PLACEMENT

A placement director and the senior faculty work with the students to identify employment opportunities.

CORRESPONDENCE

For further information or to request an application for admission, please write or call

Dr. Jim Barr, Director
Graduate Business Programs
University of Central Arkansas
Conway, Arkansas 72032
Telephone: 501-450-3190

The University of Central Florida is located in the center of the state at Orlando, a metropolitan area with a population of over 700,000. The Atlantic Ocean is less than one hour's drive away. The university has an enrollment of over 16,000 students; 4,000 of those students are in the College of Business Administration, of whom approximately 500 are pursuing master's degrees.

The Master of Business Administration (M.B.A.) has been offered since 1969. The college also offers a Master of Science degree in Accounting (M.S.A.) and a Master of Arts in Applied Economics (M.A.E.). All undergraduate and graduate programs in business administration are accredited by the American Assembly of Collegiate Schools of Business (AACSB).

PROGRAMS OF STUDY
The program leading to the Master of Business Administration at the University of Central Florida is intended to develop the student's analytical, problem-solving, and decision-making capabilities to meet the challenges of leadership in administrative positions at present and in the changing world of the future. Part I of the M.B.A. program develops a student's basic competence in the foundational areas of knowledge common to business and economic organizations and systems. Students who have recently completed academic course work in business and economics, as well as in certain quantitative areas, may have all, or a substantial portion, of the Part I foundation requirements waived. Part II of the program, the professional core, provides for intensive study in the use of analytical problem-solving approaches across a spectrum of decision areas within an organization. Courses emphasize the integrative nature of the managerial responsibilities and activities through which organizational objectives are achieved. Through appropriate elective course work, the second part of the M.B.A. program enables the student to establish some degree of specialization in one of the following areas: accounting, economics, finance, management, or marketing. The M.B.A. program does not require a thesis.

The Master of Science in Accounting program provides advanced study for those seeking careers in professional accounting. Work equivalent to an undergraduate major in accountancy is a prerequisite for enrollment in all graduate accountancy courses.

The Master of Arts in Applied Economics program provides specialization in economics for students desiring careers as economists in the academic, government, business, and financial communities.

Minimum course requirements for each of the master's degrees, in addition to the Part I requirements and the undergraduate course work in accountancy for the M.S.A., are 33 semester hours for the M.B.A. and M.S.A. and 30 semester hours for the M.A.E.

ADMISSION
A holder of a baccalaureate degree in any discipline from any regionally accredited college or university may be given immediate admission to the graduate program. Qualified applicants may be admitted for either of the two semesters or summer session. Applications should be submitted as far in advance of expected initial enrollment as possible. Primary consideration for admission is based upon an applicant's upper-division undergraduate record and the score achieved on the Graduate Management Admission Test (GMAT). For the M.A.E. only, students may submit scores on the Graduate Record Examinations (GRE). The intellectual development during prior academic work, extracurricular activities, employment experience, and other evidences of interest and motivation for graduate study may be taken into consideration in reaching admission decisions.

Other requirements consist of an end-of-program examination over the general subject areas included in the required course work. A grade-point average of B must be maintained in the overall graduate program. Applicants whose native language is not English must submit a score on the Test of English as a Foreign Language (TOEFL) of at least 575 before admission can be considered.

EXPENSES
Application fee.................. $ 15
Registration fee, per semester
   graduate hour (estimated)
      Florida resident 48
      Nonresident 136

FINANCIAL ASSISTANCE
A limited number of assistantships are awarded to promising students, as well as a waiver of the out-of-state portion of the tuition charge. Other forms of financial assistance may be obtained through the Student Financial Aid Office, University of Central Florida, Box 25000, Orlando, Florida 32816.

PLACEMENT
The university Placement Center is equipped to counsel, prepare, and assist students in making career decisions. The center is the facilitating agency that puts students into contact with both national and regional employers. Business students are also assisted in career planning and employment by the faculty and administrative officers in the College of Business Administration.

CORRESPONDENCE
For further information or to request an application for admission, please write or call
   Graduate Programs Office
   College of Business Administration
   University of Central Florida
   P.O. Box 25000
   Orlando, Florida 32816
   Telephone: 305-275-2187

The University of Chicago's Graduate School of Business, established in 1898, was the first to award the Doctor of Philosophy (Ph.D.) in business. Instruction leads to the Master of Business Administration (M.B.A.) and Ph.D. degrees. Full-time enrollment is 1,000, including approximately 90 Ph.D. students. Identical course offerings are available for the approximately 1,100 part-time evening M.B.A. students. The faculty numbers approximately 100.

PROGRAMS OF STUDY

The University of Chicago believes that it is wasteful and inefficient for a university to try to replicate on-the-job training or provide a pale substitute for business experience. What the university can do well is provide an educational experience that is complementary to business experience. Therefore, the school stresses the teaching of the basic disciplines that underlie business operations and management, and equally important, the conducting of basic research that will contribute to the understanding and solution of business problems.

The curriculum is designed to sharpen the student's critical and analytical skills as preparation for lifelong learning and decision making. Students will become proficient in the analytical skills of economics, mathematics, statistics, behavioral science, and accounting as well as the functional fields of finance, marketing, industrial relations, and production. However, no student is ever required to repeat work previously mastered merely to meet a distribution requirement. Rather, each student's program is individually designed. Students are encouraged to substitute more advanced courses for introductory offerings whenever it is appropriate and may choose either a field of concentration or a specialization. Most students will find that nearly half of the program's 20 courses are electives.

An international business program is operated in collaboration with seven foreign institutions—The London School of Economics and Political Science, The London Graduate School of Business Studies in England; Université Catholique de Louvain, Katholieke Universiteit et Leuven in Belgium; St. Gall Graduate School of Economics, Business and Public Administration in Switzerland; Ecole Supérieure des Sciences Economique et Commerciales (ESSEC) in France; and Instituto de Estudios Superiores de la Empresa (IESE) in Spain. Selected students complete the basic requirements at Chicago and enter a program of study abroad; students who complete the program receive an M.B.A. from Chicago and an advanced degree from the foreign school. With an accelerated curriculum at Chicago the total program can be completed in two calendar years.

The Graduate School of Business participates in joint degree programs with seven other schools/departments of the university—Far Eastern Studies (M.B.A./A.M.), Latin American Studies (M.B.A./A.M.), the Law School (M.B.A./J.D.), the Graduate Library School (M.B.A./A.M.), Middle Eastern Studies (M.B.A./A.M.), the Pritzker School of Medicine (M.B.A./M.D.), and the School of Social Service Administration (M.B.A./A.M.).

The programs leading to the degree of Doctor of Philosophy are flexible and are based upon the student's special interests and prior education. Qualified candidates are encouraged to enter the doctoral program immediately after completing four years of undergraduate study.

ADMISSION

Students are admitted to the school on the basis of aptitude and intellectual ability as indicated by undergraduate record, letters of evaluation, motivation and maturity, and scores on the Graduate Management Admission Test (GMAT).

Business experience is considered but not required. No special undergraduate program is prescribed, but college-level economics and mathematics are excellent preparation.

In addition to the above criteria, international students must possess an academic degree equivalent to the American four-year bachelor's degree. International students whose native language is not English and who have not completed two years of study in the U.S. must submit the results of the Test of English as a Foreign Language (TOEFL).

Full-time students may enter in June, September, or January. Part-time students may enter in any of the four quarters. Applications should be filed at least six months before the quarter for which admission is sought.

EXPENSES

Tuition and fees for 1985-86 were $11,862 per academic year for the normal program of 10 courses. A minimum budget, including tuition, for a single person for one academic year (three quarters) is $19,050. A couple should plan a budget of about $22,180; for a child, add $3,000. Tuition and fees for 1986-87 are certain to increase.

FINANCIAL ASSISTANCE

The Graduate School of Business maintains a program of financial assistance which includes both gift aid and loans. Students are selected for gift aid on the basis of academic achievement, leadership, and financial need. Applications must be made by February 3; awards are announced April 1. Loans are made on the basis of need. At the present time, the University of Chicago participates in three federal loan programs. Students requesting loans must file university applications by May 15 and the Graduate and Professional School Financial Aid Service (GAPSFAS) form no later than February 3. The school maintains a fellowship program for minority students.

PLACEMENT

The Graduate School of Business maintains its own placement office. Resumes of graduating students are published in book form and distributed widely. Over 300 companies actively recruit and hire graduates of the program.

CORRESPONDENCE

For further information on the programs offered by the Graduate School of Business, write or call
Director of Admissions and Aid
University of Chicago
Graduate School of Business
1101 East 58th Street
Chicago, Illinois 60637
Telephone: 312-962-7369
or 312-962-8608

UNIVERSITY OF CINCINNATI

CINCINNATI, OHIO

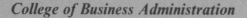

The University of Cincinnati (UC) offers the Master of Business Administration (M.B.A.), Master of Science (M.S.) and Doctor of Philosophy (Ph.D.) degrees. The M.B.A. program is available to both full- and part-time students; M.S. and Ph.D. programs are available to full-time students only. The school's bachelor's and master's programs in business are accredited by the American Assembly of Collegiate Schools of Business (AACSB).

PROGRAMS OF STUDY

The M.B.A. program provides professional management education for individuals seeking leadership positions in business and industry, government, health care, the arts, and nonprofit agencies.

The Cincinnati M.B.A. program involves two phases. Phase I is designed to provide a common body of business and economic knowledge as well as to provide the student with analytic skills. Students with an undergraduate degree from an AACSB-accredited college will normally have satisfied most of the Phase I requirements.

Phase II involves three parts. A set of nine core courses is designed to provide broad-based management skills for all M.B.A. students. Each student then elects an area of concentration designed to provide expertise in the particular area the student has targeted for his or her entry-level position. Areas of concentration in accounting, finance, management, marketing, operations management, international business, quantitative analysis and information systems are available. Two to three breadth electives are also available in Phase II to permit the student some flexibility in designing a curriculum to meet career objectives.

The M.S. program provides specialized training in business administration at the master's level. The M.S. may serve as a terminal degree or as preparation for the Ph.D. program. M.S. options are offered in marketing, taxation, quantitative analysis/information systems and human resources/labor relations.

The Ph.D. program is designed primarily for students planning careers in teaching and research. Ph.D. areas of concentration and support areas may be selected from accounting, finance, organizational behavior, operations management, marketing, quantitative analysis and information systems. Ph.D. students may also select a support area from outside the College of Business Administration.

ADMISSION

Applicants to the M.B.A. and M.S. programs must hold a bachelor's degree from an accredited college or university. Neither an undergraduate degree in business nor previous business course work is required for admission. Applicants must submit the following documents: (1) a formal application for admission with a $20 nonrefundable application fee, (2) official transcript(s) of all previous academic work, (3) two letters of appraisal from individuals qualified to judge the applicant's ability to complete graduate course work successfully, and (4) scores on the Graduate Management Admission Test (GMAT). Foreign students whose native language is not English must submit scores on the Test of English as a Foreign Language (TOEFL) and provide proof of available financial resources. Students may enter the master's programs in autumn, winter or spring quarters. Each applicant is evaluated on the basis of undergraduate record, GMAT and TOEFL scores, letters of appraisal, leadership activities, professional experiences, and career objectives.

Ph.D. applicants must provide the same documents plus one additional letter of appraisal; all three letters must come from faculty members. Ph.D. applicants are judged on academic record, test scores, appraisal letters, demonstrated commitment to original research and teaching. Ph.D. admissions are highly selective and are made by graduate faculty of the applicant's major department.

EXPENSES

1985-86

Tuition	Full-time	Part-time
Ohio resident	$1,031	$ 86 per credit hour
Nonresident	2,039	170 per credit hour
Nonrefundable application fee (all applicants) 20		

FINANCIAL ASSISTANCE

Limited aid is available to qualified full-time students through scholarships, assistantships, fellowships (including some special awards reserved for minority students), and part-time campus employment. UC also participates in college-based federal and state programs and veterans benefits. Applications for financial aid should be filed by February 15 for the following academic year.

PLACEMENT

The Career Development and Placement Office assists students in career planning, provides individual counseling, career-related workshops, and a full program of on-campus recruiting.

CORRESPONDENCE

For further information, please write or call

Director of Graduate Programs
University of Cincinnati
Cincinnati, Ohio 45221-0224
Telephone: 513-475-3437

The University of Colorado is located in Boulder, 25 miles by turnpike from downtown Denver. The university is a major institution enrolling over 20,000 students including 3,000 on-campus graduate students. Set at the foot of the Rocky Mountains in an area of dry, moderate climate and good living conditions, the university offers excellent facilities for study and research, including a fine business library and a business research division.

PROGRAMS OF STUDY

The Master of Business Administration (M.B.A.) program emphasizes breadth of training and considers business administration as a total field. The course of study is designed to develop a student's ability to integrate the work of specialists in the field of business. A company-wide point of view is used.

The minimum course of study required for the M.B.A. degree is 30 semester hours, as outlined below. For students who have adequate undergraduate training in business administration, the program is designed so they normally will complete it in two semesters or one calendar year. Areas of emphasis are accounting, finance, information systems, management science, marketing, organization management, personnel human resources management, production and operations management, and transportation management. A student with an undergraduate degree in business administration normally will be able to enter directly into the core requirements.

Core Requirements	Semester Hours
Business and Its Environment	3
Business and Economic Analysis	3
Administrative Controls	3
Human Factors and Administration	3
Business Policy	3
Area of Emphasis	9
Functional Courses	6

A student who lacks the necessary background preparation in any of the above core areas may remedy the deficiency by taking the appropriate graduate survey courses. These total 25 semester hours.

A combined Juris Doctor/M.B.A. degree is offered in conjunction with the School of Law.

The Master of Science (M.S.) program emphasizes depth of training in particular fields within business administration. The course of study offers the student the opportunity for specialization in one of these fields. The minimum course study required for the M.S. degree is 30 semester hours, which may include a thesis (4 to 6 hours credit) based upon original research by the candidate and the background courses mentioned above. Fields available for selection as a major are accounting, finance, information systems, management science, marketing, and organization management. The Master of Science degree in accounting and information systems and the Master of Science degree in taxation are also offered.

The Doctor of Philosophy (Ph.D.) program in business administration is designed to prepare students for careers in research and teaching at colleges or universities. Students must demonstrate proficiency in two fields. One field must be in a business discipline. In addition, students must demonstrate competence in quantitative analysis and economic theory. The fields of study offered in the Graduate School of Business are accounting, administrative policy, finance, management science/information systems, marketing, and organization management. Finally, in one of the fields of business, doctoral candidates must complete a dissertation that shows ability to do independent, original scholarly research. All doctoral students for whom English is the native language are required to demonstrate at least second year college proficiency in a foreign language of their choice. The doctoral program normally will require three or more years.

ADMISSION

To be admitted to graduate study, a student must have a bachelor's degree from an institution accredited by a regional accrediting association and otherwise meet the general requirements for admission to the Graduate School of the University of Colorado. In addition, the applicant must be accepted by the Graduate Committee of the Graduate School of Business Administration, which will consider his or her qualifications as evidenced by college transcripts and scores on the Graduate Management Admission Test (GMAT). In addition to the above, letters of recommendation are required from Ph.D. applicants.

EXPENSES

Tuition and fees (1985-86) for a full-time graduate student attending the fall and spring semesters at Boulder are $2,025 for a Colorado resident and $5,697 for a nonresident.

FINANCIAL ASSISTANCE

The University of Colorado has available a limited number of graduate scholarships, graduate assistantships, and research assistantships. In addition, for doctoral students, the College of Business offers opportunities for teaching as part-time instructors.

PLACEMENT

The university maintains a placement center to assist students in identifying, preparing for, and securing positions.

CORRESPONDENCE

For further information or to request an application for admission, please write to
Director of Graduate Studies
Graduate School of Business
Administration
University of Colorado
Boulder, Colorado 80309-0419

UNIVERSITY OF COLORADO AT DENVER

DENVER, COLORADO

The University of Colorado at Denver (CU-Denver), one of four institutions in the University of Colorado system, is an urban commuter campus located in downtown Denver. CU-Denver is part of the 169-acre Auraria Higher Education Center and close to major business and government offices in Denver, as well as to civic and cultural centers. An average of 11,500 students are enrolled at CU-Denver, with many of these students working full time or part time while pursuing degrees. The diversity of their backgrounds, interests, occupations, and ages stimulates a unique learning experience for the men and women enrolled at CU-Denver.

PROGRAMS OF STUDY

The Graduate School of Business Administration offers the degrees of Master of Business Administration (M.B.A.) and Master of Science (M.S.) in business. Master's degree programs are accredited by the American Assembly of Collegiate Schools of Business (AACSB). All graduate business courses are offered in the evening.

Students applying for graduate programs in business do not need to have taken their undergraduate degrees in business. The M.B.A. program specifically is designed so that all required courses cover the material needed for completion of the degree. There are no prerequisites needed to enter the M.B.A. program, and there is every reason to believe that students with nonbusiness backgrounds have equal chances for success. Applicants for the M.S. degree, however, may be required to take prerequisite courses, depending on the individual's academic and professional background.

The Master of Business Administration program is devoted to the concepts, analytical tools, and communication skills required for competent and responsible administration. The administration of an enterprise is viewed in its entirety and within its social, political, and economic environment.

M.B.A. Degree Requirements	Semester Hours
Marketing Management	3
Quantitative Business Analysis	3
Human Behavior in Organizations	3
Accounting for Managers	3
Legal and Ethical Environment of Business	3
Management Information Systems	3
Management of Operations	3
Managerial Economics	3
Economic Environment of Business	3
Financial Management	3
Business Policy and Strategic Management	3
Total Core Semester Hours	33
Elective Hours	15
Total Semester Hours	48

Students have a wide range of options available in selecting their elective hours. No area of emphasis is required for the M.B.A. degree, permitting students to choose a combination of courses appropriate for their individual career needs. If a student wishes to pursue an area of emphasis, several are available including accounting, finance, organization management, marketing, management science/ information systems, production and operations management, and transportation and distribution management.

The Master of Science program allows for specialization in particular fields within business administration. The minimum requirements for the degree, after any prerequisite courses have been completed, is 30 semester hours (which may include an optional thesis of 4 to 6 hours of credit). The following major fields are available: accounting, accounting and information systems, finance, health administration, management, management science and information systems, and marketing.

ADMISSION

Admission to the M.B.A. or M.S. programs is based on the following criteria: (1) the applicant's total academic record (the bachelor's degree must be from a regionally accredited college or university), (2) the applicant's scores on the Graduate Management Admission Test (GMAT), (3) such other criteria submitted by an applicant that would indicate high promise for success in a master's program (included would be work experience, recommendations, or other evidence of maturity and motivation).

EXPENSES

Tuition and fees for full-time and part-time students, 1986-87, are estimated as follows:

1986 Tuition/Fees	Colorado Resident	Nonresident
Full-time	$700	$2,500
Part-time	380	1,340

FINANCIAL ASSISTANCE

CU-Denver has various forms of financial assistance available for students, including fellowships, scholarships, graduate assistantships, research assistantships, and various student loan programs.

PLACEMENT

CU-Denver students and alumni use the Office of Career Planning and Placement Services of the Auraria Higher Education Center in planning their careers and securing employment.

CORRESPONDENCE

For further information or to request an application for admission, please write or call

Student Services
Graduate School of Business
Administration
University of Colorado at Denver
1475 Lawrence Street, Suite 300
Denver, Colorado 80202-2219
Telephone: 303-623-4436

The University of Connecticut was established in 1881. The main campus is located in the town of Mansfield (post office: Storrs), approximately 25 miles east of Hartford. The university operates on a semester plan with 2 six-week summer sessions.

The School of Business Administration was established in 1941. The Master of Business Administration (M.B.A.) was first offered in 1957. The M.B.A. programs are offered evenings at Danbury, Hartford, and Stamford, and full time at Storrs. The M.B.A. programs are accredited by the American Assembly of Collegiate Schools of Business (AACSB); of the 800 institutions offering an M.B.A. program only 216 have this recognition. Additionally, the accounting program is accredited by the AACSB, one of 30 in the country and the only one in New England to achieve this status.

PROGRAMS OF STUDY
The School of Business Administration offers professional education for business leadership through courses leading to the degree of Master of Business Administration. The objective is to prepare students for responsible roles in the management of all types of organized activities.

The M.B.A. program requires 57 credits; 45 of these credits are courses specified to meet AACSB requirements. Candidates are required to include managerial economics, management information systems, managerial computing, and managerial communications plus 12 elective credits. The program can be completed in 16 or 21 months, full time without summer school. Part-time students average three and a half years for completion.

An M.B.A. degree with health care management specialization requires 57 credits, including a clinical internship. With summer classes, the program can be completed in two years.

An M.B.A. degree with an accounting specialization, which prepares students to take the C.P.A. and C.M.A. professional examinations, requires 66 credits. With summer classes, the program can be completed in two years.

Three joint programs are offered: Master of Business Administration/Juris Doctor (M.B.A./J.D.), Master of Business Administration/Master of Social Work (M.B.A./M.S.W.), and Master of Business Administration/Master of Arts (M.B.A./M.A.) in international studies. Admission requirements of both schools involved must be met independently. One year of full-time study at the Storrs campus is recommended in each case.

ADMISSION
Applicants from a diversity of academic backgrounds with bachelor's degrees from accredited schools are considered. Consideration is also given to potential for success, relevant work experience, writing ability, leadership, and maturity. Applicants must submit academic transcripts and scores from the Graduate Management Admission Test (GMAT). Students from countries where English is not the native language are required to take the Test of English as a Foreign Language (TOEFL). Additional elements include the written application, a personal letter of intent, and recommendations.

The M.B.A. program is committed to attracting qualified applicants from underrepresented groups, including minorities and women.

Candidates planning to attend full time at Storrs must begin with the fall semester and are urged to apply during the fall and winter as admissions decisions start in January. At Danbury, Hartford, and Stamford, candidates may start in September, January, or May. Completed applications and GMAT scores should be submitted prior to June 1 for September entry, October 15 for January entry, and March 1 for May entry. Students are accepted before these deadlines.

EXPENSES
On the Storrs campus, the total fees for in-state students per semester are $1,030; for out-of-state students these fees are $2,275. Danbury, Hartford, and Stamford evening M.B.A. students pay $193 per credit with no maximum. Room and board, available on the Storrs campus only, costs $1,345 per semester. Many students live off campus. Total cost for nine months attendance at Storrs is estimated at $7,050 for in-state students and $9,200 for out-of-state students. All university charges are subject to change.

FINANCIAL ASSISTANCE
Tuition remission, student loans, and work-study are available. Contact the Student Financial Aid Office (Box U-116) on the Storrs campus for application forms. Several research and teaching assistantships are available on the Storrs campus.

PLACEMENT
The School of Business Administration Placement Services and the university's Department of Career Services cooperate to serve the M.B.A. students. The M.B.A. Placement Coordinator participates in preparing a student resume catalog and arranging paid summer internships and on-campus/off-campus job interviews.

CORRESPONDENCE
Additional information may be obtained by writing to
  Assistant Dean for Graduate Programs
  School of Business Administration
  University of Connecticut
  368 Fairfield Road U-41D
  Storrs, Connecticut 06268
  Telephone: 203-486-2872

In 1966, the University of Dallas introduced its first graduate program with the opening of the Braniff Graduate School of Management (GSM) and an enrollment of fewer than 100 students. Today, GSM is one of the largest schools of management in the Southwest with an enrollment of 1,500 students. The school is centrally located on 1,000 acres in the Dallas/Ft. Worth metroplex; its faculty and students come from numerous institutions and countries.

The major objective of the Graduate School of Management is academic excellence in teaching and research. The school relies on the following external criteria for judging its academic standards:
- market acceptance of its graduate students,
- quality of students applying for admission into GSM programs,
- nationwide recognition of the GSM faculty by academic and business communities.

Philosophically, GSM maintains that the study of the American free enterprise system is essential to management education. Technically, management education at GSM introduces students to the nature of decision making, the implementation of decisions, and the interaction of the private and public sectors.

Essentially an evening school, GSM, in addition to its full-time students, attracts many part-time students already well into their careers, people whose varied business backgrounds also provide practical classroom input.

PROGRAMS OF STUDY
The University of Dallas offers seven Master of Business Administration (M.B.A.) degrees: business management, international management, management information systems, engineering management, acquisition and contract management, industrial management, and health services management.

Each program consists of a course curriculum of 48 semester hours plus a one-hour seminar. All programs may be pursued on a full- or part-time basis in evening courses or on weekends.

Applicants holding a bachelor's degree in business administration from an accredited university may have up to 12 credit hours waived from GSM's M.B.A. degree programs.

ADMISSION
A bachelor's degree is required. Generally, a grade-point average (GPA) of 3.0 (B) may be regarded as indicative of an applicant's ability to pursue graduate studies. Consideration is also given to indicators of professional growth and upward mobility.

In addition to the bachelor's degree, GSM applicants must take the Graduate Management Admission Test (GMAT). Prospective full-time students must submit their GMAT scores prior to enrollment. Part-time students must submit their GMAT scores prior to registering for the second semester. All students must apply for candidacy while enrolled in their fourth 3-credit-hour course.

Admission to candidacy is determined by the following formula: GMAT score + $(200 \times GPA) = 1,000$. The GPA in the above formula is based on courses taken at GSM.

All international students applying to the Graduate School of Management are subject to the foregoing requirements and, in addition, they must furnish proof of proficiency in the English language and of sufficient finances to fund their entire course of study.

Proof of proficiency in English is furnished through submission of a Test of English as a Foreign Language (TOEFL) score of at least 500. Students who have completed an undergraduate or graduate degree from a university with English as the language of instruction may request an exemption from this requirement. Applicants whose native language is English are exempt from the TOEFL requirement. All applicants whose native language is not English are required to take a one-credit course, English Oral Communications.

None of the M.B.A. programs requires a thesis. No undergraduate prerequisite courses are necessary for admission. A maximum of six graduate hours may be transferred toward the M.B.A. degree. In addition, certain courses can be waived by the Admissions Committee when prior academic knowledge of the subject is determined. The M.B.A. program may be completed in four semesters of full-time study.

EXPENSES
Tuition for the M.B.A. programs is $165 per credit hour. All are three-credit-hour courses except the one-hour seminar.

FINANCIAL ASSISTANCE
The University of Dallas offers several types of government loans through the Financial Aid Office. In addition, numerous graduate assistantships are available through GSM. Most assistantships require 10 hours of service per week to GSM. Information and applications for graduate assistantships may be obtained from the Office of Admissions, Graduate School of Management.

PLACEMENT
Since many Graduate School of Management students are already employed, GSM does not maintain a placement service but does, on an individual basis, offer counseling to graduating students in an effort to guide them toward job opportunities.

CORRESPONDENCE
For further information on the program of study offered by the Graduate School of Management, please write
    Office of Admissions
    Graduate School of Management
    University of Dallas
    1845 East Northgate
    Irving, Texas 75062-4799

The University of Dayton is a private, medium-sized university founded in 1850. It attracts students from the local community, the state of Ohio, most other states, and 40 foreign countries. The 600 full-time members of the faculty provide instruction to 6,200 undergraduate and 3,000 graduate students. Most of the latter are enrolled part time in the evening programs.

The School of Business Administration was founded in 1924 and includes the departments of Accounting, Economics and Finance, Management, Marketing, and Decision Sciences. Graduate studies leading to the Master of Business Administration (M.B.A.) degree began in 1963. The Graduate Program is administered by a Director with a Graduate Committee providing academic policy guidance.

Over 700 students are currently enrolled in the M.B.A. program. The majority are studying on a part-time basis. Classes are conducted in Miriam Hall, the School of Business Administration's new building. This building provides excellent facilities for all types of classroom situations, including lectures, seminars, and laboratories. Supporting computer facilities are also located in Miriam. These include a microcomputer facility and a terminal center for the exclusive use of the business student and access to three large time-sharing computers. An extensive business library is located in the new university library. The M.B.A. program is also offered at two sites in Columbus, Ohio: Otterbein College and Franklin University.

The University of Dayton is accredited by the North Central Association of Colleges and Secondary Schools and by a variety of other accrediting agencies.

PROGRAM OF STUDY

The objective of the M.B.A. program is to develop creative and effective managers by providing the student with administrative, behavioral, and technical knowledge and skills required for career and personal enhancement. These skills are developed through courses in the functional disciplines and courses designed to achieve an integration and synthesis of knowledge. The emphasis of the program is on the application of theory to the practical problems faced by administrators. Case studies, research, lectures, and computer support provide the basis of teaching by a faculty committed to a "tradition of excellence." Thirty-three graduate credit hours are required for the degree, of which 30

hours are specified. The other 3 hours are electives, providing the student with the opportunity for additional course work in an area of choice.

Applicants whose baccalaureate degree is in business administration normally will have completed all prerequisite requirements for the program. The holders of degrees in other fields may find it necessary to complete preparatory survey courses prior to entering the core program. A thesis is not required. There is no comprehensive exam at the end of the program.

Since the University of Dayton is on a trimester system, the graduate student in business is afforded a great deal of flexibility in scheduling a program. Three full terms are offered during the year, and a full schedule of graduate courses is offered in every term. The time it takes to complete the requirements for the degree ranges from one calendar year to a maximum of five. Full-time students can complete the work in one year. Most part-time students extend the program over two and one-half years. Classes are conducted in the evening and on Saturday morning.

The Juris Doctor/M.B.A. program is offered jointly by the School of Business Administration and the School of Law. This program is designed to meet the increasing demand for lawyers in the business sector. Information may be obtained from either the School of Business Administration or the School of Law.

ADMISSION

Applications for the M.B.A. program are accepted from students who hold bachelor's degrees from regionally accredited colleges and universities. The degree need not have been in business or related fields. Approximately half the students hold degrees in fields other than business administration. Admission to the program is granted to students showing high promise for success in postgraduate business study. Factors considered for admission include scores on the Graduate Management Admission Test (GMAT), collegiate records and grade trends, and significant responsibilities or experience. Students may begin their studies in any one of the three trimesters which begin in late August, January, and May.

EXPENSES

Tuition for the 1985-86 year was $148 per credit hour. Estimated total program cost for the student with a business background is $5,000.

FINANCIAL ASSISTANCE

The university offers a number of financial aid programs to qualifying students, ranging from loans to work-study. A limited number of graduate assistantships are available. These carry a stipend of approximately $2,000 per term and include remission of tuition and fees. Assistants contribute half-time services in administration, research, or teaching. In addition, a limited number of Dean's Fellowships are awarded periodically on the basis of both academic merit and financial need.

PLACEMENT

The university maintains a placement office which assists students in securing part-time work to help them financially while attending school. The placement office also maintains a continuing liaison with business and industry throughout the nation and arranges interview sessions between recruiters and graduate students, assisting the student in his or her choice of prospective employment. This same service is also provided to the university's alumni without charge.

CORRESPONDENCE

For further information, please write or call

Director of M.B.A. Program
University of Dayton
Dayton, Ohio 45469
Telephone: 513-229-3732

The University of Delaware is located in Newark, Delaware, adjoining a major research complex of the chemical industry and an emerging financial center. The proximity to Philadelphia, New York, and Washington provides additional educational and cultural opportunities.

A Master of Business Administration (M.B.A.), a Master of Arts (M.A.) in economics, a Master of Science (M.S.) in accounting, a Master of Business Administration/Master of Arts (M.B.A./M.A.) in economics, and a Master of Science/Doctor of Philosophy (M.S./Ph.D.) in operations research are offered, drawing both full-time and part-time students.

PROGRAMS OF STUDY

The M.B.A. program, established in 1953, is accredited by the American Assembly of Collegiate Schools of Business (AACSB). The program meets a variety of intellectual and professional needs by offering courses that help students:
- understand the diverse problems of managing a complex organization;
- understand specific business functions and their interrelationships;
- understand the behavior of organizations, groups, and individuals;
- become aware of modern techniques for analyzing data and measuring performance;
- appreciate the problems and techniques for implementing decisions in business and other types of organizations; and
- appreciate the changing economic, technological, social, and legal environments in which business organizations operate.

Use of state-of-the-art computing equipment, including microcomputers, supplements theoretical and case-oriented instruction. Class size averages 25, increasing the opportunity for student involvement. Candidates must complete 48 semester hours, which may be accomplished in two years of full-time study. Part-time study will require from three to five years, depending on course loads. Students who have had sufficient instruction in accounting, finance, marketing, operations, or administration may waive up to four courses, thereby reducing the total number of credits required for graduation. A thesis or comprehensive examination is not required; satisfactory completion of the prescribed course work fulfills degree requirements.

The Master of Arts program in economics serves a dual purpose: to provide a sound foundation in economics for students who will pursue a Ph.D. and to provide a terminal program for those entering the job market. Two variants, a quantitative nonthesis option and a thesis option, are offered in this 30-credit-hour program to provide maximum flexibility. A combined M.B.A./M.A. in economics is also offered with a 57-credit-hour program.

The objective of the M.S. in accounting is to continue students' development in careers as professional accountants. The program requires 30 hours of graduate study in addition to the equivalent of an undergraduate degree with a major in accounting from an AACSB-accredited school.

The M.S. program in operations research is designed to provide students with a strong relevant background in mathematics and statistics along with an in-depth background in one functional area of business administration. For the M.S. program, at least 30 credit hours of study are required, including 6 credits of thesis study.

The Ph.D. program, which expands the M.S. background study in quantitative areas and in business administration, requires 60 credit hours of study, including 9 credits of thesis study.

ADMISSION

Admission to the M.B.A. program is open to qualified graduates of accredited colleges and universities. Calculus, statistics, and macroeconomics are prerequisites, although provisional admission may be granted until requirements are satisfied. Previous courses in business subjects are not required for nonbusiness majors. In general, a predictive formula is used to evaluate applicants which is a combination of two measures: grade-point average and scores on the Graduate Management Admission Test (GMAT). The GMAT is also required for admission to the accounting program. Candidates for admission to the programs in operations research and economics should submit Graduate Record Examinations (GRE) scores rather than GMAT scores.

Information concerning admission to the other graduate programs will be supplied on request.

Applicants should submit applications, transcripts of all academic work, and test scores to the Office of Graduate Studies prior to July 1 for September admission and prior to December 1 for admission in February.

EXPENSES

Tuition and fees are subject to annual revision. Applicants should request a current graduate catalog for confirmation of tuition fees.

FINANCIAL ASSISTANCE

A limited number of graduate assistantships and scholarships are available. Applications should be requested from the Administrator of the M.B.A. Program.

PLACEMENT

The university's Placement Office assists prospective graduates in finding suitable positions.

CORRESPONDENCE

Application forms and catalogs as well as additional information may be obtained from
Graduate Program
Department of Accounting, Economics, Business Administration or Operations Research
University of Delaware
Newark, Delaware 19716
Telephone: 302-451-2221

UNIVERSITY OF DENVER

DENVER, COLORADO

The University of Denver's College of Business Administration is one of the oldest collegiate schools of business in the United States. The Graduate School of Business and Public Management, the graduate unit of the college, is a member of the National Association of Schools of Public Administration and Affairs (NASPAA). Its programs are accredited by the American Assembly of Collegiate Schools of Business (AACSB). The university is a private, nonsectarian, coeducational institution, accredited by the North Central Association of Colleges and Secondary Schools.

Over 600 students are enrolled in the Graduate School of Business and Public Management, which offers innovative programs of professional education for people seeking careers in business and government. The faculty is highly qualified and alert to current and significant developments in business and government. Courses are taught by the case method, lecture, and seminar. Business and government experts serve as lecturers and consultants, and the Executive-in-Residence program brings to campus top executives of national and international firms and government agencies.

PROGRAMS OF STUDY

The Graduate School offers the Master of Business Administration (M.B.A.), the Executive Master of Business Administration (E.M.B.A.), and the Master of Accountancy (M.Acc.). The Master of International Management (M.I.M.) is offered in conjunction with the Graduate School of International Studies, and the School of Accountancy offers the Master of Taxation in conjunction with the College of Law. In addition, a combined degree with the College of Law (M.B.A./Juris Doctor) is available.

The M.B.A. program is offered for students desiring a broad professional education in all business areas in anticipation of moving into executive or administrative positions. Designed to provide concepts and techniques useful in the management of a business enterprise as a whole or any of its functional parts, it is essentially a 92-quarter-hour program, with variation in length allowed for previously completed academic work. Although the purpose of the program is broad management education, students may elect one of the following areas of concentration: finance, human

resource and productivity management, marketing, management information systems, accounting, hotel and restaurant management, business economics, and real estate finance. In addition, there are two unique and exciting programs—energy management and real estate and construction management—which reflect Denver's emergence as an energy center of the nation with a concomitant growth.

The Master of Accountancy is for students with undergraduate accounting emphasis. This program is designed for the student preparing for a career as a professional accountant, either as a member of a large C.P.A. firm or serving business as an auditor, tax adviser, or consultant. Students are able to emphasize audit/finance, managerial/information systems, tax, and general accounting.

The Master of International Management program requires a maximum of 95 quarter hours. The program's purpose is to provide a wide range of practical skills in management-related areas and to combine these skills with an understanding of international political and economic systems, international organization and law, and the cultural dynamics of societies.

The Master of Taxation is designed to train specialists in both the legal and accounting professions and is appropriately an interdisciplinary program. Applications for this program should be directed to the College of Law.

ADMISSION

A bachelor's degree from an accredited institution normally is a minimum requirement for entrance to a graduate program in business or public administration. A student is admitted on the basis of probable success as judged by previous college record and work experience, appropriate recommendations, and performance on the Graduate Management Admission Test (GMAT).

Foreign students must submit scores from the Test of English as a Foreign Language (TOEFL) unless they obtained their undergraduate degree from an institution where English is the language of instruction.

EXPENSES

Tuition and fees for the academic year of nine months (1985-86) is $7,920 for a full-time student. Tuition for part-time students is $210 per quarter hour. University housing is available for single and married students, and private housing close to the campus is generally available.

FINANCIAL ASSISTANCE

Full- or partial-tuition scholarships, teaching and research assistantships, deferred-payment loans, and work-study aid are available. Individual awards may consist of one or more of the above and are based on academic merit and financial need. The Graduate and Professional School Financial Aid Service (GAPSFAS) form is required.

PLACEMENT

The university's Counseling and Placement Centers provide all students with comprehensive placement service. The Director of Graduate Business Placements and Employer Relations works with all graduate business students. About 200 companies and government agencies interview students each year.

CORRESPONDENCE

For further information, write
  Graduate School of Business and
    Public Management
  University of Denver
  Denver, Colorado 80208
  Telephone: 303-871-3416

University of Detroit is a Catholic, Jesuit institution founded in 1877. Its schools and colleges include Architecture, Business and Administration, Dentistry, Education and Human Services, Engineering and Sciences, Law, and Liberal Arts. Its student body is comprised of approximately 6,400, across four campuses. The McNichols campus in northwest Detroit is the home of the Master of Business Administration (M.B.A.) program. This campus also houses the residence halls.

PROGRAMS OF STUDY
University of Detroit currently offers three graduate business degrees: the M.B.A., the Juris Doctor (J.D.)/M.B.A., and the Master of Arts (M.A.) in economics.

The M.B.A. program, initiated in the late 1940s, is accredited by the American Assembly of Collegiate Schools of Business (AACSB). The program is designed to appeal to full-time employees who seek the M.B.A. on a part-time basis. Approximately 75 percent of the students undertake the program on this basis. However, a smaller, yet growing, number of full-time students have been enrolling in the program. To accommodate both part-time and full-time students, all courses are scheduled in the evening hours, Monday through Thursday. Part-time students enroll in evening classes for three to six credit hours per term. Full-time students enroll in the same classes for 9 to 12 hours per term.

The M.B.A. program is designed to both broaden and deepen the student's knowledge and competence in the principal aspects of managing work organizations: businesses, hospitals, governmental units, health care agencies, and industrial firms.

The program instruction is performed by a designated corps of graduate faculty members, as assisted by academically qualified specialists from local, leading work organizations.

The program is made up of graduate-only courses. Program requirements may vary from 36 to 57 hours, depending upon the student's undergraduate/graduate educational experience. Individuals whose undergraduate/graduate experience includes successful course grades in areas of the business curriculum may be granted advanced standing and/or waivers in the curriculum structure, which would normally call for a maximum of 57 credit hours. For example, an engineering, architecture, or liberal arts major—with little or no exposure to business courses—would tend to enter the M.B.A. program with maximum requirements (57 hours). On the other hand, an undergraduate business major with a 3.00 average might "swing" toward the minimum program requirement of 36 credit hours.

The program is three-tiered in its structure: precore, core, and postcore levels. The core level of 21 hours is viewed as the principal integrative portion of the curriculum. It is composed of courses in accounting, financial management, management, marketing, statistical modeling, and corporate social responsibility.

The precore level is prerequisite to the core and is composed of courses in economics, accounting, legal environment, production, information systems, and statistics. These courses may be given advanced standing if the subject areas have been successfully completed through equivalent courses at the undergraduate level.

The postcore level is composed of one required strategic planning course and 18 hours of electives. The electives are intended to allow the student, in consultation with an adviser, to develop a cohesive plan of study designed to meet his or her professional ambitions as well as the goals of the M.B.A. program. The student must maintain a grade-point average of 3.00 (on a 4.00 scale). No comprehensive examinations are required.

ADMISSION
Admission criteria include the applicant's academic background and scholastic record, as well as performance on the Graduate Management Admission Test (GMAT).

Applications for admission are accepted through August 1 for Term I and through November 15 for Term II. An official transcript, sent by the institution to the Graduate School of the University of Detroit, is required from each college or university previously attended.

EXPENSES
Tuition is $210 per credit hour. Other fees are minimal. A nonrefundable application fee of $25 must accompany the application. Information on the university residence halls is furnished upon request.

FINANCIAL ASSISTANCE
A limited number of graduate fellowships are available. They carry a tuition waiver for up to nine credit hours in each of Terms I and II.

The Co-op/Placement office provides assistance to students in obtaining part-time and summer employment while attending the university.

PLACEMENT
M.B.A. students are invited to register with the Co-op/Placement Office, which aids in locating suitable positions offered by hundreds of employers within the metro-Detroit area.

CORRESPONDENCE
Inquiries to the program should be directed to
  Director
  Graduate Business Programs Office
  University of Detroit
  4001 West McNichols Road
  Detroit, Michigan 48221
  Telephone: 313-927-1202

The University of the District of Columbia came into being on August 1, 1976, with the merger of the existing public institutions of higher learning: District of Columbia Teachers College, Federal City College, and Washington Technical Institute. The university has three main campuses. The College of Business and Public Management is located on the Mount Vernon Square campus, only a few blocks from the White House and other main government buildings. The students have access to some of the world's largest depositories of research materials, including the U.S. Library of Congress.

The university offers a full complement of baccalaureate degrees in addition to a number of graduate programs. All programs in the university are accredited by the Middle States Association of Colleges and Secondary Schools. The College of Business and Public Management is a member of the American Assembly of Collegiate Schools of Business (AACSB).

The College of Business and Public Management offers master's degrees in business administration, business education, and public administration. The objective of the Master of Business Education degree program is to provide professional preparation on the graduate level for teachers of business education courses on the secondary, postsecondary, technical, and two- and four-year college levels. Moreover, the program can also serve as preparation for personnel such as business education supervisors, department heads, counselors, and research directors. The purpose of the Master of Public Administration program is to develop in the participants a background and working level of skills, knowledge, and attitudes that will prepare them for responsibilities in decision making in public organizations. Other degree programs such as Master of Office Administration are being planned.

PROGRAM OF STUDY
The Master of Business Administration (M.B.A.) program prepares qualified generalists for leadership roles in business, industry, finance, and all levels of governmental organizations. Although the emphasis is on providing the broad understanding of business concepts, the curriculum is designed to allow a modest specialization in areas such as accounting, business economics, business finance, business management, computer information and systems science, international business, marketing, public management, and quantitative business analysis.

The university has an outstanding computer facility that is used by faculty and students in connection with business games. Other teaching methods employed include extensive case studies, audiovisual aids, lecture-discussions, and individualized instruction.

The M.B.A. degree requires the successful completion of 36 hours (12 courses). The program consists of M.B.A. core courses and an area of emphasis. Students with baccalaureate degrees in fields other than business administration are required to complete prerequisites that include course work in accounting, economics, business finance, business law, management, marketing, and business statistics before being permitted to take M.B.A. courses. The M.B.A. core calls for completion of 27 semester hours. A student must select an area of emphasis and undertake nine hours of study from the offerings of the selected area. A written comprehensive examination is required for completion of the M.B.A. program.

The submission of an acceptable thesis, in lieu of six course credits, may be approved for a student whose particular objectives make such action appropriate. A student electing the thesis option will be required to complete one course (three hours) in the area of emphasis in addition to the M.B.A. core requirements. A student may transfer up to six semester hours for comparable courses completed at other accredited institutions.

Graduate classes in the college are offered only in the late afternoons or evenings. A student pursuing full-time studies may finish requirements in three semesters. Of course, part-time students will require longer, but the college demands completion within five years.

ADMISSION
Admission to the M.B.A. program is open to all qualified men and women who hold baccalaureate degrees from regionally accredited institutions. Admission is determined by an Admissions Committee, which considers a combination of factors. Specifically, the committee's decision is based upon (1) overall grade-point average of 2.5 on a four-point scale; (2) potential for leadership as indicated by past experience, attitudes, and aspirations; (3) two letters of recommendation; and (4) scores on the Graduate Management Admission Test (GMAT).

Admission may be accomplished in any one of the three semesters. The college admits a limited number of international students each semester; however, only those students residing in the United States are eligible to apply.

EXPENSES
Residents of the District of Columbia pay a tuition fee of $61 per semester hour, to a maximum of $545 per semester. Nonresidents are charged $129 per semester hour, to a maximum of $1,155 per semester. All students, in addition, pay a student activities fee of $17.

FINANCIAL ASSISTANCE
Students may qualify for financial assistance through a combination of scholarship aid, National Direct Student Loan, or work-study arrangements. The Director of Financial Aid attempts to match the needs of the student with the right funds and support available through the university and outside sources, including part-time work.

PLACEMENT
The University Placement Office assists students in finding part-time and career employment.

CORRESPONDENCE
For additional information, write or call
Dr. Jag Mohan S. Pabley
Associate Dean for Graduate Programs
College of Business and Public
  Management
University of the District of Columbia
900 F Street, N.W.
Washington, DC 20004
Telephone: 202-727-1051

The University of Edinburgh celebrated its 400th anniversary in 1983 and currently has some 8,500 undergraduate and 1,300 postgraduate students enrolled. The Department of Business Studies, founded in 1918, is one of the oldest in the United Kingdom. There are some 700 undergraduates and about 165 postgraduates registered with the department. About 40 postgraduates are taking the full-time Master of Business Administration (M.B.A.) program, 105 are enrolled in the part-time M.B.A. program, and around 15 are registered for research degrees.

The university is located in the historic capital city of Scotland, which is the major cultural, financial, and administrative center of the country. The location of the Department of Business Studies in George Square places it right in the heart of university activity, including its social life.

PROGRAMS OF STUDY

The M.B.A. program is constructed around a first term of compulsory courses in managerial economics, organizational behavior, accounting and business law, statistics, computing, and business policy. In the second and third terms students elect to take four options from finance and investment, managerial accounting, managerial economics, industrial relations, personnel management, general marketing, marketing research, management science, and international business. To help integrate the student's understanding of the different functional specialties and to introduce the idea of strategic management and the ethical and political issues involved in the activities of organizations, all students take a course in general management. Students also have to carry out preliminary work in preparation for their dissertations. After the degree examination in June, those passing are permitted to work on their M.B.A. dissertation, which must be submitted by September 30.

While disciplinary teaching is primarily through formal lectures, business policy and general management is primarily taught through group exercises and case studies. A considerable emphasis is placed on learning teamwork skills and the ability to present an argument in class. The school's ability to attract a wide diversity of nationalities to make up the overseas group of students provides scope for acquiring interpersonal skills necessary in international firms.

The part-time M.B.A. program, designed for people who hold jobs, is taught entirely in the evening. It is strictly comparable with the full-time degree in its academic level, but the structure is different and the courses are separate. The program recognizes the heavy pressure on a student's time; it builds on, and does not ignore, a student's knowledge of the real world of business.

Doctoral students in business are assigned research supervisors in the Department of Business Studies who advise on topics, methodology, analysis, and dissertation preparation. Students also attend the taught doctoral program, which is organized jointly by the three divisions of the Scottish Business School, during their first year of study. Additional information may be obtained from the Director, Research Degree Program.

ADMISSION

The school's aim is to have a student mix that is broken down approximately into one third new British graduates, one third British graduates with work experience, and one third overseas graduates with work experience. The selection committee also aims to recruit students from a wide disciplinary background and to have women compose not less than a third of the participants in the program.

Candidates should normally have an honors degree or an ordinary degree with evidence of good passes in any subject. Practical work experience since graduating is desirable, though not essential if other qualifications are good.

Applicants with degree-equivalent professional qualifications (for example, CA, or CEng) will be considered if they have good relevant experience. All candidates should have a satisfactory score on the Graduate Management Admission Test (GMAT).

The successful completion of the program necessitates mastery of English. Such evidence may be adduced by requiring the candidates to take the Test of English as a Foreign Language (TOEFL) or ELTS test available through British Council offices worldwide.

EXPENSES

Tuition for the M.B.A. program is currently (1985) £3,325 for one year for those not qualifying as U.K. or E.E.C. residents. The fee for the latter is £1,650. Fees are subject to revision. Expenses for accommodations, books, and miscellaneous are estimated at £3,800.

FINANCIAL ASSISTANCE

A number of awards for applicants resident in Scotland are available through the university from the Scottish Education Department. A few ESRC part-awards are also made on an open basis to applicants resident in the U.K. ESRC studentships, which are limited to good honors graduates resident in Britain, are available through a national pool competition.

Several of the national banks, in conjunction with the Business Graduates Association, operate loan schemes. Lloyds, First National City, and National Westminster Banks are among those participating. The Bank of Scotland also operates a loan scheme in conjunction with the Scottish Business School. Details may be obtained from the Scottish Business School, 79 St. George's Place, Glasgow, Scotland, G2 1EU (Telephone: 041-2213124).

PLACEMENT

The university's Career Advisory Service is staffed by professional counselors and offers M.B.A. students information and services related to career development.

CORRESPONDENCE

For further information, please contact
Director of MBA Program
The Scottish Business School
—Edinburgh Division
University of Edinburgh
Department of Business Studies
50 George Square
Edinburgh EH8 9JY Scotland
Telephone: 031 667 1011, extension 6823
TELEX: UNIVED G 727442

UNIVERSITY OF EVANSVILLE

EVANSVILLE, INDIANA

The University of Evansville traces its history from 1854 when a charter was granted to Moore's Hill College in Dearborn County, Indiana. In 1915 the school was moved to Evansville and became Evansville College. Continued growth resulted in university status being granted in 1968. Current enrollment is approximately 4,000 with the majority being full-time undergraduate students. Average enrollment in the M.B.A. program, which has been operative since 1968, varies between 125 and 175.

The beautiful 74-acre campus is located in a residential neighborhood within the city limits of Evansville. The focal point of the campus is the new Bower-Suhrheinrich Library that expands the Clifford Memorial Library to a total of 84,000 square feet. The combined space allows the library's collection to number more than 700,000 bound volumes and microforms. The university structure includes the College of Arts and Sciences, School of Business Administration, School of Education, College of Engineering and Computing Sciences, College of Fine Arts, School of Nursing and Health Sciences, and College of Graduate and Continuing Studies.

The Evansville metropolitan area has a population of 250,000 and is served by over 4,000 diversified business firms ranging in size from corner proprietorships to large drug, metal, and appliance producers. The Advisory Board to the School of Business Administration includes about 20 business leaders from the region, including representatives of large international corporations.

PROGRAMS OF STUDY

The objectives of the Master of Business Administration (M.B.A.) program at the University of Evansville are to develop (1) an understanding of the interrelationships of the various functional fields within a business, (2) an understanding of the nature and use of modern quantitative and behavioral tools of business analysis and decision making, and (3) an articulate personal rationale concerning the role of business decisions in American society.

All M.B.A. courses are held in the evening and are designed to meet the needs of both part-time and full-time students. This arrangement permits a graduate student to supplement his or her income and also encourages the student to experience real-life management situations.

The M.B.A. program is 36 semester hours in length. Nine core courses totaling 27 semester hours are required of all students and are designed to provide graduate-level coverage of all the major functional areas of business. The remaining nine semester hours may be selected to meet the individual needs of the student. No thesis is required.

Graduate course work assumes an undergraduate body of knowledge consisting of accounting, economics, finance, management, marketing, quantitative business analysis, calculus, and computing science. Students who lack portions of this body of knowledge may either take the appropriate undergraduate courses or establish competency through a testing procedure.

The program concentrates on theoretical rather than vocational aspects of business, and it emphasizes broad philosophical relationships between business decisions and society rather than technical skill in a restricted area of business.

ADMISSION

Applicants for the M.B.A. program are required to have a bachelor's degree (in any field or discipline) from an accredited college or university. Admission to the program requires an undergraduate grade-point average of at least 2.7 on a 4-point scale, as well as a composite score of at least 1,000. An applicant's composite score is determined by taking 200 times the undergraduate grade-point average and then adding the Graduate Management Admission Test (GMAT) score. Occasionally students who do not meet one or both of these conditions are admitted to the program if there is concrete evidence of significant promise for success in graduate study. For international students, a Test of English as a Foreign Language (TOEFL) score of at least 550 is also required.

EXPENSES

The application fee to all degree programs is $20; the tuition rate for the 1985-86 academic year was $150 per semester hour of credit.

FINANCIAL ASSISTANCE

A limited number of assistantships are available to full-time graduate students. These take the form of partial tuition remission. Assistantships are granted on the basis of previous academic record and the needs of the School of Business Administration.

CORRESPONDENCE

For further information or to request an application for admission, please write or call

M.B.A. Program Director
School of Business Administration
University of Evansville
1800 Lincoln Avenue
Evansville, Indiana 47714
Telephone: 812-479-2853

The University of Florida, with a student enrollment of 35,000 and a faculty numbering more than 1,200, is the largest of nine universities in the State University System. Only two other universities in the nation equal the number and breadth of programs offered on one campus. Ranging in scope from the fine arts to agriculture, they cover most of the professional fields including law, business administration, medicine and health-related professions, engineering, and architecture. The 2,000-acre campus is situated in Gainesville, a community of approximately 125,000 people located about 75 miles southwest of Jacksonville and 100 miles northeast of Tampa, within an hour's drive of the Gulf Coast and an hour and a half from the Atlantic coast.

PROGRAMS OF STUDY
The principal objective of the Master of Business Administration (M.B.A.) program is to prepare promising students for successful careers in management. The program is designed to give students the conceptual knowledge for understanding the functions and behavior common to all organizations and the analytical, problem-solving, and decision-making skills essential for effective management. Several teaching methods are utilized. Courses are taught using the method most effective for communicating their basic content. For example, managerial courses such as marketing and business policy use the case method. More conceptual courses such as quantitative methods and economics use a lecture-discussion format. Still other courses use experiential exercises and field work.

The program involves two years (four semesters) of rigorous study with an internship suggested between the first and second year. During the first year students enter and proceed through the program as a group. Course work includes financial accounting, computer information systems, managerial economics, organizational behavior, statistics, managerial accounting, finance, marketing, international management, operations management, and problem analysis and presentation.

In the second year the student takes business policy. The remaining courses are determined by the student's individual needs and interests. Students may develop a specialized area with the help of specific concentration advisers. In addition, students must select a quantitative elective and an elective dealing with the legal environment of business. The specific courses selected will depend on the individual interests of the student. Available concentrations include accounting, computer information systems, economics, finance, health and hospital administration, insurance, management, marketing, management science, and real estate and urban land studies. Some concentrations offer more than one track.

Two doctoral programs are available: the Doctor of Philosophy (Ph.D.) in economics and the Ph.D. in business administration. The latter offers majors in accounting, finance, management, marketing, and real estate. Both programs are designed to prepare individuals for careers in teaching, academic research, or applied research with governmental or private organizations. Master of Arts (M.A.) programs are offered in economics and business administration. In addition, the School of Accounting offers a Master of Accounting with areas of specialization in financial/auditing, managerial/cost, systems, and taxation.

ADMISSION
The Graduate School of Business welcomes applications from college graduates of any accredited college or university in the United States and abroad. Applicants for admission must submit satisfactory scores on the Graduate Management Admission Test (GMAT) as well as transcripts for all previous academic work. Applicants whose native language is not English are required to submit, in addition, scores on the Test of English as a Foreign Language (TOEFL).

The curriculum assumes no previous academic work in managerial disciplines or business administration. However, it is strongly recommended that students establish a background in calculus, introductory statistics, and microeconomics prior to entering the program.

Students are admitted in the fall semester only. All students are admitted on a full-time basis. Applications should be made as early as possible during the preceding academic year. Applications received after April 1 will be considered on a "space available" basis.

EXPENSES
Tuition for non-Florida residents is approximately $4,600 for the academic year. Tuition for Florida residents is approximately $1,600. Books and supplies will cost about $700 per year. Some university housing is available for graduate students ranging in rates from $200 per month for a one-bedroom apartment to $350 for two bedrooms, unfurnished. Furnished apartments are available for slightly higher costs. Rent in the dormitories for single students is approximately $1,326 per calendar year ($663 per semester for a double, air-conditioned room).

FINANCIAL ASSISTANCE
A variety of financial aid is available including graduate fellowships, special fellowships for minority and economically disadvantaged and for women in nontraditional careers, graduate assistantships, and special minority assistantships. Fellowships and assistantships may carry "out-of-state" tuition waivers. Information concerning financial assistance may be obtained from the Director of Graduate Studies.

PLACEMENT
Placement services are available through the M.B.A. Placement Center. Additional services and interview schedules are provided by the centralized University Career Resource Center.

CORRESPONDENCE
For further information or to request an application for admission, please write or call

Director of the M.B.A. Program
201 New Business Building
University of Florida
Gainesville, Florida 32611
Telephone: 904-392-7992

Established in 1785, the University of Georgia is the oldest chartered state university in America. The university began offering graduate instruction in business administration in 1923, and its bachelor's and master's programs in business are accredited by the American Assembly of Collegiate Schools of Business (AACSB). The program emphasizes excellence in teaching, research, and service. This emphasis is made possible through a distinguished faculty, excellent library holdings, and advanced computer facilities. There are over 126 faculty members teaching 4,000 B.B.A., 120 M.B.A., 80 M.Acc., 30 M.A., and 120 Ph.D. students.

PROGRAMS OF STUDY
Seven graduate degree programs are offered—Master of Business Administration (M.B.A.), Master of Accountancy (M.Acc.), Master of Marketing Research (M.M.R.), Master of Arts in both business administration and economics (M.A.), and Doctor of Philosophy in both business administration and economics (Ph.D.). The M.B.A., M.Acc., and M.M.R. degrees lead to professional and managerial careers. The M.A. programs are used for intensive specialization or as a path to the Ph.D. The Ph.D. programs lead to research and/or teaching careers. For additional information concerning the M.Acc., M.M.R., M.A., and Ph.D. programs, contact the Director of Graduate Programs.

It is the intent of the faculty that the M.B.A. candidate should receive a rich and challenging educational experience, closely monitored by the faculty. The faculty expects that a graduate of the program will be skilled in the use of a wide spectrum of analytical tools and techniques and accustomed to the discipline of systematic thinking. The faculty expects that a graduate of the M.B.A. program will be able to communicate his or her ideas clearly in both written and oral expression.

The M.B.A. degree takes two years for applicants without a B.B.A., or its equivalent, from an AACSB-accredited institution. Students with a B.B.A. degree from an AACSB-accredited institution will require only one year to complete the M.B.A. program.

The two-year student, who enters in the fall quarter, takes 96 quarter hours of course work. The first year consists of 48 hours of core work. The core courses have a professional managerial focus and provide a professional orientation of management tasks. They emphasize the development and application of analytical tools and address sophisticated, challenging problems. In the second year, the student takes 11 electives and the required Business Policy course. The Business Policy course integrates the first and second years, providing a capstone to the M.B.A. program.

The four quarter (one-year) student enters in the summer quarter. During the summer, the student takes five core courses. In the fall, winter, and spring quarters, he or she will join the second year students and take 11 electives and the Business Policy course.

Areas of specialization are carefully integrated, cumulative, and systematically built upon earlier courses. Students will take three courses in two areas of specialization. The additional five electives will support and strengthen their chosen areas.

ADMISSION
Individuals with a baccalaureate in any field are eligible to apply. Each applicant submits an application for admission, an M.B.A. supplemental application, two official transcripts of all undergraduate and graduate work, scores on the Graduate Management Admission Test (GMAT), and three letters of recommendation. Foreign applicants must also submit scores on the Test of English as a Foreign Language (TOEFL).

Admission is selective. The selection is based on a balanced appraisal of aptitude, ability, and achievement. Potential for management and leadership qualities are considered. The M.B.A. students have diversified undergraduate backgrounds from liberal arts, science, engineering, business administration, and other disciplines. The average age of M.B.A. students is 24, and approximately half have two or more years of full-time work experience. Applications should be filed at least six months before the quarter for which admission is sought.

EXPENSES
For Georgia residents tuition for 1985-86 was $518 per quarter. Nonresident graduate students paid $1,272 per quarter. Books are estimated to cost $200 per quarter. Personal expenses vary widely, but a realistic budget (including tuition) for a single person runs approximately $1,800-$2,500 per quarter.

FINANCIAL ASSISTANCE
Approximately a fourth of the graduate students receive assistantships awarded on the basis of merit in amounts ranging from $3,500 to $5,700 plus a waiver of out-of-state fees. Applications should be submitted by February 15 for the following academic year. Students will receive an assistantship application after they have been officially admitted to the M.B.A. program.

Loans are available through application to the Student Financial Aid Office, Academic Building.

PLACEMENT
The college provides individualized career counseling and coordinates job opportunities through the College of Business Administration as well as through the Office of Career Planning and Placement. An M.B.A. directory of graduating students is published and distributed to over 600 corporations nationwide. Over 600 organizations interview on campus each year.

CORRESPONDENCE
For further information, write or call
    Director of the M.B.A. Program
    Graduate School of Business
        Administration
    The University of Georgia
    Athens, Georgia 30602
    Telephone: 404-542-5671

The Barney School of Business and Public Administration is descended from Hillyer College, founded in 1879. It is one of the University of Hartford's seven colleges. Approximately 700 students are studying business or public administration. Courses are offered in late afternoon and evening on the 200-acre suburban campus.

Mortenson Library, the university's central collection, houses some 348,000 books, 2,400 periodical subscriptions, and 57,500 microfilm and microfiche items. The Barney School houses a substantial computer facility, with both stand-alone microcomputers and terminals that give students direct access to the university's mainframe. Tutors, user consultants, software, and other support encourage Barney students to draw on computer resources in a wide range of individual and group work on problems, cases, and reports.

PROGRAMS OF STUDY

Degree programs are open to both full-time and part-time students. More than half of the 700 graduate management students attend classes part time. Some have substantial managerial or other professional experience.

New students are encouraged to consult with an academic adviser in the Graduate Office in designing their personal programs of study. Applicants may request exemption or transfer of credit for some required courses on the basis of successful completion of comparable courses elsewhere.

Men and women interested in general management usually see significant career advantages in earning the Master of Business Administration (M.B.A.) or the Master of Public Administration (M.P.A.) degree. For those with specialized professional interests, the Barney School also offers programs leading to the Master of Science degrees in insurance (M.S.I.), organizational behavior (M.S.O.B.), professional accounting (M.S.P.A.), and taxation (M.S.T.).

The M.B.A. program requires 48 credits (usually 16 three-credit courses). Students without a background in economics and calculus are expected to complete those prerequisites before taking advanced courses. Advanced courses and electives are available in some 25 fields of specialized concentration.

The M.B.A. Co-op Program offers students an opportunity to earn the M.B.A. degree in 15 months while receiving 6 months of part-time work experience in a chosen area of specialization. Corporations affiliated with the Co-op Program include insurance companies, high-tech manufacturing firms, major utilities, financial institutions, retail chains, and hospitals. Students begin the program in September by attending traditional M.B.A. courses in one of the Barney School Executive Classrooms. Application information is listed under the Admission section. Applications for the program are due April 30.

The M.P.A. program requires 36 credits (usually 12 courses). The curriculum is designed to meet the special career needs of managers in government and not-for-profit organizations. In addition to the core courses and electives in a field of concentration, M.P.A. candidates prepare a qualifying paper. Students without prior work experience also complete an internship.

The Master of Science in Professional Accounting (M.S.P.A.) program normally requires 48 credits. Applicants with a strong accounting background may be able to complete the M.S.P.A. requirements with as few as 30 credits. This program satisfies the educational requirements for C.P.A., C.M.A., and C.I.A. certification.

The M.S.O.B. program requires 36 credits (12 three-credit courses). Eight required courses focus on topics in organizational development and management of human resources; the remainder are electives.

The Master of Science in Taxation (M.S.T.) program requires 30 credits. Successful applicants generally have professional experience in taxation or the law.

The Master of Science in Insurance program requires 36 credits. Students select their electives from a management concentration, such as finance, marketing, or public administration.

ADMISSION

New students enter the Barney School at the beginning of fall, spring, and summer classes. No prior courses in management or business are required: among current students are graduates of programs in accounting, engineering and science, the humanities, law, and nursing—as well as graduates of business curricula.

The Admission Committee considers academic transcripts, letters of recommendation, scores on the Graduate Management Admission Test (GMAT), and the application form. A statement of personal goals is part of the application for admission; applicants with substantial work experience may substitute a resume of their professional background for this statement.

EXPENSES

Tuition is $190 per semester credit hour ($570 for each three-credit course). Full-time students may apply for loans, part-time work, and assistantships. Most employers offer tuition grants and reimbursement for part-time students.

CORRESPONDENCE

For further information or to request an application for admission, please write
Office of Graduate Studies
Barney School of Business and
    Public Administration
University of Hartford
West Hartford, Connecticut 06117
Telephone: 203-243-4309 or 243-4444

The University of Hawaii at Manoa (UHM) is the principal campus in Hawaii's nine-campus system of higher education. More than 21,000 students attend the 300-acre campus which is located in Manoa Valley, a residential area close to the heart of metropolitan Honolulu.

As a multicultural center, Honolulu is the ideal setting for an internationally oriented business program. Consequently, the UHM College of Business Administration's distinctive competence is in serving as the leading educational bridge between East and West in business management.

The East-West Center, a federally funded institution adjacent to the university, brings together scholars from Asia, the Pacific nations, and the United States in a variety of cooperative programs. Master of Business Administration (M.B.A.) students may apply for East-West Center grants (December 1 deadline).

The bachelor's and master's programs offered by the College of Business are accredited by the American Assembly of Collegiate Schools of Business (AACSB). The college offers concentrations in international business, finance, marketing, accounting, management, decision sciences, business economics, and personnel and industrial relations. The Pacific Asian Management Institute (PAMI) is offered each summer by the College of Business. PAMI provides specialized training and M.B.A. courses in the context of the Pacific-Asian environment. A limited number of fellowships to study at the Institute for International Studies and Training in Japan are also offered each spring semester. The College of Business Administration also offers a 36-credit-hour Master of Accountancy program.

The college encourages applicants from various academic backgrounds and also encourages dual degrees with such disciplines as public health, law, engineering, Asian studies, and urban planning.

PROGRAM OF STUDY
The M.B.A. program provides a solid educational foundation for business leadership. It is ideally designed for students seeking graduate degrees in business administration to complement their undergraduate degrees in other fields; however, it can be modified to meet the needs of students with undergraduate business degrees desiring to extend their education into advanced areas of analysis and problem solving. Prerequisites to the program are limited to courses in microeconomics and macroeconomics and passage of a computer competency exam. Students requiring additional undergraduate work in written skills are informed before registration.

The M.B.A. program is primarily a nonthesis program of 54 graduate semester credit hours. It consists of nine basic, seven concentration and elective, and two integrative policy courses. All basic courses include an international component. A thesis program is also available. Current enrollment is approximately 350. Slightly more than half are employed full time.

ADMISSION
Applicants must hold a bachelor's degree from a recognized university or college, or its equivalent. Admission decisions are based on the applicant's past academic performance, Graduate Management Admission Test (GMAT) score, career goals, and at least one year of postbaccalaureate work experience. All applicants from countries where English is not the usual means of communication are required to take the Test of English as a Foreign Language (TOEFL). A grade-point average of 3.0 or better in the last two years of undergraduate work and a GMAT score of at least 500 are preferred.

Applications should be filed with the Graduate Division by March 1 for admission in the fall semester and by September 1 for admission in the spring semester.

EXPENSES
Graduate tuition is $555 per semester for resident and military students; $2,010 per semester for nonresidents. Resident and military graduate students enrolled for fewer than 12 hours are charged $47 per credit hour; nonresident students, $168 per credit hour.

Limited room and board accommodations are available on campus. Honolulu is a high-cost area and off-campus living expenses can be relatively high. An estimated minimum cost for meals, housing, personal expenses, health insurance, books and supplies, and transportation for a student living off campus with a roommate is $650 per month.

FINANCIAL ASSISTANCE
The Office of Financial Aids assists students with financial needs to continue or complete their education at the UHM. Assistance may take the form of scholarships, grants, loans, and student employment. Address correspondence to Director, Office of Financial Aids, 2442 Campus Road, Honolulu, Hawaii 96822.

A few graduate assistantships and tuition waivers are available directly through the College of Business Administration for students with outstanding scholastic records who have an adequate academic background in the field of business, economics, mathematics, statistics, or travel industry and demonstrate a high level of English proficiency. Graduate assistantships and other financial aids to students are not awarded until students arrive in Hawaii, and usually such awards do not occur until the student has completed at least one semester of graduate work at UHM.

PLACEMENT
The services of the University Office of Placement and Career Planning are available for M.B.A. students. In addition, the College of Business has established institutional relationships that provide a number of Asian-Pacific placement opportunities.

CORRESPONDENCE
For further information or to request an application for admission, please write or call
Office of Graduate Programs
College of Business Administration
University of Hawaii at Manoa
2404 Maile Way
Honolulu, Hawaii 96822
Telephone: 808-948-8266

Hong Kong University, one of the two universities in Hong Kong, was founded in 1911 as a development of the Medical School which was founded in the 1880s. It consists of nine faculties: Arts, Science, Medicine, Engineering, Social Science, Dentistry, Law, Education, and Architecture. Current full-time student enrollment is just under 7,000; to accommodate future growth a major construction program has been in progress to provide additional teaching and research facilities. The university is well-equipped with facilities necessary to provide good university-level education. The Main Library has over 400,000 bound volumes, and the Fung Ping Shan Library has an additional 250,000 volumes, which constitute one of the largest collections of Chinese books in Asia outside China. Computing facilities range from Univac and PDP mainframes to numerous microcomputers. The university also provides recreational facilities and a health service to students.

PROGRAM OF STUDY

The Master of Business Administration (M.B.A.) program is offered by the Department of Management Studies. Since its introduction in September 1976, it has evolved into one of the largest of the university's master's level programs. The program is offered part time in order to attract students who are also active managers. The program has an annual intake of about 35 students.

The Department of Management Studies is one of the largest departments within the Faculty of Social Sciences, and in addition to its postgraduate work, teaches 300 full-time undergraduate students majoring in management studies, and another 300 taking management courses as part of their studies. The department is active in a number of fields of management research, for example, international management, cross-cultural research, finance, accountancy, consumer behavior, production, and personnel. In addition to essential teaching facilities, the department has also developed, with the help of a generous donation by Mr. William Mong, the Mong Kwok Ping Management Data Bank, which contains essential reference data for research on management and business in East Asia. This important research base contributes to the department's development into a leading center of business education.

Students attend the program on a part-time basis over a three-year period (nine hours per week spread over two evenings and a Saturday morning or, in the first year, a Wednesday afternoon).

The academic year is divided into two semesters, the first running from September to December and the second from January to April; three courses are taught each semester. The first year of the course is designed to teach students the basic technical management skills and disciplines necessary for understanding business. It contains courses in Accounting, Economic Analysis of Business, Quantitative Analysis, Organization Theory, Behavioral Science, and Computing/The Economic Environment. The second year continues this skill development with the emphasis shifting to the functional specialisms of management, that is, finance, marketing, personnel, production, and international management. Also, at this point the student is introduced to research methods. The final year of the program is aimed quite specifically at the application of these skills in real-world situations, and in particular, the business world of Asia, and includes courses in Financial Aspects of Policy, Marketing Aspects of Policy, Human and Cross-Cultural Aspects of Policy, Strategic Management, and Management Skills. A dissertation on a research topic of the student's choice is also part of the final year.

ADMISSION

Applications are processed by the Registrar of the University of Hong Kong. To be eligible for admission to the course leading to the degree of Master of Business Administration, a candidate must:
- comply with the General Regulations of Hong Kong University;
- hold a degree of the University of Hong Kong or another qualification of equivalent standard from the University of Hong Kong or from another university or comparable institution accepted for this purpose, or a professional qualification as well as membership in an appropriate professional body accepted for this purpose;
- have performed satisfactorily on the Graduate Management Admission Test (GMAT);
- satisfy the examiners in a qualifying examination if required.

Candidates for the Hong Kong University M.B.A. program will normally have three or more years of full-time business experience since graduation. The term "business experience" is interpreted broadly, and students with a background from government and other nonbusiness organizations are welcome. Under certain circumstances, such as exceptional performance in business, the requirement of a university degree may be waived.

There is no rigid age requirement but a person under 25 is unlikely to possess the necessary qualifications. Most applicants are between 25 and 35.

EXPENSES

The following fees are payable to the University of Hong Kong:

Composition fee, per year	$1,800
Caution money (refundable)	125
Application fee (nonrefundable)	50

A graduation fee of $125 applies at the end of the course.

A very limited number of postgraduate students and overseas staff can be housed in the Robert Black College, a modern building constructed in the traditional Chinese style and well situated on the university campus. Private rented accommodation is expensive and may be difficult to obtain.

CORRESPONDENCE

M.B.A. inquiries should be sent to
The Registrar
University of Hong Kong
Hong Kong

Following its statewide study of higher education needs, the Coordinating Board, Texas College and University System, recommended in 1968 that a second campus of the University of Houston should be created. In 1971 the 61st Legislature authorized the creation of the University of Houston—Clear Lake (UH-CL) and subsequently provided funds for academic and physical facilities at the new institution. In December 1976, the Southern Association of Colleges and Schools granted UH-CL accreditation. The university, which opened for its first regular classes in the fall of 1974, is located in facilities adjacent to the Johnson Space Center in southeast Houston.

Approximately 80 percent of the graduate students attend part time in the evening. Both full- and part-time offerings are available. Teaching approaches utilize the case method whenever appropriate along with lectures, discussions, and investigations of actual situations. Graduate programs in business are planned to prepare students to assume the responsibilities of middle- and upper-level administrators and managers. Entering graduate students may select accounting, business administration, or finance as their primary concentration.

PROGRAMS OF STUDY

The programs in accounting or finance lead to the Master of Science (M.S.) degree. Programs in accounting and finance are designed to prepare students to assume administration, managerial, and professional positions in their respective fields. The candidate plan of study for accounting and finance students will include a minimum of 30 semester hours. Candidates are generally expected to complete a thesis, a special project, or six additional credit hours of course work.

The programs in business administration lead to the Master of Business Administration (M.B.A.) degree. Programs in business administration are designed to prepare middle- and higher-echelon administrators and managers. All candidates must complete the core requirement of 27 semester hours. In addition to the core requirement, students will select 9 hours with the approval of their adviser to complete the 36-semester-hour requirement. Candidates may elect to complete a thesis, a project, or a minimum of course work for the M.B.A. degree.

ADMISSION

All students seeking a Master of Science degree in accounting or finance, or the Master of Business Administration degree, must submit scores on the Graduate Management Admission Test (GMAT). This score must be submitted before enrolling for the first semester. Once the GMAT score is received by the Dean of the School of Business and Public Administration, a candidate plan of study will be prepared by an appropriate faculty adviser. The GMAT score and candidate plan of study will conform to all standards and policies of the School of Business and Public Administration. Admission to candidacy is based on a minimum index number of 1,000; this number is computed as follows: grade-point average (last 60 hours) × 200 + GMAT score = Index Number.

FINANCIAL ASSISTANCE

The Office of Admissions and Records coordinates all aid programs; these include the college-based federal programs, state programs, veterans' benefits, and on- and off-campus employment. On-campus employment will be reserved for students who demonstrate financial need. To determine need, the university uses the need-analysis system developed by the College Scholarship Service of the College Board. Persons interested in some form of financial assistance should contact the Director of Admissions and Records.

PLACEMENT

On-campus interviews with both local and national companies are conducted for students seeking employment. Other services available include career counseling and planning, employment readiness seminars, alumni placement, part-time and summer job placement, and credential service. The university also has a Vocational Library and supplies local and national salary surveys.

CORRESPONDENCE

For additional information on the programs of study offered at UH-CL, please write or call

Dr. William A. Staples
Associate Dean
Office of Graduate Studies
School of Business and Public
 Administration
University of Houston—Clear Lake
2700 Bay Area Boulevard
Houston, Texas 77058
Telephone: 713-488-9530

The University of Houston—University Park is a nationally recognized, comprehensive research university which plays a leading role in the state-supported system of higher education in Texas. University Park is the oldest and largest of the four campuses in the University of Houston System. Located in the nation's fourth largest city, it is ideally situated to utilize the research, business, and cultural facilities of metropolitan Houston. Opportunities abound for study, applied research, and employment.

PROGRAMS OF STUDY
The graduate programs of the College of Business Administration are designed to provide lasting educational experiences that can serve as the basis for a lifetime of continuing professional development. Their main focus is on the development of skills in managerial problem analysis, solution, and implementation. Each student is exposed to the important behavioral, economic and quantitative principles and techniques that support the administrative decision process. The systems approach, interpreted through diverse teaching methods, is used to integrate the elements of administration and to link managerial decisions to the political, social, economic, and cultural framework. Academic prerequisites to the programs include course work in finite math, calculus, at least one programming language, and management information systems.

The Master of Business Administration (M.B.A.) program is a 48-hour curriculum designed to prepare students for management positions in business organizations. Admission is open to qualified holders of bachelor's degrees, regardless of the undergraduate field of study. Areas of concentration are available in accountancy and taxation, finance, international business, marketing, management information systems, organizational behavior and management, operations management, and quantitative management science.

The Master of Science in Accountancy program is a 36- to 54-hour curriculum designed for individuals who plan to concentrate in the fields of financial, managerial, and tax accounting. It is intended to provide a well-rounded background in business administration in addition to specific competence in the area of accounting.

The program leading to the Doctor of Philosophy is research-oriented and directed toward the development of teachers and researchers for academic, industrial, government, and social organizations. Individualized programs, tailored to suit the research interests of a candidate, are planned jointly by the student and a graduate advisory committee within the student's primary area. Primary fields include accountancy and taxation, finance, marketing, operations management, management information systems, organizational behavior and management, and quantitative management science. Details concerning the program and admission can be obtained by writing to the Graduate Programs Administrator.

ADMISSION
Admission screenings consider those elements of an applicant's background that show evidence of achievement and potential to complete successfully and benefit from the program. The following minimum standards are applied for admission to the master's programs:
- bachelor's degree earned in an accredited institution with a grade-point average of 3.0 in the last 60 semester hours of course work and
- a score of 525 on the Graduate Management Admission Test (GMAT).

Applicants with a GMAT score between 475 and 525 whose grade-point average is at least 2.75 but below 3.00 will be considered by an Admission Review Committee.

Applicants having completed graduate-level course work must present a minimum 3.00 grade-point average on that course work. If at least 21 hours of graduate-level course work has been completed, the major focus in regard to grade-point average will be based on that work.

All documents (application form, two official copies of transcripts from previous college or university attended, and GMAT score) should be on file by June 7 for the fall term, November 7 for the spring term, and March 12 for the summer terms. All international applicants must submit a Test of English as a Foreign Language (TOEFL) score of 600 or above with the exception of those completing a four-year degree at a university in the United States. Citizens of Australia, Canada, New Zealand, and the United Kingdom are excluded from this TOEFL requirement.

EXPENSES
Tuition for 12 semester hours is $144 for Texas residents and $1,440 for out-of-state and international students. In addition, university fees amount to approximately $150 per semester. Tuition and fee assessments are subject to change without notice.

FINANCIAL ASSISTANCE
A number of graduate fellowships are awarded on the basis of merit to students enrolled in the program. They include the Clayton Fellowship in Systems Analysis and the Fred J. Heyne Fellowships in Business Administration. Research assistantships and teaching assistantships are available in all departments for doctoral students.

Applications for fellowships and assistantships (awards effective September 1) should be filed by April 15. Information concerning student loans may be obtained by writing to the Office of Financial Aid.

Part-time employment opportunities are available both within the university and in the local business community. The University Placement Service assists students in finding such positions.

PLACEMENT
The UH—University Park operates a placement center serving students in all colleges and departments. A professional business placement counselor is assigned to the College of Business. Both students and alumni may secure data relating to future careers and may arrange for interviews with the many recruiters who visit the campus.

CORRESPONDENCE
For additional information, direct inquiries to
Graduate Programs Office
College of Business Administration
University of Houston—University Park
Houston, Texas 77004
Telephone: 713-749-2893

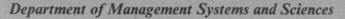

Founded in 1927, the University of Hull has an attractive campus in the historic city of Kingston upon Hull. Situated two and a half miles north of the city, the university has benefited from its location. Expansion in the 1960s was extensive but possible within the spaciousness of the immediate environment. The result is a compact, unified campus, displaying an attractive blend of old and new, with no obtrusive, high-rise buildings.

The popularity of Hull University has increased significantly in recent years. Among applicants for undergraduate entry, it is now among the five most popular universities in the United Kingdom. The total student population of the university exceeds 5,000. Of these, approximately one in five is reading for a higher degree. For the postgraduate, the university offers both an attractive environment in which to work as well as excellent library, computer, accommodation, and other support facilities.

Management teaching and research at Hull is organized by the Department of Management Systems and Sciences. This is a multidisciplinary group with interests spanning systems theory, cybernetics, organizational analysis and development, operational research, and computer applications including the development of knowledge-based decision support systems. Current research activities in these areas involve practical applications in a variety of organizational settings and, at the theoretical level, relate to the use of systems ideas and methodologies and to problem solving in organizations. The academic staff of the department have considerable full-time employment experience in a wide variety of organizations.

PROGRAMS OF STUDY

The Department of Management Systems and Sciences offers two master's degree programs and a course of study leading to a postgraduate diploma.

The Master of Arts (M.A.) Management Systems is especially suitable for graduates in business or management studies, the social sciences, or modern languages. The courses provide students with knowledge and expertise relevant to the process of management. Emphasis is placed on decision making and problem solving. The application of appropriate theory drawn from systems thinking and from the social and behavioral sciences receives full attention.

The Master of Science (M.Sc.) Management Sciences is designed to meet the needs of those students who have some knowledge of operational research/management science. Education and training is provided in those areas of management science which are of increasing importance. Particular emphasis is placed upon the design of decision-support systems and on current developments in information technology. Knowledge of these technical skills is supplemented by study of problem solving in organizations and of consulting practice.

Both of these programs run full time for 12 months and begin in late September. Students take five courses in each of the first two terms of the degrees, and these are assessed by examination. The final six months are spent working on a project, usually in a local company, or writing a dissertation. The report of work undertaken in this period forms a significant part of the overall assessment of the student.

The postgraduate Diploma in Management Systems and Sciences is a full-time course of study during the period late September to June. It is a qualification in its own right, but also provides a means of entry to the master's programs for students whose first degrees do not provide suitable background.

In addition, the department offers supervision to students pursuing studies leading to the degree of Ph.D.

At the undergraduate level, the department offers degrees in management systems (organizational analysis), management sciences (operations analysis), and management sciences (mathematical methods).

ADMISSION

Applicants should possess a good first degree from a British University, a postgraduate diploma, or suitable professional qualifications. Overseas candidates should have equivalent credentials. All will be required to take the Graduate Management Admission Test (GMAT). Candidates whose mother tongue is not English must provide evidence of their proficiency in this language. The Test of English as a Foreign Language (TOEFL) is recommended for this purpose.

EXPENSES

In 1985-86 tuition fees for British and E.E.C. full-time students were £1,632, and, for overseas students, £3,310. Students should allow at least £5,000 additional for living expenses.

FINANCIAL ASSISTANCE

Information on grants available to British students is available from the Research Councils.

PLACEMENT

The University Careers service offers information and advice on all aspects of employment and further study.

CORRESPONDENCE

For further details, including a departmental brochure, contact

The Department of Management
   Systems and Sciences
Postgraduate Studies
University of Hull
Cottingham Road
HULL, HU6 7RX, England

The Graduate School embraces 9 colleges and nearly 50 departments and subject areas. Enrollments are large enough to provide the critical mass of students and faculty necessary for graduate programs and yet sufficiently small to permit close faculty-student relationships. Interdepartmental cooperation is an important factor on the Idaho campus, which is also the research center for the state.

The university enjoys a unique location and offers the advantages of adjacent institutions, a large city nearby, and a vast expanse of outdoor recreational areas in close proximity. Cultural and scholarly exchange is common with Washington State University, eight miles distant, and a number of other colleges in Spokane and adjacent communities. Spokane, the second largest city in the state of Washington, is 80 miles from Moscow. In contrast, one of the largest wilderness and mountain areas in the country is within a short driving distance.

PROGRAMS OF STUDY
Graduate degrees offered by the College of Business and Economics are the Master of Business Administration (M.B.A.) and the Master of Science (M.S.) in economics. The M.B.A. is designed to provide a broad education based on a common body of knowledge with a competency in general management as the primary objective. It is especially adapted to students who have earned their bachelor's degree in the applied sciences of agriculture, forestry, and engineering as well as other nonbusiness areas.

The M.B.A. is a nonthesis degree requiring 30 semester hours of course work beyond the common body of knowledge. Nine of these credits must be taken in a specialty area which can be satisfied through courses within the college or through other colleges such as agriculture, forestry, or engineering. Applicants are expected to have demonstrated proficiency in elementary economics, statistics, and computer programming prior to admission. Elementary calculus is also recommended. Any deficiency at the time of admission in the foundation areas of finance, marketing, management (one course each), and accounting (one year sequence) must be removed before graduate courses in corresponding areas may be taken. A comprehensive examination is administered near the completion of the student's program. The examination stresses integration of the student's work in the eight areas covered in the required courses.

The Master of Science in economics has both thesis and nonthesis options. The emphasis in this program is on applied policy analysis.

ADMISSION
Applicants for admission must be graduates of an accredited college or university. A completed application form and transcripts of all college-level work should be forwarded to the Admissions Office. Acceptance for the M.B.A. program is based on the applicant's previous college record and scores on the Graduate Management Admission Test (GMAT); for the Master of Science in economics program, applicants should take the Graduate Record Examinations (GRE). Consideration is given to all aspects of the student's record in determining final admission.

International students must provide official or certified copies in English of all their transcripts. A score of 550 on the Test of English as a Foreign Language (TOEFL) is required for students from countries where English is not the native language.

EXPENSES

Per semester, estimated	Resident	Nonresident
Tuition	None	$1,000
Institutional fees	$ 672	672
Board and room	1,200	1,200
Books and supplies	175	175
	$2,047	$3,047

Graduate fees are $70.25 per credit hour.

FINANCIAL ASSISTANCE
Financial assistance is available in the form of loans which should be applied for through the financial aid office of the university. Also available are instructional assistantships through the graduate director in accounting, economics, and business. Scholarship monies may be applied for through the Office of Student Affairs. The Elbert S. Rawls Fellowship is offered to a graduate student who must maintain a grade-point average of at least 3.0 while in graduate school. The amount of the scholarship is $6,000. Interested students should write to the Dean's Office. A limited number of out-of-state tuition waivers for foreign students are available through the foreign student adviser.

PLACEMENT
The Career Planning and Placement Center is organized to assist all university graduates in obtaining employment according to their preparation, ability, and experience. Normally, the service is open to all students and alumni who have completed two semesters of accredited study in upper-division or graduate work at the university or who will have completed such work by the time placement information is to be utilized.

CORRESPONDENCE
For further information, please write or call
M.B.A. Director
College of Business and Economics
University of Idaho
Moscow, Idaho 83843
Telephone: 208-885-6071

UNIVERSITY OF ILLINOIS AT CHICAGO

CHICAGO, ILLINOIS

The University of Illinois at Chicago's College of Business Administration offers programs leading to the Master of Business Administration (M.B.A.), Master of Science in Accounting (M.S.A.), Master of Arts (M.A.) in economics, and Doctor of Philosophy (Ph.D.) in public policy analysis degrees. Graduate enrollment is approximately 550 students. The M.B.A. program is available on either a full-time or part-time basis, with identical course offerings and degree requirements.

PROGRAMS OF STUDY

The M.B.A. program provides a balance of theoretical knowledge and practical training, building a foundation for future managerial growth while equipping the student to meet the day-to-day challenges of the workplace. Accredited by the American Assembly of Collegiate Schools of Business (AACSB), the program is designed to meet the needs of students with undergraduate backgrounds in either business or nonbusiness areas. A minimum of 20 courses in approved graduate work is required unless the entering student holds a baccalaureate in business from an institution accredited by the AACSB, in which case the requirement may be reduced to 16 courses.

The core curriculum consists of a series of integrated required courses that lead to advanced work in the elective area. The required courses emphasize the fundamental tools of managerial decision making, whereas the elective area of the curriculum stresses the application of advanced management knowledge. Courses in the elective portion are divided into two categories: concentration courses and free elective courses. Students select two fields of concentration from the following nine: accounting, economics, finance, human resource management, international business, management information systems, marketing, operations management, and strategic management. The free electives may be selected from a wide range of disciplines to support the student's chosen fields of concentration or to explore entirely new areas. The degree must be completed within six calendar years of the date of first enrollment. Transfer credit may be granted for up to 10 courses in the required core. Transfer credit is accepted only from AACSB-accredited graduate programs. The entire program can be completed on either a full-time or part-time basis through a day/evening combination or evening only.

The complementary nature of theory and practice in the curriculum is also demonstrated in the M.B.A. Co-op program. This option allows a student to alternate periods of full-time study with full-time employment in a salaried position. Many of the companies participating in the Co-op program rank as Fortune 500 companies.

ADMISSION

The M.B.A. program is open to students who wish to pursue graduate study in business regardless of undergraduate major. A student must have a baccalaureate degree from an accredited college or university. Applicants are considered for admission on an individual basis. Evaluation for admission is based on the applicant's previous academic work, test scores on the Graduate Management Admission Test (GMAT), letters of recommendation, and a statement of objectives. Professional work experience is considered but not required. A minimum score of 570 on the Test of English as a Foreign Language (TOEFL) and a statement of financial support are required of foreign applicants.

It is recommended that applications for full-time study be submitted for the fall quarter by the 20-course-program applicant and for the summer or fall session by the 16-course-program applicant. Part-time students may apply for entrance in the fall, winter, spring, or summer quarters.

EXPENSES

The 1985-86 schedule of fees for each quarter for a typical part-time course load of two courses and a full-time course load of three or more courses was as follows:

Tuition and Fees*	Part-time	Full-time
Illinois resident	$ 622	$ 823
Nonresident	1,448	2,051

*Subject to change without notice.

FINANCIAL ASSISTANCE

A limited number of graduate research assistantships and tuition and fee waivers are awarded by the College of Business Administration on a competitive basis. Awards require students to be enrolled for a minimum of 12 credit hours per quarter. Each assistantship carries a stipend of over $3,000 and tuition and fee waiver for the academic year.

PLACEMENT

The Co-op Office within the College of Business Administration is responsible for placing interested M.B.A. students in co-op positions. The Office of Career Placement Services of the university is available to assist students in career decisions and placement. Special attention is given the placement needs of the M.B.A. program students.

CORRESPONDENCE

For information, write, call, or visit
M.B.A. Program Office
College of Business Administration
University of Illinois at Chicago
P.O. Box 4348, Grant Hall 103
Chicago, Illinois 60680
Telephone: 312-996-4573

The College of Commerce and Business Administration, through its Department of Business Administration, provides degree programs leading to the Master of Business Administration (M.B.A.), the Master of Science in Business Administration (M.S.B.A.), and the Doctor of Philosophy (Ph.D.) in business administration. Joint professional degrees are offered with architecture (M.Arch./M.B.A.), law (J.D./M.B.A.), medicine (M.D./M.B.A.), public administration (M.A.P.A./M.B.A.), engineering (M.S.E.E./M.B.A., M.S.I.E./M.B.A., M.S.M.E./M.B.A.), and computer science (M.C.S./M.B.A.). Enrollments total about 300. The college is adjacent to one of the world's largest libraries and maintains extensive computer facilities and a behavioral science laboratory for education and research purposes. The college has renowned faculties in accounting, marketing, organizational behavior, and management science. Degree programs in the Department of Business Administration are consistently rated among the top 15 in the country.

PROGRAMS OF STUDY
The professional M.B.A. program strives for diversity with quality. It recognizes that management represents a general set of skills and knowledge applied to a specific set of problems and realities. Individuals come from diverse geographic, educational, and national backgrounds. The program prepares them for analytically grounded management in diverse careers. The faculty's approach to management education is to blend the pragmatic concerns of business and nonbusiness organizations with rigorous analytic approaches to decision making and problem solving. Quality is maintained by hiring and promoting faculty according to their renowned scholarship. Diversity is maintained by integrating the fundamental management core with administratively relevant electives from specific professional fields.

The M.B.A. program is a 2-year, 16-course program composed of 12 core courses (6 from the fundamental areas of the behavioral, economic, and quantitative sciences; 6 from the functional areas of accounting, marketing, finance, production, operations, law, and policy and planning); and 4 electives. No evening or correspondence courses are offered. The department grants exemptions from the core courses for students whose prior education included core-area course work,
thereby allowing students to take additional electives in place of the exempted courses.

A two-year Executive M.B.A. Program is offered to experienced managers. Details may be obtained from the Executive M.B.A. Program, 218 Commerce West, 1206 S. Sixth St., Champaign, Illinois 61820, Telephone: 217-333-4510.

The M.S.B.A. is designed for students who desire additional specialized graduate education. The program requires 12 courses: 6 in the fundamental behavioral, economic, and quantitative sciences; 4 in the major area of concentration; and a 2-course minor or a thesis. The M.S.B.A. for International Managers is a 12-unit, 14-month program designed to familiarize participants with American and international business practices.

The Ph.D. program is designed to meet career needs for research, teaching, and problem solving in academic as well as business, government, and other types of organizations. The program has no foreign language requirement. It consists of 16 units of course work and 8 units of dissertation work. Those who enter from a master's degree in business generally complete eight units of course work and eight units of dissertation work.

Major areas of specialization within the Ph.D. program include decision and information science, marketing, organizational behavior, management information systems, international business, and business economics. A minor area usually accompanies the major area. A comprehensive examination follows the major and minor and is provided by the faculty in the selected major and minor areas. A dissertation completes the program.

ADMISSION
Admission to the M.B.A. and M.S.B.A. programs is dependent upon an undergraduate degree, acceptable scores on the Graduate Management Admission Test (GMAT), a scholastic average of at least B for the last 60 hours, letters of recommendation, and a statement of career goals. (The average GMAT for the fall 1985 class was 600.)

Admission to the Ph.D. program requires acceptable scores on the GMAT and a scholastic average of B+ on approximately the last two years of course work.
Foreign applicants for all programs are also required to submit scores from the Test of English as a Foreign Language (TOEFL) and the Test of Spoken English (TSE). A minimum score of 580 must be achieved.

The master's programs may be started only in August. The Ph.D. program may be started in August, January, or June. Application deadlines are April 15 for August and June admission, and October 1 for January admission.

EXPENSES
The 1985-86 schedule of tuition and fees, per semester, was as follows: residents of Illinois, $1,113; nonresidents of Illinois, $2,865.

FINANCIAL ASSISTANCE
Fellowships, assistantships in both teaching and research, and tuition and fee waivers are available. Approximately 10 percent of the current master's degree candidates and all Ph.D. candidates receive some form of financial aid.

PLACEMENT
The College of Commerce and Business Administration maintains a separate placement facility for its students. Approximately 300 diverse and national firms recruit regularly at the college.

CORRESPONDENCE
For further information, write or call
Director of the M.B.A. Program
University of Illinois
315 Commerce West
1206 South Sixth Street
Champaign, Illinois 61820
Telephone: 217-333-4555

The University of Iowa is located in Iowa City along the banks of the Iowa River and close to Interstate Highway 80. Current enrollment exceeds 29,000 with 7,700 in either the graduate college or in one of the three professional colleges.

The bachelor's and master's programs in business offered by the College of Business Administration are accredited by the American Assembly of Collegiate Schools of Business (AACSB). The college offers programs leading to these degrees: Master of Business Administration (M.B.A.), Master of Arts (M.A.) in accounting or in business administration, and Doctor of Philosophy (Ph.D.) in business administration. Students may concurrently earn an M.A. in accounting or business administration, or an M.B.A. and a J.D. from the College of Law, or an M.A. from the School of Library and Information Science. The Department of Economics offers an M.A. and Ph.D. in economics.

PROGRAMS OF STUDY

The M.B.A. program is designed to prepare men and women for administrative positions in business and public sectors. In this nonthesis program students learn how to analyze organizational situations, identify problems, develop and evaluate solutions, and then implement the solutions. Experience in research and writing is obtained through assigned projects and reports required in specific courses. Evening classes are available for part-time students.

The M.B.A. curriculum is designed for college graduates in any field. Previous courses in business are not required for admission. Depending upon a student's academic background, 38-62 semester hours of graduate courses in business, economics, and related fields are required.

The M.A. degree in accounting is designed to prepare candidates for careers in all areas of accounting. The M.A. in business administration permits students to specialize in one of the following: administrative studies, finance, industrial relations and human resources, insurance, or management systems. A minimum of 35 semester hours is required for the nonthesis program and 30 semester hours for the thesis program.

Students admitted to the Ph.D. program select majors from the following: accounting, finance, human resources, industrial relations, insurance, management information systems, management science, marketing, or organizational behavior. Candidates must pass written comprehensive examinations in both a major and a minor area and an oral examination covering the entire program. A completed dissertation must be defended in a final oral examination. A minimum of 72 semester hours of graduate credit (including graduate courses taken before entering the Ph.D. program) are required.

ADMISSION

As a guideline to M.B.A. applicants, a total score of 500 or better on the Graduate Management Admission Test (GMAT) and a grade-point average of 3.0 or better on the last two years of undergraduate work would be representative of students currently in the program. Median scores for recently admitted students are a total GMAT score of 560 and a 3.3 grade-point average.

For Ph.D. applicants, a total GMAT score in the range of 600 and a grade-point average of 3.5 or better on previous graduate work and on the last two years of undergraduate work would be representative of students currently in the program.

Applicants must submit a completed application form, official transcripts of all undergraduate and graduate work taken, official GMAT scores, and three references. Applications must be complete by July 1 for fall semester, November 15 for spring semester, and April 15 for summer session.

Foreign applications must be complete by March 1 for fall, spring, or summer sessions. Applicants whose native language is not English are required to take the Test of English as a Foreign Language (TOEFL) and submit an official score of 580 or better. Foreign applicants are urged to begin the application process at least 12 months in advance.

EXPENSES

Estimated tuition for the 1986-87 academic year for full-time graduate students is $1,546 for residents and $3,996 for nonresidents. Dormitory room and board (double room) is estimated at $2,100 per academic year. Inquiries concerning dormitory or university family housing should be directed to University Residence Services, Burge Hall, The University of Iowa, Iowa City, Iowa 52242.

FINANCIAL ASSISTANCE

Financial aid is available to superior M.B.A. students in the form of either research or teaching assistantships or fellowships. Ph.D. students may be eligible for research or teaching assistantships, fellowships, and tuition scholarships. Research assistants are appointed to various college institutes or centers and to faculty. Teaching assistants are assigned to introductory level courses and are supervised by faculty. Financial assistance is awarded by the following departments in the College of Business Administration: Accounting, Economics, Finance, Industrial Relations and Human Resources, Management Sciences, and Marketing. Applicants must complete their admission file and must submit an Application for Graduate Awards and resume to the Graduate Programs in Business Office by March 1.

Inquiries about student loans and other forms of aid should be directed to the Student Financial Aid Office, Calvin Hall, The University of Iowa, Iowa City, Iowa 52242.

PLACEMENT

The University Careers Office provides placement services for students and alumni. National and regional firms interview on campus each year. Ph.D. graduates seeking academic positions receive extensive assistance from departmental faculty.

CORRESPONDENCE

Inquiries should be directed to
    Graduate Programs in Business
    121 Phillips Hall
    The University of Iowa
    Iowa City, Iowa 52242
    Telephone: 319-353-3158
    Toll free in Iowa:
        800-272-6412, extension 3158
    Toll free from contiguous states:
        800-553-6380, extension 3158

UNIVERSITY OF JUDAISM

LOS ANGELES, CALIFORNIA

The University of Judaism (UJ) was founded in 1947 as the first major institution of Jewish higher education in the West. Since it is a center for research, its faculty and students engage in the disciplined exploration of a wide range of areas in Judaica and the humanities.

At the University of Judaism, training and scholarship are one. A philosophy of an integrated, holistic culture, combining the best of Jewish and Western civilizations, pervades every aspect of the institution.

The University of Judaism is accredited by the Accrediting Commission for Senior Colleges and Universities of the Western Association of Schools and Colleges. The university does not discriminate on the basis of race, color, sex, religion, national or ethnic origin, or physical handicap in the administration of its policies on admission, financial aid, or education.

PROGRAM OF STUDY

The University of Judaism's Graduate Management Programs offer a unique Master of Business Administration (M.B.A.) degree, focusing on the leadership needs of Jewish community institutions and not-for-profit, human services organizations. Students planning on careers in middle and upper management for cultural, social service, and health-care fields—in development, budgeting and planning, personnel training, marketing, and public relations—can acquire sophisticated management skills in a humanistic, ethical context.

The University of Judaism M.B.A. program can be completed in two years and one summer (full time) or three years and two summers (part time, evenings only). Students can specialize in either management for the Jewish community or management for the general not-for-profit sector.

All programs include an examination of not-for-profit organizations and how their needs differ from those of the private sector. Students study the history, sociology, and values of the community they intend to serve, in order to balance effective management skills with equally vital social and moral principles. The curriculum (72 units) covers the range of managerial techniques now employed by all types of public and private organizations, both profit and nonprofit.

All students, regardless of option, will be expected to complete 27 units in basic management skills in such disciplines as managerial accounting, marketing, financial planning and control, and organizational behavior. Students who have completed parallel courses as part of their undergraduate education may apply for advanced standing.

Students interested in careers within the Jewish community will specialize in public relations, financial development (fund raising), and management, while building their expertise in Jewish communal service and Judaica (45 units).

Students who wish to prepare for employment in the broader not-for-profit sector will also specialize in public relations, financial development (fund raising), and management. In consultation with an adviser, students choosing this option will enroll in 12 units of electives. Students concerned with broadening their understanding of the communities served by not-for-profit organizations can elect courses in the social sciences and humanities. Students may also use these units to further refine their management skills (45 units).

Each option includes an internship or field study with an appropriate organization.

ADMISSION

Admission is open to those who hold a bachelor's degree from an accredited college or university. Applicants must submit official transcripts indicating a strong academic record, as well as scores on the Graduate Management Admission Test (GMAT). Applicants whose native language is not English must demonstrate English language proficiency through achievement of a satisfactory score on the Test of English as a Foreign Language (TOEFL).

Applicants must submit two letters of recommendation, one from a faculty member with whom the applicant has studied (if possible), and one from a non-faculty member. In addition, the applicant must submit a statement of personal motivation, purposes, and goals as they are relevant to this program.

A personal interview with the Director of the Program, Professor Judith Glass, or a member of the university staff is highly desirable. The applicant should request such an interview.

EXPENSES

Tuition for all students admitted to the David Lieber School of Graduate Studies, M.B.A. Program, is $140 per credit up to a maximum of $2,100 per semester.

There is a registration fee of $20 each semester and a $25 application fee. All fees are subject to change without notice.

On-campus housing and a Kosher meal plan are available.

FINANCIAL ASSISTANCE

Scholarship funds are available to full-time UJ students from a variety of sources, including government grants, private funds, and tuition waivers from the university. In addition, work-study programs are offered to qualified students. Application forms for tuition scholarships are available from the Financial Aid Administrator.

CORRESPONDENCE

Students who have any further questions or want to talk over the opportunities available, please contact
Professor Judith Glass
Director of Management Programs
or
Miriam Prum
Director of Admissions
University of Judaism
15600 Mulholland Drive
Los Angeles, California 90077
Telephone: 213-476-9777 or 213-879-4114

The School of Business, founded in 1925, offers three programs of graduate study. The Master of Business Administration (M.B.A.) program is designed for those who desire a general management education; Master of Science (M.S.) in business is for those who desire to further their study in a specific area of business; and the Ph.D. program is for those with interests in teaching and research. The bachelor's and master's programs in business are accredited by the American Assembly of Collegiate Schools of Business (AACSB).

PROGRAMS OF STUDY

The Master of Business Administration program is designed for graduates seeking positions with managerial responsibilities in both the public and the private sectors and requires no prior college work in business. The School of Business at the University of Kansas provides two routes leading to this degree. The Regular Program requires a minimum of 56 hours of graduate credit consisting of 16 course units of 3 or more credit hours each. Included in the total are 12 required courses totaling 44 hours and 4 advanced business elective courses. Where prior academic work satisfies any of the required courses, the program may be reduced by a maximum of 3 courses (9-12 hours). The Accelerated Program requires prior academic work satisfying the required courses in the Regular Program and consists of 10 courses selected from the advanced business electives. A maximum of two course deficiencies among the required courses will be allowed.

The required core develops a sound understanding of the basic disciplines that underlie the study of business, the functional areas of business, and the economic and legal environment in which businesses operate. The student applies these concepts to the diagnosis and analysis of business problems in the areas of marketing, finance, labor relations, and operations research. The student may develop an area of concentration by selecting elective courses that most effectively build upon the individual student's background and fit his or her career interests. No thesis is required in this program.

The M.B.A. program is offered as a day program for full-time students on the Lawrence campus. The required courses of the program plus selected electives are also offered at night at The University of Kansas Regents Center in Overland Park,

Kansas, to serve persons who are able to further their graduate study only on a part-time basis at night.

The joint M.B.A. and Juris Doctor (J.D.) degree program combines into four years of postbaccalaureate study the three-year J.D. and the two-year M.B.A. programs. This program provides an opportunity to acquire academic training in the convergent fields of business management and law. It requires the prescribed portions of both the J.D. and M.B.A. programs and permits limited electives within each area.

The Master of Science program is designed for the student who has completed a baccalaureate degree in business and desires to do concentrated study in a specific area within business. The program requires a minimum of 30 hours, a thesis or research seminar, and a comprehensive examination over the area of concentration. Deficiencies in the student's undergraduate program or prerequisites for required courses in the concentration add additional total hours to the degree. Concentrations are provided in the areas of accounting, finance, human resources, marketing, operations research, and organization behavior.

ADMISSION

Selection of participants is based upon an evaluation of the applicant's demonstrated capacity to complete graduate study and potential for continued intellectual development. This appraisal considers a combination of previous academic achievement, scores on the Graduate Management Admission Test (GMAT), and work or other experience. Applicants from non-English-speaking countries who have not earned a degree from an American university must also submit an acceptable score on the Test of English as a Foreign Language (TOEFL). Applications completed after the following dates will be considered only as vacancies arise: for fall semester—May 1, for spring semester—October 1, for summer session—March 15.

EXPENSES

Fees*(Per semester) —in-state students: $675; out-of-state students: $1,577.
Room and board**—$2,107

For academic year 1985-86, subject to change.
**Based upon dormitory rates for double occupancy, nine-month contract.

FINANCIAL ASSISTANCE

Limited aid is available through scholarships, teaching and research assistantships, loans, and employment in various university offices and research groups. Financial aid, except for loans, is granted primarily on the basis of scholastic achievement or potential. Applications for teaching and research assistantships must be received no later than April 1.

PLACEMENT

The School of Business maintains its own placement office to assist graduates in obtaining positions in business, industry, and government. Over 180 national, regional, and local firms conduct on-campus interviews annually. The center also maintains a career-job listing program, a part-time and summer employment program, and a career information resource library. Publication of a student resume book, referral of students to companies with specific requirements, special career information programs, and an alumni placement service are all integral parts of the total placement program.

CORRESPONDENCE

For further information, contact
Director of Master's Programs
School of Business,
206 Summerfield Hall
The University of Kansas
Lawrence, Kansas 66045
Telephone: 913-864-4254

UNIVERSITY OF KENTUCKY

LEXINGTON, KENTUCKY

The University of Kentucky celebrated its centennial in 1965; the College of Business and Economics was founded in 1925. The university operates on a semester system with the first semester beginning in late August and ending before Christmas; the second semester begins in the middle of January and ends in early May. The bachelor's and master's programs offered by the College of Business and Economics are accredited by the American Assembly of Collegiate Schools of Business (AACSB). An air-conditioned building contains all offices and classrooms. A business library is part of the University Library which contains over 2,000,000 volumes. The Computing Center operates an IBM 3083 with three million bytes of storage, which is available for research projects, and a DEC-system-10 for interactive capabilities through KACNET networks. The university also has three PRIME computer systems, with more than 100 terminals strategically located around the campus. This system is reserved exclusively for student use. The college has a Wang VS 75 system with WANG PC terminals, and an IBM-PC classroom and laboratory.

PROGRAMS OF STUDY
The Master of Business Administration (M.B.A.) program is designed to enable the candidate to acquire an educational foundation for a career in business administration or professional employment in a specialized field. Specifically, students develop (1) an understanding of the analytical methods and processes of business administration, (2) a knowledge of the economics of business enterprise and the environmental setting in which business firms operate, (3) skills in using quantitative analysis in business decisions, (4) an understanding of organizational behavior, (5) the ability to solve business problems, and (6) an understanding of the functional areas of production, marketing, and finance. The program is 48 credit hours for nonbusiness undergraduates and 36 hours for business undergraduates.

The Master of Science (M.S.) in accounting offers a flexible 30-hour program in which students can undertake advanced studies in accounting, thus enhancing their opportunities for employment in professional public practice, government, industry, or teaching.

The Master of Public Administration (M.P.A.) offers a 45-hour program for administrative careers in public agencies. The program includes an administrative core of economics, finance, accounting, research methodology, and political and legal environment, and a technical component in special areas of interest, including health care, higher education, general government, and urban and regional development.

The Doctor of Business Administration (D.B.A.) is designed primarily for students interested in teaching and research. The D.B.A. requires course work in administrative science, research methodology, economic theory, and quantitative analysis. Major fields may be selected from accounting, finance, management and organizational behavior, management science, and marketing.

ADMISSION
Admission is through the Graduate School. Applications and required transcripts must be received at least one month prior to the date of enrollment for U.S. students, while international students must have applications completed seven months prior to enrollment. The Graduate Management Admission Test (GMAT) is required of all applicants. A student who is a graduate of a fully accredited institution of higher learning is eligible to be considered for admission. Admission to the M.B.A. program presumes six hours of accounting and three hours of calculus. For further information on this program, students may contact the Graduate Center Director. Admission to the D.B.A. program presumes completion of an M.B.A. or its equivalent. Entrance into the D.B.A. may be in August, January, or June. Entrance into the M.B.A. program is primarily in August.

EXPENSES
Full-time tuition for one semester is $672 for Kentucky residents and $1,931 for nonresidents. A wide variety of apartments are available beginning at $195 per month. A University Housing Office supervises on-campus housing.

FINANCIAL ASSISTANCE
Graduate students are offered financial aid through graduate fellowships, assistantships, and loans. Applications for university-wide fellowships should be made to the Dean of the Graduate School by February 1. These applications will also be considered for departmental assistantships in the College of Business and Economics. Students requesting financial aid should have taken the GMAT prior to applying. The Office of Student Financial Aid administers loans.

PLACEMENT
The programs cooperate with the Career Planning and Placement Center, giving all students the opportunity to meet with a large number of firms that recruit on campus each year. Doctoral candidates are assisted in locating teaching positions by being introduced to prospective employers at professional meetings. The college's Graduate Center Director aids this cooperation and facilitates job placement activities for graduate students.

CORRESPONDENCE
For further information, please write to
Graduate Center Director
College of Business and Economics
331 B&E Building
University of Kentucky
Lexington, Kentucky 40506-0034

UNIVERSITY OF LA VERNE

LA VERNE, CALIFORNIA

The University of La Verne, which traces its heritage back to 1891, is a coeducational, liberal arts institution offering bachelor's, master's, law, and doctoral degrees. It is accredited by the Accrediting Commission for Senior Colleges and Universities of the Western Association of Schools and Colleges and is a member of the American Assembly of Collegiate Schools of Business (AACSB). The university is located in the city of La Verne, 30 miles east of Los Angeles, near the foothills of the San Gabriel Mountains.

The university's School of Business and Economics offers associate, bachelor's and master's degree programs. In cooperation with the School of Continuing Education, the school also offers business degree programs for working professionals at various off-campus locations. Currently approximately 3,000 professionals at 19 different locations are enrolled in courses leading to degrees.

In order to strengthen and enhance the educational program, the school has an Advisory Board that maintains a close relationship with numerous business leaders and individual corporations.

PROGRAMS OF STUDY
The business programs have been designed by the School of Business and Economics in conjunction with practicing managers in industry to emphasize both the theoretical and applied aspects of business. Currently, three master's degree programs are offered: Master of Business Administration (M.B.A.), Master of Science in Business Management (M.S.:B.M.) and Master of Science in Business Organizational Management (M.S.:B.O.M.).

The M.B.A. program is designed to give a high level of competence in the broad areas of administration and executive management. It aims at developing advanced skills in the diagnosis of business problems, the identification of alternate solutions, decision making, and decision implementation. Consequently, the student must demonstrate competency in business fundamentals by having fulfilled 10 prerequisites, namely 2 courses in accounting, and a course each in finance, management, marketing, business law, macroeconomics, microeconomics, business statistics, and data processing/computer programming. The graduate degree program consists of six required graduate courses, three electives, and a final culminating activity of either a thesis or seminar for a total of 30 to 32 units.

The Master of Science in Business Management is designed for those individuals holding responsible positions in U.S. industry, commerce, and related fields who need to develop techniques for identifying and solving management or organizational problems. The student must have had five years of administrative experience and fulfilled the prerequisites of one course each in accounting, economics, business law, finance, management, marketing, and statistics. The actual program consists of 4 required courses, 18 semester hours of electives, and the culminating activity of thesis or seminar for a total of 33 units.

The Master of Science in Business Organizational Management degree program is designed for individuals holding responsible positions in industry who have previous educational background in either a technical field, the liberal arts, or business and who are now seeking a higher management level in business. The student must have had three years of professional experience and fulfilled two prerequisites, namely one course each in accounting and management. The degree program has 4 required courses, 21 units of electives, plus the final culminating activity of thesis or seminar for a total of 36 units.

Students who have not had the prerequisites may choose to take the appropriate undergraduate course, take a standardized test to demonstrate competency, or take the foundation course (two units). By pursuing the studies on a part-time basis, students who are working can complete the graduate degree program in about two years. Up to six units of credit may be transferred into the program from other accredited colleges or universities. Transfer credit must be appropriate for the degree, merited a grade of B or better, and earned within the last five years.

International students meeting admission standards may also be required to complete the following courses and such other remedial requirements as may be established by the school on an individual basis: Concepts and Environment of U.S. Business, Writing and Study Skills for International Graduate Students, and American Culture and Oral English for International Students.

ADMISSION
The university has a continuous admissions policy, admitting new students in any new term. The off-campus program has four terms per year. The admission requirement for all three degree programs is a bachelor's degree from a regionally accredited institution. In addition, a satisfactory grade-point average is required. For the M.B.A. and the M.S.:B.M. the grade-point average is 3.0. Students with a grade-point average of 2.5 or above may be considered for admission with appropriate materials and a satisfactory GMAT score. For the MS:BOM the required grade-point average is 2.5 and similarly if it is lower, the applicant will be considered upon a submittal of a GMAT score of 450 or above.

International applicants must also submit verification of English competence (minimum 550 score on TOEFL or two years of academic study at an institution where English is the primary language of instruction, or a verbal score of 400 on the GRE) and verification of financial support.

EXPENSES
There is a $20 application fee and a $20 registration fee per semester or term. A deferred payment plan is available. Tuition is $195 per semester hour for full-time students, $180 per semester hour for part-time students, and $150 per semester hour for part-time students at off-campus locations (subject to change).

FINANCIAL ASSISTANCE
A student loan program is available to American citizens and some scholarship funds may be awarded. In addition, the school fosters internship opportunities with firms in the region which may help to pay part of a student's expenses.

PLACEMENT
The School of Business and Economics and the university's Placement Office assist current students and alumni in career counseling and in finding suitable positions. In recent years, the school has sponsored a Career Fair, inviting leading companies to interview and to recruit on campus. Private firms and public agencies frequently notify the School of Business and Economics of job opportunities.

CORRESPONDENCE
For further information, please write or call the Graduate Office or
School of Business and Economics
University of La Verne
1950 Third Street
La Verne, California 91750
Telephone: 714-593-3511

UNIVERSITY OF LOUISVILLE

LOUISVILLE, KENTUCKY

The Master of Business Administration (M.B.A.) program at the School of Business at the University of Louisville was established in 1950. It is the oldest Master of Business Administration program in the Louisville Metropolitan area. Seventy-five percent of the M.B.A. course work is taught by doctorally qualified faculty members. Classrooms and facilities for the graduate student are in a newly constructed School of Business building. In addition to a university computer center in the School of Business building, the school has a microcomputer lab and classroom.

PROGRAM OF STUDY

The primary purpose of the School of Business is to provide a quality graduate program that will give the student sufficient background to achieve a responsible position in business and/or to provide for a higher achievement of excellence for the business person in his or her present position.

The specific aims are as follows:
- to ensure a basic knowledge of business and economic principles,
- to develop refined analytical and problem-solving abilities,
- to develop techniques of applying computers as a problem-solving tool in business situations,
- to provide an understanding of the political, social, and economic environment, and to create an awareness of the responsibilities of business to society,
- to instill a desire for continued self-development through education.

The curriculum of the M.B.A. program is designed to meet the needs of applicants who have a baccalaureate degree in business administration. An applicant whose undergraduate curriculum did not include an appropriate foundation in business courses may be admitted on a conditional status and be required to complete the needed undergraduate preparatory courses. Applicants who have an equivalent academic background in the undergraduate preparatory courses may receive a waiver of those courses. The M.B.A. courses total 36 hours and must be completed by all applicants.

ADMISSION

Students are admitted for the fall term beginning in late August, the spring term beginning in mid-January, and the summer term beginning in mid-May. The classes meet one night a week in the regular sessions. In the summer, a single, eight-week term is held with classes meeting twice a week. Classes are held Monday through Thursday from 5:30 until 8:15 p.m.

The applicant's admission file, which consists of Graduate Management Admission Test (GMAT) scores, transcripts of previous academic work, a personal statement (optional, but highly recommended for the marginal applicant), and letters of recommendation, must be received before the School of Business can evaluate and make an admission decision.

Admission to the M.B.A. program is highly competitive because of limited enrollment. Thus, the applicant's grade-point average and GMAT scores are expected to be above average.

EXPENSES

Tuition for out-of-state students is $214 a credit hour, and $74 a credit hour for Kentucky residents.

PLACEMENT

The University of Louisville operates a Placement Office for its students, and the campus is visited by representatives of various national, regional, and local companies.

CORRESPONDENCE

For further information, write or call
M.B.A. Program
School of Business
University of Louisville
Louisville, Kentucky 40292
Telephone: 502-588-6439

The University of Lowell was established in 1975 by the merger of Lowell State College and Lowell Technological Institute—two Massachusetts, publicly supported institutes, with roots to the 1890s. On three campuses in the Merrimack Valley, situated in a city planned as the first industrial center of the United States, the university has a current enrollment of about 16,000 students. Offerings of the colleges of Education, Engineering, Health Professions, Liberal Arts, Music, and Pure and Applied Science are complemented by a physical plant encompassing some 100 acres. Special facilities on the campus include the CYBER-71 Computer System and the Pinanski Nuclear Center, housing a one-megawatt research reactor and Van de Graaff accelerator. The modern center is the only one operated by the Commonwealth of Massachusetts within its system of higher education. Programs of the Graduate School and Division of Continuing Education are widely attended by students both throughout New England and the nation.

The College of Management Science has an enrollment of 2,100, including 300 graduate students. It maintains close ties with the business community, especially through the Business Advisory Council, the Small Business Development Center, and the Strategic Business Group. Through these, the college sponsors programs in executive and supervisory development for interested personnel and industries in the greater Lowell community. Plans underway to expand these operations to eastern Massachusetts involve graduate research and appropriate extensions of the M.B.A. program.

The University of Lowell is an Affirmative Action/Equal Opportunity university and does not discriminate on the basis of sex or handicap status in its educational programs, activities, or employment policies as required by Title IX of the Education Amendments of 1972 and Section 504 of the Rehabilitation Act of 1973, as amended.

PROGRAM OF STUDY

The College of Management Science offers a Master of Business Administration (M.B.A.) program. The program provides graduates of baccalaureate programs with the knowledge of the basic concepts and tools of management. It seeks to develop managers of business and government organizations. An opportunity is provided for individuals to concentrate in the area of management that suits their interests and professional objectives. Emphasis is placed on the individual's ability to respond to the changing economic, business, and societal environment.

The first year is devoted to common body of knowledge core courses in accounting, quantitative analysis, economics, and management functional areas. The second year offers concentrations in accounting, finance, human resources, marketing, operations, and general management. Students also select a mix of courses that reflects their professional goals and breadth of management knowledge. Students with appropriate backgrounds may have some of the requirements waived.

Full-time students may complete the degree in two years or less. Courses will be offered at hours that will enable part-time students to complete the program in three or four years.

ADMISSION

Admission is open to individuals who have a baccalaureate degree from an accredited college or university. The Graduate Management Admission Test (GMAT) is required. Foreign students must take the Test of English as a Foreign Language (TOEFL). The admission decision is based primarily on a student's undergraduate grade-point average and the results of the GMAT. Applications should be returned by June 15 for September admission. January and summer admissions are available.

EXPENSES

Tuition for the fall semester of 1985 was $630 per semester for Massachusetts residents. For nonresidents, including foreign students, tuition was $3,732 per year. In addition, fees ranged from $35 to $90. Total costs for state residents approximated $4,000; for nonresidents, $6,300; and for foreign students, $7,000.

FINANCIAL ASSISTANCE

Students who need financial aid should request an application for a National Direct Student Loan from the Financial Aid Office. Teaching and research assistantships are available to full-time students. Those who wish to be considered for an assistantship must have their application completed by February 1; assistantship applications will be furnished to accepted students.

PLACEMENT

The University Placement Office maintains records of all students in a placement file and arranges interviews with representatives of businesses recruiting employees. The college has established a close relationship with the business community.

CORRESPONDENCE

Inquiries should be addressed to
   Dean of the Graduate School
   University of Lowell
   Lowell, Massachusetts 01854
   Telephone: 617-452-5000, extension 2206

The College of Business Administration is located on the main campus of the University of Maine at Orono, an attractive town of about 10,000 population. The extensive campus of over 1,100 acres is situated about a mile from the business section of Orono and approximately eight miles from Bangor, the third largest city in the state.

The College of Business Administration was established in 1965 as an autonomous college within the university. Since its establishment, the Master of Business Administration (M.B.A.) program has grown rapidly. Both the undergraduate and graduate programs in business administration are accredited by the American Assembly of Collegiate Schools of Business (AACSB).

PROGRAM OF STUDY

The general purpose of the Master of Business Administration program at the university is the education of men and women, at the graduate level, for professional careers in business administration. The courses emphasize the development of foundational knowledge and executive skills rather than specialized functional techniques appropriate only for initial positions in business.

All classes are reserved exclusively for students who have been formally admitted to the Graduate School. Candidates for the degree must complete 30 semester hours of graduate courses with at least a B (3.0) average. Two courses, involving six semester hours of work, are required as an analytical and conceptual core. They include quantitative methods and information systems, and behavioral analysis for administrative decisions. Additionally, three courses (nine semester hours) are required in the functional core. These include managerial accounting, financial management, and marketing management. Students who have had extensive background in any of these functional areas may be permitted to substitute a more advanced course in the same area. One course in production management is required. (If taken at the undergraduate level, an additional graduate elective must be added.) One course, management policy, is required as an integrative core. Beyond the required core, students can choose to specialize by taking 9 (or 12) additional hours of electives in any one of the four functional areas of accounting, finance, marketing, and production and

human resource management. The present size of the program permits a close working relationship with the faculty.

ADMISSION

All applicants must present an undergraduate degree from an acceptable college or university. Applicants who have had little or no undergraduate work in business or related subjects are required to supplement their programs with appropriate undergraduate courses in business. Such students must earn or have earned, in total, the equivalent of 36 semester hours in the following areas (at least one course each except as indicated): accounting (two courses required), computers and programming, management information systems, economics, finance, political and social environment of business, management, marketing, and quantitative methods (course or courses must include probability, statistical inference, and advanced college mathematics).

Students who do not present acceptable total credit for all the above prerequisite courses, or their equivalents, may be given nondegree admission to allow completion of these prerequisites.

The program is designed so that students can enter in the fall, spring, or summer. Applications, together with letters of recommendation from academic and professional sources and official transcripts of all previous academic work, must be filed at least six weeks before the opening of the semester in which the candidate desires to enter.

The admission decision is based on the total application rather than any one aspect. Consideration is given to a candidate's academic record, scores on the Graduate Management Admission Test (GMAT), letters of recommendation on forms provided in the application material, work experience, and potential for leadership in business.

EXPENSES

Tuition for resident graduate students attending the regular session is $57.90 per credit hour (subject to change). Nonresident tuition is $174.80 per credit hour (subject to change). A graduate student dorm is reserved for single graduate students. A limited number of university apartments for married students are also available. Inquiries should be directed to the Housing Office.

FINANCIAL ASSISTANCE

M.B.A. students are eligible for tuition scholarships which are competitive and awarded on a university-wide basis. In addition, a limited number of assistantships are available. If interested, applicants should indicate this on their application. The university will assist students in securing employment in the library, residence halls, and other university-related jobs.

PLACEMENT

Job placement is handled by the Career Planning and Placement Office. More than 200 representatives from companies throughout the country interview on campus annually.

CORRESPONDENCE

For application forms, write or call
Graduate School
2 Winslow Hall
University of Maine
Orono, Maine 04469
Telephone: 207-581-3218

For additional information, write or call
Office of the Graduate Program
College of Business Administration
University of Maine
Orono, Maine 04469
Telephone: 207-581-1973

The Department of Management Sciences evolved from the Department of Industrial Administration, the first in Britain, established with the support of local industrialists in 1918. It is large by British standards, having 520 undergraduate and 124 full-time postgraduate students. The faculty exceeds 50 and there are 6 full-time professors in accounting, industrial relations, industrial economics, marketing, organizational psychology, and operations management.

PROGRAMS OF STUDY

The Department of Management Sciences offers three Master of Science (M.Sc.) degree courses, each lasting 12 months and composed of a six-month taught element followed by a period of six months of research. These are specialist courses related either to business functions or business disciplines. Each course involves the study of four modules plus research methodology in which research proposals are developed. The dissertation is prepared under the supervision of an appropriate member of staff.

The M.Sc. in Management Sciences offers a set of modules that allows students to specialize in one of the following areas: business economics, business finance, international business, industrial relations and personnel policies, and operations management. The emphasis is upon analytical techniques and their contribution to management decision making. Students take two or more units in their specialist areas and select their other modules from the remainder of the program. In addition, all students take a core course in research methodology.

The business economics modules include managerial economics, industrial economics, economics of public sector organizations, and management and the macroeconomic environment. The industrial relations and personnel policies modules include personnel policies and management practice, industrial relations, and industrial organizational sociology. The international business modules include international business management and international economics. The operations management modules include operations and logistics management, production management, and management of innovation.

In the M.Sc. in marketing program, all students take two compulsory courses in marketing management and marketing planning and select two options from international marketing, industrial marketing, and consumer and service marketing.

In the M.Sc. program in organizational psychology, all students take courses in behavioral change in organizations, organizations and people, individual and interpersonal psychology, selection and assessment in organizations, and research methodology.

The degree of Master of Science can also be secured by a minimum 12-month period of research. The degree of Doctor of Philosophy normally requires a minimum period of study and original research of 36 months, which may be reduced for candidates holding a master's degree that included a substantial research element. A doctoral candidate without a master's degree must register for an M.Sc. and after 12 months research will write a transfer report, which if judged satisfactory will enable the student to transfer to the Ph.D. program.

ADMISSION

Applicants should possess a good first degree (2.1 or better, or equivalent) or a graduate equivalent professional qualification acceptable to the university, and a score in excess of 500 on the Graduate Management Admission Test (GMAT). Applicants whose first language is not English must show sufficient competence in the language by obtaining an appropriate score on the Test of English as a Foreign Language (TOEFL), British Council, or other approved tests.

FINANCIAL ASSISTANCE

Industrially sponsored and Research Council studentships are available, and the department is also able to provide a number of part-time teaching assistantships and buraries.

The university provides residential accommodations for around 45 percent of its 14,000 students, but early application for such accommodation is advised.

PLACEMENT

The University of Manchester Careers and Appointments Service is available to students.

CORRESPONDENCE

For further information, please contact
Postgraduate Admissions Tutor
Department of Management Sciences
University of Manchester Institute of
  Science and Technology
P.O. Box 88
Manchester M60 1QD Great Britain

The University of Manitoba is a coeducational, nondenominational, government-supported institution. Founded in 1877, it is the senior university in western Canada.

The main campus of the university, consisting of approximately 600 acres bordered on the east by the Red River, is located approximately six miles from the center of the city of Winnipeg. Winnipeg has a population of some 585,000, including St. Boniface, the largest French-speaking community in Canada outside the Province of Quebec.

A graduate program in management education was established in 1967, and the Faculty of Administrative Studies offers a variety of undergraduate and graduate courses. The Master of Business Administration (M.B.A.) enrollment in the 1984-85 academic year was 129 full-time and 118 part-time students.

M.B.A. students have access to the data banks and program packages supported by the Financial Research Institute (FRI) through a Decwriter II as well as a computer link to the Amdahl 470 and 580 through terminals housed in the Faculty of Administrative Studies building. The terminal room is also equipped with a high-speed printer.

The Faculty of Administrative Studies has a full-time academic staff of 65, plus a number of sessional lecturers. Undergraduate enrollment in the faculty is approximately 1,600 full-time students.

Each academic session at the university consists of two terms: the first term begins in September and ends in December, and the second term begins early in January and ends in late April. First-year M.B.A. courses are offered on a rotation during the summer session and in the evening.

PROGRAM OF STUDY
The purpose of the M.B.A. program is to develop professional managers and administrators for both the private and public sectors. Consequently, the development of a broad range of conceptual, analytical, and behavioral skills relevant to organizational leadership is stressed.

The curriculum includes a broad range of integrated courses which provide the breadth of knowledge required of those desiring to become effective decision makers. At the same time, opportunity is provided for some degree of specialization in keeping with the candidates' aptitudes and interests.

The M.B.A. program normally requires two academic years of study. Successful entrants to the program will have a wide variety of accredited undergraduate degree backgrounds. The first year of the program is designed to provide a common base for all students and consists of 30 credit hours of course work. All students must complete a program of 60 credit hours regardless of undergraduate degree. A variety of instructional methods are utilized—lectures, seminars, case studies, management games, and others.

The M.B.A. program has been designed to recognize the needs of students and the business community. One of the important needs is that of part-time students' studies. To facilitate part-time students, two courses are offered in the evening each term on a rotating basis and one each summer in the first year of the program. Many students plan to complete the first year of the program on a part-time basis and the second year as full-time students.

There are two options available in the advanced year of the M.B.A. program, one being 30 credit hours of course work and a comprehensive examination. The areas of specialization are accounting, finance, marketing, management, personnel/industrial relations, public policy, quantitative methods, and generalist. The second option is 18 credit hours of course work and a master's thesis. Option II is restricted to students with a strong undergraduate background in the proposed thesis area.

ADMISSION
Applications for admission to the M.B.A. program will be considered from individuals who have achieved the following:
- a bachelor's degree or its equivalent from an accredited university and
- satisfactory performance on the Graduate Management Admission Test (GMAT).

Applications must be submitted by May 1 and should include three letters of reference, an official transcript of the applicant's complete academic record, an employment resume, and a brief statement of purpose. In addition, students whose native language is not English must present a minimum score of 550 on the Test of English as a Foreign Language (TOEFL).

EXPENSES
Tuition and student organization fees for a full-time student are $1,500 per year. Living and other incidental costs are approximately $7,500 for the eight-month term.

FINANCIAL ASSISTANCE
Financial assistance is limited and highly competitive. All applicants are automatically considered for scholarships and fellowships which are based on academic excellence.

PLACEMENT
The Canada Manpower Centre Student Placement Office located on campus cooperates with the Faculty of Administrative Studies to assist students in finding suitable employment after graduation.

CORRESPONDENCE
Inquiries should be addressed to
M.B.A. Program
Faculty of Administrative Studies
University of Manitoba
Winnipeg, Manitoba R3T 2N2
Canada
Telephone: 204-474-8448

The University of Maryland was established in 1807. A program in business administration was begun in 1921, and the College of Business and Public Administration was organized in 1938. A separate College of Business and Management was organized in 1973 to offer a more flexible, dynamic program in management. The college is located in College Park, Maryland, a residential community about 25 minutes from downtown Washington, D.C., and about 35 minutes from downtown Baltimore. About 600 graduate students are majoring in business at the university. There are 72 graduate faculty members.

The university is coeducational and operates on a semester plan. Both day and evening classes are conducted on the College Park campus.

PROGRAMS OF STUDY

The Master of Business Administration (M.B.A.) program emphasizes an orderly comprehension of a broad field of inquiry and a ready familiarity with the central arts and skills of management. Course work is designed to develop analytical, validating, and reporting abilities relevant to business policy analysis, planning, and decision making.

Instructional methods include case analysis, seminar discussion, and decision simulation. Computer familiarization is provided. A core of 13 courses covers the strategic areas of business decision central to the firm's operation, relevant analytical methods, behavioral factors affecting the managerial task, and the environment in which business functions, especially its relationships with government. Beyond the core, a concentration may be undertaken in one of the following fields: accounting, business and public policy, finance, human resources management, information systems, international business, marketing, operations research and statistics, organizational behavior and organization theory, personnel and labor relations, and transportation and physical distribution.

Fifty-four semester hours must be completed in courses open only to graduate students, and a minimum average of B must be earned in these courses. In addition to the core courses, five courses may be taken in a major subject. The first year of the full-time program, ten courses, is a highly integrated and sequenced set of requirements, with 40 students in each of six sections. The second year is less struc-

tured, offering students a wide range of electives.

Joint programs offered by the college are the M.B.A./ Juris Doctor (J.D.) with the university's Law School and the M.B.A./Master of Public Management (M.P.M.) with the School of Public Affairs. The former takes four academic years to complete, the latter takes three.

The Doctor of Philosophy (Ph.D.) program is offered for students who contemplate careers in university and college teaching and research and in professional or research positions in business and government. The program embraces a single major and two minor areas of study. These minors may include areas inside or outside of the College of Business and Management. In addition, an option involving a double major is available.

Areas available for Ph.D. concentrations include accounting, finance, information systems, marketing, management science and statistics, organizational behavior and theory, personnel and labor relations, strategy and planning, and transportation and physical distribution. Training in research methodology is provided.

There are no foreign language requirements. However, candidates are required to become proficient in mathematics through the elementary aspects of differential and integral calculus, matrix algebra, and probability theory before undertaking related graduate work. The program requires approximately three years of full-time study.

The Master of Science in Business Administration program is offered to provide in-depth specialization within four areas of concentration. The program is 30 credit hours for the statistics, information systems, or operations research major; 33 credit hours for the accounting systems major. All four areas offer a thesis and a nonthesis option.

ADMISSION

Among the factors considered in admission of a student for graduate work in business are an undergraduate record evidencing high scholastic attainment and satisfactory scores on the required Graduate Management Admission Test (GMAT). Entering students must have a working knowledge of calculus and computer programming. Students are admitted only in the fall.

EXPENSES

A matriculation fee of $20 is paid once only upon application. The tuition fee is a fixed charge of $154 per credit hour for nonresident students and $87 for students who are Maryland residents. A graduate student may not carry more than 15 hours each semester.

There are many apartments adjacent to the campus for single and married graduate students. In addition, the university has apartments available for married students. Graduate students may utilize university dining hall facilities or off-campus dining facilities. Information about off-campus facilities may be obtained from the Office of the Executive Dean of Student Life.

FINANCIAL ASSISTANCE

Graduate assistantships for Ph.D. students carry stipends of approximately $7,000 for the academic year. Graduate assistants aid in teaching, research, and administration of programs. They may register for 10 credit hours per semester, free of tuition. Most master's level assistantships carry stipends of $3,500 per academic year and include five hours of tuition waiver per semester. Some scholarships and fellowships are also available, and can be as much as $7,000 per year and include waived tuition.

PLACEMENT

More than 90 companies participate in the recruiting activities for M.B.A. and M.S. students. The placement office generated 77 percent of the jobs offered to students in 1984-85. The major employers seeking M.B.A. and M.S. graduates represent the following growth-oriented industries: consulting (general and systems), computers, high-tech, telecommunications, and banking. Additional services to students include corporate presentations, workshops on salary negotiation, resume writing, and interviewing skills.

CORRESPONDENCE

For further information, write or call
  Director of the Masters' Programs
  Director of the Ph.D. Program
  College of Business and Management
  University of Maryland
  College Park, Maryland 20742
  Telephone: 301-454-5140

A Placement Profile is available from the Placement Office at the same address.

All graduate degree programs of the School of Management are accredited by the American Assembly of Collegiate Schools of Business (AACSB). The graduate student population of the school totals approximately 200 master's degree students and 60 doctoral students. An evening master's degree program (part-time) is offered in Holyoke, Massachusetts.

Founded in 1863, the University of Massachusetts is state-supported, with a total student population on the Amherst campus of about 26,000. Amherst is within a two-hour drive of Boston and three hours from New York.

Applications for the graduate degree programs of the School of Business Administration are welcome from students holding any undergraduate degree.

PROGRAMS OF STUDY

The Master of Business Administration (M.B.A.) degree combines preparation in general management theory and practice with specialization in such areas as finance, accounting, marketing, personnel and industrial relations, management science, and public-sector management. Joint program arrangements also exist or may be developed individually with other professional units of the university, including engineering, education, health sciences, sports administration, and hotel, restaurant, and travel administration. The M.B.A. degree requires the completion with a B average of 54 credits of graduate course work (a 39-credit core plus 15 credits in a specialization) and normally requires four regular semesters of full-time study. A final comprehensive examination (written or oral) also is required. Admission is possible only in September, with each entering class limited to approximately 100 candidates.

A concentration in management information systems (M.I.S.) is available for M.B.A. candidates. The program emphasizes analytical skills such as statistics and management science for a career in management systems analysis and design.

Applications to the M.B.A. program are accepted equally from all areas of undergraduate study. Prerequisites to be completed prior to entering the program are limited to micro- and macroeconomics, mathematics through calculus, and statistics. Courses in these areas are available on campus during the summer. Regardless of undergraduate major, required core courses are not waived.

The Master of Science (M.S.) program in accounting requires 30 approved graduate credits, provided the student has completed undergraduate requirements in business administration and accounting. Students lacking this background complete a 54-credit Master of Science (M.S.) in accounting program. Program requirements are flexible to permit career preparation in public accounting, management accounting, information systems, taxation, teaching, or other related areas.

The Doctor of Philosophy (Ph.D.) program is designed to produce scholars capable of teaching and doing research for managing organizations. During the first year, the student prepares to take qualifying examinations in behavioral science, research methodology, statistics, and economics. A program of study in a major and a minor field of concentration and a course in research preparation are completed in the second year. A comprehensive examination in the fields of concentration must be passed before proceeding with a doctoral dissertation in the third year. Each candidate also must have one year's teaching experience and a residence requirement completed prior to graduation. The Ph.D. program normally consists of 42 credit hours of course preparation and 18 credit hours for the dissertation.

ADMISSION

Important factors in the admission process are quality of past academic record, letters of recommendation, personal statement of graduate study intent and commitment, score on the Graduate Management Admission Test (GMAT), and nature of accumulated life experiences. A personal interview is recommended but not required. The application deadline for September admission (all programs) is March 1; for January admission to the Ph.D. program and the M.S. program in accounting, the deadline is October 1. The application fee for Massachusetts residents is $10; for out-of-state residents, $40. Applications and Graduate Bulletins are obtained from the Graduate School, University of Massachusetts, Amherst, Massachusetts 01003.

EXPENSES

Tuition and fees per semester (full-time students)

Massachusetts residents, approximately $1,150
Out-of-state residents, approximately 2,300

A few university apartments are available for married students, and a graduate dormitory is available to single students. Graduate students, however, generally find private housing in Amherst or nearby towns.

FINANCIAL ASSISTANCE

A limited number of assistantships and fellowships are available for qualified graduate students. These stipends are a minimum of $900 per semester and include a waiver of tuition.

PLACEMENT

Graduate students use the services of the university placement office and the in-house counseling and placement services of the school.

CORRESPONDENCE

For further information, contact
Director of Master's Program
School of Management
University of Massachusetts
Amherst, Massachusetts 01003
Telephone: 413-549-4930, extension 266

Part of a three-campus, state-wide system, the University of Massachusetts at Boston was established in 1964 to serve commuting students in the Boston area; the university currently enrolls 11,000 students in both day and evening classes. The College of Management, which offers both a Bachelor of Science in management and a Master of Business Administration (M.B.A.) degree, is located on the Harbor Campus of UMass/Boston, overlooking Boston Harbor and adjacent to the John F. Kennedy Library and the Commonwealth of Massachusetts Archives.

The Harbor Campus is 10 minutes from downtown Boston by public or private transportation, with garage and parking lot facilities for more than 2,000 cars. Full-service cafeterias are open during the evening for the convenience of students who are on campus for evening classes and for study at the Healey Library, which also remains open into the evening. The campus offers pleasant walks along the edge of Dorchester Bay, full recreational facilities including the Clark Center's gymnasium and pool, and, for the more adventurous, access to the university's small fleet of sailboats.

PROGRAM OF STUDY
To earn an M.B.A. degree at the University of Massachusetts at Boston, students follow a curriculum totaling 54 credits, which includes both required and elective courses. The required portion of the curriculum is composed of 10 management core courses, which provide a common foundation for all students in the program before they go on to upper-level electives. Students may use some of their eight elective courses to specialize in a particular area of management. The program offers specializations in accounting, finance, public management, health management, marketing, international management, human resource management, operations management, decision sciences, and management information systems. Students are encouraged to develop individual programs of study, to strengthen and extend their own professional education in ways that will benefit their careers. Most electives are drawn from within the program itself, but some may be chosen, when appropriate, from among offerings of the university's other graduate programs.

The M.B.A. program is available to either part-time or full-time students. Classes are scheduled so as to be compatible with the needs of students who are pursuing their professional careers during the day: each M.B.A. course meets once a week for an extended evening session, so that the entire curriculum of the program is easily accessible to those who are holding full-time jobs.

ADMISSION
Admission will be offered to applicants who show evidence of high promise of success in the M.B.A. program of study. Such evidence must include the following:
- results of the Graduate Management Admission Test (GMAT),
- a minimum grade-point average of 3.0 in the last 60 semester hours of undergraduate courses,
- a statement of 1,200 words by the applicant about his or her preparation for graduate study in business administration.

The M.B.A. Admissions Committee will consider, in addition to the above requirements, the contributions of an employment record at appropriate and increasing levels of responsibility. Applicants for whom such consideration is appropriate are encouraged to include in the above statement an employment history and an account of how that work experience has contributed to their preparation for graduate study in business administration.

EXPENSES
Tuition, per academic year, subject to change:

In-state residents, per credit (maximum of $810.00) . . . . . . $ 67.50
Out-of-state residents, per credit (maximum of $2,262.00) 188.50
Fees, per academic year (required and subject to change):
One to six credits 111.00
Seven or more credits 165.00

The university provides no housing, but there is an office on campus that assists students in locating accommodations.

FINANCIAL ASSISTANCE
Graduate assistantships are available to qualified M.B.A. students who are registered for at least six graduate credits. The stipends are $2,000 per semester for the full-time assistant and $1,000 per semester for the half-time assistant. Tuition is waived for both full- and half-time assistants.

A limited amount of financial assistance is available for full-time students.

PLACEMENT
The university's Office of Career Services assists graduates in obtaining full-time employment. In addition, faculty members assist in placing graduates.

CORRESPONDENCE
For further information or to request an application, please write or call
Director, M.B.A. Program
University of Massachusetts at Boston
Harbor Campus
Boston, Massachusetts 02125-3393
Telephone: 617-929-8140

The Graduate School of Management was established in 1984, following the Commonwealth Inquiry into Management Education. The school fulfills a requirement for a national school of excellence in management education. It offers Master of Business Administration (M.B.A.), executive development, and research programs. Although the school has been recently established as a separate entity within the University of Melbourne, its precursor, the Graduate School of Business Administration was founded in 1963. Over 700 people have been graduated from the M.B.A. program run by the foregoing schools and several thousand managers have participated in the six- and four-week residential, general management programs for senior executives. Many graduates and participants from these programs belong to a strong and lively alumni organization, known as the Melbourne University Business School Association.

The Graduate School of Management has a newly constructed school building, which includes a library designed to serve specialized reference and research needs, computer facilities, lecture theaters, and 47 rooms for residential executive programs. The school has established the Melbourne Case Library of Australian case studies, and it acts as a distributor of cases from the Harvard University Graduate School of Business Administration.

PROGRAMS OF STUDY

The M.B.A. program at the University of Melbourne is designed to foster the development of future general managers. The school aims to enhance the skills of managers who have a sound academic background by providing them with a broad exposure to the fundamentals of management. The emphasis is placed on equipping a manager, or potential manager, with a comprehensive understanding of management functions and policy. This will not only have an immediate practical value, but it will also enable a manager to deal with a changing business environment.

Applicants must have had at least two years working experience before they can be accepted as M.B.A. candidates. This requirement enables students to relate the course material to their own personal experience in the workplace.

The course has a preliminary and a final year component. The preliminary year subjects are mainly concerned with analyt-ical concepts and techniques relating to the fields of accounting, economics, statistics, and human behavior. In the final year a candidate studies six subjects: three are compulsory and the others are chosen from a list of specializations that cover the fields of business policy, marketing management, organization theory, decision analysis, industrial relations, and financial management. The subjects are problem focused and increase in complexity, with the emphasis changing during the year from analysis to problem solving. Candidates are also required to submit a report on an independent field study of a managerial problem.

The M.B.A. teaching methods include individual and syndicate case studies, reading and research assignments, formal presentations, role playing, seminars with visiting speakers from senior management in industry and government, as well as formal lectures.

The M.B.A. program is a two-year postgraduate course if taken on a full-time basis. If the course is attempted on a part-time basis, it must be completed within four years. The final year must be completed full time. Classes for the preliminary year of the M.B.A. program begin at 8:00 a.m. and end at 5:30 p.m.

The school offers two six-week residential programs for senior executives. These are designed to focus on major issues in general management. A four-week management development program is also offered for middle managers.

The Ph.D. program is designed to encourage the development of first-rate research in a wide range of management-related fields. Although it is primarily a research degree, a course work component may be prescribed.

ADMISSION

Admission to the M.B.A. program is open to all qualified men and women who hold a bachelor's degree in any field from an approved undergraduate institution and who have worked for at least two years. All applicants are considered for selection by a committee that meets in November.

The Graduate Management Admission Test (GMAT) is required of all applicants, and students are advised to take the test in the first half of the calendar year and to arrange to have their scores reported directly to the school in time for the beginning of the selection process. Selection is based on the applicant's academic record, score on the GMAT, evaluation of referees' reports, employment experience, and other tests that may be prescribed.

Applications for admission to the program should be filed with the Graduate School of Management by October 31 and should be accompanied by a detailed official transcript of university studies. Overseas applicants should check initially with an Australian Diplomatic Office regarding visa requirements and English language assessment.

Applicants are advised of the result of their applications in December or January. The program commences in the first week of March.

EXPENSES

No tuition fees are payable, although overseas students must pay the overseas student charge to the Australian Government. In 1986, this charge will be $A3,500 increasing to approximately $A4,500 in 1987. All students are required by the university to pay a student activities fee (approximately $250 per year). Living expenses vary with the choice of housing and the circumstances of the student.

FINANCIAL ASSISTANCE

Details of scholarships and fellowships available (including Commonwealth Postgraduate Course Awards) may be obtained from the Scholarships Officer, Office for Research, University of Melbourne.

CORRESPONDENCE

For further information, write to
Assistant Registrar
The Graduate School of Management
University of Melbourne
Parkville, Victoria 3052, Australia
Cable: UNIMELB
Telex: AA35185 UNIMELB

The University of Miami is located in Coral Gables, a residential area adjacent to Miami which has recently become a major location for executive offices of international firms. Over 175 multinational firms have offices in Coral Gables and downtown Miami. In addition, Miami has become one of the leading banking centers in the world.

The University of Miami is a private, independent, international university and an equal opportunity employer. The undergraduate and graduate programs of the school are accredited by the American Assembly of Collegiate Schools of Business (AACSB). Additionally, the undergraduate accounting program and the Master of Professional Accounting program of the school are accredited under the special accounting accreditation standards of the AACSB.

PROGRAMS OF STUDY

At the School of Business Administration, there are four Master of Business Administration (M.B.A.) tracks. Track I is the traditional program for the student who holds an undergraduate degree in business, leading to completion of all requirements for graduation in 10 months. A student who did not major in business or who graduated from a foreign university follows Track II, taking the basic core courses during a special nine-week summer Program in Management Studies, completing all requirements in 14 months. In addition to the fast track for business and nonbusiness undergraduates, there are two other options available: Track III, in-depth specialization and a paid summer internship; and Track IV, the most comprehensive track—a paid summer internship and a concentration leading to a second degree. Students may pursue areas of interest through a variety of electives and concentrations, such as international business, economics, finance, health administration, marketing, and management.

The School of Business Administration confers the Master of Business Administration, the Master of Public Administration, the Master of Professional Accounting, the Master of Arts in Economics, Master of Science in Operations Research/Statistics, Master of Science in Taxation, Doctor of Arts in Economics, and Doctor of Philosophy in Psychology/Organizational Behavior. The majority of the students are enrolled in the M.B.A. program.

The goal of the school is to provide students from around the nation and the world with a sound background in the functional areas of business. To this end a variety of teaching methods are used: lecture, discussion, the case method, and team learning. Classes are kept small enough to encourage frequent exchange between teacher and student, and among students. Part-time evening programs are also offered.

ADMISSION

The Admissions Committee considers applications from men and women who hold bachelor's degrees from accredited colleges and universities. The admission decision is based upon a careful evaluation of all credentials presented by the applicant. The undergraduate record, scores on the Graduate Management Admission Test (GMAT), evidence of ability and motivation to do graduate work, maturity, and leadership qualities are all considered. Foreign students must submit scores from the Test of English as a Foreign Language (TOEFL).

Full-time students are encouraged to apply for June admission if they have a nonbusiness background, and for late August admission if they have a business background. Part-time students may apply for late August or January admission. Deadlines for admission are May 1 for June admission and June 30 for August admission. Foreign students must apply by April 1.

EXPENSES

Tuition for the summer Program in Management Studies was $3,500 in 1986. Tuition for the M.B.A. program in 1985-86 was $324 per credit. This does not include the cost of books, supplies, and health and activity fees, and is subject to change.

FINANCIAL ASSISTANCE

A limited number of graduate assistantships, available to qualified students, usually carry 22 credits of tuition remission plus a stipend of $3,000 for the 1985-86 academic year. Teaching and research assistantships are also available in some departments. Graduate students are also eligible to apply for scholarships, student loans, and work-study assistance through the university's Financial Aid Office.

PLACEMENT

The Graduate Business Career Resource Center provides placement services for all graduate business students. The staff offers counseling, assistance with resume writing and interviewing, workshops on career-related topics, and an internship program that includes a paid summer option. Two recruitment seasons—fall and spring—are held so that students may interview with major national and local firms. In addition, a resume book is compiled and distributed to 1,500 corporations.

CORRESPONDENCE

For further information or to request an application for admission, write or call
Harold W. Berkman, Ph.D.
Associate Dean
Graduate Business Programs and
    Research Administration
School of Business Administration
University of Miami
P.O. Box 248702
Coral Gables, Florida 33124
Telephone: 305-284-2510

The University of Michigan School of Business Administration in Ann Arbor prepares men and women for leadership roles in management in both the private and public sectors. A strong program meshes highly qualified students and faculty in an environment dedicated to learning. In addition, the full resources of a great university are available to students in the Master of Business Administration (M.B.A.) program.

Approximately 750 students are enrolled in full-time graduate study and 750 in the part-time evening program. Activities are housed in a growing complex of buildings, distinguished by the recent additions of a new library and computer center.

PROGRAMS OF STUDY

At Michigan, the teaching style reflects a balance between theory and practice and includes an active mix of cases, lectures, and discussions, enhanced by interaction between students and business leaders.

The M.B.A. program provides students the flexibility to engage in either a general course of study or concentrate in a particular field. The 10-course core curriculum occupies most of the first year and includes work in finance, accounting, marketing, corporate strategy and operations management, economics, organizational behavior, and computer techniques. These classes develop critical, analytical problem-solving and decision-making capabilities.

The remainder of the 60-credit-hour requirement for the program consists of 10 electives. Students can select courses according to personal interests and career goals. Each student can develop a program choosing from available areas of concentration, such as finance, accounting, business economics, international business, marketing, computer information systems, organizational behavior, and statistics and management science. Also, the program offers a wide variety of additional electives to strengthen an understanding of the problem areas confronting the modern manager.

The M.B.A. evening program offers people who work an educational experience that can become an important part of their career development. The outstanding faculty, the curriculum, and the teaching methods are held in common with the full-time program. Completion of the program requires four to six years at the rate of one to two courses per term. The program is offered at the Ann Arbor campus and at the Village Plaza Study Center in Dearborn.

The Michigan doctoral program is characterized by demanding studies in preparation for academic positions in leading schools of business and for research-oriented pursuits in business and government. Additional information may be obtained by writing to the Director, Doctoral Studies Program.

ADMISSION

Prior study in business is not a requirement for admission. Indeed, the precise content of the applicant's earlier educational program is of less concern to the Admissions Committee than evidence of sound scholarship and potential for responsible leadership in management. Applicants must have completed an undergraduate degree that included at least one term of calculus. Besides the application, applicants must submit official scores on the Graduate Management Admission Test (GMAT), and foreign applicants are also required to submit official results from the Test of English as a Foreign Language (TOEFL). Students enter the full-time program in September, while the evening program begins in September and January.

The median age of admitted students is 25, with nearly 75 percent having prior work experience. Students come from all over the nation and 30 foreign countries.

EXPENSES

Costs are estimated for the 1985-86 academic year, and an increase of 10 percent per year should be assumed.

	Michigan Resident	Out-of-State
Tuition and fees	$4,788	$ 9,228
Living expenses	4,800	4,800
Books and supplies	400	400
Total	$9,988	$14,428

FINANCIAL ASSISTANCE

Approximately 30 percent of incoming M.B.A. candidates receive scholarships awarded on the basis of need and merit in amounts ranging from $1,000 to $5,000. Applications should be submitted to the school through the Graduate and Professional School Financial Aid Service (GAPSFAS) by February 1 for the fall term. Loans are awarded through the university Office of Financial Aid, 2011 Student Activities Building. Michigan is also a member of the Consortium for Graduate Study in Management, which helps minority students finance their management education.

PLACEMENT

Under the auspices of the Placement Office, over 300 national and international companies recruit Michigan M.B.A. graduates each year, at competitive salaries, for both permanent and summer employment. In addition, the office offers career counseling, seminars in interviewing techniques, and resume workshops.

CORRESPONDENCE

For further information, write or call
Office of Admissions and
Student Services
School of Business Administration
The University of Michigan
Ann Arbor, Michigan 48109-1234
Telephone: 313-763-5796

The Graduate School of Management
THE UNIVERSITY OF MICHIGAN—DEARBORN
DEARBORN, MICHIGAN

The University of Michigan—Dearborn (UMD) is one of the three campuses of The University of Michigan. Founded in 1959 through a gift from the Ford Motor Company, the 202-acre urban campus is located in a rural setting on the former estate of the late Henry Ford. Eight buildings, including a student housing unit and the Fair Lane Conference Center, provide the current facilities for an expanding full-time faculty of 200 and a student enrollment of 7,000.

The UM—Dearborn academic units include the College of Arts, Sciences, and Letters, School of Engineering, School of Management, Division of Interdisciplinary Studies, and Division of Urban Education. The Master of Business Administration (M.B.A.) graduate program is offered by the resident graduate faculty of the School of Management. Graduate students have access to the UMD library and computer facilities as well as the four-million-volume university library system and university computing center.

PROGRAM OF STUDY
The M.B.A. program is offered to individuals whose achievement and aptitude match the requirements of leadership positions in modern complex organizations. The program will impart the knowledge and skill necessary both for early career success and for continued professional growth.

The M.B.A. degree program is presented by the faculty of the Graduate School of Management at UMD. The M.B.A. program is designed as a "crossover" vehicle for those whose previous college preparation lies in areas other than management or administration but whose aspirations or present responsibilities are in management. Those whose baccalaureate degree is business administration cannot be considered for admission to the M.B.A. program. The program is offered on a full- and part-time basis during the day and late afternoon hours year round. Courses are sequenced for admission in September and January.

Successful completion of 60 semester credit hours (or the equivalent) is required for the M.B.A. degree as follows:

	Credit hours
Required courses	48
Elective courses	12

The required core of 48 credit hours is distributed over 16 sequenced and integrated courses as follows:

	Courses
Analytical Foundations for Management	27
Functional Applications of Management	12
Management Planning, Control, and Environment	9

The selection of electives can be approached from two standpoints: a general management option and a concentration option. Concentrations are presently offered in finance, human resource management, management information systems, and production and operations management.

After admission to the M.B.A. program and on presentation of appropriate credentials, a student may seek up to six hours credit under any combination of these special credit provisions: course credit by examination and transfer credit for prior graduate work. The Management Internship Program is an optional feature of the M.B.A. program. Students choosing this option may take up to two internships, each of which earns three credit hours, which can be added to the basic 60 hours of the M.B.A. program.

ADMISSION
Those who wish admission to the program should make application to the Graduate School of Management. Information and application forms may be requested from the M.B.A. Program Chairman (correspondence address given below).

In general, each applicant for regular admission must have earned a bachelor's degree (in a discipline other than business or management), have attained an acceptable score on the Graduate Management Admission Test (GMAT), have successfully completed a first course in calculus and a course in computer programming. Qualified part-time applicants deficient in calculus and/or programming may be granted conditional admission for the fall term. The academic prerequisites must then be completed concurrent with their first term of enrollment. All applicants for the winter term must have both academic prerequisites satisfied prior to entry.

EXPENSES
Graduate fees for the academic year 1985-86 per 16-week term for Michigan residents and nonresidents:

	Resident	Nonresident
Full program (8-12 hours)	$887	$2,875
Six hours	680	2,180
Three hours	365	1,160

Books, room and board, and other expenses depend upon the student's full- or part-time enrollment and standard of living.

FINANCIAL ASSISTANCE
A limited number of scholarships and assistantships are available. Loans, part-time employment, and, of course, remunerated management internships may also provide financial assistance.

PLACEMENT
A full array of placement and career planning assistance is available from the UMD Career Planning and Placement Office. In addition, graduate students have access to the university-wide placement facilities. Management internships and the close proximity to major national organizations in the southeastern Michigan area provide other placement opportunities.

CORRESPONDENCE
Please address all inquiries about the Master of Business Administration degree program to

M.B.A. Program Chairman
The Graduate School of Management
The University of Michigan—Dearborn
4901 Evergreen Road
Dearborn, Michigan 48128
Telephone: 313-593-5460

The University of Michigan—Flint (UM-Flint) is one of the three campuses of The University of Michigan. From its founding in 1956, UM-Flint has represented the combined efforts of the university, the State of Michigan, and the Flint community to develop and maintain a distinguished educational program for persons of outstanding ambition, ability, and potential for leadership.

The University of Michigan—Flint serves its 6,000 full-time and part-time students on its new 42-acre campus located on the Flint River, adjacent to the new downtown development area and the cultural center. In addition to use of the library and computing center on campus, graduate students have access to the university's extensive facilities in Ann Arbor.

The School of Management is an upper-division professional school offering programs leading to the Bachelor of Business Administration (B.B.A.) and the Master of Business Administration (M.B.A.) degrees. Established as a separate school in 1975, its faculty members have had extensive experience in working with business and with government and in teaching management programs.

PROGRAM OF STUDY
The M.B.A. program is designed for those individuals who have distinguished themselves in their previous college studies, who show a high aptitude for management studies, and who have, or who soon may have, responsible positions in management. The program is a balanced one providing an in-depth coverage of the basic fields underlying management decisions as well as of the functional areas of management. In this way it provides a solid background for general management. To this broad foundation has been added a concentration designed to assist those who manage functional operations in manufacturing organizations and in service organizations such as health, financial, and not-for-profit institutions. This emphasis is called operations management. In combination with the more general subjects covered, it will provide the candidate with strong support for his or her next 10 years in management and also a solid background for higher levels of responsibility which may be assumed thereafter.

The three-year program is unlike typical evening offerings in that an entering group will stay together throughout the program. Students can profit not only from a close relationship to the faculty, but also through extended association with other managers. Every effort is made to make this interaction an effective learning experience.

The M.B.A. program is designed to educate individuals to think effectively about solutions for management problems. Its emphasis is on learning and applying the principles of problem solving which lead to effective decision making. Emphasis is also given to developing skills and techniques required in implementing decisions, in "making it happen." The approach to decision making is quantitative and analytical. Participants will learn to identify variables important in solving a problem, to collect and analyze relevant data, to evaluate solutions, and to select the best alternative.

ADMISSION
The program is designed for those who show high promise for graduate study in management. Suitability of a candidate for the M.B.A. program will be based on a review of
- job experience as indicated through a resume,
- prior educational background,
- scores on the Graduate Management Admission Test (GMAT), and
- letters of recommendation.
An interview may be requested if it appears useful to either the applicant or the admission committee.

Every effort is made to balance the composition of the class so that participants will be exposed to a range of points of view. Participants will be drawn from diverse organizations so that they may learn from exposure to others coming from different organizational settings.

Participants are expected to have differing levels of preparation. It is desirable to have some background in economics, statistics, mathematics, accounting, and computer use. Only college mathematics is required for entrance. Although no specific course is required, an exposure to calculus and/or matrix algebra is helpful. Those with serious deficiencies will be asked to correct them before admission to the program.

Participants are admitted for the fall term beginning in early September and for the winter term beginning in early January. Completed applications should be submitted by July 1 for the fall term and by November 1 for winter term.

EXPENSES
The tuition rate for 1985 is $128 per credit hour. This fee includes campus parking but does not include textbooks, supplies, or other expenses. Part-time students typically register for six or seven semester hours. The one-time application fee is $20.

FINANCIAL ASSISTANCE
A limited number of partial tuition scholarships are available to persons of exceptional ability who might otherwise be unable to attend. Also, student loans under various loan programs are available to persons who qualify.

PLACEMENT
Placement assistance provided by the university's Counseling Center includes career guidance, information on job market trends, resume writing, interviewing skills, job listings, and on-campus interviews. In addition, graduate students have access to university-wide placement services.

CORRESPONDENCE
For further information or to request an application for admission, please write or call

M.B.A. Director
School of Management
The University of Michigan—Flint
Flint, Michigan 48502-2186
Telephone: 313-762-3160

UNIVERSITY OF MINNESOTA

MINNEAPOLIS, MINNESOTA

Founded in 1851, the University of Minnesota is located in the center of the Minneapolis and St. Paul metropolitan area. The School of Management was established in 1919, and master's and Ph.D. degrees have been offered since its inception. Some 1,750 master's candidates and 138 doctoral candidates are now enrolled.

PROGRAMS OF STUDY

The Master of Business Administration (M.B.A.) degree program prepares students for rewarding positions of responsibility in the business world and increasingly in the nonprofit sector. The M.B.A. degree program requires as prerequisites an undergraduate degree in any field, plus introductory courses in microeconomics and calculus or finite mathematics.

The M.B.A. program consists of a regular program of 74 credits for students without prior education in business administration and an accelerated program of 50 credits for students with a business undergraduate degree. The regular and accelerated programs are offered in both the full-time day and the part-time evening M.B.A. programs. The regular M.B.A. program consists of a group of core courses in the first year followed by a concentration in one area and a sequence of three required courses in the second year. The regular M.B.A. requires the following graduate courses: MBA 8005, Computer Access and Programming for Business Analysis; MBA 8010, Management and Organizational Behavior; MBA 8015, Human Resources Management; MBA 8020, Business Statistics, Sources, Presentation, and Analysis; MBA 8025, Decision Sciences and Information Systems; MBA 8030, Financial Accounting; MBA 8035, Managerial Economics and Accounting; MBA 8040, Financial Management; MBA 8045, Marketing Management; MBA 8050, Operations Management; MBA 8055, Business, Government, and Macroeconomics; MBA 8060, Strategy and Policy; MBA 8065, Field Project; plus six concentration courses totaling 24 credits. The full-time regular program takes two years to complete and begins in the fall quarter each year.

Part-time evening regular program students who take two courses per quarter may complete the program in nine quarters or three years.

The accelerated program consists of an introductory quarter that complements the student's background followed by a concentration in one area and a sequence of three required courses. It requires 13 courses to be completed; 3 of the following 6: MBA 8015, MBA 8025, MBA 8035, MBA 8040, MBA 8045, MBA 8050, MBA 8005, MBA 8055, MBA 8060, MBA 8065, and 6 concentration courses totaling 24 credits. In the day program, which is full-time, this is a four-quarter program (summer-fall-winter-spring).

Part-time evening students, who register for two courses per quarter, may complete the program in six quarters or two years.

Each day and part-time student must select an area of concentration at the time of application for admission. The concentrations are as follows (concentrations designated with an asterisk are available to part-time evening students): accounting*, advertising management, auditing*, business, government and society, controllership*, finance*, general management*, insurance, line management, logistics management, management support systems*, management information systems*, marketing management*, marketing research*, operations management*, organizational leadership, quantitative analysis.

Two projects are required for the M.B.A. degree (these are called Plan B projects). A Plan B project is a written report, comparable in quality to a master's thesis, but of reduced length. One project is part of MBA 8065, Field Project (for day students) or MBA 8070, Problem Formulation and Decision Making (for part-time evening students). This project enables students to work on problems of actual organizations. A second project must be completed in a course within the student's area of concentration.

The Ph.D. in business administration is designed for students contemplating careers in university teaching and research and professional positions in business and government. Each Ph.D. student develops a program of study that reflects his or her interests, background, and special abilities.

ADMISSION

M.B.A. admission will be based primarily on three factors: an applicant's aptitude for graduate work in business, the quality of prior academic experience, and a statement of career goals. Managerial or administrative experience is given positive weight. Applicants are encouraged to apply four to six months in advance of the quarter they wish to enter; they should take the Graduate Management Admission Test (GMAT) early and not wait until the test administration immediately preceding the quarter in which they wish to enter.

EXPENSES

Estimated expenses, per quarter credit:

Resident tuition $110.78
Nonresident tuition,
  per credit 170.00
Room and board 650.00-700.00
Books 150.00
Incidental fee 91.10
Evening M.B.A. (E.M.B.A) . . . 110.00

FINANCIAL ASSISTANCE

Teaching assistantships are available to students in all graduate programs with a stipend of $3,700 for a nine-month, one-quarter-time appointment. Graduate fellowships are available each year to outstanding students.

PLACEMENT

Services of a full-time placement office and M.B.A. Placement Coordinator are available to graduate students. Several hundred companies from all sections of the United States send representatives to visit the school.

CORRESPONDENCE

For further information, write or call
  Director, Marketing and Admissions
  Graduate School of Management,
    M.B.A. Program
  295 HHH
  University of Minnesota
  271 19th Avenue South
  Minneapolis, Minnesota 55455
  Telephone: 612-373-5505

UNIVERSITY OF MINNESOTA DULUTH

DULUTH, MINNESOTA

Established in 1947, the University of Minnesota Duluth has several colleges and schools, including the College of Letters and Science, the School of Business and Economics, the School of Medicine, the College of Education, the School of Fine Arts, and the School of Social Development. The Duluth campus is an integral part of the University of Minnesota, and the Master of Business Administration (M.B.A.) program on the Duluth campus is under the direction of the University of Minnesota Graduate School.

PROGRAM OF STUDY
The Master of Business Administration program is intended for the person who desires to build competence in administration. It is directed to the improvement of ability in analyzing and solving problems and to the understanding of the nature and management of organizations.

The Master of Business Administration program requires the completion of the minimum of 45 quarter credits of graduate courses. These courses include an integrated core of required courses totaling 27 quarter credits, 9 credits in electives, 3 credits in research methodology, and 6 credits in management research. The program requires the research project which includes the submission of a written report and oral defense of the project. A related research project requirement is that students must complete research methodology and management research courses.

Students who have had limited or no undergraduate course work in business administration are required to take prerequisite courses in accounting, legal environment, management, management science, finance, marketing, and economics.

The M.B.A. courses are offered in the evening and at other special hours during the academic year. A variety of instructional methods are utilized: lectures, seminars, case studies, role playing, and guest speakers.

ADMISSION
To be considered for admission to the M.B.A. program an applicant must have a bachelor's degree from a recognized college or university, take the Graduate Management Admission Test (GMAT), and submit a completed application to the Graduate School of the University of Minnesota, Duluth, Duluth, Minnesota 55812, at least three weeks prior to the beginning of an academic quarter. The bachelor's degree may be in any subject field, such as engineering, education, the social sciences, business, the arts, or others.

Application for admission should be made as early as possible because the size of each class is limited to approximately 35 a year. The applicant's previous academic record and GMAT score are the two principal criteria used in making admission decisions.

Application forms for admission to the Graduate School may be secured from the Graduate School, University of Minnesota Duluth, Duluth, Minnesota 55812, or Director, M.B.A. Program, School of Business and Economics, University of Minnesota Duluth, Duluth, Minnesota 55812.

EXPENSES
Tuition, per quarter, for both resident and nonresident students is $110.75 per credit for the 1985-86 academic year. Room and board ranges from $900 to $1,000 per quarter, and cost of textbooks is comparable to other institutions.

FINANCIAL ASSISTANCE
A few graduate assistantships, which may involve research and teaching, are available. The amount of stipend is $7,245 for a nine-month, half-time appointment.

PLACEMENT
Services of a full-time placement office are available to graduate students.

CORRESPONDENCE
For further information, please write or call
Director
M.B.A. Program
School of Business and Economics
104 School of Business and Economics Building
University of Minnesota Duluth
Duluth, Minnesota 55812
Telephone: 218-726-7281

The University of Mississippi was founded in 1848 and its School of Business Administration in 1917. The first degree of Master of Business Administration (M.B.A.) was awarded in 1946, and the first degree of Doctor of Philosophy in business administration in 1964. The School of Business Administration has 2,200 students in its undergraduate programs and 100 students in its graduate programs. Both the graduate and undergraduate curricula are accredited by the American Assembly of Collegiate Schools of Business (AACSB).

PROGRAMS OF STUDY

The M.B.A. program is a course of study designed to prepare students to be future administrative leaders in private or public organizations. While the program is designed to be rigorous and broad in nature, an individual has the opportunity to select courses that satisfy specific professional objectives. Students are engaged in developing skills in both quantitative and qualitative courses during their educational experience. Emphasis is on providing students with the managerial skills and educational experiences that will enable them to be immediate contributors to an organization. The M.B.A. program embraces a multiple learning process that involves lecture, discussion, case analysis, and experiential learning. Through these various modes of learning, the student should acquire the ability to solve many of the problems that will be encountered in a decision-making environment, and be ready to assume a position of responsibility in any number of organizations. Ole Miss strives to have its graduates actively sought by firms that are leaders in their industry.

Students must complete the following courses (33 hours), or their equivalents, before being allowed to take a full load of graduate courses: Introduction to Accounting Principles, Principles of Economics, Economics Statistics, Business Finance, Introduction to Business Law, Information Processing, Principles of Management, Marketing Principles, and Calculus.

Ten courses are included in the program as the core requirement: Managerial Accounting, Managerial Economics, Business Conditions Analysis, Statistical Methods for Business and Economics, Financial Management, Advanced Organizational Behavior, Business Policy and Strategic Management, Management Information Systems, Production and Operations Management, Marketing Management, and six hours of electives.

A Master of Business Administration/ Juris Doctor program is offered for those students who desire training in both business and law. By meeting requirements for the two degrees simultaneously, students are able to earn the degrees in a shorter length of time than would be the case if each degree were pursued consecutively.

The degree of Doctor of Philosophy (Ph.D.) in business administration with major fields in management, marketing, and finance is awarded for scholarly attainment and represents the highest degree that the university may bestow on a business student. The basic purpose of the Ph.D. program is to enable persons who are seeking careers in institutions of higher learning or in research or staff positions in business, industry, or government to acquire a comprehensive, professional education. The doctoral program provides a broad understanding of business administration and affords an opportunity for in-depth study in a major field. A personalized program is designed for each student based upon the individual's background, experience, and needs. Students seeking the degree of Doctor of Philosophy in business administration make an unequivocal personal commitment to intellectual integrity and scholarship.

For the Ph.D. degree, students must complete at least 60 hours of approved graduate courses beyond the bachelor's degree or at least 30 hours of approved courses numbered above 600 beyond the master's degree. Moreover, students must take at least 12 hours in a major field beyond the master's degree and at least 9 hours (preferably 12) in each of the two minor fields beyond the bachelor's degree. Students must also satisfy the tool or language requirement of the major field.

ADMISSION

Applicants for admission to the M.B.A. program must hold a bachelor's degree from an accredited institution. This degree may be in any field. Admission is based primarily on the applicant's undergraduate record and the score made on the Graduate Management Admission Test (GMAT). A minimum overall grade-point average of 2.75, or 3.00 on the last 60 hours, and at least a 450 GMAT score are required for admission in full standing. The attainment of these grade-point averages and GMAT score does not constitute a guarantee of admission; additional credentials such as trend of grades and employment experiences are also considered in admission decisions.

An applicant for the Ph.D. program must submit a score of at least 450 on the GMAT. In addition, the applicant must possess an undergraduate grade-point average of 2.75, or at least a 3.10 on the last 60 hours attempted at either the undergraduate or graduate level.

EXPENSES

Tuition is $700.50 a semester for residents of Mississippi and $1,238.50 for nonresidents.

FINANCIAL ASSISTANCE

Fellowships, assistantships, loans, and other financial aids are available to graduate students. Graduate assistantships usually range from $3,000 to $6,400.

PLACEMENT

An aggressive program of placement provides students an extensive schedule of employment interviews throughout the academic year. Other services are provided for the student, such as seminars on resume writing, interviewing skills, and career counseling.

CORRESPONDENCE

For further information, please write or call

Associate Dean
School of Business Administration
University of Mississippi
University, Mississippi 38677
Telephone: 601-232-5820

The University of Missouri—Columbia (UMC) is the oldest state university west of the Mississippi River and largest of the four campuses of the University of Missouri. With a total enrollment of about 50,000 students, the University of Missouri ranks high in the top 20 in enrollment among accredited higher-learning institutions in the United States. Approximately 24,500 of these students are enrolled at the Columbia campus of the University of Missouri.

The College of Business and Public Administration, which was established in 1914 as a senior professional school, offers a variety of curricula placing emphasis upon educating students for their growing responsibilities in business, government, and society as a whole. Situated in Middlebush Hall, with 64,000 square feet of floor space, the college is located in the heart of the Columbia campus. The U-shaped structure has an auditorium and classroom space to accommodate approximately 2,400 students. In addition to classroom and office space, there is a remote job entry terminal to the university computer network which operates two Amdahl 470 computers. Ellis Library, which contains more than 2,600,000 volumes and 21,000 periodicals, and the Memorial Union are both located less than a block away.

PROGRAMS OF STUDY

The Master of Business Administration (M.B.A.) program, offered through the School of Business, is designed for superior students whose primary interest is preparation for managerial careers in business. At the same time, it provides a strong educational background for persons who plan to continue their academic training in preparation for teaching and research.

The M.B.A. program emphasizes broad problems confronting administrators of business enterprises, mastery of tools and analysis, and the cultivation of judgment required for sound decision making and competent management. Although the essential unity of all business operations within the economic, social, and political environment is stressed, opportunity exists for concentration.

The program is open to applicants who hold a baccalaureate or equivalent degree in any discipline from an accredited college or university. It is essentially a two-year program; however, first-year courses may be waived if a student has satisfactorily completed equivalent course work. Consequently, the total semester hours required for the M.B.A. may vary from a minimum of 30 to a maximum of 54 hours. Approximately two thirds of those students currently enrolled in the M.B.A. program hold bachelor's degrees in disciplines other than business administration, accounting, or economics. A thesis is not required.

The School of Accountancy offers two master's degrees—a Master of Arts (M.A.) and a Master of Science (M.S.). The M.A. in accountancy is designed for students with undergraduate degrees in business or accountancy who wish to prepare more fully for professional careers in accounting. Completion of the degree requires approximately one year.

The M.S. in accountancy is a two-year professional degree designed primarily for individuals who have completed undergraduate degrees in specializations other than accounting. The first year consists of foundation courses, while the second-year courses cover the technical requirements of the professional accountant or accounting-oriented manager. A thesis is not required.

The Master of Science degree in public administration offered through the Department of Public Administration provides professional education in preparation for administrative careers in the public service. The degree normally can be completed in two years, with a summer internship between the first and second years. The first year is devoted to foundation courses, while the second year gives students an opportunity to specialize in selected areas.

The college offers Doctor of Philosophy (Ph.D.) degrees in business administration and accountancy. The Ph.D. in business administration is designed to provide (1) a broad understanding of the major areas of business; the role of the business manager as analyst, planner, and decision maker; and the mutual dependence between the firm and its environment; (2) intensive preparation for teaching in a specialized area at the college or university level; and (3) competence for original and meaningful research.

The program for the Ph.D. degree in accountancy is designed to prepare students for research, college teaching, or other advanced professional careers in accounting. This program consists of (1) a course of study, (2) practical experience in teaching and research, (3) examination covering accumulated knowledge in a major and two supporting fields, and (4) demonstration of research and writing ability by completing a doctoral dissertation on an approved research topic.

ADMISSION

Applicants to all programs must submit official transcripts of previous undergraduate and graduate work. To be considered for admission to business administration and accountancy programs, applicants must submit scores from the Graduate Management Admission Test (GMAT). Applicants to the public administration program must submit scores from the Graduate Record Examinations (GRE).

EXPENSES

Semester expenses for tuition and incidental fees for full-time students are $884.10 for in-state students and $2,396.10 for out-of-state students.

FINANCIAL ASSISTANCE

Teaching and research assistantships range from $2,775 for master's candidates to $5,550 for Ph.D. candidates. Out-of-state tuition is waived for individuals on assistantships. Extensive scholarship money for which no work is required is also available to outstanding students.

PLACEMENT

More than 350 business, accountancy, and government employers visit the Placement Office each year.

CORRESPONDENCE

For additional information, write or call the director of the program concerned.

College of Business and Public Administration
University of Missouri—Columbia
Columbia, Missouri 65211
Telephone: 314-882-2750

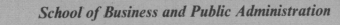
The purpose of the Master of Business Administration (M.B.A.) degree program at the University of Missouri—Kansas City (UMKC) is to develop qualified business administrators for positions of management responsibility in a changing society. The general administration courses that are required of every candidate stress the substantive knowledge and skills necessary for a professional administrator in dealing with the organization as a social-technical system composed of individuals, groups, and other subunits. The business functional courses develop the specialized knowledge and skills necessary for the economic maintenance and growth of the organization. In addition to these goals, the program stresses the social and public responsibilities of men and women in business. The program utilizes a number of special educational procedures, including the case method, seminars, T-group laboratories, simulation of business operation, and individual research.

The Master of Business Administration is designed to prepare students holding bachelor's degrees in the arts, sciences, engineering, or business administration for professional careers in business administration. To accomplish this objective, the program is organized to maximize the development of practicing administrators and is considered terminal. However, sufficient flexibility exists in the curriculum to allow a student to transfer with reasonable ease to doctoral work emphasizing the research and teaching of administration.

PROGRAMS OF STUDY
Students are required to complete 30 to 57 hours of graduate study, with the total depending on the student's undergraduate preparation. The normal full-time course load is 12 hours per semester. A thesis is not required but may be permitted with faculty approval. The curriculum for the M.B.A. contains two stages.

Stage I consists of 27 credit hours, including the basic core requirements of the American Assembly of Collegiate Schools of Business (AACSB), and is designed to develop the student's command of basic analytical tools and research skills, establish an understanding of the broader socioeconomic-cultural framework within which business behavior occurs, and ensure that the student acquires an adequate understanding of business operations. Stage II includes five

required breadth courses, three or more courses in an area of specialization, and electives to complete a minimum of 30 hours.

Concentrations are currently available in finance, (banking option available), personnel and industrial relations, marketing (an option in direct marketing is currently available), organizational behavior, policy and planning, quantitative analysis, operations management, and accounting and control.

An M.B.A. degree can be earned by attending evening classes only. A Master of Science (M.S.) in accounting and a Master of Public Administration degree are also available.

ADMISSION
Satisfactory completion of the Graduate Management Admission Test (GMAT) is a prerequisite to admission to the M.B.A. program. Students may be admitted for graduate study in business by achieving a total of at least 950 points based on the formula: 200 × undergraduate grade-point average (4.0) system + GMAT total score; or at least 1,000 points based on the formula: 200 × upper-division grade-point average (4.0) system + GMAT total score.

An applicant who has been out of school for four years or more and who does not satisfy the above criteria may enroll as a postbachelor student in a limited number of undergraduate courses. Such work shall not be counted for graduate credit. Upon satisfactory completion of such courses, and having attained a satisfactory score on the GMAT, the student may submit his or her record as evidence of ability to engage in graduate work. Such action does not obligate the school to admit the student to graduate study.

Applications must be received by the Admissions Office at least four weeks prior to the beginning of the semester.

EXPENSES
Incidental fee, per semester
Less than 12 hours,
per hour . . . . $ 63.15
Student center and activity fee (nonrefundable)
Ten or more credit hours. . . . 55.00
Less than 10 hours,
per hour 5.50
Out-of-state tuition fee
Fourteen or more semester
hours. 2,451.10
Twelve semester hours 2,108.80
Nine semester hours 1,589.85
Fees are subject to change.

FINANCIAL ASSISTANCE
The school offers students financial assistance in various forms, including scholarships, fellowships, and research assistantships. All scholarships and fellowships are awarded on the basis of scholastic merit. Loans are made to students in good standing on the basis of need. Applications should be submitted to the Financial Aids Office, 4825 Troost, Kansas City, MO 64110.

PLACEMENT
The School of Administration cooperates with the UMKC Placement Office, business firms, the U.S. Civil Service Commission, and various local associations and institutions in providing information and introductions for graduates seeking employment.

CORRESPONDENCE
For further information or to request an application for admission, please write or call
Academic Advising Office
School of Business and Public
Administration
University of Missouri—Kansas City
5110 Cherry
Kansas City, Missouri 64110
Telephone: 816-276-2215

The University of Missouri—St. Louis was established in 1963 as one of the four autonomous campuses of the University of Missouri system. The School of Business Administration was formed as an independent academic division in 1967 and began to offer a course of study leading to the Master of Business Administration (M.B.A.) degree in the fall of 1969. Initially, this graduate offering was directed toward the needs of the part-time evening student, although a full-time program began with the fall semester of 1971. The M.B.A. program is accredited by the American Assembly of Collegiate Schools of Business (AACSB). In 1981, degree programs in management information systems and accounting were added.

PROGRAMS OF STUDY

The university offers three graduate degree programs: the Master of Business Administration, the Master of Science in Management Information Systems, and the Master of Accounting. The M.B.A. degree program at the university provides a terminal professional management education. It is designed for those holding a four-year baccalaureate degree or its equivalent from accredited institutions, including those whose undergraduate education is in the sciences, humanities, or the arts.

The course of study provides exposure to the fundamental areas of management education in a 60-semester-hour or two-year program. There is no thesis requirement.

The following basic courses or their equivalent are required of all degree candidates:

	Hours
Financial Accounting Theory and Practice	3
Managerial Economic Analysis	3
Analysis of National Economic Environment	3
Public Policies toward Business	3
Financial Management	3
Organizational Behavior and Administrative Processes	3
Contemporary Marketing Concepts	3
Computer Programming and Applications	3
Statistical Analysis for Management Decisions	3
Operations Research Methods	3
Policy Formulation and Administration	3
Total credits for basic courses	33

Students are required to take at least three of the following required second-level courses:

Concepts in Management Accounting	3
Advanced Financial Management	3
Managing Human Resources	3
Marketing Planning and Strategy	3
Production and Operations Management	3
Total credits for second-level courses	9
Electives	18
Total M.B.A. program	60

The Master of Science in Management Information Systems (M.S. in M.I.S.) degree program requires a broad exposure both to the functional business areas and to the various managerial and analytical skills required in any organization. Building upon this foundation, a specialized program in computer-based management information is required. The overall objective of the program is to offer the student sufficient technical and managerial knowledge and skills to operate successfully in a computer-oriented environment.

The M.S. in M.I.S. program requires the same 33 hours of required core courses as the M.B.A. program. In addition, the following four courses are required:

Business Information Systems	3
Computer-Based Information Systems: Theory and Practice	3
Information System Design	3
Data Base Management Systems	3

Five more courses chosen primarily from a group of quantitative management science courses complete the 60-hour degree program.

The Master of Accounting (M.Acc.) program provides a fifth year of study in accounting and related business subjects. Although the 30-hour M.Acc. program is oriented toward the student with an undergraduate accounting major, the program will also be of interest to students with other backgrounds who want to prepare for a career in accounting. Such students must fulfill the equivalent of 36 credit hours of general business courses and 15 credit hours of advanced accounting background requirements prior to entering the program. The minimum requirements for the Master of Accounting degree consist of 30 credit hours of advanced accounting and business courses.

ADMISSION

To be eligible for admission, the student must hold a baccalaureate degree from an accredited college and must show high promise of academic success, as indicated by undergraduate grade-point average, scores on the Graduate Management Admission Test (GMAT), and rank in class.

EXPENSES

The fee for a resident of the state of Missouri is $68.83 per credit hour with a maximum charge per semester of $963.60. A nonresident taking more than six hours is subject to an additional nonresident tuition of $108.00 per credit hour with a maximum charge per semester of $2,475.60.

PLACEMENT

The services of the Career Planning and Placement Office are available to all graduate students and alumni. Representatives from numerous regional and national firms and governmental agencies visit the university each year to interview candidates for jobs in all sections of the country.

CORRESPONDENCE

An application for admission may be obtained by writing
Graduate Admissions
University of Missouri—St. Louis
8001 Natural Bridge Road
St. Louis, Missouri 63121

For additional information, write or call
Office of the Director of Graduate Studies in Business
School of Business Administration
University of Missouri—St. Louis
8001 Natural Bridge Road
St. Louis, Missouri 63121
Telephone: 314-553-5885

The University of Montana is the major university in the state, with a student body of 8,500. The School of Business Administration, founded in 1918, is the largest professional school of the University of Montana. The school is located on the main campus of the university near the computer facility. The Bureau of Business and Economic Research is under the administrative jurisdiction of the School of Business Administration and provides services for faculty and graduate student research.

PROGRAMS OF STUDY

The Master of Business Administration (M.B.A.) program leads to the professional management degree. The curriculum is composed of preprofessional and professional parts. Students without extensive experience or undergraduate work in business will be expected to enter a three-quarter preprofessional program. The preprofessional program includes course work in both tool and functional areas and is designed to provide the common body of knowledge needed prior to entering the professional part of the M.B.A. program. Previous appropriate academic course work or applicable experience may be substituted for any (or all) of the courses in the preprofessional program.

The M.B.A. professional (second-year) program has two parts: the first is a block of 12 required courses and the second is the completion of an option. Two options are available for completion of the Master of Business Administration, in addition to the required core:

• professional paper option—a professional paper for a minimum of 5 credits, plus elective courses, is required in addition to the 36 hours of core courses (the total requirement is 45 credit hours for the professional paper option);

• elective course work option—12 credit hours of approved elective courses are required in addition to the 36 hours of core courses, for a total of 48 credit hours (no more than 6 credits of the 48 may be in 300/400 level courses).

The Master of Accountancy (M.Acc.) program prepares the student for careers in public, private, and nonprofit accounting. For students who do not have an undergraduate degree in accounting, the requirements are as follows: all preprofessional courses (50 credits), required accounting classes taken for graduate credit (39 credits), and required management and finance classes (27 credits). Students must also pass a comprehensive exit exam. For students who have an undergraduate degree in accounting the requirements include all preprofessional courses (if not already taken as an undergraduate), all required accounting classes (if not already taken), all required finance and management classes, a thesis in an accounting subject (6 credits), and an approved accounting elective to make up a total of 45 graduate credits.

ADMISSION

Students admitted to the Graduate School must hold a bachelor's degree from a regionally accredited college or university. Admission to graduate study in business administration requires evidence of ability and aptitude based on undergraduate scholastic performance and scores on the Graduate Management Admission Test (GMAT).

EXPENSES

Estimated expenses, per quarter:

Fees (resident)	$ 383
Board and room	800
Books and supplies	200
Total, Montana resident	$1,383
Fees (nonresident)	588

FINANCIAL ASSISTANCE

A number of graduate assistantships and fellowships are available each year, including nine-month stipends of $4,750 and the remission of most fees. In some instances, part-time instructorships are awarded to exceptional students with remuneration related to teaching load. Various loan funds and a limited number of waivers of nonresident fees are also available to eligible applicants. Occasionally, privately endowed or federal research grants are awarded to graduate students in connection with the research for their professional papers.

PLACEMENT

Representatives from numerous national and regional firms and government agencies visit the Career Planning and Placement Services annually to interview qualified graduates for various types of positions.

CORRESPONDENCE

For additional information or to request an application for admission, write or call
Director of Graduate Studies
School of Business Administration
University of Montana
Missoula, Montana 59812
Telephone: 406-243-4831

UNIVERSITY OF NEBRASKA AT OMAHA

OMAHA, NEBRASKA

The University of Nebraska at Omaha offers programs leading to the following degrees: Master of Business Administration (M.B.A.), the Master of Professional Accounting (M.P.A.), and the Master of Arts and Master of Science in Economics (M.A./M.S.). To accommodate students holding full-time positions, courses are offered only during evening hours.

PROGRAMS OF STUDY

The Master of Business Administration degree program is designed to provide educational experience for students who wish to assume positions of responsibility in business. M.B.A. students must complete a minimum of 36 hours of graduate-level courses. The following are required: managerial economics, human behavior in organizations, quantitative analysis, managerial accounting, business and society, and policy, planning, and strategy. Twelve hours of concentration are taken in one of the following: business administration, marketing, real estate, management, banking and finance, economics, decision sciences, or industrial psychology. Six hours of approved electives are also included. A thesis is required in one option (real estate). The M.B.A. program is accredited by the American Assembly of Collegiate Schools of Business (AACSB).

The Master of Professional Accounting program provides a graduate-level education as a basis for a career in professional accounting. The program is broad-based in order to prepare graduates for careers in public, private, and not-for-profit organizations.

The Master of Arts program in economics consists of core courses in theory and quantitative methods, an elective specialization, and a thesis. The Master of Science program in economics consists of a similar core in theory and quantitative methods, an elected specialization, and free electives, but no thesis. Both programs require a comprehensive examination in the area of specialization.

ADMISSION

An applicant must hold a bachelor's degree from an accredited institution to be considered for admission. An official transcript must be provided showing all undergraduate and graduate credit earned by the student. Appropriate undergraduate preparation is required by each program, although deficiencies can be made up upon admission. The Graduate Management Admission Test (GMAT) is required for admission to the M.B.A. and M.P.A. programs, and the Graduate Record Examinations (GRE) are required by the first semester of enrollment in the M.A. and M.S. programs. Foreign applicants are also required to submit official Test of English as a Foreign Language (TOEFL) scores.

EXPENSES

Costs are estimated for the 1985-86 academic year. Tuition and fee assessments are subject to change without notice.

	Nebraska Resident	Nonresident
Application fee	$10.00	$ 10.00
Tuition, per credit hour	54.25	129.50
Fees (12 credit hours or more per semester)	54.25	54.25
Fees (Less than 12 credit hours per semester)	33.00	33.00

FINANCIAL ASSISTANCE

Graduate assistantships, which include tuition remission and a monthly stipend, are available.

PLACEMENT

Services of a full-time placement office are available to all graduate students.

CORRESPONDENCE

For further information, please write or call

M.B.A. Program Director
University of Nebraska at Omaha
Omaha, Nebraska 68182
Telephone: 402-554-2597

UNIVERSITY OF NEBRASKA—LINCOLN

LINCOLN, NEBRASKA

The University of Nebraska—Lincoln is the original and largest of the three campuses of the University of Nebraska system. In the fall of 1985, 24,000 students enrolled in classes on the Lincoln campus. The College of Business Administration was established in 1919 and began to offer a Master of Arts (M.A.) degree in 1923. Doctor of Philosophy (Ph.D.) programs in business and economics were started in 1932; the Master of Business Administration (M.B.A.) program was added in 1966; and the Master of Professional Accountancy (M.P.A.) in 1983. There are currently 400 students enrolled in these graduate degree programs.

The university is located in the state's capital city of Lincoln which has a population of approximately 166,400. The university and the city of Lincoln provide a full range of educational, cultural, and business opportunities.

The College of Business Administration is an equal opportunity employer.

PROGRAMS OF STUDY

The College of Business Administration offers programs of study leading to the Master of Business Administration, Master of Arts, Master of Professional Accountancy, Master of Business Administration-Juris Doctorate (M.B.A.-J.D.), and Doctor of Philosophy degrees in business administration.

The M.B.A. degree program is a broadly based, structured program intended to give the student exposure to management skills as well as to the various functional components of business administration. This program is primarily designed for those individuals who expect to pursue careers in the management of both private- and public-sector organizations. Students are expected to complete a number of courses to satisfy the Common Body of Knowledge (CBK). This consists of 24 hours of graduate credit in selected courses from the departments of economics, finance, management, and marketing, and the School of Accountancy. (A course in calculus must also be completed.) Students with no previous course work to fulfill the CBK would be required to complete a 60-hour program consisting of 24 hours of CBK courses, 21 hours of core requirements, and 15 hours of electives. Students whose previous background completely satisfies the CBK would have a 36-hour program consisting of 21 hours of core requirements and 15 hours of electives. The core requirement section con-

sists of managerial courses in accounting, economics, and finance; marketing management; management theory and practice; decision science; and administration policy and practice. The 15 hours of electives may be completed in an area of concentration or by selecting a combination of graduate electives offered by the Business Interdepartmental Area.

Students who are interested in pursuing a career in corporate law, general law practice, government regulation, business management, or other business-related fields, should consider the M.B.A.-J.D. program. The first year of course work consists of law courses. The second, third, and fourth years of schooling consist of the 21 hours of M.B.A. core courses, 9 hours of electives, and 51 hours of upper-class law courses.

The M.A. degree program, on the other hand, is characterized by flexibility and specialization within a particular field. In addition to completing the CBK courses, the student develops a program in consultation with a faculty adviser consisting of either 30 hours of course work (with thesis) or 36 hours of course work (without thesis). Students who wish to pursue the M.A. degree will normally have a bachelor's degree in business administration from a recognized college of business. Areas of specialization include banking, business history, finance, insurance, investments, management information systems, marketing, organization and management theory, management science, organizational behavior, personnel and labor relations, production, promotion, and strategic policy and planning. Students interested in the accounting field should consider the Master of Professional Accountancy program.

The Ph.D. program requires 90 hours beyond the bachelor's degree, 45 of which must be completed at the University of Nebraska. Approximately 18 of the total 90 hours required are allowed for the dissertation. Neither the courses carried nor the time spent in study determines the granting of the degree. The Ph.D. degree is given primarily for high attainment in specialized fields of scholarship and for demonstrated power of independent research. The majority of graduates from the Ph.D. program pursue careers in university teaching and research.

ADMISSION

The basic requirements for admission include a baccalaureate degree from an accredited college or university, an undergraduate record of approximately B, and satisfactory scores on the Graduate Management Admission Test (GMAT). These admission requirements are established for all graduate programs.

Applicants are expected to apply for admission at least 90 days prior to the date on which they intend to enter. Such admission will be considered only if applicants are able to submit transcripts of undergraduate work and scores on the Graduate Management Admission Test.

EXPENSES

Tuition for residents of Nebraska is $54.25 per credit hour. Nonresidents pay $129.50 per credit hour. Housing is available both on and off campus at varying costs. For information concerning on-campus housing (apartments and dormitories), applicants are requested to contact the Housing Office of the university.

FINANCIAL ASSISTANCE

A limited number of fellowships are available for graduate programs in general.

Most doctoral students receive teaching assistantships. Research assistantships are usually available to some M.A. and Ph.D. students through either the Bureau of Business Research or individual faculty research projects.

PLACEMENT

The services of the Career Planning and Placement Center on campus are available to all graduate students and alumni. Representatives from all types of business firms and governmental agencies visit the university each year to interview candidates for jobs in all sections of the country.

CORRESPONDENCE

For further information, please write or call

Director of Advising
College of Business Administration
University of Nebraska—Lincoln
Lincoln, Nebraska 68588-0405
Telephone: 402-472-2310

In 1957, the University of Nevada, Las Vegas (UNLV) constructed its first building on a 60-acre plot of desert and opened its doors to a pioneer class of 300 students. Enrollment today stands at more than 11,000. Students attend classes at an attractive 300-acre campus in one of the newest sections of metropolitan Las Vegas.

PROGRAMS OF STUDY
The primary objective of the evening Master of Business Administration (M.B.A.) program at UNLV, which the College of Business and Economics offers through the Graduate College, is to provide an opportunity for qualified men and women to develop knowledge, abilities, and attitudes that will constitute a firm and broad foundation for their growth as effective and creative leaders in business, government, and related organizations. A balanced program of learning is the goal of UNLV's program. It embraces no one teaching method or approach but uses that combination of methods suited to the objectives of each stage of the program.

The M.B.A. program for students holding baccalaureates in fields other than business is basically a two-year course of study for the full-time student. The first year of the program normally consists of preparatory courses designed to ready the student for the required advanced core courses. The total program will vary, depending upon the background of the student, up to a total of 58 credit hours.

The student who begins the program with a baccalaureate in business and who needs no preparatory courses has a 30-hour program, which a full-time student can complete in one year. The 30-hour program consists of the seven required advanced core courses (21 hours) and three approved electives (9 credits). Students interested in concentrating in a specific area may choose from accounting, economics, finance, management, or marketing.

The Master of Science (M.S.) in accountancy requires a minimum of 30 credit hours above the bachelor's degree. A minimum of 18 hours must be in accounting, exclusive of the thesis. All students are required to take MGT 560, Organization Theory; ACC 581, Seminar in Accounting; and ACC 503, Federal Taxes and Decision Making. Each student's program of study is personally tailored to meet his or her individual goals. There are several options

available. The student may elect to write a thesis or elect to take a sequence of courses in federal taxation. Normally it will not be possible to complete this program in a one-year period.

The Master of Public Administration (M.P.A.) program is designed to meet the needs of professional public administrators. It is a 36-semester-hour program, which includes courses in public administration and management.

The Master of Arts (M.A.) in economics, which the College of Business and Economics offers through the Graduate College, is supervised by the Department of Economics. Candidates must complete 30 semester credits. The M.A. program consists of a minimum of 21 credits in 500-level courses, which includes 6 credits of thesis. Students must pass a comprehensive examination upon the completion of course requirements and thesis.

ADMISSION
To be eligible for admission to the M.B.A. or M.S. in accountancy programs, students must have a baccalaureate degree from an approved college or university with a total of at least 950 points based on the formula: 200 × the overall grade-point average (GPA) plus the Graduate Management Admission Test (GMAT) score; or at least 1,000 points based on the formula: 200 × the upper-division GPA plus the GMAT score.

Admission to the M.P.A. program requires a B average in an acceptable field of undergraduate study and a satisfactory score on the GMAT (450 points) or the Graduate Record Examinations (900 points on the verbal and quantitative sections).

Applicants for the Master of Arts in economics should have a baccalaureate with a major in economics. Students lacking necessary credits in economics may be admitted after they have removed these deficiencies as determined by their adviser. Applicants must have a 3.0 or higher GPA in their undergraduate studies or have a total score of 1,500 points on the verbal, quantitative, and advanced economics sections of the Graduate Record Examinations.

Foreign students must have a minimum of 550 points on the Test of English as a Foreign Language (TOEFL).

The deadlines for submitting applications are June 15 for the fall, November 15 for the spring, and April 15 for either summer term. Applications are available upon request from the Graduate College.

EXPENSES
Graduate students are assessed fees of $41 per credit hour, and nonresidents pay an additional $1,100 per semester. The university does not provide living facilities, but there are numerous apartment complexes nearby.

FINANCIAL ASSISTANCE
Graduate assistantships, available to selected students, normally provide sufficient funds to cover the minimum expenses of an unmarried student, permitting full-time academic effort. Assistants receive a stipend of $5,000 plus a tuition waiver. Applications must be filed by March 1 for the following academic year. Off-campus employment opportunities are also readily available.

PLACEMENT
About 185 companies and organizations come to the campus annually to recruit students.

CORRESPONDENCE
Address correspondence to
Dr. James F. Adams, Dean
The Graduate College
University of Nevada, Las Vegas
Las Vegas, Nevada 89154

The University of Nevada, Reno (UNR), founded in 1874, is a land-grant institution which offers an opportunity for higher education to qualified applicants regardless of race, sex, or social status. The main campus is located on rolling hills north of the main Reno business district overlooking the picturesque expanses of the Truckee Meadows.

Reno is a small and energetic city with a metropolitan area population of about 200,000. Contrast best marks the city of Reno, for the much-publicized "White Way" often focuses attention away from the city's importance as a center of retail and wholesale trade and as an active participant in farming, ranching, mining, and summer and winter sports. Per capita personal income in Nevada is one of the highest in the nation. The city enjoys a rapidly maturing economy, an impressive rate of growth, and a dry, moderate climate distinctly marked by the seasons.

Culture is also a part of life in Reno, as art, music, and drama groups provide frequent accomplished productions to the city and university community. Within only a few miles are found unique mixtures of mountain, desert, lake, sun, and snow for nearly all recreational interests.

Bachelor's and master's degree programs of the College of Business Administration are accredited by the American Assembly of Collegiate Schools of Business (AACSB), and the University of Nevada is accredited by the Northwest Association. The graduate programs of the college provide the opportunity for small classes and close individual counseling with the teaching staff. Students enjoy the congenial atmosphere of a small, yet modern, university.

PROGRAM OF STUDY
The Master of Business Administration (M.B.A.) degree is offered by the College of Business Administration. The program is fully self-contained at the graduate level and totals 60 semester credits for those electing the thesis option or 63 credits for the nonthesis plan. As many as 30 credits of foundation courses may be waived for students who feel they have sufficient undergraduate preparation to pass a proficiency examination in the elementary subjects. These basic courses are designed to provide a broad conceptual background in accounting, business statistics, computer information systems, economics, finance, management, marketing, operations management, and ancillary topics, primarily for those students who do not hold a recent business baccalaureate degree. Students with undergraduate degrees in fields other than business comprise 60 percent of the current enrollment.

The UNR M.B.A. degree program requires advanced course work—much of it case-oriented—in all of the major business subjects and strategic management policy. Students may undertake limited specialization in a specific discipline, since four electives are required as part of the nonthesis option.

Approximately 40 percent of the student body is enrolled full time; the remainder attend part time while pursuing careers. All core courses are offered in the evenings Monday through Thursday.

ADMISSION
Applicants must have a baccalaureate degree from an accredited institution with a satisfactory combination of undergraduate grade-point average and scores on the Graduate Management Admission Test (GMAT). Foreign applicants also are required to submit official Test of English as a Foreign Language (TOEFL) scores. Over two thirds of the master's students have at least one year of full-time work or military experience. Applications are accepted for the fall term only and must be submitted by July 1.

EXPENSES
The registration fee for graduate courses is $41 per semester credit. In addition, nonresidents registered for seven or more credits pay $1,100 tuition per semester. (All subject to change.)

A limited number of modest apartments are available for married students on a first-come, first-served basis. Rooms and apartments are available in private accommodations in the vicinity of the campus. The cost of board and room in university residence halls is $1,060 per semester (subject to change).

FINANCIAL ASSISTANCE
A limited number of graduate assistantships are awarded each year to promising Nevada and out-of-state students. Assistants may be assigned to work a total of 20 hours each week (with a stipend of $5,000 per year) in the Bureau of Business and Economic Research or assisting instructors in research or laboratories. Graduate assistants receive a waiver of most registration and tuition fees, in addition to the stipend.

PLACEMENT
The graduate placement office offers assistance to students seeking part-time or full-time employment. Recruiting schedules include national and local businesses, government agencies, and institutions.

CORRESPONDENCE
For further information or to request an application for admission, write or call

Director of Graduate Programs
College of Business Administration
University of Nevada, Reno
Reno, Nevada 89557-0016
Telephone: 702-784-4912

The Whittemore School of Business and Economics, established in 1962, offers programs leading to undergraduate and graduate degrees in business administration and economics. The school is one of the six schools and colleges of the University of New Hampshire, which was founded in 1866. The university has an enrollment of about 10,500, over 1,000 of whom are graduate students.

Located 60 miles north of Boston, the university is a cultural and scientific center encompassing such service activities as the New England Center for Continuing Education, the Resources Development Center, the Space Science Center, and the Paul Arts Center.

The Whittemore School program leading to the degree of Master of Business Administration (M.B.A.) is designed to prepare its graduates for professional administrative careers in industrial and other organizations in a rapidly changing world. It provides knowledge and understanding of management principles and practices through study of the increasing body of relevant knowledge drawn from the behavioral sciences, mathematics, and economics, and through study of the functional fields of business and the role of business and other organizations in a complex society.

A close association with industry, government, and other educational institutions is encouraged. An active concern for current social issues is maintained through the school's involvement in research and consulting with industry and other institutions throughout the country. The school encourages close cooperation with related academic disciplines at the University of New Hampshire and other educational institutions.

PROGRAM OF STUDY

The program consists of an integrated sequence of required and elective courses which takes two years of full-time study. Applicants may enroll in the program only in the fall semester.

In the first year, the curriculum consists of required courses designed to build a base of understanding and analytical competence. The common course schedule followed during this first year also provides an opportunity for students to work together in groups; this emphasis reflects work in organizations that often requires group decision making, and it also fosters a significant degree of class cohesiveness. The Whittemore faculty numbers close to

50 and the current M.B.A. student body about 100, equally divided between the first- and second-year classes. An executive M.B.A. program was established in January 1978 to provide the same course content to qualified employees in area industry. The relatively small size of each M.B.A. class contributes to close, informal relationships among students and between students and faculty.

During the second year of the M.B.A. program, students complete two required courses and a complement of elective courses. The required courses in the second year give special attention to the integration and application of the student's studies to the development of overall management policy for an organization. Through the use of appropriate elective courses, the student may design the second year of study to fit his or her individual career goals. In addition to advanced courses in the various fields of business, students are encouraged to select electives from the economics curriculum and, where appropriate to individual career objectives, from graduate courses offered by other departments of the university. New concentrations in health administration and hotel management will begin in 1986. Independent study and field internships are encouraged.

ADMISSION

The Whittemore School welcomes applicants with above-average academic records in any undergraduate specialty other than business administration. Because of the increasing use of mathematical concepts, models, and notation in the practice and study of administration, applicants should normally have successfully completed one year of college mathematics through an introduction to calculus or be willing to do so before entering. In all cases, the applicant's entire educational background, relevant experience, references, and professional aims will be considered in the admission process.

Candidates for admission must possess a bachelor's degree from an accredited college or university. Scores on the Graduate Management Admission Test (GMAT) will be considered in conjunction with averages and trends in the candidate's academic record.

EXPENSES

Tuition for the day M.B.A. program for the first and second years is $2,180 for New Hampshire residents. Nonresident tuition for the first and second years is $6,050.

FINANCIAL ASSISTANCE

Students whose academic backgrounds and career interests fit the Whittemore School M.B.A. program, but who are deterred from applying because of financial need, are encouraged to submit applications for financial aid through the Graduate School. Applicants with strong academic records may qualify for appointment and service as graduate assistants. Graduate assistants receive a stipend of $2,500 per academic year plus waiver of one-half tuition and fees at the in-state rate.

PLACEMENT

The employment services of the Placement Office are available to all degree candidates who have completed at least 12 semester hours of work toward their degree. In addition to receiving recruiters from industrial, business, and governmental concerns on campus, the Placement Office is able to forward, on request, a placement registrant's papers to any potential employer.

CORRESPONDENCE

Inquiries should be addressed to
  Assistant Dean
  Whittemore School of Business and
    Economics
  Box G
  University of New Hampshire
  Durham, New Hampshire 03824
  Telephone: 603-862-1981

The Robert O. Anderson School of Business and Administrative Sciences was established at The University of New Mexico (UNM) in 1947; The Robert O. Anderson Graduate School of Management achieved accreditation of its bachelor's and master's degree programs by the American Assembly of Collegiate Schools of Business (AACSB) in 1975 and independent status with UNM in 1977. Graduate enrollment in the school is approximately 400 men and women, permitting a close relationship between students and faculty.

PROGRAMS OF STUDY

As the name of the school is intended to stress, the Anderson School of Management at The University of New Mexico is committed to an effective integration of the administrative sciences and the professional skills and personal values essential for management leadership in business, government, or service organizations. The school's programs, therefore, emphasize conceptual frameworks that link normative and empirical administrative theory with interdisciplinary contributions from the physical, biological, and social sciences. Team teaching, computer simulations, in-depth tutorials, field research, and internship programs are utilized to achieve the essential integration of management scholarship and professional practice in a diversity of areas.

The Master of Business Administration (M.B.A.) degree may be based on a bachelor's degree in any discipline. The curriculum consists of a two-year (60 semester credit hours) program. The first-year core program encompasses the basic areas of managerial economics, accounting and managerial information systems, quantitative methods, organizational behavior, organizational ecology, and organizational intelligence systems. Students who have recently completed an undergraduate program in business may be able to have a portion of the first-year core waived.

The second-year program consists of 5 required courses plus 15 hours of electives which may be used to specialize in a chosen area or to obtain additional breadth. Electives may be taken in courses offered by the school or in other graduate departments of the university. Areas of concentration offered include management science, management information systems,

organizational economics and environment, marketing management, human resources management, accounting, financial management, tax accounting, and international management.

Joint programs with the other colleges and departments are available leading to the M.B.A. with Juris Doctor (J.D.), Master of Science (M.S.) in nuclear engineering, and a Master of Arts (M.A.) in Latin American studies. In August 1984, the Anderson Schools began offering an M.S. in accounting.

A Doctor of Philosophy (Ph.D.) program in international management emphasizing Latin America was begun in 1974.

ADMISSION

Application for admission should be made to the Anderson Graduate School of Management. Admission to the M.B.A. program is based upon a record of sound scholarship and promise of development. Students from any discipline are admitted to the program, and no courses in business administration are required.

Applicants must also submit their scores on the Graduate Management Admission Test (GMAT) and a statement of purpose and are invited to have letters of recommendation sent to the school.

Students are admitted for either the fall term beginning in late August or the spring term beginning in mid-January. A summer session of eight weeks is also available. Those wishing to enter in the fall should submit applications no later than July 1; those for the spring term by November 15; for the summer session by April 15.

EXPENSES

Per semester,
exclusive of

summer session	Resident	Nonresident
Tuition and fees, credit hour	$ 34	$ 116
Health and accident insurance	50	50
Books and supplies	250	250
Board and room	1,200	1,200
Clothing, laundry, etc.	800	800

FINANCIAL ASSISTANCE

Financial assistance is available through several channels:
- graduate assistantships carrying a stipend of $4,950 are available to a limited number of qualified students;
- a limited number of scholarships are provided in varying amounts, and the number is being expanded as financial resources are available;
- loan funds are available through the National Direct Student Loans and a state-sponsored program;
- internships are arranged for qualified students with local business firms which enable the student to work part time and receive up to three hours credit per semester;
- students with outstanding scholarship records are eligible for university fellowships;
- the university assists in providing employment in the resident halls, libraries, and laboratories.

PLACEMENT

The university maintains a full-scale placement center visited annually by representatives of large numbers of companies from all sections of the United States. The school also acts as a referral center for handling requests from prospective employers.

CORRESPONDENCE

For further information or to request an application for admission, please write or call

Sue Podeyn
Director, Graduate Student Affairs
The Robert O. Anderson Graduate
 School of Management
The University of New Mexico
Albuquerque, New Mexico 87131
Telephone: 505-277-3147

The University of New Orleans, a member of the Louisiana State University System, is located on the shores of Lake Pontchartrain in an attractive residential area that is convenient to the financial, commercial, and port sections of the city of New Orleans. The university was founded in 1958 and was originally named "Louisiana State University in New Orleans."

The university has an enrollment of over 16,000 students, including approximately 2,700 students in the College of Business Administration. Special facilities include the Division of Business and Economic Research, the Center for Economic Development, and the University Computer Research Center.

PROGRAMS OF STUDY

At the graduate level, the College of Business Administration offers programs leading to the Master of Business Administration (M.B.A.), Master of Arts (M.A.) in economics, Master of Science (M.S.) in accounting, Master of Science in accounting (taxation option), and Doctor of Philosophy (Ph.D.) in financial economics degrees. The M.B.A. degree program was begun in 1964 and currently has over 300 students. The M.A. in economics program was started in 1967. The M.S. in accounting program was initiated in 1970 with a taxation option being added in 1979. The Ph.D. in financial economics program was begun in 1984. The M.B.A. and M.S. programs are accredited by the American Assembly of Collegiate Schools of Business (AACSB).

The M.B.A. degree program is designed to give students a broad preparation in business administration while allowing for some concentration in specific business areas. The program is designed to satisfy the needs of students with undergraduate degrees in areas other than business administration as well as those with business administration degrees. For students lacking sufficient preparatory studies in business, a series of foundation courses is available to provide the background needed for the successful study of business at the graduate level. Students who hold undergraduate degrees in business usually have satisfied all or most of the foundation course requirements. Exclusive of foundation courses, the program contains a minimum of 33 semester hours (21 of which are required courses).

The Master of Science in accounting program prepares students for careers in public, industrial, and governmental accounting. It also serves as a foundation for doctoral study. The program is open to students with undergraduate degrees in areas other than accounting as well as those with accounting degrees. A preparatory program is available to students with inadequate or no preparation in accounting. Both thesis and nonthesis options are offered. The taxation option (a nonthesis option) prepares persons for positions as tax specialists.

The Master of Arts in economics program contains both thesis and nonthesis options. The program contains an environmental concentration and an international concentration.

ADMISSION

A satisfactory score on the Graduate Management Admission Test (GMAT) and an acceptable undergraduate average are required for admission to either the M.B.A. program or the M.S. in accounting program.

For admission to the master's program in economics a combined score of at least 1,000 on the verbal and quantitative parts of the Graduate Record Examinations (GRE) is required.

Applicants whose native language is not English must achieve an acceptable score on the Test of English as a Foreign Language (TOEFL). However, the TOEFL requirement may be waived if the applicant has earned a degree in a country where English is the principal language.

EXPENSES

Fees for full-time graduate students who are Louisiana residents are $612 per semester, for non-Louisiana residents, $1,175 per semester. Fees for part-time enrollment and for summer-term enrollment are proportionately lower. Dormitory rooms are $620 a semester (double occupancy) and $300 a summer term. Married student apartments rent for $275 per month for one bedroom and $325 per month for two bedrooms.

FINANCIAL ASSISTANCE

A limited number of graduate assistantships involving half-time work assignments are available in the Division of Business and Economic Research, the Center for Economic Development, and in the various academic departments of the College of Business Administration.

PLACEMENT

The University Career Placement Office assists students in finding employment. Major corporations, accounting firms, and government agencies regularly schedule recruiting interviews on the campus.

CORRESPONDENCE

For further information or to request an application for admission, please write or call

Coordinator of Graduate Business
  Programs
College of Business Administration
University of New Orleans
Lakefront
New Orleans, Louisiana 70148
Telephone: 504-286-6393

The University of New South Wales has provided graduate-level university education in business administration since 1963. The original programs were offered by the School of Business Administration and later by the Graduate School of Business.

The Australian Graduate School of Management (AGSM) was established in response to the findings of the Committee of Inquiry into Postgraduate Education for Management, established in 1969 by the Australian Government under the chairmanship of Dr. Richard M. Cyert.

The AGSM's basic goal is to enhance the effectiveness of Australian professional management now and in the future and to foster, in appropriate ways, the development of management education elsewhere, particularly in Australia's neighboring countries. As a national school, the AGSM is charged with offering programs comparable in quality with those of business/management schools of international standing.

In 1981 the AGSM moved to its permanent home on the campus of the University of New South Wales. The new AGSM building provides facilities needed for a national management school, with 5 lecture theaters, 11 syndicate and tutorial rooms, a library containing the most comprehensive collection of management information in Australia, the school's own computer installation, common rooms, and dining facilities. It incorporates the Rupert Myers Hall of Residence, a 43-room residential complex for participants in the school's executive courses.

PROGRAM OF STUDY

The Master of Business Administration (M.B.A.) is a generalist degree, designed to train managers rather than specialists. The M.B.A. program gives students a grounding in several distinctly different disciplines, each contributing its own perspective on management. The program encourages students to develop a general management outlook on various aspects of an organization's performance and the environment within which it operates.

The M.B.A. program at AGSM is a two-year, full-time degree, which will bring to students a number of disciplines and professional techniques essential to the efficient and effective manager. Thus equipped, the successful M.B.A. graduate will continue to grow—personally, professionally, and intellectually.

The first term of the first year is devoted to the single subject, Management Foundations and Perspectives (MFP). This subject is taken by all M.B.A. students without exemption or substitution.

MFP is presently taught in five parallel streams—Accounting, Data Analysis, Organizational Behavior, Management in Society, and Markets and Command Structures. In addition, students are expected to become effective users of the computer facilities of the school.

In the remaining two terms of the first year, students undertake a spread of subjects that provides several different exposures to key management subjects and skills. Students must satisfy a "Distribution Requirement," that is, to complete at least one subject in at least six different fields.

In the second year of the program, students choose subjects that build upon the skills developed in the first year. Every student is required to undertake a sequence of two subjects in the field of general management, which form strong integrative links across various management skills or disciplines. The AGSM operates on a three-term academic year. Students enroll in four subjects per term.

ADMISSION

Admission is open to anyone holding a bachelor's degree, in any field, from an approved undergraduate institution who has worked for at least two years. Work experience is not necessary if a four-year degree has been completed. In exceptional cases, an applicant may be admitted without a degree if he or she has achieved acceptable general and professional attainments.

The Graduate Management Admission Test (GMAT) is required of all applicants. Selection is based on the applicant's academic record, score on the GMAT, evaluation of referees' reports, and employment experience.

Applications for admission to the program should be filed with the AGSM by November 30 and should be accompanied by a detailed official transcript of university studies. Overseas applicants should check initially with an Australian Diplomatic Office regarding visa requirements.

Applicants should take the Graduate Management Admission Test no later than October and arrange to have their scores reported directly to AGSM. Applications are considered progressively, and applicants are advised within one month after receipt of all necessary information. The program begins in March.

EXPENSES

No tuition fees are payable. All students are required by the university to pay student activities fees (approximately $240 Australian per year). Living expenses vary with the choice of housing and the circumstances of the student.

Overseas students, except New Zealand citizens, are required to pay a visa fee, currently $3,500 per year.

FINANCIAL ASSISTANCE

Details of scholarships and fellowships available (including Commonwealth Postgraduate Course Awards) may be obtained from AGSM.

CORRESPONDENCE

For further information or to request an application for admission, write or call

The Admissions Officer
Australian Graduate School of
Management
The University of New South Wales
P.O. Box 1
Kensington, New South Wales 2033
Australia
Telephone: Sydney (02) 662-0300

The University of North Alabama is a state-owned institution operated under the direction of a Board of Trustees. Major purposes of the institution include the pre-professional and professional preparation of students in a variety of fields in the arts and sciences, business, education, social work, and nursing and allied health science.

The university occupies a beautiful campus of 80 acres in a residential section of Florence, Alabama. With a population of 37,000, Florence, located just north of the Tennessee River, is the largest city in a four-city area that includes Tuscumiba, Sheffield, and Muscle Shoals City, all located south of the river.

Abundant electrical power provided by the Tennessee Valley Authority and the navigation provided by the Tennessee River combined with fine highway and rail transportation make the area one of the most rapidly developing industrial areas in the South. In addition to the world-renowned Tennessee Valley Authority, a representative sampling of industries in the area would include manufacturers of textiles, chemicals, boats, automotive parts, metals, and rubber products.

PROGRAM OF STUDY
The primary objective of the Master of Business Administration (M.B.A.) program at the University of North Alabama is to provide students with a broad professional education that will prepare them for responsible positions in business, government, and education. The courses offered at the M.B.A. level were chosen to meet this objective. The degree requirements ensure that the student will have training in several areas including accounting, finance, marketing, economics, management, and decision theory. Nine hours of elective courses will allow the student to have an area of concentration if desired.

The program, consisting primarily of evening courses, is structured so that a student with a baccalaureate degree in a business-related field (management, marketing, economics, finance, accounting, etc.) may complete requirements for the Master of Business Administration degree with a minimum of 30 semester hours. Students with degrees in other disciplines will need to complete a program of prerequisites designed to provide a common body of knowledge in business administration prior to admission to the M.B.A. program.

ADMISSION
Admission to the program is open to graduates of accredited colleges and universities who show high promise of success in postgraduate business study. In evaluating a student's application for admission, primary emphasis will be given to undergraduate record and test scores on the Graduate Management Admission Test. Students whose native language is not English must submit acceptable scores on the Test of English as a Foreign Language (TOEFL). The applicant's extracurricular activities, employment experience, and other evidences of maturation for graduate study will also be considered.

EXPENSES
Tuition for graduate credit is $46 per credit hour or a maximum of $550 per semester. The cost of room and board for university dormitories is $960 per semester.

FINANCIAL ASSISTANCE
A limited number of assistantships and part-time employment plans are available to University of North Alabama students. The university has a full-time Office of Financial Aid.

PLACEMENT
The university maintains its own Placement Office, visited annually by representatives from a large variety of companies. The Placement Office also offers its services to interested alumni.

CORRESPONDENCE
Address correspondence relating to admission to
   Dean, School of Business
   University of North Alabama
   Florence, Alabama 35632-0001

Graduate School of Business Administration
THE UNIVERSITY OF NORTH CAROLINA AT CHAPEL HILL
CHAPEL HILL, NORTH CAROLINA

The first state university to open its doors to students, The University of North Carolina began instruction in 1795. Now more than 21,000 students are enrolled in its nationally recognized graduate and undergraduate programs.

The Graduate School of Business Administration offers a Master of Business Administration (M.B.A.) program with 325 students and a Doctor of Philosophy (Ph.D.) program with 60 resident students. Facilities for the advanced degree programs include specially designed seminar rooms and classrooms, computer facilities, and a reading room. Dormitories for single graduate students and apartments for married students are maintained on the campus.

PROGRAMS OF STUDY
At Chapel Hill, M.B.A. education is distinguished by the underlying premise that effective study of management requires viewing the organization as an integrated whole rather than as a series of separate, but related, components. Believing that traditional approaches to business education have centered too firmly in a tightly structured sequence of courses in business functions and tools, the school has restructured its curriculum to present subject matter in a more integrated and flexible form.

Students are encouraged to consider basic systems of management as they relate to all functions in the organization. Analytical tools are introduced in the context of their varied cross-functional applications. The organization is also considered in its social-economic-political setting and, finally, as a composite of individuals with varied motivations, personal needs, and productive capacities.

To achieve the desired perspective, cases are emphasized which relate decisions to multiple phases of the firm. This perspective is reinforced through individual and team research projects, written and oral reports, computer simulation, field work in actual organizational situations, and seminars with business leaders. The student's personal development is emphasized.

Electives in the second year provide opportunities for concentration in one or two areas of special interest or for continued broad exposure. A concentration in professional accounting is offered in the second year, and a joint M.B.A./Juris Doctor (J.D.) program is available. Second-year M.B.A. students have access to courses in other departments of the university—such as city and regional planning, operations research, public health—and to more technical doctoral courses. Thesis and foreign language requirements have been removed to permit greater attention to the integration of subjects. Full-time residence is required in the fall and spring semester of each year, and work experience is encouraged in the intervening summer.

For students interested in international business, an exchange program with the Instituto de Estudios Superiores de Administration (IESA) in Caracas, Venezuela, offers an opportunity to spend a semester in a distinguished South American management program. The school also participates in the Washington Campus, a 12-university program that sponsors an intensive summer session on government-business relations in Washington, D.C.

ADMISSION
Applicants for admission must submit (1) a completed application form, (2) transcripts of all college-level work showing the satisfactory completion of a bachelor's degree, (3) scores on the required Graduate Management Admission Test (GMAT), and (4) three recommendations on forms provided with the application. Interviews are encouraged and may be required. Admission is based upon test scores, the quality of the transcript rather than the subject of the undergraduate major, and demonstrated potential for responsible leadership. The Test of English as a Foreign Language (TOEFL) is required for foreign applicants. The M.B.A. program strongly emphasizes work experience after college graduation in selecting candidates. Average age of entering M.B.A. students is 26. Recently, about half of the class has come from North Carolina and half from out of state. Students are admitted in the fall semester only. Early application is encouraged. The Admissions Committee begins notifying applicants in November. Applications received after April 1 are considered on the basis of available space.

The university does not discriminate against applicants, students, or employees based on race, color, national origin, religion, sex, age, or handicap. Moreover, the university is open to people of all races and actively seeks to promote racial integration by recruiting and enrolling a larger number of Black students.

EXPENSES
Tuition and fees in 1985-86 were $855 for the academic year (two semesters) for residents of North Carolina and $3,775 for nonresidents. Books and supplies cost approximately $450-500 a year. A business school survey in fall 1983 showed that married M.B.A. students spent an average of $707 per month for food and housing (including utilities and telephone); and single students, $525 per month. Estimated expenses for a single student living in the university graduate center are $1,300 for dormitory rent and $1,200 for meals for the academic year.

FINANCIAL ASSISTANCE
Scholarships are available in the M.B.A. program to applicants who present outstanding credentials. Such scholarships do not require any service, allowing the students to give uninterrupted effort to their courses. Loans are also available. Part-time employment is not recommended for M.B.A. students. North Carolina is a member of the Consortium for Graduate Study in Management which provides financial assistance for qualified minority M.B.A. students.

PLACEMENT
An active Placement Office is maintained for students in the M.B.A. program and for alumni. In 1984-85, 130 firms conducted interviews at the School of Business Administration to recruit 131 graduates.

CORRESPONDENCE
Inquiries should be addressed to
  Director of Admissions, M.B.A.
    Program
  Graduate School of Business
    Administration
  Box 32, Carroll Hall 012-A
  The University of North Carolina
  Chapel Hill, North Carolina 27514
  Telephone: 919-962-3236

THE UNIVERSITY OF NORTH CAROLINA AT CHARLOTTE

CHARLOTTE, NORTH CAROLINA

The University of North Carolina at Charlotte (UNCC), founded in 1965, is a coeducational, state-supported urban university located in a dynamic and rapidly growing metropolitan area. The university has an enrollment of 10,500 students and continues to grow very rapidly. UNCC is a new urban-oriented university and at the same time a campus of the oldest state university in the United States.

The College of Business Administration offers three undergraduate degree programs: a Bachelor of Arts degree in economics, a Bachelor of Science degree in accounting, and a Bachelor of Arts degree in business administration. The college offers one graduate degree, the Master of Business Administration (M.B.A.). Both the undergraduate and graduate programs in business administration are accredited by the American Assembly of Collegiate Schools of Business (AACSB).

PROGRAM OF STUDY

The primary objective of graduate study in management is to develop candidates for leadership positions in the complex organizations of the future. The basic philosophy of the graduate program recognizes that managerial procedures and practices of today are subject to rapid change. For this reason the program emphasizes a process of perceiving, analyzing, and solving administrative problems. The burden is placed on the student to determine relevant facts, evaluate alternatives, and prepare for action. Organizations are analyzed as economic, social, political, and technological units operating in an environment with changing regional, national, and international dimensions. Candidates are encouraged to anticipate, innovate, and adjust in this dynamic environment.

The curriculum stresses the universal characteristics of management and administration and their application in various types of organizations. Fundamental management problems are examined from an economic, quantitative, and behavioral point of view. Courses in economic analysis and managerial accounting focus on financial performance and resource allocation, while those in administrative practice emphasize individual and group behavior. Courses in information systems make possible the integration of the economic and behavioral aspects of administrative problems with the decision-making requirements of practicing managers. These areas constitute the core courses in basic analysis required of all candidates.

After completing the basic analysis sequence, a student is allowed to select two additional courses from among those offered by the College of Business Administration. Through this process, students may choose to emphasize a particular area of interest such as marketing, finance, or organizational behavior. The finance courses now offered are designed for candidates pursuing careers in commercial banking, investment banking, consumer financing, mortgage banking, and related institutions. Marketing management courses are appropriate for students pursuing careers in manufacturing and retail organizations. Other courses will be added to the program as the need arises.

The final courses in the program are management policy and strategic planning. These courses are designed to integrate the concepts and methods of analysis developed throughout a candidate's program of study. Students are required to solve administrative problems that illustrate the interdependency of financial, industrial, government, marketing, and transportation institutions.

The methods of instruction adopted in the program are designed to prepare a candidate for the realities of a management career. These methods include simulations, role playing, written communications, lectures, and the case study method. It is the ability to analyze, to judge trends, to weigh diverse influences that leads to sound judgment. This ability can be developed only through practice. The methods of instruction employed in the program are designed to provide such practice.

Courses in the program are scheduled to accommodate part-time students. Classes are held in the early evening during the academic year. Part-time students may enroll in two courses during the fall and spring semesters. A part-time student may complete the program in three years.

ADMISSION

Admission to the Master of Business Administration program is open to qualified graduates of recognized colleges or universities accredited by a regional or general accrediting agency. There are four major requirements for admission: (1) a generally satisfactory undergraduate record, (2) acceptable scores on the Graduate Management Admission Test (GMAT), (3) a description of any significant work experience, and (4) three sup-

porting letters of recommendation from professors or employers. Applications should be completed at least three months prior to the semester in which the applicant expects to enroll.

EXPENSES

Graduate tuition and general fees per semester:

Semester hours	State Resident	Out-of-state Resident
1	$ 77	$ 433
2	77	433
3	129	840
4	129	840
5	129	840
6	222	1,289
7	222	1,289
8	222	1,289
9 or more	358	1,781

There is an application fee of $15 and a parking fee of $30.

CORRESPONDENCE

For information, write or call
Director of Graduate Studies
Master of Business Administration
The University of North Carolina
  at Charlotte
U.N.C.C. Station
Charlotte, North Carolina 28223
Telephone: 704-597-4010

The University of North Carolina at Greensboro was established in 1981. Current enrollment totals more than 10,150 (including about 2,749 graduate students), and the faculty numbers more than 655.

The School of Business and Economics offers the following graduate degree programs: Master of Business Administration (M.B.A.), Master of Science degree program in accounting, Master of Science in business education, and Master of Arts with a major in economics. The M.B.A. program is the largest, having 410 students. The school's graduate faculty totals 55; all but a relatively few hold the doctorate degree.

Students have access to the 1,250,000 volumes in the university's Jackson Library and the Academic Computer Center, featuring two VAX 11/780 minicomputers operating in a cluster environment.

Both the undergraduate and graduate programs in business administration are accredited by the American Assembly of Collegiate Schools of Business (AACSB).

PROGRAM OF STUDY
Students may enroll on either a full-time or part-time basis. All courses are taught in the evenings; in addition, a limited amount of required course work is taught during the day. Eighty percent of the M.B.A. students attend part time.

The M.B.A. program is designed for qualified students from any academic background. The program consists of 54 semester hours of course work. Twelve of these 54 hours consist of foundation courses, which may be waived if an applicant has successfully completed equivalent course work within the last five years. The areas covered by the foundation courses are accounting, quantitative analysis, the environment of business, and information systems in management.

The graduate-level course requirements include three semester hours of each of the following 10 courses: Advanced Economic and Business Statistics, Operations Research, Organizational Behavior and Management, Survey of Managerial Accounting, Managerial Economics, Economic Environment of the Firm, Marketing Management, Financial Management, Production and Operations Management, and Business Policy. Additionally, 12 semester hours of approved electives are required, providing the student with an opportunity for further study in one of the following five concentrations: financial management, marketing, personnel and industrial relations management, management organization theory, and quantitative methods.

ADMISSION
To be considered, candidates must provide all the following to the Graduate School Office (Mossman Building): a completed application, official transcripts, official score from the Graduate Management Admission Test (GMAT), and three completed recommendation forms.

A minimum requirement for admission is an attained index of 950 or above, based on the formula: 200 times the overall undergraduate grade-point average (on a 4.0 scale) plus the GMAT score. Because the admission decision also considers relevant experience and recommendations, an index between 950 and 1,050 does not ensure unconditional admission and would often lead to admission conditional upon the attainment of a B average in a specified number of hours taken.

Foreign students must indicate an ability to use the English language. Accordingly, a minimum score of 550 on the Test of English as a Foreign Language (TOEFL), a minimum verbal GMAT score above the 25th percentile, and an acceptable essay on career objectives are required for foreign students whose native language is not English.

Students may apply to enter the program for the fall semester, spring semester, or the summer session. All supporting documentation must be received by the Graduate School Office at least 30 days prior to the term of entry. All application credentials for foreign applicants must be received by June 1, November 1, or April 1 for the fall, spring, or summer terms, respectively.

EXPENSES
Tuition and fees, per semester, are as follows for full-time students:

North Carolina residents	$ 444
Out-of-state residents	1,904

FINANCIAL ASSISTANCE
Assistantships are available on a competitive basis to full-time students. Stipends are approximately $3,000 for the nine-month academic year. Assignments involve about 18 hours of service per week. Applicants with outstanding academic records may apply for a Bryan Fel-lowship which typically provides $6,000 per academic year. The deadline for applying for the fellowship is March 15. Additionally, the out-of-state tuition differential is usually waived for fellows and assistants during the fall and spring semesters.

PLACEMENT
The university operates a placement office which is available to both undergraduate and graduate students. National, regional and local firms, and government agencies recruit on the campus each year.

CORRESPONDENCE
For specific information, write or call
The Director of the M.B.A. Program
School of Business and Economics
The University of North Carolina
    at Greensboro
Greensboro, North Carolina 27412-5001
Telephone: 919-379-5928
For an application or catalog, write or call
The Graduate School
The University of North Carolina
    at Greensboro
Greensboro, North Carolina 27412-5001
Telephone: 919-379-5596

The University of North Carolina at Wilmington (UNCW) was founded in 1947 as Wilmington College and became a constituent institution of the University of North Carolina in 1969. The Cameron School of Business Administration was established in 1979, with departments of Accountancy, Management and Marketing, and Economics and Finance. University enrollment exceeds 5,500 students with over 1,000 in the Cameron School of Business Administration. The Master of Business Administration (M.B.A.) degree program was approved in 1981 and began with 75 students in 1982. Enrollment is estimated to increase to over 100 students in 1986. All M.B.A. candidates are enrolled in evening courses and attending on a part-time basis while maintaining full-time employment. The average course load per semester is six to seven semester hours.

PROGRAM OF STUDY
The objective of the M.B.A. program at the University of North Carolina at Wilmington is the development of the broadly educated professional manager. Fifty-four semester credit hours of approved graduate credit must be satisfactorily completed. The number of credit hours may be reduced for students who qualify for and are granted certain course waivers. Despite the number of waivers granted, a minimum of 42 semester hours of graduate study must be completed. Up to six semester hours of graduate study may be accepted as transfer from an accredited college or university. However, the last 36 hours of graduate study must be completed at the University of North Carolina at Wilmington.

A candidate with no waivers or transfer credit is required to complete the following program: common body of knowledge (24 semester hours including courses in financial accounting, economic analysis, quantitative methods, legal environment and business regulation, management information systems, management of organizations, managerial finance, and marketing management); professional competence and integrative applications (24 semester hours including courses in managerial accounting, economic analysis, the practice of management, production/operations management, current issues in business, financial policy, strategic marketing, and corporate policy and strategy); and electives (6 semester hours).

Waivers on common body of knowledge courses will be granted by the Dean of the Cameron School of Business Administration upon recommendation by the MBA Advisory Committee. Petitions for waiver must be in writing on forms provided by the Cameron School of Business Administration and are submitted after acceptance into the M.B.A. program. Substantial course work at the undergraduate level is the basis for waiver. Courses used to acquire waivers should have been taken within the previous five years with a grade of B or better, and all waiver petitions must be made within one calendar year after the student enrolls in the M.B.A. program. Waivers on professional competence and integrative applications courses are rare and require substantial course work and applied work experience in the specific area. No waivers or transfer credit will be granted for the practice of management, current issues in business, or corporate policy and strategy.

Only graduate-level course work taken at other institutions showing grades of B or better and taken within the allowable time limits for the degree will be considered for transfer credit. Transfer credit must be approved by the Dean of the Cameron School of Business Administration. No transfer credit will be given for correspondence courses. Petitions for transfer credit must be in writing on forms provided by the Cameron School of Business Administration and are submitted after acceptance into the M.B.A. program.

ADMISSION
The M.B.A. program is open to any qualified holder of a bachelor's degree from an accredited college or university in this country or its equivalent in a foreign institution based on a four-year program. The MBA Admissions Committee considers each applicant's undergraduate grade-point average (GPA) and score on the Graduate Management Admission Test (GMAT). Foreign students must present a satisfactory score on the Test of English as a Foreign Language (TOEFL). Applicants are also expected to have at least one year of appropriate full-time work experience. To be considered for admission, applicants should score 1,000 or more based on this formula: (200 × upper-division GPA) + (GMAT score). Applicants should plan to take the GMAT at the earliest opportunity. Information and test application forms may be obtained from the UNCW

Counseling and Testing Center or from Educational Testing Service, CN 6101, Princeton, New Jersey 08541-6101.

Though not a prerequisite to admission, all students must satisfy a minimal mathematics requirement in calculus prior to enrolling in either Quantitative Methods or Economic Analysis I.

EXPENSES
Tuition and fees in 1985-86 for full-time students, per semester, were $358 for North Carolina residents and $1,483 for nonresidents. Prospective students are advised to consult the *Graduate School Bulletin* for a complete schedule of expenses.

PLACEMENT
The Office of Career Planning and Placement is maintained as a service to students and alumni. Many national, regional, and local business firms make regular recruiting trips to the campus in search of business administration graduates.

CORRESPONDENCE
For further information, please write
M.B.A. Coordinator
Cameron School of Business Administration
University of North Carolina at Wilmington
601 South College Road
Wilmington, NC 28403-3297

College of Business and Public Administration

UNIVERSITY OF NORTH DAKOTA

GRAND FORKS, NORTH DAKOTA

The University of North Dakota (UND) is a state-supported coeducational institution with its main campus located in Grand Forks, a population center of approximately 50,000 persons in the Red River Valley on the North Dakota/Minnesota border. The university offers the largest and most diversified graduate program in the region. With an enrollment of more than 11,000 students, of whom about 1,200 are graduate students, UND is large enough to provide necessary resources for graduate study but small enough to guarantee individual attention. The largest library in the state, a computer center that is the hub of the statewide network, and a faculty active in research and creative activity all contribute to interesting and provocative graduate study.

PROGRAMS OF STUDY
The College of Business and Public Administration offers graduate instruction leading to the Master of Business Administration (M.B.A.), the Master of Public Administration (M.P.A.), the Master of Accountancy, and the Master of Arts (M.A.) and Master of Science (M.S.) degrees in economics.

The M.B.A. is an advanced professional degree in administration; although some concentration in a particular functional area is permitted, breadth in the educational experience is emphasized. The degree is a nonthesis program requiring 32 semester hours of graduate course work, including an independent study. Written comprehensive examinations must be successfully completed in the last semester.

For candidates with no prior education in business or economics, the M.B.A. program may require up to two years to complete, the first year of which is primarily devoted to preparatory course requirements. Candidates may be admitted to the M.B.A. program with deficiencies in preparatory fields. Courses are then taken to remove deficiencies. Candidates whose competence levels in prior preparatory work have been allowed to decay over time may be asked to review or retake preparatory courses before registering in graduate courses. Prior course work or work experience can be accepted in lieu of preparatory courses.

The M.P.A. degree is designed to prepare people for positions in the public service. Undergraduate work must include a minimum of nine semester hours of social science and nine hours of business and economics. A student who does not have the undergraduate requirements will be required to remove the undergraduate deficiencies in addition to completing 32 semester hours of graduate credits.

The Master of Accountancy degree is designed to provide education for a career in public accounting practice, in private business enterprises, in government service, or in the teaching of accounting in colleges and universities. Undergraduate work should include 20 semester hours in the field of business of which at least 8 hours must be in the field of accounting. A student who does not have the undergraduate requirements may be admitted on a provisional basis until the deficiencies are removed. A thesis is not required.

The M.A. and M.S. degrees in economics are designed to develop a broadly educated student equipped with knowledge of modern economics who will be prepared to continue graduate studies or pursue a professional career in government or business. For admission to the program a student must present no less than 20 hours of satisfactory undergraduate credit in economics and the social sciences. A student who is deficient in undergraduate preparation may be admitted on a provisional basis until the undergraduate deficiencies are removed. Degree requirements include 30 semester hours of graduate credit with a grade-point average of 3.00 or higher. Students may select a thesis or a nonthesis option.

ADMISSION
Regular admission to all master's programs requires that a student must
- hold a bachelor's degree from an accredited college or university,
- have a cumulative grade-point average of at least 2.75 for all undergraduate work or 3.0 for the last two years of undergraduate work (A = 4.0),
- have met all departmental requirements, and
- have applied to the Graduate School for admission.

Students desiring to enroll for the M.B.A. or Master of Accountancy degree must also submit a Graduate Management Admission Test (GMAT) score. A score of at least 450 is required for admission to the M.B.A. program. For international students, a Test of English as a Foreign Language (TOEFL) score of at least 550 is normally also required for admission to all graduate programs.

EXPENSES
Tuition and fees, per semester
Resident . . . . $ 664.50
Nonresident 1,242.00

FINANCIAL ASSISTANCE
Full-time students are eligible for a variety of scholarships as well as appointments to graduate teaching assistantships. Stipends for half-time assistantships are $5,400 for a nine-month appointment; tuition and nonresident fees are waived.

PLACEMENT
The university maintains a central career planning and placement service for graduates and alumni.

CORRESPONDENCE
Address all inquiries to
Dean, Graduate School
University of North Dakota
Grand Forks, North Dakota 58202
Telephone: 701-777-2784

The University of Notre Dame Master of Business Administration (M.B.A.) program is committed to providing graduates with the knowledge, background, attitude, and confidence to enter the contemporary world of business management. The College of Business Administration is one of the 77 member schools in the Graduate Management Admission Council. Accredited by the American Assembly of Collegiate Schools of Business (AACSB), the .M.B.A. curriculum has as its aim the development of professional managers. Emphasis in the program is on the foundation, organization, operation, and control of a business enterprise with special attention to the manager's responsibility for diagnosing, isolating, and defining problems; creating and evaluating alternative courses of action; and making practical and ethical decisions.

PROGRAMS OF STUDY
Notre Dame offers several programs leading to the Master of Business Administration degree. The two-year program (60 credit hours) is designed for individuals with little or no academic background in business. The first year is highly structured with all students enrolled in identical core course sequences each semester. These courses supply the foundation material necessary for a thorough understanding and use of the comprehensive set of knowledge required by managers. Recognizing the fact that many career interests and goals are represented in the student body, there is greater flexibility in scheduling second-year programs. Therefore, the overall sequencing of courses allows for logical progression from the basic to the highly involved, yet pragmatic, aspects of corporate activity.

In addition, M.B.A. students who have an interest in international business have an option of spending the fall semester of their second year in London, England.

The three-semester program (42 credit hours) is designed for those students who have an undergraduate degree in business. These students are presumed to be proficient in the foundation areas, and in adopting the curriculum an effort has been made to remove redundancy. This 11-month program begins with an eight-week summer semester in which students are enrolled in six intensive review courses. Upon successful completion, these students move directly into the second-year courses.

The three-semester program with a concentration in taxation (42 credit hours) was developed in response to the growing demand from public accounting firms, business corporations, financial organizations, and governmental agencies for highly trained tax professionals. This 11-month program is for individuals who have undergraduate degrees in business and who have earned at least three credit hours in a federal income tax course. This interdisciplinary professional program, which has a core of 19 hours of tax courses, is designed for those who desire to enter the tax profession as well as for present tax practitioners interested in improving their skills.

A combined M.B.A./Juris Doctor (J.D.) degree program is offered jointly by the College of Business and the Law School. This program allows the student to complete both degrees in a total of four years instead of the five years that would be required if each were taken separately. The M.B.A./ J.D. program is for individuals who have a desire to develop an expertise in both the business and legal environments.

Students may use their electives to develop a specialization in accounting, finance, human resource management, international business, management information systems, marketing, and interdisciplinary studies.

ADMISSION
Decisions on a student's admissibility into the program are guided by a thorough examination of the student's ability to become an outstanding leader and manager at the highest levels of a business organization. These qualities and capabilities are measured by the following: (1) undergraduate academic record; (2) achievement on the Graduate Management Admission Test (GMAT), which is required of all applicants; (3) executive and leadership potential; (4) personal statement of career objectives and goals; (5) recommendations from professors and/ or supervisors. Foreign applicants are required to submit scores on the Test of English as a Foreign Language (TOEFL). It is strongly recommended that all students have a working knowledge of calculus before matriculation into the program.

EXPENSES
Tuition for 1985-86 academic year was $7,750, with living expenses for the single student around $3,500. Tuition for the eight-week summer semester was $3,100. Books and supplies are approximately $500.

FINANCIAL ASSISTANCE
A limited number of scholarships are awarded each year to students of high academic achievement and promise. All students who have been accepted and requested financial assistance are automatically considered. Successful candidates will be notified beginning April 15. U.S. citizens are given preference for scholarships. Full information on loan programs can be obtained by contacting the Financial Aid Office, 103 Administration Building, University of Notre Dame.

CORRESPONDENCE
For further information, including application material, please contact
    M.B.A. Admissions Office
    133 Hayes-Healy
    University of Notre Dame
    Notre Dame, Indiana 46556
    Telephone: 219-239-5206/6500

The University of Oklahoma, founded in 1890, is located in Norman, 18 miles south of Oklahoma City, the state's capital and largest city. The graduate programs offered by the College of Business Administration are accredited by the American Assembly of Collegiate Schools of Business (AACSB).

Research facilities available to graduate students include an extensive university library, the Bass Business History Collection, the Oklahoma University Research Institute, the Center for Economic and Management Research, and modern computer facilities.

The 80 graduate faculty members have a wide range of teaching and research interests. Many have experience in executive development programs and consulting activities as well as serving as guest lecturers at U.S. and foreign universities.

PROGRAMS OF STUDY

The Master of Business Administration (M.B.A.) program is designed to give the broad perspective needed to manage an overall enterprise, while allowing sufficient flexibility to gain in-depth preparation in an elected area of concentration. The program requires that the student become familiar with the functional areas of business, the necessary tools for management decision making, and the environment in which business firms operate. All M.B.A. courses are at the graduate level. They are offered during the day, evening, and late afternoon. M.B.A. program requirements are as follows:

- knowledge prerequisites—an introduction to calculus, matrix algebra, and linear programming; computer familiarity; and communication skills;
- core courses (24 hours)—financial accounting, managerial economics, contemporary economic analysis, financial administration of the firm, production and operations analysis, organization behavior, managerial marketing, and statistics for decision making (core courses may be waived on the basis of academic background);
- required courses (6 hours)—socio-legal environment of business and integrative business policy;
- electives (24 hours)—tailored to meet career objectives (no more than 9 hours from a single area of study; up to 9 hours may be from outside the College of Business Administration; tracks of study available include energy management, financial management, human resource management, marketing management, and operations management);
- program length—varies from 36 to 54 hours, depending upon the student's academic background;
- comprehensive exam—covering the core areas of accounting, economics, finance, management, and marketing, given during the final semester of work. A course in administrative research writing and a major research paper may be substituted for the comprehensive exam.

Three dual degree programs are available. A combined M.B.A./Master of Arts (M.A.) in mathematics is offered in conjunction with the mathematics department. A combined Juris Doctor (J.D.)/M.B.A. degree is offered in conjunction with the College of Law. A combined Master of Library Science/M.B.A. is offered in conjunction with the School of Library Science. A combined M.B.A./Master of Arts in French, German, or Spanish is offered in conjunction with the College of Arts and Sciences. Dual degree applicants must apply and be admitted to both academic units separately.

The Master of Accountancy program is offered for students contemplating professional careers either in public or industrial accounting. The Master of Arts in accounting and the Master of Arts in management require theses and are intended for intensive specialization in the respective fields.

The Doctor of Philosophy (Ph.D.) program in business administration is designed to prepare students for careers in college or university teaching and for research-oriented careers. The program includes the methods of inquiry, a detailed knowledge of one or more chosen areas of concentration, and an overview of the functional areas of business administration.

ADMISSION

Admission is open to qualified individuals holding a bachelor's degree from an accredited college or university who show high promise of success in graduate study. Applicants need not have undergraduate backgrounds in business. All applicants must submit satisfactory scores on the Graduate Management Admission Test (GMAT). Applicants for a doctoral degree should indicate their major field of study and include letters of recommendation.

Students may enter the fall semester beginning late August, the spring semester beginning early January, or the eight-week summer session beginning early in June.

EXPENSES

Costs, per semester
Tuition and fees, per semester hour
    Oklahoma residents . . . . $ 30.60
    Out-of-state residents 100.60
    Apartments, per month 165-404
    Health and facilities fee,
      per semester 65.00

FINANCIAL ASSISTANCE

Graduate assistantships, special instructorships, fellowships, fee-waiver scholarships, and loans are available to qualified graduate students.

PLACEMENT

The Placement Service offers assistance to students in locating full- or part-time employment. Representatives of approximately 600 companies, agencies, and institutions visit the campus regularly to interview students.

CORRESPONDENCE

For further information, please write or call
Director of Graduate Programs
307 W. Brooks, Room 207
College of Business Administration
University of Oklahoma
Norman, Oklahoma 73019
Telephone: 405-325-4107

The University of Oregon, established by an act of the Oregon Legislature in 1872, currently consists of a College of Arts and Sciences with 22 departments and 12 professional schools covering the spectrum of typical university subjects in all areas but engineering. Full-time enrollment is about 15,000 students with a supporting faculty of approximately 1,000. The campus occupies 255 acres in Eugene, a city with a population of about 100,000 located in the Willamette Valley, 110 miles south of Portland. The Pacific Ocean is an hour's drive to the west of Eugene and the Cascade Mountains a 90-minute drive to the east.

The College of Business Administration, now consisting of the Undergraduate School of Business and the Graduate School of Management (GSM), was established in 1914; graduate work was first offered in the year 1920. Heavy emphasis is given to graduate education in business. Currently there are approximately 200 master's degree candidates and 50 doctoral candidates enrolled in the GSM. The college is a member of the American Assembly of Collegiate Schools of Business (AACSB).

PROGRAMS OF STUDY

Graduate degrees are offered at the master's and doctoral levels. Work at the master's level may lead to the Master of Business Administration (M.B.A.), Master of Science (M.S.), Master of Arts (M.A.), and Master of Business Administration/Juris Doctor (M.B.A./J.D.) degrees. The M.B.A. program emphasizes breadth of understanding of business and the management skills necessary to be effective in a complex and dynamic environment. The two-year M.B.A. program is designed for students who have earned their bachelor's degree in the social sciences, humanities, sciences, or engineering. An accelerated program is available for students with prior academic training in business. For students desiring greater specialization, programs leading to the M.S. and M.A. degrees are offered.

Although specialization is not required in the M.B.A. program, major areas of concentration are offered in accounting, decision sciences, finance, forest industries management, international business, management, and marketing. In addition, the GSM offers an M.S. program in industrial relations and a four-year M.B.A./J.D. program.

At the Ph.D. level, major areas of concentration are accounting, business policy and strategy, decision sciences, finance, human resource management, marketing, and organizational studies. Students are selected for the doctoral program only if it is possible to ensure close contact with senior faculty in the student's major area of interest. The doctoral candidate is required to demonstrate proficiency in a major area of concentration in the Graduate School of Management, a supportive area inside or outside the GSM, statistics and research skills, and a behavioral science or economics tool area. Written comprehensive examinations in the major area and one in either the supportive or statistics and research methods area are required for advancement to candidacy for the degree. An oral defense of both the dissertation proposal and the completed dissertation is required.

ADMISSION

Four criteria are used jointly, and interdependently, in evaluating an application for admission to the M.B.A. program (admission requirements for the Ph.D. program are available from the Graduate School of Management):

- Grade-point average—All applicants must hold a baccalaureate degree from an accredited institution. Their grade-point average and academic program must indicate future success in graduate study in business administration. A 3.0 cumulative grade-point average (C = 2.0) is generally considered minimal.
- Graduate Management Admission Test—No rigid cutoff is specified; however, a score of 550 or above is desirable.
- Personal recommendations—a minimum of three personal recommendations is required, preferably from faculty in a position to comment on the applicant's potential for graduate study.
- Statement of purpose—The applicant is asked to outline, in a maximum of 1,000 words, personal goals and objectives in relation to the proposed program of study.

Applicants from non-English-speaking countries must earn a minimum score of 550 on the Test of English as a Foreign Language (TOEFL).

A nonrefundable application fee of $25 is required. Deadline for application to the M.B.A. program is April 1 for fall term, October 1 for winter. Deadline for application to the Ph.D. program for fall term is March 1.

EXPENSES

Graduate tuition (1985-86) for residents of Oregon was $722.50 and for nonresidents, $1,151.50 per term. Students holding graduate teaching or research fellowships paid a reduced fee of $107.50 per term.

Room and board costs in university dormitories ranged from $2,277 to $4,041 for the academic year. Monthly rents in university facilities for married students ranged from $113 to $142.

FINANCIAL ASSISTANCE

Teaching assistantships, scholarships, and fellowships are offered through the GSM. Additional financial assistance is available through the University Financial Aid Office.

PLACEMENT

Representatives of over 200 companies annually visit the university to interview graduates.

CORRESPONDENCE

Address correspondence to
    Graduate School of Management
    University of Oregon
    Eugene, Oregon 97403-1208
    Telephone: 503-686-3306

The Advanced Business Program of the University of Otago Business School first offered a Master of Business Administration (M.B.A.) degree in 1977. This was the first M.B.A. program offered in New Zealand. Participants are drawn from New Zealand, Australia, the United States, Canada, and Pacific countries.

Dunedin is relatively small (population 110,000) and is primarily a university city. The University of Otago has an international reputation, particularly in the fields of medicine, dentistry, and lately, in business. There are over 7,000 students on the campus, which is known for its nineteenth-century buildings and attractive surroundings.

PROGRAM OF STUDY
The M.B.A. program is primarily designed to cater to the needs of the New Zealand business community, but at the same time it is based on principles established at business schools in Europe and North America. The regular participation of North American and other overseas students provides an international dimension to the program. The overriding objective of the program is to develop conceptual understanding and practical skills for those in whom managerial excellence has begun to show. For many, the program is a broadening process from functional to general management.

The program begins with a business foundation sequence of six papers in accounting and finance, economics, business law, quantitative methods, behavioral science, and general management. The first week of the program is an interactive orientation covering personal skills, group learning skills, and a business game.

This 10-week foundation program is followed by a three-month (June/July/August) general semester covering six functional fields of management: marketing, personnel, accounting and finance, information systems, operations research, and operations management. At this stage students select a field of specialization and spend two months working full time in the area of their choice.

During the first year of study a program of integrating personal skills is followed together with a series of integrating cases. The integrating program also includes fitness and leadership training as options.

The second year of study consists of an intensive 10-week corporate studies semester followed by a project requirement. The latter is designed as a consulting assignment where the participant works on a business project in a New Zealand organization and presents recommendations at the board level. Some students are able to substantially complete the consulting assignment during the summer vacation and as a result are able to complete the M.B.A. degree in 15 months. The program caters to graduates and nongraduates of acceptable ability from both the public and private sector. In view of the modular nature of the program, it is possible for students to spread their studies over a period of four years spending an average of one term at the school each year.

ADMISSION
The program is open to a limited number of men and women of exceptional ability. A degree from a recognized university is normally a minimum requirement, and two to five years of business experience will definitely improve the applicant's chances of acceptance. No particular background or areas of concentration are required for admission. Nondegree candidates possessing a minimum of five years' suitable experience and professional qualifications will also be considered as suitable applicants. The composition of the class is carefully planned so that a blend of age, experience, qualifications, and areas of expertise is maintained. The M.B.A. class is limited to a maximum of 25 students, providing high staff/student contact.

The Admissions Board evaluates each applicant on the basis of comprehensive application, two referees' reports, an interview, and scores from the Graduate Management Admission Test (GMAT). Candidates whose qualifications or experience do not meet requirements are generally advised to remedy these deficiencies before reapplying.

Candidates should ensure that their applications are mailed to reach the Director of Advanced Business Program as early as possible in the 12 months prior to projected entry and ideally no later than October 1, although some late applications may be accepted. The board sits in early December. Normally candidates will be informed of the decision of the board before January 1.

EXPENSES
The tuition fees for the full M.B.A. program are $NZ500 for New Zealand citizens. Non-New Zealand citizens pay at least $NZ1500 per year tuition (under review). There is a teaching materials fee currently of $NZ200. There are no residences that specifically cater to members of the M.B.A. program, but accommodation and board for single students is usually found in one of the adjoining halls of residence on campus ($NZ85 per week). Accommodation for married students, in partly or fully furnished houses, is normally available in Dunedin ($NZ100).

FINANCIAL ASSISTANCE
New Zealand participants as well as permanent residents generally qualify for the Standard Tertiary Bursary ($NZ50–$NZ70 per week), which is available to all university students. There are often small research funds or fees available to finance the project requirement during the summer vacation (November-February).

PLACEMENT
The school has well-developed contacts with the New Zealand business community and arranges for members to meet executives to discuss employment and project opportunities during the program. An Otago MBA Network serves graduates of the program around the world.

CORRESPONDENCE
For further information, prospective applicants should write to
  The Director
  Master of Business Administration
    Program
  University of Otago Business School
  Dunedin, New Zealand
  Telephone: Dunedin 771.640,
    extension 8756

UNIVERSITY OF OTTAWA

OTTAWA, ONTARIO, CANADA

The University of Ottawa is North America's oldest and largest bilingual university. The 83-acre campus is located along the historic Rideau Canal, in residential Sandy Hill, a few blocks from Parliament Hill and downtown Ottawa.

With francophone and anglophone students and professors working side by side, the university has in a sense become a microcosm of Canada and an example of what national unity can mean: diversity exists, but the idea is to harmonize, not polarize. Cultural and social events take place in both French and English, and make the campus an entertaining place to be.

PROGRAMS OF STUDY

The Master of Business Administration (M.B.A.) program is designed to prepare students for decision-making in the private, public, and parapublic sectors, and to develop the skills necessary to assume increasing managerial responsibilities in a constantly changing society. The M.B.A. program now has a student population close to 500, one third of these attend full time.

In two years of full-time study or four to five years part-time, a student will gain knowledge that is essential to managers and, if he or she so wishes, can focus on an area of choice from the private sector to the public and social sectors, gaining expertise in marketing, finance, and international development.

The objective of the Master of Health Administration (M.H.A.) program is to produce generalist health care administrators capable of assuming management positions in a variety of organizations at a variety of levels. The faculty members offer diversity of backgrounds and engage in a number of areas of research, publication, and service activities, which have objectives focusing on the further development of health administration in Canada as a profession and a field of knowledge.

The curriculum is designed around eight key areas of theoretical and applied skills. The program is designed so that a full-time student can complete all requirements in two academic years, with an intervening summer residency. Part-time students have a maximum of six years to complete the requirements. Part-time students find it necessary to spend at least one semester (and probably two) in full-time attendance.

ADMISSION

Candidates must hold a recognized bachelor's degree with a B average or better (or its equivalent). Each applicant must submit (1) a completed application form and admission fee, (2) Graduate Management Admission Test (GMAT) scores, (3) official transcripts from all prior postsecondary institutions attended, (4) two letters of recommendation, (5) a detailed curriculum vitae (or narrative statement for the M.H.A.) and (6) any other information the Admissions Committee may require such as a proof of proficiency in English or French for applicants whose native language is neither.

EXPENSES

Tuition fees for 1985-86 for full-time study are $611 per trimester, with incidental fees of $38 in the first trimester and $33 in the two subsequent trimesters. Tuition fees per trimester for part-time study (3 to 6 credits) are $184, with incidental fees of $5.80 per trimester.

The 1985-86 fees for residences on campus from September to April were $1,326 for a single room and $1,127 for a double room. For additional information on housing, please contact the Housing Services, 85 Hastey Street, Ottawa K1N 6N5 (613-564-7013).

FINANCIAL ASSISTANCE

Awards and scholarships are available to graduate students, as well as a few teaching assistantships. For information on scholarships, please contact the Awards Office, School of Graduate Studies, 115 Wilbrod St., Ottawa K1N 6N5 (613-564-6547).

PLACEMENT

The services of the Placement Services are available to graduate students. The Faculty of Administration's contact with the government and business community, as well as with the many health care institutions in the Ottawa area, also helps to secure challenging and attractive positions for graduating students.

CORRESPONDENCE

For further information, write or call
The Administrator
M.B.A. Program
Faculty of Administration
275 Nicholas Street
Ottawa, Ontario
K1N 6N5 Canada
Telephone: 613-564-7004

The University of Pittsburgh's Graduate School of Business, located in the nation's third largest corporate headquarter city, has since 1960 provided qualified men and women the opportunity to earn the Master of Business Administration (M.B.A.) degree in an intensive, one-calendar-year program. The total 11-month, three-term sequence includes 51 credit hours. The accelerated M.B.A. program is accredited by the American Assembly of Collegiate Schools of Business (AACSB).

The primary goal of the accelerated M.B.A. program is to prepare students for careers as successful managers in a highly complex, rapidly changing society. Central to this approach is a highly integrated curriculum which stresses general management training from an upper-level managerial perspective. Emphasis is upon development of analytical and decision-making skills.

Full-time M.B.A. enrollment is 225. Approximately 600 students are enrolled in the part-time evening M.B.A. program. The full-time Doctor of Philosophy (Ph.D.) program enrollment is 55. The 60 distinguished full-time faculty members represent a wide range of disciplines and experience.

PROGRAM OF STUDY
The M.B.A. curriculum assumes that management decisions center around the internal integration of the various functional fields: finance, marketing, operations, and human resource management together with the integration of the organization with its surrounding political, social, legal, and economic environments. Another important assumption is that each functional field deals with problems which can be managed most effectively by applying the tools, concepts, theories, and findings of such basic disciplines as economics, the behavioral sciences, quantitative analysis, and accounting. The curriculum also includes course work in integrative areas such as management policy, management systems, strategic planning, and international business. Opportunities for specialization and advanced study are provided through elective courses in 11 fields. Rather than adhering to a single method of instruction for all subject areas, various teaching methods, including lectures, case studies, seminars, group projects, and simulation exercises are used.

Because of the carefully integrated nature of the accelerated program, students enter only in September and complete the degree requirements the following August. Students enrolled in the three-year evening M.B.A. program may enter in September, January, or April.

The strategic location of the business school affords M.B.A. students maximal opportunities for interaction with corporate managers representing a great diversity of organizations and functional areas.

ADMISSION
Applicants must have completed a baccalaureate degree from an accredited college or university. Previous course work in business is not required. Successful completion of a college-level course covering integral and differential calculus is a prerequisite before matriculation.

Admission to the accelerated M.B.A. program is based on the applicant's prior academic record, letters of recommendation, score on the Graduate Management Admission Test (GMAT), indication of managerial promise, leadership, and prior work experience. The nature of the accelerated program demands a student who is particularly motivated and mature.

Applicants whose native language is not English must score 575 or higher on the Test of English as a Foreign Language (TOEFL). Foreign applicants must also demonstrate adequate financial responsibility.

Approximately half of the M.B.A. class has had one or more years of work experience. Women comprise 46 percent of the class, minority students 6 percent and foreign students 18 percent.

Rolling admission is used; thus early application to the program is encouraged. Students applying for financial aid must submit the completed applications by March 15.

EXPENSES
Tuition and fees for the one-year program (11-months) are $6,150 for residents and $12,300 for nonresidents, based on 1985-86 costs.

FINANCIAL ASSISTANCE
The Graduate School of Business makes every attempt to assist qualified students with financing the costs of their graduate education. Over 20 percent of the 1985 class received some form of financial assistance (exclusive of loans) from the school. Fellowship awards, consisting of full or partial tuition, are available based on merit. Individuals with outstanding credentials may be considered for an H. R. Young or an associate fellowship, the school's most prestigious awards, consisting of full tuition and a stipend. Qualified minority students may receive a minority fellowship. The University of Pittsburgh is a lender under federal and state guaranteed loan programs.

PLACEMENT
The Graduate School of Business maintains its own career planning and placement office to work closely with M.B.A. students in securing professional employment. Representatives from major companies visit the campus each year to recruit M.B.A. graduates. Students have accepted job offers across a wide range of organizations and functional area responsibilities.

CORRESPONDENCE
For further information or to request an application for admission, please write or call
John W. Enyart
Director of Admissions
Graduate School of Business
276 Mervis Hall
Pittsburgh, Pennsylvania 15260
Telephone: 412-648-1700

The University of Portland is an independent, urban, coeducational, campus-centered institution, dedicated to the principle of attention to the individual student and emphasizing breadth of education rather than narrow specialization. The university is committed to the liberal arts tradition of education, while offering professionally oriented programs of study.

The university is located in the north residential section of the city of Portland. A 90-acre landscaped campus overlooking the Willamette River provides a quiet, restful setting conducive to the learning process. At the same time, the proximity of metropolitan Portland offers additional educational, cultural, and recreational opportunities.

The School of Business Administration at the University of Portland has offered a Master of Business Administration (M.B.A.) program since 1959. It is the oldest M.B.A. program in the Portland community.

Graduates of the program come from a variety of backgrounds in business, industry, and the professional fields. Today, they hold many key positions in both the private and public sectors of the economy.

The program in business administration provides an opportunity for college graduates, particularly in the Portland area, to continue their education for the master's degree. Because career men and women can ordinarily attend class only in the evening, the program, at least for the immediate future, will be confined primarily to evening sessions.

PROGRAM OF STUDY

The M.B.A. program is designed to provide advanced study for persons interested in a career in professional management. The aims of the program are to develop an understanding of the nature and complexities of the business decision-making process in a world of change and uncertainty and of the place of the business organization in the larger society in which it operates.

Emphasis in the curriculum is conceptual and analytical to provide a breadth of knowledge and understanding in management and business environment. This breadth encompasses the following: the interaction of business and society—economic, social, political, and moral; the administrative process and policy making; developments in the behavioral sciences as applied to business organization and management; quantitative approaches to management decision making, including accounting controls, statistics, and operations research; and analysis of the production, marketing, and financial functions in national and international firms.

To be admitted to the Master of Business Administration degree program, all students must possess a basic undergraduate-level competency in accounting, economics, and statistics. Students who have done undergraduate work in these subjects satisfy this requirement.

Those students lacking sufficient competency in these fields may be required to take certain undergraduate courses, specifically designed for prospective M.B.A. candidates. The School of Business Administration regularly offers special accelerated courses in two of the three subject areas referred to above.

Thirty-nine to forty-five semester hours of credit are required, as follows:
- nine semester hours (required of all students regardless of background)
Bus 511—Business, Government and Society
Bus 517—Organizational Theory and Behavior
Bus 518—Policy and Administration
- three semester hours (option of either course—nonbusiness applicants will usually take both)
Bus 558—Finance and Accounting or
Bus 521—Marketing and Production
- three semester hours (option of either course—nonbusiness applicants will usually take both)
Bus 533—Management Information Systems or
Bus 532—Quantitative Methods for Management
- twenty-four semester hours of electives ordinarily to be taken in the School of Business Administration.

ADMISSION

The candidate for the M.B.A. must possess a bachelor's degree from an accredited college or university. In addition to business-degree holders, applicants with degrees in liberal arts, engineering, or science are eligible. Students should have achieved above-average academic standing and must also successfully complete the Graduate Management Admission Test (GMAT).

EXPENSES

Tuition for all graduate and postgraduate students is presently charged at the rate of $196 per semester hour of credit.

CORRESPONDENCE

For further information, write or call
Dean
School of Business Administration
University of Portland
5000 North Willamette Boulevard
Portland, Oregon 97203
Telephone: 503-283-7224

The University of Rhode Island (URI) is a state-supported, coeducational institution. The university's 1,200-acre main campus in Kingston is just a few miles from scenic Newport, 30 minutes from historic Providence, and within easy reach of Boston and New York. The College of Continuing Education is in downtown Providence.

The College of Business Administration (CBA) has offered a Master of Business Administration (M.B.A.) program that integrates academic disciplines to develop the career capability of the M.B.A. candidate since 1962. The candidate will be equipped with the skills necessary not only to solve specific problems but to interrelate issues across the whole spectrum of an organization's operations.

All CBA programs are accredited by the American Assembly of Collegiate Schools of Business (AACSB). Of the 57 faculty members, 89 percent hold doctorates. Roughly 150 graduate business students are enrolled at the main campus, and 250 are part-time students in Providence.

PROGRAMS OF STUDY
The M.B.A. curriculum prepares graduates for executive positions in business, government, and nonprofit organizations. Participative learning is emphasized through case analysis, management simulation, and classroom discussion. In addition, students have the opportunity to work with local business and governmental organizations on various management tasks. Computer concepts, quantitative analysis, and behavioral science are integrated into the program as well. Outstanding computer facilities with unlimited computer time are readily available.

The M.B.A. program requires 36 to 54 credit hours (36 credits for holders of a bachelor's degree in business administration from an AACSB-accredited school). It includes 18 credit hours of graduate electives so that a student may concentrate in finance, international business, management science, marketing, organization management, human resource management, or information systems management. Internships are available whereby a student receives three or six credits for a project completed at a company under faculty supervision.

In addition to the M.B.A., the college offers a Master of Science in accounting at Kingston.

An M.B.A. degree may be earned through full- and/or part-time study. The evening M.B.A. program is based at Providence and the day program at Kingston. A master's degree program in labor studies and labor relations is also available at both locations through URI's multicollege Labor Research Center. Candidates must take at least four-fifths of the credits required for the M.B.A. degree at the University of Rhode Island. For full-time students, the requirements for the M.B.A. degree can be met in 12 to 21 months. Part-time students not in full-time residence during any term may take three to five years.

ADMISSION
Students holding any baccalaureate degree from an accredited college or university may be admitted for graduate study if their undergraduate average approximates a B or better (3.0 on a scale of 4.0) and if they achieve satisfactory scores (50th percentile) on the Graduate Management Admission Test (GMAT). The average GMAT score for admitted students is 555 (approximately the 78th percentile). The GMAT is waived for applicants with a doctorate. Applicants for whom English is not a native language must present a score of at least 575 on the Test of English as a Foreign Language (TOEFL).

Each applicant must submit completed application forms in duplicate, three letters of recommendation, two official transcripts from each college attended, and GMAT scores. The applicant must specify whether he or she will study in Kingston or Providence.

EXPENSES
An estimate for full-time study for an academic year:

Tuition, Rhode Island residents .	$1,556
Tuition, out-of-state residents . . .	3,564
Graduate student assessment . . .	10
Health services fee	165
Medical insurance fee	140
Books and supplies	300

FINANCIAL ASSISTANCE
Graduate assistantships pay $5,600 for the academic year with tuition and fees waived. Several half-time (10 hours per week) assistantships are available. In addition, tuition scholarships and fellowships are available for qualified students. Applications for student loans and work-study are available from the financial aid office. Little Family Foundation Fellowships are available on a competitive basis to M.B.A. students who have been Junior Achievement members or advisers.

PLACEMENT
The Office of Career Planning and Placement assists graduates in obtaining positions. Over 200 representatives of industry, education, and state, local, and federal governments interview on campus. In addition, the Graduate Business Student Organization maintains an active role in assisting M.B.A. students by publishing a resume book and cosponsoring career information seminars.

CORRESPONDENCE
For further information or to request an application for admission, please write or call

Dr. Dennis W. McLeavey
Associate Dean and M.B.A.
  Program Director
College of Business Administration
University of Rhode Island
Kingston, Rhode Island 02881
Telephone: 401-792-2337

The University of Richmond, founded in 1830, is the largest private university in Virginia. It is a coeducational institution located in a greater metropolitan area of about 700,000 people. The university has an enrollment of approximately 4,600 students; about 1,300 are attending part time. Full-time undergraduate student enrollment in The E. Claiborne Robins School of Business is 375, and approximately 250 are enrolled in the graduate business programs of the Richard S. Reynolds Graduate School. The bachelor's and master's programs offered by The E. Claiborne Robins School of Business are accredited by the American Assembly of Collegiate Schools of Business (AACSB).

PROGRAMS OF STUDY
There are three programs of study: the evening Master of Business Administration (M.B.A.), the Executive Master of Business Administration (E.M.B.A.) and the Juris Doctor (J.D.)/M.B.A.

The evening M.B.A. program provides a broad, flexible background in essential areas of management and business. The program, designed for students who wish to pursue the degree on a part-time basis, requires between 30 and 51 semester credit hours. Of the total, 21 hours are foundation courses, which may be waived depending on the student's academic background; 30 hours are advanced graduate courses. Of the advanced graduate courses, 24 hours are required courses and 6 hours are elective courses. All M.B.A. courses are conducted in the evening. The number of full-time students admitted is very limited, and competition for such openings is strong. Preference is given to those applicants with several years of work experience.

The E.M.B.A. program provides an alternative approach for working managers to earn the M.B.A. degree in less than two years without career interruption. Classes meet on Fridays and Saturdays of alternating weekends for approximately 22 months. The E.M.B.A. program is aimed at mid-career executives who demonstrate potential to achieve senior management positions and at senior executives who wish to enhance their effectiveness. A bulletin for the program may be obtained by writing the Director of the Executive M.B.A. program. A class will be formed approximately every two years.

The J.D./M.B.A. program is offered through a reciprocal arrangement with The T.C. Williams School of Law. A student may pursue a dual-degree program designed to provide graduates with two degrees—the J.D. and the M.B.A. Students in the dual-degree program may complete the J.D. and M.B.A. requirements in about 12 months less time than necessary to pursue the two degrees independently. Applicants for the dual-degree program are required to meet admission standards of both the T.C. Williams School of Law and the Richard S. Reynolds Graduate School. The number of students admitted to the J.D./M.B.A. program is very limited.

ADMISSION
Persons who hold a baccalaureate degree from an accredited college or university may apply for admission to the Reynolds Graduate Division. Admission decisions are based on the applicant's undergraduate grade-point average and score on the Graduate Management Admission Test (GMAT). Applicants for the E.M.B.A. program must also be recommended by their employer.

Completed applications for the evening M.B.A. and J.D./M.B.A., along with official transcripts and GMAT score reports must be received by December 1, April 1, or August 1, in order to be considered for the ensuing academic semester. The deadline for applying to the E.M.B.A. program is given in the E.M.B.A. bulletin.

EXPENSES
Graduate tuition for the 1985-86 academic year was $133.00 per semester hour for part-time students (less than nine semester hours) and $3,627.50 per semester for full-time students (nine or more semester hours) A $20.00 nonrefundable application fee is required with each application. Information on tuition and fees for the E.M.B.A. program is detailed in the bulletin.

The University of Richmond does not provide housing for graduate students.

FINANCIAL ASSISTANCE
A limited number of graduate assistantships are available for full-time M.B.A. students. Applicants interested in applying for an assistantship should contact the Associate Dean. Other sources of financial assistance may be available through the university's Financial Aid Office.

PLACEMENT
Services of the University Placement Office are available to all graduate students. Representatives of many regional and national firms visit the campus to conduct recruiting interviews.

CORRESPONDENCE
For further information on the graduate programs offered at the University of Richmond, write or call
Associate Dean
The E. Claiborne Robins School of Business
Richard S. Reynolds Graduate School
University of Richmond
Richmond, Virginia 23173
Telephone: 804-289-8553

UNIVERSITY OF ROCHESTER

ROCHESTER, NEW YORK

The University of Rochester is coeducational, nonsectarian, and privately endowed. The Graduate School of Management (GSM) offers graduate study leading to the degree of Master of Business Administration (M.B.A.), Master of Science in Business Administration (M.S.B.A.), or Doctor of Philosophy (Ph.D.) in business administration.

PROGRAMS OF STUDY

To earn the M.B.A. degree, students must successfully complete 64 credit hours—20 quarter-courses, each of which carries 3 hours of credit. Four introductory courses also have labs, which carry one hour of credit. The M.B.A. program normally involves six quarters of full-time study. Courses include the underlying disciplines of economics, operations research, and applied statistics, as well as accounting and computers and information systems. One course is required in each of the functional areas of finance, marketing, and operations management. Emphasis is on principles, analytical methods, and problem solving, rather than on description of existing practices. Ten further courses are required, of which five or more must form a sequence of concentration. The student may choose to concentrate in corporate accounting, public accounting, accounting and information systems, computers and information systems, business environment and public policy, corporate and market organizations, finance, marketing, or operations management. Advanced courses in each concentration sequence are devoted to application, implementation, and integration of the principles learned in earlier courses. The remaining electives should be taken in fields related to the student's area of concentration. They may be taken in the GSM or in another division of the university. Near the end of the program, all students also take an integrative course in business policy or corporate strategy. The option to major in public accounting prepares students for careers in public accounting and internal auditing. Graduates may be certified as having completed the registered curriculum for admission to the C.P.A. examination.

Students interested in the areas of manufacturing management or operations management may be particularly interested in the new Master of Science of Business Administration with concentrations in these two areas. Students interested in careers in health care or educational administration may take elective courses in the School of Medicine and Dentistry or in the Graduate School of Education and Human Development. An M.B.A.-Doctor of Education (Ed.D.) in educational administration and an M.B.A.-Ph.D. in education are also offered. GSM offers an M.B.A.-M.S. joint degree program in preventive medicine and community health and a Master of Science (M.S.)-Ph.D. in business administration and biotechnology.

The GSM also offers the Executive Development Program, a two-year formal program of management education designed for company-sponsored middle- and top-management personnel from the western New York area.

The Ph.D. program prepares students for careers in teaching and research in management and related fields. Admission is limited to students who demonstrate excellent potential for academic or other research careers. All first-year students take a set of core courses in one of two basic disciplines—economics or quantitative methods. The core examinations are given in July after the first year of study. Second-year students concentrate their study in two chosen fields of specialization, a major and a minor. The fields offered are accounting, applied statistics, computers and information systems, finance, industrial organization and public economics, information systems economics, macroeconomics, marketing, operations management, and operations research. Qualifying examinations in these fields are given in July following the second year of study. During the second year of study, students also begin work on an original research paper. Early in the third year, students are evaluated for admission to Ph.D. candidacy. At this point, students begin their thesis research.

ADMISSION

Each application is considered individually. The quantitative measures of the GMAT score and the undergraduate grade-point average are important in the decision-making process; however, work experience, evidence of leadership, extracurricular and community activities, and strong letters of recommendation also play key roles. An admissions interview is encouraged.

Applicants must send the completed application forms and supporting data by August 1 for the fall quarter. If the applicant is also applying for financial aid, the application should be submitted by February 22. New students may also be admitted to the winter and summer quarters; application deadlines are December 1 and May 1, respectively.

EXPENSES

The estimated total for the academic year is $17,000. The total includes $9,500 for tuition, fees of $443, $375 for books and supplies, and living expenses of $6,700. The cost per credit hour is $317. These figures are for the 1985-86 academic year and are subject to change. More than half of the graduate management students live off campus.

FINANCIAL ASSISTANCE

Merit-based financial assistance is available from the Graduate School of Management in the form of fellowships, assistantships, scholarships and loans, and through the federal Guaranteed Student Loan and National Direct Student Loan programs. The deadline for aid application to the summer and fall quarters is February 22; to the winter quarter, December 1.

PLACEMENT

The programs of the GSM Placement Office include a noncredit career course, guest speakers, on-campus recruiting, and the New York Recruiting Program, in which firms that do not recruit on campus interview students in New York City. In 1985, the New York program resulted in over 40 second interviews and 9 job offers. The average starting salary for 1985 graduates was $29,974. Approximately 75 percent of the job offers were a result of on-campus recruiting or Placement Office contacts.

CORRESPONDENCE

For further information, write to
  John G. Baker, Assistant Dean and
    Director of Admissions
  Graduate School of Management
  University of Rochester
  Rochester, New York 14627

UNIVERSITY OF ST. THOMAS

HOUSTON, TEXAS

The University of St. Thomas is located minutes from downtown Houston. Founded in 1947 as a private, Catholic, church-related, coeducational institution, St. Thomas offers graduate programs in five separate areas of study and 33 distinct undergraduate majors leading to the degrees of Bachelor of Arts (B.A.), Bachelor of Science (B.S.), and Bachelor of Business Administration (B.B.A.). Of the university's 1,800 students, roughly one third are enrolled in the Cameron School of Business, and 400 of these are in the Master of Business Administration (M.B.A.) program. The M.B.A. courses are scheduled in the evening in order to best serve the needs of the students, most of whom are young professionals attending the university on a part-time basis.

PROGRAM OF STUDY
The M.B.A. program of the University of St. Thomas is accredited by the Commission on Colleges, Southern Association of Colleges and Schools.

The program consists of 36 semester hours of course work, of which 24 hours are the core requirements. No thesis is required. In addition to the 24-hour core, the program offers three areas of concentration: finance, marketing/management, and international business. Other elective courses include business law, operations research, business communications, and computer and information systems.

The 36-hour course requirement may be reduced on the basis of waivers granted due to appropriate combinations of courses in accounting, business, economics, statistics, and mathematics or on the basis of graduate work completed at other accredited institutions. However, the program maintains a minimum of 30-semester hours of course work completed at the University of St. Thomas. The course requirements may be increased up to 12 semester hours if the student lacks an undergraduate background in accounting, economics, mathematics and statistics, and computer science.

The program is designed to prepare the student for a successful career in management by developing the essential managerial ability and skill in analyzing, quantifying, and communicating. As such, the course offerings encompass a broad range of subjects from economic theory and quantitative techniques to social environment and business ethics. The intent of this breadth of the curriculum is to provide an educational experience not only in management techniques but also in the socioeconomic environment in which management functions.

ADMISSION
Students may enter the program with degrees in business or nonbusiness areas from accredited undergraduate and graduate institutions. All applicants must take the Graduate Management Admission Test (GMAT) to be considered for admission. Admission decisions are based upon the applicant's undergraduate record, GMAT scores, recommendations from former professors and/or employers, and motivation for graduate study.

Incoming students may begin their studies in the fall, spring, or summer terms. Deadlines for all application materials to be completed and in the office of the Cameron School of Business are June 30 (fall term), November 30 (spring term), and April 30 (summer term).

A $25 nonrefundable application fee is required of all candidates for admission.

EXPENSES
Tuition per semester hour $135
Building use fee:
    Six semester hours or less 60
    More than six semester hours . . . 110
Graduation fee 50
Late registration fee 50
Computer lab fee (if applicable) . . . 30
Tuition and fees are subject to change.

FINANCIAL ASSISTANCE
The university offers a limited number of assistantships and scholarships to qualified students enrolled full time (nine hours per semester). Additionally, the University of St. Thomas participates in a variety of federal and state loan grant programs to aid the student who can demonstrate financial need.

CORRESPONDENCE
For additional information, please write or call
    Cameron School of Business
    University of St. Thomas
    3812 Montrose Boulevard
    Houston, Texas 77006
    Telephone: 713-522-3071 or
       713-522-7911, extension 509

The University of San Diego (USD) is an independent, Catholic institution chartered in 1949, with a current enrollment of approximately 5,000. Since its inception, USD has welcomed students of all races, creeds, and cultural backgrounds. The USD campus occupies 170 tabletop acres with a commanding view of the Pacific Ocean, Mission Bay, San Diego Harbor, and the surrounding mountains. Combining beauty and weather, the environment is almost unparalleled.

With the goal of promoting state-of-the-art education in business management, the School of Business, which offers programs accredited by the American Assembly of Collegiate Schools of Business (AACSB), was established in 1972. The current enrollment of graduate students is about 350, many of whom are executives studying at night.

A friendly campus atmosphere, ample opportunity for close rapport between students and faculty, class sizes that facilitate personal attention, and instructor accessibility are characteristic of the educational environment of the University of San Diego. The School of Business building, Olin Hall (completed July 1984), houses a VAX 11-780, 80 personal computers, and a behavior laboratory equipped with sophisticated videotape facilities and advanced support equipment.

PROGRAMS OF STUDY
The Master of Business Administration (M.B.A.) program is taught by USD's distinguished full-time business faculty. Depending on a student's background, the M.B.A. program ranges from 33 to 60 semester hours, generally requiring from one to two years of academic course work. Courses are offered during the day and evening hours to accommodate the full-time student as well as students working full time. Two summer sessions are offered to help students complete the program in the shortest time possible. Neither a thesis nor comprehensive examinations are required, but independent study with faculty is offered. No specific undergraduate course prerequisites or fields of concentration are required; however, students with prior course work in business administration, economics, or mathematics may have their programs shortened through appropriate course waivers. In any event, M.B.A. degree candidates must earn a minimum of 24 semester hours of graduate credit at USD.

Course requirements for the M.B.A. program are divided into four parts (1) the preliminary core (27 hours), (2) the management core (18 hours), (3) electives (12 hours), and (4) business policy (3 hours). Students may select, as electives, a maximum of six hours of first-year law courses from the USD School of Law. A joint M.B.A.-Juris Doctor (J.D.) program is offered by the School of Business Administration and the School of Law. To be admitted to the joint program, candidates must satisfy the entrance requirements of both schools.

A Master in International Business (M.I.B.) is also offered which requires an international sequence of courses and fluency in a second language.

The School of Business operates on the 4-2-4 semester system. Fall semester classes begin in early September and end before the Christmas holidays. Spring semester classes begin in late January and end in mid-May. Students may enter the M.B.A. program in the fall, spring, or either of the two-week summer sessions.

ADMISSION
Admission to the M.B.A. program requires a baccalaureate degree from an accredited college or university, a respectable undergraduate grade-point average, acceptable performance on the Graduate Management Admission Test (GMAT), a completed application form, two complete transcripts of credits from each college or university of attendance, and at least three completed appraisal forms or letters of recommendation. Interviews are encouraged but not required. Applications for admission should be filed two months before the beginning of the semester for which admission is sought.

For applicants from non-English-speaking countries, an acceptable performance (550 minimum) on the Test of English as a Foreign Language (TOEFL) is also required. Such applicants must furnish official records covering all secondary and collegiate work. All records of previous academic work must be translated into English.

EXPENSES
A nonrefundable $25 application fee is payable when application for admission is made. Tuition for the 1985-86 academic year was $235 per semester hour, and a graduate student association fee of $15

(part time) or $25 (full time) is payable each semester. Tuition and fees for an academic year total $5,690 for the full-time student and $2,850 for the part-time student.

FINANCIAL ASSISTANCE
A limited number of research assistantships are available, but these are awarded to current students. Students in financial need may apply for a Guaranteed Student Loan (GSL) through the Director of Financial Aid at USD. California residents may also apply for California State Graduate Fellowships.

PLACEMENT
Placement assistance is provided by the USD Career Development Center.

CORRESPONDENCE
For further information, write or call
Director of Graduate Programs in
   Business
Graduate School of Business
   Administration
University of San Diego
Alcala Park
San Diego, California 92110
Telephone: 619-260-4840

For application forms and Graduate Catalog, write or call
Graduate Admissions Office
University of San Diego
Alcala Park
San Diego, California 92110
Telephone: 619-260-4524

The University of San Francisco (USF), founded in 1855, is San Francisco's first university and the third oldest in California. With 51 acres, USF is the city's largest independent university campus; it overlooks downtown, the Bay, Golden Gate Bridge, and the Pacific Ocean. The unique cosmopolitan atmosphere of the city blends a wide variety of cultures, lifestyles, and interests providing an unusual and exciting environment for studying and living. San Francisco, as a major financial and international center, provides an excellent external learning environment for business students. San Francisco's location is especially ideal for business developments with the Pacific Basin countries. The San Francisco Bay Area is famous for its cultural activities, breathtaking natural scenery, and recreational activities (from skiing in the nearby Sierra Nevada to sailing on the San Francisco Bay).

USF has about 7,000 students, 35 percent of whom are studying at the graduate levels. USF is a major university which is large enough to offer the variety of resources students desire and should have at the graduate level. This permits Master of Business Administration (M.B.A.) students to move academically in a number of directions by selecting electives from other colleges within USF.

The McLaren College of Business M.B.A. program was established in 1964 with the goal of educating forward-looking managers for a wide range of careers in business as well as industry and government. The undergraduate and graduate business programs are accredited by the American Assembly of Collegiate Schools of Business (AACSB). The McLaren College of Business has a distinguished faculty of 45 who represent varied disciplines and research interests.

The M.B.A. program has 500 students. About one third are women and two thirds attend on a full-time basis. Students' ages at the time of entry range from the early twenties to the early forties, with an average age of 26. On the average, students have had two years of full-time work experience. They come from 30 different states and 25 countries throughout the world. This diverse student population contributes substantially to the dynamic and stimulating climate for study and interchange of ideas.

Part-time students represent many companies such as Bank of America, Levi-Strauss, Pacific Bell, Bechtel, Crocker Bank, Pacific Gas and Electric, and Metropolitan Life.

PROGRAMS OF STUDY

The M.B.A. program consists of four groupings: (1) foundation courses, (2) management core courses, (3) elective concentration options, and (4) management policy courses.

The McLaren College of Business offers the M.B.A. degree with emphasis in finance and banking, marketing, management, international business, and industrial relations. Students also may design their own elective course work to create other concentrations (for example, in Management Information Systems, Telecommunications).

M.B.A. students may combine the business curriculum with that of the Law or Nursing School to obtain both Juris Doctor (J.D.)/M.B.A. or Master of Science (M.S.) in nursing/M.B.A. degrees.

Students can pursue their M.B.A. on a full-time as well as a part-time basis. A semester schedule (15 weeks) is utilized in the fall and the spring, and course work in the summer is scheduled in 2 six-week sessions.

ADMISSION

The program is open to any qualified holder of a bachelor's degree from a recognized college or university, regardless of undergraduate major field of study. Because the program has limited enrollment, admission is highly competitive and only those who can present evidence of their qualifications and potential to participate successfully in graduate-level studies will be admitted.

New M.B.A. students are accepted for three starting times: fall, spring, and summer (application deadlines are June 15, November 15, and April 15, respectively). Action on an application is taken soon after the receipt of required documents, including a Graduate Management Admission Test (GMAT) score. International students must submit a Test of English as a Foreign Language (TOEFL) score (minimum 575).

EXPENSES

For 1985-86, tuition was $255 per unit. The cost of books averages $500 per year. Room and board in the graduate dormitories on campus cost approximately $1,800 per semester. Off-campus housing is available at varying costs depending on location and desired living arrangements.

FINANCIAL ASSISTANCE

The University of San Francisco provides financial assistance to students who would not otherwise be able to attend a private university. Aid available includes merit scholarships, federal and state grant programs, federal and state private loan programs, work study, and employment. Also, many companies reimburse students for tuition and books.

Financial aid applications (the SAAC or FAF) should be submitted by February 11.

PLACEMENT

The USF Career Planning and Placement Center (CPPC) provides counseling services, workshops, and research facilities for M.B.A. students. In association with the Graduate Business Student Association, the CPPC presents M.B.A. career nights with employers, professional development panel career presentations to student organizations, information sessions with companies, and visits to Bay Area companies. Recruiters from more than 100 businesses and organizations interview graduating students during the fall and spring semesters. Many off-campus job listings are received and posted daily at CPPC, and the CPPC develops and lists part-time and full-time internships and summer positions. Also, USF has many interested alumni who actively participate in the career planning process of M.B.A. students.

CORRESPONDENCE

For further information on the M.B.A. program at the University of San Francisco, contact

Director, M.B.A. Program
McLaren College of Business
University of San Francisco
Ignatian Heights
San Francisco, California 94117-1080
Telephone: 415-666-6771

Education in business at the University of Saskatchewan commenced in 1914. The college is located in the Commerce Building which was formally opened in March 1968. A computer center, equipped with a DEC 2060, is located in the same building complex. The Saskatoon campus of the University of Saskatchewan, with 14,000 undergraduate and 1,125 graduate students, is located in Saskatoon, a city having a population of approximately 155,000.

PROGRAM OF STUDY

The objective of the program is to prepare students for managerial positions. The emphasis is directed toward the development of an ability to adjust to a changing administrative environment. Consequently, the objectives of the Master of Business Administration (M.B.A.) program are to develop intellectual curiosity, a receptive attitude to innovation, perhaps some dissatisfaction with the traditional way of doing things, a commitment to modern scientific methods, and a respect for continuing research.

In addition to providing the opportunity for advanced study to students who hold undergraduate degrees in business administration, the program is designed to supply the formal academic training for those persons whose undergraduate education has been in academic disciplines other than business, but whose future careers are likely to involve managerial activity.

The academic year (September to April) is divided into a fall and spring term. Fifteen hours per week each term constitute a normal course load. A limited number of courses may be available during the summer.

In the first year of the program, the study of economics and management provides a broad understanding of administrative decision making and the business environment. The necessary quantitative skills are introduced by classes in operations research and statistics. Courses are also offered in the functional areas of accounting, industrial relations, finance, and marketing.

The second year of the program includes two required business policy courses and one required course in management information systems. The nonthesis option requires a seminar in business research methodology and six additional courses. The thesis option requires an additional three courses and a thesis under the supervision of faculty.

Exemption from certain first-year classes may be granted upon demonstration of competence in the specific areas.

ADMISSION

The Master of Business Administration program requires no specific undergraduate degree for admission to the program. In accordance with the normal admission requirements of the College of Graduate Studies, applicants must hold a baccalaureate degree in a four-year program from an accredited institution, have maintained a B or Division II average or better in the last two years of undergraduate training, and have proficiency in the English language.

Graduates of the four-year program of the College of Commerce, or its equivalent, can normally complete the program within one year. Students whose undergraduate degrees are in disciplines other than business should plan on two years to complete the program.

As enrollment in the program is limited, admission is competitive. The Graduate Studies Committee pays particular attention to the student's undergraduate record and scores on the Graduate Management Admission Test (GMAT).

Applicants are required to submit (1) application forms for admission to the College of Graduate Studies; (2) two letters of recommendation, preferably from former professors who are in a position to assess the applicant's ability to undertake graduate study; (3) two copies of transcripts of all previous academic pursuits; and (4) scores on the GMAT. Foreign students whose native language is not English are required to demonstrate their proficiency in English by taking the Test of English as a Foreign Language (TOEFL).

EXPENSES

Single persons should plan for a minimum expenditure of $6,600. This figure includes the cost of tuition and student fees ($1,107 per year), room and board, and personal items.

Residence accommodation is available on campus for both single and married students. Since a significant demand exists, those who desire campus residence should be sure that their applications are received well in advance of the commencement of the fall term. Room with board and self-contained suites or apartments can usually be obtained within walking distance of the university or close to public transportation. Parking facilities are available on campus.

FINANCIAL ASSISTANCE

The College of Commerce offers a limited number of assistantships to graduate students to help faculty members in grading and supervising undergraduate work and in doing research. All successful applicants are automatically considered for financial assistance administered by the college. Separate application is not necessary.

CORRESPONDENCE

For further information, please write or call

Director of Graduate Business Studies
Assistant Dean, (Programs)
College of Commerce
University of Saskatchewan
Saskatoon, Saskatchewan,
 Canada S7N 0W0
Telephone: 306-966-4785

The University of Scranton, one of 28 Jesuit colleges and universities in the United States, is located approximately 120 miles from New York City and 120 miles from Philadelphia. The area offers excellent opportunities for year-round recreational activities in the Pocono Mountains and short travel times to major metropolitan areas. The campus is located in Scranton, a city of 100,000 people in northeastern Pennsylvania.

The University of Scranton, the oldest Catholic institution of higher education in northeastern Pennsylvania, was founded in 1888 as Saint Thomas College. It is chartered under the laws of the Commonwealth of Pennsylvania and empowered to confer bachelor's and master's degrees in the arts, sciences, business administration, and education. Current enrollment at the university is 4,669. The Master of Business Administration (M.B.A.) program has approximately 300 students.

Graduate courses in the M.B.A. program are predominantly taught by full-time faculty members of the School of Management who have extensive professional experience and who have earned doctoral degrees from prestigious institutions.

PROGRAM OF STUDY

M.B.A. students attend classes in the evenings on either a full-time or part-time basis. Students may specialize in accounting, finance, personnel and labor relations, operations and production, or marketing. The M.B.A. curriculum includes foundation courses, core courses, and advanced electives. The curriculum is designed for students with or without an undergraduate business degree. Students with business degrees can normally complete the M.B.A. program by satisfying the core and advanced elective requirements. Students with nonbusiness undergraduate degrees will be required to complete some or all of the foundation courses. The foundation courses include micro- and macroeconomic theory, accounting and information systems, quantitative methods and statistics, management principles, marketing, finance, and business law.

The core of the M.B.A. program is designed to give students broad-based management skills at the graduate level. Courses in managerial economics, managerial accounting, management science, organizational behavior, marketing, finance, and business policy allow students to widen their perspective and communicate more effectively with managers in other functional areas.

Advanced electives allow the student to deepen his or her knowledge in one functional area of business. The total graduate-level course requirement is 36 credits.

ADMISSION

The basic policy of the school is to select for the M.B.A. program those men and women whose intellectual ability and leadership potential qualify them for careers in management. Admission is based on the following criteria: performance on the Graduate Management Admission Test (GMAT), overall grade-point average, rank in graduating class, managerial experience, and other earned graduate degrees.

Applicants should have a total of at least 950 points based on the formula: 200 × the undergraduate grade-point average + the GMAT score. A maximum of six graduate credits may be transferred to the University of Scranton. All foundation course credits may be transferred. Foreign students whose native language is not English are required to demonstrate their proficiency in English by achieving a score of at least 500 on the Test of English as a Foreign Language (TOEFL).

Applications should be made two months in advance of the entering dates in September and February.

EXPENSES

Tuition for 1985-86 was $155 per credit hour. Full-time students should plan on an expenditure of $8,200 per year for all costs.

FINANCIAL ASSISTANCE

A limited number of graduate assistantships are available for full-time students. Students receiving an assistantship are entitled to a waiver of tuition and fees plus a stipend.

PLACEMENT

The Office of Career Services maintains a full range of services for all degree candidates.

CORRESPONDENCE

For additional information or to request an application, please write or call
The Graduate School
University of Scranton
Scranton, Pennsylvania 18510
Telephone: 717-961-7600

The Division of Economic Studies of the University of Sheffield provides both postgraduate and undergraduate programs in business studies, in addition to programs in economics and in accounting and financial management. The Postgraduate Business Program covers the usual spectrum of business disciplines, functions, and skills and is intended to provide an opportunity for men and women to develop the attitudes, knowledge, and skills that will constitute a foundation for their development into competent and responsible business managers.

The course is designed for those who have relatively little experience of the wide range of problems encountered in business today and who wish to examine some of the concepts and techniques employed. It is not intended for those with a first degree in business. It may be followed either on a part-time or a full-time basis.

PROGRAMS OF STUDY

Students may be registered initially either for the Postgraduate Diploma in Business Studies or the degree of Master of Business Administration (M.B.A.) depending on qualifications. All students follow a core of interrelated courses taught during the academic year, commencing at the beginning of October and lasting until June. The core courses are, in general, intended to provide training in the range of disciplines and functions relevant to business management and expertise in decision-making techniques useful to the executive. Emphasis is placed on the steady development of the student's analytical skills in practical business situations. The core courses of the program include organizational behavior, quantitative analysis, marketing, financial management, business economics, and business policy.

A variety of teaching methods are employed in the program. Special emphasis is placed upon student participation by the use of the case method, seminars, and syndicates. Lectures and problem-solving sessions are used where appropriate. In addition to formal teaching, a series of seminars is conducted by invited executives.

The course is assessed both by course work and examinations. Projects, exercises, problems, essays, and case analyses are used in assessing performance during the year, and a series of written examinations is held in June.

Students registered initially for the degree of M.B.A. and diploma students who achieve a Division I pass in the examinations then proceed to a research project which forms the second part of the program. The research must be undertaken during the three months immediately following the end of the academic year in which the taught courses were completed. The research project may take the form of an investigation of a particular managerial problem in one or a few firms or an analysis of statistical or documentary data, including a review of the literature concerned with a particular business problem. A dissertation based on the research project must then be presented. The degree of M.B.A. is awarded to candidates who successfully complete both parts of the program.

ADMISSION

Entry requirements are flexible. Selection for the program is based on applicants' proven academic ability, motivation, and potential as managers. The normal minimum educational requirement is a second-class honors degree in any subject from a British university or the equivalent from an overseas institution. In addition, nongraduates who hold professional qualifications approved by the Senate for entry purposes may apply. The major accountancy and engineering professional qualifications have been approved. The H.N.D. in business studies is not, however, a sufficient qualification for entry. Applicants are required to take the Graduate Management Admission Test (GMAT). The median age of recent class memberships has been 25, and about half have at least three years' business experience.

Students who hold commonwealth, overseas, or foreign qualifications should note that selection standards for places on the program are high. The successful completion of the program necessitates mastery of English, and overseas candidates may be asked to take the Test of English as a Foreign Language (TOEFL).

Applications should reach the Director no later than June 1, although later applications may be considered if places are still available. A two-year part-time M.B.A./P.G. Diploma is available for local students in employment in commerce or industry.

EXPENSES

Tuition fees are subject to revision each year, and up-to-date information will be available to applicants at the appropriate time. Current fees (1985-86) are £1,594 for United Kingdom (U.K.) students or £3,330 for overseas students. All applicants should note that the Director is unable to offer financial assistance. Applicants should therefore make their own financial arrangements and should allow at least £280 per month for living expenses.

CORRESPONDENCE

For further information, please write or call

Director
The Postgraduate Business Program
Division of Economic Studies
University of Sheffield,
 Sheffield S10 2TN
Yorks, United Kingdom
Telephone: 0742-78555

UNIVERSITY OF SOUTH ALABAMA

MOBILE, ALABAMA

The University of South Alabama is relatively young, having been created by act of the Alabama State Legislature in May 1963. The university is strategically located in the greater Mobile area which has a population of more than a million within a 100-mile radius. This area, which lies along the Gulf Coast, is semitropical with a mean temperature of 67.5 degrees; most outdoor sports and recreation are pursued 12 months of the year. Some flowers or plants are in bloom throughout the year, particularly the azaleas in early spring. The city is famous also for the Senior Bowl, the America's Junior Miss Pageant, its Mardi Gras celebration, and its beach and river activities.

The University of South Alabama occupies a large picturesque 1200-acre campus located in the western section of Mobile known as Spring Hill. It also owns 327 acres on Mobile Bay, occupied by the Brookley Center. The university maintains a subdivision of 755 homes occupied by married students attending the university. The Main Campus adjoins the 750-acre Municipal Park with its extensive recreational facilities, including the Azalea City Golf Club.

The College of Business and Management, an integral part of the university, has an enrollment of approximately 1,800 undergraduate and 140 graduate students.

PROGRAM OF STUDY

The Master of Business Administration (M.B.A.) degree program is designed to enable individuals to study advanced concepts of business, industry, and government operations. The program is intended for both the active manager or technical supervisor as well as the recent graduate who is interested in advanced study in the field of business. The program includes management, accounting, finance, quantitative methods, marketing, and economics. A concentration in accounting is available.

The M.B.A. program of the University of South Alabama is a night program which accommodates students who work full time during the day. It is designed for students to take two courses a quarter to complete the program in six quarters (exclusive of summer quarter) if they take the general option, or seven quarters if they select the accounting option. All students selecting the accounting option must attend summer school. Those without a business degree may require additional hours of work to complete foundation courses.

For the M.B.A. degree in general business 48 quarter hours are required; for the M.B.A. concentration in accounting, 48 quarter hours (available only to students who do not have an undergraduate degree in accounting).

ADMISSION

Admission to the M.B.A. program is limited to holders of baccalaureate degrees from regionally accredited institutions. Applicants must also present evidence, including admission test scores and undergraduate records, indicating high promise of success in study at the graduate level.

Applicants to the Graduate School may be admitted in two categories.

The full-standing admission requirements are as follows:
- a bachelor's degree,
- a minimal grade-point average of 3.00 on all undergraduate work (A = 4.00), and
- a satisfactory score on the Graduate Management Admission Test (GMAT).

A student with less than a 3.00 and greater than a 2.50 on all undergraduate work (A = 4.00) or 2.75 on the last 96 quarter hours of college work may be admitted conditionally provided the student has a bachelor's degree and a satisfactory GMAT score. A satisfactory GMAT score is based on the formula: undergraduate grade-point average × 200 + GMAT score = 1,000 *or* upper-division grade-point average (last 96 hours) × 200 + GMAT score = 1,050. The GMAT must have been taken within the last five years.

A conditional admission student must qualify as a student in full standing upon the completion of the first 12 quarter hours of graduate credit with a minimum grade of B in each course. Students failing to do so will be dismissed from the program.

The university operates on the quarter system. Applicants may apply for admission for fall, winter, spring, or summer quarter. Quarters begin in September, January, March, and June; completed applications and supporting documents should be in the admissions office at least five weeks prior to the beginning of classes.

EXPENSES

Current fees, on a per-quarter basis, are as follows:

Application fee, nonrefundable ...	$10
Course fee, per quarter hour......	34
Other fees, approximately........	47

Since personal expenses including books, supplies, and food and living expenses vary, no attempt is made to estimate such costs; however, they probably range at the lower end of the scale when compared with a cross section of all universities.

FINANCIAL ASSISTANCE

The College of Business and Management Studies has established a limited number of full or partial graduate assistantships for students enrolled or contemplating enrollment in its M.B.A. program. These assistantships, which require a minimum of 16 hours work per week, help defray part of a student's expense.

PLACEMENT

The University Placement Office is active in recruiting and maintains placement files for graduates.

CORRESPONDENCE

Inquiries should be directed to
Director of Graduate Studies
College of Business and Management Studies
Business and Management Building
University of South Alabama
Mobile, Alabama 36688
Telephone: 205-460-6180

UNIVERSITY OF SOUTH CAROLINA

COLUMBIA, SOUTH CAROLINA

The University of South Carolina (USC), chartered in 1801, is a state-supported, coeducational institution located in the state's capital city. Academically, the university consists of 16 schools and colleges offering degrees at the baccalaureate, master's, and doctoral levels.

The College of Business Administration occupies a modern eight-story building housing some of the finest instructional facilities and resources in the nation. Approximately 1,000 graduate students are currently enrolled in the college. Both the college's undergraduate and graduate programs are accredited by the American Assembly of Collegiate Schools of Business (AACSB).

PROGRAMS OF STUDY

As a comprehensive graduate school of business, the college offers six master's and two doctoral programs in business administration. The M.B.A. program is a two-year professional management program which requires from 54 to 69 semester hours of course work depending upon one's academic background. Course work requirements include 15 hours of foundation courses for students without a background in business administration, 33 hours of core courses, 6 hours of integrative courses, 9 hours of electives, and 6 hours for participation in a field study. A unique feature of the program is the field study which gives the student practical business experience through assigned work with a participating company.

The Master of International Business Studies (M.I.B.S.) program offers two- and three-year courses of study designed for students interested in a career with firms engaged in multinational business. The program includes intensive language study in Arabic, French, German, Japanese, Portuguese, or Spanish and course work that develops functional business skills with international concepts as well as environmental understanding. Depending upon their language track, students are assigned to a cooperating multinational firm for an internship in Japan, the Middle East, France, Belgium, Germany, Colombia, or Brazil. Foreign nationals intern in the United States.

The Master of Personnel and Employee Relations (M.P.E.R.) program is designed to train individuals for careers as personnel and employee relations professionals. Owing to the increasingly complex and sophisticated nature of employee relations, a high degree of specialization is needed by the personnel and employee relations professional. The M.P.E.R. program provides the requisite specialization through 39 semester hours of course work, a 6-semester-hour internship, and a noncredit computer skills short course.

The Master of Accountancy program is a 30-semester-hour program designed to prepare students for careers in public, private, or governmental accounting or for further graduate work. Although the Master of Accountancy program is a natural extension of study for students who have completed an undergraduate major in accounting at USC, the program is open to any person who satisfies the college's admission standards. Students without adequate undergraduate preparation in accounting and/or other areas of business are required to take additional courses as part of their program.

The Master of Science (M.S.) in business administration is designed for students seeking specialization in the marketing or management information systems fields. Course requirements include a minimum of 24 hours of approved course work plus 6 hours of thesis credit and the preparation of an acceptable thesis.

The Doctor of Philosophy (Ph.D.) in business administration is designed for students of outstanding ability who wish to do advanced work in preparation for careers in university teaching and research, business, and/or government. Possible areas of concentration in the Ph.D. and M.S. programs include accounting, banking, finance, insurance, real estate, international business, strategic management, organizational behavior, personnel operations research, production, management information systems, and marketing.

The Master of Arts and Ph.D. programs in economics prepare students for careers as professional economists in government and business or for teaching and research positions at the university level. Requirements for the master's degree in economics are the same as for the M.S. in business administration. The Ph.D. normally requires three years of full-time work beyond the bachelor's degree.

ADMISSION

Admission to all programs within the college is selective and based upon a consideration of the applicant's aptitude for successful graduate work in business or economics as indicated by (1) acceptable scores on the Graduate Management Admission Test (GMAT), (2) the quality of previous academic work, (3) letters of recommendation, and (4) work experience. Admission to most degree programs is on a semester basis with the exception of the M.B.A. and M.I.B.S. programs which have a once-a-year admissions policy. Students admitted into these programs begin either in the summer or fall depending upon course exemptions.

EXPENSES

Basic academic expenses for a single student per semester are as follows:

Tuition	$804
Business administration enrichment fee:	
In-state	250
Out-of-state	500
Computer and library fees	52
University housing: (Dormitory space is not available.) One-bedroom apartments, per month	375

FINANCIAL ASSISTANCE

A number of fellowships and assistantships are awarded each year to entering students on a competitive basis. All graduate assistants pay reduced tuition.

PLACEMENT

The college operates its own placement service as well as cooperates with the university placement bureau.

CORRESPONDENCE

For further information, write or call
Director of Graduate Studies
College of Business Administration
University of South Carolina
Columbia, South Carolina 29208
Telephone: 803-777-2306

The University of South Dakota is an institution of 5,500 students located in the extreme southeastern part of the state. The School of Business enrollments are approximately 450 upper-division undergraduates and 280 full-time and part-time graduate students. Both the undergraduate programs and the Master of Business Administration (M.B.A.) program are accredited by the American Assembly of Collegiate Schools of Business (AACSB).

PROGRAMS OF STUDY

The M.B.A. program at the University of South Dakota is aimed at development of general competence in management and the decision-making process and an understanding of the role of business in society.

Students who enter with 27 semester hours of undergraduate work in business administration, economics, and accounting can expect to complete the degree in one calendar year. These 27 hours include accounting (6 hours), economics (6 hours), business finance (3 hours), marketing (3 hours), statistics (3 hours), business law (3 hours), and management (3 hours). The time is extended from a minimum of one summer session to a maximum of one year for those who have not completed this work.

The required courses beyond the undergraduate core listed above are the following:

First Semester	Hours
Managerial Economics	3
Financial Administration	3
Elective	3
Quantitative Analysis	3
Second Semester	
Business and Its Environment	3
Managerial Accounting	3
Organization Theory and Behavior	3
Management Information Systems	3
Summer	
Production	2
Administrative Policy	3
Marketing Administration	3

At least three required graduate courses are offered each semester in the part-time evening program. The courses offered are alternated, making it convenient to complete the M.B.A. on a part-time basis.

A combined law-M.B.A. program is also offered at the university. Students enrolled in the Law School, if admitted to the M.B.A. program, may elect one required M.B.A. course a semester during their junior and senior years. Up to nine hours of this work may be used in fulfilling the requirements for the Juris Doctor (J.D.) degree. Up to nine hours of work taken in the Law School may also be counted toward the M.B.A. degree. Those who have completed the undergraduate preparation in business may be able to earn both the J.D. and M.B.A. degrees in three and one-half years. Those who do not have the undergraduate preparation may be able to complete this during the summer sessions. For further information contact either the Dean of the Law School or the Director of the M.B.A. Program.

The Master of Professional Accountancy (M.P.A.) degree is offered for those who wish to concentrate their study in accounting. Students entering this program are required to have intermediate accounting (6 hours) and federal income tax (3 hours) as part of their undergraduate core. This degree meets the South Dakota State Board of Accountancy's requirements to sit for the C.P.A. examination.

ADMISSION

Enrollment is limited to graduates of accredited colleges or universities. Students must have 1,000 points or more based on the formula: 200 times the upper-division grade-point average (4.00 system) + the score on the Graduate Management Admission Test (GMAT) and a minimum of 400 points on the GMAT.

Where the applicant's undergraduate record is unclear, a written qualifying examination may be required in one or a number of business disciplines.

EXPENSES

Approximate figures, per semester:

	S.D. resident	Nonresident
Tuition	$ 582	$1,128
Fees	215	215
Room and board	900	900
Books and supplies	200	200
	$1,897	$2,443

FINANCIAL ASSISTANCE

A limited number of graduate assistantships are available. Selection is based on academic promise. Applications should be sent to the Director of the M.B.A. Program.

PLACEMENT

The School of Business maintains its own placement office which is visited each year by representatives of approximately 100 companies from all sections of the country.

CORRESPONDENCE

Students may obtain further information by writing or calling

Director
M.B.A. Program
School of Business
University of South Dakota
Vermillion, South Dakota 57069
Telephone: 605-677-5232

UNIVERSITY OF SOUTH FLORIDA

TAMPA, FLORIDA

The University of South Florida, one of the nine state universities in the State University System, is located in the Tampa Bay and Gulf Coast area of Florida. The main campus is situated on 1,700 acres to the north of the city of Tampa, thus providing the university with the advantages of a major metropolitan area. Branch campuses are located in St. Petersburg, Sarasota, and Fort Myers.

Since its opening in 1960, the University of South Florida has graduated 55,500 students. Its current enrollment of approximately 25,000 makes it the second largest university in the state. The College of Business Administration with an enrollment of 4,800 undergraduate students and 700 graduate students is one of nine colleges within the university. The College of Business Administration is housed in the new Chester Howell Ferguson Hall, a uniquely designed and energy-efficient building. This facility is ideally designed to meet the needs of graduate education and houses the latest in modern educational support equipment.

PROGRAMS OF STUDY

The objective of the Master of Business Administration (M.B.A.) program is to prepare graduates to assume increasingly responsible positions in management, in both the private and public sectors. The program permits the student to develop analytical, problem-solving, managerial, and decision-making capabilities and to provide the knowledge essential for solving managerial problems. Although emphasis in the M.B.A. program is on preparation for general management responsibilities, students may develop specialized knowledge through choice of elective courses. The 60-semester-hour program (36-hour minimum) is designed to meet the needs of qualified men and women with degrees in the liberal arts, engineering, the sciences, and humanities as well as those with prior preparation in business administration. Prior work in business and economics may provide waivers in some of the required courses. The full-time student without course waivers will require two years to complete the program. Part-time students must complete degree requirements within five years. Courses are scheduled during the day and evenings to accommodate both full-time and part-time students.

The Master of Science in management program is designed to offer specialization in the field of management as a discipline with exposure to both quantitative and qualitative aspects of managerial activity. Students are chosen from practicing managers as well as from those aspiring to a career in management. The program is a 52-semester-hour (31-hour minimum) integrated program rather than a set of courses. Students with prior academic work in selected courses may reduce the program by waiver toward the 31-hour minimum. The full-time student without course waivers will require two years to complete the program; part-time students will require longer.

The Master of Accountancy program is designed to meet the increasing needs of business, government, and professional accounting for persons who have training in accounting as well as a background in such areas as quantitative methods, economic analysis, and management science. For the student who has the equivalency of an undergraduate major in accounting, the program consists of approximately 36 semester hours. A minimum of 15 semester hours is devoted to the study of professional accounting. Another 15 semester hours of the program consist of study in business-related fields. The remaining six hours are electives with a three-semester-hour limit in accounting.

The Master of Arts (M.A.) in economics program has been developed to equip the student for responsible positions in professional economics as well as related industrial and governmental pursuits that require an economics background. The master's program in economics is a degree in general economics built around a core of economic theory, history of economic thought, and economic statistics supplemented by additional theory and methodological requirements. Electives permit the student to pursue individual interests without sacrificing the structure necessary for substantive analysis. The student is required to complete a minimum of 30 semester hours including both course work and an optional thesis to qualify for the M.A. in economics.

ADMISSION

Admission is open to all qualified men and women who hold a bachelor's degree from an accredited institution. Prior study in business or economics is not a requirement. Admission is granted to those highly motivated applicants whose records show high academic promise and managerial talent.

The Graduate Management Admission Test (GMAT) is required of all applicants except those applying for the economics program, which requires the Graduate Record Examinations (GRE). The Test of English as a Foreign Language (TOEFL) is required of all foreign students. Students are expected to enter programs for the fall or winter semester.

EXPENSES

Per semester, estimated

Tuition, per	In-state	Out-of-state*
semester hour	$50	$145

Limited out-of-state fee waivers are available.

FINANCIAL ASSISTANCE

Financial assistance is available through fellowships, scholarships, graduate assistantships, fee waivers, loans, and on-campus or local employment.

PLACEMENT

The Career Planning and Placement Center Division of Administrative Services assists students and alumni in realizing their career objectives.

CORRESPONDENCE

For further information on the programs of study offered by the College of Business Administration, please write or call

Director of Graduate Studies
College of Business Administration
University of South Florida
Tampa, Florida 33620
Telephone: 813-974-3335

The University of Southern California (USC), a large, private, nonsectarian university, is a member of the American Association of Universities. The university's location near the center of the Los Angeles metropolitan area offers students unlimited opportunities to become thoroughly acquainted with all types of business.

The Graduate School of Business Administration (GSBA) has a present graduate enrollment of 1,290, including 610 full-time master's candidates, 680 part-time master's candidates, and 80 Ph.D. candidates.

The school has a computer center exclusively for its own use, and every graduate student has an opportunity to become proficient in computer operation and application. Graduate students may also make full use of a management laboratory equipped with one-way-vision glass, audio and video tape recorders, three experimental rooms, and an observation room; the Roy P. Crocker business library of 100,000 working volumes; and Doheney Library.

PROGRAMS OF STUDY

The Master of Business Administration (M.B.A.) programs are broad in nature and aimed at general competence for overall management and business statesmanship. Major objectives are to help each student acquire a proper orientation to business, develop skill in using tools of analysis, understand the functional areas of business, begin the development of an analytical point of view, and develop a capacity for adapting to change.

A student begins course work during the two-year M.B.A. program by completing the core program the first year. During this first year, all required courses are taught using various teaching techniques: case, lecture, simulation, and group projects. In addition, students participate in a management internship program which is designed as a problem-integrating experience with Los Angeles firms.

The second year of the M.B.A. program incorporates a final required policy course and elective tracks in such areas as management decision systems, real estate, investments, financial institutions, international finance, consumer behavior, logistics and distribution management, marketing research, marketing management, professional accounting, managerial accounting, accounting information systems, operations management, planning

and environment, human resources management, and entrepreneur and ventureship management.

Students holding bachelor's degrees in business have the opportunity to waive some of the first-year requirements through examination or evaluation of course credits, thereby reducing the total number of credits to be taken.

The school also offers the Master of Science (M.S.) degrees in management science and organizational behavior. The School of Accounting offers the Master of Accounting and Master of Business Taxation. Dual degrees are offered with law, engineering, and urban planning.

A part-time program is available for those who are employed. Requirements are identical to the full-time programs, and full-time faculty conduct most of the courses.

USC offers a special 12-month M.B.A. degree (IBEAR) designed specifically for international low- and middle-level managers who have at least two years of experience in international business as well as a bachelor's degree. Each participant is sponsored by a firm or governmental agency, and the majority are from Pacific Basic Countries.

The Doctor of Philosophy (Ph.D.) program in business administration is designed to prepare students for careers in university teaching and in research. The program consists of four phases: (1) screening, (2) advanced course work, (3) qualifying examinations, and (4) dissertation. The fields and areas include accounting, business economics, finance, corporate strategy, futures research, information systems, management science, marketing, and organizational behavior. The Ph.D. program is full time, and substantial financial aid is available.

ADMISSION

Applicants should have a bachelor's degree from an accredited institution and must take the Graduate Management Admission Test (GMAT) for all master's programs and the Graduate Record Examinations (GRE) for the Ph.D. program. No specific course prerequisites, majors, or areas of concentration are required except a knowledge of calculus. Applications should be filed at least six months prior to desired entrance.

EXPENSES

Full-time students may use the following general guide*:

Tuition (full-time) and fees,
per term $4,710
Room and board
(in university housing)....... 2,250
Books and supplies 200-225
Parking, per semester
(optional) 80
Athletic activity book
(optional) 30
Tuition, per unit (for part-time
students).................. 319

---

*Figures are estimated per semester.

FINANCIAL ASSISTANCE

Twenty-five to 30 percent of the full-time students receive a GSBA fellowship. The amounts vary with most awards covering half-tuition. Applicants who wish to be considered for fellowships must file the GSBA Application for Admission and Financial Aid before March 1. Awards are announced by April 15 and become effective in September. In addition to student loans and work-study, the school participates in the Consortium for Graduate Study in Management, a fellowship program for minority students.

PLACEMENT

Placement services are offered by the GSBA Career Services Office. Additionally, the school offers a range of career services and distributes a book of personal resumes of GSBA students to over 400 firms. Job and career seminars are held each year.

CORRESPONDENCE

For further information, write or call
Director of Admissions
Graduate School of Business
Administration BR1 101
University of Southern California
Los Angeles, California 90089-1421
Telephone: 213-743-7846

A graduate program in the College of Business Administration was established in 1959. The present graduate enrollment is over 150 with the majority attending as part-time students in the evening.

PROGRAMS OF STUDY

The College of Business Administration offers programs of study leading to the degrees of Master of Business Administration (M.B.A.) and Master of Professional Accountancy.

The primary purpose of the M.B.A. is to prepare students for responsible positions in business and industry. It is also useful as preparatory graduate work for the doctoral degree as well as for teaching in junior and senior colleges. Many part-time students with technical and other specialized undergraduate degrees use the M.B.A. as an aid in making the transition into the management area.

The School of Professional Accountancy offers the Master of Professional Accountancy degree. This program prepares students for professional accountancy positions in public accounting, industry, and government. It opens the door to additional graduate work at the doctoral level and to teaching positions in higher education. Students are well prepared to take the C.P.A. examination upon the completion of this program.

Each program requires a 33-semester-hour curriculum which includes a basic integrated core of required courses supplemented with courses in a field of emphasis and one elective. Fields of emphasis are in economics, finance, management, marketing, real estate, and public administration. One elective may be chosen within the College of Business graduate offerings or from such fields as computer science, psychology, or mathematics.

Students with an undergraduate degree from an approved school of business ordinarily complete the requirements for the master's degree in one calendar year. To serve part-time students, core requirements are offered at night at least once a year.

Other courses are also scheduled to facilitate planning a night curriculum. Students with undergraduate work in fields other than business and electing the master's may be required to complete up to 27 semester hours of prerequisites. Students may complete prerequisites while doing graduate work if the deficiencies are not too great.

ADMISSION

Admission to the graduate programs in business is open to all students who have a bachelor's degree from an accredited college and who have demonstrated through their undergraduate record and performance on the Graduate Management Admission Test (GMAT) the ability and potential to undertake graduate-level work successfully. An undergraduate degree in business is not required for admission. A score of 550 or above on the Test of English as a Foreign Language (TOEFL) is required of all foreign students.

Applications must be received no later than August 9, 1986 for fall semester; December 20, 1986 for spring semester; and May 16, 1987 for summer term.

EXPENSES

Per semester	In-state	Out-of-state
Tuition	$ 633	$1,171
Room and board		
(dormitory)	955	955
Books and supplies	85	85
	$1,673	$2,211

Part-time tuition is $70 per semester hour. Unfurnished married student housing costs $520-$610 per semester. All fees and charges are subject to change without notice.

FINANCIAL ASSISTANCE

The financial aid program consists of assistantships, loans, and part-time employment. Graduate assistantships with a stipend of $3,200 or more per academic year plus waiver of out-of-state tuition are available to students with excellent academic records. Applications for assistantships should be submitted to the Coordinator of Graduate Studies no later than March 15.

Students may borrow through federally sponsored low-interest loan programs with payment deferred until completion of the student's studies, or they may participate in the work-study program which consists of part-time work within the university.

PLACEMENT

The university maintains a placement bureau to provide assistance to graduating seniors, graduate students, and alumni in obtaining employment and to employers in recruiting qualified employees.

Throughout the year, current listings of employment opportunities, both in and out of state, in teaching, business, industry, and government are made available to the students. On-campus interviews are scheduled with personnel representatives from schools, businesses, industries, and governmental agencies.

CORRESPONDENCE

For further information about the graduate program in management offered, please write or call
    Coordinator of Graduate Studies
    College of Business Administration
    University of Southern Mississippi
    Southern Station Box 5096
    Hattiesburg, Mississippi 39401
    Telephone: 601-266-4664

The University of Southern Mississippi—Gulf Coast Regional Campus, with locations in Long Beach, Keesler Air Force Base, and in Gautier, is part of a cooperative coordinated plan to offer comprehensive higher education on the Mississippi Gulf Coast.

PROGRAM OF STUDY

The Master of Business Administration (M.B.A.) program is primarily designed to prepare the student for a position of responsibility in business or industry. Also used as preparatory graduate work for the doctoral degree or for teaching in junior colleges where a teaching certificate is not required, the program is broad in nature and aimed at developing general competence in overall management.

Research reveals that individuals with technical or other specialized degrees frequently discover that, after experiencing initially satisfying careers in their specialties, further promotions require a transition into the managerial area. The M.B.A. program supplements the education of the specialist and should enable him or her to make the transition more readily. For this reason, the M.B.A. program includes many students with undergraduate degrees in other fields as well as those who majored in business or economics.

The core requirement for the M.B.A., regardless of emphasis chosen, is as follows:

	Hours
ACC 625	3
ECO 625	3
FIN 625	3
GBA 625 or MGT 615	3
MKT 625	3
MGT 625	3
MGT 670	3
Field emphasis	9
Elective	3
	33

The student may select a field emphasis as follows:

- economics—ECO 608, plus two courses elected from ECO 610, 630, 670 (ECO 606 and GBA 625 to be selected in core);
- marketing—MKT 635, 640, 650 (GBA 625 to be selected in core);
- management—MGT 620 and two courses at the 600 level depending upon the interest and needs of the student as approved by his or her adviser (MGT 615 to be selected in core);
- real estate—REI 640, 650 and REI 534 or 560;
- finance—FIN 630, 652 and one elective approved by adviser;
- general business—three courses at the 600 level from any of the departments depending upon the interest and needs of the student as approved by his or her adviser;
- public administration—PS 700, 720, 770.

ADMISSION

The M.B.A. program covers such a broad scope that an undergraduate degree in any of a wide variety of areas from any accredited university is acceptable for admission.

The student who did undergraduate work in a field other than business administration will have to spend additional time making up deficiencies. The following courses are required as prerequisites: Principles of Accounting (6 hours) or ACC 604, Financial Accounting Analysis; Principles of Economics (6 hours) or ECO 604, Economic Analysis; MAT 312 (or equivalent) and Statistics (6 hours); Principles of Management or adequate substitute (3 hours); Principles of Marketing or adequate substitute (3 hours); Business Finance (3 hours); Legal Environment of Business (3 hours); Money and Public Policy (3 hours); Fortran or Cobal (3 hours).

Regular admission to the M.B.A. program requires a minimum of 1,000 points based on the formula: 200 times the grade-point average of the last two years of undergraduate study (4.0 scale), plus the Graduate Management Admission Test (GMAT) score.

The GMAT is not a measure of achievement or knowledge in any specific subject matter, and those who take it are neither required nor expected to have had undergraduate preparation in business subjects; it is designed to measure the potential for a student for graduate study in management. This is a standardized test administered four times a year on a world-wide basis by Educational Testing Service, Princeton, New Jersey 08541.

CORRESPONDENCE

For further information, contact
  Dr. Brooks E. Smith
  Coordinator of Graduate Business
    Studies
  University of Southern Mississippi—
    Gulf Coast
  Long Beach, Mississippi 39560
  Telephone: 601-863-6231

The University of Southwestern Louisiana was established by an act of the state legislature in 1898. Now the university is the second largest state institution with a total enrollment of more than 16,000 students, while growth in size and quality continues. There are some 130 academic undergraduate degree programs, and nearly 50 graduate degree programs, including a number of Doctor of Philosophy (Ph.D.) programs in the humanities, sciences, and engineering. The College of Business Administration offers the Bachelor of Science in business administration in 12 areas, and with an enrollment of over 4,000 it is the largest college. The Lafayette area, with a population of 151,000, offers varied and numerous recreational and cultural opportunities in its famous relaxed social atmosphere. Lafayette is always listed among the best places to live and among those with the highest quality of life. The city is the cultural, trade, and medical center of the area known as "Acadiana," and is the energy industry center for the state.

PROGRAM OF STUDY
The Graduate School offers the Master of Business Administration (M.B.A.) degree. The M.B.A. is intended to develop analytical decision-making skills for a complex and dynamic business and social environment. Breadth is emphasized and is aimed at providing a common body of knowledge and developing competence for overall management. Beyond this, students may pursue their special interests through elective courses.

Basic requirements for the M.B.A. degree consist of 36 semester hours (12 courses), 30 semester hours of core courses, and 6 semester hours of electives. The requirements increase from 3 to 15 additional semester hours (foundation courses) depending upon the undergraduate business courses previously completed. For someone with no undergraduate background in business, the maximum program length would be 51 semester hours or 17 courses.

The courses of the various components of the program are as follows: foundation courses—financial accounting, managerial finance, marketing, management, statistics; core courses—managerial accounting, economics, legal environment, operations management, human factors, quantitative methods, marketing management, information systems, financial management, policy; and electives in business selected from accounting, economics, finance, management, and marketing. There is no thesis requirement or option.

Students can begin the program at any of three points of the academic calendar: fall, spring, or summer. A full complement of courses is scheduled each semester to accommodate the part-time evening student and the full-time student. The time required to complete the degree will vary depending upon the undergraduate background and full- or part-time attendance, with the minimum being less than two calendar years.

ADMISSION
A person who holds a bachelor's degree from an accredited college or university may be considered for admission regardless of the undergraduate field of study. In order to be admitted a student must show high promise of success in postgraduate business study as indicated by testing, previous schooling, and experience. In this regard, acceptable scores on the Graduate Management Admission Test (GMAT) and an acceptable undergraduate grade-point average are required. Relevant employment experience is also expected. International students must, in addition, submit scores from the Test of English as a Foreign Language (TOEFL).

EXPENSES
The following fees, which are approximate and subject to change, are for one semester. The summer session is normally less.

| | Louisiana | |
Credit hours	Resident	Nonresident
3	$119	$119
6	214	434
9 or more	415	855

On-campus housing and food service are available. Actual expenses will vary according to individual needs and preferences, but all expenses both on and off campus are considered to be relatively inexpensive.

FINANCIAL ASSISTANCE
The University of Southwestern Louisiana operates the Student Financial Aid Office to assist students in obtaining financial assistance in the form of scholarships, assistantships, loans, grants, and/or part-time employment. A limited number of assistantships are available which carry a stipend of $4,000.

PLACEMENT
An active placement office brings to the campus a large number of companies and government agencies for interviewing. The office also provides other job and career-related services.

CORRESPONDENCE
For further information, please write or call
Director
Graduate Studies in Business
College of Business Administration
University of Southwestern Louisiana
P.O. Box 44568
Lafayette, Louisiana 70504
Telephone: 318-231-6119

University of Steubenville, a Catholic liberal arts college, was founded in 1946 by the Franciscan Friars of the Third Order Regular and serves both a local and national clientele.

The Master of Business Administration (M.B.A.) program was authorized in 1979, and the first graduate core courses were offered in the spring trimester of 1980.

PROGRAM OF STUDY

The M.B.A. program is a professional program of study intended to provide an educational foundation for personal growth and advancement in an executive career. Toward this end the degree program includes a common core of studies focusing on analytical and behavioral techniques and on institutional and environmental considerations confronting business and the businessperson.

Individual specialization is afforded through a series of electives. The student is expected to acquire a broad understanding of business concepts and operations and to develop his or her own philosophy of leadership, characterized by analysis and originality.

The M.B.A. program requires successful completion of 40 semester hours. There is no comprehensive examination or thesis. Prerequisite requirements depend on the student's undergraduate preparation and self-education. The usual graduate load is two courses each term, making possible program completion in 24 months during the trimester schedule.

Each M.B.A. program applicant will be personally counseled. To assure continuing personal attention and professional guidance, each graduate student will be assigned a faculty adviser who will provide counsel on all phases of the student's graduate program.

All M.B.A. courses and prerequisite qualifying courses are offered Monday through Thursday evenings from 6:00-9:30 p.m. with a few electives on Saturdays. The M.B.A. program requires 40 graduate semester hours including the following:

• 31 semester hours (nine courses) in the areas of managerial perspectives, analytical methods, economics for managers, behavioral sciences, managerial accounting, marketing management, financial management, production management, and business policy;
• 1 semester hour—research paper;
• 8 semester hours (four courses) in elective areas.

Appropriate graduate credit may be transferred to the M.B.A. program by presentation of official transcripts. No more than nine semester hours may be transferred to M.B.A. requirements.

The student will also gain a fuller understanding of his or her own business or industry (field) through the compilation of an in-depth research paper on the topic of his or her choice.

Each individual's capacity in interpersonal and organizational communications—an ever-increasing area of importance in all types of operations—is enhanced in the University of Steubenville M.B.A. program through small group discussions, team projects, and oral and written case presentations.

ADMISSION

Admission will be granted to those students satisfying the basic qualifications and showing high promise of success in the graduate program and the business community. The basic qualifications are

• a baccalaureate degree from an accredited college or university, with a minimum quality-point average of 2.5 on a 4-point scale;
• a knowledge of the basic concepts and terminology in the fields of economics and marketing, business law, finance and accounting, and quantitative methods: mathematics and science (qualification in each of these subject cores may be satisfied by taking a four-hour prerequisite course offered in the evenings by the University of Steubenville);
• a minimum score of 460 on the Graduate Management Admission Test (GMAT). GMAT results are to be forwarded directly to the Graduate Admissions Office, University of Steubenville. Applicants must also complete the application for M.B.A. admission form and supply official transcripts of all college work.

EXPENSES

Application fee
(to accompany application and nonrefundable) . . . . $ 15
Acceptance deposit
(due upon acceptance into the core program, by stated time; applicable to total tuition charge but not refundable) 100
M.B.A. tuition, per semester credit hour 160
Prerequisite course tuition,
per semester credit hour 115

PLACEMENT

The university's Counseling and Career Planning Office is staffed by a professional career counselor and is prepared to offer M.B.A. students information and services related to career development.

CORRESPONDENCE

Inquiries should be addressed to
Donald J. Kissinger, Jr.
Director
M.B.A. Program
University of Steubenville
Steubenville, Ohio 43952

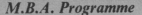

Granted its Royal Charter in September 1967, Stirling is the first entirely new university located in Scotland for over 300 years. Stirling is a short journey from Glasgow and Edinburgh with their international airports and on a main railway link to London and the rest of the United Kingdom. The university is situated around a loch on one of the most beautiful campuses in Europe. The campus, which extends to some 300 acres of mature parkland, houses the main teaching buildings, residences, shops, theater, banking, and modern sports facilities.

PROGRAMS OF STUDY

The Master of Business Administration (M.B.A.) program is mounted as a joint venture by four business departments— Business Studies, Management Science, Accountancy, and Economics—with significant contributions from other business-related departments.

The program is supported by central library and computing resources. Most of the staff who teach in the program have held senior managerial appointments in business throughout the United Kingdom and in many countries around the world. The university has close links with industry and commerce, and many staff are also working currently on a diverse range of business projects with practicing managers.

Stirling University operates on a two-semester system, the autumn semester running from mid-September to mid-December and the spring semester running from mid-February to mid-May. The taught part of the course is completed over these two semesters (eight months). Each semester's courses are separately examined. Satisfactory completion of the taught courses leads to the award of the Diploma in Business Administration. The Master of Business Administration degree is completed by adding to the taught courses a dissertation/project between June and mid-September (12 months).

The main contributing departments have considerable experience in offering taught master's and diploma programs. They already offer a well-established Master of Science (M.Sc.)/Diploma in technological economics, an M.Sc./Diploma in accounting and finance, and an M.Sc. in entrepreneurial studies.

The Stirling M.B.A./Diploma in business administration has been designed to combine a broadly based core of units covering the major functions of business with a specialized variant which will permit the study in depth of an area of particular interest to the students and of great importance to their employers.

The program, which is both intensive and challenging, will equip students with skills of a highly vocational character and enhance employment opportunities within the business world, or prepare students for further study at doctoral level.

The core courses cover financial and management accountancy, manufacturing management, business law, business economics, marketing, quantitative techniques, general management, industrial relations/personnel management, finance/capital budgeting, and business strategy. The specialist variants are in retail studies, management information systems, industrial relations and personnel management, and industry in developing countries.

Additional new variants under consideration for 1986-87 include finance, marketing, and public sector management.

ADMISSION

The normal academic admission requirement is an honors degree or equivalent from a university or college recognized by the University of Stirling or a professional qualification obtained by examination and considered by the university to be equivalent to a degree. In addition, mature managers with no formal academic qualification may be admitted as exceptions if they can satisfy the university of their ability to undertake study of a postgraduate nature.

Overseas applicants from non-English speaking countries must provide evidence of their proficiency in the use of the English language. All applicants must supply satisfactory results from the Graduate Management Admission Test (GMAT).

The course starts in mid-September of each year, and students should register at the university no later than September 17.

EXPENSES

Costs are estimated for 1986-87 academic year. Tuition and fee assessments are subject to change. The estimate attempts to take into account the likely outcome of the review to take place in 1986.

	£ Sterling	$ (1.4:£)
Tuition and Fees	*£3,655*	*$4,697*
Room (single)*	895 (12 months)	1,235
Food	1,525 (12 months)	2,135
Books	560 (12 months)	784
General	1,230 (12 months)	1,722

*Rent for married off-campus accomodations excluding running costs is around £2,500 (12 months).

CORRESPONDENCE

For further information or to receive an application, please contact
Ian F. Bird
Director M.B.A. Programme
University of Stirling
Stirling FK9 4LA, Scotland
United Kingdom
Telephone: (0786) 73171
Telex: 777759 STUNIV G

The Master of Business Administration (M.B.A.) course is intended for people with at least two years' appropriate industrial, commercial, or administrative experience and a good background of higher education, who intend to make managerial careers in business enterprises. Candidates will usually be in their twenties or early thirties. The course is broadly based and intensive, and is designed to enable participants to acquire the knowledge, attitudes, and skills requisite for managerial creativity.

PROGRAMS OF STUDY

The course extends over a period of 12 months full time, 36 months part time, and 60 months distance learning (UK students only), organized into the instructional period from mid-September to mid-June and the project period from mid-June to mid-September.

The program is aimed at an integrated presentation of the skills of management, and there is some flexibility in response to the needs of the students participating from year to year. Instruction and evaluation for the award of the degree are currently based on the following areas of study:
- foundation courses—a minimum of four from economics, quantitative methods, accountancy and finance, marketing, manufacturing management, and human resources (a class in business policy brings together work done in these foundation courses);
- electives: four from a variety of subjects including international financial management and accounting, security analysis and portfolio management, finance management, personnel management, industrial relations and labor law, commercial law, comparative industrial relations, the economics of business decisions, industry and public policy, the multinational and the world economy, management in the public sector, international business operations, decision making in operational research, business computer systems, industrial marketing, organizational development, contemporary organization theory;
- a project on an approved subject, usually consisting of an inquiry in a practical field of business supplementary to the student's own experience.

The doctoral program is available for those who wish to undertake research into the business field. There is also a Postgraduate Diploma in Business Administration (DipBA) awarded for the completion of the nine-month instructional part of the M.B.A. program; and a doctoral program is available for those who wish to undertake research into the business field, whether of an interdisciplinary or of a functionally specialized topic or area.

ADMISSION

Candidates must normally possess a first- or second-class honors degree from a British university or an acceptable equivalent qualification (for example, ACCA, CA). Applicants will be required to obtain acceptable scores on the Graduate Management Admission Test (GMAT) and most will have at least two years of appropriate experience. Selection will also depend upon provision of satisfactory references and, in some cases, on the result of an interview.

Application must be made on the standard form which may be obtained on request from the Program Secretary (see address given below). It is in the interest of applicants to submit applications before the end of April, but those received after that date may also be considered.

EXPENSES

The annual fee for full-time courses is currently £1,632 for United Kingdom students and £3,930 for overseas students. Fees are subject to periodical review. Other expenses for one year are estimated to total approximately £4,000

FINANCIAL ASSISTANCE

Applications may be made, through the university, for Economic and Social Research Council Studentships. These studentships are limited to honors graduates resident in Britain at time of application and are severely limited in number.

Candidates may also be able to obtain low-cost supplementary loans to cover the period of study from the Business Graduates Association. Applicants must have completed two years of employment in business after graduation.

The Stenhouse Scholarship is available to Scottish applicants between the ages of 20 and 35 years of age who at present are employed by, or who intend to work for a Scottish firm or business. Further conditions apply and details are available on application.

A very few postgraduate studentships are offered; these are not governed by any conditions as to nationality, but applicants should be academically well qualified.

CORRESPONDENCE

Further information on the program of study offered by the University of Strathclyde may be obtained from
The M.B.A. Administrator
Strathclyde Business School
University of Strathclyde
130 Rottenrow
Glasgow G4 0GE Great Britain
Telephone: 041-552-7141

Australia's first university, the University of Sydney, founded in 1850, is situated in close proximity to the city. The university is characterized by the Gothic architecture of the original buildings and the spacious campus adjoining a parkland area. The Graduate School of Management and Public Policy is housed in the Merewether Building, which provides library facilities, lecture rooms and study areas, and on-line computer facilities as well as a staff and student canteen.

The university has a total enrollment of approximately 18,000 students, many of whom live in residential colleges close to the campus. International House is a residence catering especially to graduate students.

PROGRAMS OF STUDY

The Graduate School offers the Master of Business Administration (M.B.A.) and Master of Public Policy degrees. Doctor of Philosophy (Ph.D.) programs are also available but can be taken only on a full-time basis by research thesis.

The M.B.A. is a specialist program concentrating on financial administration. It is offered on a three-year part-time or two-year full-time basis. The part-time program involves six hours per week of classroom attendance for 27 weeks in each year (three terms of 9 weeks). Following completion of the course work program or during the second year for full-time candidates, a dissertation of 10,000-15,000 words on an approved topic is required. The normal form of the dissertation is an in-depth report on a major company operating in Australia.

Courses offered include studies of the modern corporation, the theory and practice of decision making, the regulation of the securities markets, corporate dilemmas, frauds and failures, operations research, international financial institutions, and other areas relevant to financial administration. At the conclusion of the work part of the program, there may be a four-day, live-in school for all candidates.

Candidates are assessed by examination at the end of each course offered in the program, and regular written assignments are required. In addition, candidates are frequently called upon to give classroom presentations.

At the conclusion of the first year of course work a small number of selected candidates are nominated for a period of full-time study in Europe. This period of intensive study replaces the second year of part-time study normally undertaken in Sydney. At the conclusion of the period in Europe, candidates return to Sydney to complete their dissertation.

The European study, designed to fit in with the format and aims of the M.B.A. program, offers a small number of students the opportunity to experience the multicultural setting of European schools and to specialize in international business. While the options approved under this scheme are limited, they do increase the range of options available for those wishing to specialize in international business.

ADMISSION

Graduates of any discipline from approved universities are eligible to apply for admission, provided they have had two years of business experience since graduation. Admission is highly selective, account being taken of the applicant's score on the Graduate Management Admission Test (GMAT), undergraduate record, and subsequent experience.

A number of places are available in the program for outstanding applicants who are members of a recognized professional body and who have had at least five years of relevant business experience since gaining full professional status.

The number of applicants admitted to the M.B.A. program is small, and admission is therefore very competitive. Some attempt is made to select applicants from a wide range of business backgrounds and to develop a group in which candidates and faculty will benefit from mutual interaction.

Part-time applicants must produce written evidence of approval to undertake the course from their employer. Applications on the official form must reach the Registrar, University of Sydney, New South Wales, Australia 2006 by November 30 for admission the following year. The academic year commences early in March each year.

EXPENSES

No tuition fees are charged, but a Student Union Fee is payable each year, and a small charge is made for course materials (up to $200 per year).

FINANCIAL ASSISTANCE

No financial assistance is available, but it is anticipated that most candidates will be employed full time throughout their candidature. Overseas applicants seeking part-time enrollment will not be considered unless they already have employment in Australia or can produce evidence that they will have employment in Australia which is not dependent upon admission to the M.B.A. program.

CORRESPONDENCE

For further information, contact
The Head
Graduate School of Management
  and Public Policy
University of Sydney
New South Wales 2006, Australia
Telephone: (02) 692 3086

The Master of Business Administration (M.B.A.) program of The University of Tennessee at Chattanooga (UTC) was established in 1961 to offer a professional education in management. The primary objective is to prepare the student for a wide variety of positions requiring creative leadership ability.

The University of Tennessee at Chattanooga was founded in 1886 as Chattanooga University. For 83 years a private school, the university became a public institution in 1969 when it merged with The University of Tennessee. UTC is a major campus of The University of Tennessee. The UTC student enrollment is 8,000; about 20 percent of these are pursuing degree programs in the School of Business Administration. There are approximately 250 students in the M.B.A. program. Nearly all of these M.B.A. students attend school in the evening on a part-time basis.

The School of Business Administration has a full-time faculty of 39 professors. The faculty's teaching, publication, and research efforts are intertwined with Chattanooga's diverse business community. Chattanooga is both a manufacturing and financial center in that it has 600 manufacturers, producing more than 1,500 classified products, and two major life insurance companies. Further, Chattanooga is the geographic center of the Tennessee Valley Authority (TVA), the largest power system in the United States. The headquarters for the TVA power system is located in Chattanooga. The Chattanooga area's population is approximately 400,000.

Chattanooga is both industrial and rich in natural beauty. The city is bordered by Missionary Ridge, Lookout and Signal Mountains, and the Tennessee River. Moreover, the area's beauty is complemented by its historical significance. The city is steeped in a heritage drawn from Indian culture and the Civil War. Three city parks, two public golf courses, and a 35,000-acre lake provide the opportunity for a variety of recreational activities.

PROGRAM OF STUDY
The M.B.A. program is designed to train a manager in either the profit or not-for-profit sector. The ultimate goal is to assist students in their development as decision makers who can recognize, analyze, and solve specific problems. Also, students learn to seek and identify opportunities that provide survival and growth in a changing society and economy.

The M.B.A. program is designed both for students with undergraduate majors in business and those with majors in other fields. Previous undergraduate study in business is not required for admission. The program requires a minimum of 36 semester hours of graduate courses (eight core courses and four elective courses). However, students who have no previous academic background in business administration complete up to 24 additional semester hours (eight graduate-level foundation courses) to prepare themselves for the core program.

The minimum 36-hour program consists of eight required and four elective courses. The required courses are managerial economics or macroeconomic analysis, business research methods, managerial accounting and control, concepts in marketing, financial management, information systems, problems in operations management, and business policy.

A student may elect to concentrate in one of five areas: accounting, economics, finance, marketing, or industrial management. If a concentration is elected, three of the four elective courses must be taken in the area of concentration. The selection of a concentration is an option and not a requirement for M.B.A. students.

The program is designed for part-time evening students. A selection of courses is offered in the evening each semester, including the summer. However, full-time study is possible for those who wish a more accelerated program.

ADMISSION
The program operates year round, and entrance is possible in January, May, July, and August. Admission is open to qualified graduates of accredited colleges who meet the general admission requirements of the graduate division. Admission to the program is based on both the applicant's undergraduate grade-point average and score on the Graduate Management Admission Test (GMAT).

Applications for admission are accepted at all times. To ensure adequate consideration, the completed application and GMAT score should be received by the Graduate Admissions Office no later than one month prior to the beginning of the term for which admission is desired.

EXPENSES
Tuition and fees are as follows:
Full-time students, per semester
In-state residents .... $ 573
Out-of-state residents 1,425
Part-time students, per semester hour
In-state residents 72
(minimum charge $144)
Out-of-state residents 174
(minimum charge $348)

FINANCIAL ASSISTANCE
Limited financial assistance in the form of loans and part-time work is available to qualified students on the basis of financial need. A limited number of graduate assistantships are available on the basis of academic promise.

PLACEMENT
The University Placement Office maintains a year-round placement service which assists degree candidates and alumni in finding employment.

CORRESPONDENCE
For further information or to request an application for admission, please telephone or write
M.B.A. Program Director
School of Business Administration
The University of Tennessee at Chattanooga
Chattanooga, Tennessee 37403
Telephone: 615-755-4210

The University of Tennessee, Knoxville (UTK) has approximately 25,000 students on campus, of whom some 6,000 are graduate students. Founded in 1794, UTK is one of the oldest academic institutions west of the Appalachians. Surrounded by the Great Smokey Mountains and the TVA's "Great Lakes of the South," Knoxville is a metropolitan center of commerce, finance, high technology research and industry, science, and educational and medical services. Because of its unique attractions, Knoxville is consistently rated as one of the top 10 cities in the nation in providing gracious amenities and a high quality of life.

PROGRAMS OF STUDY
The College of Business Administration offers a two-year full-time program and a three-to-four-year part-time evening program leading to the Master of Business Administration (M.B.A.) degree. The M.B.A. experience at UTK is an individual one designed to build expertise and confidence through rigorous exposure to new ideas and sophisticated managerial techniques. This objective is achieved through an integrated program that provides analytical tools and an understanding of the fundamental areas of business enabling the student to develop and present resourceful solutions to managerial problems in an effective and concise manner. In recognition of the commitment to these goals and the college's proven ability to achieve them, the Tennessee Higher Education Commission has named the M.B.A. program at UTK a Center of Excellence.

Both the full-time and part-time programs have the same admission requirements, curriculum, and faculty. The M.B.A. program is accredited by the American Assembly of Collegiate Schools of Business (AACSB). The Colleges of Business Administration and Law also jointly offer a full-time Juris Doctor (J.D.)/M.B.A. degree program.

The Tennessee M.B.A. program consists of the core of 21 courses offered in a lock-step sequence and the concentration/elective area of 7 courses. In the concentration/elective area, at least four but not more than five courses must be in one of the following areas: controllership, economics, entrepreneurship/new venture analysis, finance, forestry industries man-

agement, management, management science, marketing, statistics, or transportation and logistics. Individualized concentrations have also been approved. All full-time students are expected to participate in the M.B.A. summer internship or an equivalent during the summer between the first and second years of study. The single prerequisite for entry into the M.B.A. program is the completion of at least one course in college calculus.

Other graduate business programs available at UTK include the Master of Accountancy (M.Acc.); the Master's and Doctor of Philosophy (Ph.D.) in economics, management science, and industrial/organizational psychology, the Master of Science (M.S.) in statistics; and the Doctor of Philosophy in business administration with concentrations in accounting, finance, management, marketing, and transportation and logistics.

ADMISSION
Applications are accepted for the summer quarter for students with nonbusiness undergraduate degrees and in the fall quarter for those who hold an undergraduate degree in business. The deadline for summer applications is April 1; for fall, July 1. The deadlines for international students are December 1 for the summer quarter and March 1 for fall.

For admission to the M.B.A. program, consideration is given to (1) the applicant's academic record, with particular attention to the last two years of undergraduate work and previous graduate studies; (2) scores on the Graduate Management Admission Test (GMAT) and for those whose native language is not English, the Test of English as a Foreign Language (TOEFL); (3) work experience and other activities that demonstrate potential for leadership; (4) recommendations from professors and work supervisors. There is no minimum cutoff for grade-point average or GMAT score. Applicants to the J.D./M.B.A. programs must be accepted independently by both programs.

EXPENSES
For 1985-86, the quarterly tuition was $346 for in-state and $1,004 for out-of-state students. In-state part-time students are charged $50 per credit hour and out-of-state students are charged $115 per credit hour. Full-time students should budget $200 per quarter for books, fees,

and supplies. The cost for food, rent, and other expenses for a single student is approximately $475 per month and approximately $600 per month for married students.

FINANCIAL ASSISTANCE
A limited number of assistantships and fellowships are available, most of which are based on merit. Federal and state programs for student loans and grants and the Student Employment Service are administered by the UTK Financial Aid Office.

PLACEMENT
The university's Career Planning and Placement Service works closely with the M.B.A. program, holding seminars and workshops as well as coordinating recruiting and interviewing activities. Approximately 350 national and regional firms and agencies recruit at the service each year. The average starting salary for UTK M.B.A. graduates in spring 1985 was $28,500.

CORRESPONDENCE
For additional information and application materials, please contact
Associate Dean for Graduate Business Programs
University of Tennessee
527 Stokely Management Center
Knoxville, Tennessee 37996-0550

The University of Texas at Arlington is one of America's most rapidly developing institutions of higher learning. This growth has been experienced not only in numbers of students but also in the quality of its programs and the strength of its faculty. The College of Business Administration has developed with the belief that the business community and its leadership play a vital role in the improvement and success of American society. Business leaders must be prepared to anticipate and, on occasion, to bring about, the essential conditions for change. Business colleges must be prepared to provide the relevant knowledge and the mastery of the processes of thought and analysis that are essential for fulfillment of this role.

PROGRAMS OF STUDY

In support of this philosophy, the college attempts to provide the graduate student with a valuable experience in learning by integrating a carefully prepared modern business curriculum with a faculty of outstanding scholarship. Seven graduate degrees are offered: Master of Business Administration (M.B.A.), Master of Arts (M.A.) in economics, Master of Science (M.S.) in personnel and human resource management, Master of Professional Accounting (M.P.A.), Master of Science (M.S.) in accounting, Master of Science (M.S.) in taxation, and Doctor of Philosophy (Ph.D.) in administration. Undergraduate and graduate programs of the college are accredited by the American Assembly of Collegiate Schools of Business (AACSB).

The M.B.A. program is designed for qualified students with any academic background. Individual student programs may range from 36 to 60 semester credit hours of graduate-level course work, depending on undergraduate preparation. Each candidate proceeds at his or her own pace, with classes available afternoons and evenings for full- and part-time students. Students may enter during the fall, spring, or summer semester.

The M.A. in economics program is designed to accommodate two basic educational and career plans, one for students who will enter the job market upon completion of the degree and the other for students who will continue graduate study in economics at the doctoral level. Thesis and nonthesis programs are offered with options in business economics, health economics, and industrial relations.

Persons with a specialized interest in personnel and human resource management may pursue the M.S. degree. This is a thesis degree program with courses emphasizing personnel strategy and policy, human resource planning and forecasting, career planning, industrial and labor relations, compensation administration, and personnel research.

Master's programs in accounting are designed to prepare students for careers as professional accountants and to provide the educational background needed for them to become Certified Public or Management Accountants. The M.P.A. program accommodates persons with undergraduate degrees in fields other than business and accounting. The M.S. degree programs in accounting and taxation are designed primarily for students with undergraduate degrees in business and accounting.

The Ph.D. in administration degree is intended to prepare individuals for teaching and research careers at the university level or in business and industry. Candidates for the degree can structure their programs to include work in the fields of accounting, economics, finance, marketing, management, information systems, and management science.

ADMISSION

To be admitted to any graduate program in the College of Business Administration, an applicant must
- hold a bachelor's degree from an accredited university;
- have demonstrated through previous academic performance the potential for graduate work;
- provide a personal statement of academic interests, strengths, and weaknesses;
- make a satisfactory score on the Graduate Management Admission Test (GMAT);
- have submitted recommendation forms from three professors, supervisors, or professional colleagues.

International applicants whose native language is not English are also required to complete the Test of English as a Foreign Language (TOEFL).

EXPENSES

Semester tuition and mandatory fees for the 1985-86 academic year were as follows:

Semester Hours	Texas	Nonresident
12	$323.00	$1,619.00
9	244.25	1,216.25
6	193.50	813.50

FINANCIAL ASSISTANCE

A limited number of graduate assistantships are available to qualified students who have been unconditionally admitted. Recipients of the assistantships are paid an annual stipend (approximately $4,500 for master's students and $7,000 for doctoral students) and are expected to work for the college about 20 hours per week as a teaching or research assistant.

PLACEMENT

The college cooperates closely with the University Placement Office and takes an active interest in the placement of its graduates. The college's central location in the Dallas/Fort Worth metroplex provides excellent career opportunities in the banking, electronics, aerospace, and transportation industries. Major accounting, consulting, and real estate firms in the areas also hire many M.B.A. graduates.

For currently enrolled students, the university operates a very active employment service through which students can secure part-time professional positions as interns.

CORRESPONDENCE

For further information, prospective applicants may write or call
Associate Dean, Graduate Studies
College of Business Administration
The University of Texas at Arlington
UTA Box 19376
Arlington, Texas 76019
Telephone: 817-273-3004

THE UNIVERSITY OF TEXAS AT AUSTIN

AUSTIN, TEXAS

The Graduate School of Business at The University of Texas at Austin awarded its first two M.B.A. degrees in 1920. Significantly, one of these degrees was awarded to a woman. These degrees followed earlier accreditation of the program by the American Assembly of Collegiate Schools of Business (AACSB) in 1916. The school is centrally located on the campus in Austin, Texas. Two Master of Business Administration (M.B.A.) degree plan options are offered (the two year full-time program and Option II which meets all day Friday and Saturday on alternate weekends for two years). A Master of Public Accountancy degree is offered, and doctoral programs in business are also available. To complete the spectrum of business education, the school offers short courses and seminars for executives in all areas of business throughout the year.

PROGRAM OF STUDY

The M.B.A. program prepares successful graduates for multiple careers and early assumption of high-level management responsibilities in a rapidly changing environment. The program is a product of intensive and continuing curriculum review and meets the future manager's educational needs as perceived by the faculty, recent graduates, and business leaders. This program accommodates students with baccalaureate degrees in either non-business or business fields. The curriculum provides training in basic disciplines underlying management, develops analytical skills, and ensures an understanding of theory and operations in the functional areas of business.

Students enrolled in the Graduate School of Business become active participants in the educational process. They are drawn into a dynamic interchange with faculty and with leaders from business and government—a process that develops both depth and breadth of understanding about the business firm and the environment within which it operates. Students also acquire and exercise skills to analyze fundamental and complex business problems. They are expected to apply both the knowledge and analytical skills in a critical, rational, and effective manner in addressing complex problems and in making "tough decisions." The faculty use a variety of instructional techniques such as seminars, case studies, laboratory training, business simulations, field research projects, computer applications, and traditional lecture methods.

The state-of-the-art classroom and computer facilities enable instructors to choose the most effective instructional medium for a particular topic. In many courses, the students are placed in diverse decision-making roles and are forced to make decisions similar to those made in actual business situations. These decisions, which are often made under deadline pressures, must be defended before critical students and instructors. Further, when managing their simulated companies, students must learn to live with the consequences of their decisions for some time into the future. Through such exercises, students have a means for assessing what they have learned by experiencing a problem; assessing its dimensions; collecting and relating relevant facts; and arriving at a responsible, reasoned solution.

Seminars complement the problem-solving orientation of the program. In these discussion groups, 10 to 20 students work closely with the instructor in reviewing and analyzing the work of both classical and contemporary experts. These special topic seminars enable students to concentrate their electives in areas of particular interest.

The M.B.A. program consists of 60 graduate hours and normally takes about two years for completion. The first year of the program is highly structured and consists of 33 hours of required courses. These courses provide the student with a strong foundation in administrative and behavioral concepts, quantitative methods, the functional areas, and the environment within which businesses operate. The second year is composed of 21 hours of electives, a 3-hour integrative course, and a professional report that carries 3 hours of academic credit. All the courses are offered from 8:00 a.m. to 5:00 p.m., Monday through Friday. There are no provisions for evening or weekend classes.

ADMISSION

Students may apply for admission to the Graduate School of Business for semesters starting in August (fall) and January (spring) each year. General requirements for admission are a bachelor's degree (or equivalent if study was done outside the United States), acceptable performance on all upper-division undergraduate and graduate courses, and a satisfactory score on the Graduate Management Admission Test (GMAT). Students who completed their undergraduate degrees at universities outside the United States must also present an acceptable score on the Test of English as a Foreign Language (TOEFL).

Selection of successful applicants is based on the student's entire past record. Evidence of substantial motivation or successful experience in business, military, or extracurricular activities is taken into consideration. Applicants are encouraged to provide resumes and personal statements when appropriate. Personal references are also welcome and given serious consideration.

Admission decisions are made on a rolling basis and early applications are encouraged. Deadline for fall admission is March 1 and for spring, October 1.

EXPENSES

The figures below reflect new tuition increases legislated for the fall 1985 semester. The other expenses are based on recent estimates of the Austin area cost of living. The figures in parentheses are for Texas residents.

	Fall Semester 12 hours	Spring Semester 12 hours	Summer Session 9 hours
Tuition and required fees	$1,606 ($310)	$1,606 ($310)	$1,217 ($245)
Other expenses	$2,324	$2,774	$1,598
Total	$3,930 ($2,634)	$4,380 ($3,084)	$2,815 ($1,843)

FINANCIAL ASSISTANCE

Students in the M.B.A. program are eligible for loans, scholarships, and teaching and research assistant positions in the Graduate School of Business. This financial assistance is provided after a careful review of the student's ability and previous academic achievement. Some minority scholarships are available directly from the Graduate School of Business, and additional minority assistance is available from the Consortium for Graduate Study in Management. The University of Texas at Austin became a member of this organization in 1985. Minority students seeking financial assistance are required to apply directly to the consortium.

CORRESPONDENCE

For further details, please write or call
Graduate School of Business
The University of Texas at Austin
Austin, Texas 78712
Telephone: 512-471-5921

THE UNIVERSITY OF TEXAS AT DALLAS

RICHARDSON, TEXAS

The University of Texas (UT) at Dallas (formerly the Southwest Center for Advanced Studies) became a component of The University of Texas System in 1969. The School of Management was established in 1972. Approximately 800 students are currently pursuing graduate study in the school. Since many of these students are employed professionals, the university offers most of its classes on weekday evenings.

The UT-Dallas campus is located in Richardson, approximately 15 miles north of the downtown business district. Dallas has one of the strongest regional economies in the nation. Approximately 1,000 million-dollar companies are headquartered in the city, offering a wide variety of employment opportunities in banking, insurance, oil and gas, public accounting and consulting, and high technology industries.

PROGRAMS OF STUDY
The University of Texas at Dallas offers five graduate degree programs: Master of Science (M.S.) in management sciences, Master of Arts (M.A.) in international management studies, Master of Business Administration (M.B.A.), and Doctor of Philosophy (Ph.D.) in both management science and international management. These programs are designed to produce students who are rigorously trained in fundamentals, concepts, and methods that are not likely to be made obsolete by changing business conditions. Beyond a set of core courses, where essential competencies are established, courses are frequently application oriented and concerned with developing the problem-solving capabilities required of modern managers.

Successful management and administrative problem solvers, it is felt, must (1) have a good foundation in the basic disciplines (for example, economics and mathematics) applicable in management and administration; (2) possess a keen understanding of the basic functions (accounting, marketing, production) involved in management and administration; (3) be skilled in both the theory of the mathematical sciences (statistics, operations research, management information systems) and their applications to management and administration; (4) be adept at applying the basic aspects of the behavioral sciences (psychology and anthropology) to problems in management and

administration; and (5) possess the ability to utilize in innovative and creative ways those four skills in a systems fashion.

The M.S. program in management and administrative sciences allows the student to concentrate in a specific discipline within management. This program consists of 21 hours of core courses and 24 hours of concentration courses. The following areas of concentration are available: accounting, behavioral management, business policy and strategy, finance, management information systems, managerial economics and analysis, marketing management, and operations research.

The M.A. program in international management studies strives to develop the highly specialized knowledge and abilities required to understand and solve the complex problems of international trade, and multinational and transnational firms. Course work in international trade, management, and cultures is prescribed. The program consists of 15 hours of basic core, 9 hours of advanced core, and 15 hours of elective courses.

The M.B.A. program provides a broad managerial education, with emphasis on professional application and problem solving. The program consists of 45 hours of core courses and 9 hours of concentration courses. The following areas of concentration are available: accounting, behavioral management, business policy and strategy, finance, international management, marketing management, and operations management.

ADMISSION
Students are encouraged to apply by January for enrollment the following June or August and by October for January enrollment. Applicants are selected on the basis of previous academic achievement, scores on the Graduate Management Admission Test (specify that grades be sent to The University of Texas at Dallas, Code 6897), and when possible a personal interview for Ph.D. students. A bachelor's degree (or its foreign equivalent) is a prerequisite. The programs of UT-Dallas generally include students with diverse backgrounds.

EXPENSES
Tuition and fees for 1985-86 for a normal 12-hour load were $321 per semester for residents of Texas, $1,617 for other U.S. citizens and foreign students. Students on

research assistantships and teaching assistantships pay in-state tuition. Some small additional fees may be required.

The University of Texas at Dallas does not own or operate any housing facilities. A wide variety of housing is available in the neighborhood. For information, contact the Director of Student Services.

FINANCIAL ASSISTANCE
Several sources of financial assistance to students are available, including part-time teaching and research assistantships, student loan funds, and partial tuition exemptions. Veterans of the U.S. armed services may apply their benefits at UT-Dallas. Research assistantships for full-time students are awarded on a competitive basis; stipends are sufficient to cover minimal living expenses and depend to some extent upon the graduate program and the level of the student.

PLACEMENT
A placement officer is available for students in the management and administration program.

CORRESPONDENCE
For general information and application forms, write or call
   Director of Admissions
   Telephone: 214-690-2341

For specific program information, consult
   Advising Office
   School of Management
   The University of Texas at Dallas
   P.O. Box 830688
   Richardson, Texas 75083-0688
   Telephone: 214-690-2750

The College of Business recognizes as its primary thrust the preparation of students for careers throughout business and other administrative environments that include various combinations of leader-manager-administrator-entrepreneur. Preparing students to face an ever-changing future encompasses a focus on organizing scarce resources to achieve a given end, mastery of written and oral communications, understanding people and how to work effectively with them, and an appreciation of the changing nature of the role of the manager. The programs offered by the College of Business at The University of Texas at San Antonio (UTSA) are accredited by the American Assembly of Collegiate Schools of Business (AACSB).

PROGRAMS OF STUDY
The Master of Business Administration (M.B.A.) degree in business is designed to provide intensive education to qualified students and is available to individuals with undergraduate degrees in the business administration areas as well as to those with specializations outside the business field. Students whose previous training has been in nonbusiness fields may be admitted to the M.B.A. program but will be required to complete a series of 24 semester hours of common body of knowledge courses or their equivalents as a condition of admission in addition to the degree requirements. Those students whose background is in business but who have completed the common body of knowledge courses or their equivalents five or more years prior to entering the program will be required to complete successfully or pass successfully tests on the common body of knowledge courses. The student may elect one of the two options to complete the M.B.A. degree: (1) option 1 which includes 24 hours of required course work and 6 hours of elective course work plus a thesis or (2) 24 hours of required course work plus 12 hours of elective course work.

In response to the geographical, commercial, and ethnic environments of UTSA, the College of Business offers the Master of Business Administration degree in inter-American management. The fundamental objective of this degree program is to offer students an opportunity to gain perspective on commercial activities in a setting which is bilingual, transnational, and cross-cultural. This program is designed to offer students from the United States or the Americas the opportunity to study business administration while developing special expertise in its international aspects. To achieve this end, specific inter-American content courses have been developed in the disciplines of management, marketing, and finance. Concurrently with the work on the M.B.A. degree in inter-American management, students are required to demonstrate reading and conversational proficiency in either Spanish or Portugese.

The Master of Professional Accounting (M.P.A.) degree is designed to accommodate applicants with a degree in any field. Such applicants must complete the equivalent of a Bachelor of Business Administration (B.B.A.) degree in accounting from an accredited institution or must enroll in the college's common body of knowledge courses plus certain accounting courses set out by the program adviser. The common body of knowledge courses may be taken simultaneously with M.P.A. requirements, subject to course prerequisites and approval of the M.P.A. program adviser. Candidates may choose to focus on taxation or public accounting.

ADMISSION
Applicants for admission to the M.B.A. or M.P.A. program must meet the following requirements:
- hold a baccalaureate degree from an accredited college or university in the United States or proof of equivalent training in a foreign institution;
- have a B average on all undergraduate and graduate-level work previously taken;
- submit an approximate total score of 500 on the Graduate Management Admission Test (GMAT);
- be in good standing at the last institution attended.

Those who do not meet all of the above stated admission requirements will be considered for admission on a conditional basis. All admission deficiencies must be removed before enrolling for the last semester before graduation and will be in addition to degree requirements.

EXPENSES
Tuition:
  Residents of Texas—$12 per semester hour of credit, minimum of $100 per semester.
  Nonresidents, including international students—$120 per semester hour of credit.

A student service fee of $7.50 per semester hour of credit with a maximum of $90 is charged. A general fee of $6 per semester hour of credit is also charged and a $10 general property deposit. The Student Union fee is $15 each regular session; $7.50 each summer session. University-owned housing is not available.

FINANCIAL ASSISTANCE
At the present time, only limited financial aid is available to qualified students. Students with definite need for financial assistance during this time should contact the Student Financial Aid Office.

PLACEMENT
UTSA maintains a placement service to assist students in locating part-time employment as well as for career placement of graduates and alumni.

CORRESPONDENCE
For further information, students should write to
  Dean
  College of Business
  The University of Texas at San Antonio
  San Antonio, Texas 78285-0631
  Telephone: 512-691-4641

Requests for catalogs or applications should be addressed to the Director of Admissions and Registrar.

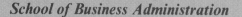
The University of Texas at Tyler (formerly Texas Eastern University) is a state-supported institution offering upper-level and graduate work. In early 1973, the first students were admitted to the institution. Currently, the enrollment consists of approximately 3,600 students. A newly constructed campus opened its doors in the fall of 1976. The site of the campus is a 207-acre wooded area located just on the southern border of the city of Tyler, Texas. Tyler has a population of over 80,000. The home of the Texas Rose Festival, Tyler is noted for its beauty.

PROGRAM OF STUDY

The goal of the Master of Business Administration (M.B.A.) program is the development of professional managers of large-scale, complex organizations. Emphasis is placed on the organization, operation, and control of a business enterprise. Special attention is directed to the manager's responsibility for defining and analyzing problems, evaluating courses of action, and making logical and ethical decisions. Emphasis is on breadth rather than specialization.

Students who have the equivalent of the basic business core (level I) via undergraduate courses take 30 semester hours of course work (level II), 21 hours of graduate business core courses, and 9 hours of approved business electives. No thesis is required.

Students who do not have undergraduate course work in business must complete 24-30 hours of basic (level I) course work before commencing level II graduate work. Credit is granted for equivalent basic business courses completed prior to enrolling in the program.

Small classes and individual instruction are stressed in the M.B.A. program, resulting in the opportunity for close association between students and faculty.

ADMISSION

Applicants for admission must submit a completed application form plus an official transcript showing completion of a baccalaureate degree from an accredited college or university. In addition, applicants are required to furnish satisfactory scores on the Graduate Management Admission Test (GMAT). Students whose native language is not English must submit acceptable scores on the Test of English as a Foreign Language (TOEFL).

EXPENSES

Expenses listed below include tuition and required fees of $6 per semester hour General Use Fee and $4 per semester hour Student Service Fee ($40 maximum).

Semester Hours	Texas Residents	Non-Texas Residents
3	$140.50	$450.00
6	180.00	801.00

FINANCIAL ASSISTANCE

The University of Texas at Tyler provides financial assistance to qualified students on the basis of both need and merit. Financial assistance consists of grants, employment, loans, and scholarships which may be awarded singly or in combination. Interested students should write in advance to the Student Financial Aid Office for applications and instructions.

CORRESPONDENCE

Inquiries concerning the M.B.A. program at The University of Texas at Tyler should be addressed to

M.B.A. Coordinator
The University of Texas at Tyler
3900 University Boulevard
Tyler, Texas 75701

The University of Toledo has grown steadily since it was founded in 1872. Today, as a state university located in an urban area with a suburban setting, it offers a metropolitan complex of business and industry balanced by cultural values as indicated by a nationally known symphony orchestra and the Toledo Museum of Art. There are over 20,000 students in attendance with over 3,000 in master's programs and nearly 350 in doctoral programs. The College of Business Administration was established in 1930; its bachelor's and master's programs are accredited by the American Assembly of Collegiate Schools of Business (AACSB). The Graduate Division of the College of Business Administration offers an excellent opportunity to earn a Master of Business Administration (M.B.A.) degree through day or evening study. Many students currently enrolled in the M.B.A. program have found the combination of a degree in a nonbusiness field and one in business administration very helpful to their individual progress.

PROGRAMS OF STUDY
The purpose of the M.B.A. program is to provide the educational foundation for an executive career. To this end, the curriculum is designed to give an integrated coverage of analytical and behavioral techniques of the institutions and environment of business. It focuses upon the pervasive functions of planning, organization, and control, and the disciplines fundamental to business operations and seeks to develop in the college graduate skill in making administrative decisions.

The curriculum is designed to allow specialization in various areas. However, the emphasis is on providing the broad understanding of business concepts and operation which is becoming increasingly important for business leadership. The student is encouraged to develop his or her own philosophy and to approach business problems with initiative and originality. A student can elect a broad (general) program or one with special emphasis in accounting, administration, health administration, business economics, business logistics, finance, international business, marketing, personnel, production, or operations analysis. The graduate curriculum may be built either on a bachelor's degree in business administration or on another baccalaureate degree.

The Master of Business Administration degree is granted to the student who satisfactorily completes a minimum of 48 quarter hours of graduate credit work in business administration beyond the Bachelor of Business of Administration (B.B.A.) with a 3.0 or better quality-point average. The required graduate program for all students consists of 36 quarter hours of work including the basic core area of business plus organization theory, research methodology, and interdisciplinary business seminar. The student can then elect course work in a general program or in his or her area of specialization to complete the requirements.

The purpose of the Master of Science (M.S.) in accounting is to develop the appropriate skills necessary for the professional accountant. This program provides a strong emphasis on the study of the content of the functional discipline of accounting. The degree is granted to the student who satisfactorily completes a minimum of 48 quarter hours. Depending upon the student's background, a maximum of 101 quarter hours may be required for the M.S. degree.

ADMISSION
To be admitted to the graduate program, a candidate must hold a baccalaureate degree from a regionally accredited institution and must show high promise of success as determined by (1) performance on the Graduate Management Admission Test (GMAT) and (2) undergraduate grade average. All applicants are required to forward the results of the GMAT to the College of Business Administration in order to be admitted to the Graduate School.

Each student must present one official transcript and two copies of all academic records. If the applicant's degree is from The University of Toledo, the college will obtain the necessary transcripts. In addition to the GMAT, international students will be required to take the Test of English as a Foreign Language (TOEFL).

EXPENSES
Graduate School tuition for a full-time student (12 to 16 quarter hours) is $630 plus a general fee of $88 for Ohio residents. The out-of-state surcharge is $705 per quarter. Campus housing costs range from $412 to $540 per quarter, and campus board is $300. Other housing is available in the university area.

FINANCIAL ASSISTANCE
Opportunity as well as feasibility characterize graduate work at The University of Toledo. There are available each year a number of graduate assistantships. Their purpose is to provide research and teaching positions to qualified students to help them finance their graduate programs and gain experience. Assistants will receive a stipend and a waiver of instructional and certain other fees. A fellowship and loan program is also available to graduate students.

PLACEMENT
Employment opportunities for students who have earned degrees are provided through faculty members and the Placement Office. The Placement Office is visited by 350 companies, businesses, and governmental agencies that conduct on-campus recruiting. Approximately 3,000 interviews are conducted yearly.

CORRESPONDENCE
For further information or to request an application for admission, please write to
Dr. Dale Sullivan
Director of the M.B.A. Program
College of Business Administration
The University of Toledo
Toledo, Ohio 43606

The Faculty of Management Studies (FMS) at the University of Toronto is now entering its 36th year as a professional school of management situated in downtown Toronto, Canada. As a graduate school of management, FMS appeals to student applicants who seek a personal challenge in four key areas: (1) intellectual capacity, (2) seriousness of purpose, (3) leadership potential, and (4) a willingness to assume managerial responsibilities in both the public and private sectors.

PROGRAMS OF STUDY

Approximately 800 students are enrolled in the full-time and part-time (evening) Master of Business Administration (M.B.A.) program, which provides a solid education in the foundation areas of economics, quantitative methods, and the behavioral sciences, and in the functional application areas of accounting, finance, marketing, information systems, and business policy. Courses in these core areas are the main elements of the first year in the M.B.A. program; they are designed to enable the student to speak the language of business and to provide students with a broad range of tools for effective business analyses.

During the second year of the M.B.A. program, an extensive array of courses is available, with more than 50 different elective courses offered each year. Students are thus provided with the opportunity to pursue either one or two specialty areas in depth or to build a broad-based general management program for themselves. A two-year weekend executive M.B.A. program for mid-career managers was launched in 1983. Currently there are 70 students in the program. This degree is intended for those interested in general management careers and includes no optional courses.

The Faculty of Management Studies offers a number of other academic and nonacademic programs which complement the M.B.A. and offer students an interesting and challenging educational environment.

For those who wish to continue with advanced studies in order to equip themselves for careers in research and teaching, the Doctor of Philosophy (Ph.D.) program is well established and offers exceptional opportunities for students wishing to work with a faculty of international reputation. Approximately 40 Ph.D. stu-

dents are enrolled in the program. Graduates of the Ph.D. program are in demand for good positions in teaching and research both in the United States and Canada where there will continue to be a serious shortage of faculty at Canadian Schools of Management and Administration.

ADMISSION

Admission to the M.B.A. program is open to men and women who have graduated from universities approved by the School of Graduate Studies with a minimum of a mid-B standing in their undergraduate work. In evaluating undergraduate standing, the greatest weight is given to the later years. No specific undergraduate major or selection of courses is required. The Admissions Committee attempts to accept candidates from a broad range of specializations in determining the composition of a class. Applicants desiring admission to the program in September must forward completed application credentials by May 31. Part-time applicants desiring admission to the program in January must forward material by October 31. The Admissions Committee makes decisions on a rolling basis; as each applicant's file is completed, it is sent to the committee for review. Notification of a decision normally occurs three to four weeks after the applicant's file is complete.

EXPENSES

Estimated annual fees for 1986-87
For Canadian residents:

M.B.A., full time	$1,600
M.B.A., part time	450

For foreign students:

Full time	7,200
Part time	2,200

FINANCIAL ASSISTANCE

Financial assistance is available for applicants to the master's and Ph.D. programs. Fellowships from the Social Sciences and Humanities Research Council, the Ontario Government Scholarship plan, and the University of Toronto are available to qualified applicants. Applicants wishing to be considered for fellowships must submit their applications for admission no later than February 1.

Teaching and research assistantships are also available. Applications for assistantships are accepted in the principal areas of accounting, economics, finance, management science, and organizational behavior after a student has been admitted to the Faculty.

PLACEMENT

The Faculty of Management Studies assumes the placement and counseling responsibility for its M.B.A. and Ph.D. students. Contacts are maintained with the business community in Toronto, throughout Canada, and elsewhere who visit the Faculty to discuss employment opportunities and to recruit graduates.

The Placement Service has experienced and trained staff who provide job and career counseling, assist in job hunting activities, and maintain the required files, information, and contacts to ensure that all graduates are effectively introduced to prospective employers. Over 100 firms visit the Faculty each year in search of graduates of the M.B.A. program.

CORRESPONDENCE

Information and application packages for the graduate management programs are available from

Faculty of Management Studies
Admissions Office
246 Bloor Street West
University of Toronto
Toronto, Ontario, Canada M5S1V4
Telephone: 416-978-3499

THE UNIVERSITY OF TULSA

TULSA, OKLAHOMA

The University of Tulsa is an accredited doctoral-degree-granting institution characterized by dynamic programs. Regular enrollment is approximately 5,000 students from all the states and many foreign countries. The faculty number 330, with 75 percent of the full-time faculty holding earned doctorates from many of the nation's outstanding universities. Located in a greater metropolitan area of some 500,000 residents, the campus is about two miles from the heart of Tulsa.

The College of Business Administration has a full-time faculty of 47, an undergraduate enrollment of 1,200 students, and 350 students pursuing the Master of Business Administration (M.B.A.) degree and the Master of Science (M.S.) in accounting. The college has been a member of the American Assembly of Collegiate Schools of Business (AACSB) since 1949.

PROGRAMS OF STUDY

The University of Tulsa's College of Business Administration offers accredited graduate programs leading to the M.B.A. and M.S. in accounting and offers with the College of Law combined M.B.A./ Juris Doctor (J.D.) and M.S./ J.D. degrees.

The primary goal of the M.B.A. program is to provide a quality graduate-level education that will prepare graduates for professional management careers and positions of leadership and responsibility in business and society. More specifically, the M.B.A. program's objectives are (1) to provide a graduate-level education program for students with a baccalaureate degree in the arts, humanities, and behavioral and technical sciences as well as business administration, who wish to prepare for professional management careers; (2) to develop and/or strengthen the managerial skills and decision-making capabilities of those in management who wish to improve their managerial effectiveness and advance their careers; and (3) to increase the quality and quantity of managerial talent available to meet the needs of private and public institutions.

M.B.A. candidates are required to complete first- and second-year programs. The first-year program is oriented toward developing students' skills and giving them a basis in theory. The first-year curriculum is composed of 30 hours in accounting, economics, finance, management, marketing, quantitative methods, management information systems, and business law.

The second year of the M.B.A. program requires completion of 30 hours of work, including 21 semester hours of core courses taken by all students and 9 semester hours of electives approved by an adviser. Students may declare concentrations in an academic area.

While the curriculum is designed to cover both quantitative and behavioral aspects of business, strong emphasis is placed on analytical decision-making tools and communication skills. Cases, reports, discussions, experiential learning and lectures all are used to reinforce such skills.

The University of Tulsa's Master of Science in accounting program is designed to build professional competence. It provides advanced studies for those seeking careers in public accounting, industry, government, and teaching. The M.S. in accounting is a nonthesis degree requiring 30 semester hours of graduate work. Not more than 18 credit hours in accounting may be counted for graduate credit. Students' programs are tailored to their individual objectives in consultation with faculty advisers. Admission is open to students with undergraduate degrees in any field. However, some background courses are required for those who did not major in accounting. Students are admitted without deficiencies if they have completed 21 hours of accounting, including introductory, intermediate, cost/managerial, tax, and auditing, and 30 hours of undergraduate business core courses in economics, finance, management, marketing, quantitative analysis, and business law.

ADMISSION

Admission to graduate study in business is based on undergraduate grade-point average, the Graduate Management Admission Test (GMAT) score, and relevant managerial experience. Preference will be given to those applicants who file a completed application and present minimum requirements by March 31 for the following fall semester or October 31 for the following spring semester. The University of Tulsa employs, advances, admits, and treats in its employment and education programs, all persons without regard to their race, color, national or ethnic origin, sex, age, religion, handicap, or status as a veteran.

EXPENSES

A fee of $30 must accompany each application. Tuition for the 1985-86 school year was $195 per semester hour.

FINANCIAL ASSISTANCE

A number of fellowships and graduate assistantships are available to qualified full-time students. These provide cash stipends and/or remission of most of the recipient's tuition. Application deadline for these awards is about February 15.

PLACEMENT

The University Planning and Placement Office offers services to aid students in planning careers and obtaining attractive positions. Each year representatives of a large number of major corporations and governmental agencies come to the campus to interview graduate students in business. Graduates receive offers for positions in both large and small firms and in a wide variety of industries in local, regional, and national markets.

CORRESPONDENCE

Admission applications may be submitted at any time. Further information concerning admission or financial aid may be obtained by writing or calling

Director of Graduate Admissions
and Advising
College of Business Administration
The University of Tulsa
600 South College
Tulsa, Oklahoma 74104
Telephone: 918-592-6000, extension 2242

The University of Utah, founded in 1850, is accredited by the Northwest Association of Schools and Colleges and is a member of the Utah System of Higher Education. The programs offered by the Graduate School of Business are accredited by the American Assembly of Collegiate Schools of Business (AACSB). The school enrolls full- and part-time students.

Located on the northeastern edge of Salt Lake City, the 1,500-acre campus with 221 academic and research buildings reaches to the foothills of the Wasatch Mountains. The U of U includes one of the region's foremost research libraries, and its 320-acre Research Park has 46 tenants.

Salt Lake City, a progressive urban and industrial center, is five minutes away. Both campus and community enjoy a year-round series of art exhibits, lectures, museum displays, theater, opera, symphony concerts, and ballet. A four-season climate invites participation in outdoor life from camping, hiking, boating, and fishing to unexcelled powder-snow skiing.

PROGRAMS OF STUDY

Master's degrees offered are the Master of Business Administration (M.B.A.), executive M.B.A., M.B.A./Health Services Administration, Master of Professional Accountancy (M.Pr.A.), Master of Science (M.S.) in finance, Master of Human Resource Management, Master of Statistics, and the following joint degree programs: Juris Doctor (J.D.)/M.B.A., M.S. in hospital pharmacy (residency)/M.B.A., M.S. architecture/M.B.A., M.S. mining engineering/M.B.A., and Bachelor of Science (B.S.) in pharmacy/M.B.A. The doctorate is a Doctor of Philosophy (Ph.D.) in business administration. Students interested in joint degrees are required to gain acceptance from both colleges.

The primary objective of the M.B.A. program is to assist students so that they will be effective managers in business firms, nonprofit institutions, or governmental units. The M.B.A. program requires two years of study (six quarters, 24 courses) for a full-time student without a degree in business. A one-year program (12 courses, three quarters) is available for those students who have bachelor's degrees from an accredited school of business. Half-time day and evening programs are also available. An executive M.B.A. program meets every weekend.

For nonbusiness graduates, the first year of study is devoted to a series of preparatory classes covering all major aspects of business activity. The second year, required of all candidates, stresses the managerial aspects of business theory and practice with some elective choices that allow for specialization.

The Master of Professional Accountancy degree builds on the technical competence students develop in undergraduate accounting programs. Special emphasis is given to developing analytical abilities, improving communication skills, and expanding professional horizons.

The M.S. in finance is an individualized program for a limited number of students; it consists of the M.B.A. core requirements and advanced work to prepare the student for a career in the areas of finance.

The Master of Human Resource Management is based on a comprehensive core of business knowledge and combines human resource management generalist and specialist courses with professional internship experience.

ADMISSION

The University of Utah is an Affirmative Action/Equal Opportunity Employer and, as such, is fully committed to nondiscrimination and equal opportunity in all programs and activities, including but not limited to student admissions and student financial assistance, without regard to age, race, color, religion, sex, national origin, or status as a handicapped individual, disabled veteran, or veteran of the Vietnam era.

The college is seeking well-qualified college graduates from all disciplines. Applications and two official transcripts of all college work must be received by March 1 for master's degree applicants for fall quarter admission. All applicants must submit scores from the Graduate Management Admission Test (GMAT). International students must also submit scores from the Test of Spoken English (TSE) and Test of English as a Foreign Language (TOEFL). Applications will be considered if scores from the January GMAT (or tests prior to that) are submitted. The general admission requirements for master's degrees are a bachelor's degree from an accredited college or university with a grade-point average of 3.0 or better and a suitable score on the GMAT. Students

interested in the special executive M.B.A. program must, in addition, have at least five years of significant experience and have employer sponsorship. For the Ph.D., one should have grades and GMAT scores in the 90th percentile. In exceptional cases those requirements are offset by particular strengths not measured by grades or test scores. Evidence of thoughtfully determined personal and professional objectives, communication skills, and initiative to conceive of and carry out significant work are requisite criteria.

EXPENSES

Per academic year (September-June)
Tuition and fees, subject to change
In state	$1,470
Out of state	4,200

Board and room
(residence halls) 2,700-3,500
Family housing (one-, two-, and three-bedroom apartments), per month 230-415
Books and supplies 400-500
Fees in the executive M.B.A. (weekend) program are different; the Director will provide details.

FINANCIAL ASSISTANCE

Assistantships, fellowships, and tuition waivers are available in limited numbers to qualified students on the basis of merit and need. Applications for financial assistance must be submitted by March 1. Applications are available from the Assistant Dean, Graduate Studies at the address listed below.

PLACEMENT

The university maintains a placement bureau visited annually by representatives of approximately 500 companies from all sections of the country. The placement bureau also keeps interested alumni informed of employment opportunities for experienced personnel.

CORRESPONDENCE

For further information, please write to
  Assistant Dean, Graduate Studies
  Graduate School of Business
  University of Utah
  Salt Lake City, Utah 84112
  Telephone: 801-581-7785

UNIVERSITY OF VERMONT

BURLINGTON, VERMONT

The University of Vermont provides graduate study leading to a Master of Business Administration (M.B.A.) degree. The program has developed from a high quality undergraduate business education offering that has been in existence for many years. Study may be full time or part time.

The 200-acre campus is located on a high point of land about four blocks above the main commercial district of Burlington and about one mile from the shores of Lake Champlain. The area is well known for its scenic beauty. Proximity to Lake Champlain and major ski areas helps provide a wide diversity of recreational activities.

PROGRAM OF STUDY

The M.B.A. program at the University of Vermont is basically designed to provide an effective educational foundation for continued growth and the development of responsible business administrators.

Candidates must present 48 credits of course work. All courses creditable toward the degree must be numbered 300. All students must complete courses in business policy, accounting, finance, marketing, organizational behavior, and quantitative methods. Courses include lecture-discussion classes, independent reading and research seminar, and case problem seminars. There is ample opportunity for close association with the faculty.

ADMISSION

A student who holds a bachelor's degree from an accredited college or university is eligible for admission to the M.B.A. program. Academic performance, professional experience and objectives, and personal qualities must indicate a high probability of success in the program. Letters of reference supporting the application are required.

Prior to being admitted to the M.B.A. program, students are expected to present as formal training courses in basic economics and calculus, and to demonstrate competence in computer programming. Transcripts and other training and experience are evaluated on an individual basis. Satisfactory scores on the Graduate Management Admission Test (GMAT) are required.

EXPENSES

Tuition rates (academic year 1985-86) were $112 per credit hour for Vermont residents with a semester maximum of $1,340. For nonresidents of Vermont, tuition was $310 per credit hour, with a semester maximum of $3,719 for 12 hours. Students enrolled for 12 credit hours or more pay a library fee of $22 and an athletic fee of $24 per semester. The health fee is $59 per semester. The above fees are under review and will likely be increased.

Limited housing for married graduate students is available through the University Housing Office. That office also maintains a listing of available off-campus rental facilities.

FINANCIAL ASSISTANCE

Graduate teaching and research fellowships are available in limited numbers. Student personnel fellowships provide both single and married graduate students with the position of a resident adviser. Students who wish to be considered for fellowships must submit applications by March 1.

PLACEMENT

The university placement service hosts a large number of representatives of business firms and government agencies who come to interview students for full-time positions. Related services include individual career counseling and preparation of confidential credentials.

CORRESPONDENCE

For copies of the Graduate Catalogue and applications for admission, write
Dean of the Graduate College
University of Vermont
Burlington, Vermont 05405

For specific curriculum information, contact
Dean, School of Business
Administration
University of Vermont
Burlington, Vermont 05405
Telephone: 802-656-4017

The Colgate Darden Graduate School of Business Administration at the University of Virginia is located in Charlottesville, an area with 100,000 people set in the foothills of the Blue Ridge Mountains. Founded in 1954, the school has a current enrollment of 450 M.B.A. students who work closely with the 60 teaching faculty in a stimulating and supportive environment. In addition to the Master of Business Administration (M.B.A.) degree, The Darden School offers several joint M.B.A./Master of Arts (M.A.) degree options, an M.B.A./Juris Doctor (J.D.), and a doctoral program.

PROGRAMS OF STUDY

The M.B.A. program prepares men and women of exceptional ability to act with determination, judgment, and integrity in responsible positions of leadership. This objective is achieved through a uniquely integrated program that develops an understanding of the fundamental areas of business while it strengthens the capacity to analyze managerial problems and present intelligent and resourceful solutions to these problems. The case method of instruction is used throughout the program to allow students the maximum opportunity to sharpen their analytical and decision-making abilities. The learning environment, characterized by the classroom discussion essential to the case method, is far removed from academic theorizing. While analyzing the problem, evaluating alternatives, making decisions, and recommending plans for implementation, the students gain knowledge and experience in the realities of a competitive environment as well as discover the underlying concepts and principles. Competence in the basic functional disciplines is treated as the means toward the more important end of personal growth in the ability to handle challenging problems wisely and responsibly.

The two-year M.B.A. program is an intensive and highly integrated course of study. All of the first-year courses are required. First-year courses in accounting, finance, marketing, quantitative analysis, operations, organizational behavior, applied macroeconomics, and written and oral communications are structured and scheduled as interrelated units. The first-year experience centers on the student's class section and informal study group. There are four sections of approximately 60 students each.

The second year of the M.B.A. program is less structured. Required courses deal with business policy, the social and political environment of business, and individually directed field work on business problems. Eight elective courses in the various disciplines make up the remainder of the program, and students may choose courses in a functional area of interest or those with a specific applicability, such as the management of small businesses. While breadth in the fundamentals of management is stressed in the program, the curriculum provides the opportunity for in-depth concentration in the second-year electives.

ADMISSION

Because of the integration of the program, students are admitted only on a full-time basis and may begin the program only in September. No credit is granted for previous course work.

The Darden School sets high standards for admission to the M.B.A. program but does not employ rigid criteria. No specific courses or undergraduate majors are required, but a baccalaureate degree is ordinarily expected. Men and women with solid academic records, proven aptitude on the Graduate Management Admission Test (GMAT), and evidence of maturity, strong interpersonal skills, and motivation for graduate work will receive first consideration. Because many aspects of the M.B.A. curriculum require competence in quantitative analysis, the ability to deal with mathematical concepts is essential. Full-time work experience is considered especially valuable preparation (95 percent of the students have over two years). Qualified applicants still in school may be offered a deferred admission.

The deadline for application is April 1, and the deadline for scholarship application is March 1. Later applicants may be placed on a waiting list.

EXPENSES

Average expenses for 1985-86 (academic year):

Tuition and fees (Virginia residents)	$3,601
Tuition and fees (out-of-state)	7,481
Room and board (single students)	6,000

FINANCIAL ASSISTANCE

Financial assistance from the school is available in the form of scholarships and an internal loan program. Scholarships are awarded on the basis of need and merit with some funds specifically designated for minority students. Students are encouraged to investigate state and federal educational loan options before relying on the school's internal loan program. About 65 percent of the students receive some financial aid. Inquiries about financial aid should be sent to the Committee of Admissions and Scholarships.

PLACEMENT

Each year more than 200 companies visit Darden to interview fewer than 200 second-year students seeking positions through the school's Placement Office. More than 5,000 on-campus interviews are conducted each year, and 95 percent of recent graduating classes have accepted positions by July 15. Graduates accept positions throughout the U.S. and abroad and consistently receive starting salaries well above the national average. In addition, the Placement Office is committed to full employment of the first-year class during the summer before their second year.

CORRESPONDENCE

For additional information, please write or call

Office of Admissions
The Colgate Darden Graduate School of Business Administration
University of Virginia
Box 6550
Charlottesville, Virginia 22906-6550
Telephone: 804-924-7281 or
800-UVA-MBA-1 (outside Virginia)

The University of Warwick is situated in pleasant countryside on the outskirts of Coventry. There are some 5,500 students, about 4,700 of these are undergraduates in a broad range of disciplines. About two thirds of the students are accommodated on the campus where there are excellent sporting, recreational, and cultural facilities. The campus is a major center for the performing arts with emphasis on music and drama. The university is at the center of England's motorway system, about 100 miles from London.

The School of Industrial and Business Studies, one of the larger schools within the university, has some 500 students. About 300 are undergraduates studying for degrees in management science or in accounting and financial analysis. Of the 140 full-time postgraduate students taking taught master's courses, about 70 are in the Master of Business Administration (M.B.A.) program; some 50 are studying for a Master of Arts (M.A.) in industrial relations, and 20 are taking a Master of Science (M.Sc.) in management science and operational research. About 50 postgraduate students are taking higher degrees by research. The school has a full-time multidisciplinary academic staff of 42. It is linked closely with the Institute for Management Research and Development and with the national Industrial Relations Research Unit which are both located at the university.

PROGRAM OF STUDY
The M.B.A. program is a rigorous course of study intended to provide an educational foundation for personal development and advancement in an executive career in the public or private sector. The course of full-time study covers a period of 12 months commencing in October. The first nine months are devoted to a mixture of compulsory and optional taught courses. These courses are taught within the university's normal academic year of three 10-week terms: autumn, spring, and summer. In the final three months, each student undertakes a project. The M.B.A. course may also be followed on a part-time basis over a period of either two or three years.

The nine-month program of taught courses is equally divided between core subjects, which everyone takes, and electives.

The first 10 weeks (autumn term) is all core and contains six subjects: Organizational Behavior, Quantitative Methods and Computing, Financial Accounting, Market Analysis, Operations Management, and Business Environment.

The second 10 weeks (spring term) contains a core course in Business Policy plus a choice of five from eight electives: The Management of the Change, Management Science, Management Information Systems, Management Accounting, Marketing Management, Production Management, Human Resource Management, and Managerial Economics.

In the third 10 weeks (spring term) students take a core course in Strategic Management and select 3 from some 20 electives, including Advanced Management Accounting, Advertising and Communications Management, Japanese-style Management, Comparative Industrial Relations, Corporate Planning, Information Management, Managing Advanced Manufacturing Technology, Service Operations Management, Small Firms—Starting and Growing Up, Financial Analysis, Financial Management, Marketing and Innovation Management, Marketing Research and Forecasting Methods, Employment Law and Personnel Policy, Industrial Relations, Information Systems, Management Economics, Manufacturing Policy, Industrial and Public Policy, and Strategic Planning Models.

The core subjects cover the basic knowledge essential to all management. The electives allow students, if they so wish, to build up an individual specialization based on their own interests and career objectives.

In the final three months (July to September) each student undertakes a project. Essentially the project puts the student in the role of a consultant on a task of significant importance to the sponsoring company. It gives students the opportunity to test their grasp of the new techniques they have learned, their judgment, and their personal skills as charge agents.

ADMISSION
Admission to the program is normally open to students who hold a good honors degree in any subject from a recognized university or an equivalent professional qualification. In judging the quality and suitability of applicants for the M.B.A.

program the school is concerned not only with their academic record and score on the Graduate Management Admission Test (GMAT), but also with evidence of achievement and motivation. Students whose native language is not English will be required to establish their proficiency. Previous work experience is highly desirable but not essential. All applicants are required to provide two references. If at all possible, students will attend an interview.

EXPENSES
The fees for 1986-87 are likely to be in the order of £1,700 for United Kingdom nationals and £3,500 for others (subject to revision each year). It is estimated that an additional £3,500 will be required for accommodation and other general living expenses for the year.

FINANCIAL ASSISTANCE
The program is recognized for awards by the Economic and Social Research Council. These awards are normally available only to citizens of the United Kingdom. Overseas applicants may consider applying to the British Council for financial support. All eligible students will be considered for the scholarships that are available. Every assistance is given to applicants wishing to take advantage of the special loan schemes offered by the leading banks in the United Kingdom in conjunction with either the Business Graduates Association or the Conference of University Management Schools.

PLACEMENT
The university's Careers Advisory Service and the school's own counseling services are available to students. Both the university and the school maintain close links with a large number of British and international companies about employment of graduates.

CORRESPONDENCE
For further information, write or call
M.B.A. Course Director
School of Industrial and Business
 Studies
University of Warwick
Coventry CV4 7AL
England
Telephone: Coventry (0203) 24011

The Graduate School of Business Administration was established in 1917 and has been a member of the American Assembly of Collegiate Schools of Business (AACSB) since 1921. Today it has a senior faculty of 110 members and an average graduate enrollment of 450 master's and 100 doctoral students.

PROGRAMS OF STUDY

The broad objective of the Master of Business Administration (M.B.A.) program is to help students develop the analytical tools for decision making and the understanding of administration that will be of value throughout their careers. The program is designed to be taken on a full-time basis by students from all academic majors. Two academic years (six quarters) are required for most students to complete the degree. College-level calculus and familiarity with the use of computers are the only prerequisites to the program.

The first year of the program is composed of required course work in accounting, finance, statistics, quantitative methods, operations management, economics, organizational behavior, marketing, human resources management, and the business context. The first year core is highly structured: students are divided into groups that take courses together from a small group of faculty. This structure encourages a high level of coordination and student interaction and cooperation.

During the second year the student takes the required policy course and 11 electives including an area of concentration and the research requirement. The latter is met through either a research paper or specially designed courses.

The Master of Professional Accounting (M.P.Acc.) degree program is aimed at preparing high-level professional accounting specialists. After completion of the first year M.B.A. core course requirements, students are provided an opportunity for in-depth accounting course work in a professionally oriented academic environment.

Joint degree programs include an M.B.A./Juris Doctor (J.D.) offered in conjunction with the School of Law and an M.B.A./Master of Arts in International Studies (M.A.I.S.) offered with the School of International Studies.

The Doctor of Philosophy (Ph.D.) program provides advanced study in business and administration suitable for teaching and research careers. The program consists of one major area of specialization and two or three additional supporting areas. The selection of subject areas and specific course work is made by the student and his or her program advisory committee. All students are expected to develop competency in research methodology. Generally, applicants must have completed a master's degree by the time of entry into the Ph.D. program. If prior work has not covered the equivalent of first year M.B.A. requirements, such courses are taken upon entry. There is no foreign language requirement. The residence requirement is three years of graduate study, two of which must be at the University of Washington. Of these two, one must be spent in continuous full-time residence at the university.

Areas of concentration are accounting; administrative theory and organizational behavior; business economics; business, government and society; business policy; finance; human resources management; information systems; international business; marketing; operations management; quantitative methods; and research methodology (minor only). Other areas may also be appropriate.

ADMISSION

New master's students are admitted for autumn quarter only. To be considered for admission an applicant must have a bachelor's degree from an accredited institution and take the Graduate Management Admission Test (GMAT). No specific undergraduate majors are given admissions preference. Beyond high demonstrated intellectual ability and excellence in academic performance, the school seeks applicants with maturity, successful experience in handling responsibility and well-developed communication skills. Applicants from non-English-speaking countries must submit scores on the Test of English as a Foreign Language (TOEFL). The application deadline for the M.B.A. and M.P.Acc. programs is April 1.

Candidates for the Ph.D. degree are also admitted for autumn quarter only. Selection is made on the basis of academic and work performance, GMAT scores, three letters of recommendation, and a brief statement of degree objectives. The application deadline for the Ph.D. program is February 15.

EXPENSES

Tuition and fees for the 1985-86 academic year (three quarters) are listed below (living costs vary widely):

Full-time, Washington resident. . $2,204
Full-time, nonresident 5,760

FINANCIAL ASSISTANCE

Entering master's students who qualify for work/study support are assured employment as research assistants to faculty members. A small number of privately sponsored tuition scholarships, fellowships, and other grants are administered through the school.

Most students admitted to the Ph.D. program receive half-time teaching appointments renewable for three years. The pay rate is competitive. Assistantship and financial aid applications should be filed concurrently with admission applications.

PLACEMENT

Employment opportunities for master's degree students are provided through the University Placement Center. Academic placement of Ph.D. students is coordinated through the Director of the Doctoral Program and interested faculty members.

CORRESPONDENCE

For further information, write or call
Graduate School of Business
    Administration
110 Mackenzie Hall (DJ-10)
University of Washington
Seattle, Washington 98195
Telephone: 206-543-4660

UNIVERSITY OF WESTERN AUSTRALIA

WESTERN AUSTRALIA

The University of Western Australia, established in 1911, began teaching in 1913. It is situated on a site of some 100 acres at Crawley-Nedlands on a bay of the Swan River about three miles from Perth, capital of the State of Western Australia. Perth has a population of about one million people and is served by international air and sea routes, which continue on to the Eastern States of Australia. Perth enjoys a delightful Mediterranean climate and is Australia's sunniest capital. Western Australia is known for its entrepreneurial spirit in mining, oil, gas, and innovative business ventures.

The master's degree in business administration began in 1973 as a new development within the Faculty of Economics and Commerce. A quota of 60 new students is applied. Both full-time and part-time courses are available. Master's degrees by course work in industrial relations, accounting, and economics, respectively, are also offered by the Faculty of Economics and Commerce, in addition to master's and Doctor of Philosophy (Ph.D.) degrees by research.

The proximity of the campus to the downtown center is convenient for part-time students. It also enhances the close relationships enjoyed among the university, the government, and the business community. The Western Australian Regional Computing Center located centrally on campus offers among the most comprehensive and powerful computer facilities available anywhere in Australia. The language of instruction is English.

PROGRAMS OF STUDY

The University of Western Australia M.B.A. program is designed to provide an environment that fosters intellectual challenge, problem solving, decision making, and action in the managerial context. The professional manager is seen as an educated, adaptive person. The manager should be at home in the scientific and scholarly world, but his or her job is to see the applications, the interactions, the costs, and the benefits among those fields of knowledge that apply to each individual situation, and to take action.

The part-time program is spread over eight semesters (four academic years). The curriculum is divided into two parts: 10 group A core half-units which are normally required of all students, and group B, the electives, from which the student chooses an additional 6 half-units. Each half-unit is studied for one semester only.

The core requirements consist of a grounding in economics, accounting, organization and management quantitative methods, finance, marketing, production, and business policy. The elective half-units permit further work in economics, finance, accounting, organization and management, and quantitative methods, and, in addition, specialization in government administration, information systems, labor relations, personnel management, innovation and entrepreneurship, and the management of small businesses. There is no thesis requirement.

Classes are held both day and evening. While the curriculum is run on a semester basis, the university calendar, which is based on a three-term structure, is observed. The academic year for the M.B.A. program normally commences in late February and finishes in early November.

Although credit may be allowed for work completed before entry, other units must be substituted for any units credited. Thus, all M.B.A. graduates complete 16 units regardless of their backgrounds.

ADMISSION

Applications for admission are considered by a selection committee which meets in the December prior to the start of the academic year. The basic admission requirement is that the student has completed an approved bachelor's degree course or its equivalent. The program is open to graduates of any faculty and in the process of student selection effort is made to preserve diversity in educational background. The criteria for selection include academic record and experience since graduation. While experience is not essential, other things being equal, the experienced person is preferred.

The October administration is the last opportunity for presenting Graduate Management Admission Test (GMAT) scores to the Selection Committee. Applicants who are not graduates of the University of Western Australia are required to apply for admission ad eundem statum and must submit an official statement of their prior academic record at the time of application.

Applications for admission, on the official form, must reach the Registrar, University of Western Australia, by September 30 of the preceding year. Successful applicants are normally notified in December prior to the year in which they are to be enrolled.

EXPENSES
On-campus accommodations (including meals) are available at a cost of approximately A$80 per week. Tuition is free, but there is an overseas student charge of A$3,500 per year.

CORRESPONDENCE
For information, write or call
M.B.A. Course Controller
Department of Management
The University of Western Australia
Nedlands, Western Australia 6009,
    Australia
Telephone: (Perth) (09) 380.2912

The fine reputation of Western's Master of Business Administration (M.B.A.) program stems in part from its unique focus. Western is concerned with the education of generalists: individuals who are prepared to launch into their immediate environment possessing the expertise essential for assuming higher management positions. While most of Western's graduates enter business careers, an increasing number are attracted to nonprofit-oriented operations such as governments, health and charitable organizations, colleges, and universities. It has become increasingly evident that skills of management are among the most effective devices for intelligent, ambitious, and optimistic young men and women to convert their ideals into meaningful reality.

The city of London, with a population of 290,000, is well known for its fine parks and recreational facilities. London is located halfway between Detroit and Toronto, a two-hour drive from either center. In addition to its proximity to these large cities, London's success in attracting a large variety of industry has made it the economic center of Southwestern Ontario. Thus the city becomes a prime location for the School of Business Administration. The university itself, situated on a campus of more than 500 acres and having an enrollment of 17,000, is representative of the physical freedom of the community and provides an excellent setting for the experience and challenge of the M.B.A. program.

PROGRAMS OF STUDY

Western's dynamic faculty have remained alert to the changing needs of organizations and the changing nature of students. In the past several years, some exciting new courses have been introduced, and the traditional courses in the curriculum have undergone considerable updating and transformation. The faculty, in conjunction with students and alumni, are constantly reevaluating the entire M.B.A. program to ensure that the school provides its students with an experience that is relevant to today's and tomorrow's world.

Western's approach to management education runs the gamut of teaching techniques. There is considerable emphasis on the use of cases, where students are faced with practical managerial problems which require action. Faculty members act both as colleagues and mentors, regularly challenging and stimulating students to analyze situations and consider alternatives, to take positions and defend these positions.

The M.B.A. program is designed to cover two academic years. The first year consists of a set of integrated courses aimed at providing extensive knowledge in the fields of finance, marketing, operations management, control, management science, economics, and organizational behavior. Beyond the compulsory business policy and political environment courses, second-year students are free to choose courses in their particular area or areas of interest.

Faculty and students remain aware that the most successful managers possess knowledge that extends well beyond the organization itself. The education and experience gained in the M.B.A. program are acquired in the context of fitting this knowledge into a multifaceted, dynamic organization with a distinct role and responsibility in the surrounding society.

In 1960, the University Senate established the program leading to a Doctor of Philosophy (Ph.D.) degree in business administration. The purpose of the doctoral program is to provide advanced training in research and teaching, as well as advanced substantive work in a special field of the candidate's choice, as preparation for an academic career. Further information may be obtained by writing to Chairman, Ph.D. Program, School of Business Administration.

ADMISSION

To be considered for admission to the M.B.A. program, a candidate must normally hold an undergraduate degree from an accredited university. Admission may be offered to candidates without an undergraduate degree if they can demonstrate that their previous work experience and leadership qualities clearly indicate a high potential for a management career. While no specific course preparation is required, candidates must be proficient in English and have a sound background in mathematics.

EXPENSES

The following is based on an academic year of 33 weeks.

	Foreign	Domestic
Tuition	$5,400	$1,500
Housing and food	3,600	3,600
Books and supplies	900	900
	$9,900	$6,000

PLACEMENT

The Placement Office at the School of Business Administration provides a variety of services to help students make meaningful career choices. Students are encouraged to become personally involved in all the career-planning activities arranged on their behalf. In addition, the school provides opportunities to master the oral and written communication skills required in job seeking efforts.

The Placement Office, supported by the M.B.A. Association, pursues an active marketing campaign on the students' behalf to expand the school's outreach to prospective employers.

CORRESPONDENCE

For further information, write to
Student Services, Room 116
School of Business Administration
The University of Western Ontario
London, Ontario, Canada N6A 3K7

The Faculty of Business Administration of the University of Windsor is committed to the preparation of men and women for leadership positions in public and private management.

To meet this objective, the faculty's M.B.A. program has been developed to allow students to acquire expertise in functional areas of business, to develop their analytical powers, and to acquire some practice and guidance in the application of these analytical powers. This is done through course work in different areas and through the M.B.A. major paper, where the student will conduct in-depth research of a topic under the guidance of a faculty committee.

This combination of course work and research both challenges the student and forces the development of business decision-making skills. Windsor M.B.A. graduates are thus prepared for managerial success or for doctoral studies.

PROGRAM OF STUDY

The M.B.A. program is a course of study accomplished in two years. Semester one of the first year consists of prerequisite courses designed to give a background in the following areas of business: accounting, administrative studies, finance, management science, and marketing. Semester two of the first year provides for limited concentration in two areas and the inclusion of an introduction to computers in management.

The second year constitutes the candidate year. Eight courses are required including Business Policy. Up to two graduate courses may be included from other faculties within the university with the approval of the Dean of the Faculty of Business Administration. In addition to course requirements, the candidate is required to prepare and orally defend a major paper.

ADMISSION

Applicants who have secured satisfactory standing (at least a B average) in their undergraduate work may be admitted. Major consideration is given to performance during the last two years of the undergraduate program. Possession of the minimum requirements for admission does not ensure acceptance. Other factors such as graduate courses taken elsewhere, suitable business experience, and Graduate Management Admission Test (GMAT) scores are considered.

Students must take the GMAT before applying for admission to the Faculty of Business Administration. (Details of the test may be obtained from Educational Testing Service, Princeton, New Jersey 08541). The Order Form for the Bulletin of Information for the GMAT is available in the Office of Graduate Studies.

Applicants must have completed at least two semesters of university-level economics and at least one semester of university-level mathematics prior to admission to the M.B.A. program. Students lacking these prerequisites may be permitted to complete the appropriate undergraduate courses in their first semester.

Graduates from a four-year honors program in commerce or business administration who, in the opinion of the Faculty of Business Administration, have completed an adequate program of studies, may be admitted to the candidate year of the program provided they have obtained satisfactory standing in their undergraduate degree. Graduates from other four-year programs may be given advanced standing for courses taken within their degree program if these courses are equivalent to 500-level courses.

Applicants whose native language is not English are required to take an English proficiency test administered by the English Language Institute of the University of Michigan or the Test of English as a Foreign Language (TOEFL). The applicant may make arrangements for taking the Michigan test in his or her own locale by contacting the center or by writing to the English Language Institute of the University of Michigan, Testing and Certification, North University Building, Ann Arbor, Michigan, 48109, U.S.A.

For information on arranging to take the Test of English as a Foreign Language, the applicant should write to TOEFL, Educational Testing Service, Princeton, New Jersey 08541, U.S.A.

EXPENSES

Per academic year	Domestic	Foreign
Tuition	$1,320	$ 7,050
Housing and food	3,000	3,000
Books and supplies	700	700
	$5,020	$10,750

FINANCIAL ASSISTANCE

Financial aid is available to well-qualified students in the form of scholarships, assistantships, Canadian student loans, and Provincial Award programs.

PLACEMENT

A Canada Manpower Centre has staff on campus who assist students in finding employment after graduation, as well as part-time and summer employment while at the school. Yearly, some 200 companies send representatives to the university to interview graduates.

CORRESPONDENCE

For catalogs and applications, write the Admissions Office, Faculty of Graduate Studies. Specific questions about curriculum should be addressed to

Dean, Faculty of Business
   Administration
University of Windsor
Windsor, Ontario, Canada N9B 3P4
Telephone: 519-253-4232, extension 3097

Frequently called "Wisconsin's Most Beautiful Campus," the University of Wisconsin—Eau Claire is located in west central Wisconsin on a 310-acre, two-level campus embracing Putnam Park on the banks of the Chippewa River. The location provides ready access to the recreational activities for which northern Wisconsin is so well known. The city of Eau Claire has a population of 55,000 and provides an attractive atmosphere for graduate study.

Founded in 1916, the University of Wisconsin—Eau Claire now enrolls over 11,000 students; faculty and academic staff total more than 640. The Master of Business Administration (M.B.A.) program is offered jointly by the School of Business and the Department of Economics. The School of Business was created in 1966. Composed of the Departments of Accountancy, Business Administration, Business Education and Administrative Management, and Management Information Systems, the School of Business currently has more than 3,500 students. There are 75 faculty members in the School of Business and Department of Economics, many of whom enjoy state, national, and international reputations.

The School of Business, through its Bureau of Management Development and Research, offers many programs to assist in business and industrial development.

PROGRAM OF STUDY
The Master of Business Administration was approved by the University of Wisconsin Board of Regents in 1975. The overall objective of the program is to prepare graduates for positions of leadership in business and public administration. The program has been designed to develop the student's critical, analytical, problem-solving, and decision-making capabilities and to provide basic knowledge useful in the solution of management problems.

The specific objectives are to provide experiences necessary to enable the student to understand the economic, social, and legal environment in which organizations exist and operate; conceptualize and analyze administrative problems; apply a wide variety of problem-solving tools and techniques in an administrative environment; communicate decisions and information; and develop the personal resources and ethical foundations required to meet the challenges and opportunities of a changing social, political, and economic environment.

Graduate M.B.A. courses are offered during late afternoons and evenings to allow students to enroll on a part-time or full-time basis. Students whose undergraduate majors were not in a business field will normally require two calendar years of full-time study to complete the program. Those who hold undergraduate degrees in business will normally require one calendar year of full-time study. Students pursuing the M.B.A. degree part time will require proportionately longer periods to complete the program.

The curriculum is composed of two segments, a foundation phase and a graduate phase. A list of the courses in each phase may be obtained from the M.B.A. Office. Students holding a baccalaureate degree in a business field normally will have satisfactorily completed all foundation courses. Other students must satisfy the foundation requirements by taking appropriate graduate or undergraduate courses prior to enrollment in the second-phase courses.

Phase II consists of a core of required courses and electives. Within the elective courses the student can specialize in order to meet particular career goals.

ADMISSION
A candidate for admission must submit the following to the Office of Admissions at least 30 days prior to the anticipated date of registration: (1) a completed application form accompanied by a $20 nonrefundable application fee, (2) an official transcript (to be sent directly from each institution at which the applicant has attempted undergraduate or graduate work), (3) official notice of the applicant's score on the Graduate Management Admission Test (GMAT), and (4) official score from the Test of English as a Foreign Language (TOEFL) for students whose native language is not English.

To be admitted to the M.B.A. program, an applicant must hold a baccalaureate degree in any major from an accredited college or university. The applicant must have an acceptable undergraduate grade-point average and must present a satisfactory GMAT score. Foreign students must obtain a TOEFL score of at least 550.

Students may apply for admission to the fall, spring, or summer terms.

EXPENSES
Tuition in the fall of 1985 was $90.45 per graduate credit for residents and $262.45 per graduate credit for nonresidents; tuition for students enrolled in nine or more graduate credits was $814.50 and $2,362.00 respectively. A reciprocity agreement allows reduction of the fees for Minnesota residents. Fees are subject to periodic change by the Board of Regents' action.

A limited number of research assistantships are available. Application is made through the office of the Dean of Graduate Studies.

PLACEMENT
The Office of Career Planning and Placement maintains contact with representatives of business and industry, governmental services, and health agencies, many of whom visit the campus to interview students each year.

CORRESPONDENCE
For catalogs and application materials contact the office of the Dean of Graduate Studies, Schofield 201. For more specific information on the M.B.A. program, contact
M.B.A. Office, Schneider 117
School of Business
University of Wisconsin—Eau Claire
Eau Claire, Wisconsin 54701
Telephone: 715-836-5473

UNIVERSITY OF WISCONSIN—LA CROSSE

LA CROSSE, WISCONSIN

In 1975, La Crosse, Wisconsin, was named the number one small city in the nation. Within the city of 50,000 are three institutions of postsecondary education, nationally recognized health care facilities, and the headquarters of two *Fortune* 500 companies. The La Crosse area is famous for its exceptional natural beauty. Abundant water, woodlands, and varying terrain provide a year-round invitation to those who enjoy outdoor activities such as skiing, sailing, hunting, fishing, skating, riding, camping, and hiking.

The University of Wisconsin—La Crosse, located in a residential area near the Mississippi River bluffs, is a public institution of higher education governed by the Board of Regents of The University of Wisconsin system. It was founded in 1909 as a normal school, authorized to grant baccalaureate degrees in 1926, and has offered graduate studies since 1956. The university has an enrollment of approximately 9,000 students and approximately 500 faculty and academic staff members.

The College of Business Administration was established in 1972 and is the fastest growing campus unit. Fifty-two faculty members instruct 2,000 undergraduate students in the majors of accounting, business administration, economics, finance, and marketing.

The Bureau of Business and Economic Research and the Small Business Development Center serve the university and the business and educational community.

PROGRAM OF STUDY

The Master of Business Administration (M.B.A.) program is designed to prepare students to achieve responsible positions in business, education, and government. It is structured as a broad preparation for managerial careers and is available to all qualified students, regardless of undergraduate major. The core curriculum provides a set of analytical tools sufficiently fundamental to be relevant to a broad range of management problems.

The curriculum is composed of two segments, a foundation and a graduate phase. Students holding a baccalaureate degree in a business field normally will have satisfied all foundation courses. Those with degrees in other fields will be required to make up any deficiencies in the foundation area prior to enrollment in graduate-level courses.

The graduate phase of the M.B.A. curriculum consists of 21 hours of core courses and 9 hours of electives. The seven required courses are taken in management, marketing, economics, accounting, and finance. The three elective courses may be taken in three different areas or as a concentration in one discipline. There is no thesis or seminar paper and no comprehensive examination. A maximum of nine credits completed satisfactorily at other institutions may be applied to the M.B.A. degree.

The program is offered on a part-time basis during the evening year round, and courses are sequenced for admission in August, January, and June.

The degree may be pursued on a part-time or full-time basis. Those who hold an undergraduate degree in business will normally require one calendar year of full-time study. Students whose undergraduate majors were not in a business field will normally require two calendar years of full-time study to complete the program.

ADMISSION

Applicants for admission to the M.B.A. program must apply through the university Admissions Office. In order to be admitted in good standing, applicants must meet the university requirements including a minimum grade-point average (GPA) of 2.85 (or 3.00 for the last half of the undergraduate work) on a 4.00 scale, and a Graduate Management Admission Test (GMAT) total score of at least 450. Applicants not meeting the minimum GPA and/or GMAT total score may be admitted on probationary status if they achieve a minimum score of 950 based on the following formula: 200 times GPA plus GMAT total score, or a minimum score of 1,000 based on 200 times GPA (upper-division) plus the GMAT total score.

A candidate for admission must submit the following at least 30 days prior to the anticipated date of registration: (1) a completed application form accompanied by a $20 nonrefundable application fee, (2) official transcripts (to be sent directly from each institution at which the applicant has attempted undergraduate or graduate work), (3) official notice of the applicant's score on the GMAT, and (4) for students whose native language is not English, an official score from the Test of English as a Foreign Language (TOEFL). Foreign students must obtain a TOEFL score of at least 550.

Students may apply for admission to the fall, spring, or summer terms.

EXPENSES

Tuition, per semester, in 1985-86 was $844 for full-time resident students and $2,391 for nonresidents.

Residence hall fees are $415 per semester for a double room. Single rooms are not available, and there is no on-campus housing for married students.

FINANCIAL ASSISTANCE

A limited number of graduate assistantships are available for students enrolled full time in the M.B.A. program.

CORRESPONDENCE

For further information, please write
Director, M.B.A. Program
College of Business Administration
University of Wisconsin—La Crosse
La Crosse, Wisconsin 54601

Graduate School of Business

UNIVERSITY OF WISCONSIN—MADISON

MADISON, WISCONSIN

Graduate work at the University of Wisconsin began informally about 1880. By 1904, departments that offered graduate work and students who were enrolled at the graduate level had so increased that the university formally established the Graduate School. In the ensuing years, graduate education at the university has grown to such a degree that the University of Wisconsin now ranks among the leading universities in the United States granting the Doctor of Philosophy (Ph.D.) degree. The Graduate School of Business enjoys full cooperation of the business community throughout Wisconsin and northern Illinois and offers students unlimited opportunity to become acquainted with financial and industrial enterprises.

The Graduate School of Business, an integral part of the University of Wisconsin Graduate School, offers programs that lead to the following degrees: Master of Business Administration (M.B.A.), Master of Science in Business, Master of Accountancy, Master of Arts in business, and Doctor of Philosophy. In 1985, there were 782 master's candidates and 108 Ph.D. candidates enrolled for full-time graduate study in the School of Business.

The Master of Business Administration program covers both the general knowledge and the special skills required for a career in business. A broad education for business includes exposure in all functional areas. Graduate students may elect the broad diversified master's degree, or they may elect a modest concentration in the following areas: accounting, actuarial science, appraisal; arts administration; business statistics; finance, investment, and banking; health care fiscal management; health services administration; information systems analysis and design; international business; management; marketing; public management; quantitative analysis; real estate appraisal and investment analysis; real estate and urban land economics; risk and insurance; and transportation and public utilities.

PROGRAMS OF STUDY
The master's degree programs vary in length from one to two years, depending upon the candidate's undergraduate major. For students who enter the program having substantially met the undergraduate requirements for the Bachelor of Business Administration (B.B.A.) degree, the master's program will usually require one calendar year. For candidates who enter the program with less than the

equivalent of a B.B.A. degree, the program will require a proportionally longer time. For example, an undergraduate English or history major would usually require two years to obtain a master's degree in business administration.

The Doctor of Philosophy, the highest earned degree conferred by any university, represents more than the mere sum of semesters during which a candidate has been in residence or the credit the student has earned for courses completed. The degree is granted only upon evidence of high proficiency, together with a recognized ability for independent investigation as demonstrated in a dissertation based upon original research or creative scholarship and communicated in a lucid, engaging writing style. Areas of specialization at the doctoral level include accounting; business statistics; finance, investment, and banking; information systems analysis and design; international business; management; marketing; public management; quantitative analysis; real estate and urban land economics; risk and insurance; and transportation and public utilities.

ADMISSION
Students admitted at the graduate level must have (1) a bachelor's degree from an approved institution; (2) an undergraduate grade-point average of 2.75 or higher (4.0 basis); and (3) satisfactory test scores from the Graduate Management Admission Test (GMAT). Foreign applicants whose national language is not English must also submit scores from the Test of English as a Foreign Language (TOEFL). Due to the increasing number of quality applications received by the School of Business, enrollment may be limited despite fulfillment of the minimum entrance requirements indicated above.

EXPENSES
In 1985-86 semester fees and tuition for candidates registered as full-time graduate students were approximately $973.00 for Wisconsin residents and $2,897.50 for nonresidents. These charges are periodically changed by the Regents. Part-time students registering for no more than seven credits may register on a per-credit basis ($121.75 resident; $362.25 nonresident). Estimated expenses for an unmarried foreign student for a calendar year of study are $15,630.00 not including travel. Tuition and fees for the summer session are based upon the number of credits carried.

FINANCIAL ASSISTANCE
Financial aid to graduate students includes fellowships, scholarships, research assistantships, teaching assistantships, and loans. Ordinarily, financial assistance is not available to foreign students in their first year of study because of the difficulty of evaluating the relative quality of their performance.

PLACEMENT
The Placement Bureau of the Graduate School of Business is available to aid candidates for advanced degrees in locating responsible and challenging management positions in business, industry, and government.

CORRESPONDENCE
For further information, please write to
Director of Graduate Admissions
Graduate School of Business
University of Wisconsin
1155 Observatory Drive
Madison, Wisconsin 53706
Telephone: 608-262-1555

The University of Wisconsin—Milwaukee is located in an urban environment; its programs are geared to both a resident and urban student body. Classes are scheduled thoughout a 14-hour day and on weekends to meet the needs of full-time and part-time students.

PROGRAMS OF STUDY

The Master of Business Administration (M.B.A.) degree offers students wide-based knowledge in five major areas, each of which contributes an essential element to the student's education as a manager. Management foundation courses provide up to 10 credits of background for those students lacking adequate preparation in the areas of economics, mathematics, statistics, accounting, and computers. Four component areas totaling 30 credits are required of all students. The management science core introduces the student to the behavioral sciences, the study of organizations, the advanced tools of analysis of modeling, operations research, and managerial economics. The functional area provides knowledge of the subject matter and operational processes in marketing, finance, and production as well as utilizing this knowledge for decision making. Integrating courses in business environment and policy provide a capstone to the managerial tools and knowledge acquired in other course work. They provide awareness of the social, cultural, legal, and ethical implications of managing an enterprise. Finally, electives allow the student to tailor a program toward research, general management, or functional area management.

The Master of Science (M.S.) program equips students with in-depth knowledge in a specialized area of their choice along with preparation in management science.

The accounting area provides professional training in the field and qualifies the student to write the Certified Public Accounting (C.P.A.) examination. Finance analysis courses equip the student with theoretical concepts and analytical tools needed for solving financial problems of the firm, the financial intermediary, and the individual investor. Health care management trains business-oriented professional administrators to assist in the management of complex health organizations and programs. The management information systems area develops a systems approach to solving informational problems, placing emphasis on the application

of information science techniques, and the use of computers in the decision context. Marketing analysis emphasizes the development of analysis, measurement, and research skills to solve problems in such areas as new product management, distribution planning, advertising media choice, and market behavior. The operations analysis area develops skills in analytical techniques, statistics, and mathematical model building for facilitation of organizational decision making. Organization science focuses on the systematic understanding of human behavior in relationships between individuals, and within and between work groups and organizational units. Taxation trains high-caliber specialists who can provide expert guidance on tax matters to business and nonbusiness organizations and to individuals.

The M.B.A.-Executive Curriculum is a special two-year program for experienced executives who have demonstrated the capacity for middle- and upper-management positions. The curriculum has been structured to meet the needs of the working manager; classes meet one full day per week on alternating Fridays and Saturdays.

The Doctor of Philosophy (Ph.D.) program leads to a doctorate in management science. The curriculum has been designed for students aspiring to research-oriented staff careers or teaching and research in academic institutions. Fields of study that may be selected by doctoral students are finance, management information systems, marketing, operations research, and organizational science.

ADMISSION

Admission to the M.B.A., M.S., and M.B.A.-Executive programs requires a bachelor's degree from an approved institution, satisfactory academic achievement, and a satisfactory score on the Graduate Management Admission Test (GMAT). It is possible for an M.S. applicant to substitute the Graduate Record Examinations (GRE). The Ph.D. program requires a minimum of a bachelor's degree for admission, as well as preparation in research skills such as mathematics, statistics, and computer programming. All applicants are reviewed by the school's Ph.D. Program Committee before a recommendation is made. Admission decisions are based on the student's achievements in prior academic work, scores on the GMAT or the GRE, assessment of the

student's analytical capabilities, stated career objectives, and the ability and potential to do independent research.

Applicants who have graduated from foreign schools must have earned the equivalent of a U.S. bachelor's degree. Foreign applicants (except those who have a degree from a U.S. institution) must attain a suitable score on the Test of English as a Foreign Language (TOEFL).

EXPENSES

Full-time tuition (effective fall 1985 and subject to change) was $1,001.60 for residents and $2,926.10 for nonresidents.

FINANCIAL ASSISTANCE

The university administers several different forms of financial aid: fellowships, scholarships, teaching assistantships, research or project assistantships, and loans. Application forms for these awards can be obtained from the Graduate School Office and must be returned to the School of Business Administration by February 10, together with complete official transcripts, scores on the GMAT or GRE, and letters of recommendation.

PLACEMENT

The school's Placement/Career Counselor complements an extensive academic advising unit providing each student with counseling and career-search opportunities.

CORRESPONDENCE

For further information write or call
    Student Services Center
    School of Business Administration
    University of Wisconsin—Milwaukee
    P.O. Box 742
    Milwaukee, Wisconsin 53201
    Telephone: 414-963-5271

Located on the Fox River near historic Lake Winnebago, the University of Wisconsin—Oshkosh is a leading institution in one of the country's great university systems. Approximately 11,000 students are enrolled with about 20 percent pursuing graduate work. The coeducational university is comprehensive in scope with schools of nursing, education, letters and science, and business. The fall semester begins in early September and terminates before Christmas. The spring semester is completed by mid-May. A comprehensive summer session is also offered.

Work leading to a Master of Business Administration (M.B.A.) degree was first offered during fall 1970, and program accreditation by the American Assembly of Collegiate Schools of Business (AACSB) was granted in 1978. Present graduate enrollment in business comprises approximately 500 students with undergraduate degrees taken in 50 major areas from 100 colleges and universities. It is possible to pursue the degree on either a full- or part-time basis. Classes are held in the evening and are offered on a selected, rotating basis throughout east-central Wisconsin. At present, programs are offered in the Green Bay and Stevens Point areas as well as on the main Oshkosh campus. Full-time, terminally qualified faculty teach at each campus.

PROGRAMS OF STUDY

The M.B.A. program is designed to provide exposure to both the conceptual and substantive facets of modern multidimensional management. Essentially, the aim is to provide broad education in management with additional graduate study in a professional area of emphasis. The curriculum is responsive to social, economic, and technological developments and applies the evolving knowledge in the social, behavioral, and quantitative sciences. The program is structured to develop the student's critical, analytical, and decision-making abilities to contribute to social change and to the growth of professional management.

There exists a critical shortage of professional managerial talent—people with the ability to organize, plan, inspire, and direct the work of others. This need involves not only competitive enterprise but also governmental organizations and nonprofit institutions as society attempts to use resources more effectively in the satisfaction of human needs. Fundamentally, the M.B.A. program is designed to help fill the need for professional managers.

Three structured levels of courses: foundations, management core, and electives, lead to the M.B.A. degree. General requirements include a minimum of 30 graduate credits in the core and elective courses. Depending on previous undergraduate training, additional graduate foundation course work may be required to provide the necessary academic background for graduate study in business.

Upon completion of the foundation requirements, M.B.A. candidates may enroll in the management core sequence. Courses that compose the management core build on the substance of the foundation study as well as provide the concepts and tools necessary for success in subsequent academic and career activities.

Management core	Credits
Financial management	3
Organization theory	3
Managerial accounting	3
Quantitative methods	3
Information systems integration	1½
Organizations and their environments	3
Corporate strategy	1½
Marketing management	3

Finally, the student must complete nine credits of graduate electives from one of the following areas of emphasis or across the following areas of emphasis: accounting, finance, operations management, manpower management, and marketing.

The school also offers a Master of Science (M.S.) in accounting program which is designed as a first professional degree in accounting. The program is structured to accommodate students with a bachelor's degree in virtually any field. Study for the M.S. in accounting degree provides preparation for employment in public accounting, business, government, and nonprofit agencies, and/or for initial employment as an instructor at the college level. The program is intended for full-time students, and all classes are held on the University of Wisconsin—Oshkosh campus during both daytime and evening hours.

ADMISSION

Applications are invited from interested persons with bachelor's degrees in any field from accredited schools. Admission is granted on either a probationary or unrestricted basis. Factors considered are scores on the Graduate Management Admission Test (GMAT), undergraduate grades and trends, and pertinent experience. Foreign students must earn an acceptable score on the Test of English as a Foreign Language (TOEFL) and meet all requirements for unrestricted admission.

EXPENSES

Tuition for fall 1985 was $92 per credit hour for Wisconsin residents and $264 per credit hour for nonresidents.

FINANCIAL ASSISTANCE

A limited number of graduate assistantships are available for full-time students. Applications for the fall term should normally be received by April 1.

PLACEMENT

The university maintains a comprehensive placement bureau to assist prospective graduates in finding desirable positions.

CORRESPONDENCE

For further information, please write or call

Director of Graduate Programs
College of Business Administration
University of Wisconsin—Oshkosh
Oshkosh, Wisconsin 54901
Telephone: 414-424-1444

The University of Wisconsin—Parkside is one of 13 degree-granting campuses in the distinguished University of Wisconsin System, one of the nation's largest. The campus opened in 1969, and currently has about 6,000 undergraduate students, 400 graduate students, and 6,000 alumni, most of whom are employed in southeastern Wisconsin. The campus is located on the outskirts of Racine and Kenosha near Lake Michigan. These two cities, together with the larger Chicago-Milwaukee urban corridor in which they are located, serve as a convenient field laboratory and employment market for the university's undergraduate and graduate students.

PROGRAM OF STUDY

The Master of Business Administration (M.B.A.) program is offered by the Division of Business and Administrative Science. The M.B.A. program is designed to prepare degree candidates for successful careers in positions of policy making and administrative responsibility in both the private and public sectors. Program focus is on the needs of mature students who have the educational background, experience, and degree of intellectual curiosity and discernment essential to graduate-level study. The program is designed to be completed in four years of part-time study, with the possibility of earlier completion depending on prior academic work or professional experience. Courses are offered in the evenings and on weekends.

The M.B.A. program admits students whose prior academic preparation in business and related areas ranges from nonexistent to extensive. The program's requirements, depending on the student's preparation, range from 30 to 54 credits divided into four functional levels: (1) fundamental concepts and methods in administration (0-12 credits), (2) analysis of problems in functional areas of business (0-24 credits), (3) professional concentration (6 credits) and electives (9-21 credits), and (4) integrative analysis and policy formulation (3 credits).

After students are admitted to the program, the M.B.A. program adviser reviews their past work with them and sets up a plan of study to meet the program requirements based on their individual needs and goals. Students with undergraduate degrees in business, economics, or related fields may be eligible for waivers of Level I and Level II foundation courses. Students without specific preparation in these fields should find that the foundation courses of the M.B.A. program will give them the fundamentals needed for the rest of the program.

ADMISSION

Candidates for admission should hold a bachelor's degree from an accredited institution. Factors considered include undergraduate academic performance, scores on the Graduate Management Admission Test (GMAT), and a personal statement (200-300 words) of the applicant's professional objectives and how graduate study in business can help in attaining them.

Applicants whose native language is not English and whose degree is not from a university in the United States must also submit scores on the Test of English as a Foreign Language (TOEFL).

All application material must be received by the following dates: fall admission—August 15, spring admission—January 1, and summer admission—June 1.

EXPENSES

Wisconsin Residents (Spring 1986)
   $816.00 per semester for nine or more credits
   $109.25 per credit for first credit less than two
   $88.25 per each subsequent credit
Nonresidents (Spring 1986)
   $2,363.50 per semester for nine or more credits
   $281.25 per credit for first credit less than two
   $260.25 per each subsequent credit

Tuition and fees are set yearly by the Board of Regents and are subject to change without notice.

FINANCIAL ASSISTANCE

Limited financial aids are available for graduate students. The Financial Aids Office can help eligible students with work-study, veterans' program benefits, fellowships, or the student loan program.

All application forms requesting grants or combinations of assistance should be submitted together with financial statements to the appropriate office before March 15 for students who expect to enter the following September. Applications are accepted throughout the school year as long as funds are available. However, a student submitting an application after the priority date will be considered only after the earlier requests have been processed. Information may be obtained from the Financial Aids Office (414-553-2291).

The university does not own student housing, but the Housing Office (414-553-2320) assists students in locating rooms, apartments, or houses in the Racine-Kenosha area. Bus service is available between Racine and Kenosha and the campus.

CORRESPONDENCE

For additional information or to request an application for admission, please contact
   M.B.A. Program
   Division of Business and Administrative Science
   University of Wisconsin—Parkside
   P.O. Box 2000
   Kenosha, Wisconsin 53141
   Telephone: 414-553-2280 or 414-553-2046

UNIVERSITY OF WISCONSIN—WHITEWATER

WHITEWATER, WISCONSIN

The College of Business and Economics was established in 1963, having grown out of a strong business program which had its inception in 1913.

The Master of Business Administration (M.B.A.) and Master of Science (M.S.) in accounting programs are accredited by the American Assembly of Collegiate Schools of Business (AACSB). It is possible to pursue either of these two degrees on a full- or part-time (night) basis. At present, classes are offered at Whitewater for full-time students, and at Whitewater, Janesville, and Waukesha for part-time (night) students. Full-time, terminally qualified faculty teach at each location.

PROGRAMS OF STUDY

The M.B.A. degree has as its main objective the preparation of men and women for careers in administration and teaching. The specific objectives are

- to provide sound preparation in foundation courses concerning basic tools and functional areas that are critical to the understanding of business,
- to study in depth those tools and functional areas that are essential to sound administrative practices,
- to give students an in-depth study of an area of concentration in which they have an interest and in which they desire to begin professional life,
- to provide the tools and knowledge for identifying problems, collecting, and analyzing data to make sound decisions in a dynamic economic environment.

The fields of concentration are accounting, business education, decision support system, finance, international business, management, managerial economics, and marketing. The program is built on a core of undergraduate requirements in the areas of accounting and finance, mathematics and statistics, economics, management, marketing, legal environment of business, and computers. The foundation courses can be completed in an undergraduate program in business or by completing specific graduate courses after having been admitted to the program. The program can be completed in one year for those who have had all foundation courses or up to two years for those who have not.

General requirements for the completion of the M.B.A. degree include a minimum of 36 graduate credits. All students are required to have adequate preparation in the common body of knowledge as defined by the AACSB. Those individuals not having sufficient preparation will be required to take additional graduate courses. Normally a program of study for those not having prior business preparation would consist of two years.

Free elective credits may be chosen from any 730-level (or above) courses offered in the departments of accounting, business education and office administration, economics, finance, management, or marketing. In consultation with the adviser these courses are chosen outside the student's emphasis area for the purpose of broadening the student's competence for overall management.

An area of emphasis will be chosen from accounting, business education, decision support system, finance, managerial economics, management (general, personnel, or production), international business, or marketing. With the approval of the student's adviser and the Associate Dean, a thesis of up to six credits may be included in the nine-credit emphasis.

An M.S. in accounting degree program is designed primarily as a first professional degree for candidates with a nonbusiness undergraduate background. Candidates with an accounting major or equivalent undergraduate background may consider either the M.B.A. program, or, if a greater degree of specialization is desired, the M.S. program. Programs for completion of the M.S. degree are designed to fit the individual needs of the student and satisfy the academic requirements to write the Certified Public Accountant examination. All candidates for the M.S. degree are required to complete a minimum of 30 credits of graduate work, depending upon their undergraduate preparation.

ADMISSION

Admission to the M.B.A. or M.S.-accounting program is limited to admission in good standing using the criteria:

- undergraduate degree from an accredited institution,
- 1,000 composite based on the formula: Graduate Management Admission Test (GMAT) + [200 × overall undergraduate grade-point average] *or* 1,050 composite based on the formula GMAT + [200 × upper-division undergraduate grade-point average].
- Foreign students must also have on record a score of at least 550 on the Test of English as a Foreign Language (TOEFL) or equivalent on another test.

An application file is not reviewed for admission consideration until official transcripts and the GMAT score are on file. Due to increasing enrollments, admission may be limited despite fulfillment of the minimum entrance requirements indicated above.

EXPENSES

Per semester	In-state	Out-of-state
Tuition (9 credits or more)	$ 750	$2,150
Room and board	1,150	1,150
Books	350	350
	$2,250	$3,650

FINANCIAL ASSISTANCE

Assistantships are available for full-time graduate students. Full graduate assistantships provide a stipend of approximately $5,200 for two semesters. Students holding an assistantship are expected to perform 20 hours of work per week. At present, graduate assistants do not teach classes. Forms are available for application for assistantships in the Graduate Office.

PLACEMENT

The College of Business and Economics works very closely with the University Placement Office. Companies come from throughout the Midwest and from other sections of the country. Representatives of approximately 230 companies interview on campus every year.

CORRESPONDENCE

For further information, please call 414-472-1945 or write to

Associate Dean, College of Business and Economics
University of Wisconsin—Whitewater
Whitewater, Wisconsin 53190

The Graduate School of Business Administration of the University of the Witwatersrand, Johannesburg, provides a center for academic and professional management education in the largest industrial and commercial area of South Africa. The school is set in spacious grounds with easy and rapid access to the commercial center of Johannesburg.

The school offers a postgraduate Master of Business Administration (M.B.A.) degree, a Doctor of Philosophy (Ph.D.) degree, a postgraduate diploma in personnel management (H.D.P.M.) leading to a master's degree in personnel management (M.P.M.), a six-week executive development program, a two-week senior executive development program, and over 20 shorter executive education programs on a continuous basis.

The Business School also controls and administers the following ancilliary organizations, which form an integral part of the school:

• The Centre for Developing Business provides a management advisory service for existing small business and arranges a variety of management training courses. It also runs the highly successful Junior Achievement Program and has established centers in the major cities of South Africa.

• The Centre for Business Studies provides a medium for informed comment on matters of interest to the business community.

PROGRAM OF STUDY

The M.B.A. degree is offered as a full-time program, a part-time program or a combination of the two. The full-time program is equivalent to two full academic years, but may be completed in 17 months since the normal university holidays are shortened. The part-time (evening) program involves a three-year period of study. A third option is that students may register for a combination of full-time and part-time study, complete 7 or 10 months full time and thereafter convert to the part-time program. The content is the same for all programs.

The primary objective of the M.B.A. program is to assist the student, firstly, to develop a professional approach to managerial problem solving, and secondly to deal in depth with the complexities of the major functional areas of management.

The first part is devoted to 11 compulsory topics aimed at developing an awareness and an understanding of the main concepts and tools of business management and involves basic studies in the fundamental areas of accounting and control, business policy, economics, financial management, human resources strategy and management, law, marketing, quantitative methods, M.I.S., and production and operations management.

In the second half of the program the student is enabled to develop competence in the use and application of what has been taught during the first half, through the study of 5 elective courses (chosen from a list of approximately 20 different courses) and secondly, through preparing and writing a research report on a relevant topic approved by the business school. During this period, students may choose to direct their studies in a more specialized direction such as financial management, marketing management, operations management, or quantitative methods, or may follow a more general program of study.

The use made of case studies, applied projects, class discussions, and field work during the core program is intensified during the second half of the program. The learning process also includes constant consultation with professors, both local and foreign, visiting businessmen, and fellow students.

ADMISSION

The M.B.A. course is open to a limited number of outstanding men and women. A degree from a recognized university in South Africa, or a degree from abroad recognized by the University Senate, is a requirement for admission. Chartered Accountants registered with the Public Accountants' and Auditors' Board of South Africa and/or similar bodies in other countries are also acceptable. No particular background, major, or area of concentration is required.

Admission to the business school is decided by an Admissions Committee which evaluates each application on the basis of the information furnished in an application form, the results obtained from the Graduate Management Admission Test (GMAT), and reports by two referees. The committee takes into account the candidate's academic record, test

scores, work experience, leadership potential, motivation, and maturity. Each candidate may be required to attend an interview if practicable.

EXPENSES

Fees are R4,830. Cost of textbooks is approximately R2,000.

FINANCIAL ASSISTANCE

A limited number of bursaries administered by the school are available for M.B.A. students. Special student bank loans are available, by private negotiation, from most of the leading commercial banks in South Africa.

CORRESPONDENCE

For information, please write or call
The Public Relations Officer
Graduate School of Business
  Administration
University of the Witwatersrand
P.O. Box 31170
Braamfontein 2017, Republic of
  South Africa
Telephone: Johannesburg (011) 643-6641
Telegrams: Embark, Johannesburg

The University of Wyoming is a fully accredited land-grant institution, founded in 1886. Located in Laramie, a city of 30,000 in the southeastern part of the state, the university remains Wyoming's only four-year institution of higher learning. Steadily increasing state revenues resulting from the growth of the energy industry in the state, has allowed the university to significantly expand its library, computer facilities, and physical plant in the last few years.

Pleasantly situated between two mountain ranges in the Medicine Bow National Forest, Laramie is less than an hour's drive from the 11,000 foot-plus Medicine Bow Range of the Rockies with all of its recreational opportunities—and less than two-and-a-half hour's drive from dynamic Denver, Colorado. Laramie's altitude of 7,200 feet provides a respite from the heat, smog, and other air pollution, humidity, and overcrowding which exists in a large part of our country. Due to the buffering action of the two mountain ranges, winters in Laramie itself are surprisingly moderate.

There are over 850 faculty serving approximately 10,000 students on a 735-acre campus containing 40 major buildings. There are approximately 200 students enrolled in graduate business programs. Of these, 70 to 80 are on the main campus, while the rest are divided between the two evening programs in Casper and Cheyenne.

PROGRAMS OF STUDY

The College of Commerce and Industry's graduate programs in business consist of a Master of Business Administration (M.B.A.) program and Master of Science (M.S.) programs in finance. Although the M.S. program tends to be more quantitative and specialized, the M.B.A. program features a mix of quantitative and more qualitative courses and emphasizes breadth and overall competence for general management. All programs emphasize individual development and personalized study through the substantial elective portions of the 30-semester-hour curriculum. Courses are taught during the day in small (10 to 25 students) sections/seminars in fall and spring semesters and a summer session. The total number of semesters depends on the student's background and course load per semester.

The M.B.A. degree program emphasizes breadth of understanding of essential information, concepts, and techniques that any contemporary general manager aspirant should be able to apply. Six three-hour graduate-level courses in accounting, general management, finance, marketing, production-operations, and business policy/strategy make up the core of the program. The flexibility inherent in the remaining 12 hours of electives is a strong point of the program because it allows students to tailor studies to their particular interests. In effect, this allows a minor area within the M.B.A. program. A student with an undergraduate background in psychology, for example, may wish to take graduate courses in psychology and have these count toward his or her M.B.A. degree. Similarly, additional concentration in accounting, finance, industrial and operations management, management, or marketing is possible. The overall program is developed in conjunction with the student's adviser.

The M.S. program is especially recommended for individuals who wish to pursue a specialty in finance. The M.S. in finance places emphasis on corporate finance, banking, investments, or real estate—with supporting areas in accounting or economics.

Students without an undergraduate degree in business or accounting must complete a standard preparatory program of common body of knowledge course work. From one to three semesters may be required, depending on the student's particular background.

ADMISSION

Applicants must have a bachelor's degree from an accredited four-year college or university. The student must achieve a satisfactory score on the Graduate Management Admission Test (GMAT) as well as have an acceptable academic record as an undergraduate. Students may enter any of the programs at the beginning of any term and may pursue their degree on either a full-time or part-time basis. There are no limits on enrollments. The application deadline is 45 days before the start of registration for any term.

EXPENSES

The 1985-86 full-time tuition per academic term was $358 for Wyoming residents and $1,113 for nonresidents. Room and board in a university residence hall is $2,544 per two-semester period. Married student housing (apartments) rates ranged from $144 to $248 per month (1985-86). Considerable off-campus housing, for both families and single students, is available in a wide range of rental rates. Inquiries regarding housing should be directed to the Director of Housing, Box 3394, The University of Wyoming, Laramie, Wyoming 82071.

FINANCIAL ASSISTANCE

There are a number of competitive half-time assistantships available to graduate students on the Laramie campus. These consist of both a stipend and a waiver of part of the tuition fees. Application deadline is the middle of the preceding semester.

Work-study assistance, National Direct Student Loans, Guaranteed Student Loans, and a limited number of fee-remission graduate scholarships are available to qualified students.

PLACEMENT

The University of Wyoming operates a very active placement service which provides assistance to graduate students in seeking both career employment and summer or part-time jobs during the school year.

CORRESPONDENCE

For further information, contact
Director, Graduate Business Programs
College of Commerce and Industry
P.O. Box 3275, University Station
The University of Wyoming
Laramie, Wyoming 82071
Telephone: 307-766-4194

Utah State University was founded in 1888 as part of the land-grant university system. Classes in commerce and business were offered in 1890, marking Utah State University as one of the oldest business schools in the country and the pioneer business school in the Intermountain West.

Utah State University is located in Logan, Utah, a community of 32,000 in northern Utah. There are approximately 10,000 full-time university students with 1,550 students in various graduate programs. An average of 120 full-time students are enrolled in the graduate business programs on campus. Two degrees are conferred: a Master of Business Administration (M.B.A.) and a Master of Accounting (M.Acc.). These programs are housed in a new business building with outstanding facilities. An additional 90-100 students are enrolled in a part-time M.B.A. program taught in Ogden, Utah, a nearby metropolitan area.

PROGRAMS OF STUDY

The M.B.A. program provides broad training which focuses attention on managerial problems and decision making. Aimed at providing a basis for long-range advancement, it is also directed at developing the character, analytical skills, and understanding of our economy and the business environment necessary to operate effectively as a manager.

The M.B.A. degree is open to qualified students with a bachelor's degree regardless of their undergraduate major. The time necessary for completion of the degree is dependent upon the individual's background and preparation.

Students with undergraduate majors in business typically require 45 quarter hours of credit or one academic year to complete the M.B.A. program. This one year consists entirely of graduate courses of a wide variety, encompassing the fields of marketing, accounting, production, finance, economics, quantitative methods, organizational behavior, social responsibility, management theory, and other related areas. Twelve hours of electives are allowed. A research requirement is satisfied through a course work option or by writing a thesis. Classes are purposely limited in size, thus allowing personal contact with the professor.

Students without an undergraduate degree in business must complete the business core courses before proceeding to the advanced or second-year program. This typically requires from one to three quarters.

The Master of Accounting program is part of a five-year professional accounting program of study which gives students the option of (1) receiving a Bachelor of Science degree after four years or (2) receiving the M.Acc. degree after completing a fifth year of study. The program emphasizes preparation for the practice of accounting in public accounting firms, industry, government, and nonprofit organizations. The M.Acc. professional program provides a choice of four areas of specialization: financial/audit, taxation, managerial accounting, and administrative services. The Certified Public Accountant (C.P.A.) examination may be taken before graduation. M.Acc. students will be expected to pass a written comprehensive examination.

Students with an undergraduate major in accounting will be expected to complete 45 credits of graduate work, 12 of which may be electives. Students with less than the equivalent of the undergraduate accounting program will be expected to make up any deficiencies.

ADMISSION

Applicants are considered who have graduated from an accredited college or university with a four-year degree. Factors considered are as follows:
- undergraduate academic record (It is desirable for a student to have achieved a 3.0 average on a 4.0 basis either during the last two years or for all four years. A student with a lower grade-point average is considered if other aspects of the credentials are highly favorable),
- Graduate Management Admission Test (GMAT) scores,
- three letters of recommendation, and
- the maturity and motivation of the student.

In addition to the above criteria, international students should achieve a minimum score of 500 on the Test of English as a Foreign Language (TOEFL). International students must also submit an I-20 form (certificate of eligibility) and a financial certificate.

Work experience is desirable but not a requirement to gain entrance to the program. Students can usually enter the program at the beginning of any quarter; however, fall quarter is preferred. The application deadline is 90 days before the start of any quarter.

EXPENSES

Full-time student tuition and fees amount to $330 per quarter for residents of Utah and $940 for nonresidents. Housing is available on campus for married and single students. Married student housing will range from $205 to $258 per month depending on the facilities desired. Single students have the option of an efficiency apartment with room and board for between $718 and $912 per quarter, depending on number of meals and living facilities. Off-campus housing is available for both married and single students. For housing information, write to the Coordinator of Student Housing, 1151 East 7 North, UMC 86, Utah State University.

FINANCIAL ASSISTANCE

Assistantships, fellowships, scholarships, and tuition waivers are available in limited numbers to qualified students.

PLACEMENT

The university provides a placement center to aid students in finding positions. Representatives from various levels of government, as well as representatives from well-known firms in industry, interview regularly.

CORRESPONDENCE

Inquiries regarding the Master of Business Administration program should be directed to
  M.B.A. Office
  College of Business, UMC 35
  Utah State University
  Logan, Utah 84322
  Telephone: 801-750-2360
Inquiries regarding the Master of Accounting program should be directed to
  Head, Department of Accounting
  College of Business, UMC 35
  Utah State University
  Logan, Utah 84322
  Telephone: 801-750-2330

Valdosta State College, founded in 1906, is a senior unit of the University System of Georgia. The undergraduate degree in business administration has been available since 1951. Graduate courses in accounting have been offered since 1971, and the Master of Business Administration (M.B.A.) program began in 1972. Present enrollment at Valdosta State College exceeds 6,000 students; business administration majors constitute about 20 percent of the enrollment. The college has modern dormitories, apartments, computer facilities, and a new library.

PROGRAM OF STUDY
The M.B.A. program is designed to provide an educational environment in which a student has the opportunity to develop administrative skills by a classroom approach as well as through interaction with an emerging industrial community. The student is made aware of the social, legal, and economic environment in which business decisions are made. The program has among its objectives the development in the student of the confidence to take risks, to innovate, and in general to assume the role of an entrepreneur in a dynamic economy.

The curriculum consists of a 50-hour core and 10 hours of approved electives. The program has been designed to give the student a general exposure to all areas of business without concentrating in a particular area. The five-hour core courses are managerial accounting, seminar in marketing, financial management, organizational behavior, quantitative methods and research, business information systems, production and operations management, managerial economics, aggregate economic theory, and business policy.

ADMISSION
M.B.A. applicants must have a bachelor's degree from an accredited or approved college or university. A satisfactory score on the Graduate Management Admission Test (GMAT) is also required, and the student must have an overall undergraduate grade-point average of 2.5 out of a possible 4.0. Certain preparatory courses (up to 50 hours) may be necessary depending upon the individual's undergraduate work. These courses are introductions to economics, management, marketing, finance, business law, statistics, computer science, and accounting.

EXPENSES

Per quarter	In-state	Out-of-state
Tuition (part time/ full time)	$135-170	$405-810
Housing	252	252
Meal tickets	315-360	315-360
Books and supplies	75	75
Health and activity fee	0-80	0-80

FINANCIAL ASSISTANCE
A number of scholarships, grants, loans, and part-time employment plans are available. There are a limited number of graduate assistantships; application forms may be obtained by writing to Director, Division of Graduate Studies, Valdosta State College, Valdosta, Georgia 31698. The only financial aid available to international students is through these graduate assistantships.

PLACEMENT
The college maintains its own Placement Office with regularly scheduled interviews by leading employers. A special placement library is available to all students.

CORRESPONDENCE
Requests for details of the program should be addressed to
Director
M.B.A. Program
Valdosta State College
Valdosta, Georgia 31698
Telephone: 912-333-5991

The Owen Graduate School of Management at Vanderbilt University is committed to teaching the art and science of management. Located in the heart of the booming Mid-South, the school seeks students who have demonstrated potential to achieve success as business managers.

Fundamentally scientific in its approach to business, the school teaches using theory, analytic methods, and the results of research. These provide the base for advanced courses in which the student deals with case studies and other real-world projects. The aim of the Owen education is to provide future managers with generalizations about sound business practices.

PROGRAMS OF STUDY

The Owen School offers a two-year M.B.A. program, a Doctor of Philosophy (Ph.D.) in management, and an executive M.B.A. program, the last designed for middle managers who are normally sponsored by their employers. The Owen School and the Vanderbilt School of Law offer a combined program that enables students to earn both an M.B.A. and a J.D. in four years. No part-time or evening degree programs are offered by the Owen School.

ADMISSION

Qualified applicants should have completed a bachelor's degree and possess a solid foundation in liberal arts; social, physical, or natural sciences; or engineering. No previous business course work is required.

Students are admitted only for the fall semester. Candidates for admission should submit an application, Graduate Management Admission Test (GMAT) results, official transcripts, and three letters of recommendation. Applicants whose native tongue is not English must submit results for the Test of English as a Foreign Language (TOEFL) and a statement of financial resources.

EXPENSES

Estimated expenses for the 1985-86 academic year:

Tuition	$10,000
Hospitalization insurance	150
Fees	50
Books	590
Room, board, other	5,710
Total	$16,500

Married students should add $1,500 to $2,500.

FINANCIAL ASSISTANCE

The Owen School offers extensive financial aid, including scholarships, fellowships, and loans. Scholarships are awarded primarily on the basis of academic merit. Loans are extended to most financial need. All candidates for financial aid are required to apply through the Graduate and Professional School Financial Aid Service (GAPSFAS).

PLACEMENT

Recently, over a hundred companies have recruited at the Owen School each year, nearly one corporation for every student seeking a job. A full-time associate dean for career planning and placement works closely with individual students throughout their two years at the school to help them develop good career opportunities.

CORRESPONDENCE

For more information, write or call
Director of Admission
Owen Graduate School of Management
Vanderbilt University
Nashville, Tennessee 37203
Telephone: 615-322-6469

Founded in 1842, Villanova University is a Roman Catholic institution sponsored by the Augustinian Fathers. The 200-acre campus is located in the suburbs of Philadelphia within easy reach of the city.

Villanova's College of Commerce and Finance was founded in 1922 and offers two graduate programs. The Master of Business Administration (M.B.A.) program is an evening program designed for those engaged in full-time employment. The M.B.A. program is accredited by the American Assembly of Collegiate Schools of Business (AACSB).

Villanova's Graduate Tax program is also a part-time evening program which is jointly sponsored by the College of Commerce and the School of Law. The entering classes are fairly evenly divided between lawyers and accountants.

PROGRAMS OF STUDY

The Villanova M.B.A. program is designed to prepare graduates for managerial responsibilities at various levels in business, government, and other organizations. To achieve the major objectives the program has been structured to

• provide knowledge and understanding of the fundamental disciplines, techniques, and ethical dimensions involved in managerial decisions;

• develop the student's proficiency in applying concepts and analytical methods in the process of identifying and analyzing problems requiring decisions; and

• give the student a broad education in domestic and international business and to develop an understanding in the behavioral, environmental, functional, and quantitative areas of management.

M.B.A. courses are offered at three levels: foundation, management core, and elective. The foundation courses provide students who hold undergraduate degrees in fields other than business with an academic background in basic business areas. The number of required courses in the foundation will vary. Specific requirements depend upon (1) the area studied at the undergraduate level, (2) the number of years since the undergraduate degree was earned, and (3) qualifying examinations. Individual work experience does not qualify for academic credit.

After a student has satisfied the requirements of the foundation, the course work leading to the M.B.A. degree may be started. Twelve courses beyond the foundation are required, including the seven management core courses and five elective courses. The core program is structured to provide a comprehensive understanding of management decision making within a framework of market, economic, social, and governmental environments. Elective courses permit a student to pursue particular areas of interest at a more advanced level.

Each student accepted into the M.B.A. program will be provided with a recommended program of study, showing the order in which foundation courses (if required) and management core courses should be taken to benefit most from the program.

The Graduate Tax program was established to provide further educational opportunities to accountants and lawyers who face substantial exposure to the subject of taxation in their professions. The university believes that an interdisciplinary approach offers a distinct advantage to the student; it makes the accountant familiar with the operation of the legal system and provides the lawyer with an understanding of fundamental principles of accounting.

At present there are 25 courses offered, all of which deal with the subject of taxation. Among the courses required for graduation are Taxation of the Individual, Tax Consequences of the Disposition of Property, Taxation of Corporations and Shareholders, Tax Accounting, Taxation of Trusts and Estates, and an Estate Planning Workshop.

Some of the elective courses are Estate and Gift Taxation, Qualified Pension and Profit Sharing Plans, Advanced Corporate Tax Problems, Consolidated Tax Returns, and a Business Planning Workshop.

All degree candidates must satisfactorily complete 24 credits. Accountants will be awarded a master's degree in taxation and lawyers will receive an LL.M.

ADMISSION

The admission standards for the M.B.A. program and the Graduate Tax program are comparable. Admission to either program is based on the student's undergraduate record, performance on the Graduate Management Admission Test (GMAT), and professional experience.

EXPENSES

Tuition, per credit hour
M.B.A. program $205
Graduate Tax program 290

CORRESPONDENCE

For further information contact

M.B.A. Program
Dennis Kuhn, Director
Bartley Hall-Room 112A
Villanova University
Villanova, Pennsylvania 19085

Graduate Tax Program
Don Llewellyn
School of Law
Villanova University
Villanova, Pennsylvania 19085

Virginia Commonwealth University traces its founding to 1838. Graduate programs in business have been offered since 1954 and are accredited by the American Assembly of Collegiate Schools of Business (AACSB). The present enrollment in the program is approximately 800 students, the majority of whom attend on a part-time basis.

PROGRAMS OF STUDY
The School of Business offers programs leading to the Master of Business Administration (M.B.A.), the Master of Science (M.S.) in business, the Master of Accountancy, the Master of Taxation, the Master of Arts (M.A.) in economics, and the Doctor of Philosophy (Ph.D.) in business degrees.

The M.B.A. program, designed for students with diverse undergraduate backgrounds, is suitable for both nonbusiness and business graduates. Normally, it is a two-year program for graduates of the curricula in the arts and humanities, in engineering, and in the sciences. The program can be completed in one year of full-time study by students who have an undergraduate degree in business.

The aim of the M.B.A. degree program is to prepare persons for the responsibilities of management in a wide variety of business endeavors. The program requires 30 credit hours of advanced work. It is intended to develop a knowledge of functions and techniques of management as well as an understanding of environmental and economic forces that influence administration and decision making.

The M.S. in business degree program is designed for those interested in concentrating in a given area. It requires 30 credit hours (10 courses) of advanced work. Some areas of concentration require additional undergraduate courses. Approximately one third of the program consists of core courses, one third of restricted electives, and one third of approved electives. Electives permit a concentration in business education, economics, finance, information systems, marketing, personnel and industrial relations, quantitative techniques, real estate and urban land development, or risk management and insurance.

The Master of Accountancy and Master of Taxation require 30 hours of advanced work.

The M.A. degree in economics is designed to provide training for business and government economists, for those now teaching in secondary schools or in junior colleges, and for those who plan doctoral study. It requires that the candidate earn at least 30 semester credits. The program provides a substantive core in economic theory and econometrics with the choice of a thesis or nonthesis option. Electives allow the student to develop the core skills and concentrate in the fields of his or her choice.

The Ph.D. program in business offers major concentrations in accounting/taxation, finance, information systems, management and organizational behavior, management science, and personnel and industrial relations. Students can select minor concentrations from any of the major areas, business education, marketing, and approved areas outside the School of Business.

ADMISSION
Both full-time and part-time students are admitted to the programs. Applicants must have earned a bachelor's degree. Selection is made on the basis of undergraduate performance, intellectual capacity, character, experience, and other indicators of the ability to successfully pursue graduate study. The Graduate Management Admission Test (GMAT) is required for admission to the M.S., M.B.A., Master of Accountancy, Master of Taxation, and Ph.D. programs. For the M.A. in economics, the Graduate Record Examinations (GRE) (verbal, quantitative, and advanced economics) are required for admittance.

Applicants to the M.B.A. and M.S. programs who have an undergraduate major other than business/economics are required to complete 24 semester hours of foundation courses in accounting, economics, management, marketing, statistics, business law, finance, and information systems. A course in calculus is also required for those who have not completed it.

The Master of Accountancy and Master of Taxation programs require 24 semester hours of foundation courses in business and economics and 21 hours of undergraduate work in accounting and taxation. Some or all of the foundation and undergraduate courses may be waived for those who have completed prior equivalent courses of study.

Students admitted to the M.A. program must have completed 12 semester credits of economics courses, including economic principles, microeconomic theory, and macroeconomic theory. A knowledge of mathematics sufficient for the study of econometrics and the advanced theory courses must be acquired before those courses may be attempted. The students' advisory committee will set the mathematical requirements for each student.

Students may begin their studies in the summer session as well as in the fall or spring semesters. Candidates should submit applications and supporting references and transcripts at least eight weeks in advance of the semester in which they wish to enroll.

EXPENSES
Tuition for Virginia residents is approximately $2,134 per year; tuition for nonresidents is $3,964 per year. Expenses for books, special equipment, and fees are extra. No campus housing is available for graduate students; housing is available in the immediate area at reasonable rates.

FINANCIAL ASSISTANCE
The School of Business offers a limited number of graduate assistantships to full-time students in the amount of $2,100 for the academic year for master's students and $6,500 plus tuition waiver for the academic year for Ph.D. students.

PLACEMENT
The university maintains a placement office, visited annually by representatives of various companies.

CORRESPONDENCE
For further information, write or call
Associate Dean of Graduate Studies
School of Business
Virginia Commonwealth University
1015 Floyd Avenue
Richmond, Virginia 23284
Telephone: 804-257-1741

Virginia Polytechnic Institute and State University, Virginia's land-grant university, has grown since its founding in 1872 into the largest university in the state. Its recent history is one of rapid, well-planned growth in size and quality of programs. The current enrollment of approximately 22,500 students includes some 3,500 graduate students, a large proportion of whom come from other states.

The programs offered by the College of Business are accredited by the American Assembly of Collegiate Schools of Business (AACSB). The college has an enrollment of approximately 4,000, including more than 300 master's and doctoral degree candidates. The college offers graduate programs leading to the following degrees: Master of Business Administration (M.B.A.); Master of Accountancy; Master of Science in business administration (areas of concentration: management, management science, and marketing); Master of Arts (economics); Doctor of Philosophy in business (major fields: accounting, finance, management, management science, and marketing); and Doctor of Philosophy in economics.

PROGRAMS OF STUDY
The Master of Business Administration degree is a professional degree designed primarily to provide the student seeking a career in industry with advanced educational experience in business administration. Unlike the Master of Science in business, the M.B.A. is not directed toward research or a high degree of specialization in one of the fields of business administration. Opportunities for specialized study are provided through the college's thesis M.S. degree programs.

Students in the M.B.A. program take a common core of 52 quarter hours, 13 of which may be waived for students who are granted advance standing. This course work spans the functional areas of accounting, economics, management, finance, marketing, and management science. Seven elective courses provide the opportunity to specialize in a variety of areas; a generalist option is also available. In total, the program consists of a minimum of 60 hours and maximum of 73 hours. Students whose background is in business can finish the program in five regular academic quarters; others can finish in six quarters. Approximately 50 percent of the students do not have a business

undergraduate degree. Course work in micro- and macroeconomics and differential/integral calculus must be completed before entering the program. Summer courses are available for students lacking this background.

The Master of Accountancy is a multi-purpose degree program. It provides a comprehensive analysis of accounting and its applications for those who seek a terminal degree at the graduate level. In addition, for those who wish to continue into a doctoral program, the Master of Accountancy provides the necessary foundation in course work and research techniques. Serving such diverse goals is made possible through the flexibility inherent in the program. The program provides basic courses that analyze the concepts that underlie this system and also consider the disciplines to which it is directly related. In addition, the program offers more intensive study of specific areas of application.

Although the program is open to students with no educational background in business or accounting, those who have an appropriate background enter with advanced standing. Students with no background in these areas can expect to spend at least two years in the program. For those who enter with advanced standing, it is possible to complete the program in four regular academic quarters.

The Doctor of Philosophy in business program is designed for students with outstanding ability to do advanced work in preparation for careers in college and university teaching and research. The student is required to take one major field, one minor field, and 12 quarter hours of methodology and research. There is no language requirement. In addition to completing the course work, students must pass field examinations and complete an acceptable dissertation under the guidance of a faculty committee.

The Master of Business Administration degree and the Master of Arts in economics degree are offered in northern Virginia, as well as on the main campus.

ADMISSION
Masters' programs are open to students who hold a bachelor's degree and present evidence of their ability to do graduate work. Evidence of ability means that successful applicants will stand well above average in most measures of graduate

promise: scores on the Graduate Management Admission Test (GMAT), undergraduate grade-point average, and standing in graduating class.

EXPENSES
Full-time graduate student tuition and fees were $777 per quarter for the 1985-86 academic year. Out-of-state tuition and fees were $848 per quarter. Adequate housing for graduate students is available in Blacksburg and the surrounding area. Housing inquiries may be made to the Director of Student Housing.

FINANCIAL ASSISTANCE
A variety of financial awards are available to qualified master's degree students. The departments offer graduate assistantships which carry stipends of up to $740 per month ($6,660 for the academic year). Financial support is awarded on a merit basis.

PLACEMENT
Comprehensive placement support is provided by the college and the University Placement Center.

CORRESPONDENCE
For further information regarding the programs of study offered at the College of Business, please write

Director of Graduate Programs
in Business Administration
Virginia Polytechnic Institute and
State University
Blacksburg, Virginia 24061

WAKE FOREST UNIVERSITY

WINSTON-SALEM, NORTH CAROLINA

Wake Forest University is located in the North Carolina Piedmont city of Winston-Salem, with a population of approximately 140,000. The city forms one apex of the area known as the Triad (Winston-Salem, Greensboro, High Point) which over the last five years has consistently been rated among the best five places in the United States to live by Rand-McNally's *Places Rated Almanac*. The Triad is the fourth most important business center in the South behind Houston, Dallas, and Atlanta. Winston-Salem offers the best of small town comforts with the amenities of larger city living. Residents enjoy a wealth of academic, cultural, entertainment, sports, and social events.

PROGRAMS OF STUDY

The Wake Forest M.B.A. program does not simply give students more knowledge and additional tools to employ. Rather, the purpose of the program is to transform the way students think. The goal of the program is that after two years at Wake Forest, students will not only have the information and tools of management but will also have a different perspective on how they identify, approach, and respond to activities and problems in management. This is accomplished in an environment that emphasizes close personal involvement and interaction between students and faculty.

The program makes use of the case method which involves active discussion of business situations to develop managerial skills and knowledge. Other pedagogical approaches include lectures, seminars, and team exercises which require students to integrate the skills and knowledge acquired in the classroom and apply them to real-world managerial problems. Students also become involved in learning situations outside the Babcock setting through field projects and internships.

During their first year, students are introduced to the fundamental concepts of management and analytical approaches to a wide range of managerial problems through the required core curriculum. In the second year, students have significant elective freedom which allows them to structure the curriculum to meet individual interests and goals. All second year students also undertake a major field study project, which allows them to act as consultants for a local or regional organization.

A combined Master of Business Administration/Juris Doctor (J.D.) degree is offered in cooperation with the Wake Forest School of Law. This program enables students to complete both degrees in four years.

A special M.B.A.-Executive program is available for current middle managers which will allow them to pursue a two-year course of study leading to the M.B.A. without interrupting their professional careers. Participants attend classes on the Winston-Salem campus one full day each week on alternate Fridays and Saturdays and engage in intensive individual and team study between formal class sessions. For further information, contact the Director of the M.B.A.-Executive Program.

ADMISSION

A candidate's academic record and scores from the Graduate Management Admission Test (GMAT) are only part of the data considered in an application. Grades or test scores alone will not guarantee acceptance or ensure rejection. The Babcock School places primary emphasis on the development of each individual's managerial potential. Consequently, admission requirements for the Babcock School cannot be reduced to a simple formula; rather, the school seeks a combination of intellect, motivation, personality, and past achievement indicating potential for the development of an effective manager.

EXPENSES

Tuition for the M.B.A. program for 1985-86 was $7,900. Books and case materials cost about $450.

FINANCIAL ASSISTANCE

All efforts are made by the school to ensure that no qualified person is denied attending the program because of financial limitations. The application for admission is considered without regard to financial needs. Decisions on financial aid are made only after a candidate has been accepted for admission. Financial assistance is available in the form of fellowships, grants, assistantships, and deferred payment loans. Awards may include a combination of these types of financial aid and are determined on the basis of merit and need. Outstanding candidates can expect some form of financial assistance, with the type and amount subject to individual circumstances.

PLACEMENT

The Babcock Graduate School maintains its own Career Planning and Placement Office. In addition to on-campus interviews, the office offers a summer internship program, individual and group career planning, and career conferences. An M.B.A. resume book, published by the office, is sent to several hundred prospective employers each year. A Job Listing Service and Alumni Relocation Service are also provided. The office is a member of the College Placement Council.

CORRESPONDENCE

For further information, please write or call

Director of Admissions
Babcock Graduate School of
   Management
Wake Forest University
7659 Reynolda Station
Winston-Salem, North Carolina 27109
Telephone: 919-761-5422

Washburn University is situated in an urban environment with diverse economic, social, and cultural features. With a population of approximately 150,000, the Topeka metropolitan area is the site of the state capital. The world-renowned Menninger Foundation plus five hospitals, including the Comerly-O'Neil Veterans Hospital, enhance Topeka's reputation as a major medical center, employing personnel and attracting patients from throughout the world.

The economic base is further broadened by the existence of large and small financial, merchandising, manufacturing, and transportation establishments. Hence, there is an excellent local job market, and roughly 70 percent of the students attending Washburn work part or full time. The local economy also offers numerous career opportunities to graduates of the School of Business.

PROGRAM OF STUDY

The Master of Business Administration (M.B.A.) program at Washburn is designed for the business professional who desires to combine an existing career with formal educational development. The courses will be offered in the evenings. Although full-time study is possible, it is expected that individuals employed in full-time occupations will enroll for a maximum of six hours of graduate course work each semester and three hours in the summer session.

ADMISSION

Admission to the M.B.A. program permits a student to pursue the degree, provided that individual continues to meet all standards in force. Admission will be granted to students showing high promise of success in postgraduate business study.

The following are the procedural steps and criteria that are utilized for evaluation:

• Applicants must hold a baccalaureate degree from an institution accredited by a Council on Postsecondary Accreditation (COPA) recognized institution accrediting agency.

• Applicants should request that two official transcripts be sent to the Graduate Adviser, School of Business, Washburn University, from all previously attended institutions.

• Applicants must take the Graduate Management Admission Test (GMAT) administered by Educational Testing Service (ETS), CN 6101, Princeton, NJ 08541-6101. The GMAT Code Number for Washburn University is 6928. Request that scores be reported to the School of Business, Washburn University.

• Admission is determined in part on the basis of a point system; the applicant should have a total of at least 950 points based on the formula: 200 times the overall grade-point average (on a 4.0 system) plus score on the Graduate Management Admission Test; or at least 1,000 points based on the formula: 200 times the upper-division grade-point average plus the GMAT score.

• The applicant must complete the common body of knowledge in business administration with a grade of C or better in each course. Recent graduates of programs accredited by the American Assembly of Collegiate Schools of Business (AACSB) will normally meet this requirement.

• The applicant should arrange for two letters to be submitted by academicians, employers, or other persons who can attest to his or her potential for success in graduate study in business. These letters should be sent to the Graduate Adviser, School of Business, Washburn University.

• The applicant must make application to both Washburn University and the Graduate School of Business. These applications should be submitted to the Graduate Adviser, School of Business, Washburn University. The School of Business will notify the registrar of the names of those accepted.

Admission to the M.B.A. program is granted on an individual basis by the Graduate Committee. A personal interview is helpful but not required for admission.

EXPENSES

Tuition for resident undergraduate and graduate courses is $53 per credit hour; nonresident tuition is $79 per credit hour.

CORRESPONDENCE

For more information and applications, please contact

Coordinator, Graduate Program
School of Business
Washburn University
Topeka, Kansas 66621
Telephone: 913-295-6307

Founded in 1890, Washington State University is the land-grant institution of the state of Washington. Approximately 16,000 students, both men and women, are enrolled in degree programs covering virtually all academic areas except law and human medicine. Washington State University is one of the largest residential universities in the western United States, and housing facilities are provided for both married and unmarried students.

PROGRAMS OF STUDY

The program leading to the Master of Business Administration (M.B.A.) degree provides a comprehensive professional education suitable for the development of careers in management. It is designed for students with undergraduate degrees in all academic areas with the first year composed of foundation courses in business for the nonbusiness majors. There is no thesis or foreign language requirement, but a rigorous mix of case courses prepares students well for entry into mid-management positions in industry. In addition to the foundation requirements, the M.B.A. degree requires 30 semester credits of graduate work. These courses are designed to combine a field of special interest with a well-rounded but in-depth program in all areas of corporate management. A final oral examination is required.

The Master of Accounting (M.Acc.) degree program is aimed at providing a greater breadth and depth in professional accounting education. Admission requires a baccalaureate degree in business administration with a field of specialization in accounting (or its equivalent). The Master of Accounting degree program entails 30 semester hours of graduate credit, an accounting research paper, and a final oral examination. There is no thesis or foreign language requirement.

The Doctor of Philosophy (Ph.D.) program is designed to prepare graduates for careers of teaching and research in colleges and universities, and for research-oriented positions in business, industry, and government. The program requirements are designed with sufficient flexibility to permit the candidate to pursue a course of study that provides a greater breadth in preparation for a university teaching career or for a greater depth in preparation for a predominantly research-oriented career. The requirements reflect the belief that all doctorally qualified persons must be competent and solidly trained in research methodology, and particularly familiar with current developments in their areas of specialization.

Generally, applicants will have completed a master's level degree prior to entry into the Ph.D. program. If prior academic work has not covered the equivalent of the M.B.A. foundation courses, these must be completed as part of the Ph.D. program. The residence requirement is three years of graduate study, two of which must be at Washington State University. Of these two, one must be spent in continuous, full-time residence at the university. There is no foreign language requirement.

A strong and academically rigorous program, the Ph.D. degree currently offers specialization in the areas of accounting, finance, human resource management, management, marketing, operations management, organizational behavior, and quantitative methods.

ADMISSION

All persons admitted for graduate study must have earned a baccalaureate degree from an academically recognized college or university. The Graduate Management Admission Test (GMAT) is required of all applicants and three academic reference letters must accompany applications. Students from non-English-speaking countries must also submit scores from the Test of English as a Foreign Language (TOEFL).

Qualified applicants can be admitted in August, January, or June, although a complete program is not offered during the summer session.

EXPENSES

Resident tuition and fees amount to $1,160 per semester; nonresident tuition and fees total $2,888 per semester. Unmarried students can obtain board and room in the graduate center for $1,335 per semester. Housing for married students varies in cost from approximately $160 to $300 per month, depending upon the size of the accommodations. Complete information on rentals can be obtained from University Housing and Food Service.

FINANCIAL ASSISTANCE

Financial support from the College of Business and Economics is available in the form of teaching assistantships. These are awarded in both the fall and spring semesters. At the present time, over 40 percent of the M.B.A. candidates and virtually all of the Ph.D. candidates are on appointment with sizable annual stipends, plus waiver of out-of-state tuition.

All Ph.D. candidates are eligible for doctoral teaching assistantship appointments, specific student scholarships, and special summer appointments. Highly qualified Ph.D. candidates often receive annual stipends ranging from $9,000 to $16,000.

PLACEMENT

The Washington State University Career Services and Placement Center is very favorably known for its service both to graduates and to employers. A large number of business firms, government agencies, and educational institutions interview graduates each year.

CORRESPONDENCE

Inquiries concerning graduate programs in accounting , economics, or business administration should be addressed to

Director of Graduate Programs
College of Business and Economics
Todd Hall, Room 244
Washington State University
Pullman, Washington 99164-4728
Telephone: 509-335-7617

Graduate School of Business Administration
WASHINGTON UNIVERSITY
ST. LOUIS, MISSOURI

The Graduate School of Business Administration offers a professional education in advanced management. The school is a division of Washington University, a private university known for the quality of its graduate programs. The campus, with its garden-like setting, is located in a fine residential suburb of St. Louis. In January 1986, the business school moved to a new building that features outstanding state-of-the-art facilities for computing, research, teaching, and placement activities.

The Business School offers a full-time M.B.A. program that enrolls 125 students each fall, an evening M.B.A. program for part-time study, an executive M.B.A. program, and a doctoral program. The undergraduate and master's programs in business offered by Washington University are accredited by the American Assembly of Collegiate Schools of Business (AACSB).

PROGRAMS OF STUDY
The major goal of the M.B.A. program is to develop excellent general managers. The curriculum is designed to enhance the students' analytical abilities and to teach decision-making strategies that will serve them during a lifelong managerial career. The school recognizes that the student must be prepared with both technical skills, which aid them in achieving their most immediate career objectives, and a broad, comprehensive education in the theoretic foundations of business, which prepares them for long-term professional growth and advancement to positions of managerial leadership.

The M.B.A. program requires 60 semester hours of study. Of the 60 hours, 15 hours may be waived through proficiency exams. Students normally take 15 hours per semester and complete the degree in two academic years. Joint degrees are offered in law, social work, and architecture. Interdisciplinary study is encouraged. Students may take elective courses in other graduate departments within the university.

ADMISSION
Washington University welcomes applications from persons holding bachelor's degrees in any field from an accredited institution. Prior study in business is not required. Students with backgrounds in the arts, education, engineering, health sciences, humanities, natural sciences, and social and behavioral sciences are encouraged to apply. The Graduate Management Admission Test (GMAT) is required. Full-time students may begin only in the fall.

When making the admission decision, the committee considers the candidate's academic aptitude, communication and interpersonal skills, maturity, leadership, work experience, motivation, and achievement orientation.

EXPENSES
Expenses for full-time study in the 1985-86 academic year were $9,200 for tuition and $8,000 for living expenses. Inexpensive housing is available within walking distance of campus. The University Housing Office assists students in finding accommodations.

FINANCIAL ASSISTANCE
The Business School makes every effort to provide financial assistance to admitted M.B.A. candidates who would otherwise be unable to attend. An application for financial assistance does not, in any way, affect the admission decision.

In 1985, when the full-time tuition was $9,200, the average financial aid award for a full-time student was $9,113 per academic year. Many scholarships, fellowships, work-study awards, and loans are available to full-time students.

The Business School sponsors an extensive scholarship program, titled the Dean's Scholarship Program, to recognize exceptional academic achievement and potential. Thirty of these scholarships are awarded annually.

Other special scholarship awards are full-tuition minority fellowships through the Consortium for Graduate Study in Management (approximately 10 annually); full-tuition fellowships through the Olin Fellowships for Women program (approximately 1 or 2 annually); full tuition plus stipend through the Finance Fellowship (1 annually) and a $10,000 Computing Scholarship/Assistantship (1 annually).

The Business School does not offer need-based aid to foreign students.

PLACEMENT
The Business School operates one of the most professional and comprehensive placement and career planning facilities in the country. Over 130 top firms recruit on-campus annually. Since a graduating M.B.A. class numbers 125 students, the number of interviews per student is very high. Average starting salaries are consistently well above average for the nation's business schools. In addition, the St. Louis business community provides many opportunities for M.B.A. student internships, both during the school year and during the summer break.

Extensive programming is offered in techniques of interviewing, firm and industry research, career selection, and resume preparation.

CORRESPONDENCE
For further information, write or call
M.B.A. Admissions Director
Graduate School of Business Administration
Washington University
Campus Box 1133
St. Louis, Missouri 63130
Telephone: 314-889-6315
within Missouri
314-MBA-3MBA toll-free
outside Missouri

Wayne State University, founded in 1868, is located in the cultural center of Detroit within walking distance of the Detroit Public Library, the Detroit Institute of Arts, the Engineering Society of Detroit, the Fisher Theater, and the international headquarters of the General Motors and Burroughs Corporations. The campus is within minutes of many other international headquarters of both automotive and nonautomotive corporations.

Wayne's 30,000 students, enrolled in 10 colleges and schools, live and work, for the most part, in the metropolitan area. . The university has continuously utilized the industrial and social complex of the city as a research laboratory. Since 1956, when the state of Michigan assumed full financial responsibility for it, Wayne has attracted an increasing number of students from out of state. Two new university apartment buildings provide housing for many of Wayne State's graduate and professional students, both single and married. Since 1956, Wayne has become one of the major graduate institutions in the country.

The School of Business Administration has offered programs leading to the bachelor's degree since 1945 and master's degree programs since 1954. There are approximately 1,000 men and women in the master's program.

PROGRAM OF STUDY
The objective of the Master of Business Administration (M.B.A.) program is to prepare men and women for managerial decision-making careers in business, government, and other types of organizations. Applicants with a baccalaureate degree in business administration will usually have completed all foundation requirements for the program and thus will begin the minimum 11-course (33 semester hours) program. Applicants with baccalaureate degrees in fields other than business administration may be required to complete certain foundation requirements from among the following areas: accounting, computer science, economics, mathematics, statistics, management, production, business law, marketing, and finance. Special accelerated foundation courses have been developed to assist entering M.B.A. students.

After completion of eight core courses and consultation with a graduate faculty adviser, the M.B.A. candidate can select from an extensive number of concentration and elective courses in accounting,

business economics, business information systems, finance, industrial relations, management and organizational behavior, personnel/human resources, marketing, and operations management. Graduate courses in other schools and colleges of the university may also be selected.

Two 15-week semesters of study are offered each academic year, plus a spring/summer semester, with a full schedule of graduate courses. Classes meet in the evening and on Saturday mornings only. A number of graduate courses are taught at suburban locations. M.B.A./C.P.A., thesis, and essay options are available.

Wayne State University operates one of the largest computer centers in the Detroit metropolitan area. The center has two Amdahl 470/V8 computers each with four megabytes of main storage. The center is part of the MERIT Computer Network which joins to Wayne State the computing facilities of the University of Michigan, Michigan State University, and Western Michigan University.

ADMISSION
The M.B.A. program is open to students with bachelor's degrees from regionally accredited institutions who demonstrate high promise of success in graduate study. A completed Application of Graduate Admission, a $20 application fee, official transcripts from all colleges or universities attended, and the results of the Graduate Management Admission Test (GMAT) are required.

Admissions are made to the M.B.A. program each term. Deadlines for receipt of materials listed above are August 1 (for fall semester), November 15 (for winter), and April 1 (for spring/summer). International students must provide materials four months before the start of the classes for the semester of application.

EXPENSES
Depending on the total number of hours elected, the 1984-85 academic year tuition rates were as listed below:

Part-time resident	$ 204-614
Full-time resident	696-1,024
Part-time nonresident	396-1,286
Full-time nonresident	1,464-2,176

FINANCIAL ASSISTANCE
Limited numbers of scholarships, fellowships, and assistantships are available. The usual government scholarship loans and some locally sponsored loan funds are also available to qualified graduate students. Contact should be made with the Office of Graduate Studies, Mackenzie Hall, Wayne State University, Detroit, Michigan 48202.

PLACEMENT
The university provides a comprehensive Placement Service to assist students in finding employment both while going to school and upon obtaining their degrees. Prospective employers, both local and national, visit the campus twice each year to recruit graduating seniors and M.B.A. students for positions with their firms. Career counseling and other placement services, including a career/placement library, are also available to students.

CORRESPONDENCE
Inquiries should be addressed to
Student Services Office
School of Business Administration
Wayne State University
Detroit, Michigan 48202
Telephone: 313-577-4510

Master of Business Administration

WEBBER COLLEGE

BABSON PARK, FLORIDA

Webber College, founded in 1927, is a four-year, private, coeducational college located on beautiful Lake Caloosa in Babson Park, Florida. Webber offers 14 undergraduate programs of study and a Master of Business Administration (M.B.A.) from the School of Commerce. Built on a strong business tradition that sets it apart from others, the college exemplifies integrity, high standards, and achievement. Webber provides an environment that encourages success through academic excellence and hard work.

PROGRAM OF STUDY

The Master of Business Administration is a professional degree program that provides students with knowledge of the functions and techniques of scientific management necessary in competitive enterprises, governmental bodies, and institutions. In addition, an understanding of environmental and economic forces that influence administration and decision making is instilled in the students. The curriculum and faculty reflect real-world concerns and are sensitive to the requirements of both public and private sector employers as well as the needs of the individual student. The classroom approach utilizes traditional lecture/discussion, the case method, simulation, model building, and laboratory techniques to give students a breadth of outlook to assist them in solving complex problems and selecting optimal courses of action. Students will be required to demonstrate mastery of written and verbal communication skills. Since a thesis is not required for an M.B.A., each course will require formal written assignments and reports that involve quantitative as well as qualitative methodology. The Webber College M.B.A. degree is recognized as a valuable professional credential, and its achievement is a meaningful personal accomplishment.

The M.B.A. degree requires a minimum of 36 hours of advanced studies. Before a student is allowed to begin the program, undergraduate business area prerequisites must be satisfied. An applicant may be admitted conditionally if some, but not all, of the undergraduate prerequisites have been met. (Undergraduate courses are taken on a pass/fail basis.) The undergraduate prerequisite areas are accounting, economics, management, marketing, finance, and mathematics.

Graduate Requirements (36 Hours)	Credit Hours
ACC 520 -Managerial Accounting Principles	3
BUS 699 -Business Policy Seminar	3
COM 521-Computer Systems Management I	3
ECO 540 -Managerial Economics	3
FIN 661 -Advanced Corporate Finance	3
MAT 511 -Business and Economic Statistics	3
MGT 609-Management Theory and Practice	3
MKT 620-Advanced Marketing Management	3
Electives	12
	36

ADMISSION

Applicants for the M.B.A. program must hold a bachelor's degree or its equivalent from an accredited institution and must have earned a 3.0 (B) or higher grade-point average for the final 60 hours of that degree. Grade-point average (based on the 4.0 system) × 200 + the Graduate Management Admission Test (GMAT) score should equal approximately 1,000. Foreign students should obtain a score of approximately 500 on the Test of English as a Foreign Language (TOEFL). Transfer credit will be given for a maximum of six hours. The applicant must submit official transcripts from all undergraduate and graduate schools attended. All applicants must take the Graduate Management Admission Test. Applicants admitted conditionally without having taken the test will be required to take it at the next available administration. Conditional students may take up to 12 credit hours. Students must submit three evaluations and a personal statement of career objectives.

EXPENSES

Costs are estimated for the 1985-86 academic year. Tuition and fee assessments are subject to change without notice.

	Florida and Non-Florida Residents
Tuition and fees	$3,650
Room and board	2,400
Books	600
Total	$6,650

Webber students will incur additional living expenses for the summer session.

PLACEMENT

A placement director and the senior faculty work with the students to identify employment opportunities. Since the state of Florida is ranked number one in industrial and business growth, and projected to be the third largest state in population by the year 2000, numerous employment opportunities are available.

CORRESPONDENCE

For further information, please write or call

Dean, Graduate School
Webber College
Babson Park, Florida 33827
Telephone: 813-638-1431, extension 210

West Georgia College is fully accredited by the Southern Association of Colleges and Schools. A senior college unit of the University System of Georgia, it enrolls students from most counties in Georgia, as well as other states and several foreign countries. Total college enrollment is over 6,000 with approximately 2,000 students in the School of Business. The Master of Business Administration (M.B.A.) program has approximately 60 students. Located in Carrollton, the county seat of Carroll County, the college is about 50 miles west of downtown Atlanta. Carrollton's population is over 15,000 and Carroll County's more than 50,000.

PROGRAM OF STUDY
The Master of Business Administration degree at West Georgia College is a nonthesis program requiring 50 quarter hours of course work. It is designed to develop competence in business and institutional administration by providing a broad background of advanced professional training. The objectives of the program are to provide terminal training for students who wish to improve their competence in economics, management, marketing, finance, and accounting for work in research, government, or business and to equip students for research and study at the doctoral level. The program is open to those students seeking the degree of Master of Business Administration.

The core curriculum consists of the following 8 five-hour courses: ACC 816, Advanced Managerial Accounting; MKT 815, Marketing Strategy; MGT 805, Quantitative Analysis for Business Decisions; ECN 830, Business Cycles and Forecasting; ECN 848, Managerial Economics; FIN 831, Advanced Financial Management; MGT 872, Theory and Philosophy of Management; and MGT 881, Seminar in Administrative Policy. Ten hours of electives are also required (2 five-hour courses).

Classes in the M.B.A. program are small, and the program can be completed at night on a part-time basis.

ADMISSION
To enter the program leading to the degree of Master of Business Administration, a person must be admitted to the Graduate School, West Georgia College. Requests for information and application materials should be made to the Dean of the Graduate School, West Georgia College, Carrollton, Georgia 30118. Applications for admission should be filed with the Graduate School at least two weeks prior to the date of registration for the quarter in which the student wishes to enroll. Applicants should have two copies of transcripts of all previous work mailed by the college concerned to the Graduate School.

International students are welcome and encouraged to apply. The same admission process and criteria are used for international students as are used for national students.

All applicants for admission are required to take the Graduate Management Admission Test (GMAT) given by Educational Testing Service, and a satisfactory score must be received before an admission decision is made. Admission is based on academic record, scores on the GMAT, work experience, and general fitness for a career in business.

Although all graduate students must have a bachelor's degree from an accredited college or university, no specific undergraduate courses are required for admission to the program. Some preparatory work may be necessary for those who do not have a bachelor's degree in business administration, or who have not covered the common body of knowledge.

EXPENSES
Fees per quarter (12 hours or more)

Regular Students	Resident	Nonresident
Matriculation	$320	$ 320
Nonresident		
Tuition	—	$ 640
Health	30	30
Student Activity	62	62
Total	$412	$1,052

Students or auditors registering for less than 12 quarter hours are charged $27 per quarter hour for matriculation. In addition, nonresidents of Georgia are charged for out-of-state tuition at the rate of $54 per quarter hour.

Room charges for Boykin, Downs, Gunn, Pritchard, Watson, Bowden, Roberts Hall, and Strozier Annex are $280 per quarter (double occupancy); for a single room, add $100. Room charges for Tyrus Hall are $290-$320 per quarter. Private rooms are also available in Tyrus Hall at additional cost. Private rooms are available on a limited basis only. A $5 annual social fee is charged to each resident and used for the purpose of residence hall programming.

Two types of meal tickets are available on an optional basis to all students. Meal charges per quarter for three meals/five days are $310; for two meals/five days the charge is $270 per quarter.

FINANCIAL ASSISTANCE
Graduate assistantships are offered.

PLACEMENT
West Georgia College provides a placement service which is available to all students.

CORRESPONDENCE
For further information, please write
   The Graduate School
   West Georgia College
   Carrollton, Georgia 30118
   Telephone: 404-834-1243

West Texas State University is a state-supported coeducational institution. Founded in 1910, it was the first institution of higher education to be located in the west Texas region. Courses in business were taught at West Texas State University in 1915. The School of Business was founded in 1943 at which time graduate courses were added to the curriculum. The School of Business has evolved into four departments: administrative services, business administration, business analysis, and financial administration.

The School of Business is housed in a new four-story, air-conditioned building. West Texas State has a student population of 6,500 with about 2,250 enrolled in undergraduate School of Business programs and 602 full- and part-time students in master's degree programs.

PROGRAMS OF STUDY

The Master of Business Administration (M.B.A.) program is designed for students who are preparing for careers as professional managers and who desire an integrated program of study. The proficiency requirements have been streamlined to seven courses for students with backgrounds in fields other than business. The M.B.A. core includes courses in areas of managerial accounting, business policy, finance, management, marketing, quantitative analysis, and economic analysis. M.B.A. candidates may choose 15 semester hours for areas of specialization.

The Master of Professional Accounting (M.P.A.) degree is designed for students who are planning careers in the field of accounting. Students with limited backgrounds in accounting may enroll in this degree program after completing proficiency requirements in introductory, intermediate, tax, and cost accounting. Leveling work in business subjects is also required. Core courses are required in accounting theory, accounting systems, auditing, and nine additional hours in accounting. Students may pursue a thesis or nonthesis program.

The Master of Business Education (M.B.E.) degree is designed for students who plan careers teaching business subjects in high schools and junior colleges or managing an office environment for businesses or governments. The curriculum includes seminars on skills to assist business teachers, courses to enlarge backgrounds in business administration subjects, advanced seminars in the field of education, and a research capability. Students pursuing the M.B.E. degree must have a background of 30 hours of undergraduate courses in business.

The Master of Arts degree in economics is a traditional degree program for students interested in employment in areas such as research, teaching, journalism, government, or law. Students may elect a thesis or nonthesis program. The graduate course offerings are concentrated in macro- and microeconomics, monetary theory, and international trade, but specialization in economic growth and development, economic analysis, and comparative economic systems is possible.

ADMISSION

Requirements for admission include a baccalaureate degree from an accredited college or university with an acceptable grade average and acceptable test scores. A grade average of 2.85 (4.0 scale) in the last 60 hours of undergraduate work or a score of 475 on the Graduate Management Admission Test (GMAT) for M.B.A. and M.P.A. candidates or 950 on the Graduate Record Examinations (GRE) for M.B.E. and Master of Arts in economics candidates will be required for admission. However, some students will be allowed entrance on a probationary basis with a B average on the first 12 hours being required. Applications must be completed at least two months prior to the start of the semester.

EXPENSES

Students may enroll in as few as 3 to as many as 15 credit hours each semester. Estimated expenses for full-time graduate students for an academic year are as follows:

	Residents	Out-of-state	Alien
Tuition and fees	$ 770	$4,010	$4,010
Books	300	300	300
Room and board	2,130	2,130	2,130
Miscellaneous	500	500	500
	$3,700	$6,940	$6,940

FINANCIAL ASSISTANCE

Assistantships carrying grants up to $4,800 per academic year may be awarded to master's degree candidates in the School of Business. Scholarships and student loans are also provided by the Financial Aid Office. Out-of-state students are encouraged to apply for scholarships, as a $200 scholarship will exempt the student from paying out-of-state tuition. For information, write to the Director of Financial Aid.

PLACEMENT

Graduate students in the School of Business are assisted in placement both by the West Texas State University Placement Office and by the faculty and administration.

CORRESPONDENCE

For further information or to request an application for admission, please write or call

Graduate Coordinator
West Texas State University
Canyon, Texas 79016
Telephone: 806-656-2317

West Virginia University (WVU) is one of only 72 land-grant institutions serving the nation. Since its founding in 1867, WVU has developed into a comprehensive university and has become the center of graduate and professional education, research, and extension programs in West Virginia.

PROGRAMS OF STUDY

The College of Business and Economics offers graduate programs in business administration, accounting, economics, and industrial relations. The program in business leads to the degree of Master of Business Administration (M.B.A.); the program in accounting leads to the degree of Master of Professional Accountancy; the program in industrial relations leads to the degree of Master of Science; and the graduate programs in economics lead to the degrees of Master of Arts and Doctor of Philosophy. A joint M.B.A./ Juris Doctor (J.D.) program is available. Students must apply to each program separately.

The M.B.A. program is offered both full time and part time on campus at Morgantown and part time off campus at Parkersburg and Wheeling. A full-time student must enter the program at the beginning of July and may complete the course of study in 13 ½ months. Part-time students may complete the program in 40 months. Admission and degree requirements are the same for students at all locations. The off-campus program is offered on weekends and is taught by the Morgantown faculty. The undergraduate and graduate programs offered by the College of Business and Economics are accredited by the American Assembly of Collegiate Schools of Business (AACSB).

The M.B.A. program is designed for individuals with varying educational and professional backgrounds. Thus, no prior course work in business is required. The program develops a managerial perspective that is primarily line- as opposed to staff-oriented and is relevant to those in both private and public organizations. The plan of study is a tightly integrated program requiring a total of 53 semester hours of graduate credit:

Hours

Preparatory courses (July-August)
Management Information
    Technology and Systems 3
Organization Behavior and
    Ethics 3
Quantitative Analysis of Business
    Data 2

Foundation courses (August-December)
Financial Accounting for
    Decision 3
Legal and Regulatory
    Environment 2
Economic Decision Making 2
Fundamentals of Finance 2
Management Information
    Systems 3
Seminar in Executive Processes . . 3
Marketing Management 2
Application Courses (January-May)
Managerial Control 2
Economic Policy 2
Corporate Financial
    Administration 3
Operations Management 2
Organization Design 3
Marketing Strategy 3
Integration and Specialization (May-August)
    Policy and Strategy 4
    Electives 9

The required courses provide the student with a broad background and the integrative perspective needed in today's business world. Conceptual, quantitative, and practical materials are combined to provide the student with the flexibility necessary for meeting present and future challenges. Electives are offered in accounting, finance, industrial relations, management, management science, and marketing. Students may take elective courses in other disciplines within the university. No thesis is required, but writing is emphasized in most courses in the M.B.A. program.

ADMISSION

To receive approval to enter the M.B.A. program, an applicant must have a baccalaureate degree from an accredited college or university, with an undergraduate average of at least 2.75 (of a possible 4.0). An applicant with a grade-point average (GPA) that falls between 2.75 and 3.0 should have a GPA of at least 3.0 based on the last 60 hours of college work. A resume citing one's experience and/or evidence of leadership potential should be attached to the application. In addition, an applicant must submit a minimum score on the Graduate Management Admission Test (GMAT) in the range of 500-550 or above, depending on academic background and record and number of applicants. No action will be taken on an application for admission until a GMAT score is submitted. Foreign applicants must submit a score of at least 580-610 on the Test of English as a Foreign Language

(TOEFL). Candidates should have completed a course in statistics before enrolling in required M.B.A. courses. All applications must be received in the WVU Office of Admissions at least two months prior to enrollment.

EXPENSES

A nonrefundable fee of $20 must accompany applications for admission. The university fees for the entire program for full-time graduate students are $2,308 for West Virginia residents and $6,927 for nonresidents. Tuition for part-time on-campus and off-campus students is $45 and $164 per semester hour for residents and nonresidents, respectively. Off-campus students must pay an additional fee of $40 per course. All students must pay a $20 graduation fee. The West Virginia Board of Regents reserves the right to increase fees without prior notice.

FINANCIAL ASSISTANCE

A number of graduate assistantships are granted each year by the College of Business and Economics as well as by some of the research organizations on campus. These typically carry a stipend of $3,915 for 9 months along with remission of tuition for the 12 months. Graduate assistants work about 15 hours per week helping professors with research and other related activities. Graduate teaching assistantships in accounting are available to qualified master's candidates. The deadline for receipt of applications for assistantships is March 31. Loans are also available on a limited basis.

PLACEMENT

The university placement service offers a complete program of placement activities to both students and alumni.

CORRESPONDENCE

Requests for information should be directed to
    Director, M.B.A. Program
    College of Business and Economics
    West Virginia University
    P.O. Box 6025
    Morgantown, West Virginia 26506-6025
    Telephone: 304-293-5408

The School of Business at Western Carolina University is dedicated to offering quality graduate business education. The curriculum provides participants with the knowledge and tools necessary for strategic planning and managerial decision making in today's complex business environment. Graduate degree programs are accredited by the American Assembly of Collegiate Schools of Business (AACSB).

The WCU campus is nestled in the Appalachian Mountains of North Carolina, approximately 50 miles west of Asheville, 100 miles southeast of Knoxville, and 150 miles northeast of Atlanta. The Blue Ridge Parkway, the Great Smoky Mountains National Park, the Cherokee Indian Reservation, and numerous resort areas offering golf, skiing, fishing, hunting, hiking, water sports, and other recreational opportunities are located near the university.

PROGRAMS OF STUDY
The School of Business offers the Master of Business Administration (M.B.A.) and Master of Project Management (M.P.M.) degrees. The M.B.A. degree consists of 39 semester hours—24 hours of core courses and 15 hours of electives. The core requirement is a set of eight interwoven courses designed to ensure the breadth of business understanding necessary for the attainment of career and organizational goals. Electives provide further breadth as well as the opportunity to concentrate in a functional area of business. Both full- and part-time students may enroll at the start of any session in the evening program in Asheville or the main campus program in Cullowhee.

The M.P.M. degree, a new program for which the first class will enter in the fall of 1986, requires a minimum of 33 semester hours. Fifteen of these hours are foundation courses to provide breadth of knowledge in business administration tools and techniques. A minimum of 18 hours are in specialized project management courses. The program is highly structured. All prerequisite courses must be taken prior to entry into the program, and students may enter only in the fall semester. The program concludes the following June after a special three-week capstone course.

Teaching methods for both degrees include lectures, cases, group projects, field study, and independent study.

ADMISSION
Applicants must hold a bachelor's degree from a recognized college or university and present Graduate Management Admission Test (GMAT) scores. To be considered for admission, applicants must attain a minimum admissions index of 950 (index = 200 × grade-point average + GMAT score). M.P.M. program applicants must present letters of reference from their prior, current, or prospective employers concerning future use of the applicant's training in project management.

In addition to meeting the admissions index, the following undergraduate course prerequisites must be satisfactorily completed for admission to either program: six semester hours each of accounting and economics and three semester hours each of business statistics, management principles, financial management, and business law. For students who meet the admissions index, the School of Business offers an accelerated option of intensive graduate-level courses to complete the prerequisites. Students who meet prerequisite requirements are admitted directly to the program

Foreign applicants whose native tongue is not English must present a Test of English as a Foreign Language (TOEFL) score of 550 or higher. A statement of financial resources is also required.

EXPENSES
Full-time, in-state graduate students pay tuition and fees of approximately $425 per semester; full-time, out-of-state students pay about $1,850 per semester. Room and board is $905 per semester. These amounts were applicable for the 1985-86 academic year and are subject to change. Books and supplies are additional.

FINANCIAL ASSISTANCE
Approximately one half of all students pursuing the M.B.A. degree full time receive a graduate assistantship. Duties include research, assisting senior faculty members with classroom instruction, and contributing services to various administrative units. Assistantship stipends ranged from $3,600 to $4,000 for the 1985-86 academic year. Out-of-state tuition waivers are limited and competition for them is keen. Other types of aid are available through the university's Financial Aid Office.

PLACEMENT
The Career Planning and Placement Center is available to assist students in job search. The Graduate Business Students Organization distributes 200 resume books to regional and national firms each year. WCU is one of the few universities in the United States to offer graduate-level cooperative education to its students. This is a program in which students alternate formal academic study with terms of practical work experience in business and government. This co-op program will commence with its first placements in 1986.

CORRESPONDENCE
For further information, please write or call

Dr. John Wade, Director
Graduate Programs in Business
School of Business
Western Carolina University
Cullowhee, North Carolina 28723
Telephone: 704-227-7401

Western Connecticut State University was founded in 1903 by state legislative enactment and has expanded over the years to include three schools: School of Arts and Science, Ancell School of Business, and School of Professional Studies. The university offers degree programs at both the baccalaureate and postbaccalaureate levels and in September 1985 was servicing a student body of approximately 6,000 students.

Western Connecticut State University began offering business courses in 1969, and the Ancell School of Business was created in 1977. The university offers a Bachelor of Business Administration degree and a Master of Science in Administration (M.S.A.) degree. It is accredited by the New England Association of Colleges and Secondary Schools, the Commission for Higher Education, and the Connecticut State Board of Education.

PROGRAM OF STUDY
The Master of Science in Administration degree offers advanced study for those students seeking specialized training in accounting, finance, health care administration, international business, marketing, human resource management, or public and nonprofit emphasis. The purpose is to provide the M.S.A. student with the analytical techniques necessary to solve business problems, to expose the student to decision-making concepts and practices, and to encourage a logical approach to the resolution of business problems. All graduate courses are offered in the evenings or on Saturday for the convenience of the students who are actively engaged in business activities during the day.

The student must earn 30 credit hours in order to receive a Master of Science in Administration degree. A research project is included within the 30 credit hours; however, a thesis is not required. The applicant whose undergraduate training has not included prerequisite studies for the graduate program will be required to take preparatory courses in addition to the 30 credit hours necessary to earn a Master of Science in Administration degree.

ADMISSION
Undergraduate preparation in business or public administration is not required for admission to the M.S.A. program. To be eligible for admission the applicant must hold a baccalaureate degree. In evaluating a student's application for admission, primary emphasis will be given to his or her undergraduate record and scores on the Graduate Management Admission Test (GMAT). A student can receive transfer credit for up to nine semester hours providing that he or she received a grade of at least a B in each of the courses and that each of the courses is equivalent to a course in the M.S.A. program.

EXPENSES
Student fee, per semester........... $ 5
Tuition, per credit hour............ 84
There is no application fee for part-time students.

FINANCIAL ASSISTANCE
Graduate assistantships are available based on the student's experience and education. Applications may be obtained from the Personnel Office.

PLACEMENT
The Placement Office will provide free placement service to students who are seeking employment opportunities.

CORRESPONDENCE
For further information, call or write
Coordinator of Graduate Studies in Business
Ancell School of Business
Western Connecticut State University
181 White Street
Danbury, Connecticut 06810
Telephone: 203-797-4204

Western Illinois University is located in Macomb, Illinois, just 40 miles east of the Mississippi River. The campus extends over 1,056 acres and contains 52 buildings including classroom structures, special facilities for students, and modern residence halls. The library is ranked among the 10 largest in the United States for non-doctoral-degree-granting universities.

The College of Business has approximately 85 full-time faculty members organized into 5 academic departments. The college is housed in Stipes Hall. This building is relatively new, containing modern classrooms, audiovisual equipment, special laboratories, computer facilities, and faculty offices. It is centrally located and provides convenient access to the library, computer center, student union, residence halls, and other campus areas.

PROGRAMS OF STUDY
The College of Business offers a professional graduate program designed to enable qualified students to become competent and responsible managers and executives. The major objective of the Master of Business Administration (M.B.A.) program is to prepare graduates for career positions in business, education, and government. A second objective of the program is to provide an appropriate background for those who plan to pursue an advanced degree in a specialized field. Emphasis is placed on providing prospective managers with a background in analytical decision-making techniques, insights into the behavioral sciences, and methods of adapting to change.

The program is open to graduates in liberal arts, engineering, science, education, and other fields as well as business. Students who have not had introductory course work in calculus, linear algebra, and computer systems will be required to remedy these deficiencies.

In addition, there may be as many as 30 semester hours in the areas of accounting, management, economics, business statistics, corporate finance, marketing, and business law. All, or part, of these requirements may be waived based on the student's undergraduate preparation.

The minimum requirements for the degree are 33 semester hours of graduate credit. They include one or more required courses in accounting, economics, finance, management, marketing, operations research, and research methodology. A student with a strong undergraduate background in one of these areas may seek approval to substitute an elective for the corresponding required course. There is a minimum of nine semester hours of electives for each student. The electives can be taken in one area or selected from a number of areas. Electives are available in several areas, including accounting, marketing, finance, management, and economics.

Two graduate programs of study are available in addition to the M.B.A. degree. They are the Master of Accountancy and the Master of Arts in economics.

ADMISSION
Application is made through the School of Graduate Studies which requires the student to hold a bachelor's degree from an accredited undergraduate institution. The Graduate Management Admission Test (GMAT) is required of all applicants to the M.B.A. program and to the Master of Accountancy program. Admission to the M.B.A. program requires an acceptable combination of an undergraduate grade-point average and the total score on the GMAT. A high score on the GMAT can offset a low grade-point average and vice versa. The minimum grade-point average for acceptance as a degree-seeking graduate student is 2.5 overall or 2.75 for the last 60 semester hours (A = 4.0). All application materials must be submitted at least three weeks before the student's first registration.

EXPENSES
Tuition and fees for full-time graduate students are approximately $730 per semester for in-state students and $1,828 per semester for out-of-state students. The university maintains residence halls for students with special floors available for graduate students. Room and board is approximately $1,000 per semester. All fees are subject to change without notice by action of the Board of Governors of State Colleges and Universities.

FINANCIAL ASSISTANCE
There are a number of research assistantships available to qualified candidates. In addition to the stipend, full remission of the tuition fee is granted. Information on loans and other forms of financial assistance available to graduate students can be obtained by writing to the Office of Financial Aids.

PLACEMENT
The Office of Occupational Information and Placement maintains a close relationship with the business and educational community. Each year a number of firms visit the campus recruiting students from the master's programs.

CORRESPONDENCE
For additional information, please write or call

Director of M.B.A. Program
College of Business
Western Illinois University
Macomb, Illinois 61455
Telephone: 309-298-2442

Western Kentucky University, established in 1906, has an enrollment of approximately 11,500 students. The campus is located approximately 110 miles south of Louisville and 65 miles north of Nashville, Tennessee. Sixty-four major buildings and an estimated 200 acres constitute the main campus.

Western's academic program seeks to provide curricula which will foster broad intellectual development as well as prepare students for careers in the arts and sciences, business, government service, allied medical arts, education, and other fields. Academic support facilities include seven libraries and a computer center. The library system currently holds 750,000 volumes and receives 3,500 periodicals. The computer center is available to both students and faculty for the conduct of research involving data samplings and complex mathematical analyses.

PROGRAM OF STUDY

The Master of Business Administration (M.B.A.) program is designed to provide professional education for successful careers in management. The program is general in approach and emphasizes the relevance of economics, quantitative methods, the behavioral sciences, and finance.

Students must complete 30 semester hours of approved graduate course work. A comprehensive final examination is also required of all students. Prerequisites are required of those students whose business backgrounds are deficient. The 30 semester hours of approved graduate work consist of the following courses:

Accounting 560, Managerial Accounting;
Business Admin. 570, Business, Government, and Law;
Business Admin. 573, International Business;
Business Admin. 575, Organization Theory;
Business Admin. 535, Advanced Management Science;
Business Admin. 520, Advanced Marketing;
Business Admin. 530, Advanced Managerial Finance;
Business Admin. 578, Administrative Policy;
Economics 580, Applied Microeconomic Theory; and
Economics 585, Applied Macroeconomic Theory.

Those students who are not required to complete prerequisite courses normally are able to finish the program in 14 months. Students whose business backgrounds are deficient may require as much as two years to complete the program. Evening classes are available for anyone wishing to pursue study part time.

ADMISSION

Admission to the program requires the approval of the Graduate College and the M.B.A. Admissions Committee. Applicants will be evaluated primarily on the basis of a combination of undergraduate grade-point average and Graduate Management Admission Test (GMAT) scores, in accordance with formulas specified by the American Assembly of Collegiate Schools of Business (AACSB).

EXPENSES

As of the fall semester 1985, the fee for students carrying nine or more semester hours was $521 for Kentucky residents and $1,494 for nonresidents. The fee for part-time students was $57 per credit hour for residents and $165 per credit hour for nonresidents.

FINANCIAL ASSISTANCE

A limited number of graduate assistantships are available for qualified students. Appointments are made each semester. In addition to the remuneration in the form of a stipend, the out-of-state portion of the graduate assistant's fees is awarded in the form of a scholarship. Student loan programs are available to qualified applicants.

PLACEMENT

The university maintains a placement office which offers a free, lifetime service to students and alumni.

CORRESPONDENCE

For additional information on the M.B.A. program, write to
Graduate College
Admissions Officer
Western Kentucky University
Bowling Green, Kentucky 42101

Western Michigan University, one of the four large universities in the state, has an on-campus enrollment of 20,000 students. Approximately 4,000 of these are graduate students in master's, specialist, and doctoral programs.

PROGRAMS OF STUDY
The College of Business has some 6,200 students of whom more than 750 are in graduate business programs. Some 80 graduate courses are offered in accounting, business education, finance, law, management, and marketing.

The Master of Business Administration (M.B.A.) program is designed to prepare graduate students to function effectively in administrative positions. This preparation emphasizes the development of the student's ability to make and execute decisions. The program of study is designed to provide the student with skills and knowledge in the areas of critical analysis, business operations, changing environments, professional development, and specialized professional interests. The program consists of prerequisites, M.B.A. core courses, and electives. The total program requires, in addition to the prerequisites, a minimum of 33 hours of course work or 27 hours and a thesis.

The prerequisites include course work in accounting, economics, finance, law, management, marketing, statistics, and computer information systems. This requirement may be satisfied by (1) waiver (in case of prior completion of appropriate undergraduate courses—Bachelor of Business Administration (B.B.A.) core courses or equivalent); (2) examination; or (3) by taking 210 and 211 Principles of Accounting, 201, 202 Economics, 320 Business Finance, 340 Legal Environment, 300 Management Fundamentals, 370 Marketing, and 200 Decision Making with Statistics.

The M.B.A. core consists of the following: 600 Applied Economics for Management, 602 Computer Information Systems, 607 Legal Controls, 607 Accounting Control and Analysis, 608 Financial Management, 607 Marketing Management, and 699 Policy Formulation and Administration (capstone core course).

With the approval of the M.B.A. program adviser, additional elective courses may be selected from economics, finance, management, marketing, paper science, and/or other areas. If desired, all of the electives may be taken from a single area provided that at least 15 hours of course work are taken outside this area.

In addition to the English usage exam required by the Graduate College, M.B.A. applicants must submit scores on the Graduate Management Admission Test (GMAT) prior to admission.

The Master of Science (M.S.) in accountancy degree program allows the student an opportunity to concentrate in accountancy at the graduate level. A knowledge and understanding of the theory, literature, and controversial concepts of accounting are developed as well as an ability to carry out research. The student's understanding of the relationship of accounting to other fields in business and to other disciplines is also stressed.

Specific requirements for the M.S. degree vary with the applicant's background (a minimum of 30 graduate hours and 21 hours of accountancy is required). The GMAT and an English test are required.

The Master of Science in business with concentrations in administrative services, finance, management, and marketing is also offered.

EXPENSES

Per semester	*In-state*	*Out-of-state*
Tuition		
(12-hour load)	$ 738	$1,797
Room and board	700*	700*
Books and supplies	90*	90*
Total	$1,528*	$2,587*

*Approximate figures.

FINANCIAL ASSISTANCE
Graduate fellowships valued at $5,000 are granted on the basis of merit to persons planning to pursue full-time work on the campus leading to advanced degrees.

Graduate associateships carrying a somewhat greater stipend than the fellowships are offered to a limited number of graduate students who have completed a master's degree and are registering for work on an advanced degree.

Graduate assistantships with stipends of approximately $5,000 are available to promising students. Students receiving an assistantship are expected to participate in approximately 15 hours per week of professional service in the department.

Graduate students who enroll for a minimum of nine hours of on-campus credit in a semester may qualify for a National Direct Student Loan or some other type of loan.

PLACEMENT
The university maintains a free placement service for students and alumni which is visited annually by several hundred business, industrial, governmental, and educational institutions and agencies.

CORRESPONDENCE
For further information, write or call
   Director of Admissions
   Graduate Business Programs
   Western Michigan University
   Kalamazoo, Michigan 49008
   Telephone: 616-383-4672

Western New England College is a private, independent, coeducational college offering undergraduate, graduate, and continuing education programs. Central to all programs is a commitment to effective instruction in an atmosphere of personal concern for the student.

The graduate program provides opportunities for the professional development of those students interested in careers in business, engineering, and law. To accomplish these goals, the college is organized into a School of Arts and Sciences, a School of Business, a School of Engineering, and a School of Continuing Higher Education, all offering a variety of undergraduate programs.

PROGRAM OF STUDY
The objective of the graduate business program leading to the Master of Business Administration (M.B.A.) is to enhance the problem-solving and decision-making capabilities of those who hold, or aspire to, positions of responsibility within organizations. The program develops managers who are capable of articulating their ideas to others, both verbally and in writing. The thinking processes that are developed include a consideration of long-range societal implications.

The M.B.A. program is composed of three areas: foundation courses, core courses, and elective courses. All students in the M.B.A. program who have no prior graduate work must take seven core courses and three electives for a total of 30 semester hours. Six foundation courses are required but may be waived depending on previous education or practical experience. The maximum number of semester hours for a student required to take all courses in the program is 48. Requests for waivers of foundation courses must be made at the time of admission.

ADMISSION
Admission to any of the graduate programs is open only to persons who hold at least a baccalaureate degree from an accredited college or university. It is possible for students to enter at midyear, as a number of courses offered each year allow students to begin a program in the second semester.

The following procedure should be completed for admission: the completed application form should be returned to the Office of Graduate Studies with a $20 application fee, along with transcripts of undergraduate degree work and any previous graduate work. Notification of decision will be forwarded to the candidate on receipt of the required documents. Details regarding registration will be sent to all accepted applicants before the registration period.

Admission to the program requires (1) a baccalaureate degree from an accredited college or university with at least one year of college mathematics and (2) results of the Graduate Management Admission Test (GMAT).

EXPENSES
Tuition per semester hour $185
Registration fee (per semester) . . .   10
General service fee (per semester
   credit hour).   5
Tuition and fees are due and payable at the time of registration unless other arrangements have been made.

FINANCIAL ASSISTANCE
Under the Deferred Payment Privilege plan, a finance charge will be computed by a "period rate" of 1 percent per month which is an annual percentage rate of 12 percent applied to the prior balance after deducting current payments and/or credits appearing on the statement.

An increasing number of companies are underwriting, in whole or in part, the cost of tuition of part-time students in their employ. In cases where the employer wishes to make direct payment to the college, the student must furnish at the time of registration or immediately thereafter, an authorization from his or her employer indicating that the company is underwriting the cost of tuition.

The college offers financial assistance through scholarships, grants, loans, and part-time employment, but resources are limited. Parents of dependent students and independent students applying for aid must submit the Financial Aid Form (FAF) to the College Scholarship Service for processing, along with the college's Application for Financial Aid. Both the FAF and the Application for Financial Aid must be received by Western New

England College before April 1 in order for the student to be considered for all forms of aid. Applicants filing after the deadline may be considered for financial aid if sufficient funds are available.

PLACEMENT
The Office of Career Planning and Placement provides instructional services such as resume writing, interview techniques, and job search strategies as well as personal career counseling. The office maintains a reference and credential service and serves as a point of contact for recruitment visits and hundreds of employer inquiries.

CORRESPONDENCE
For additional information, please write or call
   School of Continuing Higher Education
   Office of Graduate Studies
   Western New England College
   Springfield, Massachusetts 01119
   Telephone: 413-782-3111

WESTERN NEW MEXICO UNIVERSITY

SILVER CITY, NEW MEXICO

The master's programs at Western New Mexico University offer the professional person the opportunity to acquire a generalist's background, with varying degrees of specialization, in the environment of a small university.

Western was founded in 1893 as a state coeducational institution of higher learning. The university is located in the quiet mountain town of Silver City, population 12,000, which serves as the marketing and financial center for a vast three-county area that extends to Arizona on the west and south to Mexico. Located in the foothills of the Mogollon and Black Range Mountains, Silver City has a climate that is dry, mild, and invigorating. The Gila National Forest, only minutes away, provides an attractive setting for backpacking, camping, hunting, and fishing and has a number of hiking trails as well as Indian ruins which can be explored. Hot springs and ghost towns are nearby. The area has a great appeal to rock hounds, and gold panning is still practiced by some. The town is far enough removed from large urban centers to assure tranquility and a sense of freedom, yet close enough to the metropolitan areas of El Paso, Juarez, Tucson, Albuquerque, and Phoenix to enjoy them.

The university occupies a gently rolling campus of 80 acres and has an average enrollment of 1,600 students. The campus includes 25 major buildings or building complexes. These facilities include the J. Cloyd Miller Library which contains more than 117,000 paper volumes and 246,000 volumes in micro-formats. In addition, the library has access to the holdings of 5 million volumes in over 1,500 libraries across the country, through the use of an Ohio College Library Center computer network. The Fine Arts Center encompasses a 1,000-seat auditorium and multi-studio art facilities. The Health and Recreation Complex houses two basketball courts, a 25-meter indoor swimming pool, a training room, four racketball courts, a dance studio, and other recreational activities.

PROGRAMS OF STUDY

The Department of Business and Public Administration offers two graduate programs. The Master of Business Administration (M.B.A.) program is designed for persons who want to become management generalists and who do not wish to write a thesis. The Master of Arts (M.A.) in teaching program is designed for business educators who want to continue their studies in business and related areas.

The M.B.A. program is composed of a core of 18 hours of department graduate courses, plus 18 additional semester hours from approved graduate offerings. Prerequisites to the program include 24 semester hours of the following common body of knowledge courses or their equivalents: principles of economics (6), accounting (6), marketing (3), business law (3), management (3), and finance (3).

The majority of graduate courses are scheduled in the evenings to accommodate students who work. Full-time students who have the necessary prerequisites may complete the M.B.A. within one academic year. The faculty make every effort to provide students with a variety of learning experiences; cases and simulations are commonly used, and the university's computer laboratory is integrated into the quantitative course work. The computer lab has an array of microcomputers and an ample number of terminals providing access to the university's DEC VAX mainframe. Students benefit from lecture sessions that emphasize interactive exchanges between faculty and student in small, personal classes.

The minimum residence requirement for the completion of the master's degree is two semesters. Five summer sessions are accepted as an equivalent. All credit, except the permitted transfer of 12 semester hours, must be earned in residence. All graduate credit, including transfer credit, must have been earned within five years prior to issuance of the master's degree.

ADMISSION

To be admitted as a regular graduate student, the university requires the following: (1) a baccalaureate degree from an accredited institution with an overall grade-point average of at least 2.75 out of a possible 4.00 for the last 64 semester hours of undergraduate work, and at least a 3.00 grade-point average in the major field; (2) completion of the appropriate application form and payment of a $10 nonrefundable fee; and (3) submission of official transcripts of all previous college work.

In addition, the Department of Business and Public Administration requires the following: (1) evidence of completion of all prerequisite courses (A student who has not completed the necessary prerequisite courses may be approved to enter the graduate program; however, deficiencies must be removed prior to enrollment in the graduate core courses) and (2) submission of scores on the Graduate Management Admission Test (GMAT). Students who have not taken the GMAT may be admitted provisionally, contingent on the presentation of a satisfactory score from the next test administration.

EXPENSES

A major attraction of Western is its fee structure. It is the least expensive university in this beautiful southwestern region. Tuition for full-time students (12 or more credit hours) is $301 for residents and $1,099 for nonresidents. Part-time students, both resident and nonresident, pay $22 per credit. First-time registrants pay a matriculation fee of $5. All full-time students receive activity ticket privileges, university health service benefits, and accident and health insurance coverage. A limited number of assistantships are available to full-time graduate students. A stipend is paid monthly, and out-of-state tuition is waived.

CORRESPONDENCE

For further information, contact
Mr. C. Richard Scott
Chairman, Department of
    Business
Western New Mexico University
Silver City, New Mexico 88061
Telephone: 505-538-6322

Western Washington University, established in 1893, has an enrollment of about 9,200 students, of which about 1,000 are post baccalaureate students. The university is located in Bellingham, Washington, in the northwest corner of the state. Bellingham is some 90 miles north of Seattle and 55 miles south of Vancouver, British Columbia. Climate conditions are mild, ranging from a mean temperature of 36°F in January to 65°F in July. The university, from its hilltop site, overlooks Bellingham Bay and the San Juan Islands. Snow-capped Mount Baker is only 45 miles to the east of the university campus.

The College of Business and Economics is one of five semiautonomous colleges that, together with the Graduate School and School of Education, compose Western Washington University. The college is located in Parks Hall, a five-story office and classroom building completed in 1982. The college houses two computer labs (including a state-of-the-art microcomputer lab) and a management lab (complete with videotaping capabilities).

The Master of Business Administration (M.B.A.) program was added in 1978. The M.B.A. program seeks to prepare students for responsible leadership positions in private, public, and nonprofit organizations. The purpose of the program is to provide broad training in the skills needed by the professional manager. The Western M.B.A. program is a rigorous, integrated program that focuses on quantitative, theoretical, and analytical skills. It strives to provide a proper balance of theory and application essential for managerial excellence. The program is intended for both the active manager or technical supervisor as well as those looking for new opportunities at the mid-management level. Regardless of undergraduate education, the candidates will find a challenging program designed to meet their specific background and needs.

PROGRAM OF STUDY

Both a full-time and a part-time program of study are offered. The program is composed of 15 to 18 four-credit courses. Students with a nonbusiness/quantitative background are normally required to take all 18 courses. Students with an undergraduate record in business or economics may make application to waive certain foundation courses. The foundation consists of courses in accounting, management, quantitative skills, finance, economics, and computer information systems. The balance of the program is composed of advanced courses in some of the above areas and elective courses. All students are able to select at least four electives.

Classes are offered in the evening, and students attend four quarters a year. A new class is admitted for June of each year. Some students may be able to have the first summer quarter classes waived and start the program in the fall. Part-time students take two courses per quarter and require nine consecutive quarters to complete the degree. Full-time students proceed at a pace of three or four courses per quarter and will normally complete their requirements in 14 months. M.B.A. program requirements are as follows:

- knowledge prerequisites—normally an applicant must have completed a college algebra and a college calculus course prior to entering the program. Well-developed communications skills are also important.
- foundation courses (24 hours).
- core courses (28 hours), including managerial accounting, marketing management, managerial finance, managerial economics, production management, business environment, and business policy.
- elective courses (20 hours).
- a comprehensive exam is given as part of business policy.

ADMISSION

Students enter the program with diverse backgrounds, including engineering, arts and humanities, social and natural sciences, business, and accounting. The recent M.B.A. entering classes have included about 30 percent women, 10 percent minority, and 15 percent international students. The typical M.B.A. student at Western is 30 years of age and has several years of professional work experience.

Applicants must have a bachelor's degree, but that degree need not be in business or a business-related area. Applications are made to the Graduate School and must include an official application form, the results of the Graduate Management Admission Test (GMAT), official transcripts of all previous work (graduate and undergraduate), and a resume showing work experience. Applicants from non-English-speaking areas must include their scores on the Test of English as a Foreign Language (TOEFL). Letters of recommendation may be requested by the Graduate Office or M.B.A. program adviser.

EXPENSES

Graduate tuition for residents of Washington State is $567 per quarter for full-time students and $57 per credit for part-time study. Nonresident tuition is $1,695 per quarter and $170 per credit hour for part-time study. Reduced fees are available to Southeast Asian veterans. All fees are subject to change.

FINANCIAL ASSISTANCE

Financial support is available to a limited number of full-time students in the form of work-study assignments and assistantships. Graduate assistants receive a stipend of approximately $5,300 per academic year. Student loans are available to those who qualify.

CORRESPONDENCE

Applications and document submissions should be directed to
    Dean of the Graduate School
    Western Washington University
    Bellingham, Washington 98225
Requests for application materials and other information should be directed to the above address or to
    Director of the M.B.A. Program
    College of Business and Economics
    Western Washington University
    Bellingham, Washington 98225

The Wharton School—the oldest collegiate school of business in the world—offers a professional education in advanced management. The school is an integral part both academically and physically of the University of Pennsylvania, located in Philadelphia. Wharton derives its unique strength and diversity from the far-reaching educational resources of the university and the active business communities of Philadelphia and nearby New York and Washington. The total enrollment of 1,450 in the Graduate Division includes students from the continental United States and abroad. A diverse class of 650 men and women matriculate each September; 110 enter in January.

PROGRAMS OF STUDY

The Master of Business Administration (M.B.A.) program can be viewed as general management training complemented by specialization. Nineteen courses are required for the two-year M.B.A. degree, eight of which are part of the core curriculum. The core is designed to develop competence in the areas of economic analysis and policy, management and administration, accounting, statistics, quantitative methods, and problem solving using the computer. The entering class is divided into cohorts of 55 students. During the first semester, each cohort will go through four of the six core courses as a group. Students are also encouraged to take diverse elective courses during the first year. A major is selected from over 30 fields during the second year and is supplemented by elective courses which may be taken in any graduate division. A renowned faculty of over 200, recognized for both research and teaching, serve both the graduate and undergraduate divisions.

Reflecting the breadth of students' interests and the unusually broad range of the faculty's expertise, the Wharton curriculum, in sharp contrast to those found in many comparable M.B.A. programs, does not feature a lock-step pattern of prescribed courses. Rather, it establishes broad parameters and requirements within which each student selects an individual sequence of courses. This distinctive flexibility of the curriculum not only characterizes the M.B.A. program's capacity to complement any student's prior academic training or professional experience but also assures each student that his or her personal and career objectives can be satisfied.

Joint programs exist with the schools of law, medicine, dental medicine, social work, and engineering. In addition, Wharton participates in joint programs with The School of Advanced International Studies at Johns Hopkins University and the Joseph H. Lauder Institute of Management and International Studies. Admission must be granted by both participating schools.

The Public Policy Fellowship Program places selected students in Washington government agencies between their first and second years.

ADMISSION

Selection to the M.B.A. program is based on intellectual capacity, prior work experience, maturity, motivation, leadership qualities, and seriousness of purpose. A bachelor's degree or the equivalent is the minimum requirement for admission; application may be made for either September or January entry. Personal interviews are not available, but all applicants are encouraged to visit the campus and to meet with students. Group information sessions are offered on a daily basis.

Students who have completed courses similar to any of the required core courses may receive exemption either through examination or credentials, permitting them to substitute an elective in lieu of the requirement. Substitution does not reduce the number of courses needed for graduation, and credits from any other schools of business are not transferable. All students must demonstrate proficiency in elementary calculus and computer programming by passing an examination prior to matriculation or taking noncredit courses in both subjects during the first three weeks of the term.

EXPENSES

Estimated,

per academic year	Single	Married
Tuition and fees	$11,565	$11,565
Room and board	5,330	8,375
Books and supplies	700	700
Miscellaneous	1,450	2,900
Total	$19,045	$23,540

FINANCIAL ASSISTANCE

Wharton is a participant in the National Direct Student Loan Program, a five percent federally funded loan resource. Last year, assistance in the form of both fellowships and loans was allocated, on the basis of need, to approximately 50 per-

cent of the class. Wharton is a participant in the Johnson & Johnson Leadership Awards. Research opportunities, teaching assistantships, and stipends are also available to students at The Wharton Graduate School.

PLACEMENT

Over 400 companies recruited on campus. The average graduate had 22 interviews and received nearly 4 job offers. The Placement Office is instrumental in placing students in summer positions as well as in permanent career situations.

CORRESPONDENCE

For information, write or call
Wharton Graduate Division
Admissions Office
102 Vance Hall, CS
University of Pennsylvania
Philadelphia, Pennsylvania 19104
Telephone: 215-898-6182

Wheeling College is a private, coeducational institution founded in 1954 and accredited by the North Central Association. Conducted by the Jesuit order, Wheeling College offers programs of study that integrate the traditional liberal arts with a modern career-oriented curriculum. The Master of Business Administration (M.B.A.) program began in 1978 in response to a growing need in the Upper Ohio Valley for a local master's program in business. Enrollment in the program is held to approximately 120 students per semester, thus enabling each student to be known and guided as an individual.

PROGRAM OF STUDY

The M.B.A. program is structured to provide a quality program of professional education for men and women who wish to obtain responsible positions in business and other complex organizations. The program is oriented toward a general management point of view and incorporates three interrelated themes: (1) an emphasis on the functional areas of business, (2) a focus on the ability to see one's own business function in the context of the total environment, and (3) a value orientation that addresses the ethical implications of an organization's internal and external decision-making processes.

The M.B.A. program is designed for the student who wishes to combine graduate study with work experience. Therefore, classes are scheduled in the evenings and on Saturdays. Students may enroll on a full- or part-time basis.

The M.B.A. program is composed of 36-54 semester hours depending on waivers granted.

Survey of Computer Science for Management	3
Analytical Methods I	3
Analytical Methods II	3
Accounting and Financial Concepts	3
Economic Concepts	3
Management and Marketing Concepts	3
Organizational Behavior	3
Marketing Management	3
Ethical Environment of Business	3
Quantitative Business Analysis	3
Managerial Economics	3
Management of Financial Resources	3
Accounting for Management Control	3
Production and Operations Management	3
Managerial Policy and Decision Making	3
Electives	9

Students are eligible for potential waivers of tool course requirements (Survey of Computer Science for Management, Analytical and Financial Concepts, Economic Concepts, and Management and Marketing Concepts) for a total of up to 18 hours. These courses may be waived by completing comparable undergraduate courses or by examination. Thus, a student may be able to complete the degree requirements with 36-54 semester hours of course work, depending on waivers granted. No thesis is required in the program; rather, the course in Managerial Policy serves to integrate all aspects of the curriculum. Students are required to complete a minimum of 24 semester hours at Wheeling College; thus up to 12 hours may be transferred from other graduate programs.

ADMISSION

Admission to the M.B.A. program is open to men and women who hold bachelor's degrees or the equivalent from accredited institutions. Consideration in the admission decision is based on the student's academic record, Graduate Management Admission Test (GMAT) score, and letters of recommendation. Students are classified as fully or specially admitted, based on undergraduate grade-point average and GMAT score. Specially admitted students are required to meet certain specified academic standards in order to become fully admitted (or degree seeking) students.

Admission to the program is initiated by filing an application with the Graduate Office of Wheeling College. Applicants must furnish official transcripts of all previous undergraduate and graduate work, GMAT score, and three letters of recommendation. Students whose native language is not English are required to submit a score from the Test of English as a Foreign Language (TOEFL) in addition to the required documentation.

The M.B.A. program offers four sessions per year: fall (September), spring (January), summer I (May), and summer II (July). Students may enter the program in any of the four semesters. All documentation must be filed at least three weeks before the start of the semester in which the student intends to begin graduate study.

EXPENSES

The tuition fees for all graduate courses are based on a rate of $165 per semester hour. On-campus housing is available for single students at a cost of $2,925 per academic year (board included).

FINANCIAL ASSISTANCE

Financial aid through loans is available. Inquiries should be directed to the Office of Financial Aid. The M.B.A. program is approved for veterans' benefits.

PLACEMENT

Wheeling College maintains a Career Development Office which assists students with career information and job interviews.

CORRESPONDENCE

Further information may be obtained by writing

Director, M.B.A. Program
Wheeling College
Wheeling, West Virginia 26003
Telephone: 304-243-2344 or 243-2000

WHITTIER COLLEGE

WHITTIER, CALIFORNIA

Whittier College, located 20 miles east of Los Angeles, is a coeducational, liberal arts and professional institution. The 94-acre campus is situated in a suburban hillside setting. Whittier has historically attracted students from diverse geographic, ethnic, and religious backgrounds. The college recognizes its responsibility to provide for individualized instruction and creative programs. It encourages student participation and flexible learning opportunities.

Within the college vicinity lies a complex of industrial and suburban communities as diverse as any to be found in the entire southwestern United States. The diversity of business contacts available contributes a major element of strength to Whittier's graduate and undergraduate business programs.

PROGRAM OF STUDY

The Master of Business Administration (M.B.A.) degree program at Whittier is designed to assist students in developing management competence and a professional approach in applying management skills. In the context of Whittier's M.B.A., professional management requires a capacity for analytical reasoning and creative thinking. It requires behavioral skills and an appreciation of the interrelationships involved in an organizational system. It also demands an understanding of the complex environment in which the organization functions. Each of these areas is viewed as an integral part of the student's M.B.A. experience.

The program consists of three major parts, with specific requirements varying according to undergraduate background. Part I comprises the foundation and functional core requirement, including 15 units in accounting, economics, quantitative methods, and finance. If the student has completed a well-rounded undergraduate major, Part I may be waived upon entry.

The second part of the program requires 24 units of advanced and integrative courses. Included here are courses dealing with the external environments of business, management information systems, and strategic planning. In Part III, students complete 9 units of electives in either (1) financial management, (2) human resource management, (3) marketing management, or (4) a general M.B.A. option, for those who wish to design their own elective track.

M.B.A. courses are scheduled during the evening, Monday through Thursday, and are held one day per week throughout the semester.

ADMISSION

The program is open to all qualified men and women who hold a bachelor's degree from an accredited college or university. Admission to graduate standing in the program is based upon

- undergraduate grade-point average,
- Graduate Management Admission Test (GMAT) score,
- personal interview or two letters of recommendation for applicants residing outside the southern California area, and
- work experience (for those who have been employed full time in business or public organizations).

Other factors may also be considered by the Admissions Committee. Foreign students who completed their bachelor's degree outside of the United States or Canada, and whose first language is other than English must submit an official score report on the Test of English as a Foreign Language (TOEFL) administered by Educational Testing Service. Students should contact their local college or university testing advisers for further information regarding times and locations for taking this examination. No decision on admission can be made until the applicant's official TOEFL report is on file at the M.B.A. program office.

Application for admission to the M.B.A. program is made through the Office of Admissions. GMAT results and official transcripts of all previous undergraduate course work must be forwarded to the office of the M.B.A. Program Director. As soon as all material has been received and evaluated, the applicant will be notified in writing of the Graduate Committee's admission decision.

EXPENSES

Fees shown here apply to the 1985-86 academic year:

Tuition, per credit hour	$240
Application and evaluation fee	25
Matriculation and orientation fee	20
Master's degree fee	50

FINANCIAL ASSISTANCE

Through the Whittier College Loan Program for Graduate Study in Business, loans of limited size are available to U.S. students on a term-by-term basis. Financial assistance may also be available through the National Direct Student Loan, the federally guaranteed loan, and the College Work-Study programs.

PLACEMENT

The college operates a Placement Center; services of the center are available to all registered students seeking new positions. Career counseling, resume writing, practice interviewing, and many other services are available through the center, and the Placement Director also arranges on-campus interviews for numerous employer representatives and interested students.

CORRESPONDENCE

For further information, please write or call

Director
M.B.A. Program
Whittier College
Whittier, California 90608
Telephone: 213-693-0771, extension 368

The Wichita State University (WSU) is an urban institution located in Wichita, Kansas, a metropolitan area with a population of 400,000. The WSU, established in 1895, is one of six state universities in Kansas. Some 17,000 Wichita State University students enjoy a beautifully landscaped campus encompassing almost 320 acres. The WSU is a fully accredited, state-supported institution of higher learning with over 100 areas of concentration offered in seven degree-granting schools and colleges. The WSU is dedicated to providing a strong graduate program emphasizing the career-oriented master's degree. The College of Business Administration, established 60 years ago, has 2,100 undergraduate and 550 graduate students enrolled in its various academic programs.

PROGRAMS OF STUDY

The objective of graduate programs in business administration is to assist men and women who desire careers in business and other organizations or in teaching business administration, to develop those attitudes, abilities, and skills that constitute a foundation for future growth in their chosen field. The purpose, then, is to develop the student's (1) understanding of the structure and function of business organizations, (2) ability to recognize and analyze problems and to make decisions, (3) sense of responsibility for the social consequences of his or her actions, and (4) foundation for continuing self-education and growth.

Various combinations of teaching methods are used: formal and informal seminars, written and/or oral reports, case study and analysis, research projects, lectures, and discussions. Graduate instruction provides students with opportunities to develop skill and competence through individual and/or group effort and achievement.

Generally the Master of Business Administration (M.B.A.) program requires a minimum of two years regardless of the student's undergraduate field of study. The total hours required range from 30 to 63. Students who enter the M.B.A. program with no prior formal education in business administration must complete 28 hours of background fundamentals in accounting, economics, organizational behavior, statistics, marketing, finance, production, management information systems, and business and society.

Students who have recent (within the last six years) course work in business may have some of these courses waived.

All students are required to complete the 30 hours that constitute the managerial core. Included in the core are 12 hours in the basic disciplines of business (behavioral, accounting, and economics) and 3 hours in business policy. Fifteen hours of free and directed electives are allowed.

The Master in Professional Accounting program is a five-year degree designed for individuals with career objectives in professional accounting. Its purpose is to provide the additional breadth and depth of knowledge increasingly recommended for professional accountants. This nonthesis program requires a total of 151 hours, 55 taken while the student is in graduate status. A student holding a baccalaureate degree may pursue the graduate portion of this program with the addition of one background course.

The Master of Science (M.S.) in administration is oriented toward research and specialization in one of the following areas: finance, marketing, quantitative systems, or behavioral systems. The thesis program requires 30 hours, including a minimum of 9 hours of courses and a thesis in the area of specialization. The nonthesis program requires 33 hours (including a minimum of 15 hours in the area of specialization) and final oral and written exams.

The Master of Arts (M.A.) degree in economics trains economists and business managers through a grounding in the fundamentals of economics. Economic theory and statistics are emphasized. A subspecialization in business economics is available. The M.A. degree requires 30 hours, including a thesis (defended orally) or 34 hours without a thesis (which includes written comprehensive exams).

ADMISSION

Admission is granted to students who show high promise of success in postgraduate business study. Multiple criteria are considered in granting admission to all of the programs; however, special attention is given to the applicant's grade-point average for the last two years of academic work and scores on the Graduate Management Admission Test (GMAT). General minimum requirements for admission are (1) a baccalaureate degree from an

accredited institution and (2) a total of 1,050 points based on the formula of 200 × the student's overall grade-point average (4.00 system) + the GMAT scores or at least 1,100 points based on the formula of 200 × the grade-point average on the last 60 hours (4.00 system) + the GMAT score.

EXPENSES

	Resident	Nonresident
1-14 hours, per credit hour	$ 45.20	$ 105.35
15 hours and over, flat fee	$678.00	$1,580.00

FINANCIAL ASSISTANCE

Three kinds of financial assistance are available: graduate assistantships, graduate scholarships, and part-time employment. Graduate assistantships, involving teaching or research activities, are available in each of the master's programs. Stipends range from $3,800 to $4,500 per academic year. Applications must be filed by March 1.

PLACEMENT

The university maintains a placement office to serve students and alumni. This service offers information regarding career advantages, job search assistance, campus recruiting, possible job listings, and employer resource information. Alumni services are also available. The college faculty works cooperatively with the placement office to cover the transition from graduation to the job market. This year, 180 companies from all sections of the country made 450 visits to the campus to recruit.

CORRESPONDENCE

For further information, interested students may address
Dr. Robert H. Ross, Director
Graduate Studies in Business
College of Business Administration
The Wichita State University
Wichita, Kansas 67208
Telephone: 316-689-3230

Widener, a private, accredited university, offers doctoral, master's, baccalaureate, and associate degrees through its eight schools and colleges. Incorporated in both Pennsylvania and Delaware, the university's two campuses are located in Chester, Pennsylvania, and 15 miles southwest on Rt. 202, north of Wilmington, Delaware. Total university enrollment for 1984-85 is approximately 7,800. The total plant value is $100,000,000; the operating budget is $35,000,000.

The School of Management first offered graduate courses in business administration in the academic year 1967-68 with an initial class of 55 students. Currently, enrollment in all graduate programs in the School of Management is approaching 900 students, which places the school among the largest providers of management education in the area. Widener's graduate business programs are carefully selected and fully integrated; they provide comprehensive exposure to the knowledge that is essential and of lasting value to the business, institutional, industrial, or human resource manager, as well as to the professional in the specific area of taxation, accounting, or health administration. Courses are offered in the fall and spring semesters and also in the summer.

PROGRAMS OF STUDY
Graduate Business Programs of Widener University offer seven graduate degrees as well as two joint degree programs: Master of Business Administration (M.B.A.), Master of Science in taxation, Master of Science in accounting, Master of Science in industrial management, M.B.A. in health and medical services administration, and Master of Science in financial management of health institutions. Also, two joint degrees are offered: Juris Doctor (J.D.)/M.B.A. in affiliation with the Delaware Law School of Widener University; and Master of Engineering (M.E.)/M.B.A. in affiliation with Widener's School of Engineering. (Further details on specific programs may be requested from the address below.) Most of the graduate degrees can be completed on either a full- or part-time basis; classes have been scheduled during evening hours, and, recently, on weekends.

The M.B.A. program consists of the following components: (1) the Foundation Program, (2) the M.B.A. Core, and (3) the Option Courses.

● *Foundation Program* (0-24 credits). The following undergraduate course work is required of all matriculants:

	Credits
Principles of Accounting	6
Principles of Economics	6
College Mathematics	6
Managerial Accounting	3
Intermediate Economics	3
Statistics	3
Financial Management	3
Business Law	3
Marketing Research	3
Computer Science	3
Management Research Communication	3
Principles of Management	3

Students may elect to take equivalent undergraduate courses to fulfill the requirements or may select the foundation courses in the M.B.A. program.

● *The M.B.A. Core* (18 credits) seeks to furnish advanced analytical skills and helps students develop a managerial perspective. The courses are as follows:

		Credits
EC	600 Managerial Economics	3
MGT	603 Organizational Behavior	3
FIN	600 Managerial Finance	3
QA	601 Advanced Statistical Methods	3
QA	602 Management Science	3
MGT	699 Business Policy and Strategy	3

● *The Option Courses* (15 credits). The M.B.A. program offers the following options/concentrations: Managerial Accounting, Marketing Management, Production Management, Economic Analysis, Management Information Systems, and Manpower Management.

ADMISSION
Interested holders of baccalaureate degrees are invited to apply for admission to any of the graduate programs in business by (1) completing an application form, (2) paying the application fee of $15 (nonrefundable), (3) submitting two letters of recommendation, (4) having an official transcript sent from previous colleges attended, and (5) taking the Graduate Management Admission Test (GMAT). In addition to satisfying the requirements above, all applicants from non-English-speaking countries must take the Test of English as a Foreign Language (TOEFL).

EXPENSES
Tuition for the M.B.A. program is $180 per semester hour. New students are charged a registration fee of $10. All students are charged a general fee of $15 for each semester. Foreign students who are admitted must pay a deposit of $300 before receiving permission to attend (US Form I-20).

FINANCIAL ASSISTANCE
Since most graduate students attend part-time, financial assistance is generally not available. However, graduate students can receive financial aid through the Guaranteed Student Loan Program via a private bank or other participating lender. Further questions should be addressed to the Financial Aid Office, 215-499-4169.

PLACEMENT
Both undergraduate and graduate students make use of the placement office, which is visited annually by representatives of some 200 companies.

CORRESPONDENCE
For further information, contact
Office of Graduate Business Programs
School of Management
Widener University
Chester, Pennsylvania 19013
Attn: *Director of pertinent program*
Telephone: 215-499-4305
on the Pennsylvania Campus
302-478-3000, extension 225
on the Delaware Campus

The part-time Master of Business Administration (M.B.A.) program at Wilfrid Laurier University (WLU) provides its students with the current theoretical and conceptual development of the management literature and insights into today's modern practices. The program helps students acquire managerial expertise so they can accept the responsibilities of initiating and implementing operational plans. The philosophy of the M.B.A. program is to prepare managers for more responsible positions in Canadian society.

PROGRAM OF STUDY

The program provides students with
• an understanding of organizational and national policy;
• an ability to establish administrative structures to facilitate policy implementation;
• an ability to recognize, conceptualize, articulate, and resolve effectively business problems;
• an ability to research and analyze appropriate corporate/community conditions, needs, and limits for purposeful change;
• an ability to recognize and appreciate corporate/social influences on employees;
• an ability to lead and redirect employees to realize corporate policy.

The Master of Business Administration degree differs from the liberal arts degree, in that the M.B.A. is, by intent, professional in nature. WLU's M.B.A. program is designed to assure a distinct professional flavor aimed at providing advanced study in business in the greater Kitchener-Waterloo community. The program is intended to give a unique blend of the academic and the applied. It is the school's belief that the approach to problems benefits from the combination of theoretical and practical backgrounds.

Most of the students in the proposed program will come from and return to the regional business community. Thus, the M.B.A. will be a terminal degree for most. Nevertheless, recognition is given to a necessary academic environment for all students, particularly for those who may later wish to continue their education for the doctorate at another university.

The M.B.A. program structure makes maximum use of group work and faculty-student seminars. Small student groups are formed which represent a cross section of their ages and experiences. Groups are expected to prepare and present case assignments. Lectures and discussions involve faculty teams and participation of adjunct faculty from the business community. Class assignments utilize the literature of business, both academic and professional.

ADMISSION

Students will be admitted to the university by the university's Graduate Council. The School of Business and Economics will operate an M.B.A. Admissions Committee to make recommendations to the university's Graduate Council concerning specific applicant admissions.

The program size will be restricted to 50 students in each year of the program. These students will be selected as follows: (1) approximately one third will have substantial business management experience at a senior level in larger firms, (2) approximately one third will have small business management experience, and (3) approximately one third will have only limited business experience.

Admission requirements include the following:
• a minimum of three years of full-time working experience (it is assumed that all students will have full-time jobs),
• a bachelor's degree from a university or college of recognized standing,
• at least a B standing in the final year of the undergraduate program,
• personal suitability for a graduate program in business administration, including an acceptable score on the Graduate Management Admission Test (GMAT).

A limited number of applicants who do not meet all of the above requirements may be admitted. Application for the fall semester must be received by early May.

EXPENSES

Application fee.................. $ 25
An application fee of $25 must accompany each application for it to be activated. Certified check or money order should be made payable to Wilfrid Laurier University—M.B.A. This fee is not refundable and is not applicable to any other costs incurred.
Qualifying phase—per one term course..................... 133
(All qualifying year courses are one-term courses.)
Master's phase.................. 414
Per term registration fee (for first six terms)—students must maintain continuous registration—three semesters per year until graduation
Per term registration thereafter... 206

CORRESPONDENCE

Inquiries should be addressed to
M.B.A. Program Director
School of Business and Economics
Wilfrid Laurier University
Waterloo, Ontario N2L 3C5
Canada
Telephone: 519-884-1970
Telex: 069-5476
Cable: "Interbusiness"

The Atkinson Graduate School of Management was established in 1974 by Willamette University to offer an innovative program in management, combining the disciplines of business administration and public administration. Created with the goal of equipping present and future administrators with skills in the management of both public and private enterprise, the school is the first of its kind in the Northwest. Versed in the problems, concepts, and techniques of management as they appear in all types of organizations, graduates of the school are well prepared for professional managerial careers.

Located in Salem, Oregon, 45 miles south of Portland, Willamette University's campus adjoins the grounds of the Oregon State Capitol. The campus is close to state institutions, courts of law, state and city libraries, and Salem's Civic Center, and to business and other organizations in Portland and the mid-Willamette Valley. This proximity presents students at the Atkinson School with a wide variety of internship and job opportunities and the ability to observe business and government processes and meet frequently with practitioners.

Some students combine law and management studies in a four-year joint degree program carried out in cooperation with the Willamette University College of Law.

Superior teaching ability and scholarship are essential for selection and advancement of the faculty. The school's faculty have wide experience in business, government, and graduate education. The school is small enough to permit individualized attention. Enrollment in the fall term of 1985 included 85 full-time and 50 part-time students.

PROGRAM OF STUDY
The Master of Management (M.M.) is a distinctive academic degree awarded in recognition of successful completion of a demanding educational experience requiring four semesters of full-time study. Every graduate completes first-year courses in economics, finance, quantitative methods, organizational behavior, accounting, legal processes, and the relationships among government, business, and society. This core is designed to provide students with the analytic tools, skills, and concepts that are applicable in any managerial environment.

An internship or a research project is required of all students. Usually completed during the summer between the two years of the program, the internship offers each student an opportunity to apply tools, skills, and concepts in a work environment.

Each student structures his or her second-year course of study to fit individual career objectives. This flexibility permits concentration in areas such as small business, public management, organizational development, finance, accounting, and other subjects. The second year is designed to help the student further develop and apply analytic tools through the use of cases, projects, and practicums.

Throughout the program, special emphasis is placed on developing each student's understanding of the interplay of business and governmental processes. The private sector manager is equipped to deal effectively with public sector organizations, to comprehend governmental processes, and to explain his or her organization's role to labor, consumer, environmental, and other groups. The public sector manager graduates with an understanding of business and is equipped to manage public organizations with analytic tools as well as knowledge of the social and political environment.

ADMISSION
The admission decision takes into consideration important variables that reflect intellectual capacity and motivation. Applicants are evaluated on the basis of an overall achievement record, including transcripts, test scores, references, and records of leadership in extracurricular activities, employment, or military service. Maturity and a clear sense of purpose are important. There are no curriculum prerequisites; the Atkinson School seeks a diverse student body of men and women from all academic disciplines.

Specific requirements include a bachelor's degree from an accredited college. Candidates are required to take the Graduate Management Admission Test (GMAT). Candidates interested primarily in public sector management may take either the GMAT or the Graduate Record Examinations (GRE).

Applications are considered as soon as they are complete. Financial aid awards are announced by April 1. Full-time students should plan to enter the program at the beginning of the academic year only.

EXPENSES
Tuition for the 1985-86 academic year is $6,950. Single students should budget $11,700 per academic year total expenses. Students may expect to earn between $2,400 and $6,000 from their work as full-time summer interns.

FINANCIAL ASSISTANCE
Financial aid in the form of loans, grants, scholarships, and part-time employment is available and awarded on the basis of the student's qualifications and financial need. Applicants for financial assistance based on need must submit requests through the Graduate and Professional School Financial Aid Service (GAPSFAS) or College Scholarship Service Financial Aid Form.

PLACEMENT
The employment pattern of Atkinson graduates reflects the broad diversity and utility of the M.M. degree; typically 70 percent of the graduates work in business and 30 percent in government or not-for-profit organizations. The career development office offers a variety of programs to inform students about the career applications of their education, and assists in career planning, job search strategies, and internship development.

CORRESPONDENCE
For further information or to request an application for admission, please write or call

Director of Admissions
Geo. H. Atkinson Graduate School of Management
Willamette University
Salem, Oregon 97301
Telephone: 503-370-6440

William Carey College was founded in 1906 as a private coeducational institution known as South Mississippi College. The college is in the heart of the Sun Belt with aggressive business enterprise very much a part of the scene. The college is accredited by the Southern Association of Colleges and Schools and the Board of Trustees of the Institutions of Higher Learning of the state of Mississippi; it is also a member of the National Commission on Accrediting as well as the American Council on Education.

The student population includes undergraduates as well as graduate students in business education, music, and psychology. The Graduate Center for Management Development of the School of Business, William Carey College, is an integral part of the Graduate Division, offering a year-round evening program leading to the degree of Master of Business Administration (M.B.A.). Master's degree requirements can be fulfilled entirely at the center in Gulfport; additional expansion is expected in Hattiesburg in 1986.

PROGRAM OF STUDY

The program leading to the Master of Business Administration degree is aimed at preparing managers with multiple responsibilities rather than staff specialists. In addition, it is the desire of the Center for Management Development to provide managers for a widely diverse group of enterprises. Courses in the program are developed with the idea of a manager needing to be a well-rounded, vibrant purveyor of ideas and activity. In addition, a facility with both quantitative and qualitative methodology is an overriding goal.

The program requires a background in accounting principles, economic principles, money and banking, investment and corporate finance, management and marketing principles, as well as business economic statistics and business law. Students lacking the background must complete the missing foundation (prerequisite) courses or their equivalent in order to gain regular admittance to the program.

The program is specific in thrust and nature with required courses in Management, Decision Making, Business Ethics, Accounting, Quantitative Analysis, the Manager in Business and Society, Managerial Economics, Personnel and Industrial Relations, as well as Marketing, Managerial Finance, and Production. Emphasis may be on management or marketing by the selection of optional courses. The program may be completed in 18 months.

ADMISSION

Students may be admitted to the program in August, November, February, and June. The admission process requires the following steps:

● The applicant must hold a bachelor's degree from an accredited college or university.

● The applicant must submit a completed application for admission form with a nonrefundable $10 application fee.

● An official undergraduate transcript from each previous institution of higher learning is to be sent directly by that institution to the Graduate Center for Management Development, William Carey College.

● An applicant should have demonstrated in his or her undergraduate work an aptitude for study on the graduate level.

● The prospective student must take the Graduate Management Admission Test (GMAT) and submit the results to the Graduate Center for Management Development.

● International students coming from countries where English is not the major language will be required to demonstrate effective use of the English language by submitting their objective scores on the Test of English as a Foreign Language (TOEFL).

EXPENSES

Fees per semester were $99 per credit hour for 1985. Tuition and fees are subject to revision by the College Board of Trustees. Tuition is same for in-state and out-of-state students. Apartments with cooking facilities, having direct access to the beach, are available at the following rates: three persons sharing an apartment at $150 per month; two persons sharing an apartment at $210 per month. Utilities are paid, but phone is not included.

FINANCIAL ASSISTANCE

Some financial assistance is available. Further information may be obtained from the School of Business directly.

CORRESPONDENCE

For further information or to request an application for admission, please write or call

Dr. F. Ed. Weldon, Dean
Graduate Center for Management
  Development
William Carey College
Hattiesburg, Mississippi 39401
Telephone: 601-582-5051,
  extension 256 or 225
  or
Jerry Morgan
William Carey College on the Coast
1856 Beach Drive
Gulfport, Mississippi 39501
Telephone: 601-896-4455

Wilmington College, founded in 1967, is a private liberal-arts-oriented institution offering undergraduate and graduate degrees. The college's main campus is located approximately six miles from the city of Wilmington, 45 minutes from Philadelphia, and easily accessible by air, rail, and bus.

Graduate programs were introduced in 1977, beginning with the Master of Business Administration (M.B.A.) degree. The Master of Science (M.S.) degree in management and supervision followed in 1983. The programs are accredited by the Commission on Higher Education of the Middle States Association of Colleges and Schools.

PROGRAMS OF STUDY
The central objective of the Wilmington College M.B.A. program is to develop an individual, the business professional, who will understand decision-making methodology and its applications in a high risk and often uncalculable environment. This is almost always done in an atmosphere of incomplete information necessitating flexibility and creativity. These skills are applicable to either the private or public sector.

This undertaking requires an educational experience which, while providing specific tools and skills, also emphasizes creative thinking and problem solving. The program is offered through a series of closely coordinated eight-week modules, and is organized and scheduled to accommodate the needs of persons who maintain full-time employment while pursuing their degree. Classes are scheduled on weekday evenings and on Saturday mornings. Ten core courses are required for program completion. Two additional courses are to be selected from the elective offerings.

The M.S. degree program is designed to develop and refine the administrative skills of supervisors, coordinators, and managers in the private and public sectors. Both the administrative management and personnel management options provide administrators and others with the skills that are needed to function successfully in an increasingly complex work force.

To fulfill the requirements of the M.S. degree program, students must complete a common core of 18 semester hours and one of two 15-semester-hour concentrations—administrative management or personnel management. A capstone three-semester-hour independent study course is also required.

The application of the knowledge and skills acquired in the classroom is expected to be applied to the student's work as soon as possible. Courses are offered in special accelerated eight-week block formats for the convenience of the student.

ADMISSION
Wilmington College is a nondiscriminatory institution of higher learning and welcomes applications from men and women of every race, color, creed, and national origin. Admission is granted to students who show promise of success. Multiple criteria are considered for admissions and special attention is directed toward the applicant's present motivation and employment setting.

To be considered for unconditional acceptance, the applicant must have completed an admission interview and have the following on file:
● official transcript from an accredited college/university or degree-granting institution verifying completion of a bachelor's degree, and
● all forms and recommendations completed.

A minimum of three years of work experience is also preferred.

Students may be admitted on conditional status by the Academic Vice President; however, students must remove their conditional status prior to the completion of 12 semester hours from the time of their admission in order to maintain graduate standing.

The applicant should call or write for the necessary forms using the information given in the "Correspondence" section. The applicant must then complete the following steps: (1) return the completed application with a $20 application fee, (2) include all official undergraduate and/or graduate transcripts, (3) have two evaluation forms completed and returned by persons who recommend the applicant for admission, and (4) establish a date for an interview with one of the following offices: M.B.A.—Graduate and Conference Center, Georgetown or Silver Lake; M.S.—New Castle, Graduate and Conference Center, Dover Air Force Base or Georgetown.

EXPENSES
Costs for the 1985-86 school year were $430 per three-credit course. A $20 application fee and a $25 registration fee are required. Books are an additional expense. Tuition and fee assessments are subject to change without notice.

FINANCIAL ASSISTANCE
Financial aid is available in the form of low-interest loans and/or part-time work. Federally funded support includes the Guaranteed Student Loan (GSL), the National Direct Student Loan (NDSL), and the College Work-Study Program (CWS). These funds are provided to supplement the student's resources and include allowances for tuition, books and supplies, transportation, and modest living expenses.

CORRESPONDENCE
For further information and application materials, please write or call the pertinent addressee listed below.

Graduate and Conference Center
(M.S. & M.B.A. Programs)
6th and King Streets
Wilmington, Delaware 19801
Telephone: 302-655-5400

Georgetown (D.T.C.C.) (M.S. & M.B.A. Programs)
P.O. Box 610
Georgetown, Delaware 19947
Telephone: 302-865-7052

Dover Air Force Base (M.S. Program)
436 ABG/DPE
Dover, Delaware 19902-5065
Telephone: 302-736-6204

Silver Lake (M.B.A. Program)
821 Silver Lake Boulevard
Dover, Delaware 19901
Telephone: 302-734-2594

Winona State University nestles amid the bluffs of the Mississippi River which flows not more than 10 blocks from campus. Founded in 1857, Winona State is the oldest public university west of the Mississippi. It is one of the seven universities in the Minnesota State University System along with St. Cloud State, Mankato State, Bemiji State, Moorhead State, Southwest State, and Metro State Universities. The city of Winona is a city of colleges and universities. Although the city has only 26,000 in population, two private colleges along with Winona State infuse over 7,000 students into the community each fall. Winona is located in the southeastern corner of Minnesota two and a half hours from Minneapolis-St. Paul, five hours from Chicago, and three hours from Madison. It is directly across the river from Wisconsin, and less than 50 miles from the Iowa border to the south.

The College of Business offers majors in accounting, economics, business education and office administration, and business administration with concentrations in management, marketing, personnel administration, and public administration.

Winona State has satellite centers throughout the region, with a major center at Rochester, Minnesota, which boasts the Mayo Clinic and a large IBM production and development plant as major industries.

PROGRAM OF STUDY

The Master of Business Administration (M.B.A.) at Winona State is a part-time evening program developed to meet the needs of upwardly mobile middle management in both Winona and Rochester. It is a general program of study following the philosophy of the School of Business and Industry that a general rather than specialized course of study provides students with the most appropriate education to allow them to advance within their institutions. The student can, however, with the choice of electives, projects, and papers within many of the required M.B.A. core courses, study one particular industry or functional area within an industry.

The program of study has three components: the prerequisite areas of knowledge, the M.B.A. core, and the M.B.A. elective courses. The prerequisite areas of knowledge are Principles of Micro- and Macroeconomics, Principles of Financial Accounting, Principles of Marketing, Principles of Management, Statistics, Computer Programming, Finance, Business Law, and Communication Skills. These requirements may be met through undergraduate courses taken at an accredited college or university, or through an approved testing program.

The M.B.A. core includes the following courses: Accounting for Management, Macroeconomic Theory and Forecasting, Research Methodology, Management Law, Managerial Economics, Financial Management, Production Management and Inventory Control, Marketing Analysis, Human Resource Development and Administration, Business Policies, and Small Business Administration Consulting Project. The emphasis in the core is on management's role in each of the functional areas of business and on practical applications of classroom theory.

M.B.A. electives of three additional courses complete the program of study. The electives allow students to explore in depth one area of the curriculum or to take courses that add breadth to their programs

ADMISSION

The Master of Business Administration program at Winona State is open to qualified students who hold an undergraduate degree from an accredited college or university regardless of undergraduate major. Those with no background in business can expect a year of full-time study to complete the areas of knowledge outlined as prerequisites to the program.

Factors considered in admission to the program are the undergraduate gradepoint average, the score earned on the Graduate Management Admission Test (GMAT), the holding of an undergraduate degree, and evidence of an aptitude for successful completion of an advanced degree in business administration.

EXPENSES

Graduate resident tuition is $39.25 per credit hour. Graduate nonresident tuition is $68.80 per credit hour. Fees are $6.50 per credit. Classes taken off campus may have different fees. A $10 initial matriculation fee is charged.

FINANCIAL ASSISTANCE

Graduate assistantships are available. To obtain application forms, write to the Director of the M.B.A. Program at the address listed below. A variety of student loans are also available. Those interested should contact the Financial Aids Office, Winona State University.

PLACEMENT

Master of Business Administration graduates receive placement assistance through the university's Placement Office.

CORRESPONDENCE

For further information or assistance regarding the Master of Business Administration Program, write or call
M.B.A. Director
Department of Business Administration
  and Economics
Somsen Hall, Suite 324
Winona State University
Winona, Minnesota 55987
Telephone: 507-457-5183/5170

Winthrop College is a medium-sized, state-supported, coeducational institution located in South Carolina just 20 miles south of Charlotte, North Carolina. The location enables it to draw students from the established textile corporations in the area as well as from new industry moving into the Sun Belt. Winthrop's graduate programs were established in 1972 and offer evening instruction leading to the Master of Business Administration (M.B.A.) degree. The graduate enrollment is limited to 200 students, allowing frequent contact with the faculty. Both the school's graduate and undergraduate programs are accredited by the American Assembly of Collegiate Schools of Business (AACSB).

PROGRAM OF STUDY
The graduate program is designed to serve three groups of students: (1) those in management or technical positions who wish to enhance their careers; (2) those in nonbusiness fields who wish to move into the business sector; and (3) those who, having completed a baccalaureate degree program, wish to undertake advanced study before establishing a career.

The M.B.A. program is 36 semester hours in length for students who have an accredited degree in business administration. Prerequisite courses in accounting, finance, management, marketing, economics, quantitative methods, and the legal environment of business are offered for those who need them. The length of time required to complete each degree varies with the individual, depending on the student's academic background and pace of study.

All courses are offered in the evenings, and students can vary course loads from 3 to 12 hours a semester. A maximum of 12 semester hours of graduate transfer credit from an AACSB-accredited graduate program may be accepted toward the degree.

The Master of Business Administration degree program consists of eight required courses and four elective courses. The curriculum is broad-based and provides students with a generalized background in business concepts. Courses in finance, personnel, accounting, marketing, economics, quantitative methods, and public policy develop knowledge in these areas and strengthen decision-making abilities. No thesis or comprehensive examination is required; however, in a required business policy course students integrate all aspects of the program.

Winthrop's graduate instructors employ a variety of teaching methods. Lectures, case studies, team projects, individual projects, and role play enable students to develop flexibility and creativity. Interaction with faculty and exposure to the various backgrounds of other students are also key elements.

The academic year is divided into three terms: fall semester, spring semester, and summer session. Students may enter the program at the beginning of any term.

ADMISSION
Admission is limited to graduates of accredited colleges and universities who show high promise of success in graduate study. Applicants must provide (1) a completed application form, (2) transcripts of all college-level work, and (3) scores on the required Graduate Management Admission Test (GMAT). Evaluation is based primarily on a combination of the GMAT score and undergraduate grade-point average. An undergraduate degree in business administration is not required. Applicants whose native language is not English must submit a score of at least 550 on the Test of English as a Foreign Language (TOEFL).

EXPENSES
Expenses for 1985-86 were:
Application fee, one-time only	$15
Registration fee, per term	5
Tuition, per credit hour	
Residents of South Carolina	55
Nonresidents	55
Parking fee, per year	20
Books and supplies	Dependent on course load

FINANCIAL ASSISTANCE
A limited number of graduate assistantships are available in the School of Business Administration and elsewhere on campus. The stipend varies according to the number of hours worked, ranging from 5 to 20 hours per week. Graduate assistants pay tuition and fees based on rates for South Carolina residents. Applications may be obtained from the Coordinator of Graduate Studies in the School of Business Administration. The college also offers forms of financial assistance through the Winthrop Financial Aid Office.

PLACEMENT
Winthrop College maintains an active placement office to assist students in finding jobs. Representatives from business and industry regularly recruit on campus.

CORRESPONDENCE
For information about the graduate programs of study offered by Winthrop College, write or call
> Coordinator of Graduate Studies
> School of Business Administration
> Winthrop College
> Rock Hill, South Carolina 29733
> Telephone: 803-323-2186

The Graduate Management Programs at Worcester Polytechnic Institute (WPI) equip engineers and managers with the tools and training they need to manage in rapidly changing organizations, operate with limited resources, and move products through the production cycle quickly and efficiently. The programs stress the vital issues facing managers in today's technological environments—issues such as innovation, productivity management, and computer applications and information systems.

WPI's Graduate Management Program was established in 1970 with the Master of Science degree in Management (M.S.M.). In 1980 the Master of Business Administration (M.B.A.) degree was introduced. More than 300 graduate management students are enrolled in both full- and part-time programs. WPI is located on an attractive 56-acre campus within one hour's drive from Boston.

PROGRAMS OF STUDY

WPI offers two graduate management programs: Master of Business Administration and Master of Science in Management. The M.B.A. is recommended for individuals seeking to commence or advance their management careers in technological environments. The M.S.M. is recommended for those seeking to develop basic management skills while also advancing in technical specialties.

The M.B.A. program consists of 12 core courses and three electives. The core covers marketing, production, organizational science, economics, and business policy. It also includes statistics, computer applications, and quantitative methods. Beyond the core, three options are available for satisfying the 15-course requirement. Option 1 consists of advanced management courses in such areas as management information systems, productivity management, and organizational change. Option 2 is the technical option which may be satisfied through graduate courses in a field of science or engineering. Option 3, independent study, enables students to pursue in depth and under a flexible schedule a particular aspect of a core subject, integrate several of the core subjects, or perform applied research.

The M.S.M. program requires 12 courses including 7 core courses and a 5-course specialty. The core includes accounting, finance, organizational science, production, quantitative methods,

marketing, and economics. The specialty program is a cohesive set of five courses including a significant technical component. Specialty programs are available in engineering management, production/operations management, and management information systems. Additional opportunities are available in conjunction with risk management engineering and manufacturing engineering.

Throughout every course emphasis is placed on managing the technology of the 1980s with both theoretical frameworks and applications-oriented techniques. Instructors use a variety of instructional methods including lectures, discussions, case studies, computer simulations, and independent study.

All classes are held weekdays from 6:30 to 9:30 p.m. and meet once a week for 14 weeks. A seven-week summer term is also available.

ADMISSION

Admission to the Graduate Management Program is granted to applicants whose academic and professional records indicate the likelihood of success in a challenging academic program. Applicants should have the analytic aptitude and academic preparation necessary to complete a technology-oriented management program. This includes a minimum of four semesters of college-level mathematics, preferably to include two semesters of calculus, and computer programming ability. Noncredit courses will be required in mathematics and computer programming for those applicants who do not meet these standards.

Applicants are required to submit an application form, official transcripts of all college work, three letters of recommendation, and official Graduate Management Admission Test (GMAT) results. Applicants whose native language is not English must submit official results of the Test of English as a Foreign Language (TOEFL).

EXPENSES

For the academic year 1985-86, tuition for graduate courses was $741 per three-credit course. Tuition for a full-time graduate student taking eight courses per year was $5,928.

FINANCIAL ASSISTANCE

A limited number of research and teaching assistantships are available for full-time students. Specific questions on financial assistance should be directed to the Graduate Management Programs Administrator.

PLACEMENT

The many services of WPI's Office of Graduate and Career Plans are available to all WPI students and alumni. Recruiters from over 300 different organizations including large and small industrial firms, government, civic, and professional associations visit WPI annually. The office also maintains a large reference library for WPI students and alumni.

CORRESPONDENCE

For further information, please write or call

Graduate Management Programs
Worcester Polytechnic Institute
Worcester, Massachusetts 01609
Telephone: 617-793-5218

WRIGHT STATE UNIVERSITY

DAYTON, OHIO

Wright State is one of Ohio's newest and most exciting centers of learning. Beginning as a campus operated jointly by the Ohio State University and Miami University, Wright State was accredited as an independent university in 1967. Today, it offers 9 different baccalaureate degrees and 30 programs of graduate and professional study.

Located on a 618-acre campus northeast of Dayton, the university enjoys both the stimulation of a metropolitan area and the atmosphere of a rural setting. Enrollment is now approximately 15,000 with over 500 students enrolled in the Master of Business Administration (M.B.A.) program.

A central objective of the College of Business and Administration is to assist individuals to become qualified professional managers. To provide advanced professional study in business administration, the Master of Business Administration degree program was instituted in 1967. In another noteworthy step, the Master of Science (M.S.) degree program in logistics management was established in 1985. The M.B.A. and the M.S. programs are designed to serve the following two groups: those students with undergraduate degrees in business who want an in-depth program of advanced study; and those students whose undergraduate program has been in the liberal arts, sciences, or other technical or professional areas who desire advanced management education. The M.B.A. program is accredited by the American Assembly of Collegiate Schools of Business (AACSB). The college also offers a graduate program leading to the degree of Master of Science in social and applied economics.

PROGRAMS OF STUDY

The Master of Business Administration and M.S. in logistics management programs are planned on an individual basis, considering the student's background, needs, and objectives. This allows the programs to be built upon undergraduate work in business or other fields of study. The aims of the programs include the following:

- emphasize broad concepts and analytical tools rather than descriptive information and techniques;
- seek to develop and enlarge the individual's understanding of the economic, political, social, and technological environment and the manager's responsibility to these environments;

- provide the student with the opportunity to develop particular competence in a special field of his or her own choosing;
- seek to provide the student with a foundation for continuing education and development.

Completion of the programs normally requires four quarters on a full-time basis. In addition, all candidates must have or obtain a knowledge of fundamentals in the following areas: accounting, business law, economics, finance, management, marketing, mathematics, and statistics.

The curriculum of the M.B.A. program includes a minimum of 48 quarter hours with a thesis option. Areas of concentration include accountancy, finance, financial administration, health care management, logistics management, management, management science, and marketing. The program consists of required courses (30 hours), concentration area (6-12 hours), and elective (6-12 hours). Internships are available for students who could benefit from a planned program of paid business experience.

The curriculum of the M.S. in logistics management program requires a minimum of 48 quarter hours. The program includes course work in logistics, business, and systems areas with required courses (24 hours), concentration (18 hours with 6 hours for thesis), and elective (6 hours).

ADMISSION

Admission to the M.B.A. and M.S. in logistics management programs requires application to the School of Graduate Studies. All applicants must hold a baccalaureate degree from a regionally accredited institution and must submit official transcripts and Graduate Management Admission Test (GMAT) scores.

Admission is based on a variety of criteria, including prior academic performance, test scores, intellectual capacity (quantitative and analytical skills), preparedness for graduate study, and other factors that in the judgment of the College of Business and Administration indicate potential for successful graduate study.

EXPENSES

Per quarter	In-state	Out-of-state
Instructional and general fees	$680	$ 680
Nonresident tuition		541
Books and supplies, estimate	105	105
Total	$785	$1,326

Part-time fees are $64 per credit hour for Ohio residents.

The university does have limited housing for single and married students. The cost of on-campus housing starts at $595. Requests for on-campus housing should be made early to the Director of Housing.

Off-campus housing is generally available. Apartments in nearby communities are available at a cost from $200 per month.

FINANCIAL ASSISTANCE

Graduate assistantships are available for qualified students and carry a stipend of $3,000-5,000 for three quarters. Graduate assistantships also include a complete tuition waiver. All interested students should apply.

PLACEMENT

University Placement provides assistance in securing full-time career employment for graduate students. Services are offered without charge.

CORRESPONDENCE

For further information, please write to
Director of the M.B.A. (or M.S. in
Logistics Management) Program
College of Business and Administration
Wright State University
Dayton, Ohio 45435

Xavier University, established in 1831, is located in the heart of Cincinnati. Its main campus and Edgecliff campus have an enrollment of over 7,000 students in undergraduate and graduate programs. Xavier University is a private, coeducational institution with Colleges of Arts and Sciences, Business Administration, Continuing Education, and a Graduate School. The university's total enrollment is approximately 7,000 students, about evenly divided between undergraduate and graduate students. The students, faculty, and staff represent all faiths.

The McDonald Memorial Library on the main campus is a modern building with open stacks allowing users free access to most library materials. Students also have access to Brennan Memorial Library on the Edgecliff campus. The collection in McDonald numbers over 260,000 volumes of books and periodicals and over 300,000 pieces of microfilm. The library receives more than 1,700 periodical subscriptions. In addition, over 3,000 recordings, both musical and spoken word, are available in a listening area. Special collections include incunabula, rare books, manuscripts of literary and historical figures, and the University Archives.

PROGRAMS OF STUDY

The Graduate Program in Hospital and Health Administration at Xavier University offers a program leading to the degree of Master of Hospital and Health Administration. The program is fully accredited by the Accrediting Commission on Graduate Education for Hospital Administration.

The goals of the program are to develop individuals who are
- aware of the impacts of technology, socioeconomic trends, disease patterns, and individual, societal, and professional values upon the determination of health policy and health care utilization, organizing, and financing;
- competent in the application of conceptual (organizational analysis and policy development) skills, technical (financial, quantitative, and information-processing) skills, and personal development (self-discipline and leadership) skills;
- prepared to integrate these skills in working with representatives of consumer groups, professional organizations, and societal institutions, both public and private, in the development and operation of socially responsive health and medical care programs and services;

- able to assume upon graduation responsible administrative, policy development, and corporate management positions in hospitals and a variety of selected health care environments;
- motivated to apply the concepts of lifelong learning to build upon the foundation of their experience; and
- willing to assume increasing leadership roles as they progress in their career development.

The program of study is divided into two major segments. The first segment consists of four semesters spent on campus, beginning in the fall semester. During this period, 50 semester hours of graduate course work are pursued. In the second segment, students complete a minimum eight-month administrative residency in a health care facility. The student registers for 10 credit hours during the residency period and completes a thesis at this time. The program encompasses a total of 60 credit hours over the course of two calendar years.

The program's student body consists of approximately 40 students plus 40 residents. The average age of the student is 28. Students' backgrounds include health care administration, clinical and nonclinical health care, business experience, and recent undergraduate study. The variety of backgrounds provides for a rich interaction and contributes significantly to the students' learning experiences. A dual Master of Business Administration/Master of Health Administration degree program is offered.

ADMISSION

Application to the program should be completed by May 15. All applicants must take the Graduate Management Admission Test (GMAT) and must show evidence of a minimum cumulative grade-point average of 2.75 on a 4.0 scale. Students are accepted for study each fall.

EXPENSES

Tuition fees are $158 per semester hour (fees as of fall 1985). Students will ordinarily receive compensation from the health care facility in which they serve their residency during the second phase of the program.

FINANCIAL ASSISTANCE

Limited financial aid is available in the form of partial scholarships, deferred tuition payment plans, and loan funds. A limited amount may be available in Federal U.S. Public Health Service Traineeships.

PLACEMENT

To assist graduates in career development, the Alumni Office maintains a job placement service as well as a job information service. A bimonthly newsletter lists all job openings which come to the attention of the office.

CORRESPONDENCE

For further program information and applications, write to

Edward J. Arlinghas, Ph.D., Director
Graduate Program in Hospital and
  Health Administration
Xavier University, Edgecliff Campus,
  Department E
2220 Victory Parkway
Cincinnati, Ohio 45206

Xavier University was founded in 1831 and opened its first graduate program in 1946. The Master of Business Administration (M.B.A.) program was added in 1952. Total university enrollment is approximately 6,500 students including 2,700 graduate students. Approximately 1,600 students are enrolled in the M.B.A. program. Most of these students are pursuing part-time programs and maintaining full-time management-related positions. About 75 M.B.A. students are enrolled full time.

The campus of Xavier University, located 10 minutes from downtown Cincinnati, includes approximately 100 scenic acres, centered around a tree-lined mall. Graduate business classrooms and administrative offices are housed in a modern building dedicated in 1981.

Within the College of Business Administration Building, M.B.A. students have access to the university's VAX-11/780 computer system and a microcomputer laboratory. Workshops, consultants, and other supportive services enable students to utilize these computer resources in a wide range of problems, cases, and reports.

A modern library contains more than 260,000 books and 1,500 periodicals. The library also provides computer-assisted literature searches of business-related databases. Through the Greater Cincinnati Library Consortium, students also have access to the collections of most major libraries in the area.

The thriving business community of Cincinnati offers outstanding opportunities for M.B.A. students to gain practical experiences. Business people are frequent speakers in the classrooms, and at student organization meetings, and top executives serve on the dean's Advisory Council.

PROGRAM OF STUDY

The degree of Master of Business Administration is a professional degree designed to meet the needs of persons in business, preparing them for increasing executive responsibilities. Students with no previous business background take a series of eight prerequisite courses (25 semester hours), while those with sufficient undergraduate course work can accelerate their programs by commencing study at the advanced level. Requirements for the M.B.A. degree include 11 courses (33 semester hours) at the advanced level. Eighteen semester hours are in the six core areas (accounting, economics, administrative operations, marketing, quantitative business methods, and business finance) and 9 semester hours are in an area of concentration selected by the student. Three hours in a seminar on business administration problems and three hours in an elective course are also required. The lecture, case method, and incident process are all used as teaching techniques in the M.B.A. program.

Students may earn the M.B.A. degree by full- or part-time graduate work. Courses are offered days, evenings, and on Saturday mornings. In addition to its program in Cincinnati, Xavier has M.B.A. Centers for part-time students on the campuses of Ohio Dominican College in Columbus, Ohio, and Transylvania University in Lexington, Kentucky.

ADMISSION

Admission is open to the student with a baccalaureate degree from an accredited college or university. The program is open to graduates in science, liberal arts, education, engineering, or other fields. In evaluating a student's application for admission, primary emphasis will be given to undergraduate grade-point average and scores on the Graduate Management Admission Test (GMAT). However, the applicant's intellectual development during the course of his or her previous academic career, employment experience, and other evidences of motivation for graduate study will also be considered. A candidate may enter the Master of Business Administration program at the beginning of any semester or term. The fall semester begins in September, and the spring semester starts in January. Two summer terms are available for continuing students who wish to accelerate their program of study.

Applicants for admission to the M.B.A. program must submit the appropriate form, official transcripts of undergraduate credits and degree, and scores from the Graduate Management Admission Test.

EXPENSES

Tuition during the 1985-86 academic year was $158 per credit hour. Expenditures for textbooks and class materials are supplemental costs. Limited housing is available in residence halls on campus; however, most graduate students find housing in one of the pleasant residential areas nearby.

FINANCIAL ASSISTANCE

A limited number of graduate assistantships carrying tuition waiver and stipend are available. A limited number of full- and half-tuition scholarships are also available. Assistantships and scholarships are awarded on the basis of merit. Deadline for application is March 31 for the following academic year.

PLACEMENT

The Career Planning and Placement Office offers a program of courses and professional seminars to help the student construct a career plan designed to meet particular needs and complement the student's strengths. In addition, the center offers on-campus interviewing opportunities.

CORRESPONDENCE

For further information, call or write
Nancy S. Tom
College of Business Administration
M.B.A. Program
Xavier University
Cincinnati, Ohio 45207
Telephone: 513-745-3525

The Yale School of Organization and Management prepares men and women of exceptional promise, motivation, and achievement for careers as managers in business, government, and nonprofit enterprises. Through a two-year graduate program leading to the Master in Public and Private Management (M.P.P.M.) degree, the school has developed an important new approach to management education. The fundamental concerns of a traditional school of business administration and those of a school of public administration or public policy are combined in a single, rigorous, and comprehensive curriculum. Yale believes that this approach is particularly appropriate in a modern world in which the public and private sectors are increasingly intertwined. The school's objective is to develop in its graduates the skills and understanding they need to work effectively in the modern world, to move at levels of leadership from one sector to another, and to cope with new institutions and institutions undergoing rapid change.

The school is housed in a beautifully coordinated cluster of new and distinguished older buildings in the center of the Yale campus. Although most students choose to live in nearby private houses and apartments, the university maintains housing which is available to both single and married students.

PROGRAM OF STUDY

The M.P.P.M. program is a full-time, two-year course of study. There are two semesters each year, and enrollment is permitted only in the fall semester. The first-year curriculum gives a balanced emphasis to analytical and quantitative skills; individual, group, and organizational behavior; and the political, economic, and institutional environment of management. In the second year, emphasis is placed on advanced analytical skills and integrative management courses. Students may also take a wide range of elective courses both within the school and elsewhere in the university.

The M.P.P.M. program is distinctive for its comprehensiveness and rigor; for its humanist, noncompetitive atmosphere; and for the opportunity it offers to work closely with the school's distinguished faculty. There is an internship during the summer between the first and second years.

ADMISSION

The Yale School of Organization and Management seeks to enroll men and women with diverse academic and professional backgrounds and career goals. M.P.P.M. classes include students with experience and interests in public, private, and nonprofit organizations. In general terms, Yale is looking for individuals who want to assume responsibility for the management of institutions within the United States and abroad, and who have demonstrated the drive, the potential for exercising leadership, and the intellectual capacity equal to such responsibility.

While some students are admitted directly from undergraduate programs, the school gives preference to applicants with work experience and especially to those who have demonstrated leadership. The school evaluates each application according to the following criteria:

• capacity and motivation for academic achievement;

• motivation and ability to cope with the complex, practical problems of organizations, to influence the outcome of events, and to work effectively with and lead others;

• personal and professional objectives.

Candidates are required to take the Graduate Management Admission Test (GMAT). Applicants whose primary language is not English are asked to take the Test of English as a Foreign Language (TOEFL). Transcripts for academic work beyond the secondary level are required, as are letters of recommendation.

Admission is done over four separate cycles, beginning in early December and extending to May.

The School of Organization and Management, together with Yale's other professional schools and graduate departments, offers various possibilities for joint degrees. Further information regarding joint degree programs is available from the M.P.P.M. Admissions Office.

Information about the school's doctoral program in administrative sciences is available from the Director of Graduate Studies.

EXPENSES

Tuition for the 1985-86 year was $10,350, plus $580 student fees and $200 hospitalization charge. Single student (dormitory) housing currently ranges in price from $1,570 to $2,270 for the academic year; married student housing rents range from $375 per month for an efficiency to $550 per month for a three-bedroom unit.

FINANCIAL ASSISTANCE

Financial assistance is available through fellowships, long-term loan programs, and other sources. All applicants for financial assistance must submit requests through the Graduate and Professional School Financial Aid Service (GAPSFAS).

PLACEMENT

Full-time staff members in the Career Development Office assist students in choosing both summer internships and permanent positions following graduation. A full recruitment schedule of presentations by representatives of public and private organizations is maintained throughout the year to enable students to discuss careers in a wide range of settings.

CORRESPONDENCE

For further information or to request an application for admission, please write or call

M.P.P.M. Admissions
Yale School of Organization and
   Management
Box 1A
New Haven, Connecticut 06520
Telephone: 203-436-3006

YORK COLLEGE OF PENNSYLVANIA

YORK, PENNSYLVANIA

York College of Pennsylvania is located in south central Pennsylvania contiguous to the city of York, population 50,000, within a metropolitan area of approximately 250,000 population. The 78-acre campus is located approximately 25 miles south of Harrisburg, 25 miles east of Gettysburg, 25 miles west of Lancaster, and 50 miles north of Baltimore, Maryland. The campus is easily accessible from Interstate 83 and the Pennsylvania Turnpike.

York College of Pennsylvania, a private and coeducational institution, enjoys a 200-year heritage. It is the legal and academic descendent of several institutions, the earliest being founded about 1776. The college welcomes students of all ages from all racial, religious, national, and socioeconomic backgrounds.

The academic year consists of two semesters of approximately 14 weeks and three summer sessions: one 3-week and two 5-week sessions. The fall semester begins early September and ends mid-December; the spring semester begins mid-January and ends mid-May. Presently, the M.B.A. program is an evening one with classes meeting one night a week from 7 to 10 p.m. on Monday through Thursday during the fall and spring semesters only.

PROGRAM OF STUDY

The program recognizes the broad-based proficiency needed by the professional manager. Therefore, achievement of the Master of Business Administration (M.B.A.) degree requires the student to have successfully completed three bodies of knowledge:

(1) prerequisite knowledge of accounting, economics, statistics, mathematics, and introductory management;

(2) a program core of 27 hours in areas of management theory and practice, quantitative and statistical decision analysis, managerial economics and accounting, human relations in management, marketing management, operations management, and business policy; and

(3) program electives of 9 hours to be divided between two groups in areas of communication concepts and skills, personnel and industrial relations, organizational theory and practice, management finance, business and government, production management, and directed study.

ADMISSION

Applicants for admission to the M.B.A. program must submit (1) a completed application form with a $15 nonrefundable fee, (2) transcripts of all college work showing satisfactory completion of a bachelor's degree and any other documents necessary to show satisfactory completion of the prerequisite body of knowledge, and (3) an official report of his or her score on the required Graduate Management Admission Test. Applications should be filed by July 15 for the fall semester and by December 15 for the spring semester for which admission is desired.

Applicants who have not satisfied the entire prerequisite body of knowledge will be required to complete successfully undergraduate courses and/or graduate-level survey courses before admission will be considered.

EXPENSES

Graduate tuition is $110 per credit. Other charges are a $5 registration fee and a $10 general fee per semester. Textbooks and required supplies and materials are in addition to the tuition and other charges.

No on-campus housing is available. Rooms and apartments are available in the community. Full food service is available.

FINANCIAL ASSISTANCE

Requests for information about financial aid should be directed to the Student Financial Aid Office, York College of Pennsylvania, Country Club Road, York, Pennsylvania 17405.

PLACEMENT

The college's Director of Placement coordinates placement activities. Services of the placement office include the listing of job opportunities as well as the coordination of interviews with employment representatives who visit the campus.

CORRESPONDENCE

For further information concerning the M.B.A. program, contact
  M.B.A. Coordinator
  York College of Pennsylvania
  Country Club Road
  York, Pennsylvania 17405

The Faculty of Administrative Studies was founded in 1965 as a professional faculty dedicated to providing the highest quality preparation for managers of all types of organizations. The faculty accepted its first students in 1966. Since then it has grown to include 55 full-time faculty members, almost all of whom hold doctoral degrees from the finest universities and who have extensive practical business and professional experience. York University's location in metropolitan Toronto has helped to attract a faculty in administrative studies which is second to none in Canada.

York has the largest graduate program in administration in Canada. About 1,300 students are currently enrolled; 400 are full-time students. Its size permits York to offer a wider range of elective courses than any similar program in the country.

The programs require 20 one-term courses, the equivalent of two years of full-time study. There are 13 required courses which provide the basic core of knowledge and skill for the practice of management. These courses develop (1) a sound background in the principles, concepts, and approaches common to all types of administration, (2) a basis for continuing communication among practicing administrators; and (3) a lasting awareness of the various managerial roles and environments. Specialization is achieved through a broad offering of electives in the second year of the graduate program.

PROGRAMS OF STUDY

The Master of Business Administration (M.B.A.) and the Master of Public Administration (M.P.A.) at York are professional degrees, awarded upon completion of a program of studies designed to prepare the graduate for a position of responsibility within business and government. The curriculum is designed for both full- and part-time students, and many classes are scheduled in the evening for persons already engaged in business and professional work.

In addition to the regular M.B.A. and M.P.A. programs, York is offering a combined M.B.A./LL.B. program within four years of study. This accelerated program is open only to a selected group of highly qualified students.

The core courses include the environmental framework of management, accounting and control, finance, marketing, microeconomics, macroeconomics, behavioral problems and issues in organization, and quantitative methods for management.

In addition to the core, each student takes 7 elective courses chosen from more than 80 electives offered each year. These may be chosen by the student to meet his or her personal objectives. Some students choose to specialize in one or two subject areas while others forego specialization in favor of acquiring greater breadth.

The second-year integrative courses consist of (1) a case course on Strategy Formulation and Implementation and (2) a policy report to the faculty. The policy report is a comprehensive description and evaluation of an actual organization, either for profit or nonprofit, with appropriate recommendations for improved performance.

The Faculty of Administrative Studies also offers a fully funded doctoral program in business administration. Areas of specialization can be finance, marketing, organizational behavior, or industrial relations and policy.

ADMISSION

Admission to the M.B.A. program is available to those who hold an undergraduate degree from a recognized university and who present evidence indicating that they can complete the graduate program successfully. Such evidence is usually in the form of an official transcript indicating the achievement of at least second-class standing in undergraduate studies, a satisfactory test score on the Graduate Management Admission Test (GMAT), and two recommendations, at least one academic. Working experience is also an important consideration.

EXPENSES

Tuition fees for Canadian citizens and landed immigrants for the Faculty of Administrative Studies at York University are $135.90 per semester course. Students who are on a student visa are required to pay $529.20 per semester course. All students are required to pay a $15 registration fee and course material fees each semester.

The residence fees for furnished apartments are $221.00 per month for a bachelor, $321.00 per month for a one-bedroom apartment, and $370.00 for a two-bedroom apartment. Off-campus housing costs vary widely. These fees are subject to change.

FINANCIAL ASSISTANCE

Assistantships, loans, bursaries, and scholarships are available to qualified candidates. The financial aid program is a varied one; its resources include private, university, and government funds. Application forms are included in each information kit or may be obtained from the Financial Aid Office, York University, North York, Ontario M3J 2R6, Canada.

PLACEMENT

The Faculty of Administrative Studies operates a comprehensive placement program including assistance in career planning, job search strategies, permanent employment, and summer employment.

CORRESPONDENCE

For further information or to request an application for admission, please call or write

Office of Student Affairs
Faculty of Administrative Studies
York University
4700 Keele Street
North York, Ontario, Canada M3J 2R6

PROGRAMS OF STUDY

The School of Business Administration offers graduate studies leading to the Master of Business Administration (M.B.A.) degree with a concentration in accounting, management, marketing, or finance.

The program is designed to enable the graduates to cope with the increased specialization of management competence and knowledge, to develop their intellectual qualities and leadership abilities, and to provide a general breadth of understanding of the factors that affect our society.

The basic M.B.A. program consists of 53 to 59 quarter hours (equivalent 36 semester hours) of graduate work. Two thirds of these hours are in the required M.B.A. core with the remainder in the area of concentration and electives. The program may be taken on a part-time basis, and courses are most frequently offered during evening hours. Part-time students will usually complete the program in two to three years, while full-time graduate students may complete the required course work in one year.

ADMISSION

Entrance to the M.B.A. program is open to all qualified men and women who show promise of success in graduate business study. Previous academic work in business subjects is not required for admission; such deficiencies may be met through accelerated foundation courses or, when approved, by examination. Admission is based on the applicant's record of undergraduate studies and score on the Graduate Management Admission Test (GMAT). Admission to the program requires an index score of at least 950 points based on the formula: 200 × undergraduate grade average (4.0 system) plus GMAT total score; or at least 1,000 points using the last 90 quarter hours (or 60 semester hours) of upper-division or post-bachelor academic work to determine the grade average in the above formula. Regular admission requirements are (1) a baccalaureate degree from an accredited institution with an unrecalculated grade-point average of 2.7 or above, and (2) satisfactory completion of the GMAT with a score of 450 or more. Individuals who do not obtain a satisfactory index score but feel they are otherwise qualified may petition the M.B.A. Director for provisional admission. All persons must complete formal application requirements before petitioning for provisional admission.

All applicants must submit scores on the Graduate Management Admission Test. Foreign students should also submit results from the Test of English as a Foreign Language (TOEFL).

EXPENSES

Tuition for Ohio residents is $43 per quarter hour; tuition for nonresidents is an additional $27 per quarter hour. Expenses for books, special equipment, and student fees are extra.

As no special campus housing is available for graduate students, students should find living quarters in the metropolitan area. Rooms are available in the immediate area at about $40 per week and apartments from about $160 per month upwards.

FINANCIAL ASSISTANCE

Financial assistance in the form of graduate assistantships, scholarships, and student loans is available to graduate students enrolled in specific degree programs. Under no circumstances will financial aid be awarded until the student has been admitted to the Graduate School.

Depending upon qualifications, graduate assistants will be assigned three kinds of duties: instruction, research, or other academic services. Normally, graduate assistantships are awarded for a period of three quarters beginning with the fall quarter. Appointees must maintain enrollment in at least 21 quarter hours of degree-credit-hour work for the regular academic year and not less than 6 quarter hours for any one quarter.

Scholarships in varying amounts for varying periods are awarded on the basis of the student's academic achievement, potential for graduate work, and financial need. They are available to both entering and enrolled students carrying at least 12 quarter hours of degree-credit work. Student loans are made through the office of the Director of Financial Aids.

Applications for assistantships and scholarships must be accompanied or preceded by application for admission to the Graduate School. To obtain admission material and information about procedures for applying for an assistantship or scholarship, write to the Dean of the Graduate School, Youngstown State University, Youngstown, Ohio 44555.

PLACEMENT

The university maintains a placement office.

CORRESPONDENCE

For further information about the M.B.A. program at Youngstown State University, write to

Director
M.B.A. Graduate Program
School of Business Administration
Youngstown State University
Youngstown, Ohio 44555

Other Schools That Require the GMAT

The schools listed below did not choose to submit a description of their graduate management program for this publication, but all of them require the GMAT of applicants for admission.

AFIT School of Systems and Logistics
American University (Italy)
Anna Maria College for Men and Women
Atlantic Provinces Association of Chartered Accountants
Averett College
Baldwin-Wallace College
Barry University
Butler University
California State University, Fresno
California State University, Northridge
California State University, Sacramento
Centenary College of Louisiana
City University of New York
Colegio Universitario Turbado
College of the Virgin Islands
Columbus College
Dowling College
Durham University
Fitchburg State College
Florida A&M University
George Mason University
GMI Engineering and Management Institute
Hampton Institute
Harding University
Houston Baptist University
International University of Africa
Iona College
Iran Center for Management Studies
Katholieke Universiteit Leuven
Kennesaw College
Krungthep (Bangkok) University
La Grange College
Lake Superior State College
Lincoln University (California)
Lincoln University (Missouri)
Loma Linda University (Loma Linda)
Long Island University (Brooklyn)
Long Island University (Greenvale)
Macquarie University
Mary Washington College
Massey University
MBA Institute
Moorhead State University
Morgan State College
National Institute of Higher Education
North Dakota State University
Northrop University
Norwegian School of Economics and Business Administration

Pace University
Pacific Christian College
Pan American University—Brownsville
Pepperdine University
Phillips University
Prairie View A&M University
Queens University of Belfast
Quinnipiac College
Quincy College
Regis College (Colorado Springs)
Rensselaer Polytechnic Institute
Rockford College
Roosevelt University
St. Francis College
Sam Houston State University
Singapore Institute of Management
Sophia University
Southern Utah State College
State University of New York at Binghamton
Syracuse University (Corning)
Troy State University (Montgomery)
Universidade Nova de Lisboa
University College
University of Alaska—Fairbanks
University of Alaska Southeast
University of Aston Management Center
University of Auckland
University of Benin
University of Birmingham
University of Guam
University of Hartford, Paris
University of Hawaii, Hilo
University of Lagos
University of Manchester (Business School)
University of Nairobi
University of New Brunswick
University of Newcastle
University of North Dakota—Minot
University of Northern Iowa
University of Petroleum and Minerals
University of Puerto Rico
University of Reading
University of Singapore
University of Tennessee at Martin
University of Ulster
Waynesburg College
Weber State College
Webster University in Geneva
West Chester University of Pennsylvania
Western New England College Hanscom
Western State University
William Paterson College of New Jersey
World University

Order Forms for the Official Guides

Both *The Official Guide for GMAT Review* and *The Official Guide to MBA Programs* are sold in many bookstores at the list price of $9.95 each. They (and *The Official Software for GMAT Review*) may also be ordered directly from ETS. Fill out the order form and mailing label below and send it with the appropriate payment to ETS, either with your GMAT registration form or in a separate envelope addressed to Graduate Management Admission Test, Educational Testing Service, CN 6108, Princeton, NJ 08541-6108.

All orders to be sent to addresses in the United States or U.S. territories will be shipped by priority mail (first class) at no additional charge. Please allow two weeks for delivery to U.S. addresses.

For delivery outside the United States and its territories, allow about four weeks. Be sure to check the appropriate box on the order form.

- - - - - - - - - - CUT HERE TO DETACH - - - - - - - - - -

Complete the address label at the right and enclose both this order form and the address label with a check or money order made payable to Graduate Management Admission Test. **Do not send cash.** Orders received without payment cannot be processed.

My payment is enclosed for:

	U.S. Priority delivery*	Foreign Airmail**
Both books	☐ $17.00	☐ $ 33.00
The Official Guide for GMAT Review	☐ $ 9.95	☐ $ 21.95
The Official Guide to MBA Programs	☐ $ 9.95	☐ $ 21.95
The Official Software for GMAT Review (including *The Official Guide for GMAT Review*)		
Apple II version	☐ $79.95	☐ $ 95.00
IBM PC version	☐ $79.95	☐ $ 95.00
The Official Software for GMAT Review (with *The Official Guide for GMAT Review* and *The Official Guide to MBA Programs*)		
Apple II version	☐ $85.00	☐ $110.00
IBM PC version	☐ $85.00	☐ $110.00

* Airmail delivery to United States, Guam, Puerto Rico, U.S. Virgin Islands, and U.S. territories
**Airmail delivery to countries and areas other than those named above

DO NOT DETACH

(Please print.)

Name _____

Number and Street _____

City _____

State or Province _____

Zip or Postal Code _____

Country _____

Graduate Management Admission Test
Educational Testing Service
CN 6108
Princeton, NJ 08541-6108

692-82
GMAC
GUIDES

- - - - - - - - - - CUT HERE TO DETACH - - - - - - - - - -

Complete the address label at the right and enclose both this order form and the address label with a check or money order made payable to Graduate Management Admission Test. **Do not send cash.** Orders received without payment cannot be processed.

My payment is enclosed for:

	U.S. Priority delivery*	Foreign Airmail**
Both books	☐ $17.00	☐ $ 33.00
The Official Guide for GMAT Review	☐ $ 9.95	☐ $ 21.95
The Official Guide to MBA Programs	☐ $ 9.95	☐ $ 21.95
The Official Software for GMAT Review (including *The Official Guide for GMAT Review*)		
Apple II version	☐ $79.95	☐ $ 95.00
IBM PC version	☐ $79.95	☐ $ 95.00
The Official Software for GMAT Review (with *The Official Guide for GMAT Review* and *The Official Guide to MBA Programs*)		
Apple II version	☐ $85.00	☐ $110.00
IBM PC version	☐ $85.00	☐ $110.00

* Airmail delivery to United States, Guam, Puerto Rico, U.S. Virgin Islands, and U.S. territories
**Airmail delivery to countries and areas other than those named above

DO NOT DETACH

(Please print.)

Name _____

Number and Street _____

City _____

State or Province _____

Zip or Postal Code _____

Country _____

Graduate Management Admission Test
Educational Testing Service
CN 6108
Princeton, NJ 08541-6108

692-82
GMAC
GUIDES

Order Form for GMAT Bulletin of Information

Applicants to schools requiring the Graduate Management Admission Test (GMAT) may arrange with Educational Testing Service to take the test on one of four dates. If you wish to receive a **Bulletin of Information** describing arrangements for taking the test, the nature of the exam, and scoring procedures, complete the address label at the right and mail it to:

Graduate Management Admission Test
Educational Testing Service
CN 6101
Princeton, NJ 08541-6101

*Please note that, although you may receive this notice from several schools, you need only one **Bulletin** and registration form.*

A registration form and return envelope accompany each **Bulletin of Information.** Depending on where and when you want to take the test, your completed registration form and fee must be postmarked between five and eight weeks before the test date you select (requests for supplementary and Monday centers and special arrangements for the handicapped have even earlier deadlines). See the calendar on the reverse side for test dates and deadlines. It is to your advantage to send for your **Bulletin** and to complete your registration form as early as possible.

This is your mailing label. Type or print clearly.

TO _____

GRADUATE MANAGEMENT ADMISSION TEST 666-17
EDUCATIONAL TESTING SERVICE GMAT
CN 6101 BULLETIN
PRINCETON, NJ 08541-6101

Order Form for GMAT Bulletin of Information

Applicants to schools requiring the Graduate Management Admission Test (GMAT) may arrange with Educational Testing Service to take the test on one of four dates. If you wish to receive a **Bulletin of Information** describing arrangements for taking the test, the nature of the exam, and scoring procedures, complete the address label at the right and mail it to:

Graduate Management Admission Test
Educational Testing Service
CN 6101
Princeton, NJ 08541-6101

*Please note that, although you may receive this notice from several schools, you need only one **Bulletin** and registration form.*

A registration form and return envelope accompany each **Bulletin of Information.** Depending on where and when you want to take the test, your completed registration form and fee must be postmarked between five and eight weeks before the test date you select (requests for supplementary and Monday centers and special arrangements for the handicapped have even earlier deadlines). See the calendar on the reverse side for test dates and deadlines. It is to your advantage to send for your **Bulletin** and to complete your registration form as early as possible.

This is your mailing label. Type or print clearly.

TO _____

GRADUATE MANAGEMENT ADMISSION TEST 666-17
EDUCATIONAL TESTING SERVICE GMAT
CN 6101 BULLETIN
PRINCETON, NJ 08541-6101

Order Form for GMAT Bulletin of Information

Applicants to schools requiring the Graduate Management Admission Test (GMAT) may arrange with Educational Testing Service to take the test on one of four dates. If you wish to receive a **Bulletin of Information** describing arrangements for taking the test, the nature of the exam, and scoring procedures, complete the address label at the right and mail it to:

Graduate Management Admission Test
Educational Testing Service
CN 6101
Princeton, NJ 08541-6101

*Please note that, although you may receive this notice from several schools, you need only one **Bulletin** and registration form.*

A registration form and return envelope accompany each **Bulletin of Information.** Depending on where and when you want to take the test, your completed registration form and fee must be postmarked between five and eight weeks before the test date you select (requests for supplementary and Monday centers and special arrangements for the handicapped have even earlier deadlines). See the calendar on the reverse side for test dates and deadlines. It is to your advantage to send for your **Bulletin** and to complete your registration form as early as possible.

This is your mailing label. Type or print clearly.

TO _____

GRADUATE MANAGEMENT ADMISSION TEST 666-17
EDUCATIONAL TESTING SERVICE GMAT
CN 6101 BULLETIN
PRINCETON, NJ 08541-6101

Registration Calendar

Test Dates	DOMESTIC REGISTRATION GMAT administrations in the U.S., Guam, Puerto Rico, U.S. Virgin Islands, and U.S. Territories			FOREIGN REGISTRATION GMAT administrations in all other countries (including Canada)	
	REGULAR REGISTRATION	LATE REGISTRATION & CENTER CHANGE	SPECIAL REQUESTS	FINAL REGISTRATION & CENTER CHANGE	SPECIAL REQUESTS
	Registration forms postmarked after this date must be accompanied by a $10 late registration fee.	Add $10 late registration fee. Registration forms postmarked after this period will be returned.	Last postmark date for supplementary centers, Monday administrations,* and arrangements for the handicapped.	Registration forms postmarked after this date or received too late for processing will be returned.	Last postmark date for requests for supplementary centers,† Monday administrations,* and arrangements for the handicapped.
	Postmark Dates			Airmail Postmark Dates	
Oct. 18, 1986*†	Sept. 15	Sept. 16-22	Aug. 27	Aug. 27	Aug. 11
Jan. 24, 1987*	Dec. 22	Dec. 23-31	Dec. 3	Dec. 3	Nov. 17
March 21, 1987*	Feb. 17	Feb. 18-24	Jan. 28	Jan. 28	Jan. 12
June 20, 1987*	May 18	May 19-26	April 29	April 29	April 13

*Monday administration dates will be October 20, 1986, January 26, 1987, March 23, 1987, and June 22, 1987.
†No supplementary centers will be established for foreign registration for the October 1986 test date.

Registration Calendar

Test Dates	DOMESTIC REGISTRATION GMAT administrations in the U.S., Guam, Puerto Rico, U.S. Virgin Islands, and U.S. Territories			FOREIGN REGISTRATION GMAT administrations in all other countries (including Canada)	
	REGULAR REGISTRATION	LATE REGISTRATION & CENTER CHANGE	SPECIAL REQUESTS	FINAL REGISTRATION & CENTER CHANGE	SPECIAL REQUESTS
	Registration forms postmarked after this date must be accompanied by a $10 late registration fee.	Add $10 late registration fee. Registration forms postmarked after this period will be returned.	Last postmark date for supplementary centers, Monday administrations,* and arrangements for the handicapped.	Registration forms postmarked after this date or received too late for processing will be returned.	Last postmark date for requests for supplementary centers,† Monday administrations,* and arrangements for the handicapped.
	Postmark Dates			Airmail Postmark Dates	
Oct. 18, 1986*†	Sept. 15	Sept. 16-22	Aug. 27	Aug. 27	Aug. 11
Jan. 24, 1987*	Dec. 22	Dec. 23-31	Dec. 3	Dec. 3	Nov. 17
March 21, 1987*	Feb. 17	Feb. 18-24	Jan. 28	Jan. 28	Jan. 12
June 20, 1987*	May 18	May 19-26	April 29	April 29	April 13

*Monday administration dates will be October 20, 1986, January 26, 1987, March 23, 1987, and June 22, 1987.
†No supplementary centers will be established for foreign registration for the October 1986 test date.

Registration Calendar

Test Dates	DOMESTIC REGISTRATION GMAT administrations in the U.S., Guam, Puerto Rico, U.S. Virgin Islands, and U.S. Territories			FOREIGN REGISTRATION GMAT administrations in all other countries (including Canada)	
	REGULAR REGISTRATION	LATE REGISTRATION & CENTER CHANGE	SPECIAL REQUESTS	FINAL REGISTRATION & CENTER CHANGE	SPECIAL REQUESTS
	Registration forms postmarked after this date must be accompanied by a $10 late registration fee.	Add $10 late registration fee. Registration forms postmarked after this period will be returned.	Last postmark date for supplementary centers, Monday administrations,* and arrangements for the handicapped.	Registration forms postmarked after this date or received too late for processing will be returned.	Last postmark date for requests for supplementary centers,† Monday administrations,* and arrangements for the handicapped.
	Postmark Dates			Airmail Postmark Dates	
Oct. 18, 1986*†	Sept. 15	Sept. 16-22	Aug. 27	Aug. 27	Aug. 11
Jan. 24, 1987*	Dec. 22	Dec. 23-31	Dec. 3	Dec. 3	Nov. 17
March 21, 1987*	Feb. 17	Feb. 18-24	Jan. 28	Jan. 28	Jan. 12
June 20, 1987*	May 18	May 19-26	April 29	April 29	April 13

*Monday administration dates will be October 20, 1986, January 26, 1987, March 23, 1987, and June 22, 1987.
†No supplementary centers will be established for foreign registration for the October 1986 test date.

I am interested in information about your graduate management school. I will be ready to enter school in:

MONTH _____   YEAR _____

Please send me: ☐ a catalog
☐ admissions material
☐ financial aid information
☐ other _____
Please specify

NAME _____

ADDRESS _____

_____ ZIP_____

UNDERGRADUATE COLLEGE _____

These cards are for your convenience in writing to graduate management schools for information. They are not applications for admission. At the end of each school's description in this book, you will find an address to which the card should be addressed.

I am interested in information about your graduate management school. I will be ready to enter school in:

MONTH _____   YEAR _____

Please send me: ☐ a catalog
☐ admissions material
☐ financial aid information
☐ other _____
Please specify

NAME _____

ADDRESS _____

_____ ZIP_____

UNDERGRADUATE COLLEGE _____

I am interested in information about your graduate management school. I will be ready to enter school in:

MONTH _____   YEAR _____

Please send me: ☐ a catalog
☐ admissions material
☐ financial aid information
☐ other _____
Please specify

NAME _____

ADDRESS _____

_____ ZIP_____

UNDERGRADUATE COLLEGE _____

GMAC™
Graduate
Management
Admission
Council

PLACE
STAMP
HERE

_____

_____

_____

_____

GMAC™
Graduate
Management
Admission
Council

PLACE
STAMP
HERE

_____

_____

_____

_____

GMAC™
Graduate
Management
Admission
Council

PLACE
STAMP
HERE

_____

_____

_____

I am interested in information about your graduate management school. I will be ready to enter school in:

MONTH _____ YEAR _____

Please send me: ☐ a catalog
☐ admissions material
☐ financial aid information
☐ other _____
Please specify

NAME _____

ADDRESS _____

_____ ZIP_____

UNDERGRADUATE COLLEGE _____

These cards are for your convenience in writing to graduate management schools for information. They are not applications for admission. At the end of each school's description in this book, you will find an address to which the card should be addressed.

I am interested in information about your graduate management school. I will be ready to enter school in:

MONTH _____ YEAR _____

Please send me: ☐ a catalog
☐ admissions material
☐ financial aid information
☐ other _____
Please specify

NAME _____

ADDRESS _____

_____ ZIP_____

UNDERGRADUATE COLLEGE _____

I am interested in information about your graduate management school. I will be ready to enter school in:

MONTH _____ YEAR _____

Please send me: ☐ a catalog
☐ admissions material
☐ financial aid information
☐ other _____
Please specify

NAME _____

ADDRESS _____

_____ ZIP_____

UNDERGRADUATE COLLEGE _____

GMAC™
Graduate
Management
Admission
Council

PLACE
STAMP
HERE

_____

_____

_____

_____

GMAC™
Graduate
Management
Admission
Council

PLACE
STAMP
HERE

_____

_____

_____

_____

GMAC™
Graduate
Management
Admission
Council

PLACE
STAMP
HERE

_____

_____

_____

Please send me more information on the National Doctoral Fellowship Program in Business & Management, which offers significant financial assistance to qualified first-year doctoral students.

Name _____

Address _____

_____ Zip _____

☐ I would like more information about faculty careers in business. Please send me one free copy of *Business Faculty Careers: A Logical Choice.*

☐ I would like to order a copy of the *Guide to Doctoral Programs in Business & Management.* Enclosed is a check made out to AACSB for $10 ($15 outside the U.S.). Please send to:

Name _____

Address _____

_____ Zip _____

Copies of the TOEFL *Bulletin* are usually available at United States educational commissions and foundations, United States Information Service (USIS) offices, binational centers, and private organizations such as the Institute of International Education (IIE). If you are unable to obtain a *Bulletin* locally, you may enter your name and address below and mail this card. Since your request will be forwarded from the Princeton address to the agency responsible for registration in your country or area, this card should be used *only* if you have no other means of obtaining a *Bulletin*.

Please send a copy of the TOEFL *Bulletin* to:

Name _____

Address _____

_____ Zip _____

AACSB
605 Old Ballas Road, Suite 220
St. Louis, Missouri 63141 USA

AACSB
605 Old Ballas Road, Suite 220
St. Louis, Missouri 63141 USA

Test of English as a Foreign Language
CN 6151
Princeton, NJ 08541-6151 USA

634-16

Please send a GAPSFAS Financial Aid Form to:

Name _____

Address _____

_____ Zip _____

216-02

Please send a CSS Financial Aid Form (FAF) to:

Name _____

Address _____

_____ Zip _____

Please send a copy of your free publication, *The Student Guide: Five Federal Financial Aid Programs* to:

Name _____

Address _____

_____ Zip _____

634-16

Graduate and Professional Schools
  Financial Aid Service
CN 6660
Princeton, NJ 08541-6660 USA

216-02

College Scholarship Service
CN 6327
Princeton, NJ 08541-6327 USA

Public Documents Distribution Center
Department DEA-87
Pueblo, Colorado 81009 USA